D1307917

St. Thomas Aquinas
Summa Theologica

St. Thomas Aquinas
Summa Theologica

COMPLETE ENGLISH EDITION

IN FIVE VOLUMES

Translated by
Fathers of the English Dominican Province

VOLUME FIVE

IIIª QQ. 74–90

SUPPLEMENT QQ. 1–99

CHART OF THE SUMMA
ANALYTICAL INDEX

WITH SYNOPTICAL CHARTS

Christian Classics
A DIVISION OF THOMAS MORE PUBLISHING

Allen, Texas

Summa Theologica originally published in English 1911. Revised edition published 1920, London. Reissued in 3 volumes, New York, 1948. Copy right 1948 by Benziger Brothers, Inc. Reprinted 1981 by Christian Classics, under a license granted by Benziger, a division of Glencoe Publishing Co., Inc., successor in interest to Benziger Brothers, Inc. All Rights Reserved.

Send all inquiries to:
Christian Classics™
a division of Thomas More Publishing
200 East Bethany Drive
Allen, Texas 75002

Copyright © 1948 by Benziger Bros., New York, NY

LIBRARY OF CONGRESS CATALOG CARD NUMBER: 81–68580

ISBN:	CLOTH EDITION	PAPERBACK EDITION
Volume I	0–87061–064–3	0–87061–070–8
Volume II	0–87061–065–1	0–87061–071–6
Volume III	0–87061–066–X	0–87061–072–4
Volume IV	0–87061–067–8	0–87061–073–2
Volume V	0–87061–068–6	0–87061–074–0
Complete Set	0–87061–063–5	0–87061–069–4

PRINTED IN THE UNITED STATES OF AMERICA

CONTENTS

QUESTION 74

Of the Matter of This Sacrament

(In Eight Articles)

WE have now to consider the matter of this sacrament: and first of all as to its species; secondly, the change of the bread and wine into the body of Christ; thirdly, the manner in which Christ's body exists in this sacrament; fourthly, the accidents of bread and wine which continue in this sacrament.

Under the first heading there are eight points for inquiry: (1) Whether bread and wine are the matter of this sacrament? (2) Whether a determinate quantity of the same is required for the matter of this sacrament? (3) Whether the matter of this sacrament is wheaten bread? (4) Whether it is unleavened or fermented bread? (5) Whether the matter of this sacrament is wine from the grape? (6) Whether water should be mixed with it? (7) Whether water is of necessity for this sacrament? (8) Of the quantity of the water added.

FIRST ARTICLE

Whether the Matter of This Sacrament Is Bread and Wine?

We proceed thus to the First Article:—

Objection 1. It seems that the matter of this sacrament is not bread and wine. Because this sacrament ought to represent Christ's Passion more fully than did the sacraments of the Old Law. But the flesh of animals, which was the matter of the sacraments under the Old Law, shows forth Christ's Passion more fully than bread and wine. Therefore the matter of this sacrament ought rather to be the flesh of animals than bread and wine.

Obj. 2. Further, this sacrament is to be celebrated in every place. But in many lands bread is not to be found, and in many places wine is not to be found. Therefore bread and wine are not a suitable matter for this sacrament.

Obj. 3. Further, this sacrament is for both hale and weak. But to some weak persons wine is hurtful. Therefore it seems that wine ought not to be the matter of this sacrament.

On the contrary, Pope Alexander (I) says *(Ep. ad omnes Orthod.* i): *In oblations of the sacraments only bread and wine mixed with water are to be offered.*

I answer that, Some have fallen into various errors about the matter of this sacrament. Some, known as the Artotyrytæ, as Augustine says *(De Hæres.* xxviii), *offer bread and cheese in this sacrament, contending that oblations*

were celebrated by men in the first ages, from fruits of the earth and sheep. Others, called Cataphrygæ and Pepuziani, *are reputed to have made their Eucharistic bread with infants' blood drawn from tiny punctures over the entire body, and mixed with flour.* Others, styled Aquarii, under guise of sobriety, offer nothing but water in this sacrament.

Now all these and similar errors are excluded by the fact that Christ instituted this sacrament under the species of bread and wine, as is evident from Matth. xxvi. Consequently, bread and wine are the proper matter of this sacrament. And the reasonableness of this is seen, first, in the use of this sacrament, which is eating: for, as water is used in the sacrament of Baptism for the purpose of spiritual cleansing, since bodily cleansing is commonly done with water; so bread and wine, wherewith men are commonly fed, are employed in this sacrament for the use of spiritual eating.

Secondly, in relation to Christ's Passion, in which the blood was separated from the body. And therefore in this sacrament, which is the memorial of our Lord's Passion, the bread is received apart as the sacrament of the body, and the wine as the sacrament of the blood.

Thirdly, as to the effect, considered in each of the partakers. For, as Ambrose *(Mag. Sent.* iv, D. xi) says on 1 Cor. xi. 20, this sacrament *avails for the defense of soul and body;* and therefore *Christ's body is offered* under the species of bread *for the health of the body,* and the blood under the species of wine *for the health of the soul,* according to Lev. xvii. 14: *The life of the animal* (Vulg.,—*of all flesh) is in the blood.*

Fourthly, as to the effect with regard to the whole Church, which is made up of many believers, just *as bread is composed of many grains, and wine flows from many grapes,* as the gloss observes on 1 Cor. x. 17: *We being many are . . . one body,* etc.

Reply Obj. 1. Although the flesh of slaughtered animals represents the Passion more forcibly, nevertheless it is less suitable for the common use of this sacrament, and for denoting the unity of the Church.

Reply Obj. 2. Although wheat and wine are not produced in every country, yet they can easily be conveyed to every land, that is, as much as is needful for the use of this sacrament: at the same time one is not to be consecrated when the other is lacking, because it would not be a complete sacrament.

Reply Obj. 3. Wine taken in small quantity cannot do the sick much harm: yet if there be fear of harm, it is not necessary for all who take Christ's body to partake also of His blood, as will be stated later (Q. 80, A. 12).

SECOND ARTICLE

Whether a Determinate Quantity of Bread and Wine Is Required for the Matter of This Sacrament?

We proceed thus to the Second Article:—

Objection 1. It seems that a determinate quantity of bread and wine is required for the matter of this sacrament. Because the effects of grace are no less set in order than those of nature. But, *there is a limit set by nature upon all existing things, and a reckoning of size and development (De Anima.* ii). Consequently, in this sacrament, which is called *Eucharist,* that is, *a good grace,* a determinate quantity of the bread and wine is required.

Obj. 2. Further, Christ gave no power to the ministers of the Church regarding matters which involve derision of the faith and of His sacraments, according to 2 Cor. x. 8: *Of our power which the Lord hath given us unto edification, and not for your destruction.* But it would lead to mockery of this sacrament if the priest were to wish to consecrate all the bread which is sold in the market and all the wine in the cellar. Therefore he cannot do this.

Obj. 3. Further, if anyone be baptized in the sea, the entire sea-water is not sanctified by the form of baptism, but only the water wherewith the body of the baptized is cleansed. Therefore, neither in this sacrament can a superfluous quantity of bread be consecrated.

On the contrary, Much is opposed to little, and great to small. But there is no quantity, however small, of the bread and wine which cannot be consecrated. Therefore, neither is there any quantity, however great, which cannot be consecrated.

I answer that, Some have maintained that the priest could not consecrate an immense quantity of bread and wine, for instance, all the bread in the market or all the wine in a cask. But this does not appear to be true, because in all things containing matter, the reason for the determination of the matter is drawn from its disposition to an end, just as the matter of a saw is iron, so as to adapt it for cutting. But the end of this sacrament is the use of the faithful. Consequently, the quantity of the matter of this sacrament must be determined by comparison with the use of the faithful. But this cannot be determined by comparison with the use of the faithful who are actually present; otherwise the parish priest having few parishioners could not consecrate

many hosts. It remains, then, for the matter of this sacrament to be determined in reference to the number of the faithful absolutely. But the number of the faithful is not a determinate one. Hence it cannot be said that the quantity of the matter of this sacrament is restricted.

Reply Obj. 1. The matter of every natural object has its determinate quantity by comparison with its determinate form. But the number of the faithful, for whose use this sacrament is ordained, is not a determinate one. Consequently there is no comparison.

Reply Obj. 2. The power of the Church's ministers is ordained for two purposes: first for the proper effect, and secondly for the end of the effect. But the second does not take away the first. Hence, if the priest intends to consecrate the body of Christ for an evil purpose, for instance, to make mockery of it, or to administer poison through it, he commits sin by his evil intention, nevertheless, on account of the power committed to him, he accomplishes the sacrament.

Reply Obj. 3. The sacrament of Baptism is perfected in the use of the matter: and therefore no more of the water is hallowed than what is used. But this sacrament is wrought in the consecration of the matter. Consequently there is no parallel.

THIRD ARTICLE

Whether Wheaten Bread Is Required for the Matter of This Sacrament?

We proceed thus to the Third Article:—

Objection 1. It seems that wheaten bread is not requisite for the matter of this sacrament, because this sacrament is a reminder of our Lord's Passion. But barley bread seems to be more in keeping with the Passion than wheaten bread, as being more bitter, and because Christ used it to feed the multitudes upon the mountain, as narrated in John vi. Therefore wheaten bread is not the proper matter of this sacrament.

Obj. 2. Further, in natural things the shape is a sign of species. But some cereals resemble wheat, such as spelt and maize, from which in some localities bread is made for the use of this sacrament. Therefore wheaten bread is not the proper matter of this sacrament.

Obj. 3. Further, mixing dissolves species. But wheaten flour is hardly to be found unmixed with some other species of grain, except in the instance of specially selected grain. Therefore it does not seem that wheaten bread is the proper matter for this sacrament.

Obj. 4. Further, what is corrupted appears to be of another species. But some make the sacrament from bread which is corrupted, and which no longer seems to be wheaten bread. Therefore, it seems that such bread is not the proper matter of this sacrament.

On the contrary, Christ is contained in this sacrament, and He compares Himself to a grain of wheat, saying (John xii. 24): *Unless the grain of wheat falling into the ground die, itself remaineth alone.* Therefore bread from corn, i.e. wheaten bread, is the matter of this sacrament.

I answer that, As stated above (A. 1), for the use of the sacraments such matter is adopted as is commonly made use of among men. Now among other breads wheaten bread is more commonly used by men; since other breads seem to be employed when this fails. And consequently Christ is believed to have instituted this sacrament under this species of bread. Moreover this bread strengthens man, and so it denotes more suitably the effect of this sacrament. Consequently, the proper matter for this sacrament is wheaten bread.

Reply Obj. 1. Barley bread serves to denote the hardness of the Old Law; both on account of the hardness of the bread, and because, as Augustine says (Q. 83): *The flour within the barley, wrapped up as it is within a most tenacious fibre, denotes either the Law itself, which was given in such manner as to be vested in bodily sacraments; or else it denotes the people themselves, who were not yet despoiled of carnal desires, which clung to their hearts like fibre.* But this sacrament belongs to Christ's *sweet yoke,* and to the truth already manifested, and to a spiritual people. Consequently barley bread would not be a suitable matter for this sacrament.

Reply Obj. 2. A begetter begets a thing like to itself in species; yet there is some unlikeness as to the accidents, owing either to the matter, or to weakness within the generative power. And therefore, if there be any cereals which can be grown from the seed of the wheat (as wild wheat from wheat seed grown in bad ground), the bread made from such grain can be the matter of this sacrament: and this does not obtain either in barley, or in spelt, or even in maize, which is of all grains the one most resembling the wheat grain. But the resemblance as to shape in such seems to denote closeness of species rather than identity; just as the resemblance in shape between the dog and the wolf goes to show that they are allied but not of the same species. Hence from such grains, which cannot in any way be generated from wheat grain, bread cannot be made such as to be the proper matter of this sacrament.

Reply Obj. 3. A moderate mixing does not alter the species, because that little is as it were absorbed by the greater. Consequently, then, if a small quantity of another grain be mixed with a much greater quantity of wheat, bread may be made therefrom so as to be the proper matter of this sacrament; but if the mixing be notable, for instance, half and half, or nearly so, then such mixing alters the species; consequently, bread made therefrom will not be the proper matter of this sacrament.

Reply Obj. 4. Sometimes there is such corruption of the bread that the species of bread is lost, as when the continuity of its parts is destroyed, and the taste, color, and other accidents are changed; hence the body of Christ may not be made from such matter. But sometimes there is not such corruption as to alter the species, but merely disposition towards corruption, which a slight change in the savor betrays, and from such bread the body of Christ may be made: but he who does so, sins from irreverence towards the sacrament. And because starch comes of corrupted wheat, it does not seem as if the body of Christ could be made of the bread made therefrom, although some hold the contrary.

FOURTH ARTICLE

Whether This Sacrament Ought to Be Made of Unleavened Bread?

We proceed thus to the Fourth Article:—

Objection 1. It seems that this sacrament ought not to be made of unleavened bread, because in this sacrament we ought to imitate Christ's institution. But Christ appears to have instituted this sacrament in fermented bread, because, as we have read in Exod. xii, the Jews, according to the Law, began to use unleavened bread on the day of the Passover, which is celebrated on the fourteenth day of the moon; and Christ instituted this sacrament at the supper which He celebrated *before the festival day of the Pasch (John* xiii. 1, 4). Therefore we ought likewise to celebrate this sacrament with fermented bread.

Obj. 2. Further, legal observances ought not to be continued in the time of grace. But the use of unleavened bread was a ceremony of the Law, as is clear from Exod. xii. Therefore we ought not to use unfermented bread in this sacrament of grace.

Obj. 3. Further, as stated above (Q. 65, A. 1; Q. 73, A. 3), the Eucharist is the sacrament of charity just as Baptism is the sacrament of faith. But the fervor of charity is signified by fermented bread, as is declared by the gloss on Matth. xiii. 33: *The kingdom of heaven is like unto leaven,* etc. Therefore this sacrament ought to be made of leavened bread.

Obj. 4. Further, leavened or unleavened are mere accidents of bread, which do not vary the species. But in the matter for the sacrament of Baptism no difference is observed regarding the variation of the accidents, as to whether it be salt or fresh, warm or cold water. Therefore neither ought any distinction to be observed, as to whether the bread be unleav- ened or leavened.

On the contrary, According to the Decretals (Extra, *De Celebr. Miss.*), a priest is pun- ished *for presuming to celebrate, using fer- mented bread and a wooden cup.*

I answer that, Two things may be consid- ered touching the matter of this sacrament, namely, what is necessary, and what is suit- able. It is necessary that the bread be wheaten, without which the sacrament is not valid, as stated above (A. 3). It is not, however, neces-. sary for the sacrament that the bread be un- leavened or leavened, since it can be celebrated in either.

But it is suitable that every priest observe the rite of his Church in the celebration of the sacrament. Now in this matter there are various customs of the Churches: for, Gregory says: *The Roman Church offers unleavened bread, because our Lord took flesh without union of sexes: but the Greek Churches offer leavened bread, because the Word of the Father was clothed with flesh; as leaven is mixed with the flour.* Hence, as a priest sins by celebrating with fermented bread in the Latin Church, so a Greek priest celebrating with unfermented bread in a church of the Greeks would also sin, as perverting the rite of his Church.

Nevertheless the custom of celebrating with unleavened bread is more reasonable. First, on account of Christ's institution: for He in- stituted this sacrament *on the first day of the Azymes* (Matth. xxvi. 17, Mark xiv. 12, Luke xxii. 7), on which day there ought to be noth- ing fermented in the houses of the Jews, as is stated in Exod. xii. 15, 19. Secondly, because bread is properly the sacrament of Christ's body, which was conceived without corruption, rather than of His Godhead, as will be seen later (Q. 76, A. 1, *ad* 1). Thirdly, because this is more in keeping with the sincerity of the faithful, which is required in the use of this sacrament, according to 1 Cor. v. 7: *Christ our Pasch is sacrificed: therefore let us feast . . . with the unleavened bread of sincerity and truth.*

However, this custom of the Greeks is not unreasonable, both on account of its significa- tion, to which Gregory refers, and in detesta- tion of the heresy of the Nazarenes, who mixed up legal observances with the Gospel.

Reply Obj. 1. As we read in Exod. xii, the paschal solemnity began on the evening of the fourteenth day of the moon. So, then, after immolating the Paschal Lamb, Christ insti- tuted this sacrament: hence this day is said by John to precede the day of the Pasch, while the other three Evangelists call it *the first day of the Azymes,* when fermented bread was not found in the houses of the Jews, as stated above. Fuller mention was made of this in the treatise on our Lord's Passion (Q. 46, A. 9, *ad* 1).

Reply Obj. 2. Those who celebrate the sacrament with unleavened bread do not in- tend to follow the ceremonial of the Law, but to conform to Christ's institution; so they are not Judaizing; otherwise those celebrating in fermented bread would be Judaizing, because the Jews offered up fermented bread for the firstfruits.

Reply Obj. 3. Leaven denotes charity on account of one single effect, because it makes the bread more savory and larger; but it also signifies corruption from its very nature.

Reply Obj. 4. Since whatever is fermented partakes of corruption, this sacrament may not be made from corrupt bread, as stated above (A. 3, *ad* 4); consequently, there is a wider difference between unleavened and leav- ened bread than between warm and cold bap- tismal water: because there might be such corruption of fermented bread that it could not be validly used for the sacrament.

FIFTH ARTICLE

Whether Wine of the Grape Is the Proper Matter of This Sacrament?

We proceed thus to the Fifth Article:—

Objection 1. It seems that wine of the grape is not the proper matter of this sacrament. Because, as water is the matter of Baptism, so is wine the matter of this sacrament. But Baptism can be conferred with any kind of water. Therefore this sacrament can be cele- brated in any kind of wine, such as of pome- granates, or of mulberries; since vines do not grow in some countries.

Obj. 2. Further, vinegar is a kind of wine drawn from the grape, as Isidore says *(Etym.* xx). But this sacrament cannot be celebrated with vinegar. Therefore, it seems that wine from the grape is not the proper matter of this sacrament.

Obj. 3. Further, just as the clarified wine is drawn from grapes, so also are the juice of unripe grapes and must. But it does not ap- pear that this sacrament may be made from such, according to what we read in the Sixth Council *(Trull.,* Can. 28): *We have learned that in some churches the priests add grapes to the sacrifice of the oblation; and so they dispense both together to the people. Conse- quently we give order that no priest shall do this in future.* And Pope Julius I rebukes some priests *who offer wine pressed from the grape in the sacrament of the Lord's chalice.* Consequently, it seems that wine from the grape is not the proper matter of this sacrament.

On the contrary, As our Lord compared Himself to the grain of wheat, so also He compared Himself to the vine, saying (John xv. 1): *I am the true vine.* But only bread from wheat is the matter of this sacrament, as stated above (A. 3). Therefore, only wine from the grape is the proper matter of this sacrament.

I answer that, This sacrament can only be performed with wine from the grape. First of all on account of Christ's institution, since He instituted this sacrament in wine from the grape, as is evident from His own words, in instituting this sacrament (Matth. xxvi. 29): *I will not drink from henceforth of this fruit of the vine.* Secondly, because, as stated above (A. 3), that is adopted as the matter of the sacraments which is properly and universally considered as such. Now that is properly called wine, which is drawn from the grape, whereas other liquors are called wine from resemblance to the wine of the grape. Thirdly, because the wine from the grape is more in keeping with the effect of this sacrament, which is spiritual; because it is written (Ps. ciii. 15): *That wine may cheer the heart of man.*

Reply Obj. 1. Such liquors are called wine, not properly but only from their resemblance thereto. But genuine wine can be conveyed to such countries wherein the grape-vine does not flourish, in a quantity sufficient for this sacrament.

Reply Obj. 2. Wine becomes vinegar by corruption; hence there is no returning from vinegar to wine, as is said in *Metaph.* viii. And consequently, just as this sacrament may not be made from bread which is utterly corrupt, so neither can it be made from vinegar. It can, however, be made from wine which is turning sour, just as from bread turning corrupt, although he who does so sins, as stated above (A. 3).

Reply Obj. 3. The juice of unripe grapes is at the stage of incomplete generation, and therefore it has not yet the species of wine: on which account it may not be used for this sacrament. Must, however, has already the species of wine, for its sweetness* indicates fermentation which is *the result of its natural heat (Meteor.* iv); consequently this sacrament can be made from must. Nevertheless entire grapes ought not to be mixed with this sacrament, because then there would be something else besides wine. It is furthermore forbidden to offer must in the chalice, as soon as it has been squeezed from the grape, since this

is unbecoming owing to the impurity of the must. But in case of necessity it may be done: for it is said by the same Pope Julius, in the passage quoted in the argument: *If necessary, let the grape be pressed into the chalice.*

SIXTH ARTICLE

Whether Water Should Be Mixed with the Wine?

We proceed thus to the Sixth Article:—

Objection 1. It seems that water ought not to be mixed with the wine, since Christ's sacrifice was foreshadowed by that of Melchisedech, who (Gen. xiv. 18) is related to have offered up bread and wine only. Consequently, it seems that water should not be added in this sacrament.

Obj. 2. Further, the various sacraments have their respective matters. But water is the matter of Baptism. Therefore it should not be employed as the matter of this sacrament.

Obj. 3. Further, bread and wine are the matter of this sacrament. But nothing is added to the bread. Therefore neither should anything be added to the wine.

On the contrary, Pope Alexander (I) writes *(Ep. I. ad omnes Orthod.): In the sacramental oblations which in mass are offered to the Lord, only bread and wine mixed with water are to be offered in sacrifice.*

I answer that, Water ought to be mingled with the wine which is offered in this sacrament. First of all on account of its institution: for it is believed with probability that our Lord instituted this sacrament in wine tempered with water according to the custom of that country: hence it is written (Prov. ix. 5): *Drink the wine which I have mixed for you.* Secondly, because it harmonizes with the representation of our Lord's Passion: hence Pope Alexander (I) says *(loc. cit.): In the Lord's chalice neither wine only nor water only ought to be offered, but both mixed, because we read that both flowed from His side in the Passion.* Thirdly, because this is adapted for signifying the effect of this sacrament, since as Pope Julius says *(Concil. Bracarens* iii, Can. 1): *We see that the people are signified by the water, but Christ's blood by the wine. Therefore when water is mixed with the wine in the chalice, the people is made one with Christ.* Fourthly, because this is appropriate to the fourth effect of this sacrament, which is the entering into everlasting life: hence Ambrose says *(De Sacram.* v): *The water flows into the chalice, and springs forth unto everlasting life.*

Reply Obj. 1. As Ambrose says *(ibid.),* just as Christ's sacrifice is denoted by the

* *Aut dulcis musti Vulcano decoquit humorem* (Virg.,—*Georg.* i. 295).

offering of Melchisedech, so likewise it is signified by the water which flowed from the rock in the desert, according to 1 Cor. x. 4: *But they drank of the spiritual rock which came after them.*

Reply Obj. 2. In Baptism water is used for the purpose of ablution: but in this sacrament it is used by way of refreshment, according to Ps. xxii. 3: *He hath brought me up on the water of refreshment.*

Reply Obj. 3. Bread is made of water and flour; and therefore, since water is mixed with the wine, neither is without water.

SEVENTH ARTICLE

Whether the Mixing with Water Is Essential to This Sacrament?

We proceed thus to the Seventh Article:—

Objection 1. It seems that the mixing with water is essential to this sacrament. Because Cyprian says to Cecilius *(Ep.* lxiii): *Thus the Lord's chalice is not water only and wine only, but both must be mixed together: in the same way as neither the Lord's body be of flour only, except both,* i.e. the flour and the water *be united as one.* But the admixture of water with the flour is necessary for this sacrament. Consequently, for the like reason, so is the mixing of water with the wine.

Obj. 2. Further, at our Lord's Passion, of which this is the memorial, water as well as blood flowed from His side. But wine, which is the sacrament of the blood, is necessary for this sacrament. For the same reason, therefore, so is water.

Obj. 3. Further, if water were not essential to this sacrament, it would not matter in the least what kind of water was used; and so water distilled from roses, or any other kind, might be employed; which is contrary to the usage of the Church. Consequently water is essential to this sacrament.

On the contrary, Cyprian says *(loc. cit.)*: *If any of our predecessors, out of ignorance or simplicity, has not kept this usage,* i.e. of mixing water with the wine, *one may pardon his simplicity;* which would not be the case if water were essential to the sacrament, as the wine or the bread. Therefore the mingling of water with the wine is not essential to the sacrament.

I answer that, Judgment concerning a sign is to be drawn from the thing signified. Now the adding of water to the wine is for the purpose of signifying the sharing of this sacrament by the faithful, in this respect that by the mixing of the water with the wine, is signified the union of the people with Christ, as stated (A. 6). Moreover, the flowing of water from the side of Christ hanging on the cross

refers to the same, because by the water is denoted the cleansing from sins, which was the effect of Christ's Passion. Now it was observed above (Q. 73, A. 1, *ad* 3), that this sacrament is completed in the consecration of the matter: while the usage of the faithful is not essential to the sacrament, but only a consequence thereof. Consequently, then, the adding of water is not essential to the sacrament.

Reply Obj. 1. Cyprian's expression is to be taken in the same sense in which we say that a thing cannot be, which cannot be suitably. And so the comparison refers to what ought to be done, not to what is essential to be done; since water is of the essence of bread, but not of the essence of wine.

Reply Obj. 2. The shedding of the blood belonged directly to Christ's Passion: for it is natural for blood to flow from a wounded human body. But the flowing of the water was not necessary for the Passion; but merely to show its effect, which is to wash away sins, and to refresh us from the heat of concupiscence. And therefore the water is not offered apart from the wine in this sacrament, as the wine is offered apart from the bread; but the water is offered mixed with the wine to show that the wine belongs of itself to this sacrament, as of its very essence; but the water as something added to the wine.

Reply Obj. 3. Since the mixing of water with the wine is not necessary for the sacrament, it does not matter, as to the essence of the sacrament, what kind of water is added to the wine, whether natural water, or artificial, as rose-water, although, as to the propriety of the sacrament, he would sin who mixes any other than natural and true water, because true water flowed from the side of Christ hanging on the cross, and not phlegm, as some have said, in order to show that Christ's body was truly composed of the four elements; as by the flowing blood, it was shown to be composed of the four humors, as Pope Innocent III says in a certain Decree. But because the mixing of water with flour is essential to this sacrament, as making the composition of bread, if rose-water, or any other liquor besides true water, be mixed with the flour, the sacrament would not be valid, because it would not be true bread.

EIGHTH ARTICLE

Whether Water Should Be Added in Great Quantity?

We proceed thus to the Eighth Article:—

Objection 1. It seems that water ought to be added in great quantity, because as blood flowed sensibly from Christ's side, so did water: hence it is written (John xix. 35): *He that saw it, hath given testimony.* But water could not be sensibly present in this sacrament except it were used in great quantity. Consequently it seems that water ought to be added in great quantity.

Obj. 2. Further, a little water mixed with much wine is corrupted. But what is corrupted no longer exists. Therefore, it is the same thing to add a little water in this sacrament as to add none. But it is not lawful to add none. Therefore, neither is it lawful to add a little.

Obj. 3. Further, if it sufficed to add a little, then as a consequence it would suffice to throw one drop of water into an entire cask. But this seems ridiculous. Therefore it does not suffice for a small quantity to be added.

On the contrary, It is said in the Decretals (Extra, *De Celeb. Miss.*): *The pernicious abuse has prevailed in your country of adding water in greater quantity than the wine, in the sacrifice, where according to the reasonable custom of the entire Church more wine than water ought to be employed.*

I answer that, There is a threefold opinion regarding the water added to the wine, as Pope Innocent III says in a certain Decretal. For some say that the water remains by itself when the wine is changed into blood: but such an opinion cannot stand, because in the sacrament of the altar after the consecration there is nothing else save the body and the blood of Christ. Because, as Ambrose says in *De Officiis (De Mysteriis,* ix): *Before the blessing it is another species that is named, after the blessing the Body is signified;* otherwise it would not be adored with adoration of latria.

And therefore others have said that as the wine is changed into blood, so the water is changed into the water which flowed from Christ's side. But this cannot be maintained reasonably, because according to this the water would be consecrated apart from the wine, as the wine is from the bread.

And therefore as he (Innocent III, *loc. cit.*) says, the more probable opinion is that which holds that the water is changed into wine, and the wine into blood. Now, this could not be done unless so little water was used that it would be changed into wine. Consequently, it is always safer to add little water, especially if the wine be weak, because the sacrament could not be celebrated if there were such addition of water as to destroy the species of the wine. Hence Pope Julius (I) reprehends some who *keep throughout the year a linen cloth steeped in must, and at the time of sacrifice wash a part of it with water, and so make the offering.*

Reply Obj. 1. For the signification of this sacrament it suffices for the water to be appreciable by sense when it is mixed with the wine: but it is not necessary for it to be sensible after the mingling.

Reply Obj. 2. If no water were added, the signification would be utterly excluded: but when the water is changed into wine, it is signified that the people is incorporated with Christ.

Reply Obj. 3. If water were added to a cask, it would not suffice for the signification of this sacrament, but the water must be added to the wine at the actual celebration of the sacrament.

QUESTION 75

Of the Change of Bread and Wine into the Body and Blood of Christ

(In Eight Articles)

WE have now to consider the change of the bread and wine into the body and blood of Christ; under which head there are eight points of inquiry: (1) Whether the substance of bread and wine remain in this sacrament after the consecration?* (2) Whether it is annihilated? (3) Whether it is changed into the body and blood of Christ? (4) Whether the accidents remain after the change? (5) Whether the substantial form remains there? (6) Whether this change is instantaneous? (7) Whether it is more miraculous

than any other change? (8) By what words it may be suitably expressed?

FIRST ARTICLE

Whether the Body of Christ Be in This Sacrament in Very Truth, or Merely As in a Figure or Sign?

We proceed thus to the First Article:—

Objection 1. It seems that the body of Christ is not in this sacrament in very truth, but only as in a figure, or sign. For it is written (John vi. 54) that when our Lord had

---

* The titles of the Articles here given were taken by S. Thomas from his Commentary on the Sentences (iv. *Dist.* xc). However, in writing the Articles he introduced a new point of inquiry, that of the First Article; and substituted another division of the matter under discussion, as may be seen by referring to the titles of the various Articles. Most editions have ignored S. Thomas's original division, and give the one to which he subsequently adhered.

uttered these words: *Except you eat the flesh of the Son of Man, and drink His blood*, etc., *Many of His disciples on hearing it said: "this is a hard saying"*: to whom He rejoined: *"It is the spirit that quickeneth; the flesh profiteth nothing"*: as if He were to say, according to Augustine's exposition on Ps. iv*: *Give a spiritual meaning to what I have said. You are not to eat this body which you see, nor to drink the blood which they who crucify Me are to spill. It is a mystery that I put before you: in its spiritual sense it will quicken you; but the flesh profiteth nothing.*

Obj. 2. Further, our Lord said (Matth. xxviii. 20): *Behold I am with you all days even to the consummation of the world.* Now in explaining this, Augustine makes this observation *(Tract. xxx, in Joan.): The Lord is on high until the world be ended; nevertheless the truth of the Lord is here with us; for the body, in which He rose again, must be in one place; but His truth is spread abroad everywhere.* Therefore, the body of Christ is not in this sacrament in very truth, but only as in a sign.

Obj. 3. Further, no body can be in several places at the one time. For this does not even belong to an angel; since for the same reason it could be everywhere. But Christ's is a true body, and it is in heaven. Consequently, it seems that it is not in very truth in the sacrament of the altar, but only as in a sign.

Obj. 4. Further, the Church's sacraments are ordained for the profit of the faithful. But according to Gregory in a certain Homily (xxviii, *in Evang.*), the ruler is rebuked *for demanding Christ's bodily presence*. Moreover the apostles were prevented from receiving the Holy Ghost because they were attached to His bodily presence, as Augustine says on John xvi. 7: *Except I go, the Paraclete will not come to you (Tract. xciv, in Joan.).* Therefore Christ is not in the sacrament of the altar according to His bodily presence.

On the contrary, Hilary says *(De Trin.* viii): *There is no room for doubt regarding the truth of Christ's body and blood; for now by our Lord's own declaring and by our faith His flesh is truly food, and His blood is truly drink.* And Ambrose says *(De Sacram.* vi): *As the Lord Jesus Christ is God's true Son, so is it Christ's true flesh which we take, and His true blood which we drink.*

I answer that, The presence of Christ's true body and blood in this sacrament cannot be detected by sense, nor understanding, but by faith alone, which rests upon Divine authority. Hence, on Luke xxii. 19: *This is My body, which shall be delivered up for you,* Cyril

* On Ps. xcviii. 9.

says: *Doubt not whether this be true; but take rather the Saviour's words with faith; for since He is the Truth, He lieth not.*

Now this is suitable, first for the perfection of the New Law. For, the sacrifices of the Old Law contained only in figure that true sacrifice of Christ's Passion, according to Heb. x. 1: *For the law having a shadow of the good things to come, not the very image of the things.* And therefore it was necessary that the sacrifice of the New Law instituted by Christ should have something more, namely, that it should contain Christ Himself crucified, not merely in signification or figure, but also in very truth. And therefore this sacrament which contains Christ Himself, as Dionysius says *(Eccl. Hier.* iii), is perfective of all the other sacraments, in which Christ's virtue is participated.

Secondly, this belongs to Christ's love, out of which for our salvation He assumed a true body of our nature. And because it is the special feature of friendship to live together with friends, as the Philosopher says *(Ethic.* ix), He promises us His bodily presence as a reward, saying (Matth. xxiv. 28): *Where the body is, there shall the eagles be gathered together.* Yet meanwhile in our pilgrimage He does not deprive us of His bodily presence; but unites us with Himself in this sacrament through the truth of His body and blood. Hence (John vi. 57) he says: *He that eateth My flesh, and drinketh My blood, abideth in Me, and I in him.* Hence this sacrament is the sign of supreme charity, and the uplifter of our hope, from such familiar union of Christ with us.

Thirdly, it belongs to the perfection of faith, which concerns His humanity just as it does His Godhead, according to John xiv. 1: *You believe in God, believe also in Me.* And since faith is of things unseen, as Christ shows us His Godhead invisibly, so also in this sacrament He shows us His flesh in an invisible manner.

Some men accordingly, not paying heed to these things, have contended that Christ's body and blood are not in this sacrament except as in a sign, a thing to be rejected as heretical, since it is contrary to Christ's words. Hence Berengarius, who had been the first deviser of this heresy, was afterwards forced to withdraw his error, and to acknowledge the truth of the faith.

Reply Obj. 1. From this authority the aforesaid heretics have taken occasion to err from evilly understanding Augustine's words. For when Augustine says: *You are not to eat this body which you see,* he means not to exclude the truth of Christ's body, but that it was not to be eaten in this species in which it was seen by them. And by the words: *It is a mystery that I put before you; in its spiritual sense it will quicken you*, he intends not that the body of Christ is in this sacrament merely according to mystical signification, but *spiritually*, that is, invisibly, and by the power of the spirit. Hence *(Tract.* xxvii), expounding John vi. 64—*the flesh profiteth nothing*, he says: *Yea, but as they understood it, for they understood that the flesh was to be eaten as it is divided piecemeal in a dead body, or as sold in the shambles, not as it is quickened by the spirit. . . . Let the spirit draw nigh to the flesh . . . then the flesh profiteth very much: for if the flesh profiteth nothing, the Word had not been made flesh, that It might dwell among us.*

Reply Obj. 2. That saying of Augustine and all others like it are to be understood of Christ's body as it is beheld in its proper species; according as our Lord Himself says (Matth. xxvi. 11): *But Me you have not always.* Nevertheless He is invisibly under the species of this sacrament, wherever this sacrament is performed.

Reply Obj. 3. Christ's body is not in this sacrament in the same way as a body is in a place, which by its dimensions is commensurate with the place; but in a special manner which is proper to this sacrament. Hence we say that Christ's body is upon many altars, not as in different places, but *sacramentally:* and thereby we do not understand that Christ is there only as in a sign, although a sacrament is a kind of sign; but that Christ's body is here after a fashion proper to this sacrament, as stated above.

Reply Obj. 4. This argument holds good of Christ's bodily presence, as He is present after the manner of a body, that is, as it is in its visible appearance, but not as it is spiritually, that is, invisibly, after the manner and by the virtue of the spirit. Hence Augustine *(Tract.* xxvii, *in Joan.)* says: *If thou hast understood* Christ's words spiritually concerning His flesh, *they are spirit and life to thee; if thou hast understood them carnally, they are also spirit and life, but not to thee.*

SECOND ARTICLE

Whether in This Sacrament the Substance of the Bread and Wine Remains after the Consecration?

We proceed thus to the Second Article:—

Objection 1. It seems that the substance of the bread and wine does remain in this sacrament after the consecration: because Damascene says *(De Fide Orthod.* iv): *Since it is customary for men to eat bread and drink wine, God has wedded his Godhead to them, and made them His body and blood:* and further on: *The bread of communication is not simple bread, but is united to the Godhead.* But wedding together belongs to things actually existing. Therefore the bread and wine are at the same time, in this sacrament, with the body and the blood of Christ.

Obj. 2. Further, there ought to be conformity between the sacraments. But in the other sacraments the substance of the matter remains, like the substance of water in Baptism, and the substance of chrism in Confirmation. Therefore the substance of the bread and wine remains also in this sacrament.

Obj. 3. Further, bread and wine are made use of in this sacrament, inasmuch as they denote ecclesiastical unity, as *one bread is made from many grains and wine from many grapes*, as Augustine says in his book on the Creed *(Tract.* xxvi, *in Joan.).* But this belongs to the substance of bread and wine. Therefore, the substance of the bread and wine remains in this sacrament.

On the contrary, Ambrose says *(De Sacram.* iv): *Although the figure of the bread and wine be seen, still, after the Consecration, they are to be believed to be nothing else than the body and blood of Christ.*

I answer that, Some have held that the substance of the bread and wine remains in this sacrament after the consecration. But this opinion cannot stand: first of all, because by such an opinion the truth of this sacrament is destroyed, to which it belongs that Christ's true body exists in this sacrament; which indeed was not there before the consecration. Now a thing cannot be in any place, where it was not previously, except by change of place, or by the conversion of another thing into itself; just as fire begins anew to be in some house, either because it is carried thither, or because it is generated there. Now it is evident that Christ's body does not begin to be present in this sacrament by local motion. First of all, because it would follow that it would cease to be in heaven: for what is moved locally does not come anew to some place unless it quit the former one. Secondly, because every body moved locally passes through all intermediary spaces, which cannot be said here. Thirdly, because it is not possible for one movement of the same body moved locally to be terminated in different places at the one time, whereas the body of Christ under this sacrament begins at the one time to be in several places. And consequently it remains that Christ's body cannot begin to be anew in this sacrament except by change of the substance of bread into itself. But what is changed into another thing, no longer remains after such change. Hence the conclusion is that, saving the truth of this sacrament, the substance of the bread cannot remain after the consecration.

Secondly, because this position is contrary to the form of this sacrament, in which it is said: *This is My body,* which would not be true if the substance of the bread were to remain there; for the substance of bread never is the body of Christ. Rather should one say in that case: *Here is My body.*

Thirdly, because it would be opposed to the veneration of this sacrament, if any substance were there, which could not be adored with adoration of latria.

Fourthly, because it is contrary to the rite of the Church, according to which it is not lawful to take the body of Christ after bodily food, while it is nevertheless lawful to take one consecrated host after another. Hence this opinion is to be avoided as heretical.

Reply Obj. 1. God *wedded His Godhead,* i.e. His Divine power, to the bread and wine, not that these may remain in this sacrament, but in order that He may make from them His body and blood.

Reply Obj. 2. Christ is not really present in the other sacraments, as in this; and therefore the substance of the matter remains in the other sacraments, but not in this.

Reply Obj. 3. The species which remain in this sacrament, as shall be said later (A. 5), suffice for its signification; because the nature of the substance is known by its accidents.

THIRD ARTICLE

Whether the Substance of the Bread or Wine Is Annihilated after the Consecration of This Sacrament, or Dissolved into Their Original Matter?

We proceed thus to the Third Article:—

Objection 1. It seems that the substance of the bread is annihilated after the consecration of this sacrament, or dissolved into its original matter. For whatever is corporeal must be somewhere. But the substance of bread, which is something corporeal, does not remain, in this sacrament, as stated above (A. 2); nor can we assign any place where it may be. Consequently it is nothing after the consecration. Therefore, it is either annihilated, or dissolved into its original matter.

Obj. 2. Further, what is the term *wherefrom* in every change exists no longer, except in the potentiality of matter; e.g. when air is changed into fire, the form of the air remains only in the potentiality of matter; and in like fashion when what is white becomes black. But in this sacrament the substance of the bread or of the wine is the *term wherefrom,* while the body or the blood of Christ is the *term whereunto:* for Ambrose says in *De Officiis (De Myster.* ix): *Before the bless-*

ing it is called another species, after the blessing the body of Christ is signified. Therefore, when the consecration takes place, the substance of the bread or wine no longer remains, unless perchance dissolved into its (original) matter.

Obj. 3. Further, one of two contradictories must be true. But this proposition is false: *After the consecration the substance of the bread or wine is something.* Consequently, this is true: *The substance of the bread or wine is nothing.*

On the contrary, Augustine says (Q. 83): *God is not the cause of tending to nothing.* But this sacrament is wrought by Divine power. Therefore, in this sacrament the substance of the bread or wine is not annihilated.

I answer that, Because the substance of the bread and wine does not remain in this sacrament, some, deeming that it is impossible for the substance of the bread and wine to be changed into Christ's flesh and blood, have maintained that by the consecration, the substance of the bread and wine is either dissolved into the original matter, or that it is annihilated.

Now the original matter into which mixed bodies can be dissolved is the four elements. For dissolution cannot be made into primary matter, so that a subject can exist without a form, since matter cannot exist without a form. But since after the consecration nothing remains under the sacramental species except the body and the blood of Christ, it will be necessary to say that the elements into which the substance of the bread and wine is dissolved, depart from thence by local motion, which would be perceived by the senses.—In like manner also the substance of the bread or wine remains until the last instant of the consecration; but in the last instant of the consecration there is already present there the substance of the body or blood of Christ, just as the form is already present in the last instant of generation. Hence no instant can be assigned in which the original matter can be there. For it cannot be said that the substance of the bread or wine is dissolved gradually into the original matter, or that it successively quits the species, for if this began to be done in the last instant of its consecration, then at the one time under part of the host there would be the body of Christ together with the substance of bread, which is contrary to what has been said above (A. 2). But if this begin to come to pass before the consecration, there will then be a time in which under one part of the host there will be neither the substance of bread nor the body of Christ, which is not fitting. They seem indeed to have taken this into careful consideration; wherefore they formulated their proposition with an alternative, viz. that (the substance) may be annihilated. But even this cannot stand, because no way can be assigned whereby Christ's true body can begin to be in this sacrament, except by the change of the substance of bread into it, which change is excluded the moment we admit either annihilation of the substance of the bread, or dissolution into the original matter. —Likewise no cause can be assigned for such dissolution or annihilation, since the effect of the sacrament is signified by the form: *This is My body.* Hence it is clear that the aforesaid opinion is false.

Reply Obj. 1. The substance of the bread or wine, after the consecration, remains neither under the sacramental species, nor elsewhere; yet it does not follow that it is annihilated; for it is changed into the body of Christ; just as if the air, from which fire is generated, be not there or elsewhere, it does not follow that it is annihilated.

Reply Obj. 2. The form, which is the term *wherefrom*, is not changed into another form; but one form succeeds another in the subject; and therefore the first form remains only in the potentiality of matter. But here the substance of the bread is changed into the body of Christ, as stated above. Hence the conclusion does not follow.

Reply Obj. 3. Although after the consecration this proposition is false: *The substance of the bread is something*, still that into which the substance of the bread is changed, is something, and consequently the substance of the bread is not annihilated.

FOURTH ARTICLE

Whether Bread Can Be Converted into the Body of Christ?

We proceed thus to the Fourth Article:—

Objection 1. It seems that bread cannot be converted into the body of Christ. For conversion is a kind of change. But in every change there must be some subject, which from being previously in potentiality is now in act; because as is said in *Phys.* iii: *motion is the act of a thing existing in potentiality.* But no subject can be assigned for the substance of the bread and of the body of Christ, because it is of the very nature of substance for it *not to be in a subject*, as it is said in *Prædic.* iii. Therefore it is not possible for the whole substance of the bread to be converted into the body of Christ.

Obj. 2. Further, the form of the thing into which another is converted, begins anew to inhere in the matter of the thing converted into it: as when air is changed into fire not

already existing, the form of fire begins anew to be in the matter of the air; and in like manner when food is converted into non-pre-existing man, the form of the man begins to be anew in the matter of the food. Therefore, if bread be changed into the body of Christ, the form of Christ's body must necessarily begin to be in the matter of the bread, which is false. Consequently, the bread is not changed into the substance of Christ's body.

Obj. 3. Further, when two things are diverse, one never becomes the other, as whiteness never becomes blackness, as is stated in *Phys.* i. But since two contrary forms are of themselves diverse, as being the principles of formal difference, so two signate matters are of themselves diverse, as being the principles of material distinction. Consequently, it is not possible for this matter of bread to become this matter whereby Christ's body is individuated, and so it is not possible for this substance of bread to be changed into the substance of Christ's body.

On the contrary, Eusebius Emesenus says: *To thee it ought neither to be a novelty nor an impossibility that earthly and mortal things be changed into the substance of Christ.*

I answer that, As stated above (A. 2), since Christ's true body is in this sacrament, and since it does not begin to be there by local motion, nor is it contained therein as in a place, as is evident from what was stated above (A. 1, *ad* 2), it must be said then that it begins to be there by conversion of the substance of bread into itself.

Yet this change is not like natural changes, but is entirely supernatural, and effected by God's power alone. Hence Ambrose says* [(*De Sacram.* iv): *See how Christ's word changes nature's laws, as He wills: a man is not wont to be born save of man and woman: see therefore that against the established law and order a man is born of a Virgin:* and] (*De Myster.* iv): *It is clear that a Virgin begot beyond the order of nature: and what we make is the body from the Virgin. Why, then, do you look for nature's order in Christ's body, since the Lord Jesus was Himself brought forth of a Virgin beyond nature?* Chrysostom likewise (*Hom.* xlvii), commenting on John vi. 64,—*The words which I have spoken to you,* namely, of this sacrament, *are spirit and life,* says: i.e. *spiritual, having nothing carnal, nor natural consequence; but they are rent from all such necessity which exists upon earth, and from the laws here established.*

For it is evident that every agent acts according as it is in act. But every created agent is limited in its act, as being of a determinate genus and species: and consequently the action

* The passage in the brackets is not in the Leonine edition.

of every created agent bears upon some determinate act. Now the determination of every thing in actual existence comes from its form. Consequently, no natural or created agent can act except by changing the form in something; and on this account every change made according to nature's laws is a formal change. But God is infinite act, as stated in the First Part (Q. 7, A. 1; Q. 26, A. 2); hence His action extends to the whole nature of being. Therefore He can work not only formal conversion, so that diverse forms succeed each other in the same subject; but also the change of all being, so that, to wit, the whole substance of one thing be changed into the whole substance of another. And this is done by Divine power in this sacrament; for the whole substance of the bread is changed into the whole substance of Christ's body, and the whole substance of the wine into the whole substance of Christ's blood. Hence this is not a formal, but a substantial conversion; nor is it a kind of natural movement: but, with a name of its own, it can be called *transubstantiation*.

Reply Obj. 1. This objection holds good in respect of formal change, because it belongs to a form to be in matter or in a subject; but it does not hold good in respect of the change of the entire substance. Hence, since this substantial change implies a certain order of substances, one of which is changed into the other, it is in both substances as in a subject, just as order and number.

Reply Obj. 2. This argument also is true of formal conversion or change, because, as stated above (*ad* 1), a form must be in some matter or subject. But this is not so in a change of the entire substance; for in this case no subject is possible.

Reply Obj. 3. Form cannot be changed into form, nor matter into matter by the power of any finite agent. Such a change, however, can be made by the power of an infinite agent, which has control over all being, because the nature of being is common to both forms and to both matters; and whatever there is of being in the one, the author of being can change into whatever there is of being in the other, withdrawing that whereby it was distinguished from the other.

FIFTH ARTICLE

Whether the Accidents of the Bread and Wine Remain in This Sacrament after the Change?

We proceed thus to the Fifth Article:—

Objection 1. It seems that the accidents of the bread and wine do not remain in this sacrament. For when that which comes first is removed, that which follows is also taken away. But substance is naturally before acci-

dent, as is proved in *Metaph.* vii. Since, then, after consecration, the substance of the bread does not remain in this sacrament, it seems that its accidents cannot remain.

Obj. 2. Further, there ought not to be any deception in a sacrament of truth. But we judge of substance by accidents. It seems, then, that human judgment is deceived, if, while the accidents remain, the substance of the bread does not. Consequently this is unbecoming to this sacrament.

Obj. 3. Further, although our faith is not subject to reason, still it is not contrary to reason, but above it, as was said in the beginning of this work (P. I., Q. 1, A. 6, *ad* 2; A. 8). But our reason has its origin in the senses. Therefore our faith ought not to be contrary to the senses, as it is when sense judges that to be bread which faith believes to be the substance of Christ's body. Therefore it is not befitting this sacrament for the accidents of bread to remain subject to the senses, and for the substance of bread not to remain.

Obj. 4. Further, what remains after the change has taken place seems to be the subject of change. If therefore the accidents of the bread remain after the change has been effected, it seems that the accidents are the subject of the change. But this is impossible; for *an accident cannot have an accident* (*Metaph.* iii). Therefore the accidents of the bread and wine ought not to remain in this sacrament.

On the contrary, Augustine says in his book on the Sentences of Prosper (Lanfranc, *De Corp. et Sang. Dom.* xiii): *Under the species which we behold, of bread and wine, we honor invisible things,* i.e. *flesh and blood.*

I answer that, It is evident to sense that all the accidents of the bread and wine remain after the consecration. And this is reasonably done by Divine providence. First of all, because it is not customary, but horrible, for men to eat human flesh, and to drink blood. And therefore Christ's flesh and blood are set before us to be partaken of under the species of those things which are the more commonly used by men, namely, bread and wine. Secondly, lest this sacrament might be derided by unbelievers, if we were to eat our Lord under His own species. Thirdly, that while we receive our Lord's body and blood invisibly, this may redound to the merit of faith.

Reply Obj. 1. As is said in the book *De Causis*, an effect depends more on the first cause than on the second. And therefore by God's power, which is the first cause of all things, it is possible for that which follows to remain, while that which is first is taken away.

Reply Obj. 2. There is no deception in this sacrament; for the accidents which are discerned by the senses are truly present. But the intellect, whose proper object is substance, as is said in *De Anima* iii, is preserved by faith from deception.

And this serves as answer to the third argument; because faith is not contrary to the senses, but concerns things to which sense does not reach.

Reply Obj. 4. This change has not properly a subject, as was stated above (A. 4, *ad* 1); nevertheless the accidents which remain have some resemblance of a subject.

SIXTH ARTICLE

Whether the Substantial Form of the Bread Remains in This Sacrament after the Consecration?

We proceed thus to the Sixth Article:—

Objection 1. It seems that the substantial form of the bread remains in this sacrament after the consecration. For it has been said (A. 5) that the accidents remain after the consecration. But since bread is an artificial thing, its form is an accident. Therefore it remains after the consecration.

Obj. 2. Further, the form of Christ's body is His soul: for it is said in *De Anima* ii, that the soul *is the act of a physical body which has life in potentiality.* But it cannot be said that the substantial form of the bread is changed into the soul. Therefore it appears that it remains after the consecration.

Obj. 3. Further, the proper operation of a things follows its substantial form. But what remains in this sacrament, nourishes, and performs every operation which bread would do were it present. Therefore the substantial form of the bread remains in this sacrament after the consecration.

On the contrary, The substantial form of bread is of the substance of bread. But the substance of the bread is changed into the body of Christ, as stated above (AA. 2, 3, 4). Therefore the substantial form of the bread does not remain.

I answer that, Some have contended that after the consecration not only do the accidents of the bread remain, but also its substantial form. But this cannot be. First of all, because if the substantial form of the bread were to remain, nothing of the bread would be changed into the body of Christ, excepting the matter; and so it would follow that it would be changed, not into the whole body of Christ, but into its matter, which is repugnant to the form of the sacrament, wherein it is said: *This is My body.*

Secondly, because if the substantial form of the bread were to remain, it would remain either in matter, or separated from matter. The first cannot be, for if it were to remain

in the matter of the bread, then the whole substance of the bread would remain, which is against what was said above (A. 2). Nor could it remain in any other matter, because the proper form exists only in its proper matter.—But if it were to remain separate from matter, it would then be an actually intelligible form, and also an intelligence; for all forms separated from matter are such.

Thirdly, it would be unbefitting this sacrament: because the accidents of the bread remain in this sacrament, in order that the body of Christ may be seen under them, and not under its proper species, as stated above (A. 5).

And therefore it must be said that the substantial form of the bread does not remain.

Reply Obj. 1. There is nothing to prevent art from making a thing whose form is not an accident, but a substantial form; as frogs and serpents can be produced by art: for art produces such forms not by its own power, but by the power of natural energies. And in this way it produces the substantial forms of bread, by the power of fire baking the matter made up of flour and water.

Reply Obj. 2. The soul is the form of the body, giving it the whole order of perfect being, i.e. being, corporeal being, and animated being, and so on. Therefore the form of the bread is changed into the form of Christ's body, according as the latter gives corporeal being, but not according as it bestows animated being.

Reply Obj. 3. Some of the operations of bread follow it by reason of the accidents, such as to affect the senses, and such operations are found in the species of the bread after the consecration on account of the accidents which remain. But some other operations follow the bread either by reason of the matter, such as that it is changed into something else, or else by reason of the substantial form, such as an operation consequent upon its species, for instance, that it *strengthens man's heart* (Ps. ciii. 15); and such operations are found in this sacrament, not on account of the form or matter remaining, but because they are bestowed miraculously upon the accidents themselves, as will be said later (Q. 77, A. 3, *ad* 2, 3; AA. 5, 6).

SEVENTH ARTICLE

Whether This Change Is Wrought Instantaneously?

We proceed thus to the Seventh Article:—

Objection 1. It seems that this change is not wrought instantaneously, but successively. For in this change there is first the substance of bread, and afterwards the substance of Christ's body. Neither, then, is in the same instant, but in two instants. But there is a mid-time between every two instants. Therefore this change must take place according to the succession of time, which is between the last instant in which the bread is there, and the first instant in which the body of Christ is present.

Obj. 2. Further, in every change something is *in becoming* and something is *in being.* But these two things do not exist at the one time, for, what is *in becoming,* is not yet, whereas what is *in being,* already is. Consequently, there is a before and an after in such change: and so necessarily the change cannot be instantaneous, but successive.

Obj. 3. Further, Ambrose says *(De Sacram.* iv) that this sacrament *is made by the words of Christ.* But Christ's words are pronounced successively. Therefore the change takes place successively.

On the contrary, This change is effected by a power which is infinite, to which it belongs to operate in an instant.

I answer that, A change may be instantaneous from a threefold reason. First on the part of the form, which is the terminus of the change. For, if it be a form that receives more and less, it is acquired by its subject successively, such as health; and therefore because a substantial form does not receive more and less, it follows that its introduction into matter is instantaneous.

Secondly on the part of the subject, which sometimes is prepared successively for receiving the form; thus water is heated successively. When, however, the subject itself is in the ultimate disposition for receiving the form, it receives it suddenly, as a transparent body is illuminated suddenly. Thirdly on the part of the agent, which possesses infinite power: wherefore it can instantly dispose the matter for the form. Thus it is written (Mark vii. 34) that when Christ had said, *"Ephpheta," which is "Be thou opened," immediately his ears were opened, and the string of his tongue was loosed.*

For these three reasons this conversion is instantaneous. First, because the substance of Christ's body which is the term of this conversion, does not receive more or less.—Secondly, because in this conversion there is no subject to be disposed successively.—Thirdly, because it is effected by God's infinite power.

Reply Obj. 1. Some* do not grant simply that there is a mid-time between every two instants. For they say that this is true of two instants referring to the same movement, but not if they refer to different things. Hence between the instant that marks the close of

rest, and another which marks the beginning of movement, there is no mid-time. But in this they are mistaken, because the unity of time and of instant, or even their plurality, is not taken according to movements of any sort, but according to the first movement of the heavens, which is the measure of all movement and rest.

Accordingly others grant this of the time which measures movement depending on the movement of the heavens. But there are some movements which are not dependent on tne movement of the heavens, nor measured by it, as was said in the First Part (Q. 53, A. 3) concerning the movements of the angels. Hence between two instants responding to those movements there is no mid-time.—But this is not to the point, because although the change in question has no relation of itself to the movement of the heavens, still it follows the pronouncing of the words, which (pronouncing) must necessarily be measured by the movement of the heavens. And therefore there must of necessity be a mid-time between every two signate instants in connection with that change.

Some say therefore that the instant in which the bread was last, and the instant in which the body of Christ is first, are indeed two in comparison with the things measured, but are one comparatively to the time measuring; as when two lines touch, there are two points on the part of the two lines, but one point on the part of the place containing them. But here there is no likeness, because instant and time is not the intrinsic measure of particular movements, as a line and point are of a body, but only the extrinsic measure, as place is to bodies.

Hence others say that it is the same instant in fact, but another according to reason. But according to this it would follow that things really opposite would exist together; for diversity of reason does not change a thing objectively.

And therefore it must be said that this change, as stated above, is wrought by Christ's words which are spoken by the priest, so that the last instant of pronouncing the words is the first instant in which Christ's body is in the sacrament; and that the substance of the bread is there during the whole preceding time. Of this time no instant is to be taken as proximately preceding the last one, because time is not made up of successive instants, as is proved in *Phys.* vi. And therefore a first instant can be assigned in which Christ's body is present; but a last instant cannot be assigned in which the substance of bread is there, but a last time can be assigned. And the

* *Cf.* Albert the Great, IV, Sent., Dist. xi; S. Bonaventure, IV, Sent., Dist. xi.

same holds good in natural changes, as is evident from the Philosopher (*Phys.* viii).

Reply Obj. 2. In instantaneous changes a thing is *in becoming,* and is *in being* simultaneously; just as becoming illuminated and to be actually illuminated are simultaneous: for in such, a thing is said to be *in being* according as it now is; but to be *in becoming,* according as it was not before.

Reply Obj. 3. As stated above (*ad* 1), this change comes about in the last instant of the pronouncing of the words; for then the meaning of the words is finished, which meaning is efficacious in the forms of the sacraments. And therefore it does not follow that this change is successive.

EIGHTH ARTICLE

Whether This Proposition Is False: The Body of Christ Is Made out of Bread?

We proceed thus to the Eighth Article:—

Objection 1. It seems that this proposition is false: *The body of Christ is made out of bread.* For everything out of which another is made, is that which is made the other; but not conversely: for we say that a black thing is made out of a white thing, and that a white thing is made black: and although we may say that a man becomes black, still we do not say that a black thing is made out of a man, as is shown in *Phys.* i. If it be true, then, that Christ's body is made out of bread, it will be true to say that bread is made the body of Christ. But this seems to be false, because the bread is not the subject of the making, but rather its term. Therefore, it is not said truly that Christ's body is made out of bread.

Obj. 2. Further, the term of *becoming* is something that *is,* or something that *is made.* But this proposition is never true: *The bread is the body of Christ;* or *The bread is made the body of Christ;* or again, *The bread will be the body of Christ.* Therefore it seems that not even this is true: *The body of Christ is made out of bread.*

Obj. 3. Further, everything out of which another is made is converted into that which is made from it. But this proposition seems to be false: *The bread is converted into the body of Christ,* because such conversion seems to be more miraculous than the creation of the world, in which it is not said that non-being is converted into being. Therefore it seems that this proposition likewise is false: *The body of Christ is made out of bread.*

Obj. 4. Further, that out of which something is made, can be that thing. But this proposition is false: *Bread can be the body of Christ.* Therefore this is likewise false: *The body of Christ is made out of bread.*

On the contrary, Ambrose says (*De Sa-*

cram. iv): *When the consecration takes place, the body of Christ is made out of the bread.*

I answer that, This conversion of bread into the body of Christ has something in common with creation, and with natural transmutation, and in some respect differs from both. For the order of the terms is common to these three; that is, that after one thing there is another (for, in creation there is being after non-being; in this sacrament, Christ's body after the substance of bread; in natural transmutation white after black, or fire after air); and that the aforesaid terms are not coexistent.

Now the conversion, of which we are speaking, has this in common with creation, that in neither of them is there any common subject belonging to either of the extremes; the contrary of which appears in every natural transmutation.

Again, this conversion has something in common with natural transmutation in two respects, although not in the same fashion. First of all because in both, one of the extremes passes into the other, as bread into Christ's body, and air into fire; whereas non-being is not converted into being. But this comes to pass differently on the one side and on the other; for in this sacrament the whole substance of the bread passes into the whole body of Christ; whereas in natural transmutation the matter of the one receives the form of the other, the previous form being laid aside. Secondly, they have this in common, that on both sides something remains the same; whereas this does not happen in creation: yet differently; for the same matter or subject remains in natural transmutation; whereas in this sacrament the same accidents remain.

From these observations we can gather the various ways of speaking in such matters. For, because in no one of the aforesaid three things are the extremes coexistent, therefore in none of them can one extreme be predicated of the other by the substantive verb of the present tense: for we do not say, *Non-being is being,* or, *Bread is the body of Christ,* or, *Air is fire,* or, *White is black.* Yet because of the relationship of the extremes in all of them we can use the preposition *ex* (*out of*), which denotes order; for we can truly and properly say that *being is made out of non-being,* and *out of bread, the body of Christ,* and *out of air, fire,* and *out of white, black.* But because in creation one of the extremes does not pass into the other, we cannot use the word *conversion* in creation, so as to say that *non-being is converted into being:* we can, however, use the word in this sacrament, just as in natural transmutation. But since in this sacrament the whole substance is converted into the whole substance, on that account this conversion is properly termed transubstantiation.

Again, since there is no subject of this conversion, the things which are true in natural conversion by reason of the subject, are not to be granted in this conversion. And in the first place indeed it is evident that potentiality to the opposite follows a subject, by reason whereof we say that *a white thing can be black,* or that *air can be fire;* although the latter is not so proper as the former: for the subject of whiteness, in which there is potentiality to blackness, is the whole substance of the white thing; since whiteness is not a part thereof; whereas the subject of the form of air is part thereof: hence when it is said, *Air can be fire,* it is verified by synecdoche by reason of the part. But in this conversion, and similarly in creation, because there is no subject, it is not said that one extreme can be the other, as that *non-being can be being,* or that *bread can be the body of Christ:* and for the same reason it cannot be properly said that *being is made of (de) non-being,* or that *the body of Christ is made of bread,* because this preposition *of (de)* denotes a consubstantial cause, which consubstantiality of the extremes in natural transmutations is considered according to something common in the subject. And for the same reason it is not granted that *bread will be the body of Christ,* or that it *may become the body of Christ,* just as it is not granted in creation that *non-being will be being,* or that *non-being may become being,* because this manner of speaking is verified in natural transmutations by reason of the subject: for instance, when we say that *a white thing becomes black,* or *a white thing will be black.*

Nevertheless, since in this sacrament, after the change, something remains the same, namely, the accidents of the bread, as stated above (A. 5), some of these expressions may be admitted by way of similitude, namely, that *bread is the body of Christ,* or, *bread will be the body of Christ,* or *the body of Christ is made of bread;* provided that by the word *bread* is not understood the substance of bread,

but in general *that which is contained under the species of bread,* under which species there is first contained the substance of bread, and afterwards the body of Christ.

Reply Obj. 1. That out of which something else is made, sometimes implies together with the subject, one of the extremes of the transmutation, as when it is said *a black thing is made out of a white one;* but sometimes it implies only the opposite or the extreme, as when it is said—*out of morning comes the day.* And so it is not granted that the latter becomes the former, that is, *that morning becomes the day.* So likewise in the matter in hand, although it may be said properly that *the body of Christ is made out of bread,* yet it is not said properly that *bread becomes the body of Christ,* except by similitude, as was said above.

Reply Obj. 2. That out of which another is made, will sometimes be that other because of the subject which is implied. And therefore, since there is no subject of this change, the comparison does not hold.

Reply Obj. 3. In this change there are many more difficulties than in creation, in which there is but this one difficulty, that something is made out of nothing; yet this belongs to the proper mode of production of the first cause, which presupposes nothing else. But in this conversion not only is it difficult for this whole to be changed into that whole, so that nothing of the former may remain (which does not belong to the common mode of production of a cause), but furthermore it has this difficulty that the accidents remain while the substance is destroyed, and many other difficulties of which we shall treat hereafter (Q. 77). Nevertheless the word *conversion* is admitted in this sacrament, but not in creation, as stated above.

Reply Obj. 4. As was observed above, potentiality belongs to the subject, whereas there is no subject in this conversion. And therefore it is not granted that bread can be the body of Christ: for this conversion does not come about by the passive potentiality of the creature, but solely by the active power of the Creator.

QUESTION 76

Of the Way in Which Christ Is in This Sacrament

(In Eight Articles)

WE have now to consider the manner in which Christ exists in this sacrament; and under this head there are eight points of inquiry: (1) Whether the whole Christ is under this sacrament? (2) Whether the entire Christ is under each species of the sacrament? (3) Whether the entire Christ is under every part of the species? (4) Whether all the dimensions of Christ's body are in this sacrament? (5) Whether the body of Christ is in this sacrament locally? (6) Whether after the consecration, the body of Christ is moved when the host or chalice is moved? (7) Whether Christ's body, as it is in this sacrament, can be seen by the eye? (8) Whether the true body of Christ remains in this sacrament when He is seen under the appearance of a child or of flesh?

FIRST ARTICLE

Whether the Whole Christ Is Contained under This Sacrament?

We proceed thus to the First Article:—

Objection 1. It seems that the whole Christ is not contained under this sacrament, because Christ begins to be in this sacrament by conversion of the bread and wine. But it is evident that the bread and wine cannot be changed either into the Godhead or into the soul of Christ. Since therefore Christ exists in three substances, namely, the Godhead, soul and body, as shown above (Q. 2, A. 5; Q. 5, AA. 1, 3), it seems that the entire Christ is not under this sacrament.

Obj. 2. Further, Christ is in this sacrament, forasmuch as it is ordained to the refection of the faithful, which consists in food and drink, as stated above (Q. 74, A. 1). But our Lord said (John vi. 56): *My flesh is meat indeed, and My blood is drink indeed.* Therefore, only the flesh and blood of Christ are contained in this sacrament. But there are many other parts of Christ's body, for instance, the nerves, bones, and such like. Therefore the entire Christ is not contained under this sacrament.

Obj. 3. Further, a body of greater quantity cannot be contained under the measure of a lesser. But the measure of the bread and wine is much smaller than the measure of Christ's body. Therefore it is impossible that the entire Christ be contained under this sacrament.

On the contrary, Ambrose says *(De Offic.): Christ is in this sacrament.*

I answer that, It is absolutely necessary to confess according to Catholic faith that the entire Christ is in this sacrament. Yet we must know that there is something of Christ in this sacrament in a twofold manner: first, as it were, by the power of the sacrament; secondly, from natural concomitance. By the power of the sacrament, there is under the species of this sacrament that into which the pre-existing substance of the bread and wine is changed, as expressed by the words of the form, which are effective in this as in the other sacraments; for instance, by the words —*This is My body,* or, *This is My blood.* But from natural concomitance there is also in this sacrament that which is really united with that thing wherein the aforesaid conversion is terminated. For if any two things be really united, then wherever the one is really, there

must the other also be: since things really united together are only distinguished by an operation of the mind.

Reply Obj. 1. Because the change of the bread and wine is not terminated at the Godhead or the soul of Christ, it follows as a consequence that the Godhead or the soul of Christ is in this sacrament not by the power of the sacrament, but from real concomitance. For since the Godhead never set aside the assumed body, wherever the body of Christ is, there, of necessity, must the Godhead be; and therefore it is necessary for the Godhead to be in this sacrament concomitantly with His body. Hence we read in the profession of faith at Ephesus (P. I., chap. xxvi): *We are made partakers of the body and blood of Christ, not as taking common flesh, nor as of a holy man united to the Word in dignity, but the truly life-giving flesh of the Word Himself.*

On the other hand, His soul was truly separated from His body, as stated above (Q. 50, A. 5). And therefore had this sacrament been celebrated during those three days when He was dead, the soul of Christ would not have been there, neither by the power of the sacrament, nor from real concomitance. But since *Christ rising from the dead dieth now no more* (Rom. vi. 9), His soul is always really united with His body. And therefore in this sacrament the body indeed of Christ is present by the power of the sacrament, but His soul from real concomitance.

Reply Obj. 2. By the power of the sacrament there is contained under it, as to the species of the bread, not only the flesh, but the entire body of Christ, that is, the bones, the nerves, and the like. And this is apparent from the form of this sacrament, wherein it is not said: *This is My flesh,* but—*This is My body.* Accordingly, when our Lord said (John vi. 56): *My flesh is meat indeed,* there the word flesh is put for the entire body, because according to human custom it seems to be more adapted for eating, as men commonly are fed on the flesh of animals, but not on the bones or the like.

Reply Obj. 3. As has been already stated (Q. 75, A. 5), after the consecration of the bread into the body of Christ, or of the wine into His blood, the accidents of both remain. From which it is evident that the dimensions of the bread or wine are not changed into the dimensions of the body of Christ, but substance into substance. And so the substance of Christ's body or blood is under this sacrament by the power of the sacrament, but not the dimensions of Christ's body or blood. Hence it is clear that the body of Christ is in this sacrament *by way of substance,* and not by way of quantity. But the proper totality of substance is contained indifferently in a small or large quantity; as the whole nature of air in a great or small amount of air, and the whole nature of a man in a big or small individual. Wherefore, after the consecration, the whole substance of Christ's body and blood is contained in this sacrament, just as the whole substance of the bread and wine was contained there before the consecration.

SECOND ARTICLE

Whether the Whole Christ Is Contained under Each Species of This Sacrament?

We proceed thus to the Second Article:—

Objection 1. It seems that the whole Christ is not contained under both species of this sacrament. For this sacrament is ordained for the salvation of the faithful, not by virtue of the species, but by virtue of what is contained under the species, because the species were there even before the consecration, from which comes the power of this sacrament. If nothing, then, be contained under one species, but what is contained under the other, and if the whole Christ be contained under both, it seems that one of them is superfluous in this sacrament.

Obj. 2. Further, it was stated above (A. 1, *ad* 1) that all the other parts of the body, such as the bones, nerves, and the like, are comprised under the name of flesh. But the blood is one of the parts of the human body, as Aristotle proves *(De Anima. Histor.* i). If, then, Christ's blood be contained under the species of bread, just as the other parts of the body are contained there, the blood ought not to be consecrated apart, just as no other part of the body is consecrated separately.

Obj. 3. Further, what is once *in being* cannot be again *in becoming*. But Christ's body has already begun to be in this sacrament by the consecration of the bread. Therefore, it cannot begin again to be there by the consecration of the wine; and so Christ's body will not be contained under the species of the wine, and accordingly neither the entire Christ. Therefore the whole Christ is not contained under each species.

On the contrary, The gloss on 1 Cor. xi. 25, commenting on the word *Chalice,* says that *under each species,* namely, of the bread and wine, *the same is received;* and thus it seems that Christ is entire under each species.

I answer that, After what we have said above (A. 1), it must be held most certainly that the whole Christ is under each sacramental species yet not alike in each. For the body of Christ is indeed present under the species of bread by the power of the sacrament, while the blood is there from real concomitance, as stated above (A. 1, *ad* 1) in regard to the soul and Godhead of Christ; and under the species of wine the blood is present by the power of the sacrament, and His body by real concomitance, as is also His soul and Godhead: because now Christ's blood is not separated from His body, as it was at the time of His Passion and death. Hence if this sacrament had been celebrated then, the body of Christ would have been under the species of the bread, but without the blood; and, under the species of the wine, the blood would have been present without the body, as it was then, in fact.

Reply Obj. 1. Although the whole Christ is under each species, yet it is so not without purpose. For in the first place this serves to represent Christ's Passion, in which the blood was separated from the body; hence in the form for the consecration of the blood mention is made of its shedding. Secondly, it is in keeping with the use of this sacrament, that Christ's body be shown apart to the faithful as food, and the blood as drink. Thirdly, it is in keeping with its effect, in which sense it was stated above (Q. 74, A. 1) that *the body is offered for the salvation of the body, and the blood for the salvation of the soul.*

Reply Obj. 2. In Christ's Passion, of which this is the memorial, the other parts of the body were not separated from one another, as the blood was, but the body remained entire, according to Exod. xii. 46: *You shall not break a bone thereof.* And therefore in this sacrament the blood is consecrated apart from the body, but no other part is consecrated separately from the rest.

Reply Obj. 3. As stated above, the body of Christ is not under the species of wine by the power of the sacrament, but by real concomitance: and therefore by the consecration of the wine the body of Christ is not there of itself, but concomitantly.

THIRD ARTICLE

Whether Christ Is Entire under Every Part of the Species of the Bread and Wine?

We proceed thus to the Third Article:—

Objection 1. It seems that Christ is not entire under every part of the species of bread and wine. Because those species can be divided infinitely. If therefore Christ be entirely under every part of the said species, it would follow that He is in this sacrament an infinite number of times: which is unreasonable; because the infinite is repugnant not only to nature, but likewise to grace.

Obj. 2. Further, since Christ's is an organic body, it has parts determinately distant; for a determinate distance of the individual parts from each other is of the very nature of an organic body, as that of eye from eye, and eye from ear. But this could not be so, if Christ were entire under every part of the species; for every part would have to be under every other part, and so where one part would be, there another part would be. It cannot be then that the entire Christ is under every part of the host or of the wine contained in the chalice.

Obj. 3. Further, Christ's body always retains the true nature of a body, nor is it ever changed into a spirit. Now it is the nature of a body for it to be *quantity having position (Predic.* iv). But it belongs to the nature of this quantity that the various parts exist in various parts of place. Therefore, apparently it is impossible for the entire Christ to be under every part of the species.

On the contrary, Augustine says in a sermon (Gregory, *Sacramentarium*): *Each receives Christ the Lord, Who is entire under every morsel, nor is He less in each portion, but bestows Himself entire under each.*

I answer that, As was observed above (A. 1, *ad* 3), because the substance of Christ's body is in this sacrament by the power of the sacrament, while dimensive quantity is there by reason of real concomitance, consequently Christ's body is in this sacrament substantively, that is, in the way in which substance is under dimensions, which means, not in the way in which the dimensive quantity of a body is under the dimensive quantity of place.

Now it is evident that the whole nature of a substance is under every part of the dimensions under which it is contained; just as the entire nature of air is under every part of air, and the entire nature of bread under every part of bread; and this indifferently, whether the dimensions be actually divided (as when the air is divided or the bread cut), or whether they be actually undivided, but potentially divisible. And therefore it is manifest that the entire Christ is under every part of the species of the bread, even while the host remains entire, and not merely when it is broken, as some say, giving the example of an image which appears in a mirror, which appears as one in the unbroken mirror, whereas when the mirror is broken, there is an image in each part of the broken mirror: for the comparison is not perfect, because the multiplying of such images results in the broken mirror on account of the various reflections in the various parts of the mirror; but here there is only one consecration, whereby Christ's body is in this sacrament.

Reply Obj. 1. Number follows division, and therefore so long as quantity remains actually undivided, neither is the substance of any thing several times under its proper di-

mensions, nor is Christ's body several times under the dimensions of the bread; and consequently not an infinite number of times, but just as many times as it is divided into parts.

Reply Obj. 2. The determinate distance of parts in an organic body is based upon its dimensive quantity; but the nature of substance precedes even dimensive quantity. And since the conversion of the substance of the bread is terminated at the substance of the body of Christ, and since according to the manner of substance the body of Christ is properly and directly in this sacrament; such distance of parts is indeed in Christ's true body, which, however, is not compared to this sacrament according to such distance, but according to the manner of its substance, as stated above (A. 1, *ad* 3).

Reply Obj. 3. This argument is based on the nature of a body, arising from dimensive quantity. But it was said above (*ad* 2) that Christ's body is compared with this sacrament not by reason of dimensive quantity, but by reason of its substance, as already stated.

FOURTH ARTICLE

Whether the Whole Dimensive Quantity of Christ's Body Is in This Sacrament?

We proceed thus to the Fourth Article:—

Objection 1. It seems that the whole dimensive quantity of Christ's body is not in this sacrament. For it was said (A. 3) that Christ's entire body is contained under every part of the consecrated host. But no dimensive quantity is contained entirely in any whole, and in its every part. Therefore it is impossible for the entire dimensive quantity of Christ's body to be there.

Obj. 2. Further, it is impossible for two dimensive quantities to be together, even though one be separate from its subject, and the other in a natural body, as is clear from the Philosopher (*Metaph.* iii). But the dimensive quantity of the bread remains in this sacrament, as is evident to our senses. Consequently, the dimensive quantity of Christ's body is not there.

Obj. 3. Further, if two unequal dimensive quantities be set side by side, the greater will overlap the lesser. But the dimensive quantity of Christ's body is considerably larger than the dimensive quantity of the consecrated host, according to every dimension. Therefore, if the dimensive quantity of Christ's body be in this sacrament together with the dimensive quantity of the host, the dimensive quantity of Christ's body is extended beyond the quantity of the host, which nevertheless is not without the substance of Christ's body. Therefore, the substance of Christ's body will be in this sacrament even outside the species of the bread, which is unreasonable, since the substance of Christ's body is in this sacrament, only by the consecration of the bread, as stated above (A. 2). Consequently, it is impossible for the whole dimensive quantity of Christ's body to be in this sacrament.

On the contrary, The existence of the dimensive quantity of any body cannot be separated from the existence of its substance. But in this sacrament the entire substance of Christ's body is present, as stated above (AA. 1, 3). Therefore the entire dimensive quantity of Christ's body is in this sacrament.

I answer that, As stated above (A. 1), any part of Christ is in this sacrament in two ways: in one way, by the power of the sacrament; in another, from real concomitance. By the power of the sacrament the dimensive quantity of Christ's body is not in this sacrament; for, by the power of the sacrament that is present in this sacrament, whereat the conversion is terminated. But the conversion which takes place in this sacrament is terminated directly at the substance of Christ's body, and not at its dimensions; which is evident from the fact that the dimensive quantity of the bread remains after the consecration, while only the substance of the bread passes away.

Nevertheless, since the substance of Christ's body is not really deprived of its dimensive quantity and its other accidents, hence it comes that by reason of real concomitance the whole dimensive quantity of Christ's body and all its other accidents are in this sacrament.

Reply Obj. 1. The manner of being of every thing is determined by what belongs to it of itself, and not according to what is coupled accidentally with it: thus an object is present to the sight, according as it is white, and not according as it is sweet, although the same object may be both white and sweet; hence sweetness is in the sight after the manner of whiteness, and not after that of sweetness. Since, then, the substance of Christ's body is present on the altar by the power of this sacrament, while its dimensive quantity is there concomitantly and as it were accidentally, therefore the dimensive quantity of Christ's body is in this sacrament, not according to its proper manner (namely, that the whole is in the whole, and the individual parts in individual parts), but after the manner of substance, whose nature is for the whole to be in the whole, and the whole in every part.

Reply Obj. 2. Two dimensive quantities cannot naturally be in the same subject at the same time, so that each be there according to the proper manner of dimensive quantity. But in this sacrament the dimensive quantity of the bread is there after its proper manner, that is, according to commensuration: not so the dimensive quantity of Christ's body, for that is there after the manner of substance, as stated above (*ad* 1).

Reply Obj. 3. The dimensive quantity of Christ's body is in this sacrament not by way of commensuration, which is proper to quantity, and to which it belongs for the greater to be extended beyond the lesser; but in the way mentioned above (*ad* 1, 2).

FIFTH ARTICLE

Whether Christ's Body Is in This Sacrament As in a Place?

We proceed thus to the Fifth Article:—

Objection 1. It seems that Christ's body is in this sacrament as in a place. Because, to be in a place definitively or circumscriptively belongs to being in a place. But Christ's body seems to be definitively in this sacrament, because it is so present where the species of the bread and wine are, that it is nowhere else upon the altar: likewise it seems to be there circumscriptively, because it is so contained under the species of the consecrated host, that it neither exceeds it nor is exceeded by it. Therefore Christ's body is in this sacrament as in a place.

Obj. 2. Further, the place of the bread and wine is not empty, because nature abhors a vacuum; nor is the substance of the bread there, as stated above (Q. 75, A. 2); but only the body of Christ is there. Consequently the body of Christ fills that place. But whatever fills a place is there locally. Therefore the body of Christ is in this sacrament locally.

Obj. 3. Further, as stated above (A. 4), the body of Christ is in this sacrament with its dimensive quantity, and with all its accidents. But to be in a place is an accident of a body; hence *where* is numbered among the nine kinds of accidents. Therefore Christ's body is in this sacrament locally.

On the contrary, The place and the object placed must be equal, as is clear from the Philosopher *(Phys.* iv). But the place, where this sacrament is, is much less than the body of Christ. Therefore Christ's body is not in this sacrament as in a place.

I answer that, As stated above (A. 1, *ad* 3; A. 3), Christ's body is in this sacrament not after the proper manner of dimensive quantity, but rather after the manner of substance. But every body occupying a place is in the place according to the manner of dimensive quantity, namely, inasmuch as it is commensurate with the place according to its dimensive quantity. Hence it remains that Christ's body is not in this sacrament as in a place, but after the manner of substance, that is to say, in that way in which substance is contained by dimensions; because the substance of Christ's body succeeds the substance of bread in this sacrament: hence as the substance of bread was not locally under its dimensions, but after the manner of substance, so neither is the substance of Christ's body. Nevertheless the substance of Christ's body is not the subject of those dimensions, as was the substance of the bread: and therefore the substance of the bread was there locally by reason of its dimensions, because it was compared with that place through the medium of its own dimensions; but the substance of Christ's body is compared with that place through the medium of foreign dimensions, so that, on the contrary, the proper dimensions of Christ's body are compared with that place through the medium of substance; which is contrary to the notion of a located body.

Hence in no way is Christ's body locally in this sacrament.

Reply Obj. 1. Christ's body is not in this sacrament definitively, because then it would be only on the particular altar where this sacrament is performed; whereas it is in heaven under its own species, and on many other altars under the sacramental species. Likewise it is evident that it is not in this sacrament circumscriptively, because it is not there according to the commensuration of its own quantity, as stated above. But that it is not outside the superficies of the sacrament, nor on any other part of the altar, is due not to its being there definitively or circumscriptively, but to its being there by consecration and conversion of the bread and wine, as stated above (A. 1; Q. 75, A. 2 *sqq.*).

Reply Obj. 2. The place in which Christ's body is, is not empty; nor yet is it properly filled with the substance of Christ's body, which is not there locally, as stated above; but it is filled with the sacramental species, which have to fill the place either because of the nature of dimensions, or at least miraculously, as they also subsist miraculously after the fashion of substance.

Reply Obj. 3. As stated above (A. 4), the accidents of Christ's body are in this sacrament by real concomitance. And therefore those accidents of Christ's body which are intrinsic to it are in this sacrament. But to be in a place is an accident when compared with the extrinsic container. And therefore it is not necessary for Christ to be in this sacrament as in a place.

Whether Christ's Body Is in This Sacrament Movably?

We proceed thus to the Sixth Article:—

Objection 1. It seems that Christ's body is movably in this sacrament, because the Philosopher says (*Topic.* ii) that *when we are moved, the things within us are moved:* and this is true even of the soul's spiritual substance. *But Christ is in this sacrament,* as shown above (Q. 74, A. 1). Therefore He is moved when it is moved.

Obj. 2. Further, the truth ought to correspond with the figure. But, according to the commandment (Exod. xii. 10), concerning the Paschal Lamb, a figure of this sacrament, *there remained nothing until the morning.* Neither, therefore, if this sacrament be reserved until morning, will Christ's body be there; and so it is not immovably in this sacrament.

Obj. 3. Further, if Christ's body were to remain under this sacrament even until the morrow, for the same reason it will remain there during all coming time; for it cannot be said that it ceases to be there when the species pass, because the existence of Christ's body is not dependent on those species. Yet Christ does not remain in this sacrament for all coming time. It seems, then, that straightway on the morrow, or after a short time, He ceases to be under this sacrament. And so it seems that Christ is in this sacrament movably.

On the contrary, it is impossible for the same thing to be in motion and at rest, else contradictories would be verified of the same subject. But Christ's body is at rest in heaven. Therefore it is not movably in this sacrament.

I answer that, When any thing is one, as to subject, and manifold in being, there is nothing to hinder it from being moved in one respect, and yet to remain at rest in another just as it is one thing for a body to be white, and another thing, to be large; hence it can be moved as to its whiteness, and yet continue unmoved as to its magnitude. But in Christ, being in Himself and being under the sacrament are not the same thing, because when we say that He is under this sacrament, we express a kind of relationship to this sacrament. According to this being, then, Christ is not moved locally of Himself, but only accidentally, because Christ is not in this sacrament as in a place, as stated above (A. 5). But what is not in a place, is not moved of itself locally, but only according to the motion of the subject in which it is.

In the same way neither is it moved of itself according to the being which it has in this sacrament, by any other change whatever, as for instance, that it ceases to be under this sacrament: because whatever possesses unfailing existence of itself, cannot be the principle of failing; but when something else fails, then it ceases to be in it; just as God, Whose existence is unfailing and immortal, ceases to be in some corruptible creature because such corruptible creature ceases to exist. And in this way, since Christ has unfailing and incorruptible being, He ceases to be under this sacrament, not because He ceases to be, nor yet by local movement of His own, as is clear from what has been said, but only by the fact that the sacramental species cease to exist.

Hence it is clear that Christ, strictly speaking, is immovably in this sacrament.

Reply Obj. 1. This argument deals with accidental movement, whereby things within us are moved together with us. But with things which can of themselves be in a place, like bodies, it is otherwise than with things which cannot of themselves be in a place, such as forms and spiritual substances. And to this mode can be reduced what we say of Christ, being moved accidentally, according to the existence which He has in this sacrament, in which He is not present as in a place.

Reply Obj. 2. It was this argument which seems to have convinced those who held that Christ's body does not remain under this sacrament if it be reserved until the morrow. It is against these that Cyril says (*Ep.* lxxxiii): *Some are so foolish as to say that the mystical blessing departs from the sacrament, if any of its fragments remain until the next day: for Christ's consecrated body is not changed, and the power of the blessing, and the life-giving grace is perpetually in it.* Thus are all other consecrations irremovable so long as the consecrated things endure; on which account they are not repeated.—And although the truth corresponds with the figure, still the figure cannot equal it.

Reply Obj. 3. The body of Christ remains in this sacrament not only until the morrow, but also in the future, so long as the sacramental species remain: and when they cease, Christ's body ceases to be under them, not because it depends on them, but because the relationship of Christ's body to those species is taken away, in the same way as God ceases to be the Lord of a creature which ceases to exist.

SEVENTH ARTICLE

Whether the Body of Christ, As It Is in This Sacrament, Can Be Seen by Any Eye, at Least by a Glorified One?

We proceed thus to the Seventh Article:—

Objection 1. It seems that the body of Christ, as it is in this sacrament, can be seen by the eye, at least by a glorified one. For our eyes are hindered from beholding Christ's body in this sacrament, on account of the sacramental species veiling it. But the glorified eye cannot be hindered by anything from seeing bodies as they are. Therefore, the glorified eye can see Christ's body as it is in this sacrament.

Obj. 2. Further, the glorified bodies of the saints will be *made like to the body* of Christ's *glory,* according to Phil. iii. 21. But Christ's eye beholds Himself as He is in this sacrament. Therefore, for the same reason, every other glorified eye can see Him.

Obj. 3. Further, in the resurrection the saints will be equal to the angels, according to Luke xx. 36. But the angels see the body of Christ as it is in this sacrament, for even the devils are found to pay reverence thereto, and to fear it. Therefore, for like reason, the glorified eye can see Christ as He is in this sacrament.

On the contrary, As long as a thing remains the same, it cannot at the same time be seen by the same eye under diverse species. But the glorified eye sees Christ always, as He is in His own species, according to Isa. xxxiii. 17: *(His eyes) shall see the king in his beauty.* It seems, then, that it does not see Christ, as He is under the species of this sacrament.

I answer that, The eye is of two kinds, namely, the bodily eye properly so-called, and the intellectual eye, so-called by similitude. But Christ's body as it is in this sacrament cannot be seen by any bodily eye. First of all, because a body which is visible brings about an alteration in the medium, through its accidents. Now the accidents of Christ's body are in this sacrament by means of the substance; so that the accidents of Christ's body have no immediate relationship either to this sacrament or to adjacent bodies; consequently they do not act on the medium so as to be seen by any corporeal eye. Secondly, because, as stated above (A. 1, *ad* 3; A. 3), Christ's body is substantially present in this sacrament. But substance, as such, is not visible to the bodily eye, nor does it come under any one of the senses, nor under the imagination, but solely under the intellect, whose object is *what a thing is* (*De Anima.* iii).

And therefore, properly speaking, Christ's body, according to the mode of being which it has in this sacrament, is perceptible neither by the sense nor by the imagination, but only by the intellect, which is called the spiritual eye.

Moreover it is perceived differently by different intellects. For since the way in which Christ is in this sacrament is entirely supernatural, it is visible in itself to a supernatural, i.e. the Divine, intellect, and consequently to a beatified intellect, of angel or of man, which, through the participated glory of the Divine intellect, sees all supernatural things in the vision of the Divine Essence. But it can be seen by a wayfarer through faith alone, like other supernatural things. And not even the angelic intellect of its own natural power is capable of beholding it; consequently the devils cannot by their intellect perceive Christ in this sacrament, except through faith, to which they do not pay willing assent; yet they are convinced of it from the evidence of signs, according to James ii. 19: *The devils believe, and tremble.*

Reply Obj. 1. Our bodily eye, on account of the sacramental species, is hindered from beholding the body of Christ underlying them, not merely as by way of veil (just as we are hindered from seeing what is covered with any corporeal veil), but also because Christ's body bears a relation to the medium surrounding this sacrament, not through its own accidents, but through the sacramental species.

Reply Obj. 2. Christ's own bodily eye sees Himself existing under the sacrament, yet it cannot see the way in which it exists under the sacrament, because that belongs to the intellect. But it is not the same with any other glorified eye, because Christ's eye is under this sacrament, in which no other glorified eye is conformed to it.

Reply Obj. 3. No angel, good or bad, can see anything with a bodily eye, but only with the mental eye. Hence there is no parallel reason, as is evident from what was said above.

EIGHTH ARTICLE

Whether Christ's Body Is Truly There When Flesh or a Child Appears Miraculously in This Sacrament?

We proceed thus to the Eighth Article:—

Objection 1. It seems that Christ's body is not truly there when flesh or a child appears miraculously in this sacrament. Because His body ceases to be under this sacrament when the sacramental species cease to be present, as stated above (A. 6). But when flesh or a child appears, the sacramental species cease to be present. Therefore Christ's body is not truly there.

Obj. 2. Further, wherever Christ's body is, it is there either under its own species, or under those of the sacrament. But when such apparitions occur, it is evident that Christ is not present under His own species, because the entire Christ is contained in this sacrament, and He remains entire under the form in which He ascended to heaven: yet what appears miraculously in this sacrament is sometimes seen as a small particle of flesh, or at times as a small child. Now it is evident that He is not there under the sacramental species,

which is that of bread or wine. Consequently, it seems that Christ's body is not there in any way.

Obj. 3. Further, Christ's body begins to be in this sacrament by consecration and conversion, as was said above (Q. 75, AA. 2, 3, 4). But the flesh and blood which appear by miracle are not consecrated, nor are they converted into Christ's true body and blood. Therefore the body or the blood of Christ is not under those species.

On the contrary, When such apparition takes place, the same reverence is shown to it as was shown at first, which would not be done if Christ were not truly there, to Whom we show reverence of *latria.* Therefore, when such apparition occurs, Christ is under the sacrament.

I answer that, Such apparition comes about in two ways, when occasionally in this sacrament flesh, or blood, or a child, is seen. Sometimes it happens on the part of the beholders, whose eyes are so affected as if they outwardly saw flesh, or blood, or a child, while no change takes place in the sacrament. And this seems to happen when to one person it is seen under the species of flesh or of a child, while to others it is seen as before under the species of bread; or when to the same individual it appears for an hour under the appearance of flesh or a child, and afterwards under the appearance of bread. Nor is there any deception there, as occurs in the feats of magicians, because such species is divinely formed in the eye in order to represent some truth, namely, for the purpose of showing that Christ's body is truly under this sacrament; just as Christ without deception appeared to the disciples who were going to Emmaus. For Augustine says (*De Qq. Evang.* ii) that *when our pretense is referred to some significance, it is not a lie, but a figure of the truth.* And since in this way no change is made in the sacrament, it is manifest that, when such apparition occurs, Christ does not cease to be under this sacrament.

But it sometimes happens that such apparition comes about not merely by a change wrought in the beholders, but by an appearance which really exists outwardly. And this indeed is seen to happen when it is beheld by everyone under such an appearance, and it remains so not for an hour, but for a considerable time; and, in this case some think that it is the proper species of Christ's body. Nor does it matter that sometimes Christ's entire body is not seen there, but part of His flesh, or else that it is not seen in youthful guise, but in the semblance of a child, because it lies within the power of a glorified body for it to be seen by a non-glorified eye either entirely or in part, and under its own semblance or in strange guise, as will be said later (Suppl. Q. 85, AA. 2, 3).

But this seems unlikely. First of all, because Christ's body under its proper species can be seen only in one place, wherein it is definitively contained. Hence since it is seen in its proper species, and is adored in heaven, it is not seen under its proper species in this sacrament. Secondly, because a glorified body, which appears at will, disappears when it wills after the apparition; thus it is related (Luke xxiv. 31) that our Lord *vanished out of sight* of the disciples. But that which appears under the likeness of flesh in this sacrament, continues for a long time; indeed, one reads of its being sometimes enclosed, and, by order of many bishops, preserved in a pyx, which it would be wicked to think of Christ under His proper semblance.

Consequently, it remains to be said, that, while the dimensions remain the same as before, there is a miraculous change wrought in the other accidents, such as shape, color, and the rest, so that flesh, or blood, or a child, is seen. And, as was said already, this is not deception, because it is done *to represent the truth,* namely, to show by this miraculous apparition that Christ's body and blood are truly in this sacrament. And thus it is clear that as the dimensions remain, which are the foundation of the other accidents, as we shall see later on (Q. 77, A. 2), the body of Christ truly remains in this sacrament.

Reply Obj. 1. When such apparition takes place, the sacramental species sometimes continue entire in themselves; and sometimes only as to that which is principal, as was said above.

Reply Obj. 2. As stated above, during such apparitions Christ's proper semblance is not seen, but a species miraculously formed either in the eyes of the beholders, or in the sacramental dimensions themselves, as was said above.

Reply Obj. 3. The dimensions of the consecrated bread and wine continue, while a miraculous change is wrought in the other accidents, as stated above.

QUESTION 77

Of the Accidents Which Remain in This Sacrament

(In Eight Articles)

WE must now consider the accidents which remain in this sacrament; under which head there are eight points of inquiry: (1) Whether the accidents which remain are without a subject? (2) Whether dimensive quantity is the subject of the other accidents? (3) Whether such accidents can affect an extrinsic body? (4) Whether they can be corrupted? (5) Whether anything can be generated from them? (6) Whether they can nourish? (7) Of the breaking of the consecrated bread? (8) Whether anything can be mixed with the consecrated wine?

FIRST ARTICLE

Whether the Accidents Remain in This Sacrament without a Subject?

We proceed thus to the First Article:—

Objection 1. It seems that the accidents do not remain in this sacrament without a subject, because there ought not to be anything disorderly or deceitful in this sacrament of truth. But for accidents to be without a subject is contrary to the order which God established in nature; and furthermore it seems to savor of deceit, since accidents are naturally the signs of the nature of the subject. Therefore the accidents are not without a subject in this sacrament.

Obj. 2. Further, not even by miracle can the definition of a thing be severed from it, or the definition of another thing be applied to it; for instance, that, while man remains a man, he can be an irrational animal. For it would follow that contradictories can exist at the one time: for the *definition of a thing is what its name expresses,* as is said in *Metaph.* iv. But it belongs to the definition of an accident for it to be in a subject, while the definition of substance is that it must subsist of itself, and not in another. Therefore it cannot come to pass, even by miracle, that the accidents exist without a subject in this sacrament.

Obj. 3. Further, an accident is individuated by its subject. If therefore the accidents remain in this sacrament without a subject, they will not be individual, but general, which is clearly false, because thus they would not be sensible, but merely intelligible.

Obj. 4. Further, the accidents after the consecration of this sacrament do not obtain any composition. But before the consecration they were not composed either of matter and form, nor of existence *(quo est)* and essence *(quod est).* Therefore, even after consecration, they are not composite in either of these ways. But this is unreasonable, for thus they would be simpler than angels, whereas at the same time these accidents are perceptible to the senses. Therefore, in this sacrament the accidents do not remain without a subject.

On the contrary, Gregory says in an Easter Homily (Lanfranc, *De Corp. et Sang. Dom.* xx) that *the sacramental species are the names of those things which were there before, namely, of the bread and wine.* Therefore since the substance of the bread and the wine does not remain, it seems that these species remain without a subject.

I answer that, The species of the bread and wine, which are perceived by our senses to remain in this sacrament after consecration, are not subjected in the substance of the bread and wine, for that does not remain, as stated above (Q. 75, A. 2); nor in the substantial form, for that does not remain *(ibid.,* A. 6), and if it did remain, *it could not be a subject,* as Boëthius declares *(De Trin.* i). Furthermore it is manifest that these accidents are not subjected in the substance of Christ's body and blood, because the substance of the human body cannot in any way be affected by such accidents; nor is it possible for Christ's glorious and impassible body to be altered so as to receive these qualities.

Now there are some who say that they are in the surrounding atmosphere as in a subject. But even this cannot be: in the first place, because atmosphere is not susceptive of such accidents. Secondly, because these accidents are not where the atmosphere is, nay more, the atmosphere is displaced by the motion of these species. Thirdly, because accidents do not pass from subject to subject, so that the same identical accident which was first in one subject be afterwards in another; because an accident is individuated by the subject; hence it cannot come to pass for an accident remaining identically the same to be at one time in one subject, and at another time in another. Fourthly, since the atmosphere is not deprived of its own accidents, it would have at the one time its own accidents and others foreign to it. Nor can it be maintained that this is done miraculously in virtue of the consecration, because the words of consecration do not signify this, and they effect only what they signify.

Therefore it follows that the accidents continue in this sacrament without a subject. This can be done by Divine power: for since an effect depends more upon the first cause than on the second, God Who is the first cause both of substance and accident, can by His unlimited power preserve an accident in existence when the substance is withdrawn whereby it was preserved in existence as by its proper cause, just as without natural causes He can produce other effects of natural causes, even as He formed a human body in the Virgin's womb, *without the seed of man (Hymn for Christmas, First Vespers).*

Reply Obj. 1. There is nothing to hinder the common law of nature from ordaining a thing, the contrary of which is nevertheless ordained by a special privilege of grace, as is evident in the raising of the dead, and in the restoring of sight to the blind: even thus in human affairs, to some individuals some things are granted by special privilege which are outside the common law. And so, even though it be according to the common law of nature for an accident to be in a subject, still for a special reason, according to the order of grace, the accidents exist in this sacrament without a subject, on account of the reasons given above (Q. 75, A. 5).

Reply Obj. 2. Since being is not a genus, then being cannot be of itself the essence of either substance or accident. Consequently, the definition of substance is not—*a being of itself without a subject,* nor is the definition of accident—*a being in a subject;* but it belongs to the quiddity or essence of substance *to have existence not in a subject;* while it belongs to the quiddity or essence of accident *to have existence in a subject.* But in this sacrament it is not in virtue of their essence that accidents are not in a subject, but through the Divine power sustaining them; and consequently they do not cease to be accidents, because neither is the definition of accident withdrawn from them, nor does the definition of substance apply to them.

Reply Obj. 3. These accidents acquired individual being in the substance of the bread and wine; and when this substance is changed into the body and blood of Christ, they remain in that individuated being which they possessed before, hence they are individual and sensible.

Reply Obj. 4. These accidents had no being of their own nor other accidents, so long as the substance of the bread and wine remained; but their subjects had *such* being through them, just as snow is *white* through whiteness. But after the consecration the accidents which remain have being; hence they are compounded of existence and essence, as was said of the angels, in the First Part (Q. 50, A. 2, *ad* 3); and besides they have composition of quantitative parts.

SECOND ARTICLE

Whether in This Sacrament the Dimensive Quantity of the Bread or Wine Is the Subject of the Other Accidents?

We proceed thus to the Second Article:—

Objection 1. It seems that in this sacrament the dimensive quantity of the bread or wine is not the subject of the other accidents. For accident is not the subject of accident; because no form can be a subject, since to be a subject is a property of matter. But dimensive quantity is an accident. Therefore dimensive quantity cannot be the subject of the other accidents.

Obj. 2. Further, just as quantity is individuated by substance, so also are the other accidents. If, then, the dimensive quantity of the bread or wine remains individuated according to the being it had before, in which it is preserved, for like reason the other accidents remain individuated according to the existence which they had before in the substance. Therefore they are not in dimensive quantity as in a subject, since every accident is individuated by its own subject.

Obj. 3. Further, among the other accidents that remain, of the bread and wine, the senses perceive also rarity and density, which cannot be in dimensive quantity existing outside matter; because a thing is rare which has little matter under great dimensions; while a thing is dense which has much matter under small dimensions, as is said in *Phys.* iv. It does not seem, then, that dimensive quantity can be the subject of the accidents which remain in this sacrament.

Obj. 4. Further, quantity abstract from matter seems to be mathematical quantity, which is not the subject of sensible qualities. Since, then, the remaining accidents in this sacrament are sensible, it seems that in this sacrament they cannot be subjected in the dimensive quantity of the bread and wine that remains after consecration.

On the contrary, Qualities are divisible only accidentally, that is, by reason of the subject. But the qualities remaining in this sacrament are divided by the division of dimensive quantity, as is evident through our senses. Therefore, dimensive quantity is the subject of the accidents which remain in this sacrament.

I answer that, It is necessary to say that the other accidents which remain in this sacrament are subjected in the dimensive quantity of the bread and wine that remains: first of all, because something having quantity and color and affected by other accidents is perceived by the senses; nor is sense deceived in such. Secondly, because the first disposition of matter is dimensive quantity, hence Plato also assigned *great* and *small* as the first differences of matter (Aristotle, *Metaph.* iv). And because the first subject is matter, the consequence is that all other accidents are related to their subject through the medium of dimensive quantity; just as the first subject of color is said to be the surface, on which ac-

count some have maintained that dimensions are the substances of bodies, as is said in *Metaph.* iii. And since, when the subject is withdrawn, the accidents remain according to the being which they had before, it follows that all accidents remain founded upon dimensive quantity.

Thirdly, because, since the subject is the principle of individuation of the accidents, it is necessary for what is admitted as the subject of some accidents to be somehow the principle of individuation: for it is of the very notion of an individual that it cannot be in several; and this happens in two ways. First, because it is not natural to it to be in any one; and in this way immaterial separated forms, subsisting of themselves, are also individuals of themselves. Secondly, because a form, be it substantial or accidental, is naturally in someone indeed, not in several, as this whiteness, which is in this body. As to the first, matter is the principle of individuation of all inherent forms, because, since these forms, considered in themselves, are naturally in something as in a subject, from the very fact that one of them is received in matter, which is not in another, it follows that neither can the form itself thus existing be in another. As to the second, it must be maintained that the principle of individuation is dimensive quantity. For that something is naturally in another one solely, is due to the fact that that other is undivided in itself, and distinct from all others. But it is on account of quantity that substance can be divided, as is said in *Phys.* i. And therefore dimensive quantity itself is a particular principle of individuation in forms of this kind, namely, inasmuch as forms numerically distinct are in different parts of the matter. Hence also dimensive quantity has of itself a kind of individuation, so that we can imagine several lines of the same species, differing in position, which is included in the notion of this quantity; for it belongs to dimension for it to be *quantity having position* (Aristotle.—*Categ.* iv), and therefore dimensive quantity can be the subject of the other accidents, rather than the other way about.

Reply Obj. 1. One accident cannot of itself be the subject of another, because it does not exist of itself. But inasmuch as an accident is received in another thing, one is said to be the subject of the other, inasmuch as one is received in a subject through another, as the surface is said to be the subject of color. Hence when God makes an accident to exist of itself, it can also be of itself the subject of another.

Reply Obj. 2. The other accidents, even as they were in the substance of the bread, were individuated by means of dimensive quantity, as stated above. And therefore dimensive quantity is the subject of the other accidents remaining in this sacrament, rather than conversely.

Reply Obj. 3. Rarity and density are particular qualities accompanying bodies, by reason of their having much or little matter under dimensions; just as all other accidents likewise follow from the principles of substance. And consequently, as the accidents are preserved by Divine power when the substance is withdrawn, so, when matter is withdrawn, the qualities which go with matter, such as rarity and density, are preserved by Divine power.

Reply Obj. 4. Mathematical quantity abstracts not from intelligible matter, but from sensible matter, as is said in *Metaph.* vii. But matter is termed sensible because it underlies sensible qualities. And therefore it is manifest that the dimensive quantity, which remains in this sacrament without a subject, is not mathematical quantity.

THIRD ARTICLE

Whether the Species Remaining in This Sacrament Can Change External Objects?

We proceed thus to the Third Article:—

Objection 1. It seems that the species which remain in this sacrament cannot affect external objects. For it is proved in *Phys.* vii. that forms which are in matter are produced by forms that are in matter, but not from forms which are without matter, because like makes like. But the sacramental species are species without matter, since they remain without a subject, as is evident from what was said above (A. 1). Therefore they cannot affect other matter by producing any form in it.

Obj. 2. Further, when the action of the principal agent ceases, then the action of the instrument must cease, as when the carpenter rests, the hammer is moved no longer. But all accidental forms act instrumentally in virtue of the substantial form as the principal agent. Therefore, since the substantial form of the bread and wine does not remain in this sacrament, as was shown above (Q. 75, A. 6), it seems that the accidental forms which remain cannot act so as to change external matter.

Obj. 3. Further, nothing acts outside its species, because an effect cannot surpass its cause. But all the sacramental species are accidents. Therefore they cannot change external matter, at least as to a substantial form.

On the contrary, If they could not change external bodies, they could not be felt; for a thing is felt from the senses being changed by a sensible thing, as is said in *De Anima.* ii.

I answer that, Because everything acts in so far as it is an actual being, the consequence is that everything stands in the same relation to action as it does to being. Therefore, because, according to what was said above (A. 1), it is an effect of the Divine power that the sacramental species continue in the being which they had when the substance of the bread and wine was present, it follows that they continue in their action. Consequently they retain every action which they had while the substance of the bread and wine remained, now that the substance of the bread and wine has passed into the body and blood of Christ. Hence there is no doubt but that they can change external bodies.

Reply Obj. 1. The sacramental species, although they are forms existing without matter, still retain the same being which they had before in matter, and therefore as to their being they are like forms which are in matter.

Reply Obj. 2. The action of an accidental form depends upon the action of a substantial form in the same way as the being of accident depends upon the being of substance; and therefore, as it is an effect of Divine power that the sacramental species exist without substance, so is it an effect of Divine power that they can act without a substantial form, because every action of a substantial or accidental form depends upon God as the first agent.

Reply Obj. 3. The change which terminates in a substantial form is not effected by a substantial form directly, but by means of the active and passive qualities, which act in virtue of the substantial form. But by Divine power this instrumental energy is retained in the sacramental species, just as it was before: and consequently their action can be directed to a substantial form instrumentally, just in the same way as anything can act outside its species, not as by its own power, but by the power of the chief agent.

FOURTH ARTICLE

Whether the Sacramental Species Can Be Corrupted?

We proceed thus to the Fourth Article:—

Objection 1. It seems that the sacramental species cannot be corrupted, because corruption comes of the separation of the form from the matter. But the matter of the bread does not remain in this sacrament, as is clear from what was said above (Q. 75, A. 2). Therefore these species cannot be corrupted.

Obj. 2. Further, no form is corrupted except accidentally, that is, when its subject is corrupted; hence self-subsisting forms are incorruptible, as is seen in spiritual substances. But the sacramental species are forms without a subject. Therefore they cannot be corrupted.

Obj. 3. Further, if they be corrupted, it will either be naturally or miraculously. But they cannot be corrupted naturally, because no subject of corruption can be assigned as remaining after the corruption has taken place. Neither can they be corrupted miraculously, because the miracles which occur in this sacrament take place in virtue of the consecration, whereby the sacramental species are preserved: and the same thing is not the cause of preservation and of corruption. Therefore, in no way can the sacramental species be corrupted.

On the contrary, We perceive by our senses that the consecrated hosts become putrefied and corrupted.

I answer that, Corruption is *movement from being into non-being* (Aristotle, *Phys.* v). Now it has been stated (A. 3) that the sacramental species retain the same being as they had before when the substance of the bread was present. Consequently, as the being of those accidents could be corrupted while the substance of the bread and wine was present, so likewise they can be corrupted now that the substance has passed away.

But such accidents could have been previously corrupted in two ways: in one way, of themselves; in another way, accidentally. They could be corrupted of themselves, as by alteration of the qualities, and increase or decrease of the quantity, not in the way in which increase or decrease is found only in animated bodies, such as the substances of the bread and wine are not, but by addition or division; for, as is said in *Metaph.* iii, one dimension is dissolved by division, and two dimensions result; while on the contrary, by addition, two dimensions become one. And in this way such accidents can be corrupted manifestly after consecration, because the dimensive quantity which remains can receive division and addition; and since it is the subject of sensible qualities, as stated above (A. 1), it can likewise be the subject of their alteration, for instance, if the color or the savor of the bread or wine be altered.

An accident can be corrupted in another way, through the corruption of its subject, and in this way also they can be corrupted after consecration; for although the subject does not remain, still the being which they had in the subject does remain, which being is proper, and suited to the subject. And therefore such being can be corrupted by a contrary agent, as the substance of the bread or wine was subject to corruption, and, moreover, was not corrupted except by a preceding alteration regarding the accidents.

Nevertheless, a distinction must be made between each of the aforesaid corruptions;

because, when the body and the blood of Christ succeed in this sacrament to the substance of the bread and wine, if there be such change on the part of the accidents as would not have sufficed for the corruption of the bread and wine, then the body and blood of Christ do not cease to be under this sacrament on account of such change, whether the change be on the part of the quality, as for instance, when the color or the savor of the bread or wine is slightly modified; or on the part of the quantity, as when the bread or the wine is divided into such parts as to keep in them the nature of bread or of wine. But if the change be so great that the substance of the bread or wine would have been corrupted, then Christ's body and blood do not remain under this sacrament; and this either on the part of the qualities, as when the color, savor, and other qualities of the bread and wine are so altered as to be incompatible with the nature of bread or of wine; or else on the part of the quantity, as, for instance, if the bread be reduced to fine particles, or the wine divided into such tiny drops that the species of bread or wine no longer remain.

Reply Obj. 1. Since it belongs essentially to corruption to take away the being of a thing, in so far as the being of some form is in matter, it results that by corruption the form is separated from the matter. But if such being were not in matter, yet like such being as is in matter, it could be taken away by corruption, even where there is no matter; as takes place in this sacrament, as is evident from what was said above.

Reply Obj. 2. Although the sacramental species are forms not in matter, yet they have the being which they had in matter.

Reply Obj. 3. This corruption of species is not miraculous, but natural; nevertheless, it presupposes the miracle which is wrought in the consecration, namely, that those sacramental species retain without a subject, the same being as they had in a subject; just as a blind man, to whom sight is given miraculously, sees naturally.

FIFTH ARTICLE

Whether Anything Can Be Generated from the Sacramental Species?

We proceed thus to the Fifth Article:—

Objection 1. It seems that nothing can be generated from the sacramental species: because, whatever is generated, is generated out of some matter: for nothing is generated out of nothing, although by creation something is made out of nothing. But there is no matter underlying the sacramental species except that of Christ's body, and that body is incorruptible. Therefore it seems that nothing can be generated from the sacramental species.

Obj. 2. Further, things which are not of the same genus cannot spring from one another: thus a line is not made of whiteness. But accident and substance differ generically. Therefore, since the sacramental species are accidents, it seems that no substance can be generated from them.

Obj. 3. Further, if any corporeal substance be generated from them, such substance will not be without accident. Therefore, if any corporeal substance be generated from the sacramental species, then substance and accident would be generated from accident, namely, two things from one, which is impossible. Consequently, it is impossible for any corporeal substance to be generated out of the sacramental species.

On the contrary, The senses are witness that something is generated out of the sacramental species, either ashes, if they be burned, worms if they putrefy, or dust if they be crushed.

I answer that, Since *the corruption of one thing is the generation of another (De Gener.* i), something must be generated necessarily from the sacramental species if they be corrupted, as stated above (A. 4); for they are not corrupted in such a way that they disappear altogether, as if reduced to nothing; on the contrary, something sensible manifestly succeeds to them.

Nevertheless, it is difficult to see how anything can be generated from them. For it is quite evident that nothing is generated out of the body and blood of Christ which are truly there, because these are incorruptible. But if the substance, or even the matter, of the bread and wine were to remain in this sacrament, then, as some have maintained, it would be easy to account for this sensible object which succeeds to them. But that supposition is false, as was stated above (Q. 75, AA. 2, 4, 8).

Hence it is that others have said that the things generated have not sprung from the sacramental species, but from the surrounding atmosphere. But this can be shown in many ways to be impossible. In the first place, because when a thing is generated from another, the latter at first appears changed and corrupted; whereas no alteration or corruption appeared previously in the adjacent atmosphere; hence the worms or ashes are not generated therefrom.—Secondly, because the nature of the atmosphere is not such as to permit of such things being generated by such alterations. —Thirdly, because it is possible for many consecrated hosts to be burned or putrefied; nor would it be possible for an earthen body, large enough to be generated from the atmosphere,

unless a great and, in fact, exceedingly sensible condensation of the atmosphere took place.— Fourthly, because the same thing can happen to the solid bodies surrounding them, such as iron or stone, which remain entire after the generation of the aforesaid things. Hence this opinion cannot stand, because it is opposed to what is manifest to our senses.

And therefore others have said that the substance of the bread and wine returns during the corruption of the species, and so from the returning substance of the bread and wine, ashes or worms or something of the kind are generated.—But this explanation seems an impossible one. First of all, because if the substance of the bread and wine be converted into the body and blood of Christ, as was shown above (Q. 75, AA. 2, 4), the substance of the bread and wine cannot return, except the body and blood of Christ be again changed back into the substance of bread and wine, which is impossible: thus if air be turned into fire, the air cannot return without the fire being again changed into air. But if the substance of bread or wine be annihilated, it cannot return again, because what lapses into nothing does not return numerically the same. Unless perchance it be said that the said substance returns, because God creates anew another new substance to replace the first.—Secondly, this seems to be impossible, because no time can be assigned when the substance of the bread returns. For, from what was said above (A. 4; Q. 76, A. 6, *ad* 3), it is evident that while the species of the bread and wine remain, there remain also the body and blood of Christ, which are not present together with the substance of the bread and wine in this sacrament, according to what was stated above (Q. 75, A. 2). Hence the substance of the bread and wine cannot return while the sacramental species remain; nor, again, when these species pass away; because then the substance of the bread and wine would be without their proper accidents, which is impossible.—Unless perchance it be said that in the last instant of the corruption of the species there returns (not, indeed, the substance of bread and wine, because it is in that very instant that they have the being of the substance generated from the species, but) the matter of bread and wine; which matter, properly speaking, would be more correctly described as created anew, than as returning. And in this sense the aforesaid position might be held.

However, since it does not seem reasonable to say that anything takes place miraculously in this sacrament, except in virtue of the consecration itself, which does not imply either creation or return of matter, it seems better to say that in the actual consecration it is miraculously bestowed on the dimensive quantity of the bread and wine to be the subject of subsequent forms. Now this is proper to matter; and therefore as a consequence everything which goes with matter is bestowed on dimensive quantity; and therefore everything which could be generated from the matter of bread or wine, if it were present, can be generated from the aforesaid dimensive quantity of the bread or wine, not, indeed, by a new miracle, but by virtue of the miracle which has already taken place.

Reply Obj. 1. Although no matter is there out of which a thing may be generated, nevertheless dimensive quantity supplies the place of matter, as stated above.

Reply Obj. 2. Those sacramental species are indeed accidents, yet they have the act and power of substance, as stated above (A. 3).

Reply Obj. 3. The dimensive quantity of the bread and wine retains its own nature, and receives miraculously the power and property of substance; and therefore it can pass to both, that is, into substance and dimension.

SIXTH ARTICLE

Whether the Sacramental Species Can Nourish?

We proceed thus to the Sixth Article:—

Objection 1. It seems that the sacramental species cannot nourish, because, as Ambrose says *(De Sacram.* v), *it is not this bread that enters into our body, but the bread of everlasting life, which supports the substance of our soul.* But whatever nourishes enters into the body. Therefore this bread does not nourish: and the same reason holds good of the wine.

Obj. 2. Further, as is said in *De Gener.* ii, *We are nourished by the very things of which we are made.* But the sacramental species are accidents, whereas man is not made of accidents, because accident is not a part of substance. Therefore it seems that the sacramental species cannot nourish.

Obj. 3. Further, the Philosopher says *(De Anima* ii) that *food nourishes according as it is a substance, but it gives increase by reason of its quantity.* But the sacramental species are not a substance. Consequently they cannot nourish.

On the contrary, The Apostle speaking of this sacrament says (1 Cor. xi. 21): *One, indeed, is hungry, and another is drunk:* upon which the gloss observes that *he alludes to those who after the celebration of the sacred mystery, and after the consecration of the bread and wine, claimed their oblations, and not sharing them with others, took the whole, so as even to become intoxicated thereby.* But

this could not happen if the sacramental species did not nourish Therefore the sacramental species do nourish.

I answer that, This question presents no difficulty, now that we have solved the preceding question. Because, as stated in *De Anima.* ii, food nourishes by being converted into the substance of the individual nourished. Now it has been stated (A. 5) that the sacramental species can be converted into a substance generated from them. And they can be converted into the human body for the same reason as they can into ashes or worms. Consequently, it is evident that they nourish.

But the senses witness to the untruth of what some maintain; viz. that the species do not nourish as though they were changed into the human body, but merely refresh and hearten by acting upon the senses (as a man is heartened by the odor of meat, and intoxicated by the fumes of wine). Because such refreshment does not suffice long for a man, whose body needs repair owing to constant waste: and yet a man could be supported for long if he were to take hosts and consecrated wine in great quantity.

In like manner the statement advanced by others cannot stand, who hold that the sacramental species nourish owing to the remaining substantial form of the bread and wine: both because the form does not remain, as stated above (Q. 75, A. 6): and because to nourish is the act not of a form but rather of matter, which takes the form of the one nourished, while the form of the nourishment passes away: hence it is said in *De Anima* ii that nourishment is at first unlike, but at the end is like.

Reply Obj. 1. After the consecration bread can be said to be in this sacrament in two ways. First, as to the species, which retain the name of the previous substance, as Gregory says in an Easter Homily (Lanfranc,— *De Corp. et Sang. Dom.* xx). Secondly, Christ's very body can be called bread, since it is the mystical bread *coming down from heaven.* Consequently, Ambrose uses the word *bread* in this second meaning, when he says that *this bread does not pass into the body,* because, to wit, Christ's body is not changed into man's body, but nourishes his soul. But he is not speaking of bread taken in the first acceptation.

Reply Obj. 2. Although the sacramental species are not those things out of which the human body is made, yet they are changed into those things stated above.

Reply Obj. 3. Although the sacramental species are not a substance, still they have the virtue of a substance, as stated above.

SEVENTH ARTICLE

Whether the Sacramental Species Are Broken in This Sacrament?

We proceed thus to the Seventh Article:—

Objection 1. It seems that the sacramental species are not broken in this sacrament, because the Philosopher says in *Meteor.* iv that bodies are breakable owing to a certain disposition of the pores; a thing which cannot be attributed to the sacramental species. Therefore the sacramental species cannot be broken.

Obj. 2. Further, breaking is followed by sound. But the sacramental species emit no sound: because the Philosopher says (*De Anima* ii), that what emits sound is a hard body, having a smooth surface. Therefore the sacramental species are not broken.

Obj. 3. Further, breaking and mastication are seemingly of the same object. But it is Christ's true body that is eaten, according to John vi. 57: *He that eateth My flesh, and drinketh My blood.* Therefore it is Christ's body that is broken and masticated: and hence it is said in the confession of Berengarius: *I agree with the Holy Catholic Church, and with heart and lips I profess, that the bread and wine which are placed on the altar, are the true body and blood of Christ after consecration, and are truly handled and broken by the priest's hands, broken and crushed by the teeth of believers.* Consequently, the breaking ought not to be ascribed to the sacramental species.

On the contrary, Breaking arises from the division of that which has quantity. But nothing having quantity except the sacramental species is broken here, because neither Christ's body is broken, as being incorruptible, nor is the substance of the bread, because it no longer remains. Therefore the sacramental species are broken.

I answer that, Many opinions prevailed of old on this matter. Some held that in this sacrament there was no breaking at all in reality, but merely in the eyes of the beholders. But this contention cannot stand, because in this sacrament of truth the sense is not deceived with regard to its proper object of judgment, and one of these objects is breaking, whereby from one thing arise many: and these are common sensibles, as is stated in *De Anima* ii.

Others accordingly have said that there was indeed a genuine breaking, but without any subject. But this again contradicts our senses; because a quantitative body is seen in this sacrament, which formerly was one, and is now divided into many, and this must be the subject of the breaking.

But it cannot be said that Christ's true body

is broken. First of all, because it is incorruptible and impassible: secondly, because it is entire under every part, as was shown above (Q. 76, A. 3), which is contrary to the nature of a thing broken.

It remains, then, that the breaking is in the dimensive quantity of the bread, as in a subject, just as the other accidents. And as the sacramental species are the sacrament of Christ's true body, so is the breaking of these species the sacrament of our Lord's Passion, which was in Christ's true body.

Reply Obj. 1. As rarity and density remain under the sacramental species, as stated above (A. 2, *ad* 3), so likewise porousness remains, and in consequence breakableness.

Reply Obj. 2. Hardness results from density; therefore, as density remains under the sacramental species, hardness remains there too, and the capability of sound as a consequence.

Reply Obj. 3. What is eaten under its own species, is also broken and masticated under its own species; but Christ's body is eaten not under its proper, but under the sacramental species. Hence in explaining John vi. 64, *The flesh profiteth nothing,* Augustine (*Tract.* xxvii *in Joan.*) says that this is to be taken as referring to those who understood carnally: *for they understood the flesh thus, as it is divided piecemeal, in a dead body, or as sold in the shambles.* Consequently, Christ's very body is not broken, except according to its sacramental species. And the confession made by Berengarius is to be understood in this sense, that the breaking and the crushing with the teeth is to be referred to the sacramental species, under which the body of Christ truly is.

EIGHTH ARTICLE

Whether Any Liquid Can Be Mingled with the Consecrated Wine?

We proceed thus to the Eighth Article:—

Objection 1. It seems that no liquid can be mingled with the consecrated wine, because everything mingled with another partakes of its quality. But no liquid can share in the quality of the sacramental species, because those accidents are without a subject, as stated above (A. 1). Therefore it seems that no liquid can be mingled with the sacramental species of the wine.

Obj. 2. Further, if any kind of liquid be mixed with those species, then some one thing must be the result. But no one thing can result from the liquid, which is a substance, and the sacramental species, which are accidents; nor from the liquid and Christ's blood, which owing to its incorruptibility suffers neither increase nor decrease. Therefore no liquid can be mixed with the consecrated wine.

Obj. 3. Further, if any liquid be mixed with the consecrated wine, then that also would appear to be consecrated; just as water added to holy-water becomes holy. But the consecrated wine is truly Christ's blood. Therefore the liquid added would likewise be Christ's blood otherwise than by consecration, which is unbecoming. Therefore no liquid can be mingled with the consecrated wine.

Obj. 4. Further, if one of two things be entirely corrupted, there is no mixture *(De Gener.* i). But if we mix any liquid, it seems that the entire species of the sacramental wine is corrupted, so that the blood of Christ ceases to be beneath it; both because great and little are difference of quantity, and alter it, as white and black cause a difference of color; and because the liquid mixed, as having no obstacle, seems to permeate the whole, and so Christ's blood ceases to be there, since it is not there with any other substance. Consequently, no liquid can be mixed with the consecrated wine.

On the contrary, It is evident to our senses that another liquid can be mixed with the wine after it is consecrated, just as before.

I answer that, The truth of this question is evident from what has been said already. For it was said above (A. 3; A. 5, *ad* 2) that the species remaining in this sacrament, as they acquire the manner of being of substance in virtue of the consecration, so likewise do they obtain the mode of acting and of being acted upon, so that they can do or receive whatever their substance could do or receive, were it there present. But it is evident that if the substance of wine were there present, then some other liquid could be mingled with it.

Nevertheless there would be a different effect of such mixing both according to the form and according to quantity of the liquid. For if sufficient liquid were mixed so as to spread itself all through the wine, then the whole would be a mixed substance. Now what is made up of things mixed is neither of them, but each passes into a third resulting from both: hence it would result that the former wine would remain no longer. But if the liquid added were of another species, for instance, if water were mixed, the species of the wine would be dissolved, and there would be a liquid of another species. But if liquid of the same species were added, for instance, wine with wine, the same species would remain, but the wine would not be the same numerically, as the diversity of the accidents shows: for instance, if one wine were white and the other red.

But if the liquid added were of such minute quantity that it could not permeate the whole, the entire wine would not be mixed, but only part of it, which would not remain the same numerically owing to the blending of extraneous matter: still it would remain the same specifically, not only if a little liquid of the same species were mixed with it, but even if it were of another species, since a drop of water blended with much wine passes into the species of wine *(De Gener.* i).

Now it is evident that the body and blood of Christ abide in this sacrament so long as the species remain numerically the same, as stated above (A. 4; Q. 76, A. 6, *ad* 3); because it is this bread and this wine which is consecrated. Hence, if the liquid of any kind whatsoever added be so much in quantity as to permeate the whole of the consecrated wine, and be mixed with it throughout, the result will be something numerically distinct, and the blood of Christ will remain there no longer. But if the quantity of the liquid added be so slight as not to permeate throughout, but to reach only a part of the species, Christ's blood will cease to be under that part of the consecrated wine, yet will remain under the rest.

Reply Obj. 1. Pope Innocent III in a Decretal writes thus: *The very accidents appear to affect the wine that is added, because, if water be added, it takes the savor of the wine. The result is, then, that the accidents change the subject, just as subject changes accidents; for nature yields to miracle, and power works beyond custom.* But this must not be understood as if the same identical accident, which was in the wine previous to consecration, is afterwards in the wine that is added; but such change is the result of action; because the remaining accidents of the wine retain the action of substance, as stated above, and so they act upon the liquid added, by changing it.

Reply Obj. 2. The liquid added to the consecrated wine is in no way mixed with the substance of Christ's blood. Nevertheless it is mixed with the sacramental species, yet so that after such mixing the aforesaid species are corrupted entirely or in part, after the way mentioned above (A. 5), whereby something can be generated from those species. And if they be entirely corrupted, there remains no further question, because the whole will be uniform. But if they be corrupted in part, there will be one dimension according to the continuity of quantity, but not one according to the mode of being, because one part thereof will be without a subject while the other is in a subject; as in a body that is made up of two metals, there will be one body quantitatively, but not one as to the species of the matter.

Reply Obj. 3. As Pope Innocent says in the aforesaid Decretal, *if after the consecration other wine be put in the chalice, it is not changed into the blood, nor is it mingled with the blood, but, mixed with the accidents of the previous wine, it is diffused throughout the body which underlies them, yet without wetting what surrounds it.* Now this it to be understood when there is not sufficient mixing of extraneous liquid to cause the blood of Christ to cease to be under the whole; because a thing is said to be *diffused throughout,* not because it touches the body of Christ according to its proper dimensions, but according to the sacramental dimensions, under which it is contained. Now it is not the same with holy water, because the blessing works no change

in the substance of the water, as the consecration of the wine does.

Reply Obj. 4. Some have held that however slight be the mixing of extraneous liquid, the substance of Christ's blood ceases to be under the whole, and for the reason given above *(Obj.* 4); which, however, is not a cogent one; because *more* or *less* diversify dimensive quantity, not as to its essence, but as to the determination of its measure. In like manner the liquid added can be so small as on that account to be hindered from permeating the whole, and not simply by the dimensions; which, although they are present without a subject, still they are opposed to another liquid, just as substance would be if it were present, according to what was said at the beginning of the article.

QUESTION 78

Of the Form of This Sacrament

(In Six Articles)

WE must now consider the form of this sacrament; concerning which there are six points of inquiry: (1) What is the form of this sacrament? (2) Whether the form for the consecration of the bread is appropriate? (3) Whether the form for the consecration of the blood is appropriate? (4) Of the power of each form? (5) Of the truth of the expression? (6) Of the comparison of the one form with the other?

FIRST ARTICLE

Whether This Is the Form of This Sacrament: "This Is My Body," and, "This Is the Chalice of My Blood"?

We proceed thus to the First Article:—

Objection 1. It seems that this is not the form of this sacrament: *This is My body,* and, *This is the chalice of My blood.* Because those words seem to belong to the form of this sacrament, wherewith Christ consecrated His body and blood. But Christ first blessed the bread which He took, and said afterwards: *Take ye and eat; this is My body* (Matth. xxvi. 26). Therefore the whole of this seems to belong to the form of this sacrament: and the same reason holds good of the words which go with the consecration of the blood.

Obj. 2. Further, Eusebius Emissenus (Pseudo-Hieron.,—*Ep.* xxxix: Pseudo-Isid.,— *Hom.* iv) says: *The invisible Priest changes visible creatures into His own body, saying: "Take ye and eat; this is My body."* Therefore, the whole of this seems to belong to the form of this sacrament: and the same holds good of the words appertaining to the blood.

Obj. 3. Further, in the form of Baptism both the minister and his act are expressed, when it is said, *I baptize thee.* But in the words set forth above there is no mention made either of the minister or of his act. Therefore the form of the sacrament is not a suitable one.

Obj. 4. Further, the form of the sacrament suffices for its perfection; hence the sacrament of Baptism can be performed sometimes by pronouncing the words of the form only, omitting all the others. Therefore, if the aforesaid words be the form of this sacrament, it would seem as if this sacrament could be performed sometimes by uttering those words alone, while leaving out all the others which are said in the mass; yet this seems to be false, because, were the other words to be passed over, the said words would be taken as spoken in the person of the priest saying them, whereas the bread and wine are not changed into his body and blood. Consequently, the aforesaid words are not the form of this sacrament.

On the contrary, Ambrose says (*De Sacram.* iv): *The consecration is accomplished by the words and expressions of the Lord Jesus. Because, by all the other words spoken, praise is rendered to God, prayer is put up for the people, for kings, and others; but when the time comes for perfecting the sacrament, the priest uses no longer his own words, but the words of Christ. Therefore, it is Christ's words that perfect this sacrament.*

I answer that, This sacrament differs from the other sacraments in two respects. First of all, in this, that this sacrament is accomplished by the consecration of the matter, while the rest are perfected in the use of the consecrated matter. Secondly, because in the other sacraments the consecration of the matter consists only in a blessing, from which the matter consecrated derives instrumentally a spiritual power, which through the priest who is an animated instrument, can pass on to inanimate instruments. But in this sacrament the consecration of the matter consists in the miraculous change of the substance, which can only be done by God; hence the minister in performing this sacrament has no other act save the pronouncing of the words. And because the form should suit the thing, therefore the form of this sacrament differs from the forms of the other sacraments in two respects. First, because the form of the other sacraments implies the use of the matter, as for instance, baptizing, or signing; but the form of this sacrament implies merely the consecration of the matter, which consists in transubstantiation, as when it is said, *This is My body*, or, *This is the chalice of My blood*. Secondly, because the forms of the other sacraments are pronounced in the person of the minister, whether by way of exercising an act, as when it is said, *I baptize thee*, or *I confirm thee*, etc.; or by way of command, as when it is said in the sacrament of Order, *Take the power*, etc.; or by way of entreaty, as when in the sacrament of Extreme Unction it is said, *By this anointing and our intercession*, etc. But the form of this sacrament is pronounced as if Christ were speaking in person, so that it is given to be understood that the minister does nothing in perfecting this sacrament, except to pronounce the words of Christ.

Reply Obj. 1. There are many opinions on this matter. Some have said that Christ, Who had power of excellence in the sacraments, performed this sacrament without using any form of words, and that afterwards He pronounced the words under which others were to consecrate thereafter. And the words of Pope Innocent III seem to convey the same sense *(De Sacr. Alt. Myst. iv)*, where he says: *In good sooth it can be said that Christ accomplished this sacrament by His Divine power, and subsequently expressed the form under which those who came after were to consecrate*. But in opposition to this view are the words of the Gospel in which it is said that Christ *blessed*, and this blessing was effected by certain words. Accordingly those words of Innocent are to be considered as expressing an opinion, rather than determining the point.

Others, again, have said that the blessing was effected by other words not known to us. But this statement cannot stand, because the blessing of the consecration is now performed by reciting the things which were then accomplished; hence, if the consecration was not performed then by these words, neither would it be now.

Accordingly, others have maintained that this blessing was effected by the same words as are used now; but that Christ spoke them twice, at first secretly, in order to consecrate, and afterwards openly, to instruct others. But even this will not hold good, because the priest in consecrating uses these words, not as spoken in secret, but as openly pronounced. Accordingly, since these words have no power except from Christ pronouncing them, it seems that Christ also consecrated by pronouncing them openly.

And therefore others said that the Evangelists did not always follow the precise order in their narrative as that in which things actually happened, as is seen from Augustine *(De Consens. Evang.* ii). Hence it is to be understood that the order of what took place can be expressed thus: *Taking the bread He blessed it, saying: This is My body, and then He broke it, and gave it to His disciples*. But the same sense can be had even without changing the words of the Gospel; because the participle *saying* implies sequence of the words uttered with what goes before. And it is not necessary for the sequence to be understood only with respect to the last word spoken, as if Christ had just then pronounced those words, when He gave it to His disciples; but the sequence can be understood with regard to all that had gone before; so that the sense is: *While He was blessing, and breaking, and giving it to His disciples, He spoke the words, "Take ye,"* etc.

Reply Obj. 2. In these words, *Take ye and eat*, the use of the consecrated matter is indicated, which is not of the necessity of this sacrament, as stated above (Q. 74, A. 7). And therefore not even these words belong to the substance of the form. Nevertheless, because the use of the consecrated matter belongs to a certain perfection of the sacrament, in the same way as operation is not the first but the second perfection of a thing, consequently, the whole perfection of this sacrament is expressed by all those words: and it was in this way that Eusebius understood that the sacrament was accomplished by those words, as to its first and second perfection.

Reply Obj. 3. In the sacrament of Baptism the minister exercises an act regarding the use of the matter, which is of the essence of the sacrament: such is not the case in this sacrament; hence there is no parallel.

Reply Obj. 4. Some have contended that this sacrament cannot be accomplished by uttering the aforesaid words, while leaving out the rest, especially the words in the Canon of the Mass. But that this is false can be seen both from Ambrose's words quoted above, as well as from the fact that the Canon of the Mass is not the same in all places or times, but various portions have been introduced by various people.

Accordingly it must be held that if the priest were to pronounce only the aforesaid words with the intention of consecrating this sacrament, this sacrament would be valid because the intention would cause these words to be understood as spoken in the person of Christ, even though the words were pronounced without those that precede. The priest, however, would sin gravely in consecrating the sacrament thus, as he would not be observing the rite of the Church. Nor does the comparison with Baptism prove anything; for it is a sacrament of necessity: whereas the lack of this sacrament can be supplied by the spiritual partaking thereof, as Augustine says (cf. Q. 73, A. 3, ad 1).

SECOND ARTICLE

Whether This Is the Proper Form for the Consecration of the Bread: This Is My Body?

We proceed thus to the Second Article:—

Objection 1. It seems that this is not the proper form of this sacrament: *This is My body.* For the effect of a sacrament ought to be expressed in its form. But the effect of the consecration of the bread is the change of the substance of the bread into the body of Christ, and this is better expressed by the word *becomes* than by *is.* Therefore, in the form of the consecration we ought to say: *This becomes My body.*

Obj. 2. Further, Ambrose says (*De Sacram.* iv), *Christ's words consecrate this sacrament. What word of Christ? This word, whereby all things are made. The Lord commanded, and the heavens and earth were made.* Therefore, it would be a more proper form of this sacrament if the imperative mood were employed, so as to say: *Be this My body.*

Obj. 3. Further, that which is changed is implied in the subject of this phrase, just as the term of the change is implied in the predicate. But just as that into which the change is made is something determinate, for the change is into nothing else but the body of Christ, so also that which is converted is determinate, since only bread is converted into the body of Christ. Therefore, as a noun is inserted on the part of the predicate, so also should a noun be inserted in the subject, so that it be said: *This bread is My body.*

Obj. 4. Further, just as the term of the change is determinate in nature, because it is

a body, so also is it determinate in person. Consequently, in order to determine the person, it ought to be said: *This is the body of Christ.*

Obj. 5. Further, nothing ought to be inserted in the form except what is substantial to it. Consequently, the conjunction *for* is improperly added in some books, since it does not belong to the substance of the form.

On the contrary, Our Lord used this form in consecrating, as is evident from Matth. xxvi. 26.

I answer that, This is the proper form for the consecration of the bread. For it was said (A. 1) that this consecration consists in changing the substance of bread into the body of Christ. Now the form of a sacrament ought to denote what is done in the sacrament. Consequently the form for the consecration of the bread ought to signify the actual conversion of the bread into the body of Christ. And herein are three things to be considered: namely, the actual conversion, the term *whence,* and the term *whereunto.*

Now the conversion can be considered in two ways: first, in *becoming,* secondly, in *being.* But the conversion ought not to be signified in this form as in *becoming,* but as in *being.* First, because such conversion is not successive, as was said above (Q. 75, A. 7), but instantaneous; and in such changes the *becoming* is nothing else than the *being.*— Secondly, because the sacramental forms bear the same relation to the signification of the sacramental effect as artificial forms to the representation of the effect of art. Now an artificial form is the likeness of the ultimate effect, on which the artist's intention is fixed; just as the art-form in the builder's mind is principally the form of the house constructed, and secondarily of the constructing. Accordingly, in this form also the conversion ought to be expressed as in *being,* to which the intention is referred.

And since the conversion is expressed in this form as in *being,* it is necessary for the extremes of the conversion to be signified as they exist in the fact of conversion. But then the term *whereunto* has the proper nature of its own substance; whereas the term *whence* does not remain in its own substance, but only as to the accidents whereby it comes under the senses, and can be determined in relation to the senses. Hence the term *whence* of the conversion is conveniently expressed by the demonstrative pronoun, relative to the sensible accidents which continue; but the term *whereunto* is expressed by the noun signifying the nature of the thing which terminates the conversion, and this is Christ's entire body, and not merely His flesh; as was said above (Q. 76,

A. 1, *ad* 2). Hence this form is most appropriate: *This is My body.*

Reply Obj. 1. The ultimate effect of this conversion is not a *becoming* but a *being*, as stated above, and consequently prominence should be given to this in the form.

Reply Obj. 2. God's word operated in the creation of things, and it is the same which operates in this consecration, yet each in different fashion: because here it operates effectively and sacramentally, that is, in virtue of its signification. And consequently the last effect of the consecration must needs be signified in this sentence by a substantive verb of the indicative mood and present time. But in the creation of things it worked merely effectively, and such efficiency is due to the command of His wisdom; and therefore in the creation of things the Lord's word is expressed by a verb in the imperative mood, as in Gen. i. 3: *Let there be light, and light was made.*

Reply Obj. 3. The term *whence* does not retain the nature of its substance in the *being* of the conversion, as the term *whereunto* does. Therefore there is no parallel.

Reply Obj. 4. The pronoun *My*, which implicitly points to the chief person, i.e. the person of the speaker, sufficiently indicates Christ's person, in Whose person these words are uttered, as stated above (A. 1).

Reply Obj. 5. The conjunction *for* is set in this form according to the custom of the Roman Church, who derived it from Peter the Apostle; and this on account of the sequence with the words preceding: and therefore it is not part of the form, just as the words preceding the form are not.

THIRD ARTICLE

Whether This Is the Proper Form for the Consecration of the Wine: This Is the Chalice of My Blood, etc.?

We proceed thus to the Third Article:—

Objection 1. It seems that this is not the proper form for the consecration of the wine. *This is the chalice of My blood, of the New and Eternal Testament, the Mystery of Faith, which shall be shed for you and for many unto the forgiveness of sins.* For as the bread is changed by the power of consecration into Christ's body, so is the wine changed into Christ's blood, as is clear from what was said above (Q. 76, AA. 1, 2, 3). But in the form of the consecration of the bread, the body of Christ is expressly mentioned, without any addition. Therefore in this form the blood of Christ is improperly expressed in the oblique case, and the chalice in the nominative, when it is said: *This is the chalice of My blood.*

Obj. 2. Further, the words spoken in the consecration of the bread are not more efficacious than those spoken in the consecration

of the wine, since both are Christ's words. But directly the words are spoken—*This is My body*, there is perfect consecration of the bread. Therefore, directly these other words are uttered—*This is the chalice of My blood*, there is perfect consecration of the blood; and so the words which follow do not appear to be of the substance of the form, especially since they refer to the properties of this sacrament.

Obj. 3. Further, the New Testament seems to be an internal inspiration, as is evident from the Apostle quoting the words of Jeremias (xxxi. 31): *I will perfect unto the house of Israel a New Testament . . . , I will give My laws into their mind* (Heb. viii. 8). But a sacrament is an outward visible act. Therefore, in the form of the sacrament the words *of the New Testament* are improperly added.

Obj. 4. Further, a thing is said to be new which is near the beginning of its existence. But what is eternal has no beginning of its existence. Therefore it is incorrect to say *of the New and Eternal*, because it seems to savor of a contradiction.

Obj. 5. Further, occasions of error ought to be withheld from men, according to Isa. lvii. 14: *Take away the stumbling blocks out of the way of My people.* But some have fallen into error in thinking that Christ's body and blood are only mystically present in this sacrament. Therefore it is out of place to add *the mystery of faith.*

Obj. 6. Further, it was said above (Q. 73, A. 3, *ad* 3), that as Baptism is the sacrament of faith, so is the Eucharist the sacrament of charity. Consequently, in this form the word *charity* ought rather to be used than *faith*.

Obj. 7. Further, the whole of this sacrament, both as to body and blood, is a memorial of our Lord's Passion, according to 1 Cor. xi. 26: *As often as you shall eat this bread and drink the chalice, you shall show the death of the Lord.* Consequently, mention ought to be made of Christ's Passion and its fruit rather in the form of the consecration of the blood, than in the form of the consecration of the body, especially since our Lord said: *This is My body, which shall be delivered up for you* (Luke xxii. 19).

Obj. 8. Further, as was already observed (Q. 48, A. 2; Q. 49, A. 3), Christ's Passion sufficed for all; while as to its efficacy it was profitable for many. Therefore it ought to be said: *Which shall be shed for all*, or else *for many*, without adding, *for you.*

Obj. 9. Further, the words whereby this sacrament is consecrated draw their efficacy from Christ's institution. But no Evangelist narrates that Christ spoke all these words. Therefore this is not an appropriate form for the consecration of the wine.

On the contrary, The Church, instructed by the apostles, uses this form.

I answer that, There is a twofold opinion regarding this form. Some have maintained that the words *This is the chalice of My blood* alone belong to the substance of this form, but not those words which follow. Now this seems incorrect, because the words which follow them are determinations of the predicate, that is, of Christ's blood; consequently they belong to the integrity of the expression.

And on this account others say more accurately that all the words which follow are of the substance of the form down to the words, *As often as ye shall do this,* which belong to the use of this sacrament, and consequently do not belong to the substance of the form. Hence it is that the priest pronounces all these words, under the same rite and manner, namely, holding the chalice in his hands. Moreover, in Luke xxii. 20, the words that follow are interposed with the preceding words: *This is the chalice, the new testament in My blood.*

Consequently it must be said that all the aforesaid words belong to the substance of the form; but that by the first words, *This is the chalice of My blood,* the change of the wine into blood is denoted, as explained above (A. 2) in the form for the consecration of the bread; but by the words which come after is shown the power of the blood shed in the Passion, which power works in this sacrament, and is ordained for three purposes. First and principally for securing our eternal heritage, according to Heb. x. 19: *Having confidence in the entering into the holies by the blood of Christ;* and in order to denote this, we say, *of the New and Eternal Testament.* Secondly, for justifying by grace, which is by faith according to Rom. iii. 25, 26: *Whom God hath proposed to be a propitiation, through faith in His blood, . . . that He Himself may be just, and the justifier of him who is of the faith of Jesus Christ:* and on this account we add, *The Mystery of Faith.* Thirdly, for removing sins which are the impediments to both of these things, according to Heb. ix. 14: *The blood of Christ . . . shall cleanse our conscience from dead works,* that is, from sins; and on this account, we say, *which shall be shed for you and for many unto the forgiveness of sins.*

Reply Obj. 1. The expression *This is the chalice of My blood* is a figure of speech, which can be understood in two ways. First, as a figure of metonymy; because the container is put for the contained, so that the meaning is: *This is My blood contained in the chalice;* of which mention is now made, because Christ's blood is consecrated in this sacrament, inasmuch as it is the drink of the

faithful, which is not implied under the notion of blood; consequently this had to be denoted by the vessel adapted for such usage.

Secondly, it can be taken by way of metaphor, so that Christ's Passion is understood by the chalice by way of comparison, because, like a cup, it inebriates, according to Lam. iii. 15: *He hath filled me with bitterness, he hath inebriated me with wormwood:* hence our Lord Himself spoke of His Passion as a chalice, when He said (Matth. xxvi. 39): *Let this chalice pass away from Me:*—so that the meaning is: *This is the chalice of My Passion.* This is denoted by the blood being consecrated apart from the body; because it was by the Passion that the blood was separated from the body.

Reply Obj. 2. As was said above (*ad* 1; Q. 76, A. 2, *ad* 1), the blood consecrated apart expressly represents Christ's Passion, and therefore mention is made of the fruits of the Passion in the consecration of the blood rather than in that of the body, since the body is the subject of the Passion. This is also pointed out in our Lord's saying, *which shall be delivered up for you,* as if to say, *which shall undergo the Passion for you.*

Reply Obj. 3. A testament is the disposal of a heritage. But God disposed of a heavenly heritage to men, to be bestowed through the virtue of the blood of Jesus Christ; because, according to Heb. ix. 16: *Where there is a testament the death of the testator must of necessity come in.* Now Christ's blood was exhibited to men in two ways. First of all in figure, and this belongs to the Old Testament; consequently the Apostle concludes (*ibid.*): *Whereupon neither was the first indeed dedicated without blood,* which is evident from this, that as related in Exod. xxiv. 7, 8, *when every commandment of the law had been read* by Moses, *he sprinkled all the people* saying: *This is the blood of the testament which the Lord hath enjoined unto you.*

Secondly, it was shown in very truth; and this belongs to the New Testament. This is what the Apostle premises when he says (*ibid.* 15): *Therefore He is the Mediator of the New Testament, that by means of His death . . . they that are called may receive the promise of eternal inheritance.* Consequently, we say here, *The blood of the New Testament,* because it is shown now not in figure but in truth; and therefore we add, *which shall be shed for you.*—But the internal inspiration has its origin in the power of this blood, according as we are justified by Christ's Passion.

Reply Obj. 4. This Testament is a *new* one by reason of its showing forth: yet it is called *eternal* both on account of God's eternal preordination, as well as on account of the eternal heritage which is prepared by this testament. Moreover, Christ's Person is eternal, in Whose blood this testament is appointed.

Reply Obj. 5. The word *mystery* is inserted, not in order to exclude reality, but to show that the reality is hidden, because Christ's blood is in this sacrament in a hidden manner, and His Passion was dimly foreshadowed in the Old Testament.

Reply Obj. 6. It is called the *Sacrament of Faith,* as being an object of faith: because by faith alone do we hold the presence of Christ's blood in this sacrament. Moreover Christ's Passion justifies by faith. Baptism is called the *Sacrament of Faith* because it is a profession of faith.—This is called the *Sacrament of Charity,* as being figurative and effective thereof.

Reply Obj. 7. As stated above (*ad* 2), the blood consecrated apart represents Christ's blood more expressively; and therefore mention is made of Christ's Passion and its fruits, in the consecration of the blood rather than in that of the body.

Reply Obj. 8. The blood of Christ's Passion has its efficacy not merely in the elect among the Jews, to whom the blood of the Old Testament was exhibited, but also in the Gentiles; nor only in priests who consecrate this sacrament, and in those others who partake of it; but likewise in those for whom it is offered. And therefore He says expressly, *for you,* the Jews, *and for many,* namely the Gentiles; or, *for you* who eat of it, and *for many,* for whom it is offered.

Reply Obj. 9. The Evangelists did not intend to hand down the forms of the sacraments, which in the primitive Church had to be kept concealed, as Dionysius observes at the close of his book on the ecclesiastical hierarchy; their object was to write the story of Christ. Nevertheless nearly all these words can be culled from various passages of the Scriptures. Because the words, *This is the chalice,* are found in Luke xxii. 20, and 1 Cor. xi. 25, while Matthew says in chapter xxvi. 28: *This is My blood of the New Testament, which shall be shed for many unto the remission of sins.* The words added, namely, *eternal* and *mystery of faith,* were handed down to the Church by the apostles, who received them from our Lord, according to 1 Cor. xi. 23: *I have received of the Lord that which also I delivered unto you.*

FOURTH ARTICLE

Whether in the Aforesaid Words of the Forms There Be Any Created Power Which Causes the Consecration?

We proceed thus to the Fourth Article:—

Objection 1. It seems that in the aforesaid words of the forms there is no created power which causes the consecration. Because Damascene says (*De Fide Orthod.* iv): *The change of the bread into Christ's body is caused solely by the power of the Holy Ghost.* But the power of the Holy Ghost is uncreated. Therefore this sacrament is not caused by any created power of those words.

Obj. 2. Further, miraculous works are wrought not by any created power, but solely by Divine power, as was stated in the First Part (Q. 110, A. 4). But the change of the bread and wine into Christ's body and blood is a work not less miraculous than the creation of things, or than the formation of Christ's body in the womb of a virgin: which things could not be done by any created power. Therefore, neither is this sacrament consecrated by any created power of the aforesaid words.

Obj. 3. Further, the aforesaid words are not simple, but composed of many; nor are they uttered simultaneously, but successively. But, as stated above (Q. 75, A. 7), this change is wrought instantaneously; hence it must be done by a simple power. Therefore it is not effected by the power of those words.

On the contrary, Ambrose says (*De Sacram.* iv): *If there be such might in the word of the Lord Jesus that things non-existent came into being, how much more efficacious is it to make things existing to continue, and to be changed into something else? And so, what was bread before consecration is now the body of Christ after consecration, because Christ's word changes a creature into something different.*

I answer that, Some have maintained that neither in the above words is there any created power for causing the transubstantiation, nor in the other forms of the sacraments, or even in the sacraments themselves, for producing the sacramental effects.—This, as was shown above (Q. 62, A. 1), is both contrary to the teachings of the saints, and detracts from the dignity of the sacraments of the New Law. Hence, since this sacrament is of greater worth than the others, as stated above (Q. 65, A. 3), the result is that there is in the words of the form of this sacrament a created power which causes the change to be wrought in it: instrumental, however, as in the other sacraments, as stated above (Q. 62, AA. 3, 4). For since these words are uttered in the person of Christ, it is from His command that they receive their instrumental power from Him, just as His other deeds and sayings derive their salutary power instrumentally, as was observed above (Q. 48, A. 6; Q. 56, A. 1, *ad* 3).

Reply Obj. 1. When the bread is said to be changed into Christ's body solely by the power of the Holy Ghost, the instrumental power which lies in the form of this sacrament is not excluded: just as when we say that the smith alone makes a knife we do not deny the power of the hammer.

Reply Obj. 2. No creature can work miracles as the chief agent; yet it can do so instrumentally, just as the touch of Christ's hand healed the leper. And in this fashion Christ's words change the bread into His body. But in Christ's conception, whereby His body was fashioned, it was impossible for anything derived from His body to have the instrumental power of forming that very body. Likewise in creation there was no term wherein the instrumental action of a creature could be received. Consequently there is no comparison.

Reply Obj. 3. The aforesaid words, which work the consecration, operate sacramentally. Consequently, the converting power latent under the forms of these sacraments follows the meaning, which is terminated in the uttering of the last word. And therefore the aforesaid words have this power in the last instant of their being uttered, taken in conjunction with those uttered before. And this power is simple by reason of the thing signified, although there be composition in the words uttered outwardly.

FIFTH ARTICLE

Whether the Aforesaid Expressions Are True?

We proceed thus to the Fifth Article:—

Objection 1. It seems that the aforesaid expressions are not true. Because when we say: *This is My body,* the word *this* designates a substance. But according to what was said above (AA. 1, 4, *ad* 3; Q. 75, AA. 2, 7), when the pronoun *this* is spoken, the substance of the bread is still there, because the transubstantiation takes place in the last instant of pronouncing the words. But it is false to say: *Bread is Christ's body.* Consequently this expression, *This is My body,* is false.

Obj. 2. Further, the pronoun *this* appeals to the senses. But the sensible species in this sacrament are neither Christ's body nor even its accidents. Therefore this expression, *This is My body,* cannot be true.

Obj. 3. Further, as was observed above (A. 4, *ad* 3), these words, by their signification, effect the change of the bread into the body of Christ. But an effective cause is understood as preceding its effect. Therefore the meaning of these words is understood as preceding the change of the bread into the body of Christ. But previous to the change this expression, *This is My body,* is false. Therefore the expression is to be judged as false simply; and the same reason holds

good of the other phrase: *This is the chalice of My blood,* etc.

On the contrary, These words are pronounced in the person of Christ, Who says of Himself (John xiv. 6): *I am the truth.*

I answer that, There have been many opinions on this point. Some have said that in this expression, *This is My body,* the word *this* implies demonstration as conceived, and not as exercised, because the whole phrase is taken materially, since it is uttered by a way of narration: for the priest relates that Christ said: *This is My body.*

But such a view cannot hold good, because then these words would not be applied to the corporeal matter present, and consequently the sacrament would not be valid: for Augustine says *(Tract.* lxxx, *in Joan.): The word is added to the element, and this becomes a sacrament.*—Moreover this solution ignores entirely the difficulty which this question presents: for there is still the objection in regard to the first uttering of these words by Christ; since it is evident that then they were employed, not materially, but significatively. And therefore it must be said that even when spoken by the priest they are taken significatively, and not merely materially.—Nor does it matter that the priest pronounces them by way of recital, as though they were spoken by Christ, because owing to Christ's infinite power, just as through contact with His flesh the regenerative power entered not only into the waters which came into contact with Christ, but into all waters throughout the whole world and during all future ages, so likewise from Christ's uttering these words they derived their consecrating power, by whatever priest they be uttered, as if Christ present were saying them.

And therefore others have said that in this phrase the word *this* appeals, not to the senses, but to the intellect; so that the meaning is, *This is My body*—i.e. *The thing signified by "this" is My body.* But neither can this stand, because, since in the sacraments the effect is that which is signified, from such a form it would not result that Christ's body was in very truth in this sacrament, but merely as in a sign, which is heretical, as stated above (Q. 85, A. 1).

Consequently, others have said that the word *this* appeals to the senses; not at the precise instant of its being uttered, but merely at the last instant thereof; as when a man says, *Now I am silent,* this adverb *now* points to the instant immediately following the speech: because the sense is: *Directly these words are spoken I am silent.*—But neither can this hold good, because in that case the meaning of the sentence would be: *My body is My body,* which the above phrase does not effect, because this was so even before the utterance of the words: hence neither does the aforesaid sentence mean this.

Consequently, then, it remains to be said, as stated above (A. 4), that this sentence possesses the power of effecting the conversion of the bread into the body of Christ. And therefore it is compared to other sentences, which have power only of signifying and not of producing, as the concept of the practical intellect, which is productive of the thing, is compared to the concept of our speculative intellect, which is drawn from things; because *words are signs of concepts,* as the Philosopher says *(Peri Herm.* i). And therefore as the concept of the practical intellect does not presuppose the thing understood, but makes it, so the truth of this expression does not presuppose the thing signified, but makes it; for such is the relation of God's word to the things made by the Word. Now this change takes place not successively, but in an instant, as stated above (Q. 77, A. 7). Consequently one must understand the aforesaid expression with reference to the last instant of the words being spoken, yet not so that the subject may be understood to have stood for that which is the term of the conversion; viz. that the body of Christ is the body of Christ; nor again that the subject be understood to stand for that which it was before the conversion, namely, the bread; but for that which is commonly related to both, i.e. that which is contained in general under those species. For these words do not make the body of Christ to be the body of Christ, nor do they make the bread to be the body of Christ; but what was contained under those species, and was formerly bread, they make to be the body of Christ. And therefore expressly our Lord did not say: *This bread is My body,* which would be the meaning of the second opinion; nor—*This My body is My body,* which would be the meaning of the third opinion: but in general: *This is My body,* assigning no noun on the part of the subject, but only a pronoun, which signifies substance in common, without quality, that is, without a determinate form.

Reply Obj. 1. The term *this* points to a substance, yet without determining its proper nature, as stated above.

Reply Obj. 2. The pronoun *this* does not indicate the accidents, but the substance underlying the accidents, which at first was bread, and is afterwards the body of Christ, which body, although not informed by those accidents, is yet contained under them.

Reply Obj. 3. The meaning of this expression is, in the order of nature, understood before the thing signified, just as a cause is

naturally prior to the effect; but not in order of time, because this cause has its effect with it at the same time, and this suffices for the truth of the expression.

SIXTH ARTICLE

Whether the Form of the Consecration of the Bread Accomplishes Its Effect before the Form of the Consecration of the Wine Be Completed?

We proceed thus to the Sixth Article:—

Objection 1. It seems that the form of the consecration of the bread does not accomplish its effect until the form for the consecration of the wine be completed. For, as Christ's body begins to be in this sacrament by the consecration of the bread, so does His blood come to be there by the consecration of the wine. If, then, the words for consecrating the bread were to produce their effect before the consecration of the wine, it would follow that Christ's body would be present in this sacrament without the blood, which is improper.

Obj. 2. Further, one sacrament has one completion: hence although there be three immersions in Baptism, yet the first immersion does not produce its effect until the third be completed. But all this sacrament is one, as stated above (Q. 73, A. 2). Therefore the words whereby the bread is consecrated do not bring about their effect without the sacramental words whereby the wine is consecrated.

Obj. 3. Further, there are several words in the form for consecrating the bread, the first of which do not secure their effect until the last be uttered, as stated above (A. 4, *ad* 3). Therefore, for the same reason, neither do the words for the consecration of Christ's body produce their effect, until the words for consecrating Christ's blood are spoken.

On the contrary, Directly the words are uttered for consecrating the bread, the consecrated host is shown to the people to be adored, which would not be done if Christ's body were not there, for that would be an act of idolatry. Therefore the consecrating words of the bread produce their effect before the words are spoken for consecrating the wine.

I answer that, Some of the earlier doctors said that these two forms, namely, for consecrating the bread and the wine, await each other's action, so that the first does not produce its effect until the second be uttered.

But this cannot stand, because, as stated above (A. 5, *ad* 3), for the truth of this phrase, *This is My body,* wherein the verb is in the present tense, it is required for the thing signified to be present simultaneously in time with the signification of the expression used; otherwise, if the thing signified had to be awaited for afterwards, a verb of the future tense would be employed, and not one of the present tense, so that we should not say, *This is My body*, but—*This will be My body*: But the signification of this speech is complete directly those words are spoken. And therefore the thing signified must be present instantaneously, and such is the effect of this sacrament; otherwise it would not be a true speech. —Moreover, this opinion is against the rite of the Church, which forthwith adores the body of Christ after the words are uttered.

Hence it must be said that the first form does not await the second in its action, but has its effect on the instant.

Reply Obj. 1. It is on this account that they who maintained the above opinion seem to have erred. Hence it must be understood that directly the consecration of the bread is complete, the body of Christ is indeed present

by the power of the sacrament, and the blood by real concomitance; but afterwards by the consecration of the wine, conversely, the blood of Christ is there by the power of the sacrament, and the body by real concomitance, so that the entire Christ is under either species, as stated above (Q. 76, A. 2).

Reply Obj. 2. This sacrament is one in perfection, as stated above (Q. 73, A. 2), namely, inasmuch as it is made up of two things, that is, of food and drink, each of which of itself has its own perfection; but the three immersions of Baptism are ordained to one simple effect, and therefore there is no resemblance.

Reply Obj. 3. The various words in the form for consecrating the bread constitute the truth of one speech, but the words of the different forms do not, and consequently there is no parallel.

QUESTION 79

Of the Effects of This Sacrament

(In Eight Articles)

WE must now consider the effects of this sacrament, and under this head there are eight points of inquiry: (1) Whether this sacrament bestows grace? (2) Whether the attaining of glory is an effect of this sacrament? (3) Whether the forgiveness of mortal sin is an effect of this sacrament? (4) Whether venial sin is forgiven by this sacrament? (5) Whether the entire punishment due for sin is forgiven by this sacrament? (6) Whether this sacrament preserves man from future sins? (7) Whether this sacrament benefits others besides the recipients? (8) Of the obstacles to the effect of this sacrament.

FIRST ARTICLE

Whether Grace Is Bestowed through This Sacrament?

We proceed thus to the First Article:—

Objection 1. It seems that grace is not bestowed through this sacrament. For this sacrament is spiritual nourishment. But nourishment is only given to the living. Therefore since the spiritual life is the effect of grace, this sacrament belongs only to one in the state of grace. Therefore grace is not bestowed through this sacrament for it to be had in the first instance. In like manner neither is it given so as grace may be increased, because spiritual growth belongs to the sacrament of Confirmation, as stated above (Q. 72, A. 1). Consequently, grace is not bestowed through this sacrament.

Obj. 2. Further, this sacrament is given as a spiritual refreshment. But spiritual refreshment seems to belong to the use of grace rather than to its bestowal. Therefore it seems that grace is not given through this sacrament.

Obj. 3. Further, as was said above (Q. 74, A. 1), *Christ's body is offered up in this sacrament for the salvation of the body, and His blood for that of the soul.* Now it is not the body which is the subject of grace, but the soul, as was shown in the Second Part (I-II, Q. 110, A. 4). Therefore grace is not bestowed through this sacrament, at least so far as the body is concerned.

On the contrary, Our Lord says (John vi. 52): *The bread which I will give, is My flesh for the life of the world.* But the spiritual life is the effect of grace. Therefore grace is bestowed through this sacrament.

I answer that, The effect of this sacrament ought to be considered, first of all and principally, from what is contained in this sacrament, which is Christ; Who, just as by coming into the world, He visibly bestowed the life of grace upon the world, according to John i. 17: *Grace and truth came by Jesus Christ,* so also, by coming sacramentally into man, causes the life of grace, according to John vi. 58: *He that eateth Me, the same also shall live by Me.* Hence Cyril says on Luke xxii. 19: *God's life-giving Word by uniting Himself with His own flesh, made it to be productive of life. For it was becoming that He should be united somehow with bodies through His sacred flesh and precious blood, which we receive in a life-giving blessing in the bread and wine.*

Secondly, it is considered on the part of what is represented by this sacrament, which is Christ's Passion, as stated above (Q. 74, A. 1; Q. 76, A. 2, *ad* 1). And therefore this sacrament works in man the effect which Christ's Passion wrought in the world. Hence, Chrysostom says on the words, *Immediately there came out blood and water* (John xix. 34): *Since the sacred mysteries derive their origin from thence, when you draw nigh to the awe-inspiring chalice, so approach as if you were going to drink from Christ's own side.* Hence our Lord Himself says (Matth. xxvi. 28: *This is My blood . . . which shall be shed for many unto the remission of sins.*

Thirdly, the effect of this sacrament is considered from the way in which this sacrament is given; for it is given by way of food and drink. And therefore this sacrament does for the spiritual life all that material food does for the bodily life, namely, by sustaining, giving increase, restoring, and giving delight. Accordingly, Ambrose says *(De Sacram. v)*: *This is the bread of everlasting life, which supports the substance of our soul.* And Chrysostom says *(Hom.* xlvi, *in Joan.)*: *When we desire it, He lets us feel Him, and eat Him, and embrace Him.* And hence our Lord says (John vi. 56): *My flesh is meat indeed, and My blood is drink indeed.*

Fourthly, the effect of this sacrament is considered from the species under which it is given. Hence Augustine says *(Tract.* xxvi, *in Joan.)*: *Our Lord betokened His body and blood in things which out of many units are made into some one whole: for out of many grains is one thing made,* viz. bread; *and many grapes flow into one thing,* viz. wine. And therefore he observes elsewhere *(ibid.)*: *O sacrament of piety, O sign of unity, O bond of charity!*

And since Christ and His Passion are the cause of grace; and since spiritual refreshment, and charity cannot be without grace, it is clear from all that has been set forth that this sacrament bestows grace.

Reply Obj. 1. This sacrament has of itself the power of bestowing grace; nor does anyone possess grace before receiving this sacrament except from some desire thereof; from his own desire, as in the case of the adult; or from the Church's desire in the case of children, as stated above (Q. 73, A. 3). Hence it is due to the efficacy of its power, that even from desire thereof a man procures grace whereby he is enabled to lead the spiritual life. It re-

mains, then, that when the sacrament itself is really received, grace is increased, and the spiritual life perfected: yet in different fashion from the sacrament of Confirmation, in which grace is increased and perfected for resisting the outward assaults of Christ's enemies. But by this sacrament grace receives increase, and the spiritual life is perfected, so that man may stand perfect in himself by union with God.

Reply Obj. 2. This sacrament confers grace spiritually together with the virtue of charity. Hence Damascene *(De Fide Orthod.* iv) compares this sacrament to the burning coal which Isaias saw (vi. 6): *For a live ember is not simply wood, but wood united to fire; so also the bread of communion is not simple bread, but bread united with the Godhead.* But as Gregory observes in a Homily for Pentecost, *God's love is never idle; for, wherever it is, it does great works.* And consequently through this sacrament, as far as its power is concerned, not only is the habit of grace and of virtue bestowed, but it is furthermore aroused to act, according to 2 Cor. v. 14: *The charity of Christ presseth us.* Hence it is that the soul is spiritually nourished through the power of this sacrament, by being spiritually gladdened, and as it were inebriated with the sweetness of the Divine goodness, according to Cant. v. 1: *Eat, O friends, and drink, and be inebriated, my dearly beloved.*

Reply Obj. 3. Because the sacraments operate according to the similitude by which they signify, therefore by way of assimilation it is said that in this sacrament *the body is offered for the salvation of the body, and the blood for the salvation of the soul,* although each works for the salvation of both, since the entire Christ is under each, as stated above (Q. 76, A. 2). And although the body is not the immediate subject of grace, still the effect of grace flows into the body while in the present life we present *our* (Vulg.,—*your*) *members* as *instruments of justice unto God* (Rom. vi. 13), and in the life to come our body will share in the incorruption and the glory of the soul.

SECOND ARTICLE

Whether the Attaining of Glory Is an Effect of This Sacrament?

We proceed thus to the Second Article:—

Objection 1. It seems that the attaining of glory is not an effect of this sacrament. For an effect is proportioned to its cause. But this sacrament belongs to *wayfarers (viatoribus),* and hence it is termed *Viaticum.* Since, then, wayfarers are not yet capable of glory, it seems that this sacrament does not cause the attaining of glory.

Obj. 2. Further, given sufficient cause, the

effect follows. But many take this sacrament who will never come to glory, as Augustine declares *(De Civ. Dei* xxi). Consequently, this sacrament is not the cause of attaining unto glory.

Obj. 3. Further, the greater is not brought about by the lesser, for nothing acts outside its species. But it is the lesser thing to receive Christ under a strange species, which happens in this sacrament, than to enjoy Him in His own species, which belongs to glory. Therefore this sacrament does not cause the attaining of glory.

On the contrary, It is written (John vi. 52): *If any man eat of this bread, he shall live for ever.* But eternal life is the life of glory. Therefore the attaining of glory is an effect of this sacrament.

I answer that, In this sacrament we may consider both that from which it derives its effect, namely, Christ contained in it, as also His Passion represented by it; and that through which it works its effect, namely, the use of the sacrament, and its species.

Now as to both of these it belongs to this sacrament to cause the attaining of eternal life. Because it was by His Passion that Christ opened to us the approach to eternal life, according to Heb. ix. 15: *He is the Mediator of the New Testament; that by means of His death . . . they that are called may receive the promise of eternal inheritance.* Accordingly in the form of this sacrament it is said: *This is the chalice of My blood, of the New and Eternal Testament.*

In like manner the refreshment of spiritual food and the unity denoted by the species of the bread and wine are to be had in the present life, although imperfectly; but perfectly in the state of glory. Hence Augustine says on the words, *My flesh is meat indeed* (John vi. 56): *Seeing that in meat and drink, men aim at this, that they hunger not nor thirst, this verily nought doth afford save only this meat and drink which maketh them who partake thereof to be immortal and incorruptible, in the fellowship of the saints, where shall be peace, and unity, full and perfect.*

Reply Obj. 1. As Christ's Passion, in virtue whereof this sacrament is accomplished, is indeed the sufficient cause of glory, yet not so that we are thereby forthwith admitted to glory, but we must first *suffer with Him in order that we may also be glorified afterwards with Him* (Rom. viii. 17), so this sacrament does not at once admit us to glory, but bestows on us the power of coming unto glory. And therefore it is called *Viaticum,* a figure whereof we read in 3 Kings xix. 8: *Elias ate and drank, and walked in the strength of that*

food forty days and forty nights unto the mount of God, Horeb.

Reply Obj. 2. Just as Christ's Passion has not its effect in them who are not disposed towards it as they should be, so also they do not come to glory through this sacrament who receive it unworthily. Hence Augustine *(Tract.* xxvi, *in Joan.),* expounding the same passage, observes: *The sacrament is one thing, the power of the sacrament another. Many receive it from the altar . . . and by receiving . . . die. . . . Eat, then, spiritually the heavenly bread, bring innocence to the altar.* It is no wonder, then, if those who do not keep innocence, do not secure the effect of this sacrament.

Reply Obj. 3. That Christ is received under another species belongs to the nature of a sacrament, which acts instrumentally. But there is nothing to prevent an instrumental cause from producing a more mighty effect, as is evident from what was said above (Q. 77, A. 3, *ad* 3).

THIRD ARTICLE

Whether the Forgiveness of Mortal Sin Is an Effect of This Sacrament?

We proceed thus to the Third Article:—

Objection 1. It seems that the forgiveness of mortal sin is an effect of this sacrament. For it is said in one of the Collects (Postcommunion, *Pro vivis et defunctis): May this sacrament be a cleansing from crimes.* But mortal sins are called crimes. Therefore mortal sins are blotted out by this sacrament.

Obj. 2. Further, this sacrament, like Baptism, works by the power of Christ's Passion. But mortal sins are forgiven by Baptism, as stated above (Q. 69, A. 1). Therefore they are forgiven likewise by this sacrament, especially since in the form of this sacrament it is said: *Which shall be shed for many unto the forgiveness of sins.*

Obj. 3. Further, grace is bestowed through this sacrament, as stated above (A. 1). But by grace a man is justified from mortal sins, according to Rom. iii. 24: *Being justified freely by His grace.* Therefore mortal sins are forgiven by this sacrament.

On the contrary, It is written (1 Cor. xi. 29): *He that eateth and drinketh unworthily, eateth and drinketh judgment to himself:* and a gloss of the same passage makes the following commentary: *He eats and drinks unworthily who is in the state of sin, or who handles (the sacrament) irreverently; and such a one eats and drinks judgment, i.e. damnation, unto himself.* Therefore, he that is in mortal sin, by taking the sacrament heaps sin upon sin, rather than obtains forgiveness of his sin.

I answer that, The power of this sacrament can be considered in two ways. First of all, in itself: and thus this sacrament has from Christ's Passion the power of forgiving all sins, since the Passion is the fount and cause of the forgiveness of sins.

Secondly, it can be considered in comparison with the recipient of the sacrament, in so far as there is, or is not, found in him an obstacle to receiving the fruit of this sacrament. Now whoever is conscious of mortal sin, has within him an obstacle to receiving the effect of this sacrament; since he is not a proper recipient of this sacrament, both because he is not alive spiritually, and so he ought not to eat the spiritual nourishment, since nourishment is confined to the living; and because he cannot be united with Christ, which is the effect of this sacrament, as long as he retains an attachment towards mortal sin. Consequently, as is said in the book *De Eccles. Dogmat.: If the soul leans towards sin, it is burdened rather than purified from partaking of the Eucharist.* Hence, in him who is conscious of mortal sin, this sacrament does not cause the forgiveness of sin.

Nevertheless this sacrament can effect the forgiveness of sin in two ways. First of all, by being received, not actually, but in desire; as when a man is first justified from sin. Secondly, when received by one in mortal sin of which he is not conscious, and for which he has no attachment; since possibly he was not sufficiently contrite at first, but by approaching this sacrament devoutly and reverently he obtains the grace of charity, which will perfect his contrition and bring forgiveness of sin.

Reply Obj. 1. We ask that this sacrament may be the *cleansing of crimes,* or of those sins of which we are unconscious, according to Ps. xviii. 13: *Lord, cleanse me from my hidden sins;* or that our contrition may be perfected for the forgiveness of our sins; or that strength be bestowed on us to avoid sin.

Reply Obj. 2. Baptism is spiritual generation, which is a transition from spiritual non-being into spiritual being, and is given by way of ablution. Consequently, in both respects he who is conscious of mortal sin does not improperly approach Baptism. But in this sacrament man receives Christ within himself by way of spiritual nourishment, which is unbecoming to one that lies dead in his sins. Therefore the comparison does not hold good.

Reply Obj. 3. Grace is the sufficient cause of the forgiveness of mortal sin; yet it does not forgive sin except when it is first bestowed on the sinner. But it is not given so in this sacrament. Hence the argument does not prove.

FOURTH ARTICLE

Whether Venial Sins Are Forgiven through This Sacrament?

We proceed thus to the Fourth Article:—

Objection 1. It seems that venial sins are not forgiven by this sacrament, because this is the *sacrament of charity,* as Augustine says *(Tract.* xxvi, *in Joan.).* But venial sins are not contrary to charity, as was shown in the Second Part (I-II, Q. 88, AA. 1, 2; II-II, Q. 24, A. 10). Therefore, since contrary is taken away by its contrary, it seems that venial sins are not forgiven by this sacrament.

Obj. 2. Further, if venial sins be forgiven by this sacrament, then all of them are forgiven for the same reason as one is. But it does not appear that all are forgiven, because thus one might frequently be without any venial sin, against what is said in 1 John i. 8: *If we say that we have no sin, we deceive ourselves.* Therefore no venial sin is forgiven by this sacrament.

Obj. 3. Further, contraries mutually exclude each other. But venial sins do not forbid the receiving of this sacrament: because Augustine says on the words, *If any man eat of it, he shall* (Vulg.,—*may) not die* for ever (John vi. 50): *Bring innocence to the altar: your sins, though they be daily, . . . let them not be deadly.* Therefore neither are venial sins taken away by this sacrament.

On the contrary, Innocent III says *(De S. Alt. Myst.* iv) that this sacrament *blots out venial sins, and wards off mortal sins.*

I answer that, Two things may be considered in this sacrament, to wit, the sacrament itself, and the reality of the sacrament: and it appears from both that this sacrament has the power of forgiving venial sins. For this sacrament is received under the form of nourishing food. Now nourishment from food is requisite for the body to make good the daily waste caused by the action of natural heat. But something is also lost daily of our spirituality from the heat of concupiscence through venial sins, which lessen the fervor of charity, as was shown in the Second Part (II-II, Q. 24, A. 10). And therefore it belongs to this sacrament to forgive venial sins. Hence Ambrose says *(De Sacram.* v) that this daily bread is taken *as a remedy against daily infirmity.*

The reality of this sacrament is charity, not only as to its habit, but also as to its act, which is kindled in this sacrament; and by this means venial sins are forgiven. Consequently, it is manifest that venial sins are forgiven by the power of this sacrament.

Reply Obj. 1. Venial sins, although not opposed to the habit of charity, are nevertheless opposed to the fervor of its act, which act is kindled by this sacrament; by reason of which act venial sins are blotted out.

Reply Obj. 2. The passage quoted is not to be understood as if a man could not at some time be without all guilt of venial sin: but that the just do not pass through this life without committing venial sins.

Reply Obj. 3. The power of charity, to which this sacrament belongs, is greater than that of venial sins: because charity by its act takes away venial sins, which nevertheless cannot entirely hinder the act of charity. And the same holds good of this sacrament.

FIFTH ARTICLE

Whether the Entire Punishment Due to Sin Is Forgiven through This Sacrament?

We proceed thus to the Fifth Article:—

Objection 1. It seems that the entire punishment due to sin is forgiven through this sacrament. For through this sacrament man receives the effect of Christ's Passion within himself, as stated above (AA. 1, 2), just as he does through Baptism. But through Baptism man receives forgiveness of all punishment, through the virtue of Christ's Passion, which satisfied sufficiently for all sins, as was explained above (Q. 69, A. 2). Therefore it seems the whole debt of punishment is forgiven through this sacrament.

Obj. 2. Further, Pope Alexander (I) says (*Ep. ad omnes Orthod.*): *No sacrifice can be greater than the body and the blood of Christ.* But man satisfied for his sins by the sacrifices of the Old Law: for it is written (Lev. iv and v): *If a man shall sin, let him offer* (so and so) *for his sin, and it shall be forgiven him.* Therefore this sacrament avails much more for the forgiveness of all punishment.

Obj. 3. Further, it is certain that some part of the debt of punishment is forgiven by this sacrament; for which reason it is sometimes enjoined upon a man, by way of satisfaction, to have masses said for himself. But if one part of the punishment is forgiven, for the same reason is the other forgiven: owing to Christ's infinite power contained in this sacrament. Consequently, it seems that the whole punishment can be taken away by this sacrament.

On the contrary, In that case no other punishment would have to be enjoined; just as none is imposed upon the newly baptized.

I answer that, This sacrament is both a sacrifice and a sacrament; it has the nature of a sacrifice inasmuch as it is offered up; and it has the nature of a sacrament inasmuch as it is received. And therefore it has the effect of a sacrament in the recipient, and the effect of a sacrifice in the offerer, or in them for whom it is offered.

If, then, it be considered as a sacrament, it produces its effect in two ways: first of all directly through the power of the sacrament; secondly as by a kind of concomitance, as was said above regarding what is contained in the sacrament (Q. 76, AA. 1, 2). Through the power of the sacrament it produces directly that effect for which it was instituted. Now it was instituted not for satisfaction, but for nourishing spiritually through union between Christ and His members, as nourishment is united with the person nourished. But because this union is the effect of charity, from the fervor of which man obtains forgiveness, not only of guilt but also of punishment, hence it is that as a consequence, and by concomitance with the chief effect, man obtains forgiveness of the punishment, not indeed of the entire punishment, but according to the measure of his devotion and fervor.

But in so far as it is a sacrifice, it has a satisfactory power. Yet in satisfaction, the affection of the offerer is weighed rather than the quantity of the offering. Hence our Lord says (Mark xii. 43: *cf.* Luke xxi. 4) of the widow who offered *two mites* that she *cast in more than all.* Therefore, although this offering suffices of its own quantity to satisfy for all punishment, yet it becomes satisfactory for them for whom it is offered, or even for the offerers, according to the measure of their devotion, and not for the whole punishment.

Reply Obj. 1. The sacrament of Baptism is directly ordained for the remission of punishment and guilt: not so the Eucharist, because Baptism is given to man as dying with Christ, whereas the Eucharist is given as by way of nourishing and perfecting him through Christ. Consequently there is no parallel.

Reply Obj. 2. Those other sacrifices and oblations did not effect the forgiveness of the whole punishment, neither as to the quantity of the thing offered, as this sacrament does, nor as to personal devotion; from which it comes to pass that even here the whole punishment is not taken away.

Reply Obj. 3. If part of the punishment and not the whole be taken away by this sacrament, it is due to a defect not on the part of Christ's power, but on the part of man's devotion.

SIXTH ARTICLE

Whether Man Is Preserved by This Sacrament from Future Sins?

We proceed thus to the Sixth Article:—

Objection 1. It seems that man is not preserved by this sacrament from future sins.

For there are many that receive this sacrament worthily, who afterwards fall into sin. Now this would not happen if this sacrament were to preserve them from future sins. Consequently, it is not an effect of this sacrament to preserve from future sins.

Obj. 2. Further, the Eucharist is the sacrament of charity, as stated above (A. 4). But charity does not seem to preserve from future sins, because it can be lost through sin after one has possessed it, as was stated in the Second Part (II-II, Q. 24, A. 11). Therefore it seems that this sacrament does not preserve man from sin.

Obj. 3. Further, the origin of sin within us is *the law of sin, which is in our members,* as declared by the Apostle (Rom. vii. 23). But the lessening of the fomes, which is the law of sin, is set down as an effect not of this sacrament, but rather of Baptism. Therefore preservation from sin is not an effect of this sacrament.

On the contrary, Our Lord said (John vi. 50): *This is the bread which cometh down from heaven; that if any man eat of it, he may not die:* which manifestly is not to be understood of the death of the body. Therefore it is to be understood that this sacrament preserves from spiritual death, which is through sin.

I answer that, Sin is the spiritual death of the soul. Hence man is preserved from future sin in the same way as the body is preserved from future death of the body: and this happens in two ways. First of all, in so far as man's nature is strengthened inwardly against inner decay, and so by means of food and medicine he is preserved from death. Secondly, by being guarded against outward assaults; and thus he is protected by means of arms by which he defends his body.

Now this sacrament preserves man from sin in both of these ways. For, first of all, by uniting man with Christ through grace, it strengthens his spiritual life, as spiritual food and spiritual medicine, according to Ps. ciii. 5 *(That) bread strengthens* (Vulg., — *may strengthen) man's heart.* Augustine likewise says *(Tract.* xxvi, *in Joan.): Approach without fear; it is bread, not poison.* Secondly, inasmuch as it is a sign of Christ's Passion, whereby the devils are conquered, it repels all the assaults of demons. Hence Chrysostom says *(Hom.* xlvi, *in Joan.): Like lions breathing forth fire, thus do we depart from that table, being made terrible to the devil.*

Reply Obj. 1. The effect of this sacrament is received according to man's condition: such is the case with every active cause in that its effect is received in matter according to the condition of the matter. But such is the con-

dition of man on earth that his free-will can be bent to good or evil. Hence, although this sacrament of itself has the power of preserving from sin, yet it does not take away from man the possibility of sinning.

Reply Obj. 2. Even charity of itself keeps man from sin, according to Rom. xiii. 10: *The love of our neighbor worketh no evil:* but it is due to the mutability of free-will that a man sins after possessing charity, just as after receiving this sacrament.

Reply Obj. 3. Although this sacrament is not ordained directly to lessen the fomes, yet it does lessen it as a consequence, inasmuch as it increases charity, because, as Augustine says (Q. 83), *the increase of charity is the lessening of concupiscence.* But it directly strengthens man's heart in good; whereby he is also preserved from sin.

SEVENTH ARTICLE

Whether This Sacrament Benefits Others Besides the Recipients?

We proceed thus to the Seventh Article:—

Objection 1. It seems that this sacrament benefits only the recipients. For this sacrament is of the same genus as the other sacraments, being one of those into which that genus is divided. But the other sacraments only benefit the recipients; thus the baptized person alone receives effect of Baptism. Therefore, neither does this sacrament benefit others than the recipients.

Obj. 2. Further, the effects of this sacrament are the attainment of grace and glory, and the forgiveness of sin, at least of venial sin. If therefore this sacrament were to produce its effects in others besides the recipients, a man might happen to acquire grace and glory and forgiveness of sin without doing or receiving anything himself, through another receiving or offering this sacrament.

Obj. 3. Further, when the cause is multiplied, the effect is likewise multiplied. If therefore this sacrament benefit others besides the recipients, it would follow that it benefits a man more if he receive this sacrament through many hosts being consecrated in one mass, whereas this is not the Church's custom: for instance, that many receive communion for the salvation of one individual. Consequently, it does not seem that this sacrament benefits anyone but the recipient.

On the contrary, Prayer is made for many others during the celebration of this sacrament; which would serve no purpose were the sacrament not beneficial to others. Therefore, this sacrament is beneficial not merely to them who receive it.

I answer that, As stated above (A. 3), this

sacrament is not only a sacrament, but also a sacrifice. For, it has the nature of a sacrifice inasmuch as in this sacrament Christ's Passion is represented, whereby Christ *offered Himself a Victim to God* (Eph. v. 2), and it has the nature of a sacrament inasmuch as invisible grace is bestowed in this sacrament under a visible species. So, then, this sacrament benefits recipients by way both of sacrament and of sacrifice, because it is offered for all who partake of it. For it is said in the Canon of the Mass: *May as many of us as, by participation at this Altar, shall receive the most sacred body and blood of Thy Son, be filled with all heavenly benediction and grace.*

But to others who do not receive it, it is beneficial by way of sacrifice, inasmuch as it is offered for their salvation. Hence it is said in the Canon of the Mass: *Be mindful, O Lord, of Thy servants, men and women . . . for whom we offer, or who offer up to Thee, this sacrifice of praise for themselves and for all their own, for the redemption of their souls, for the hope of their safety and salvation.* And our Lord expressed both ways, saying (Matth. xxvi. 28, with Luke xxii. 20): *Which for you,* i.e. who receive it, *and for many,* i.e. others, *shall be shed unto remission of sins.*

Reply Obj. 1. This sacrament has this in addition to the others, that it is a sacrifice: and therefore the comparison fails.

Reply Obj. 2. As Christ's Passion benefits all, for the forgiveness of sin and the attaining of grace and glory, whereas it produces no effect except in those who are united with Christ's Passion through faith and charity, so likewise this sacrifice, which is the memorial of our Lord's Passion, has no effect except in those who are united with this sacrament through faith and charity. Hence Augustine says to Renatus (*De Anima et ejus origine,* i): *Who may offer Christ's body except for them who are Christ's members?* Hence in the Canon of the Mass no prayer is made for them who are outside the pale of the Church. But it benefits them who are members, more or less, according to the measure of their devotion.

Reply Obj. 3. Receiving is of the very nature of the sacrament, but offering belongs to the nature of sacrifice: consequently, when one or even several receive the body of Christ, no help accrues to others. In like fashion even when the priest consecrates several hosts in one mass, the effect of this sacrament is not increased, since there is only one sacrifice; because there is no more power in several hosts than in one, since there is only one Christ present under all the hosts and under one. Hence, neither will any one receive greater effect from the sacrament by taking many

consecrated hosts in one mass. But the oblation of the sacrifice is multiplied in several masses, and therefore the effect of the sacrifice and of the sacrament is multiplied.

EIGHTH ARTICLE

Whether the Effect of This Sacrament Is Hindered by Venial Sin?

We proceed thus to the Eighth Article:—

Objection 1. It seems that the effect of this sacrament is not hindered by venial sin. For Augustine (*Tract.* xxvi, *in Joan.*), commenting on John vi. 52, *If any man eat of this bread,* etc., says: *Eat the heavenly bread spiritually; bring innocence to the altar; your sins, though they be daily, let them not be deadly.* From this it is evident that venial sins, which are called daily sins, do not prevent spiritual eating. But they who eat spiritually, receive the effect of this sacrament. Therefore, venial sins do not hinder the effect of this sacrament.

Obj. 2. Further, this sacrament is not less powerful than Baptism. But, as stated above (Q. 69, AA. 9, 10), only pretense checks the effect of Baptism, and venial sins do not belong to pretense; because according to Wis. i. 5: *the Holy Spirit of discipline will flee from the deceitful,* yet He is not put to flight by venial sins. Therefore neither do venial sins hinder the effect of this sacrament.

Obj. 3. Further, nothing which is removed by the action of any cause, can hinder the effect of such cause. But venial sins are taken away by this sacrament. Therefore, they do not hinder its effect.

On the contrary, Damascene says (*De Fide Orthod.* iv): *The fire of that desire which is within us, being kindled by the burning coal,* i.e. this sacrament, *will consume our sins, and enlighten our hearts, so that we shall be inflamed and made godlike.* But the fire of our desire or love is hindered by venial sins, which hinder the fervor of charity, as was shown in the Second Part (I-II, Q. 81, A. 4; II-II, Q. 24, A. 10). Therefore venial sins hinder the effect of this sacrament.

I answer that, Venial sins can be taken in two ways: first of all as past, secondly as in the act of being committed. Venial sins taken in the first way do not in any way hinder the effect of this sacrament. For it can come to pass that after many venial sins a man may approach devoutly to this sacrament and fully secure its effect. Considered in the second way, venial sins do not utterly hinder the effect of this sacrament, but merely in part. For, it has been stated above (A. 1), that the effect of this sacrament is not only the obtaining of habitual grace or charity, but also a certain actual refreshment of spiritual sweetness: which is indeed hindered if anyone approach to this sacrament with mind distracted through venial sins; but the increase of habitual grace or of charity is not taken away.

Reply Obj. 1. He that approaches this sacrament with actual venial sin, eats spiritually indeed, in habit but not in act: and therefore he shares in the habitual effect of the sacrament, but not in its actual effect.

Reply Obj. 2. Baptism is not ordained, as this sacrament is, for the fervor of charity as its actual effect. Because Baptism is spiritual regeneration, through which the first perfection is acquired, which is a habit or form; but this sacrament is spiritual eating, which has actual delight.

Reply Obj. 3. This argument deals with past venial sins, which are taken away by this sacrament.

QUESTION 80

Of the Use or Receiving of This Sacrament in General

(In Twelve Articles)

WE have now to consider the use or receiving of this sacrament, first of all in general; secondly, how Christ used this sacrament.

Under the first heading there are twelve points of inquiry: (1) Whether there are two ways of eating this sacrament, namely, sacramentally and spiritually? (2) Whether it belongs to man alone to eat this sacrament spiritually? (3) Whether it belongs to the just man only to eat it sacramentally? (4) Whether the sinner sins in eating it sacramentally? (5) Of the degree of this sin. (6) Whether this sacrament should be refused to the sinner that approaches it? (7) Whether nocturnal pollution prevents man from receiving this sacrament? (8) Whether it is to be received only when one is fasting? (9) Whether it is to be given to them who lack the use of reason? (10) Whether it is to be received daily? (11) Whether it is lawful to refrain from it altogether? (12) Whether it is lawful to receive the body without the blood?

FIRST ARTICLE

Whether There Are Two Ways to Be Distinguished of Eating Christ's Body?

We proceed thus to the First Article:—

Objection 1. It seems that two ways ought not to be distinguished of eating Christ's body, namely, sacramentally and spiritually. For, as Baptism is spiritual regeneration, according to John iii. 5: *Unless a man be born again of water and the Holy Ghost,* etc., so also this sacrament is spiritual food: hence our Lord, speaking of this sacrament, says (John vi. 64): *The words that I have spoken to you are spirit and life.* But there are no two distinct ways of receiving Baptism, namely, sacramentally and spiritually. Therefore neither ought this distinction to be made regarding this sacrament.

Obj. 2. Further, when two things are so related that one is on account of the other, they should not be put in contradistinction to one another, because the one derives its species from the other. But sacramental eating is ordained for spiritual eating as its end. Therefore sacramental eating ought not to be divided in contrast with spiritual eating.

Obj. 3. Further, things which cannot exist without one another ought not to be divided in contrast with each other. But it seems that no one can eat spiritually without eating sacramentally; otherwise the fathers of old would have eaten this sacrament spiritually. Moreover, sacramental eating would be to no purpose, if the spiritual eating could be had without it. Therefore it is not right to distinguish a twofold eating, namely, sacramental and spiritual.

On the contrary, The gloss says on 1 Cor. xi. 29: *He that eateth and drinketh unworthily,* etc.: *We hold that there are two ways of eating, the one sacramental, and the other spiritual.*

I answer that, There are two things to be considered in the receiving of this sacrament, namely, the sacrament itself, and its fruits, and we have already spoken of both (QQ. 73, 79). The perfect way, then, of receiving this sacrament is when one takes it so as to partake of its effect. Now, as was stated above (Q. 79, AA. 3, 8), it sometimes happens that a man is hindered from receiving the effect of this sacrament; and such receiving of this sacrament is an imperfect one. Therefore, as the perfect is divided against the imperfect, so sacramental eating, whereby the sacrament only is received without its effect, is divided against spiritual eating, by which one receives the effect of this sacrament, whereby a man is spiritually united with Christ through faith and charity.

Reply Obj. 1. The same distinction is made regarding Baptism and the other sacraments: for, some receive the sacrament only, while others receive the sacrament and the reality of the sacrament. However, there is a difference, because, since the other sacraments are accomplished in the use of the matter, the receiving of the sacrament is the actual perfection of the sacrament; whereas this sacrament is accomplished in the consecration of the matter: and consequently both uses follow the sacrament. On the other hand, in Baptism and in the other sacraments that imprint a character, they who receive the sacrament receive some spiritual effect, that is, the character; which is not the case in this sacrament. And therefore, in this sacrament, rather than in Baptism, the sacramental use is distinguished from the spiritual use.

Reply Obj. 2. That sacramental eating which is also a spiritual eating is not divided in contrast with spiritual eating, but is included under it; but that sacramental eating which does not secure the effect, is divided in contrast with spiritual eating; just as the imperfect, which does not attain the perfection of its species, is divided in contrast with the perfect.

Reply Obj. 3. As stated above (Q. 73, A. 3), the effect of the sacrament can be secured by every man if he receive it in desire, though not in reality. Consequently, just as some are baptized with the Baptism of desire, through their desire of baptism, before being baptized in the Baptism of water; so likewise some eat this sacrament spiritually ere they receive it sacramentally. Now this happens in two ways. First of all, from desire of receiving the sacrament itself, and thus are said to be baptized, and to eat spiritually, and not sacramentally, they who desire to receive these sacraments since they have been instituted. Secondly, by a figure: thus the Apostle says (1 Cor. x. 2), that the fathers of old were *baptized in the cloud and in the sea,* and that *they did eat . . . spiritual food, and . . . drank . . . spiritual drink.* Nevertheless sacramental eating is not without avail, because the actual receiving of the sacrament produces more fully the effect of the sacrament than does the desire thereof, as stated above of Baptism (Q. 69, A. 4, *ad* 2).

SECOND ARTICLE

Whether It Belongs to Man Alone to Eat This Sacrament Spiritually?

We proceed thus to the Second Article:—

Objection 1. It seems that it does not belong to man alone to eat this sacrament spiritually, but likewise to angels. Because on Ps. lxxvii. 25: *Man ate the bread of angels,* the gloss says,—*that is, the body of Christ, Who is truly the food of angels.* But it would not be so unless the angels were to eat Christ spiritually. Therefore the angels eat Christ spiritually.

Obj. 2. Further, Augustine (*Tract.* xxvi, *Joan.*) says: *By this meat and drink, He would have us to understand the fellowship of His body and members, which is the Church in His predestinated ones.* But not only men, but also the holy angels belong to that fellowship. Therefore the holy angels eat of it spiritually.

Obj. 3. Further, Augustine in his book *De Verbis Domini (Serm.* cxlii) says: *Christ is to be eaten spiritually, as He Himself declares:* "*He that eateth My flesh and drinketh My blood, abideth in Me, and I in him.*" But this belongs not only to men, but also to the holy angels, in whom Christ dwells by charity, and they in Him. Consequently, it seems that to eat Christ spiritually is not for men only, but also for the angels.

On the contrary, Augustine (*Tract.* xxvi, *in Joan.*) says: *Eat the bread* of the altar *spiritually; take innocence to the altar.* But angels do not approach the altar as for the purpose of taking something therefrom. Therefore the angels do not eat spiritually.

I answer that, Christ Himself is contained in this sacrament, not under His proper species, but under the sacramental species. Consequently there are two ways of eating spiritually. First, as Christ Himself exists under His proper species, and in this way the angels eat Christ spiritually inasmuch as they are united with Him in the enjoyment of perfect charity, and in clear vision (and this is the bread we hope for in heaven), and not by faith, as we are united with Him here.

In another way one may eat Christ spiritually, as He is under the sacramental species, inasmuch as a man believes in Christ, while desiring to receive this sacrament; and this is not merely to eat Christ spiritually, but likewise to eat this sacrament; which does not fall to the lot of the angels. And therefore although the angels feed on Christ spiritually, yet it does not belong to them to eat this sacrament spiritually.

Reply Obj. 1. The receiving of Christ under this sacrament is ordained to the enjoyment of heaven, as to its end, in the same way as the angels enjoy it; and since the means are gauged by the end, hence it is that such eating of Christ whereby we receive Him under this sacrament, is, as it were, derived from that eating whereby the angels enjoy Christ in heaven. Consequently, man is said to eat the *bread of angels,* because it belongs to the angels to do so firstly and principally, since they enjoy Him in his proper species; and secondly it belongs to men, who receive Christ under this sacrament.

Reply Obj. 2. Both men and angels belong to the fellowship of His mystical body; men by faith, and angels by manifest vision. But the sacraments are proportioned to faith, through which the truth is seen *through a glass* and *in a dark manner*. And therefore, properly speaking, it does not belong to angels, but to men, to eat this sacrament spiritually.

Reply Obj. 3. Christ dwells in men through faith, according to their present state, but He is in the blessed angels by manifest vision. Consequently the comparison does not hold, as stated above (*ad 2*).

THIRD ARTICLE

Whether the Just Man Alone May Eat Christ Sacramentally?

We proceed thus to the Third Article:—

Objection 1. It seems that none but the just man may eat Christ sacramentally. For Augustine says in his book *De Remedio Penitentiæ (cf. Tract. in Joan.* xxv, *n.* 12; xxvi, *n.* 1): *Why make ready tooth and belly? Believe, and thou hast eaten. . . . For to believe in Him, this it is, to eat the living bread.* But the sinner does not believe in Him; because he has not living faith, to which it belongs to believe *in God*, as stated above in the Second Part (II-II, Q. 2, A. 2; Q. 4, A. 5). Therefore the sinner cannot eat this sacrament, which is the living bread.

Obj. 2. Further, this sacrament is specially called *the sacrament of charity*, as stated above (Q. 78, A. 3, *ad* 6). But as unbelievers lack faith, so all sinners lack charity. Now unbelievers do not seem to be capable of eating this sacrament, since in the sacramental form it is called the *Mystery of Faith*. Therefore, for like reason, the sinner cannot eat Christ's body sacramentally.

Obj. 3. Further, the sinner is more abominable before God than the irrational creature: for it is said of the sinner (Ps. xlviii. 21): *Man when he was in honor did not understand; he hath been compared to senseless beasts, and made like to them.* But an irrational animal, such as a mouse or a dog, cannot receive this sacrament, just as it cannot receive the sacrament of Baptism. Therefore it seems that for the like reason neither may sinners eat this sacrament.

On the contrary, Augustine (*Tract.* xxvi, *in Joan.*), commenting on the words, *that if any man eat of it he may not die,* says: *Many receive from the altar, and by receiving die: whence the Apostle saith, "eateth and drinketh judgment to himself."* But only sinners die by receiving. Therefore sinners eat the body of Christ sacramentally, and not the just only.

I answer that, In the past, some have erred upon this point, saying that Christ's body is not received sacramentally by sinners; but that directly the body is touched by the lips of sinners, it ceases to be under the sacramental species.

But this is erroneous; because it detracts from the truth of this sacrament, to which truth it belongs that so long as the species last, Christ's body does not cease to be under them, as stated above (Q. 76, A. 6, *ad* 3; Q. 77, A. 8). But the species last so long as the substance of the bread would remain, if it were there, as was stated above (Q. 77, A. 4). Now it is clear that the substance of bread taken by a sinner does not at once cease to be, but it continues until digested by natural heat: hence Christ's body remains just as long under the sacramental species when taken by sinners. Hence it must be said that the sinner, and not merely the just, can eat Christ's body.

Reply Obj. 1. Such words and similar expressions are to be understood of spiritual eating, which does not belong to sinners. Consequently, it is from such expressions being misunderstood that the above error seems to have arisen, through ignorance of the distinction between corporeal and spiritual eating.

Reply Obj. 2. Should even an unbeliever receive the sacramental species, he would receive Christ's body under the sacrament: hence he would eat Christ sacramentally, if the word *sacramentally* qualify the verb on the part of the thing eaten. But if it qualify the verb on the part of the one eating, then, properly speaking, he does not eat sacramentally, because he uses what he takes, not as a sacrament, but as simple food. Unless perchance the unbeliever were to intend to receive what the Church bestows; without having proper faith regarding the other articles, or regarding this sacrament.

Reply Obj. 3. Even though a mouse or a dog were to eat the consecrated host, the substance of Christ's body would not cease to be under the species, so long as those species remain, and that is, so long as the substance of bread would have remained; just as if it were to be cast into the mire. Nor does this turn to any indignity regarding Christ's body, since He willed to be crucified by sinners without detracting from His dignity; especially since the mouse or dog does not touch Christ's body in its proper species, but only as to its sacramental species.

Some, however, have said that Christ's body would cease to be there, directly it were touched by a mouse or a dog; but this again detracts from the truth of the sacrament, as stated above.

None the less it must not be said that the irrational animal eats the body of Christ sacramentally; since it is incapable of using it as a sacrament. Hence it eats Christ's body *accidentally*, and not sacramentally, just as if anyone not knowing a host to be consecrated were to consume it. And since no genus is divided by an accidental difference, therefore this manner of eating Christ's body is not set down as a third way besides sacramental and spiritual eating.

FOURTH ARTICLE

Whether the Sinner Sins in Receiving Christ's Body Sacramentally?

We proceed thus to the Fourth Article:—

Objection 1. It seems that the sinner does not sin in receiving Christ's body sacramentally, because Christ has no greater dignity under the sacramental species than under His own. But sinners did not sin when they touched Christ's body under its proper species; nay, rather they obtained forgiveness of their sins, as we read in Luke vii of the woman who was a sinner; while it is written (Matth. xiv. 36) that *as many as touched the hem of His garment were healed.* Therefore, they do not sin, but rather obtain salvation, by receiving the body of Christ.

Obj. 2. Further, this sacrament, like the others, is a spiritual medicine. But medicine is given to the sick for their recovery, according to Matth. ix. 12: *They that are in health need not a physician.* Now they that are spiritually sick or infirm are sinners. Therefore this sacrament can be received by them without sin.

Obj. 3. Further, this sacrament is one of our greatest gifts, since it contains Christ. But according to Augustine *(De Lib. Arb.* ii), the greatest gifts are those *which no one can abuse.* Now no one sins except by abusing something. Therefore no sinner sins by receiving this sacrament.

Obj. 4. Further, as this sacrament is perceived by taste and touch, so also is it by sight. Consequently, if the sinner sins by receiving the sacrament, it seems that he would sin by beholding it, which is manifestly untrue, since the Church exposes this sacrament to be seen and adored by all. Therefore the sinner does not sin by eating this sacrament.

Obj. 5. Further, it happens sometimes that the sinner is unconscious of his sin. Yet such a one does not seem to sin by receiving the body of Christ, for according to this all who receive it would sin, as exposing themselves to danger, since the Apostle says (1 Cor. iv. 4): *I am not conscious to myself of anything, yet I am not hereby justified.* Therefore, the sinner, if he receive this sacrament, does not appear to be guilty of sin.

On the contrary, The Apostle says (1 Cor. xi. 29): *He that eateth and drinketh unworthily, eateth and drinketh judgment to himself.* Now the gloss says on this passage: *He eats and drinks unworthily who is in sin, or who handles it irreverently.* Therefore, if anyone, while in mortal sin, receives this sacrament, he purchases damnation, by sinning mortally.

I answer that, In this sacrament, as in the others, that which is a sacrament is a sign of the reality of the sacrament. Now there is a twofold reality of this sacrament, as stated above (Q. 73, A. 6): one which is signified and contained, namely, Christ Himself; while the other is signified but not contained, namely, Christ's mystical body, which is the fellowship of the saints. Therefore, whoever receives this sacrament, expresses thereby that he is made one with Christ, and incorporated in His members; and this is done by living faith, which no one has who is in mortal sin. And therefore it is manifest that whoever receives this sacrament while in mortal sin, is guilty of lying to this sacrament, and consequently of sacrilege, because he profanes the sacrament: and therefore he sins mortally.

Reply Obj. 1. When Christ appeared under His proper species, He did not give Himself to be touched by men as a sign of spiritual union with Himself, as He gives Himself to be received in this sacrament. And therefore sinners in touching Him under His proper species did not incur the sin of lying to Godlike things, as sinners do in receiving this sacrament.

Furthermore, Christ still bore the likeness of the body of sin; consequently He fittingly allowed Himself to be touched by sinners. But as soon as the body of sin was taken away by the glory of the Resurrection, he forbade the woman to touch Him, for her faith in Him was defective, according to John xx. 17: *Do not touch Me, for I am not yet ascended to My Father,* i.e. *in your heart,* as Augustine explains *(Tract.* cxxi, *in Joan.).* And therefore sinners, who lack living faith regarding Christ are not allowed to touch this sacrament.

Reply Obj. 2. Every medicine does not suit every stage of sickness; because the tonic given to those who are recovering from fever would be hurtful to them if given while yet in their feverish condition. So likewise Baptism and Penance are as purgative medicines, given to take away the fever of sin; whereas this sacrament is a medicine given to strengthen, and it ought not to be given except to them who are quit of sin.

Reply Obj. 3. By the *greatest gifts* Augustine understands the soul's virtues, *which no one uses to evil purpose,* as though they were principles of evil. Nevertheless sometimes a man makes a bad use of them, as objects of an evil use, as is seen in those who are proud of their virtues. So likewise this sacrament, so far as the sacrament is concerned, is not the principle of an evil use, but the object thereof. Hence Augustine says *(Tract. lxii, in Joan.)*: *Many receive Christ's body unworthily; whence we are taught what need there is to beware of receiving a good thing evilly. . . . For behold, of a good thing, received evilly, evil is wrought:* just as on the other hand, in the Apostle's case, *good was wrought through evil well received,* namely, by bearing patiently the sting of Satan.

Reply Obj. 4. Christ's body is not received by being seen, but only its sacrament, because sight does not penetrate to the substance of Christ's body, but only to the sacramental species, as stated above (Q. 76, A. 7). But he who eats, receives not only the sacramental species, but likewise Christ Himself Who is under them. Consequently, no one is forbidden to behold Christ's body, when once he has received Christ's sacrament, namely, Baptism: whereas the non-baptized are not to be allowed even to see this sacrament, as is clear from Dionysius *(Eccl. Hier.* vii). But only those are to be allowed to share in the eating who are united with Christ not merely sacramentally, but likewise really.

Reply Obj. 5. The fact of a man being unconscious of his sin can come about in two ways. First of all through his own fault, either because through ignorance of the law (which ignorance does not excuse him), he thinks something not to be sinful which is a sin, as for example if one guilty of fornication were to deem simple fornication not to be a mortal sin; or because he neglects to examine his conscience, which is opposed to what the Apostle says (1 Cor. xi. 28): *Let a man prove himself, and so let him eat of that bread, and drink of the chalice.* And in this way nevertheless the sinner who receives Christ's body commits sin, although unconscious thereof, because the very ignorance is a sin on his part.

Secondly, it may happen without fault on his part, as, for instance, when he has sorrowed over his sin, but is not sufficiently contrite: and in such a case he does not sin in receiving the body of Christ, because a man cannot know for certain whether he is truly contrite. It suffices, however, if he find in himself the marks of contrition, for instance, if he *grieve over past sins,* and *propose to avoid them in the future.** But if he be ignorant that what he did was a sinful act, through ignorance of the fact, which excuses, for instance, if a man approach a woman whom he believed to be his wife whereas she was not, he is not to be called a sinner on that

account; in the same way if he has utterly forgotten his sin, general contrition suffices for blotting it out, as will be said hereafter (Suppl., Q. 2, A. 3, *ad* 2) ; hence he is no longer to be called a sinner.

FIFTH ARTICLE

ether to Approach This Sacrament with Consciousness of Sin Is the Gravest of All Sins?

We proceed thus to the Fifth Article:—

Objection 1. It seems that to approach this sacrament with consciousness of sin is the gravest of all sins; because the Apostle says (1 Cor. xi. 27): *Whosoever shall eat this bread, or drink the chalice of the Lord unworthily, shall be guilty of the body and of the blood of the Lord:* upon which the gloss observes: *He shall be punished as though he slew Christ.* But the sin of them who slew Christ seems to have been most grave. Therefore this sin, whereby a man approaches Christ's table with consciousness of sin, appears to be the gravest.

Obj. 2. Further, Jerome says in an Epistle (xlix): *What hast thou to do with women, thou that speakest familiarly with God at the altar?†* Say, priest, say, cleric, how dost thou kiss the Son of God with the same lips wherewith thou hast kissed the daughter of a harlot? "Judas, thou betrayest the Son of Man with a kiss!" And thus it appears that the fornicator approaching Christ's table sins as Judas did, whose sin was most grave. But there are many other sins which are graver than fornication, especially the sin of unbelief. Therefore the sin of every sinner approaching Christ's table is the gravest of all.

Obj. 3. Further, spiritual uncleanness is more abominable to God than corporeal. But if anyone was to cast Christ's body into mud or a cess-pool, his sin would be reputed a most grave one. Therefore, he sins more deeply by receiving it with sin, which is spiritual uncleanness, upon his soul.

On the contrary, Augustine says on the words, *If I had not come, and had not spoken to them, they would be without sin (Tract.* lxxxix, *in Joan.),* that this is to be understood of the sin of unbelief, *in which all sins are comprised,* and so the greatest of all sins appears to be, not this, but rather the sin of unbelief.

I answer that, As stated in the Second Part (I-II, Q. 73, AA. 3, 6; II-II, Q. 73, A. 3), one sin can be said to be graver than another in two ways: first of all essentially, secondly accidentally. Essentially, in regard to its species, which is taken from its object: and so a sin is greater according as that against which it is committed is greater. And since Christ's

---

* Cf. Rule of St. Augustine.   † The remaining part of the quotation is not from S. Jerome.

Godhead is greater than His humanity, and His humanity greater than the sacraments of His humanity, hence it is that those are the gravest sins which are committed against the Godhead, such as unbelief and blasphemy. The second degree of gravity is held by those sins which are committed against His humanity: hence it is written (Matth. xii. 32): *Whosoever shall speak a word against the Son of Man, it shall be forgiven him; but he that shall speak against the Holy Ghost, it shall not be forgiven him, neither in this world nor in the world to come.* In the third place come sins committed against the sacraments, which belong to Christ's humanity; and after these are the other sins committed against mere creatures.

Accidentally, one sin can be graver than another on the sinner's part; for example, the sin which is the result of ignorance or of weakness is lighter than one arising from contempt, or from sure knowledge; and the same reason holds good of other circumstances. And according to this, the above sin can be graver in some, as happens in them who from actual contempt and with consciousness of sin approach this sacrament: but in others it is less grave; for instance, in those who from fear of their sin being discovered, approach this sacrament with consciousness of sin.

So, then, it is evident that this sin is specifically graver than many others, yet it is not the greatest of all.

Reply Obj. 1. The sin of the unworthy recipient is compared to the sin of them who slew Christ, by way of similitude, because each is committed against Christ's body; but not according to the degree of the crime. Because the sin of Christ's slayers was much graver, first of all, because their sin was against Christ's body in its own species, while this sin is against it under sacramental species; secondly, because their sin came of the intent of injuring Christ, while this does not.

Reply Obj. 2. The sin of the fornicator receiving Christ's body is likened to Judas kissing Christ, as to the resemblance of the sin, because each outrages Christ with the sign of friendship; but not as to the extent of the sin, as was observed above (*ad* 1). And this resemblance in crime applies no less to other sinners than to fornicators: because by other mortal sins, sinners act against the charity of Christ, of which this sacrament is the sign, and all the more according as their sins are graver. But in a measure the sin of fornication makes one more unfit for receiving this sacrament, because thereby especially the spirit becomes enslaved by the flesh, which is a hindrance to the fervor of love required for this sacrament.

However, the hindrance to charity itself weighs more than the hindrance to its fervor. Hence the sin of unbelief, which fundamentally severs a man from the unity of the Church, simply speaking, makes him to be utterly unfit for receiving this sacrament; because it is the sacrament of the Church's unity, as stated above (Q. 67, A. 2). Hence the unbeliever who receives this sacrament sins more grievously than the believer who is in sin; and shows greater contempt towards Christ Who is in the sacrament, especially if he does not believe Christ to be truly in this sacrament; because, so far as lies in him, he lessens the holiness of the sacrament, and the power of Christ acting in it, and this is to despise the sacrament in itself. But the believer who receives the sacrament with consciousness of sin, by receiving it unworthily despises the sacrament, not in itself, but in its use. Hence the Apostle (1 Cor. xi. 29) in assigning the cause of this sin, says, *not discerning the body of the Lord,* that is, not distinguishing it from other food: and this is what he does who disbelieves Christ's presence in this sacrament.

Reply Obj. 3. The man who would throw this sacrament into the mire would be guilty of more heinous sin than another approaching the sacrament fully conscious of mortal sin. First of all, because he would intend to outrage the sacrament, whereas the sinner receiving Christ's body unworthily has no such intent; secondly, because the sinner is capable of grace; hence he is more capable of receiving this sacrament than any irrational creature. Hence he would make a most revolting use of this sacrament who would throw it to dogs to eat, or fling it in the mire to be trodden upon.

SIXTH ARTICLE

Whether the Priest Ought to Deny the Body of Christ to the Sinner Seeking It?

We proceed thus to the Sixth Article:—

Objection 1. It seems that the priest should deny the body of Christ to the sinner seeking it. For Christ's precept is not to be set aside for the sake of avoiding scandal or on account of infamy to anyone. But (Matth. vii. 6) our Lord gave this command: *Give not that which is holy to dogs.* Now it is especially casting holy things to dogs to give this sacrament to sinners. Therefore, neither on account of avoiding scandal or infamy should this sacrament be administered to the sinner who asks for it.

Obj. 2. Further, one must choose the lesser of two evils. But it seems to be the lesser evil if the sinner incur infamy; or if an unconsecrated host be given to him; than for him to sin mortally by receiving the body of Christ. Consequently, it seems that the course to be adopted is either that the sinner seeking the body of Christ be exposed to infamy, or that an unconsecrated host be given to him.

Obj. 3. Further, the body of Christ is sometimes given to those suspected of crime in order to put them to proof. Because we read in the Decretals: *It often happens that thefts are perpetrated in monasteries of monks; wherefore we command that when the brethren have to exonerate themselves of such acts, that the abbot shall celebrate Mass, or someone else deputed by him, in the presence of the community; and so, when the Mass is over, all shall communicate under these words: "May the body of Christ prove thee today."* And further on: *If any evil deed be imputed to a bishop or priest, for each charge he must say Mass and communicate, and show that he is innocent of each act imputed.* But secret sinners must not be disclosed, for, once the blush of shame is set aside, they will indulge the more in sin, as Augustine says *(De Verbis Dom.; cf. Serm.* lxxxii). Consequently, Christ's body is not to be given to occult sinners, even if they ask for it.

On the contrary, On Ps. xxi. 30: *All the fat ones of the earth have eaten and have adored,* Augustine says: *Let not the dispenser hinder the fat ones of the earth,* i.e. sinners, *from eating at the table of the Lord.*

I answer that, A distinction must be made among sinners: some are secret; others are notorious, either from evidence of the fact, as public usurers, or public robbers, or from being denounced as evil men by some ecclesiastical or civil tribunal. Therefore Holy Communion ought not to be given to open sinners when they ask for it. Hence Cyprian writes to someone *(Ep.* lxi): *You were so kind as to consider that I ought to be consulted regarding actors, and that magician who continues to practice his disgraceful arts among you; as to whether I thought that Holy Communion ought to be given to such with the other Christians. I think that it is beseeming neither the Divine majesty, nor Christian discipline, for the Church's modesty and honor to be defiled by such shameful and infamous contagion.*

But if they be not open sinners, but occult, the Holy Communion should not be denied them if they ask for it. For since every Christian, from the fact that he is baptized, is admitted to the Lord's table, he may not be robbed of his right, except from some open cause. Hence on 1 Cor. v. 11, *If he who is called a brother among you,* etc., Augustine's gloss remarks: *We cannot inhibit any person from Communion, except he has openly confessed, or has been named and convicted by some ecclesiastical or lay tribunal.* Nevertheless a priest who has knowledge of the crime can privately warn the secret sinner, or warn all openly in public, from approaching the Lord's table, until they have repented of their sins and have been reconciled to the Church; because after repentance and reconciliation, Communion must not be refused even to public sinners, especially in the hour of death. Hence in the (3rd) Council of Carthage *(Can.* xxxv) we read: *Reconciliation is not to be denied to stage-players or actors, or others of the sort, or to apostates, after their conversion to God.*

Reply Obj. 1. Holy things are forbidden to be given to dogs, that is, to notorious sinners: whereas hidden deeds may not be published, but are to be left to the Divine judgment.

Reply Obj. 2. Although it is worse for the secret sinner to sin mortally in taking the body of Christ, rather than be defamed, nevertheless for the priest administering the body of Christ it is worse to commit mortal sin by unjustly defaming the hidden sinner than that the sinner should sin mortally; because no one ought to commit mortal sin in order to keep another out of mortal sin. Hence Augustine says *(Quæst, super Gen.* xlii): *It is a most dangerous exchange, for us to do evil lest another perpetrate a greater evil.* But the secret sinner ought rather to prefer infamy than approach the Lord's table unworthily.

Yet by no means should an unconsecrated host be given in place of a consecrated one; because the priest by so doing, so far as he is concerned, makes others, either the bystanders or the communicant, commit idolatry by believing that it is a consecrated host; because, as Augustine says on Ps. xcviii. 5: *Let no one eat Christ's flesh, except he first adore it.* Hence in the Decretals (Extra, *De Celeb. Miss.,* Ch. *De Homine)* it is said: *Although he who reputes himself unworthy of the Sacrament, through consciousness of his sin, sins gravely, if he receive; still he seems to offend more deeply who deceitfully has presumed to simulate it.*

Reply Obj. 3. Those decrees were abolished by contrary enactments of Roman Pontiffs: because Pope Stephen (V) writes as follows: *The Sacred Canons do not allow of a confession being extorted from any person by trial made by burning iron or boiling water; it belongs to our government to judge of public crimes committed, and that by means of confession made spontaneously, or by proof of witnesses: but private and unknown crimes are to be left to Him Who alone knows the hearts of the sons of men.* And the same is found in the Decretals (Extra, *De Purgationibus,* Ch. *Ex tuarum).* Because in all such practices there seems to be a tempting of God; hence such things cannot be done without sin. And it would seem graver still if anyone were to incur judgment of death through this sacrament, which was instituted as a means of salvation. Consequently, the body of Christ should never be given to anyone suspected of crime, as by way of examination.

SEVENTH ARTICLE

Whether the Seminal Loss That Occurs during Sleep Hinders Anyone from Receiving This Sacrament?

We proceed thus to the Seventh Article:—

Objection 1. It seems that seminal loss does not hinder anyone from receiving the body of Christ: because no one is prevented from receiving the body of Christ except on account of sin. But seminal loss happens without sin: for Augustine says *(Gen. ad lit.* xii) that *the same image that comes into the mind of a speaker may present itself to the mind of the sleeper, so that the latter be unable to distinguish the image from the reality, and is moved carnally and with the result that usually follows such motions; and there is as little sin in this as there is in speaking and therefore thinking about such things.* Consequently these motions do not prevent one from receiving this sacrament.

Obj. 2. Further, Gregory says in a Letter to Augustine, Bishop of the English *(Regist.* xi): *Those who pay the debt of marriage not from lust, but from desire to have children, should be left to their own judgment, as to whether they should enter the church and receive the mystery of our Lord's body, after such intercourse: because they ought not to be forbidden from receiving it, since they have passed through the fire unscorched.*

From this it is evident that seminal loss even of one awake, if it be without sin, is no hindrance to receiving the body of Christ. Consequently, much less is it in the case of one asleep.

Obj. 3. Further, these movements of the flesh seem to bring with them only bodily uncleanness. But there are other bodily defilements which according to the Law forbade entrance into the holy places, yet which under the New Law do not prevent receiving this sacrament: as, for instance, in the case of a woman after child-birth, or in her periods, or suffering from issue of blood, as Gregory writes to Augustine, Bishop of the English *(loc. cit.).* Therefore it seems that neither do these movements of the flesh hinder a man from receiving this sacrament.

Obj. 4. Further, venial sin is no hindrance to receiving the sacrament, nor is mortal sin after repentance. But even supposing that

seminal loss arises from some foregoing sin, whether of intemperance, or of bad thoughts, for the most part such sin is venial; and if occasionally it be mortal, a man may repent of it by morning and confess it. Consequently, it seems that he ought not to be prevented from receiving this sacrament.

Obj. 5. Further, a sin against the Fifth Commandment is greater than a sin against the Sixth. But if a man dream that he has broken the Fifth or Seventh or any other Commandment, he is not on that account debarred from receiving this sacrament. Therefore it seems that much less should he be debarred through defilement resulting from a dream against the Sixth Commandment.

On the contrary, It is written (Lev. xv. 16): *The man from whom the seed of copulation goeth out . . . shall be unclean until evening.* But for the unclean there is no approaching to the sacraments. Therefore, it seems that owing to such defilement of the flesh a man is debarred from taking this which is the greatest of the sacraments.

I answer that, There are two things to be weighed regarding the aforesaid movements: one on account of which they necessarily prevent a man from receiving this sacrament; the other, on account of which they do so, not of necessity, but from a sense of propriety.

Mortal sin alone necessarily prevents anyone from partaking of this sacrament: and although these movements during sleep, considered in themselves, cannot be a mortal sin, nevertheless, owing to their cause, they have mortal sin connected with them; which cause, therefore, must be investigated. Sometimes they are due to an external spiritual cause, viz. the deception of the demons, who can stir up phantasms, as was stated in the First Part (Q. 111, A. 3), through the apparition of which, these movements occasionally follow. Sometimes they are due to an internal spiritual cause, such as previous thoughts. At other times they arise from some internal corporeal cause, as from abundance or weakness of nature, or even from surfeit of meat or drink. Now every one of these three causes can be without sin at all, or else with venial sin, or with mortal sin. If it be without sin, or with venial sin, it does not necessarily prevent the receiving of this sacrament, so as to make a man guilty of the body and blood of the Lord: but should it be with mortal sin, it prevents it of necessity.

For such illusions on the part of demons sometimes come from one's not striving to receive fervently; and this can be either a mortal or a venial sin. At other times it is due to malice alone on the part of the demons who wish to keep men from receiving this sacrament. So we read in the Conferences of the Fathers (Cassian,—*Collat.* xxii) that when a certain one always suffered thus on those feast-days on which he had to receive Communion, his superiors, discovering that there was no fault on his part, ruled that he was not to refrain from communicating on that account, and the demoniacal illusion ceased.

In like fashion previous evil thoughts can sometimes be without any sin whatever, as when one has to think of such things on account of lecturing or debating; and if it be done without concupiscence and delectation, the thoughts will not be unclean but honest; and yet defilement can come of such thoughts, as is clear from the authority of Augustine (*Obj.* 1). At other times such thoughts come of concupiscence and delectation, and should there be consent, it will be a mortal sin: otherwise it will be a venial sin.

In the same way too the corporeal cause can be without sin, as when it arises from bodily debility, and hence some individuals suffer seminal loss without sin even in their wakeful hours; or it can come from the abundance of nature: for, just as blood can flow without sin, so also can the semen which is superfluity of the blood, according to the Philosopher (*De Gener. Animal.* i). But occasionally it is with sin, as when it is due to excess of food or drink. And this also can be either venial or mortal sin; although more frequently the sin is mortal in the case of evil thoughts on account of the proneness to consent, rather than in the case of consumption of food and drink. Hence Gregory, writing to Augustine, Bishop of the English (*loc. cit.*), says that one ought to refrain from Communion when this arises from evil thoughts, but not when it arises from excess of food or drink, especially if necessity call for Communion. So, then, one must judge from its cause whether such bodily defilement of necessity hinders the receiving of this sacrament.

At the same time a sense of decency forbids Communion on two accounts. The first of these is always verified, viz. the bodily defilement, with which, out of reverence for the sacrament, it is unbecoming to approach the altar (and hence those who wish to touch any sacred object, wash their hands): except perchance such uncleanness be perpetual or of long standing, such as leprosy or issue of blood, or anything else of the kind. The other reason is the mental distraction which follows after the aforesaid movements, especially when they take place with unclean imaginings. Now this obstacle, which arises from a sense of decency, can be set aside owing to any necessity, as Gregory says (*ibid.*): *As when per-*

chance either a festival day calls for it, or necessity compels one to exercise the ministry because there is no other priest at hand.

Reply Obj. 1. A person is hindered necessarily, only by mortal sin, from receiving this sacrament: but from a sense of decency one may be hindered through other causes, as stated above.

Reply Obj. 2. Conjugal intercourse, if it be without sin, (for instance, if it be done for the sake of begetting offspring, or of paying the marriage debt), does not prevent the receiving of this sacrament for any other reason than do those movements in question which happen without sin, as stated above; namely, on account of the defilement to the body and distraction to the mind. On this account Jerome expresses himself in the following terms in his commentary on Matthew (*Epist.* xxviii, among S. Jerome's works): *If the loaves of Proposition might not be eaten by them who had known their wives carnally, how much less may this bread which has come down from heaven be defiled and touched by them who shortly before have been in conjugal embraces? It is not that we condemn marriages, but that at the time when we are going to eat the flesh of the Lamb, we ought not to indulge in carnal acts.* But since this is to be understood in the sense of decency, and not of necessity, Gregory says that such a person *is to be left to his own judgment. But if,* as Gregory says (*ibid.*), *it be not desire of begetting offspring, but lust that prevails,* then such a one should be forbidden to approach this sacrament.

Reply Obj. 3. As Gregory says in his Letter quoted above to Augustine, Bishop of the English, in the old Testament some persons were termed polluted figuratively, which the people of the New Law understand spiritually. Hence such bodily uncleannesses, if perpetual or of long standing, do not hinder the receiving of this saving sacrament, as they prevented approaching those figurative sacraments; but if they pass speedily, like the uncleanness of the aforesaid movements, then from a sense of fittingness they hinder the receiving of this sacrament during the day on which it happens. Hence it is written (Deut. xxiii. 10): *If there be among you any man, that is defiled in a dream by night, he shall go forth out of the camp; and he shall not return before he be washed with water in the evening.*

Reply Obj. 4. Although the stain of guilt be taken away by contrition and confession, nevertheless the bodily defilement is not taken away, nor the mental distraction which follows therefrom.

Reply Obj. 5. To dream of homicide brings

no bodily uncleanness, nor such distraction of mind as fornication, on account of its intense delectation; still if the dream of homicide comes of a cause sinful in itself, especially if it be mortal sin, then owing to its cause it hinders the receiving of this sacrament.

EIGHTH ARTICLE

Whether Food or Drink Taken Beforehand Hinders the Receiving of This Sacrament?

We proceed thus to the Eighth Article:—

Objection 1. It seems that food or drink taken beforehand does not hinder the receiving of this sacrament. For this sacrament was instituted by our Lord at the supper. But when the supper was ended our Lord gave the sacrament to His disciples, as is evident from Luke xxii. 20, and from 1 Cor. xi. 25. Therefore it seems that we ought to take this sacrament after receiving other food.

Obj. 2. Further, it is written (1 Cor. xi. 33): *When you come together to eat,* namely, the Lord's body, *wait for one another; if any man be hungry, let him eat at home:* and thus it seems that after eating at home a man may eat Christ's body in the Church.

Obj. 3. Further, we read in the (3rd) Council of Carthage *(Can.* xxix): *Let the sacraments of the altar be celebrated only by men who are fasting, with the exception of the anniversary day on which the Lord's Supper is celebrated.* Therefore, at least on that day, one may receive the body of Christ after partaking of other food.

Obj. 4. Further, the taking of water or medicine, or of any other food or drink in very slight quantity, or of the remains of food continuing in the mouth, neither breaks the Church's fast, nor takes away the sobriety required for reverently receiving this sacrament. Consequently, one is not prevented by the above things from receiving this sacrament.

Obj. 5. Further, some eat and drink late at night, and possibly after passing a sleepless night receive the sacred mysteries in the morning when the food it not digested. But it would savor more of moderation if a man were to eat a little in the morning and afterwards receive this sacrament about the ninth hour, since also there is occasionally a longer interval of time. Consequently, it seems that such taking of food beforehand does not keep one from this sacrament.

Obj. 6. Further, there is no less reverence due to this sacrament after receiving it, than before. But one may take food and drink after receiving the sacrament. Therefore one may do so before receiving it.

On the contrary, Augustine says *(Resp. ad Januar.,—Ep.* liv): *It has pleased the Holy Ghost that, out of honor for this great sacrament, the Lord's body should enter the mouth of a Christian before other foods.*

I answer that, A thing may prevent the receiving of this sacrament in two ways: first of all in itself, like mortal sin, which is repugnant to what is signified by this sacrament, as stated above (A. 4): secondly, on account of the Church's prohibition; and thus a man is prevented from taking this sacrament after receiving food or drink, for three reasons. First, as Augustine says *(loc. cit.), out of respect for this sacrament,* so that it may enter into a mouth not yet contaminated by any food or drink. Secondly, because of its signification, i.e. to give us to understand that Christ, Who is the reality of this sacrament, and His charity, ought to be first of all established in our hearts, according to Matth. vi. 33: *Seek first the kingdom of God.* Thirdly, on account of the danger of vomiting and intemperance, which sometimes arise from over-indulging in food, as the Apostle says (1 Cor. xi. 21): *One, indeed, is hungry, and another is drunk.*

Nevertheless the sick are exempted from this general rule, for they should be given Communion at once, even after food, should there be any doubt as to their danger, lest they die without Communion, because necessity has no law. Hence it is said in the Canon de Consecratione: *Let the priest at once take Communion to the sick person, lest he die without Communion.*

Reply Obj. 1. As Augustine says in the same book, *the fact that our Lord gave this sacrament after taking food is no reason why the brethren should assemble after dinner or supper in order to partake of it, or receive it at meal-time, as did those whom the Apostle reproves and corrects. For our Saviour, in order the more strongly to commend the depth of this mystery, wished to fix it closely in the hearts and memories of the disciples; and on that account He gave no command for it to be received in that order, leaving this to the apostles, to whom He was about to entrust the government of the churches.*

Reply Obj. 2. The text quoted is thus paraphrased by the gloss: *If any man be hungry and loath to await the rest, let him partake of his food at home, that is, let him fill himself with earthly bread, without partaking of the Eucharist afterwards.*

Reply Obj. 3. The wording of this decree is in accordance with the former custom observed by some of receiving the body of Christ on that day after breaking their fast, so as to represent the Lord's supper. But this is now abrogated, because as Augustine says *(loc.*

cit.), it is customary throughout the whole world for Christ's body to be received before breaking the fast.

Reply Obj. 4. As stated in the Second Part (II-II, Q. 147, A. 6, *ad* 2), there are two kinds of fast. First, there is the natural fast, which implies privation of everything taken beforehand by way of food or drink: and such fast is required for this sacrament for the reasons given above. And therefore it is never lawful to take this sacrament after taking water, or other food or drink, or even medicine, no matter how small the quantity be. Nor does it matter whether it nourishes or not, whether it be taken by itself or with other things, provided it be taken by way of food or drink. But the remains of food left in the mouth, if swallowed accidentally, do not hinder receiving this sacrament, because they are swallowed not by way of food but by way of saliva. The same holds good of the unavoidable remains of the water or wine wherewith the mouth is rinsed, provided they be not swallowed in great quantity, but mixed with saliva.

Secondly, there is the fast of the Church, instituted for afflicting the body: and this fast is not hindered by the things mentioned (in the objection), because they do not give much nourishment, but are taken rather as an alterative.

Reply Obj. 5. *That this sacrament ought to enter into the mouth of a Christian before any other food* must not be understood absolutely of all time, otherwise he who had once eaten or drunk could never afterwards take this sacrament: but it must be understood of the same day; and although the beginning of the day varies according to different systems of reckoning (for some begin their day at noon, some at sunset, others at midnight, and others at sunrise), the Roman Church begins it at midnight. Consequently, if any person takes anything by way of food or drink after midnight, he may not receive this sacrament on that day; but he can do so if the food was taken before midnight. Nor does it matter, so far as the precept is concerned, whether he has slept after taking food or drink, or whether he has digested it; but it does matter as to the mental disturbance which one suffers from want of sleep or from indigestion, for, if the mind be much disturbed, one becomes unfit for receiving this sacrament.

Reply Obj. 6. The greatest devotion is called for at the moment of receiving this sacrament, because it is then that the effect of the sacrament is bestowed, and such devotion is hindered more by what goes before it than by what comes after it. And therefore it was ordained that men should fast before receiving the sacrament rather than after. Nevertheless there ought to be some interval between receiving this sacrament and taking other food. Consequently, both the Postcommunion prayer of thanksgiving is said in the Mass, and the communicants say their own private prayers.

However, according to the ancient Canons, the following ordination was made by Pope Clement (I), (*Ep.* ii), *If the Lord's portion be eaten in the morning, the ministers who have taken it shall fast until the sixth hour, and if they take it at the third or fourth hour, they shall fast until evening.* For in olden times, the priest celebrated Mass less frequently, and with greater preparation: but now, because the sacred mysteries have to be celebrated oftener, the same could not be easily observed, and so it has been abrogated by contrary custom.

NINTH ARTICLE

Whether Those Who Have Not the Use of Reason Ought to Receive This Sacrament?

We proceed thus to the Ninth Article:—

Objection 1. It seems that those who have not the use of reason ought not to receive this sacrament. For it is required that man should approach this sacrament with devotion and previous self-examination, according to 1 Cor. xi. 28: *Let a man prove himself, and so let him eat of that bread, and drink of the chalice.* But this is not possible for those who are devoid of reason. Therefore this sacrament should not be given to them.

Obj. 2. Further, among those who have not the use of reason are the possessed, who are called energumens. But such persons are kept from even beholding this sacrament, according to Dionysius (*Eccl. Hier.* iii). Therefore this sacrament ought not to be given to those who have not the use of reason.

Obj. 3. Further, among those that lack the use of reason are children, the most innocent of all. But this sacrament is not given to children. Therefore much less should it be given to others deprived of the use of reason.

On the contrary, We read in the First Council of Orange, (Canon 13); and the same is to be found in the Decretals (xxvi. 6): *All things that pertain to piety are to be given to the insane:* and consequently, since this is the *sacrament of piety,* it must be given to them.

I answer that, Men are said to be devoid of reason in two ways. First, when they are feeble-minded, as a man who sees dimly is said not to see: and since such persons can conceive some devotion towards this sacrament, it is not to be denied them.

In another way men are said not to possess

fully the use of reason. Either, then, they never had the use of reason, and have remained so from birth; and in that case this sacrament is not to be given to them, because in no way has there been any preceding devotion towards the sacrament: or else, they were not always devoid of reason, and then, if when they formerly had their wits they showed devotion towards this sacrament, it ought to be given to them in the hour of death; unless danger be feared of vomiting or spitting it out. Hence we read in the acts of the Fourth Council of Carthage (Canon 76); and the same is to be found in the Decretals (xxvi. 6): *If a sick man ask to receive the sacrament of Penance, and if, when the priest who has been sent for comes to him, he be so weak as to be unable to speak, or becomes delirious, let them, who heard him ask, bear witness, and let him receive the sacrament of Penance; then if it be thought that he is going to die shortly, let him be reconciled by imposition of hands, and let the Eucharist be placed in his mouth.*

Reply Obj. 1. Those lacking the use of reason can have devotion towards the sacrament; actual devotion in some cases, and past in others.

Reply Obj. 2. Dionysius is speaking there of energumens who are not yet baptized, in whom the devil's power is not yet extinct, since it thrives in them through the presence of original sin. But as to baptized persons who are vexed in body by unclean spirits, the same reason holds good of them as of others who are demented. Hence Cassian says *(Collat.* vii): *We do not remember the most Holy Communion to have ever been denied by our elders to them who are vexed by unclean spirits.*

Reply Obj. 3. The same reason holds good of newly born children as of the insane who never have had the use of reason: consequently, the sacred mysteries are not to be given to them. Although certain Greeks do the contrary, because Dionysius says *(Eccl. Hier.* ii) that Holy Communion is to be given to them who are baptized; not understanding that Dionysius is speaking there of the Baptism of adults. Nor do they suffer any loss of life from the fact of our Lord saying (John vi. 54), *Except you eat the flesh of the Son of Man, and drink His blood, you shall not have life in you;* because, as Augustine writes to Boniface (Pseudo-Beda *Comment. in 1 Cor.* x. 17), *then every one of the faithful becomes a partaker,* i.e. spiritually, *of the body and blood of the Lord, when he is made a member of Christ's body in Baptism.* But when children once begin to have some use of reason so as to be able to conceive some devotion for the sacrament, then it can be given to them.

TENTH ARTICLE

Whether It Is Lawful to Receive This Sacrament Daily?

We proceed thus to the Tenth Article:—

Objection 1. It does not appear to be lawful to receive this sacrament daily, because, as Baptism shows forth our Lord's Passion, so also does this sacrament. Now one may not be baptized several times, but only once, because *Christ died once* only *for our sins,* according to 1 Pet. iii. 18. Therefore, it seems unlawful to receive this sacrament daily.

Obj. 2. Further, the reality ought to answer to the figure. But the Paschal Lamb, which was the chief figure of this sacrament, as was said above (Q. 73, A. 9) was eaten only once in the year; while the Church once a year commemorates Christ's Passion, of which this sacrament is the memorial. It seems, then, that it is lawful to receive this sacrament not daily, but only once in the year.

Obj. 3. Further, the greatest reverence is due to this sacrament as containing Christ. But it is a token of reverence to refrain from receiving this sacrament; hence the Centurion is praised for saying (Matth. viii. 8), *Lord, I am not worthy that Thou shouldst enter under my roof;* also Peter, for saying (Luke v. 8), *Depart from me, for I am a sinful man, O Lord.* Therefore, it is not praiseworthy for a man to receive this sacrament daily.

Obj. 4. Further, if it were a praiseworthy custom to receive this sacrament frequently, then the oftener it were taken the more praiseworthy it would be. But there would be greater frequency if one were to receive it several times daily; and yet this is not the custom of the Church. Consequently, it does not seem praiseworthy to receive it daily.

Obj. 5. Further, the Church by her statutes intends to promote the welfare of the faithful. But the Church's statute only requires Communion once a year; hence it is enacted (Extra, *De Pœnit. et Remiss.* xii): *Let every person of either sex devoutly receive the sacrament of the Eucharist at least at Easter; unless by the advice of his parish priest, and for some reasonable cause, he considers he ought to refrain from receiving for a time.* Consequently, it is not praiseworthy to receive this sacrament daily.

On the contrary, Augustine says *(De Verb. Dom., Serm.* xxviii): *This is our daily bread; take it daily, that it may profit thee daily.*

I answer that, There are two things to be considered regarding the use of this sacrament. The first is on the part of the sacrament itself, the virtue of which gives health to men; and consequently it is profitable to receive it daily so as to receive its fruits daily. Hence Ambrose says *(De Sacram.* iv): *If, whenever Christ's blood is shed, it is shed for the forgiveness of sins, I who sin often, should receive it often: I need a frequent remedy.* The second thing to be considered is on the part of the recipient, who is required to approach this sacrament with great reverence and devotion. Consequently, if anyone finds that he has these dispositions every day, he will do well to receive it daily. Hence, Augustine, after saying, *Receive daily, that it may profit thee daily,* adds: *So live, as to deserve to receive it daily.* But because many persons are lacking in this devotion, on account of the many drawbacks both spiritual and corporal from which they suffer, it is not expedient for all to approach this sacrament every day; but they should do so as often as they find themselves properly disposed. Hence it is said in *De Eccles. Dogmat.* liii: *I neither praise nor blame daily reception of the Eucharist.*

Reply Obj. 1. In the sacrament of Baptism a man is conformed to Christ's death, by receiving His character within him. And therefore, as Christ died but once, so a man ought to be baptized but once. But a man does not receive Christ's character in this sacrament; He receives Christ Himself, Whose virtue endures for ever. Hence it is written (Heb. x. 14): *By one oblation He hath perfected for ever them that are sanctified.* Consequently, since man has daily need of Christ's health-giving virtue, he may commendably receive this sacrament every day.

And since Baptism is above all a spiritual regeneration, therefore, as a man is born naturally but once, so ought he by Baptism to be reborn spiritually but once, as Augustine says *(Tract.* xi, *in Joan.),* commenting on John iii. 4, *How can a man be born again, when he is grown old?* But this sacrament is spiritual food; hence, just as bodily food is taken every day, so is it a good thing to receive this sacrament every day. Hence it is that our Lord (Luke xi. 3), teaches us to pray, *Give us this day our daily bread:* in explaining which words Augustine observes *(De Verb. Dom., loc. cit.): If you receive it,* i.e. this sacrament, every day, every day is today for thee, and Christ rises again every day in thee, for when Christ riseth it is today.

Reply Obj. 2. The Paschal Lamb was the figure of this sacrament chiefly as to Christ's Passion represented therein; and therefore it was partaken of once a year only, since Christ died but once. And on this account the Church celebrates once a year the remembrance of Christ's Passion. But in this sacrament the memorial of His Passion is given by way of

food which is partaken of daily; and therefore in this respect it is represented by the manna which was given daily to the people in the desert.

Reply Obj. 3. Reverence for this sacrament consists in fear associated with love; consequently reverential fear of God is called filial fear, as was said in the Second Part (I-II, Q. 67, A. 4, *ad* 2; II-II, Q. 19, AA. 9, 11, 12); because the desire of receiving arises from love, while the humility of reverence springs from fear. Consequently, each of these belongs to the reverence due to this sacrament; both as to receiving it daily, and as to refraining from it sometimes. Hence Augustine says *(Ep.* liv)): *If one says that the Eucharist should not be received daily, while another maintains the contrary, let each one do as according to his devotion he thinketh right; for Zaccheus and the Centurion did not contradict one another while the one received the Lord with joy, whereas the other said: "Lord, I am not worthy that Thou shouldst enter under my roof"; since both honored our Saviour, though not in the same way.* But love and hope, whereunto the Scriptures constantly urge us, are preferable to fear. Hence, too, when Peter had said, *Depart from me, for I am a sinful man, O Lord,* Jesus answered: *Fear not.*

Reply Obj. 4. Because our Lord said (Luke xi. 3), *Give us this day our daily bread,* we are not on that account to communicate several times daily, for, by one daily communion the unity of Christ's Passion is set forth.

Reply Obj. 5. Various statutes have emanated according to the various ages of the Church. In the primitive Church, when the devotion of the Christian faith was more flourishing, it was enacted that the faithful should communicate daily: hence Pope Anaclete says *(Ep.* i): *When the consecration is finished, let all communicate who do not wish to cut themselves off from the Church; for so the apostles have ordained, and the holy Roman Church holds.* Later on, when the fervor of faith relaxed, Pope Fabian (Third Council of Tours, Canon 1) gave permission *that all should communicate, if not more frequently, at least three times in the year, namely, at Easter, Pentecost, and Christmas.* Pope Soter likewise (Second Council of Chalon, *Canon* xlvii) declares that Communion should be received *on Holy Thursday,* as is set forth in the Decretals *(De Consecratione,* dist. 2). Later on, when *iniquity abounded and charity grew cold* (Matth. xxiv. 12), Pope Innocent III commanded that the faithful should communicate *at least once a year,* namely, *at Easter.* However, in *De Eccl. Dogmat.* xxiii, the faithful are counseled *to communicate on all Sundays.*

ELEVENTH ARTICLE

Whether It Is Lawful to Abstain Altogether from Communion?

We proceed thus to the Eleventh Article:—

Objection 1. It seems to be lawful to abstain altogether from Communion. Because the Centurion is praised for saying (Matth. viii. 8): *Lord, I am not worthy that Thou shouldst enter under my roof;* and he who deems that he ought to refrain entirely from Communion can be compared to the Centurion, as stated above (A. 10, *ad* 3). Therefore, since we do not read of Christ entering his house, it seems to be lawful for any individual to abstain from Communion his whole life long.

Obj. 2. Further, it is lawful for anyone to refrain from what is not of necessity for salvation. But this sacrament is not of necessity for salvation, as was stated above (Q. 73, A. 3). Therefore it is permissible to abstain from Communion altogether.

Obj. 3. Further, sinners are not bound to go to Communion: hence Pope Fabian (*loc. cit.*, A. 10, *ad* 5) after saying, *Let all communicate thrice each year*, adds: *Except those who are hindered by grievous crimes.* Consequently, if those who are not in the state of sin are bound to go to Communion, it seems that sinners are better off than good people, which is unfitting. Therefore, it seems lawful even for the godly to refrain from Communion.

On the contrary, Our Lord said (John vi. 54): *Except ye eat the flesh of the Son of Man, and drink His blood, you shall not have life in you.*

I answer that, As stated above (A. 1), there are two ways of receiving this sacrament, namely, spiritually and sacramentally. Now it is clear that all are bound to eat it at least spiritually, because this is to be incorporated in Christ, as was said above (Q. 73, A. 3, *ad* 1). Now spiritual eating comprises the desire or yearning for receiving this sacrament, as was said above (A. 1, *ad* 3, A. 2). Therefore, a man cannot be saved without desiring to receive this sacrament.

Now a desire would be vain except it were fulfilled when opportunity presented itself. Consequently, it is evident that a man is bound to receive this sacrament, not only by virtue of the Church's precept, but also by virtue of the Lord's command (Luke xxii. 19): *Do this in memory of Me.* But by the precept of the Church there are fixed times for fulfilling Christ's command.

Reply Obj. 1. As Gregory says: *He is truly humble, who is not obstinate in rejecting what is commanded for his good.* Consequently, humility is not praiseworthy if anyone abstains altogether from Communion against the precept of Christ and the Church. Again the Centurion was not commanded to receive Christ into his house.

Reply Obj. 2. This sacrament is said not to be as necessary as Baptism, with regard to children, who can be saved without the Eucharist, but not without the sacrament of Baptism: both, however, are of necessity with regard to adults.

Reply Obj. 3. Sinners suffer great loss in being kept back from receiving this sacrament, so that they are not better off on that account; and although while continuing in their sins they are not on that account excused from transgressing the precept, nevertheless, as Pope Innocent (III) says, penitents, *who refrain on the advice of their priest,* are excused.

TWELFTH ARTICLE

Whether It Is Lawful to Receive the Body of Christ without the Blood?

We proceed thus to the Twelfth Article:—

Objection 1. It seems unlawful to receive the body of Christ without the blood. For Pope Gelasius says (*cf. De Consecr.* ii): *We have learned that some persons after taking only a portion of the sacred body, abstain from the chalice of the sacred blood. I know not for what superstitious motive they do this: therefore let them either receive the entire sacrament, or let them be withheld from the sacrament altogether.* Therefore it is not lawful to receive the body of Christ without His blood.

Obj. 2. Further, the eating of the body and the drinking of the blood are required for the perfection of this sacrament, as stated above (Q. 73, A. 2; Q. 76, A. 2, *ad* 1). Consequently, if the body be taken without the blood, it will be an imperfect sacrament, which seems to savor of sacrilege; hence Pope Gelasius adds (*cf. Obj.* 1), *because the dividing of one and the same mystery cannot happen without a great sacrilege.*

Obj. 3. Further, this sacrament is celebrated in memory of our Lord's Passion, as stated above (Q. 73, AA. 4, 5; Q. 74, A. 1), and is received for the health of soul. But the Passion is expressed in the blood rather than in the body; moreover, as stated above (Q. 74, A. 1), the blood is offered for the health of the soul. Consequently, one ought to refrain from receiving the body rather than the blood. Therefore, such as approach this sacrament ought not to take Christ's body without His blood.

On the contrary, It is the custom of many churches for the body of Christ to be given to the communicant without His blood.

I answer that, Two points should be observed regarding the use of this sacrament, one on the part of the sacrament, the other on the part of the recipients. On the part of the sacrament it is proper for both the body and the blood to be received, since the perfection of the sacrament lies in both, and consequently, since it is the priest's duty both to consecrate and finish the sacrament, he ought on no account to receive Christ's body without the blood.

But on the part of the recipient the greatest reverence and caution are called for, lest anything happen which is unworthy of so great a mystery. Now this could especially happen in receiving the blood, for, if incautiously handled, it might easily be spilt. And because the multitude of the Christian people increased, in which there are old, young, and children, some of whom have not enough discretion to observe due caution in using this sacrament, on that account it is a prudent custom in some churches for the blood not to be offered to the reception of the people, but to be received by the priest alone.

Reply Obj. 1. Pope Gelasius is speaking of priests, who, as they consecrate the entire sacrament, ought to communicate in the entire sacrament. For, as we read in the (Twelfth) Council of Toledo, *What kind of a sacrifice is that, wherein not even the sacrificer is known to have a share?*

Reply Obj. 2. The perfection of this sacrament does not lie in the use of the faithful, but in the consecration of the matter. And hence there is nothing derogatory to the perfection of this sacrament; if the people receive the body without the blood, provided that the priest who consecrates receive both.

Reply Obj. 3. Our Lord's Passion is represented in the very consecration of this sacrament, in which the body ought not to be consecrated without the blood. But the body can be received by the people without the blood: nor is this detrimental to the sacrament. Because the priest both offers and consumes the blood on behalf of all; and Christ is fully contained under either species, as was shown above (Q. 76, A. 2).

QUESTION 81

Of the Use Which Christ Made of This Sacrament at Its Institution

(In Four Articles)

WE have now to consider the use which Christ made of this sacrament at its institution; under which heading there are four points of inquiry: (1) Whether Christ received His own body and blood? (2) Whether He gave it to Judas? (3) What kind of body did He receive or give, namely, was it passible or impassible? (4) What would have been the condition of Christ's body under this sacrament, if it had been reserved or consecrated during the three days He lay dead?

FIRST ARTICLE

Whether Christ Received His Own Body and Blood?

We proceed thus to the First Article:—

Objection 1. It seems that Christ did not receive His own body and blood, because nothing ought to be asserted of either Christ's doings or sayings, which is not handed down by the authority of Sacred Scripture. But it is not narrated in the gospels that He ate His own body or drank His own blood. Therefore we must not assert this as a fact.

Obj. 2. Further, nothing can be within itself except perchance by reason of its parts, for instance, as one part is in another, as is stated in *Phys.* iv. But what is eaten and drunk is in the eater and drinker. Therefore, since the entire Christ is under each species of the sac-

rament, it seems impossible for Him to have received this sacrament.

Obj. 3. Further, the receiving of this sacrament is twofold, namely, spiritual and sacramental. But the spiritual was unsuitable for Christ, as He derived no benefit from the sacrament; and in consequence so was the sacramental, since it is imperfect without the spiritual, as was observed above (Q. 80, A. 1). Consequently, in no way did Christ partake of this sacrament.

On the contrary, Jerome says (*Ad Hedib., Ep.* xxx), *The Lord Jesus Christ, Himself the guest and banquet, is both the partaker and what is eaten.*

I answer that, Some have said that Christ during the supper gave His body and blood to His disciples, but did not partake of it Himself. But this seems improbable. Because Christ Himself was the first to fulfill what He required others to observe: hence He willed first to be baptized when imposing Baptism upon others: as we read in Acts i. 1: *Jesus began to do and to teach.* Hence He first of all took His own body and blood, and afterwards gave it to be taken by the disciples. And hence the gloss upon Ruth iii. 7, *When he had eaten and drunk,* says: *Christ ate and drank at the supper, when He gave to the disciples the sacrament of His body and blood. Hence,* *"because the children partook* of His flesh and blood, He also hath been partaker in the same."*

Reply Obj. 1. We read in the Gospels how Christ *took the bread . . . and the chalice;* but it is not to be understood that He took them merely into His hands, as some say; but that He took them in the same way as He gave them to others to take. Hence when He said to the disciples, *Take ye and eat,* and again, *Take ye and drink,* it is to be understood that He Himself, in taking it, both ate and drank. Hence some have composed this rhyme:

> *The King at supper sits,*
> *The twelve as guests He greets,*
> *Clasping Himself in His hands,*
> *The food Himself now eats.*

Reply Obj. 2. As was said above (Q. 76, A. 5), Christ as contained under this sacrament stands in relation to place, not according to His own dimensions, but according to the dimensions of the sacramental species; so that Christ is Himself in every place where those species are. And because the species were able to be both in the hands and the mouth of Christ, the entire Christ could be in both His hands and mouth. Now this could not come to pass were His relation to place to be according to His proper dimensions.

Reply Obj. 3. As was stated above (Q. 79, A. 1, *ad* 2), the effect of this sacrament is not merely an increase of habitual grace, but furthermore a certain actual delectation of spiritual sweetness. But although grace was not increased in Christ through His receiving this sacrament, yet He had a certain spiritual delectation from the new institution of this sacrament. Hence He Himself said (Luke xxii. 15): *With desire I have desired to eat this Pasch with you,* which words Eusebius explains of the new mystery of the New Testament, which He gave to the disciples. And therefore He ate it both spiritually and sacramentally, inasmuch as He received His own body under the sacrament, which sacrament of His own body He both understood and prepared; yet differently from others who partake of it both sacramentally and spiritually, for these receive an increase of grace, and they have need of the sacramental signs for perceiving its truth.

SECOND ARTICLE

Whether Christ Gave His Body to Judas?

We proceed thus to the Second Article:—

Objection 1. It seems that Christ did not give His body to Judas. Because, as we read (Matth. xxvi. 29), our Lord, after giving His body and blood to the disciples, said to them: *I will not drink from henceforth of this fruit*

* Vulg., *are partakers* (Heb. ii. 14).

of the vine, until that day when I shall drink it with you new in the kingdom of My Father.* From this it appears that those to whom He had given His body and blood were to drink of it again with Him. But Judas did not drink of it afterwards with Him. Therefore he did not receive Christ's body and blood with the other disciples.

Obj. 2. Further, what the Lord commanded, He Himself fulfilled, as is said in Acts i. 1: *Jesus began to do and to teach.* But He gave the command (Matth. vii. 6): *Give not that which is holy to dogs.* Therefore, knowing Judas to be a sinner, seemingly He did not give him His body and blood.

Obj. 3. Further, it is distinctly related (John xiii. 26) that Christ gave dipped bread to Judas. Consequently, if He gave His body to him, it appears that He gave it him in the morsel, especially since we read *(ibid.)* that *after the morsel, Satan entered into him.* And on this passage Augustine says *(Tract.* lxii, *in Joan.): From this we learn how we should beware of receiving a good thing in an evil way. . . . For if he be "chastised" who does "not discern," i.e. distinguish, the body of the Lord from other meats, how must he be "condemned" who, feigning himself a friend, comes to His table a foe?* But (Judas) did not receive our Lord's body with the dipped morsel; thus Augustine commenting on John xiii. 26, *When He had dipped the bread, He gave it to Judas, the son of Simon the Iscariot* (Vulg.,—*to Judas Iscariot, the son of Simon*), says *(loc. cit.): Judas did not receive Christ's body then, as some think who read carelessly.* Therefore it seems that Judas did not receive the body of Christ.

On the contrary, Chrysostom says *(Hom.* lxxxii, *in Matth.): Judas was not converted while partaking of the sacred mysteries: hence on both sides his crime becomes the more heinous, both because imbued with such a purpose he approached the mysteries, and because he became none the better for approaching, neither from fear, nor from the benefit received, nor from the honor conferred on him.*

I answer that, Hilary, in commenting on Matth. xxvi. 17, held that Christ did not give His body and blood to Judas. And this would have been quite proper, if the malice of Judas be considered. But since Christ was to serve us as a pattern of justice, it was not in keeping with His teaching authority to sever Judas, a hidden sinner, from Communion with the others without an accuser and evident proof; lest the Church's prelates might have an example for doing the like, and lest Judas himself being exasperated might take occasion of sinning. Therefore, it remains to be said that Judas received our Lord's body and blood with the other disciples, as Dionysius says (*Eccl. Hier.* iii), and Augustine (*Tract.* lxii, *in Joan.*).

Reply Obj. 1. This is Hilary's argument, to show that Judas did not receive Christ's body. But it is not cogent; because Christ is speaking to the disciples, from whose company Judas separated himself: and it was not Christ that excluded him. Therefore Christ for His part drinks the wine even with Judas in the kingdom of God; but Judas himself repudiated this banquet.

Reply Obj. 2. The wickedness of Judas was known to Christ as God; but it was unknown to Him, after the manner in which men know it. Consequently, Christ did not repel Judas from Communion; so as to furnish an example that such secret sinners are not to be repelled by other priests.

Reply Obj. 3. Without any doubt Judas did not receive Christ's body in the dipped bread; he received mere bread. Yet as Augustine observes (*ibid.*), *perchance the feigning of Judas is denoted by the dipping of the bread; just as some things are dipped to be dyed. If, however, the dipping signifies here anything good* (for instance, the sweetness of the Divine goodness, since bread is rendered more savory by being dipped), *then, not undeservedly, did condemnation follow his ingratitude for that same good.* And owing to that ingratitude, *what is good became evil to him,* as happens to them who receive Christ's body unworthily.

And as Augustine says (*ibid.*), *it must be understood that our Lord had already distributed the sacrament of His body and blood to all His disciples, among whom was Judas also, as Luke narrates: and after that, we came to this, where, according to the relation of John, our Lord, by dipping and handing the morsel, does most openly declare His betrayer.*

THIRD ARTICLE

Whether Christ Received and Gave to the Disciples His Impassible Body?

We proceed thus to the Third Article:—

Objection 1. It seems that Christ both received and gave to the disciples His impassible body. Because on Matth. xvii. 2, *He was transfigured before them,* the gloss says: *He gave to the disciples at the supper that body which He had through nature, but neither mortal nor passible.* And again, on Lev. ii. 5, *if thy oblation be from the frying-pan,* the gloss says: *The Cross mightier than all things made Christ's flesh fit for being eaten, which before the Passion did not seem so suited.* But Christ gave His body as suited for eating. Therefore He gave it just as it was after the Passion, that is, impassible and immortal.

Obj. 2. Further, every possible body suffers by contact and by being eaten. Consequently, if Christ's body was passible, it would have suffered both from contact and from being eaten by the disciples.

Obj. 3. Further, the sacramental words now spoken by the priest in the person of Christ are not more powerful than when uttered by Christ Himself. But now by virtue of the sacramental words it is Christ's impassible and immortal body which is consecrated upon the altar. Therefore, much more so was it then.

On the contrary, As Innocent III says (*De Sacr. Alt. Myst.* iv), *He bestowed on the disciples His body such as it was.* But then He had a passible and a mortal body. Therefore, He gave a passible and mortal body to the disciples.

I answer that, Hugh of Saint Victor (Innocent III, *ibid.*) maintained, that before the Passion, Christ assumed at various times the four properties of a glorified body—namely, subtlety in His birth, when He came forth from the closed womb of the Virgin; agility, when He walked dryshod upon the sea; clarity, in the Transfiguration; and impassibility at the Last Supper, when He gave His body to the disciples to be eaten. And according to this He gave His body in an impassible and immortal condition to His disciples.

But whatever may be the case touching the other qualities, concerning which we have already stated what should be held (Q. 28, A. 2, ad 3; Q. 45, A. 2), nevertheless the above opinion regarding impassibility is inadmissible. For it is manifest that the same body of Christ which was then seen by the disciples in its own species, was received by them under the sacramental species. But as seen in its own species it was not impassible; nay more, it was ready for the Passion. Therefore, neither was Christ's body impassible when given under the sacramental species.

Yet there was present in the sacrament, in an impassible manner, that which was passible of itself; just as that was there invisibly which of itself was visible. For as sight requires that the body seen be in contact with the adjacent medium of sight, so does passion require contact of the suffering body with the active agents. But Christ's body, according as it is under the sacrament, as stated above (A. 1, ad 2; Q. 76, A. 5), is not compared with its surroundings through the intermediary of its own dimensions, whereby bodies touch each other, but through the dimensions of the bread and wine; consequently, it is those species which are acted upon and are seen, but not Christ's own body.

Reply Obj. 1. Christ is said not to have given His mortal and passible body at the supper, because He did not give it in mortal and passible fashion. But the Cross made His flesh adapted for eating, inasmuch as this sacrament represents Christ's Passion.

Reply Obj. 2. This argument would hold, if Christ's body, as it was passible, were also present in a passible manner in this sacrament.

Reply Obj. 3. As stated above (Q. 76, A. 4), the accidents of Christ's body are in this sacrament by real concomitance, but not by the power of the sacrament, whereby the substance of Christ's body comes to be there. And therefore the power of the sacramental words extends to this, that the body, i.e. Christ's, is under this sacrament, whatever accidents really exist in it.

FOURTH ARTICLE

Whether, If This Sacrament Had Been Reserved in a Pyx, or Consecrated at the Moment of Christ's Death by One of the Apostles, Christ Himself Would Have Died There?

We proceed thus to the Fourth Article:—

Objection 1. It seems that if this sacrament had been reserved in a pyx at the moment of Christ's death, or had then been consecrated by one of the apostles, that Christ would not have died there. For Christ's death happened through His Passion. But even then He was in this sacrament in an impassible manner. Therefore, He could not die in this sacrament.

Obj. 2. Further, on the death of Christ, His blood was separated from the body. But His flesh and blood are together in this sacrament. Therefore He could not die in this sacrament.

Obj. 3. Further, death ensues from the separation of the soul from the body. But both the body and the soul of Christ are contained in this sacrament. Therefore Christ could not die in this sacrament.

On the contrary, The same Christ Who was upon the cross would have been in this sacrament. But He died upon the cross. Therefore, if this sacrament had been reserved, He would have died therein.

I answer that, Christ's body is substantially the same in this sacrament, as in its proper species, but not after the same fashion; be-

cause in its proper species it comes in contact with surrounding bodies by its own dimensions: but it does not do so as it is in this sacrament, as stated above (A. 3). And therefore, all that belongs to Christ, as He is in Himself, can be attributed to Him both in His proper species, and as He exists in the sacrament; such as to live, to die, to grieve, to be animate or inanimate, and the like; while all that belongs to Him in relation to outward bodies, can be attributed to Him as He exists in His proper species, but not as He is in this sacrament; such as to be mocked, to be spat upon, to be crucified, to be scourged, and the rest. Hence some have composed this verse:

Our Lord can grieve beneath the sacramental veils
But cannot feel the piercing of the thorns and nails.

Reply Obj. 1. As was stated above, suffering belongs to a body that suffers in respect of some extrinsic body. And therefore Christ, as in this sacrament, cannot suffer; yet He can die.

Reply Obj. 2. As was said above (Q. 76, A. 2), in virtue of the consecration, the body of Christ is under the species of bread, while His blood is under the species of wine. But now that His blood is not really separated from His body; by real concomitance, both His blood is present with the body under the species of the bread, and His body together with the blood under the species of the wine. But at the time when Christ suffered, when His blood was really separated from His body, if this sacrament had been consecrated, then the body only would have been present under the species of the bread, and the blood only under the species of the wine.

Reply Obj. 3. As was observed above (Q. 76, A. 1, *ad* 1), Christ's soul is in this sacrament by real concomitance; because it is not without the body: but it is not there in virtue of the consecration. And therefore, if this sacrament had been consecrated then, or reserved, when His soul was really separated from His body, Christ's soul would not have been under this sacrament, not from any defect in the form of the words, but owing to the different dispositions of the thing contained

QUESTION 82

Of the Minister of This Sacrament

(In Ten Articles)

WE now proceed to consider the minister of this sacrament: under which head there are ten points for our inquiry: (1) Whether it belongs to a priest alone to consecrate this

sacrament? (2) Whether several priests can at the same time consecrate the same host? (3) Whether it belongs to the priest alone to dispense this sacrament? (4) Whether it is lawful for the priest consecrating to refrain from communicating? (5) Whether a priest in sin can perform this sacrament? (6) Whether the Mass of a wicked priest is of less value than that of a good one? (7) Whether those who are heretics, schismatics, or excommunicated, can perform this sacrament? (8) Whether degraded priests can do so? (9) Whether communicants receiving at their hands are guilty of sinning? (10) Whether a priest may lawfully refrain altogether from celebrating?*

FIRST ARTICLE

Whether the Consecration of This Sacrament Belongs to a Priest Alone?

We proceed thus to the First Article:—

Objection 1. It seems that the consecration of this sacrament does not belong exclusively to a priest. Because it was said above (Q. 78, A. 4) that this sacrament is consecrated in virtue of the words, which are the form of this sacrament. But those words are not changed, whether spoken by a priest or by anyone else. Therefore, it seems that not only a priest, but anyone else, can consecrate this sacrament.

Obj. 2. Further, the priest performs this sacrament in the person of Christ. But a devout layman is united with Christ through charity. Therefore, it seems that even a layman can perform this sacrament. Hence Chrysostom *(Op. imperf. in Matth., Hom.* xliii) says that *every holy man is a priest.*

Obj. 3. Further, as Baptism is ordained for the salvation of mankind, so also is this sacrament, as is clear from what was said above (Q. 74, A. 1; Q. 79, A. 2). But a layman can also baptize, as was stated above (Q. 67, A. 3). Consequently, the consecration of this sacrament is not proper to a priest.

Obj. 4. Further, this sacrament is completed in the consecration of the matter. But the consecration of other matters such as the chrism, the holy oil, and blessed oil, belongs exclusively to a bishop; yet their consecration does not equal the dignity of the consecration of the Eucharist, in which the entire Christ is contained. Therefore it belongs, not to a priest, but only to a bishop, to perform this sacrament.

On the contrary, Isidore says in an Epistle to Ludifred *(Decret., dist.* 25): *It belongs to a priest to consecrate this sacrament of the Lord's body and blood upon God's altar.*

I answer that, As stated above (Q. 78, AA. 1, 4), such is the dignity of this sacrament that it is performed only as in the person of Christ. Now whoever performs any act in

another's stead, must do so by the power bestowed by such a one. But as the power of receiving this sacrament is conceded by Christ to the baptized person, so likewise the power of consecrating this sacrament on Christ's behalf is bestowed upon the priest at his ordination: for thereby he is put upon a level with them to whom the Lord said (Luke xxii. 19): *Do this for a commemoration of Me.* Therefore, it must be said that it belongs to priests to accomplish this sacrament.

Reply Obj. 1. The sacramental power is in several things, and not merely in one: thus the power of Baptism lies both in the words and in the water. Accordingly the consecrating power is not merely in the words, but likewise in the power delivered to the priest in his consecration and ordination, when the bishop says to him: *Receive the power of offering up the Sacrifice in the Church for the living as well as for the dead.* For instrumental power lies in several instruments through which the chief agent acts.

Reply Obj. 2. A devout layman is united with Christ by spiritual union through faith and charity, but not by sacramental power: consequently he has a spiritual priesthood for offering spiritual sacrifices, of which it is said (Ps. l. 19): *A sacrifice to God is an afflicted spirit;* and (Rom. xii. 1): *Present your bodies a living sacrifice.* Hence, too, it is written (1 Pet. ii. 5): *A holy priesthood, to offer up spiritual sacrifices.*

Reply Obj. 3. The receiving of this sacrament is not of such necessity as the receiving of Baptism, as is evident from what was said above (Q. 65, AA. 3, 4; Q. 80, A. 11, *ad* 2). And therefore, although a layman can baptize in case of necessity, he cannot perform this sacrament.

Reply Obj. 4. The bishop receives power to act on Christ's behalf upon His mystical body, that is, upon the Church; but the priest receives no such power in his consecration, although he may have it by commission from the bishop. Consequently all such things as do not belong to the mystical body are not reserved to the bishop, such as the consecration of this sacrament. But it belongs to the bishop to deliver, not only to the people, but likewise to priests, such things as serve them in the fulfillment of their respective duties. And because the blessing of the chrism, and of the holy oil, and of the oil of the sick, and other consecrated things, such as altars, churches, vestments, and sacred vessels, makes such things fit for use in performing the sacraments which belong to the priestly duty, therefore such consecrations are reserved to

* This is the order observed by S. Thomas in writing the Articles; but in writing this prologue, he placed Article 10 immediately after Article 4 (*cf.* Leonine ed.).

the bishop as the head of the whole ecclesiastical order.

SECOND ARTICLE

Whether Several Priests Can Consecrate One and the Same Host?

We proceed thus to the Second Article:—

Objection 1. It seems that several priests cannot consecrate one and the same host. For it was said above (Q. 67, A. 6), that several cannot at the same time baptize one individual. But the power of a priest consecrating is not less than that of a man baptizing. Therefore, several priests cannot consecrate one host at the same time.

Obj. 2. Further, what can be done by one, is superfluously done by several. But there ought to be nothing superfluous in the sacraments. Since, then, one is sufficient for consecrating, it seems that several cannot consecrate one host.

Obj. 3. Further, as Augustine says *(Tract.* xxvi, *in Joan.)*, this is *the sacrament of unity.* But multitude seems to be opposed to unity. Therefore it seems inconsistent with the sacrament for several priests to consecrate the same host.

On the contrary, It is the custom of some Churches for priests newly ordained to co-celebrate with the bishop ordaining them.

I answer that, As stated above (A. 1), when a priest is ordained he is placed on a level with those who received consecrating power from our Lord at the Supper. And therefore, according to the custom of some Churches, as the apostles supped when Christ supped, so the newly ordained co-celebrate with the ordaining bishop. Nor is the consecration, on that account, repeated over the same host, because as Innocent III says *(De Sac. Alt. Myst.* iv), *the intention of all should be directed to the same instant of the consecration.*

Reply Obj. 1. We do not read of Christ baptizing with the apostles when He committed to them the duty of baptizing; consequently there is no parallel.

Reply Obj. 2. If each individual priest were acting in his own power, then other celebrants would be superfluous, since one would be sufficient. But whereas the priest does not consecrate except as in Christ's stead; and since many are *one in Christ* (Gal. iii. 28); consequently it does not matter whether this sacrament be consecrated by one or by many, except that the rite of the Church must be observed.

Reply Obj. 3. The Eucharist is the sacrament of ecclesiastical unity, which is brought about by many being *one in Christ.*

THIRD ARTICLE

Whether the Dispensing of This Sacrament Belongs to a Priest Alone?

We proceed thus to the Third Article:—

Objection 1. It seems that the dispensing of this sacrament does not belong to a priest alone. For Christ's blood belongs to this sacrament no less than His body. But Christ's blood is dispensed by deacons: hence the blessed Lawrence said to the blessed Sixtus *(Office of S. Lawrence, Resp. at Matins): Try whether you have chosen a fit minister, to whom you have entrusted the dispensing of the Lord's blood.* Therefore, with equal reason the dispensing of Christ's body does not belong to priests only.

Obj. 2. Further, priests are the appointed ministers of the sacraments. But this sacrament is completed in the consecration of the matter, and not in the use, to which the dispensing belongs. Therefore it seems that it does not belong to a priest to dispense the Lord's body.

Obj. 3. Further, Dionysius says *(Eccl. Hier.,* iii, iv) that this sacrament, like chrism, has the power of perfecting. But it belongs, not to priests, but to bishops, to sign with the chrism. Therefore likewise, to dispense this sacrament belongs to the bishop and not to the priest.

On the contrary, It is written *(De Consecr.,* dist. 12): *It has come to our knowledge that some priests deliver the Lord's body to a layman or to a woman to carry it to the sick: The synod therefore forbids such presumption to continue; and let the priest himself communicate the sick.*

I answer that, The dispensing of Christ's body belongs to the priest for three reasons. First, because, as was said above (A. 1), he consecrates as in the person of Christ. But as Christ consecrated His body at the supper, so also He gave it to others to be partaken of by them. Accordingly, as the consecration of Christ's body belongs to the priest, so likewise does the dispensing belong to him. Secondly, because the priest is the appointed intermediary between God and the people; hence as it belongs to him to offer the people's gifts to God, so it belongs to him to deliver consecrated gifts to the people. Thirdly, because out of reverence towards this sacrament, nothing touches it, but what is consecrated; hence the corporal and the chalice are consecrated, and likewise the priest's hands, for touching this sacrament. Hence it is not lawful for anyone else to touch it except from necessity, for instance, if it were to fall upon the ground, or else in some other case of urgency.

Reply Obj. 1. The deacon, as being nigh to

the priestly order, has a certain share in the latter's duties, so that he may dispense the blood; but not the body, except in case of necessity, at the bidding of a bishop or of a priest. First of all, because Christ's blood is contained in a vessel, hence there is no need for it to be touched by the dispenser, as Christ's body is touched.—Secondly, because the blood denotes the redemption derived by the people from Christ; hence it is that water is mixed with the blood, which water denotes the people. And because deacons are between priest and people, the dispensing of the blood is in the competency of deacons, rather than the dispensing of the body.

Reply Obj. 2. For the reason given above, it belongs to the same person to dispense and to consecrate this sacrament.

Reply Obj. 3. As the deacon, in a measure, shares in the priest's *power of enlightening (Eccl. Hier.* v), inasmuch as he dispenses the blood; so the priest shares in the *perfective dispensing (ibid.)* of the bishop, inasmuch as he dispenses this sacrament whereby man is perfected in himself by union with Christ. But other perfections whereby a man is perfected in relation to others, are reserved to the bishop.

FOURTH ARTICLE

Whether the Priest Who Consecrates Is Bound to Receive This Sacrament?

We proceed thus to the Fourth Article:—

Objection 1. It seems that the priest who consecrates is not bound to receive this sacrament. Because, in the other consecrations, he who consecrates the matter does not use it, just as the bishop consecrating the chrism is not anointed therewith. But this sacrament consists in the consecration of the matter. Therefore, the priest performing this sacrament need not use the same, but may lawfully refrain from receiving it.

Obj. 2. Further, in the other sacraments the minister does not give the sacrament to himself: for no one can baptize himself, as stated above (Q. 66, A. 5, *ad* 4). But as Baptism is dispensed in due order, so also is this sacrament. Therefore the priest who consecrates this sacrament ought not to receive it at his own hands.

Obj. 3. Further, it sometimes happens that Christ's body appears upon the altar under the guise of flesh, and the blood under the guise of blood; which are unsuited for food and drink: hence, as was said above (Q. 75, A. 5), it is on that account that they are given under another species, lest they beget revulsion in the communicants. Therefore the priest who consecrates is not always bound to receive this sacrament.

On the contrary, We read in the acts of the (Twelfth) Council of Toledo (Can. v), and again *(De Consecr.,* dist. 2): *It must be strictly observed that as often as the priest sacrifices the body and blood of our Lord Jesus Christ upon the altar, he must himself be a partaker of Christ's body and blood.*

I answer that, As stated above (Q. 79, AA. 5, 7), the Eucharist is not only a sacrament, but also a sacrifice. Now whoever offers sacrifice must be a sharer in the sacrifice, because the outward sacrifice he offers is a sign of the inner sacrifice whereby he offers himself to God, as Augustine says *(De Civ. Dei* x). Hence by partaking of the sacrifice he shows that the inner one is likewise his. In the same way also, by dispensing the sacrifice to the people he shows that he is the dispenser of Divine gifts, of which he ought himself to be the first to partake, as Dionysius says *(Eccl. Hier.* iii). Consequently, he ought to receive before dispensing it to the people. Accordingly we read in the chapter mentioned above (Arg., *On the contrary):* "What kind of sacrifice is that wherein not even the sacrificer is known to have a share?" But it is by partaking of the sacrifice that he has a share in it, as the Apostle says (1 Cor. x. 18): *Are not they that eat of the sacrifices, partakers of the altar?* Therefore it is necessary for the priest, as often as he consecrates, to receive this sacrament in its integrity.

Reply Obj. 1. The consecration of chrism or of anything else is not a sacrifice, as the consecration of the Eucharist is: consequently there is no parallel.

Reply Obj. 2. The sacrament of Baptism is accomplished in the use of the matter, and consequently no one can baptize himself, because the same person cannot be active and passive in a sacrament. Hence neither in this sacrament does the priest consecrate himself, but he consecrates the bread and wine, in which consecration the sacrament is completed. But the use thereof follows the sacrament, and therefore there is no parallel.

Reply Obj. 3. If Christ's body appears miraculously upon the altar under the guise of flesh, or the blood under the guise of blood, it is not to be received. For Jerome says upon Leviticus *(cf. De Consecr.,* dist. 2): *It is lawful to eat of this sacrifice which is wonderfully performed in memory of Christ: but it is not lawful for anyone to eat of that one which Christ offered on the altar of the cross.* Nor does the priest transgress on that account, because miraculous events are not subject to human laws. Nevertheless the priest would be well advised to consecrate again and receive the Lord's body and blood.

FIFTH ARTICLE

Whether a Wicked Priest Can Consecrate the Eucharist?

We proceed thus to the Fifth Article:—

Objection 1. It seems that a wicked priest cannot consecrate the Eucharist. For Jerome, commenting on *Sophon.* iii. 4, says: *The priests who perform the Eucharist, and who distribute our Lord's blood to the people, act wickedly against Christ's law, in deeming that the Eucharist is consecrated by a prayer rather than by a good life; and that only the solemn prayer is requisite, and not the priest's merits: of whom it is said: "Let not the priest, in whatever defilement he may be, approach to offer oblations to the Lord"* (Lev. xxi. 21; *Sept. version*). But the sinful priest, being defiled, has neither the life nor the merits befitting this sacrament. Therefore a sinful priest cannot consecrate the Eucharist.

Obj. 2. Further, Damascene says *(De Fide Orthod.* iv) that *the bread and wine are changed supernaturally into the body and blood of our Lord, by the coming of the Holy Ghost.* But Pope Gelasius (I) says *(Ep. ad Elphid., cf.* Decret. i, q. 1): *How shall the Holy Spirit, when invoked, come for the consecration of the Divine Mystery, if the priest invoking him be proved full of guilty deeds?* Consequently, the Eucharist cannot be consecrated by a wicked priest.

Obj. 3. Further, this sacrament is consecrated by the priest's blessing. But a sinful priest's blessing is not efficacious for consecrating this sacrament, since it is written (Mal. ii. 2): *I will curse your blessings.* Again, Dionysius says in his Epistle (viii) to the monk Demophilus: *He who is not enlightened has completely fallen away from the priestly order; and I wonder that such a man dare to employ his hands in priestly actions, and in the person of Christ to utter, over the Divine symbols, his unclean infamies, for I will not call them prayers.*

On the contrary, Augustine (Paschasius) says *(De Corp. Dom.* xii): *Within the Catholic Church, in the mystery of the Lord's body and blood, nothing greater is done by a good priest, nothing less by an evil priest, because it is not by the merits of the consecrator that the sacrament is accomplished, but by the Creator's word, and by the power of the Holy Spirit.*

I answer that, As was said above (AA. 1, 3), the priest consecrates this sacrament not by his own power, but as the minister of Christ, in Whose person he consecrates this sacrament. But from the fact of being wicked he does not cease to be Christ's minister; because our Lord has good and wicked ministers or servants. Hence (Matth. xxiv. 45) our Lord says: *Who, thinkest thou, is a faithful and wise servant?* and afterwards He adds: *But if that evil servant shall say in his heart,* etc. And the Apostle (1 Cor. iv. 1) says: *Let a man so account of us as of the ministers of Christ;* and afterwards he adds: *I am not conscious to myself of anything; yet am I not hereby justified.* He was therefore certain that he was Christ's minister; yet he was not certain that he was a just man. Consequently, a man can be Christ's minister even though he be not one of the just. And this belongs to Christ's excellence, Whom, as the true God, things both good and evil serve, since they are ordained by His providence for His glory. Hence it is evident that priests, even though they be not godly, but sinners, can consecrate the Eucharist.

Reply Obj. 1. In those words Jerome is condemning the error of priests who believed they could consecrate the Eucharist worthily, from the mere fact of being priests, even though they were sinners; and Jerome condemns this from the fact that persons defiled are forbidden to approach the altar; but this does not prevent the sacrifice, which they offer, from being a true sacrifice, if they do approach.

Reply Obj. 2. Previous to the words quoted, Pope Gelasius expresses himself as follows: *That most holy rite, which contains the Catholic discipline, claims for itself such reverence that no one may dare to approach it except with clean conscience.* From this it is evident that his meaning is that the priest who is a sinner ought not to approach this sacrament. Hence when he resumes, *How shall the Holy Spirit come when summoned,* it must be understood that He comes, not through the priest's merits, but through the power of Christ, Whose words the priest utters.

Reply Obj. 3. As the same action can be evil, inasmuch as it is done with a bad intention of the servant; and good from the good intention of the master; so the blessing of a sinful priest, inasmuch as he acts unworthily is deserving of a curse, and is reputed an infamy and a blasphemy, and not a prayer; whereas, inasmuch as it is pronounced in the person of Christ, it is holy and efficacious. Hence it is said with significance: *I will curse your blessings.*

SIXTH ARTICLE

Whether the Mass of a Sinful Priest Is of Less Worth Than the Mass of a Good Priest?

We proceed thus to the Sixth Article:—

Objection 1. It seems that the mass of a sinful priest is not of less worth than that of a good priest. For Pope Gregory says in the

Register: Alas, into what a great snare they fall who believe that the Divine and hidden mysteries can be sanctified more by some than by others; since it is the one and the same Holy Ghost Who hallows those mysteries in a hidden and invisible manner. But these hidden mysteries are celebrated in the mass. Therefore the mass of a sinful priest is not of less value than the mass of a good priest.

Obj. 2. Further, as Baptism is conferred by a minister through the power of Christ Who baptizes, so likewise this sacrament is consecrated in the person of Christ. But Baptism is no better when conferred by a better priest, as was said above (Q. 64, A. 1, *ad* 2). Therefore neither is a mass the better, which is celebrated by a better priest.

Obj. 3. Further, as the merits of priests differ in the point of being good and better, so they likewise differ in the point of being good and bad. Consequently, if the mass of a better priest be itself better, it follows that the mass of a bad priest must be bad. Now this is unreasonable, because the malice of the ministers cannot affect Christ's mysteries, as Augustine says in his work on Baptism *(Contra Donat.* xii). Therefore neither is the mass of a better priest the better.

On the contrary, It is stated in (Decretal) i, q. 1: *The worthier the priest, the sooner is he heard in the needs for which he prays.*

I answer that, There are two things to be considered in the mass; namely, the sacrament itself, which is the chief thing; and the prayers which are offered up in the mass for the quick and the dead. So far as the mass itself is concerned, the mass of a wicked priest is not of less value than that of a good priest, because the same sacrifice is offered by both.

Again, the prayer put up in the mass can be considered in two respects: first of all, in so far as it has its efficacy from the devotion of the priest interceding, and in this respect there is no doubt but that the mass of the better priest is the more fruitful. In another respect, inasmuch as the prayer is said by the priest in the mass in the place of the entire Church, of which the priest is the minister; and this ministry remains even in sinful men, as was said above (A. 5) in regard to Christ's ministry. Hence, in this respect the prayer even of the sinful priest is fruitful, not only that which he utters in the mass, but likewise all those he recites in the ecclesiastical offices, wherein he takes the place of the Church. On the other hand, his private prayers are not fruitful, according to Prov. xxviii. 9: *He that turneth away his ears from hearing the law, his prayer shall be an abomination.*

Reply Obj. 1. Gregory is speaking there of the holiness of the Divine sacrament.

Reply Obj. 2. In the sacrament of Baptism solemn prayers are not made for all the faithful, as in the mass; therefore there is no parallel in this respect. There is, however, a resemblance as to the effect of the sacrament.

Reply Obj. 3. By reason of the power of the Holy Ghost, Who communicates to each one the blessings of Christ's members on account of their being united in charity, the private blessing in the mass of a good priest is fruitful to others. But the private evil of one man cannot hurt another, except the latter, in some way, consent, as Augustine says *(Contra Parmen.* ii).

SEVENTH ARTICLE

Whether Heretics, Schismatics, and Excommunicated Persons Can Consecrate?

We proceed thus to the Seventh Article:—

Objection 1. It seems that heretics, schismatics, and excommunicated persons are not able to consecrate the Eucharist. For Augustine says *(Liber sentent. Prosperi,* xv) that *there is no such thing as a true sacrifice outside the Catholic Church:* and Pope Leo (I) says *(Ep.* lxxx; *cf.* Decret. i, q. 1) : Elsewhere (i.e. *than in the Church which is Christ's body) there is neither valid priesthood nor true sacrifice.* But heretics, schismatics, and excommunicated persons are severed from the Church. Therefore they are unable to offer a true sacrifice.

Obj. 2. Further *(ibid.,* caus. i, q. 1), Innocent (I) is quoted as saying: *Because we receive the laity of the Arians and other pestilential persons, if they seem to repent; it does not follow that their clergy have the dignity of the priesthood or of any other ministerial office, for we allow them to confer nothing save Baptism.* But none can consecrate the Eucharist, unless he have the dignity of the priesthood. Therefore heretics and the like cannot consecrate the Eucharist.

Obj. 3. Further, it does not seem feasible for one outside the Church to act on behalf of the Church. But when the priest consecrates the Eucharist, he does so in the person of the entire Church, as is evident from the fact of his putting up all prayers in the person of the Church. Therefore, it seems that those who are outside the Church, such as those who are heretics, schismatics, and excommunicate, are not able to consecrate the Eucharist.

On the contrary, Augustine says *(Contra Parmen.* ii) : *Just as Baptism remains in them,* i.e. in heretics, schismatics, and those who are excommunicate, *so do their Orders remain intact.* Now, by the power of his ordination, a priest can consecrate the Eucharist. Therefore, it seems that heretics, schismatics, and those who are excommunicate, can consecrate the

Eucharist, since their Orders remain entire.

I answer that, Some have contended that heretics, schismatics, and the excommunicate, who are outside the pale of the Church, cannot perform this sacrament. But herein they are deceived, because, as Augustine says *(Contra Parmen.* ii), *it is one thing to lack something utterly, and another to have it improperly;* and in like fashion, *it is one thing not to bestow, and quite another to bestow, but not rightly.* Accordingly, such as, being within the Church, received the power of consecrating the Eucharist through being ordained to the priesthood, have such power rightly indeed; but they use it improperly if afterwards they be separated from the Church by heresy, schism, or excommunication. But such as are ordained while separated from the Church, have neither the power rightly, nor do they use it rightly. But that in both cases they have the power, is clear from what Augustine says *(ibid.),* that when they return to the unity of the Church, they are not re-ordained, but are received in their Orders. And since the consecration of the Eucharist is an act which follows the power of Order, such persons as are separated from the Church by heresy, schism, or excommunication, can indeed consecrate the Eucharist, which on being consecrated by them contains Christ's true body and blood; but they act wrongly, and sin by doing so; and in consequence they do not receive the fruit of the sacrifice, which is a spiritual sacrifice.

Reply Obj. 1. Such and similar authorities are to be understood in this sense, that the sacrifice is offered wrongly outside the Church. Hence outside the Church there can be no spiritual sacrifice that is a true sacrifice with the truth of its fruit, although it be a true sacrifice with the truth of the sacrament; thus it was stated above (Q. 80, A. 3), that the sinner receives Christ's body sacramentally, but not spiritually.

Reply Obj. 2. Baptism alone is allowed to be conferred by heretics, and schismatics, because they can lawfully baptize in case of necessity; but in no case can they lawfully consecrate the Eucharist, or confer the other sacraments.

Reply Obj. 3. The priest, in reciting the prayers of the mass, speaks instead of the Church, in whose unity he remains; but in consecrating the sacrament he speaks as in the person of Christ, Whose place he holds by the power of his Orders. Consequently, if a priest severed from the unity of the Church celebrates mass, not having lost the power of Order, he consecrates Christ's true body and blood; but because he is severed from the unity of the Church, his prayers have no efficacy.

EIGHTH ARTICLE

Whether a Degraded Priest Can Consecrate This Sacrament?

We proceed thus to the Eighth Article:—

Objection 1. It seems that a degraded priest cannot consecrate this sacrament. For no one can perform this sacrament except he have the power of consecrating. But the priest *who has been degraded has no power of consecrating, although he has the power of baptizing* (App. Gratiani). Therefore it seems that a degraded priest cannot consecrate the Eucharist.

Obj. 2. Further, he who gives can take away. But the bishop in ordaining gives to the priest the power of consecrating. Therefore he can take it away by degrading him.

Obj. 3. Further, the priest, by degradation, loses either the power of consecrating, or the use of such power. But he does not lose merely the use, for thus the degraded one would lose no more than one excommunicated, who also lacks the use. Therefore it seems that he loses the power to consecrate, and in consequence that he cannot perform this sacrament.

On the contrary, Augustine *(Contra Parmen.* ii) proves that *apostates* from the faith *are not deprived of their Baptism,* from the fact that *it is not restored to them when they return repentant; and therefore it is deemed that it cannot be lost.* But in like fashion, if the degraded man be restored, he has not to be ordained over again. Consequently, he has not lost the power of consecrating, and so the degraded priest can perform this sacrament.

I answer that, The power of consecrating the Eucharist belongs to the character of the priestly Order. But every character is indelible, because it is given with a kind of consecration, as was said above (Q. 63, A. 5), just as the consecrations of all other things are perpetual, and cannot be lost or repeated. Hence it is clear that the power of consecrating is not lost by degradation. For, again, Augustine says *(ibid.): Both are sacraments,* namely Baptism and Order, *and both are given to a man with a kind of consecration; the former, when he is baptized; the latter when he is ordained; and therefore it is not lawful for Catholics to repeat either of them.* And thus it is evident that the degraded priest can perform this sacrament.

Reply Obj. 1. That Canon is speaking, not as by way of assertion, but by way of inquiry, as can be gleaned from the context.

Reply Obj. 2. The bishop gives the priestly power of Order, not as though coming from himself, but instrumentally, as God's minister. and its effect cannot be taken away by man. according to Matth. xix. 6: *What God hath joined together, let no man put asunder.* And therefore the bishop cannot take this power away, just as neither can he who baptizes take away the baptismal character.

Reply Obj. 3. Excommunication is medicinal. And therefore the ministry of the priestly power is not taken away from the excommunicate, as it were, perpetually, but only for a time, that they may mend; but the exercise is withdrawn from the degraded, as though condemned perpetually.

NINTH ARTICLE

Whether It Is Permissible to Receive Communion from Heretical, Excommunicate, or Sinful Priests, and to Hear Mass Said by Them?

We proceed thus to the Ninth Article:—

Objection 1. It seems that one may lawfully receive Communion from heretical, excommunicate, or even sinful priests, and to hear mass said by them. Because, as Augustine says *(Contra Petilian.* iii), *we should not avoid God's sacraments, whether they be given by a good man or by a wicked one.* But priests, even if they be sinful, or heretics, or excommunicate, perform a valid sacrament. Therefore it seems that one ought not to refrain from receiving Communion at their hands, or from hearing their mass.

Obj. 2. Further, Christ's true body is figurative of His mystical body, as was said above (Q. 67, A. 2). But Christ's true body is consecrated by the priests mentioned above. Therefore it seems that whoever belongs to His mystical body can communicate in their sacrifices.

Obj. 3. Further, there are many sins graver than fornication. But it is not forbidden to hear the masses of priests who sin otherwise. Therefore, it ought not to be forbidden to hear the masses of priests guilty of this sin.

On the contrary, The Canon says (Dist. 32): *Let no one hear the mass of a priest whom he knows without doubt to have a concubine.* Moreover, Gregory says *(Dial.* iii) that *the faithless father sent an Arian bishop to his son, for him to receive sacrilegiously the consecrated Communion at his hands. But, when the Arian bishop arrived, God's devoted servant rebuked him, as was right for him to do.*

I answer that, As was said above (AA. 5, 7), heretical, schismatical, excommunicate, or even sinful priests, although they have the power to consecrate the Eucharist, yet they do not make a proper use of it; on the contrary, they sin by using it. But whoever communicates with another who is in sin, becomes a sharer in his sin. Hence we read in John's Second Canonical Epistle (11) that *He that saith unto him, God speed you, communicateth with his wicked works.* Consequently, it is not lawful to receive Communion from them, or to assist at their mass.

Still there is a difference among the above, because heretics, schismatics, and excommunicates, have been forbidden, by the Church's sentence, to perform the Eucharistic rite. And therefore whoever hears their mass or receives the sacraments from them, commits sin. But not all who are sinners are debarred by the Church's sentence from using this power: and so, although suspended by the Divine sentence, yet they are not suspended in regard to others by any ecclesiastical sentence: consequently, until the Church's sentence is pronounced, it is lawful to receive Communion at their hands, and to hear their mass. Hence on 1 Cor. v. 11, *with such a one not so much as to eat,* Augustine's gloss runs thus: *In saying this he was unwilling for a man to be judged by his fellow man on arbitrary suspicion, or even by usurped extraordinary judgment, but rather by God's law, according to the Church's ordering, whether he confess of his own accord, or whether he be accused and convicted.*

Reply Obj. 1. By refusing to hear the masses of such priests, or to receive Communion from them, we are not shunning God's sacraments; on the contrary, by so doing we are giving them honor (hence a host consecrated by such priests is to be adored, and if it be reserved, it can be consumed by a lawful priest): but what we shun is the sin of the unworthy ministers.

Reply Obj. 2. The unity of the mystical body is the fruit of the true body received. But those who receive or minister unworthily, are deprived of the fruit, as was said above (A. 7; Q. 80, A. 4). And therefore, those who belong to the unity of the Faith are not to receive the sacrament from their dispensing.

Reply Obj. 3. Although fornication is not graver than other sins, yet men are more prone to it, owing to fleshly concupiscence. Consequently, this sin is specially inhibited to priests by the Church, lest anyone hear the mass of one living in concubinage. However, this is to be understood of one who is notorious, either from being convicted and sentenced, or from having acknowledged his guilt in legal form, or from it being impossible to conceal his guilt by any subterfuge.

TENTH ARTICLE

Whether It Is Lawful for a Priest to Refrain Entirely from Consecrating the Eucharist?

We proceed thus to the Tenth Article:—

Objection 1. It seems to be lawful for a

priest to refrain entirely from consecrating the Eucharist. Because, as it is the priest's office to consecrate the Eucharist, so it is likewise to baptize and administer the other sacraments. But the priest is not bound to act as a minister of the other sacraments, unless he has undertaken the care of souls. Therefore, it seems that likewise he is not bound to consecrate the Eucharist except he be charged with the care of souls.

Obj. 2. Further, no one is bound to do what is unlawful for him to do; otherwise he would be in two minds. But it is not lawful for the priest who is in a state of sin, or excommunicate, to consecrate the Eucharist, as was said above (A. 7). Therefore it seems that such men are not bound to celebrate, and so neither are the others; otherwise they would be gainers by their fault.

Obj. 3. Further, the priestly dignity is not lost by subsequent weakness: because Pope Gelasius (I) says *(cf.* Decret., Dist. 55): *As the canonical precepts do not permit them who are feeble in body to approach the priesthood, so if anyone be disabled when once in that state, he cannot lose what he received at the time he was well.* But it sometimes happens that those who are already ordained as priests incur defects whereby they are hindered from celebrating, such as leprosy or epilepsy, or the like. Consequently, it does not appear that priests are bound to celebrate.

On the contrary, Ambrose says in one of his Orations (xxxiii): *It is a grave matter if we do not approach Thy altar with clean heart and pure hands; but it is graver still if while shunning sins we also fail to offer our sacrifice.*

I answer that, Some have said that a priest may lawfully refrain altogether from consecrating, except he be bound to do so, and to give the sacraments to the people, by reason of his being entrusted with the care of souls.

But this is said quite unreasonably, because everyone is bound to use the grace entrusted to him, when opportunity serves, according to 2 Cor. vi. 1: *We exhort you that you receive not the grace of God in vain.* But the opportunity of offering sacrifice is considered not merely in relation to the faithful of Christ to whom the sacraments must be administered, but chiefly with regard to God to Whom the sacrifice of this sacrament is offered by consecrating. Hence, it is not lawful for the priest, even though he has not the care of souls, to refrain altogether from celebrating; and he seems to be bound to celebrate at least on the chief festivals, and especially on those days on which the faithful usually communicate. And hence it is that (2 Machab. iv. 14) it is said against some priests that they *were not now occupied about the offices of the altar, . . . despising the temple and neglecting the sacrifices.*

Reply Obj. 1. The other sacraments are accomplished in being used by the faithful, and therefore he alone is bound to administer them who has undertaken the care of souls. But this sacrament is performed in the consecration of the Eucharist, whereby a sacrifice is offered to God, to which the priest is bound from the Order he has received.

Reply Obj. 2. The sinful priest, if deprived by the Church's sentence from exercising his Order, simply or for a time, is rendered incapable of offering sacrifice; consequently, the obligation lapses. But if not deprived of the power of celebrating, the obligation is not removed; nor is he in two minds, because he can repent of his sin and then celebrate.

Reply Obj. 3. Weakness or sickness contracted by a priest after his Ordination does not deprive him of his Orders; but hinders him from exercising them, as to the consecration of the Eucharist: sometimes by making it impossible to exercise them, as, for example, if he lose his sight, or his fingers, or the use of speech; and sometimes on account of danger, as in the case of one suffering from epilepsy, or indeed any disease of the mind; and sometimes, on account of loathsomeness, as is evident in the case of a leper, who ought not to celebrate in public: he can, however, say mass privately, unless the leprosy has gone so far that it has rendered him incapable owing to the wasting away of his limbs.

QUESTION 83

Of the Rite of This Sacrament

(In Six Articles)

WE have now to consider the Rite of this sacrament, under which head there are six points of inquiry. (1) Whether Christ is sacrificed in the celebration of this mystery? (2) Of the time of celebrating. (3) Of the place and other matters relating to the equipment for this celebration. (4) Of the words uttered in celebrating this mystery. (5) Of the actions performed in celebrating this mystery. (6) Of the defects which occur in the celebration of this sacrament.

FIRST ARTICLE

Whether Christ Is Sacrificed in This Sacrament?

We proceed thus to the First Article:—

Objection 1. It seems that Christ is not sacrificed in the celebration of this sacrament. For it is written (Heb. x. 14) that *Christ by one oblation hath perfected for ever them that are sanctified.* But that oblation was His oblation. Therefore Christ is not sacrificed in the celebration of this sacrament.

Obj. 2. Further, Christ's sacrifice was made upon the cross, whereon *He delivered Himself for us, an oblation and a sacrifice to God for an odor of sweetness,* as is said in Eph. v. 2. But Christ is not crucified in the celebration of this mystery. Therefore, neither is He sacrificed.

Obj. 3. Further, as Augustine says (*De Trin.* iv), in Christ's sacrifice the priest and the victim are one and the same. But in the celebration of this sacrament the priest and the victim are not the same. Therefore, the celebration of this sacrament is not a sacrifice of Christ.

On the contrary, Augustine says in the *Liber Sentent. Prosp.* (cf. *Ep.* xcviii): *Christ was sacrificed once in Himself, and yet He is sacrificed daily in the Sacrament.*

I answer that, The celebration of this sacrament is called a sacrifice for two reasons. First, because, as Augustine says (*Ad Simplician.* ii), *the images of things are called by the names of the things whereof they are the images; as when we look upon a picture or a fresco, we say, "This is Cicero and that is Sallust."* But, as was said above (Q. 79, A. 1), the celebration of this sacrament is an image representing Christ's Passion, which is His true sacrifice. Accordingly the celebration of this sacrament is called Christ's sacrifice. Hence it is that Ambrose, in commenting on Heb. x. 1, says: *In Christ was offered up a sacrifice capable of giving eternal salvation; what then do we do? Do we not offer it up every day in memory of His death?*

Secondly it is called a sacrifice, in respect of the effect of His Passion: because, to wit, by this sacrament, we are made partakers of the fruit of our Lord's Passion. Hence in one of the Sunday *Secrets* (Ninth Sunday after Pentecost) we say: *Whenever the commemoration of this sacrifice is celebrated, the work of our redemption is enacted.* Consequently, according to the first reason, it is true to say that Christ was sacrificed, even in the figures of the Old Testament: hence it is stated in the Apocalypse (xiii. 8): *Whose names are not written in the Book of Life of the Lamb, which was slain from the beginning of the world.* But according to the second reason, it is proper to this sacrament for Christ to be sacrificed in its celebration.

Reply Obj. 1. As Ambrose says (*ibid.*), *there is but one victim,* namely that which Christ offered, and which we offer, *and not many victims, because Christ was offered but once: and this latter sacrifice is the pattern of the former. For, just as what is offered everywhere is one body, and not many bodies, so also is it but one sacrifice.*

Reply Obj. 2. As the celebration of this sacrament is an image representing Christ's Passion, so the altar is representative of the cross itself, upon which Christ was sacrificed in His proper species.

Reply Obj. 3. For the same reason (cf. *Reply Obj.* 2) the priest also bears Christ's image, in Whose person and by Whose power he pronounces the words of consecration, as is evident from what was said above (Q. 82, AA. 1, 3). And so, in a measure, the priest and victim are one and the same.

SECOND ARTICLE

Whether the Time for Celebrating This Mystery Has Been Properly Determined?

We proceed thus to the Second Article:—

Objection 1. It seems that the time for celebrating this mystery has not been properly determined. For as was observed above (A. 1), this sacrament is representative of our Lord's Passion. But the commemoration of our Lord's Passion takes place in the Church once in the year: because Augustine says (*Enarr.* ii, in Ps. xxi): *Is not Christ slain as often as the Pasch is celebrated? Nevertheless, the anniversary remembrance represents what took place in bygone days; and so it does not cause us to be stirred as if we saw our Lord hanging upon the cross.* Therefore this sacrament ought to be celebrated but once a year.

Obj. 2. Further, Christ's Passion is commemorated in the Church on the Friday before Easter, and not on Christmas Day. Consequently, since this sacrament is commemorative of our Lord's Passion, it seems unsuitable for this sacrament to be celebrated thrice on Christmas Day, and to be entirely omitted on Good Friday.

Obj. 3. Further, in the celebration of this sacrament the Church ought to imitate Christ's institution. But it was in the evening that Christ consecrated this sacrament. Therefore it seems that this sacrament ought to be celebrated at that time of day.

Obj. 4. Further, as is set down in the Decretals (*De Consecr.,* dist. i), Pope Leo (I) wrote to Dioscorus, Bishop of Alexandria, that *it is permissible to celebrate mass in the first part of the day.* But the day begins at midnight, as was said above (Q. 80, A. 8, *ad* 5). Therefore it seems that after midnight it is lawful to celebrate.

Obj. 5. Further, in one of the Sunday *Secrets* (Ninth Sunday after Pentecost) we say: *Grant us, Lord, we beseech Thee, to frequent these mysteries.* But there will be greater frequency if the priest celebrates several times a day. Therefore it seems that the priest ought not to be hindered from celebrating several times daily.

On the contrary is the custom which the Church observes according to the statutes of the Canons.

I answer that, As stated above (A. 1), in the celebration of this mystery, we must take into consideration the representation of our Lord's Passion, and the participation of its fruits; and the time suitable for the celebration of this mystery ought to be determined by each of these considerations. Now since, owing to our daily defects, we stand in daily need of the fruits of our Lord's Passion, this sacrament is offered regularly every day in the Church. Hence our Lord teaches us to pray (Luke xi. 3): *Give us this day our daily bread:* in explanation of which words Augustine says *(De Verb. Dom.* xxviii): *If it be a daily bread, why do you take it once a year, as the Greeks have the custom in the east? Receive it daily that it may benefit you every day.*

But since our Lord's Passion was celebrated from the third to the ninth hour, therefore this sacrament is solemly celebrated by the Church in that part of the day.

Reply Obj. 1. Christ's Passion is recalled in this sacrament, inasmuch as its effect flows out to the faithful; but at Passion-tide Christ's Passion is recalled inasmuch as it was wrought in Him Who is our Head. This took place but once; whereas the faithful receive daily the fruits of His Passion: consequently, the former is commemorated but once in the year, whereas the latter takes place every day, both that we may partake of its fruit and in order that we may have a perpetual memorial.

Reply Obj. 2. The figure ceases on the advent of the reality. But this sacrament is a figure and a representation of our Lord's Passion, as stated above. And therefore on the day on which our Lord's Passion is recalled as it was really accomplished, this sacrament is not consecrated. Nevertheless, lest the Church be deprived on that day of the fruit of the Passion offered to us by this sacrament, the body of Christ consecrated the day before is reserved to be consumed on that day; but the blood is not reserved, on account of danger, and because the blood is more specially the image of our Lord's Passion, as stated

above (Q. 78, A. 3, *ad* 2). Nor is it true, as some affirm, that the wine is changed into blood when the particle of Christ's body is dropped into it. Because this cannot be done otherwise than by consecration under the due form of words.

On Christmas Day, however, several masses are said on account of Christ's threefold nativity. Of these the first is His eternal birth, which is hidden in our regard; and therefore one mass is sung in the night, in the *Introit* of which we say: *The Lord said unto Me: Thou art My Son, this day have I begotten Thee.* The second is His nativity in time, and the spiritual birth, whereby Christ rises *as the day-star in our* (Vulg.,—*your*) *hearts* (2 Pet. i. 19), and on this account the mass is sung at dawn, and in the *Introit* we say: *The light will shine on us today.* The third is Christ's temporal and bodily birth, according as He went forth from the virginal womb, becoming visible to us through being clothed with flesh: and on that account the third mass is sung in broad daylight, in the *Introit* of which we say: *A child is born to us.* Nevertheless, on the other hand, it can be said that His eternal generation, of itself, is in the full light, and on this account in the gospel of the third mass mention is made of His eternal birth. But regarding His birth in the body, He was literally born during the night, as a sign that He came to the darknesses of our infirmity; hence also in the midnight mass we say the gospel of Christ's nativity in the flesh.

Likewise on other days upon which many of God's benefits have to be recalled or besought, several masses are celebrated on one day, as for instance, one for the feast, and another for a fast or for the dead.

Reply Obj. 3. As already observed (Q. 73, A. 5). Christ wished to give this sacrament last of all, in order that it might make a deeper impression on the hearts of the disciples; and therefore it was after supper, at the close of day, that He consecrated this sacrament and gave it to His disciples. But we celebrate at the hour when our Lord suffered, i.e. either, as on feast-days, at the hour of Terce, when He was crucified by the tongues of the Jews (Mark xv. 25), and when the Holy Ghost descended upon the disciples (Acts ii. 15); or, as when no feast is kept, at the hour of Sext, when He was crucified at the hands of the soldiers (John xix. 14), or, as on fasting days, at None, when crying out with a loud voice He gave up the ghost (Matth. xxvii. 46, 50).

Nevertheless the mass can be postponed, especially when Holy Orders have to be conferred, and still more on Holy Saturday; both on account of the length of the Office, and also because Orders belong to the Sunday, as is set forth in the Decretals (dist. 75).

Masses, however, can be celebrated *in the first part of the day*, owing to any necessity; as is stated *De Consecr.*, dist. 1.

Reply Obj. 4. As a rule mass ought to be said in the day and not in the night, because Christ is present in this sacrament, Who says (John ix. 4, 5): *I must work the works of Him that sent Me, whilst it is day: because the night cometh when no man can work; as long as I am in the world, I am the light of the world.* Yet this should be done in such a manner that the beginning of the day is not to be taken from midnight; nor from sunrise, that is, when the substance of the sun appears above the earth; but when the dawn begins to show: because then the sun is said to be risen when the brightness of his beams appears. Accordingly it is written (Mark xvi. 1) that *the women came to the tomb, the sun being now risen;* though, as John relates (xx. 1), *while it was yet dark they came to the tomb.* It is in this way that Augustine explains this difference *(De Consens. Evang. iii).*

Exception is made on the night of Christmas eve, when mass is celebrated, because our Lord was born in the night *(De Consecr.,* dist. 1). And in like manner it is celebrated on Holy Saturday towards the beginning of the night, since our Lord rose in the night, that is, *when it was yet dark,* before the sun's rising was manifest.

Reply Obj. 5. As is set down in the decree *(De Consecr.,* dist. 1), in virtue of a decree of Pope Alexander (II), *it is enough for a priest to celebrate one mass each day, because Christ suffered once and redeemed the whole world; and very happy is he who can worthily celebrate one mass. But there are some who say one mass for the dead, and another of the day, if need be. But I do not deem that those escape condemnation who presume to celebrate several masses daily, either for the sake of money, or to gain flattery from the laity.* And Pope Innocent III says (Extra, *De Celebr. Miss.,* chap. *Consuluisti) that except on the day of our Lord's birth, unless necessity urges, it suffices for a priest to celebrate only one mass each day.*

THIRD ARTICLE

Whether This Sacrament Ought to Be Celebrated in a House and with Sacred Vessels?

We proceed thus to the Third Article:—

Objection 1. It seems that this sacrament ought not to be celebrated in a house and with sacred vessels. For this sacrament is a representation of our Lord's Passion. But Christ did not suffer in a house, but outside the city gate, according to Heb. i. 12: *Jesus, that He might sanctify the people by His own blood, suffered without the gate.* Therefore, it seems that this sacrament ought not to be celebrated in a house, but rather in the open air.

Obj. 2. Further, in the celebration of this sacrament the Church ought to imitate the custom of Christ and the apostles. But the house wherein Christ first wrought this sacrament was not consecrated, but merely an ordinary supper-room prepared by the master of the house, as related in Luke xxii. 11, 12. Moreover, we read (Acts ii. 46) that *the apostles were continuing daily with one accord in the temple; and, breaking bread from house to house, they took their meat with gladness.* Consequently, there is no need for houses, in which this sacrament is celebrated, to be consecrated.

Obj. 3. Further, nothing that is to no purpose ought to be done in the Church, which is governed by the Holy Ghost. But it seems useless to consecrate a church, or an altar, or such like inanimate things, since they are not capable of receiving grace or spiritual virtue. Therefore it is unbecoming for such consecrations to be performed in the Church.

Obj. 4. Further, only Divine works ought to be recalled with solemnity, according to Ps. xci. 5: *I shall rejoice in the works of Thy hands.* Now the consecration of a church or altar, is the work of a man; as is also the consecration of the chalice, and of the ministers, and of other such things. But these latter consecrations are not commemorated in the Church. Therefore neither ought the consecration of a church or of an altar to be commemorated with solemnity.

Obj. 5. Further, the truth ought to correspond with the figure. But in the Old Testament, which was a figure of the New, the altar was not made of hewn stones: for, it is written (Exod. xx. 24): *You shall make an altar of earth unto Me, . . . and if thou make an altar of stone unto Me, thou shalt not build it of hewn stones.* Again, the altar is commanded to be made of *setim-wood,* covered *with brass* (Exod. xxvii. 1, 2), or *with gold (ibid.,* xxv). Consequently, it seems unfitting for the Church to make exclusive use of altars made of stone.

Obj. 6. Further, the chalice with the paten represents Christ's tomb, which was *hewn in a rock,* as is narrated in the Gospels. Consequently, the chalice ought to be of stone, and not of gold or of silver or tin.

Obj. 7. Further, just as gold is the most precious among the materials of the altar vessels, so are cloths of silk the most precious among other cloths. Consequently, since the chalice is of gold, the altar cloths ought to be made of silk and not of linen.

Obj. 8. Further, the dispensing and ordering of the sacraments belong to the Church's ministers, just as the ordering of temporal affairs is subject to the ruling of secular princes; hence the Apostle says (1 Cor. iv. 1): *Let a man so esteem us as the ministers of Christ and the dispensers of the mysteries of God.* But if anything be done against the ordinances of princes it is deemed void. Therefore, if the various items mentioned above are suitably commanded by the Church's prelates, it seems that the body of Christ could not be consecrated unless they be observed; and so it appears to follow that Christ's words are not sufficient of themselves for consecrating this sacrament: which is contrary to the fact. Consequently, it does not seem fitting for such ordinances to be made touching the celebration of this sacrament.

On the contrary, The Church's ordinances are Christ's own ordinances; since He said (Matth. xviii. 20): *Wherever two or three are gathered together in My name, there am I in the midst of them.*

I answer that, There are two things to be considered regarding the equipment of this sacrament: one of these belongs to the representation of the events connected with our Lord's Passion; while the other is connected with the reverence due to the sacrament, in which Christ is contained verily, and not in figure only.

Hence we consecrate those things which we make use of in this sacrament; both that we may show our reverence for the sacrament, and in order to represent the holiness which is the effect of the Passion of Christ, according to Heb. xiii. 12: *Jesus, that He might sanctify the people by His own blood,* etc.

Reply Obj. 1. This sacrament ought as a rule to be celebrated in a house, whereby the Church is signified, according to 1 Tim. iii. 15: *That thou mayest know how thou oughtest to behave thyself in the house of God, which is the Church of the living God.* Because outside the Church there is no place for the true sacrifice, as Augustine says *(Liber Sent. Prosp. xv).* And because the Church was not to be confined within the territories of the Jewish people, but was to be established throughout the whole world, therefore Christ's Passion was not celebrated within the city of the Jews, but in the open country, that so the whole world might serve as a house for Christ's Passion. Nevertheless, as is said in *De Consecr.,* dist. 1, *if a church be not to hand, we permit travelers to celebrate mass in the open air, or in a tent, if there be a consecrated altar-table* to hand, and the other requisites belonging to the sacred function.

Reply Obj. 2. The house in which this sacrament is celebrated denotes the Church, and is termed a church; and so it is fittingly consecrated, both to represent the holiness which the Church acquired from the Passion, as well as to denote the holiness required of them who have to receive this sacrament.—By the altar Christ Himself is signified, of Whom the Apostle says (Heb. xiii. 15): *Through Him we offer a sacrifice of praise to God.* Hence the consecration of the altar signifies Christ's holiness, of which it was said (Luke i. 35): *The Holy One born of thee shall be called the Son of God.* Hence we read in *De Consecr.,* dist. 1: *It has seemed pleasing for the altars to be consecrated not merely with the anointing of chrism, but likewise with the priestly blessing.*

And therefore, as a rule, it is not lawful to celebrate this sacrament except in a consecrated house. Hence it is enacted *(De Consecr.,* dist. 1): *Let no priest presume to say mass except in places consecrated by the bishop.* And furthermore because pagans and other unbelievers are not members of the Church, therefore we read *(ibid.): It is not lawful to bless a church in which the bodies of unbelievers are buried, but if it seem suitable for consecration, then, after removing the corpses and tearing down the walls or beams, let it be rebuilt. If, however, it has been already consecrated, and the faithful lie in it, it is lawful to celebrate mass therein.* Nevertheless in a case of necessity this sacrament can be performed in houses which have not been consecrated, or which have been profaned; but with the bishop's consent. Hence we read in the same distinction: *We deem that masses are not to be celebrated everywhere, but in places consecrated by the bishop, or where he gives permission.* But not without a portable altar consecrated by the bishop: hence in the same distinction we read: *We permit that, if the churches be devastated or burned, masses may be celebrated in chapels, with a consecrated altar.* For because Christ's holiness is the fount of all the Church's holiness, therefore in necessity a consecrated altar suffices for performing this sacrament. And on this account a church is never consecrated without consecrating the altar. Yet sometimes an altar is consecrated apart from the church, with the relics of the saints, *whose lives are hidden with Christ in God* (Col. iii. 3). Accordingly under the same distinction we read: *It is our pleasure that altars, in which no relics of saints are found enclosed, be thrown down, if possible, by the bishops presiding over such places.*

Reply Obj. 3. The church, altar, and other

like inanimate things are consecrated, not because they are capable of receiving grace, but because they acquire special spiritual virtue from the consecration, whereby they are rendered fit for the Divine worship, so that man derives devotion therefrom, making him more fitted for Divine functions, unless this be hindered by want of reverence. Hence it is written (2 Mach. iii. 38): *There is undoubtedly in that place a certain power of God; for He that hath His dwelling in the heavens is the visitor, and the protector of that place.*

Hence it is that such places are cleansed and exorcised before being consecrated, that the enemy's power may be driven forth. And for the same reason churches defiled by shedding of blood or seed are reconciled: because some machination of the enemy is apparent on account of the sin committed there. And for this reason we read in the same distinction: *Wherever you find churches of the Arians, consecrate them as Catholic churches without delay by means of devout prayers and rites.* Hence, too, it is that some say with probability, that by entering a consecrated church one obtains forgiveness of venial sins, just as one does by the sprinkling of holy water; alleging the words of Ps. lxxxiv. 2, 3: *Lord, Thou hast blessed Thy land. . . . Thou hast forgiven the iniquity of Thy people.* And therefore, in consequence of the virtue acquired by a church's consecration, the consecration is never repeated. Accordingly we find in the same distinction the following words quoted from the Council of Nicæa: *Churches which have once been consecrated, must not be consecrated again, except they be devastated by fire, or defiled by shedding of blood or of anyone's seed; because, just as a child once baptized in the name of the Father, and of the Son, and of the Holy Ghost, ought not to be baptized again, so neither ought a place, once dedicated to God, to be consecrated again, except owing to the causes mentioned above; provided that the consecrators held faith in the Holy Trinity:* in fact, those outside the Church cannot consecrate. But, as we read in the same distinction: *Churches or altars of doubtful consecration are to be consecrated anew.*

And since they acquire special spiritual virtue from their consecration, we find it laid down in the same distinction that *the beams of a dedicated church ought not to be used for any other purpose, except it be for some other church, or else they are to be burned, or put to the use of brethren in some monastery: but on no account are they to be discarded for works of the laity.* We read there, too, that *the altar covering, chair, candlesticks, and veil, are to be burned when worn out; and*

their ashes are to be placed in the baptistery, or in the walls, or else cast into the trenches beneath the flag-stones, so as not to be defiled by the feet of those that enter.

Reply Obj. 4. Since the consecration of the altar signifies Christ's holiness, and the consecration of a house the holiness of the entire Church, therefore the consecration of a church or of an altar is more fittingly commemorated. And on this account the solemnity of a church dedication is observed for eight days, in order to signify the happy resurrection of Christ and of the Church's members. Nor is the consecration of a church or altar man's doing only, since it has a spiritual virtue. Hence in the same distinction *(De Consecr.)* it is said: *The solemnities of the dedication of churches are to be solemnly celebrated each year: and that dedications are to be kept up for eight days, you will find in the third book of Kings* (viii. 66).

Reply Obj. 5. As we read in *De Consecr.,* dist. 1, *altars, if not of stone, are not to be consecrated with the anointing of chrism.* And this is in keeping with the signification of this sacrament; both because the altar signifies Christ, for in 1 Cor. x. 3, it is written, *But the rock was Christ:* and because Christ's body was laid in a stone sepulchre. This is also in keeping with the use of the sacrament. Because stone is solid, and may be found everywhere; which was not necessary in the Old Law, when the altar was made in one place.—As to the commandment to make the altar of earth, or of unhewn stones, this was given in order to remove idolatry.

Reply Obj. 6. As is laid down in the same distinction, *formerly the priests did not use golden but wooden chalices; but Pope Zephyrinus ordered the mass to be said with glass patens; and subsequently Pope Urban had everything made of silver.* Afterwards it was decided that *the Lord's chalice with the paten should be made entirely of gold, or of silver, or at least of tin. But it is not to be made of brass, or copper, because the action of the wine thereon produces verdigris, and provokes vomiting. But no one is to presume to sing mass with a chalice of wood or of glass,* because as the wood is porous, the consecrated blood would remain in it; while glass is brittle, and there might arise danger of breakage; and the same applies to stone. Consequently, out of reverence for the sacrament, it was enacted that the chalice should be made of the aforesaid materials.

Reply Obj. 7. Where it could be done without danger, the Church gave order for that thing to be used which more expressively represents Christ's Passion. But there was not so much danger regarding the body which is placed on the corporal, as there is with the blood contained in the chalice. And consequently, although the chalice is not made of stone, yet the corporal is made of linen, since Christ's body was wrapped therein. Hence we read in an Epistle of Pope Silvester, quoted in the same distinction: *By a unanimous decree we command that no one shall presume to celebrate the sacrifice of the altar upon a cloth of silk, or dyed material, but upon linen consecrated by the bishop; as Christ's body was buried in a clean linen winding-sheet.* Moreover, linen material is becoming, owing to its cleanness, to denote purity of conscience, and, owing to the manifold labor with which it is prepared, to denote Christ's Passion.

Reply Obj. 8. The dispensing of the sacraments belongs to the Church's ministers; but their consecration is from God Himself. Consequently, the Church's ministers can make no ordinances regarding the form of the consecration, and the manner of celebrating. And therefore, if the priest pronounces the words of consecration over the proper matter with the intention of consecrating, then, without every one of the things mentioned above,—namely, without house, and altar, consecrated chalice and corporal, and the other things instituted by the Church, — he consecrates Christ's body in very truth; yet he is guilty of grave sin, in not following the rite of the Church.

FOURTH ARTICLE

Whether the Words Spoken in This Sacrament Are Properly Framed?

We proceed thus to the Fourth Article:—

Objection 1. It seems that the words spoken in this sacrament are not properly framed. For, as Ambrose says *(De Sacram.* iv), *this sacrament is consecrated with Christ's own words.* Therefore no other words besides Christ's should be spoken in this sacrament.

Obj. 2. Further, Christ's words and deeds are made known to us through the Gospel. But in consecrating this sacrament words are used which are not set down in the Gospels: for we do not read in the Gospel, of Christ lifting up His eyes to heaven while consecrating this sacrament: and similarly it is said in the Gospel: *Take ye and eat (comedite)* without the addition of the word *all,* whereas in celebrating this sacrament we say: *Lifting up His eyes to heaven,* and again, *Take ye and eat (manducate) of this.* Therefore such words as these are out of place when spoken in the celebration of this sacrament.

Obj. 3. Further, all the other sacraments are ordained for the salvation of all the faithful. But in the celebration of the other sacraments there is no common prayer put up for the salvation of all the faithful and of the departed. Consequently it is unbecoming in this sacrament.

Obj. 4. Further, Baptism especially is called the sacrament of faith. Consequently, the truths which belong to instruction in the faith ought rather to be given regarding Baptism than regarding this sacrament, such as the doctrine of the apostles and of the Gospels.

Obj. 5. Further, devotion on the part of the faithful is required in every sacrament. Consequently, the devotion of the faithful ought not to be stirred up in this sacrament more than in the others by Divine praises and by admonitions, such as, *Lift up your hearts.*

Obj. 6. Further, the minister of this sacrament is the priest, as stated above (Q. 82, A. 1). Consequently, all the words spoken in this sacrament ought to be uttered by the priest, and not some by the ministers, and some by the choir.

Obj. 7. Further, the Divine power works this sacrament unfailingly. Therefore it is to no purpose that the priest asks for the perfecting of this sacrament, saying: *Which oblation do thou, O God, in all,* etc.

Obj. 8. Further, the sacrifice of the New Law is much more excellent than the sacrifice of the fathers of old. Therefore it is unfitting for the priest to pray that this sacrifice may be as acceptable as the sacrifice of Abel, Abraham, and Melchisedech.

Obj. 9. Further, just as Christ's body does not begin to be in this sacrament by change of place, as stated above (Q. 75, A. 2), so likewise neither does it cease to be there. Consequently, it is improper for the priest to ask: *Bid these things be borne by the hands of thy holy angel unto Thine altar on high.*

On the contrary, We find it stated in *De Consecr.,* dist. 1, that *James, the brother of the Lord according to the flesh, and Basil, bishop of Cæsarea, edited the rite of celebrating the mass:* and from their authority it is manifest that whatever words are employed in this matter, are chosen becomingly.

I answer that, Since the whole mystery of our salvation is comprised in this sacrament, therefore is it performed with greater solemnity than the other sacraments. And since it is written (Eccles. iv. 17): *Keep thy foot when thou goest into the house of God;* and (Ecclus. xviii. 23): *Before prayer prepare thy soul,* therefore the celebration of this mystery is preceded by a certain preparation in order that we may perform worthily that which follows after. The first part of this preparation is Divine praise, and consists in the *Introit:* according to Ps. xlix. 23: *The sacrifice of praise shall glorify me; and there is the way by which I will show him the salvation of God:* and this is taken for the most part from the Psalms, or, at least, is sung with a Psalm, because, as Dionysius says *(Eccl. Hier.* iii): *The Psalms comprise by way of praise whatever is contained in Sacred Scripture.*

The second part contains a reference to our present misery, by reason of which we pray for mercy, saying: *Lord, have mercy on us,* thrice for the Person of the Father, and *Christ, have mercy on us,* thrice for the Person of the Son, and *Lord, have mercy on us,* thrice for the Person of the Holy Ghost; against the threefold misery of ignorance, sin, and punishment; or else to express the *circuminsession* of all the Divine Persons.

The third part commemorates the heavenly glory, to the possession of which, after this life of misery, we are tending, in the words, *Glory be to God on high,* which are sung on festival days, on which the heavenly glory is commemorated, but are omitted in those sorrowful offices which commemorate our unhappy state.

The fourth part contains the prayer which the priest makes for the people, that they may be made worthy of such great mysteries.

There precedes, in the second place, the instruction of the faithful, because this sacrament is *a mystery of faith,* as stated above (Q. 78, A. 3, *ad* 5). Now this instruction is given *dispositively,* when the Lectors and Subdeacons read aloud in the church the teachings of the prophets and apostles: after this *lesson,* the choir sing the *Gradual,* which signifies progress in life; then the *Alleluia* is intoned, and this denotes spiritual joy; or in mournful Offices the *Tract,* expressive of spiritual sighing; for all these things ought to result from the aforesaid teaching. But the people are instructed *perfectly* by Christ's teaching contained in the Gospel, which is read by the higher ministers, that is, by the Deacons. And because we believe Christ as the Divine truth, according to John viii. 46, *If I tell you the truth, why do you not believe Me?* after the Gospel has been read, the *Creed* is sung in which the people show that they assent by faith to Christ's doctrine. And it is sung on those festivals of which mention is made therein, as on the festivals of Christ, of the Blessed Virgin, and of the apostles, who laid the foundations of this faith, and on other such days.

So then, after the people have been prepared and instructed, the next step is to proceed to the celebration of the mystery, which is both offered as a sacrifice, and consecrated and received as a sacrament: since first we have the oblation; then the consecration of the matter offered; and thirdly, its reception.

In regard to the oblation, two things are done, namely, the people's praise in singing the *Offertory,* expressing the joy of the offerers, and the priest's prayer asking for the people's oblation to be made acceptable to God. Hence David said (1 Para. xxix. 17): *In the simplicity of my heart, I have . . . offered all these things: and I have seen with great joy Thy people which are here present, offer Thee their offerings:* and then he makes the following prayer: *O Lord God . . . keep . . . this will.*

Then, regarding the consecration, performed by supernatural power, the people are first of all excited to devotion in the *Preface,* hence they are admonished *to lift up their hearts to the Lord,* and therefore when the *Preface* is ended the people devoutly praise Christ's Godhead, saying with the angels: *Holy, Holy, Holy;* and His humanity, saying with the children: *Blessed is he that cometh.* In the next place the priest makes a *commemoration,* first of those for whom this sacrifice is offered, namely, for the whole Church, and *for those set in high places* (1 Tim. ii. 2), and, in a special manner, of them *who offer, or for whom the mass is offered.* Secondly, he commemorates the saints, invoking their patronage for those mentioned above, when he says: —*Communicating with, and honoring the memory,* etc. Thirdly, he concludes the petition when he says: *Wherefore that this oblation,* etc., in order that the oblation may be salutary to them for whom it is offered.

Then he comes to the consecration itself. Here he asks first of all for the effect of the consecration, when he says: *Which oblation do Thou, O God,* etc. Secondly, he performs the consecration using our Saviour's words, when he says: *Who the day before,* etc. Thirdly, he makes excuse for his presumption in obeying Christ's command, saying: *Wherefore, calling to mind,* etc. Fourthly, he asks that the sacrifice accomplished may find favor with God, when he says: *Look down upon them with a propitious,* etc. Fifthly, he begs for the effect of this sacrifice and sacrament, first for the partakers, saying: *We humbly beseech Thee;* then for the dead, who can no longer receive it, saying: *Be mindful also, O Lord,* etc.; thirdly, for the priests themselves who offer, saying: *And to us sinners,* etc.

Then follows the act of receiving the sacrament. First of all, the people are prepared for Communion; first, by the common prayer of the congregation, which is the Lord's Prayer, in which we ask for our daily bread to be given us; and also by private prayer, which the priest puts up specially for the people, when he says: *Deliver us, we beseech Thee, O Lord,* etc. Secondly, the people are prepared by the *Pax* which is given with the words, *Lamb of God*, etc., because this is the sacrament of unity and peace, as stated above (Q. 73, A. 4; Q. 79, A. 1). But in masses for the dead, in which the sacrifice is offered not for present peace, but for the repose of the dead, the *Pax* is omitted.

Then follows the reception of the sacrament, the priest receiving first, and afterwards giving it to others, because, as Dionysius says *(Eccl. Hier.* iii), he who gives Divine things to others, ought first to partake thereof himself.

Finally, the whole celebration of mass ends with the thanksgiving, the people rejoicing for having received the mystery (and this is the meaning of the singing after the Communion); and the priest returning thanks by prayer, as Christ, at the close of the supper with His disciples, *said a hymn* (Matth. xxvi. 30).

Reply Obj. 1. The consecration is accomplished by Christ's words only; but the other words must be added to dispose the people for receiving it, as stated above.

Reply Obj. 2. As is stated in the last chapter of John *(verse* 25), our Lord said and did many things which are not written down by the Evangelists; and among them is the uplifting of His eyes to heaven at the supper; nevertheless the Roman Church had it by tradition from the apostles. For it seems reasonable that He Who lifted up His eyes to the Father in raising Lazarus to life, as related in John xi. 41, and in the prayer which He made for the disciples (John xvii. 1), had more reason to do so in instituting this sacrament, as being of greater import.

The use of the word *manducate* instead of *comedite* makes no difference in the meaning, nor does the expression signify, especially since those words are no part of the form, as stated above (Q. 78, A. 1, *ad* 2, 4).

The additional word *all* is understood in the Gospels, although not expressed, because He had said (John vi. 54): *Except you eat the flesh of the Son of Man, . . . you shall not have life in you.*

Reply Obj. 3. The Eucharist is the sacrament of the unity of the whole Church: and therefore in this sacrament, more than in the others, mention ought to be made of all that belongs to the salvation of the entire Church.

Reply Obj. 4. There is a twofold instruction in the Faith: the first is for those receiving it for the first time, that is to say, for catechumens, and such instruction is given in connection with Baptism. The other is the instruction of the faithful who take part in this sacrament; and such instruction is given in connection with this sacrament. Nevertheless catechumens and unbelievers are not excluded therefrom. Hence in *De Consecr.*, dist.

1, it is laid down: *Let the bishop hinder no one from entering the church, and hearing the word of God, be they Gentiles, heretics, or Jews, until the mass of the Catechumens begins,* in which the instruction regarding the Faith is contained.

Reply Obj. 5. Greater devotion is required in this sacrament than in the others, for the reason that the entire Christ is contained therein. Moreover, this sacrament requires a more general devotion, i.e. on the part of the whole people, since for them it is offered; and not merely on the part of the recipients, as in the other sacraments. Hence Cyprian observes *(De Orat. Domin.* 31), *The priest, in saying the Preface, disposes the souls of the brethren by saying, "Lift up your hearts," and when the people answer—"We have lifted them up to the Lord," let them remember that they are to think of nothing else but God.*

Reply Obj. 6. As was said above (*ad* 3), those things are mentioned in this sacrament which belong to the entire Church; and consequently some things which refer to the people are sung by the choir, and some of these words are all sung by the choir, as though inspiring the entire people with them; and there are other words which the priest begins and the people take up, the priest then acting as in the person of God; to show that the things they denote have come to the people through Divine revelation, such as faith and heavenly glory; and therefore the priest intones the *Creed* and the *Gloria in excelsis Deo.* Other words are uttered by the ministers, such as the doctrine of the Old and New Testament, as a sign that this doctrine was announced to the peoples through ministers sent by God. And there are other words which the priest alone recites, namely, such as belong to his personal office, *that he may offer up gifts and prayers for the people* (Heb. v. 1). Some of these, however, he says aloud, namely, such as are common to priest and people alike, such as the *common prayers;* other words, however, belong to the priest alone, such as the oblation and the consecration; consequently, the prayers that are said in connection with these have to be said by the priest in secret. Nevertheless, in both he calls the people to attention by saying: *The Lord be with you,* and he waits for them to assent by saying *Amen.* And therefore before the secret prayers he says aloud, *The Lord be with you,* and he concludes, *For ever and ever.*—Or the priest secretly pronounces some of the words as a token that regarding Christ's Passion the disciples acknowledged Him only in secret.

Reply Obj. 7. The efficacy of the sacramental words can be hindered by the priest's intention. Nor is there anything unbecoming in our asking of God for what we know He will do, just as Christ (John xvii. 1, 5) asked for His glorification.

But the priest does not seem to pray there for the consecration to be fulfilled, but that it may be fruitful in our regard, hence he says expressively: *That it may become "to us" the body and the blood.* Again, the words preceding these have that meaning, when he says: *Vouchsafe to make this oblation blessed,* i.e. according to Augustine (Paschasius, *De Corp. et Sang. Dom.* xii), *that we may receive a blessing,* namely, through grace; *"enrolled,"* i.e. *that we may be enrolled in heaven; "ratified,"* i.e. *that we may be incorporated in Christ; "reasonable,"* i.e. *that we may be stripped of our animal sense; "acceptable,"* i.e. *that we who in ourselves are displeasing, may, by its means, be made acceptable to His only Son.*

Reply Obj. 8. Although this sacrament is of itself preferable to all ancient sacrifices, yet the sacrifices of the men of old were most acceptable to God on account of their devotion. Consequently the priest asks that this sacrifice may be accepted by God through the devotion of the offerers, just as the former sacrifices were accepted by Him.

Reply Obj. 9. The priest does not pray that the sacramental species may be borne up to heaven; nor that Christ's true body may be borne thither, for it does not cease to be there; but he offers this prayer for Christ's mystical body, which is signified in this sacrament, that the angel standing by at the Divine mysteries may present to God the prayers of both priest and people, according to Apoc. viii. 4: *And the smoke of the incense of the prayers of the saints ascended up before God, from the hand of the angel.* But God's *altar on high* means either the Church triumphant, unto which we pray to be translated, or else God Himself, in Whom we ask to share; because it is said of this altar (Exod. xx. 26): *Thou shalt not go up by steps unto My altar,* i.e. *thou shalt make no steps towards the Trinity.* Or else by the angel we are to understand Christ Himself, Who is the *Angel of great counsel* (Isa. ix. 6: *Septuag. version),* Who unites His mystical body with God the Father and the Church triumphant.

And from this the mass derives its name *(missa)*; because the priest sends *(mittit)* his prayers up to God through the angel, as the people do through the priest. Or else because Christ is the victim sent *(missa)* to us: accordingly the deacon on festival days *dismisses* the people at the end of the mass, by saying: *Ite, missa est,* that is, the victim has been sent *(missa est)* to God through the angel, so that it may be accepted by God.

FIFTH ARTICLE

Whether the Actions Performed in Celebrating This Sacrament Are Becoming?

We proceed thus to the Fifth Article:—

Objection 1. It seems that the actions performed in celebrating this mystery are not becoming. For, as is evident from its form, this sacrament belongs to the New Testament. But under the New Testament the ceremonies of the Old are not to be observed, such as that the priests and ministers were purified with water when they drew nigh to offer up the sacrifice: for we read (Exod. xxx. 19, 20): *Aaron and his sons shall wash their hands and feet . . . when they are going into the tabernacle of the testimony, . . . and when they are to come to the altar.* Therefore it is not fitting that the priest should wash his hands when celebrating mass.

Obj. 2. Further, *(ibid. 7),* the Lord commanded Aaron to *burn sweet-smelling incense* upon the altar which was *before the propitiatory:* and the same action was part of the ceremonies of the Old Law. Therefore it is not fitting for the priest to use incense during mass.

Obj. 3. Further, the ceremonies performed in the sacraments of the Church ought not to be repeated. Consequently it is not proper for the priest to repeat the sign of the cross many times over this sacrament.

Obj. 4. Further, the Apostle says (Heb. vii. 7): *And without all contradiction, that which is less, is blessed by the better.* But Christ, Who is in this sacrament after the consecration, is much greater than the priest. Therefore quite unseemingly the priest, after the consecration, blesses this sacrament, by signing it with the cross.

Obj. 5. Further, nothing which appears ridiculous ought to be done in one of the Church's sacraments. But it seems ridiculous to perform gestures, e.g. for the priest to stretch out his arms at times, to join his hands, to join together his fingers, and to bow down. Consequently, such things ought not to be done in this sacrament.

Obj. 6. Further, it seems ridiculous for the priest to turn round frequently towards the people, and often to greet the people. Consequently, such things ought not to be done in the celebration of this sacrament.

Obj. 7. Further, the Apostle (1 Cor. xiii) deems it improper for Christ to be divided. But Christ is in this sacrament after the consecration. Therefore it is not proper for the priest to divide the host.

Obj. 8. Further, the ceremonies performed in this sacrament represent Christ's Passion. But during the Passion Christ's body was divided in the places of the five wounds. Therefore Christ's body ought to be broken into five parts rather than into three.

Obj. 9. Further, Christ's entire body is consecrated in this sacrament apart from the blood. Consequently, it is not proper for a particle of the body to be mixed with the blood.

Obj. 10. Further, just as, in this sacrament, Christ's body is set before us as food, so is His blood, as drink. But in receiving Christ's body no other bodily food is added in the celebration of the mass. Therefore, it is out of place for the priest, after taking Christ's blood, to receive other wine which is not consecrated.

Obj. 11. Further, the truth ought to be conformable with the figure. But regarding the Paschal Lamb, which was a figure of this sacrament, it was commanded that nothing of it should *remain until the morning.* It is improper therefore for consecrated hosts to be reserved, and not consumed at once.

Obj. 12. Further, the priest addresses in the plural number those who are hearing mass, when he says, *The Lord be with you:* and, *Let us return thanks.* But it is out of keeping to address one individual in the plural number, especially an inferior. Consequently it seems unfitting for a priest to say mass with only a single server present. Therefore in the celebration of this sacrament it seems that some of the things done are out of place.

On the contrary, The custom of the Church stands for these things: and the Church cannot err, since she is taught by the Holy Ghost.

I answer that, As was said above (Q. 60, A. 6), there is a twofold manner of signification in the sacraments, by words, and by actions, in order that the signification may thus be more perfect. Now, in the celebration of this sacrament words are used to signify things pertaining to Christ's Passion, which is represented in this sacrament; or again, pertaining to Christ's mystical body, which is signified therein; and again, things pertaining to the use of this sacrament, which use ought to be devout and reverent. Consequently, in the celebration of this mystery some things are done in order to represent Christ's Passion, or the disposing of His mystical body, and some others are done which pertain to the devotion and reverence due to this sacrament.

Reply Obj. 1. The washing of the hands is done in the celebration of mass out of reverence for this sacrament; and this for two reasons: first, because we are not wont to handle precious objects except the hands be washed; hence it seems indecent for anyone to approach so great a sacrament with hands that are, even literally, unclean. Secondly, on

account of its signification, because, as Dionysius says *(Eccl. Hier.* iii), the washing of the extremities of the limbs denotes cleansing from even the smallest sins, according to John xiii. 10: *He that is washed needeth not but to wash his feet.* And such cleansing is required of him who approaches this sacrament; and this is denoted by the confession which is made before the *Introit* of the mass. Moreover, this was signified by the washing of the priests under the Old Law, as Dionysius says *(ibid.).* However, the Church observes this ceremony, not because it was prescribed under the Old Law, but because it is becoming in itself, and therefore instituted by the Church. Hence it is not observed in the same way as it was then: because the washing of the feet is omitted, and the washing of the hands is observed; for this can be done more readily, and suffices for denoting perfect cleansing. For, since the hand is the *organ of organs (De Anima* iii), all works are attributed to the hands: hence it is said in Ps. xxv. 6: *I will wash my hands among the innocent.*

Reply Obj. 2. We use incense, not as commanded by a ceremonial precept of the Law, but as prescribed by the Church; accordingly we do not use it in the same fashion as it was ordered under the Old Law. It has reference to two things: first, to the reverence due to this sacrament, i.e. in order by its good odor, to remove any disagreeable smell that may be about the place; secondly, it serves to show the effect of grace, wherewith Christ was filled as with a good odor, according to Gen. xxvii. 27: *Behold, the odor of my son is like the odor of a ripe field;* and from Christ it spreads to the faithful by means of His ministers, according to 2 Cor. ii. 14: *He manifesteth the odor of his knowledge by us in every place;* and therefore when the altar which represents Christ, has been incensed on every side, then all are incensed in their proper order.

Reply Obj. 3. The priest, in celebrating the mass, makes use of the sign of the cross to signify Christ's Passion which was ended upon the cross. Now, Christ's Passion was accomplished in certain stages. First of all there was Christ's betrayal, which was the work of God, of Judas, and of the Jews; and this is signified by the triple sign of the cross at the words, *These gifts, these presents, these holy unspotted sacrifices.*

Secondly, there was the selling of Christ. Now he was sold to the Priests, to the Scribes, and to the Pharisees: and to signify this the threefold sign of the cross is repeated, at the words, *blessed, enrolled, ratified.* Or again, to signify the price for which He was sold, viz. thirty pence. And a double cross is added at the words—*that it may become to us the Body and the Blood,* etc., to signify the person of Judas the seller, and of Christ Who was sold.

Thirdly, there was the foreshadowing of the Passion at the last supper. To denote this, in the third place, two crosses are made, one in consecrating the body, the other in consecrating the blood; each time while saying, *He blessed.*

Fourthly, there was Christ's Passion itself. And so in order to represent His five wounds, in the fourth place, there is a fivefold signing of the cross at the words, *a pure Victim, a holy Victim, a spotless Victim, the holy bread of eternal life, and the cup of everlasting salvation.*

Fifthly, the outstretching of Christ's body, and the shedding of the blood, and the fruits of the Passion, are signified by the triple signing of the cross at the words, *as many as shall receive the body and blood, may be filled with every blessing,* etc.

Sixthly, Christ's threefold prayer upon the cross is represented; one for His persecutors when He said, *Father, forgive them;* the second for deliverance from death, when He cried, *My God, My God, why hast Thou forsaken Me?* the third referring to His entrance into glory, when He said, *Father, into Thy hands I commend My spirit;* and in order to denote these there is a triple signing with the cross made at the words, *Thou dost sanctify, quicken, bless.*

Seventhly, the three hours during which He hung upon the cross, that is, from the sixth to the ninth hour, are represented; in signification of which we make once more a triple sign of the cross at the words, *Through Him, and with Him, and in Him.*

Eighthly, the separation of His soul from the body is signified by the two subsequent crosses made over the chalice.

Ninthly, the resurrection on the third day is represented by the three crosses made at the words—*May the peace of the Lord be ever with you.*

In short, we may say that the consecration of this sacrament, and the acceptance of this sacrifice, and its fruits, proceed from the virtue of the cross of Christ, and therefore wherever mention is made of these, the priest makes use of the sign of the cross.

Reply Obj. 4. After the consecration, the priest makes the sign of the cross, not for the purpose of blessing and consecrating, but only for calling to mind the virtue of the cross, and the manner of Christ's suffering, as is evident from what has been said (*ad* 3).

Reply Obj. 5. The actions performed by the priest in mass are not ridiculous gestures, since they are done so as to represent something else. The priest in extending his arms signifies the outstretching of Christ's arms upon the cross.—He also lifts up his hands as he prays, to point out that his prayer is directed to God for the people, according to Lament. iii. 41: *Let us lift up our hearts with our hands to the Lord in the heavens:* and Exod. xvii. 11: *And when Moses lifted up his hands Israel overcame.* That at times he joins his hands, and bows down, praying earnestly and humbly, denotes the humility and obedience of Christ, out of which He suffered.—He closes his fingers, i.e. the thumb and first finger, after the consecration, because, with them, he had touched the consecrated body of Christ; so that if any particle cling to the fingers, it may not be scattered: and this belongs to the reverence for this sacrament.

Reply Obj. 6. Five times does the priest turn round towards the people, to denote that our Lord manifested Himself five times on the day of His Resurrection, as stated above in the treatise on Christ's Resurrection (Q. 55, A. 3, *Obj.* 3).—But the priest greets the people seven times, namely, five times, by turning round to the people, and twice without turning round, namely, when he says, *The Lord be with you* before the *Preface,* and again when he says, *May the peace of the Lord be ever with you:* and this is to denote the sevenfold grace of the Holy Ghost. But a bishop, when he celebrates on festival days, in his first greeting says, *Peace be to you,* which was our Lord's greeting after Resurrection, Whose person the bishop chiefly represents.

Reply Obj. 7. The breaking of the host denotes three things: first, the rending of Christ's body, which took place in the Passion; secondly, the distinction of His mystical body according to its various states; and thirdly, the distribution of the graces which flow from Christ's Passion, as Dionysius observes *(Eccl. Hier.* iii). Hence this breaking does not imply severance in Christ.

Reply Obj. 8. As Pope Sergius says, and it is to be found in the Decretals *(De Consecr.,* dist. ii), *the Lord's body is threefold; the part offered and put into the chalice signifies Christ's risen body,* namely, Christ Himself, and the Blessed Virgin, and the other saints, if there be any, who are already in glory with their bodies. *The part consumed denotes those still walking upon earth,* because while living upon earth they are united together by this sacrament; and are bruised by the passions, just as the bread eaten is bruised by the teeth. *The part reserved on the altar till the close of the mass, is His body hidden in the sepulchre, because the bodies of the saints will be in their graves until the end of the world:* though their souls are either in purgatory, or in heaven. However, this rite of reserving one part on the altar till the close of the mass is no longer observed, on account of the danger; nevertheless, the same meaning of the parts continues, which some persons have expressed in verse, thus:

> The host being rent—
> What is dipped, means the blest;
> What is dry, means the living;
> What is kept, those at rest.

Others, however, say that the part put into the chalice denotes those still living in this world; while the part kept outside the chalice denotes those fully blessed both in soul and body; while the part consumed means the others.

Reply Obj. 9. Two things can be signified by the chalice: first, the Passion itself, which is represented in this sacrament, and according to this, by the part put into the chalice are denoted those who are still sharers of Christ's sufferings; secondly, the enjoyment of the Blessed can be signified, which is likewise foreshadowed in this sacrament; and therefore those whose bodies are already in full beatitude, are denoted by the part put into the chalice. And it is to be observed that the part put into the chalice ought not to be given to the people to supplement the communion, because Christ gave dipped bread only to Judas the betrayer.

Reply Obj. 10. Wine, by reason of its humidity, is capable of washing, consequently it is received in order to rinse the mouth after receiving this sacrament, lest any particles remain: and this belongs to reverence for the sacrament. Hence (*Extra, De Celebratione missæ*, chap. *Ex parte*), it is said: *The priest should always cleanse his mouth with wine after receiving the entire sacrament of Eucharist: except when he has to celebrate another mass on the same day, lest from taking the ablution-wine he be prevented from celebrating again;* and it is for the same reason that wine is poured over the fingers with which he had touched the body of Christ.

Reply Obj. 11. The truth ought to be conformable with the figure, in some respect: namely, because a part of the host consecrated, of which the priest and ministers or even the people communicate, ought not to be reserved until the day following. Hence, as is laid down (*De Consecr.*, dist. ii), Pope Clement (I) ordered that *as many hosts are to be offered on the altar as shall suffice for the people; should any be left over, they are not to be reserved until the morrow, but let the clergy carefully consume them with fear and trembling.* Nevertheless, since this sacrament is to be received daily, whereas the Paschal Lamb was not, it is therefore necessary for other hosts to be reserved for the sick. Hence we read in the same distinction: *Let the priest always have the Eucharist ready, so that, when anyone fall sick, he may take Communion to him at once, lest he die without it.*

Reply Obj. 12. Several persons ought to be present at the solemn celebration of the mass. Hence Pope Soter says (*De Consecr.* dist. 1): *It has also been ordained, that no priest is to presume to celebrate solemn mass, unless two others be present answering him, while he himself makes the third; because when he says in the plural, "The Lord be with you," and again in the Secrets, "Pray ye for me," it is most becoming that they should answer his greeting.* Hence it is for the sake of greater solemnity that we find it decreed (*ibid.*) that a bishop is to solemnize mass with several assistants. Nevertheless, in private masses it suffices to have one server, who takes the place of the whole Catholic people, on whose behalf he makes answer in the plural to the priest.

SIXTH ARTICLE

Whether the Defects Occurring during the Celebration of This Sacrament Can Be Sufficiently Met by Observing the Church's Statutes?

We proceed thus to the Sixth Article:—

Objection 1. It seems that the defects occurring during the celebration of this sacrament cannot be sufficiently met by observing the statutes of the Church. For it sometimes happens that before or after the consecration the priest dies or goes mad, or is hindered by some other infirmity from receiving the sacrament and completing the mass. Consequently it seems impossible to observe the Church's statute, whereby the priest consecrating must communicate of his own sacrifice.

Obj. 2. Further, it sometimes happens that, before the consecration, the priest remembers that he has eaten or drunk something, or that he is in mortal sin, or under excommunication, which he did not remember previously. Therefore, in such a dilemma a man must necessarily commit mortal sin by acting against the Church's statute, whether he receives or not.

Obj. 3. Further, it sometimes happens that a fly or a spider, or some other poisonous creature falls into the chalice after the consecration; or even that the priest comes to know that poison has been put in by some evilly disposed person in order to kill him. Now in this instance, if he takes it, he appears to sin by killing himself, or by tempting God: also in like manner if he does not take it, he sins by acting against the Church's statute. Consequently, he seems to be perplexed, and under necessity of sinning, which is not becoming.

Obj. 4. Further, it sometimes happens from

the server's want of heed that water is not added to the chalice, or even the wine overlooked, and that the priest discovers this. Therefore he seems to be perplexed likewise in this case, whether he receives the body without the blood, thus making the sacrifice to be incomplete, or whether he receives neither the body nor the blood.

Obj. 5. Further, it sometimes happens that the priest cannot remember having said the words of consecration, or other words which are uttered in the celebration of this sacrament. In this case he seems to sin, whether he repeats the words over the same matter, which words possibly he has said before, or whether he uses bread and wine which are not consecrated, as if they were consecrated.

Obj. 6. Further, it sometimes comes to pass owing to the cold that the host will slip from the priest's hands into the chalice, either before or after the breaking. In this case then the priest will not be able to comply with the Church's rite, either as to the breaking, or else as to this, that only a third part is put into the chalice.

Obj. 7. Further, sometimes, too, it happens, owing to the priest's want of care, that Christ's blood is spilled, or that he vomits the sacrament received, or that the consecrated hosts are kept so long that they become corrupt, or that they are nibbled by mice, or lost in any manner whatsoever; in which cases it does not seem possible for due reverence to be shown towards this sacrament, as the Church's ordinances require. It does not seem then that such defects or dangers can be met by keeping to the Church's statutes.

On the contrary, Just as God does not command an impossibility, so neither does the Church.

I answer that, Dangers or defects happening to this sacrament can be met in two ways: first, by preventing any such mishaps from occurring: secondly, by dealing with them in such a way, that what may have happened amiss is put right, either by employing a remedy, or at least by repentance on his part who has acted negligently regarding this sacrament.

Reply Obj. 1. If the priest be stricken by death or grave sickness before the consecration of our Lord's body and blood, there is no need for it to be completed by another. But if this happens after the consecration is begun, for instance, when the body has been consecrated and before the consecration of the blood, or even after both have been consecrated, then the celebration of the mass ought to be finished by someone else. Hence, as is laid down (Decret. vii, q. 1), we read the following decree of the (Seventh) Council of Toledo: *We consider it to be fitting that when the sacred mysteries are consecrated by priests during the time of mass, if any sickness supervenes, in consequence of which they cannot finish the mystery begun, let it be free for the bishop or another priest to finish the consecration of the office thus begun. For nothing else is suitable for completing the mysteries commenced, unless the consecration be completed either by the priest who began it, or by the one who follows him: because they cannot be completed except they be performed in perfect order. For since we are all one in Christ, the change of persons makes no difference, since unity of faith insures the happy issue of the mystery. Yet let not the course we propose for cases of natural debility, be presumptuously abused: and let no minister or priest presume ever to leave the Divine offices unfinished, unless he be absolutely prevented from continuing. If anyone shall have rashly presumed to do so, he will incur sentence of excommunication.*

Reply Obj. 2. Where difficulty arises, the less dangerous course should always be followed. But the greatest danger regarding this sacrament lies in whatever may prevent its completion, because this is a heinous sacrilege; while that danger is of less account which regards the condition of the receiver. Consequently, if after the consecration has been begun the priest remembers that he has eaten or drunk anything, he ought nevertheless to complete the sacrifice and receive the sacrament. Likewise, if he recalls a sin committed, he ought to make an act of contrition, with the firm purpose of confessing and making satisfaction for it: and thus he will not receive the sacrament unworthily, but with profit. The same applies if he calls to mind that he is under some excommunication; for he ought to make the resolution of humbly seeking absolution; and so he will receive absolution from the invisible High Priest Jesus Christ for his act of completing the Divine mysteries.

But if he calls to mind any of the above facts previous to the consecration, I should deem it safer for him to interrupt the mass begun, especially if he has broken his fast, or is under excommunication, unless grave scandal were to be feared.

Reply Obj. 3. If a fly or a spider falls into the chalice before consecration, or if it be discovered that the wine is poisoned, it ought to be poured out, and after purifying the chalice, fresh wine should be served for consecration. —But if anything of the sort happen after the consecration, the insect should be caught carefully and washed thoroughly, then burned, and the *ablution*, together with the ashes, thrown into the sacrarium. If it be discovered that the wine has been poisoned, the priest should neither receive it nor administer it to others on any account, lest the life-giving chalice become one of death, but it ought to be kept in a suitable vessel with the relics: and in order that the sacrament may not remain incomplete, he ought to put other wine into the chalice, resume the mass from the consecration of the blood, and complete the sacrifice.

Reply Obj. 4. If before the consecration of the blood, and after the consecration of the body the priest detect that either the wine or the water is absent, then he ought at once to add them and consecrate. But if after the words of consecration he discover that the water is absent, he ought notwithstanding to proceed straight on, because the addition of the water is not necessary for the sacrament, as stated above (Q. 74, A. 7): nevertheless the person responsible for the neglect ought to be punished. And on no account should water be mixed with the consecrated wine, because corruption of the sacrament would ensue in part, as was said above (Q. 77, A. 8). But if after the words of consecration the priest perceive that no wine has been put in the chalice, and if he detect it before receiving the body, then rejecting the water, he ought to pour in wine with water, and begin over again the consecrating words of the blood. But if he notice it after receiving the body, he ought to procure another host which must be consecrated together with the blood; and I say so for this reason, because if he were to say only the words of consecration of the blood, the proper order of consecrating would not be observed; and, as is laid down by the Council of Toledo, quoted above (*ad* 1), *sacrifices cannot be perfect, except they be performed in perfect order.* But if he were to begin from the consecration of the blood, and were to repeat all the words which follow, it would not suffice, unless there was a consecrated host present, since in those words there are things to be said and done not only regarding the blood, but also regarding the body; and at the close he ought once more to receive the consecrated host and blood, even if he had already taken the water which was in the chalice, because the precept of the completing this sacrament is of greater weight than the precept of receiving the sacrament while fasting, as stated above (Q. 80, A. 8).

Reply Obj. 5. Although the priest may not recollect having said some of the words he ought to say, he ought not to be disturbed mentally on that account; for a man who utters many words cannot recall to mind all that he has said; unless perchance in uttering them he adverts to something connected with the consecration; for so it is impressed on the memory. Hence, if a man pays attention to what he is saying, but without adverting to

the fact that he is saying these particular words, he remembers soon after that he has said them; for, a thing is presented to the memory under the formality of the past (*De Mem. et Remin.* i).

But if it seem to the priest that he has probably omitted some of the words that are not necessary for the sacrament, I think that he ought not to repeat them on that account, changing the order of the sacrifice, but that he ought to proceed: but if he is certain that he has left out any of those that are necessary for the sacrament, namely, the form of the consecration, since the form of the consecration is necessary for the sacrament, just as the matter is, it seems that the same thing ought to be done as was stated above (*ad* 4) with regard to defect in the matter, namely, that he should begin again with the form of the consecration, and repeat the other things in order, lest the order of the sacrifice be altered.

Reply Obj. 6. The breaking of the consecrated host, and the putting of only one part into the chalice, regards the mystical body, just as the mixing with water signifies the people, and therefore the omission of either of them causes no such imperfection in the sacrifice, as calls for repetition regarding the celebration of this sacrament.

Reply Obj. 7. According to the decree, *De Consecr.,* dist. ii, quoting a decree of Pope Pius (I), *If from neglect any of the blood falls upon a board which is fixed to the ground, let it be taken up with the tongue, and let the board be scraped. But if it be not a board, let the ground be scraped, and the scrapings burned, and the ashes buried inside the altar, and let the priest do penance for forty days. But if a drop fall from the chalice on to the altar, let the minister suck up the drop, and do penance during three days; if it falls upon the altar cloth and penetrates to the second altar cloth, let him do four days' penance; if it penetrates to the third, let him do nine days' penance; if to the fourth, let him do twenty days' penance; and let the altar linens which the drop touched be washed three times by the priest, holding the chalice below, then let the water be taken and put away nigh to the altar.* It might even be drunk by the minister, unless it might be rejected from nausea. Some persons go further, and cut out that part of the linen, which they burn, putting the ashes in the altar or down the sacrarium. And the Decretal continues with a quotation from the Penitential of Bede the Priest: *If, owing to drunkenness or gluttony, anyone vomits up the Eucharist, let him do forty days' penance, if he be a layman; but let clerics or monks, deacons and priests, do seventy days' penance; and let a bishop do ninety days'. But if they vomit from sickness, let them do penance for seven days.* And in the same distinction, we read a decree of the (Fourth) Council of Arles: *They who do not keep proper custody over the sacrament, if a mouse or other animal consume it, must do forty days' penance: he who loses it in a church, or if a part fall and be not found, shall do thirty days' penance.* And the priest seems to deserve the same penance, who from neglect allows the hosts to putrefy. And on those days the one doing penance ought to fast, and abstain from Communion. However, after weighing the circumstances of the fact and of the person, the said penances may be lessened or increased. But it must be observed that wherever the species are found to be entire, they must be preserved reverently, or consumed; because Christ's body is there so long as the species last, as stated above (Q. 77, AA. 4, 5). But if it can be done conveniently, the things in which they are found are to be burned, and the ashes put in the sacrarium, as was said of the scrapings of the altar-table, here above.

QUESTION 84

Of the Sacrament of Penance

(In Ten Articles)

WE must now consider the Sacrament of Penance. We shall consider (1) Penance itself; (2) Its effect; (3) Its Parts; (4) The recipients of this sacrament; (5) The power of the ministers, which pertains to the keys; (6) The solemnization of this sacrament.

The first of these considerations will be twofold: (1) Penance as a sacrament; (2) Penance as a virtue.

Under the first head there are ten points of inquiry: (1) Whether Penance is a sacrament? (2) Of its proper matter. (3) Of its form. (4) Whether imposition of hands is necessary for this sacrament? (5) Whether this sacrament is necessary for salvation? (6) Of its relation to the other sacraments. (7) Of its institution. (8) Of its duration. (9) Of its continuance. (10) Whether it can be repeated?

FIRST ARTICLE

Whether Penance Is a Sacrament?

We proceed thus to the First Article:—

Objection 1. It would seem that Penance is not a sacrament. For Gregory* says: *The sacraments are Baptism, Chrism, and the Body and Blood of Christ; which are called sacraments because under the veil of corporeal things the Divine power works out salvation in a hidden manner.* But this does not happen in Penance, because therein corporeal things are not employed that, under them, the power of God may work our salvation. Therefore Penance is not a sacrament.

Obj. 2. Further, the sacraments of the Church are shown forth by the ministers of Christ, according to 1 Cor. iv. 1: *Let a man so account of us as of the ministers of Christ, and the dispensers of the mysteries of God.* But Penance is not conferred by the ministers of Christ, but is inspired inwardly into man by God, according to Jerem. xxxi. 19: *After Thou didst convert me, I did penance.* Therefore it seems that Penance is not a sacrament.

Obj. 3. Further, in the sacraments of which we have already spoken above, there is something that is sacrament only, something that is both reality and sacrament, and something that is reality only, as is clear from what has been stated (Q. 66, A. 1). But this does not apply to Penance. Therefore Penance is not a sacrament.

On the contrary, As Baptism is conferred

* Cf. Isidore, *Etym.* vi, ch. 19.

that we may be cleansed from sin, so also is Penance: wherefore Peter said to Simon Magus (Acts viii. 22): *Do penance . . . from this thy wickedness.* But Baptism is a sacrament as stated above (Q. 66, A. 1). Therefore for the same reason Penance is also a sacrament.

I answer that, As Gregory says *(loc. cit.), a sacrament consists in a solemn act, whereby something is so done that we understand it to signify the holiness which it confers.* Now it is evident that in Penance something is done so that something holy is signified both on the part of the penitent sinner, and on the part of the priest absolving, because the penitent sinner, by deed and word, shows his heart to have renounced sin, and in like manner the priest, by his deed and word with regard to the penitent, signifies the work of God Who forgives his sins. Therefore it is evident that Penance, as practiced in the Church, is a sacrament.

Reply Obj. 1. By corporeal things taken in a wide sense we may understand also external sensible actions, which are to this sacrament what water is to Baptism, or chrism to Confirmation. But it is to be observed that in those sacraments, whereby an exceptional grace surpassing altogether the proportion of a human act, is conferred, some corporeal matter is employed externally, e.g. in Baptism, which confers full remission of all sins, both as to guilt and as to punishment, and in Confirmation, wherein the fulness of the Holy Ghost is bestowed, and in Extreme Unction, which confers perfect spiritual health derived from the virtue of Christ as from an extrinsic principle. Wherefore, such human acts as are in these sacraments, are not the essential matter of the sacrament, but are dispositions thereto. On the other hand, in those sacraments whose effect corresponds to that of some human act, the sensible human act itself takes the place of matter, as in the case of Penance and Matrimony, even as in bodily medicines, some are applied externally, such as plasters and drugs, while others are acts of the person who seeks to be cured, such as certain exercises.

Reply Obj. 2. In those sacraments which have a corporeal matter, this matter needs to be applied by a minister of the Church, who stands in the place of Christ, which denotes that the excellence of the power which operates in the sacraments is from Christ. But in the sacrament of Penance, as stated above (*ad* 1), human actions take the place of matter. and these actions proceed from internal inspiration, wherefore the matter is not applied by the minister, but by God working inwardly; while the minister furnishes the complement of the sacrament, when he absolves the penitent.

Reply Obj. 3. In Penance also, there is something which is sacrament only, viz. the acts performed outwardly both by the repentant sinner, and by the priest in giving absolution; that which is reality and sacrament is the sinner's inward repentance; while that which is reality, and not sacrament, is the forgiveness of sin. The first of these taken altogether is the cause of the second; and the first and second together are the cause of the third.

SECOND ARTICLE

Whether Sins Are the Proper Matter of This Sacrament?

We proceed thus to the Second Article:—

Objection 1. It would seem that sins are not the proper matter of this sacrament. Because, in the other sacraments, the matter is hallowed by the utterance of certain words, and being thus hallowed produces the sacramental effect. Now sins cannot be hallowed, for they are opposed to the effect of the sacrament, viz. grace which blots out sin. Therefore sins are not the proper matter of this sacrament.

Obj. 2. Further, Augustine says in his book *De Pœnitentia:** No one can begin a new life, unless he repent of the old.* Now not only sins but also the penalties of the present life belong to the old life. Therefore sins are not the proper matter of Penance.

Obj. 3. Further, sin is either original, mortal or venial. Now the sacrament of Penance is not ordained against original sin, for this is taken away by Baptism, [nor against mortal sin, for this is taken away by the sinner's confession],† nor against venial sin, which is taken away by the beating of the breast and the sprinkling of holy water and the like. Therefore sins are not the proper matter of Penance.

On the contrary, The Apostle says (2 Cor. xii. 21): *(Who) have not done penance for the uncleanness and fornication and lasciviousness, that they have committed.*

I answer that, Matter is twofold, viz. proximate and remote: thus the proximate matter of a statue is a metal, while the remote matter is water. Now it has been stated (A. 1, *ad* 1, *ad* 2), that the proximate matter of this sacra-

ment consists in the acts of the penitent, the matter of which acts are the sins over which he grieves, which he confesses, and for which he satisfies. Hence it follows that sins are the remote matter of Penance, as a matter, not for approval, but for detestation, and destruction.

Reply Obj. 1. This argument considers the proximate matter of a sacrament.

Reply Obj. 2. The old life that was subject to death is the object of Penance, not as regards the punishment, but as regards the guilt connected with it.

Reply Obj. 3. Penance regards every kind of sin in a way, but not each in the same way. Because Penance regards actual mortal sin properly and chiefly; properly, since, properly speaking, we are said to repent of what we have done of our own will; chiefly, since this sacrament was instituted chiefly for the blotting out of mortal sin. Penance regards venial sins, properly speaking indeed, in so far as they are committed of our own will, but this was not the chief purpose of its institution. But as to original sin, Penance regards it neither chiefly, since Baptism, and not Penance, is ordained against original sin, nor properly, because original sin is not done of our own will, except in so far as Adam's will is looked upon as ours, in which sense the Apostle says (Rom. v. 12): *In whom all have sinned.* Nevertheless, Penance may be said to regard original sin, if we take it in a wide sense for any detestation of something past: in which sense Augustine uses the term in his book *De Pœnitentia (loc. cit.).*

THIRD ARTICLE

Whether the Form of This Sacrament Is: "I Absolve Thee?"

We proceed thus to the Third Article:—

Objection 1. It would seem that the form of this sacrament is not: *I absolve thee.* Because the forms of the sacraments are received from Christ's institution and the Church's custom. But we do not read that Christ instituted this form. Nor is it in common use; in fact in certain absolutions which are given publicly in church (e.g. at Prime and Compline and on Maund Thursday), absolution is given not in the indicative form by saying: *I absolve thee,* but in the deprecatory form, by saying: *May Almighty God have mercy on you,* or: *May Almighty God grant you absolution and forgiveness.* Therefore the form of this sacrament is not: *I absolve thee.*

Obj. 2. Further, Pope Leo says (*Ep.* cviii) that God's forgiveness cannot be obtained

* Cf. Serm. cccli.   † The words in brackets are omitted in the Leonine edition.

without the priestly supplications: and he is speaking there of God's forgiveness granted to the penitent. Therefore the form of this sacrament should be deprecatory.

Obj. 3. Further, to absolve from sin is the same as to remit sin. But God alone remits sin, for He alone cleanses man inwardly from sin, as Augustine says *(Contra Donatist.* v. 21). Therefore it seems that God alone absolves from sin. Therefore the priest should say not: *I absolve thee,* as neither does he say: *I remit thy sins.*

Obj. 4. Further, just as our Lord gave His disciples the power to absolve from sins, so also did He give them the power *to heal infirmities, to cast out devils,* and *to cure diseases* (Matth. x. 1: Luke ix. 1). Now the apostles, in healing the sick, did not use the words: *I heal thee,* but: *The Lord Jesus Christ heal* (Vulg.,—*heals) thee,* as Peter said to the palsied man (Acts ix. 34). Therefore since priests have the power which Christ gave His apostles, it seems that they should not use the form: *I absolve thee,* but: *May Christ absolve thee.*

Obj. 5. Further, some explain this form by stating that when they say: *I absolve thee,* they mean *I declare you to be absolved.* But neither can this be done by a priest unless it be revealed to him by God, wherefore, as we read in Matth. xvi. 19 before it was said to Peter: *Whatsoever thou shalt bind upon earth,* etc., it was said to him *(verse* 17): *Blessed art thou Simon Bar-Jona: because flesh and blood have not revealed it to thee, but My Father Who is in heaven.* Therefore it seems presumptuous for a priest, who has received no revelation on the matter, to say: *I absolve thee,* even if this be explained to mean: *I declare thee absolved.*

On the contrary, As our Lord said to His disciples (Matth. xxviii. 19): *Going . . . teach ye all nations, baptizing them,* etc., so did He say to Peter (Matth. xvi. 19): *Whatsoever thou shalt loose on earth,* etc. Now the priest, relying on the authority of those words of Christ, says: *I baptize thee.* Therefore on the same authority he should say in this sacrament: *I absolve thee.*

I answer that, The perfection of a thing is ascribed to its form. Now it has been stated above (A. 1, *ad* 2) that this sacrament is perfected by that which is done by the priest. Wherefore the part taken by the penitent, whether it consist of words or deeds, must needs be the matter of this sacrament, while the part taken by the priest, takes the place of the form.

Now since the sacraments of the New Law accomplish what they signify, as stated above

(Q. 62, A. 1, *ad* 1), it behooves the sacramental form to signify the sacramental effect in a manner that is in keeping with the matter. Hence the form of Baptism is: *I baptize thee,* and the form of Confirmation is: *I sign thee with the sign of the cross, and I confirm thee with the chrism of salvation,* because these sacraments are perfected in the use of their matter: while in the sacrament of the Eucharist, which consists in the very consecration of the matter, the reality of the consecration is expressed in the words: *This is My Body.*

Now this sacrament, namely the sacrament of Penance, consists not in the consecration of a matter, nor in the use of a hallowed matter, but rather in the removal of a certain matter, viz. sin, in so far as sins are said to be the matter of Penance, as explained above (A. 2). This removal is expressed by the priest saying: *I absolve thee:* because sins are fetters, according to Prov. v. 22. *His own iniquities catch the wicked, and he is fast bound with the ropes of his own sins.* Wherefore it is evident that this is the most fitting form of this sacrament: *I absolve thee.*

Reply Obj. 1. This form is taken from Christ's very words which He addressed to Peter (Matth. xvi. 19): *Whatsoever thou shalt loose on earth,* etc., and such is the form employed by the Church in sacramental absolution. But such absolutions as are given in public are not sacramental, but are prayers for the remission of venial sins. Wherefore in giving sacramental absolution it would not suffice to say: *May Almighty God have mercy on thee,* or: *May God grant thee absolution and forgiveness,* because by such words the priest does not signify the giving of absolution, but prays that it may be given. Nevertheless the above prayer is said before the sacramental absolution is given, lest the sacramental effect be hindered on the part of the penitent, whose acts are as matter in this sacrament, but not in Baptism or Confirmation.

Reply Obj. 2. The words of Leo are to be understood of the prayer that precedes the absolution, and do not exclude the fact that the priest pronounces absolution.

Reply Obj. 3. God alone absolves from sin and forgives sins authoritatively; yet priests do both ministerially, because the words of the priest in this sacrament work as instruments of the Divine power, as in the other sacraments: because it is the Divine power that works inwardly in all the sacramental signs, be they things or words, as shown above (Q. 62, A. 4; Q. 64, AA. 1, 2). Wherefore our Lord expressed both: for He said to Peter (Matth. xvi. 19): *Whatsoever thou shalt loose on earth,* etc., and to His disciples (Jo. xx. 23): *Whose sins you shall forgive, they are forgiven them.* Yet the priest says: *I absolve thee,* rather than: *I forgive thee thy sins,* because it is more in keeping with the words of our Lord, by expressing the power of the keys whereby priests absolve. Nevertheless, since the priest absolves ministerially, something is suitably added in reference to the supreme authority of God, by the priest saying: *I absolve thee in the name of the Father, and of the Son, and of the Holy Ghost,* or by the power of Christ's Passion, or by the authority of God. However, as this is not defined by the words of Christ, as it is for Baptism, this addition is left to the discretion of the priest.

Reply Obj. 4. Power was given to the apostles, not that they themselves might heal the sick, but that the sick might be healed at the prayer of the apostles: whereas power was given to them to work instrumentally or ministerially in the sacraments; wherefore they could express their own agency in the sacramental forms rather than in the healing of infirmities. Nevertheless in the latter case they did not always use the deprecatory form, but sometimes employed the indicative or imperative: thus we read (Acts iii. 6) that Peter said to the lame man: *What I have, I give thee: In the name of Jesus Christ of Nazareth, arise and walk.*

Reply Obj. 5. It is true in a sense that the words, *I absolve thee* mean *I declare thee absolved,* but this explanation is incomplete. Because the sacraments of the New Law not only signify, but effect what they signify. Wherefore, just as the priest in baptizing anyone, declares by deed and word that the person is washed inwardly, and this not only significatively but also effectively, so also when he says: *I absolve thee,* he declares the man to be absolved not only significatively but also effectively. And yet he does not speak as of something uncertain, because just as the other sacraments of the New Law have, of themselves, a sure effect through the power of Christ's Passion, which effect, nevertheless, may be impeded on the part of the recipient, so is it with this sacrament. Hence Augustine says *(De Adult. Conjug.* ii); *There is nothing disgraceful or onerous in the reconciliation of husband and wife, when adultery committed has been washed away, since there is no doubt that remission of sins is granted through the keys of the kingdom of heaven.* Consequently there is no need for a special revelation to be made to the priest, but the general revelation of faith suffices, through which sins are forgiven. Hence the revelation of faith is said to have been made to Peter.

It would be a more complete explanation to say that the words, *I absolve thee* mean: *I grant thee the sacrament of absolution.*

FOURTH ARTICLE

Whether the Imposition of the Priest's Hands Is Necessary for This Sacrament?

We proceed thus to the Fourth Article:—

Objection 1. It would seem that the imposition of the priest's hands is necessary for this sacrament. For it is written (Mark xvi. 18): *They shall lay hands upon the sick, and they shall recover.* Now sinners are sick spiritually, and obtain recovery through this sacrament. Therefore an imposition of hands should be made in this sacrament.

Obj. 2. Further, in this sacrament man regains the Holy Ghost Whom he had lost, wherefore it is said in the person of the penitent (Ps. l. 14): *Restore unto me the joy of Thy salvation, and strengthen me with a perfect spirit.* Now the Holy Ghost is given by the imposition of hands; for we read (Acts viii. 17) that the apostles *laid their hands upon them, and they received the Holy Ghost;* and (Matth. xix. 13) that *little children were presented* to our Lord, *that He should impose hands upon them.* Therefore an imposition of hands should be made in this sacrament.

Obj. 3. Further, the priest's words are not more efficacious in this than in the other sacraments. But in the other sacraments the words of the minister do not suffice, unless he perform some action: thus, in Baptism, the priest while saying: *I baptize thee,* has to perform a bodily washing. Therefore, also while saying: *I absolve thee,* the priest should perform some action in regard to the penitent, by laying hands on him.

On the contrary, When our Lord said to Peter (Matth. xvi. 19): *Whatsoever thou shalt loose on earth,* etc., He made no mention of an imposition of hands; nor did He when He said to all the apostles (Jo. xx. 13): *Whose sins you shall forgive, they are forgiven them.* Therefore no imposition of hands is required for this sacrament.

I answer that, In the sacraments of the Church the imposition of hands is made, to signify some abundant effect of grace, through those on whom the hands are laid being, as it were, united to the ministers in whom grace should be plentiful. Wherefore an imposition of hands is made in the sacrament of Confirmation, wherein the fulness of the Holy Ghost is conferred; and in the sacrament of Order, wherein is bestowed a certain excellence of power over the Divine mysteries; hence it is written (2 Tim. i. 6): *Stir up the grace of God which is in thee, by the imposition of my hands.*

Now the sacrament of Penance is ordained, not that man may receive some abundance of grace, but that his sins may be taken away;

and therefore no imposition of hands is required for this sacrament, as neither is there for Baptism, wherein nevertheless a fuller remission of sins is bestowed.

Reply Obj. 1. That imposition of hands is not sacramental, but is intended for the working of miracles, namely, that by the contact of a sanctified man's hand, even bodily infirmity might be removed; even as we read of our Lord (Mark vi. 5) that He cured the sick, *laying His hands upon them,* and (Matth. viii. 3) that He cleansed a leper by touching him.

Reply Obj. 2. It is not every reception of the Holy Ghost that requires an imposition of hands, since even in Baptism man receives the Holy Ghost, without any imposition of hands: it is at the reception of the fulness of the Holy Ghost which belongs to Confirmation that an imposition of hands is required.

Reply Obj. 3. In those sacraments which are perfected in the use of the matter, the minister has to perform some bodily action on the recipient of the sacrament, e.g. in Baptism, Confirmation, and Extreme Unction; whereas this sacrament does not consist in the use of matter employed outwardly, the matter being supplied by the part taken by the penitent: wherefore, just as in the Eucharist the priest perfects the sacrament by merely pronouncing the words over the matter, so the mere words which the priest while absolving pronounces over the penitent perfect the sacrament of absolution. If, indeed, any bodily act were necessary on the part of the priest, the sign of the cross, which is employed in the Eucharist, would not be less becoming than the imposition of hands, in token that sins are forgiven through the blood of Christ crucified; and yet this is not essential to this sacrament as neither is it to the Eucharist.

FIFTH ARTICLE

Whether This Sacrament Is Necessary for Salvation?

We proceed thus to the Fifth Article:—

Objection 1. It would seem that this sacrament is not necessary for salvation. Because on Ps. cxxv. 5, *They that sow in tears,* etc., the gloss says: *Be not sorrowful, if thou hast a good will, of which peace is the meed.* But sorrow is essential to Penance, according to 2 Cor. vii. 10: *The sorrow that is according to God worketh penance steadfast unto salvation.* Therefore a good will without Penance suffices for salvation.

Obj. 2. Further, it is written (Prov. x. 12): *Charity covereth all sins,* and further on (xv. 27): *By mercy and faith sins are purged away.*

But this sacrament is for nothing else but the purging of sins. Therefore if one has charity, faith, and mercy, one can obtain salvation, without the sacrament of Penance.

Obj. 3. Further, the sacraments of the Church take their origin from the institution of Christ. But according to John viii. Christ absolved the adulterous woman without Penance. Therefore it seems that Penance is not necessary for salvation.

On the contrary, Our Lord said (Luke xiii. 3): *Unless you shall do penance, you shall all likewise perish.*

I answer that, A thing is necessary for salvation in two ways: first, absolutely; secondly, on a supposition. A thing is absolutely necessary for salvation, if no one can obtain salvation without it, as, for example, the grace of Christ, and the sacrament of Baptism, whereby a man is born again in Christ. The sacrament of Penance is necessary on a supposition, for it is necessary, not for all, but for those who are in sin. For it is written (2 Paral. xxxvii),* *Thou, Lord, God of the righteous, hast not appointed repentance to the righteous, to Abraham, Isaac and Jacob, nor to those who sinned not against Thee.* But *sin, when it is completed, begetteth death* (James i. 15). Consequently it is necessary for the sinner's salvation that sin be taken away from him; which cannot be done without the sacrament of Penance, wherein the power of Christ's Passion operates through the priest's absolution and the acts of the penitent, who co-operates with grace unto the destruction of his sin. For as Augustine says *(Tract.* lxxii, *in Joan.*†), *He Who created thee without thee, will not justify thee without thee.* Therefore it is evident that after sin the sacrament of Penance is necessary for salvation, even as bodily medicine after man has contracted a dangerous disease.

Reply Obj. 1. This gloss should apparently be understood as referring to the man who has a good will unimpaired by sin, for such a man has no cause for sorrow: but as soon as the good will is forfeited through sin, it cannot be restored without that sorrow whereby a man sorrows for his past sin, and which belongs to Penance.

Reply Obj. 2. As soon as a man falls into sin, charity, faith, and mercy do not deliver him from sin, without Penance. Because charity demands that a man should grieve for the offense committed against his friend, and that he should be anxious to make satisfaction to his friend; faith requires that he should seek to be justified from his sins through the power of Christ's Passion which operates in the sacraments of the Church; and well-ordered pity

---

* The prayer of Manasses, among the Apocrypha.
† Implicitly in the passage referred to, but explicitly *Serm.* xv, *de verb. Apost.*

necessitates that man should succor himself by repenting of the pitiful condition into which sin has brought him, according to Prov. xiv. 34: *Sin maketh nations miserable;* wherefore it is written (Ecclus. xxx. 24): *Have pity on thy own soul, pleasing God.*

Reply Obj. 3. It was due to His power of *excellence,* which He alone had, as stated above (Q. 64, A. 3), that Christ bestowed on the adulterous woman the effect of the sacrament of Penance, viz. the forgiveness of sins, without the sacrament of Penance, although not without internal repentance, which He operated in her by grace.

SIXTH ARTICLE

Whether Penance Is a Second Plank after Shipwreck?

We proceed thus to the Sixth Article:—

Objection 1. It would seem that Penance is not a second plank after shipwreck. Because on Isa. iii. 9, *They have proclaimed abroad their sin as Sodom,* a gloss says: *The second plank after shipwreck is to hide one's sins.* Now Penance does not hide sins, but reveals them. Therefore Penance is not a second plank.

Obj. 2. Further, in a building the foundation takes the first, not the second place. Now in the spiritual edifice, Penance is the foundation, according to Heb. vi. 1: *Not laying again the foundation of Penance from dead works;* wherefore it precedes even Baptism, according to Acts ii. 38: *Do penance, and be baptized every one of you.* Therefore Penance should not be called a second plank.

Obj. 3. Further, all the sacraments are planks, i.e. helps against sin. Now Penance holds, not the second but the fourth, place among the sacraments, as is clear from what has been said above (Q. 65, AA. 1, 2). Therefore Penance should not be called a second plank after shipwreck.

On the contrary, Jerome says *(Ep.* cxxx) that *Penance is a second plank after shipwreck.*

I answer that, That which is of itself precedes naturally that which is accidental, as substance precedes accident. Now some sacraments are, of themselves, ordained to man's salvation, e.g. Baptism, which is the spiritual birth, Confirmation which is the spiritual growth, the Eucharist which is the spiritual food; whereas Penance is ordained to man's salvation accidentally as it were, and on something being supposed, viz. sin: for unless man were to sin actually, he would not stand in need of Penance, and yet he would need Baptism, Confirmation, and the Eucharist; even as in the life of the body, man would need no medical treatment, unless he were ill, and yet

life, birth, growth, and food are, of themselves, necessary to man.

Consequently Penance holds the second place with regard to the state of integrity which is bestowed and safeguarded by the aforesaid sacraments, so that it is called metaphorically *a second plank after shipwreck.* For just as the first help for those who cross the sea is to be safeguarded in a whole ship, while the second help when the ship is wrecked, is to cling to a plank; so too the first help in this life's ocean is that man safeguard his integrity, while the second help is, if he lose his integrity through sin, that he regain it by means of Penance.

Reply Obj. 1. To hide one's sins may happen in two ways: first, in the very act of sinning. Now it is worse to sin in public than in private, both because a public sinner seems to sin more from contempt, and because by sinning he gives scandal to others. Consequently in sin it is a kind of remedy to sin secretly, and it is in this sense that the gloss says that *to hide one's sins is a second plank after shipwreck;* not that it takes away sin, as Penance does, but because it makes the sin less grievous. Secondly, one hides one's sin previously committed, by neglecting to confess it: this is opposed to Penance, and to hide one's sins thus is not a second plank, but is the reverse, since it is written (Prov. xxviii. 13): *He that hideth his sins shall not prosper.*

Reply Obj. 2. Penance cannot be called the foundation of the spiritual edifice simply, i.e. in the first building thereof; but it is the foundation in the second building which is accomplished by destroying sin, because man, on his return to God, needs Penance first. However, the Apostle is speaking there of the foundation of spiritual doctrine. Moreover, the penance which precedes Baptism is not the sacrament of Penance.

Reply Obj. 3. The three sacraments which precede Penance refer to the ship in its integrity, i.e. to man's state of integrity, with regard to which Penance is called a second plank.

SEVENTH ARTICLE

Whether This Sacrament Was Suitably Instituted in the New Law?

We proceed thus to the Seventh Article:—

Objection 1. It would seem that this sacrament was unsuitably instituted in the New Law. Because those things which belong to the natural law need not to be instituted. Now it belongs to the natural law that one should repent of the evil one has done: for it is impossible to love good without grieving for its contrary. Therefore Penance was unsuitably instituted in the New Law.

Obj. 2. Further, that which existed in the Old Law had not to be instituted in the New. Now there was Penance in the Old Law, wherefore the Lord complains (Jer. viii. 6) saying: *There is none that doth penance for his sin, saying: What have I done?* Therefore Penance should not have been instituted in the New Law.

Obj. 3. Further, Penance comes after Baptism, since it is a second plank, as stated above (A. 6). Now it seems that our Lord instituted Penance before Baptism, because we read that at the beginning of His preaching He said (Matth. iv. 17): *Do penance, for the kingdom of heaven is at hand.* Therefore this sacrament was not suitably instituted in the New Law.

Obj. 4. Further, the sacraments of the New Law were instituted by Christ, by Whose power they work, as stated above (Q. 62, A. 5; Q. 64, A. 1). But Christ does not seem to have instituted this sacrament, since He made no use of it, as of the other sacraments which He instituted. Therefore this sacrament was unsuitably instituted in the New Law.

On the contrary, Our Lord said (Luke xxiv. 46, 47): *It behooved Christ to suffer, and to rise again from the dead the third day: and that penance and remission of sins should be preached in His name unto all nations.*

I answer that, As stated above (A. 1, *ad* 1, *ad* 2), in this sacrament the acts of the penitent are as matter, while the part taken by the priest, who works as Christ's minister, is the formal and completive element of the sacrament. Now in the other sacraments the matter pre-exists, being provided by nature, as water, or by art, as bread: but that such and such a matter be employed for a sacrament requires to be decided by the institution; while the sacrament derives its form and power entirely from the institution of Christ, from Whose Passion the power of the sacraments proceeds.

Accordingly the matter of this sacrament pre-exists, being provided by nature; since it is by a natural principle of reason that man is moved to repent of the evil he has done: yet it is due to Divine institution that man does penance in this or that way. Wherefore at the outset of His preaching, our Lord admonished men, not only to repent, but also to *do penance,* thus pointing to the particular manner of actions required for this sacrament. As to the part to be taken by the ministers, this was fixed by our Lord when He said to Peter (Matth. xvi. 19): *To thee will I give the keys of the kingdom of heaven,* etc.; but it was after His resurrection that He made known the efficacy of this sacrament and the source of its power, when He said (Luke xxiv. 47) that *penance and remission of sins should be preached in His name unto all nations,* after

speaking of His Passion and resurrection. Because it is from the power of the name of Jesus Christ suffering and rising again that this sacrament is efficacious unto the remission of sins.

It is therefore evident that this sacrament was suitably instituted in the New Law.

Reply Obj. 1. It is a natural law that one should repent of the evil one has done, by grieving for having done it, and by seeking a remedy for one's grief in some way or other, and also that one should show some signs of grief, even as the Ninevites did, as we read in Jon. iii. And yet even in their case there was also something of faith which they had received through Jonas' preaching, inasmuch as they did these things in the hope that they would receive pardon from God, according as we read *(ibid.* 9): *Who can tell if God will turn and forgive, and will turn away from His fierce anger, and we shall not perish?* But just as other matters which are of the natural law were fixed in detail by the institution of the Divine law, as we have stated in the Second Part (I-II, Q. 91, A. 4; Q. 95, A. 2; Q. 99), so was it with Penance.

Reply Obj. 2. Things which are of the natural law were determined in various ways in the Old and in the New Law, in keeping with the imperfection of the Old, and the perfection of the New. Wherefore Penance was fixed in a certain way in the Old Law,—with regard to sorrow, that it should be in the heart rather than in external signs, according to Joel ii. 13: *Rend your hearts and not your garments;*—and with regard to seeking a remedy for sorrow, that they should in some way confess their sins, at least in general, to God's ministers. Wherefore the Lord said (Levit. v. 17, 18): *If anyone sin through ignorance, . . . he shall offer of the flocks a ram without blemish to the priest, according to the measure and estimation of the sin, and the priest shall pray for him, because he did it ignorantly, and it shall be forgiven him;* since by the very fact of making an offering for his sin, a man, in a fashion, confessed his sin to the priest. And accordingly it is written (Prov. xxviii. 13): *He that hideth his sins, shall not prosper: but he that shall confess, and forsake them, shall obtain mercy.* Not yet, however, was the power of the keys instituted, which is derived from Christ's Passion, and consequently it was not yet ordained that a man should grieve for his sin, with the purpose of submitting himself by confession and satisfaction to the keys of the Church, in the hope of receiving forgiveness through the power of Christ's Passion.

Reply Obj. 3. If we note carefully what our Lord said about the necessity of Baptism (Jo. iii. 3, *seqq.),* we shall see that this was said before His words about the necessity of Penance (Matth. iv. 17); because He spoke to Nicodemus about Baptism before the imprisonment of John, of whom it is related afterwards (Jo. iii. 23, 24) that he baptized, whereas His words about Penance were said after John was cast into prison.

If, however, He had admonished men to do penance before admonishing them to be baptized, this would be because also before Baptism some kind of penance is required, according to the words of Peter (Acts ii. 38): *Do penance, and be baptized, every one of you.*

Reply Obj. 4. Christ did not use the Baptism which He instituted, but was baptized with the baptism of John, as stated above (Q. 39, AA. 1, 2). Nor did He use it actively by administering it Himself, because He *did not baptize* as a rule, *but His disciples* did, as related in Jo. iv. 2, although it is to be believed that He baptized His disciples, as Augustine asserts (*Ep.* cclxv, *ad Seleuc.*). But with regard to His institution of this sacrament it was nowise fitting that He should use it, neither by repenting Himself, in Whom there was no sin, nor by administering the sacrament to others, since, in order to show His mercy and power, He was wont to confer the effect of this sacrament without the sacrament itself, as stated above (A. 5, *ad* 3). On the other hand, He both received and gave to others the sacrament of the Eucharist, both in order to commend the excellence of that sacrament, and because that sacrament is a memorial of His Passion, in which Christ is both priest and victim.

EIGHTH ARTICLE

Whether Penance Should Last Till the End of Life?

We proceed thus to the Eighth Article:—

Objection 1. It would seem that Penance should not last till the end of life. Because Penance is ordained for the blotting out of sin. Now the penitent receives forgiveness of his sins at once, according to Ezech. xviii. 21: *If the wicked do penance for all his sins which he hath committed . . . he shall live and shall not die.* Therefore there is no need for Penance to be further prolonged.

Obj. 2. Further, Penance belongs to the state of beginners. But man ought to advance from that state to the state of the proficient, and, from this, on to the state of the perfect. Therefore man need not do Penance till the end of his life.

Obj. 3. Further, man is bound to observe the laws of the Church in this as in the other sacraments. But the duration of repentance is fixed by the canons, so that, to wit, for such

and such a sin one is bound to do penance for so many years. Therefore it seems that Penance should not be prolonged till the end of life.

On the contrary, Augustine says in his book, *De Pœnitentia:* * *What remains for us to do, save to sorrow ever in this life? For when sorrow ceases, repentance fails; and if repentance fails, what becomes of pardon?*

I answer that, Penance is twofold, internal and external. Internal penance is that whereby one grieves for a sin one has committed, and this penance should last until the end of life. Because man should always be displeased at having sinned, for if he were to be pleased thereat, he would for this very reason fall into sin and lose the fruit of pardon. Now displeasure causes sorrow in one who is susceptible to sorrow, as man is in this life; but after this life the saints are not susceptible to sorrow, wherefore they will be displeased at, without sorrowing for, their past sins, according to Isa. lxv. 16. *The former distresses are forgotten.*

External penance is that whereby a man shows external signs of sorrow, confesses his sins verbally to the priest who absolves him, and makes satisfaction for his sins according to the judgment of the priest. Such penance need not last until the end of life, but only for a fixed time according to the measure of the sin.

Reply Obj. 1. True penance not only removes past sins, but also preserves man from future sins. Consequently, although a man receives forgiveness of past sins in the first instant of his true penance, nevertheless he must persevere in his penance, lest he fall again into sin.

Reply Obj. 2. To do penance both internal and external belongs to the state of beginners, of those, to wit, who are making a fresh start from the state of sin. But there is room for internal penance even in the proficient and the perfect, according to Ps. lxxxiii. 7: *In his heart he hath disposed to ascend by steps, in the vale of tears.* Wherefore Paul says (1 Cor. xv. 9): *I . . . am not worthy to be called an apostle because I persecuted the Church of God.*

Reply Obj. 3. These durations of time are fixed for penitents as regards the exercise of external penance.

NINTH ARTICLE

Whether Penance Can Be Continuous?

We proceed thus to the Ninth Article:—

Objection 1. It would seem that penance cannot be continuous. For it is written (Jerem.

---

* *De vera et falsa Pœnitentia.* the authorship of which is unknown.

xxxi. 16): *Let thy voice cease from weeping, and thy eyes from tears.* But this would be impossible if penance were continuous, for it consists in weeping and tears. Therefore penance cannot be continuous.

Obj. 2. Further, man ought to rejoice at every good work, according to Ps. xcix. 1: *Serve ye the Lord with gladness.* Now to do penance is a good work. Therefore man should rejoice at it. But man cannot rejoice and grieve at the same time, as the Philosopher declares *(Ethic.* ix. 4). Therefore a penitent cannot grieve continually for his past sins, which is essential to penance. Therefore penance cannot be continuous.

Obj. 3. Further, the Apostle says (2 Cor. ii. 7): *Comfort him,* viz. the penitent, *lest perhaps such an one be swallowed up with overmuch sorrow.* But comfort dispels grief, which is essential to penance. Therefore penance need not be continuous.

On the contrary, Augustine says in his book on Penance:* *In doing penance grief should be continual.*

I answer that, One is said to repent in two ways, actually and habitually. It is impossible for a man continually to repent actually; for the acts, whether internal or external, of a penitent must needs be interrupted by sleep and other things which the body needs. Secondly, a man is said to repent habitually; and thus he should repent continually, both by never doing anything contrary to penance, so as to destroy the habitual disposition of the penitent, and by being resolved that his past sins should always be displeasing to him.

Reply Obj. 1. Weeping and tears belong to the act of external penance, and this act needs neither to be continuous, nor to last until the end of life, as stated above (A. 8): wherefore it is significantly added: *For there is a reward for thy work.* Now the reward of the penitent's work is the full remission of sin both as to guilt and as to punishment; and after receiving this reward there is no need for man to proceed to acts of external penance. This, however, does not prevent penance being continual, as explained above.

Reply Obj. 2. Of sorrow and joy we may speak in two ways: first, as being passions of the sensitive appetite; and thus they can nowise be together, since they are altogether contrary to one another, either on the part of the object (as when they have the same object), or at least on the part of the movement, for joy is with expansion† of the heart, whereas sorrow is with contraction; and it is in this sense that the Philosopher speaks in *Ethic.* ix. Secondly, we may speak of joy and sorrow as being simple acts of the will, to which

* Cf. footnote, p. 2530.   † Cf. I-II, Q. 33, A. 1.

something is pleasing or displeasing. Accordingly, they cannot be contrary to one another, except on the part of the object, as when they concern the same object in the same respect, in which way joy and sorrow cannot be simultaneous, because the same thing in the same respect cannot be pleasing and displeasing. If, on the other hand, joy and sorrow, understood thus, be not of the same object in the same respect, but either of different objects, or of the same object in different respects, in that case joy and sorrow are not contrary to one another, so that nothing hinders a man from being joyful and sorrowful at the same time, —for instance, if we see a good man suffer, we both rejoice at his goodness and at the same time grieve for his suffering. In this way a man may be displeased at having sinned, and be pleased at his displeasure together with his hope for pardon, so that his very sorrow is a matter of joy. Hence Augustine says *(loc. cit.): The penitent should ever grieve and rejoice at his grief.*

If, however, sorrow were altogether incompatible with joy, this would prevent the continuance, not of habitual penance, but only of actual penance.

Reply Obj. 3. According to the Philosopher *(Ethic.* ii. 3, 6, 7, 9) it belongs to virtue to establish the mean in the passions. Now the sorrow which, in the sensitive appetite of the penitent, arises from the displeasure of his will, is a passion; wherefore it should be moderated according to virtue, and if it be excessive it is sinful, because it leads to despair, as the Apostle teaches *(ibid.),* saying: *Lest such an one be swallowed up with overmuch sorrow.* Accordingly comfort, of which the Apostle speaks, moderates sorrow but does not destroy it altogether.

TENTH ARTICLE

Whether the Sacrament of Penance May Be Repeated?

We proceed thus to the Tenth Article:—

Objection 1. It would seem that the sacrament of Penance should not be repeated. For the Apostle says (Heb. vi. 4, *seqq.): It is impossible for those, who were once illuminated, have tasted also the heavenly gift, and were made partakers of the Holy Ghost . . . and are fallen away, to be renewed again to penance.* Now whosoever have done penance, have been illuminated, and have received the gift of the Holy Ghost. Therefore whosoever sin after doing penance, cannot do penance again.

Obj. 2. Further, Ambrose says *(De Pœnit.* ii): *Some are to be found who think they ought often to do penance, who take liberties with Christ: for if they were truly penitent, they would not think of doing penance over again, since there is but one Penance even as there is but one Baptism.* Now Baptism is not repeated. Neither, therefore, is Penance to be repeated.

Obj. 3. Further, the miracles whereby our Lord healed bodily diseases, signify the healing of spiritual diseases, whereby men are delivered from sins. Now we do not read that our Lord restored the sight to any blind man twice, or that He cleansed any leper twice, or twice raised any dead man to life. Therefore it seems that He does not twice grant pardon to any sinner.

Obj. 4. Further, Gregory says (*Hom.* xxxiv, *in Evang.*): *Penance consists in deploring past sins, and in not committing again those we have deplored:* and Isidore says (*De Summo Bono,* ii): *He is a mocker and no penitent who still does what he has repented of.* If, therefore, a man is truly penitent, he will not sin again. Therefore Penance cannot be repeated.

Obj. 5. Further, just as Baptism derives its efficacy from the Passion of Christ, so does Penance. Now Baptism is not repeated, on account of the unity of Christ's Passion and death. Therefore in like manner Penance is not repeated.

Obj. 6. Further, Ambrose says on Ps. cxviii. 58, *I entreated Thy face,* etc., that *facility of obtaining pardon is an incentive to sin.* If, therefore, God frequently grants pardon through Penance, it seems that He affords man an incentive to sin, and thus He seems to take pleasure in sin, which is contrary to His goodness. Therefore Penance cannot be repeated.

On the contrary, Man is induced to be merciful by the example of Divine mercy, according to Luke vi. 36: *Be ye . . . merciful, as your Father also is merciful.* Now our Lord commanded His disciples to be merciful by frequently pardoning their brethren who had sinned against them; wherefore, as related in Matth. xviii. 21, when Peter asked: *How often shall my brother offend against me, and I forgive him? till seven times?* Jesus answered: *I say not to thee, till seven times, but till seventy times seven times.* Therefore also God over and over again, through Penance, grants pardon to sinners, especially as He teaches us to pray (Matth. vi. 12): *Forgive us our trespasses, as we forgive them that trespass against us.*

I answer that, As regards Penance, some have erred, saying that a man cannot obtain pardon of his sins through Penance a second time. Some of these, viz. the Novatians, went so far as to say that he who sins after the first

Penance which is done in Baptism, cannot be restored again through Penance. There were also other heretics who, as Augustine relates in *De Pœnitentia,** said that, after Baptism, Penance is useful, not many times, but only once.

These errors seem to have arisen from a twofold source: first from not knowing the nature of true Penance. For since true Penance requires charity, without which sins are not taken away, they thought that charity once possessed could not be lost, and that, consequently, Penance, if true, could never be removed by sin, so that it should be necessary to repeat it. But this was refuted in the Second part (II-II, Q. 24, A. 11), where it was shown that on account of free-will charity, once possessed, can be lost, and that, consequently, after true Penance, a man can sin mortally.—Secondly, they erred in their estimation of the gravity of sin. For they deemed a sin committed by a man after he had received pardon, to be so grave that it could not be forgiven. In this they erred not only with regard to sin which, even after a sin has been forgiven, can be either more or less grievous than the first, which was forgiven, but much more did they err against the infinity of Divine mercy, which surpasses any number and magnitude of sins, according to Ps. l. 1, 2: *Have mercy on me, O God, according to Thy great mercy: and according to the multitude of Thy tender mercies, blot out my iniquity.* Wherefore the words of Cain were reprehensible, when he said (Gen. iv. 13): *My iniquity is greater than that I may deserve pardon.* And so God's mercy, through Penance, grants pardon to sinners without any end, wherefore it is written (2 *Paralip.* xxxvii†): *Thy merciful promise is unmeasurable and unsearchable . . . (and Thou repentest) for the evil brought upon man.* It is therefore evident that Penance can be repeated many times.

Reply Obj. 1. Some of the Jews thought that a man could be washed several times in the laver of Baptism, because among them the Law prescribed certain washing-places where they were wont to cleanse themselves repeatedly from their uncleannesses. In order to disprove this the Apostle wrote to the Hebrews that *it is impossible for those who were once illuminated,* viz. through Baptism, *to be renewed again to penance,* viz. through Baptism, which is *the laver of regeneration, and renovation of the Holy Ghost,* as stated in Tit. iii. 5: and he declares the reason to be that by Baptism man dies with Christ, wherefore he adds (Heb. vi. 6): *Crucifying again to themselves the Son of God.*

---

* Cf. footnote, p. 2530.   † Prayer of Manasses, among the Apocrypha. S. Thomas is evidently quoting from memory, and omits the words in brackets.

Reply Obj. 2. Ambrose is speaking of solemn Penance, which is not repeated in the Church, as we shall state further on (Suppl., Q. 28, A. 2).

Reply Obj. 3. As Augustine says *(loc. cit.)*, *Our Lord gave sight to many blind men at various times, and strength to many infirm, thereby showing, in these different men, that the same sins are repeatedly forgiven, at one time healing a man from leprosy and afterwards from blindness. For this reason He healed so many stricken with fever, so many feeble in body, so many lame, blind, and withered, that the sinner might not despair; for this reason He is not described as healing anyone but once, that every one might fear to link himself with sin; for this reason He declares Himself to be the physician welcomed not of the hale, but of the unhealthy. What sort of a physician is he who knows not how to heal a recurring disease? For if a man ail a hundred times it is for the physician to heal him a hundred times: and if he failed where others succeed, he would be a poor physician in comparison with them.*

Reply Obj. 4. Penance is to deplore past sins, and, *while deploring them,* not to commit again, either by act or by intention, those which we have to deplore. Because a man is a mocker and not a penitent, who, *while doing penance,* does what he repents having done, or intends to do again what he did before, or even commits actually the same or another kind of sin. But if a man sin afterwards either by act or intention, this does not destroy the fact that his former penance was real, because the reality of a former act is never destroyed by a subsequent contrary act: for even as he truly ran who afterwards sits, so he truly repented who subsequently sins.

Reply Obj. 5. Baptism derives its power from Christ's Passion, as a spiritual regeneration, with a spiritual death, of a previous life. Now *it is appointed unto man once to die* (Heb. ix. 27), and to be born once, wherefore man should be baptized but once. On the other hand, Penance derives its power from Christ's Passion, as a spiritual medicine, which can be repeated frequently.

Reply Obj. 6. According to Augustine *(loc. cit.), it is evident that sins displease God exceedingly, for He is always ready to destroy them, lest what He created should perish, and what He loved be lost,* viz. by despair.

QUESTION 85

Of Penance As a Virtue

(In Six Articles)

WE must now consider penance as a virtue, under which head there are six points of inquiry: (1) Whether penance is a virtue? (2) Whether it is a special virtue? (3) To what species of virtue does it belong? (4) Of its subject. (5) Of its cause. (6) Of its relation to the other virtues.

FIRST ARTICLE

Whether Penance Is a Virtue?

We proceed thus to the First Article:—

Objection 1. It would seem that penance is not a virtue. For penance is a sacrament numbered among the other sacraments, as was shown above (Q. 84, A. 1; Q. 65, A. 1). Now no other sacrament is a virtue. Therefore neither is penance a virtue.

Obj. 2. Further, according to the Philosopher *(Ethic.* iv. 9), *shame is not a virtue,* both because it is a passion accompanied by a bodily alteration, and because it is not the disposition of a perfect thing, since it is about an evil act, so that it has no place in a virtuous man. Now, in like manner, penance is a passion accompanied by a bodily alteration, viz.

tears, according to Gregory, who says *(Hom. xxxiv, in Evang.)* that *penance consists in deploring past sins:* moreover it is about evil deeds, viz. sins, which have no place in a virtuous man. Therefore penance is not a virtue.

Obj. 3. Further, according to the Philosopher *(Ethic.* iv. 3), *no virtuous man is foolish.* But it seems foolish to deplore what has been done in the past, since it cannot be otherwise, and yet this is what we understand by penance. Therefore penance is not a virtue.

On the contrary, The precepts of the Law are about acts of virtue, because *a lawgiver intends to make the citizens virtuous (Ethic.* ii. 1). But there is a precept about penance in the Divine law, according to Matth. iv. 17: *Do penance,* etc. Therefore penance is a virtue.

I answer that, As stated above *(Obj. 2, Q.* 84, A. 10, *ad* 4), to repent is to deplore something one has done. Now it has been stated above (Q. 84, A. 9) that sorrow or sadness is twofold. First, it denotes a passion of the sensitive appetite, and in this sense penance is not a virtue, but a passion. Secondly, it denotes an act of the will, and in this way it implies choice, and if this be right, it must, of necessity, be an act of virtue. For it is stated in *Ethic.* ii. 6 that virtue is a habit of choosing according to right reason. Now it belongs to right reason than one should grieve for a proper object of grief as one ought to grieve, and for an end for which one ought to grieve. And this is observed in the penance of which we are speaking now; since the penitent assumes a moderated grief for his past sins, with the intention of removing them. Hence it is evident that the penance of which we are speaking now, is either a virtue or the act of a virtue.

Reply Obj. 1. As stated above (Q. 84, A. 1, *ad* 1; AA. 2, 3), in the sacrament of Penance, human acts take the place of matter, which is not the case in Baptism and Confirmation. Wherefore, since virtue is a principle of an act, penance is either a virtue or accompanies a virtue, rather than Baptism or Confirmation.

Reply Obj. 2. Penance, considered as a passion, is not a virtue, as stated above, and it is thus that it is accompanied by a bodily alteration. On the other hand, it is a virtue, according as it includes a right choice on the part of the will; which, however, applies to penance rather than to shame. Because shame regards the evil deed as present, whereas penance regards the evil deed as past. Now it is contrary to the perfection of virtue that one should have an evil deed actually present, of which one ought to be ashamed; whereas it is not contrary to the perfection of virtue that we should have previously committed evil deeds, of which it behooves us to repent, since a man from being wicked becomes virtuous.

Reply Obj. 3. It would indeed be foolish to grieve for what has already been done, with the intention of trying to make it not done. But the penitent does not intend this: for his sorrow is displeasure or disapproval with regard to the past deed, with the intention of removing its result, viz. the anger of God and the debt of punishment: and this is not foolish.

SECOND ARTICLE

Whether Penance Is a Special Virtue?

We proceed thus to the Second Article:—

Objection 1. It would seem that penance is not a special virtue. For it seems that to rejoice at the good one has done, and to grieve for the evil one has done are acts of the same nature. But joy for the good one has done is not a special virtue, but is a praiseworthy emotion proceeding from charity, as Augustine states *(De Civ. Dei,* xiv. 7, 8, 9): wherefore the Apostle says (1 Cor. xiii. 6) that charity *rejoiceth not at iniquity, but rejoiceth with the truth.* Therefore, in like manner, neither

is penance, which is sorrow for past sins, a special virtue, but an emotion resulting from charity.

Obj. 2. Further, every special virtue has its special matter, because habits are distinguished by their acts, and acts by their objects. But penance has no special matter, because its matter is past sins in any matter whatever. Therefore penance is not a special virtue.

Obj. 3. Further, nothing is removed except by its contrary. But penance removes all sins. Therefore it is contrary to all sins, and consequently is not a special virtue.

On the contrary, The Law has a special precept about penance, as stated above (Q. 84, AA. 5, 7).

I answer that, As stated in the Second Part (I-II, Q. 54, A. 1, *ad* 1, A. 2), habits are specifically distinguished according to the species of their acts, so that whenever an act has a special reason for being praiseworthy, there must needs be a special habit. Now it is evident that there is a special reason for praising the act of penance, because it aims at the destruction of past sin, considered as an offense against God, which does not apply to any other virtue. We must therefore conclude that penance is a special virtue.

Reply Obj. 1. An act springs from charity in two ways: first as being elicited by charity, and a like virtuous act requires no other virtue than charity, e.g. to love the good, to rejoice therein, and to grieve for what is opposed to it. Secondly, an act springs from charity, being, so to speak, commanded by charity; and thus, since charity commands all the virtues, inasmuch as it directs them to its own end, an act springing from charity may belong even to another special virtue. Accordingly, if in the act of the penitent we consider the mere displeasure in the past sin, it belongs to charity immediately, in the same way as joy for past good acts; but the intention to aim at the destruction of past sin requires a special virtue subordinate to charity.

Reply Obj. 2. In point of fact, penance has indeed a general matter, inasmuch as it regards all sins; but it does so under a special aspect, inasmuch as they can be remedied by an act of man in co-operating with God for his justification.

Reply Obj. 3. Every special virtue removes formally the habit of the opposite vice, just as whiteness removes blackness from the same subject: but penance removes every sin effectively, inasmuch as it works for the destruction of sins, according as they are pardonable through the grace of God if man co-operate therewith. Wherefore it does not follow that it is a general virtue.

THIRD ARTICLE

Whether the Virtue of Penance Is a Species of Justice?

We proceed thus to the Third Article:—

Objection 1. It would seem that the virtue of penance is not a species of justice. For justice is not a theological but a moral virtue, as was shown in the Second Part (II-II, Q. 62, A. 3). But penance seems to be a theological virtue, since God is its object, for it makes satisfaction to God, to Whom, moreover, it reconciles the sinner. Therefore it seems that penance is not a species of justice.

Obj. 2. Further, since justice is a moral virtue it observes the mean. Now penance does not observe the mean, but rather goes to the extreme, according to Jerem. vi. 26: *Make thee mourning as for an only son, a bitter lamentation.* Therefore penance is not a species of justice.

Obj. 3. Further, there are two species of justice, as stated in *Ethic.* v. 4, viz. *distributive* and *commutative.* But penance does not seem to be contained under either of them. Therefore it seems that penance is not a species of justice.

Obj. 4. Further, a gloss on Luke vi. 21, *Blessed are ye that weep now,* says: *It is prudence that teaches us the unhappiness of earthly things and the happiness of heavenly things.* But weeping is an act of penance. Therefore penance is a species of prudence rather than of justice.

On the contrary, Augustine says in *De Pœnitentia:** Penance is the vengeance of the sorrowful, ever punishing in them what they are sorry for having done.* But to take vengeance is an act of justice, wherefore Tully says *(De Inv. Rhetor.* ii) that one kind of justice is called vindictive. Therefore it seems that penance is a species of justice.

I answer that, As stated above (A. 1, *ad* 2), penance is a special virtue not merely because it sorrows for evil done (since charity would suffice for that), but also because the penitent grieves for the sin he has committed, inasmuch as it is an offense against God, and purposes to amend. Now amendment for an offense committed against anyone is not made by merely ceasing to offend, but it is necessary to make some kind of compensation, which obtains in offenses committed against another, just as retribution does, only that compensation is on the part of the offender, as when he makes satisfaction, whereas retribution is on the part of the person offended against. Each of these belongs to the matter of justice, because each is a kind of commutation. Wherefore it is evident that penance, as a virtue, is a part of justice.

It must be observed, however, that according to the Philosopher *(Ethic.* v. 6) a thing is said to be just in two ways, simply and relatively. A thing is just simply when it is between equals, since justice is a kind of equality, and he calls this the politic or civil just, because all citizens are equal, in the point of being immediately under the ruler, retaining their freedom. But a thing is just relatively when it is between parties of whom one is subject to the other, as a servant under his master, a son under his father, a wife under her husband. It is this kind of just that we consider in penance. Wherefore the penitent has recourse to God with a purpose of amendment, as a servant to his master, according to Ps. cxxii. 2: *Behold, as the eyes of servants are on the hands of their masters, . . . so are our eyes unto the Lord our God, until He have mercy on us;* and as a son to his father, according to Luke xv. 21: *Father, I have sinned against heaven and before thee;* and as a wife to her husband, according to Jerem. iii. 1: *Thou hast prostituted thyself to many lovers; nevertheless return to Me, saith the Lord.*

Reply Obj. 1. As stated in *Ethic.* v. 1, justice is a virtue towards another person, and the matter of justice is not so much the person to whom justice is due as the thing which is the subject of distribution or commutation. Hence the matter of penance is not God, but human acts, whereby God is offended or appeased; whereas God is as one to whom justice is due. Wherefore it is evident that penance is not a theological virtue, because God is not its matter or object.

Reply Obj. 2. The mean of justice is the equality that is established between those between whom justice is, as stated in *Ethic.* v. But in certain cases perfect equality cannot be established, on account of the excellence of one, as between father and son, God and man, as the Philosopher states *(Ethic.* viii. 14), wherefore in such cases, he that falls short of the other must do whatever he can. Yet this will not be sufficient simply, but only according to the acceptance of the higher one; and this is what is meant by ascribing excess to penance.

Reply Obj. 3. As there is a kind of commutation in favors, when, to wit, a man gives thanks for a favor received, so also is there commutation in the matter of offenses, when, on account of an offense committed against another, a man is either punished against his will, which pertains to vindictive justice, or makes amends of his own accord, which belongs to penance, which regards the person of the sinner, just as vindictive justice regards

* *De vera et falsa Pœnitentia,* the authorship of which is unknown.

the person of the judge. Therefore it is evident that both are comprised under commutative justice.

Reply Obj. 4. Although penance is directly a species of justice, yet, in a fashion, it comprises things pertaining to all the virtues; for inasmuch as there is a justice of man towards God, it must have a share in matter pertaining to the theological virtues, the object of which is God. Consequently penance comprises faith in Christ's Passion, whereby we are cleansed of our sins, hope for pardon, and hatred of vice, which pertains to charity. Inasmuch as it is a moral virtue, it has a share of prudence, which directs all the moral virtues: but from the very nature of justice, it has not only something belonging to justice, but also something belonging to temperance and fortitude, inasmuch as those things which cause pleasure, and which pertain to temperance, and those which cause terror, which fortitude moderates, are objects of commutative justice. Accordingly it belongs to justice both to abstain from pleasure, which belongs to temperance, and to bear with hardships, which belongs to fortitude.

FOURTH ARTICLE

Whether the Will Is Properly the Subject of Penance?

We proceed thus to the Fourth Article:—

Objection 1. It would seem that the subject of penance is not properly the will. For penance is a species of sorrow. But sorrow is in the concupiscible part, even as joy is. Therefore penance is in the concupiscible faculty.

Obj. 2. Further, penance is a kind of vengeance, as Augustine states in *De Pœnitentia (loc. cit.,* A. 3). But vengeance seems to regard the irascible faculty, since anger is the desire for vengeance. Therefore it seems that penance is in the irascible part.

Obj. 3. Further, the past is the proper object of the memory, according to the Philosopher *(De Memoria,* i). Now penance regards the past, as stated above (A. 1, *ad 2, ad* 3). Therefore penance is subjected in the memory.

Obj. 4. Further, nothing acts where it is not. Now penance removes sin from all the powers of the soul. Therefore penance is in every power of the soul, and not only in the will.

On the contrary, Penance is a kind of sacrifice, according to Ps. l. 19: *A sacrifice to God is an afflicted spirit.* But to offer a sacrifice is an act of the will, according to Ps. liii. 8: *I will freely sacrifice to Thee.* Therefore penance is in the will.

I answer that, We can speak of penance in

* The Septuagint.

two ways: first, in so far as it is a passion, and thus, since it is a kind of sorrow, it is in the concupiscible part as its subject; secondly, in so far as it is a virtue, and thus, as stated above (A. 3), it is a species of justice. Now justice, as stated in the Second Part (I-II, Q. 56, A. 6), is subjected in the rational appetite which is the will. Therefore it is evident that penance, in so far as it is a virtue, is subjected in the will, and its proper act is the purpose of amending what was committed against God.

Reply Obj. 1. This argument considers penance as a passion.

Reply Obj. 2. To desire vengeance on another, through passion, belongs to the irascible appetite, but to desire or take vengeance on oneself or on another, through reason, belongs to the will.

Reply Obj. 3. The memory is a power that apprehends the past. But penance belongs not to the apprehensive but to the appetitive power, which presupposes an act of the apprehension. Wherefore penance is not in the memory, but presupposes it.

Reply Obj. 4. The will, as stated above (P. I., Q. 82, A. 4; P. I-II, Q. 9, A. 1), moves all the other powers of the soul; so that it is not unreasonable for penance to be subjected in the will, and to produce an effect in each power of the soul.

FIFTH ARTICLE

Whether Penance Originates from Fear?

We proceed thus to the Fifth Article:—

Objection 1. It would seem that penance does not originate from fear. For penance originates in displeasure at sin. But this belongs to charity, as stated above (A. 3). Therefore penance originates from love rather than fear.

Obj. 2. Further, men are induced to do penance, through the expectation of the heavenly kingdom, according to Matth. iii. 2 and iv. 17: *Do penance, for the kingdom of heaven is at hand.* Now the kingdom of heaven is the object of hope. Therefore penance results from hope rather than from fear.

Obj. 3. Further, fear is an internal act of man. But penance does not seem to arise in us through any work of man, but through the operation of God, according to Jerem. xxxi. 19: *After Thou didst convert me I did penance.* Therefore penance does not result from fear.

On the contrary, It is written (Isa. xxvi. 17): *As a woman with child, when she draweth near the time of her delivery, is in pain, and crieth out in her pangs, so are we become,* by penance, to wit; and according to another*

version the text continues: *Through fear of Thee, O Lord, we have conceived, and been as it were in labor, and have brought forth the spirit of salvation,* i.e. of salutary penance, as is clear from what precedes. Therefore penance results from fear.

I answer that, We may speak of penance in two ways: first, as to the habit, and then it is infused by God immediately without our operating as principal agents, but not without our co-operating dispositively by certain acts. Secondly, we may speak of penance, with regard to the acts whereby in penance we co-operate with God operating, the first principle* of which acts is the operation of God in turning the heart, according to Lament. v. 21: *Convert us, O Lord, to Thee, and we shall be converted;* the second, an act of faith; the third, a movement of servile fear, whereby a man is withdrawn from sin through fear of punishment; the fourth, a movement of hope, whereby a man makes a purpose of amendment, in the hope of obtaining pardon; the fifth, a movement of charity, whereby sin is displeasing to man for its own sake and no longer for the sake of the punishment; the sixth, a movement of filial fear whereby a man, of his own accord, offers to make amends to God through fear of Him.

Accordingly it is evident that the act of penance results from servile fear as from the first movement of the appetite in this direction and from filial fear as from its immediate and proper principle.

Reply Obj. 1. Sin begins to displease a man, especially a sinner, on account of the punishments which servile fear regards, before it displeases him on account of its being an offense against God, or on account of its wickedness, which pertains to charity.

Reply Obj. 2. When the kingdom of heaven is said to be at hand, we are to understand that the king is on his way, not only to reward but also to punish. Wherefore John the Baptist said (Matth. iii. 7): *Ye brood of vipers, who hath showed you to flee from the wrath to come?*

Reply Obj. 3. Even the movement of fear proceeds from God's act in turning the heart; wherefore it is written (Deut. v. 29): *Who shall give them to have such a mind, to fear Me?* And so the fact that penance results from fear does not hinder its resulting from the act of God in turning the heart.

SIXTH ARTICLE

Whether Penance Is the First of the Virtues?

We proceed thus to the Sixth Article:—

Objection 1. It would seem that penance is the first of the virtues. Because, on Matth.

*Cf. I-II, Q. 113.

iii. 2, *Do penance,* etc., a gloss says: *The first virtue is to destroy the old man, and hate sin by means of penance.*

Obj. 2. Further, withdrawal from one extreme seems to precede approach to the other. Now all the other virtues seem to regard approach to a term, because they all direct man to do good; whereas penance seems to direct him to withdraw from evil. Therefore it seems that penance precedes all the other virtues.

Obj. 3. Further, before penance, there is sin in the soul. Now no virtue is compatible with sin in the soul. Therefore no virtue precedes penance, which is itself the first of all, and opens the door to the others by expelling sin.

On the contrary, Penance results from faith, hope, and charity, as already stated (AA. 2, 5). Therefore penance is not the first of the virtues.

I answer that, In speaking of the virtues, we do not consider the order of time with regard to the habits, because, since the virtues are connected with one another, as stated in the Second Part (I-II, Q. 65, A. 1), they all begin at the same time to be in the soul; but one is said to precede the other in the order of nature, which order depends on the order of their acts, in so far as the act of one virtue presupposes the act of another. Accordingly, then, one must say that, even in the order of time, certain praiseworthy acts can precede the act and the habit of penance, e.g. acts of dead faith and hope, and an act of servile fear; while the act and habit of charity are, in point of time, simultaneous with the act and habit of penance, and with the habits of the other virtues. For, as was stated in the Second Part (I-II, Q. 113, AA. 7, 8), in the justification of the ungodly, the movement of the free-will towards God, which is an act of faith quickened by charity, and the movement of the free-will towards sin, which is the act of penance, are simultaneous. Yet of these two acts, the former naturally precedes the latter, because the act of the virtue of penance is directed against sin, through love of God; where the first-mentioned act is the reason and cause of the second.

Consequently penance is not simply the first of the virtues, either in the order of time, or in the order of nature, because, in the order of nature, the theological virtues precede it simply. Nevertheless, in a certain respect, it is the first of the other virtues in the order of time, as regards its act, because this act is the first in the justification of the ungodly; whereas in the order of nature, the other virtues seem to precede, as that which is natural precedes that which is accidental; because the other virtues seem to be necessary for man's good, by reason of their very nature, whereas penance is only necessary if something, viz. sin, be presupposed, as stated above (Q. 55, A. 2), when we spoke of the relation of the sacrament of penance to the other sacraments aforesaid.

Reply Obj. 1. This gloss is to be taken as meaning that the act of penance is the first in point of time, in comparison with the acts of the other virtues.

Reply Obj. 2. In successive movements withdrawal from one extreme precedes approach to the other, in point of time; and also in the order of nature, if we consider the subject, i.e. the order of the material cause; but if we consider the order of the efficient and

final causes, approach to the end is first, for it is this that the efficient cause intends first of all: and it is this order which we consider chiefly in the acts of the soul, as stated in *Phys.* ii.

Reply Obj. 3. Penance opens the door to the other virtues, because it expels sin by the virtues of faith, hope and charity, which precede it in the order of nature; yet it so opens the door to them that they enter at the same time as it: because, in the justification of the ungodly, at the same time as the free-will is moved towards God and against sin, the sin is pardoned and grace infused, and with grace all the virtues, as stated in the Second Part (I-II, Q. 65, AA. 3, 5).

QUESTION 86

Of the Effect of Penance, As Regards the Pardon of Mortal Sin

(In Six Articles)

WE must now consider the effect of Penance; and (1) as regards the pardon of mortal sins; (2) as regards the pardon of venial sins; (3) as regards the return of sins which have been pardoned; (4) as regards the recovery of the virtues.

Under the first head there are six points of inquiry: (1) Whether all mortal sins are taken away by Penance? (2) Whether they can be taken away without Penance? (3) Whether one can be taken away without the other? (4) Whether Penance takes away the guilt while the debt remains? (5) Whether any remnants of sin remain? (6) Whether the removal of sin is the effect of Penance as a virtue, or as a sacrament?

FIRST ARTICLE

Whether All Sins Are Taken Away by Penance?

We proceed thus to the First Article:—

Objection 1. It would seem that not all sins are taken away by Penance. For the Apostle says (Heb. xii. 17) that Esau *found no place of repentance, although with tears he had sought it,* which a gloss explains as meaning that *he found no place of pardon and blessing through Penance:* and it is related (2 Machab. ix. 13) of Antiochus, that *this wicked man prayed to the Lord, of Whom he was not to obtain mercy.* Therefore it does not seem that all sins are taken away by Penance.

Obj. 2. Further, Augustine says (*De Serm. Dom. in Monte,* i) that *so great is the stain of that sin* (namely, *when a man, after coming to the knowledge of God through the grace of Christ, resists fraternal charity, and by the brands of envy combats grace itself) that he is unable to humble himself in prayer,* although

he is forced by his wicked consience to acknowledge and confess his sin. Therefore not every sin can be taken away by Penance.

Obj. 3. Further, our Lord said (Matth. xii. 32): *He that shall speak against the Holy Ghost, it shall not be forgiven him, neither in this world nor in the world to come.* Therefore not every sin can be pardoned through Penance.

On the contrary, It is written (Ezech. xviii. 22): *I will not remember* any more *all his iniquities that he hath done.*

I answer that, The fact that a sin cannot be taken away by Penance may happen in two ways: first, because of the impossibility of repenting of sin; secondly, because of Penance being unable to blot out a sin. In the first way the sins of the demons and of men who are lost, cannot be blotted out by Penance, because their will is confirmed in evil, so that sin cannot displease them as to its guilt, but only as to the punishment which they suffer, by reason of which they have a kind of repentance, which yet is fruitless, according to Wis. v. 3: *Repenting, and groaning for anguish of spirit.* Consequently such Penance brings no hope of pardon, but only despair. Nevertheless no sin of a wayfarer can be such as that, because his will is flexible to good and evil. Wherefore to say that in this life there is any sin of which one cannot repent, is erroneous, first, because this would destroy free-will, secondly, because this would be derogatory to the power of grace, whereby the heart of any sinner whatsoever can be moved to repent, according to Prov. xxi. 1: *The heart of the king is in the hand of the Lord: whithersoever He will He shall turn it.*

It is also erroneous to say that any sin cannot be pardoned through true Penance. First, because this is contrary to Divine mercy, of which it is written (Joel ii. 13) that God *is gracious and merciful, patient, and rich in mercy, and ready to repent of the evil;* for, in a manner, God would be overcome by man, if man wished a sin to be blotted out, which God were unwilling to blot out. Secondly, because this would be derogatory to the power of Christ's Passion, through which Penance produces its effect, as do the other sacraments, since it is written (1 Jo. ii. 2): *He is the propitiation for our sins, and not for ours only, but also for those of the whole world.*

Therefore we must say simply that, in this life, every sin can be blotted out by true Penance.

Reply Obj. 1. Esau did not truly repent. This is evident from his saying (Gen. xxvii. 41): *The days will come of the mourning of my father, and I will kill my brother Jacob.* Likewise neither did Antiochus repent truly; since he grieved for his past sin, not because he had offended God thereby, but on account of the sickness which he suffered in his body.

Reply Obj. 2. These words of Augustine should be understood thus: *So great is the stain of that sin, that man is unable to humble himself in prayer,* i.e. it is not easy for him to do so; in which sense we say that a man cannot be healed, when it is difficult to heal him. Yet this is possible by the power of God's grace, which sometimes turns men even *into the depths of the sea* (Ps. lxvii. 23).

Reply Obj. 3. The word or blasphemy spoken against the Holy Ghost is final impenitence, as Augustine states *(De Verb. Dom.* xi), which is altogether unpardonable, because after this life is ended, there is no pardon of sins. Or, if by the blasphemy against the Holy Ghost, we understand sin committed through certain malice, this means either that the blasphemy itself against the Holy Ghost is unpardonable, i.e. not easily pardonable, or that such a sin does not contain in itself any motive for pardon, or that for such a sin a man is punished both in this and in the next world, as we explained in the Second Part (II-II, Q. 14, A. 3).

SECOND ARTICLE

Whether Sin Can Be Pardoned without Penance?

We proceed thus to the Second Article:—

Objection 1. It would seem that sin can be pardoned without Penance. For the power of God is no less with regard to adults than with regard to children. But He pardons the sins of children without Penance. Therefore He also pardons adults without penance.

Obj. 2. Further, God did not bind His power to the sacraments. But Penance is a sacrament. Therefore by God's power sin can be pardoned without Penance.

Obj. 3. Further, God's mercy is greater than man's. Now man sometimes forgives another for offending him, without his repenting: wherefore our Lord commanded us (Matth. v. 44): *Love your enemies, do good to them that hate you.* Much more, therefore, does God pardon men for offending him, without their repenting.

On the contrary, The Lord said (Jerem. xviii. 8): *If that nation . . . shall repent of their evil* which they have done, *I also will repent of the evil that I have thought to do them,* so that, on the other hand, if man *do not penance,* it seems that God will not pardon him his sin.

I answer that, It is impossible for a mortal actual sin to be pardoned without penance, if we speak of penance as a virtue. For, as sin is an offense against God, He pardons sin in the same way as he pardons an offense committed against Him. Now an offense is directly opposed to grace, since one man is said to be offended with another, because he excludes him from his grace. Now, as stated in the Second Part (I-II, Q. 110, A. 1), the difference between the grace of God and the grace of man, is that the latter does not cause, but presupposes true or apparent goodness in him who is graced, whereas the grace of God causes goodness in the man who is graced, because the good-will of God, which is denoted by the word *grace,* is the cause of all created good. Hence it is possible for a man to pardon an offense, for which he is offended with someone, without any change in the latter's will; but it is impossible that God pardon a man for an offense, without his will being changed. Now the offense of mortal sin is due to man's will being turned away from God, through being turned to some mutable good. Consequently, for the pardon of this offense against God, it is necessary for man's will to be so changed as to turn to God and to renounce having turned to something else in the aforesaid manner, together with a purpose of amendment; all of which belongs to the nature of penance as a virtue. Therefore it is impossible for a sin to be pardoned anyone without penance as a virtue.

But the sacrament of Penance, as stated above (Q. 88, A. 3), is perfected by the priestly office of binding and loosing, without which God can forgive sins, even as Christ pardoned the adulterous woman, as related in Jo. viii, and the woman that was a sinner, as related in Luke vii, whose sins, however, He did not forgive without the virtue of penance: for as

Gregory states (*Hom. xxxiii, in Evang.*), *He drew inwardly by grace*, i.e. by penance, *her whom He received outwardly by His mercy.*

Reply Obj. 1. In children there is none but original sin, which consists, not in an actual disorder of the will, but in a habitual disorder of nature, as explained in the Second Part (I-II, Q. 82, A. 1), and so in them the forgiveness of sin is accompanied by a habitual change resulting from the infusion of grace and virtues, but not by an actual change. On the other hand, in the case of an adult, in whom there are actual sins, which consist in an actual disorder of the will, there is no remission of sins, even in Baptism, without an actual change of the will, which is the effect of Penance.

Reply Obj. 2. This argument takes Penance as a sacrament.

Reply Obj. 3. God's mercy is more powerful than man's, in that it moves man's will to repent, which man's mercy cannot do.

THIRD ARTICLE

Whether by Penance One Sin Can Be Pardoned without Another?

We proceed thus to the Third Article:—

Objection 1. It would seem that by Penance one sin can be pardoned without another. For it is written (Amos iv. 7): *I caused it to rain upon one city, and caused it not to rain upon another city; one piece was rained upon: and the piece whereupon I rained not, withered.* These words are expounded by Gregory, who says (*Hom. x, super Ezech.*): *When a man who hates his neighbor, breaks himself of other vices, rain falls on one part of the city, leaving the other part withered, for there are some men who, when they prune some vices, become much more rooted in others.* Therefore one sin can be forgiven by Penance, without another.

Obj. 2. Further, Ambrose in commenting on Ps. cxviii, *Blessed are the undefiled in the way*, after expounding verse 136 (*My eyes have sent forth springs of water*), says that *the first consolation is that God is mindful to have mercy; and the second, that He punishes, for although faith be wanting, punishment makes satisfaction and raises us up.* Therefore a man can be raised up from one sin, while the sin of unbelief remains.

Obj. 3. Further, when several things are not necessarily together, one can be removed without the other. Now it was stated in the Second Part (I-II, Q. 73, A. 1) that sins are not connected together, so that one sin can be without another. Therefore also one sin can

be taken away by Penance without another being taken away.

Obj. 4. Further, sins are the debts, for which we pray for pardon when we say in the Lord's Prayer: *Forgive us our trespasses*, etc. Now man sometimes forgives one debt without forgiving another. Therefore God also, by Penance, forgives one sin without another.

Obj. 5. Further, man's sins are forgiven him through the love of God, according to Jerem. xxxi. 3: *I have loved thee with an everlasting love, therefore have I drawn thee, taking pity on thee.* Now there is nothing to hinder God from loving a man in one respect, while being offended with him in another, even as He loves the sinner as regards his nature, while hating him for his sin. Therefore it seems possible for God, by Penance, to pardon one sin without another.

On the contrary, Augustine says in *De Pœnitentia:* * *There are many who repent having sinned, but not completely; for they except certain things which give them pleasure, forgetting that our Lord delivered from the devil the man who was both dumb and deaf, whereby He shows us that we are never healed unless it be from all sins.*

I answer that, It is impossible for Penance to take one sin away without another. First because sin is taken away by grace removing the offense against God. Wherefore it was stated in the Second Part (I-II, Q. 109, A. 7; Q. 113, A. 2) that without grace no sin can be forgiven. Now every mortal sin is opposed to grace and excludes it. Therefore it is impossible for one sin to be pardoned without another. Secondly, because, as shown above (A. 2) mortal sin cannot be forgiven without true Penance, to which it belongs to renounce sin, by reason of its being against God, which is common to all mortal sins: and where the same reason applies, the result will be the same. Consequently a man cannot be truly penitent, if he repent of one sin and not of another. For if one particular sin were displeasing to him, because it is against the love of God above all things (which motive is necessary for true repentance), it follows that he would repent of all. Whence it follows that it is impossible for one sin to be pardoned through Penance, without another. Thirdly, because this would be contrary to the perfection of God's mercy, since His works are perfect, as stated in Deut. xxxii. 4; wherefore whomsoever He pardons, He pardons altogether. Hence Augustine says (*loc. cit.*), that *it is irreverent and heretical to expect half a pardon from Him Who is just and justice itself.*

Reply Obj. 1. These words of Gregory do

---

* *De vera et falsa Pœnitentia,* the authorship of which is unknown.

not refer to the forgiveness of the guilt, but to the cessation from act, because sometimes a man who has been wont to commit several kinds of sin, renounces one and not the other; which is indeed due to God's assistance, but does not reach to the pardon of the sin.

Reply Obj. 2. In this saying of Ambrose *faith* cannot denote the faith whereby we believe in Christ, because, as Augustine says on Jo. xv. 22, *If I had not come, and spoken to them, they would not have sin* (viz. unbelief): *for this is the sin which contains all others:* but it stands for consciousness, because sometimes a man receives pardon for a sin of which he is not conscious, through the punishment which he bears patiently.

Reply Obj. 3. Although sins are not connected in so far as they turn towards a mutable good, yet they are connected in so far as they turn away from the immutable Good, which applies to all mortal sins in common; and it is thus that they have the character of an offense which needs to be removed by Penance.

Reply Obj. 4. Debt as regards external things, e.g. money, is not opposed to friendship through which the debt is pardoned; hence one debt can be condoned without another. On the other hand, the debt of sin is opposed to friendship, and so one sin or offense is not pardoned without another; for it would seem absurd for anyone to ask even a man to forgive him one offense and not another.

Reply Obj. 5. The love whereby God loves man's nature, does not ordain man to the good of glory from which man is excluded by any mortal sin; but the love of grace, whereby mortal sin is forgiven, ordains man to eternal life, according to Rom. vi. 23: *The grace of God* (is) *life everlasting.* Hence there is no comparison.

FOURTH ARTICLE

Whether the Debt of Punishment Remains after the Guilt Has Been Forgiven through Penance?

We proceed thus to the Fourth Article:—

Objection 1. It would seem that no debt of punishment remains after the guilt has been forgiven through Penance. For when the cause is removed, the effect is removed. But the guilt is the cause of the debt of punishment: since a man deserves to be punished because he has been guilty of a sin. Therefore when the sin has been forgiven, no debt of punishment can remain.

Obj. 2. Further, according to the Apostle (Rom. v) the gift of Christ is more effective than the sin of Adam. Now, by sinning, man incurs at the same time guilt and the debt of punishment. Much more therefore, by the

gift of grace, is the guilt forgiven and at the same time the debt of punishment remitted.

Obj. 3. Further, the forgiveness of sins is effected in Penance through the power of Christ's Passion, according to Rom. iii. 25: *Whom God hath proposed to be a propitiation, through faith in His Blood, . . . for the remission of former sins.* Now Christ's Passion made satisfaction sufficient for all sins, as stated above (QQ. 48, 49, 79, A. 5). Therefore after the guilt has been pardoned, no debt of punishment remains.

On the contrary, It is related (2 Kings xii. 13) that when David penitent had said to Nathan: *I have sinned against the Lord,* Nathan said to him: *The Lord also hath taken away thy sin, thou shalt not die. Nevertheless . . . the child that is born to thee shall surely die,* which was to punish him for the sin he had committed, as stated in the same place. Therefore a debt of some punishment remains after the guilt has been forgiven.

I answer that, As stated in the Second Part (I-II, Q. 87, A. 4), in mortal sin there are two things, namely, a turning from the immutable Good, and an inordinate turning to mutable good. Accordingly, in so fas as mortal sin turns away from the immutable Good, it induces a debt of eternal punishment, so that whosoever sins against the eternal Good should be punished eternally. Again, in so far as mortal sin turns inordinately to a mutable good, it gives rise to a debt of some punishment, because the disorder of guilt is not brought back to the order of justice, except by punishment: since it is just that he who has been too indulgent to his will, should suffer something against his will, for thus will equality be restored. Hence it is written (Apoc. xviii. 7): *As much as she hath glorified herself, and lived in delicacies, so much torment and sorrow give ye to her.*

Since, however, the turning to mutable good is finite, sin does not, in this respect, induce a debt of eternal punishment. Wherefore, if man turns inordinately to a mutable good, without turning from God, as happens in venial sins, he incurs a debt, not of eternal but of temporal punishment. Consequently when guilt is pardoned through grace, the soul ceases to be turned away from God, through being united to God by grace: so that at the same time, the debt of punishment is taken away, albeit a debt of some temporal punishment may yet remain.

Reply Obj. 1. Mortal sin both turns away from God and turns to a created good. But, as stated in the Second Part (I-II, Q. 71, A. 6), the turning away from God is as its form, while the turning to created good is as its matter. Now if the formal element of anything be removed, the species is taken away: thus, if you take away rational, you take away the human species. Consequently mortal sin is said to be pardoned from the very fact that, by means of grace, the aversion of the mind from God is taken away together with the debt of eternal punishment: and yet the material element remains, viz. the inordinate turning to a created good, for which a debt of temporal punishment is due.

Reply Obj. 2. As stated in the Second Part (I-II, Q. 109, AA. 7, 8; Q. 111, A. 2), it belongs to grace to operate in man by justifying him from sin, and to co-operate with man that his work may be rightly done. Consequently the forgiveness of guilt and of the debt of eternal punishment belongs to operating grace, while the remission of the debt of temporal punishment belongs to co-operating grace, in so far as man, by bearing punishment patiently with the help of Divine grace, is released also from the debt of temporal punishment. Consequently just as the effect of operating grace precedes the effect of co-operating grace, so too, the remission of guilt and of eternal punishment precedes the complete release from temporal punishment, since both are from grace, but the former, from grace alone, the latter, from grace and free-will.

Reply Obj. 3. Christ's Passion is of itself sufficient to remove all debt of punishment, not only eternal, but also temporal; and man is released from the debt of punishment according to the measure of his share in the power of Christ's Passion. Now in Baptism man shares the Power of Christ's Passion fully, since by water and the Spirit of Christ, he dies with Him to sin, and is born again in Him to a new life, so that, in Baptism, man receives the remission of all debt of punishment. In Penance, on the other hand, man shares in the power of Christ's Passion according to the measure of his own acts, which are the matter of Penance, as water is of Baptism, as stated above (Q. 84, AA. 1, 3). Wherefore the entire debt of punishment is not remitted at once after the first act of Penance, by which act the guilt is remitted, but only when all the acts of Penance have been completed.

FIFTH ARTICLE

Whether the Remnants of Sin Are Removed When a Mortal Sin Is Forgiven?

We proceed thus to the Fifth Article:—

Objection 1. It would seem that all the remnants of sin are removed when a mortal sin is forgiven. For Augustine says in *De Pœnitentia:** Our Lord never healed anyone without delivering him wholly; for He wholly*

healed the man on the Sabbath, since He delivered his body from all disease, and his soul from all taint.* Now the remnants of sin belong to the disease of sin. Therefore it does not seem possible for any remnants of sin to remain when the guilt has been pardoned.

Obj. 2. Further, according to Dionysius *(Div. Nom.* iv), *good is more efficacious than evil, since evil does not act save in virtue of some good.* Now, by sinning, man incurs the taint of sin all at once. Much more, therefore, by repenting, is he delivered also from all remnants of sin.

Obj. 3. Further, God's work is more efficacious than man's. Now by the exercise of good human works the remnants of contrary sins are removed. Much more, therefore, are they taken away by the remission of guilt, which is a work of God.

On the contrary, We read (Mark viii) that the blind man whom our Lord enlightened, was restored first of all to imperfect sight, wherefore he said *(verse* 24): *I see men, as it were trees, walking;* and afterwards he was restored perfectly, *so that he saw all things clearly.* Now the enlightenment of the blind man signifies the delivery of the sinner. Therefore after the first remission of sin, whereby the sinner is restored to spiritual sight, there still remain in him some remnants of his past sin.

I answer that, Mortal sin, in so far as it turns inordinately to a mutable good, produces in the soul a certain disposition, or even a habit, if the acts be repeated frequently. Now it has been said above (A. 4) that the guilt of mortal sin is pardoned through grace removing the aversion of the mind from God. Nevertheless when that which is on the part of the aversion has been taken away by grace, that which is on the part of the inordinate turning to a mutable good can remain, since this may happen to be without the other, as stated above (A. 4). Consequently, there is no reason why, after the guilt has been forgiven, the dispositions caused by preceding acts should not remain, which are called the remnants of sin. Yet they remain weakened and diminished, so as not to domineer over man, and they are after the manner of dispositions rather than of habits, like the *fomes* which remains after Baptism.

Reply Obj. 1. God heals the whole man perfectly; but sometimes suddenly, as Peter's mother-in-law was restored at once to perfect health, so that *rising she ministered to them* (Luke iv. 39), and sometimes by degrees, as we said above (Q. 44, A. 3, *ad* 2) about the blind man who was restored to sight (Matth

* *De vera et falsa Pœnitentia,* the authorship of which is unknown.

viii). And so too, He sometimes turns the heart of man with such power, that it receives at once perfect spiritual health, not only the guilt being pardoned, but all remnants of sin being removed, as was the case with Magdalen (Luke vii) ; whereas at other times He sometimes first pardons the guilt by operating grace, and afterwards, by co-operating grace, removes the remnants of sin by degrees.

Reply Obj. 2. Sin too, sometimes induces at once a weak disposition, such as is the result of one act, and sometimes a stronger disposition, the result of many acts.

Reply Obj. 3. One human act does not remove all the remnants of sin, because, as stated in the *Predicaments (Categor.* viii) *a vicious man by doing good works will make but little progress so as to be any better, but if he continue in good practice, he will end in being good as to acquired virtue.* But God's grace does this much more effectively, whether by one or by several acts.

SIXTH ARTICLE

Whether the Forgiveness of Guilt Is an Effect of Penance?

We proceed thus to the Sixth Article:—

Objection 1. It would seem that the forgiveness of guilt is not an effect of penance as a virtue. For penance is said to be a virtue, in so far as it is a principle of a human action. But human action does nothing towards the remission of guilt, since this is an effect of operating grace. Therefore the forgiveness of guilt is not an effect of penance as a virtue.

Obj. 2. Further, certain other virtues are more excellent than penance. But the forgiveness of sin is not said to be the effect of any other virtue. Neither, therefore, is it the effect of penance as a virtue.

Obj. 3. Further, there is no forgiveness of sin except through the power of Christ's Passion, according to Heb. ix. 22: *Without shedding of blood there is no remission.* Now Penance, as a sacrament, produces its effect through the power of Christ's Passion, even as the other sacraments do, as was shown above (Q. 62, AA. 4, 5). Therefore the forgiveness of sin is the effect of Penance, not as a virtue, but as a sacrament.

On the contrary, Properly speaking, the cause of a thing is that without which it cannot be, since every defect depends on its cause. Now forgiveness of sin can come from God without the sacrament of Penance, but not without the virtue of penance, as stated above (Q. 84, A. 5, *ad* 3; Q. 85, A. 2); so that, even before the sacraments of the New Law were

instituted, God pardoned the sins of the penitent. Therefore the forgiveness of sin is chiefly the effect of penance as a virtue.

I answer that, Penance is a virtue in so far as it is a principle of certain human acts. Now the human acts, which are performed by the sinner, are the material element in the sacrament of Penance. Moreover every sacrament produces its effect, in virtue not only of its form, but also of its matter; because both these together make the one sacrament, as stated above (Q. 60, A. 6, *ad* 2, A. 7). Hence in Baptism forgiveness of sin is effected, in virtue not only of the form (but also of the matter, viz. water, albeit chiefly in virtue of the form)* from which the water receives its power—and, similarly, the forgiveness of sin is the effect of Penance, chiefly by the power of the keys, which is vested in the ministers, who furnish the formal part of the sacrament, as stated above (Q. 84, A. 3), and secondarily by the instrumentality of those acts of the penitent which pertain to the virtue of penance, but only in so far as such acts are, in some way, subordinate to the keys of the Church. Accordingly it is evident that the forgiveness of sin is the effect of penance as a virtue, but still more of Penance as a sacrament.

Reply Obj. 1. The effect of operating grace is the justification of the ungodly (as stated in the Second Part, I-II, Q. 113), wherein there is, as was there stated (AA. 1, 2, 3), not only infusion of grace and forgiveness of sin, but also a movement of the free-will towards God, which is an act of faith quickened by charity, and a movement of the free-will against sin, which is the act of penance. Yet these human acts are there as the effects of operating grace, and are produced at the same time as the forgiveness of sin. Consequently the forgiveness of sin does not take place without an act of the virtue of penance, although it is the effect of operating grace.

Reply Obj. 2. In the justification of the ungodly there is not only an act of penance, but also an act of faith, as stated above (*ad* 1: I-II, Q. 113, A. 4). Wherefore the forgiveness of sin is accounted the effect not only of the virtue of penance, but also, and that chiefly, of faith and charity.

Reply Obj. 3. The act of the virtue of penance is subordinate to Christ's Passion both by faith, and by its relation to the keys of the Church; and so, in both ways, it causes the forgiveness of sin, by the power of Christ's Passion.

To the argument advanced in the contrary sense we reply that the act of the virtue of penance is necessary for the forgiveness of

* The words in brackets are omitted in the Leonine edition.

sin, through being an inseparable effect of grace, whereby chiefly is sin pardoned, and which produces its effect in all the sacraments. Consequently it only follows that grace is a higher cause of the forgiveness of sin than the sacrament of Penance. Moreover, it must be observed that, under the Old Law and the law of nature, there was a sacrament of Penance after a fashion, as stated above (Q. 84, A. 7, *ad* 2).

QUESTION 87

Of the Remission of Venial Sin

(In Four Articles)

WE must now consider the forgiveness of venial sins, under which head there are four points of inquiry: (1) Whether venial sin can be forgiven without Penance? (2) Whether it can be forgiven without the infusion of grace? (3) Whether venial sins are forgiven by the sprinkling of holy water, a bishop's blessing, the beating of the breast, the Lord's Prayer, and the like? (4) Whether a venial sin can be taken away without a mortal sin?

FIRST ARTICLE

Whether Venial Sin Can Be Forgiven without Penance?

We proceed thus to the First Article:—

Objection 1. It would seem that venial sin can be forgiven without penance. For, as stated above (Q. 84, A. 10, *ad* 4), it is essential to true penance that man should not only sorrow for his past sins, but also that he should purpose to avoid them for the future. Now venial sins are forgiven without any such purpose, for it is certain that man cannot lead the present life without committing venial sins. Therefore venial sins can be forgiven without penance.

Obj. 2. Further, there is no penance without actual displeasure at one's sins. But venial sins can be taken away without any actual displeasure at them, as would be the case if a man were to be killed in his sleep, for Christ's sake, since he would go to heaven at once, which would not happen if his venial sins remained. Therefore venial sins can be forgiven without penance.

Obj. 3. Further, venial sins are contrary to the fervor of charity, as stated in the Second Part (II-II, Q. 24, A. 10). Now one contrary is removed by another. Therefore forgiveness of venial sins is caused by the fervor of charity, which may be without actual displeasure at venial sin.

On the contrary, Augustine says in *De Pœnitentia,** that *there is a penance which is done for venial sins in the Church every day,* which would be useless if venial sins could be forgiven without Penance.

I answer that, Forgiveness of sin, as stated above (Q. 86, A. 2), is effected by man being united to God from Whom sin separates him in some way. Now this separation is made complete by mortal sin, and incomplete by venial sin: because, by mortal sin, the mind through acting against charity is altogether turned away from God; whereas by venial sin man's affections are clogged, so that they are slow in tending towards God. Consequently both kinds of sin are taken away by penance, because by both of them man's will is disordered through turning inordinately to a created good; for just as mortal sin cannot be forgiven so long as the will is attached to sin, so neither can venial sin, because while the cause remains, the effect remains.

Yet a more perfect penance is requisite for the forgiveness of mortal sin, namely that man should detest actually the mortal sin which he committed, so far as lies in his power, that is to say, he should endeavor to remember each single mortal sin, in order to detest each one. But this is not required for the forgiveness of venial sins; although it does not suffice to have habitual displeasure, which is included in the habit of charity or of penance as a virtue, since then venial sin would be incompatible with charity, which is evidently untrue. Consequently it is necessary to have a certain virtual displeasure, so that, for instance, a man's affections so tend to God and Divine things, that whatever might happen to him to hamper that tendency would be displeasing to him, and would grieve him, were he to commit it, even though he were not to think of it actually: and this is not sufficient for the remission of mortal sin, except as regards those sins which he fails to remember after a careful examination.

Reply Obj. 1. When man is in a state of grace, he can avoid all mortal sins, and each single one; and he can avoid each single venial sin, but not all, as was explained in the Second Part (I-II, Q. 74, A. 3, *ad* 2: Q. 109, A. 8). Consequently penance for mortal sins requires man to purpose abstaining from mortal sins, all and each; whereas penance for venial sins requires man to purpose abstaining from each,

* *De vera et falsa Pœnitentia,* the authorship of which is unknown.

but not from all, because the weakness of this life does not allow of this. Nevertheless he needs to have the purpose of taking steps to commit fewer venial sins, else he would be in danger of falling back, if he gave up the desire of going forward, or of removing the obstacles to spiritual progress, such as venial sins are.

Reply Obj. 2. Death for Christ's sake, as stated above (Q. 66, A. 11), obtains the power of Baptism, wherefore it washes away all sin, both venial and mortal, unless it find the will attached to sin.

Reply Obj. 3. The fervor of charity implies virtual displeasure at venial sins, as stated above (Q. 79, A. 4).

SECOND ARTICLE

Whether Infusion of Grace Is Necessary for the Remission of Venial Sins?

We proceed thus to the Second Article:—

Objection 1. It would seem that infusion of grace is necessary for the remission of venial sins. Because an effect is not produced without its proper cause. Now the proper cause of the remission of sins is grace; for man's sins are not forgiven through his own merits; wherefore it is written (Eph. ii. 4, 5): *God, Who is rich in mercy, for His exceeding charity, wherewith He loved us, even when we were dead in sins, hath quickened us together in Christ, by Whose grace you are saved.* Therefore venial sins are not forgiven without infusion of grace.

Obj. 2. Further, venial sins are not forgiven without Penance. Now grace is infused, in Penance as in the other sacraments of the New Law. Therefore venial sins are not forgiven without infusion of grace.

Obj. 3. Further, venial sin produces a stain on the soul. Now a stain is not removed save by grace which is the spiritual beauty of the soul. Therefore it seems that venial sins are not forgiven without infusion of grace.

On the contrary, The advent of venial sin neither destroys nor diminishes grace, as stated in the Second Part (II-II, Q. 24, A. 10). Therefore, in like manner, an infusion of grace is not necessary in order to remove venial sin.

I answer that, Each thing is removed by its contrary. But venial sin is not contrary to habitual grace or charity, but hampers its act, through man being too much attached to a created good, albeit not in opposition to God, as stated in the Second Part (I-II, Q. 88, A. 1; II-II, Q. 24, A. 10). Therefore, in order that venial sin be removed, it is not necessary that habitual grace be infused, but a movement of grace or charity suffices for its forgiveness. Nevertheless, since in those who have the

use of free-will (in whom alone can there be venial sins), there can be no infusion of grace without an actual movement of the free-will towards God and against sin, consequently whenever grace is infused anew, venial sins are forgiven.

Reply Obj. 1. Even the forgiveness of venial sins is an effect of grace, in virtue of the act which grace produces anew, but not through any habit infused anew into the soul.

Reply Obj. 2. Venial sin is never forgiven without some act, explicit or implicit, of the virtue of penance, as stated above (A. 1): it can, however, be forgiven without the sacrament of Penance, which is formally perfected by the priestly absolution, as stated above (Q. 87, A. 2). Hence it does not follow that infusion of grace is required for the forgiveness of venial sin, for although this infusion takes place in every sacrament, it does not occur in every act of virtue.

Reply Obj. 3. Just as there are two kinds of bodily stain, one consisting in the privation of something required for beauty, e.g. the right color or the due proportion of members, and another by the introduction of some hindrance to beauty, e.g. mud or dust; so too, a stain is put on the soul, in one way, by the privation of the beauty of grace through mortal sin, in another, by the inordinate inclination of the affections to some temporal thing, and this is the result of venial sin. Consequently, an infusion of grace is necessary for the removal of mortal sin, but in order to remove venial sin, it is necessary to have a movement proceeding from grace, removing the inordinate attachment to the temporal thing.

THIRD ARTICLE

Whether Venial Sins Are Removed by the Sprinkling of Holy Water and the Like?

We proceed thus to the Third Article:—

Objection 1. It would seem that venial sins are not removed by the sprinkling of holy water, a bishop's blessing, and the like. For venial sins are not forgiven without Penance, as stated above (A. 1). But Penance suffices by itself for the remission of venial sins. Therefore the above have nothing to do with the remission of venial sins.

Obj. 2. Further, each of the above bears the same relation to one venial sin as to all. If therefore, by means of one of them, some venial sin is remitted, it follows that in like manner all are remitted, so that by beating his breast once, or by being sprinkled once with holy water, a man would be delivered from all his venial sins, which seems unreasonable.

Obj. 3. Further, venial sins occasion a debt of some punishment, albeit temporal; for it is written (1 Cor. iii. 12, 15) of him that builds up *wood, hay, stubble* that *he shall be saved, yet so as by fire.* Now the above things whereby venial sins are said to be taken away, contain either no punishment at all, or very little. Therefore they do not suffice for the full remission of venial sins.

On the contrary, Augustine says in *De Pœnitentia** that *for our slight sins we strike our breasts, and say: Forgive us our trespasses,* and so it seems that striking one's breast, and the Lord's Prayer cause the remission of venial sins: and the same seems to apply to the other things.

I answer that, As stated above (A. 2), no infusion of fresh grace is required for the forgiveness of a venial sin, but it is enough to have an act proceeding from grace, in detestation of that venial sin, either explicit or at least implicit, as when one is moved fervently to God. Hence, for three reasons, certain things cause the remission of venial sins: first, because they imply the infusion of grace, since the infusion of grace removes venial sins, as stated above (A. 2); and so, by the Eucharist, Extreme Unction, and by all the sacraments of the New Law without exception, wherein grace is conferred, venial sins are remitted. Secondly, because they imply a movement of detestation for sin, and in this way the general confession,† the beating of one's breast, and the Lord's Prayer conduce to the remission of venial sins, for we ask in the Lord's Prayer: *Forgive us our trespasses.* Thirdly, because they include a movement of reverence for God and Divine things; and in this way a bishop's blessing, the sprinkling of holy water, any sacramental anointing, a prayer said in a dedicated church, and anything else of the kind, conduce to the remission of venial sins.

Reply Obj. 1. All these things cause the remission of venial sins, in so far as they incline the soul to the movement of penance, viz., the implicit or explicit detestation of one's sins.

Reply Obj. 2. All these things, so far as they are concerned, conduce to the remission of all venial sins: but the remission may be hindered as regards certain venial sins, to which the mind is still actually attached, even as insincerity sometimes impedes the effect of Baptism.

Reply Obj. 3. By the above things, venial sins are indeed taken away as regards the guilt, both because those things are a kind of satisfaction, and through the virtue of charity whose movement is aroused by such things.

* Cf. *Hom.* 30 inter 1.: Ep. cclxv. † i.e. the recital of the *Confiteor* or of an act of contrition.

Yet it does not always happen that, by means of each one, the whole guilt of punishment is taken away, because, in that case, whoever was entirely free from mortal sin, would go straight to heaven if sprinkled with holy water: but the debt of punishment is remitted by means of the above, according to the movement of fervor towards God, which fervor is aroused by such things, sometimes more, sometimes less.

FOURTH ARTICLE

Whether Venial Sin Can be Taken Away without Mortal Sin?

We proceed thus to the Fourth Article:—

Objection 1. It would seem that venial sin can be taken away without mortal sin. For, on Jo. viii. 7: *He that is without sin among you, let him first cast a stone at her,* a gloss says that *all those men were in a state of mortal sin: for venial offenses were forgiven them through the legal ceremonies.* Therefore venial sin can be taken away without mortal sin.

Obj. 2. Further, no infusion of grace is required for the remission of venial sin: but it is required for the forgiveness of mortal sin. Therefore venial sin can be taken away without mortal sin.

Obj. 3. Further, a venial sin differs from a mortal sin more than from another venial sin. But one venial sin can be pardoned without another, as stated above (A. 3, *ad* 2; Q. 87, A. 3). Therefore a venial sin can be taken away without a mortal sin.

On the contrary, It is written (Matth. v. 26): *Amen I say to thee, thou shalt not go out from thence,* viz., from the prison, into which a man is cast for mortal sin, *till thou repay the last farthing,* by which venial sin is denoted. Therefore a venial sin is not forgiven without mortal sin.

I answer that, As stated above (Q. 87, A. 3), there is no remission of any sin whatever except by the power of grace, because, as the Apostle declares (Rom. iv. 8), it is owing to God's grace that He does not impute sin to a man, which a gloss on that passage expounds as referring to venial sin. Now he that is in a state of mortal sin is without the grace of God. Therefore no venial sin is forgiven him.

Reply Obj. 1. Venial offenses, in the passage quoted, denote the irregularities or uncleannesses which men contracted in accordance with the Law.

Reply Obj. 2. Although no new infusion of habitual grace is requisite for the remission of venial sin, yet it is necessary to exercise some act of grace, which cannot be in one who is a subject of mortal sin.

Reply Obj. 3. Venial sin does not preclude every act of grace whereby all venial sins can be removed; whereas mortal sin excludes altogether the habit of grace, without which no sin, either mortal or venial, is remitted. Hence the comparison fails.

QUESTION 88

Of the Return of Sins Which Have Been Taken Away by Penance

(In Four Articles)

WE must now consider the return of sins which have been taken away by Penance: under which head there are four points of inquiry: (1) Whether sins which have been taken away by Penance return simply through a subsequent sin? (2) Whether more specially as regards certain sins they return, in a way, on account of ingratitude? (3) Whether the debt of punishment remains the same for sins thus returned? (4) Whether this ingratitude, on account of which sins return, is a special sin?

FIRST ARTICLE

Whether Sins Once Forgiven Return through a Subsequent Sin?

We proceed thus to the First Article:—

Objection 1. It would seem that sins once forgiven return through a subsequent sin. For Augustine says (*De Bapt. contra Donat.,* i. 12): *Our Lord teaches most explicitly in the Gospel that sins which have been forgiven return, when fraternal charity ceases, in the example of the servant from whom his master exacted the payment of the debt already forgiven, because he had refused to forgive the debt of his fellow-servant.* Now fraternal charity is destroyed through each mortal sin. Therefore sins already taken away through Penance, return through each subsequent mortal sin.

Obj. 2. Further, on Luke xi. 24, *I will return into my house, whence I came out,* Bede says: *This verse should make us tremble, we should not endeavor to explain it away lest through carelessness we give place to the sin which we thought to have been taken away, and become its slave once more.* Now this would not be so unless it returned. Therefore a sin returns after once being taken away by Penance.

Obj. 3. Further, the Lord said (Ezech. xviii. 24): *If the just man turn himself away from his justice, and do iniquity . . . all his justices which he hath done, shall not be remembered.* Now among the other *justices* which he had done, is also his previous penance, since it was said above (Q. 85, A. 3) that penance is a part of justice. Therefore

* Prosper, *Responsiones ad Capitula Gallorum,* ii.

when one who has done penance, sins, his previous penance, whereby he received forgiveness of his sins, is not imputed to him. Therefore his sins return.

Obj. 4. Further, past sins are covered by grace, as the Apostle declares (Rom. iv. 7) where he quotes Ps. xxxi. 1: *Blessed are they whose iniquities are forgiven, and whose sins are covered.* But a subsequent mortal sin takes away grace. Therefore the sins committed previously, become uncovered: and so, seemingly, they return.

On the contrary, The Apostle says (Rom. xi. 29): *The gifts and the calling of God are without repentance.* Now the penitent's sins are taken away by a gift of God. Therefore the sins which have been taken away do not return through a subsequent sin, as though God repented His gift of forgiveness.

Moreover, Augustine says (*Lib. Resp. Prosperi,* i*): *When he that turns away from Christ, comes to the end of this life a stranger to grace, whither does he go, except to perdition? Yet he does not fall back into that which had been forgiven, nor will he be condemned for original sin.*

I answer that, As stated above (Q. 86, A. 4), mortal sin contains two things, aversion from God and adherence to a created good. Now, in mortal sin, whatever attaches to the aversion, is, considered in itself, common to all mortal sins, since man turns away from God by every mortal sin, so that, in consequence, the stain resulting from the privation of grace, and the debt of everlasting punishment are common to all mortal sins. This is what is meant by what is written (James ii. 10): *Whosoever . . . shall offend in one point, is become guilty of all.* On the other hand, as regards their adherence they are different from, and sometimes contrary to one another. Hence it is evident, that on the part of the adherence, a subsequent mortal sin does not cause the return of mortal sins previously dispelled, else it would follow that by a sin of wastefulness a man would be brought back to the habit or disposition of avarice previously dispelled, so that one contrary would be the cause of another, which is impossible. But if in mortal sins we consider that which attaches to the aversion absolutely, then a subsequent mortal sin [causes the return of that which was comprised in the mortal sins before they were pardoned, in so far as the subsequent mortal sin]* deprives man of grace, and makes him deserving of everlasting punishment, just as he was before. Nevertheless, since the aversion of mortal sin is [in a way, caused by the adherence, those things which attach to the aversion are]* diversified somewhat in relation to various adherences, as it were to various causes, so that there will be a different aversion, a different stain, a different debt of punishment, according to the different acts of mortal sin from which they arise; hence the question is moved whether the stain and the debt of eternal punishment, as caused by acts of sins previously pardoned, return through a subsequent mortal sin.

Accordingly some have maintained that they return simply even in this way. But this is impossible, because what God has done cannot be undone by the work of man. Now the pardon of the previous sins was a work of Divine mercy, so that it cannot be undone by man's subsequent sin, according to Rom. iii. 3: *Shall their unbelief make the faith of God without effect?*

Wherefore others who maintained the possibility of sins returning, said that God pardons the sins of a penitent who will afterwards sin again, not according to His foreknowledge, but only according to His present justice: since He foresees that He will punish such a man eternally for his sins, and yet, by His grace, He makes him righteous for the present. But this cannot stand: because if a cause be placed absolutely, its effect is placed absolutely; so that if the remission of sins were effected by grace and the sacraments of grace, not absolutely but under some condition dependent on some future event, it would follow that grace and the sacraments of grace are not the sufficient causes of the remission of sins, which is erroneous, as being derogatory to God's grace.

Consequently it is in no way possible for the stain of past sins and the debt of punishment incurred thereby, to return, as caused by those acts. Yet it may happen that a subsequent sinful act virtually contains the debt of punishment due to the previous sin, in so far as when a man sins a second time, for this very reason he seems to sin more grievously than before, as stated in Rom. ii. 5: *According to thy hardness and impenitent heart, thou treasurest up to thyself wrath against the day of wrath,* from the mere fact, namely, that God's goodness, which waits for us to repent, is despised. And so much the more is God's

goodness despised, if the first sin is committed a second time after having been forgiven, as it is a greater favor for the sin to be forgiven than for the sinner to be endured.

Accordingly the sin which follows repentance brings back, in a sense, the debt of punishment due to the sins previously forgiven, not as caused by those sins already forgiven, but as caused by this last sin being committed, on account of its being aggravated in view of those previous sins. This means that those sins return, not simply, but in a restricted sense, viz., in so far as they are virtually contained in the subsequent sin.

Reply Obj. 1. This saying of Augustine seems to refer to the return of sins as to the debt of eternal punishment considered in itself, namely, that he who sins after doing penance incurs a debt of eternal punishment, just as before, but not altogether for the same *reason. Wherefore Augustine,*† *after saying* (*Lib. Resp. Prosperi,* i) that *he does not fall back into that which was forgiven, nor will he be condemned for original sin,* adds: *Nevertheless, for these last sins he will be condemned to the same death, which he deserved to suffer for the former,* because he incurs the punishment of eternal death which he deserved for his previous sins.

Reply Obj. 2. By these words Bede means that the guilt already forgiven enslaves man, not by the return of his former debt of punishment, but by the repetition of his act.

Reply Obj. 3. The effect of a subsequent sin is that the former *justices* are not remembered, in so far as they were deserving of eternal life, but not in so far as they were a hindrance to sin. Consequently if a man sins mortally after making restitution, he does not become guilty as though he had not paid back what he owed; and much less is penance previously done forgotten as to the pardon of the guilt, since this is the work of God rather than of man.

Reply Obj. 4. Grace removes the stain and the debt of eternal punishment simply; but it covers the past sinful acts, lest, on their account, God deprive man of grace, and judge him deserving of eternal punishment; and what grace has once done, endures for ever.

SECOND ARTICLE

Whether Sins That Have Been Forgiven, Return through Ingratitude Which Is Shown Especially in Four Kinds of Sin?

We proceed thus to the Second Article:—

Objection 1. It would seem that sins do not return through ingratitude, which is shown especially in four kinds of sin, viz., hatred of

* The words in brackets are omitted in the Leonine edition.   † See footnote, p. 2547.

one's neighbor, apostasy from faith, contempt of confession and regret for past repentance, and which have been expressed in the following verse:

> Fratres odit, apostata fit, spernitque, fateri,
> Poenituisse piget, pristina culpa redit.

For the more grievous the sin committed against God after one has received the grace of pardon, the greater the ingratitude. But there are sins more grievous than these, such as blasphemy against God, and the sin against the Holy Ghost. Therefore it seems that sins already pardoned do not return through ingratitude as manifested in these sins, any more than as shown in other sins.

Obj. 2. Further, Rabanus says: *God delivered the wicked servant to the torturers, until he should pay the whole debt, because a man will be deemed punishable not only for the sins he commits after Baptism, but also for original sin which was taken away when he was baptized.* Now venial sins are reckoned among our debts, since we pray in their regard: *Forgive us our trespasses (debita).* Therefore they too return through ingratitude; and, in like manner seemingly, sins already pardoned return through venial sins, and not only through those sins mentioned above.

Obj. 3. Further, ingratitude is all the greater, according as one sins after receiving a greater favor. Now innocence whereby one avoids sin is a Divine favor, for Augustine says *(Conf.* ii): *Whatever sins I have avoided committing, I owe it to Thy grace.* Now innocence is a greater gift, than even the forgiveness of all sins. Therefore the first sin committed after innocence is no less an ingratitude to God, than a sin committed after repentance, so that seemingly ingratitude in respect of the aforesaid sins is not the chief cause of sins returning.

On the contrary, Gregory says *(Moral.* xviii*): *It is evident from the words of the Gospel that if we do not forgive from our hearts the offenses committed against us, we become once more accountable for what we rejoiced in as forgiven through Penance:* so that ingratitude implied in the hatred of one's brother is a special cause of the return of sins already forgiven: and the same seems to apply to the others.

I answer that, As stated above (A. 1), sins pardoned through Penance are said to return, in so far as their debt of punishment, by reason of ingratitude, is virtually contained in the subsequent sin. Now one may be guilty of ingratitude in two ways: first by doing something against the favor received, and, in this way, man is ungrateful to God in every mortal

* Cf. *Dial* iv.

sin whereby he offends God Who forgave his sins, so that by every subsequent mortal sin, the sins previously pardoned return, on account of the ingratitude. Secondly, one is guilty of ingratitude, by doing something not only against the favor itself, but also against the form of the favor received. If this form be considered on the part of the benefactor, it is the remission of something due to him; wherefore he who does not forgive his brother when he asks pardon, and persists in his hatred, acts against this form. If, however, this form be taken in regard to the penitent who receives this favor, we find on his part a twofold movement of the free-will. The first is the movement of the free-will towards God, and is an act of faith quickened by charity; and against this a man acts by apostatizing from the faith. The second is a movement of the free-will against sin, and is the act of penance. This act consists first, as we have stated above (Q. 85, AA. 2, 5) in man's detestation of his past sins; and against this a man acts when he regrets having done penance. Secondly, the act of penance consists in the penitent purposing to subject himself to the keys of the Church by confession, according to Ps. xxxi. 5: *I said: I will confess against myself my injustice to the Lord: and Thou hast forgiven the wickedness of my sin:* and against this a man acts when he scorns to confess as he had purposed to do.

Accordingly it is said that the ingratitude of sinners is a special cause of the return of sins previously forgiven.

Reply Obj. 1. This is not said of these sins as though they were more grievous than others, but because they are more directly opposed to the favor of the forgiveness of sin.

Reply Obj. 2. Even venial sins and original sin return in the way explained above, just as mortal sins do, in so far as the favor conferred by God in forgiving those sins is despised. A man does not, however, incur ingratitude by committing a venial sin, because by sinning venially man does not act against God, but apart from Him, wherefore venial sins nowise cause the return of sins already forgiven.

Reply Obj. 3. A favor can be weighed in two ways. First by the quantity of the favor itself, and in this way innocence is a greater favor from God than penance, which is called the second plank after shipwreck (cf. Q. 84, A. 6). Secondly, a favor may be weighed with regard to the recipient, who is less worthy, wherefore a greater favor is bestowed on him, so that he is the more ungrateful if he scorns it. In this way the favor of the pardon of sins is greater when bestowed on one who is altogether unworthy, so that the ingratitude which follows is all the greater.

THIRD ARTICLE

Whether the Debt of Punishment That Arises through Ingratitude in Respect of a Subsequent Sin Is As Great As That of the Sins Previously Pardoned?

We proceed thus to the Third Article:—

Objection 1. It would seem that the debt of punishment arising through ingratitude in respect of a subsequent sin is as great as that of the sins previously pardoned. Because the greatness of the favor of the pardon of sins is according to the greatness of the sin pardoned, and so too, in consequence, is the greatness of the ingratitude whereby this favor is scorned. But the greatness of the consequent debt of punishment is in accord with the greatness of the ingratitude. Therefore the debt of punishment arising through ingratitude in respect of a subsequent sin is as great as the debt of punishment due for all the previous sins.

Obj. 2. Further, it is a greater sin to offend God than to offend man. But a slave who is freed by his master returns to the same state of slavery from which he was freed, or even to a worse state. Much more therefore he that sins against God after being freed from sin, returns to the debt of as great a punishment as he had incurred before.

Obj. 3. Further, it is written (Matth. xviii. 34) that *his lord being angry, delivered him* (whose sins returned to him on account of his ingratitude) *to the torturers, until he paid all the debt.* But this would not be so unless the debt of punishment incurred through ingratitude were as great as that incurred through all previous sins. Therefore an equal debt of punishment returns through ingratitude.

On the contrary, It is written (Deut. xxv. 2): *According to the measure of the sin shall the measure also of the stripes be,* whence it is evident that a great debt of punishment does not arise from a slight sin. But sometimes a subsequent mortal sin is much less grievous than any one of those previously pardoned. Therefore the debt of punishment incurred through subsequent sins is not equal to that of sins previously forgiven.

I answer that, Some have maintained that the debt of punishment incurred through ingratitude in respect of a subsequent sin is equal to that of the sins previously pardoned, in addition to the debt proper to this subsequent sin. But there is no need for this, because, as stated above (A. 1), the debt of punishment incurred by previous sins does not return on account of a subsequent sin, as resulting from the acts of the subsequent sin. Wherefore the amount of the debt that returns must be according to the gravity of the subsequent sin.

It is possible, however, for the gravity of the subsequent sin to equal the gravity of all previous sins. But it need not always be so, whether we speak of the gravity which a sin has from its species (since the subsequent sin may be one of simple fornication, while the previous sins were adulteries, murders, or sacrileges); or of the gravity which it incurs through the ingratitude connected with it. For it is not necessary that the measure of ingratitude should be exactly equal to the measure of the favor received, which latter is measured according to the greatness of the sins previously pardoned. Because it may happen that in respect of the same favor, one man is very ungrateful, either on account of the intensity of his scorn for the favor received, or on account of the gravity of the offense committed against the benefactor, while another man is slightly ungrateful, either because his scorn is less intense, or because his offense against the benefactor is less grave. But the measure of ingratitude is proportionately equal to the measure of the favor received: for supposing an equal contempt of the favor, or an equal offense against the benefactor, the ingratitude will be so much the greater, as the favor received is greater.

Hence it is evident that the debt of punishment incurred by a subsequent sin need not always be equal to that of previous sins; but it must be in proportion thereto, so that the more numerous or the greater the sins previously pardoned, the greater must be the debt of punishment incurred by any subsequent mortal sin whatever.

Reply Obj. 1. The favor of the pardon of sins takes its absolute quantity from the quantity of the sins previously pardoned: but the sin of ingratitude does not take its absolute quantity from the measure of the favor bestowed, but from the measure of the contempt or of the offense, as stated above: and so the objection does not prove.

Reply Obj. 2. A slave who has been given his freedom is not brought back to his previous state of slavery for any kind of ingratitude, but only when this is grave.

Reply Obj. 3. He whose forgiven sins return to him on account of subsequent ingratitude, incurs the debt for all, in so far as the measure of his previous sins is contained proportionally in his subsequent ingratitude, but not absolutely, as stated above.

FOURTH ARTICLE

Whether the Ingratitude Whereby a Subsequent Sin Causes the Return of Previous Sins, Is a Special Sin?

We proceed thus to the Fourth Article:—

Objection 1. It would seem that the ingratitude, whereby a subsequent sin causes the return of sins previously forgiven, is a special sin. For the giving of thanks belongs to counterpassion which is a necessary condition of justice, as the Philosopher shows *(Ethic.* v. 5). But justice is a special virtue. Therefore this ingratitude is a special sin.

Obj. 2. Further, Tully says *(De Inv. Rhetor.* ii) that thanksgiving is a special virtue. But ingratitude is opposed to thanksgiving. Therefore ingratitude is a special sin.

Obj. 3. Further, a special effect proceeds from a special cause. Now ingratitude has a special effect, viz. the return, after a fashion, of sins already forgiven. Therefore ingratitude is a special sin.

On the contrary, That which is a sequel to every sin is not a special sin. Now by any mortal sin whatever, a man becomes ungrateful to God, as evidenced from what has been said (A. 1). Therefore ingratitude is not a special sin.

I answer that, The ingratitude of the sinner is sometimes a special sin; and sometimes it is not, but a circumstance arising from all mortal sins in common committed against God. For a sin takes its species according to the sinner's intention, wherefore the Philosopher says *(Ethic.* v. 2) that *he who commits adultery in order to steal is a thief rather than an adulterer.*

If, therefore, a sinner commits a sin in contempt of God and of the favor received from Him, that sin is drawn to the species of ingratitude, and in this way a sinner's ingratitude is a special sin. If, however, a man, while intending to commit a sin, e.g. murder or adultery, is not withheld from it on account of its implying contempt of God, his ingratitude will not be a special sin, but will be drawn to the species of the other sin, as a circumstance thereof. And, as Augustine observes *(De Nat. et Grat.* xxix), not every sin is committed through contempt, although every sin implies contempt of God in His commandments. Therefore it is evident that the sinner's ingratitude is sometimes a special sin, sometimes not.

This suffices for the *Replies* to the *Objections:* for the first (three) objections prove that ingratitude is in itself a special sin; while the last objection proves that ingratitude, as included in every sin, is not a special sin.

QUESTION 89

Of the Recovery of Virtue by Means of Penance

(In Six Articles)

WE must now consider the recovery of virtues by means of Penance, under which head there are six points of inquiry: (1) Whether virtues are restored through Penance? (2) Whether they are restored in equal measure? (3) Whether equal dignity is restored to the penitent? (4) Whether works of virtue are deadened by subsequent sin? (5) Whether works deadened by sin revive through Penance? (6) Whether dead works, i.e. works that are done without charity, are quickened by Penance?

FIRST ARTICLE

Whether the Virtues Are Restored through Penance?

We proceed thus to the First Article:—

Objection 1. It would seem that the virtues are not restored through penance. Because lost virtue cannot be restored by penance, unless penance be the cause of virtue. But, since penance is itself a virtue, it cannot be the cause of all the virtues, and all the more, since some virtues naturally precede penance, viz., faith, hope, and charity, as stated above (Q. 85, A. 6). Therefore the virtues are not restored through penance.

Obj. 2. Further, Penance consists in certain acts of the penitent. But the gratuitous virtues are not caused through any act of ours: for Augustine says *(De Lib. Arb.* ii. 18: *In Ps.* cxviii) that *God forms the virtues in us without us.* Therefore it seems that the virtues are not restored through Penance.

Obj. 3. Further, he that has virtue performs works of virtue with ease and pleasure: wherefore the Philosopher says *(Ethic.* i. 8) that *a man is not just if he does not rejoice in just deeds.* Now many penitents find difficulty in performing deeds of virtue. Therefore the virtues are not restored through Penance.

On the contrary, We read (Luke xv. 22) that the father commanded his penitent son to be clothed in *the first robe,* which, according to Ambrose *(Expos. in Luc.,* vii), is the *mantle of wisdom,* from which all the virtues flow together, according to Wis. viii. 7: *She teacheth temperance, and prudence, and justice, and fortitude, which are such things as men can have nothing more profitable in life.* Therefore all the virtues are restored through Penance.

I answer that, Sins are pardoned through Penance, as stated above (Q. 86, A. 1). But there can be no remission of sins except through the infusion of grace. Wherefore it follows that grace is infused into man through Penance. Now all the gratuitous virtues flow from grace, even as all the powers result from the essence of the soul, as stated in the Second Part (I-II, Q. 110, A. 4, *ad* 1). Therefore all the virtues are restored through Penance.

Reply Obj. 1. Penance restores the virtues in the same way as it causes grace, as stated above (Q. 86, A. 1). Now it is a cause of grace, in so far as it is a sacrament, because, in so far as it is a virtue, it is rather an effect of grace. Consequently it does not follow that penance, as a virtue, needs to be the cause of all the other virtues, but that the habit of penance together with the habits of the other virtues is caused through the sacrament of Penance.

Reply Obj. 2. In the sacrament of Penance human acts stand as matter, while the formal power of this sacrament is derived from the power of the keys. Consequently the power of the keys causes grace and virtue effectively indeed, but instrumentally; and the first act of the penitent, viz., contrition, stands as ultimate disposition to the reception of grace, while the subsequent acts of Penance proceed from the grace and virtues which are already there.

Reply Obj. 3. As stated above (Q. 86, A. 5), sometimes after the first act of Penance, which is contrition, certain remnants of sin remain, viz. dispositions caused by previous acts, the result being that the penitent finds difficulty in doing deeds of virtue. Nevertheless, so far as the inclination itself of charity and of the other virtues is concerned, the penitent performs works of virtue with pleasure and ease; even as a virtuous man may accidentally find it hard to do an act of virtue, on account of sleepiness or some indisposition of the body.

SECOND ARTICLE

Whether, after Penance, Man Rises Again to Equal Virtue?

We proceed thus to the Second Article:—

Objection 1. It would seem that, after Penance, man rises again to equal virtue. For the Apostle says (Rom. viii. 28): *To them that love God all things work together unto good,* whereupon a gloss of Augustine says that *this is so true that, if any such man goes astray and wanders from the path, God makes even this conduce to his good.* But this would not be true if he rose again to lesser virtue. Therefore it seems that a penitent never rises again to lesser virtue.

Obj. 2. Further, Ambrose says* that *Penance is a very good thing, for it restores every defect to a state of perfection.* But this would

not be true unless virtues were recovered in equal measure. Therefore equal virtue is always recovered through Penance.

Obj. 3. Further, on Gen. i. 5: *There was evening and morning, one day,* a gloss says: *The evening light is that from which we fall, the morning light is that to which we rise again.* Now the morning light is greater than the evening light. Therefore a man rises to greater grace or charity than that which he had before; which is confirmed by the Apostle's words (Rom. v. 20): *Where sin abounded, grace did more abound.*

On the contrary, Charity whether proficient or perfect is greater than incipient charity. But sometimes a man falls from proficient charity, and rises again to incipient charity. Therefore man always rises again to less virtue.

I answer that, As stated above (Q. 86, A. 6, *ad* 3; Q. 89, A. 1, *ad* 2), the movement of the free-will, in the justification of the ungodly, is the ultimate disposition to grace; so that in the same instant there is infusion of grace together with the aforesaid movement of the free-will, as stated in the Second Part (I-II, Q. 113, AA. 5, 7), which movement includes an act of penance, as stated above (Q. 86, A. 2). But it is evident that forms which admit of being more or less, become intense or remiss, according to the different dispositions of the subject, as stated in the Second Part (Q. 52, AA. 1, 2; Q. 66, A. 1). Hence it is that, in Penance, according to the degree of intensity or remissness in the movement of the free-will, the penitent receives greater or lesser grace. Now the intensity of the penitent's movement may be proportionate sometimes to a greater grace than that from which man fell by sinning, sometimes to an equal grace, sometimes to a lesser. Wherefore the penitent sometimes arises to a greater grace than that which he had before, sometimes to an equal, sometimes to a lesser grace: and the same applies to the virtues, which flow from grace.

Reply Obj. 1. The very fact of falling away from the love of God by sin, does not work unto the good of all those who love God, which is evident in the case of those who fall and never rise again, or who rise and fall yet again; but only to the good of *such as according to His purpose are called to be saints,* viz. the predestined, who, however often they may fall, yet rise again finally. Consequently good comes of their falling, not that they always rise again to greater grace, but that they rise to more abiding grace, not indeed on the part of grace itself, because the greater the grace, the more abiding it is, but on the part of man, who, the more careful and humble he is,

* Cf. *Hypognosticon* iii, an anonymous work falsely ascribed to S. Augustine.

abides the more steadfastly in grace. Hence the same gloss adds that *their fall conduces to their good, because they rise more humble and more enlightened.*

Reply Obj. 2. Penance, considered in itself, has the power to bring all defects back to perfection, and even to advance man to a higher state; but this is sometimes hindered on the part of man, whose movement towards God and in detestation of sin is too remiss, just as in Baptism adults receive a greater or a lesser grace, according to the various ways in which they prepare themselves.

Reply Obj. 3. This comparison of the two graces to the evening and morning light is made on account of a likeness of order, since the darkness of night follows after the evening light, and the light of day after the light of morning, but not on account of a likeness of greater or lesser quantity.—Again, this saying of the Apostle refers to the grace of Christ, which abounds more than any number of man's sins. Nor is it true of all, that the more their sins abound, the more abundant grace they receive, if we measure habitual grace by the quantity. Grace is, however, more abundant, as regards the very notion of grace, because to him who sins more a more *gratuitous* favor is vouchsafed by his pardon; although sometimes those whose sins abound, abound also in sorrow, so that they receive a more abundant habit of grace and virtue, as was the case with Magdalen.

To the argument advanced in the contrary sense it must be replied that in one and the same man proficient grace is greater than incipient grace, but this is not necessarily the case in different men, for one begins with a greater grace than another has in the state of proficiency: thus Gregory says *(Dial.* ii. 1): *Let all, both now and hereafter, acknowledge how perfectly the boy Benedict turned to the life of grace from the very beginning.*

THIRD ARTICLE

Whether, by Penance, Man Is Restored to His Former Dignity?

We proceed thus to the Third Article:—

Objection 1. It would seem that man is not restored by Penance to his former dignity: because a gloss on Amos v. 2, *The virgin of Israel is cast down,* observes: *It is not said that she cannot rise up, but that the virgin of Israel shall not rise; because the sheep that has once strayed, although the shepherd bring it back on his shoulder, has not the same glory as if it had never strayed.* Therefore man does not, through Penance, recover his former dignity.

Obj. 2. Further, Jerome says: *Whoever fail to preserve the dignity of the sacred order, must be content with saving their souls; for it is a difficult thing to return to their former degree.* Again, Pope Innocent I says *(Ep.* vi, *ad Agapit.)* that *the canons framed at the council of Nicæa exclude penitents from even the lowest orders of clerics.* Therefore man does not, through Penance, recover his former dignity.

Obj. 3. Further, before sinning a man can advance to a higher sacred order. But this is not permitted to a penitent after his sin, for it is written (Ezech. xliv. 10, 13): *The Levites that went away . . . from Me . . . shall never* (Vulg.,—*not) come near to Me, to do the office of priest:* and as laid down in the Decretals (Dist. l, *ch.* 52), and taken from the council of Lerida: *If those who serve at the Holy Altar fall suddenly into some deplorable weakness of the flesh, and by God's mercy do proper penance, let them return to their duties, yet so as not to receive further promotion.* Therefore Penance does not restore man to his former dignity.

On the contrary, As we read in the same *Distinction,* Gregory writing to Secundinus *(Regist.* vii) says: *We consider that when a man has made proper satisfaction, he may return to his honorable position:* and moreover we read in the acts of the council of Agde: *Contumacious clerics, so far as their position allows, should be corrected by their bishops; so that when Penance has reformed them, they may recover their degree and dignity.*

I answer that, By sin, man loses a twofold dignity, one in respect of God, the other in respect of the Church. In respect of God he again loses a twofold dignity. One is his principal dignity, whereby he was counted among the children of God, and this he recovers by Penance, which is signified (Luke xv) in the prodigal son, for when he repented, his father commanded that the first garment should be restored to him, together with a ring and shoes. The other is his secondary dignity, viz. innocence, of which, as we read in the same chapter, the elder son boasted saying *(verse* 29): *Behold, for so many years do I serve thee, and I have never transgressed thy commandments:* and this dignity the penitent cannot recover. Nevertheless he recovers something greater sometimes; because as Gregory says *(Hom. de centum Ovibus,* 34 *in Ev.),* those who acknowledge themselves to have strayed away from God, make up for their past losses, by subsequent gains: so that there is more joy in heaven on their account, even as in battle, the commanding officer thinks more of the soldier who, after running away, returns and bravely attacks the foe, than of one who has *never turned his back, but has done nothing brave.*

By sin man loses his ecclesiastical dignity, because thereby he becomes unworthy of those things which appertain to the exercise of the ecclesiastical dignity. This he is debarred from recovering: first, because he fails to repent; wherefore Isidore wrote to the bishop Masso, and as we read in the *Distinction* quoted above (*Obj.* 3): *The canons order those to be restored to their former degree, who by repentance have made satisfaction for their sins, or have made worthy confession of them. On the other hand, those who do not mend their corrupt and wicked ways are neither allowed to exercise their order, nor received to the grace of communion.*

Secondly, because he does penance negligently, wherefore it is written in the same *Distinction: We can be sure that those who show no signs of humble compunction, or of earnest prayer, who avoid fasting or study, would exercise their former duties with great negligence if they were restored to them.*

Thirdly, if he has committed a sin to which an irregularity is attached; wherefore it is said in the same *Distinction*, quoting the council of Pope Martin*: *If a man marry a widow or the relict of another, he must not be admitted to the ranks of the clergy: and if he has succeeded in creeping in, he must be turned out. In like manner, if anyone after Baptism be guilty of homicide, whether by deed, or by command, or by counsel, or in self-defense.* But this is in consequence not of sin, but of irregularity.

Fourthly, on account of scandal, wherefore it is said in the same *Distinction: Those who have been publicly convicted or caught in the act of perjury, robbery, fornication, and of such like crimes, according to the prescription of the sacred canons must be deprived of the exercise of their respective orders, because it is a scandal to God's people that such persons should be placed over them. But those who commit such sins occultly and confess them secretly to a priest, may be retained in the exercise of their respective orders, with the assurance of God's merciful forgiveness, provided they be careful to expiate their sins by fasts and alms, vigils and holy deeds.* The same is expressed (Extra, *De Qual. Ordinand.*): *If the aforesaid crimes are not proved by a judicial process, or in some other way made notorious, those who are guilty of them must not be hindered, after they have done penance, from exercising the orders they have received, or from receiving further orders, except in cases of homicide.*

Reply Obj. 1. The same is to be said of

* Martin, bishop of Braga.

the recovery of virginity as of the recovery of innocence which belongs to man's secondary dignity in the sight of God.

Reply Obj. 2. In these words Jerome does not say that it is impossible, but that it is difficult, for man to recover his former dignity after having sinned, because this is allowed to none but those who repent perfectly, as stated above. To those canonical statutes, which seem to forbid this, Augustine replies in his letter to Boniface (*Ep.* clxxxv): *If the law of the Church forbids anyone, after doing penance for a crime, to become a cleric, or to return to his clerical duties, or to retain them, the intention was not to deprive him of the hope of pardon, but to preserve the rigor of discipline; else we should have to deny the keys given to the Church, of which it was said: "Whatsoever you shall loose on earth shall be loosed in heaven."* And further on he adds: *For holy David did penance for his deadly crimes, and yet he retained his dignity; and Blessed Peter by shedding most bitter tears did indeed repent him of having denied his Lord, and yet he remained an apostle. Nevertheless we must not deem the care of later teachers excessive, who without endangering a man's salvation, exacted more from his humility, having, in my opinion, found by experience, that some assumed a pretended repentance through hankering after honors and power.*

Reply Obj. 3. This statute is to be understood as applying to those who do public penance, for these cannot be promoted to a higher order. For Peter, after his denial, was made shepherd of Christ's sheep, as appears from Jo. xxi. 21, where Chrysostom comments as follows: *After his denial and repentance Peter gives proof of greater confidence in Christ: for whereas, at the supper, he durst not ask Him, but deputed John to ask in his stead, afterwards he was placed at the head of his brethren, and not only did not depute another to ask for him, what concerned him, but henceforth asks the Master instead of John.*

FOURTH ARTICLE

Whether Virtuous Deeds Done in Charity Can Be Deadened?

We proceed thus to the Fourth Article:—

Objection 1. It would seem that virtuous deeds done in charity cannot be deadened. For that which is not cannot be changed. But to be deadened is to be changed from life to death. Since therefore virtuous deeds, after being done, are no more, it seems that they cannot afterwards be deadened.

Obj. 2. Further, by virtuous deeds done in charity, man merits eternal life. But to take away the reward from one who has merited it is an injustice, which cannot be ascribed to God. Therefore it is not possible for virtuous deeds done in charity to be deadened by a subsequent sin.

Obj. 3. Further, the strong is not corrupted by the weak. Now works of charity are stronger than any sins, because, as it is written (Prov. x. 12), *charity covereth all sins.* Therefore it seems that deeds done in charity cannot be deadened by a subsequent mortal sin.

On the contrary, It is written (Ezech. xviii. 24): *If the just man turn himself away from his justice . . . all his justices which he hath done shall not be remembered.*

I answer that, A living thing, by dying, ceases to have vital operations: for which reason, by a kind of metaphor, a thing is said to be deadened when it is hindered from producing its proper effect or operation.

Now the effect of virtuous works, which are done in charity, is to bring man to eternal life; and this is hindered by a subsequent mortal sin, inasmuch as it takes away grace. Wherefore deeds done in charity are said to be deadened by a subsequent mortal sin.

Reply Obj. 1. Just as sinful deeds pass as to the act but remain as to guilt, so deeds done in charity, after passing, as to the act, remain as to merit, in so far as they are acceptable to God. It is in this respect that they are deadened, inasmuch as man is hindered from receiving his reward.

Reply Obj. 2. There is no injustice in withdrawing the reward from him who has deserved it, if he has made himself unworthy by his subsequent fault, since at times a man justly forfeits through his own fault, even that which he has already received.

Reply Obj. 3. It is not on account of the strength of sinful deeds that deeds, previously done in charity, are deadened, but on account of the freedom of the will which can be turned away from good to evil.

FIFTH ARTICLE

Whether Deeds Deadened by Sin, Are Revived by Penance?

We proceed thus to the Fifth Article:—

Objection 1. It would seem that deeds deadened by sin are not revived by Penance. Because just as past sins are remitted by subsequent Penance, so are deeds previously done in charity, deadened by subsequent sin. But sins remitted by Penance do not return, as stated above (Q. 88, AA. 1, 2). Therefore it seems that neither are dead deeds revived by charity.

Obj. 2. Further, deeds are said to be deadened by comparison with animals who die, as stated above (A. 4). But a dead animal cannot be revived. Therefore neither can dead works be revived by Penance.

Obj. 3. Further, deeds done in charity are deserving of glory according to the quantity of grace or charity. But sometimes man arises through Penance to lesser grace or charity. Therefore he does not receive glory according to the merit of his previous works; so that it seems that deeds deadened by sin are not revived.

On the contrary, On Joel ii. 25, *I will restore to you the years, which the locust . . . hath eaten,* a gloss says: *I will not suffer to perish the fruit which you lost when your soul was disturbed.* But this fruit is the merit of good works which was lost through sin. Therefore meritorious deeds done before are revived by Penance.

I answer that, Some have said that meritorious works deadened by subsequent sin are not revived by the ensuing Penance, because they deemed such works to have passed away, so that they could not be revived. But that is no reason why they should not be revived: because they are conducive to eternal life (wherein their life consists) not only as actually existing, but also after they cease to exist actually, and as abiding in the Divine acceptance. Now, they abide thus, so far as they are concerned, even after they have been deadened by sin, because those works, according as they were done, will ever be acceptable to God and give joy to the saints, according to Apoc. iii. 11: *Hold fast that which thou hast, that no man take thy crown.* That they fail in their efficacy to bring the man, who did them, to eternal life, is due to the impediment of the supervening sin whereby he is become unworthy of eternal life. But this impediment is removed by Penance, inasmuch as sins are taken away thereby. Hence it follows that deeds previously deadened, recover, through Penance, their efficacy in bringing him, who did them, to eternal life, and, in other words, they are revived. It is therefore evident that deadened works are revived by Penance.

Reply Obj. 1. The very works themselves of sin are removed by Penance, so that, by God's mercy, no further stain or debt of punishment is incurred on their account: on the other hand, works done in charity are not removed by God, since they abide in His acceptance, but they are hindered on the part of the man who does them; wherefore if this hindrance, on the part of the man who does those works, be removed, God on His side fulfills what those works deserved.

Reply Obj. 2. Deeds done in charity are not in themselves deadened, as explained above, but only with regard to a supervening impediment on the part of the man who does them. On the other hand, an animal dies in itself, through being deprived of the principle of life: so that the comparison fails.

Reply Obj. 3. He who, through Penance, arises to lesser charity, will receive the essential reward according to the degree of charity in which he is found. Yet he will have greater joy for the works he had done in his former charity, than for those which he did in his subsequent charity: and this joy belongs to the accidental reward.

SIXTH ARTICLE

Whether the Effect of Subsequent Penance Is to Quicken Even Dead Works?

We proceed thus to the Sixth Article:—

Objection 1. It would seem that the effect of subsequent Penance is to quicken even dead works, those, namely, that were not done in charity. For it seems more difficult to bring to life that which has been deadened, since this is never done naturally, than to quicken that which never had life, since certain living things are engendered naturally from things without life. Now deadened works are revived by Penance, as stated above (A. 5). Much more, therefore, are dead works revived.

Obj. 2. Further, if the cause be removed, the effect is removed. But the cause of the lack of life in works generically good done without charity, was the lack of charity and grace; which lack is removed by Penance. Therefore dead works are quickened by charity.

Obj. 3. Further, Jerome in commenting on Agg. i. 6: *You have sowed much,* says: *If at any time you find a sinner, among his many evil deeds, doing that which is right, God is not so unjust as to forget the few good deeds on account of his many evil deeds.* Now this seems to be the case chiefly when past evil *deeds* are removed by Penance. Therefore it seems that through Penance, God rewards the former deeds done in the state of sin, which implies that they are quickened.

On the contrary, The Apostle says (1 Cor. xiii. 3): *If I should distribute all my goods to feed the poor, and if I should deliver my body to be burned, and have not charity, it profiteth me nothing.* But this would not be true, if, at least by subsequent Penance, they were quickened. Therefore Penance does not quicken works which before were dead.

I answer that, A work is said to be dead in two ways: first, effectively, because, to wit, it is a cause of death, in which sense sinful works

are said to be dead, according to Heb. ix. 14: *The blood of Christ . . . shall cleanse our conscience from dead works.* These dead works are not quickened but removed by Penance, according to Heb. vi. 1: *Not laying again the foundation of Penance from dead works.* Secondly, works are said to be dead privatively, because, to wit, they lack spiritual life, which is founded on charity, whereby the soul is united to God, the result being that it is quickened as the body by the soul: in which sense too, faith, if it lack charity, is said to be dead, according to James ii. 20: *Faith without works is dead.* In this way also, all works that are generically good, are said to be dead, if they be done without charity, inasmuch as they fail to proceed from the principle of life; even as we might call the sound of a harp, a dead voice. Accordingly, the difference of life and death in works is in relation to the principle from which they proceed. But works cannot proceed a second time from a principle, because they are transitory, and the same identical deed cannot be resumed. Therefore it is impossible for dead works to be quickened by Penance.

Reply Obj. 1. In the physical order things whether dead or deadened lack the principle of life. But works are said to be deadened, not in relation to the principle whence they proceeded, but in relation to an extrinsic impediment; while they are said to be dead in relation to a principle. Consequently there is no comparison.

Reply Obj. 2. Works generically good done without charity are said to be dead on account of the lack of grace and charity, as principles. Now the subsequent Penance does not supply that want, so as to make them proceed from such a principle. Hence the argument does not prove.

Reply Obj. 3. God remembers the good deeds a man does when in a state of sin, not by rewarding them in eternal life, which is due only to living works, i.e. those done from charity, but by a temporal reward: thus Gregory declares (*Hom. de Divite et Lazaro,* 41 *in Ev.*) that *unless that rich man had done some good deed, and had received his reward in this world, Abraham would certainly not have said to him: "Thou didst receive gooa things in thy lifetime."*—Or again, this may mean that he will be judged less severely: wherefore Augustine says (*De Patientia* xxvi) *We cannot say that it would be better for the schismatic that by denying Christ he should suffer none of those things which he suffered by confessing Him; but we must believe that he will be judged with less severity, than if by denying Christ, he had suffered none of those things. Thus the words of the Apostle,*

"If I should deliver my body to be burned, and have not charity, it profiteth me nothing," refer to the obtaining of the kingdom of heaven, and do not exclude the possibility of being sentenced with less severity at the last judgment.

QUESTION 90

Of the Parts of Penance, in General

(In Four Articles)

WE must now consider the parts of Penance: (1) in general; (2) each one in particular.

Under the first head there are four points of inquiry: (1) Whether Penance has any parts? (2) Of the number of its parts. (3) What kind of parts are they? (4) Of its division into subjective parts.

FIRST ARTICLE

Whether Penance Should Be Assigned Any Parts?

We proceed thus to the First Article:—

Objection 1. It would seem that parts should not be assigned to Penance. For it is the Divine power that works our salvation most secretly in the sacraments. Now the Divine power is one and simple. Therefore Penance, being a sacrament, should have no parts assigned to it.

Obj. 2. Further, Penance is both a virtue and a sacrament. Now no parts are assigned to it as a virtue, since virtue is a habit, which is a simple quality of the mind. In like manner, it seems that parts should not be assigned to Penance as a sacrament, because no parts are assigned to Baptism and the other sacraments. Therefore no parts at all should be assigned to Penance.

Obj. 3. Further, the matter of Penance is sin, as stated above (Q. 84, A. 2). But no parts are assigned to sin. Neither, therefore, should parts be assigned to Penance.

On the contrary, The parts of a thing are those out of which the whole is composed. Now the perfection of Penance is composed of several things, viz. contrition, confession, and satisfaction. Therefore Penance has parts.

I answer that, The parts of a thing are those into which the whole is divided materially, for the parts of a thing are to the whole, what matter is to the form; wherefore the parts are reckoned as a kind of material cause, and the whole as a kind of formal cause (*Phys.* ii). Accordingly wherever, on the part of matter, we find a kind of plurality, there we shall find a reason for assigning parts.

Now it has been stated above (Q. 84, AA. 2, 3), that, in the sacrament of Penance, human actions stand as matter: and so, since several actions are requisite for the perfection of Penance, viz., contrition, confession, and satisfac-tion, as we shall show further on (A. 2), it follows that the sacrament of Penance has parts.

Reply Obj. 1. Every sacrament is some-thing simple by reason of the Divine power, which operates therein: but the Divine power is so great that it can operate both through one and through many, and by reason of these many, parts may be assigned to a particular sacrament.

Reply Obj. 2. Parts are not assigned to penance as a virtue: because the human acts of which there are several in penance, are related to the habit of virtue, not as its parts, but as its effects. It follows, therefore, that parts are assigned to Penance as a sacrament, to which the human acts are related as matter: whereas in the other sacraments the matter does not consist of human acts, but of some one external thing, either simple, as water or oil, or compound, as chrism, and so parts are not assigned to the other sacraments.

Reply Obj. 3. Sins are the remote matter of Penance, inasmuch, to wit, as they are the matter or object of the human acts, which are the proper matter of Penance as a sacrament.

SECOND ARTICLE

Whether Contrition, Confession, and Satisfaction Are Fittingly Assigned As Parts of Penance?

We proceed thus to the Second Article:—

Objection 1. It would seem that contrition, confession, and satisfaction are not fittingly assigned as parts of Penance. For contrition is in the heart, and so belongs to interior pen-ance; while confession consists of words, and satisfaction in deeds; so that the two latter belong to interior penance. Now interior pen-ance is not a sacrament, but only exterior pen-ance which is perceptible by the senses. There-fore these three parts are not fittingly assigned to the sacrament of Penance.

Obj. 2. Further, grace is conferred in the sacraments of the New Law, as stated above (Q. 62, AA. 1, 3). But no grace is conferred in satisfaction. Therefore satisfaction is not part of a sacrament.

Obj. 3. Further, the fruit of a thing is not the same as its part. But satisfaction is a fruit of penance, according to Luke iii. 8:

Bring forth . . . fruits worthy of penance. Therefore it is not a part of Penance.

Obj. 4. Further, Penance is ordained against sin. But sin can be completed merely in the thought by consent, as stated in the Second Part (I-II, Q. 72, A. 7): therefore Penance can also. Therefore confession in word and satisfaction in deed should not be reckoned as parts of Penance.

On the contrary, It seems that yet more parts should be assigned to Penance. For not only is the body assigned as a part of man, as being the matter, but also the soul, which is his form. But the aforesaid three, being the acts of the penitent, stand as matter, while the priestly absolution stands as form. Therefore the priestly absolution should be assigned as a fourth part of Penance.

I answer that, A part is twofold, essential and quantitative. The essential parts are naturally the form and the matter, and logically the genus and the difference. In this way, each sacrament is divided into matter and form as its essential parts. Hence it has been said above (Q. 60, AA. 5, 6) that sacraments consist of things and words. But since quantity is on the part of matter, quantitative parts are parts of matter: and, in this way, as stated above (A. 1), parts are assigned specially to the sacrament of Penance, as regards the acts of the penitent, which are the matter of this sacrament.

Now it has been said above (Q. 85, A. 3, *ad* 3) that an offense is atoned otherwise in Penance than in vindictive justice. Because, in vindictive justice the atonement is made according to the judge's decision, and not according to the discretion of the offender or of the person offended; whereas, in Penance, the offense is atoned according to the will of the sinner, and the judgment of God against Whom the sin was committed, because in the latter case we seek not only the restoration of the equality of justice, as in vindictive justice, but also and still more the reconciliation of friendship, which is accomplished by the offender making atonement according to the will of the person offended. Accordingly the first requisite on the part of the penitent is the will to atone, and this is done by contrition; the second is that he submit to the judgment of the priest standing in God's place, and this is done in confession; and the third is that he atone according to the decision of God's minister, and this is done in satisfaction: and so contrition, confession, and satisfaction are assigned as parts of Penance.

Reply Obj. 1. Contrition, as to its essence, is in the heart, and belongs to interior penance; yet, virtually, it belongs to exterior penance, inasmuch as it implies the purpose of confessing and making satisfaction.

Reply Obj. 2. Satisfaction confers grace, in so far as it is in man's purpose, and it increases grace, according as it is accomplished, just as Baptism does in adults, as stated above (Q. 68, A. 2; Q. 69, A. 8).

Reply Obj. 3. Satisfaction is a part of Penance as a sacrament, and a fruit of penance as a virtue.

Reply Obj. 4. More things are required for good, *which proceeds from a cause that is entire,* than for evil, *which results from each single defect,* as Dionysius states (*Div. Nom.* iv). And thus, although sin is completed in the consent of the heart, yet the perfection of Penance requires contrition of the heart, together with confession in word and satisfaction in deed.

The *Reply to the Fifth Objection* is clear from what has been said.

THIRD ARTICLE
Whether These Three Are Integral Parts of Penance?

We proceed thus to the Third Article:—

Objection 1. It would seem that these three are not integral parts of Penance. For, as stated above (Q. 84, A. 3), Penance is ordained against sin. But sins of thought, word, and deed are the subjective and not integral parts of sin, because sin is predicated of each one of them. Therefore in Penance also, contrition in thought, confession in word, and satisfaction in deed are not integral parts.

Obj. 2. Further, no integral part includes within itself another that is condivided with it. But contrition includes both confession and satisfaction in the purpose of amendment. Therefore they are not integral parts.

Obj. 3. Further, a whole is composed of its integral parts, taken at the same time and equally, just as a line is made up of its parts. But such is not the case here. Therefore these are not integral parts of Penance.

On the contrary, Integral parts are those by which the perfection of the whole is integrated. But the perfection of Penance is integrated by these three. Therefore they are integral parts of Penance.

I answer that, Some have said that these three are subjective parts of Penance. But this is impossible, because the entire power of the whole is present in each subjective part at the same time and equally, just as the entire power of an animal, as such, is assured to each animal species, all of which species divide the animal genus at the same time and equally: which does not apply to the point in question. Wherefore others have said that these are potential parts: yet neither can this be true, since the whole is present, as to the entire essence, in each potential part, just as the entire essence of the soul is present in each of its powers: which does not apply to the case in point. Therefore it follows that these three are integral parts of Penance, the nature of which is that the whole is not present in each of the parts, either as to its entire power, or as to its entire essence, but that it is present to all of them together at the same time.

Reply Obj. 1. Sin, forasmuch as it is an evil, can be completed in one single point, as stated above (A. 2, *ad* 4) ; and so the sin which is completed in thought alone, is a special kind of sin. Another species is the sin that is completed in thought and word: and yet a third species is the sin that is completed in thought, word, and deed; and the quasi-integral parts of this last sin, are that which is in thought, that which is in word, and that which is in deed. Wherefore these three are the integral parts of Penance, which is completed in them.

Reply Obj. 2. One integral part can include the whole, though not as to its essence: because the foundation, in a way, contains virtually the whole building. In this way contrition includes virtually the whole of Penance.

Reply Obj. 3. All integral parts have a certain relation of order to one another: but some are only related as to position, whether in sequence as the parts of an army, or by contact, as the parts of a heap, or by being fitted together, as the parts of a house, or by continuation, as the parts of a line; while some are related, in addition, as to power, as the parts of an animal, the first of which is the heart, the others in a certain order being dependent on one another: and thirdly some are related in the order of time: as the parts of time and movement. Accordingly the parts of Penance are related to one another in the order of power and time, since they are actions, but not in the order of position, since they do not occupy a place.

FOURTH ARTICLE

Whether Penance Is Fittingly Divided into Penance before Baptism, Penance for Mortal Sins, and Penance for Venial Sins?

We proceed thus to the Fourth Article:—

Objection 1. It would seem that penance is unfittingly divided into penance before Baptism, penance for mortal, and penance for venial sins. For Penance is the second plank after shipwreck, as stated above (Q. 84, A. 6), while Baptism is the first. Therefore that which precedes Baptism should not be called a species of penance.

* Cf. *Hom.* 30 inter 1.

Obj. 2. Further, that which can destroy the greater, can destroy the lesser. Now mortal sin is greater than venial; and penance which regards mortal sins regards also venial sins. Therefore they should not be considered as different species of penance.

Obj. 3. Further, just as after Baptism man commits venial and mortal sins, so does he before Baptism. If therefore penance for venial sins is distinct from penance for mortal sins after Baptism, in like manner they should be distinguished before Baptism. Therefore penance is not fittingly divided into these species.

On the contrary, Augustine says in *De Pœnitentia** that these three are species of Penance.

I answer that, This is a division of penance as a virtue. Now it must be observed that every virtue acts in accordance with the time being, as also in keeping with other due circumstances, wherefore the virtue of penance has its act at this time, according to the requirements of the New Law.

Now it belongs to penance to detest one's past sins, and to purpose, at the same time, to change one's life for the better, which is the end, so to speak, of penance. And since moral matters take their species from the end, as stated in the Second Part (I-II, Q. 1, A. 3; Q. 18, AA. 4, 6), it is reasonable to distinguish various species of penance, according to the various changes intended by the penitent.

Accordingly there is a threefold change intended by the penitent. The first is by regeneration unto a new life, and this belongs to that penance which precedes Baptism. The second is by reforming one's past life after it has been already destroyed, and this belongs to penance for mortal sins committed after Baptism. The third is by changing to a more perfect operation of life, and this belongs to penance for venial sins, which are remitted through a fervent act of charity, as stated above (Q. 87, AA. 2, 3).

Reply Obj. 1. The penance which precedes Baptism is not a sacrament, but an act of virtue disposing one to that sacrament.

Reply Obj. 2. The penance which washes away mortal sins, washes away venial sins also, but the converse does not hold. Wherefore these two species of penance are related to one another as perfect and imperfect.

Reply Obj. 3. Before Baptism there are no venial sins without mortal sins. And since a venial sin cannot be remitted without mortal sin, as stated above (Q. 87, A. 4), before Baptism, penance for mortal sins is not distinct from penance for venial sins.

AFTER writing these few questions of the treatise on Penance, St. Thomas was called to the heavenly reward which he had merited by writing so well of his Divine Master. The remainder of the "Summa Theologica," known as the Supplement, was compiled probably by Fra Rainaldo da Piperno, companion and friend of the Angelic Doctor, and was gathered from St. Thomas's commentary on the Fourth Book of the Sentences of Peter Lombard. This commentary was written in the years 1235-1253, while St. Thomas was under thirty years of age. Everywhere it reveals the influence of him whom St. Thomas always called the Master. But that influence was not to be always supreme. That the mind of the Angelic Doctor moved forward to positions which directly contradicted the Master may be seen by any student of the "Summa Theologica." The compiler of the Supplement was evidently well acquainted with the commentary on the Sentences, which had been in circulation for some twenty years or more, but it is probable that he was badly acquainted with the "Summa Theologica." This will be realized and must be borne in mind when we read the Supplement, notably (in this volume) Q. 62, A. 1: also Q. 43, A. 3 *ad* 2 of the Supplement.

SUPPLEMENT

To the Third Part of the "Summa Theologica" of St. Thomas Aquinas Gathered from His Commentary on Book IV "of the Sentences."

QUESTION 1

Of the Parts of Penance, in Particular, and First of Contrition

(In Three Articles)

WE must now consider each single part of Penance, and (1) Contrition; (2) Confession; (3) Satisfaction. The consideration about Contrition will be fourfold: (1) What is it? (2) What should it be about? (3) How great should it be? (4) Of its duration. (5) Of its effect.

Under the first head there are three points of inquiry: (1) Whether Contrition is suitably defined? (2) Whether it is an act of virtue? (3) Whether attrition can become contrition?

FIRST ARTICLE

Whether Contrition Is an Assumed Sorrow for Sins, Together with the Purpose of Confessing Them and of Making Satisfaction for Them?

We proceed thus to the First Article:—

Objection 1. It would seem that contrition is not *an assumed sorrow for sins, together with the purpose of confessing them and of making satisfaction for them,* as some define it. For, as Augustine states *(De Civ. Dei,* xiv. 6), *sorrow is for those things that happen against our will.* But this does not apply to sin. Therefore contrition is not sorrow for sins.

Obj. 2. Further, contrition is given us by God. But what is given is not assumed. Therefore contrition is not an assumed sorrow.

Obj. 3. Further, satisfaction and confession are necessary for the remission of the punishment which was not remitted by contrition. But sometimes the whole punishment is remitted in contrition. Therefore it is not always necessary for the contrite person to have the purpose of confessing and of making satisfaction.

On the contrary, stands the definition.

I answer that, As stated in Ecclus. x. 15, *pride is the beginning of all sin,* because thereby man clings to his own judgment, and strays from the Divine commandments. Consequently that which destroys sin must needs make man give up his own judgment. Now he that persists in his own judgment, is called metaphorically rigid and hard: wherefore anyone is said to be broken when he is torn from his own judgment. But, in material things, whence these expressions are transferred to spiritual things, there is a difference between breaking and crushing or contrition, as stated in *Meteor.* iv, in that we speak of breaking when a thing is sundered into large parts, but of crushing or contrition when that which was in itself solid is reduced to minute particles. And since, for the remission of sin, it is necessary that man should put aside entirely his attachment to sin, which implies a certain state of continuity and solidity in his mind, therefore it is that the act through which sin is cast aside is called contrition metaphorically.

In this contrition several things are to be observed, viz. the very substance of the act, the way of acting, its origin and its effect: in respect of which we find that contrition has been defined in various ways. For, as regards the substance of the act, we have the definition given above: and since the act of contrition is both an act of virtue, and a part of the sacrament of Penance, its nature as an act of virtue is explained in this definition by mentioning its genus, viz. *sorrow,* its object by the words *for sins,* and the act of choice which is necessary for an act of virtue, by the word *assumed:* while, as a part of the sacrament, it is made manifest by pointing out its relation to the other parts, in the words, *together with the purpose of confessing and of making satisfaction.*

Tnere is another definition which defines contrition, only as an act of virtue; but at the same time including the difference which confines it to a special virtue, viz. penance, for it is thus expressed: *Contrition is voluntary sorrow for sin whereby man punishes in himself that which he grieves to have done,* because the addition of the word *punishes* confines the definition to a special virtue.—Another definition is given by Isidore *(De Sum. Bono, ii. 12)* as follows: *Contrition is a tearful sorrow and humility of mind, arising from remembrance of sin and fear of the Judgment.* Here we have an allusion to the derivation of the word, when it is said that it is *humility of the mind,* because just as pride makes the mind rigid, so is a man humbled, when contrition leads him to give up his mind. Also the external manner is indicated by the word *tearful,* and the origin of contrition, by the words, *arising from remembrance of sin,* etc. —Another definition is taken from the words of Augustine,* and indicates the effect of contrition. It runs thus: *Contrition is the sorrow which takes away sin.*—Yet another is gathered from the words of Gregory *(Moral. xxxiii. 11)* as follows: *Contrition is humility of the soul, crushing sin between hope and fear.* Here the derivation is indicated by saying that contrition is *humility of the soul;* the effect, by the words, *crushing sin;* and the origin, by the words, *between hope and fear.* Indeed, it includes not only the principal cause, which is fear, but also its joint cause, which is hope, without which, fear might lead to despair.

Reply Obj. 1. Although sins, when committed, were voluntary, yet when we are contrite for them, they are no longer voluntary, so that they occur against our will; not indeed in respect of the will that we had when we consented to them, but in respect of that which we have now, so as to wish they had never been.

Reply Obj. 2. Contrition is from God alone as to the form that quickens it, but as to the substance of the act, it is from the free-will and from God, Who operates in all works both of nature and of will.

Reply Obj. 3. Although the entire punishment may be remitted by contrition, yet confession and satisfaction are still necessary, both because man cannot be sure that his contrition was sufficient to take away all, and because confession and satisfaction are a matter of precept: wherefore he becomes a trans-

* Implicitly, on Ps. xlvi.

gressor, who confesses not and makes not satisfaction.

<h3>SECOND ARTICLE</h3>

<h4>Whether Contrition Is an Act of Virtue?</h4>

We proceed thus to the Second Article:—

Objection 1. It would seem that contrition is not an act of virtue. For passions are not acts of virtue, since *they bring us neither praise nor blame (Ethic.* ii. 5). But sorrow is a passion. As therefore contrition is sorrow, it seems that it is not an act of virtue.

Obj. 2. Further, as contrition is so called from its being a crushing, so is attrition. Now all agree in saying that attrition is not an act of virtue. Neither, therefore, is contrition an act of virtue.

On the contrary, Nothing but an act of virtue is meritorious. But contrition is a meritorious act. Therefore it is an act of virtue.

I answer that, Contrition as to the literal signification of the word, does not denote an act of virtue, but a corporeal passion. But the question in point does not refer to contrition in this sense, but to that which the word is employed to signify by way of metaphor. For just as the inflation of one's own will unto wrong-doing implies, in itself, a generic evil, so the utter undoing and crushing of that same will implies something generically good, for this is to detest one's own will whereby sin was committed. Wherefore contrition, which signifies this, implies rectitude of the will; and so it is the act of that virtue to which it belongs to detest and destroy past sins, the act, to wit, of penance, as is evident from what was said above *(Sentent.* iv, D. 14. Q. 1, A. 1: P. iii, Q. 85, AA. 2, 3).

Reply Obj. 1. Contrition includes a twofold sorrow for sin. One is in the sensitive part, and is a passion. This does not belong essentially to contrition as an act of virtue, but is rather its effect. For just as the virtue of penance inflicts outward punishment on the body, in order to compensate for the offense done to God through the instrumentality of the bodily members, so does it inflict on the concupiscible part of the soul a punishment, viz. the aforesaid sorrow, because the concupiscible also co-operated in the sinful deeds. Nevertheless this sorrow may belong to contrition taken as part of the sacrament, since the nature of a sacrament is such that it consists not only of internal but also of external acts and sensible things.—The other sorrow is in the will, and is nothing else save displeasure for some evil, for the emotions of the will are named after the passions, as stated above *(Sentent.* iii, D. 26, Q. 1, A. 5: I-II, Q. 22, A. 3, *ad* 3). Accordingly, contrition is essentially a kind of sorrow, and is an act of the virtue of penance.

Reply Obj. 2. Attrition denotes approach to perfect contrition, wherefore in corporeal matters, things are said to be attrite, when they are worn away to a certain extent, but not altogether crushed to pieces; while they are said to be contrite, when all the parts are crushed *(tritæ)* minutely. Wherefore, in spiritual matters, attrition signifies a certain but not a perfect displeasure for sins committed, whereas contrition denotes perfect displeasure.

THIRD ARTICLE

Whether Attrition Can Become Contrition?

We proceed thus to the Third Article:—

Objection 1. It would seem that attrition can become contrition. For contrition differs from attrition, as living from dead. Now dead faith becomes living. Therefore attrition can become contrition.

Obj. 2. Further, matter receives perfection when privation is removed. Now sorrow is to grace, as matter to form, because grace quickens sorrow. Therefore the sorrow that was previously lifeless, while guilt remained, receives perfection through being quickened by grace: and so the same conclusion follows as above.

On the contrary, Things which are caused by principles altogether diverse cannot be changed, one into the other. Now the principle of attrition is servile fear, while filial fear is the cause of contrition. Therefore attrition cannot become contrition.

I answer that, There are two opinions on this question: for some say that attrition may become contrition, even as lifeless faith becomes living faith. But, seemingly, this is impossible; since, although the habit of lifeless faith becomes living, yet never does an act of lifeless faith become an act of living faith, because the lifeless act passes away and remains no more, as soon as charity comes. Now attrition and contrition do not denote a habit, but an act only: and those habits of infused virtue which regard the will cannot be lifeless, since they result from charity, as stated above *(Sentent.* iii, D. 27, Q. 2, A. 4: I-II, 65, A. 4). Wherefore until grace be infused, there is no habit by which afterwards the act of contrition may be elicited; so that attrition can nowise become contrition: and this is the other opinion.

Reply Obj. 1. There is no comparison between faith and contrition, as stated above.

Reply Obj. 2. When the privation is removed from matter, the matter is quickened if it remains when the perfection comes. But the sorrow which was lifeless, does not remain when charity comes, wherefore it cannot be quickened.

It may also be replied that matter does not take its origin from the form essentially, as an act takes its origin from the habit which quickens it. Wherefore nothing hinders matter being quickened anew by some form, whereby it was not quickened previously: whereas this cannot be said of an act, even as it is impossible for the identically same thing to arise from a cause wherefrom it did not arise before, since a thing is brought into being but once.

QUESTION 2

Of the Object of Contrition

(In Six Articles)

WE must now consider the object of contrition. Under this head there are six points of inquiry: (1) Whether a man should be contrite on account of his punishment? (2) Whether, on account of original sin? (3) Whether, for every actual sin he has committed? (4) Whether, for actual sins he will commit? (5) Whether, for the sins of others? (6) Whether, for each single mortal sin?

FIRST ARTICLE

Whether Man Should Be Contrite on Account of the Punishment, and Not Only on Account of His Sin?

We proceed thus to the First Article:—

Objection 1. It would seem that man should

be contrite on account of the punishment, and not only on account of his sin. For Augustine says in *De Pœnitentia:** No man desires life everlasting unless he repent of this mortal life. But the mortality of this life is a punishment. Therefore the penitent should be contrite on account of his punishments also.

Obj. 2. Further, the Master says *(Sentent.* iv, D. 16, cap. i), quoting Augustine *(De vera et falsa Pœnitentia†),* that the penitent should be sorry for having deprived himself of virtue. But privation of virtue is a punishment. Therefore contrition is sorrow for punishments also.

On the contrary, No one holds to that for which he is sorry. But a penitent, by the very

* Cf. *Hom* 50 *inter* 1.   † Work of an unknown author.

signification of the word, is one who holds to his punishment.* Therefore he is not sorry on account of his punishment, so that contrition which is penitential sorrow is not on account of punishment.

I answer that, As stated above (Q. 1, A. 1), contrition implies the crushing of something hard and whole. Now this wholeness and hardness is found in the evil of fault, since the will, which is the cause thereof in the evildoer, sticks to its own ground,† and refuses to yield to the precept of the law, wherefore displeasure at a suchlike evil is called metaphorically *contrition.* But this metaphor cannot be applied to evil of punishment, because punishment simply denotes a lessening, so that it is possible to have sorrow for punishment but not contrition.

Reply Obj. 1. According to Augustine, penance should be on account of this mortal life, not by reason of its mortality (unless penance be taken broadly for every kind of sorrow); but by reason of sins, to which we are prone on account of the weakness of this life.

Reply Obj. 2. Sorrow for the loss of virtue through sin is not essentially the same as contrition, but is its principle. For just as we are moved to desire a thing on account of the good we expect to derive from it, so are we moved to be sorry for something, on account of the evil accruing to us therefrom.

SECOND ARTICLE

Whether Contrition Should Be on Account of Original Sin?

We proceed thus to the Second Article:—

Objection 1. It would seem that contrition should be on account of original sin. For we ought to be contrite on account of actual sin; not by reason of the act, considered as a kind of being, but by reason of its deformity, since the act, regarded in its substance, is a good, and is from God. Now original sin has a deformity, even as actual sin has. Therefore we should be contrite on its account also.

Obj. 2. Further, by original sin man has been turned away from God, since in punishment thereof he was to be deprived of seeing God. But every man should be displeased at having been turned away from God. Therefore man should be displeased at original sin; and so he ought to have contrition for it.

On the contrary, The medicine should be proportionate to the disease. Now we contracted original sin without willing to do so. Therefore it is not necessary that we should be cleansed from it by an act of the will, such as contrition is.

I answer that, Contrition is sorrow, as stated above (Q. 1, AA. 1, 2), respecting and, so to speak, crushing the hardness of the will. Consequently it can regard those sins only which result in us through the hardness of our will. And as original sin was not brought upon us by our own will, but contracted from the origin of our infected nature, it follows that, properly speaking, we cannot have contrition on its account, but only displeasure or sorrow.

Reply Obj. 1. Contrition is for sin, not by reason of the mere substance of the act, because it does not derive the character of evil therefrom; nor again, by reason of its deformity alone, because deformity, of itself, does not include the notion of guilt, and sometimes denotes a punishment. But contrition ought to be on account of sin, as implying deformity resulting from an act of the will; and this does not apply to original sin, so that contrition does not regard it.

The same *Reply* avails for the *Second Objection,* because contrition is due to aversion of the will.

THIRD ARTICLE

Whether We Should Have Contrition for Every Actual Sin?

We proceed thus to the Third Article:—

Objection 1. It would seem that we have no need to have contrition for every actual sin we have committed. For contraries are healed by their contraries. Now some sins are committed through sorrow, e.g. sloth and envy. Therefore their remedy should not be sorrow, such as contrition is, but joy.

Obj. 2. Further, contrition is an act of the will, which cannot refer to that which is not known. But there are sins of which we have no knowledge, such as those we have forgotten. Therefore we cannot have contrition for them.

Obj. 3. Further, by voluntary contrition those sins are blotted out which we committed voluntarily. But ignorance takes away voluntariness, as the Philosopher declares *(Ethic.* iii. 1). Therefore contrition need not cover things which have occurred through ignorance.

Obj. 4. Further, we need not be contrite for a sin which is not removed by contrition. Now some sins are not removed by contrition, e.g. venial sins, that remain after the grace of contrition. Therefore there is no need to have contrition for all one's past sins.

On the contrary, Penance is a remedy for all actual sins. But penance cannot regard some sins, without contrition regarding them

* *Pœnitens,* i.e. *Pœnam tenens.*   † There is a play on the words here,—*integer* (whole) and *in suis terminis* (to its own ground).

also, for it is the first part of Penance. Therefore contrition should be for all one's past sins.

Further, no sin is forgiven a man unless he be justified. But justification requires contrition, as stated above (Q. 1, A. 1: I-II, Q. 113). Therefore it is necessary to have contrition for all one's sins.

I answer that, Every actual sin is caused by our will not yielding to God's law, either by transgressing it, or by omitting it, or by acting beside it: and since a hard thing is one that is disposed not to give way easily, hence it is that a certain hardness of the will is to be found in every actual sin. Wherefore, if a sin is to be remedied, it needs to be taken away by contrition which crushes it.

Reply Obj. 1. As clearly shown above (A. 2, *ad* 1), contrition is opposed to sin, in so far as it proceeds from the choice of the will that had failed to obey the command of God's law, and not as regards the material part of sin: and it is on this that the choice of the will falls. Now the will's choice falls not only on the acts of the other powers, which the will uses for its own end, but also on the will's own proper act: for the will wills to will something. Accordingly the will's choice falls on that pain or sadness which is to be found in the sin of envy and the like, whether such pain be in the senses or in the will itself. Consequently the sorrow of contrition is opposed to those sins.

Reply Obj. 2. One may forget a thing in two ways, either so that it escapes the memory altogether, and then one cannot search for it; or so that it escapes from the memory in part, and in part remains, as when I remember having heard something in general, but know not what it was in particular, and then I search my memory in order to discover it. Accordingly a sin also may be forgotten in two ways, either so as to remain in a general, but not in a particular remembrance, and then a man is bound to bethink himself in order to discover the sin, because he is bound to have contrition for each individual mortal sin. And if he is unable to discover it, after applying himself with due care, it is enough that he be contrite for it, according as it stands in his knowledge, and indeed he should grieve not only for the sin, but also for having forgotten it, because this is owing to his neglect. If, however, the sin has escaped from his memory altogether, then he is excused from his duty through being unable to fulfill it, and it is enough that he be contrite in general for everything wherein he has offended God. But when this inability is removed, as when the sin is recalled to his memory, then he is bound to have contrition for that sin in particular, even as a poor man,

* S. Basil asserts this implicitly (*De Vera Virgin.*).

who cannot pay a debt, is excused, and yet is bound to, as soon as he can.

Reply Obj. 3. If ignorance were to remove altogether the will to do evil, it would excuse, and there would be no sin: but sometimes it does not remove the will altogether, and then it does not altogether excuse, but only to a certain extent: wherefore a man is bound to be contrite for a sin committed through ignorance.

Reply Obj. 4. A venial sin can remain after contrition for a mortal sin, but not after contrition for the venial sin: wherefore contrition should also cover venial sins even as penance does, as stated above (*Sentent.* iv, D. 16, Q. 2, A. 2, qu. 2; P. III, Q. 87, A. 1).

FOURTH ARTICLE

Whether a Man Is Bound to Have Contrition for His Future Sins?

We proceed thus to the Fourth Article:—

Objection 1. It would seem that a man is bound to have contrition for his future sins also. For contrition is an act of the free-will: and the free-will extends to the future rather than to the past, since choice, which is an act of the free-will, is about future contingents, as stated in *Ethic.* iii. Therefore contrition is about future sins rather than about past sins.

Obj. 2. Further, sin is aggravated by the result that ensues from it: wherefore Jerome says* that the punishment of Arius is not yet ended, for it is yet possible for some to be ruined through his heresy, by reason of whose ruin his punishment would be increased: and the same applies to a man who is judged guilty of murder, if he has committed a murderous assault, even before his victim dies. Now the sinner ought to be contrite during that intervening time. Therefore the degree of his contrition ought to be proportionate not only to his past act, but also to its eventual result: and consequently contrition regards the future.

On the contrary, Contrition is a part of penance. But penance always regards the past: and therefore contrition does also, and consequently is not for a future sin.

I answer that, In every series of things moving and moved ordained to one another, we find that the inferior mover has its proper movement, and besides this, it follows, in some respect, the movement of the superior mover: this is seen in the movement of the planets, which, in addition to their proper movements, follow the movement of the first heaven. Now, in all the moral virtues, the first mover is prudence, which is called the charioteer of the virtues. Consequently each moral virtue, in addition to its proper movement, has something of the movement of prudence: and therefore, since penance is a moral virtue, as it is a part of justice, in addition to its own act, it acquires the movement of prudence. Now its proper movement is towards its proper object, which is a sin committed. Wherefore its proper and principal act, viz. contrition, essentially regards past sins alone; but, inasmuch as it acquires something of the act of prudence, it regards future sins indirectly, although it is not essentially moved towards those future sins. For this reason, he that is contrite, is sorry for his past sins, and is cautious of future sins. Yet we do not speak of contrition for future sins, but of caution, which is a part of prudence conjoined to penance.

Reply Obj. 1. The free-will is said to regard future contingents, in so far as it is concerned with acts, but not with the object of acts: because, of his own free-will, a man can think about past and necessary things, and yet the very act of thinking, in so far as it is subject to the free-will, is a future contingent. Hence the act of contrition also is a future contingent, in so far as it is subject to the free-will; and yet its object can be something past.

Reply Obj. 2. The consequent result which aggravates a sin was already present in the act as in its cause; wherefore when the sin was committed, its degree of gravity was already complete, and no further guilt accrued to it when the result took place. Nevertheless some accidental punishment accrues to it, in respect of which the damned will have the more motives of regret for the more evils that have resulted from their sins. It is in this sense that Jerome (Basil) speaks. Hence there is no need for contrition to be for other than past sins.

FIFTH ARTICLE

Whether a Man Ought to Have Contrition for Another's Sin?

We proceed thus to the Fifth Article:—

Objection 1. It would seem that a man ought to have contrition for another's sin. For one should not ask forgiveness for a sin unless one is contrite for it. Now forgiveness is asked for another's sin in Ps. xviii. 13: *From those of others spare thy servant.* Therefore a man ought to be contrite for another's sins.

Obj. 2. Further, man is bound, out of charity, to love his neighbor as himself. Now, through love of himself, he both grieves for his ills, and desires good things. Therefore, since we are bound to desire the goods of grace for our neighbor, as for ourselves, it seems that we ought to grieve for his sins, even as for our own. But contrition is nothing else than sorrow for sins. Therefore man should be contrite for the sins of others.

On the contrary, Contrition is an act of the virtue of penance. But no one repents save for what he has done himself. Therefore no one is contrite for others' sins.

I answer that, The same thing is crushed *(conteritur)* which hitherto was hard and whole. Hence contrition for sin must needs be in the same subject in which the hardness of sin was hitherto: so that there is no contrition for the sins of others.

Reply Obj. 1. The prophet prays to be spared from the sins of others, in so far as, through fellowship with sinners, a man contracts a stain by consenting to their sins: thus it is written (Ps. xvii. 27): *With the perverse thou wilt be perverted.*

Reply Obj. 2. We ought to grieve for the sins of others, but not to have contrition for them, because not all sorrow for past sins is contrition, as is evident from what has been said already.

SIXTH ARTICLE

Whether It Is Necessary to Have Contrition for Each Mortal Sin?

We proceed thus to the Sixth Article:—

Objection 1. It would seem that it is not necessary to have contrition for each mortal sin. For the movement of contrition in justification is instantaneous: whereas a man cannot think of every mortal sin in an instant. Therefore it is not necessary to have contrition for each mortal sin.

Obj. 2. Further, contrition should be for sins, inasmuch as they turn us away from God, because we need not be contrite for turning to creatures without turning away from God. Now all mortal sins agree in turning us away from God. Therefore one contrition for all is sufficient.

Obj. 3. Further, mortal sins have more in common with one another, than actual and original sin. Now one Baptism blots out all sins both actual and original. Therefore one general contrition blots out all mortal sins.

On the contrary, For diverse diseases there are diverse remedies, since *what heals the eye will not heal the foot,* as Jerome says (*Super Marc.* ix. 28). But contrition is the special remedy for one mortal sin. Therefore one general contrition for all mortal sins does not suffice.

Further, contrition is expressed by confession. But it is necessary to confess each mortal sin. Therefore it is necessary to have contrition for each mortal sin.

I answer that, Contrition may be considered in two ways, as to its origin, and as to its term. By origin of contrition I mean the process of thought, when a man thinks of his sin and is sorry for it, albeit not with the sorrow of contrition, yet with that of attrition. The term of contrition is when that sorrow is already quickened by grace. Accordingly, as regards the origin of contrition, a man needs to be contrite for each sin that he calls to mind; but as regards its term, it suffices for him to have one general contrition for all, because then the movement of his contrition acts in virtue of all his preceding dispositions.

This suffices for the *Reply* to the *First Objection*

Reply Obj. 2. Although all mortal sins agree in turning man away from God, yet they differ in the cause and mode of aversion, and in the degree of separation from God; and this regards the different ways in which they turn us to creatures.

Reply Obj. 3. Baptism acts in virtue of Christ's merit, Who had infinite power for the blotting out of all sins; and so for all sins one Baptism suffices. But in contrition, in addi-

tion to the merit of Christ, an act of ours is requisite, which must, therefore, correspond to each sin, since it has not infinite power for contrition.

It may also be replied that Baptism is a spiritual generation; whereas Penance, as regards contrition and its other parts, is a kind of spiritual healing by way of some alteration. Now it is evident in the generation of a body, accompanied by corruption of another body, that all the accidents contrary to the thing generated, and which were the accidents of the thing corrupted, are removed by the one generation: whereas in alteration, only that accident is removed which was contrary to the accident which is the term of the alteration. In like manner, one Baptism blots out all sins together and introduces a new life; whereas Penance does not blot out each sin, unless it be directed to each. For this reason it is necessary to be contrite for, and to confess each sin.

QUESTION 3

Of the Degree of Contrition

(In Three Articles)

We must now consider the degree of contrition: under which head there are three points of inquiry: (1) Whether contrition is the greatest possible sorrow in the world? (2) Whether the sorrow of contrition can be too great? (3) Whether sorrow for one sin ought to be greater than for another?

FIRST ARTICLE

Whether Contrition Is the Greatest Possible Sorrow in the World?

We proceed thus to the First Article:—

Objection 1. It would seem that contrition is not the greatest possible sorrow in the world. For sorrow is the sensation of hurt. But some hurts are more keenly felt than the hurt of sin, e.g. the hurt of a wound. Therefore contrition is not the greatest sorrow.

Obj. 2. Further, we judge of a cause according to its effect. Now the effect of sorrow is tears. Since therefore sometimes a contrite person does not shed outward tears for his sins, whereas he weeps for the death of a friend, or for a blow, or the like, it seems that contrition is not the greatest sorrow.

Obj. 3. Further, the more a thing is mingled with its contrary, the less its intensity. But the sorrow of contrition has a considerable admixture of joy, because the contrite man rejoices in his delivery, in the hope of pardon, and in many like things. Therefore his sorrow is very slight.

Obj. 4. Further, the sorrow of contrition is a kind of displeasure. But there are many things more displeasing to the contrite than their past sins; for they would not prefer to suffer the pains of hell rather than to sin; nor to have suffered, nor yet to suffer all manner of temporal punishment; else few would be found contrite. Therefore the sorrow of contrition is not the greatest.

On the contrary, According to Augustine *(De Civ. Dei,* xiv. 7, 9), *all sorrow is based on love.* Now the love of charity, on which the sorrow of contrition is based, is the greatest love. Therefore the sorrow of contrition is the greatest sorrow.

Further, sorrow is for evil. Therefore the greater the evil, the greater the sorrow. But the fault is a greater evil than its punishment. Therefore contrition which is sorrow for fault, surpasses all other sorrow.

I answer that, As stated above (Q. 1, A. 2, *ad* 1), there is a twofold sorrow in contrition: one is in the will, and is the very essence of contrition, being nothing else than displeasure at past sin, and this sorrow, in contrition, surpasses all other sorrows. For the more pleasing a thing is, the more displeasing is its contrary. Now the last end is above all things pleasing: wherefore sin, which turns us away from the last end, should be, above all things displeasing.—The other sorrow is in the sensitive part, and is caused by the former sorrow either from natural necessity, in so far as the lower powers follow the movements of the higher, or from choice, in so far as a penitent excites in himself this sorrow for his sins. In neither of these ways is such sorrow, of necessity, the greatest, because the lower powers are more deeply moved by their own objects than through redundance from the higher powers. Wherefore the nearer the operation of the higher powers approaches to the objects of the lower powers, the more do the latter follow the movement of the former. Consequently there is greater pain in the sensitive part, on account of a sensible hurt, than that which redounds into the sensitive part from the reason; and likewise, that which redounds from the reason when it deliberates on corporeal things, is greater than that which redounds from the reason in considering spiritual things. Therefore the sorrow which results in the sensitive part from the reason's displeasure at sin, is not greater than the other sorrows of which that same part is the subject: and likewise, neither is the sorrow which is assumed voluntarily greater than other sorrows,—both because the lower appetite does not obey the higher appetite infallibly, as though in the lower appetite there should arise a passion of such intensity and of such a kind as the higher appetite might ordain,—and because the passions are employed by the reason, in acts of virtue, according to a certain measure, which the sorrow that is without virtue sometimes does not observe, but exceeds.

Reply Obj. 1. Just as sensible sorrow is on account of the sensation of hurt, so interior sorrow is on account of the thought of something hurtful. Therefore, although the hurt of sin is not perceived by the external sense, yet it is perceived to be the most grievous hurt by the interior sense or reason.

Reply Obj. 2. Affections of the body are the immediate result of the sensitive passions and, through them, of the emotions of the higher appetite. Hence it is that bodily tears flow more quickly from sensible sorrow, or even from a thing that hurts the senses, than from the spiritual sorrow of contrition.

Reply Obj. 3. The joy which a penitent has for his sorrow does not lessen his displeasure (for it is not contrary to it), but increases it, according as every operation is increased by the delight which it causes, as stated in *Ethic.* x. 5. Thus he who delights in learning a science, learns the better, and, in like manner, he who rejoices in his displeasure, is the more intensely displeased. But it may well happen that this joy tempers the sorrow that results from the reason in the sensitive part.

Reply Obj. 4. The degree of displeasure at a thing should be proportionate to the degree of its malice. Now the malice of mortal sin is measured from Him against Whom it is committed, inasmuch as it is offensive to Him; and from him who sins, inasmuch as it is hurtful to him. And, since man should love God more than himself, therefore he should hate sin, as an offense against God, more than as being hurtful to himself. Now it is hurtful to him chiefly because it separates him from God; and in this respect the separation from God which is a punishment, should be more displeasing than the sin itself, as causing this hurt (since what is hated on account of something else, is less hated), but less than the sin, as an offense against God. Again, among all the punishments of malice a certain order is observed according to the degree of the hurt. Consequently, since this is the greatest hurt, inasmuch as it consists in privation of the greatest good, the greatest of all punishments will be separation from God.

Again, with regard to this displeasure, it is necessary to observe that there is also an accidental degree of malice, in respect of the present and the past; since what is past, is no more, whence it has less of the character of malice or goodness. Hence it is that a man shrinks from suffering an evil at the present, or at some future time, more than he shudders at the past evil: wherefore also, no passion of the soul corresponds directly to the past, as sorrow corresponds to present evil, and fear to future evil. Consequently, of two past evils, the mind shrinks the more from that one which still produces a greater effect at the present time, or which, it fears, will produce a greater effect in the future, although in the past it was the lesser evil. And, since the effect of the past sin is sometimes not so keenly felt as the effect of the past punishment, both because sin is more perfectly remedied than punishment, and because bodily defect is more manifest than spiritual defect, therefore even a man, who is well disposed, sometimes feels a greater abhorrence of his past punishment than of his past sin, although he would be ready to suffer the same punishment over again rather than commit the same sin.

We must also observe, in comparing sin with punishment, that some punishments are inseparable from offense of God, e.g. separation from God; and some also are everlasting, e.g. the punishment of hell. Therefore the punishment to which is connected offense of God is to be shunned in the same way as sin; whereas that which is everlasting is simply to be shunned more than sin. If, however, we separate from these punishments the notion of offense, and consider only the notion of punishment, they have the character of malice, less than sin has as an offense against God:

and for this reason should cause less displeasure.

We must, however, take note that, although the contrite should be thus disposed, yet he should not be questioned about his feelings, because man cannot easily measure them. Sometimes that which displeases least seems to displease most, through being more closely connected with some sensible hurt, which is more known to us.

SECOND ARTICLE

Whether the Sorrow of Contrition Can Be Too Great?

We proceed thus to the Second Article:—

Objection 1. It would seem that the sorrow of contrition cannot be too great. For no sorrow can be more immoderate than that which destroys its own subject. But the sorrow of contrition, if it be so great as to cause death or corruption of the body, is praiseworthy. For Anselm says *(Orat.* lii) : *Would that such were the exuberance of my inmost soul, as to dry up the marrow of my body;* and Augustine* confesses that *he deserves to blind his eyes with tears.* Therefore the sorrow of contrition cannot be too great.

Obj. 2. Further, the sorrow of contrition results from the love of charity. But the love of charity cannot be too great. Neither, therefore, can the sorrow of contrition be too great.

Obj. 3. *On the contrary,* Every moral virtue is destroyed by excess and deficiency. But contrition is an act of a moral virtue, viz. penance, since it is a part of justice. Therefore sorrow for sins can be too great.

I answer that, Contrition, as regards the sorrow in the reason, i.e. the displeasure, whereby the sin is displeasing through being an offense against God, cannot be too great; even as neither can the love of charity be too great, for when this is increased the aforesaid displeasure is increased also. But, as regards the sensible sorrow, contrition may be too great, even as outward affliction of the body may be too great. In all these things the rule should be the safeguarding of the subject, and of that general well-being which suffices for the fulfillment of one's duties; hence it is written (Rom. xii. 1): *Let your sacrifice be reasonable.†*

Reply Obj. 1. Anselm desired the marrow of his body to be dried up by the exuberance of his devotion, not as regards the natural humor, but as to his bodily desires and concupiscences. And, although Augustine acknowledged that he deserved to lose the use of his bodily eyes on account of his sins, because every sinner deserves not only eternal, but also temporal death, yet he did not wish his eyes to be blinded.

Reply Obj. 2. This objection considers the sorrow which is in the reason: while the *Third* considers the sorrow of the sensitive part.

THIRD ARTICLE

Whether Sorrow for One Sin Should Be Greater Than for Another?

We proceed thus to the Third Article:—

Objection 1. It would seem that sorrow for one sin need not be greater than for another. For Jerome *(Ep.* cviii) commends Paula for that *she deplored her slightest sins as much as great ones.* Therefore one need not be more sorry for one sin than for another.

Obj. 2. Further, the movement of contrition is instantaneous. Now one instantaneous movement cannot be at the same time more intense and more remiss. Therefore contrition for one sin need not be greater than for another.

Obj. 3. Further, contrition is for sin chiefly as turning us away from God. But all mortal sins agree in turning us away from God, since they all deprive us of grace whereby the soul is united to God. Therefore we should have equal contrition for all mortal sins.

On the contrary, It is written (Deut. xxv. 2) : *According to the measure of the sin, shall the measure also of the stripes be.* Now, in contrition, the stripes are measured according to the sins, because to contrition is united the purpose of making satisfaction. Therefore contrition should be for one sin more than for another.

Further, man should be contrite for that which he ought to have avoided. But he ought to avoid one sin more than another, if that sin is more grievous, and it be necessary to do one or the other. Therefore, in like manner, he ought to be more sorry for one, viz. the more grievous, than for the other.

I answer that, We may speak of contrition in two ways: first, in so far as it corresponds to each single sin, and thus, as regards the sorrow in the higher appetite, a man ought to be more sorry for a more grievous sin, because there is more reason for sorrow, viz. the offense against God, in such a sin than in another, since the more inordinate the act is, the more it offends God. In like manner, since the greater sin deserves a greater punishment, the sorrow also of the sensitive part, in so far as it is voluntarily undergone for sin, as the punishment thereof, ought to be greater where the sin is greater. But in so far as the emotions of the lower appetite result from the impres-

---

* *De Contritione Cordis,* work of an unknown author.
† Vulg.,—*Present your bodies . . . a reasonable sacrifice.*

sion of the higher appetite, the degree of sorrow depends on the disposition of the lower faculty to the reception of impressions from the higher faculty, and not on the greatness of the sin.

Secondly, contrition may be taken in so far as it is directed to all one's sins together, as in the act of justification. Such contrition arises either from the consideration of each single sin, and thus although it is but one act, yet the distinction of the sins remains virtually therein; or, at least, it includes the purpose of thinking of each sin; and in this way too it is habitually more for one than for another.

Reply Obj. 1. Paula is commended, not for deploring all her sins equally, but because she grieved for her slight sins as much as though they were grave sins, in comparison with other persons who grieve for their sins: but for graver sins she would have grieved much more.

Reply Obj. 2. In that instantaneous movement of contrition, although it is not possible to find an actually distinct intensity in respect of each individual sin, yet it is found in the way explained above; and also in another way, in so far as, in this general contrition, each individual sin is related to that particular motive of sorrow which occurs to the contrite person, viz. the offense against God. For he who loves a whole, loves its parts potentially although not actually, and accordingly he loves some parts more and some less, in proportion to their relation to the whole; thus he who loves a community, virtually loves each one more or less according to their respective relations to the common good. In like manner he who is sorry for having offended God, implicitly grieves for his different sins in different ways, according as by them he offended God more or less.

Reply Obj. 3. Although each mortal sin turns us away from God and deprives us of His grace, yet some remove us further away than others, inasmuch as through their inordinateness they become more out of harmony with the order of the Divine goodness, than others do.

QUESTION 4

Of the Time for Contrition

(In Three Articles)

WE must now consider the time for contrition: under which head there are three points of inquiry: (1) Whether the whole of this life is the time for contrition? (2) Whether it is expedient to grieve continually for our sins? (3) Whether souls grieve for their sins even after this life?

FIRST ARTICLE

Whether the Whole of This Life Is the Time for Contrition?

We proceed thus to the First Article:—

Objection 1. It would seem that the time for contrition is not the whole of this life. For as we should be sorry for a sin committed, so should we be ashamed of it. But shame for sin does not last all one's life, for Ambrose says (*De Pœnit.* ii) that *he whose sin is forgiven has nothing to be ashamed of.* Therefore it seems that neither should contrition last all one's life, since it is sorrow for sin.

Obj. 2. Further, it is written (1 Jo. iv. 18) that *perfect charity casteth out fear, because fear hath pain.* But sorrow also has pain. Therefore the sorrow of contrition cannot remain in the state of perfect charity.

Obj. 3. Further, there cannot be any sorrow for the past (since it is, properly speaking, about a present evil) except in so far as something of the past sin remains in the present time. Now, in this life, sometimes one attains to a state in which nothing remains of a past sin, neither disposition, nor guilt, nor any debt of punishment. Therefore there is no need to grieve any more for that sin.

Obj. 4. Further, it is written (Rom. viii. 28) that *to them that love God all things work together unto good,* even sins as a gloss declares.* Therefore there is no need for them to grieve for sin after it has been forgiven.

Obj. 5. Further, contrition is a part of Penance, condivided with satisfaction. But there is no need for continual satisfaction. Therefore contrition for sin need not be continual.

On the contrary, Augustine in *De Pœnitentia*† says that *when sorrow ceases, penance fails, and when penance fails, no pardon remains.* Therefore, since it behooves one not to lose the forgiveness which has been granted, it seems that one ought always to grieve for one's sins.

Further, it is written (Ecclus. v. 5): *Be not without fear about sin forgiven.* Therefore man should always grieve, that his sins may be forgiven him.

I answer that, As stated above (Q. 3, A. 1),

* Augustine, *De Correp. et Grat.*   † *De vera et falsa Pœnitentia,* work of an unknown author

there is a twofold sorrow in contrition: one is in the reason, and is detestation of the sin committed; the other is in the sensitive part, and results from the former: and as regards both, the time for contrition is the whole of the present state of life. For as long as one is a wayfarer, one detests the obstacles which retard or hinder one from reaching the end of the way. Wherefore, since past sin retards the course of our life towards God (because the time which was given to us for the course cannot be recovered), it follows that the state of contrition remains during the whole of this lifetime, as regards the detestation of sin. The same is to be said of the sensible sorrow, which is assumed by the will as a punishment: for since man, by sinning, deserved everlasting punishment, and sinned against the eternal God, the everlasting punishment being commuted into a temporal one, sorrow ought to remain during the whole of man's eternity, i.e. during the whole of the state of this life. For this reason Hugh of S. Victor says* that *when God absolves a man from eternal guilt and punishment, He binds him with a chain of eternal detestation of sin.*

Reply Obj. 1. Shame regards sin only as a disgraceful act; wherefore after sin has been taken away as to its guilt, there is no further motive for shame; but there does remain a motive of sorrow, which is for the guilt, not only as being something disgraceful, but also as having a hurt connected with it.

Reply Obj. 2. Servile fear which charity casts out, is opposed to charity by reason of its servility, because it regards the punishment. But the sorrow of contrition results from charity, as stated above (Q. 3, A. 2): wherefore the comparison fails.

Reply Obj. 3. Although, by penance, the sinner returns to his former state of grace and immunity from the debt of punishment, yet he never returns to his former dignity of innocence, and so something always remains from his past sin.

Reply Obj. 4. Just as a man ought not to do evil that good may come of it, so he ought not to rejoice in evil, for the reason that good may perchance come from it through the agency of Divine grace or providence, because his sins did not cause but hindered those goods; rather was it Divine providence that was their cause, and in this man should rejoice, whereas he should grieve for his sins.

Reply Obj. 5. Satisfaction depends on the punishment appointed, which should be enjoined for sins; hence it can come to an end, so that there be no further need of satisfaction. But that punishment is proportionate to

sin chiefly on the part of its adherence to a creature whence it derives its finiteness. On the other hand, the sorrow of contrition corresponds to sin on the part of the aversion, whence it derives a certain infinity; wherefore contrition ought to continue always; nor is it unreasonable if that which precedes remains, when that which follows is taken away.

SECOND ARTICLE

Whether It Is Expedient to Grieve for Sin Continually?

We proceed thus to the Second Article:—

Objection 1. It would seem that it is not expedient to grieve for sin continually. For it is sometimes expedient to rejoice, as is evident from Philip. iv. 4, where the gloss on the words, *Rejoice in the Lord always*, says that *it is necessary to rejoice*. Now it is not possible to rejoice and grieve at the same time. Therefore it is not expedient to grieve for sin continually.

Obj. 2. Further, that which, in itself, is an evil and a thing to be avoided should not be taken upon oneself, except in so far as it is necessary as a remedy against something, as in the case of burning or cutting a wound. Now sorrow is in itself an evil; wherefore it is written (Ecclus. xxx. 24): *Drive away sadness far from thee*, and the reason is given *(verse* 25): *For sadness hath killed many, and there is no profit in it.* Moreover the Philosopher says the same *(Ethic.* vii. 13, 14, x. 5). Therefore one should not grieve for sin any longer than suffices for the sin to be blotted out. Now sin is already blotted out after the first sorrow of contrition. Therefore it is not expedient to grieve any longer.

Obj. 3. Further, Bernard says *(Serm.* xi, *in Cant.): Sorrow is a good thing, if it is not continual; for honey should be mingled with wormwood.* Therefore it seems that it is inexpedient to grieve continually.

On the contrary, Augustine† says: *The penitent should always grieve, and rejoice in his grief.*

Further, it is expedient always to continue, as far as it is possible, those acts in which beatitude consists. Now such is sorrow for sin, as is shown by the words of Matth. v. 5, *Blessed are they that mourn.* Therefore it is expedient for sorrow to be as continual as possible.

I answer that, We find this condition in the acts of the virtues, that in them excess and defect are not possible, as is proved in *Ethic.* ii. 6, 7. Wherefore, since contrition, so far as it is a kind of displeasure seated in the rational

---

* Richard of S. Victor, *De Pot. Lig. et Solv.*, 3, 5, 13.
† *De vera et falsa Pœnitentia,* work of an unknown author.

appetite, is an act of the virtue of penance, there can never be excess in it, either as to its intensity, or as to its duration, except in so far as the act of one virtue hinders the act of another which is more urgent for the time being. Consequently the more continually a man can perform acts of this displeasure, the better it is, provided he exercises the acts of other virtues when and how he ought to. On the other hand, passions can have excess and defect, both in intensity and in duration. Wherefore, as the passion of sorrow, which the will takes upon itself, ought to be moderately intense, so ought it to be of moderate duration, lest, if it should last too long, man fall into despair, cowardice, and such like vices.

Reply Obj. 1. The sorrow of contrition is a hindrance to worldly joy, but not to the joy which is about God, and which has sorrow itself for object.

Reply Obj. 2. The words of Ecclesiasticus refer to worldly joy: and the Philosopher is referring to sorrow as a passion, of which we should make moderate use, according as the end, for which it is assumed, demands.

Reply Obj. 3. Bernard is speaking of sorrow as a passion.

THIRD ARTICLE

Whether Our Souls Are Contrite for Sins Even after This Life?

We proceed thus to the Third Article:—

Objection 1. It would seem that our souls are contrite for sins even after this life. For the love of charity causes displeasure at sin. Now, after this life, charity remains in some, both as to its act and as to its habit, since *charity never falleth away.* Therefore the displeasure at the sin committed, which is the essence of contrition, remains.

Obj. 2. Further, we should grieve more for sin than for punishment. But the souls in purgatory grieve for their sensible punishment and for the delay of glory. Much more, therefore, do they grieve for the sins they committed.

Obj. 3. Further, the pain of purgatory satisfies for sin. But satisfaction derives its efficacy from the power of contrition. Therefore contrition remains after this life.

On the contrary, contrition is a part of the sacrament of Penance. But the sacraments do not endure after this life. Neither, therefore, does contrition.

Further, contrition can be so great as to blot out both guilt and punishment. If therefore the souls in purgatory could have contrition, it would be possible for their debt of punishment to be remitted through the power of their contrition, so that they would be delivered from their sensible pain, which is false.

I answer that, Three things are to be observed in contrition: first, its genus, viz. sorrow; secondly, its form, for it is an act of virtue quickened by charity; thirdly, its efficacy, for it is a meritorious and sacramental act, and, to a certain extent, satisfactory. Accordingly, after this life, those souls which dwell in the heavenly country, cannot have contrition, because they are void of sorrow by reason of the fulness of their joy: those which are in hell, have no contrition, for although they have sorrow, they lack the grace which quickens sorrow; while those which are in purgatory have a sorrow for their sins, that is quickened by grace; yet it is not meritorious, for they are not in the state of meriting. In this life, however, all these three can be found.

Reply Obj. 1. Charity does not cause this sorrow, save in those who are capable of it; but the fulness of joy in the Blessed excludes all capability of sorrow from them: wherefore, though they have charity, they have no contrition.

Reply Obj. 2. The souls in purgatory grieve for their sins; but their sorrow is not contrition, because it lacks the efficacy of contrition.

Reply Obj. 3. The pain which the souls suffer in purgatory, cannot, properly speaking, be called satisfaction, because satisfaction demands a meritorious work; yet, in a broad sense, the payment of the punishment due may be called satisfaction.

QUESTION 5

Of the Effect of Contrition

(In Three Articles)

WE must now consider the effect of contrition: under which head there are three points of inquiry: (1) Whether the remission of sin is the effect of contrition? (2) Whether contrition can take away the debt of punishment entirely? (3) Whether slight contrition suffices to blot out great sins?

FIRST ARTICLE

Whether the Forgiveness of Sin Is the Effect of Contrition?

We proceed thus to the First Article:—

Objection 1. It would seem that the forgiveness of sin is not the effect of contrition.

For God alone forgives sins. But we are somewhat the cause of contrition, since it is an act of our own. Therefore contrition is not the cause of forgiveness.

Obj. 2. Further, contrition is an act of virtue. Now virtue follows the forgiveness of sin: because virtue and sin are not together in the soul. Therefore contrition is not the cause of the forgiveness of sin.

Obj. 3. Further, nothing but sin is an obstacle to receiving the Eucharist. But the contrite should not go to Communion before going to confession. Therefore they have not yet received the forgiveness of their sins.

On the contrary, a gloss on Ps. l. 19, *A sacrifice to God is an afflicted spirit,* says: *A hearty contrition is the sacrifice by which sins are loosed.*

Further, virtue and vice are engendered and corrupted by the same causes, as stated in *Ethic.* ii. 1, 2. Now sin is committed through the heart's inordinate love. Therefore it is destroyed by sorrow caused by the heart's ordinate love; and consequently contrition blots out sin.

I answer that, Contrition can be considered in two ways, either as part of a sacrament, or as an act of virtue, and in either case it is the cause of the forgiveness of sin, but not in the same way. Because, as part of a sacrament, it operates primarily as an instrument for the forgiveness of sin, as is evident with regard to the other sacraments (cf. *Sent.* iv, D. 1, Q. 1, A. 4: P. III, Q. 62, A. 1); while, as an act of virtue, it is the quasi-material cause of sin's forgiveness. For a disposition is, as it were, a necessary condition for justification, and a disposition is reduced to a material cause, if it be taken to denote that which disposes matter to receive something. It is otherwise in the case of an agent's disposition to act, because this is reduced to the genus of efficient cause.

Reply Obj. 1. God alone is the principal efficient cause of the forgiveness of sin: but the dispositive cause can be from us also, and likewise the sacramental cause, since the sacramental forms are words uttered by us, having an instrumental power of conferring grace whereby sins are forgiven.

Reply Obj. 2. The forgiveness of sin precedes virtue and the infusion of grace, in one way, and, in another, follows: and in so far as it follows, the act elicited by the virtue can be a cause of the forgiveness of sin.

Reply Obj. 3. The dispensation of the Eucharist belongs to the ministers of the Church: wherefore a man should not go to Communion until his sin has been forgiven through the ministers of the Church, although his sin may be forgiven him before God.

SECOND ARTICLE

Whether Contrition Can Take Away the Debt of Punishment Entirely?

We proceed thus to the Second Article:—

Objection 1. It would seem that contrition cannot take away the debt of punishment entirely. For satisfaction and confession are ordained for man's deliverance from the debt of punishment. Now no man is so perfectly contrite as not to be bound to confession and satisfaction. Therefore contrition is never so great as to blot out the entire debt of punishment.

Obj. 2. Further, in Penance the punishment should in some way compensate for the sin. Now some sins are accomplished by members of the body. Therefore, since it is for the due compensation for sin that *by what things a man sinneth, by the same also he is tormented* (Wis. xi. 17), it seems that the punishment for suchlike sins can never be remitted by contrition.

Obj. 3. Further, the sorrow of contrition is finite. Now an infinite punishment is due for some, viz. mortal, sins. Therefore contrition can never be so great as to remit the whole punishment.

On the contrary, The affections of the heart are more acceptable to God than external acts. Now man is absolved from both punishment and guilt by means of external actions; and therefore he is also by means of the heart's affections, such as contrition is.

Further, we have an example of this in the thief, to whom it was said (Luke xxiii. 43): *This day shalt thou be with Me in paradise,* on account of his one act of repentance.

As to whether the whole debt of punishment is always taken away by contrition, this question has already been considered above (*Sent.* iv, D. 14, Q. 2, AA. 1, 2; P. III, Q. 86, A. 4), where the same question was raised with regard to Penance.

I answer that, The intensity of contrition may be regarded in two ways. First, on the part of charity, which causes the displeasure, and in this way it may happen that the act of charity is so intense that the contrition resulting therefrom merits not only the removal of guilt, but also the remission of all punishment. Secondly, on the part of the sensible sorrow, which the will excites in contrition: and since this sorrow is also a kind of punishment, it may be so intense as to suffice for the remission of both guilt and punishment.

Reply Obj. 1. A man cannot be sure that his contrition suffices for the remission of both punishment and guilt: wherefore he is bound to confess and to make satisfaction, especially since his contrition would not be true contrition, unless he had the purpose of confessing united thereto: which purpose must also be carried into effect, on account of the precept given concerning confession.

Reply Obj. 2. Just as inward joy redounds into the outward parts of the body, so does interior sorrow show itself in the exterior members: wherefore it is written (Prov. xvii. 22): *A sorrowful spirit drieth up the bones.*

Reply Obj. 3. Although the sorrow of contrition is finite in its intensity, even as the punishment due for mortal sin is finite; yet it derives infinite power from charity, whereby it is quickened, and so it avails for the remission of both guilt and punishment.

THIRD ARTICLE

Whether Slight Contrition Suffices to Blot Out Great Sins?

We proceed thus to the Third Article:—

Objection 1. It would seem that slight contrition does not suffice to blot out great sins. For contrition is the remedy for sin. Now a bodily remedy, that heals a lesser bodily infirmity, does not suffice to heal a greater. Therefore the least contrition does not suffice to blot out very great sins.

Obj. 2. Further, it was stated above (Q. 3, A. 3) that for greater sins one ought to have greater contrition. Now contrition does not blot out sin, unless it fulfills the requisite conditions. Therefore the least contrition does not blot out all sins.

On the contrary, Every sanctifying grace blots out every mortal sin, because it is incompatible therewith. Now every contrition is quickened by sanctifying grace. Therefore, however slight it be, it blots out all sins.

I answer that, As we have often said (Q. 1, A. 2, *ad* 1; Q. 3, A. 1; Q. 4, A. 1), contrition includes a twofold sorrow. One is in the reason, and is displeasure at the sin committed. This can be so slight as not to suffice for real contrition, e.g. if a sin were less displeasing to a man, than separation from his last end ought to be; just as love can be so slack as not to suffice for real charity. The other sorrow is in the senses, and the slightness of this is no hindrance to real contrition, because it does not, of itself, belong essentially to contrition, but is connected with it accidentally: nor again is it under our control. Accordingly we must say that sorrow, however slight it be, provided it suffice for true contrition, blots out all sin.

Reply Obj. 1. Spiritual remedies derive infinite efficacy from the infinite power which operates in them: wherefore the remedy which suffices for healing a slight sin, suffices also to heal a great sin. This is seen in Baptism which looses great and small: and the same applies to contrition provided it fulfill the necessary conditions.

Reply Obj. 2. It follows of necessity that a man grieves more for a greater sin than for a lesser, according as it is more repugnant to the love which causes his sorrow. But if one has the same degree of sorrow for a greater sin, as another has for a lesser, this would suffice for the remission of the sin.

QUESTION 6

Of Confession, As Regards Its Necessity

(In Six Articles)

WE must now consider confession, about which there are six points for our consideration: (1) The necessity of confession: (2) Its nature: (3) Its minister: (4) Its quality: (5) Its effect: (6) The seal of confession.

Under the first head there are six points of inquiry: (1) Whether confession is necessary for salvation? (2) Whether confession is according to the natural law? (3) Whether all are bound to confession? (4) Whether it is lawful to confess a sin of which one is not guilty? (5) Whether one is bound to confess at once? (6) Whether one can be dispensed from confessing to another man?

FIRST ARTICLE

Whether Confession Is Necessary for Salvation?

We proceed thus to the First Article:—

Objection 1. It would seem that confession is not necessary for salvation. For the sacrament of Penance is ordained for the sake of the remission of sin. But sin is sufficiently remitted by the infusion of grace. Therefore confession is not necessary in order to do penance for one's sins.

Obj. 2. Further, we read of some being forgiven their sins without confession, e.g. Peter, Magdalen and Paul. But the grace that remits sins is not less efficacious now than it was then. Therefore neither is it necessary for salvation now that man should confess.

Obj. 3. Further, a sin which is contracted from another, should receive its remedy from another. Therefore actual sin, which a man has committed through his own act, must take its remedy from the man himself. Now Penance is ordained against such sins. Therefore confession is not necessary for salvation.

Obj. 4. Further, confession is necessary for a judicial sentence, in order that punishment may be inflicted in proportion to the offense. Now a man is able to inflict on himself a greater punishment than that which might be inflicted on him by another. Therefore it seems that confession is not necessary for salvation.

On the contrary, Boëthius says (*De Consol.* i): *If you want the physician to be of assistance to you, you must make your disease known to him.* But it is necessary for salvation that man should take medicine for his sins. Therefore it is necessary for salvation that man should make his disease known by means of confession.

Further, in a civil court the judge is distinct from the accused. Therefore the sinner who is the accused ought not to be his own judge, but should be judged by another and consequently ought to confess to him.

I answer that, Christ's Passion, without whose power, neither original nor actual sin is remitted, produces its effect in us through the reception of the sacraments which derive their efficacy from it. Wherefore for the remission of both actual and original sin, a sacrament of the Church is necessary, received either actually, or at least in desire, when a man fails to receive the sacrament actually, through an unavoidable obstacle, and not through contempt. Consequently those sacraments which are ordained as remedies for sin which is incompatible with salvation, are necessary for salvation: and so just as Baptism, whereby original sin is blotted out, is necessary for salvation, so also is the sacrament of Penance. And just as a man through asking to be baptized, submits to the ministers of the Church, to whom the dispensation of that sacrament belongs, even so, by confessing his sin, a man submits to a minister of the Church, that, through the sacrament of Penance dispensed by him, he may receive the pardon of his sins: nor can the minister apply a fitting remedy, unless he be acquainted with the sin, which knowledge he acquires through the penitent's confession. Wherefore confession is necessary for the salvation of a man who has fallen into a mortal actual sin.

Reply Obj. 1. The infusion of grace suffices for the remission of sin; but after the sin has been forgiven, the sinner still owes a debt of temporal punishment. Moreover, the sacraments of grace are ordained in order that man may receive the infusion of grace, and before he receives them, either actually or in his intention, he does not receive grace. This is evident in the case of Baptism, and applies to Penance likewise. Again, the penitent expiates his temporal punishment by undergoing the

shame of confession, by the power of the keys to which he submits, and by the enjoined satisfaction which the priest moderates according to the kind of sins made known to him in confession. Nevertheless the fact that confession is necessary for salvation is not due to its conducing to the satisfaction for sins, because this punishment to which one remains bound after the remission of sin, is temporal, wherefore the way of salvation remains open, without such punishment being expiated in this life: but it is due to its conducing to the remission of sin, as explained above.

Reply Obj. 2. Although we do not read that they confessed, it may be that they did; for many things were done which were not recorded in writing. Moreover Christ has the power of excellence in the sacraments; so that He could bestow the reality of the sacrament without using the things which belong to the sacrament.

Reply Obj. 3. The sin that is contracted from another, viz. original sin, can be remedied by an entirely extrinsic cause, as in the case of infants: whereas actual sin, which a man commits of himself, cannot be expiated without some operation on the part of the sinner. Nevertheless man is not sufficient to expiate his sin by himself, though he was sufficient to sin by himself, because sin is finite on the part of the thing to which it turns, in which respect the sinner returns to self; while, on the part of the aversion, sin derives infinity, in which respect the remission of sin must needs begin from someone else, because *that which is last in order of generation is first in the order of intention (Ethic.* iii). Consequently actual sin also must needs take its remedy from another.

Reply Obj. 4. Satisfaction would not suffice for the expiation of sin's punishment, by reason of the severity of the punishment which is enjoined in satisfaction, but it does suffice as being a part of the sacrament having the sacramental power; wherefore it ought to be imposed by the dispensers of the sacraments, and consequently confession is necessary.

SECOND ARTICLE

Whether Confession Is According to the Natural Law?

We proceed thus to the Second Article:—

Objection 1. It would seem that confession is according to the natural law. For Adam and Cain were bound to none but the precepts of the natural law, and yet they are reproached for not confessing their sin. Therefore confession of sin is according to the natural law.

Obj. 2. Further, those precepts which are common to the Old and New Law are according to the natural law. But confession was prescribed in the Old Law, as may be gathered from Isa. xliii. 26: *Tell, if thou hast anything to justify thyself.* Therefore it is according to the natural law.

Obj. 3. Further, Job was subject only to the natural law. But he confessed his sins, as appears from his words (xxxi. 33) *If, as a man, I have hid my sin.* Therefore confession is according to the natural law.

On the contrary, Isidore says *(Etym.* v.) that the natural law is the same in all. But confession is not in all in the same way. Therefore it is not according to the natural law.

Further, confession is made to one who has the keys. But the keys of the Church are not an institution of the natural law; neither, therefore, is confession.

I answer that, The sacraments are professions of faith, wherefore they ought to be proportionate to faith. Now faith surpasses the knowledge of natural reason, whose dictate is therefore surpassed by the sacraments. And since *the natural law is not begotten of opinion, but a product of a certain innate power,* as Tully states *(De Inv. Rhet.* ii), consequently the sacraments are not part of the natural law, but of the Divine law which is above nature. This latter, however, is sometimes called natural, in so far as whatever a thing derives from its Creator is natural to it, although, properly speaking, those things are said to be natural which are caused by the principles of nature. But such things are above nature as God reserves to Himself; and these are wrought either through the agency of nature, or in the working of miracles, or in the revelation of mysteries, or in the institution of the sacraments. Hence confession, which is of sacramental necessity, is according to Divine, but not according to natural law.

Reply Obj. 1. Adam is reproached for not confessing his sin before God: because the confession which is made to God by the acknowledgment of one's sin, is according to the natural law; whereas here we are speaking of confession made to a man.—We may also reply that in such a case confession of one's sin is according to the natural law, namely when one is called upon by the judge to confess in a court of law, for then the sinner should not lie by excusing or denying his sin, as Adam and Cain are blamed for doing. But confession made voluntarily to a man in order to receive from God the forgiveness of one's sins, is not according to the natural law.

Reply Obj. 2. The precepts of the natural law avail in the same way in the law of Moses and in the New Law. But although there was a kind of confession in the law of Moses, yet it was not after the same manner as in the

* Cf. Gregory, *Moral.* xxii. 9.

New Law, nor as in the law of nature; for in the law of nature it was sufficient to acknowledge one's sin inwardly before God; while in the law of Moses it was necessary for a man to declare his sin by some external sign, as by making a sin-offering, whereby the fact of his having sinned became known to another man; but it was not necessary for him to make known what particular sin he had committed, or what were its circumstances, as in the New Law.

Reply Obj. 3. Job is speaking of the man who hides his sin by denying it or excusing himself when he is accused thereof, as we may gather from a gloss* on the passage.

THIRD ARTICLE

Whether All Are Bound to Confession?

We proceed thus to the Third Article:—

Objection 1. It would seem that not all are bound to confession, for Jerome says on Isa. iii. 9 *(They have proclaimed abroad),* their sin, etc.: *Penance is the second plank after shipwreck.* But some have not suffered shipwreck after Baptism. Therefore Penance is not befitting them, and consequently neither is confession which is a part of Penance.

Obj. 2. Further, it is to the judge that confession should be made in any court. But some have no judge over them. Therefore they are not bound to confession.

Obj. 3. Further, some have none but venial sins. Now a man is not bound to confess such sins. Therefore not everyone is bound to confession.

On the contrary, Confession is condivided with satisfaction and contrition. Now all are bound to contrition and satisfaction. Therefore all are bound to confession also.

Further, this appears from the Decretals *(De Pœnit. et Remiss.* xii), where it is stated that *all of either sex are bound to confess their sins as soon as they shall come to the age of discretion.*

I answer that, We are bound to confession on two counts: first, by the Divine law, from the very fact that confession is a remedy, and in this way not all are bound to confession, but those only who fall into mortal sin after Baptism; secondly, by a precept of positive law, and in this way all are bound by the precept of the Church laid down in the general council (Later. iv: *Can.* 21) under Innocent III, both in order that everyone may acknowledge himself to be a sinner, because *all have sinned and need the grace of God* (Rom. iii. 23); and that the Eucharist may be approached with greater reverence; and lastly, that parish priests may know their flock, lest a wolf may hide therein.

Reply Obj. 1. Although it is possible for a man, in this mortal life, to avoid shipwreck, i.e. mortal sin, after Baptism, yet he cannot avoid venial sins, which dispose him to shipwreck, and against which also Penance is ordained; wherefore there is still room for Penance, and consequently for confession, even in those who do not commit mortal sins.

Reply Obj. 2. All must acknowledge Christ as their judge, to Whom they must confess in the person of His vicar; and although the latter may be the inferior if the penitent be a prelate, yet he is the superior, in so far as the penitent is a sinner, while the confessor is the minister of Christ.

Reply Obj. 3. A man is bound to confess his venial sins, not in virtue of the sacrament, but by the institution of the Church, and that, when he has no other sins to confess.—We may also, with others, answer that the Decretal quoted above does not bind others than those who have mortal sins to confess. This is evident from the fact that it orders all sins to be confessed, which cannot apply to venial sins, because no one can confess all his venial sins. Accordingly, a man who has no mortal sins to confess, is not bound to confess his venial sins, but it suffices for the fulfillment of the commandment of the Church that he present himself before the priest, and declare himself to be unconscious of any mortal sin: and this will count for his confession.

FOURTH ARTICLE

Whether It Is Lawful for a Man to Confess a Sin Which He Has Not Committed?

We proceed thus to the Fourth Article:—

Objection 1. It would seem that it is lawful for a man to confess a sin which he has not committed. For, as Gregory says *(Regist.* xii), *it is the mark of a good conscience to acknowledge a fault where there is none.* Therefore it is the mark of a good conscience to accuse oneself of those sins which one has not committed.

Obj. 2. Further, by humility a man deems himself worse than another, who is known to be a sinner, and in this he is to be praised. But it is lawful for a man to confess himself to be what he thinks he is. Therefore it is lawful to confess having committed a more grievous sin than one has.

Obj. 3. Further, sometimes one doubts about a sin, whether it be mortal or venial, in which case, seemingly, one ought to confess it as mortal. Therefore a person must sometimes confess a sin which he has not committed.

Obj. 4. Further, satisfaction originates from confession. But a man can do satisfaction for a sin which he has not committed. Therefore he can also confess a sin which he has not done.

On the contrary, Whosoever says he has done what he did not, tells an untruth. But no one ought to tell an untruth in confession, since every untruth is a sin. Therefore no one should confess a sin which he has not committed.

Further, in the public court of justice, no one should be accused of a crime which cannot be proved by means of proper witnesses. Now the witness, in the tribunal of Penance, is the conscience. Therefore a man ought not to accuse himself of a sin which is not on his conscience.

I answer that, The penitent should, by his confession, make his state known to his confessor. Now he who tells the priest something other than what he has on his conscience, whether it be good or evil, does not make his state known to the priest, but hides it; wherefore his confession is unavailing: and in order for it to be effective his words must agree with his thoughts, so that his words accuse him only of what is on his conscience.

Reply Obj. 1. To acknowledge a fault where there is none, may be understood in two ways: first, as referring to the substance of the act, and then it is untrue; for it is a mark, not of a good, but of an erroneous conscience, to acknowledge having done what one has not done.—Secondly, as referring to the circumstances of the act, and thus the saying of Gregory is true, because a just man fears lest, in any act which is good in itself, there should be any defect on his part; thus it is written (Job ix. 28): *I feared all my works.* Wherefore it is also the mark of a good conscience that a man should accuse himself in words of this fear which he holds in his thoughts.

From this may be gathered the *Reply* to the *Second Objection*, since a just man, who is truly humble, deems himself worse not as though he had committed an act generically worse, but because he fears lest in those things which he seems to do well, he may by pride sin more grievously.

Reply Obj. 3. When a man doubts whether a certain sin be mortal, he is bound to confess it, so long as he remains in doubt, because he sins mortally by committing or omitting anything, while doubting of its being a mortal sin, and thus leaving the matter to chance; and, moreover, he courts danger, if he neglect to confess that which he doubts may be a mortal sin. He should not, however, affirm that it was a mortal sin, but speak doubtfully, leaving the verdict to the priest, whose business it is to discern between what is leprosy and what is not.

Reply Obj. 4. A man does not commit a falsehood by making satisfaction for a sin which he did not commit, as when anyone confesses a sin which he thinks he has not committed. And if he mentions a sin that he has not committed, believing that he has, he does not lie; wherefore he does not sin, provided his confession thereof tally with his conscience.

FIFTH ARTICLE

Whether One Is Bound to Confess at Once?

We proceed thus to the Fifth Article:—

Objection 1. It would seem that one is bound to confess at once. For Hugh of S. Victor says *(De Sacram.* ii) : *The contempt of confession is inexcusable, unless there be an urgent reason for delay.* But everyone is bound to avoid contempt. Therefore everyone is bound to confess as soon as possible.

Obj. 2. Further, everyone is bound to do more to avoid spiritual disease than to avoid bodily disease. Now if a man who is sick in body were to delay sending for the physician, it would be detrimental to his health. Therefore it seems that it must needs be detrimental to a man's health if he omits to confess immediately to a priest if there be one at hand.

Obj. 3. Further, that which is due always, is due at once. But man owes confession to God always. Therefore he is bound to confess at once.

On the contrary, A fixed time both for confession and for receiving the Eucharist is determined by the Decretals (Cap. *Omnis utriusque sexus: De Pœnit. et Remiss.).* Now a man does not sin by failing to receive the Eucharist before the fixed time. Therefore he does not sin if he does not confess before that time.

Further, it is a mortal sin to omit doing what a commandment bids us to do. If therefore a man is bound to confess at once, and omits to do so, with a priest at hand, he would commit a mortal sin; and in like manner at any other time, and so on, so that he would fall into many mortal sins for the delay in confessing one, which seems unreasonable.

I answer that, As the purpose of confessing is united to contrition, a man is bound to have this purpose when he is bound to have contrition, viz. when he calls his sins to mind, and chiefly when he is in danger of death, or when he is so circumstanced that unless his sin be forgiven, he must fall into another sin: for instance, if a priest be bound to say Mass, and a confessor is at hand, he is bound to confess, or, if there be no confessor, he is bound at least to contrition and to have the purpose of confessing.

But to actual confession a man is bound in two ways. First, accidentally, viz. when he is bound to do something which he cannot do without committing a mortal sin, unless he go to confession first: for then he is bound to confess; for instance, if he has to receive the Eucharist, to which no one can approach, after committing a mortal sin, without confessing first, if a priest be at hand, and there be no urgent necessity. Hence it is that the Church obliges all to confess once a year; because she commands all to receive Holy Communion once a year, viz. at Easter, wherefore all must go to confession before that time.

Secondly, a man is bound absolutely to go to confession; and here the same reason applies to delay of confession as to delay of Baptism, because both are necessary sacraments. Now a man is not bound to receive Baptism as soon as he makes up his mind to be baptized; and so he would not sin mortally, if he were not baptized at once: nor is there any fixed time beyond which, if he defer Baptism, he would incur a mortal sin. Nevertheless the delay of Baptism may amount to a mortal sin, or it may not, and this depends on the cause of the delay, since, as the Philosopher says *(Phys.* viii, text. 15), the will does not defer doing what it wills to do, except for a reasonable cause. Wherefore if the cause of the delay of Baptism has a mortal sin connected with it, e.g. if a man put off being baptized through contempt, or some like motive, the delay will be a mortal sin, but otherwise not: and the same seems to apply to confession, which is not more necessary than Baptism. Moreover, since man is bound to fulfill in this life those things that are necessary for salvation, therefore, if he be in danger of death, he is bound, even absolutely, then and there to make his confession or to receive Baptism. For this reason too, James proclaimed at the same time the commandment about making confession and that about receiving Extreme Unction (James v. 14, 16). Therefore the opinion seems probable of those who say that a man is not bound to confess at once, though it is dangerous to delay.

Others, however, say that a contrite man is bound to confess at once, as soon as he has a reasonable and proper opportunity. Nor does it matter that the Decretal fixes the time limit to an annual confession, because the Church does not favor delay, but forbids the neglect involved in a further delay. Wherefore by this Decretal the man who delays is excused, not from sin in the tribunal of conscience, but from punishment in the tribunal of the Church; so that such a person would not be deprived of proper burial if he were to die before that time. But this seems too severe, because affirmative precepts bind, not at once, but at a fixed time; and this, not because it is most convenient to fulfill them then (for in that case if a man were not to give alms of his superfluous goods, whenever he met with a man in need, he would commit a mortal sin, which is false), but because the time involves urgency. Consequently, if he does not confess at the very first opportunity, it does not follow that he commits a mortal sin, even though he does not await a better opportunity; unless it becomes urgent for him to confess through being in danger of death. Nor is it on account of the Church's indulgence that he is not bound to confess at once, but on account of the nature of an affirmative precept, so that before the commandment was made, there was still less obligation.

Others again say that secular persons are not bound to confess before Lent, which is the time of penance for them; but that religious are bound to confess at once, because, for them, all time is a time for penance. But this is not to the point; for religious have no obligations besides those of other men, with the exception of such as they are bound to by vow.

Reply Obj. 1. Hugh is speaking of those who die without this sacrament.

Reply Obj. 2. It is not necessary for bodily health that the physician be sent for at once, except when there is necessity for being healed: and the same applies to spiritual disease.

Reply Obj. 3. The retaining of another's property against the owner's will is contrary to a negative precept, which binds always and for always, and therefore one is always bound to make immediate restitution. It is not the same with the fulfillment of an affirmative precept, which binds always, but not for always, wherefore one is not bound to fulfill it at once.

SIXTH ARTICLE

Whether One Can Be Dispensed from Confession?

We proceed thus to the Sixth Article:—

Objection 1. It would seem that one can be dispensed from confessing his sins to a man. For precepts of positive law are subject to dispensation by the prelates of the Church. Now such is confession, as appears from what was said above (A. 3). Therefore one may be dispensed from confession.

Obj. 2. Further, a man can grant a dispensation in that which was instituted by a man. But we read of confession being instituted, not by God, but by a man (James v. 16): *Confess your sins, one to another.* Now the Pope has the power of dispensation in things instituted by the apostles, as appears in the matter of bigamists. Therefore he can also dispense a man from confessing.

On the contrary, Penance, whereof confession is a part, is a necessary sacrament, even as Baptism is. Since therefore no one can be dispensed from Baptism, neither can one be dispensed from confession.

I answer that, The ministers of the Church are appointed in the Church which is founded by God. Wherefore they need to be appointed by the Church before exercising their ministry, just as the work of creation is presupposed to the work of nature. And since the Church is founded on faith and the sacraments, the ministers of the Church have no power to publish new articles of faith, or to do away with those which are already published, or to institute new sacraments, or to abolish those that are instituted, for this belongs to the power of excellence, which belongs to Christ alone, Who is the foundation of the Church. Consequently, the Pope can neither dispense a man so that he may be saved without Baptism, nor that he be saved without confession, in so far as it is obligatory in virtue of the sacrament. He can, however, dispense from confession, in so far as it is obligatory in virtue of the commandment of the Church; so that a man may delay confession longer than the limit prescribed by the Church.

Reply Obj. 1. The precepts of the Divine law do not bind less than those of the natural law: wherefore, just as no dispensation is possible from the natural law, so neither can there be from positive Divine law.

Reply Obj. 2. The precept about confession was not instituted by a man first of all, though it was promulgated by James: it was instituted by God, and although we do not read it explicitly, yet it was somewhat foreshadowed in the fact that those who were being prepared by John's Baptism for the grace of Christ, confessed their sins to him, and that the Lord sent the lepers to the priests, and though they were not priests of the New Testament, yet the priesthood of the New Testament was foreshadowed in them.

QUESTION 7

Of the Nature of Confession

(In Three Articles)

WE must now consider the nature of confession, under which head there are three points of inquiry: (1) Whether Augustine fittingly defines confession? (2) Whether confession is an act of virtue? (3) Whether confession is an act of the virtue of penance?

FIRST ARTICLE

Whether Augustine Fittingly Defines Confession?

We proceed thus to the First Article:—

Objection 1. It would seem that Augustine defines confession unfittingly, when he says *(Super Ps.* xxi) that confession *lays bare the hidden disease by the hope of pardon.* For the disease against which confession is ordained, is sin. Now sin is sometimes manifest. Therefore it should not be said that confession is the remedy for a *hidden* disease.

Obj. 2. Further, the beginning of penance is fear. But confession is a part of Penance. Therefore fear rather than *hope* should be set down as the cause of confession.

Obj. 3. Further, that which is placed under a seal, is not laid bare, but closed up. But the sin which is confessed is placed under the seal of confession. Therefore sin is not laid bare in confession, but closed up.

Obj. 4. Further, other definitions are to be found differing from the above. For Gregory says *(Hom.* xl, *in Evang.)* that confession is *the uncovering of sins, and the opening of the wound.* Others say that *confession is a legal declaration of our sins in the presence of a priest.* Others define it thus: *Confession is the sinner's sacramental self-accusation through shame for what he has done, which through the keys of the Church makes satisfaction for his sins, and binds him to perform the penance imposed on him.* Therefore it seems that the definition in question is insufficient, since it does not include all that these include.

I answer that, Several things offer themselves to our notice in the act of confession: first, the very substance or genus of the act, which is a kind of manifestation; secondly, the matter manifested, viz. sin; thirdly, the person to whom the manifestation is made, viz. the priest; fourthly, its cause, viz. hope of pardon; fifthly, its effect, viz. release from part of the punishment, and the obligation to pay the other part. Accordingly the first definition, given by Augustine, indicates the substance of the act, by saying that *it lays bare,* —the matter of confession, by saying that it

is a *hidden disease,*—its cause, which is *the hope of pardon;* while the other definitions include one or other of the five things aforesaid, as may be seen by anyone who considers the matter.

Reply Obj. 1. Although the priest, as a man, may sometimes have knowledge of the penitent's sin, yet he does not know it as a vicar of Christ (even as a judge sometimes knows a thing, as a man, of which he is ignorant, as a judge), and in this respect it is made known to him by confession. Or we may reply that although the external act may be in the open, yet the internal act, which is the cause of the external act, is hidden; so that it needs to be revealed by confession.

Reply Obj. 2. Confession presupposes charity, which gives us life, as stated in the text (iv. *Sent.,* D. 17). Now it is in contrition that charity is given; while servile fear, which is void of hope, is previous to charity: yet he that has charity is moved more by hope than by fear. Hence hope rather than fear is set down as the cause of confession.

Reply Obj. 3. In every confession sin is laid bare to the priest, and closed to others by the seal of confession.

Reply Obj. 4. It is not necessary that every definition should include everything connected with the thing defined: and for this reason we find some definitions or descriptions that indicate one cause, and some that indicate another.

SECOND ARTICLE

Whether Confession Is an Act of Virtue?

We proceed thus to the Second Article:—

Objection 1. It would seem that confession is not an act of virtue. For every act of virtue belongs to the natural law, since *we are naturally capable of virtue,* as the Philosopher says *(Ethic.* ii. 1). But confession does not belong to the natural law. Therefore it is not an act of virtue.

Obj. 2. Further, an act of virtue is more befitting one who is innocent than one who has sinned. But the confession of a sin, which is the confession of which we are speaking now, cannot be befitting an innocent man. Therefore it is not an act of virtue.

Obj. 3. Further, the grace which is in the sacraments differs somewhat from the grace which is in the virtues and gifts. But confession is part of a sacrament. Therefore it is not an act of virtue.

On the contrary, The precepts of the law are about acts of virtue. But confession comes under a precept. Therefore it is an act of virtue.

Further, we do not merit except by acts of virtue. But confession is meritorious, for *it opens the gate of heaven,* as the Master says (iv. *Sent.,* D. 17). Therefore it seems that it is an act of virtue.

I answer that, As stated above (I-II, Q. 18, AA. 6, 7; II-II, Q. 80; Q. 85, A. 3; Q. 109, A. 3), for an act to belong to a virtue it suffices that it be of such a nature as to imply some condition belonging to virtue. Now, although confession does not include everything that is required for virtue, yet its very name implies the manifestation of that which a man has on his conscience: for thus his lips and heart agree. For if a man professes with his lips what he does not hold in his heart, it is not a confession but a fiction. Now to express in words what one has in one's thoughts is a condition of virtue; and, consequently, confession is a good thing generically, and is an act of virtue: yet it can be done badly, if it be devoid of other due circumstances.

Reply Obj. 1. Natural reason, in a general way, inclines a man to make confession in the proper way, to confess as he ought, what he ought, and when he ought, and in this way confession belongs to the natural law. But it belongs to the Divine law to determine the circumstances, when, how, what, and to whom, with regard to the confession of which we are speaking now. Accordingly it is evident that the natural law inclines a man to confession, by means of the Divine law, which determines the circumstances, as is the case with all matters belonging to the positive law.

Reply Obj. 2. Although an innocent man may have the habit of the virtue whose object is a sin already committed, he has not the act, so long as he remains innocent. Wherefore the confession of sins, of which confession we are speaking now, is not befitting an innocent man, though it is an act of virtue.

Reply Obj. 3. Though the grace of the sacraments differs from the grace of the virtues, they are not contrary but disparate; hence there is nothing to prevent that which is an act of virtue, in so far as it proceeds from the free-will quickened by grace, from being a sacrament, or part of a sacrament, in so far as it is ordained as a remedy for sin.

THIRD ARTICLE

Whether Confession Is an Act of the Virtue of Penance?

We proceed thus to the Third Article:—

Objection 1. It would seem that confession is not an act of the virtue of penance. For an act belongs to the virtue which is its cause. Now the cause of confession is the hope of pardon, as appears from the definition given above (A. 1). Therefore it seems that it is an act of hope and not of penance.

Obj. 2. Further, shame is a part of temperance. But confession arises from shame, as appears in the definition given above (A. 1, *Obj.* 4). Therefore it is an act of temperance and not of penance.

Obj. 3. Further, the act of penance leans on Divine mercy. But confession leans rather on Divine wisdom, by reason of the truth which is required in it. Therefore it is not an act of penance.

Obj. 4. Further, we are moved to penance by the article of the Creed which is about the Judgment, on account of fear, which is the origin of penance. But we are moved to confession by the article which is about life everlasting, because it arises from hope of pardon. Therefore it is not an act of penance.

Obj. 5. Further, it belongs to the virtue of truth that a man shows himself to be what he is. But this is what a man does when he goes to confession. Therefore confession is an act of that virtue which is called truth, and not of penance.

On the contrary, Penance is ordained for the destruction of sin. Now confession is ordained to this also. Therefore it is an act of penance.

I answer that, It must be observed with regard to virtues, that when a special reason of goodness or difficulty is added over and above the object of a virtue, there is need of a special virtue: thus the expenditure of large sums is the object of magnificence, although the ordinary kind of average expenditure and gifts belongs to liberality, as appears from *Ethic.* ii. 7, iv. 1. The same applies to the confession of truth, which, although it belongs to the virtue of truth absolutely, yet, on account of the additional reason of goodness, begins to belong to another kind of virtue. Hence the Philosopher says *(Ethic.* iv. 7) that a confession made in a court of justice belongs to the virtue of justice rather than to truth. In like manner the confession of God's favors in praise of God, belongs not to truth, but to religion: and so too the confession of sins, in order to receive pardon for them, is not the elicited act of the virtue of truth, as some say, but of the virtue of penance. It may, however, be the commanded act of many virtues, in so far as the act of confession can be directed to the end of many virtues.

Reply Obj. 1. Hope is the cause of confession, not as eliciting but as commanding.

Reply Obj. 2. In that definition shame is not mentioned as the cause of confession, since it is more of a nature to hinder the act of confession, but rather as the joint cause of delivery from punishment (because shame is in itself a punishment), since also the keys of the Church are the joint cause with confession, to the same effect.

Reply Obj. 3. By a certain adaptation the parts of Penance can be ascribed to three Personal Attributes, so that contrition may correspond to mercy or goodness, by reason of its being sorrow for evil,—confession to wisdom, by reason of its being a manifestation of the truth,—and satisfaction to power, on account of the labor it entails. And since contrition is the first part of Penance, and renders the other parts efficacious, for this reason the same is to be said of Penance as a whole, as of contrition.

Reply Obj. 4. Since confession results from hope rather than from fear, as stated above (A. 1, *ad* 2), it is based on the article about eternal life which hope looks to, rather than on the article about the Judgment, which fear considers; although penance, in its aspect of contrition, is the opposite.

The *Reply* to the *Fifth Objection* is to be gathered from what has been said.

QUESTION 8

Of the Minister of Confession

(In Seven Articles)

WE must now consider the minister of confession, under which head there are seven points of inquiry: (1) Whether it is necessary to confess to a priest? (2) Whether it is ever lawful to confess to another than a priest? (3) Whether outside a case of necessity one who is not a priest can hear the confession of venial sins? (4) Whether it is necessary for a man to confess to his own priest? (5) Whether it is lawful for anyone to confess to another than his own priest, in virtue of a privilege or of the command of a superior? (6) Whether a penitent, in danger of death, can be absolved by any priest? (7) Whether the temporal punishment should be enjoined in proportion to the sin?

FIRST ARTICLE

Whether It Is Necessary to Confess to a Priest?

We proceed thus to the First Article:—

Objection 1. It would seem that it is not necessary to confess to a priest. For we are not bound to confession, except in virtue of its Divine institution. Now its Divine institution is made known to us (James v. 16): *Confess your sins, one to another,* where there is no mention of a priest. Therefore it is not necessary to confess to a priest.

Obj. 2. Further, Penance is a necessary sacrament, as is also Baptism. But any man is the minister of Baptism, on account of its necessity. Therefore any man is the minister of Penance. Now confession should be made to the minister of Penance. Therefore it suffices to confess to anyone.

Obj. 3. Further, confession is necessary in order that the measure of satisfaction should be imposed on the penitent. Now, sometimes another than a priest might be more discreet than many priests are in imposing the measure of satisfaction on the penitent. Therefore it is not necessary to confess to a priest.

Obj. 4. Further, confession was instituted in the Church in order that the rectors might know their sheep by sight. But sometimes a rector or prelate is not a priest. Therefore confession should not always be made to a priest.

On the contrary, The absolution of the penitent, for the sake of which he makes his confession, is imparted by none but priests to whom the keys are intrusted. Therefore confession should be made to a priest.

Further, confession is foreshadowed in the raising of the dead Lazarus to life. Now our Lord commanded none but the disciples to loose Lazarus (Jo. xi. 44). Therefore confession should be made to a priest.

I answer that, The grace which is given in the sacraments, descends from the Head to the members. Wherefore he alone who exercises a ministry over Christ's true body is a minister of the sacraments, wherein grace is given; and this belongs to a priest alone, who can consecrate the Eucharist. Therefore, since grace is given in the sacrament of Penance, none but a priest is the minister of the sacrament: and consequently sacramental confession which should be made to a minister of the Church, should be made to none but a priest.

Reply Obj. 1. James speaks on the presupposition of the Divine institutions: and since confession had already been prescribed by God to be made to a priest, in that He empowered them, in the person of the apostles, to forgive sins, as related in Jo. xx. 23, we must take the words of James as conveying an admonishment to confess to priests.

Reply Obj. 2. Baptism is a sacrament of greater necessity than Penance, as regards confession and absolution, because sometimes

Baptism cannot be omitted without loss of eternal salvation, as in the case of children who have not come to the use of reason: whereas this cannot be said of confession and absolution, which regard none but adults, in whom contrition, together with the purpose of confessing and the desire of absolution, suffices to deliver them from everlasting death. Consequently there is no parity between Baptism and confession.

Reply Obj. 3. In satisfaction we must consider not only the quantity of the punishment but also its power, inasmuch as it is part of a sacrament. In this way it requires a dispenser of the sacraments, though the quantity of the punishment may be fixed by another than a priest.

Reply Obj. 4. It may be necessary for two reasons to know the sheep by sight. First, in order to register them as members of Christ's flock, and to know the sheep by sight thus belongs to the pastoral charge and care, which is sometimes the duty of those who are not priests. Secondly, that they may be provided with suitable remedies for their health; and to know the sheep by sight thus belongs to the man, i.e. the priest, whose business it is to provide remedies conducive to health, such as the sacrament of the Eucharist, and other like things. It is to this knowledge of the sheep that confession is ordained.

SECOND ARTICLE

Whether It Is Ever Lawful to Confess to Another Than a Priest?

We proceed thus to the Second Article:—

Objection 1. It would seem that it is never lawful to confess to another than a priest. For confession is a sacramental accusation, as appears from the definition given above (Q. 7, A. 1). But the dispensing of a sacrament belongs to none but the minister of a sacrament. Since then the proper minister of Penance is a priest, it seems that confession should be made to no one else.

Obj. 2. Further, in every court of justice confession is ordained to the sentence. Now in a disputed case the sentence is void if pronounced by another than the proper judge; so that confession should be made to none but a judge. But, in the court of conscience, the judge is none but a priest, who has the power of binding and loosing. Therefore confession should be made to no one else.

Obj. 3. Further, in the case of Baptism, since anyone can baptize, if a layman has baptized, even without necessity, the Baptism should not be repeated by a priest. But if anyone confess to a layman in a case of neces-

sity, he is bound to repeat his confession to a priest, when the cause for urgency has passed. Therefore confession should not be made to a layman in a case of necessity.

On the contrary, is the authority of the text (iv. *Sent.*, D. 17).

I answer that, Just as Baptism is a necessary sacrament, so is Penance. And Baptism, through being a necessary sacrament has a twofold minister: one whose duty it is to baptize, in virtue of his office, viz. the priest, and another, to whom the conferring of Baptism is committed, in a case of necessity. In like manner the minister of Penance, to whom, in virtue of his office, confession should be made, is a priest; but in a case of necessity even a layman may take the place of a priest, and hear a person's confession.

Reply Obj. 1. In the sacrament of Penance there is not only something on the part of the minister, viz. the absolution and imposition of satisfaction, but also something on the part of the recipient, which is also essential to the sacrament, viz. contrition and confession. Now satisfaction originates from the minister in so far as he enjoins it, and from the penitent who fulfills it; and, for the fulness of the sacrament, both these things should concur when possible. But when there is reason for urgency, the penitent should fulfill his own part, by being contrite and confessing to whom he can; and although this person cannot perfect the sacrament, so as to fulfill the part of the priest by giving absolution, yet this defect is supplied by the High Priest. Nevertheless confession made to a layman, through lack* of a priest, is quasi-sacramental, although it is not a perfect sacrament, on account of the absence of the part which belongs to the priest.

Reply Obj. 2. Although a layman is not the judge of the person who confesses to him, yet, on account of the urgency, he does take the place of a judge over him, absolutely speaking, in so far as the penitent submits to him, through lack of a priest.

Reply Obj. 3. By means of the sacraments man must needs be reconciled not only to God, but also to the Church. Now he cannot be reconciled to the Church, unless the hallowing of the Church reach him. In Baptism the hallowing of the Church reaches a man through the element itself applied externally, which is sanctified by *the word of life* (Eph. v. 26), by whomsoever it is conferred: and so when once a man has been baptized, no matter by whom, he must not be baptized again. On the other hand, in Penance the hallowing of the Church reaches man by the minister alone, because in that sacrament there is no bodily element applied externally, through the hallowing of

* Here and in the *Reply* to the *Second Objection* the Leonine edition reads *through desire for a priest.*

which grace may be conferred. Consequently although the man who, in a case of necessity, has confessed to a layman, has received forgiveness from God, for the reason that he fulfilled, so far as he could, the purpose which he conceived in accordance with God's command, he is not yet reconciled to the Church, so as to be admitted to the sacraments, unless he first be absolved by a priest, even as he who has received the Baptism of desire, is not admitted to the Eucharist. Wherefore he must confess again to a priest, as soon as there is one at hand, and the more so since, as stated above (*ad* 1), the sacrament of Penance was not perfected, and so it needs yet to be perfected, in order that by receiving the sacrament, the penitent may receive a more plentiful effect, and that he may fulfill the commandment about receiving the sacrament of Penance.

THIRD ARTICLE

Whether, Outside a Case of Necessity, Anyone Who Is Not a Priest May Hear the Confession of Venial Sins?

We proceed thus to the Third Article :—

Objection 1. It would seem that, outside a case of necessity, no one but a priest may hear the confession of venial sins. For the dispensation of a sacrament is committed to a layman by reason of necessity. But the confession of venial sins is not necessary. Therefore it is not committed to a layman.

Obj. 2. Further, Extreme Unction is ordained against venial sin, just as Penance is. But the former may not be given by a layman, as appears from James v. 14. Therefore neither can the confession of venial sins be made to a layman.

On the contrary, is the authority of Bede (on James v. 16, *Confess . . . one to another*) quoted in the text (iv. *Sent.*, D. 17).

I answer that, By venial sin man is separated neither from God nor from the sacraments of the Church: wherefore he does not need to receive any further grace for the forgiveness of such a sin, nor does he need to be reconciled to the Church. Consequently a man does not need to confess his venial sins to a priest. And since confession made to a layman is a sacramental, although it is not a perfect sacrament, and since it proceeds from charity, it has a natural aptitude to remit sins, just as the beating of one's breast, or the sprinkling of holy water (cf. P. III, Q. 87, A. 3).

This suffices for the *Reply* to the *First Objection,* because there is no need to receive a sacrament for the forgiveness of venial sins; and a sacramental, such as holy water or the like, suffices for the purpose.

Reply Obj. 2. Extreme Unction is not given directly as a remedy for venial sin, nor is any other sacrament.

FOURTH ARTICLE

Whether It Is Necessary for One to Confess to One's Own Priest?

We proceed thus to the Fourth Article :—

Objection 1. It would seem that it is not necessary to confess to one's own priest. For Gregory* says: *By our apostolic authority and in discharge of our solicitude we have decreed that priests, who as monks imitate the example of the apostles, may preach, baptize, give communion, pray for sinners, impose penances, and absolve from sins.* Now monks are not the proper priests of anyone, since they have not the care of souls. Since, therefore, confession is made for the sake of absolution it suffices for it to be made to any priest.

Obj. 2. Further, the minister of this sacrament is a priest, as also of the Eucharist. But any priest can perform the Eucharist. Therefore any priest can administer the sacrament of Penance. Therefore there is no need to confess to one's own priest.

Obj. 3. Further, when we are bound to one thing in particular it is not left to our choice. But the choice of a discreet priest is left to us, as appears from the authority of Augustine quoted in the text (ix. *Sent.*, D. 17): for he says in *De vera et falsa Pœnitentia :*† *He who wishes to confess his sins, in order to find grace, must seek a priest who knows how to loose and to bind.* Therefore it seems unnecessary to confess to one's own priest.

Obj. 4. Further, there are some, such as prelates, who seem to have no priest of their own, since they have no superior: yet they are bound to confession. Therefore a man is not always bound to confess to his own priest.

Obj. 5. Further, *That which is instituted for the sake of charity, does not militate against charity,* as Bernard observes (*De Praecept. et Dispens.* ii). Now confession, which was instituted for the sake of charity, would militate against charity, if a man were bound to confess to any particular priest: e.g. if the sinner know that his own priest is a heretic, or a man of evil influence, or weak and prone to the very sin that he wishes to confess to him, or reasonably suspected of breaking the seal of confession, or if the penitent has to confess a sin committed against his confessor. Therefore it seems that one need not always confess to one's own priest.

Obj. 6. Further, men should not be straitened in matters necessary for salvation, lest they be hindered in the way of salvation. But

* Cf. *Can. Ex auctoritate* xvi, Q. 1.   † Work of an unknown author.

it seems a great inconvenience to be bound of necessity to confess to one particular man, and many might be hindered from going to confession, through either fear, shame, or something else of the kind. Therefore, since confession is necessary for salvation, men should not be straitened, as apparently they would be, by having to confess to their own priest.

On the contrary, stands a decree of Pope Innocent III in the Fourth Lateran Council (Can. 21), who appointed *all of either sex to confess once a year to their own priest.*

Further, as a bishop is to his diocese, so is a priest to his parish. Now it is unlawful, according to canon law (Can. *Nullus primas* ix, Q. 2; and Can. *Si quis episcoporum* xvi, Q. 5), for a bishop to exercise the episcopal office in another diocese. Therefore it is not lawful for one priest to hear the confession of another's parishioner.

I answer that, The other sacraments do not consist in an action of the recipient, but only in his receiving something, as is evident with regard to Baptism and so forth; though the action of the recipient is required as removing an obstacle, i.e. insincerity, in order that he may receive the benefit of the sacrament, if he has come to the use of his free-will. On the other hand, the action of the man who approaches the sacrament of Penance is essential to the sacrament, since contrition, confession, and satisfaction, which are acts of the penitent, are parts of Penance. Now our actions, since they have their origin in us, cannot be dispensed by others, except through their command. Hence whoever is appointed a dispenser of this sacrament, must be such as to be able to command something to be done. Now a man is not competent to command another unless he have jurisdiction over him. Consequently it is essential to this sacrament, not only for the minister to be in orders, as in the case of the other sacraments, but also for him to have jurisdiction: wherefore he that has no jurisdiction cannot administer this sacrament any more than one who is not a priest. Therefore confession should be made not only to a priest, but to one's own priest; for since a priest does not absolve a man except by binding him to do something, he alone can absolve, who, by his command, can bind the penitent to do something.

Reply Obj. 1. Gregory is speaking of those monks who have jurisdiction, through having charge of a parish; about whom some had maintained that from the very fact that they were monks, they could not absolve or impose penance, which is false.

Reply Obj. 2. The sacrament of the Eucharist does not require the power of command over a man, whereas this sacrament does, as stated above: and so the argument proves nothing. Nevertheless it is not lawful to receive the Eucharist from another than one's own priest, although it is a real sacrament that one receives from another.

Reply Obj. 3. The choice of a discreet priest is not left to us in such a way that we can do just as we like; but it is left to the permission of a higher authority, if perchance one's own priest happens to be less suitable for applying a salutary remedy to our sins.

Reply Obj. 4. Since it is the duty of prelates to dispense the sacraments, which the clean alone should handle, they are allowed by law *(De Pœnit. et Remiss.,* Cap. *Ne pro dilatione)* to choose a priest for their confessor; who in this respect is the prelate's superior; even as one physician is cured by another, not as a physician but as a patient.

Reply Obj. 5. In those cases wherein the penitent has reason to fear some harm to himself or to the priest by reason of his confessing to him, he should have recourse to the higher authority, or ask permission of the priest himself to confess to another; and if he fails to obtain permission, the case is to be decided as for a man who has no priest at hand; so that he should rather choose a layman and confess to him. Nor does he disobey the law of the Church by so doing, because the precepts of positive law do not extend beyond the intention of the lawgiver, which is the end of the precept, and in this case, is charity, according to the Apostle (1 Tim. i. 5). Nor is any slur cast on the priest, for he deserves to forfeit his privilege, for abusing the power intrusted to him.

Reply Obj. 6. The necessity of confessing to one's own priest does not straiten the way of salvation, but determines it sufficiently. A priest, however, would sin if he were not easy in giving permission to confess to another, because many are so weak that they would rather die without confession than confess to such a priest. Wherefore those priests who are too anxious to probe the consciences of their subjects by means of confession, lay a snare of damnation for many, and consequently for themselves.

FIFTH ARTICLE

Whether It Is Lawful for Anyone to Confess to Another Than His Own Priest, in Virtue of a Privilege or a Command Given by a Superior?

We proceed thus to the Fifth Article:—

Objection 1. It would seem that it is not lawful for anyone to confess to another than his own priest, even in virtue of a privilege or command given by a superior. For no privilege should be given that wrongs a third party. Now it would be prejudicial to the subject's own priest, if he were to confess to another. Therefore this cannot be allowed by a superior's privilege, permission, or command.

Obj. 2. Further, that which hinders the observance of a Divine command cannot be the subject of a command or privilege given by man. Now it is a Divine command to the rectors of churches to *know the countenance of their own cattle* (Prov. xxvii. 23); and this is hindered if another than the rector hear the confession of his subjects. Therefore this cannot be prescribed by any human privilege or command.

Obj. 3. Further, he that hears another's confession is the latter's own judge, else he could not bind or loose him. Now one man cannot have several priests or judges of his own, for then he would be bound to obey several men, which would be impossible, if their commands were contrary or incompatible. Therefore one may not confess to another than one's own priest, even with the superior's permission.

Obj. 4. Further, it is derogatory to a sacrament, or at least useless, to repeat a sacrament over the same matter. But he who has confessed to another priest, is bound to confess again to his own priest, if the latter requires him to do so, because he is not absolved from his obedience, whereby he is bound to him in this respect. Therefore it cannot be lawful for anyone to confess to another than his own priest.

On the contrary, He that can perform the actions of an order can depute the exercise thereof to anyone who has the same order. Now a superior, such as a bishop, can hear the confession of anyone belonging to a priest's parish, for sometimes he reserves certain cases to himself, since he is the chief rector. Therefore he can also depute another priest to hear that man.

Further, a superior can do whatever his subject can do. But the priest himself can give his parishioner permission to confess to another. Much more, therefore, can his superior do this.

Further, the power which a priest has among his people, comes to him from the bishop. Now it is through that power that he can hear confessions. Therefore, in like manner, another can do so, to whom the bishop gives the same power.

I answer that, A priest may be hindered in two ways from hearing a man's confession: first, through lack of jurisdiction; secondly, through being prevented from exercising his order, as those who are excommunicate, degraded, and so forth. Now whoever has juris-

diction, can depute to another whatever comes under his jurisdiction; so that if a priest is hindered from hearing a man's confession through want of jurisdiction, anyone who has immediate jurisdiction over that man, priest, bishop, or Pope, can depute that priest to hear his confession and absolve him. If, on the other hand, the priest cannot hear the confession, on account of an impediment to the exercise of his order, anyone who has the power to remove that impediment can permit him to hear confessions.

Reply Obj. 1. No wrong is done to a person unless what is taken away from him was granted for his own benefit. Now the power of jurisdiction is not granted a man for his own benefit, but for the good of the people and for the glory of God. Wherefore if the higher prelates deem it expedient for the furthering of the people's salvation and God's glory, to commit matters of jurisdiction to others, no wrong is done to the inferior prelates, except to those who *seek the things that are their own; not the things that are Jesus Christ's* (Philip. ii. 21), and who rule their flock, not by feeding it, but by feeding on it.

Reply Obj. 2. The rector of a church should *know the countenance of his own cattle* in two ways. First, by an assiduous attention to their external conduct, so as to watch over the flock committed to his care: and in acquiring this knowledge he should not believe his subject, but, as far as possible, inquire into the truth of facts. Secondly, by the manifestation of confession; and with regard to this knowledge, he cannot arrive at any greater certainty than by believing his subject, because this is necessary that he may help his subject's conscience. Consequently in the tribunal of confession, the penitent is believed whether he speak for himself or against himself, but not in the court of external judgment: wherefore it suffices for this knowledge that he believe the penitent when he says that he has confessed to one who could absolve him. It is therefore clear that this knowledge of the flock is not hindered by a privilege granted to another to hear confessions.

Reply Obj. 3. It would be inconvenient, if two men were placed equally over the same people, but there is no inconvenience if over the same people two are placed one of whom is over the other. In this way the parish priest, the bishop, and the Pope are placed immediately over the same people, and each of them can commit matters of jurisdiction to some other. Now a higher superior delegates a man in two ways: first, so that the latter takes the superior's place, as when the Pope or a bishop appoints his penitentiaries; and then the man thus delegated is higher than the inferior prelate, as the Pope's penitentiary is higher than a bishop, and the bishop's penitentiary than a parish priest, and the penitent is bound to obey the former rather than the latter. Secondly, so that the delegate is appointed the coadjutor of this other priest; and since a co-adjutor is subordinate to the person he is appointed to help, he holds a lower rank, and the penitent is not so bound to obey him as his own priest.

Reply Obj. 4. No man is bound to confess sins that he has no longer. Consequently, if a man has confessed to the bishop's penitentiary, or to someone else having faculties from the bishop, his sins are forgiven both before the Church and before God, so that he is not bound to confess them to his own priest, however much the latter may insist: but on account of the Ecclesiastical precept *(De Pœnit. et Remiss.,* Cap. *Omnis utriusque)* which prescribes confession to be made once a year to one's own priest, he is under the same obligation as one who has committed none but venial sins. For such a one, according to some, is bound to confess none but venial sins, or he must declare that he is free from mortal sin, and the priest, in the tribunal of conscience, ought, and is bound, to believe him. If, however, he were bound to confess again, his first confession would not be useless, because the more priests one confesses to, the more is the punishment remitted, both by reason of the shame in confessing, which is reckoned as a satisfactory punishment, and by reason of the power of the keys: so that one might confess so often as to be delivered from all punishment. Nor is repetition derogatory to a sacrament, except in those wherein there is some kind of sanctification, either by the impressing of a character, or by the consecration of the matter, neither of which applies to Penance. Hence it would be well for him who hears confessions by the bishop's authority, to advise the penitent to confess to his own priest, yet he must absolve him, even if he declines to do so.

SIXTH ARTICLE

Whether a Penitent, at the Point of Death, Can Be Absolved by Any Priest?

We proceed thus to the Sixth Article:—

Objection 1. It would seem that a penitent, at the point of death, cannot be absolved by any priest. For absolution requires jurisdiction, as stated above (A. 5). Now a priest does not acquire jurisdiction over a man who repents at the point of death. Therefore he cannot absolve him.

Obj. 2. Further, he that receives the sacrament of Baptism, when in danger of death, from another than his own priest, does not need to be baptized again by the latter. If, therefore, any priest can absolve, from any sin, a man who is in danger of death, the penitent, if he survive the danger, need not go to his own priest; which is false, since otherwise the priest would not *know the countenance of his cattle.*

Obj. 3. Further, when there is danger of death, Baptism can be conferred not only by a strange priest, but also by one who is not a priest. But one who is not a priest can never absolve in the tribunal of Penance. Therefore neither can a priest absolve a man who is not his subject, when he is in danger of death.

On the contrary, Spiritual necessity is greater than bodily necessity. But it is lawful in a case of extreme necessity, for a man to make use of another's property, even against the owner's will, in order to supply a bodily need. Therefore in danger of death, a man may be absolved by another than his own priest, in order to supply his spiritual need.

Further, the authorities quoted in the text prove the same (iv. *Sent.,* D. 20, Cap. *Non Habet).*

I answer that, If we consider the power of the keys, every priest has power over all men equally and over all sins: and it is due to the fact that by the ordination of the Church, he has a limited jurisdiction or none at all, that he cannot absolve all men from all sins. But since *necessity knows no law,** in cases of necessity the ordination of the Church does not hinder him from being able to absolve, since he has the keys sacramentally: and the penitent will receive as much benefit from the absolution of this other priest as if he had been absolved by his own. Moreover a man can then be absolved by any priest not only from his sins, but also from excommunication, by whomsoever pronounced, because such absolution is also a matter of that jurisdiction which by the ordination of the Church is confined within certain limits.

Reply Obj. 1. One person may act on the jurisdiction of another according to the latter's will, since matters of jurisdiction can be deputed. Since, therefore, the Church recognizes absolution granted by any priest at the hour of death, from this very fact a priest has the use of jurisdiction though he lack the power of jurisdiction.

Reply Obj. 2. He needs to go to his own priest, not that he may be absolved again from the sins, from which he was absolved when in danger of death, but that his own priest may know that he is absolved. In like manner, he who has been absolved from excommunication needs to go to the judge, who in other circum-

* Cap. *Consilium, De observ. jejun.; De reg. jur.* (v, Decretal.).

stances could have absolved him, not in order to seek absolution, but in order to offer satisfaction.

Reply Obj. 3. Baptism derives its efficacy from the sanctification of the matter itself, so that a man receives the sacrament whosoever baptizes him: whereas the sacramental power of Penance consists in a sanctification pronounced by the minister, so that if a man confess to a layman, although he fulfills his own part of the sacramental confession, he does not receive sacramental absolution. Wherefore his confession avails him somewhat, as to the lessening of his punishment, owing to the merit derived from his confession and to his repentance; but he does not receive that diminution of his punishment which results from the power of the keys; and consequently he must confess again to a priest; and one who has confessed thus, is more punished hereafter than if he had confessed to a priest.

SEVENTH ARTICLE

Whether the Temporal Punishment Is Imposed According to the Degree of the Fault?

We proceed thus to the Seventh Article:—

Objection 1. It would seem that the temporal punishment, the debt of which remains after Penance, is not imposed according to the degree of fault. For it is imposed according to the degree of pleasure derived from the sin, as appears from Apoc. xviii. 7: *As much as she hath glorified herself and lived in delicacies, so much torment and sorrow give ye her.* Yet sometimes where there is greater pleasure, there is less fault, since *carnal sins, which afford more pleasure than spiritual sins, are less guilty,* according to Gregory *(Moral.* xxxiii. 2). Therefore the punishment is not imposed according to the degree of fault.

Obj. 2. Further, in the New Law one is bound to punishment for mortal sins, in the same way as in the Old Law. Now in the Old Law the punishment for sin was due to last seven days, in other words, they had to remain unclean seven days for one mortal sin. Since therefore, in the New Testament, a punishment of seven years is imposed for one mortal sin, it seems that the quantity of the punishment does not answer to the degree of fault.

Obj. 3. Further, the sin of murder in a layman is more grievous than that of fornication in a priest, because the circumstance which is taken from the species of a sin, is more aggravating than that which is taken from the person of the sinner. Now a punishment of seven years' duration is appointed for a layman guilty of murder, while for fornication a priest is punished for ten years, according to Can. *Presbyter,* Dist. lxxxii. Therefore

punishment is not imposed according to the degree of fault.

Obj. 4. Further, a sin committed against the very body of Christ is most grievous, because the greater the person sinned against, the more grievous the sin. Now for spilling the blood of Christ in the sacrament of the altar a punishment of forty days or a little more is enjoined, while a punishment of seven years is prescribed for fornication, according to the Canons *(ibid.).* Therefore the quantity of the punishment does not answer to the degree of fault.

On the contrary, It is written (Isa. xxvii. 8): *In measure against measure, when it shall be cast off, thou shalt judge it.* Therefore the quantity of punishment adjudicated for sin answers the degree of fault.

Further, man is reduced to the equality of justice by the punishment inflicted on him. But this would not be so if the quantity of the fault and of the punishment did not mutually correspond. Therefore one answers the other.

I answer that, After the forgiveness of sin, a punishment is required for two reasons, viz. to pay the debt, and to afford a remedy. Hence the punishment may be imposed in consideration of two things. First, in consideration of the debt, and in this way the quantity of the punishment corresponds radically to the quantity of the fault, before anything of the latter is forgiven: yet the more there is remitted by the first of those things which are of a nature to remit punishment, the less there remains to be remitted or paid by the other, because the more contrition remits of the punishment, the less there remains to be remitted by confession. Secondly, in consideration of the remedy, either as regards the one who sinned, or as regards others: and thus sometimes a greater punishment is enjoined for a lesser sin; either because one man's sin is more difficult to resist than another's (thus a heavier punishment is imposed on a young man for fornication, than on an old man, though the former's sin be less grievous), or because one man's sin, for instance, a priest's, is more dangerous to others, than another's sin, or because the people are more prone to that particular sin, so that it is necessary by the punishment of the one man to deter others. Consequently, in the tribunal of Penance, the punishment has to be imposed with due regard to both these things: and so a greater punishment is not always imposed for a greater sin. On the other hand, the punishment of Purgatory is only for the payment of the debt, because there is no longer any possibility of sinning, so that this punishment is meted only according to the measure of sin, with due consideration however for the degree of contrition, and for confession and absolution, since all these lessen the punishment somewhat: wherefore the priest in enjoining satisfaction should bear them in mind.

Reply Obj. 1. In the words quoted two things are mentioned with regard to the sin, viz. *glorification* and *delicacies* or *delectation;* the first of which regards the uplifting of the sinner, whereby he resists God; while the second regards the pleasure of sin: and though sometimes there is less pleasure in a greater sin, yet there is greater uplifting; wherefore the argument does not prove.

Reply Obj. 2. This punishment of seven days did not expiate the punishment due for the sin, so that even if the sinner died after that time, he would be punished in Purgatory: but it was in expiation of the irregularity incurred, from which all the legal sacrifices expiated. Nevertheless, other things being equal, a man sins more grievously under the New Law than under the Old, on account of the more plentiful sanctification received in Baptism, and on account of the more powerful blessings bestowed by God on the human race. This is evident from Heb. 29: *How much more, do you think, he deserveth worse punishments,* etc.—And yet it is not universally true that a seven years' penance is exacted for every mortal sin: but it is a kind of general rule applicable to the majority of cases, which must, nevertheless, be disregarded, with due consideration for the various circumstances of sins and penitents.

Reply Obj. 3. A bishop or priest sins with greater danger to others or to himself; wherefore the canons are more anxious to withdraw him from sin, by inflicting a greater punishment, in as much as it is intended as a remedy; although sometimes so great a punishment is not strictly due. Hence he is punished less in Purgatory.

Reply Obj. 4. This punishment refers to the case when this happens against the priest's will: for if he spilled it willingly, he would deserve a much heavier punishment.

QUESTION 9

Of the Quality of Confession

(In Four Articles)

WE must now consider the quality of confession: under which head there are four points of inquiry: (1) Whether confession can be lacking in form? (2) Whether confession ought to be entire? (3) Whether one can confess through another, or by writing? (4) Whether the sixteen conditions, which are assigned by the masters, are necessary for confession?

FIRST ARTICLE

Whether Confession Can Be Lacking in Form?

We proceed thus to the First Article:—

Objection 1. It would seem that confession cannot be lacking in form. For it is written (Ecclus. xvii. 26): *Praise (confession) perisheth from the dead as nothing.* But a man without charity is dead, because charity is the life of the soul. Therefore there can be no confession without charity.

Obj. 2. Further, confession is condivided with contrition and satisfaction. But contrition and satisfaction are impossible without charity. Therefore confession is also impossible without charity.

Obj. 3. Further, it is necessary in confession that the word should agree with the thought, for the very name of confession requires this. Now if a man confess while remaining attached to sin, his word is not in accord with his thought, since in his heart he holds to sin, while he condemns it with his lips. Therefore such a man does not confess.

On the contrary, Every man is bound to confess his mortal sins. Now if a man in mortal sin has confessed once, he is not bound to confess the same sins again, because, as no man knows himself to have charity, no man would know of him that he had confessed. Therefore it is not necessary that confession should be quickened by charity.

I answer that, Confession is an act of virtue, and is part of a sacrament. In so far as it is an act of virtue, it has the property of being meritorious, and thus is of no avail without charity, which is the principle of merit. But in so far as it is part of a sacrament, it subordinates the penitent to the priest who has the keys of the Church, and who by means of the confession knows the conscience of the person confessing. In this way it is possible for confession to be in one who is not contrite, for he can make his sins known to the priest, and subject himself to the keys of the Church: and though he does not receive the fruit of absolution then, yet he will begin to receive it, when he is sincerely contrite, as happens in the other sacraments: wherefore he is not bound to repeat his confession, but to confess his lack of sincerity.

Reply Obj. 1. These words must be understood as referring to the receiving of the fruit of confession, which none can receive who is not in the state of charity.

Reply Obj. 2. Contrition and satisfaction are offered to God: but confession is made to man: hence it is essential to contrition and satisfaction, but not to confession, that man should be united to God by charity.

Reply Obj. 3. He who declares the sins which he has, speaks the truth; and thus his thought agrees with his lips or words, as to the substance of confession, though it is discordant with the purpose of confession.

SECOND ARTICLE

Whether Confession Should Be Entire?

We proceed thus to the Second Article:—

Objection 1. It would seem that it is not necessary for confession to be entire, namely, for a man to confess all his sins to one priest. For shame conduces to the diminution of punishment. Now the greater the number of priests to whom a man confesses, the greater his shame. Therefore confession is more fruitful if it be divided among several priests.

Obj. 2. Further, confession is necessary in Penance in order that punishment may be enjoined for sin according to the judgment of the priest. Now a sufficient punishment for different sins can be imposed by different priests. Therefore it is not necessary to confess all one's sins to one priest.

Obj. 3. Further, it may happen that a man after going to confession and performing his penance, remembers a mortal sin, which escaped his memory while confessing, and that his own priest to whom he confessed first is no longer available, so that he can only confess that sin to another priest, and thus he will confess different sins to different priests.

Obj. 4. Further, the sole reason for confessing one's sins to a priest is in order to receive absolution. Now sometimes, the priest who hears a confession can absolve from some of the sins, but not from all. Therefore in such a case at all events the confession need not be entire.

On the contrary, Hypocrisy is an obstacle to Penance. But it savors of hypocrisy to divide one's confession, as Augustine says.* Therefore confession should be entire. Further, confession is a part of Penance. But Penance should be entire. Therefore confession also should be entire.

I answer that, In prescribing medicine for the body, the physician should know not only the disease for which he is prescribing, but also the general constitution of the sick person, since one disease is aggravated by the addition of another, and a medicine which

would be adapted to one disease, would be harmful to another. The same is to be said in regard to sins, for one is aggravated when another is added to it; and a remedy which would be suitable for one sin, might prove an incentive to another, since sometimes a man is guilty of contrary sins, as Gregory says (*Pastoral.* iii. 3). Hence it is necessary for confession that man confess all the sins that he calls to mind, and if he fails to do this, it is not a confession, but a pretense of confession.

Reply Obj. 1. Although a man's shame is multiplied when he makes a divided confession to different confessors, yet all his different shames together are not so great as that with which he confesses all his sins together: because one sin considered by itself does not prove the evil disposition of the sinner, as when it is considered in conjunction with several others, for a man may fall into one sin through ignorance or weakness, but a number of sins proves the malice of the sinner, or his great corruption.

Reply Obj. 2. The punishment imposed by different priests would not be sufficient, because each would only consider one sin by itself, and not the gravity which it derives from being in conjunction with another. Moreover sometimes the punishment which would be given for one sin would foster another. Again the priest in hearing a confession takes the place of God, so that confession should be made to him just as contrition is made to God: wherefore as there would be no contrition unless one were contrite for all the sins which one calls to mind, so is there no confession unless one confess all the sins that one remembers committing.

Reply Obj. 3. Some say that when a man remembers a sin which he had previously forgotten, he ought to confess again the sins which he had confessed before, especially if he cannot go to the same priest to whom his previous confession was made, in order that the total quantity of his sins may be made known to one priest. But this does not seem necessary, because sin takes its quantity both from itself and from the conjunction of another; and as to the sins which he confessed he had already manifested their quantity which they have of themselves, while as to the sin which he had forgotten, in order that the priest may know the quantity which it has under both the above heads, it is enough that the penitent declare it explicitly, and confess the others in general, saying that he had confessed many sins in his previous confession, but had forgotten this particular one.

Reply Obj. 4. Although the priest may be

* *De vera et falsa Pœnitentia,* work of an unknown author.

unable to absolve the penitent from all his sins, yet the latter is bound to confess all to him, that he may know the total quantity of his guilt, and refer him to the superior with regard to the sins from which he cannot absolve him.

THIRD ARTICLE

Whether One May Confess through Another, or by Writing?

We proceed thus to the Third Article:—

Objection 1. It would seem that one may confess through another, or by writing. For confession is necessary in order that the penitent's conscience may be made known to the priest. But a man can make his conscience known to the priest, through another or by writing. Therefore it is enough to confess through another or by writing.

Obj. 2. Further, some are not understood by their own priests on account of a difference of language, and consequently cannot confess save through others. Therefore it is not essential to the sacrament that one should confess by oneself, so that if anyone confesses through another in any way whatever, it suffices for his salvation.

Obj. 3. Further, it is essential to the sacrament that a man should confess to his own priest, as appears from what has been said (Q. 8, A. 5). Now sometimes a man's own priest is absent, so that the penitent cannot speak to him with his own voice. But he could make his conscience known to him by writing. Therefore it seems that he ought to manifest his conscience to him by writing to him.

On the contrary, Man is bound to confess his sins even as he is bound to confess his faith. But confession of faith should be made *with the mouth,* as appears from Rom. x. 10: therefore confession of sins should also.

Further, who sinned by himself should, by himself, do penance. But confession is part of penance. Therefore the penitent should confess his own sins.

I answer that, Confession is not only an act of virtue, but also part of a sacrament. Now, though, in so far as it is an act of virtue it matters not how it is done, even if it be easier to do it in one way than in another, yet, in so far as it is part of a sacrament, it has a determinate act, just as the other sacraments have a determinate matter. And as in Baptism, in order to signify the inward washing, we employ that element which is chiefly used in washing, so in the sacramental act which is intended for manifestation we generally make use of that act which is most commonly employed for the purpose of manifestation, viz. our own words; for other ways have been introduced as supplementary to this.

Reply Obj. 1. Just as in Baptism it is not enough to wash with anything, but it is necessary to wash with a determinate element, so neither does it suffice, in Penance, to manifest one's sins anyhow, but they must be declared by a determinate act.

Reply Obj. 2. It is enough for one who is ignorant of a language, to confess by writing, or by signs, or by an interpreter, because a man is not bound to do more than he can: although a man is not able or obliged to receive Baptism, except with water, which is from an entirely external source and is applied to us by another: whereas the act of confession is from within and is performed by ourselves, so that when we cannot confess in one way, we must confess as we can.

Reply Obj. 3. In the absence of one's own priest, confession may be made even to a layman, so that there is no necessity to confess in writing, because the act of confession is more essential than the person to whom confession is made.

FOURTH ARTICLE

Whether the Sixteen Conditions Usually Assigned Are Necessary for Confession?

We proceed thus to the Fourth Article:—

Objection 1. It would seem that the conditions assigned by masters, and contained in the following lines, are not requisite for confession:

> Simple, humble, pure, faithful,
> Frequent, undisguised, discreet, voluntary, shamefaced,
> Entire, secret, tearful, not delayed,
> Courageously accusing, ready to obey.

For fidelity, simplicity, and courage are virtues by themselves, and therefore should not be reckoned as conditions of confession.

Obj. 2. Further, a thing is *pure* when it is not mixed with anything else: and *simplicity,* in like manner, removes composition and admixture. Therefore one or the other is superfluous.

Obj. 3. Further, no one is bound to confess more than once a sin which he has committed but once. Therefore if a man does not commit a sin again, his penance need not be *frequent.*

Obj. 4. Further, confession is directed to satisfaction. But satisfaction is sometimes public. Therefore confession should not always be *secret.*

Obj. 5. Further, that which is not in our power is not required of us. But it is not in our power to shed *tears.* Therefore it is not required of those who confess.

On the contrary, We have the authority of the masters who assigned the above.

I answer that, Some of the above conditions are essential to confession, and some are requisite for its well-being. Now those things which are essential to confession belong to it either as to an act of virtue, or as to part of a sacrament. If in the first way, it is either by reason of virtue in general, or by reason of the special virtue of which it is the act, or by reason of the act itself. Now there are four conditions of virtue in general, as stated in *Ethic.* ii. 4. The first is knowledge, in respect of which confession is said to be *discreet,* inasmuch as prudence is required in every act of virtue: and this discretion consists in giving greater weight to greater sins. The second condition is choice, because acts of virtue should be voluntary, and in this respect confession is said to be *voluntary.* The third condition is that the act be done for a particular purpose, viz. the due end, and in this respect confession is said to be *pure,* i.e. with a right intention. The fourth condition is that one should act immovably, and in this respect it is said that confession should be *courageous,* viz. that the truth should not be forsaken through shame.

Now confession is an act of the virtue of penance. First of all it takes its origin in the horror which one conceives for the shamefulness of sin, and in this respect confession should be *full of shame,* so as not to be a boastful account of one's sins, by reason of some worldly vanity accompanying it. Then it goes on to deplore the sin committed, and in this respect it is said to be *tearful.* Thirdly, it culminates in self-abjection, and in this respect it should be *humble,* so that one confesses one's misery and weakness.

By reason of its very nature, viz. confession, this act is one of manifestation: which manifestation can be hindered by four things: first, by falsehood, and in this respect confession is said to be *faithful,* i.e. true. Secondly, by the use of vague words, and against this confession is said to be *open,* so as not to be wrapped up in vague words; thirdly, by *multiplicity* of words, in which respect it is said to be *simple,* indicating that the penitent should relate only such matters as affect the gravity of the sin; fourthly none of those things should be suppressed which should be made known, and in this respect confession should be *entire.*

In so far as confession is part of a sacrament it is subject to the judgment of the priest who is the minister of the sacrament. Wherefore it should be an *accusation* on the part of the penitent, should manifest his *readiness to obey* the priest, should be *secret* as regards the nature of the court wherein the hidden affairs of conscience are tried.

The well-being of confession requires that it should be *frequent;* and *not delayed,* i.e. that the sinner should confess at once.

Reply Obj. 1. There is nothing unreasonable in one virtue being a condition of the act of another virtue, through this act being commanded by that virtue; or through the mean which belongs to one virtue principally, belonging to other virtues by participation.

Reply Obj. 2. The condition *pure* excludes perversity of intention, from which man is cleansed: but the condition *simple* excludes the introduction of unnecessary matter.

Reply Obj. 3. This is not necessary for confession, but is a condition of its well-being.

Reply Obj. 4. Confession should be made not publicly but privately. lest others be scandalized, and led to do evil through hearing the sins confessed. On the other hand, the penance enjoined in satisfaction does not give rise to scandal, since like works of satisfaction are done sometimes for slight sins, and sometimes for none at all.

Reply Obj. 5. We must understand this to refer to tears of the heart.

QUESTION 10

Of the Effect of Confession

(In Five Articles)

WE must now consider the effect of confession: under which head there are five points of inquiry: (1) Whether confession delivers one from the death of sin? (2) Whether confession delivers one in any way from punishment? (3) Whether confession opens Paradise to us? (4) Whether confession gives hope of salvation? (5) Whether a general confession blots out mortal sins that one has forgotten?

FIRST ARTICLE

Whether Confession Delivers One from the Death of Sin?

We proceed thus to the First Article:—

Objection 1. It would seem that confession does not deliver one from the death of sin. For confession follows contrition. But contrition sufficiently blots out guilt. Therefore confession does not deliver one from the death of sin.

Obj. 2. Further, just as mortal sin is a fault, so is venial. Now confession renders venial that which was mortal before, as stated in the text (iv. *Sent.*, D. 17). Therefore confession does not blot out guilt, but one guilt is changed into another.

On the contrary, Confession is part of the sacrament of Penance. But Penance delivers from guilt. Therefore confession does also.

I answer that, Penance, as a sacrament, is perfected chiefly in confession, because by the latter a man submits to the ministers of the Church, who are the dispensers of the sacraments: for contrition has the desire of confession united thereto, and satisfaction is enjoined according to the judgment of the priest who hears the confession. And since in the sacrament of Penance, as in Baptism, that grace is infused whereby sins are forgiven, therefore confession in virtue of the absolution granted remits guilt, even as Baptism does. Now Baptism delivers one from the death of sin, not only by being received actually, but also by being received in desire, as is evident with regard to those who approach the sacrament of Baptism after being already sanctified. And unless a man offers an obstacle, he receives, through the very fact of being baptized, grace whereby his sins are remitted, if they are not already remitted. The same is to be said of confession, to which absolution is added, because it delivered the penitent from guilt through being previously in his desire. Afterwards at the time of actual confession and absolution he receives an increase of grace, and forgiveness of sins would also be granted to him, if his previous sorrow for sin was not sufficient for contrition, and if at the time he offered no obstacle to grace. Consequently just as it is said of Baptism that it delivers from death, so can it be said of confession.

Reply Obj. 1. Contrition has the desire of confession attached to it, and therefore it delivers penitents from death in the same way as the desire of Baptism delivers those who are going to be baptized.

Reply Obj. 2. In the text venial does not designate guilt, but punishment that is easily expiated; and so it does not follow that one guilt is changed into another, but that it is wholly done away. For *venial* is taken in three senses:* first, for what is venial generically, e.g. an idle word: secondly, for what is venial in its cause, i.e. having within itself a motive of pardon, e.g. sins due to weakness: thirdly, for what is venial in the result, in which sense it is understood here, because the

result of confession is that man's past guilt is pardoned.

SECOND ARTICLE

Whether Confession Delivers from Punishment in Some Way?

We proceed thus to the Second Article:—

Objection 1. It would seem that confession nowise delivers from punishment. For sin deserves no punishment but what is either eternal or temporal. Now eternal punishment is remitted by contrition, and temporal punishment by satisfaction. Therefore nothing of the punishment is remitted by confession.

Obj. 2. Further, *the will is taken for the deed,*† as stated in the text (iv. *Sent.*, D. 17). Now he that is contrite has the intention to confess; wherefore his intention avails him as though he had already confessed, and so the confession which he makes afterwards remits no part of the punishment.

On the contrary, Confession is a penal work. But all penal works expiate the punishment due to sin. Therefore confession does also.

I answer that, Confession together with absolution has the power to deliver from punishment, for two reasons. First, from the power of absolution itself: and thus the very desire of absolution delivers a man from eternal punishment, as also from the guilt. Now this punishment is one of condemnation and total banishment: and when a man is delivered therefrom he still remains bound to a temporal punishment, in so far as punishment is a cleansing and perfecting remedy; and so this punishment remains to be suffered in Purgatory by those who also have been delivered from the punishment of hell. Which temporal punishment is beyond the powers of the penitent dwelling in this world, but is so far diminished by the power of the keys, that it is within the ability of the penitent, and he is able, by making satisfaction, to cleanse himself in this life.—Secondly, confession diminishes the punishment in virtue of the very nature of the act of the one who confesses, for this act has the punishment of shame attached to it, so that the oftener one confesses the same sins, the more is the punishment diminished.

This suffices for the *Reply* to the *First Objection.*

Reply Obj. 2. The will is not taken for the deed, if this is done by another, as in the case of Baptism: for the will to receive Baptism is not worth as much as the reception of Baptism. But a man's will is taken for the deed, when the latter is something done by him

* Cf. I-II, Q. 88, A. 2.   † Cf. Can. *Magna Pietas, De Pœnit.* Dist. i.

entirely. Again, this is true of the essential reward, but not of the removal of punishment and the like, which come under the head of accidental and secondary reward. Consequently one who has confessed and received absolution will be less punished in Purgatory than one who has gone no further than contrition.

THIRD ARTICLE
Whether Confession Opens Paradise?

We proceed thus to the Third Article:—

Objection 1. It would seem that confession does not open Paradise. For different sacraments have different effects. But it is the effect of Baptism to open Paradise. Therefore it is not the effect of confession.

Obj. 2. Further, it is impossible to enter by a closed door before it be opened. But a dying man can enter heaven before making his confession. Therefore confession does not open Paradise.

On the contrary, Confession makes a man submit to the keys of the Church. But Paradise is opened by those keys. Therefore it is opened by confession.

I answer that, Guilt and the debt of punishment prevent a man from entering into Paradise: and since confession removes these obstacles, as shown above (AA. 1, 2), it is said to open Paradise.

Reply Obj. 1. Although Baptism and Penance are different sacraments, they act in virtue of Christ's one Passion, whereby a way was opened unto Paradise.

Reply Obj. 2. If the dying man was in mortal sin Paradise was closed to him before he conceived the desire to confess his sin, although afterwards it was opened by contrition implying a desire for confession, even before he actually confessed. Nevertheless the obstacle of the debt of punishment was not entirely removed before confession and satisfaction.

FOURTH ARTICLE
Whether Confession Gives Hope of Salvation?

We proceed thus to the Fourth Article:—

Objection 1. It would seem that hope of salvation should not be reckoned an effect of confession. For hope arises from all meritorious acts. Therefore, seemingly, it is not the proper effect of confession.

Obj. 2. Further, we arrive at hope through tribulation, as appears from Rom. v. 3, 4. Now man suffers tribulation chiefly in satisfaction. Therefore, satisfaction rather than confession gives hope of salvation.

On the contrary, Confession makes a man more humble and more wary, as the Master states in the text (iv. *Sent.,* D. 17). But the result of this is that man conceives a hope of salvation. Therefore it is the effect of confession to give hope of salvation.

I answer that, We can have no hope for the forgiveness of our sins except through Christ: and since by confession a man submits to the keys of the Church which derive their power from Christ's Passion, therefore do we say that confession gives hope of salvation.

Reply Obj. 1. It is not our actions, but the grace of our Redeemer, that is the principal cause of the hope of salvation: and since confession relies upon the grace of our Redeemer, it gives hope of salvation, not only as a meritorious act, but also as part of a sacrament.

Reply Obj. 2. Tribulation gives hope of salvation, by making us exercise our own virtue, and by paying off the debt of punishment: while confession does so also in the way mentioned above.

FIFTH ARTICLE
Whether a General Confession Suffices to Blot Out Forgotten Mortal Sins?

We proceed thus to the Fifth Article:—

Objection 1. It would seem that a general confession does not suffice to blot out forgotten mortal sins. For there is no necessity to confess again a sin which has been blotted out by confession. If, therefore, forgotten sins were forgiven by a general confession, there would be no need to confess them when they are called to mind.

Obj. 2. Further, whoever is not conscious of sin, either is not guilty of sin, or has forgotten his sin. If, therefore, mortal sins are forgiven by a general confession, whoever is not conscious of a mortal sin, can be certain that he is free from mortal sin, whenever he makes a general confession: which is contrary to what the Apostle says (1 Cor. iv. 4), *I am not conscious to myself of anything, yet am I not hereby justified.*

Obj. 3. Further, no man profits by neglect. Now a man cannot forget a mortal sin without neglect, before it is forgiven him. Therefore he does not profit by his forgetfulness so that the sin is forgiven him without special mention thereof in confession.

Obj. 4. Further, that which the penitent knows nothing about is further from his knowledge than that which he has forgotten. Now a general confession does not blot out sins committed through ignorance, else heretics, who are not aware that certain things they have done are sinful, and certain simple people, would be absolved by a general confession, which is false. Therefore a general confession does not take away forgotten sins.

On the contrary, It is written (Ps. xxxiii. 6): *Come ye to Him and be enlightened, and your faces shall not be confounded.* Now he who confesses all the sins of which he is conscious, approaches to God as much as he can: nor can more be required for him. Therefore he will not be confounded by being repelled, but will be forgiven.

Further, he that confesses is pardoned unless he be insincere. But he who confesses all the sins that he calls to mind, is not insincere through forgetting some, because he suffers from ignorance of fact, which excuses from sin. Therefore he receives forgiveness, and then the sins which he has forgotten, are loosened, since it is wicked to hope for half a pardon.

I answer that, Confession produces its effect, on the presupposition that there is contrition which blots out guilt: so that confession is directly ordained to the remission of punishment, which it causes in virtue of the shame which it includes, and by the power of the keys to which a man submits by confessing. Now it happens sometimes that by previous contrition a sin has been blotted out as to the guilt, either in a general way (if it was not remembered at the time) or in particular (and yet is forgotten before confession): and then general sacramental confession works for the remission of the punishment in virtue of the keys, to which man submits by confessing, provided he offers no obstacle so far as he is concerned: but so far as the shame of confessing a sin diminishes its punishment, the punishment for the sin for which a man does not express his shame, through failing to confess it to the priest, is not diminished.

Reply Obj. 1. In sacramental confession, not only is absolution required, but also the judgment of the priest who imposes satisfaction is awaited. Wherefore although the latter has given absolution, nevertheless the penitent is bound to confess in order to supply what was wanting to the sacramental confession.

Reply Obj. 2. As stated above, confession does not produce its effect, unless contrition be presupposed; concerning which no man can know whether it be true contrition, even as neither can one know for certain if he has grace. Consequently a man cannot know for certain whether a forgotten sin has been forgiven him in a general confession, although he may think so on account of certain conjectural signs.

Reply Obj. 3. He does not profit by his neglect, since he does not receive such full pardon, as he would otherwise have received, nor is his merit so great. Moreover he is bound to confess the sin when he calls it to mind.

Reply Obj. 4. Ignorance of the law does not excuse, because it is a sin by itself: but ignorance of fact does excuse. Therefore if a man omits to confess a sin, because he does not know it to be a sin, through ignorance of the Divine law, he is not excused from insincerity. On the other hand, he would be excused, if he did not know it to be a sin, through being unaware of some particular circumstance, for instance, if he had knowledge of another's wife, thinking her his own. Now forgetfulness of an act of sin comes under the head of ignorance of fact, wherefore it excuses from the sin of insincerity in confession, which is an obstacle to the fruit of absolution and confession.

QUESTION 11

Of the Seal of Confession

(In Five Articles)

WE must now inquire about the seal of confession, about which there are five points of inquiry: (1) Whether in every case a man is bound to hide what he knows under the seal of confession? (2) Whether the seal of confession extends to other matters than those which have reference to confession? (3) Whether the priest alone is bound by the seal of confession? (4) Whether, by permission of the penitent, the priest can make known to another, a sin of his which he knew under the seal of confession? (5) Whether he is bound to hide even what he knows through other sources besides?

FIRST ARTICLE

Whether in Every Case the Priest Is Bound to Hide the Sins Which He Knows under the Seal of Confession?

We proceed thus to the First Article:—

Objection 1. It would seem that the priest is not bound in every case to hide the sins which he knows under the seal of confession. For, as Bernard says (*De Præcep. et Dispens.* ii), *that which is instituted for the sake of charity does not militate against charity.* Now the secret of confession would militate against charity in certain cases: for instance, if a man knew through confession that a certain man was a heretic, whom he cannot persuade to desist from misleading the people; or, in like manner, if a man knew, through confession, that certain people who wish to marry are related to one another. Therefore such ought to reveal what they know through confession.

Obj. 2. Further, that which is obligatory solely on account of a precept of the Church need not be observed, if the commandment be changed to the contrary. Now the secret of confession was introduced solely by a precept of the Church. If therefore the Church were to prescribe that anyone who knows anything about such and such a sin must make it known, a man that had such knowledge through confession would be bound to speak.

Obj. 3. Further, a man is bound to safeguard his conscience rather than the good name of another, because there is order in charity. Now it happens sometimes that a man by hiding a sin injures his own conscience, —for instance, if he be called upon to give witness of a sin of which he has knowledge through confession, and is forced to swear to tell the truth, — or when an abbot knows through confession the sin of a prior who is subject to him, which sin would be an occasion of ruin to the latter, if he suffers him to retain his priorship, wherefore he is bound to deprive him of the dignity of his pastoral charge, and yet in depriving him he seem to divulge the secret of confession. Therefore it seems that in certain cases it is lawful to reveal a confession.

Obj. 4. Further, it is possible for a priest through hearing a man's confession to be conscious that the latter is unworthy of ecclesiastical preferment. Now everyone is bound to prevent the promotion of the unworthy, if it is his business. Since then by raising an objection he seems to raise a suspicion of sin, and so to reveal the confession somewhat, it seems that it is necessary sometimes to divulge a confession.

On the contrary, The Decretal says *(De Pœnit. et Remiss. Cap. Omnis utriusque): Let the priest beware lest he betray the sinner, by word, or sign, or in any other way whatever.*

Further, the priest should conform himself to God, Whose minister he is. But God does not reveal the sins which are made known to Him in confession, but hides them. Neither, therefore, should the priest reveal them.

I answer that, Those things which are done outwardly in the sacraments are the signs of what takes place inwardly: wherefore confession, whereby a man subjects himself to a priest, is a sign of the inward submission, whereby one submits to God. Now God hides the sins of those who submit to Him by Pen-

ance; wherefore this also should be signified in the sacrament of Penance, and consequently the sacrament demands that the confession should remain hidden, and he who divulges a confession sins by violating the sacrament. Besides this there are other advantages in this secrecy, because thereby men are more attracted to confession, and confess their sins with greater simplicity.

Reply Obj. 1. Some say that the priest is not bound by the seal of confession to hide other sins than those in respect of which the penitent promises amendment; otherwise he may reveal them to one who can be a help and not a hindrance. But this opinion seems erroneous, since it is contrary to the truth of the sacrament; for just as, though the person baptized be insincere, yet his Baptism is a sacrament, and there is no change in the essentials of the sacrament on that account, so confession does not cease to be sacramental, although he that confesses, does not purpose amendment. Therefore, this notwithstanding, it must be held secret; nor does the seal of confession militate against charity on that account, because charity does not require a man to find a remedy for a sin which he knows not: and that which is known in confession, is, as it were, unknown, since a man knows it, not as man, but as God knows it. Nevertheless in the cases quoted one should apply some kind of remedy, so far as this can be done without divulging the confession, e.g. by admonishing the penitent, and by watching over the others lest they be corrupted by heresy. He can also tell the prelate to watch over his flock with great care, yet so as by neither word nor sign to betray the penitent.

Reply Obj. 2. The precept concerning the secret of confession follows from the sacrament itself. Wherefore just as the obligation of making a sacramental confession is of Divine law, so that no human dispensation or command can absolve one therefrom, even so, no man can be forced or permitted by another man to divulge the secret of confession. Consequently if he be commanded under pain of excommunication to be incurred *ipso facto*, to say whether he knows anything about such and such a sin, he ought not to say it, because he should assume that the intention of the person in commanding him thus, was that he should say what he knew as man. And even if he were expressly interrogated about a confession, he ought to say nothing, nor would he incur the excommunication, for he is not subject to his superior, save as a man, and he knows this not as a man, but as God knows it.

Reply Obj. 3. A man is not called upon to witness except as a man, wherefore without wronging his conscience he can swear that he knows not, what he knows only as God knows it. In like manner a superior can, without wronging his conscience, leave a sin unpunished which he knows only as God knows it, or he may forbear to apply a remedy, since he is not bound to apply a remedy, except according as it comes to his knowledge. Wherefore with regard to matters which come to his knowledge in the tribunal of Penance, he should apply the remedy, as far as he can, in the same court: thus as to the case in point, the abbot should advise the prior to resign his office, and if the latter refuse, he can absolve him from the priorship on some other occasion, yet so as to avoid all suspicion of divulging the confession.

Reply Obj. 4. A man is rendered unworthy of ecclesiastical preferment, by many other causes besides sin, for instance, by lack of knowledge, age, or the like: so that by raising an objection one does not raise a suspicion of crime or divulge the secret of confession.

SECOND ARTICLE

Whether the Seal of Confession Extends to Other Matters Than Those Which Have Reference to Confession?

We proceed thus to the Second Article:—

Objection 1. It would seem that the seal of confession extends to other matters besides those which have reference to confession. For sins alone have reference to confession. Now sometimes besides sins other matters are told which have no reference to confession. Therefore, since such things are told to the priest, as to God, it seems that the seal of confession extends to them also.

Obj. 2. Further, sometimes one person tells another a secret, which the latter receives under the seal of confession. Therefore the seal of confession extends to matters having no relation to confession.

On the contrary, The seal of confession is connected with sacramental confession. But those things which are connected with a sacrament, do not extend outside the bounds of the sacrament. Therefore the seal of confession does not extend to matters other than those which have reference to sacramental confession.

I answer that, The seal of confession does not extend directly to other matters than those which have reference to sacramental confession, yet indirectly matters also which are not connected by the seal of confession, those, for instance, which might lead to the discovery of a sinner or of his sin. Nevertheless these matters also must be most carefully hidden, both

on account of scandal, and to avoid leading others into sin through their becoming familiar with it.

This suffices for the *Reply* to the *First Objection.*

Reply Obj. 2. A confidence ought not easily to be accepted in this way: but if it be done, the secret must be kept in the way promised, as though one had the secret through confession, though not through the seal of confession.

THIRD ARTICLE

Whether the Priest Alone Is Bound by the Seal of Confession?

We proceed thus to the Third Article:—

Objection 1. It would seem that not only the priest is bound by the seal of confession. For sometimes a priest hears a confession through an interpreter, if there be an urgent reason for so doing. But it seems that the interpreter is bound to keep the confession secret. Therefore one who is not a priest knows something under the seal of confession.

Obj. 2. Further, it is possible sometimes in cases of urgency for a layman to hear a confession. But he is bound to secrecy with regard to those sins, since they are told to him as to God. Therefore not only the priest is bound by the seal of confession.

Obj. 3. Further, it may happen that a man pretends to be a priest, so that by this deceit he may know what is on another's conscience: and it would seem that he also sins if he divulges the confession. Therefore not only the priest is bound by the seal of confession.

On the contrary, A priest alone is the minister of this sacrament. But the seal of confession is connected with this sacrament. Therefore the priest alone is bound by the seal of confession.

Further, the reason why a man is bound to keep secret what he hears in confession, is because he knows them, not as man but as God knows them. But the priest alone is God's minister. Therefore he alone is bound to secrecy.

I answer that, The seal of confession affects the priest as minister of this sacrament: which seal is nothing else than the obligation of keeping the confession secret, even as the key is the power of absolving. Yet, as one who is not a priest, in a particular case has a kind of share in the act of the keys, when he hears a confession in a case of urgency, so also does he have a certain share in the act of the seal of confession, and is bound to secrecy, though, properly speaking, he is not bound by the seal of confession.

This suffices for the *Replies* to the *Objections.*

Whether by the Penitent's Permission, a Priest May Reveal to Another a Sin Which He Knows under the Seal of Confession?

We proceed thus to the Fourth Article:—

Objection 1. It would seem that a priest may not, by the penitent's permission, reveal to another a sin which he knows under the seal of confession. For an inferior may not do what his superior may not. Now the Pope cannot give permission for anyone to divulge a sin which he knows through confession. Neither therefore can the penitent give him such a permission.

Obj. 2. Further, that which is instituted for the common good of the Church cannot be changed at the will of an individual. Now the secrecy of confession was instituted for the good of the whole Church, in order that men might have greater confidence in approaching the confessional. Therefore the penitent cannot allow the priest to divulge his confession.

Obj. 3. Further, if the priest could grant such a permission, this would seem to palliate the wickedness of bad priests, for they might pretend to have received the permission and so they might sin with impunity, which would be unbecoming. Therefore it seems that the penitent cannot grant this permission.

Obj. 4. Further, the one to whom this sin is divulged does not know that sin under the seal of confession, so that he may publish a sin which is already blotted out, which is unbecoming. Therefore this permission cannot be granted.

On the contrary, If the sinner consent, a superior may refer him by letter to an inferior priest. Therefore with the consent of the penitent, the priest may reveal a sin of his to another.

Further, whosoever can do a thing of his own authority, can do it through another. But the penitent can by his own authority reveal his sin to another. Therefore he can do it through the priest.

I answer that, There are two reasons for which the priest is bound to keep a sin secret: first and chiefly, because this very secrecy is essential to the sacrament, in so far as the priest knows that sin, as it is known to God, Whose place he holds in confession: secondly, in order to avoid scandal. Now the penitent can make the priest know, as a man, what he knew before only as God knows it, and he does this when he allows him to divulge it: so that if the priest does reveal it, he does not break the seal of confession. Nevertheless he should beware of giving scandal by revealing the sin, lest he be deemed to have broken the seal.

Reply Obj. 1. The Pope cannot permit a priest to divulge a sin, because he cannot make him to know it as a man, whereas he that has confessed it, can.

Reply Obj. 2. When that is told which is known through another source, that which is instituted for the common good is not done away with, because the seal of confession is not broken.

Reply Obj. 3. This does not bestow impunity on wicked priests, because they are in danger of having to prove that they had the penitent's permission to reveal the sin, if they should be accused of the contrary.

Reply Obj. 4. He that is informed of a sin through the priest with the penitent's consent, shares in an act of the priest's, so that the same applies to him as to an interpreter, unless perchance the penitent wish him to know it unconditionally and freely.

Whether a Man May Reveal That Which He Knows through Confession and through Some Other Source Besides?

We proceed thus to the Fifth Article:—

Objection 1. It would seem that a man may not reveal what he knows through confession and through some other source besides. For the seal of confession is not broken unless one reveals a sin known through confession. If therefore a man divulges a sin which he knows through confession, no matter how he knows it otherwise, he seems to break the seal.

Obj. 2. Further, whoever hears someone's confession, is under obligation to him not to divulge his sins. Now if one were to promise someone to keep something secret, he would be bound to do so, even if he knew it through some other source. Therefore a man is bound to keep secret what he knows through the confession, no matter how he knows it otherwise.

Obj. 3. Further, the stronger of two things draws the other to itself. Now the knowledge whereby a man knows a sin as God knows it, is stronger and more excellent than the knowledge whereby he knows a sin as man. Therefore it draws the latter to itself: and consequently a man cannot reveal that sin, because this is demanded by his knowing it as God knows it.

Obj. 4. Further, the secrecy of confession was instituted in order to avoid scandal, and to prevent men being shy of going to confession. But if a man might say what he had heard in confession, though he knew it otherwise, scandal would result all the same. Therefore he can nowise say what he has heard.

On the contrary, No one can put another

under a new obligation, unless he be his superior, who can bind him by a precept. Now he who knew of a sin by witnessing it was not bound to keep it secret. Therefore he that confesses to him, not being his superior, cannot put him under an obligation of secrecy by confessing to him.

Further, the justice of the Church would be hindered if a man, in order to escape a sentence of excommunication, incurred on account of some sin, of which he has been convicted, were to confess to the person who has to sentence him. Now the execution of justice falls under a precept. Therefore a man is not bound to keep a sin secret, which he has heard in confession, but knows from some other source.

I answer that, There are three opinions about this question. For some say that a man can by no means tell another what he has heard in confession, even if he knew it from some other source either before or after the confession: while others assert that the confession debars him from speaking of what he knew already, but not from saying what he knew afterwards and in another way. Now both these opinions, by exaggerating the seal of confession, are prejudicial to the truth and to the safeguarding of justice. For a man might be more inclined to sin, if he had no fear of being accused by his confessor supposing that he repeated the sin in his presence: and furthermore it would be most prejudicial to justice if a man could not bear witness to a deed which he has seen committed again after being confessed to him. Nor does it matter that, as some say, he ought to declare that he cannot keep it secret, for he cannot make such a declaration until the sin has already been confessed to him, and then every priest could, if he wished, divulge a sin, by making such a declaration, if this made him free to divulge it. Consequently there is a third and truer opinion, viz. that what a man knows through another source either before or after confession, he is not bound to keep secret, in so far as he knows it as a man, for he can say: *I know so and so since I saw it.* But he is bound to keep it secret in so far as he knows it as God knows it, for he cannot say: *I heard so and so in confession.* Nevertheless, on account of the scandal he should refrain from speaking of it unless there is an urgent reason.

Reply Obj. 1. If a man says that he has seen what he has heard in the confessional, he does not reveal what he heard in confession, save indirectly: even as one who knows something through hearing and seeing it, does not. properly speaking, divulge what he saw, if he says he heard it, but only indirectly, because he says he has heard what he incidentally saw. Wherefore he does not break the seal of confession.

Reply Obj. 2. The confessor is not forbidden to reveal a sin simply, but to reveal it as heard in confession: for in no case is he allowed to say that he has heard it in the confessional.

Reply Obj. 3. This is true of things that are in opposition to one another: whereas to know a sin as God knows it, and to know it as man knows it, are not in opposition; so that the argument proves nothing.

Reply Obj. 4. It would not be right to avoid scandal so as to desert justice: for the truth should not be gainsayed for fear of scandal. Wherefore when justice and truth are in the balance, a man should not be deterred by the fear of giving scandal, from divulging what he has heard in confession, provided he knows it from some other source: although he ought to avoid giving scandal, as far as he is able.

QUESTION 12

Of Satisfaction, As to Its Nature

(In Three Articles)

WE must now consider satisfaction; about which four things have to be considered: (1) Its nature; (2) Its possibility; (3) Its quality; (4) The means whereby man offers satisfaction to God.

Under the first head there are three points of inquiry: (1) Whether satisfaction is a virtue or an act of virtue? (2) Whether it is an act of justice? (3) Whether the definition of satisfaction contained in the text is suitable?

FIRST ARTICLE

Whether Satisfaction Is a Virtue or an Act of Virtue?

We proceed thus to the First Article:—

Objection 1. It would seem that satisfaction is neither a virtue nor an act of virtue. For every act of virtue is meritorious; whereas, seemingly, satisfaction is not, since merit is gratuitous, while satisfaction answers to a debt. Therefore satisfaction is not an act of virtue.

Obj. 2. Further, every act of virtue is voluntary. But sometimes a man has to make satisfaction for something against his will, as when anyone is punished by the judge for an offense against another. Therefore satisfaction is not an act of virtue.

Obj. 3. Further, according to the Philosopher *(Ethic.* viii. 13): *Choice holds the chief place in moral virtue.* But satisfaction is not an act of choice but regards chiefly external works. Therefore it is not an act of virtue.

On the contrary, Satisfaction belongs to penance. Now penance is a virtue. Therefore satisfaction is also an act of virtue.

Further, none but an act of virtue has the effect of blotting out sin, for one contrary is destroyed by the other. Now satisfaction destroys sin altogether. Therefore it is an act of virtue.

I answer that, An act is said to be the act of a virtue in two ways. First, materially; and thus any act which implies no malice, or defect of a due circumstance, may be called an act of virtue, because virtue can make use of any such act for its end, e.g. to walk, to speak, and so forth. Secondly, an act is said to belong to a virtue formally, because its very name implies the form and nature of virtue; thus to suffer courageously is an act of courage. Now the formal element in every moral virtue is the observance of a mean: wherefore every act that implies the observance of a mean is formally an act of virtue. And since equality is the mean implied in the name of satisfaction (for a thing is said to be satisfied by reason of an equal proportion to something), it is evident that satisfaction also is formally an act of virtue.

Reply Obj. 1. Although to make satisfaction is due in itself, yet, in so far as the deed is done voluntarily by the one who offers satisfaction, it becomes something gratuitous on the part of the agent, so that he makes a virtue of necessity. For debt diminishes merit through being necessary and consequently against the will, so that if the will consent to the necessity, the element of merit is not forfeited.

Reply Obj. 2. An act of virtue demands voluntariness not in the patient but in the agent, for it is his act. Consequently since he on whom the judge wreaks vengeance is the patient and not the agent as regards satisfaction, it follows that satisfaction should be voluntary not in him but in the judge as agent.

Reply Obj. 3. The chief element of virtue can be understood in two ways. First, as being the chief element of virtue as virtue, and thus the chief element of virtue denotes whatever belongs to the nature of virtue or is most akin

* Cf. next article, *Obj.* 1.

thereto; thus choice and other internal acts hold the chief place in virtue. Secondly, the chief element of virtue may be taken as denoting that which holds the first place in such and such a virtue; and then the first place belongs to that which gives its determination. Now the interior act, in certain virtues, is determined by some external act, since choice, which is common to all virtues, becomes proper to such and such a virtue through being directed to such and such an act. Thus it is that external acts hold the chief place in certain virtues; and this is the case with satisfaction.

<h2 style="text-align:center">SECOND ARTICLE</h2>

Whether Satisfaction Is an Act of Justice?

We proceed thus to the Second Article:—

Objection 1. It would seem that satisfaction is not an act of justice. Because the purpose of satisfaction is that one may be reconciled to the person offended. But reconciliation, being an act of love, belongs to charity. Therefore satisfaction is an act of charity and not of justice.

Obj. 2. Further, the causes of sin in us are the passions of the soul, which incline us to evil. But justice, according to the Philosopher *(Ethic.* v. 2, 3), is not about passions, but about operations. Since therefore satisfaction aims at removing the causes of sin, as stated in the text (iv. *Sent.,* D. 15), it seems that it is not an act of justice.

Obj. 3. Further, to be careful about the future is not an act of justice but of prudence, of which caution is a part. But it belongs to satisfaction, *to give no opening to the suggestions of sin.** Therefore satisfaction is not an act of justice.

On the contrary, No virtue but justice considers the notion of that which is due. But satisfaction gives due honor to God, as Anselm states *(Cur Deus Homo,* i). Therefore satisfaction is an act of justice.

Further, no virtue save justice establishes equality between external things. But this is done by satisfaction which establishes equality between amendment and the previous offense. Therefore satisfaction is an act of justice.

I answer that, According to the Philosopher *(Ethic.* v. 3, 4), the mean of justice is considered with regard to an equation between thing and thing according to a certain proportion. Wherefore, since the very name of satisfaction implies an equation of the kind, because the adverb *satis (enough)* denotes an equality of proportion, it is evident that satisfaction is formally an act of justice. Now the act of justice, according to the Philosopher *(Ethic.* v. 2, 4), is either an act done by one man to another, as when a man pays another what he owes him, or an act done by one man between two others, as when a judge does justice between two men. When it is an act of justice of one man to another, the equality is set up in the agent, while when it is something done between two others, the equality is set up in the subject that has suffered an injustice. And since satisfaction expresses equality in the agent, it denotes, properly speaking, an act of justice of one man to another. Now a man may do justice to another either in actions and passions or in external things; even as one may do an injustice to another, either by taking something away, or by a hurtful action. And since to give is to use an external thing, the act of justice, in so far as it establishes equality between external things, signifies, properly speaking, a giving back: but to make satisfaction clearly points to equality between actions, although sometimes one is put for the other. Now equalization concerns only such things as are unequal, wherefore satisfaction presupposes inequality among actions, which inequality constitutes an offense; so that satisfaction regards a previous offense. But no part of justice regards a previous offense, except vindictive justice, which establishes equality indifferently, whether the patient be the same subject as the agent, as when anyone punishes himself, or whether they be distinct, as when a judge punishes another man, since vindictive justice deals with both cases. The same applies to penance, which implies equality in the agent only, since it is the penitent who holds to the penance *(poenam tenet)*, so that penance is in a way a species of vindictive justice. This proves that satisfaction, which implies equality in the agent with respect to a previous offense, is a work of justice, as to that part which is called penance.

Reply Obj. 1. Satisfaction, as appears from what has been said, is compensation for injury inflicted. Wherefore as the injury inflicted entailed of itself an inequality of justice, and consequently an inequality opposed to friendship, so satisfaction brings back directly equality of justice, and consequently equality of friendship. And since an act is elicited by the habit to whose end it is immediately directed, but is commanded by that habit to whose end it is directed ultimately, hence satisfaction is elicited by justice but is commanded by charity.

Reply Obj. 2. Although justice is chiefly about operations, yet it is consequently about passions, in so far as they are the causes of operations. Wherefore as justice curbs anger, lest it inflict an unjust injury on another, and

concupiscence from invading another's marriage right, so satisfaction removes the causes of other sins.

Reply Obj. 3. Each moral virtue shares in the act of prudence, because this virtue completes in it the conditions essential to virtue, since each moral virtue takes its mean according to the ruling of prudence, as is evident from the definition of virtue given in *Ethic.* ii. 6.

THIRD ARTICLE

Whether the Definition of Satisfaction Given in the Text Is Suitable?

We proceed thus to the Third Article:—

Objection 1. It would seem that the definition of satisfaction given in the text (iv. *Sent.*, D. 15) and quoted from Augustine* is unsuitable,—viz. that *satisfaction is to uproot the causes of sins, and to give no opening to the suggestions thereof.* For the cause of actual sin is the *fomes.*† But we cannot remove the *fomes* in this life. Therefore satisfaction does not consist in removing the causes of sins.

Obj. 2. Further, the cause of sin is stronger than sin itself. But man by himself cannot remove sin. Much less therefore can he remove the cause of sin; and so the same conclusion follows.

Obj. 3. Further, since satisfaction is a part of Penance, it regards the past and not the future. Now *to give no opening to the suggestions of sin* regards the future. Therefore it should not be put in the definition of satisfaction.

Obj. 4. Further, satisfaction regards a past offense. Yet no mention is made of this. Therefore the definition of satisfaction is unsuitable.

Obj. 5. Further, Anselm gives another definition *(Cur Deus homo,* i): *Satisfaction consists in giving God due honor,* wherein no reference is made to the things mentioned by Augustine (Gennadius) in this definition. Therefore one or the other is unsuitable.

Obj. 6. Further, an innocent man can give due honor to God: whereas satisfaction is not compatible with innocence. Therefore Anselm's definition is faulty.

I answer that, Justice aims not only at removing inequality already existing, by punishing the past fault, but also at safeguarding equality for the future, because according to the Philosopher *(Ethic.* ii. 3) *punishments are medicinal.* Wherefore satisfaction which is the act of justice inflicting punishment, is a medicine healing past sins and preserving from future sins: so that when one man makes

---

* Gennadius Massiliensis,—*De Eccl. Dogm.* liv.

† *Fomes* signifies literally *fuel,* and metaphorically, *incentive.* As used by theologians, it denotes the quasimaterial element and effect of original sin, and sometimes goes under the name of *concupiscence,* (Cf. I-II, Q. 82, A. 3).

satisfaction to another, he offers compensation for the past, and takes heed for the future. Accordingly satisfaction may be defined in two ways, first with regard to past sin, which it heals by making compensation, and thus it is defined as *compensation for an inflicted injury according to the equality of justice.* The definition of Anselm amounts to the same, for he says that *satisfaction consists in giving God due honor;* where duty is considered in respect of the sin committed.—Secondly, satisfaction may be defined, considered as preserving us from future sins; and as Augustine (Cf. *Obj.* 1) defines it. Now preservation from bodily sickness is assured by removing the causes from which the sickness may ensue, for if they be taken away the sickness cannot follow. But it is not thus in spiritual diseases, for the free-will cannot be forced, so that even in the presence of their causes, they can, though with difficulty, be avoided, while they can be incurred even when their causes are removed. Hence he puts two things in the definition of satisfaction, viz. removal of the causes, as to the first, and the free-will's refusal to sin.

Reply Obj. 1. By *causes* we must understand the proximate causes of actual sin, which are twofold: viz. the lust of sin through the habit or act of a sin that has been given up, and those things which are called the remnants of past sin; and external occasions of sin, such as place, bad company and so forth. Such causes are removed by satisfaction in this life, albeit the *fomes,* which is the remote cause of actual sin, is not entirely removed by satisfaction in this life though it is weakened.

Reply Obj. 2. Since the cause of evil or of privation (according as it has a cause) is nothing else than a defective good, and since it is easier to destroy good than to set it up, it follows that it is easier to uproot the causes

of privation and of evil than to remove the evil itself, which can only be removed by setting up good, as may be seen in the case of blindness and its causes. Yet the aforesaid are not sufficient causes of sin, for sin does not, of necessity, ensue therefrom, but they are occasions of sin. Nor again can satisfaction be made without God's help, since it is not possible without charity, as we shall state further on (Q. 14, A. 2).

Reply Obj. 3. Although Penance was primarily instituted and intended with a view to the past, yet, as a consequence, it regards the future, in so far as it is a safeguarding remedy; and the same applies to satisfaction.

Reply Obj. 4. Augustine* defined satisfaction, as made to God, from Whom, in reality, nothing can be taken, though the sinner, for his own part, takes something away. Consequently in such like satisfaction, amendment for future time is of greater weight than compensation for the past. Hence Augustine defines satisfaction from this point of view. And yet it is possible to gauge the compensation for the past from the heed taken for the future, for the latter regards the same object as the former, but in the opposite way: since when looking at the past we detest the causes of sins on account of the sins themselves, which are the starting-point of the movement of detestation: whereas when taking heed of the future, we begin from the causes, that by their removal we may avoid sins the more easily.

Reply Obj. 5. There is no reason why the same thing should not be described in different ways according to the various things found in it: and such is the case here, as explained above.

Reply Obj. 6. By debt is meant the debt we owe to God by reason of the sins we have committed, because Penance regards a debt, as stated above (A. 2).

QUESTION 13

Of the Possibility of Satisfaction

(In Two Articles)

WE must now consider the possibility of satisfaction, under which head there are two points of inquiry: (1) Whether man can make satisfaction to God? (2) Whether one man can make satisfaction for another?

FIRST ARTICLE

Whether Man Can Make Satisfaction to God?

We proceed thus to the First Article:—

Objection 1. It would seem that man can-

    * See footnote, p. 2601

not make satisfaction to God. For satisfaction should balance the offense, as shown above (Q. 12, AA. 2, 3). But an offense against God is infinite, since it is measured by the person against whom it is committed, for it is a greater offense to strike a prince than anyone else. Therefore, as no action of man can be infinite, it seems that he cannot make satisfaction to God.

Obj. 2. Further, a slave cannot make compensation for a debt, since all that he has is his master's. But we are the slaves of God, and whatever good we have, we owe to Him. Therefore, as satisfaction is compensation for a past offense, it seems that we cannot offer it to God.

Obj. 3. Further, if all that a man has suffices not to pay one debt, he cannot pay another debt. Now all that man is, all that he can do, and all that he has, does not suffice to pay what he owes for the blessing of creation, wherefore it is written (Isa. xl. 16) that *the wood of Libanus shall not be enough for a burnt offering.** Therefore by no means can he make satisfaction for the debt resulting from the offense committed.

Obj. 4. Further, man is bound to spend all his time in the service of God. Now time once lost cannot be recovered, wherefore, as Seneca observes *(Lib.* i, *Ep.* i, *ad Lucilium)* loss of time is a very grievous matter. Therefore man cannot make compensation to God, and the same conclusion follows as before.

Obj. 5. Further, mortal actual sin is more grievous than original sin. But none could satisfy for original sin unless he were both God and man. Neither, therefore, can he satisfy for actual sin.

On the contrary, Jerome† says: *Whoever maintains that God has commanded anything impossible to man, let him be anathema.* But satisfaction is commanded (Luke iii. 8): *Bring forth . . . fruits worthy of penance.* Therefore it is possible to make satisfaction to God.

Further, God is more merciful than any man. But it is possible to make satisfaction to a man. Therefore it is possible to make satisfaction to God.

Further, there is due satisfaction when the punishment balances the fault, since *justice is the same as counterpassion,* as the Pythagoreans said.‡ Now punishment may equal the pleasure contained in a sin committed. Therefore satisfaction can be made to God.

I answer that, Man becomes God's debtor in two ways; first, by reason of favors received, secondly, by reason of sin committed: and just as thanksgiving or worship or the like regard the debt for favors received, so satisfaction regards the debt for sin committed. Now in giving honor to one's parents or to the gods, as indeed the Philosopher says *(Ethic.* viii. 14), it is impossible to repay them measure for measure, but it suffices that man repay as much as he can, for friendship does not demand measure for measure, but what is possible. Yet even this is equal somewhat, viz. according to proportion, for as the debt due to God is, in comparison with God, so is what man can do, in comparison with himself, so that in another way the form of justice

is preserved. It is the same as regards satisfaction. Consequently man cannot make satisfaction to God if *satis (enough)* denotes quantitative equality; but he can, if it denote proportionate equality, as explained above, and as this suffices for justice, so does it suffice for satisfaction.

Reply Obj. 1. Just as the offense derived a certain infinity from the infinity of the Divine majesty, so does satisfaction derive a certain infinity from the infinity of Divine mercy, in so far as it is quickened by grace, whereby whatever man is able to repay becomes acceptable.—Others, however, say that the offense is infinite as regards the aversion, and in this respect it is pardoned gratuitously, but that it is finite as turning to a mutable good, in which respect it is possible to make satisfaction for it. But this is not to the point, since satisfaction does not answer to sin, except as this is an offense against God, which is a matter, not of turning to a creature but of turning away from God.—Others again say that even as regards the aversion it is possible to make satisfaction for sin in virtue of Christ's merit, which was, in a way, infinite. And this comes to the same as what we said before, since grace is given to believers through faith in the Mediator. If, however, He were to give grace otherwise, satisfaction would suffice in the way explained above.

Reply Obj. 2. Man, who was made to God's image, has a certain share of liberty, in so far as he is master of his actions through his free-will; so that, through acting by his free-will, he can make satisfaction to God, for though it belongs to God, in so far as it was bestowed on him by God, yet it was freely bestowed on him, that he might be his own master, which cannot be said of a slave.

Reply Obj. 3. This argument proves that it is impossible to make equivalent satisfaction to God, but not that it is impossible to make sufficient satisfaction to Him. For though man owes God all that he is able to give Him, yet it is not necessary for his salvation that he should actually do the whole of what he is able to do, for it is impossible for him, according to his present state of life, to put forth his whole power into any one single thing, since he has to be heedful about many things. And so his conduct is subject to a certain measure, viz. the fulfillment of God's commandments, over and above which he can offer something by way of satisfaction.

Reply Obj. 4. Though man cannot recover the time that is past, he can in the time that follows make compensation for what he should have done in the past, since the commandment

---

* Vulg.,—*Libanus shall not be enough to burn, nor the beasts thereof for a burnt offering.*
† Pelagius, *Expos. Fidei ad Damasum.*   ‡ Aristotle, *Ethic.* v. 5. Cf. II-II, Q. 61, A. 4.

did not exact from him the fulfillment of his whole power, as stated above (*ad* 3).

Reply Obj. 5. Though original sin has less of the nature of sin than actual sin has, yet it is a more grievous evil, because it is an infection of human nature itself, so that, unlike actual sin, it could not be expiated by the satisfaction of a mere man.

SECOND ARTICLE

Whether One Man Can Fulfill Satisfactory Punishment for Another?

We proceed thus to the Second Article:—

Objection 1. It would seem that one man cannot fulfill satisfactory punishment for another. Because merit is requisite for satisfaction. Now one man cannot merit or demerit for another, since it is written (Ps. lxi. 12): *Thou wilt render to every man according to his works.* Therefore one man cannot make satisfaction for another.

Obj. 2. Further, satisfaction is condivided with contrition and confession. But one man cannot be contrite or confess for another. Neither therefore can one make satisfaction for another.

Obj. 3. Further, by praying for another one merits also for oneself. If therefore a man can make satisfaction for another, he satisfies for himself by satisfying for another, so that if a man satisfy for another he need not make satisfaction for his own sins.

Obj. 4. Further, if one can satisfy for another, as soon as he takes the debt of punishment on himself, this other is freed from his debt. Therefore the latter will go straight to heaven, if he die after the whole of his debt of punishment has been taken up by another; else, if he be punished all the same, a double punishment will be paid for the same sin, viz. by him who has begun to make satisfaction, and by him who is punished in Purgatory.

On the contrary, It is written (Gal. vi. 2): *Bear ye one another's burdens.* Therefore it seems that one can bear the burden of punishment laid upon another.

Further, charity avails more before God than before man. Now before man, one can pay another's debt for love of him. Much more, therefore, can this be done before the judgment seat of God.

I answer that, Satisfactory punishment has a twofold purpose, viz. to pay the debt, and to serve as a remedy for the avoidance of sin. Accordingly, as a remedy against future sin, the satisfaction of one does not profit another, for the flesh of one man is not tamed by another's fast; nor does one man acquire the habit of well-doing, through the actions of another, except accidentally, in so far as a

man, by his good actions, may merit an increase of grace for another, since grace is the most efficacious remedy for the avoidance of sin. But this is by way of merit rather than of satisfaction. On the other hand, as regards the payment of the debt, one man can satisfy for another, provided he be in a state of charity, so that his works may avail for satisfaction. Nor is it necessary that he who satisfies for another should undergo a greater punishment than the principal would have to undergo (as some maintain, who argue that a man profits more by his own punishment than by another's), because punishment derives its power of satisfaction chiefly from charity whereby man bears it. And since greater charity is evidenced by a man satisfying for another than for himself, less punishment is required of him who satisfies for another, than of the principal: wherefore we read in the *Lives of the Fathers* (v. 5) of one who for love of his brother did penance for a sin which his brother had not committed, and that on account of his charity his brother was released from a sin which he had committed. Nor is it necessary that the one for whom satisfaction is made should be unable to make satisfaction himself, for even if he were able, he would be released from his debt when the other satisfied in his stead. But this is necessary in so far as the satisfactory punishment is medicinal: so that a man is not to be allowed to do penance for another, unless there be evidence of some defect in the penitent, either bodily, so that he is unable to bear it, or spiritual, so that he is not ready to undergo it.

Reply Obj. 1. The essential reward is bestowed on a man according to his disposition, because the fulness of the sight of God will be according to the capacity of those who see Him. Wherefore just as one man is not disposed thereto by another's act, so one man does not merit the essential reward for another, unless his merit has infinite efficacy, as the merit of Christ, whereby children come to eternal life through Baptism. On the other hand, the temporal punishment due to sin after the guilt has been forgiven is not measured according to the disposition of the man to whom it is due, since sometimes the better man owes a greater debt of punishment. Consequently one man can merit for another as regards release from punishment, and one man's act becomes another's, by means of charity whereby we are *all one in Christ* (Gal. iii. 28).

Reply Obj. 2. Contrition is ordained against the guilt which affects a man's disposition to goodness or malice, so that one man is not freed from guilt by another's contrition. In like manner by confession a man submits to the sacraments of the Church: nor can one man receive a sacrament instead of another, since in a sacrament grace is given to the recipient, not to another. Consequently there is no comparison between satisfaction and contrition and confession.

Reply Obj. 3. In the payment of the debt we consider the measure of the punishment, whereas in merit we regard the root which is charity: wherefore he that, through charity, merits for another, at least congruously, merits more for himself; yet he that satisfies for another does not also satisfy for himself, because the measure of the punishment does not suf-

fice for the sins of both, although by satisfying for another he merits something greater than the release from punishment, viz. eternal life.

Reply Obj. 4. If this man bound himself to undergo a certain punishment, he would not be released from the debt before paying it: wherefore he himself will suffer the punishment, as long as the other makes satisfaction for him: and if he do not this, both are debtors in respect of fulfilling this punishment, one for the sin committed, the other for his omission, so that it does not follow that one sin is twice punished.

QUESTION 14

Of the Quality of Satisfaction

(In Five Articles)

WE must now consider the quality of satisfaction, under which head there are five points of inquiry: (1) Whether a man can satisfy for one sin without satisfying for another? (2) Whether if a man fall into sin after being contrite for all his sins, he can, now that he has lost charity, satisfy for his other sins which were pardoned him through his contrition? (3) Whether a man's previous satisfaction begins to avail when he recovers charity? (4) Whether works done without charity merit any good? (5) Whether such works avail for the mitigation of the pains of hell?

FIRST ARTICLE

Whether a Man Can Satisfy for One Sin without Satisfying for Another?

We proceed thus to the First Article:—

Objection 1. It would seem that a man can satisfy for one sin without satisfying for another. Because when several things are not connected together one can be taken away without another. Now sins are not connected together, else whoever had one would have them all. Therefore one sin can be expiated by satisfaction, without another.

Obj. 2. Further, God is more merciful than man. But man accepts the payment of one debt without the payment of another. Therefore God accepts satisfaction for one sin without the other.

Obj. 3. Further, as stated in the text (iv. *Sent.*, D. 15), *satisfaction is to uproot the causes of sin, and give no opening to the suggestions thereof.* Now this can be done with regard to one sin and not another, as when a man curbs his lust and perseveres in covetousness. Therefore we can make satisfaction for one sin without satisfying for another.

On the contrary, The fast of those who

fasted *for debates and strifes* (Isa. lviii. 4, 5) was not acceptable to God, though fasting be a work of satisfaction. Now satisfaction cannot be made save by works that are acceptable to God. Therefore he that has a sin on his conscience cannot make satisfaction to God.

Further, satisfaction is a remedy for the healing of past sins, and for preserving from future sins, as stated above (Q. 12, A. 3). But without grace it is impossible to avoid sins. Therefore, since each sin excludes grace, it is not possible to make satisfaction for one sin and not for another.

I answer that, Some have held that it is possible to make satisfaction for one sin and not for another, as the Master states (iv. *Sent.*, 15). But this cannot be. For since the previous offense has to be removed by satisfaction, the mode of satisfaction must needs be consistent with the removal of the offense. Now removal of offense is renewal of friendship: wherefore if there be anything to hinder the renewal of friendship there can be no satisfaction. Since, therefore, every sin is a hindrance to the friendship of charity, which is the friendship of man for God, it is impossible for man to make satisfaction for one sin while holding to another; even as neither would a man make satisfaction to another for a blow, if while throwing himself at his feet he were to give him another.

Reply Obj. 1. As sins are not connected together in some single one, a man can incur one without incurring another; whereas all sins are remitted by reason of one same thing, so that the remissions of various sins are connected together. Consequently satisfaction cannot be made for one and not for another.

Reply Obj. 2. When a man is under obligation to another by reason of a debt, the only inequality between them is that which is opposed to justice, so that for restitution nothing further is required than that the equality of justice should be reinstated, and this can be done in respect of one debt without another. But when the obligation is based on an offense, there is inequality not only of justice but also of friendship, so that for the offense to be removed by satisfaction, not only must the equality of justice be restored by the payment of a punishment equal to the offense, but also the equality of friendship must be reinstated, which is impossible so long as an obstacle to friendship remains.

Reply Obj. 3. *By its weight, one sin drags us down to another,* as Gregory says *(Moral.* xxv)*:* so that when a man holds to one sin, he does not sufficiently cut himself off from the causes of further sin.

SECOND ARTICLE

Whether, When Deprived of Charity, a Man Can Make Satisfaction for Sins for Which He Was Previously Contrite?

We proceed thus to the Second Article:—

Objection 1. It would seem that if a man fall into sin after being contrite for all his sins, he can, now that he has lost charity, satisfy for his other sins which were already pardoned him through his contrition. For Daniel said to Nabuchodonosor (Dan. iv. 24): *Redeem thou thy sins with alms.* Yet he was still a sinner, as is shown by his subsequent punishment. Therefore a man can make satisfaction while in a state of sin.

Obj. 2. Further, *Man knoweth not whether he be worthy of love or hatred* (Eccle. ix. 1). If therefore one cannot make satisfaction unless one be in a state of charity, it would be impossible to know whether one had made satisfaction, which would be unseemly.

Obj. 3. Further, a man's entire action takes its form from the intention which he had at the beginning. But a penitent is in a state of charity when he begins to repent. Therefore his whole subsequent satisfaction will derive its efficacy from the charity which quickens his intention.

Obj. 4. Further, satisfaction consists in a certain equalization of guilt to punishment. But these things can be equalized even in one who is devoid of charity. Therefore, etc.

On the contrary, Charity covereth all sins (Prove. x. 12). But satisfaction has the power of blotting out sins. Therefore it is powerless without charity.

Further, the chief work of satisfaction is almsdeeds. But alms given by one who is devoid of charity avail nothing, as is clearly stated 1 Cor. xiii. 3, *If I should distribute all my goods to feed the poor . . . and have not charity, it profiteth me nothing.* Therefore there can be no satisfaction with mortal sin.

I answer that, Some have said that if, when all a man's sins have been pardoned through contrition, and before he has made satisfaction for them, he falls into sin, and then makes satisfaction, such satisfaction will be valid, so that if he die in that sin, he will not be punished in hell for the other sins.

But this cannot be, because satisfaction requires the reinstatement of friendship and the restoration of the equality of justice, the contrary of which destroys friendship, as the Philosopher states *(Ethic.* ix. 1, 3). Now in satisfaction made to God, the equality is based, not on equivalence but rather on God's acceptation: so that, although the offense be already removed by previous contrition, the works of satisfaction must be acceptable to God, and for this they are dependent on charity. Consequently works done without charity are not satisfactory.

Reply Obj. 1. Daniel's advice meant that he should give up sin and repent, and so make satisfaction by giving alms.

Reply Obj. 2. Even as man knows not for certain whether he had charity when making satisfaction, or whether he has it now, so too he knows not for certain whether he made full satisfaction: wherefore it is written (Ecclus. v. 5): *Be not without fear about sin forgiven.* And yet man need not, on account of that fear, repeat the satisfaction made, if he is not conscious of a mortal sin. For although he may not have expiated his punishment by that satisfaction, he does not incur the guilt of omission through neglecting to make satisfaction; even as he who receives the Eucharist without being conscious of a mortal sin of which he is guilty, does not incur the guilt of receiving unworthily.

Reply Obj. 3. His intention was interrupted by his subsequent sin, so that it gives no virtue to the works done after that sin.

Reply Obj. 4. Sufficient equalization is impossible both as to the Divine acceptation and as to equivalence: so that the argument proves nothing.

THIRD ARTICLE

Whether Previous Satisfaction Begins to Avail after Man Is Restored to Charity?

We proceed thus to the Third Article:—

Objection 1. It would seem that when a man has recovered charity his previous satisfaction begins to avail, because a gloss on Levit. xxv. 25, *If thy brother being impoverished,* etc., says that *the fruit of a man's good works should be counted from the time when he sinned.* But they would not be counted, unless they derived some efficacy from his subsequent charity. Therefore they begin to avail after he recovers charity.

Obj. 2. Further, as the efficacy of satisfaction is hindered by sin, so the efficacy of Baptism is hindered by insincerity. Now Baptism begins to avail when insincerity ceases. Therefore satisfaction begins to avail when sin is taken away.

Obj. 3. Further, if a man is given as a penance for the sins he has committed, to fast for several days, and then, after falling again into sin, he completes his penance, he is not told, when he goes to confession a second time, to fast once again. But he would be told to do so, if he did not fulfill his duty of satisfaction by them. Therefore his previous works become valid unto satisfaction, through his subsequent repentance.

On the contrary, Works done without charity were not satisfactory, through being dead works. But they are not quickened by penance. Therefore they do not begin to be satisfactory.

Further, charity does not quicken a work, unless in some way that work proceeds therefrom. But works cannot be acceptable to God, and therefore cannot be satisfactory, unless they be quickened by charity. Since then the works done without charity, in no way proceeded from charity, nor ever can proceed therefrom, they can by no means count towards satisfaction.

I answer that, Some have said that works done while in a state of charity, which are called living works, are meritorious in respect of eternal life, and satisfactory in respect of paying off the debt of punishment; and that by subsequent charity, works done without charity are quickened so as to be satisfactory, but not so as to be meritorious of eternal life. But this is impossible, because works done in charity produce both these effects for the same reason, viz. because they are pleasing to God: wherefore just as charity by its advent cannot make works done without charity to be pleasing in one respect, so neither can it make them pleasing in the other respect.

Reply Obj. 1. This means that the fruits are reckoned, not from the time when he was first in sin, but from the time when he ceased to sin, when, to wit, he was last in sin; unless he was contrite as soon as he had sinned, and did many good actions before he confessed.— Or we may say that the greater the contrition, the more it alleviates the punishment, and the more good actions a man does while in sin, the more he disposes himself to the grace of contrition, so that it is probable that he owes a smaller debt of punishment. For this reason the priest should use discretion in taking them

into account, so as to give him a lighter penance, according as he finds him better disposed.

Reply Obj. 2. Baptism imprints a character on the soul, whereas satisfaction does not. Hence on the advent of charity, which removes both insincerity and sin, it causes Baptism to have its effect, whereas it does not do this for satisfaction. Moreover Baptism confers justification in virtue of the deed (*ex opere operato*) which is not man's deed but God's, wherefore it does not become a lifeless deed as satisfaction does, which is a deed of man.

Reply Obj. 3. Sometimes satisfaction is such as to leave an effect in the person who makes satisfaction, even after the act of satisfaction has been done; thus fasting leaves the body weak, and almsdeeds result in a diminution of a person's substance, and so on. In such cases there is no need to repeat the works of satisfaction if they have been done while in a state of sin, because through penance they are acceptable to God in the result they leave behind. But when a work of satisfaction leaves behind no effect in the person that does satisfaction, it needs to be repeated, as in the case of prayer and so forth. Interior works, since they pass away altogether, are nowise quickened, and must be repeated.

FOURTH ARTICLE

Whether Works Done without Charity Merit Any, at Least Temporal, Good?

We proceed thus to the Fourth Article:—

Objection 1. It would seem that works done without charity merit some, at least a temporal, good. For as punishment is to the evil act, so is reward to a good act. Now no evil deed is unpunished by God the just judge. Therefore no good deed is unrewarded, and so every good deed merits some good.

Obj. 2. Further, reward is not given except for merit. Now some reward is given for works done without charity, wherefore it is written (Matth. vi. 2, 5, 16) of those who do good actions for the sake of human glory, that *they have received their reward.* Therefore those works merit some good.

Obj. 3. Further, if there be two men both in sin, one of whom does many deeds that are good in themselves and in their circumstances, while the other does none, they are not equally near to the reception of good things from God, else the latter need not be advised to do any good deeds. Now he that is nearer to God receives more of His good things. Therefore the former, on account of his good works, merits some good from God.

On the contrary, Augustine says that *the sinner is not worthy of the bread he eats.* Therefore he cannot merit anything from God.

Further, he that is nothing, can merit nothing. But a sinner, through not having charity, is nothing in respect of spiritual being, according to 1 Cor. xiii. 2. Therefore he can merit nothing.

I answer that, Properly speaking a merit is an action on account of which it is just that the agent should be given something. Now justice is twofold: first, there is justice properly so called, which regards something due on the part of the recipient. Secondly, there is metaphorical justice, so to speak, which regards something due on the part of the giver, for it may be right for the giver to give something to which the receiver has no claim. In this sense the *fitness of the Divine goodness* is justice; thus Anselm says (*Proslog.* x) that *God is just when He spares the sinner, because this is befitting.* And in this way merit is also twofold. The first is an act in respect of which the agent himself has a claim to receive something, and this is called merit of *condignity.* The second is an act the result of which is that there is a duty of giving in the giver by reason of fittingness, wherefore it is called merit of *congruity.* Now since in all gratuitous givings, the primary reason of the giving is love, it is impossible for anyone, properly speaking, to lay claim to a gift, if he lack friendship. Wherefore, as all things, whether temporal or eternal, are bestowed on us by the bounty of God, no one can acquire a claim to any of them, save through charity towards God: so that works done without charity are not condignly meritorious of any good from God, either eternal or temporal. But since it is befitting the goodness of God, that wherever He finds a disposition He should grant the perfection, a man is said to merit congruously some good by means of good works done without charity. Accordingly suchlike works avail for a threefold good, acquisition of temporal goods, disposition to grace, habituation to good works. Since, however, this is not merit properly so called, we should grant that such works are not meritorious of any good, rather than that they are.

Reply Obj. 1. As the Philosopher states (*Ethic.* viii. 14), since no matter what a son may do, he can never give back to his father the equal of what he has received from him, a father can never become his son's debtor: and much less can man make God his debtor on account of equivalence of work. Consequently no work of ours can merit a reward by reason of its measure of goodness, but it can by reason of charity, which makes friends hold their possessions in common. Therefore, no matter how good a work may be, if it be done without charity, it does not give man a claim to receive anything from God. On the other hand,

an evil deed deserves an equivalent punishment according to the measure of its malice, because no evil has been done to us on the part of God, like the good which He has done. Therefore, although an evil deed deserves condign punishment, nevertheless a good deed without charity does not merit condign reward.

Reply Obj. 2 and 3. These arguments consider merit of congruity; while the other arguments consider merit of condignity.

FIFTH ARTICLE

Whether the Aforesaid Works Avail for the Mitigation of the Pains of Hell?

We proceed thus to the Fifth Article:—

Objection 1. It would seem that the aforesaid works do not avail for the mitigation of the pains of hell. For the measure of punishment in hell will answer to the measure of guilt. But works done without charity do not diminish the measure of guilt. Neither, therefore, do they lessen the pains of hell.

Obj. 2. Further, the pain of hell, though infinite in duration, is nevertheless finite in intensity. Now anything finite is done away with by finite subtraction. If therefore works done without charity canceled any of the punishment due for sins, those works might be so numerous, that the pain of hell would be done away with altogether: which is false.

Obj. 3. Further, the suffrages of the Church are more efficacious than works done without charity. But, according to Augustine (*Enchir.* cx), *the suffrages of the Church do not profit the damned in hell.* Much less therefore are those pains mitigated by works done without charity.

On the contrary, Augustine also says (*Enchir. ibid.*): *Whomsoever they profit, either receive a full pardon, or at least find damnation itself more tolerable.*

Further, it is a greater thing to do a good deed than to omit an evil deed. But the omission of an evil deed always avoids a punishment, even in one who lacks charity. Much more, therefore, do good deeds void punishment.

I answer that, Mitigation of the pains of hell can be understood in two ways: first, as though one were delivered from the punishment which he already deserved, and thus, since no one is delivered from punishment unless he be absolved from guilt, (for an effect is not diminished or taken away unless its cause be diminished or taken away), the pain of hell cannot be mitigated by works done without charity, since they are unable to remove or diminish guilt. Secondly, so that the demerit of punishment is hindered; and thus the aforesaid works diminish the pain of hell,—first because he who does such works escapes being guilty of omitting them,—secondly, because such works dispose one somewhat to good, so that a man sins from less contempt, and indeed is drawn away from many sins thereby.

These works do, however, merit a diminution or postponement of temporal punishment, as in the case of Achab (3 Kings xxi. 27 *seqq.*), as also the acquisition of temporal goods.

Some, however, say that they mitigate the pains of hell, not by subtracting any of their substance, but by strengthening the subject, so that he is more able to bear them. But this is impossible, because there is no strengthening without a diminution of passibility. Now passibility is according to the measure of guilt, wherefore if guilt is not removed, neither can the subject be strengthened.

Some again say that the punishment is mitigated as to the remorse of conscience, though not as to the pain of fire. But neither will this stand, because as the pain of fire is equal to the guilt, so also is the pain of the remorse of conscience: so that what applies to one applies to the other.

This suffices for the *Replies* to the *Objections.*

QUESTION 15

Of the Means of Making Satisfaction

(In Three Articles)

WE must now consider the means of making satisfaction, under which head there are three points of inquiry: (1) Whether satisfaction must be made by means of penal works? (2) Whether the scourges whereby God punishes man in this life, are satisfactory? (3) Whether the works of satisfaction are suitably reckoned, by saying that there are three, viz. almsdeeds, fasting, and prayer?

FIRST ARTICLE

Whether Satisfaction Must Be Made by Means of Penal Works?

We proceed thus to the First Article:—

Objection 1. It would seem that satisfaction need not be made by means of penal works. For satisfaction should make compensation for the offense committed against God. Now, seemingly, no compensation is given to God by penal works, for God does not delight in our sufferings, as appears from Tob. iii. 22. Therefore satisfaction need not be made by means of penal works.

Obj. 2. Further, the greater the charity from which a work proceeds, the less penal is that work, for *charity hath no pain** according to 1 Jo. iv. 18. If therefore works of satisfaction need to be penal, the more they proceed from charity, the less satisfactory will they be: which is false.

Obj. 3. Further, *Satisfaction,* as Anselm states *(Cur Deus homo* i) *consists in giving due honor to God.* But this can be done by other means than penal works. Therefore satisfaction needs not to be made by means of penal works.

On the contrary, Gregory says *(Hom. in Evang.* xx): *It is just that the sinner, by his repentance, should inflict on himself so much the greater suffering, as he has brought greater harm on himself by his sin.*

Further, the wound caused by sin should be perfectly healed by satisfaction. Now punishment is the remedy for sins, as the Philosopher says *(Ethic.* ii. 3). Therefore satisfaction should be made by means of penal works.

I answer that, As stated above (Q. 12, A. 3), satisfaction regards both the past offense, for which compensation is made by its means, and also future sin wherefrom we are preserved thereby: and in both respects satisfaction needs to be made by means of penal works. For compensation for an offense implies equality, which must needs be between the offender and the person whom he offends. Now equalization in human justice consists in taking away from one that which he has too much of, and giving it to the person from whom something has been taken. And, although nothing can be taken away from God, so far as He is concerned, yet the sinner, for his part, deprives Him of something by sinning, as stated above (Q. 12, AA. 3, 4). Consequently, in order that compensation be made, something by way of satisfaction that may conduce to the glory of God must be taken away from the sinner. Now a good work, as such, does not deprive the agent of anything, but perfects him: so that the deprivation cannot be effected by a good work unless it be penal. Therefore, in order that a work be satisfactory it needs to be good, that it may conduce to God's honor, and it must be penal, so that something may be taken away from the sinner thereby.

Again punishment preserves from future sin,

* Vulg.,—*Perfect charity casteth out fear, because fear hath pain.*

because a man does not easily fall back into sin when he has had experience of the punishment. Wherefore, according to the Philosopher *(loc. cit.)* punishments are medicinal.

Reply Obj. 1. Though God does not delight in our punishments as such, yet He does, in so far as they are just, and thus they can be satisfactory.

Reply Obj. 2. Just as, in satisfaction, we have to note the penality of the work, so, in merit, we must observe its difficulty. Now if the difficulty of the work itself be diminshed, other things being equal, the merit is also diminished; but if the difficulty be diminished on the part of the promptitude of the will, this does not diminish the merit, but increases it; and, in like manner, diminution of the penality of a work, on account of the will being made more prompt by charity, does not lessen the efficacy of satisfaction, but increases it.

Reply Obj. 3. That which is due for sin is compensation for the offense, and this cannot be done without punishment of the sinner. It is of this debt that Anselm speaks.

SECOND ARTICLE

Whether the Scourges of the Present Life Are Satisfactory?

We proceed thus to the Second Article:—

Objection 1. It would seem that the scourges whereby we are punished by God in this life, cannot be satisfactory. For nothing but what is meritorious can be satisfactory, as is clear from what has been said (Q. 14, A. 2). But we do not merit except by what is in our own power. Since therefore the scourges with which God punishes us are not in our power, it seems that they cannot be satisfactory.

Obj. 2. Further, only the good make satisfaction. But these scourges are inflicted on the wicked also, and are deserved by them most of all. Therefore they cannot be satisfactory.

Obj. 3. Further, satisfaction regards past sins. But these scourges are sometimes inflicted on those who have no sins, as in the case of Job. Therefore it seems that they are not satisfactory.

On the contrary, It is written (Rom. v. 3, 4): *Tribulation worketh patience, and patience trial,* i.e. *deliverance from sin,* as a gloss explains it.

Further, Ambrose says *(Super Ps.* cxviii): *Although faith,* i.e. the consciousness of sin, *be lacking, the punishment satisfies.* Therefore the scourges of this life are satisfactory.

I answer that, Compensation for a past offense can be enforced either by the offender or by another. When it is enforced by another, such compensation is of a vindictive rather than of a satisfactory nature, whereas when it is made by the offender, it is also satisfactory. Consequently, if the scourges, which are inflicted by God on account of sin, become in some way the act of the sufferer they acquire a satisfactory character. Now they become the act of the sufferer in so far as he accepts them for the cleansing of his sins, by taking advantage of them patiently. If, however, he refuse to submit to them patiently, then they do not become his personal act in any way, and are not of a satisfactory, but merely of a vindictive character.

Reply Obj. 1. Although these scourges are not altogether in our power, yet in some respect they are, in so far as we use them patiently. In this way man makes a virtue of necessity, so that such things can become both meritorious and satisfactory.

Reply Obj. 2. As Augustine observes *(De Civ. Dei,* i. 8), even as *the same fire makes gold glisten and straw reek,* so by the same scourges are the good cleansed and the wicked worsened on account of their impatience. Hence, though the scourges are common to both, satisfaction is only on the side of the good.

Reply Obj. 3. These scourges always regard past guilt, not always the guilt of the person, but sometimes the guilt of nature. For had there not been guilt in human nature, there would have been no punishment. But since guilt preceded in nature, punishment is inflicted by God on a person without the person's fault, that his virtue may be meritorious, and that he may avoid future sin. Moreover, these two things are necessary in satisfaction. For the work needs to be meritorious, that honor may be given to God, and it must be a safeguard of virtue, that we may be preserved from future sins.

THIRD ARTICLE

Whether the Works of Satisfaction Are Suitably Enumerated?

We proceed thus to the Third Article:—

Objection 1. It would seem that the works of satisfaction are unsuitably enumerated by saying that there are three, viz. almsdeeds, fasting, and prayer. For a work of satisfaction should be penal. But prayer is not penal, since it is a remedy against penal sorrow, and is a source of pleasure, wherefore it is written (James v. 13): *Is any of you sad? Let him pray. Is he cheerful in mind? Let him sing.* Therefore prayer should not be reckoned among the works of satisfaction.

Obj. 2. Further, every sin is either carnal or spiritual. Now, as Jerome says on Mark ix. 28, *This kind* of demons *can go out by nothing, but by prayer and fasting:—Diseases of the body are healed by fasting, diseases of the mind, by prayer.* Therefore no other work of satisfaction is necessary.

Obj. 3. Further, satisfaction is necessary in order for us to be cleansed from our sins. But almsgiving cleanses from all sins, according to Luke xi. 41: *Give alms, and behold all things are clean unto you.* Therefore the other two are in excess.

Obj. 4. *On the other hand,* it seems that there should be more. For contrary heals contrary. But there are many more than three kinds of sin. Therefore more works of satisfaction should be enumerated.

Obj. 5. Further, pilgrimages and scourgings are also enjoined as works of satisfaction, and are not included among the above. Therefore they are not sufficiently enumerated.

I answer that, Satisfaction should be of such a nature as to involve something taken away from us for the honor of God. Now we have but three kinds of goods, bodily, spiritual, and goods of fortune, or external goods. By almsdeeds we deprive ourselves of some goods of fortune, and by fasting we retrench goods of the body. As to goods of the soul, there is no need to deprive ourselves of any of them, either in whole or in part, since thereby we become acceptable to God, but we should submit them entirely to God, which is done by prayer.

This number is shown to be suitable in so far as satisfaction uproots the causes of sin, for these are reckoned to be three (1 Jo. ii. 16), viz. *concupiscence of the flesh, concupiscence of the eyes,* and *pride of life.* Fasting is directed against concupiscence of the *flesh,* almsdeeds against concupiscence of the *eyes,* and *prayer* against *pride of life,* as Augustine says (*Enarr. in Ps.* xlii).

This number is also shown to be suitable in so far as satisfaction does not open a way to the suggestions of sin, because every sin is committed either against God, and this is prevented by *prayer,* or against our neighbor, and this is remedied by *almsdeeds,* or against ourselves, and this is forestalled by *fasting.*

Reply Obj. 1. According to some, prayer is twofold. There is the prayer of contempla-

tives whose *conversation is in heaven:* and this, since it is altogether delightful, is not a work of satisfaction. The other is a prayer which pours forth sighs for sin; this is penal and a part of satisfaction.

It may also be replied, and better, that every prayer has the character of satisfaction, for though it be sweet to the soul it is painful to the body, since, as Gregory says (*Super Ezech., Hom.* xiv), *doubtless, when our soul's love is strengthened, our body's strength is weakened;* hence we read (Gen. xxxii. 25) that the sinew of Jacob's thigh shrank through his wrestling with the angel.

Reply Obj. 2. Carnal sin is twofold; one which is completed in carnal delectation, as gluttony and lust; and, another which is completed in things relating to the flesh, though it be completed in the delectation of the soul rather than of the flesh, as covetousness. Hence such like sins are between spiritual and carnal sins, so that they need a satisfaction proper to them, viz. almsdeeds.

Reply Obj. 3. Although each of these three, by a kind of likeness, is appropriated to some particular kind of sin because it is reasonable that, whereby a man sins, in that he should be punished, and that satisfaction should cut out the very root of the sin committed, yet each of them can satisfy for any kind of sin. Hence if a man is unable to perform one of the above, another is imposed on him, chiefly almsdeeds, which can take the place of the others, in so far as in those to whom a man gives alms he purchases other works of satisfaction thereby. Consequently even if almsgiving washes all sins away, it does not follow that other works are in excess.

Reply Obj. 4. Though there are many kinds of sins, all are reduced to those three roots or to those three kinds of sin, to which, as we have said, the aforesaid works of satisfaction correspond.

Reply Obj. 5. Whatever relates to affliction of the body is all referred to fasting, and whatever is spent for the benefit of one's neighbor is a kind of alms, and whatever act of worship is given to God becomes a kind of prayer, so that even one work can be satisfactory in several ways.

QUESTION 16

Of Those Who Receive the Sacrament of Penance

(In Three Articles)

WE must now consider the recipients of the sacrament of Penance: under which head there are three points of inquiry: (1) Whether penance can be in the innocent? (2) Whether it can be in the saints in glory? (3) Whether in the good or bad angels?

FIRST ARTICLE

Whether Penance Can Be in the Innocent?

We proceed thus to the First Article:—

Objection 1. It would seem that penance cannot be in the innocent. For penance consists in bewailing one's evil deeds: whereas the innocent have done no evil. Therefore penance cannot be in them.

Obj. 2. Further, the very name of penance (*pœnitentia*) implies punishment (*pœna*). But the innocent do not deserve punishment. Therefore penance is not in them.

Obj. 3. Further, penance coincides with vindictive justice. But if all were innocent, there would be no room for vindictive justice. Therefore there would be no penance, so that there is none in the innocent.

On the contrary, All the virtues are infused together. But penance is a virtue. Since, therefore, other virtues are infused into the innocent at Baptism, penance is infused with them.

Further, a man is said to be curable though he has never been sick in body: therefore in like manner, one who has never been sick spiritually. Now even as there can be no actual cure from the wound of sin without an act of penance, so is there no possibility of cure without the habit of penance. Therefore one who has never had the disease of sin, has the habit of penance.

I answer that, Habit comes between power and act: and since the removal of what precedes entails the removal of what follows, but not conversely, the removal of the habit ensues from the removal of the power to act, but not from the removal of the act. And because removal of the matter entails the removal of the act, since there can be no act without the matter into which it passes, hence the habit of a virtue is possible in one for whom the matter is not available, for the reason that it can be available, so that the habit can proceed to its act,—thus a poor man can have the habit of magnificence, but not the act, because he is not possessed of great wealth which is the matter of magnificence, but he can be possessed thereof.

Reply Obj. 1. Although the innocent have committed no sin, nevertheless they can, so that they are competent to have the habit of penance. Yet this habit can never proceed to its act, except perhaps with regard to their venial sins, because mortal sins destroy the habit. Nevertheless it is not without its purpose, because it is a perfection of the natural power.

Reply Obj. 2. Although they deserve no punishment actually, yet it is possible for something to be in them for which they would deserve to be punished.

Reply Obj. 3. So long as the power to sin remains, there would be room for vindictive justice as to the habit, though not as to the act, if there were no actual sins.

SECOND ARTICLE

Whether the Saints in Glory Have Penance?

We proceed thus to the Second Article:—

Objection 1. It would seem that the saints in glory have not penance. For, as Gregory says (*Moral.* iv), *the blessed remember their sins, even as we, without grief, remember our griefs after we have been healed.* But penance is grief of the heart. Therefore the saints in heaven have not penance.

Obj. 2. Further, the saints in heaven are conformed to Christ. But there was no penance in Christ, since there was no faith which is the principle of penance. Therefore there will be no penance in the saints in heaven.

Obj. 3. Further, a habit is useless if it is not reduced to its act. But the saints in heaven will not repent actually, because, if they did, there would be something in them against their wish. Therefore the habit of penance will not be in them.

Obj. 4. *On the other hand,* penance is a part of justice. But justice is *perpetual and immortal* (Wis. i. 15), and will remain in heaven. Therefore penance will also.

Obj. 5. Further, we read in the *Lives of the Fathers,* that one of them said that even Abraham will repent of not having done more good. But one ought to repent of evil done more than of good left undone, and which one was not bound to do, for such is the good in question. Therefore repentance will be there of evil done.

I answer that, The cardinal virtues will remain in heaven, but only as regards the acts which they exercise in respect of their end. Wherefore, since the virtue of penance is a part of justice which is a cardinal virtue, whoever has the habit of penance in this life, will have it in the life to come: but he will not have the same act as now, but another, viz. thanksgiving to God for His mercy in pardoning his sins.

Reply Obj. 1. This argument proves that they do not have the same act as penance has now; and we grant this.

Reply Obj. 2. Christ could not sin, wherefore the matter of this virtue was lacking in His respect both actually and potentially: so that there is no comparison between Him and others.

Reply Obj. 3. Repentance, properly speaking, considered as that act of penance which is in this life, will not be in heaven: and yet the habit will not be without its use, for it will have another act.

Reply Obj. 4, 5. We grant the Fourth argument. But since the Fifth Objection proves that there will be the same act of penance in heaven as now, we answer the latter by saying that in heaven one will be altogether conformed to the will of God. Wherefore, as God, by His antecedent will, but not by His consequent will, wishes that all things should be good, and therefore that there should be no evil, so is it with the blessed. It is this will that this holy father improperly calls penance.

THIRD ARTICLE

Whether an Angel Can Be the Subject of Penance?

We proceed thus to the Third Article:—

Objection 1. It would seem that even a good or bad angel can be a subject of penance. For fear is the beginning of penance. But fear is in the angels, according to James ii. 19: *The devils . . . believe and tremble.* Therefore there can be penance in them.

Obj. 2. Further, the Philosopher says *(Ethic.* ix. 4) that *evil men are full of repentance, and this is a great punishment for them.* Now the devils are exceeding evil, nor is there any punishment that they lack. Therefore they can repent.

Obj. 3. Further, a thing is more easily moved to that which is according to its nature than to that which is against its nature: thus water which has by violence been heated, of itself returns to its natural property. Now angels can be moved to sin which is contrary to their common nature. Much more therefore can they return to that which is in accord with their nature. But this is done by penance. Therefore they are susceptible to penance.

Obj. 4. Further, what applies to angels, applies equally to separated souls, as Damascene says *(De Fide Orthod.* ii. 4). But there can be penance in separated souls, as some say, as in the souls of the blessed in heaven. Therefore there can be penance in the angels.

On the contrary, By penance man obtains pardon for the sin he has committed. But this is impossible in the angels. Therefore they are not subjects of penance.

Further, Damascene says *(loc. cit.)* that man is subject to penance on account of the weakness of his body. But the angels are not united to a body. Therefore no penance can be in them.

I answer that, In us, penance is taken in two senses; first, as a passion, and thus it is nothing but pain or sorrow on account of a sin committed: and though, as a passion it is only in the concupiscible part, yet, by way of comparison, the name of penance is given to that act of the will, whereby a man detests what he has done, even as love and other passions are spoken of as though they were in the intellectual appetite. Secondly, penance is taken as a virtue, and in this way its act consists in the detestation of evil done, together with the purpose of amendment and the intention of expiating the evil, or of placating God for the offense committed. Now detestation of evil befits a person according as he is naturally ordained to good. And since this order or inclination is not entirely destroyed in any creature, it remains even in the damned, and consequently the passion of repentance, or something like it, remains in them too, as stated in Wis. v. 3 *(saying) within themselves, repenting,* etc. This repentance, as it is not a habit, but a passion or act, can by no means be in the blessed angels, who have not committed any sins: but it is in the wicked angels, since the same applies to them as to the lost souls, for, according to Damascene *(loc. cit.), death is to man what sin is to an angel.* But no forgiveness is possible for the sin of an angel. Now sin is the proper object of the virtue itself which we call penance, in so far as it can be pardoned or expiated. Therefore, since the wicked angels cannot have the matter, they have not the power to produce the act, so that neither can they have the habit. Hence the angels cannot be subjects of the virtue of penance.

Reply Obj. 1. A certain movement of penance is engendered in them from fear, but not such as is a virtue.

This suffices for the *Reply* to the *Second Objection.*

Reply Obj. 3. Whatever is natural in them is entirely good, and inclines to good: but their free-will is fixed on evil. And since the movement of virtue and vice follows the inclination, not of nature, but of the free-will, there is no need that there should be movements of virtue in them either actually or possibly, although they are inclined to good by nature.

Reply Obj. 4. There is no parity between the holy angels and the beatified souls, because in the latter there has been or could have been a sin that could be pardoned, but not in the former: so that though they are like as to their present state, they differ as to their previous states, which penance regards directly.

QUESTION 17

Of the Power of the Keys

(In Three Articles)

WE must now consider the power of the ministers of this sacrament, which power depends on the keys. As to this matter, in the first place we shall treat of the keys, secondly, of excommunication, thirdly, of indulgences, since these two things are connected with the power of the keys. The first of these considerations will be fourfold: (1) the nature and meaning of the keys; (2) the use of the keys; (3) the ministers of the keys; (4) those on whom the use of the keys can be exercised.

Under the first head there are three points of inquiry: (1) Whether there ought to be keys in the Church? (2) Whether the key is the power of binding and loosing, etc.? (3) Whether there are two keys or only one?

FIRST ARTICLE

Whether There Should Be Keys in the Church?

We proceed thus to the First Article:—

Objection 1. It would seem that there is no necessity for keys in the Church. For there is no need for keys that one may enter a house the door of which is open. But it is written (*Apoc.* iv. 1): *I looked and behold a door was opened in heaven,* which door is Christ, for He said of Himself (Jo. x. 7): *I am the door.* Therefore the Church needs no keys for the entrance into heaven.

Obj. 2. Further, a key is needed for opening and shutting. But this belongs to Christ alone, *Who openeth and no man shutteth, shutteth and no man openeth* (Apoc. iii. 7). Therefore the Church has no keys in the hands of her ministers.

Obj. 3. Further, hell is opened to whomever heaven is closed, and vice versa. Therefore whoever has the keys of heaven, has the keys of hell. But the Church is not said to have the keys of hell. Therefore neither has she the keys of heaven.

On the contrary, It is written (Matth. xvi. 19): *To thee will I give the keys of the kingdom of heaven.*

Further, every dispenser should have the keys of the things that he dispenses. But the ministers of the Church are the dispensers of the divine mysteries, as appears from 1 Cor. iv. 1. Therefore they ought to have the keys.

I answer that, In material things a key is an instrument for opening a door. Now the door of the kingdom is closed to us through sin, both as to the stain and as to the debt of

* Augustine,—*Enarr. in Ps.* cxxxviii.

punishment. Wherefore the power of removing this obstacle is called a key. Now this power is in the Divine Trinity by authority; hence some say that God has the key of *authority.* But Christ Man had the power to remove the above obstacle, through the merit of His Passion, which also is said to open the door; hence some say that He has the keys of *excellence.* And since *the sacraments of which the Church is built, flowed from the side of Christ while He lay asleep on the cross,** the efficacy of the Passion abides in the sacraments of the Church. Wherefore a certain power for the removal of the aforesaid obstacle is bestowed on the ministers of the Church, who are the dispensers of the sacraments, not by their own, but by a Divine power and by the Passion of Christ. This power is called metaphorically the Church's key, and is the key of *ministry.*

Reply Obj. 1. The door of heaven, considered in itself, is ever open, but it is said to be closed to someone, on account of some obstacle against entering therein, which is in himself. The obstacle which the entire human nature inherited from the sin of the first man, was removed by Christ's Passion; hence, after the Passion, John saw an opened door in heaven. Yet that door still remains closed to this or that man, on account of the original sin which he has contracted, or the actual sin which he has committed: hence we need the sacraments and the keys of the Church.

Reply Obj. 2. This refers to His closing Limbo, so that thenceforth no one should go there, and to His opening of Paradise, the obstacle of nature being removed by His Passion.

Reply Obj. 3. The key whereby hell is opened and closed, is the power of bestowing grace, whereby hell is opened to man, so that he is taken out from sin which is the door of hell, and closed, so that by the help of grace man should no more fall into sin. Now the power of bestowing grace belongs to God alone, wherefore He kept this key to Himself. But the key of the kingdom is also the power to remit the debt of temporal punishment, which debt prevents man from entering the kingdom. Consequently the key of the kingdom can be given to man rather than the key of hell, for they are not the same, as is clear from what has been said. For a man may be set free from hell by the remission of the debt of eternal punishment, without being at once admitted to the kingdom, on account of his yet owing a debt of temporal punishment.

It may also be replied, as some state, that the key of heaven is also the key of hell, since if one is opened to a man, the other, for that very reason, is closed to him, but it takes its name from the better of the two.

SECOND ARTICLE

Whether the Key Is the Power of Binding and Loosing, etc.?

We proceed thus to the Second Article:—

Objection 1. It would seem that the key is not the power of binding and loosing, whereby *the ecclesiastical judge has to admit the worthy to the kingdom and exclude the unworthy therefrom*, as stated in the text (iv. *Sent.*, D. 16). For the spiritual power conferred in a sacrament is the same as the character. But the key and the character do not seem to be the same, since by the character man is referred to God, whereas by the key he is referred to his subjects. Therefore the key is not a power.

Obj. 2. Further, an ecclesiastical judge is only one who has jurisdiction, which is not given at the same time as Orders. But the keys are given in the conferring of Orders. Therefore there should have been no mention of the ecclesiastical judge in the definition of the keys.

Obj. 3. Further, when a man has something of himself, he needs not to be reduced to act by some active power. Now a man is admitted to the kingdom from the very fact that he is worthy. Therefore it does not concern the power of the keys to admit the worthy to the kingdom.

Obj. 4. Further, sinners are unworthy of the kingdom. But the Church prays for sinners, that they may go to heaven. Therefore she does not exclude the unworthy, but admits them, so far as she is concerned.

Obj. 5. Further, in every ordered series of agents, the last end belongs to the principal and not to the instrumental agent. But the principal agent in view of man's salvation is God. Therefore admission to the kingdom, which is the last end, belongs to Him, and not to those who have the keys, who are as instrumental or ministerial agents.

I answer that, According to the Philosopher (*De Anima,* ii, text 33), *powers are defined from their acts.* Wherefore, since the key is a kind of power, it should be defined from its act or use, and reference to the act should include its object from which it takes its species, and the mode of acting whereby the power is shown to be well-ordered. Now the act of the spiritual power is to open heaven, not absolutely, since it is already open, as stated above (A. 1, *ad* 1), but for this or that man; and this cannot be done in an orderly manner without due consideration of the worthiness of the one to be admitted to heaven. Hence the aforesaid definition of the key gives the genus, viz. *power,* the subject of the power, viz. the *ecclesiastical judge,* and the act, viz. *of excluding or admitting,* corresponding to the two acts of a material key which are to open and shut; the object of which act is referred to in the words *from the kingdom,* and the mode, in the words, *worthy* and *unworthy,* because account is taken of the worthiness or unworthiness of those on whom the act is exercised.

Reply Obj. 1. The same power is directed to two things, of which one is the cause of the other, as heat, in fire, is directed to make a thing hot and to melt it. And since every grace and remission in a mystical body comes to it from its head, it seems that it is essentially the same power whereby a priest can consecrate, and whereby he can loose and bind, if he has jurisdiction, and that there is only a logical difference, according as it is referred to different effects, even as fire in one respect is said to have the power of heating, and in another, the power of melting. And because the character of the priestly order is nothing else than the power of exercising that act to which the priestly order is chiefly ordained (if we maintain that it is the same as a spiritual power), therefore the character, the power of consecrating, and the power of the keys are one and the same essentially, but differ logically.

Reply Obj. 2. All spiritual power is conferred by some kind of consecration. Therefore the key is given together with the order: yet the use of the key requires due matter, i.e. a people subject through jurisdiction, so that until he has jurisdiction, the priest has the keys, but he cannot exercise the act of the keys. And since the key is defined from its act, its definition contains a reference to jurisdiction.

Reply Obj. 3. A person may be worthy to have something in two ways, either so as to have a right to possess it, and thus whoever is worthy has heaven already opened to him,— or so that it is meet that he should receive it, and thus the power of the keys admits those who are worthy, but to whom heaven is not yet altogether opened.

Reply Obj. 4. Even as God hardens not by imparting malice, but by withholding grace, so a priest is said to exclude, not as though he placed an obstacle to entrance, but because he does not remove an obstacle which is there, since he cannot remove it unless God has already removed it.* Hence God is prayed that He may absolve, so that there may be room for the priest's absolution.

Reply Obj. 5. The priest's act does not bear immediately on the kingdom, but on the sacraments, by means of which man wins to the kingdom.

THIRD ARTICLE

Whether There Are Two Keys or Only One?

We proceed thus to the Third Article:—

Objection 1. It would seem that there are not two keys but only one. For one lock requires but one key. Now the lock for the removal of which the keys of the Church are required, is sin. Therefore the Church does not require two keys for one sin.

Obj. 2. Further, the keys are given when Orders are conferred. But knowledge is not always due to infusion, but sometimes is acquired, nor is it possessed by all those who are ordained, and is possessed by some who are not ordained. Therefore knowledge is not a key, so that there is but one key, viz. the power of judging.

Obj. 3. Further, the power which the priest has over the mystic body of Christ flows from the power which he has over Christ's true body. Now the power of consecrating Christ's true body is but one. Therefore the power which regards Christ's mystic body is but one. But this is a key. Therefore, etc.

Obj. 4. **On the other hand,** It seems that there are more than two keys. For just as knowledge and power are requisite for man to act, so is will. But the knowledge of discretion is reckoned as a key, and so is the power of judging. Therefore the will to absolve should be counted as a key.

Obj. 5. Further, all three Divine Persons remit sins. Now the priest, through the keys, is the minister for the remission of sins. Therefore he should have three keys, so that he may be conformed to the Trinity.

I answer that, Whenever an act requires fitness on the part of the recipient, two things are necessary in the one who has to perform the act, viz. judgment of the fitness of the recipient, and accomplishment of the act. Therefore in the act of justice whereby a man is given what he deserves, there needs to be a judgment in order to discern whether he deserves to receive. Again, an authority or power is necessary for both these things, for we cannot give save what we have in our power; nor can there be judgment, without the right to enforce it, since judgment is determined to one particular thing, which determination it derives, in speculative matters, from the first

* See footnote, p. 2617

principles which cannot be gainsaid, and, in practical matters, from the power of command vested in the one who judges. And since the act of the key requires fitness in the person on whom it is exercised,—because the ecclesiastical judge, by means of the key, *admits the worthy and excludes the unworthy,* as may be seen from the definition given above (A. 2),—therefore the judge requires both judgment of discretion whereby he judges a man to be worthy, and also the very act of receiving (that man's confession); and for both these things a certain power or authority is necessary. Accordingly we may distinguish two keys, the first of which regards the judgment about the worthiness of the person to be absolved, while the other regards the absolution.

These two keys are distinct, not in the essence of authority, since both belong to the minister by virtue of his office, but in comparison with their respective acts, one of which presupposes the other.

Reply Obj. 1. One key is ordained immediately to the opening of one lock, but it is not unfitting that one key should be ordained to the act of another. Thus it is in the case in point. For it is the second key, which is the power of binding and loosing, that opens the lock of sin immediately, but the key of knowledge shows to whom that lock should be opened.

Reply Obj. 2. There are two opinions about the key of knowledge. For some say that knowledge considered as a habit, acquired or infused, is the key in this case, and that it is not the principal key, but is called a key through being subordinate to another key: so that it is not called a key when the other key is wanting, for instance, in an educated man who is not a priest. And although priests lack this key at times, through being without knowledge, acquired or infused, of loosing and binding, yet sometimes they make use of their natural endeavors, which they who hold this opinion call a little key, so that although knowledge be not bestowed together with Orders, yet with the conferring of Orders the knowledge becomes a key which it was not before. This seems to have been the opinion of the Master (iv. *Sent.,* D. 19).

But this does not seem to agree with the words of the Gospel, whereby the keys are promised to Peter (Matth. xvi. 19), so that not only one but two are given in Orders. For which reason the other opinion holds that the key is not knowledge considered as a habit, but the authority to exercise the act of knowledge, which authority is sometimes without knowledge, while the knowledge is sometimes present without the authority. This may be seen even in secular courts, for a secular judge may have the authority to judge, without having the knowledge of the law, while another man, on the contrary, has knowledge of the law without having the authority to judge. And since the act of judging, to which a man is bound through the authority which is vested in him, and not through his habit of knowledge, cannot be well performed without both of the above, the authority to judge, which is the key of knowledge, cannot be accepted without sin by one who lacks knowledge; whereas knowledge void of authority can be possessed without sin.

Reply Obj. 3. The power of consecrating is directed to only one act of another kind, wherefore it is not numbered among the keys, nor is it multiplied as the power of the keys, which is directed to different acts, although as to the essence of power and authority it is but one, as stated above.

Reply Obj. 4. Everyone is free to will, so that no one needs authority to will; wherefore will is not reckoned as a key.

Reply Obj. 5. All three Persons remit sins in the same way as one Person, wherefore there is no need for the priest, who is the minister of the Trinity, to have three keys: and all the more, since the will, which is appropriated to the Holy Ghost, requires no key, as stated above (*ad* 4).

QUESTION 18

Of the Effect of the Keys

(In Four Articles)

WE must now consider the effect of the keys, under which head there are four points of inquiry: (1) Whether the power of the keys extends to the remission of guilt? (2) Whether a priest can remit sin as to the punishment? (3) Whether a priest can bind in virtue of the power of the keys? (4) Whether he can loose and bind according to his own judgment?

FIRST ARTICLE

Whether the Power of the Keys Extends to the Remission of Guilt? *

We proceed thus to the First Article:—

Objection 1. It would seem that the power of the keys extends to the remission of guilt. For it was said to the disciples (Jo. xx. 23): *Whose sins you shall forgive, they are forgiven them.* Now this was not said in reference to the declaration only, as the Master states (iv. *Sent.*, D. 18), for in that case the priest of the New Testament would have no more power than the priest of the Old Testament. Therefore he exercises a power over the remission of the guilt.

Obj. 2. Further, in Penance grace is given for the remission of sin. Now the priest is the dispenser of this sacrament by virtue of the keys. Therefore, since grace is opposed to sin, not on the part of the punishment, but on the part of the guilt, it seems that the priest operates unto the remission of sin by virtue of the keys.

Obj. 3. Further, the priest receives more power by his consecration than the baptismal water by its sanctification. Now the baptismal water receives the power *to touch the body and cleanse the heart,* as Augustine says (*Tract.* lxxx, *in Joan.*). Much more, therefore, does the priest, in his consecration, receive the power to cleanse the heart from the stain of sin.

On the contrary, The Master stated above (iv, *Sent.*, D. 18) that God has not bestowed on the minister the power to co-operate with Him in the inward cleansing. Now if he remitted sins as to the guilt, he would co-operate with God in the inward cleansing. Therefore the power of the keys does not extend to the remission of guilt.

Further, sin is not remitted save by the Holy Ghost. But no man has the power to give the Holy Ghost, as the Master said above (i, *Sent.*, D. 14). Neither therefore can he remit sins as to their guilt.

I answer that, According to Hugh (*De Sacram.* ii), *the sacraments, by virtue of their sanctification, contain an invisible grace.* Now this sanctification is sometimes essential to the sacrament both as regards the matter and as regards the minister, as may be seen in Confirmation, and then the sacramental virtue is in both together. Sometimes, however, the essence of the sacrament requires only sanctification of the matter, as in Baptism, which has no fixed minister on whom it depends necessarily, and then the whole virtue of the sacrament is in the matter. Again, sometimes the essence of the sacrament requires the consecration or sanctification of the minister without any sanctification of the matter, and then the entire sacramental virtue is in the minister,

---

* St. Thomas here follows the opinion of Peter Lombard, and replies in the negative. Later in life he altered his opinion. (Cf. P. iii, Q. 62, A. 1; Q. 64, A. 1; Q. 86, A. 6).

as in Penance. Hence the power of the keys which is in the priest, stands in the same relation to the effect of Penance, as the virtue in the baptismal water does to the effect of Baptism. Now Baptism and the sacrament of Penance agree somewhat in their effect, since each is directly ordained against guilt, which is not the case in the other sacraments: yet they differ in this, that the sacrament of Penance, since the acts of the recipient are as its matter, cannot be given save to adults, who need to be disposed for the reception of the sacramental effect; whereas Baptism is given, sometimes to adults, sometimes to children and others who lack the use of reason, so that by Baptism children receive grace and remission of sin without any previous disposition, while adults do not, for they require to be disposed by the removal of insincerity. This disposition sometimes precedes their Baptism by priority of time, being sufficient for the reception of grace, before they are actually baptized, but not before they have come to the knowledge of the truth and have conceived the desire for Baptism. At other times this disposition does not precede the reception of Baptism by a priority of time, but is simultaneous with it, and then the grace of the remission of guilt is bestowed through the reception of Baptism. On the other hand, grace is never given through the sacrament of Penance unless the recipient be disposed either simultaneously or before. Hence the power of the keys operates unto the remision of guilt, either through being desired or through being actually exercised, even as the waters of Baptism. But just as Baptism acts, not as a principal agent but as an instrument, and does not go so far as to cause the reception itself of grace, even instrumentally,* but merely disposes the recipient to the grace whereby his guilt is remitted, so is it with the power of the keys. Wherefore God alone directly remits guilt, and Baptism acts through His power instrumentally, as an inanimate instrument, and the priest as an animate instrument, such as a servant is, according to the Philosopher (*Ethic.* viii. 11): and consequently the priest acts as a minister. Hence it is clear that the power of the keys is ordained, in a manner, to the remission of guilt, not as causing that remission, but as disposing thereto. Consequently if a man, before receiving absolution, were not perfectly disposed for the reception of grace, he would receive grace at the very time of sacramental confession and absolution, provided he offered no obstacle. For if the key were in no way ordained to the remission of guilt, but only to the remission of punishment, as some hold, it would not be necessary to have a desire of

* Cf. footnote on p. 2617

receiving the effect of the keys in order to have one's sins forgiven, just as it is not necessary to have a desire of receiving the other sacraments which are ordained, not to the remission of guilt, but against punishment. But this enables us to see that it is not ordained unto the remission of guilt, because the use of the keys, in order to be effective, always requires a disposition on the part of the recipient of the sacrament. And the same would apply to Baptism, were it never given save to adults.

Reply Obj. 1. As the Master says in the text (iv. *Sent.*, D. 18), the power of forgiving sins was entrusted to priests, not that they may forgive them, by their own power, for this belongs to God, but that, as ministers, they may declare* the operation of God Who forgives. Now this happens in three ways. First, by a declaration, not of present, but of future forgiveness, without co-operating therein in any way: and thus the sacraments of the Old Law signified the Divine operation, so that the priest of the Old Law did but declare and did not operate the forgiveness of sins. Secondly, by a declaration of present forgiveness without co-operating in it at all: and thus some say that the sacraments of the New Law signify the bestowal of grace, which God gives when the sacraments are conferred, without the sacraments containing any power productive of grace, according to which opinion, even the power of the keys would merely declare the Divine operation that has its effect in the remission of guilt when the sacrament is conferred. Thirdly, by signifying the Divine operation causing then and there the remission of guilt, and by co-operating towards this effect dispositively and instrumentally: and then, according to another and more common opinion, the sacraments of the New Law declare the cleansing effected by God. In this way also the priest of the New Testament declares the recipient to be absolved from guilt, because in speaking of the sacraments, what is ascribed to the power of the ministers must be consistent with the sacrament. Nor is it unreasonable that the keys of the Church should dispose the penitent to the remission of his guilt, from the fact that the guilt is already remitted, even as neither is it unreasonable that Baptism, considered in itself, causes a disposition in one who is already sanctified.

Reply Obj. 2. Neither the sacrament of Penance, nor the sacrament of Baptism, by its operation, causes grace, or the remission of guilt, directly, but only dispositively.* Hence the *Reply* to the *Third Objection* is evident.

The other arguments show that the power of the keys does not effect the remission of guilt directly, and this is to be granted.

**Whether a Priest Can Remit Sin
As to the Punishment?**

We proceed thus to the Third Article:—

Objection 1. It would seem that a priest cannot remit sin as to the punishment. For sin deserves eternal and temporal punishment. But after the priest's absolution the penitent is still obliged to undergo temporal punishment either in Purgatory or in this world. Therefore the priest does not remit the punishment in any way.

Obj. 2. Further, the priest cannot anticipate the judgment of God. But Divine justice appoints the punishment which penitents have to undergo. Therefore the priest cannot remit any part of it.

Obj. 3. Further, a man who has committed a slight sin, is not less susceptible to the power of the keys, than one who has committed a graver sin. Now if the punishment for the graver sin be lessened in any way through the priestly administrations, it would be possible for a sin to be so slight that the punishment which it deserves is no greater than that which has been remitted for the graver sin. Therefore the priest would be able to remit the entire punishment due for the slight sin: which is false.

Obj. 4. Further, the whole of the temporal punishment due for a sin is of one kind. If, therefore, by a first absolution something is taken away from the punishment, it will be possible for something more to be taken away by a second absolution, so that the absolution can be so often repeated, that by virtue of the keys the whole punishment will be taken away, since the second absolution is not less efficacious than the first: and consequently that sin will be altogether unpunished, which is absurd.

On the contrary, The key is the power of binding and loosing. But the priest can enjoin a temporal punishment. Therefore he can absolve from punishment.

Further, the priest cannot remit sin either as to the guilt,* as stated in the text (iv, *Sent.*, D. 18), or as to the eternal punishment, for a like reason. If therefore he cannot remit sin as to the temporal punishment, he would be unable to remit sin in any way, which is altogether contrary to the words of the Gospel.

I answer that, Whatever may be said of the effect of Baptism conferred on one who has already received grace, applies equally to the effect of the actual exercise of the power of the keys on one who has already been contrite. For a man may obtain the grace of the remission of his sins as to their guilt, through faith

* Cf. footnote on p. 2617

and contrition, previous to Baptism; but when, afterwards, he actually receives Baptism, his grace is increased, and he is entirely absolved from the debt of punishment, since he is then made a partaker of the Passion of Christ. In like manner when a man, through contrition, has received the pardon of his sins as to their guilt, and consequently as to the debt of eternal punishment, (which is remitted together with the guilt) by virtue of the keys which derive their efficacy from the Passion of Christ, his grace is increased and the temporal punishment is remitted, the debt of which remained after the guilt had been forgiven. However, this temporal punishment is not entirely remitted, as in Baptism, but only partly, because the man who is regenerated in Baptism is conformed to the Passion of Christ, by receiving into himself entirely the efficacy of Christ's Passion, which suffices for the blotting out of all punishment, so that nothing remains of the punishment due to his preceding actual sins. For nothing should be imputed to a man unto punishment, save what he has done himself, and in Baptism man begins a new life, and by the baptismal water becomes a new man, as that no debt for previous sin remains in him. On the other hand, in Penance, a man does not take on a new life, since therein he is not born again, but healed. Consequently by virtue of the keys which produce their effect in the sacrament of Penance, the punishment is not entirely remitted, but something is taken off the temporal punishment, the debt of which could remain after the eternal punishment had been remitted. Nor does this apply only to the temporal punishment which the penitent owes at the time of confession, as some hold, (for then confession and sacramental absolution would be mere burdens, which cannot be said of the sacraments of the New Law), but also to the punishment due in Purgatory, so that one who has been absolved and dies before making satisfaction, is less punished in Purgatory, than if he had died before receiving absolution.

Reply Obj. 1. The priest does not remit the entire temporal punishment, but part of it; wherefore the penitent still remains obliged to undergo satisfactory punishment.

Reply Obj. 2. Christ's Passion was sufficiently satisfactory for the sins of the whole world, so that without prejudice to Divine justice something can be remitted from the punishment which a sinner deserves, in so far as the effect of Christ's Passion reaches him through the sacraments of the Church.

Reply Obj. 3. Some satisfactory punishment must remain for each sin, so as to provide a remedy against it. Wherefore though, by virtue of the absolution some measure of the punishment due to a grave sin is remitted, it does not follow that the same measure of punishment is remitted for each sin, because in that case some sin would remain without any punishment at all: but, by virtue of the keys, the punishments due to various sins are remitted in due proportion.

Reply Obj. 4. Some say that at the first absolution, as much as possible is remitted by virtue of the keys, and that, nevertheless, the second confession is valid, on account of the instruction received, on account of the additional surety, on account of the prayers of the priest or confessor, and lastly on account of the merit of the shame.

But this does not seem to be true, for though there might be a reason for repeating the confession, there would be no reason for repeating the absolution, especially if the penitent has no cause to doubt about his previous absolution; for he might just as well doubt after the second as after the first absolution: even as we see that the sacrament of Extreme Unction is not repeated during the same sickness, for the reason that all that could be done through the sacrament, has been done once. Moreover, in the second confession, there would be no need for the confessor to have the keys, if the power of the keys had no effect therein.

For these reasons others say that even in the second absolution something of the punishment is remitted by virtue of the keys, because when absolution is given a second time, grace is increased, and the greater the grace received, the less there remains of the blemish of the previous sin, and the less punishment is required to remove that blemish. Wherefore even when a man is first absolved, his punishment is more or less remitted by virtue of the keys, according as he disposes himself more or less to receive grace; and this disposition may be so great, that even by virtue of his contrition the whole punishment is remitted, as we have already stated (Q. 5, A. 2). Consequently it is not unreasonable, if by frequent confession even the whole punishment be remitted, that a sin remain altogether unpunished, since Christ made satisfaction for its punishment.

THIRD ARTICLE

Whether the Priest Can Bind through the Power of the Keys?

We proceed thus to the Third Article:—

Objection 1. It would seem that the priest cannot bind by virtue of the power of the keys. For the sacramental power is ordained as a remedy against sin. Now binding is not a remedy for sin, but seemingly is rather con-

ducive to an aggravation of the disease. Therefore, by the power of the keys, which is a sacramental power, the priest cannot bind.

Obj. 2. Further, just as to loose or to open is to remove an obstacle, so to bind is to place an obstacle. Now an obstacle to heaven is sin, which cannot be placed on us by an extrinsic cause, since no sin is committed except by the will. Therefore the priest cannot bind.

Obj. 3. Further, the keys derive their efficacy from Christ's Passion. But binding is not an effect of the Passion. Therefore the priest cannot bind by the power of the keys.

On the contrary, It is written (Matth. xvi. 19): *Whatsoever thou shalt bind on earth, shall be bound also in heaven.*

Further, rational powers are directed to opposites. But the power of the keys is a rational power, since it has discretion connected with it. Therefore it is directed to opposites. Therefore if it can loose, it can bind.

I answer that, The operation of the priest in using the keys, is conformed to God's operation, Whose minister he is. Now God's operation extends both to guilt and to punishment; to the guilt indeed, so as to loose it directly, but to bind it indirectly, in so far as He is said to harden, when He withholds His grace; whereas His operation extends to punishment directly, in both respects, because He both spares and inflicts it. In like manner, therefore, although the priest, in absolving, exercises an operation ordained to the remission of guilt, in the way mentioned above (A. 1), nevertheless, in binding, he exercises no operation on the guilt; (unless he be said to bind by not absolving the penitent and by declaring him to be bound), but he has the power both of binding and of loosing with regard to the punishment. For he looses from the punishment which he remits, while he binds as to the punishment which remains. This he does in two ways,—first as regards the quantity of the punishment considered in general, and thus he does not bind save by not loosing, and declaring the penitent to be bound, secondly, as regards this or that particular punishment, and thus he binds to punishment by imposing it.

Reply Obj. 1. The remainder of the punishment to which the priest binds the penitent, is the medicine which cleanses the latter from the blemish of sin.

Reply Obj. 2. Not only sin, but also punishment is an obstacle to heaven: and how the latter is enjoined by the priest, has been said in the article.

Reply Obj. 3. Even the Passion of Christ binds us to some punishment whereby we are conformed to Him.

FOURTH ARTICLE

Whether the Priest Can Bind and Loose According to His Own Judgment?

We proceed thus to the Fourth Article:—

Objection 1. It seems that the priest can bind and loose according to his own judgment. For Jerome* says: *The canons do not fix the length of time for doing penance so precisely as to say how each sin is to be amended, but leave the decision of this matter to the judgment of a discreet priest.* Therefore it seems that he can bind and loose according to his own judgment.

Obj. 2. Further, *The Lord commended the unjust steward, forasmuch as he had done wisely* (Luke xvi. 5), because he had allowed a liberal discount to his master's debtors. But God is more inclined to mercy than any temporal lord. Therefore it seems that the more punishment the priest remits, the more he is to be commended.

Obj. 3. Further, Christ's every action is our instruction. Now on some sinners He imposed no punishment, but only amendment of life, as in the case of the adulterous woman (Jo. viii). Therefore it seems that the priest also, who is the vicar of Christ, can, according to his own judgment, remit the punishment, either wholly or in part.

On the contrary, Gregory VII† says: *We declare it a mock penance if it is not imposed according to the authority of the holy fathers in proportion to the sin.* Therefore it seems that it does not altogether depend on the priest's judgment.

Further, the act of the keys requires discretion. Now if the priest could remit and impose as much as he liked of a penance, he would have no need of discretion, because there would be no room for indiscretion. Therefore it does not altogether depend on the priest's judgment.

I answer that, In using the keys, the priest acts as the instrument and minister of God. Now no instrument can have an efficacious act, except in so far as it is moved by the principal agent. Wherefore, Dionysius says *(Hier. Eccl.,* cap. ult.) that *priests should use their hierarchical powers, according as they are moved by God.* A sign of this is that before the power of the keys was conferred on Peter (Matth. xvi. 19) mention is made of the revelation vouchsafed to him of the Godhead; and the gift of the Holy Ghost, whereby *the sons of God are led* (Rom. viii. 14), is mentioned before power was given to the apostles to forgive sins. Consequently if anyone were to presume to use his power against that Divine motion, he would not realize the effect, as Dionysius states *(ibid.),* and, besides, he would be turned away from the Divine order, and consequently would be guilty of a sin. Moreover, since satisfactory punishments are medicinal, just as the medicines prescribed by the medical art are not suitable to all, but have to be changed according to the judgment of a medical man, who follows not his own will, but his medical science, so the satisfactory punishments appointed by the canons are not suitable to all, but have to be varied according to the judgment of the priest guided by the Divine instinct. Therefore just as sometimes the physician prudently refrains from giving a medicine sufficiently efficacious to heal the disease, lest a greater danger should arise on account of the weakness of nature, so the priest, moved by Divine instinct, sometimes refrains from enjoining the entire punishment due to one sin, lest by the severity of the punishment, the sick man come to despair and turn away altogether from repentance.

Reply Obj. 1. This judgment should be guided entirely by the Divine instinct.

Reply Obj. 2. The steward is commended also for having done wisely. Therefore in the remission of the due punishment, there is need for discretion.

Reply Obj. 3. Christ had the power of *excellence* in the sacraments, so that, by His own authority, He could remit the punishment wholly or in part, just as He chose. Therefore there is no comparison between Him and those who act merely as ministers.

QUESTION 19

Of the Ministers of the Keys

(In Six Articles)

WE must now consider the ministers and the use of the keys: under which head there are six points of inquiry: (1) Whether the priest of the Law had the keys? (2) Whether Christ had the keys? (3) Whether priests alone have the keys? (4) Whether holy men who are not priests have the keys or their use? (5) Whether wicked priests have the effective use of the keys? (6) Whether those who are schismatics, heretics, excommunicate, suspended or degraded, have the use of the keys?

* Cf. Can. 86 *Mensuram, De Pœnit.,* Dist. i. † Cf. *Act. Concil. Rom.* v, Can. 5.

FIRST ARTICLE

Whether the Priest of the Law Had the Keys?

We proceed thus to the First Article:—

Objection 1. It would seem that the priests of the Law had the keys. For the possession of the keys results from having Orders. But they had Orders since they were called priests. Therefore the priests of the Law had the keys.

Obj. 2. Further, as the Master states (iv, *Sent.*, D. 18), there are two keys, knowledge of discretion, and power of judgment. But the priests of the Law had authority for both of these: therefore they had the keys.

Obj. 3. Further, the priests of the Law had some power over the rest of the people, which power was not temporal, else the kingly power would not have differed from the priestly power. Therefore it was a spiritual power; and this is the key. Therefore they had the key.

On the contrary, The keys are ordained to the opening of the heavenly kingdom, which could not be opened before Christ's Passion. Therefore the priest of the Law had not the keys.

Further, the sacraments of the Old Law did not confer grace. Now the gate of the heavenly kingdom could not be opened except by means of grace. Therefore it could not be opened by means of those sacraments, so that the priests who administered them, had not the keys of the heavenly kingdom.

I answer that, Some have held that, under the Old Law, the keys of the kingdom were in the hands of the priests, because the right of imposing punishment for sin was conferred on them, as related in Levit. v, which right seems to belong to the keys; but that these keys were incomplete then, whereas now they are complete as bestowed by Christ on the priests of the New Law.

But this seems to be contrary to the intent of the Apostle in the Epistle to the Hebrews (ix. 11-12). For there the priesthood of Christ is given the preference over the priesthood of the Law, inasmuch as Christ came, *a high priest of the good things to come,* and brought us *by His own blood* into a tabernacle not made with hand, whither the priesthood of the Old Law brought men *by the blood of goats and of oxen.* Hence it is clear that the power of that priesthood did not reach to heavenly things but to the shadow of heavenly things: and so, we must say with others that they had not the keys, but that the keys were fore-shadowed in them.

Reply Obj. 1. The keys of the kingdom go with the priesthood whereby man is brought into the heavenly kingdom, but such was not the priesthood of Levi; hence it had the keys, not of heaven, but of an earthly tabernacle.

Reply Obj. 2. The priests of the Old Law had authority to discern and judge, but not to admit those they judged into heaven, but only into the shadow of heavenly things.

Reply Obj. 3. They had no spiritual power, since, by the sacraments of the Law, they cleansed men not from their sins but from irregularities, so that those who were cleansed by them could enter into a tabernacle which was *made with hand.*

SECOND ARTICLE

Whether Christ Had the Key?

We proceed thus to the Second Article:—

Objection 1. It would seem that Christ did not have the key. For the key goes with the character of Order. But Christ did not have a character. Therefore He had not the key.

Obj. 2. Further, Christ had power of *excellence* in the sacraments, so that He could produce the sacramental effect without the sacramental rite. Now the key is something sacramental. Therefore He needed no key, and it would have been useless to Him to have it.

On the contrary, It is written (Apoc. iii. 7): *These things saith . . . He that hath the key of David,* etc.

I answer that, The power to do a thing is both in the instrument and in the principal agent, but not in the same way since it is more perfectly in the latter. Now the power of the keys which we have, like other sacramental powers, is instrumental: whereas it is in Christ as principal agent in the matter of our salvation, by authority, if we consider Him as God, by merit, if we consider Him as man.[*] But the very notion of a key expresses a power to open and shut, whether this be done by the principal agent or by an instrument. Consequently we must admit that Christ had the key, but in a higher way than His ministers, wherefore He is said to have the key of *excellence.*

Reply Obj. 1. A character implies the notion of something derived from another, hence the power of the keys which we receive from Christ results from the character whereby we are conformed to Christ, whereas in Christ it results not from a character, but from the principal form.

Reply Obj. 2. The key, which Christ had was not sacramental, but the origin of the sacramental key.

[*] For St. Thomas's later teaching on this point, cf. P. III, Q. 48, A. 6; I-II, Q. 112, A. 1, *ad* 1.

THIRD ARTICLE

Whether Priests Alone Have the Keys?

We proceed thus to the Third Article:—

Objection 1. It would seem that not only priests have the keys. For Isidore says *(Etym.* vii. 12) that the *doorkeepers have to tell the good from the bad, so as to admit the good and keep out the bad.* Now this is the definition of the keys, as appears from what has been said (Q. 17, A. 2). Therefore not only priests but even doorkeepers have the keys.

Obj. 2. Further, the keys are conferred on priests when by being anointed they receive power from God. But kings of Christian peoples also receive power from God and are consecrated by being anointed. Therefore not only priests have the keys.

Obj. 3. Further, the priesthood is an Order belonging to an individual person. But sometimes a number of people together seem to have the key, because certain Chapters can pass a sentence of excommunication, which pertains to the power of the keys. Therefore not only priests have the key.

Obj. 4. Further, a woman is not capable of receiving the priesthood, since she is not competent to teach, according to the Apostle (1 Cor. xiv. 34). But some women (abbesses, for instance, who exercise a spiritual power over their subjects), seem to have the keys. Therefore not only priests have the keys.

On the contrary, Ambrose says *(De Pœnit.* i): *This right,* viz. of binding and loosing, *is granted to priests alone.*

Further, by receiving the power of the keys, a man is set up between the people and God. But this belongs to the priest alone, who *is ordained . . . in the things that appertain to God, that he may offer up gifts and sacrifices for sins* (Heb. v. 1). Therefore only priests have the keys.

I answer that, There are two kinds of key. One reaches to heaven itself directly, by remitting sin and thus removing the obstacles to the entrance into heaven; and this is called the key of *Order.* Priests alone have this key, because they alone are ordained for the people in the things which appertain to God directly. The other key reaches to heaven, not directly but through the medium of the Church Militant. By this key a man goes to heaven, since, by its means, a man is shut out from or admitted to the fellowship of the Church Militant, by excommunication or absolution. This is called the key of *jurisdiction* in the external court, wherefore even those who are not priests can have this key, e.g. archdeacons, bishops elect, and others who can excommunicate. But it is not properly called a key of heaven, but a disposition thereto.

Reply Obj. 1. The doorkeepers have the key for taking care of those things which are contained in a material temple, and they have to judge whether a person should be excluded from or admitted to that temple; which judgment they pronounce, not by their own authority, but in pursuance to the priest's judgment, so that they appear to be the administrators of the priestly power.

Reply Obj. 2. Kings have no power in spiritual matters, so that they do not receive the key of the heavenly kingdom. Their power is confined to temporal matters, and this too can only come to them from God, as appears from Rom. xiii. 1. Nor are they consecrated by the unction of a sacred Order: their anointing is merely a sign that the excellence of their power comes down to them from Christ, and that, under Christ, they reign over the Christian people.

Reply Obj. 3. Just as in civil matters the whole power is sometimes vested in a judge, as in a kingdom, whereas sometimes it is vested in many exercising various offices but acting together with equal rights *(Ethic.* viii. 10, 11), so too, spiritual jurisdiction may be exercised both by one alone, e.g. a bishop, and by many together, e.g. by a Chapter, and thus they have the key of jurisdiction, but they have not all together the key of Order.

Reply Obj. 4. According to the Apostle (1 Tim. ii. 11, Tit. ii. 5), woman is in a state of subjection: wherefore she can have no spiritual jurisdiction, since the Philosopher also says *(Ethic.* viii) that it is a corruption of public life when the government comes into the hands of a woman. Consequently a woman has neither the key of Order nor the key of jurisdiction. Nevertheless a certain use of the keys is allowed to women, such as the right to correct other women who are under them, on account of the danger that might threaten if men were to dwell under the same roof.

FOURTH ARTICLE

Whether Holy Men Who Are Not Priests Have the Keys?

We proceed thus to the Fourth Article:—

Objection 1. It would seem that holy men, even those who are not priests, have the use of the keys. For loosing and binding, which are the effects of the keys, derive their efficacy from the merit of Christ's Passion. Now those are most conformed to Christ's Passion, who follow Christ, suffering by patience and other virtues. Therefore it seems that even if they have not the priestly Order, they can bind and loose.

Obj. 2. Further, it is written (Heb. vii. 7):

Without all contradiction, that which is less is blessed by the greater (Vulg.,—*better*). Now *in spiritual matters*, according to Augustine (*De Trin.* vi. 8), *to be better is to be greater.* Therefore those who are better, i.e. who have more charity, can bless others by absolving them. Hence the same conclusion follows.

On the contrary, Action belongs to that which has the power, as the Philosopher says (*De Somno et Vigil.* i). But the key which is a spiritual power belongs to priests alone. Therefore priests alone are competent to have the use of the keys.

I answer that, There is this difference between a principal and an instrumental agent, that the latter does not produce, in the effect, its own likeness, but the likeness of the principal agent, whereas the principal agent produces its own likeness. Consequently a thing becomes a principal agent through having a form, which it can reproduce in another, whereas an instrumental agent is not constituted thus, but through being applied by the principal agent in order to produce a certain effect. Since therefore in the act of the keys the principal agent by authority is Christ as God, and by merit is Christ as man,* it follows that on account of the very fulness of Divine goodness in Him, and of the perfection of His grace, He is competent to exercise the act of the keys. But another man is not competent to exercise this act as principal agent, since neither can he give another man grace whereby sins are remitted, nor can he merit sufficiently; so that he is nothing more than an instrumental agent. Consequently the recipient of the effect of the keys, is likened, not to the one who uses the keys, but to Christ. Therefore, no matter how much grace a man may have, he cannot produce the effect of the keys, unless he be appointed to that purpose by receiving Orders.

Reply Obj. 1. Just as between instrument and effect there is need or likeness, not of a similar form, but of aptitude in the instrument for the effect, so is it as regards the instrument and the principal agent. The former is the likeness between holy men and the suffering Christ, nor does it bestow on them the use of the keys.

Reply Obj. 2. Although a mere man cannot merit grace for another man condignly, yet the merit of one man can co-operate in the salvation of another. Hence there is a twofold blessing. One proceeds from a mere man, as meriting by his own act: this blessing can be conferred by any holy person, in whom Christ dwells by His grace, in so far as he excels in goodness the person whom he blesses. The other blessing is when a man blesses, as apply-

* See footnote, p. 2622

ing a blessing instrumentally through the merit of Christ, and this requires excellence of Order and not of virtue.

Whether Wicked Priests Have the Use of the Keys?

We proceed thus to the Fifth Article:—

Objection 1. It would seem that wicked priests have not the use of the keys. For in the passage where the use of the keys is bestowed on the apostles (Jo. xx. 22, 23), the gift of the Holy Ghost is promised. But wicked men have not the Holy Ghost. Therefore they have not the use of the keys.

Obj. 2. Further, no wise king entrusts his enemy with the dispensation of his treasure. Now the use of the keys consists in dispensing the treasure of the King of heaven, Who is Wisdom itself. Therefore the wicked, who are His enemies on account of sin, have not the use of the keys.

Obj. 3. Further, Augustine says (*De Bapt.* v. 21) that *God gives the sacrament of grace even through wicked men, but grace itself only by Himself or through His saints. Hence He forgives sin by Himself, or by those who are members of the Dove.* But the remission of sins is the use of the keys. Therefore sinners, who are not *members of the Dove,* have not the use of the keys.

Obj. 4. Further, the prayer of a wicked priest cannot effect reconciliation, for, as Gregory says (*Pastor.* i. 11), *if an unacceptable person is sent to intercede, anger is provoked to yet greater severity.* But the use of the keys implies a kind of intercession, as appears in the form of absolution. Therefore wicked priests cannot use the keys effectively.

On the contrary, No man can know whether another man is in the state of grace. If, therefore, no one could use the keys in giving absolution unless he were in a state of grace, no one would know that he had been absolved, which would be very unfitting.

Further, the wickedness of the minister cannot void the liberality of his lord. But the priest is no more than a minister. Therefore he cannot by his wickedness take away from us the gift which God has given through him.

I answer that, Just as participation of a form to be induced into an effect does not make a thing to be an instrument, so neither does the loss of that form prevent that thing being used as an instrument. Consequently, since man is merely an instrument in the use of the keys, however much he may through sin be deprived of grace, whereby sins are forgiven, yet he is by no means deprived of the use of the keys.

Reply Obj. 1. The gift of the Holy Ghost is requisite for the use of the keys, not as being indispensable for the purpose, but because it is unbecoming for the user to use them without it, though he that submits to them receives their effect.

Reply Obj. 2. An earthly king can be cheated and deceived in the matter of his treasure, and so he does not entrust his enemy with the dispensation thereof. But the King of heaven cannot be cheated, because all tends to His own glory, even the abuse of the keys by some, for He can make good come out of evil, and produce many good effects through evil men. Hence the comparison fails.

Reply Obj. 3. Augustine speaks of the remission of sins, in so far as holy men cooperate therein, not by virtue of the keys, but by merit of congruity. Hence He says that God confers the sacraments even through evil men, and among the other sacraments, absolution which is the use of the keys should be reckoned: but that through *members of the Dove*, i.e. holy men, He grants forgiveness of sins, in so far as He remits sins on account of their intercession.

We might also reply that by *members of the Dove* he means all who are not cut off from the Church, for those who receive the sacraments from them, receive grace, whereas those who receive the sacraments from those who are cut off from the Church, do not receive grace, because they sin in so doing, except in the case of Baptism, which, in cases of necessity, may be received even from one who is excommunicate.

Reply Obj. 4. The prayer which the wicked priest proffers on his own account, is not efficacious: but that which he makes as a minister of the Church, is efficacious through the merit of Christ. Yet in both ways the priest's prayer should profit those who are subject to him.

SIXTH ARTICLE

Whether Those Who Are Schismatics, Heretics, Excommunicate, Suspended or Degraded Have the Use of the Keys?

We proceed thus to the Sixth Article:—

Objection 1. It would seem that those who are schismatics, heretics, excommunicate, suspended or degraded have the use of the keys. For just as the power of the keys results from Orders, so does the power of consecration. But the above cannot lose the use of the power of consecration, since if they do consecrate it is valid, though they sin in doing so. Therefore neither can they lose the use of the keys.

Obj. 2. Further, any active spiritual power in one who has the use of his free-will can be exercised by him when he wills. Now the power of the keys remains in the aforesaid, for, since it is only conferred with Orders, they would have to be reordained when they return to the Church. Therefore, since it is an active power, they can exercise it when they will.

Obj. 3. Further, spiritual grace is hindered by guilt more than by punishment. Now excommunication, suspension and degradation are punishments. Therefore, since a man does not lose the use of the keys on account of guilt, it seems that he does not lose it on account of the aforesaid.

On the contrary, Augustine says (*Tract.* cxxi, *in Joan.*) that the *charity of the Church forgives sins.* Now it is the charity of the Church which unites its members. Since therefore the above are disunited from the Church, it seems that they have not the use of the keys in remitting sins.

Further, no man is absolved from sin by sinning. Now it is a sin for anyone to seek absolution of his sins from the above, for he disobeys the Church in so doing. Therefore he cannot be absolved by them: and so the same conclusion follows.

I answer that, In all the above the power of the keys remains as to its essence, but its use is hindered on account of the lack of matter. For since the use of the keys requires in the user authority over the person on whom they are used, as stated above (Q. 17, A. 2, *ad* 2), the proper matter on whom one can exercise the use of the keys is a man under one's authority. And since it is by appointment of the Church that one man has authority over another, so a man may be deprived of his authority over another by his ecclesiastical superiors. Consequently, since the Church deprives heretics, schismatics and the like, by withdrawing their subjects from them either altogether or in some respect, in so far as they are thus deprived, they cannot have the use of the keys.

Reply Obj. 1. The matter of the sacrament of the Eucharist, on which the priest exercises his power, is not a man but wheaten bread, and in Baptism, the matter is simply a man. Wherefore, just as, were a heretic to be without wheaten bread, he could not consecrate, so neither can a prelate absolve if he be deprived of his authority, yet he can baptize and consecrate, albeit to his own damnation.

Reply Obj. 2. The assertion is true, provided matter be not lacking as it is in the case in point.

Reply Obj. 3. Sin, of itself, does not remove matter, as certain punishments do: so that punishment is a hindrance not because it is contrary to the effect, but for the reason stated.

QUESTION 20

Of Those on Whom the Power of the Keys Can Be Exercised

(In Three Articles)

WE must now consider those on whom the power of the keys can be exercised. Under this head there are three points of inquiry: (1) Whether a priest can use the key, which he has, on any man? (2) Whether a priest can always absolve his subject? (3) Whether anyone can use the keys on his superior?

FIRST ARTICLE

Whether a Priest Can Use the Key Which He Has, on Any Man?

We proceed thus to the First Article:—

Objection 1. It would seem that a priest can use the key which he has, on any man. For the power of the keys was bestowed on priests by Divine authority in the words: *Receive ye the Holy Ghost; whose sins you shall forgive, they are forgiven them* (Jo. xx. 22, 23). But this was said without any restriction. Therefore he that has the key, can use it on any without restriction.

Obj. 2. Further, a material key that opens one lock, opens all locks of the same pattern. Now every sin of every man is the same kind of obstacle against entering into heaven. Therefore if a priest can, by means of the key which he has, absolve one man, he can do the same for all others.

Obj. 3. Further, the priesthood of the New Testament is more perfect than that of the Old Testament. But the priest of the Old Testament could use the power which he had of discerning between different kinds of leprosy, with regard to all indiscriminately. Much more therefore can the priest of the Gospel use his power with regard to all.

On the contrary, It is written in the Appendix of Gratian: *It is not lawful for every priest to loose or bind another priest's parishioner.* Therefore a priest cannot absolve everybody.

Further, judgment in spiritual matters should be better regulated than in temporal matters. But in temporal matters a judge cannot judge everybody. Therefore, since the use of the keys is a kind of judgment, it is not within the competency of a priest to use his key with regard to everyone.

I answer that, That which has to do with singular matters is not equally in the power of all. Thus, even as besides the general principles of medicine, it is necessary to have physicians, who adapt those general principles to individual patients or diseases, according to their various requirements, so in every kingdom, besides that one who proclaims the universal precepts of law, there is need for others to adapt those precepts to individual cases, according as each case demands. For this reason, in the heavenly hierarchy also, under the Powers who rule indiscriminately, a place is given to the Principalities, who are appointed to individual kingdoms, and to the Angels who are given charge over individual men, as we have explained above (P. I., Q. 113, AA. 1, 2). Consequently there should be a like order of authority in the Church Militant, so that an indiscriminate authority over all should be vested in one individual, and that there should be others under him, having distinct authority over various people. Now the use of the keys implies a certain power to exercise authority, whereby the one on whom the keys are used, becomes the proper matter of that act. Therefore he that has power over all indiscriminately, can use the keys on all, whereas those who have received authority over distinct persons, cannot use the keys on everyone, but only on those over whom they are appointed, except in cases of necessity, when the sacraments should be refused to no one.

Reply Obj. 1. A twofold power is required in order to absolve from sins, namely, power of order and power of jurisdiction. The former power is equally in all priests, but not the latter. And therefore, when our Lord (John xx. 23) gave all the apostles in general, the power of forgiving sins, this is to be understood of the power which results from receiving Orders, wherefore these words are addressed to priests when they are ordained. But to Peter in particular He gave the power of forgiving sins (Matth. xvi. 19), that we may understand that he has the power of jurisdiction before the others. But the power of Orders, considered in itself, extends to all who can be absolved: wherefore our Lord said indeterminately, *Whose sins you shall forgive, they are forgiven them,* on the understanding that this power should be used in dependence on the power given to Peter, according to His appointment.

Reply Obj. 2. A material key can open only its own lock, nor can any active force act save on its own matter. Now a man becomes the matter of the power of Order by jurisdiction: and consequently no one can use the key in respect of another over whom he has not jurisdiction.

Reply Obj. 3. The people of Israel were one

people, and had but one temple, so that there was no need for a distinction in priestly jurisdiction, as there is now in the Church which comprises various peoples and nations.

SECOND ARTICLE

Whether a Priest Can Always Absolve His Subject?

We proceed thus to the Second Article:—

Objection 1. It would seem that a priest cannot always absolve his subject. For, as Augustine says *(De vera et falsa Pœnit.),** *no man should exercise the priestly office, unless he be free from those things which he condemns in others.* But a priest might happen to share in a sin committed by his subject, e.g. by knowledge of a woman who is his subject. Therefore it seems that he cannot always use the power of the keys on his subjects.

Obj. 2. Further, by the power of the keys a man is healed of all his shortcomings. Now it happens sometimes that a sin has attached to it a defect of irregularity or a sentence of excommunication, from which a simple priest cannot absolve. Therefore it seems that he cannot use the power of the keys on such as are shackled by these things in the above manner.

Obj. 3. Further, the judgment and power of our priesthood was foreshadowed by the judgment of the ancient priesthood. Now according to the Law, the lesser judges were not competent to decide all cases, and had recourse to the higher judges, according to Exod. xxiv. 14: *If any question shall arise among you, you shall refer it to them.* It seems, therefore, that a priest cannot absolve his subject from graver sins, but should refer him to his superior.

On the contrary, Whoever has charge of the principal has charge of the accessory. Now priests are charged with the dispensation of the Eucharist to their subjects, to which sacrament the absolution of sins is subordinate.† Therefore, as far as the power of the keys is concerned, a priest can absolve his subject from any sins whatever.

Further, grace, however small, removes all sin. But a priest dispenses sacraments whereby grace is given. Therefore, as far as the power of the keys is concerned, he can absolve from all sins.

I answer that, The power of Order, considered in itself, extends to the remission of all sins. But since, as stated above, the use of this power requires jurisdiction which inferiors derive from their superiors, it follows that the superior can reserve certain matters to himself, the judgment of which he does not commit to

his inferior; otherwise any simple priest who has jurisdiction can absolve from any sin. Now there are five cases in which a simple priest must refer his penitent to his superior. The first is when a public penance has to be imposed, because in that case the bishop is the proper minister of the sacrament. The second is the case of those who are excommunicated, when the inferior priest cannot absolve a penitent through the latter being excommunicated by his superior. The third case is when he finds that an irregularity has been contracted, for the dispensation of which he has to have recourse to his superior. The fourth is the case of arson. The fifth is when it is the custom in a diocese for the more heinous crimes to be reserved to the bishop, in order to inspire fear, because custom in these cases either gives the power or takes it away.

Reply Obj. 1. In this case the priest should not hear the confession of his accomplice, with regard to that particular sin, but must refer her to another: nor should she confess to him, but should ask permission to go to another, or should have recourse to his superior if he refused, both on account of the danger, and for the sake of less shame. If, however, he were to absolve her it would be valid:‡ because when Augustine says that they should not be guilty of the same sin, he is speaking of what is congruous, not of what is essential to the sacrament.

Reply Obj. 2. Penance delivers man from all defects of guilt, but not from all defects of punishment, since even after doing penance for murder, a man remains irregular. Hence a priest can absolve from a crime, but for the remission of the punishment he must refer the penitent to the superior, except in the case of excommunication, absolution from which should precede absolution from sin, for as long as a man is excommunicated, he cannot receive any sacrament of the Church.

Reply Obj. 3. This objection considers those cases in which superiors reserve the power of jurisdiction to themselves.

THIRD ARTICLE

Whether a Man Can Use the Keys with Regard to His Superior?

We proceed thus to the Third Article:—

Objection 1. It would seem that a man cannot use the keys in respect of a superior. For every sacramental act requires its proper matter. Now the proper matter for the use of the keys, is a person who is subject, as stated above (Q. 19, A. 6). Therefore a priest cannot use the keys in respect of one who is not his subject.

---

* Work of an unknown author.

† Cf. Q. 17, A. 2, *ad* 1.

‡ Benedict XIV declared the absolution of an accomplice *in materia turpi* to be invalid.

Obj. 2. Further, the Church Militant is an image of the Church Triumphant. Now in the heavenly Church an inferior angel never cleanses, enlightens or perfects a higher angel. Therefore neither can an inferior priest exercise on a superior a hierarchical action such as absolution.

Obj. 3. Further, the judgment of Penance should be better regulated than the judgment of an external court. Now in the external court an inferior cannot excommunicate or absolve his superior. Therefore, seemingly, neither can he do so in the penitential court.

On the contrary, The higher prelate is also *compassed with infirmity,* and may happen to sin. Now the power of the keys is the remedy for sin. Therefore, since he cannot use the key on himself, for he cannot be both judge and accused at the same time, it seems that an inferior can use the power of the keys on him.

Further, absolution which is given through the power of the keys, is ordained to the reception of the Eucharist. But an inferior can give Communion to his superior, if the latter asks him to. Therefore he can use the power of the keys on him if he submit to him.

I answer that, The power of the keys, considered in itself, is applicable to all, as stated above (A. 2): and that a priest is unable to use the keys on some particular person is due to his power being limited to certain individuals. Therefore he who limited his power can extend it to whom he wills, so that he can give him power over himself, although he cannot use the power of the keys on himself, because this power requires to be exercised on a subject, and therefore on someone else, for no man can be subject to himself.

Reply Obj. 1. Although the bishop whom a simple priest absolves is his superior absolutely speaking, yet he is beneath him in so far as he submits himself as a sinner to him.

Reply Obj. 2. In the angels there can be no defect by reason of which the higher angel can submit to the lower, such as there can happen to be among men; and so there is no comparison.

Reply Obj. 3. External judgment is according to men, whereas the judgment of confession is according to God, in Whose sight a man is lessened by sinning, which is not the case in human prelacy. Therefore just as in external judgment no man can pass sentence of excommunication on himself, so neither can he empower another to excommunicate him. On the other hand, in the tribunal of conscience he can give another the power to absolve him, though he cannot use that power himself.

It may also be replied that absolution in the tribunal of the confessional belongs principally to the power of the keys and consequently to the power of jurisdiction, whereas excommunication regards jurisdiction exclusively. And, as to the power of Orders, all are equal, but not as to jurisdiction. Wherefore there is no comparison.

QUESTION 21

Of the Definition, Congruity and Cause of Excommunication

(In Four Articles)

WE must now treat of excommunication: we shall consider: (1) the definition, congruity and cause of excommunication; (2) who has the power to excommunicate; (3) communication with excommunicated persons; (4) absolution from excommunication.

Under the first head there are four points of inquiry: (1) Whether excommunication is suitably defined? (2) Whether the Church should excommunicate anyone? (3) Whether anyone should be excommunicated for inflicting temporal harm? (4) Whether an excommunication unjustly pronounced has any effect?

FIRST ARTICLE

Whether Excommunication Is Suitably Defined As Separation from the Communion of the Church, etc.?

We proceed thus to the First Article:—

Objection 1. It would seem that excommunication is unsuitably defined by some thus: *Excommunication is separation from the communion of the Church, as to fruit and general suffrages.* For the suffrages of the Church avail for those for whom they are offered. But the Church prays for those who are outside the Church, as, for instance, for heretics and pagans. Therefore she prays also for the excommunicated, since they are outside the Church, and so the suffrages of the Church avail for them.

Obj. 2. Further, no one loses the suffrages of the Church except by his own fault. Now excommunication is not a fault, but a punishment. Therefore excommunication does not deprive a man of the general suffrages of the Church.

Obj. 3. Further, the fruit of the Church seems to be the same as the Church's suffrages, for it cannot mean the fruit of temporal goods, since excommunication does not deprive a man of these. Therefore there is no reason for mentioning both.

Obj. 4. Further, there is a kind of excommunication called minor,* by which man is not deprived of the suffrages of the Church. Therefore this definition is unsuitable.

I answer that, When a man enters the Church by Baptism, he is admitted to two things, viz. the body of the faithful and the participation of the sacraments; and this latter presupposes the former, since the faithful are united together in the participation of the sacraments. Consequently a person may be expelled from the Church in two ways. First, by being deprived merely of the participation of the sacraments, and this is the minor excommunication. Secondly, by being deprived of both, and this is the major excommunication, of which the above is the definition. Nor can there be a third, consisting in the privation of communion with the faithful, but not of the participation of the sacraments, for the reason already given, because, to wit, the faithful communicate together in the sacraments. Now communion with the faithful is twofold. One consists in spiritual things, such as their praying for one another, and meeting together for the reception of sacred things; while another consists in certain legitimate bodily actions. These different manners of communion are signified in the verse which declares that those who are excommunicate are deprived of,—

os, orare, vale, communio, mensa.

Os, i.e. we must not give them tokens of goodwill; *orare,* i.e. we must not pray with them; *vale,* we must not give them marks of respect; *communio,* i.e. we must not communicate with them in the sacraments; *mensa,* i.e. we must not take meals with them. Accordingly the above definition includes privation of the sacraments in the words *as to the fruit,* and from partaking together with the faithful in spiritual things, in the words, *and the general prayers of the Church.*

Another definition is given which expresses the privation of both kinds of acts, and is as follows: *Excommunication is the privation of all lawful communion with the faithful.*

Reply Obj. 1. Prayers are said for unbelievers, but they do not receive the fruit of those prayers unless they be converted to the faith. In like manner prayers may be offered up for those who are excommunicated, but not among the prayers that are said for the members of the Church. Yet they do not receive the fruit so long as they remain under the excommunication, but prayers are said for them that they may receive the spirit of re-

pentance, so that they may be loosed from excommunication.

Reply Obj. 2. One man's prayers profit another in so far as they can reach to him. Now the action of one man may reach to another in two ways. First, by virtue of charity which unites all the faithful, making them one in God, according to Ps. cxviii. 63: *I am a partaker with all them that fear Thee.* Now excommunication does not interrupt this union, since no man can be justly excommunicated except for a mortal sin, whereby a man is already separated from charity, even without being excommunicated. An unjust excommunication cannot deprive a man of charity, since this is one of the greatest of all goods, of which a man cannot be deprived against his will. Secondly, through the intention of the one who prays, which intention is directed to the person he prays for, and this union is interrupted by excommunication, because by passing sentence of excommunication, the Church severs a man from the whole body of the faithful, for whom she prays. Hence those prayers of the Church which are offered up for the whole Church, do not profit those who are excommunicated. Nor can prayers be said for them among the members of the Church, as speaking in the Church's name, although a private individual may say a prayer with the intention of offering it for their conversion.

Reply Obj. 3. The spiritual fruit of the Church is derived not only from her prayers, but also from the sacraments received and from the faithful dwelling together.

Reply Obj. 4. The minor excommunication does not fulfill all the conditions of excommunication but only a part of them, hence the definition of excommunication need not apply to it in every respect, but only in some.

SECOND ARTICLE

Whether the Church Should Excommunicate Anyone?

We proceed thus to the Second Article:—

Objection 1. It would seem that the Church ought not to excommunicate anyone, because excommunication is a kind of curse, and we are forbidden to curse (Rom. xii. 14). Therefore the Church should not excommunicate.

Obj. 2. Further, the Church Militant should imitate the Church Triumphant. Now we read in the epistle of Jude *(verse 9)* that *when Michael the Archangel disputing with the devil contended about the body of Moses, he durst not bring against him the judgment of railing speech, but said: The Lord command thee* Therefore the Church Militant ought not to judge any man by cursing or excommunicating him.

---

* Minor excommunication is no longer recognized by Canon Law.

Obj. 3. Further, no man should be given into the hands of his enemies, unless there be no hope for him. Now by excommunication a man is given into the hands of Satan, as is clear from 1 Cor. v. 5. Since then we should never give up hope about anyone in this life, the Church should not excommunicate anyone.

On the contrary, The Apostle (1 Cor. v. 5) ordered a man to be excommunicated.

Further, it is written (Matth. xviii. 17) about the man who refuses to hear the Church: *Let him be to thee as the heathen or publican.* But heathens are outside the Church. Therefore they also who refuse to hear the Church, should be banished from the Church by excommunication.

I answer that, The judgment of the Church should be conformed to the judgment of God. Now God punishes the sinner in many ways, in order to draw him to good, either by chastising him with stripes, or by leaving him to himself, so that being deprived of those helps whereby he was kept out of evil, he may acknowledge his weakness, and humbly return to God Whom he had abandoned in his pride. In both these respects the Church by passing sentence of excommunication imitates the judgment of God. For by severing a man from the communion of the faithful that he may blush with shame, she imitates the judgment whereby God chastises man with stripes; and by depriving him of prayers and other spiritual things, she imitates the judgment of God in leaving man to himself, in order that by humility he may learn to know himself and return to God.

Reply Obj. 1. A curse may be pronounced in two ways: first, so that the intention of the one who curses is fixed on the evil which he invokes or pronounces, and cursing in this sense is altogether forbidden. Secondly, so that the evil which a man invokes in cursing is intended for the good of the one who is cursed, and thus cursing is sometimes lawful and salutary: thus a physician makes a sick man undergo pain, by cutting him, for instance, in order to deliver him from his sickness.

Reply Obj. 2. The devil cannot be brought to repentance, wherefore the pain of excommunication cannot do him any good.

Reply Obj. 3. From the very fact that a man is deprived of the prayers of the Church, he incurs a triple loss, corresponding to the three things which a man acquires through the Church's prayers. For they bring an increase of grace to those who have it, or merit grace for those who have it not; and in this respect the Master of the Sentences says (iv, *Sent.,* D. 18): *The grace of God is taken away by excommunication.* They also prove a safe-

guard of virtue; and in this respect he says that *protection is taken away,* not that the excommunicated person is withdrawn altogether from God's providence, but that he is excluded from that protection with which He watches over the children of the Church in a more special way. Moreover, they are useful as a defense against the enemy, and in this respect he says that *the devil receives greater power of assaulting the excommunicated person, both spiritually and corporally.* Hence in the early Church, when men had to be enticed to the faith by means of outward signs (thus the gift of the Holy Ghost was shown openly by a visible sign), so too excommunication was evidenced by a person being troubled in his body by the devil. Nor is it unreasonable that one, for whom there is still hope, be given over to the enemy, for he is surrendered, not unto damnation, but unto correction, since the Church has the power to rescue him from the hands of the enemy, whenever he is willing.

THIRD ARTICLE

Whether Anyone Should Be Excommunicated for Inflicting Temporal Harm?

We proceed thus to the Third Article:—

Objection 1. It would seem that no man should be excommunicated for inflicting a temporal harm. For the punishment should not exceed the fault. But the punishment of excommunication is the privation of a spiritual good, which surpasses all temporal goods. Therefore no man should be excommunicated for temporal injuries.

Obj. 2. Further, we should render to no man evil for evil, according to the precept of the Apostle (Rom. xii. 17). But this would be rendering evil for evil, if a man were to be excommunicated for doing such an injury. Therefore this ought by no means to be done.

On the contrary, Peter sentenced Ananias and Saphira to death for keeping back the price of their piece of land (Acts v. 1-10). Therefore it is lawful for the Church to excommunicate for temporal injuries.

I answer that, By excommunication the ecclesiastical judge excludes a man, in a sense, from the kingdom. Wherefore, since he ought not to exclude from the kingdom others than the unworthy, as was made clear from the definition of the keys (Q. 17, A. 2), and since no one becomes unworthy, unless, through committing a mortal sin, he lose charity which is the way leading to the kingdom, it follows that no man should be excommunicated except for a mortal sin. And since by injuring a man in his body or in his temporalities, one may sin mortally and act against charity, the Church can excommunicate a man for having inflicted temporal injury on anyone. Yet, as excommunication is the most severe punishment, and since punishments are intended as remedies, according to the Philosopher (*Ethic.* ii), and again since a prudent physician begins with lighter and less risky remedies, therefore excommunication should not be inflicted, even for a mortal sin, unless the sinner be obstinate, either by not coming up for judgment, or by going away before judgment is pronounced, or by failing to obey the decision of the court. For then, if, after due warning, he refuse to obey, he is reckoned to be obstinate, and the judge, not being able to proceed otherwise against him, must excommunicate him.

Reply Obj. 1. A fault is not measured by the extent of the damage a man does, but by the will with which he does it, acting against charity. Wherefore, though the punishment of excommunication exceeds the harm done, it does not exceed the measure of the sin.

Reply Obj. 2. When a man is corrected by being punished, evil is not rendered to him, but good: since punishments are remedies, as stated above.

FOURTH ARTICLE

Whether an Excommunication Unjustly Pronounced Has Any Effect?

We proceed thus to the Fourth Article:—

Objection 1. It would seem that an excommunication which is pronounced unjustly has no effect at all. Because excommunication deprives a man of the protection and grace of God, which cannot be forfeited unjustly. Therefore excommunication has no effect if it be unjustly pronounced.

Obj. 2. Further, Jerome says (on Matth. xvi. 19, *I will give to thee the keys*): *It is a pharisaical severity to reckon as really bound or loosed, that which is bound or loosed unjustly.* But that severity was proud and erroneous. Therefore an unjust excommunication has no effect.

On the contrary, According to Gregory (*Hom.* xxvi, *in Evang.*), *the sentence of the pastor is to be feared whether it be just or unjust.* Now there would be no reason to fear an unjust excommunication if it did not hurt. Therefore, etc.

I answer that, An excommunication may be unjust for two reasons. First, on the part of its author, as when anyone excommunicates through hatred or anger, and then, nevertheless, the excommunication takes effect, though its author sins, because the one who is excommunicated suffers justly, even if the author act wrongly in excommunicating him. Secondly, on the part of the excommunication, through there being no proper cause, or through the sentence being passed without the forms of law being observed. In this case, if the error, on the part of the sentence, be such as to render the sentence void, this has no effect, for there is no excommunication; but if the error does not annul the sentence, this takes effect, and the person excommunicated should humbly submit (which will be credited to him as a merit), and either seek absolution from the person who has excommunicated him, or appeal to a higher judge. If, however, he were to contemn the sentence, he would *ipso facto* sin mortally.

But sometimes it happens that there is sufficient cause on the part of the excommunicator, but not on the part of the excommunicated, as when a man is excommunicated for a crime which he has not committed, but which has been proved against him: in this case, if he submit humbly, the merit of his humility will compensate him for the harm of excommunication.

Reply Obj. 1. Although a man cannot lose God's grace unjustly, yet he can unjustly lose those things which on our part dispose us to receive grace; for instance, a man may be deprived of the instruction which he ought to have. It is in this sense that excommunication is said to deprive a man of God's grace, as was explained above (A. 2, *ad* 3).

Reply Obj. 2. Jerome is speaking of sin, not of its punishments, which can be inflicted unjustly by ecclesiastical superiors.

QUESTION 22

Of Those Who Can Excommunicate or Be Excommunicated

(In Six Articles)

WE must now consider those who can excommunicate or be excommunicated. Under this head there are six points of inquiry: (1) Whether every priest can excommunicate? (2) Whether one who is not a priest can excommunicate? (3) Whether one who is excommunicated or suspended, can excommunicate? (4) Whether anyone can excommunicate himself, or an equal, or a superior? (5) Whether a multitude can be excommunicated? (6) Whether one who is already excommunicated can be excommunicated again?

FIRST ARTICLE

Whether Every Priest Can Excommunicate?

We proceed thus to the First Article:—

Objection 1. It would seem that every priest can excommunicate. For excommunication is an act of the keys. But every priest has the keys. Therefore every priest can excommunicate.

Obj. 2. Further, it is a greater thing to loose and bind in the tribunal of penance than in the tribunal of judgment. But every priest can loose and bind his subjects in the tribunal of Penance. Therefore every priest can excommunicate his subjects.

On the contrary, Matters fraught with danger should be left to the decision of superiors. Now the punishment of excommunication is fraught with many dangers, unless it be inflicted with moderation. Therefore it should not be entrusted to every priest.

I answer that, In the tribunal of conscience the plea is between man and God, whereas in the outward tribunal it is between man and man. Wherefore the loosing or binding of one man in relation to God alone, belongs to the tribunal of Penance, whereas the binding or loosing of a man in relation to other men, belongs to the public tribunal of external judgment. And since excommunication severs a man from the communion of the faithful, it belongs to the external tribunal. Consequently those alone can excommunicate who have jurisdiction in the judicial tribunal. Hence, of their own authority, only bishops and higher prelates, according to the more common opinion, can excommunicate, whereas parish priests can do so only by commission or in certain cases, as those of theft, rapine and the like, in which the law allows them to excommunicate. Others, however, have maintained that even parish priests can excommunicate: but the former opinion is more reasonable.

Reply Obj. 1. Excommunication is an act of the keys, not directly, but with respect to the external judgment. The sentence of excommunication, however, though it is promulgated by an external verdict, still, as it belongs somewhat to the entrance to the kingdom, in so far as the Church Militant is the way to the Church Triumphant, this jurisdiction whereby a man is competent to excommunicate, can be called a key. It is in this sense that some distinguish between the key of Orders, which all priests have, and the key of jurisdiction in the tribunal of judgment, which none have but the judges of the external tribunal. Nevertheless God bestowed both on Peter (Matth. xvi. 19), from whom they are

* Cf. A. 1, *ad* 2, Q. 24, A. 1, *ad* 1.

derived by others, whichever of them they have.

Reply Obj. 2. Parish priests have jurisdiction indeed over their subjects, in the tribunal of conscience, but not in the judicial tribunal, for they cannot summons them in contentious cases. Hence they cannot excommunicate, but they can absolve them in the tribunal of Penance. And though the tribunal of Penance is higher, yet more solemnity is requisite in the judicial tribunal, because therein it is necessary to make satisfaction not only to God but also to man.

SECOND ARTICLE

Whether Those Who Are Not Priests Can Excommunicate?

We proceed thus to the Second Article:—

Objection 1. It would seem that those who are not priests cannot excommunicate. Because excommunication is an act of the keys, as stated in iv, *Sent.*, D. 18. But those who are not priests have not the keys. Therefore they cannot excommunicate.

Obj. 2. Further, more is required for excommunication than for absolution in the tribunal of Penance. But one who is not a priest cannot absolve in the tribunal of Penance. Neither therefore can he excommunicate.

On the contrary, Archdeacons, legates and bishops-elect excommunicate, and yet sometimes they are not priests. Therefore not only priests can excommunicate.

I answer that, Priests alone are competent to dispense the sacraments wherein grace is given: wherefore they alone can loose and bind in the tribunal of Penance. On the other hand, excommunication regards grace, not directly but consequently, in so far as it deprives a man of the Church's prayers, by which he is disposed for grace or preserved therein. Consequently even those who are not priests, provided they have jurisdiction in a contentious court, can excommunicate.

Reply Obj. 1. Though they have not the key of Orders, they have the key of jurisdiction.

Reply Obj. 2. These two are related to one another as something exceeding and something exceeded,* and consequently one of them may be within the competency of someone while the other is not.

THIRD ARTICLE

Whether a Man Who Is Excommunicated or Suspended Can Excommunicate Another?

We proceed thus to the Third Article:—

Objection 1. It would seem that one who is excommunicated or suspended can excommunicate another. For such a one has lost neither Orders nor jurisdiction, since neither is he ordained anew when he is absolved, nor is his jurisdiction renewed. But excommunication requires nothing more than Orders or jurisdiction. Therefore even one who is excommunicated or suspended can excommunicate.

Obj. 2. Further, it is a greater thing to consecrate the body of Christ than to excommunicate. But such persons can consecrate. Therefore they can excommunicate.

On the contrary, One whose body is bound cannot bind another. But spiritual gyves are stronger than bodily fetters. Therefore one who is excommunicated cannot excommunicate another, since excommunication is a spiritual chain.

I answer that, Jurisdiction can only be used in relation to another man. Consequently, since every excommunicated person is severed from the communion of the faithful, he is deprived of the use of jurisdiction. And as excommunication requires jurisdiction, an excommunicated person cannot excommunicate, and the same reason applies to one who is suspended from jurisdiction. For if he be suspended from Orders only, then he cannot exercise his Order, but he can use his jurisdiction, while, on the other hand, if he be suspended from jurisdiction and not from Orders, he cannot use his jurisdiction, though he can exercise his Order: and if he be suspended from both, he can exercise neither.

Reply Obj. 1. Although an excommunicated or suspended person does not lose his jurisdiction, yet he does lose its use.

Reply Obj. 2. The power of consecration results from the power of the character which is indelible, wherefore, from the very fact that a man has the character of Order, he can always consecrate, though not always lawfully. It is different with the power of excommunication which results from jurisdiction, for this can be taken away and bound.

FOURTH ARTICLE

Whether a Man Can Excommunicate Himself, His Equal, or His Superior?

We proceed thus to the Fourth Article:—

Objection 1. It would seem that a man can excommunicate himself, his equal, or his superior. For an angel of God was greater than Paul, according to Matth. xi. 11: *He that is lesser in the kingdom of heaven is greater than he,* a greater than whom *hath not risen among men that are born of women.* Now Paul excommunicated an angel from heaven (Gal. i. 8). Therefore a man can excommunicate his superior.

Obj. 2. Further, sometimes a priest pronounces a general excommunication for theft or the like. But it might happen that he, or his equal, or a superior has done such things. Therefore a man can excommunicate himself, his equal, or a superior.

Obj. 3. Further, a man can absolve his superior or his equal in the tribunal of Penance, as when a bishop confesses to his subject, or one priest confesses venial sins to another. Therefore it seems that a man may also excommunicate his superior, or his equal.

On the contrary, Excommunication is an act of jurisdiction. But no man has jurisdiction over himself (since one cannot be both judge and defendant in the same trial), or over his superior, or over an equal. Therefore a man cannot excommunicate his superior, or his equal, or himself.

I answer that, Since, by jurisdiction, a man is placed above those over whom he has jurisdiction, through being their judge, it follows that no man has jurisdiction over himself, his superior, or his equal, and that, consequently, no one can excommunicate either himself, or his superior, or his equal.

Reply Obj. 1. The Apostle is speaking hypothetically, i.e. supposing an angel were to sin, for in that case he would not be higher than the Apostle, but lower. Nor is it absurd that, if the antecedent of a conditional sentence be impossible, the consequence be impossible also.

Reply Obj. 2. In that case no one would be excommunicated, since no man has power over his peer.

Reply Obj. 3. Loosing and binding in the tribunal of confession affects our relation to God only, in Whose sight a man from being above another sinks below him through sin; while on the other hand excommunication is the affair of an external tribunal in which a man does not forfeit his superiority on account of sin. Hence there is no comparison between the two tribunals. Nevertheless, even in the tribunal of confession, a man cannot absolve himself, or his superior, or his equal, unless the power to do so be committed to him. This does not apply to venial sins, because they can be remitted through any sacraments which confer grace, hence remission of venial sins follows the power of Orders.

FIFTH ARTICLE

Whether Sentence of Excommunication Can Be Passed on a Body of Men?

We proceed thus to the Fifth Article:—

Objection 1. It would seem that sentence

of excommunication can be passed on a body of men. Because it is possible for a number of people to be united together in wickedness. Now when a man is obstinate in his wickedness he should be excommunicated. Therefore a body of men can be excommunicated.

Obj. 2. Further, the most grievous effect of an excommunication is privation of the sacraments of the Church. But sometimes a whole country is laid under an interdict. Therefore a body of people can be excommunicated.

On the contrary, A gloss of Augustine* on Matth. xii. asserts that the sovereign and a body of people cannot be excommunicated.

I answer that, No man should be excommunicated except for a mortal sin. Now sin consists in an act: and acts do not belong to communities, but, generally speaking, to individuals. Wherefore individual members of a community can be excommunicated, but not the community itself. And although sometimes an act belongs to a whole multitude, as when many draw a boat, which none of them could draw by himself, yet it is not probable that a community would so wholly consent to evil that there would be no dissentients. Now God, Who judges all the earth, does not condemn the just with the wicked (Gen. xviii. 25). Therefore the Church, who should imitate the judgments of God, prudently decided that a community should not be excommunicated, lest the wheat be uprooted together with the tares and cockle.

The *Reply* to the *First Objection* is evident from what has been said.

Reply Obj. 2. Suspension is not so great a punishment as excommunication, since those who are suspended are not deprived of the prayers of the Church, as the excommunicated are. Wherefore a man can be suspended without having committed a sin himself, just as a whole kingdom is laid under an interdict on account of the king's crime. Hence there is no comparison between excommunication and suspension.

SIXTH ARTICLE

Whether a Man Can Be Excommunicated Who Is Already under Sentence of Excommunication?

We proceed thus to the Sixth Article:—

Objection 1. It would seem that a man who is already under sentence of excommunication cannot be excommunicated any further. For the Apostle says (1 Cor. v. 12): *What have I to do to judge them that are without?* Now those who are excommunicated are already outside the Church. Therefore the Church cannot exercise any further judgment on them, so as to excommunicate them again.

Obj. 2. Further, excommunication is privation of divine things and of the communion of the faithful. But when a man has been deprived of a thing, he cannot be deprived of it again. Therefore one who is excommunicated cannot be excommunicated again.

On the contrary, Excommunication is a punishment and a healing medicine. Now punishments and medicines are repeated when necessary. Therefore excommunication can be repeated.

I answer that, A man who is under sentence of one excommunication, can be excommunicated again, either by a repetition of the same excommunication, for his greater confusion, so that he may renounce sin, or for some other cause. And then there are as many principal excommunications, as there are causes for his being excommunicated.

Reply Obj. 1. The Apostle is speaking of heathens and of other unbelievers who have no (sacramental) character, whereby they are numbered among the people of God. But since the baptismal character whereby a man is numbered among God's people, is indelible, one who is baptized always belongs to the Church in some way, so that the Church is always competent to sit in judgment on him.

Reply Obj. 2. Although privation does not receive more or less in itself, yet it can, as regards its cause. In this way an excommunication can be repeated, and a man who has been excommunicated several times is further from the Church's prayers than one who has been excommunicated only once.

QUESTION 23

Of Communication with Excommunicated Persons

(In Three Articles)

WE must now consider communication with those who are excommunicated. Under this head there are three points of inquiry: (1) Whether it is lawful to communicate in matters purely corporal with one who is ex-

communicated? (2) Whether one who communicates with an excommunicated person is excommunicated? (3) Whether it is always a mortal sin to communicate with an excommunicated person in matters not permitted by law?

* Cf. *Ep.* ccl.

FIRST ARTICLE

Whether It Is Lawful, in Matters Purely Corporal, to Communicate with an Excommunicated Person?

We proceed thus to the First Article:—

Objection 1. It would seem that it is lawful, in matters purely corporal, to communicate with an excommunicated person. For excommunication is an act of the keys. But the power of the keys extends only to spiritual matters. Therefore excommunication does not prevent one from communicating with another in matters corporal.

Obj. 2. Further, *What is instituted for the sake of charity, does not militate against charity.* (Cf. Q. 11, A. 1, *Obj.* 1). But we are bound by the precept of charity to succor our enemies, which is impossible without some sort of communication. Therefore it is lawful to communicate with an excommunicated person in corporal matters.

On the contrary, It is written (1 Cor. v. 11): *With such an one not so much as to eat.*

I answer that, Excommunication is twofold: there is minor excommunication, which deprives a man merely of a share in the sacraments, but not of the communion of the faithful. Wherefore it is lawful to communicate with a person lying under an excommunication of this kind, but not to give him the sacraments. The other is major excommunication, which deprives a man of the sacraments of the Church and of the communion of the faithful. Wherefore it is not lawful to communicate with one who lies under such an excommunication. But, since the Church resorts to excommunication to repair and not to destroy, exception is made from this general law, in certain matters wherein communication is lawful, viz. in those which concern salvation, for one is allowed to speak of such matters with an excommunicated person; and one may even speak of other matters so as to put him at his ease and to make the words of salvation more acceptable. Moreover exception is made in favor of certain people whose business it is to be in attendance on the excommunicated person, viz. his wife, child, slave, vassal or subordinate. This, however, is to be understood of children who have not attained their majority, else they are forbidden to communicate with their father: and as to the others, the exception applies to them if they have entered his service before his excommunication, but not if they did so afterwards.

Some understand this exception to apply in the opposite way, viz. that the master can communicate with his subjects: while others hold the contrary. At any rate it is lawful for them to communicate with others in matters wherein they are under an obligation to them, for just as subjects are bound to serve their master, so is the master bound to look after his subjects. Again certain cases are excepted; as when the fact of the excommunication is unknown, or in the case of strangers or travelers in the country of those who are excommunicated, for they are allowed to buy from them, or to receive alms from them. Likewise if anyone were to see an excommunicated person in distress; for then he would be bound by the precept of charity to assist him. These are all contained in the following line:

Utility, law, lowliness, ignorance of fact, necessity,

where *utility* refers to salutary words, *law* to marriage, *lowliness* to subjection. The others need no explanation.

Reply Obj. 1. Corporal matters are subordinate to spiritual matters. Wherefore the power which extends to spiritual things, can also extend to matters touching the body: even as the art which considers the end commands in matters ordained to the end.

Reply Obj. 2. In a case where one is bound by the precept of charity to hold communication, the prohibition ceases, as is clear from what has been said.

SECOND ARTICLE

Whether a Person Incurs Excommunication for Communicating with One Who Is Excommunicated?

We proceed thus to the Second Article:—

Objection 1. It would seem that a person does not incur excommunication for communicating with one who is excommunicated. For a heathen or a Jew is more separated from the Church than a person who is excommunicated. But one does not incur excommunication for communicating with a heathen or a Jew. Neither, therefore, does one for communicating with an excommunicated Christian.

Obj. 2. Further, if a man incurs excommunication for communicating with an excommunicated person, for the same reason a third would incur excommunication for communicating with him, and thus one might go on indefinitely, which would seem absurd. Therefore one does not incur excommunication for communicating with one who is excommunicated.

On the contrary, An excommunicated person is banished from communion. Therefore whoever communicates with him leaves the communion of the Church: and hence he seems to be excommunicated.

I answer that, A person may incur excommunication in two ways. First, so that the excommunication includes both himself and whosoever communicates with him: and then, without any doubt, whoever communicates with him, incurs a major excommunication. Secondly, so that the excommunication is simply pronounced on him; and then a man may communicate with him either in his crime, by counsel, help or favor, in which case again he incurs the major excommunication, or he may communicate with him in other things by speaking to him, greeting him, or eating with him, in which case he incurs the minor excommunication.

Reply Obj. 1. The Church has no intention of correcting unbelievers as well as the faithful who are under her care: hence she does not sever those, whom she excommunicates, from the fellowship of unbelievers, as she does from the communion of the faithful over whom she exercises a certain power.

Reply Obj. 2. It is lawful to hold communion with one who has incurred a minor excommunication, so that excommunication does not pass on to a third person.

THIRD ARTICLE

Whether It Is Always a Mortal Sin to Communicate with an Excommunicated Person in Other Cases Than Those in Which It Is Allowed?

We proceed thus to the Third Article:—

Objection 1. It would seem that it is always a mortal sin to hold communion with an excommunicated person in other cases than those in which it is allowed. Because a certain decretal (Cap. *Sacris: De his quæ vi, metuve,* etc.) declares that *not even through fear of death should anyone hold communion with an excommunicated person, since one ought to die rather than commit a mortal sin.* But this would be no reason unless it were always a mortal sin to hold communion with an excommunicated person. Therefore, etc.

Obj. 2. Further, it is a mortal sin to act against a commandment of the Church. But the Church forbids anyone to hold communion with an excommunicated person. Therefore it is a mortal sin to hold communion with one who is excommunicated.

Obj. 3. Further, no man is debarred from receiving the Eucharist on account of a venial sin. But a man who holds communion with an excommunicated person, outside those cases in which it is allowed, is debarred from receiving the Eucharist, since he incurs a minor excommunication. Therefore it is a mortal sin to hold communion with an excommunicated person, save in those cases in which it is allowed.

Obj. 4. Further, no one should incur a major excommunication save for a mortal sin. Now according to the law (Can. *Præcipue, seqq.,* caus. xi) a man may incur a major excommunication for holding communion with an excommunicated person. Therefore it is a mortal sin to hold communion with one who is excommunicated.

On the contrary, None can absolve a man from mortal sin unless he have jurisdiction over him. But any priest can absolve a man for holding communion with those who are excommunicated. Therefore it is not a mortal sin.

Further, the measure of the penalty should be according to the measure of the sin, as stated in Deut. xxv. 3. Now the punishment appointed by common custom for holding communion with an excommunicated person is not that which is inflicted for mortal sin, but rather that which is due for venial sin. Therefore it is not a mortal sin.

I answer that, Some hold that it is always a mortal sin to hold communion with an excommunicated person, by word or in any of the forbidden ways mentioned above (A. 2), except in those cases allowed by law (Cap. *Quoniam*). But since it seems very hard that a man should be guilty of a mortal sin by uttering just a slight word to an excommunicated person, and that by excommunicating a person one would endanger the salvation of many, and lay a snare which might turn to one's own hurt, it seems to others more probable that he is not always guilty of a mortal sin, but only when he holds communion with him in a criminal deed, or in an act of Divine worship, or through contempt of the Church.

Reply Obj. 1. This decretal is speaking of holding communion in Divine worship. It may also be replied that the same reason applies both to mortal and venial sin, since just as one cannot do well by committing a mortal sin, so neither can one by committing a venial sin: so that just as it is a man's duty to suffer death rather than commit a mortal sin, so is it his duty to do so sooner than commit a venial sin, inasmuch as it is his duty to avoid venial sin.

Reply Obj. 2. The commandment of the Church regards spiritual matters directly, and legitimate actions as a consequence: hence by holding communion in Divine worship one acts against the commandment, and commits a mortal sin; but by holding communion in other matters, one acts beside the commandment, and sins venially.

Reply Obj. 3. Sometimes a man is debarred from the Eucharist even without his own fault, as in the case of those who are suspended or under an interdict, because these penalties are sometimes inflicted on one person for the sin of another who is thus punished.

Reply Obj. 4. Although it is a venial sin to hold communion with one who is excommunicated, yet to do so obstinately is a mortal sin : and for this reason one may be excommunicated according to the law.

QUESTION 24

Of Absolution from Excommunication

(In Three Articles)

WE must now consider absolution from excommunication: under which head there are three points of inquiry: (1) Whether any priest can absolve his subject from excommunication? (2) Whether a man can be absolved from excommunication against his will? (3) Whether a man can be absolved from one excommunication without being absolved from another?

FIRST ARTICLE

Whether Any Priest Can Absolve His Subject from Excommunication?

We proceed thus to the First Article:—

Objection 1. It would seem that any priest can absolve his subject from excommunication. For the chains of sin are stronger than those of excommunication. But any priest can absolve his subject from sin. Therefore much more can he absolve him from excommunication.

Obj. 2. Further, if the cause is removed the effect is removed. But the cause of excommunication is a mortal sin. Therefore since any priest can absolve (his subject) from that mortal sin, he is able likewise to absolve him from the excommunication.

On the contrary, It belongs to the same power to excommunicate as to absolve from excommunication. But priests of inferior degree cannot excommunicate their subjects. Neither, therefore, can they absolve them.

I answer that, Anyone can absolve from minor excommunication who can absolve from the sin of participation in the sin of another. But in the case of a major excommunication, this is pronounced either by a judge, and then he who pronounced sentence or his superior can absolve,—or it is pronounced by law, and then the bishop or even a priest can absolve except in the six cases which the Pope, who is the maker of laws, reserves to himself:—the first is the case of a man who lays hands on a cleric or a religious; the second is of one who breaks into a church and is denounced for so doing; the third is of the man who sets fire to a church and is denounced for the deed; the fourth is of one who knowingly communicates in the Divine worship with those whom the Pope has excommunicated by name; the fifth is the case of one who tampers with the letters of the Holy See; the sixth is the case of one who communicates in a crime of one who is excommunicated. For he should not be absolved except by the person who excommunicated him, even though he be not subject to him, unless, by reason of the difficulty of appearing before him, he be absolved by the bishop or by his own priest, after binding himself by oath to submit to the command of the judge who pronounced the excommunication on him.

There are however eight exceptions to the first case: (1) In the hour of death, when a person can be absolved by any priest from any excommunication; (2) if the striker be the doorkeeper of a man in authority, and the blow be given neither through hatred nor of set purpose; (3) if the striker be a woman; (4) if the striker be a servant, whose master is not at fault and would suffer from his absence; (5) if a religious strike a religious, unless he strike him very grievously; (6) if the striker be a poor man; (7) if he be a minor, an old man, or an invalid; (8) if there be a deadly feud between them.

There are, besides, seven cases in which the person who strikes a cleric does not incur excommunication: (1) if he do it for the sake of discipline, as a teacher or a superior; (2) if it be done for fun; (3) if the striker find the cleric behaving with impropriety towards his wife, his mother, his sister or his daughter; (4) if he return blow for blow at once; (5) if the striker be not aware that he is striking a cleric; (6) if the latter be guilty of apostasy after the triple admonition; (7) if the cleric exercise an act which is altogether contrary to the clerical life, e.g. if he become a soldier, or if he be guilty of bigamy.*

Reply Obj. 1. Although the chains of sin are in themselves greater than those of excommunication, yet in a certain respect the chains of excommunication are greater, inasmuch as they bind a man not only in the sight of God, but also in the eye of the Church. Hence ab-

---

* Namely, that which is known by canonists as *similar bigamy.*

solution from excommunication requires jurisdiction in the external forum, whereas absolution from sin does not. Nor is there need of giving one's word by oath, as in the case of absolution from excommunication, because, as the Apostle declares (Heb. vi. 16), controversies between men are decided by oath.

Reply Obj. 2. As an excommunicated person has no share in the sacraments of the Church, a priest cannot absolve him from his guilt, unless he be first absolved from excommunication.

SECOND ARTICLE

Whether Anyone Can Be Absolved against His Will?

We proceed thus to the Second Article:—

Objection 1. It would seem that no man can be absolved against his will. For spiritual things are not conferred on anyone against his will. Now absolution from excommunication is a spiritual favor. Therefore it cannot be granted to a man against his will.

Obj. 2. Further, the cause of excommunication is contumacy. But when, through contempt of the excommunication, a man is unwilling to be absolved, he shows a high degree of contumacy. Therefore he cannot be absolved.

On the contrary, Excommunication can be pronounced on a man against his will. Now things that happen to a man against his will, can be removed from him against his will, as in the case of the goods of fortune. Therefore excommunication can be removed from a man against his will.

I answer that, Evil of fault and evil of punishment differ in this, that the origin of fault is within us, since all sin is voluntary, whereas the origin of punishment is sometimes without, since punishment does not need to be voluntary, in fact the nature of punishment is rather to be against the will. Wherefore, just as a man commits no sin except willingly, so no sin is forgiven him against his will. On the other hand just as a person can be excommunicated against his will, so can he be absolved therefrom.

Reply Obj. 1. The assertion is true of those spiritual goods which depend on our will, such as the virtues, which we cannot lose unwillingly; for knowledge, although a spiritual good, can be lost by a man against his will through sickness. Hence the argument is not to the point.

Reply Obj. 2. It is possible for excommunication to be removed from a man even though he be contumacious, if it seem to be for the good of the man for whom the excommunication was intended as a medicine.

THIRD ARTICLE

Whether a Man Can Be Absolved from One Excommunication without Being Absolved from All?

We proceed thus to the Third Article:—

Objection 1. It would seem that a man cannot be absolved from one excommunication without being absolved from all. For an effect should be proportionate to its cause. Now the cause of excommunication is a sin. Since then a man cannot be absolved from one sin without being absolved from all, neither can this happen as regards excommunication.

Obj. 2. Further, absolution from excommunication is pronounced in the Church. But a man who is under the ban of one excommunication is outside the Church. Therefore so long as one remains, a man cannot be loosed from another.

On the contrary, Excommunication is a punishment. Now a man can be loosed from one punishment, while another remains. Therefore a man can be loosed from one excommunication and yet remain under another.

I answer that, Excommunications are not connected together in any way, and so it is possible for a man to be absolved from one, and yet remain under another.

It must be observed however that sometimes a man lies under several excommunications pronounced by one judge; and then, when he is absolved from one, he is understood to be absolved from all, unless the contrary be expressed, or unless he ask to be absolved from excommunication on one count only, whereas he was excommunicated under several. On the other hand sometimes a man lies under several sentences of excommunication pronounced by several judges; and then, when absolved from one excommunication, he is not therefore absolved from the others, unless at his prayer they all confirm his absolution, or unless they all depute one to absolve him.

Reply Obj. 1. All sins are connected together in aversion from God, which is incompatible with the forgiveness of sin: wherefore one sin cannot be forgiven without another. But excommunications have no such connection. Nor again is absolution from excommunication hindered by contrariety of the will, as stated above (A. 2). Hence the argument does not prove.

Reply Obj. 2. Just as such a man was for several reasons outside the Church so is it possible for his separation to be removed on one count and to remain on another.

QUESTION 25

Of Indulgences

(In Three Articles)

WE must now consider indulgence: (1) in itself; (2) those who grant indulgence; (3) those who receive it.

Under the first head there are three points of inquiry: (1) Whether an indulgence remits any part of the punishment due for the satisfaction of sins? (2) Whether indulgences are as effective as they claim to be? (3) Whether an indulgence should be granted for temporal assistance?

FIRST ARTICLE

Whether an Indulgence Can Remit Any Part of the Punishment Due for the Satisfaction of Sins?

We proceed thus to the First Article:—

Objection 1. It would seem that an indulgence cannot remit any part of the punishment due for the satisfaction of sins. Because a gloss on 2 Tim. ii. 13, *He cannot deny Himself,* says: *He would do this if He did not keep His word.* Now He said (Deut. xxv. 2): *According to the measure of the sin shall the measure also of the stripes be.* Therefore nothing can be remitted from the satisfactory punishment which is appointed according to the measure of sin.

Obj. 2. Further, an inferior cannot absolve from an obligation imposed by his superior. But when God absolves us from sin He binds us to temporal punishment, as Hugh of S. Victor declares *(Tract.* vi, *Sum. Sent.).** Therefore no man can absolve from that punishment, by remitting any part of it.

Obj. 3. Further, the granting of the sacramental effect without the sacraments belongs to the power of excellence. Now none but Christ has the power of excellence in the sacraments. Since then satisfaction is a part of the sacrament of Penance, conducing to the remission of the punishment due, it seems that no mere man can remit the debt of punishment without satisfaction.

Obj. 4. Further, the power of the ministers of the Church was given them, not *unto destruction,* but *unto edification* (2 Cor. x. 8). But it would be conducive to destruction, if satisfaction, which was intended for our good, inasmuch as it serves for a remedy, were done away with. Therefore the power of the ministers of the Church does not extend to this.

On the contrary, It is written (2 Cor. ii. 10): *For, what I have pardoned, if I have pardoned anything, for your sakes have I done*

* Of doubtful authenticity.

it in the person of Christ, and a gloss adds: i.e. *as though Christ Himself had pardoned.* But Christ could remit the punishment of a sin without any satisfaction, as evidenced in the case of the adulterous woman (Jo. viii). Therefore Paul could do so likewise. Therefore the Pope can too, since his power in the Church is not less than Paul's.

Further, the universal Church cannot err, since He Who *was heard for His reverence* (Heb. v. 7) said to Peter, on whose profession of faith the Church was founded (Luke xxii. 32): *I have prayed for thee that thy faith fail not.* Now the universal Church approves and grants indulgences. Therefore indulgences have some value.

I answer that, All admit that indulgences have some value; for it would be blasphemy to say that the Church does anything in vain. But some say that they do not avail to free a man from the debt of punishment which he has deserved in Purgatory according to God's judgment, and that they merely serve to free him from the obligation imposed on him by the priest as a punishment for his sins, or from the canonical penalties he has incurred. But this opinion does not seem to be true. First, because it is expressly opposed to the privilege granted to Peter, to whom it was said (Matth. xvi. 19) that whatsoever he should loose on earth should be loosed also in heaven. Wherefore whatever remission is granted in the court of the Church holds good in the court of God. Moreover the Church by granting such indulgences would do more harm than good, since, by remitting the punishment she had enjoined on a man, she would deliver him to be punished more severely in Purgatory.

Hence we must say on the contrary that indulgences hold good both in the Church's court and in the judgment of God, for the remission of the punishment which remains after contrition, absolution, and confession, whether this punishment be enjoined or not. The reason why they so avail is the oneness of the mystical body in which many have performed works of satisfaction exceeding the requirements of their debts; in which, too, many have patiently borne unjust tribulations whereby a multitude of punishments would have been paid, had they been incurred. So great is the quantity of such merits that it exceeds the entire debt of punishment due to those who are living at this moment: and this is especially due to the merits of Christ: for though He acts through the sacraments, yet His efficacy is nowise restricted to them, but infinitely surpasses their efficacy.

Now one man can satisfy for another, as we have explained above (Q. 13, A. 2). And the saints in whom this super-abundance of satisfactions is found, did not perform their good works for this or that particular person, who needs the remission of his punishment (else he would have received this remission without any indulgence at all), but they performed them for the whole Church in general, even as the Apostle declares that he fills up *those things that are wanting of the sufferings of Christ . . . for His body, which is the Church* to whom he wrote (Col. i. 24). These merits, then, are the common property of the whole Church. Now those things which are the common property of a number are distributed to the various individuals according to the judgment of him who rules them all. Hence, just as one man would obtain the remission of his punishment if another were to satisfy for him, so would he too if another's satisfactions be applied to him by one who has the power to do so.

Reply Obj. 1. The remission which is granted by means of indulgences does not destroy the proportion between punishment and sin, since someone has spontaneously taken upon himself the punishment due for another's guilt, as explained above.

Reply Obj. 2. He who gains an indulgence is not, strictly speaking, absolved from the debt of punishment, but is given the means whereby he may pay it.

Reply Obj. 3. The effect of sacramental absolution is the removal of a man's guilt, an effect which is not produced by indulgences. But he who grants indulgences pays the debt of punishment which a man owes, out of the common stock of the Church's goods, as explained above.

Reply Obj. 4. Grace affords a better remedy for the avoidance of sin than does habituation to (good) works. And since he who gains an indulgence is disposed to grace through the love which he conceives for the cause for which the indulgence is granted, it follows that indulgences provide a remedy against sin. Consequently it is not harmful to grant indulgences unless this be done without discretion. Nevertheless those who gain indulgences should be advised, not, on this account, to omit the penitential works imposed on them, so that they may derive a remedy from these also, even though they may be quit of the debt of punishment; and all the more, seeing that they are often more in debt than they think.

SECOND ARTICLE

Whether Indulgences Are As Effective As They Claim to Be?

We proceed thus to the Second Article:—

Objection 1. It would seem that indulgences are not as effective as they claim to be. For indulgences have no effect save from the power of the keys. Now by the power of the keys, he who has that power can only remit some fixed part of the punishment due for sin, after taking into account the measure of the sin and of the penitent's sorrow. Since then indulgences depend on the mere will of the grantor, it seems that they are not as effective as they claim to be.

Obj. 2. Further, the debt of punishment keeps man back from the attainment of glory, which he ought to desire above all things. Now, if indulgences are as effective as they claim to be, a man by setting himself to gain indulgences might become immune from all debt of temporal punishment. Therefore it would seem that a man ought to put aside all other kinds of works, and devote himself to gain indulgences.

Obj. 3. Further, sometimes an indulgence whereby a man is remitted a third part of the punishment due for his sins is granted if he contribute towards the erection of a certain building. If, therefore, indulgences produce the effect which is claimed for them, he who gives a penny, and then another, and then again another, would obtain a plenary absolution from all punishment due for his sins, which seems absurd.

Obj. 4. Further, sometimes an indulgence is granted, so that for visiting a church a man obtains a seven years' remission. If, then, an indulgence avails as much as is claimed for it, a man who lives near that church, or the clergy attached thereto who go there every day, obtain as much indulgence as one who comes from a distance (which would appear unjust); moreover, seemingly, they would gain the indulgence several times a day, since they go there repeatedly.

Obj. 5. Further, to remit a man's punishment beyond a just estimate, seems to amount to the same as to remit it without reason; because in so far as he exceeds that estimate, he limits the compensation. Now he who grants an indulgence cannot without cause remit a man's punishment either wholly or partly, even though the Pope were to say to anyone: *I remit to all the punishment you owe for your sins.* Therefore it seems that he cannot remit anything beyond the just estimate. Now indulgences are often published which exceed that just estimate. Therefore they do not avail as much as is claimed for them.

On the contrary, It is written (Job xiii. 7): *Hath God any need of your lie, that you should speak deceitfully for Him?* Therefore the Church, in publishing indulgences, does not lie; and so they avail as much as is claimed for them.

Further, the Apostle says (1 Cor. xv. 14): *If . . . our preaching is vain, your faith is also vain.* Therefore whoever utters a falsehood in preaching, so far as he is concerned, makes faith void; and so sins mortally. If therefore indulgences are not as effective as they claim to be, all who publish indulgences would commit a mortal sin: which is absurd.

I answer that, On this point there are many opinions. For some maintain that indulgences have not the efficacy claimed for them, but that they simply avail each individual in proportion to his faith and devotion. And consequently those who maintain this, say that the Church publishes her indulgences in such a way as, by a kind of pious fraud, to induce men to do well, just as a mother entices her child to walk by holding out an apple. But this seems a very dangerous assertion to make. For as Augustine states *(Ep. ad Hieron.* lxxviii), *if any error were discovered in Holy Writ, the authority of Holy Writ would perish.* In like manner, if any error were to be found in the Church's preaching, her doctrine would have no authority in settling questions of faith.

Hence others have maintained that indulgences avail as much as is claimed for them, according to a just estimate, not of him who grants it,—who perhaps puts too high a value on it,—nor of the recipient,—for he may prize too highly the gift he receives, but a just estimate according to the estimate of good men who consider the condition of the person affected, and the utility and needs of the Church, for the Church's needs are greater at one time than at another. Yet, neither, seemingly, can this opinion stand. First, because in that case indulgences would no longer be a remission, but rather a mere commutation. Moreover the preaching of the Church would not be excused from untruth, since, at times, indulgences are granted far in excess of the requirements of this just estimate, taking into consideration all the aforesaid conditions, as, for example, when the Pope granted to anyone who visited a certain church, an indulgence of seven years, which indulgence was granted by Blessed Gregory for the Roman Stations.

Hence others say that the quantity of remission accorded in an indulgence is not to be measured by the devotion of the recipient, as the first opinion suggested, nor according to the quantity of what is given, as the second

* S. Bonaventure, *Sent.* IV, D. 20.

opinion held; but according to the cause for which the indulgence is granted, and according to which a person is held deserving of obtaining such an indulgence. Thus according as a man approached near to that cause, so would he obtain remission in whole or in part. But neither will this explain the custom of the Church, who assigns, now a greater, now a lesser indulgence, for the same cause: thus, under the same circumstances, now a year's indulgence, now one of only forty days, according to the graciousness of the Pope, who grants the indulgence, is granted to those who visit a church. Wherefore the amount of the remission granted by the indulgence is not to be measured by the cause for which a person is worthy of an indulgence.

We must therefore say otherwise that the quantity of an effect is proportionate to the quantity of the cause. Now the cause of the remission of punishment effected by indulgences is no other than the abundance of the Church's merits, and this abundance suffices for the remission of all punishment. The effective cause of the remission is not the devotion, or toil, or gift of the recipient; nor, again, is it the cause for which the indulgence was granted. We cannot, then, estimate the quantity of the remission by any of the foregoing, but solely by the merits of the Church —and these are always superabundant. Consequently, according as these merits are applied to a person so does he obtain remission. That they should be so applied demands, firstly, authority to dispense this treasure; secondly, union between the recipient and Him Who merited it—and this is brought about by charity; thirdly, there is required a reason for so dispensing this treasury, so that the intention, namely, of those who wrought these meritorious works is safeguarded, since they did them for the honor of God and for the good of the Church in general. Hence whenever the cause assigned tends to the good of the Church and the honor of God, there is sufficient reason for granting an indulgence.

Hence, according to others, indulgences have precisely the efficacy claimed for them, provided that he who grants them have the authority, that the recipient have charity, and that, as regards the cause, there be piety which includes the honor of God and the profit of our neighbor. Nor in this view have we *too great a market of the Divine mercy,** as some maintain, nor again does it derogate from Divine justice, for no punishment is remitted, but the punishment of one is imputed to another.

Reply Obj. 1. As stated above (Q. 19, A. 3) there are two keys, the key of Orders and the key of jurisdiction. The key of Orders is a sacramental: and as the effects of the sacraments are fixed, not by men but by God, the priest cannot decide in the tribunal of confession how much shall be remitted by means of the key of Orders from the punishment due; it is God Who appoints the amount to be remitted. On the other hand the key of jurisdiction is not something sacramental, and its effect depends on a man's decision. The remission granted through indulgences is the effect of this key, since it does not belong to the dispensation of the sacraments, but to the distribution of the common property of the Church:—hence it is that legates, even though they be not priests, can grant indulgences. Consequently the decision of how much punishment is to be remitted by an indulgence depends on the will of the one who grants that indulgence. If, however, he remits punishment without sufficient reason, so that men are enticed to substitute mere nothings, as it were, for works of penance, he sins by granting such indulgences, although the indulgence is gained fully.

Reply Obj. 2. Although indulgences avail much for the remission of punishment, yet works of satisfaction are more meritorious in respect of the essential reward, which infinitely transcends the remission of temporal punishment.

Reply Obj. 3. When an indulgence is granted in a general way to anyone that helps towards the building of a church, we must understand this to mean a help proportionate to the giver: and in so far as he approaches to this, he will gain the indulgence more or less fully. Consequently a poor man by giving one penny would gain the full indulgence, not so a rich man, whom it would not become to give so little to so holy and profitable a work; just as a king would not be said to help a man if he gave him an *obol*.

Reply Obj. 4. A person who lives near the church, and the priest and clergy of the church, gain the indulgence as much as those who come perhaps a distance of a thousand days' journey: because the remission, as stated above, is proportionate, not to the toil, but to the merits which are applied. Yet he who toils most gains most merit. This, however, is to be understood of those cases in which an indulgence is given in an undeterminate manner. For sometimes a distinction is expressed: thus the Pope at the time of general absolution grants an indulgence of five years to those who come from across the seas, and one of three years to those who come from across the mountains, to others an indulgence of one year. Nor does a person gain the indulgence each time he visits the church during the term of indulgence, because sometimes it is granted for a fixed time; thus when it is said, *Whoever*

visits such and such a church until such and such a day, shall gain so much indulgence, we must understand that it can be gained only once. On the other hand if there be a continual indulgence in a certain church, as the indulgence of forty days to be gained in the church of the Blessed Peter, then a person gains the indulgence as often as he visits the church.

Reply Obj. 5. An indulgence requires a cause, not as a measure of the remission of punishment, but in order that the intention of those whose merits are applied, may reach to this particular individual. Now one person's good is applied to another in two ways:— first, by charity; and in this way, even without indulgences, a person shares in all the good deeds done, provided he have charity: secondly, by the intention of the person who does the good action; and in this way, provided there be a lawful cause, the intention of a person who has done something for the profit of the Church, may reach to some individual through indulgences.

THIRD ARTICLE

Whether an Indulgence Ought to Be Granted for Temporal Help?

We proceed thus to the Third Article:—

Objection 1. It would seem that an indulgence ought not to be granted for temporal help. Because the remission of sins is something spiritual. Now to exchange a spiritual for a temporal thing is simony. Therefore this ought not to be done.

Obj. 2. Further, spiritual assistance is more necessary than temporal. But indulgences do not appear to be granted for spiritual assistance. Much less therefore ought they to be granted for temporal help.

On the contrary, stands the common custom of the Church in granting indulgences for pilgrimages and almsgiving.

I answer that, Temporal things are subordinate to spiritual matters, since we must make use of temporal things on account of spiritual things. Consequently an indulgence must not be granted for the sake of temporal matters as such, but in so far as they are subordinate to spiritual things: such as the quelling of the Church's enemies, who disturb her peace; or such as the building of a church, of a bridge, and other forms of almsgiving. It is therefore evident that there is no simony in these transactions, since a spiritual thing is exchanged, not for a temporal but for a spiritual commodity.

Hence the *Reply* to the *First Objection* is clear.

Reply Obj. 2. Indulgences can be, and sometimes are, granted even for purely spiritual matters. Thus Pope Innocent IV granted an indulgence of ten days to all who prayed for the king of France; and in like manner sometimes the same indulgence is granted to those who preach a crusade as to those who take part in it.

QUESTION 26

Of Those Who Can Grant Indulgences

(In Four Articles)

WE must now consider those who can grant indulgences: under which head there are four points of inquiry: (1) Whether every parish priest can grant indulgences? (2) Whether a deacon or another, who is not a priest, can grant indulgences? (3) Whether a bishop can grant them? (4) Whether they can be granted by one who is in mortal sin?

FIRST ARTICLE

Whether Every Parish Priest Can Grant Indulgences?

We proceed thus to the First Article:—

Objection 1. It would seem that every parish priest can grant indulgences. For an indulgence derives its efficacy from the superabundance of the Church's merits. Now there is no congregation without some superabundance of merits. Therefore every priest, who has charge of a congregation, can grant indulgences, and, in like manner, so can every prelate.

Obj. 2. Further, every prelate stands for a multitude, just as an individual stands for himself. But any individual can assign his own goods to another and thus offer satisfaction for a third person. Therefore a prelate can assign the property of the multitude subject to him, and so it seems that he can grant indulgences.

On the contrary, To excommunicate is less than to grant indulgences. But a parish priest cannot do the former. Therefore he cannot do the latter.

I answer that, Indulgences are effective, in as much as the works of satisfaction done by one person are applied to another, not only by virtue of charity, but also by the intention of the person who did them being directed in some way to the person to whom they are applied. Now a person's intention may be directed to another in three ways, specifically, generically and individually. Individually, as when one person offers satisfaction for another particular person; and thus anyone can apply his works to another. Specifically, as when a person prays for the congregation to which he belongs, for the members of his household, or for his benefactors, and directs his works of satisfaction to the same intention: in this way the superior of a congregation can apply those works to some other person, by applying the intention of those who belong to his congregation to some fixed individual. Generically, as when a person directs his works for the good of the Church in general; and thus he who presides over the whole Church can communicate those works, by applying his intention to this or that individual. And since a man is a member of a congregation, and a congregation is a part of the Church, hence the intention of private good includes the intention of the good of the congregation, and of the good of the whole Church. Therefore he who presides over the Church can communicate what belongs to an individual congregation or to an individual man: and he who presides over a congregation can communicate what belongs to an individual man, but not conversely. Yet neither the first nor the second communication is called an indulgence, but only the third; and this for two reasons. First, because, although those communications loose man from the debt of punishment in the sight of God, yet he is not freed from the obligation of fulfilling the satisfaction enjoined, to which he is bound by a commandment of the Church; whereas the third communication frees man even from this obligation. Secondly, because in one person or even in one congregation there is not such an unfailing supply of merits as to be sufficient both for the one person or congregation and for all others; and consequently the individual is not freed from the entire debt of punishment unless satisfaction is offered for him individually, to the very amount that he owes. On the other hand, in the whole Church there is an unfailing supply of merits, chiefly on account of the merit of Christ. Consequently he alone who is at the head of the Church can grant indulgences. Since, however, the Church is the congregation of the faithful, and since a congregation of men is of two kinds, the domestic, composed of members of the same family, and the civil, composed of members of the same nationality, the Church is like to a civil congregation, for the people themselves are called the Church; while the various assemblies, or parishes of one diocese are likened to a congregation in the various families and services. Hence a bishop alone is properly called a prelate of the Church, wherefore he alone, like a bridegroom, receives the ring of the Church. Consequently full power in the dispensation of the sacraments, and jurisdiction in the public tribunal, belong to him alone as the public person, but to others by delegation from him. Those priests who have charge of the people are not prelates strictly speaking, but assistants, hence, in consecrating priests the bishop says: *The more fragile we are, the more we need these assistants:* and for this reason they do not dispense all the sacraments. Hence parish priests, or abbots or other like prelates cannot grant indulgences.

This suffices for the *Replies* to the *Objections.*

SECOND ARTICLE

Whether a Deacon or Another Who Is Not a Priest Can Grant an Indulgence?

We proceed thus to the Second Article:—

Objection 1. It would seem that a deacon, or one that is not a priest cannot grant an indulgence. Because remission of sins is an effect of the keys. Now none but a priest has the keys. Therefore a priest alone can grant indulgences.

Obj. 2. Further, a fuller remission of punishment is granted by indulgences than by the tribunal of Penance. But a priest alone has power in the latter, and, therefore, he alone has power in the former.

On the contrary, The distribution of the Church's treasury is entrusted to the same person as the government of the Church. Now this is entrusted sometimes to one who is not a priest. Therefore he can grant indulgences, since they derive their efficacy from the distribution of the Church's treasury.

I answer that, The power of granting indulgences follows jurisdiction, as stated above (Q. 25, A. 2). And since deacons and others, who are not priests, can have jurisdiction either delegated, as legates, or ordinary, as bishops-elect, it follows that even those who are not priests can grant indulgences, although they cannot absolve in the tribunal of Penance, since this follows the reception of Orders. This suffices for the *Replies* to the *Objections,* because the granting of indulgences belongs to the key of jurisdiction and not to the key of Orders.

THIRD ARTICLE

Whether a Bishop Can Grant Indulgences?

We proceed thus to the Third Article:—

Objection 1. It would seem that even a bishop cannot grant indulgences. Because the treasury of the Church is the common property of the whole Church. Now the common property of the whole Church cannot be distributed save by him who presides over the whole Church. Therefore the Pope alone can grant indulgences.

Obj. 2. Further, none can remit punishments fixed by law, save the one who has the power to make the law. Now punishments in satisfaction for sins are fixed by law. Therefore the Pope alone can remit these punishments, since he is the maker of the law.

On the contrary, stands the custom of the Church in accordance with which bishops grant indulgences.

I answer that, The Pope has the plenitude of pontifical power, being like a king in his kingdom: whereas the bishops are appointed to a share in his solicitude, like judges over each city. Hence them alone the Pope, in his letters, addresses as *brethren,* whereas he calls all others his *sons.* Therefore the plenitude of the power of granting indulgences resides in the Pope, because he can grant them, as he lists, provided the cause be a lawful one: while, in bishops, this power resides subject to the Pope's ordination, so that they can grant them within fixed limits and not beyond.

This suffices for the *Replies* to the *Objections.*

FOURTH ARTICLE

Whether Indulgences Can Be Granted by One Who Is in Mortal Sin?

We proceed thus to the Fourth Article:—

Objection 1. It would seem that indulgences cannot be granted by one who is in mortal sin. For a stream can no longer flow if cut off from its source. Now the source of grace which is the Holy Ghost is cut off from one who is in mortal sin. Therefore such a one can convey nothing to others by granting indulgences.

Obj. 2. Further, it is a greater thing to grant an indulgence than to receive one. But one who is in mortal sin cannot receive an indulgence, as we shall show presently (Q. 27, A. 1). Neither, therefore, can he grant one.

On the contrary, Indulgences are granted in virtue of the power conferred on the prelates of the Church. Now mortal sin takes away, not power but goodness. Therefore one who is in mortal sin can grant indulgences.

I answer that, The granting of indulgences belongs to jurisdiction. But a man does not, through sin, lose jurisdiction. Consequently indulgences are equally valid, whether they be granted by one who is in mortal sin, or by a most holy person; since he remits punishment, not by virtue of his own merits, but by virtue of the merits laid up in the Church's treasury.

Reply Obj. 1. The prelate who, while in a state of mortal sin, grants an indulgence, does not pour forth anything of his own, and so it is not necessary that he should receive an inflow from the source, in order that he may grant a valid indulgence.

Reply Obj. 2. Further, to grant an indulgence is more than to receive one, if we consider the power, but it is less, if we consider the personal profit.

QUESTION 27

Of Those Whom Indulgences Avail

(In Four Articles)

WE must now consider those whom indulgences avail: under which head there are four points of inquiry: (1) Whether indulgences avail those who are in mortal sin? (2) Whether they avail religious? (3) Whether they avail a person who does not fulfill the conditions for which the indulgence is given? (4) Whether they avail him who grants them?

FIRST ARTICLE

Whether an Indulgence Avails Those Who Are in Mortal Sin?

We proceed thus to the First Article:—

Objection 1. It would seem that an indulgence avails those who are in mortal sin. For one person can merit grace and many other good things for another, even though he be in mortal sin. Now indulgences derive their efficacy from the application of the saints' merits to an individual. Therefore they are effective in one who is in mortal sin.

Obj. 2. Further, the greater the need, the more room there is for pity. Now a man who is in mortal sin is in very great need. Therefore all the more should pity be extended to him by indulgence.

On the contrary, A dead member receives no inflow from the other members that are living. But one who is in mortal sin, is like a dead member. Therefore he receives no inflow, through indulgences, from the merits of living members.

I answer that, Some hold that indulgences avail those even who are in mortal sin, for the acquiring of grace, but not for the remission of their punishment, since none can be freed from punishment who is not yet freed from guilt. For he who has not yet been reached by God's operation unto the remission of guilt, cannot receive the remission of his punishment from the minister of the Church, neither by indulgences nor in the tribunal of Penance.

But this opinion seems to be untrue. Because, although those merits which are applied by means of an indulgence, might possibly avail a person so that he could merit grace (by way of congruity and impetration), yet it is not for this reason that they are applied, but for the remission of punishment. Hence they do not avail those who are in mortal sin, and consequently, true contrition and confession are demanded as conditions for gaining all indulgences. If however the merits were applied by such a form as this: *I grant you a share in the merits of the whole Church,—or of one congregation, or of one specified person,* then they might avail a person in mortal sin so that he could merit something, as the foregoing opinion holds.

This suffices for the *Reply* to the *First Objection.*

Reply Obj. 2. Although he who is in mortal sin is in greater need of help, yet he is less capable of receiving it.

SECOND ARTICLE

Whether Indulgences Avail Religious?

We proceed thus to the Second Article:—

Objection 1. It would seem that indulgences do not avail religious. For there is no reason to bring supplies to those who supply others out of their own abundance. Now indulgences are derived from the abundance of works of satisfaction to be found in religious. Therefore it is unreasonable for them to profit by indulgences.

Obj. 2. Further, nothing detrimental to religious life should be done in the Church. But, if indulgences were to avail religious, this would be detrimental to regular discipline, because religious would become lax on account of indulgences, and would neglect the penances imposed in chapter. Therefore indulgences do not avail religious.

On the contrary, Good brings harm to no man. But the religious life is a good thing. Therefore it does not take away from religious the profit to be derived from indulgences.

I answer that, Indulgences avail both seculars and religious, provided they have charity and satisfy the conditions for gaining the indulgences: for religious can be helped by indulgences no less than persons living in the world.

Reply Obj. 1. Although religious are in the state of perfection, yet they cannot live without sin: and so if at times they are liable to punishment on account of some sin, they can expiate this debt by means of indulgences. For it is not unreasonable that one who is well off absolutely speaking, should be in want at times and in some respect, and thus need to be supplied with what he lacks. Hence it is written (Gal. vi. 2): *Bear ye one another's burdens.*

Reply Obj. 2. There is no reason why indulgences should be detrimental to religious observance, because, as to the reward of eternal life, religious merit more by observing their rule than by gaining indulgences; although, as to the remission of punishment, which is a lesser good, they merit less. Nor again do indulgences remit the punishment enjoined in chapter, because the chapter is a judicial rather than a penitential tribunal; hence even those who are not priests hold chapter. Absolution from punishment enjoined or due for sin is given in the tribunal of Penance.

THIRD ARTICLE

Whether an Indulgence Can Ever Be Granted to One Who Does Not Fulfill the Conditions Required?

We proceed thus to the Third Article:—

Objection 1. It would seem that an indulgence can sometimes be granted to one who does not fulfill the required conditions. Because when a person is unable to perform a certain action his will is taken for the deed. Now sometimes an indulgence is to be gained by giving an alms, which a poor man is unable to do, though he would do so willingly. Therefore he can gain the indulgence.

Obj. 2. Further, one man can make satisfaction for another. Now an indulgence is directed to the remission of punishment, just as satisfaction is. Therefore one man can gain an indulgence for another; and so a man can gain an indulgence without doing that for which the indulgence is given.

On the contrary, If the cause is removed, the effect is removed. If therefore a person fails to do that for which an indulgence is granted, and which is the cause of the indulgence, he does not gain the indulgence.

I answer that, Failing the condition of a grant, no grant ensues. Hence, as an indulgence is granted on the condition that a person does or gives a certain thing, if he fails in this, he does not gain the indulgence.

Reply Obj. 1. This is true of the essential reward, but not of certain accidental rewards, such as the remission of punishment and the like.

Reply Obj. 2. A person can by his intention apply his own action to whomever he lists, and so he can make satisfaction for whomever he chooses. On the other hand, an indulgence cannot be applied to someone, except in accordance with the intention of the grantor. Hence, since he applies it to the doer or giver of a particular action or thing, the doer cannot transfer this intention to another. If, however, the indulgence were expressed thus: *Whosoever does this, or for whomsoever this is done, shall gain so much indulgence,* it would avail the person for whom it is done. Nor would the person who does this action, give the indulgence to another, but he who grants the indulgence in this form.

FOURTH ARTICLE

Whether an Indulgence Avails the Person Who Grants It?

We proceed thus to the Fourth Article:—

Objection 1. It would seem that an indulgence does not avail him who grants it. For the granting of an indulgence belongs to jurisdiction. Now no one can exercise jurisdiction on himself; thus no one can excommunicate himself. Therefore no one can participate in an indulgence granted by himself.

Obj. 2. Further, if this were possible, he who grants an indulgence might gain the remission of the punishment of all his sins for some small deed, so that he would sin with impunity, which seems senseless.

Obj. 3. Further, to grant indulgences and to excommunicate belong to the same power. Now a man cannot excommunicate himself. Therefore he cannot share in the indulgence of which he is the grantor.

On the contrary, He would be worse off than others if he could not make use of the Church's treasury which he dispenses to others.

I answer that, An indulgence should be given for some reason, in order for anyone to be enticed by the indulgence to perform some action that conduces to the good of the Church and to the honor of God. Now the prelate to whom is committed the care of the Church's good and of the furthering of God's honor, does not need to entice himself thereto. Therefore he cannot grant an indulgence to himself alone; but he can avail himself of an indulgence that he grants for others, since it is based on a cause for granting it to them.

Reply Obj. 1. A man cannot exercise an act of jurisdiction on himself, but a prelate can avail himself of those things which are granted to others by the authority of his jurisdiction, both in temporal and in spiritual matters: thus also a priest gives himself the Eucharist which he gives to others. And so a bishop too can apply to himself the suffrages of the Church which he dispenses to others, the immediate effect of which suffrages, and not of his jurisdiction, is the remission of punishment by means of indulgences.

The *Reply* to the *Second Objection* is clear from what had been said.

Reply Obj. 3. Excommunication is pronounced by way of sentence, which no man can pronounce on himself, for the reason that in the tribunal of justice the same man cannot be both judge and accused. On the other hand an indulgence is not given under the form of a sentence, but by way of dispensation, which a man can apply to himself.

QUESTION 28

Of the Solemn Rite of Penance

(In Three Articles)

WE must now consider the solemn rite of Penance: under which head there are three points of inquiry: (1) Whether a penance can be published or solemnized? (2) Whether a solemn penance can be repeated? (3) Whether public penance should be imposed on women?

FIRST ARTICLE

Whether a Penance Should Be Published or Solemnized?

We proceed thus to the First Article:—

Objection 1. It would seem that a penance should not be published or solemnized. Because it is not lawful for a priest, even through fear, to divulge anyone's sin, however notorious it may be. Now a sin is published by a solemn penance. Therefore a penance should not be solemnized.

Obj. 2. Further, the judgment should follow the nature of the tribunal. Now penance is a judgment pronounced in a secret tribunal. Therefore it should not be published or solemnized.

Obj. 3. Further, *Every deficiency is made good by penance* as Ambrose* states. Now solemnization has a contrary effect, since it involves the penitent in many deficiencies: for a layman cannot be promoted to the ranks of the clergy nor can a cleric be promoted to higher orders, after doing solemn penance. Therefore Penance should not be solemnized.

On the contrary, Penance is a sacrament. Now some kind of solemnity is observed in every sacrament. Therefore there should be some solemnity in Penance.

Further, the medicine should suit the disease. Now a sin is sometimes public, and by its example draws many to sin. Therefore the penance which is its medicine should also be public and solemn so as to give edification to many.

I answer that, Some penances should be public and solemn for four reasons. First, so that a public sin may have a public remedy; secondly, because he who has committed a very grave crime deserves the greatest confusion even in this life; thirdly, in order that it may deter others; fourthly, that he may be an example of repentance, lest those should despair, who have committed grievous sins.

Reply Obj. 1. The priest does not divulge the confession by imposing such a penance, though people may suspect the penitent of having committed some great sin. For a man is not certainly taken to be guilty, because he is punished, since sometimes one does penance for another: thus we read in the *Lives of the Fathers* of a certain man who, in order to incite his companion to do penance, did penance together with him. And if the sin be public, the penitent, by fulfilling his penance, shows that he has been to confession.

Reply Obj. 2. A solemn penance, as to its imposition, does not go beyond the limits of a secret tribunal, since, just as the confession is made secretly, so the penance is imposed secretly. It is the execution of the penance, that goes beyond the limits of the secret tribunal: and there is nothing objectionable in this.

Reply Obj. 3. Although Penance cancels all deficiencies, by restoring man to his former state of grace, yet it does not always restore him to his former dignity. Hence women after doing penance for fornication are not given the veil, because they do not recover the honor of virginity. In like manner, after doing public penance, a sinner does not recover his former dignity so as to be eligible for the clerical state, and a bishop who would ordain such a one ought to be deprived of the power of ordaining, unless perhaps the needs of the Church or custom require it. In that case such a one would be admitted to minor orders by way of exception, but not to the sacred orders.

* Cf. *Hypognost.* iii, among the spurious works ascribed to S. Augustine.

First, on account of the dignity of the latter; secondly, for fear of relapse; thirdly, in order to avoid the scandal which the people might take through recollection of his former sins; fourthly, because he would not have the face to correct others, by reason of the publicity of his own sin.

SECOND ARTICLE

Whether a Solemn Penance Can Be Repeated?

We proceed thus to the Second Article:—

Objection 1. It would seem that a solemn penance can be repeated. For those sacraments which do not imprint a character, can be solemnized a second time, such as the Eucharist, Extreme Unction and the like. But Penance does not imprint a character, therefore it can be solemnized over again.

Obj. 2. Further, penance is solemnized on account of the gravity and publicity of the sin. Now, after doing penance, a person may commit the same sins over again, or even more grievous sins. Therefore the solemn penance should be imposed again.

On the contrary, Solemn penance signifies the expulsion of the first man from paradise. Now this was done but once. Therefore solemn penance should be imposed once only.

I answer that, Solemn penance ought not to be repeated, for three reasons. First, lest frequency bring it into contempt. Secondly, on account of its signification; for it signifies the expulsion of the first man from paradise, which happened only once; thirdly, because the solemnization indicates, in a way, that one makes profession of continual repentance. Wherefore repetition is inconsistent with solemnization. And if the sinner fall again, he is not precluded from doing penance, but a solemn penance should not be imposed on him again.

Reply Obj. 1. In those sacraments which are solemnized again and again, repetition is not inconsistent with solemnity, as it is in the present case. Hence the comparison fails.

Reply Obj. 2. Although, if we consider his crime, he ought to do the same penance again, yet the repeated solemnization is not becoming, for the reasons stated above.

THIRD ARTICLE

Whether Solemn Penance Should Be Imposed on Women and Clerics, and Whether Any Priest Can Impose It?

We proceed thus to the Third Article:—

Objection 1. It would seem that solemn penance should not be imposed on women. Because, when this penance is imposed on a

man, he has to cut his hair off. But this becomes not a woman, according to 1 Cor. xi. 15. Therefore she should not do solemn penance.

Obj. 2. It also seems that it ought to be imposed on clerics. For it is enjoined on account of a grievous crime. Now the same sin is more grievous in a cleric than in a layman. Therefore it ought to be imposed on a cleric more than on a layman.

Obj. 3. It also seems that it can be imposed by any priest. Because to absolve in the tribunal of Penance belongs to one who has the keys. Now an ordinary priest has the keys. Therefore he can administer this penance.

I answer that, Every solemn penance is public, but not vice versa. For solemn penance is done as follows: *On the first day of Lent, these penitents clothed in sackcloth, with bare feet, their faces to the ground, and their hair shorn away, accompanied by their priests, present themselves to the bishop of the city at the door of the church. Having brought them into the church the bishop with all his clergy recites the seven penitential psalms, and then imposes his hand on them, sprinkles them with holy water, puts ashes on their heads, covers their shoulders with a hair-shirt, and sorrowfully announces to them that as Adam was expelled from paradise, so are they expelled from the church. He then orders the ministers to put them out of the church, and the clergy follow reciting the responsory: "In the sweat of thy brow, etc." Every year on the day of Our Lord's Supper they are brought back into the church by their priests, and there shall they be until the octave day of Easter, without however being admitted to Communion or to the kiss of peace. This shall be done every year as long as entrance into the church is forbidden them. The final reconciliation is reserved to the bishop, who alone can impose solemn penance.**

This penance can be imposed on men and women; but not on clerics, for fear of scandal. Nor ought such a penance to be imposed except for a crime which has disturbed the whole of the city.

On the other hand public but not solemn penance is that which is done in the presence of the Church, but without the foregoing solemnity, such as a pilgrimage throughout the world with a staff. A penance of this kind can be repeated, and can be imposed by a mere priest, even on a cleric. Sometimes however a solemn penance is taken to signify a public one: so that authorities speak of solemn penance in different senses.

Reply Obj. 1. The woman's hair is a sign of her subjection, a man's is not. Hence it is

* Cap. lxiv, dist. 50.

not proper for a woman to put aside her hair when doing penance, as it is for a man.

Reply Obj. 2. Although in the same kind of sin, a cleric offends more grievously than a layman, yet a solemn penance is not imposed on him, lest his Orders should be an object of contempt. Thus deference is given not to the person but to his Orders.

Reply Obj. 3. Grave sins need great care in their cure. Hence the imposition of a solemn penance, which is only applied for the most grievous sins, is reserved to the bishop.

2651

QUESTION 29

Of Extreme Unction, As Regards Its Essence and Institution

(In Nine Articles)

WE must now consider the sacrament of Extreme Unction: in respect of which five points have to be considered: (1) Its essentials and institution; (2) Its effect; (3) Its minister; (4) On whom should it be conferred and in what parts; (5) Its repetition.

Under the first head there are nine points of inquiry: (1) Whether Extreme Unction is a sacrament? (2) Whether it is one sacrament? (3) Whether this sacrament was instituted by Christ? (4) Whether olive oil is a suitable matter for this sacrament? (5) Whether the oil ought to be consecrated? (6) Whether the matter of this sacrament should be consecrated by a bishop? (7) Whether this sacrament has any form? (8) Whether the form of this sacrament should take the shape of a deprecatory phrase? (9) Whether this is a suitable form for this sacrament?

FIRST ARTICLE

Whether Extreme Unction Is a Sacrament?

We proceed thus to the First Article:—

Objection 1. It would seem that Extreme Unction is not a sacrament. For just as oil is used on sick people, so is it on catechumens. But anointing of catechumens with oil is not a sacrament. Therefore neither is the Extreme Unction of the sick with oil.

Obj. 2. Further, the sacraments of the Old Law were figures of the sacraments of the New Law. But there was no figure of Extreme Unction in the Old Law. Therefore it is not a sacrament of the New Law:

Obj. 3. Further, according to Dionysius *(Eccl. Hier.* iii. v) every sacrament aims at either cleansing, or enlightening, or perfecting. Now Extreme Unction does not aim at either cleansing, or enlightening, for this is ascribed to Baptism alone, or perfecting, for according to Dionysius *(ibid.* ii), this belongs to Confirmation and the Eucharist. Therefore Extreme Unction is not a sacrament.

On the contrary, The sacraments of the Church supply man's defects sufficiently with respect to every state of life. Now no other than Extreme Unction does this for those who are departing from this life. Therefore it is a sacrament.

Further, the sacraments are neither more nor less than spiritual remedies. Now Extreme Unction is a spiritual remedy, since it avails for the remission of sins, according to James v. 15. Therefore it is a sacrament.

I answer that, Among the visible operations of the Church, some are sacraments, as Baptism, some are sacramentals, as Exorcism. The difference between these is that a sacrament is an action of the Church that reaches to the principal effect intended in the administration of the sacraments, whereas a sacramental is an action which, though it does not reach to that effect, is nevertheless directed towards that principal action. Now the effect intended in the administration of the sacraments is the healing of the disease of sin: wherefore it is written (Isa. xxvii. 9): *This is all the fruit, that the sin . . . should be taken away.* Since then Extreme Unction reaches to this effect, as is clear from the words of James, and is not ordained to any other sacrament as an accessory thereto, it is evident that Extreme Unction is not a sacramental but a sacrament.

Reply Obj. 1. The oil with which catechumens are anointed does not convey the remission of sins to them by its unction, for that belongs to Baptism. It does, however, dispose them to receive Baptism, as stated above (P. III, Q. 71, A. 3). Hence that unction is not a sacrament as Extreme Unction is.

Reply Obj. 2. This sacrament prepares man for glory immediately, since it is given to those who are departing from this life. And as, under the Old Law, it was not yet time to enter into glory, because *the Law brought nobody* (Vulg.,—*nothing) to perfection* (Heb. vii. 19), so this sacrament had not to be foreshadowed therein by some corresponding sacrament, as by a figure of the same kind. Nevertheless it was somewhat foreshadowed remotely by all the healings related in the Old Testament.

Reply Obj. 3. Dionysius makes no mention of Extreme Unction, as neither of Penance, nor of Matrimony, because he had no intention to decide any question about the sacraments, save in so far as they serve to illustrate the orderly disposition of the ecclesiastical hierarchy, as regards the ministers, their actions, and the recipients. Nevertheless since Extreme Unction confers grace and remission of sins, there is no doubt that it possesses an enlightening and cleansing power, even as Baptism, though not so copious.

SECOND ARTICLE

Whether Extreme Unction Is One Sacrament?

We proceed thus to the Second Article:—

Objection 1. It would seem that Extreme Unction is not one sacrament. Because the oneness of a thing depends on its matter and form, since being and oneness are derived from the same source. Now the form of this sacrament is said several times during the one administration, and the matter is applied to the person anointed in respect of various parts of his body. Therefore it is not one sacrament.

Obj. 2. Further, the unction itself is a sacrament, for it would be absurd to say that the oil is a sacrament. But there are several unctions. Therefore there are several sacraments.

Obj. 3. Further, one sacrament should be performed by one minister. But the case might occur that Extreme Unction could not be conferred by one minister: thus if the priest die after the first unction, another priest would have to proceed with the others. Therefore Extreme Unction is not one sacrament.

On the contrary, As immersion is in relation to Baptism, so is unction to this sacrament. But several immersions are but one sacrament of Baptism. Therefore the several unctions in Extreme Unction are also one sacrament.

Further, if it were not one sacrament, then after the first unction, it would not be essential for the perfection of the sacrament that the second unction should be performed, since each sacrament has perfect being of itself. But that is not true. Therefore it is one sacrament.

I answer that, Strictly speaking, a thing is one numerically in three ways. First, as something indivisible, which is neither actually nor potentially several,—as a point, and unity. Secondly, as something continuous, which is actually one, but potentially several,—as a line. Thirdly, as something complete, that is composed of several parts,—as a house, which is, in a way, several things, even actually, although those several things go together towards making one. In this way each sacrament is said to be one thing, in as much as the many things which are contained in one sacrament, are united together for the purpose of signifying or causing one thing, because a sacrament is a sign of the effect it produces. Hence when one action suffices for a perfect signification, the unity of the sacrament consists in that action only, as may be seen in Confirmation. When, however, the signification of the sacrament can be both in one and in several actions, then the sacrament can be complete both in one and in several actions, even as Baptism in one immersion and in three, since washing which is signified in Baptism,

can be completed by one immersion and by several. But when the perfect signification cannot be expressed except by means of several actions, then these several actions are essential for the perfection of the sacrament, as is exemplified in the Eucharist, for the refreshment of the body which signifies that of the soul, can only be attained by means of meat and drink. It is the same in this sacrament, because the healing of the internal wounds cannot be perfectly signified save by the application of the remedy to the various sources of the wounds. Hence several actions are essential to the perfection of this sacrament.

Reply Obj. 1. The unity of a complete whole is not destroyed by reason of a diversity of matter or form in the parts of that whole. Thus it is evident that there is neither the same matter nor the same form in the flesh and in the bones of which one man is composed. In like manner too, in the sacrament of the Eucharist, and in this sacrament, the diversity of matter and form does not destroy the unity of the sacrament.

Reply Obj. 2. Although those actions are several simply, yet they are united together in one complete action, viz. the anointing of all the external senses, whence arises the infernal malady.

Reply Obj. 3. Although, in the Eucharist, if the priest die after the consecration of the bread, another priest can go on with the consecration of the wine, beginning where the other left off, or can begin over again with fresh matter, in Extreme Unction he cannot begin over again, but should always go on, because to anoint the same part a second time would produce as much effect as if one were to consecrate a host a second time, which ought by no means to be done. Nor does the plurality of ministers destroy the unity of this sacrament, because they only act as instruments, and the unity of a smith's work is not destroyed by his using several hammers.

THIRD ARTICLE

Whether This Sacrament Was Instituted by Christ?

We proceed thus to the Third Article:—

Objection 1. It would seem that this sacrament was not instituted by Christ. For mention is made in the Gospel of the institution of those sacraments which Christ instituted, for instance the Eucharist and Baptism. But no mention is made of Extreme Unction. Therefore it was not instituted by Christ.

Obj. 2. Further, the Master says explicitly (iv, *Sent.*, D. 23) that it was instituted by the apostles. Therefore Christ did not institute it Himself.

Obj. 3. Further, Christ showed forth the sacraments which He instituted, as in the case of the Eucharist and Baptism. But He did not bestow this sacrament on anyone. Therefore He did not institute it Himself.

On the contrary, The sacraments of the New Law are more excellent than those of the Old Law. But all the sacraments of the Old Law were instituted by God. Therefore much more do all the sacraments of the New Law owe their institution to Christ Himself.

Further, to make an institution and to remove it belongs to the same authority. Now the Church, who enjoys the same authority in the successors of the apostles, as the apostles themselves possessed, cannot do away with the sacrament of Extreme Unction. Therefore the apostles did not institute it, but Christ Himself.

I answer that, There are two opinions on this point. For some hold that this sacrament and Confirmation were not instituted by Christ Himself, but were left by Him to be instituted by the apostles; for the reason that these two sacraments, on account of the plenitude of grace conferred in them, could not be instituted before the mission of the Holy Ghost in perfect plenitude. Hence they are sacraments of the New Law in such a way as not to be foreshadowed in the Old Law. But this argument is not very cogent, since, just as Christ, before His Passion, promised the mission of the Holy Ghost in His plenitude, so could He institute these sacraments.

Wherefore others hold that Christ Himself instituted all the sacraments, but that He Himself published some, which present greater difficulty to our belief, while he reserved some to be published by the apostles, such as Extreme Unction and Confirmation. This opinion seems so much the more probable, as the sacraments belong to the foundation of the Law, wherefore their institution pertains to the lawgiver; besides, they derive their efficacy from their institution, which efficacy is given them by God alone.

Reply Obj. 1. Our Lord did and said many things which are not related in the Gospel. For the evangelists were intent on handing down chiefly those things that were necessary for salvation or concerned the building of the ecclesiastical edifice. Hence they related the institution by Christ of Baptism, Penance, the Eucharist and Orders, rather than of Extreme Unction and Confirmation, which are not necessary for salvation, nor do they concern the building or division of the Church. As a matter of fact however an anointing done by the apostles is mentioned in the Gospel (Mark vi. 13) where it is said that they *anointed the sick with oil.*

Reply Obj. 2. The Master says it was instituted by the apostles because its institution was made known to us by the teaching of the apostles.

Reply Obj. 3. Christ did not show forth any sacrament except such as He received by way of example: but He could not be a recipient of Penance and Extreme Unction, since there was no sin in Him: hence He did not show them forth.

FOURTH ARTICLE

Whether Olive Oil Is a Suitable Matter for This Sacrament?

We proceed thus to the Fourth Article:—

Objection 1. It would seem that olive oil is not a suitable matter for this sacrament. For this sacrament is ordained immediately to the state of incorruption. Now incorruption is signified by balsam which is contained in chrism. Therefore chrism would be a more suitable matter for this sacrament.

Obj. 2. Further, this sacrament is a spiritual healing. Now spiritual healing is signified by the use of wine, as may be gathered from the parable of the wounded man (Luke x. 34). Therefore wine also would be more suitable a matter for this sacrament.

Obj. 3. Further, where there is the greater danger, the remedy should be a common one. But olive oil is not a common remedy, since the olive is not found in every country. Therefore, since this sacrament is given to the dying, who are in the greatest danger, it seems that olive oil is not a suitable matter.

On the contrary, Oil is appointed (James v. 14) as the matter of this sacrament. Now, properly speaking, oil is none but olive oil. Therefore this is the matter of this sacrament.

Further, spiritual healing is signified by anointing with oil, as is evident from Isa. i. 6 where we read: . . . *swelling sores: they are not . . . dressed nor fomented with oil.* Therefore the suitable matter for this sacrament is oil.

I answer that, The spiritual healing, which is given at the end of life, ought to be complete, since there is no other to follow; it ought also to be gentle, lest hope, of which the dying stand in utmost need, be shattered rather than fostered. Now oil has a softening effect, it penetrates to the very heart of a thing, and spreads over it. Hence, in both the foregoing respects, it is a suitable matter for this sacrament. And since oil is, above all, the name of the liquid extract of olives, for other liquids are only called oil from their likeness to it, it follows that olive oil is the matter which should be employed in this sacrament.

Reply Obj. 1. The incorruption of glory is

something not contained in this sacrament: and there is no need for the matter to signify such a thing. Hence it is not necessary for balsam to be included in the matter of this sacrament, because on account of its fragrance it is indicative of a good name, which is no longer necessary, for its own sake, to those who are dying; they need only a clear conscience which is signified by oil.

Reply Obj. 2. Wine heals by its roughness, oil by its softness, wherefore healing with wine pertains to Penance rather than to this sacrament.

Reply Obj. 3. Though olive oil is not produced everywhere, yet it can easily be transported from one place to another. Moreover this sacrament is not so necessary that the dying cannot obtain salvation without it.

FIFTH ARTICLE

Whether the Oil Ought to Be Consecrated?

We proceed thus to the Fifth Article:—

Objection 1. It would seem that the oil need not be consecrated. Because there is a sanctification in the use of this sacrament, through the form of words. Therefore another sanctification is superfluous if it be applied to the matter.

Obj. 2. Further, the efficacy and signification of the sacraments are in their very matter. But the signification of the effect of this sacrament, is suitable to oil on account of its natural properties, and the efficacy thereof is due to the Divine institution. Therefore its matter does not need to be sanctified.

Obj. 3. Further, Baptism is a more perfect sacrament than Extreme Unction. But, so far as the essentials of the sacrament are concerned, the baptismal matter needs no sanctification. Neither therefore does the matter of Extreme Unction need to be sanctified.

On the contrary, In all other anointings the matter is previously consecrated. Therefore since this sacrament is an anointing, it requires consecrated matter.

I answer that, Some hold that mere oil is the matter of this sacrament, and that the sacrament itself is perfected in the consecration of the oil by the bishop. But this is clearly false since we proved when treating of the Eucharist that that sacrament alone consists in the consecration of the matter. (Q. 2, A. 1, *ad* 2).

We must therefore say that this sacrament consists in the anointing itself, just as Baptism consists in the washing, and that the matter of this sacrament is consecrated oil. Three reasons may be assigned why consecrated matter is needed in this sacrament and in certain others. The first is that all sacramental efficacy is derived from Christ: wherefore those sacraments which He Himself used, derived their efficacy from His use of them, even as, by the contact of His flesh, He bestowed the force of regeneration on the waters. But He did not use this sacrament, nor any bodily anointing, wherefore in all anointings a consecrated matter is required. The second reason is that this sacrament confers a plenitude of grace, so as to take away not only sin but also the remnants of sin, and bodily sickness. The third reason is that its effect on the body, viz. bodily health, is not caused by a natural property of the matter; wherefore it has to derive this efficacy from being consecrated.

Reply Obj. 1. The first consecration sanctifies the matter in itself, but the second regards rather the use of the matter considered as actually producing its effect. Hence neither is superfluous, because instruments also receive their efficacy from the craftsman, both when they are made, and when they are used for action.

Reply Obj. 2. The efficacy which the sacrament derives from its institution, is applied to this particular matter when it is consecrated.

The *Reply* to the *Third Objection* is gathered from what has been said.

SIXTH ARTICLE

Whether the Matter of This Sacrament Need Be Consecrated by a Bishop?

We proceed thus to the Sixth Article:—

Objection 1. It would seem that the matter of this sacrament need not be consecrated by a bishop. Because the consecration of the Eucharistic elements surpasses that of the matter in this sacrament. But a priest can consecrate the matter in the Eucharist. Therefore he can do so in this sacrament also.

Obj. 2. Further, in material works the higher art never prepares the matter for the lower, because the art which applies the matter is more excellent than that which prepares it, as stated in *Phys.* ii, text. 25. Now a bishop is above a priest. Therefore he does not prepare the matter of a sacrament which is applied by a priest. But a priest dispenses this sacrament, as we shall state further on (Q. 31). Therefore the consecration of the matter does not belong to a bishop.

On the contrary, In other anointings also the matter is consecrated by a bishop. Therefore the same applies to this.

I answer that, The minister of a sacrament produces the effect, not by his own power, as though he were the principal agent, but by the efficacy of the sacrament which he dispenses. This efficacy comes, in the first place, from Christ, and from Him flows down to others in due order, viz. to the people through the medium of the ministers who dispense the sacraments, and to the lower ministers through the medium of the higher ministers who sanctify the matter. Wherefore, in all the sacraments which require a sanctified matter, the first consecration of the matter is performed by a bishop, and the application thereof sometimes by a priest, in order to show that the priest's power is derived from the bishop's, according to Ps. cxxxii. 2: *Like the precious ointment on the head,* i.e. Christ, *that ran down upon the beard of Aaron* first, and then *to the skirt of his garment.*

Reply Obj. 1. The sacrament of the Eucharist consists in the consecration of the matter and not in its use. Consequently, strictly speaking, that which is the matter of the sacrament is not a consecrated thing. Hence no consecration of the matter by a bishop is required beforehand: but the altar and such like things, even the priest himself, need to be consecrated, all of which can be done by none but a bishop: so that in this sacrament also, the priest's power is shown to be derived from the bishop's, as Dionysius observes *(Eccl. Hier.* iii). The reason why a priest can perform that consecration of matter which is a sacrament by itself, and not that which, as a sacramental, is directed to a sacrament consisting in something used by the faithful, is that in respect of Christ's true body no order is above the priesthood, whereas, in respect of Christ's mystic body the episcopate is above the priesthood, as we shall state further on (Q. 40, A. 4).

Reply Obj. 2. The sacramental matter is not one that is made into something else by him that uses it, as occurs in the mechanical arts: it is one, in virtue of which something is done, so that it partakes somewhat of the nature of an efficient cause, in so far as it is the instrument of a Divine operation. Hence the matter needs to acquire this virtue from a higher art or power, since among efficient causes, the more prior the cause the more perfect it is, whereas in material causes, the more prior the matter, the more imperfect it is.

SEVENTH ARTICLE

Whether This Sacrament Has a Form?

We proceed thus to the Seventh Article:—

Objection 1. It would seem that this sacrament has no form. Because, since the efficacy of the sacraments is derived from their institution, as also from their form, the latter must needs be appointed by the institutor of the sacrament. But there is no account of the form of this sacrament being instituted either by Christ or by the apostles. Therefore this sacrament has no form.

Obj. 2. Further, whatever is essential to a sacrament is observed everywhere in the same way. Now nothing is so essential to a sacrament that has a form, as that very form. Therefore, as in this sacrament there is no form commonly used by all, since various words are in use, it seems that this sacrament has no form.

Obj. 3. Further, in Baptism no form is needed except for the sanctification of the matter, because the water *is sanctified by the word of life so as to wash sin away,* as Hugh states *(De Sacram.* ii). Now the matter of this sacrament is already consecrated. Therefore it needs no form of words.

On the contrary, The Master says (iv, *Sent.,* D. 1) that every sacrament of the New Law consists in things and words. Now the words are the sacramental form. Therefore, since this is a sacrament of the New Law, it seems that it has a form.

Further, this is confirmed by the rite of the Universal Church, who uses certain words in the bestowal of this sacrament.

I answer that, Some have held that no form is essential to this sacrament. This, however, seems derogatory to the effect of this sacrament, since every sacrament signifies its effect. Now the matter is indifferent as regards its effect, and consequently cannot be determined to any particular effect save by the form of words. Hence in all the sacraments of the New Law, since they effect what they signify, there must needs be things and words. Moreover James (v. 14, 15) seems to ascribe the whole force of this sacrament to prayer, which is the form thereof, as we shall state further on (*ad* 2: AA. 8, 9). Wherefore the foregoing opinion seems presumptuous and erroneous; and for that reason we should hold with the common opinion that this, like all the other sacraments, has a fixed form.

Reply Obj. 1. Holy Writ is proposed to all alike: and so, the form of Baptism, which can be conferred by all, should be expressed in Holy Writ, as also the form of the Eucharist, which in regard to that sacrament, expresses faith which is necessary for salvation. Now the forms of the other sacraments are not contained in Holy Writ, but were handed down to the Church by the apostles, who received them from Our Lord, as the Apostle declares (1 Cor. xi. 23): *For I have received of the Lord that which also I delivered to you,* etc.

Reply Obj. 2. The words which are essential to the form, viz. the prayer of deprecation, are said by all; but other words which pertain to the well-being thereof, are not said by all.

Reply Obj. 3. The matter of Baptism has

a certain sanctification of its own from the very contact of our Saviour's flesh; but the form of words sanctifies it so that it has a sanctifying force. In like manner when the matter of this sacrament has been sanctified in itself, it requires sanctification in its use, so that it may sanctify actually.

EIGHTH ARTICLE

Whether the Form of This Sacrament Should Be Expressed by Way of Assertion or of Petition?

We proceed thus to the Eighth Article:—

Objection 1. It would seem that the form of this sacrament should be expressed by way of assertion rather than of petition. Because all the sacraments of the New Law have a sure effect. But sureness of effect is not expressed in the sacramental forms except by way of assertion, as when we say: *This is My body*, or *I baptize thee*. Therefore the form of this sacrament should be expressed as an assertion.

Obj. 2. Further, the intention of the minister should be expressed in the sacramental forms, because it is essential to the sacrament. But the intention of conferring a sacrament is not expressed except by an assertion. Therefore, etc.

Obj. 3. Further, in some churches the following words are said in the conferring of this sacrament: *I anoint these eyes with consecrated oil in the name of the Father*, etc., which is in keeping with the forms of the other sacraments. Therefore it seems that such is the form of this sacrament.

On the contrary, The form of a sacrament must needs be one that is observed everywhere. Now the words employed according to the custom of all the churches are not those quoted above, but take the form of a petition, viz.: *Through this holy unction, and His most tender mercy, may the Lord pardon thee whatever sins thou hast committed, by sight,* etc. Therefore the form of this sacrament is expressed as a petition.

Further, this seems to follow from the words of James, who ascribes the effect of this sacrament to prayer: *The prayer of faith,* says he (v. 15), *shall save the sick man*. Since then a sacrament takes its efficacy from its form, it seems that the form of this sacrament is expressed as a petition.

I answer that, The form of this sacrament is expressed by way of a petition, as appears from the words of James, and from the custom of the Roman Church, who uses no other than words of supplication in conferring this sacrament. Several reasons are assigned for this: first, because the recipient of this sacrament is deprived of his strength, so that he needs to be helped by prayers; secondly, because it

is given to the dying, who are on the point of quitting the courts of the Church, and rest in the hands of God alone, for which reason they are committed to Him by prayer; thirdly, because the effect of this sacrament is not such that it always results from the minister's prayer, even when all essentials have been duly observed, as is the case with the character in Baptism and Confirmation, transubstantiation in the Eucharist, remission of sin in Penance (given contrition) which remission is essential to the sacrament of Penance but not to this sacrament. Consequently the form of this sacrament cannot be expressed in the indicative mood, as in the sacraments just mentioned.

Reply Obj. 1. This sacrament, like the others mentioned, considered in itself, is sure of its effect; yet this effect can be hindered through the insincerity of the recipient (though by his intention he submit to the sacrament), so that he receives no effect at all. Hence there is no parity between this sacrament, and the others wherein some effect always ensues.

Reply Obj. 2. The intention is sufficiently expressed by the act which is mentioned in the form, viz.: *By this holy unction*.

Reply Obj. 3. These words in the indicative mood, which some are wont to say before the prayer, are not the sacramental form, but are a preparation for the form, in so far as they determine the intention of the minister.

NINTH ARTICLE

Whether the Foregoing Prayer Is a Suitable Form for This Sacrament?

We proceed thus to the Ninth Article:—

Objection 1. It would seem that the foregoing prayer is not a suitable form for this sacrament. For in the forms of the other sacraments mention is made of the matter, for instance in Confirmation, whereas this is not done in the aforesaid words. Therefore it is not a suitable form.

Obj. 2. Further, just as the effect of this sacrament is bestowed on us by the mercy of God, so are the effects of the other sacraments. But mention is made in the forms of the other sacraments, not of the Divine mercy, but rather of the Trinity and of the Passion. Therefore the same should be done here.

Obj. 3. Further, this sacrament is stated in the text (iv, *Sent.*, D. 23) to have a twofold effect. But in the foregoing words mention is made of only one effect, viz. the remission of sins, and not of the healing of the body, to which end James directs the prayer of faith to be made (v. 15): *The prayer of faith shall save the sick man*. Therefore the above form is unsuitable.

I answer that, The prayer given above (A. 8) is a suitable form for this sacrament, for it includes the sacrament by the words: *By this holy unction,* and that which works in the sacrament, viz. *the mercy of God,* and the effect, viz. *remission of sins.*

Reply Obj. 1. The matter of this sacrament may be understood in the act of anointing, whereas the matter of Confirmation cannot be implied by the act expressed in the form. Hence there is no parity.

Reply Obj. 2. The object of mercy is misery: and because this sacrament is given when we are in a state of misery, i.e. of sickness, mention of mercy is made in this rather than in other sacraments.

Reply Obj. 3. The form should contain mention of the principal effect, and of that which always ensues in virtue of the sacrament, unless there be something lacking on the part of the recipient. Now bodily health is not an effect of this kind, as we shall state further on (Q. 30, AA. 1, 2), though it does ensue at times, for which reason James ascribes this effect to the prayer which is the form of this sacrament.

QUESTION 30

Of the Effect of This Sacrament

(In Three Articles)

WE must now consider the effect of this sacrament: under which head there are three points of inquiry: (1) Whether Extreme Unction avails for the remission of sins? (2) Whether bodily health is an effect of this sacrament? (3) Whether this sacrament imprints a character?

FIRST ARTICLE

Whether Extreme Unction Avails for the Remission of Sins?

We proceed thus to the First Article:—

Objection 1. It would seem that Extreme Unction does not avail for the remission of sins. For when a thing can be attained by one means, no other is needed. Now repentance is required in the recipient of Extreme Unction, for the remission of his sins. Therefore sins are not remitted by Extreme Unction.

Obj. 2. Further, there are no more than three things in sin, the stain, the debt of punishment, and the remnants of sin. Now Extreme Unction does not remit the stain without contrition, and this remits sin even without Unction; nor does it remit the punishment, for if the recipient recover, he is still bound to fulfill the satisfaction enjoined; nor does it take away the remnants of sin, since the dispositions remaining from preceding acts still remain, as may easily be seen after recovery. Therefore remission of sins is by no means the effect of Extreme Unction.

Obj. 3. Further, remission of sins takes place, not successively, but instantaneously. On the other hand, Extreme Unction is not done all at once, since several anointings are required. Therefore the remission of sins is not its effect.

On the contrary, It is written (James v. 15): *If he be in sins, they shall be forgiven him.*

Further, every sacrament of the New Law confers grace. Now grace effects the forgiveness of sins. Therefore since Extreme Unction is a sacrament of the New Law, its effect is the remission of sins.

I answer that, Each sacrament was instituted for the purpose of one principal effect, though it may, in consequence, produce other effects besides. And since a sacrament causes what it signifies, the principal effect of a sacrament must be gathered from its signification. Now this sacrament is conferred by way of a kind of medicament, even as Baptism is conferred by way of washing, and the purpose of a medicament is to expel sickness. Hence the chief object of the institution of this sacrament is to cure the sickness of sin. Therefore, just as Baptism is a spiritual regeneration, and Penance, a spiritual resurrection, so Extreme Unction is a spiritual healing or cure. Now just as a bodily cure presupposes bodily life in the one who is cured, so does a spiritual cure presuppose spiritual life. Hence this sacrament is not an antidote to those defects which deprive man of spiritual life, namely, original and mortal sin, but is a remedy for such defects as weaken man spiritually, so as to deprive him of perfect vigor for acts of the life of grace or of glory; which defects consist in nothing else but a certain weakness and unfitness, the result in us of actual or original sin; against which weakness man is strengthened by this sacrament. Since, however, this strength is given by grace, which is incompatible with sin, it follows that, in consequence, if it finds any sin, either mortal or venial, it removes it as far as the guilt is concerned, provided there be no obstacle on the part of the recipient; just as we have stated to be the case with regard to the Eucharist and Confirmation (P. III, Q. 73, A. 7; Q. 79, A. 3). Hence, too, James speaks of the remission of sin as being conditional, for he says: *If he be in sins, they shall be forgiven him,* viz. as to the guilt. Because it does not always blot out sin, since it does not always find any: but it always remits in respect of the aforesaid weakness which some call the remnants of sin. Some, however, maintain that it is instituted chiefly as a remedy for venial sin which cannot be cured perfectly in this liftime: for which reason the sacrament of the dying is ordained specially against venial sin. But this does not seem to be true, since Penance also blots out venial sins sufficiently during this life as to their guilt, and that we cannot avoid them after doing penance, does not cancel the effect of the previous penance; moreover this is part of the weakness mentioned above.

Consequently we must say that the principal effect of this sacrament is the remission of sin, as to its remnants, and, consequently, even as to its guilt, if it find it.

Reply Obj. 1. Although the principal effect of a sacrament can be obtained without actually receiving that sacrament (either without any sacrament at all, or indirectly by means of some other sacrament), yet it never can be obtained without the purpose of receiving that sacrament. And so, since Penance was instituted chiefly against actual sin, whichever other sacrament may blot out sin indirectly, it does not exclude the necessity of Penance.

Reply Obj. 2. Extreme Unction remits sin in some way as to those three things. For, although the stain of sin is not washed out without contrition, yet this sacrament, by the grace which it bestows, makes the movement of the free will towards sin to be one of contrition, just as may occur in the Eucharist and Confirmation. Again it diminishes the debt of temporal punishment; and this indirectly, in as much as it takes away weakness, for a strong man bears the same punishment more easily than a weak man. Hence it does not follow that the measure of satisfaction is diminished. As to the remnants of sin, they do not mean here those dispositions which result from acts, and are inchoate habits so to speak, but a certain spiritual debility in the mind, which debility being removed, though such like habits or dispositions remain, the mind is not so easily prone to sin.

Reply Obj. 3. When many actions are ordained to one effect, the last is formal with respect to all the others that precede, and acts by virtue of them: wherefore by the last anointing is infused grace which gives the sacrament its effect.

SECOND ARTICLE

**Whether Bodily Health Is an Effect
of This Sacrament?**

We proceed thus to the Second Article:—

Objection 1. It would seem that bodily health is not an effect of this sacrament. For every sacrament is a spiritual remedy. Now a spiritual remedy is ordained to spiritual health, just as a bodily remedy is ordained to health of the body. Therefore bodily health is not an effect of this sacrament.

Obj. 2. Further, the sacraments always produce their effect in those who approach them in the proper dispositions. Now sometimes the recipient of this sacrament does not receive bodily health, no matter how devoutly he receives it. Therefore bodily health is not its effect.

Obj. 3. Further, the efficacy of this sacrament is notified to us in the fifth chapter of James. Now healing is ascribed there as the effect, not of the anointing, but of the prayer, for he says: *The prayer of faith shall save the sick man.* Therefore bodily healing is not an effect of this sacrament.

On the contrary, The operation of the Church is more efficacious since Christ's Passion than before. Now, before the Passion, those whom the apostles anointed with oil were healed (Mark vi. 13). Therefore unction has its effect now in healing bodies.

Further, the sacraments produce their effect by signifying it. Now Baptism signifies and effects a spiritual washing, through the bodily washing in which it consists outwardly. Therefor Extreme Unction signifies and causes a spiritual healing through the bodily healing which it effects externally.

I answer that, Just as Baptism causes a spiritual cleansing from spiritual stains by means of a bodily washing, so this sacrament causes an inward healing by means of an outward sacramental healing: and even as the baptismal washing has the effect of a bodily washing, since it effects even a bodily cleansing, so too, Extreme Unction has the effect of a bodily remedy, namely a healing of the body. But there is a difference, for as much as the bodily washing causes a bodily cleansing by a natural property of the bodily element, and consequently always causes it, whereas Extreme Unction causes a bodily healing, not by a natural property of the matter, but by the Divine power which works reasonably. And since reasonable working never produces a secondary effect, except in so far as it is required for the principal effect, it follows that a bodily healing does not always ensue from this sacrament, but only when it is requisite for the spiritual healing: and then it produces it always, provided there be no obstacle on the part of the recipient.

Reply Obj. 1. This objection proves that bodily health is not the principal effect of this sacrament: and this is true.

The *Reply* to the *Second Objection* is clear from what has been said above (cf. Q. 29, A. 8).

Reply Obj. 3. This prayer is the form of this sacrament as stated above (Q. 29, AA. 8, 9). Hence, so far as its form is concerned, this sacrament derives from it its efficacy in healing the body.

THIRD ARTICLE

Whether This Sacrament Imprints a Character?

We proceed thus to the Third Article:—

Objection 1. It would seem that this sacrament imprints a character. For a character is a distinctive sign. Now just as one who is baptized is distinguished from one who is not, so is one who is anointed, from one who is not. Therefore, just as Baptism imprints a character so does Extreme Unction.

Obj. 2. Further, there is an anointing in the sacraments or Order and Confirmation, as there is in this sacrament. But a character is imprinted in those sacraments. Therefore a character is imprinted in this one also.

Obj. 3. Further, every sacrament contains something that is a reality only, something that is a sacrament only, and something that is both reality and sacrament. Now nothing in this sacrament can be assigned as both reality and sacrament except a character. Therefore in this sacrament also, a character is imprinted.

On the contrary, No sacrament·that imprints a character is repeated. But this sacrament is repeated as we shall state further on (Q. 33). Therefore it does not imprint a character.

Further, a sacramental character causes a distinction among those who are in the present Church. But Extreme Unction is given to one who is departing from the present Church. Therefore it does not imprint a character.

I answer that, A character is not imprinted except in those sacraments whereby man is deputed to some sacred duty. Now this sacrament is for no other purpose than a remedy, and man is not deputed thereby to do or receive anything holy. Therefore it does not imprint a character.

Reply Obj. 1. A character marks a distinction of states with regard to duties which have to be performed in the Church, a distinction which a man does not receive by being anointed.

Reply Obj. 2. The unction of Orders and Confirmation, is the unction of consecration whereby a man is deputed to some sacred duty, whereas this unction is remedial. Hence the comparison fails.

Reply Obj. 3. In this sacrament, that which is both reality and sacrament is not a character, but a certain inward devotion which is a kind of spiritual anointing.

QUESTION 31

Of the Minister of This Sacrament

(In Three Articles)

WE must now consider the minister of this sacrament: under which head there are three points of inquiry: (1) Whether a layman can confer this sacrament? (2) Whether a deacon can? (3) Whether none but a bishop can confer it?

FIRST ARTICLE

Whether a Layman Can Confer This Sacrament?

We proceed thus to the First Article:—

Objection 1. It would seem that even a layman can confer this sacrament. For this sacrament derives its efficacy from prayer, as James declares (v. 15). But a layman's prayer is sometimes as acceptable to God as a priest's. Therefore he can confer this sacrament.

Obj. 2. Further, we read of certain fathers in Egypt that they sent the oil to the sick, and that these were healed. It is also related of the Blessed Geneviève that she anointed the sick with oil. Therefore this sacrament can be conferred even by lay people.

On the contrary, Remission of sins is given in this sacrament. But laymen have not the power to forgive sins. Therefore, etc.

I answer that, According to Dionysius (*Eccl. Hier.* v) there are some who exercise hierarchical actions, and some who are recipients only. Hence laymen are officially incompetent to dispense any sacrament: and that they can baptize in cases of necessity, is due to the Divine dispensation, in order that no one may be deprived of spiritual regeneration.

Reply Obj. 1. This prayer is not said by the priest in his own person, for since sometimes he is in sin, he would not in that case be heard. But it is said in the person of the whole Church, in whose person he can pray as a public official, whereas a layman cannot, for he is a private individual.

Reply Obj. 2. These unctions were not sacramental. It was due to the devotion of the recipients of the unction, and to the merits of those who anointed them that they procured the effects of bodily health, through the *grace of healing* (1 Cor. xii. 9) but not through sacramental grace.

SECOND ARTICLE

Whether Deacons Can Confer This Sacrament?

We proceed thus to the Second Article:—

Objection 1. It would seem that deacons can confer this sacrament. For, according to Dionysius *(Eccl. Hier.* v) *deacons have the power to cleanse.* Now this sacrament was instituted precisely to cleanse from sickness of the mind and body. Therefore deacons also can confer it.

Obj. 2. Further, Baptism is a more excellent sacrament than the one of which we are speaking. But deacons can baptize, as instanced by the Blessed Laurence. Therefore they can confer this sacrament also.

On the contrary, It is written (James v. 14): *Let him bring in the priests of the Church.*

I answer that, A deacon has the power to cleanse but not to enlighten. Hence, since enlightenment is an effect of grace, no sacrament whereby grace is conferred can be given by a deacon in virtue of his office: and so he cannot confer this sacrament, since grace is bestowed therein.

Reply Obj. 1. This sacrament cleanses by enlightening through the bestowal of grace: wherefore a deacon is not competent to confer it.

Reply Obj. 2. This is not a necessary sacrament, as Baptism is. Hence its bestowal is not committed to all in cases of necessity, but only to those who are competent to do so in virtue of their office. Nor are deacons competent to baptize in virtue of their office.

THIRD ARTICLE

Whether None But a Bishop Can Confer This Sacrament?

We proceed thus to the Third Article:—

Objection 1. It would seem that none but a bishop can confer this sacrament. For this sacrament consists in an anointing, just as Confirmation does. Now none but a bishop can confirm. Therefore only a bishop can confer this sacrament.

Obj. 2. Further, he who cannot do what is less cannot do what is greater. Now the use of consecrated matter surpasses the act of consecrating the matter, since the former is the end of the latter. Therefore since a priest cannot consecrate the matter, neither can he use the matter after it has been consecrated.

On the contrary, The minister of this sacrament has to be brought in to the recipient as is clear from James v. 14. Now a bishop cannot go to all the sick people of his diocese. Therefore the bishop is not the only one who can confer this sacrament.

I answer that, According to Dionysius *(Eccl. Hier.* v), the office of perfecting belongs to a bishop, just as it belongs to a priest to enlighten. Wherefore those sacraments are reserved to a bishop's dispensation, which place the recipient in a state of perfection above others. But this is not the case with this sacrament, for it is given to all. Consequently it can be given by ordinary priests.

Reply Obj. 1. Confirmation imprints a character, whereby man is placed in a state of perfection, as stated above (P. III, Q. 63 AA. 1, 2, 6). But this does not take place in this sacrament; hence there is no comparison.

Reply Obj. 2. Although the use of consecrated matter is of more importance than the consecration of the matter, from the point of view of the final cause; nevertheless, from the point of view of efficient cause, the consecration of the matter is the more important since the use of the matter is dependent thereon, as on its active cause: hence the consecration of the matter demands a higher power than the use of the matter does.

QUESTION 32

On Whom Should This Sacrament Be Conferred and on What Part of the Body?

(In Seven Articles)

WE must now consider on whom this sacrament should be conferred and on what part of the body: under which head there are seven points of inquiry: (1) Whether this sacrament should be conferred on those who are in good health? (2) Whether it should be conferred in any kind of sickness? (3) Whether it should be conferred on madmen and imbeciles? (4) Whether it should be given to children? (5) Whether, in this sacrament, the whole body should be anointed? (6) Whether certain parts are suitably assigned to be anointed?

(7) Whether those who are deformed in the above parts ought to be anointed thereon?

FIRST ARTICLE

Whether This Sacrament Ought to Be Conferred on Those Who Are in Good Health?

We proceed thus to the First Article:—

Objection 1. It would seem that this sacrament should be conferred even on those who are in good health. For the healing of the mind is a more important effect of this sacrament than the healing of the body, as stated above (Q. 30, A. 2). Now even those who are healthy in body need to be healed in mind. Therefore this sacrament should be conferred on them also.

Obj. 2. Further, this is the sacrament of those who are departing this life, just as Baptism is the sacrament of those who are entering this life. Now Baptism is given to all who enter. Therefore this sacrament should be given to all who are departing. But sometimes those who are near departure are in good health, for instance those who are to be beheaded. Therefore this sacrament should be conferred on them.

On the contrary, It is written 'James v. 14): *Is any man sick among you,* etc. Therefore none but the sick are competent to receive this sacrament.

I answer that, This sacrament is a spiritual healing, as stated above (Q. 30, AA. 1, 2), and is signified by way of a healing of the body. Hence this sacrament should not be conferred on those who are not subjects for bodily healing, those namely, who are in good health.

Reply Obj. 1. Although spiritual health is the principal effect of this sacrament, yet this same spiritual healing needs to be signified by a healing of the body, although bodily health may not actually ensue. Consequently spiritual health can be conferred by this sacrament on those alone who are competent to receive bodily healing, viz. the sick; even as he alone can receive Baptism who is capable of a bodily washing, and not a child yet in its mother's womb.

Reply Obj. 2. Even those who are entering into life cannot receive Baptism unless they are capable of a bodily washing. And so those who are departing this life cannot receive this sacrament, unless they be subjects for a bodily healing.

SECOND ARTICLE

Whether This Sacrament Ought to Be Given in Any Kind of Sickness?

We proceed thus to the Second Article:—

Objection 1. It would seem that this sacrament should be given in any kind of sickness. For no kind of sickness is determined in the fifth chapter of James where this sacrament is delivered to us. Therefore this sacrament should be given in all kinds of sickness.

Obj. 2. Further, the more excellent a remedy is, the more generally should it be available. Now this sacrament is more excellent than bodily medicine. Since then bodily medicine is given to all manner of sick persons, it seems that this sacrament should be given in like manner to all.

On the contrary, This sacrament is called by all Extreme Unction. Now it is not every sickness that brings man to the extremity of his life, since some ailments prolong life, according to the Philosopher (*De Long. et Brev. Vitæ* i). Therefore this sacrament should not be given in every case of sickness.

I answer that, This sacrament is the last remedy that the Church can give, since it is an immediate preparation for glory. Therefore it ought to be given to those only, who are so sick as to be in a state of departure from this life, through their sickness being of such a nature as to cause death, the danger of which is to be feared.

Reply Obj. 1. Any sickness can cause death, if it be aggravated. Hence if we consider the different kinds of disease, there is none in which this sacrament cannot be given; and for this reason the apostle does not determine any particular one. But if we consider the degree and the stage of the complaint, this sacrament should not be given to every sick person.

Reply Obj. 2. The principal effect of bodily medicine is bodily health, which all sick people lack, whatever be the stage of their sickness. But the principal effect of this sacrament is that immunity from disorder which is needed by those who are taking their departure from this life and setting out for the life of glory. Hence the comparison fails.

THIRD ARTICLE

Whether This Sacrament Ought to Be Given to Madmen and Imbeciles?

We proceed thus to the Third Article:—

Objection 1. It would seem that this sacrament should be given to madmen and imbeciles. For these diseases are full of danger and cause death quickly. Now when there is danger it is the time to apply the remedy. Therefore this sacrament, which was intended as a remedy to human weakness, should be given to such people.

Obj. 2. Further, Baptism is a greater sacrament than this. Now Baptism is conferred on mad people as stated above (P. III, Q. 68,

A. 12). Therefore this sacrament also should be given to them.

On the contrary, This sacrament should be given to none but such as acknowledge it. Now this does not apply to madmen and imbeciles. Therefore it should not be given to them.

I answer that, The devotion of the recipient, the personal merit of the minister, and the general merits of the whole Church, are of great account towards the reception of the effect of this sacrament. This is evident from the fact that the form of this sacrament is pronounced by way of a prayer. Hence it should not be given those who cannot acknowledge it, and especially to madmen and imbeciles, who might dishonor the sacrament by their offensive conduct, unless they have lucid intervals, when they would be capable of acknowledging the sacrament, for then the sacrament should be given to children the same in that state.

Reply Obj. 1. Although such people are sometimes in danger of death, yet the remedy cannot be applied to them, on account of their lack of devotion. Hence it should not be given to them.

Reply Obj. 2. Baptism does not require a movement of the free-will, because it is given chiefly as a remedy for original sin, which, in us, is not taken away by a movement of the free-will. On the other hand this sacrament requires a movement of the free-will; wherefore the comparison fails. Moreover Baptism is a necessary sacrament, while Extreme Unction is not.

FOURTH ARTICLE

Whether This Sacrament Should Be Given to Children?

We proceed thus to the Fourth Article:—

Objection 1. It would seem that this sacrament ought to be given to children. Because children suffer from the same ailments sometimes as adults. Now the same disease requires the same remedy. Therefore this sacrament should be given to children the same as to adults.

Obj. 2. Further, this sacrament is given in order to remove the remnants of sin, whether original or actual, as stated above (Q. 30, A. 1). Now the remnants of original sin are in children. Therefore this sacrament should be given to them.

On the contrary, This sacrament should be given to none but those to whom the form applies. But the form of this sacrament does not apply to children, since they have not sinned by sight and hearing; as expressed in the form. Therefore this sacrament should not be given to them.

I answer that, This sacrament, like the Eucharist, requires actual devotion in the recipient. Therefore, just as the Eucharist ought not to be given to children, so neither ought this sacrament to be given to them.

Reply Obj. 1. Children's infirmities are not caused by actual sin, as in adults, and this sacrament is given chiefly as a remedy for infirmities that result from sins, being the remnants of sin, as it were.

Reply Obj. 2. This sacrament is not given as a remedy for the remnants of original sin, except in so far as they gather strength, so to speak, from actual sins. Hence from the very form it appears that it is given chiefly as a remedy for actual sins, which are not in children.

FIFTH ARTICLE

Whether the Whole Body Should Be Anointed in This Sacrament?

We proceed thus to the Fifth Article:—

Objection 1. It would seem that the whole body should be anointed in this sacrament. For, according to Augustine *(De Trin.* vi. 6), *the whole soul is in every part of the body.* Now this sacrament is given chiefly in order to heal the soul. Therefore the whole body ought to be anointed.

Obj. 2. Further, the remedy should be applied to the part affected by the disease. But sometimes the disease is general, and affects the whole body, as a fever does. Therefore the whole body should be anointed.

Obj. 3. Further, in Baptism the whole body is dipped under the water. Therefore in this sacrament the whole body should be anointed.

On the contrary, stands the rite observed throughout the Church, according to which in this sacrament the sick man is anointed, only in certain fixed parts of the body.

I answer that, This sacrament is shown to us under the form of a healing. Now bodily healing has to be effected, by applying the remedy, not to the whole body, but to those parts where the root of the disease is seated. Consequently the sacramental unction also ought to be applied to those parts only in which the spiritual sickness is rooted.

Reply Obj. 1. Although the whole soul is as to its essence, in each part of the body, it is not as to its powers which are the roots of sinful acts. Hence certain fixed parts have to be anointed, those, namely, in which powers have their being.

Reply Obj. 2. The remedy is not always applied to the part affected by the disease, but, with greater reason, to the part where the root of the disease is seated.

Reply Obj. 3. Baptism is given under the

form of washing: and a bodily washing cleanses only the part to which it is applied; for this reason Baptism is applied to the whole body. It is different with Extreme Unction, for the reason given above.

SIXTH ARTICLE

Whether the Parts to Be Anointed Are Suitably Assigned?

We proceed thus to the Sixth Article:—

Objection 1. It would seem that these parts are unsuitably assigned, namely, that the eyes, nose, ears, lips, hands, and feet should be anointed. For a wise physician heals the disease in its root. Now *from the heart come forth thoughts . . . that defile a man* (Matth. xv. 19, 20). Therefore the breast ought to be anointed.

Obj. 2. Further, purity of mind is not less necessary to those who are departing this life than to those who are entering therein. Now those who are entering are anointed with chrism on the head by the priest, to signify purity of mind. Therefore in this sacrament those who are departing should be anointed on the head.

Obj. 3. Further, the remedy should be applied where the disease is most virulent. Now spiritual sickness is most virulent in the loins in men, and in the navel in women, according to Job. xl. 11: *His strength is in his loins, and his force in the navel of his belly,* as Gregory expounds the passage *(Moral.* xxxii. 11). Therefore these parts should be anointed.

Obj. 4. Further, sins are committed with other parts of the body, no less than with the feet. Therefore, as the feet are anointed, so ought other members of the body to be anointed.

I answer that, The principles of sinning are the same in us as the principles of action, for a sin is an act. Now there are in us three principles of action; the first is the directing principle, namely, the cognitive power; the second is the commanding principle, namely, the appetitive power; the third is the executive principle, namely, the motive power.

Now all our knowledge has its origin in the senses. And, since the remedy for sin should be applied where sin originates in us first, for that reason the places of the five senses are anointed; the eyes, to wit, on account of the sight, the ears on account of hearing, the nostrils on account of the smell, the mouth on account of the taste, the hands on account of the touch which is keenest in the finger tips, (in some places too the loins are anointed on account of the appetite), and the feet are anointed on account of the motive power of

which they are the chief instrument. And since the cognitive power is the first principle of human activity, the anointing of the five senses is observed by all, as being essential to the sacrament. But some do not observe the other unctions,—some also anoint the feet but not the loins,—because the appetitive and motive powers are secondary principles.

Reply Obj. 1. No thought arises in the heart without an act of the imagination which is a movement proceeding from sensation *(De Anima* ii). Hence the primary root of thought is not the heart, but the sensory organs, except in so far as the heart is a principle of the whole body, albeit a remote principle.

Reply Obj. 2. Those who enter have to receive purity of the mind, whereas those who are departing have to cleanse the mind. Hence the latter need to be anointed in those parts in respect of which the mind's purity may be sullied.

Reply Obj. 3. Some are wont to anoint the loins, because they are the chief seat of the concupiscible appetite: however, as stated above, the appetitive power is not the primary root.

Reply Obj. 4. The bodily organs which are the instruments of sin, are the feet, hands, and tongue, all of which are anointed, and the organs of generation which it would be unbecoming to anoint, on account of their uncleanliness, and out of respect for the sacrament.

SEVENTH ARTICLE

Whether Those Who Are Deformed in Those Parts Should Be Anointed?

We proceed thus to the Seventh Article:—

Objection 1. It would seem that those who are deformed should not be anointed in those parts. For just as this sacrament demands a certain disposition on the part of the recipient, viz. that he should be sick, so it demands that he should be anointed in a certain part of the body. Now he that is not sick cannot be anointed. Therefore neither can he be anointed who lacks the part to be anointed.

Obj. 2. Further, a man born blind does not sin by his sight. Yet in the anointing of the eyes mention is made of sins by sight. Therefore this anointing ought not to be applied to one born blind, and in like manner as regards the other senses.

On the contrary, Bodily deformity is not an impediment to any other sacrament. Therefore it should not be an impediment to this one. Now each of the anointings is essential to the sacrament. Therefore all should be applied to those who are deformed.

I answer that, Even those who are deformed

should be anointed, and that as near as possible to the part which ought to have been anointed. For though they have not the members, nevertheless, they have, at least radically, the powers of the soul, corresponding to those members, and they may commit inwardly the sins that pertain to those members, though they cannot outwardly.

This suffices for the *Replies* to the *Objections*.

QUESTION 33

Of the Repetition of This Sacrament

(In Two Articles)

WE must now consider the repetition of this sacrament: under which head there are two points of inquiry: (1) Whether this sacrament ought to be repeated? (2) Whether it ought to be repeated during the same sickness?

FIRST ARTICLE

Whether This Sacrament Ought to Be Repeated?

We proceed thus to the First Article:—

Objection 1. It would seem that this sacrament ought not to be repeated. For the anointing of a man is of greater import than the anointing of a stone. But the anointing of an altar is not repeated, unless the altar be shattered. Neither, therefore, should Extreme Unction, whereby a man is anointed, be repeated.

Obj. 2. Further, nothing comes after what is extreme. But this unction is called extreme. Therefore it should not be repeated.

On the contrary, This sacrament is a spiritual healing applied under the form of a bodily cure. But a bodily cure is repeated. Therefore this sacrament also can be repeated.

I answer that, No sacramental or sacrament, having an effect that lasts for ever, can be repeated, because this would imply that the sacrament had failed to produce that effect; and this would be derogatory to the sacrament. On the other hand a sacrament whose effect does not last for ever, can be repeated without disparaging that sacrament, in order that the lost effect may be recovered. And since health of body and soul, which is the effect of this sacrament, can be lost after it has been effected, it follows that this sacrament can, without disparagement thereto, be repeated.

Reply Obj. 1. The stone is anointed in order that the altar may be consecrated, and the stone remains consecrated, as long as the altar remains, hence it cannot be anointed again. But a man is not consecrated by being anointed, since it does not imprint a character on him. Hence there is no comparison.

Reply Obj. 2. What men think to be extreme is not always extreme in reality. It is thus that this sacrament is called Extreme Unction, because it ought not to be given save to those whose death men think to be nigh.

SECOND ARTICLE

Whether This Sacrament Ought to Be Repeated During the Same Sickness?

We proceed thus to the Second Article:—

Objection 1. It would seem that this sacrament ought not to be repeated during the same sickness. For one disease demands one remedy. Now this sacrament is a spiritual remedy. Therefore it ought not to be repeated for one sickness.

Obj. 2. Further, if a sick man could be anointed more than once during one disease, this might be done for a whole day: which is absurd.

On the contrary, Sometimes a disease lasts long after the sacrament has been received, so that the remnants of sin, against which chiefly this sacrament is given, would be contracted. Therefore it ought to be given again.

I answer that, This sacrament regards not only the sickness, but also the state of the sick man, because it ought not to be given except to those sick people who seem, in man's estimation, to be nigh to death. Now some diseases do not last long; so that if this sacrament is given at the time that the sick man is in a state of danger of death, he does not leave that state except the disease be cured, and thus he needs not to be anointed again. But if he has a relapse, it will be a second sickness, and he can be anointed again. On the other hand some diseases are of long duration, as hectic fever, dropsy and the like, and those who lie sick of them should not be anointed until they seem to be in danger of death. And if the sick man escape that danger while the disease continues, and be brought again thereby to the same state of danger, he can be anointed again, because it is, as it were, another state of sickness, although strictly speaking, it is not another sickness. This suffices for the *Replies* to the *Objections*.

QUESTION 34

Of the Sacrament of Order As to Its Essence and Its Parts

(In Five Articles)

IN the next place we must consider the sacrament of Order: (1) Order in general; (2) the difference of Orders; (3) those who confer Orders; (4) the impediments to receiving Orders; (5) things connected with Orders.

Concerning Order in general three points have to be considered: (1) Its essence, quiddity, and parts. (2) Its effect. (3) The recipients of Orders.

Under the first head there are five points of inquiry: (1) Whether there should be Order in the Church? (2) Whether it is fittingly defined? (3) Whether it is a sacrament? (4) Whether its form is expressed properly? (5) Whether this sacrament has any matter?

FIRST ARTICLE

Whether There Should Be Order in the Church?

We proceed thus to the First Article:—

Objection 1. It would seem that there should not be Order in the Church. For Order requires subjection and preëminence. But subjection seemingly is incompatible with the liberty whereunto we are called by Christ. Therefore there should not be Order in the Church.

Obj. 2. Further, he who has received an Order becomes another's superior. But in the Church everyone should deem himself lower than another (Phil. ii. 3): *Let each esteem others better than themselves.* Therefore Order should not be in the Church.

Obj. 3. Further, we find Order among the angels on account of their differing in natural and gratuitous gifts. But all men are one in nature, and it is not known who has the higher gifts of grace. Therefore Order should not be in the Church.

On the contrary, Those things that are of God, are in order.* Now the Church is of God, for He Himself built it with His blood. Therefore there ought to be Order in the Church.

Further, the state of the Church is between the state of nature and the state of glory. Now we find order in nature, in that some things are above others, and likewise in glory, as in the angels. Therefore there should be Order in the Church.

I answer that, God wished to produce His works in likeness to Himself, as far as possible, in order that they might be perfect, and that He might be known through them. Hence, that He might be portrayed in His works, not only according to what He is in Himself, but also according as He acts on others, He laid this natural law on all things, that last things should be reduced and perfected by middle things, and middle things by the first, as Dionysius says *(Eccl. Hier.* v). Wherefore that this beauty might not be lacking to the Church, He established Order in her so that some should deliver the sacraments to others, being thus made like to God in their own way, as co-operating with God; even as in the natural body, some members act on others.

Reply Obj. 1. The subjection of slavery is incompatible with liberty; for slavery consists in lording over others and employing them for one's own profit. Such subjection is not required in Order, whereby those who preside have to seek the salvation of their subjects and not their own profit.

Reply Obj. 2. Each one should esteem himself lower in merit, not in office; and Orders are a kind of office.

Reply Obj. 3. Order among the angels does not arise from difference of nature, unless accidentally, in so far as difference of grace results in them from difference of nature. But in them it results directly from their difference in grace; because their orders regard their participation of divine things, and their communicating them in the state of glory, which is according to the measure of grace, as being the end and effect, so to speak, of grace. On the other hand, the Orders of the Church militant regard the participation in the sacraments and the communication thereof, which are the cause of grace and, in a way, precede grace; and consequently our Orders do not require sanctifying grace, but only the power to dispense the sacraments; for which reason Order does not correspond to the difference of sanctifying grace, but to the difference of power.

SECOND ARTICLE

Whether Order Is Properly Defined?

We proceed thus to the Second Article:—

Objection 1. It would seem that Order is improperly defined by the Master (iv. *Sent.* D. 53), where it is said *Order is a seal of the Church, whereby spiritual power is conferred on the person ordained.* For a part should not be described as the genus of the whole. Now the character which is denoted by the seal in

* Vulg.,—*Those* (powers) *that are, are ordained of God.*

a subsequent definition is a part of order, since it is placed in contradistinction with that which is either reality only, or sacrament only, since it is both reality and sacrament. Therefore seal should not be mentioned as the genus of Order.

Obj. 2. Further, just as a character is imprinted in the sacrament of Order, so is it in the sacrament of Baptism. Now character was not mentioned in the definition of Baptism. Therefore neither should it be mentioned in the definition of Order.

Obj. 3. Further, in Baptism there is also given a certain spiritual power to approach the sacraments; and again it is a seal, since it is a sacrament. Therefore this definition is applicable to Baptism; and consequently it is improperly applied to Order.

Obj. 4. Further, Order is a kind of relation, and relation is realized in both its terms. Now the terms of the relation of Order are the superior and the inferior. Therefore inferiors have Order as well as superiors. Yet there is no power of preëminence in them, such as is mentioned here in the definition of Order, as appears from the subsequent explanation *(loc. cit.)*, where promotion to power is mentioned. Therefore Order is improperly defined there.

I answer that, The Master's definition of Order applies to Order as a sacrament of the Church. Hence he mentions two things, namely the outward sign, a *kind of seal,* i.e. a kind of sign, and the inward effect, *whereby spiritual power,* etc.

Reply Obj. 1. Seal stands here, not for the inward character, but for the outward action, which is the sign and cause of inward power; and this is also the sense of character in the other definition. If, however, it be taken for the inward character, the definition would not be unsuitable; because the division of a sacrament into those three things is not a division into integral parts, properly speaking; since what is reality only is not essential to the sacrament, and that which is the sacrament is transitory; while that which is sacrament and reality is said to remain. Wherefore it follows that inward character itself is essentially and principally the sacrament of Order.

Reply Obj. 2. Although in Baptism there is conferred a spiritual power to receive the other sacraments, for which reason it imprints a character, nevertheless this is not its principal effect, but the inward cleansing; wherefore Baptism would be given even though the former motive did not exist. On the other hand, Order denotes power principally. Wherefore the character which is a spiritual power is included in the definition of Order, but not in that of Baptism.

Reply Obj. 3. In Baptism there is given a

certain spiritual potentiality to receive, and consequently a somewhat passive potentiality. But power properly denotes active potentiality, together with some kind of preëminence. Hence this definition is not applicable to Baptism.

Reply Obj. 4. The word "order" is used in two ways. For sometimes it denotes the relation itself, and thus it is both in the inferior and in the superior, as the objection states; but it is not thus that we use the word here. On the other hand, it denotes the degree which results in the order taken in the first sense. And since the notion of order as relation is observed where we first meet with something higher than another, it follows that this degree of preëminence by spiritual power is called Order.

THIRD ARTICLE

Whether Order Is a Sacrament?

We proceed thus to the Third Article:—

Objection 1. It would seem that Order is not a sacrament. For a sacrament, according to Hugh of S. Victor *(De Sacram.* i) is *a material element.* Now Order denotes nothing of the kind, but rather relation or power; since Order is a part of power according to Isidore. Therefore it is not a sacrament.

Obj. 2. Further, the sacraments do not concern the Church triumphant. Yet Order is there, as in the angels. Therefore it is not a sacrament.

Obj. 3. Further, just as spiritual authority, which is Order, is given by means of consecration, so is secular authority, since kings also are anointed, as stated above (Q. 19, A. 3, *ad* 2). But the kingly power is not a sacrament. Therefore neither is Order of which we speak now.

On the contrary, It is mentioned by all among the seven sacraments of the Church.

Further, *the cause of a thing being such, is still more so.* Now Order is the cause of man being the dispenser of the other sacraments. Therefore Order has more reason for being a sacrament than the others.

I answer that, As stated above (Q. 29, A. 1; P. III, Q. 60), a sacrament is nothing else than a sanctification conferred on man with some outward sign. Wherefore, since by receiving Orders a consecration is conferred on man by visible signs, it is clear that Order is a sacrament.

Reply Obj. 1. Although Order does not by its name express a material element, it is not conferred without some material element.

Reply Obj. 2. Power must needs be proportionate to the purpose for which it is intended. Now the communication of divine things, which is the purpose for which spiritual power is given, is not effected among the angels by means of sensible signs, as is the case among men. Hence the spiritual power that is Order is not bestowed on the angels by visible signs, as on men. Wherefore Order is a sacrament among men, but not among angels.

Reply Obj. 3. Not every blessing or consecration given to men is a sacrament, for both monks and abbots are blessed, and yet such blessings are not sacraments, and in like manner neither is the anointing of a king; because by such blessings men are not ordained to the dispensing of the divine sacraments, as by the blessing of Order. Hence the comparison fails.

FOURTH ARTICLE

Whether the Form of This Sacrament Is Suitably Expressed?

We proceed thus to the Fourth Article:—

Objection 1. It would seem that the form of this sacrament is unsuitably set forth in the text (iv. *Sent.* D. 24). Because the sacraments take their efficacy from their form. Now the efficacy of the sacraments is from the divine power, which works our salvation in them in a most hidden manner. Therefore the form of this sacrament should include a mention of the divine power by the invocation of the Trinity, as in the other sacraments.

Obj. 2. Further, to command pertains to one who has authority. Now the dispenser of the sacrament exercises no authority, but only ministry. Therefore he should not use the imperative mood by saying: *Do* or *Receive* this or that, or some similar expression.

Obj. 3. Further, mention should not be made in the sacramental form, except of such things as are essential to the sacrament. But the use of the power received is not essential to this sacrament, but is consequent upon it. Therefore it should not be mentioned in the form of this sacrament.

Obj. 4. Further, all the sacraments direct us to an eternal reward. But the forms of the other sacraments make no mention of a reward. Therefore neither should any mention be made thereof in the form of this sacrament, as in the words: *Since thou wilt have a share, if faithfully,* etc.

I answer that, This sacrament consists chiefly in the power conferred. Now power is conferred by power, as like proceeds from like; and again power is made known by its use, since powers are manifested by their acts. Wherefore in the form of Order the use of Order is expressed by the act which is commanded; and the conferring of power is expressed by employing the imperative mood.

Reply Obj. 1. The other sacraments are not

ordained chiefly to effects similar to the power whereby the sacraments are dispensed, as this sacrament is. Hence in this sacrament there is a kind of universal communication. Wherefore in the other sacraments something is expressed on the part of the divine power to which the effect of the sacrament is likened, but not in this sacrament.

Reply Obj. 2. [There is a special reason why this sacrament, rather than the others, is conferred by employing the imperative mood. For]* although the bishop who is the minister of this sacrament has no authority in respect of the conferring of this sacrament, nevertheless he has some power with regard to the power of Order, which power he confers, in so far as it is derived, from his.

Reply Obj. 3. The use of power is the effect of power in the genus of efficient cause, and from this point of view it has no reason to be mentioned in the definition of Order. But it is somewhat a cause in the genus of final cause, and from this point of view it can be placed in the definition of Order.

Reply Obj. 4. There is here a difference between this and the other sacraments. Because by this sacrament an office or the power to do something is conferred; and so it is fitting that mention be made of the reward to be obtained if it be administered faithfully. But in the other sacraments no such office or power to act is conferred, and so no mention of reward is made in them. Accordingly the recipient is somewhat passive in relation to the other sacraments, because he receives them for the perfecting of his own state only, whereas in relation to this sacrament he holds himself somewhat actively, since he receives it for the sake of exercising hierarchical duties in the Church. Wherefore although the other sacraments, from the very fact that they give grace, direct the recipient to salvation, properly speaking they do not direct him to a reward, in the same way as this sacrament does.

FIFTH ARTICLE

Whether This Sacrament Has Any Matter?

We proceed thus to the Fifth Article:—

Objection 1. It would seem that this sacrament has no matter. Because in every sacrament that has a matter the power that works in the sacrament is in the matter. But in the material objects which are used here, such as keys, candlesticks, and so forth, there is not apparently any power of sanctification. Therefore it has no matter.

Obj. 2. Further, in this sacrament the fulness of sevenfold grace is conferred, as stated in the text (iv. *Sent.* D. 24), just as in Con-

* The sentence in brackets is not in the Leonine edition.

firmation. But the matter of Confirmation requires to be consecrated beforehand. Since then the things which appear to be material in this sacrament are not consecrated beforehand, it would seem that they are not the matter of the sacrament.

Obj. 3. Further, in any sacrament that has matter there needs to be contact of matter with the recipient of the sacrament. Now, as some say, it is not essential to this sacrament that there be contact between the aforesaid material objects and the recipient of the sacrament, but only that they be presented to him. Therefore the aforesaid material objects are not the matter of this sacrament.

On the contrary, Every sacrament consists of things and words. Now in any sacrament the thing is the matter. Therefore the things employed in this sacrament are its matter.

Further, more is requisite to dispense the sacraments than to receive them. Yet Baptism, wherein the power is given to receive the sacraments, needs a matter. Therefore Order also does, wherein the power is given to dispense them.

I answer that, The matter employed outwardly in the sacraments signifies that the power which works in the sacraments comes entirely from without. Wherefore, since the effect proper to this sacrament, namely the character, is not received through any operation of the one who approaches the sacrament, as was the case in Penance, but comes wholly from without, it is fitting that it should have

a matter, yet otherwise than the other sacraments that have matter; because that which is bestowed in the other sacraments comes from God alone, and not from the minister who dispenses the sacrament; whereas that which is conferred in this sacrament, namely the spiritual power, comes also from him who gives the sacrament, as imperfect from perfect power. Hence the efficacy of the other sacraments resides chiefly in the matter which both signifies and contains the divine power through the sanctification applied by the minister; whereas the efficacy of this sacrament resides chiefly with him who dispenses the sacrament. And the matter is employed to show the powers conferred in particular by one who has it completely, rather than to cause power; and this is clear from the fact that the matter is in keeping with the use of power. This suffices for the *Reply* to the *First Objection.*

Reply Obj. 2. It is necessary for the matter to be consecrated in the other sacraments, on account of the power it contains; but it is not so in the case in point.

Reply Obj. 3. If we admit this assertion, the reason for it is clear from what we have said; for since the power of Order is received from the minister and not from the matter, the presenting of the matter is more essential to the sacrament than contact therewith. However, the words themselves of the form would seem to indicate that contact with the matter is essential to the sacrament, for it is said: *Receive* this or that.

QUESTION 35

Of the Effect of This Sacrament

(In Five Articles)

WE must next consider the effect of this sacrament. Under this head there are five points of inquiry: (1) Whether sanctifying grace is conferred in the sacrament of Order? (2) Whether a character is imprinted in connection with all the Orders? (3) Whether the character of Order presupposes of necessity the character of Baptism? (4) Whether it presupposes of necessity the character of Confirmation? (5) Whether the character of one Order presupposes of necessity the character of another Order?

FIRST ARTICLE

Whether Sanctifying Grace Is Conferred in the Sacrament of Order?

We proceed thus to the First Article:—

Objection 1. It would seem that sanctifying grace is not conferred in the sacrament of

Order. For it is commonly agreed that the sacrament of Order is directed to counteract the defect of ignorance. Now not sanctifying grace but gratuitous grace is given to counteract ignorance, for sanctifying grace has more to do with the will. Therefore sanctifying grace is not given in the sacrament of Order.

Obj. 2. Further, Order implies distinction. Now the members of the Church are distinguished, not by sanctifying but by gratuitous grace, of which it is said (1 Cor. xii. 4): *There are diversities of graces.* Therefore sanctifying grace is not given in Order.

Obj. 3. Further, no cause presupposes its effect. But grace is presupposed in one who receives Orders, so that he may be worthy to receive them. Therefore this same grace is not given in the conferring of Orders.

On the contrary, The sacraments of the New Law cause what they signify. Now Order by its sevenfold number signifies the seven gifts of the Holy Ghost, as stated in the text (iv. *Sent.* D. 24). Therefore the gifts of the Holy Ghost, which are not apart from sanctifying grace, are given in Orders.

Further, Order is a sacrament of the New Law. Now the definition of a sacrament of that kind includes the words, *that it may be a cause of grace.* Therefore it causes grace in the recipient.

I answer that, The works of God are perfect (Deut. xxxii. 4); and consequently whoever receives power from above receives also those things that render him competent to exercise that power. This is also the case in natural things, since animals are provided with members, by which their soul's powers are enabled to proceed to their respective actions unless there be some defect on the part of matter. Now just as sanctifying grace is necessary in order that man receive the sacraments worthily, so is it that he may dispense them worthily. Wherefore as in Baptism, whereby a man is adapted to receive the other sacraments, sanctifying grace is given, so is it in the sacrament of Order whereby man is ordained to the dispensation of the other sacraments.

Reply Obj. 1. Order is given as a remedy, not to one person but to the whole Church. Hence, although it is said to be given in order to counteract ignorance, it does not mean that by receiving Orders a man has his ignorance driven out of him, but that the recipient of Orders is set in authority to expel ignorance from among the people.

Reply Obj. 2. Although the gifts of sanctifying grace are common to all the members of the Church, nevertheless a man cannot be the worthy recipient of those gifts, in respect of which the members of the Church are distinguished from one another, unless he have charity, and this cannot be apart from sanctifying grace.

Reply Obj. 3. The worthy exercise of Orders requires not any kind of goodness but excellent goodness, in order that as they who receive Orders are set above the people in the degree of Order, so may they be above them by the merit of holiness. Hence they are required to have the grace that suffices to make them worthy members of Christ's people, but when they receive Orders they are given a yet greater gift of grace, whereby they are rendered apt for greater things.

SECOND ARTICLE

Whether in the Sacrament of Order a Character Is Imprinted in Connection with All the Orders?

We proceed thus to the Second Article:—

Objection 1. It would seem that in the sacrament of Order a character is not imprinted in connection with all the Orders. For the character of Order is a spiritual power. Now some Orders are directed only to certain bodily acts, for instance those of the doorkeeper or of the acolyte. Therefore a character is not imprinted in these Orders.

Obj. 2. Further, every character is indelible. Therefore a character places a man in a state whence he cannot withdraw. Now those who have certain Orders can lawfully return to the laity. Therefore a character is not imprinted in all the Orders.

Obj. 3. Further, by means of a character a man is appointed to give or to receive some sacred thing. Now a man is sufficiently adapted to the reception of the sacraments by the character of Baptism, and a man is not appointed to dispense the sacraments except in the Order of priesthood. Therefore a character is not imprinted in the other Orders.

On the contrary, Every sacrament in which a character is not imprinted can be repeated. But no order can be repeated. Therefore a character is imprinted in each Order.

Further, a character is a distinctive sign. Now there is something distinct in every Order. Therefore every Order imprints a character.

I answer that, There have been three opinions on this point. For some have said that a character is imprinted only in the Order of priesthood; but this is not true, since none but a deacon can exercise the act of the diaconate, and so it is clear that in the dispensation of the sacraments, he has a spiritual power which others have not. For this reason others have said that a character is impressed in the sacred, but not in the minor, Orders. But this again comes to nothing, since each Order sets a man above the people in some degree of authority directed to the dispensation of the sacraments. Wherefore since a character is a sign whereby one thing is distinguished from another, it follows that a character is imprinted in each Order. And this is confirmed by the fact that they remain for ever and are never repeated. This is the third and more common opinion.

Reply Obj. 1. Each Order either has an act connected with the sacrament itself, or adapts a man to the dispensation of the sacraments; thus doorkeepers exercise the act of admitting men to witness the Divine sacraments, and so forth; and consequently a spiritual power is required in each.

Reply Obj. 2. For all that a man may return to the laity, the character always remains in him. This is evident from the fact that if he return to the clerical state, he does not receive again the Order which he had already.

The *Reply* to the *Third Objection* is the same as to the *First*.

THIRD ARTICLE

Whether the Character of Order Presupposes the Baptismal Character?

We proceed thus to the Third Article:—

Objection 1. It would seem that the character of Order does not presuppose the character of Baptism. For the character of Order makes a man a dispenser of the sacraments; while the character of Baptism makes him a recipient of them. Now active power does not necessarily presuppose passive power, for it can be without it, as in God. Therefore the character of Order does not necessarily presuppose the character of Baptism.

Obj. 2. Further, it may happen that a man is not baptized, and yet think with probability that he has been baptized. If therefore such a person present himself for Orders, he will not receive the character of Order, supposing the character of Order to presuppose the character of Baptism; and consequently whatever he does by way of consecration or absolution will be invalid, and the Church will be deceived therein, which is inadmissible.

On the contrary, Baptism is the door of the sacraments. Therefore since Order is a sacrament, it presupposes Baptism.

I answer that, No one can receive what he has not the power to receive. Now the character of Baptism gives a man the power to receive the other sacraments. Wherefore he that has not the baptismal character, can receive no other sacrament; and consequently the character of Order presupposes the character of Baptism.

Reply Obj. 1. In one who has active power of himself, the active does not presuppose the passive power; but in one who has active power from another, passive power, whereby he is enabled to receive the active power, is prerequisite to active power.

Reply Obj. 2. Such a man if he be ordained to the priesthood is not a priest, and he can neither consecrate, nor absolve in the tribunal of Penance. Wherefore according to the canons he must be baptized, and reordained (Extra, *De Presbyt. non Bapt.,* cap. *Si quis;* cap. *Veniens*). And even though he be raised to the episcopate, those whom he ordains receive not the Order. Yet it may piously be believed that as regards the ultimate effects of the sacraments, the High Priest will supply the defect, and that He would not allow this to be so hidden as to endanger the Church.

FOURTH ARTICLE

Whether the Character of Order Necessarily Presupposes the Character of Confirmation?

We proceed thus to the Fourth Article:—

Objection 1. It would seem that the character of Order necessarily presupposes the character of Confirmation. For in things subordinate to one another, as the middle presupposes the first, so does the last presuppose the middle. Now the character of Confirmation presupposes that of Baptism as being the first. Therefore the character of Order presupposes that of Confirmation as being in the middle.

Obj. 2. Further, those who are appointed to confirm should themselves be most firm. Now those who receive the sacrament of Order are appointed to confirm others. Therefore they especially should have received the sacrament of Confirmation.

On the contrary, The apostles received the power of Order before the Ascension (Jo. xx. 22), where it is said: *Receive the Holy Ghost.* But they were confirmed after the Ascension by the coming of the Holy Ghost. Therefore Order does not presuppose Confirmation.

I answer that, For the reception of Orders something is prerequisite for the validity of the sacrament, and something as congruous to the sacrament. For the validity of the sacrament it is required that one who presents himself for Orders should be capable of receiving them, and this is competent to him through Baptism; wherefore the baptismal character is prerequisite for the validity of the sacrament, so that the sacrament of Order cannot be conferred without it. On the other hand, as congruous to the sacrament a man is required to have every perfection whereby he becomes adapted to the exercise of Orders, and one of these is that he be confirmed. Wherefore the character of Order presupposes the character of Confirmation as congruous but not as necessary.

Reply Obj. 1. In this case the middle does not stand in the same relation to the last as the first to the middle, because the character of Baptism enables a man to receive the sacrament of Confirmation, whereas the character of Confirmation does not enable a man to receive the sacrament of Order. Hence the comparison fails.

Reply Obj. 2. This argument considers aptness by way of congruity.

FIFTH ARTICLE

Whether the Character of One Order Necessarily Presupposes the Character of Another Order?

We proceed thus to the Fifth Article:—

Objection 1. It would seem that the character of one Order necessarily presupposes the character of another Order. For there is more in common between one Order and another, than between Order and another sacrament. But the character of Order presupposes the character of another sacrament, namely Baptism. Much more therefore does the character of one Order presuppose the character of another.

Obj. 2. Further, the Orders are degrees of a kind. Now no one can reach a further degree, unless he first mount the previous degree. Therefore no one can receive the character of a subsequent Order unless he has first received the preceding Order.

On the contrary, If anything necessary for a sacrament be omitted in that sacrament, the sacrament must be repeated. But if one receive a subsequent Order, without receiving a preceding Order, he is not reordained, but receives what was lacking, according to the canonical statutes (cap. *Tuæ literæ,* De clerico per salt. prom.). Therefore the preceding Order is not necessary for the following.

I answer that, It is not necessary for the higher Orders that one should have received the minor Orders, because their respective powers are distinct, and one, considered in its essentials, does not require another in the same subject. Hence even in the early Church some were ordained priests without having previously received the lower Orders, and yet they could do all that the lower Orders could, because the lower power is comprised in the higher, even as sense in understanding, and dukedom in kingdom. Afterwards, however, it was decided by the legislation of the Church that no one should present himself to the higher Orders who had not previously humbled himself in the lower offices. And hence it is that according to the Canons *(loc. cit.)* those who are ordained without receiving a preceding Order are not reordained, but receive what was lacking to them of the preceding Orders.

Reply Obj. 1. Orders have more in common with one another as regards specific likeness, than Order has with Baptism. But as regards proportion of power to action, Baptism has more in common with Order, than one Order with another, because Baptism confers on man the passive power to receive Orders, whereas a lower Order does not give him the passive power to receive higher Orders.

Reply Obj. 2. Orders are not degrees combining in one action or in one movement, so that it be necessary to reach the last through the first; but they are like degrees consisting in things of different kinds, such as the degrees between man and angel, and it is not necessary that one who is an angel be first of all a man. Such also are the degrees between the head and all members of the body; nor is it necessary that that which is the head should be previously a foot; and thus it is in the case in point.

QUESTION 36

Of the Qualities Required of Those Who Receive This Sacrament

(In Five Articles)

WE must next consider the qualities required of those who receive the sacrament of Order. Under this head there are five points of inquiry: (1) Whether goodness of life is required of those who receive this sacrament? (2) Whether the knowledge of the whole of Sacred Writ is required? (3) Whether the degree of Orders is obtained by mere merit of life? (4) Whether he who raises the unworthy to Orders sins? (5) Whether one who is in sin can without committing a sin exercise the Order he has received?

FIRST ARTICLE

Whether Goodness of Life Is Required of Those Who Receive Orders?

We proceed thus to the First Article:—

Objection 1. It would seem that goodness of life is not required of those who receive Orders. For by Orders a man is ordained to the dispensation of the sacraments. But the

* Vulg.,—*Say to Aaron: Whosoever of thy seed,* etc.

sacraments can be administered by good and wicked. Therefore goodness of life is not requisite.

Obj. 2. Further, the service of God in the sacraments is no greater than service offered to Him in the body. Now our Lord did not cast aside the sinful and notorious woman from rendering Him a bodily service (Luke vii). Therefore neither should the like be debarred from His service in the sacraments.

Obj. 3. Further, by every grace a remedy is given against sin. Now those who are in sin should not be refused a remedy that may avail them. Since then grace is given in the sacrament of Order, it would seem that this sacrament ought also to be conferred on sinners.

On the contrary, Whosoever of the seed of Aaron* throughout their families hath a blemish, he shall not offer bread to his God neither shall he approach to minister to him (Lev.

xxi. 17, 18). Now *blemish signifies all kinds of vice* according to a gloss. Therefore he who is shackled by any vice should not be admitted to the ministry of Orders.

Further, Jerome commenting on the words of Tit. ii. 15, *Let no man despise thee,* says that *not only should bishops, priests, and deacons take very great care to be examples of speech and conduct to those over whom they are placed, but also the lower grades, and without exception all who serve the household of God, since it is most disastrous to the Church if the laity be better than the clergy.* Therefore holiness of life is requisite in all the Orders.

I answer that, As Dionysius says (*Eccl. Hier.* iii), *even as the more subtle and clear essences, being filled by the outpouring of the solar radiance, like the sun enlighten other bodies with their brilliant light, so in all things pertaining to God a man must not dare to become a leader of others, unless in all his habits he be most deiform and godlike.* Wherefore, since in every Order a man is appointed to lead others in Divine things, he who being conscious of mortal sin presents himself for Orders is guilty of presumption and sins mortally. Consequently holiness of life is requisite for Orders, as a matter of precept, but not as essential to the sacrament; and if a wicked man be ordained, he receives the Order none the less, and yet with sin withal.

Reply Obj. 1. Just as the sinner dispenses sacraments validly, so does he receive validly the sacrament of Orders, and as he dispenses unworthily, even so he receives unworthily.

Reply Obj. 2. The service in point consisted only in the exercise of bodily homage, which even sinners can offer lawfully. It is different with the spiritual service to which the ordained are appointed, because thereby they are made to stand between God and the people. Wherefore they should shine with a good conscience before God, and with a good name before men.

Reply Obj. 3. Certain medicines require a robust constitution, else it is mortally dangerous to take them; others can be given to the weakly. So too in spiritual things certain sacraments are ordained as remedies for sin, and the like are to be given to sinners, as Baptism and Penance, while others, which confer the perfection of grace, require a man made strong by grace.

SECOND ARTICLE

Whether Knowledge of All Holy Writ Is Required?

We proceed thus to the Second Article:—

Objection 1. It would seem that knowledge of all Holy Writ is required. For one from whose lips we seek the law, should have knowledge of the law. Now the laity seek the law at the mouth of the priest (Malach. ii. 7). Therefore he should have knowledge of the whole law.

Obj. 2. Further, *being always ready to satisfy everyone that asketh you a reason of that faith** *and hope which is in you.* Now to give a reason for things pertaining to faith and hope belongs to those who have perfect knowledge of Holy Writ. Therefore the like knowledge should be possessed by those who are placed in Orders, and to whom the aforesaid words are addressed.

Obj. 3. Further, no one is competent to read what he understands not, since to *read without intelligence is negligence,*† as Cato declares (*Rudiment.*). Now it belongs to the reader (which is the lower Order) to read the Old Testament, as stated in the text (iv. *Sent.* D. 24). Therefore he should understand the whole of the Old Testament; and much more those in the higher Orders.

On the contrary, Many are raised to the priesthood even who know nothing at all of these things, even in many religious Orders. Therefore apparently this knowledge is not required.

Further, we read in the *Lives of the Fathers* that some who were monks were raised to the priesthood, being of a most holy life. Therefore the aforesaid knowledge is not required in those to be ordained.

I answer that, For any human act to be rightly ordered there must needs be the direction of reason. Wherefore in order that a man exercise the office of an Order, it is necessary for him to have as much knowledge as suffices for his direction in the act of that Order. And consequently one who is to be raised to Orders is required to have that knowledge, and to be instructed in Sacred Scripture, not the whole, but more or less, according as his office is of a greater or lesser extent—to wit, that those who are placed over others, and receive the care of souls, know things pertaining to the doctrine of faith and morals, and that others know whatever concerns the exercise of their Order.

Reply Obj. 1. A priest exercises a twofold action: the one, which is principal, over the true body of Christ; the other, which is secondary, over the mystical body of Christ. The second act depends on the first, but not conversely. Wherefore some are raised to the priesthood, to whom the first act alone is deputed, for instance those religious who are not empowered with the care of souls. The law is not sought at the mouth of these, they

---

* Vulg.,—*Of that hope which is in you.* S. Thomas apparently took his reading from Bede.
† *Legere et non intelligere est negligere.* The play on the words is more evident in the Latin.

are required only for the celebration of the sacraments; and consequently it is enough for them to have such knowledge as enables them to observe rightly those things that regard the celebration of the sacrament. Others are raised to exercise the other act which is over the mystical body of Christ, and it is at the mouth of these that the people seek the law; wherefore they ought to possess knowledge of the law, not indeed to know all the difficult points of the law (for in these they should have recourse to their superiors), but to know what the people have to believe and fulfill in the law. To the higher priests, namely the bishops, it belongs to know even those points of the law which may offer some difficulty, and to know them the more perfectly according as they are in a higher position.

Reply Obj. 2. The reason that we have to give for our faith and hope does not denote one that suffices to prove matters of faith and hope, since they are both of things invisible; it means that we should be able to give general proofs of the probability of both, and for this there is not much need of great knowledge.

Reply Obj. 3. The reader has not to explain Holy Writ to the people (for this belongs to the higher Orders), but merely to voice the words. Therefore he is not required to have so much knowledge as to understand Holy Writ, but only to know how to pronounce it correctly. And since such knowledge is obtained easily and from many persons, it may be supposed with probability that the ordained will acquire that knowledge even if he have it not already, especially if it appear that he is on the road to acquire it.

THIRD ARTICLE

Whether a Man Obtains the Degrees of Order by the Merit of One's Life?

We proceed thus to the Third Article:—

Objection 1. It would seem that a man obtains the degrees of Order by the mere merit of his life. For, according to Chrysostom,* *not every priest is a saint, but every saint is a priest.* Now a man becomes a saint by the merit of his life. Consequently he thereby also becomes a priest, and *a fortiori* has he the other Orders.

Obj. 2. Further, in natural things, men obtain a higher degree from the very fact that they are near God, and have a greater share of His favors, as Dionysius says *(Eccl. Hier.* iv). Now it is by merit of holiness and knowledge that a man approaches nearer to God and receives more of His favors. Therefore by this alone he is raised to the degree of Orders.

On the contrary, Holiness once possessed

can be lost. But when once a man is ordained he never loses his Order. Therefore Order does not consist in the mere merit of holiness.

I answer that, A cause should be proportionate to its effect. And consequently as in Christ, from Whom grace comes down on all men, there must needs be fulness of grace; so in the ministers of the Church, to whom it belongs, not to give grace, but to give the sacraments of grace, the degree of Order does not result from their having grace, but from their participating in a sacrament of grace.

Reply Obj. 1. Chrysostom is speaking of the priest in reference to the reason for which he is so called, the word *sacerdos* signifying dispenser of holy things *(sacra dans):* for in this sense every righteous man, in so far as he assists others by the sacraments, may be called a priest. But he is not speaking according to the actual meaning of the words; for this word *sacerdos* (priest) is employed to signify one who gives sacred things by dispensing the sacraments.

Reply Obj. 2. Natural things acquire a degree of superiority over others, from the fact that they are able to act on them by virtue of their form; wherefore from the very fact that they have a higher form, they obtain a higher degree. But the ministers of the Church are placed over others, not to confer anything on them by virtue of their own holiness (for this belongs to God alone), but as ministers, and as instruments, so to say, of the outpouring from the Head to the members. Hence the comparison fails as regards the dignity of Order, although it applies as to congruity.

FOURTH ARTICLE

Whether He Who Raises the Unworthy to Orders Commits a Sin?

We proceed thus to the Fourth Article:—

Objection 1. It would seem that he who raises the unworthy to Orders commits no sin. For a bishop needs assistants appointed to the lesser offices. But he would be unable to find them in sufficient number, if he were to require of them such qualifications as the saints enumerate. Therefore if he raise some who are not qualified, he would seem to be excusable.

Obj. 2. Further, the Church needs not only ministers for the dispensation of things spiritual, but also for the supervision of temporalities. But sometimes men without knowledge or holiness of life may be useful for the conduct of temporal affairs, either because of their worldly power, or on account of their natural industry. Therefore seemingly the like can be promoted without sin.

Obj. 3. Further, everyone is bound to avoid

---

* *Hom.* xliii, in the *Opus Imperfectum,* wrongly ascribed to S. John Chrysostom.

sin, as far as he can. If therefore a bishop sins in promoting the unworthy, he is bound to take the utmost pains to know whether those who present themselves for Orders be worthy, by making a careful inquiry about their morals and knowledge, and yet seemingly this is not done anywhere.

On the contrary, It is worse to raise the wicked to the sacred minstry, than not to correct those who are raised already. But Heli sinned mortally by not correcting his sons for their wickedness; wherefore *he fell backwards . . . and died* (1 Kings iv. 18). Therefore he who promotes the unworthy does not escape sin.

Further, spiritual things must be set before temporal things in the Church. Now a man would commit a mortal sin were he knowingly to endanger the temporalities of the Church. Much more therefore is it a mortal sin to endanger spiritual things. But whoever promotes the unworthy endangers spiritual things, since according to Gregory *(Hom. xii, in Ev.) if a man's life is contemptible, his preaching is liable to be despised;* and for the same reason all the spiritual things that he dispenses. Therefore he who promotes the unworthy sins mortally.

I answer that, Our Lord describes the faithful servant whom He has set *over His household to give them their measure of wheat.* Hence he is guilty of unfaithfulness who gives any man Divine things above his measure: and whoso promotes the unworthy does this. Wherefore he commits a mortal crime, as being unfaithful to his sovereign Lord, especially since this is detrimental to the Church and to the Divine honor which is promoted by good ministers. For a man would be unfaithful to his earthly lord were he to place unworthy subjects in his offices.

Reply Obj. 1. God never so abandons His Church that apt ministers are not to be found sufficient for the needs of the people, if the worthy be promoted and the unworthy set aside. And though it were impossible to find as many ministers as there are now, it were better to have few good ministers than many bad ones, as the blessed Clement declares in his second epistle to James the brother of the Lord.

Reply Obj. 2. Temporal things are not to be sought but for the sake of spiritual things. Wherefore all temporal advantage should count for nothing, and all gain be despised for the advancement of spiritual good.

Reply Obj. 3. It is at least required that the ordainer know that nothing contrary to holiness is in the candidate for ordination. But besides this he is required to take the greatest

* Cf. P. III, Q. 64, A. 6.

care, in proportion to the Order or office to be enjoined, so as to be certain of the qualifications of those to be promoted, at least from the testification of others. This is the meaning of the Apostle when he says (1 Tim. v. 22): *Impose not hands lightly on any man.*

FIFTH ARTICLE

Whether a Man Who Is in Sin Can without Sin Exercise the Order He Has Received? *

We proceed thus to the Fifth Article:—

Objection 1. It would seem that one who is in sin can without sin exercise the Order he has received. For since, by virtue of his office, he is bound to exercise his Order, he sins if he fails to do so. If therefore he sins by exercising it, he cannot avoid sin: which is inadmissible.

Obj. 2. Further, a dispensation is a relaxation of the law. Therefore although by rights it would be unlawful for him to exercise the Order he has received, it would be lawful for him to do so by dispensation.

Obj. 3. Further, whoever co-operates with another in a mortal sin, sins mortally. If therefore a sinner sins mortally by exercising his Order, he who receives or demands any Divine thing from him also sins mortally: and this seems absurd.

Obj. 4. Further, if he sins by exercising his Order, it follows that every act of his Order that he performs is a mortal sin; and consequently since many acts concur in the one exercise of his Order, it would seem that he commits many mortal sins: which seems very hard.

On the contrary, Dionysius says *(Ep. ad Demophil.): It seems presumptuous for such a man, one to wit who is not enlightened, to lay hands on priestly things; he is not afraid nor ashamed, all unworthy that he is, to take part in Divine things, with the thought that God does not see what he sees in himself; he thinks, by false pretense, to cheat Him Whom he falsely calls his Father; he dares to utter in the person of Christ, words polluted by his infamy, I will not call them prayers, over the Divine symbols.* Therefore a priest is a blasphemer and a cheat if he exercises his Order unworthily, and thus he sins mortally: and in like manner any other person in Orders.

Further, holiness of life is required in one who receives an Order, that he may be qualified to exercise it. Now a man sins mortally if he present himself for Orders in mortal sin. Much more therefore does he sin mortally whenever he exercises his Order.

I answer that, The law prescribes (Deut. xvi. 20) that *man should follow justly after that which is just.* Wherefore whoever fulfills unworthily the duties of his Order follows unjustly after that which is just, and acts contrary to a precept of the law, and thereby sins mortally. Now anyone who exercises a sacred office in mortal sin, without doubt does so unworthily. Hence it is clear that he sins mortally.

Reply Obj. 1. He is not perplexed as though he were in the necessity of sinning; for he can renounce his sin, or resign his office whereby he was bound to the exercise of his Order.

Reply Obj. 2. The natural law allows of no dispensation; and it is of natural law that man handle holy things holily. Therefore no one can dispense from this.

Reply Obj. 3. So long as a minister of the Church who is in mortal sin is recognized by the Church, his subject must receive the sacraments from him, since this is the purpose for which he is bound to him. Nevertheless, outside the case of necessity, it would not be safe to induce him to an execution of his Order, as long as he is conscious of being in mortal sin, which conscience, however, he can lay aside since a man is repaired in an instant by Divine grace.

Reply Obj. 4. When any man performs an action as a minister of the Church while in a state of mortal sin, he sins mortally, and as often as he performs that action, since, as Dionysius says (*Eccl. Hier.* i), *it is wrong for the unclean even to touch the symbols*, i.e. the sacramental signs. Hence when they touch sacred things in the exercise of their office they sin mortally. It would be otherwise if they were to touch some sacred thing or perform some sacred duty in a case of necessity, when it would be allowable even to a layman, for instance if they were to baptize in a case of urgency, or gather up the Lord's body should it be cast to the ground.

QUESTION 37

Of the Distinction of Orders, of Their Acts, and the Imprinting of the Character

(In Five Articles)

In the next place we must consider the distinction of the Orders and their acts, and the imprinting of the character. Under this head there are five points of inquiry: (1) Whether Order should be divided into several kinds? (2) How many are there? (3) Whether they ought to be divided into those that are sacred and those that are not? (4) Whether the acts of the Orders are rightly assigned in the text? (5) When are the characters of the Orders imprinted?

FIRST ARTICLE

Whether We Ought to Distinguish Several Orders?

We proceed thus to the First Article:—

Objection 1. It would seem that we ought not to distinguish several Orders. For the greater a power is, the less is it multiplied. Now this sacrament ranks above the others in so far as it places its recipients in a degree above other persons. Since then the other sacraments are not divided into several of which the whole is predicated, neither ought this sacrament to be divided into several Orders.

Obj. 2. Further, if it be divided, the parts of the division are either integral or subjective. But they are not integral, for then the whole would not be predicated of them. Therefore it is a division into subjective parts. Now subjective parts can have the remote genus predicated of them in the plural in the same way as the proximate genus; thus man and ass are several animals, and are several animated bodies. Therefore also priesthood and diaconate, as they are several Orders, even so are several sacraments, since sacrament is the genus, so to speak, in respect of Orders.

Obj. 3. Further, according to the Philosopher (*Ethic.* viii. 10) the form of authority in which one alone governs is a better government of the common weal than aristocracy, where different persons occupy different offices. But the government of the Church should be the best of all. Therefore in the Church there should be no distinction of Orders for different acts, but the whole power should reside in one person; and consequently there ought to be only one Order.

On the contrary, The Church is Christ's mystical body, like to our natural body, according to the Apostle (Rom. xii. 5; 1 Cor. xii. 12, 27; Eph. i. 22, 23; Col. i. 24). Now in the natural body there are various offices of the members. Therefore in the Church also there should be various Orders.

Further, the ministry of the New Testament is superior to that of the Old Testament (2 Cor. iii). Now in the Old Testament not only the priests, but also their ministers, the Levites, were consecrated. Therefore likewise in the New Testament not only the priests but also their ministers should be consecrated by the sacrament of Order; and consequently there ought to be several Orders.

I answer that, Multiplicity of Orders was introduced into the Church for three reasons.

First to show forth the wisdom of God, which is reflected in the orderly distinction of things both natural and spiritual. This is signified in the statement of 3 Kings. x. 4, 5 that *when the queen of Saba saw . . . the order of* Solomon's *servants . . . she had no longer any spirit in her,* for she was breathless from admiration of his wisdom. Secondly, in order to succor human weakness, because it would be impossible for one man, without his being heavily burdened, to fulfill all things pertaining to the Divine mysteries; and so various orders are severally appointed to the various offices; and this is shown by the Lord giving Moses seventy ancients to assist him. Thirdly, that men may be given a broader way for advancing (to perfection), seeing that the various duties are divided among many men, so that all become the co-operators of God; than which nothing is more God-like, as Dionysius says *(Eccles. Hier.* iii).

Reply Obj. 1. The other sacraments are given that certain effects may be received; but this sacrament is given chiefly that certain acts may be performed. Hence it behooves the sacrament of Order to be differentiated according to the diversity of acts, even as powers are differentiated by their acts.

Reply Obj. 2. The division of Order is not that of an integral whole into its parts, nor of a universal whole, but of a potential whole, the nature of which is that the notion of the whole is found to be complete in one part, but in the others by some participation thereof. Thus it is here: for the entire fulness of the sacrament is in one Order, namely the priesthood, while in the other sacraments there is a participation of Order. And this is signified by the Lord saying (Num. xi. 17): *I will take of thy spirit and give to them, that they may bear with thee the burden of the people.* Therefore all the Orders are one sacrament.

Reply Obj. 3. In a kingdom, although the entire fulness of power resides in the king, this does not exclude the ministers having a power which is a participation of the kingly power. It is the same in Order. In the aristocratic form of government, on the contrary, the fulness of power resides in no one, but in all.

SECOND ARTICLE

Whether There Are Seven Orders?

We proceed thus to the Second Article:—

Objection 1. It would seem that there are not seven Orders. For the Orders of the Church are directed to the hierarchical acts. But there are only three hierarchical acts, namely *to cleanse, to enlighten, and to perfect,* for which reason Dionysius distinguishes three

* Cf. Q. 40, A. 5.

Orders *(Eccles. Hier.* v). Therefore there are not seven.

Obj. 2. Further, all the sacraments derive their efficacy and authenticity from their institution by Christ, or at least by His apostles. But no mention except of priests and deacons is made in the teaching of Christ and His apostles. Therefore seemingly there are no other Orders.

Obj. 3. Further, by the sacrament of Order a man is appointed to dispense the other sacraments. But there are only six other sacraments. Therefore there should be only six Orders.

Obj. 4. *On the other hand,* It would seem that there ought to be more. For the higher a power is, the less is it subject to multiplication. Now the hierarchical power is in the angels in a higher way than in us, as Dionysius says *(Eccles. Hier.* i). Since then there are nine orders in the angelic hierarchy, there should be as many, or more, in the Church.

Obj. 5. Further, the prophecy of the Psalms is the most noble of all the prophecies. Now there is one Order, namely of readers, for reading the other prophecies in the Church. Therefore there ought to be another Order for reading the Psalms, especially since (Decret., Dist. xxi, cap. *Cleros)* the *psalmist* is reckoned as the second Order after the doorkeeper.

I answer that, Some show the sufficiency of the Orders from their correspondence with the gratuitous graces which are indicated 1 Cor. xii. For they say that the *word of wisdom* belongs to the bishop, because he is the ordainer of others, which pertains to wisdom; the *word of knowledge* to the priest, for he ought to have the key of knowledge; *faith* to the deacon, for he preaches the Gospel; the *working of miracles* to the subdeacon, who sets himself to do deeds of perfection by the vow of continency; *interpretation of speeches* to the acolyte, this being signified by the light which he bears; the *grace of healing* to the exorcist; *diverse kinds of tongues* to the psalmist; *prophecy* to the reader; and the *discerning of spirits* to the doorkeeper, for he excludes some and admits others. But this is of no account, for the gratuitous graces are not given, as the Orders are, to one same man. For it is written (1 Cor. xii. 4): *There are distributions* (Douay,—*diversities) of graces.* Moreover the episcopate* and the office of psalmist are included, which are not Orders. Wherefore others account for the Orders by likening them to the heavenly hierarchy, where the orders are distinguished in reference to cleansing, enlightening, and perfecting. Thus they say that the doorkeeper cleanses outwardly, by separating even in the body the good from the wicked; that the acolyte cleanses inwardly, because by the light which he bears, he signifies that he dispels inward darkness; and that the exorcist cleanses both ways, for he casts out the devil who disturbs a man both ways. But enlightening, which is effected by teaching, is done by readers as regards prophetic doctrine; by subdeacons as to apostolic doctrine; and by deacons as to the gospel doctrine; while ordinary perfection, such as the perfection of Penance, Baptism, and so forth, is the work of the priest; excellent perfection, such as the consecration of priests and virgins, is the work of the bishop; while the most excellent perfection is the work of the Sovereign Pontiff in whom resides the fulness of authority. But this again is of no account; both because the orders of the heavenly hierarchy are not distinguished by the aforesaid hierarchical actions, since each of them is applicable to every order; and because, according to Dionysius (Eccles. Hier. v), perfecting belongs to the bishops alone, enlightening to the priests, and cleansing to all the ministers.—Wherefore others suit the Orders to the seven gifts, so that the priesthood corresponds to the gift of wisdom, which feeds us with the bread of life and understanding, even as the priest refreshes us with the heavenly bread; fear to the doorkeeper, for he separates us from the wicked; and thus the intermediate Orders to the intermediate gifts. But this again is of no account, since the sevenfold grace is given in each one of the Orders. Consequently we must answer differently by saying that the sacrament of Order is directed to the sacrament of the Eucharist, which is the sacrament of sacraments, as Dionysius says (Eccles. Hier. iii). For just as temple, altar, vessels, and vestments need to be consecrated, so do the ministers who are ordained for the Eucharist; and this consecration is the sacrament of Order. Hence the distinction of Orders is derived from their relation to the Eucharist. For the power of Order is directed either to the consecration of the Eucharist itself, or to some ministry in connection with this sacrament of the Eucharist. If in the former way, then it is the Order of priests; hence when they are ordained, they receive the chalice with wine, and the paten with the bread, because they are receiving the power to consecrate the body and blood of Christ. The co-operation of the ministers is directed either to the sacrament itself, or to the recipients. If the former, this happens in three ways. For in the first place, there is the ministry whereby the minister co-operates with the priest in the sacrament itself, by dispensing, but not by consecrating, for this is done by the priest alone; and this belongs to the deacon. Hence in the text (iv. Sent. D. 24) it is said that it belongs to the deacon to minister to the priests in whatever is done in Christ's sacraments, wherefore he dispenses Christ's blood. Secondly, there is the ministry directed to the disposal of the sacramental matter in the sacred vessels of the sacrament; and this belongs to subdeacons. Wherefore it is stated in the text (ibid.) that they carry the vessels of our Lord's body and blood, and place the oblation on the altar; hence, when they are ordained, they receive the chalice, empty however, from the bishop's hands. Thirdly, there is the ministry directed to the proffering of the sacramental matter, and this belongs to the acolyte. For he, as stated in the text (ibid.), prepares the cruet with wine and water; wherefore he receives an empty cruet. The ministry directed to the preparation of the recipients can be exercised only over the unclean, since those who are clean are already apt for receiving the sacraments. Now the unclean are of three kinds, according to Dionysius (ibid.). For some are absolute unbelievers and unwilling to believe; and these must be altogether debarred from beholding Divine things and from the assembly of the faithful; this belongs to the doorkeepers. Some, however, are willing to believe, but are not as yet instructed, namely catechumens, and to the instruction of such persons the Order of readers is directed, who are therefore entrusted with the reading of the first rudiments of the doctrine of faith, namely the Old Testament. But some are believers and instructed, yet lie under an impediment through the power of the devil, namely those who are possessed: and to this ministry the Order of exorcists is directed. Thus the reason and number of the degrees of Orders is made clear.

Reply Obj. 1. Dionysius is speaking of the Orders not as sacraments, but as directed to hierarchical actions. Wherefore he distinguishes three Orders corresponding to those actions. The first of these Orders, namely the bishop, has all three actions; the second, namely the priest, has two; while the third has one, namely to cleanse; this is the deacon who is called a minister: and under this last all the lower Orders are comprised. But the Orders derive their sacramental nature from their relation to the greatest of the sacraments, and consequently the number of Orders depends on this.

Reply Obj. 2. In the early Church, on account of the fewness of ministers, all the lower ministries were entrusted to the deacons, as Dionysius says (Eccles. Hier. iii), where he says: *Some of the ministers stand at the closed door of the Church, others are otherwise occupied in the exercise of their own Order; others place the sacred bread and the chalice of benediction on the altar and offer them to the priests.* Nevertheless all the power to do all these things was included in the one power of the deacon, though implicitly. But afterwards the Divine worship developed, and the Church committed expressly to several persons that which had hitherto been committed implicitly in one Order. This is what the Master means, when He says in the text *(ibid.)* that the Church instituted other Orders.

Reply Obj. 3. The Orders are directed to the sacrament of the Eucharist chiefly, and to the other sacraments consequently, for even the other sacraments flow from that which is contained in that sacrament. Hence it does not follow that the Orders ought to be distinguished according to the sacraments.

Reply Obj. 4. The angels differ specifically:* for this reason it is possible for them to have various modes of receiving Divine things, and hence also they are divided into various hierarchies. But in men there is only one hierarchy, because they have only one mode of receiving Divine things, which results from the human species, namely through the images of sensible objects. Consequently the distinction of Orders in the angels cannot bear any relation to a sacrament as it is with us, but only a relation to the hierarchical actions which among them each Order exercises on the Orders below. In this respect our Orders correspond to theirs; since in our hierarchy there are three Orders, distinguished according to the three hierarchical actions, even as in each angelic hierarchy.

Reply Obj. 5. The office of psalmist is not an Order, but an office annexed to an Order. For the psalmist is also styled precentor because the psalms are recited with chant. Now precentor is not the name of a special Order, both because it belongs to the whole choir to sing, and because he has no special relation to the sacrament of the Eucharist. Since, however, it is a particular office, it is sometimes reckoned among the Orders, taking these in a broad sense.

THIRD ARTICLE

Whether the Order Should Be Divided into Those That Are Sacred and Those That Are Not?

We proceed thus to the Third Article:—

Objection 1. It would seem that the Orders ought not to be divided into those that are sacred and those that are not. For all the Orders are sacraments, and all the sacraments are sacred. Therefore all the Orders are sacred.

Obj. 2. Further, by the Orders of the Church a man is not appointed to any other than Divine offices. Now all these are sacred. Therefore all the Orders also are sacred.

* Cf. P. I, Q. 50, A. 4.

On the contrary, The sacred Orders are an impediment to the contracting of marriage and annul the marriage that is already contracted. But the four lower Orders neither impede the contracting nor annul the contract. Therefore these are not sacred Orders.

I answer that, An Order is said to be sacred in two ways. First, in itself, and thus every Order is sacred, since it is a sacrament. Secondly, by reason of the matter about which it exercises an act, and thus an Order is called sacred, if it exercises an act about some consecrated thing. In this sense there are only three sacred Orders, namely the priesthood and diaconate, which exercise an act about the consecrated body and blood of Christ, and the subdiaconate, which exercises an act about the consecrated vessels. Wherefore continency is enjoined them, that they who handle holy things may themselves be holy and clean.

This suffices for the *Replies* to the *Objections.*

FOURTH ARTICLE

Whether the Acts of the Orders Are Rightly Assigned in the Text?

We proceed thus to the Fourth Article:—

Objection 1. It would seem that the acts of the Orders are not rightly assigned in the text (iv. *Sent.* D. 24). Because a person is prepared by absolution to receive Christ's body. Now the preparation of the recipients of a sacrament belongs to the lower Orders. Therefore absolution from sins is unfittingly reckoned among the acts of a priest.

Obj. 2. Further, man is made like to God immediately in Baptism, by receiving the character which causes this likeness. But prayer and the offering of oblations are acts directed immediately to God. Therefore every baptized person can perform these acts, and not priests alone.

Obj. 3. Further, different Orders have different acts. But it belongs to the subdeacon to place the oblations on the altar, and to read the epistle; and subdeacons carry the cross before the Pope. Therefore these acts should not be assigned to the deacon.

Obj. 4. Further, the same truth is contained in the Old and in the New Testament. But it belongs to the readers to read the Old Testament. Therefore it should belong to them likewise, and not to deacons, to read the New Testament.

Obj. 5. Further, the apostles preached naught else but the gospel of Christ (Rom. i. 15). But the teaching of the apostles is entrusted to subdeacons to be read by them. Therefore the Gospel teaching should be also.

Obj. 6. Further, according to Dionysius

(Eccles Hier. v) that which belongs to a higher Order should not be applicable to a lower Order. But it is an act of subdeacons to minister with the cruets. Therefore it should not be assigned to acolytes.

Obj. 7. Further, spiritual actions should rank above bodily actions. But the acolyte's act is merely corporeal. Therefore the exorcist has not the spiritual act of casting out devils, since he is of inferior rank.

Obj. 8. Further, things that have most in common should be placed beside one another. Now the reading of the Old Testament must needs have most in common with the reading of the New Testament, which latter belongs to the higher ministers. Therefore the reading of the Old Testament should be reckoned the act, not of the reader, but rather of the acolyte; especially since the bodily light which the acolytes carry signifies the light of spiritual doctrine.

Obj. 9. Further, in every act of a special Order, there should be some special power, which the person ordained has to the exclusion of other persons. But in opening and shutting doors the doorkeeper has no special power that other men have not. Therefore this should not be reckoned their act.

I answer that, Since the consecration conferred in the sacrament of Orders is directed to the sacrament of the Eucharist, as stated above (A. 2), the principal act of each Order is that whereby it is most nearly directed to the sacrament of the Eucharist. In this respect, too, one Order ranks above another, in so far as one act is more nearly directed to that same sacrament. But because many things are directed to the Eucharist, as being the most exalted of the sacraments, it follows that unfittingly that one Order has many acts besides its principal act, and all the more, as it ranks higher, since a power extends to the more things, the higher it is.

Reply Obj. 1. The preparation of the recipients of a sacrament is twofold. One is remote and is effected by the ministers: another is proximate, whereby they are rendered apt at once for receiving the sacraments. This latter belongs to priests, since even in natural things matter receives from one and the same agent both the ultimate disposition to the form, and the form itself. And since a person acquires the proximate disposition to the Eucharist by being cleansed from sin, it follows that the priest is the proper minister of all those sacraments which are chiefly instituted for the cleansing of sins, namely Baptism, Penance, and Extreme Unction.

Reply Obj. 2. Acts are directed immediately to God in two ways; in one way on the part of one person only, for instance the prayers of individuals, vows, and so forth: such acts befit any baptized person. In another way on the part of the whole Church, and thus the priest alone exercises acts immediately directed to God; because to impersonate the whole Church belongs to him alone who consecrates the Eucharist, which is the sacrament of the universal Church.

Reply Obj. 3. The offerings made by the people are offered through the priest. Hence a twofold ministry is necessary with regard to offerings. One on the part of the people: and this belongs to the subdeacon who receives the offerings from the people and places them on the altar or offers them to the deacon; the other is on the part of the priest, and belongs to the deacon, who hands the offerings to the priest. This is the principal act of both Orders, and for this reason the deacon's Order is the higher. But to read the epistle does not belong to a deacon, except as the acts of lower Orders are ascribed to the higher; and in like manner to carry the cross. Moreover, this depends on the customs of Churches, because in secondary acts it is not unfitting for customs to vary.

Reply Obj. 4. Doctrine is a remote preparation for the reception of a sacrament; wherefore the announcement of doctrine is entrusted to the ministers. But the doctrine of the Old Testament is more remote than that of the New Testament, since it contains no instruction about this sacrament except in figures. Hence announcing of the New Testament is entrusted to the higher ministers, and that of the Old Testament to the lower ministers. Moreover the doctrine of the New Testament is more perfect as delivered by our Lord Himself, than as made known by His apostles. Wherefore the Gospel is committed to deacons, and the Epistle to subdeacons.

This suffices for the *Reply* to the *Fifth Objection.*

Reply Obj. 6. Acolytes exercise an act over the cruet alone, and not over the contents of the cruet; whereas the subdeacon exercises an act over the contents of the cruet, because he handles the water and wine to the end that they be put into the chalice,* and again he pours the water over the hands of the priest; and the deacon, like the subdeacon, exercises an act over the chalice only, not over its contents, whereas the priest exercises an act over the contents. Wherefore as the subdeacon at his ordination receives an empty chalice, while the priest receives a full chalice, so the acolyte receives an empty cruet, but the subdeacon a

---

* The wording of S. Thomas is sufficiently vague to refer either to the Roman rite, where the priest pours the wine and water into the chalice, or to the Dominican rite, where this is done by the subdeacon.

full one. Thus there is a certain connection among the Orders.

Reply Obj. 7. The bodily acts of the acolyte are more intimately connected with the act of Holy Orders than the act of the exorcist, although the latter is, in a fashion, spiritual. For the acolytes exercise a ministry over the vessels in which the sacramental matter is contained, as regards the wine, which needs a vessel to hold it on account of its humidity. Hence of all the minor Orders the Order of acolytes is the highest.

Reply Obj. 8. The act of the acolyte is more closely connected with the principal acts of the higher ministers, than the acts of the other minor Orders, as is self-evident; and again as regards the secondary acts whereby they prepare the people by doctrine. For the acolyte by bearing a light represents the doctrine of the New Testament in a visible manner, while the reader by his recital represents it differently, wherefore the acolyte is of higher rank. It is the same with the exorcist, for as the act of the reader is compared with the secondary act of the deacon and subdeacon, so is the act of the exorcist compared with the secondary act of the priest, namely to bind and to loose, by which man is wholly freed from the slavery of the devil. This, too, shows the degrees of Order to be most orderly; since only the three higher Orders co-operate with the priest in his principal act which is to consecrate the body of Christ, while both the higher and lower Orders co-operate with him in his secondary act, which is to loose and bind.

Reply Obj. 9. Some say that in receiving the Order the doorkeeper is given a Divine power to debar others from entering the Church, even as Christ had, when He cast out the sellers from the Temple. But this belongs to a gratuitous grace rather than to a sacramental grace. Wherefore we should reply that he receives the power to do this by virtue of his office, although others may do so, but not officially. It is the case in all the acts of the minor Orders, that they can be lawfully exercised by others, even though these have no office to that effect: just as Mass may be said in an unconsecrated building, although the consecration of a church is directed to the purpose that Mass be said there.

FIFTH ARTICLE

Whether the Character Is Imprinted on a Priest When the Chalice Is Handed to Him?

We proceed thus to the Fifth Article:—

Objection 1. It would seem that the character is not imprinted on the priest at the moment when the chalice is handed to him.

For the consecration of a priest is done by anointing as in Confirmation. Now in Confirmation the character is imprinted at the moment of anointing; and therefore in the priesthood also and not at the handing of the chalice.

Obj. 2. Further, our Lord gave His disciples the priestly power when He said (Jo. xx. 22, 23): *Receive ye the Holy Ghost: whose sins you shall forgive,* etc. Now the Holy Ghost is given by the imposition of hands. Therefore the character of Order is given at the moment of the imposition of hands.

Obj. 3. Further, as the ministers are consecrated, even so are the ministers' vestments. Now the blessing alone consecrates the vestments. Therefore the consecration of the priest also is effected by the mere blessing of the bishop.

Obj. 4. Further, as a chalice is handed to the priest, even so is the priestly vestment. Therefore if a character is imprinted at the giving of the chalice, so likewise is there at the giving of the chasuble, and thus a priest would have two characters: but this is false.

Obj. 5. Further, the deacon's Order is more closely allied to the priest's Order than is the subdeacon's. But if a character is imprinted on the priest at the moment of the handing of the chalice, the subdeacon would be more closely allied to the priest than the deacon; because the subdeacon receives the character at the handing of the chalice and not the deacon. Therefore the priestly character is not imprinted at the handing of the chalice.

Obj. 6. Further, the Order of acolytes approaches nearer to the priestly act by exercising an act over the cruet than by exercising an act over the torch. Yet the character is imprinted on the acolytes when they receive the torch rather than when they receive the cruet, because the name of acolyte signifies candle-bearer. Therefore the character is not imprinted on the priest when he receives the chalice.

On the contrary, The principal act of the priest's Order is to consecrate Christ's body. Now he receives the power to this effect at the handing of the chalice. Therefore the character is imprinted on him then.

I answer that, As stated above (A. 4, *ad* 1), to cause the form and to give the matter its proximate preparation for the form belong to the same agent. Wherefore the bishop in conferring Orders does two things; for he prepares the candidates for the reception of Orders, and delivers to them the power of Order. He prepares them, both by instructing them in their respective offices and by doing something to them, so that they may be adapted to receive the power. This preparation consists of three things, namely blessing, imposition of hands, and anointing. By the blessing they are enlisted in the Divine service, wherefore the blessing is given to all. By the imposition of hands the fulness of grace is given, whereby they are qualified for exalted duties, wherefore only deacons and priests receive the imposition of hands, because they are competent to dispense the sacraments, although the latter as principal dispensers, the former as ministers. But by the anointing they are consecrated for the purpose of handling the sacrament, wherefore the anointing is done to the priests alone who touch the body of Christ with their own hands; even as a chalice is anointed because it holds the blood, and the paten because it holds the body.

The conferring of power is effected by giving them something pertaining to their proper act. And since the principal act of a priest is to consecrate the body and blood of Christ, the priestly character is imprinted at the very giving of the chalice under the prescribed form of words.

Reply Obj. 1. In Confirmation there is not given the office of exercising an act on an exterior matter, wherefore the character is not imprinted in that sacrament at the handing of some particular thing, but at the mere imposition of hands and anointing. But it is otherwise in the priestly Order, and consequently the comparison fails.

Reply Obj. 2. Our Lord gave His disciples the priestly power, as regards the principal act, before His passion at the supper when He said: *Take ye and eat* (Matth. xxvi. 26), wherefore He added: *Do this for a commemoration of Me* (Luke xxii. 19). After the resurrection, however, He gave them the priestly power, as to its secondary act, which is to bind and loose.

Reply Obj. 3. Vestments require no other consecration except to be set aside for the Divine worship, wherefore the blessing suffices for their consecration. But it is different with those who are ordained, as explained above.

Reply Obj. 4. The priestly vestment signifies, not the power given to the priest, but the aptitude required of him for exercising the act of that power. Wherefore a character is imprinted neither on the priest nor on anyone else at the giving of a vestment.

Reply Obj. 5. The deacon's power is midway between the subdeacon's and the priest's. For the priest exercises a power directly on Christ's body, the subdeacon on the vessels only, and the deacon on Christ's body contained in a vessel. Hence it is not for him to touch Christ's body, but to carry the body on the paten, and to dispense the blood with the chalice. Consequently his power, as to the principal act, could not be expressed, either by the giving of the vessel only, or by the giving of the matter; and his power is expressed as to the secondary act alone, by his receiving the book of the Gospels, and this power is understood to contain the other; wherefore the character is impressed at the handing of the book.

Reply Obj. 6. The act of the acolyte whereby he serves with the cruet ranks before his act of carrying the torch; although he takes his name from the secondary act, because it is better known and more proper to him. Hence the acolyte receives the character when he is given the cruet, by virtue of the words uttered by the bishop.

QUESTION 38

Of Those Who Confer This Sacrament

(In Two Articles)

WE must now consider those who confer this sacrament. Under this head there are two points of inquiry: (1) Whether a bishop alone can confer this sacrament? (2) Whether a heretic or any other person cut off from the Church can confer this sacrament?

FIRST ARTICLE

Whether a Bishop Alone Confers the Sacrament of Order?

We proceed thus to the First Article:—

Objection 1. It would seem that not only a bishop confers the sacrament of Order. For the imposition of hands has something to do with the consecration. Now not only the bishop but also the assisting priests lay hands on the priests who are being ordained. Therefore not only a bishop confers the sacrament of Order.

Obj. 2. Further, a man receives the power of Order, when that which pertains to the act of his Order is handed to him. Now the cruet with water, bowl* and towel, are given to the subdeacon by the archdeacon; as also the candlestick with candle, and the empty cruet

---

* *Bacili.* The rubric has *aquamanili.* Some texts of the Summa have *mantili* (*maniple*), but the archdeacon does not give the maniple to the subdeacon.

to the acolyte. Therefore not only the bishop confers the sacrament of Order.

Obj. 3. Further, that which belongs to an Order cannot be entrusted to one who has not the Order. Now the conferring of minor Orders is entrusted to certain persons who are not bishops, for instance to Cardinal priests. Therefore the conferring of Orders does not belong to the episcopal Order.

Obj. 4. Further, whoever is entrusted with the principal is entrusted with the accessory also. Now the sacrament of Order is directed to the Eucharist, as accessory to principal. Since then a priest consecrates the Eucharist, he can also confer Orders.

Obj. 5. Further, there is a greater distinction between a priest and a deacon than between bishop and bishop. But a bishop can consecrate a bishop. Therefore a priest can ordain a deacon.

On the contrary, Ministers are applied by their Orders to the Divine worship in a more noble way than the sacred vessels. But the consecration of the vessels belongs to a bishop only. Much more therefore does the consecration of ministers.

Further, the sacrament of Order ranks higher than the sacrament of Confirmation. Now a bishop alone confirms. Much more therefore does a bishop alone confer the sacrament of Order.

Further, virgins are not placed in a degree of spiritual power by their consecration, as the ordained are. Yet a bishop alone can consecrate a virgin. Therefore much more can he alone ordain.

I answer that, The episcopal power stands in the same relation to the power of the lower Orders, as political science, which seeks the common good, to the lower acts and virtues which seek some special good, as appears from what was said above (Q. 37, A. 1). Now political science, as stated in *Ethic.* i. 2, lays down the law to lower sciences, namely what science each one ought to cultivate, and how far he should pursue it and in what way. Wherefore it belongs to a bishop to assign others to places in all the Divine services. Hence he alone confirms, because those who are confirmed receive the office, as it were, of confessing the faith; again he alone blesses virgins who are images of the Church, Christ's spouse, the care of which is entrusted chiefly to him; and he it is who consecrates the candidates for ordination to the ministry of Orders, and, by his consecration, appoints the vessels that they are to use; even as secular offices in various cities are allotted by him who holds the highest power, for instance by the king.

Reply Obj. 1. As stated above (Q. 37, A. 5),
* Cf. P. III, Q. 64, AA. 5, 9.

at the imposition of hands there is given, not the character of the priestly Order, but grace which makes a man fit to exercise his Order. And since those who are raised to the priesthood need most copious grace, the priests together with the bishop lay hands on them, but the bishop alone lays hands on deacons.

Reply Obj. 2. Since the archdeacon is as it were minister-in-chief, all things pertaining to the ministry are handed by him, for instance the candle with which the acolyte serves the deacon by carrying it before him at the Gospel, and the cruet with which he serves the subdeacon; and in like manner he gives the subdeacon the things with which the latter serves the higher Orders. And yet the principal act of the subdeacon does not consist in these things, but in his co-operation as regards the matter of the sacrament; wherefore he receives the character through the chalice being handed to him by the bishop. On the other hand, the acolyte receives the character by virtue of the words of the bishop when the aforesaid things—the cruet rather than the candlestick—are handed to him by the archdeacon. Hence it does not follow that the archdeacon ordains.

Reply Obj. 3. The Pope, who has the fulness of episcopal power, can entrust one who is not a bishop with things pertaining to the epicopal dignity, provided they bear no immediate relation to the true body of Christ. Hence by virtue of his commission a simple priest can confer the minor Orders and confirm; but not one who is not a priest. Nor can a priest confer the higher Orders which bear an immediate relation to Christ's body, over the consecration of which the Pope's power is no greater than that of a simple priest.

Reply Obj. 4. Although the Eucharist is in itself the greatest of the sacraments, it does not place a man in an office as does the sacrament of Order. Hence the comparison fails.

Reply Obj. 5. In order to bestow what one has on another, it is necessary not only to be near him but also to have fulness of power. And since a priest has not fulness of power in the hierarchical offices, as a bishop has, it does not follow that he can raise others to the diaconate, although the latter Order is near to his.

SECOND ARTICLE

Whether Heretics and Those Who Are Cut Off from the Church Can Confer Orders? *

We proceed thus to the Second Article:—

Objection 1. It would seem that heretics and those who are cut off from the Church cannot confer Orders. For to confer Orders is a greater thing than to loose or bind anyone

But a heretic cannot loose or bind. Neither therefore can he ordain.

Obj. 2. Further, a priest that is separated from the Church can consecrate, because the character whence he derives this power remains in him indelibly. But a bishop receives no character when he is raised to the episcopate. Therefore he does not necessarily retain the episcopal power after his separation from the Church.

Obj. 3. Further, in no community can one who is expelled therefrom dispose of the offices of the community. Now Orders are offices of the Church. Therefore one who is outside the Church cannot confer Orders.

Obj. 4. Further, the sacraments derive their efficacy from Christ's passion. Now a heretic is not united to Christ's passion; neither by his own faith, since he is an unbeliever, nor by the faith of the Church, since he is severed from the Church. Therefore he cannot confer the sacrament of Orders.

Obj. 5. Further, a blessing is necessary in the conferring of Orders. But a heretic cannot bless; in fact his blessing is turned into a curse, as appears from the authorities quoted in the text (iv. *Sent.* D. 25). Therefore he cannot ordain.

On the contrary, When a bishop who has fallen into heresy is reconciled he is not reconsecrated. Therefore he did not lose the power which he had of conferring Orders.

Further, the power to ordain is greater than the power of Orders. But the power of Orders is not forfeited on account of heresy and the like. Neither therefore is the power to ordain.

Further, as the one who baptizes exercises a merely outward ministry, so does one who ordains, while God works inwardly. But one who is cut off from the Church by no means loses the power to baptize. Neither therefore does he lose the power to ordain.

I answer that, On this question four opinions are mentioned in the text *(loc. cit.).* For some said that heretics, so long as they are tolerated by the Church, retain the power to ordain, but not after they have been cut off from the Church; as neither do those who have been degraded and the like. This is the first opinion. Yet this is impossible, because, happen what may, no power that is given with a consecration can be taken away so long as the thing itself remains, any more than the consecration itself can be annulled, for even an altar or chrism once consecrated remains consecrated for ever. Wherefore, since the episcopal power is conferred by consecration, it must needs endure for ever, however much a man may sin or be cut off from the Church. For this reason others said that those who are

cut off from the Church after having episcopal power in the Church, retain the power to ordain and raise others, but that those who are raised by them have not this power. This is the fourth opinion. But this again is impossible, for if those who were ordained in the Church retain the power they received, it is clear that by exercising their power they consecrate validly, and therefore they validly confer whatever power is given with that consecration, and thus those who receive ordination or promotion from them have the same power as they. Wherefore others said that even those who are cut off from the Church can confer Orders and the other sacraments, provided they observe the due form and intention, both as to the first effect, which is the conferring of the sacrament, and as to the ultimate effect, which is the conferring of grace. This is the second opinion. But this again is inadmissible, since by the very fact that a person communicates in the sacraments with a heretic who is cut off from the Church, he sins, and thus approaches the sacrament insincerely and cannot obtain grace, except perhaps in Baptism in a case of necessity. Hence others say that they confer the sacraments validly, but do not confer grace with them, not that the sacraments are lacking in efficacy, but on account of the sins of those who receive the sacraments from such persons despite the prohibition of the Church. This is the third and the true opinion.

Reply Obj. 1. The effect of absolution is nothing else but the forgiveness of sins which results from grace, and consequently a heretic cannot absolve, as neither can he confer grace in the sacraments. Moreover in order to give absolution it is necesary to have jurisdiction, which one who is cut off from the Church has not.

Reply Obj. 2. When a man is raised to the episcopate he receives a power which he retains for ever. This, however, cannot be called a character, because a man is not thereby placed in direct relation to God, but to Christ's mystical body. Nevertheless it remains indelibly, even as the character, because it is given by consecration.

Reply Obj. 3. Those who are ordained by heretics, although they receive an Order, do not receive the exercise thereof, so as to minister lawfully in their Orders, for the very reason indicated in the *Objection.*

Reply Obj. 4. They are united to the passion of Christ by the faith of the Church, for although in themselves they are severed from it, they are united to it as regards the form of the Church which they observe.

Reply Obj. 5. This refers to the ultimate effect of the sacraments, as the third opinion maintains.

QUESTION 39

Of the Impediments to This Sacrament

(In Six Articles)

WE must next consider the impediments to this sacrament. Under this head there are six points of inquiry: (1) Whether the female sex is an impediment to receiving this sacrament? (2) Whether lack of the use of reason is? (3) Whether the state of slavery is? (4) Whether homicide is? (5) Whether illegitimate birth is? (6) Whether lack of members is?

FIRST ARTICLE

Whether the Female Sex Is an Impediment to Receiving Orders?

We proceed thus to the First Article:—

Objection 1. It would seem that the female sex is no impediment to receiving Orders. For the office of prophet is greater than the office of priest, since a prophet stands midway between God and priests, just as the priest does between God and people. Now the office of prophet was sometimes granted to women, as may be gathered from 4 Kings xxii. 14. Therefore the office of priest also may be competent to them.

Obj. 2. Further, just as Order pertains to a kind of pre-eminence, so does a position of authority as well as martyrdom and the religious state. Now authority is entrusted to women in the New Testament, as in the case of abbesses, and in the Old Testament, as in the case of Debbora, who judged Israel (Judges ii). Moreover martyrdom and the religious life are also befitting to them. Therefore the Orders of the Church are also competent to them.

Obj. 3. Further, the power of Orders is founded in the soul. But sex is not in the soul. Therefore difference in sex makes no difference to the reception of Orders.

On the contrary, It is said (1 Tim. ii. 12): *I suffer not a woman to teach (in the Church),* nor to use authority over the man.*

Further, the crown is required previous to receiving Orders, albeit not for the validity of the sacrament. But the crown or tonsure is not befitting to women according to 1 Cor. xi. Neither therefore is the receiving of Orders.

I answer that, Certain things are required in the recipient of a sacrament as being requisite for the validity of the sacrament, and if such things be lacking, one can receive neither the sacrament nor the reality of the sacrament. Other things, however, are required, not for the validity of the sacrament, but for its lawfulness, as being congruous to the sacrament; and without these one receives the sacrament, but not the reality of the sacrament. Accordingly we must say that the male sex is required for receiving Orders not only in the second, but also in the first way. Wherefore even though a woman were made the object of all that is done in conferring Orders, she would not receive Orders, for since a sacrament is a sign, not only the thing, but the signification of the thing, is required in all sacramental actions; thus it was stated above (Q. 32, A. 2) that in Extreme Unction it is necessary to have a sick man, in order to signify the need of healing. Accordingly, since it is not possible in the female sex to signify eminence of degree, for a woman is in the state of subjection it follows that she cannot receive the sacrament of Order. Some, however, have asserted that the male sex is necessary for the lawfulness and not for the validity of the sacrament because even in the Decretals (cap. *Mulieres* dist. 32; cap. *Diaconissam,* 27, qu. i) mention is made of deaconesses and priestesses. But *deaconess* there denotes a woman who shares in some act of a deacon, namely who reads the homilies in the Church; and *priestess (presbytera)* means a widow, for the word *presbyter* means elder.

Reply Obj. 1. Prophecy is not a sacrament but a gift of God. Wherefore there it is not the signification, but only the thing which is necessary. And since in matters pertaining to the soul woman does not differ from man as to the thing (for sometimes a woman is found to be better than many men as regards the soul), it follows that she can receive the gift of prophecy and the like, but not the sacrament of Orders.

And thereby appears the *Reply* to the *Second* and *Third Objections.* However, as to abbesses, it is said that they have not ordinary authority, but delegated as it were, on account of the danger of men and women living together. But Debbora exercised authority in temporal, not in priestly matters, even as now woman may have temporal power.

SECOND ARTICLE

Whether Boys and Those Who Lack the Use of Reason Can Receive Orders?

We proceed thus to the Second Article:—

Objection 1. It would seem that boys and

---

* The words in parenthesis are from 1 Cor. xiv. 34, *Let women keep silence in the churches.*

those who lack the use of reason cannot receive Orders. For, as stated in the text (iv. *Sent.* D. 25), the sacred canons have appointed a certain fixed age in those who receive Orders. But this would not be if boys could receive the sacrament of Orders. Therefore, etc.

Obj. 2. Further, the sacrament of Orders ranks above the sacrament of matrimony. Now children and those who lack the use of reason cannot contract matrimony. Neither therefore can they receive Orders.

Obj. 3. Further, act and power are in the same subject, according to the Philosopher (*De Somn. et Vigil.* i). Now the act of Orders requires the use of reason. Therefore the power of Orders does also.

On the contrary, One who is raised to Orders before the age of discretion is sometimes allowed to exercise them without being reordained, as appears from Extra., *De Cler. per salt. prom.* But this would not be the case if he had not received Orders. Therefore a boy can receive Orders.

Further, boys can receive other sacraments in which a character is imprinted, namely Baptism and Confirmation. Therefore in like manner they can receive Orders.

I answer that, Boyhood and other defects which remove the use of reason occasion an impediment to act. Wherefore the like are unfit to receive all those sacraments which require an act on the part of the recipient of the sacrament, such as Penance, Matrimony, and so forth. But since infused powers like natural powers precede acts — although acquired powers follow acts—and the removal of that which comes after does not entail the removal of what comes first, it follows that children and those who lack the use of reason can receive all the sacraments in which an act on the part of the recipient is not required for the validity of the sacrament, but some spiritual power is conferred from above; with this difference, however, that in the minor Orders the age of discretion is required out of respect for the dignity of the sacrament, but not for its lawfulness, nor for its validity. Hence some can without sin be raised to the minor Orders before the years of discretion, if there be an urgent reason for it and hope of their proficiency, and they are validly ordained; for although at the time they are not qualified for the offices entrusted to them, they will become qualified by being habituated thereto. For the higher Orders, however, the use of reason is required both out of respect for, and for the lawfulness of, the sacrament, not only on account of the vow of continency annexed thereto, but also because the handling of the sacraments is entrusted to them.* But for the

* See Acts of the Council of Trent (*De Reform.*, Sess. xxiii, cap. 4, 11, 12).

episcopate whereby a man receives power also over the mystical body, the act of accepting the pastoral care of souls is required; wherefore the use of reason is necessary for the validity of episcopal consecration. Some, however, maintain that the use of reason is necessary for the validity of the sacrament in all the Orders; but this statement is not confirmed either by authority or by reason.

Reply Obj. 1. As stated in the *Article,* not all that is necessary for the lawfulness of a sacrament is required for its validity.

Reply Obj. 2. The cause of matrimony is consent, which cannot be without the use of reason. Whereas in the reception of Orders no act is required on the part of the recipients since no act on their part is expressed in their consecration. Hence there is no comparison.

Reply Obj. 3. Act and power are in the same subject; yet sometimes a power, such as the free-will, precedes its act; and thus it is in the case in point.

THIRD ARTICLE

Whether the State of Slavery Is an Impediment to Receiving Orders?

We proceed thus to the Third Article:—

Objection 1. It would seem that the state of slavery is not an impediment to receiving Orders. For corporal subjection is not incompatible with spiritual authority. But in a slave there is corporal subjection. Therefore he is not hindered from receiving the spiritual authority which is given in Orders.

Obj. 2. Further, that which is an occasion for humility should not be an impediment to the reception of a sacrament. Now such is slavery, for the Apostle counsels a man, if possible, rather to remain in slavery (1 Cor. vii. 21). Therefore it should not hinder him from being raised to Orders.

Obj. 3. Further, it is more disgraceful for a cleric to become a slave than for a slave to be made a cleric. Yet a cleric may lawfully be sold as a slave; for a bishop of Nola, Paulinus, to wit, sold himself as a slave as related by Gregory (*Dial.* iii). Much more therefore can a slave be made a cleric.

Obj. 4. *On the contrary,* It would seem that it is an impediment to the validity of the sacrament. For a woman, on account of her subjection, cannot receive the sacrament of Orders. But greater still is the subjection in a slave; since woman was not given to man as his handmaid (for which reason she was not made from his feet). Therefore neither can a slave receive this sacrament.

Obj. 5. Further, a man, from the fact that he receives an Order, is bound to minister in that Order. But he cannot at the same time serve his carnal master and exercise his spiritual ministry. Therefore it would seem that he cannot receive Orders, since the master must be indemnified.

I answer that, By receiving Orders a man pledges himself to the Divine offices. And since no man can give what is not his, a slave who has not the disposal of himself, cannot be raised to Orders. If, however, he be raised, he receives the Order, because freedom is not required for the validity of the sacrament, although it is requisite for its lawfulness, since it hinders not the power, but the act only. The same reason applies to all who are under an obligation to others, such as those who are in debt and like persons.

Reply Obj. 1. The reception of spiritual power involves also an obligation to certain bodily actions, and consequently it is hindered by bodily subjection.

Reply Obj. 2. A man may take an occasion for humility from many other things which do not prove a hindrance to the exercise of Orders.

Reply Obj. 3. The blessed Paulinus did this out of the abundance of his charity, being led by the spirit of God; as was proved by the result of his action, since by his becoming a slave, many of his flock were freed from slavery. Hence we must not draw a conclusion from this particular instance, since *where the spirit of the Lord is, there is liberty* (2 Cor. iii. 17).

Reply Obj. 4. The sacramental signs signify by reason of their natural likeness. Now a woman is a subject by her nature, whereas a slave is not. Hence the comparison fails.

Reply Obj. 5. If he be ordained, his master knowing and not dissenting, by this very fact he becomes a freedman. But if his master be in ignorance, the bishop and he who presented him are bound to pay the master double the slave's value, if they knew him to be a slave. Otherwise if the slave has possessions of his own, he is bound to buy his freedom, else he would have to return to the bondage of his master, notwithstanding the impossibility of his exercising his Order.

FOURTH ARTICLE

Whether a Man Should Be Debarred from Receiving Orders on Account of Homicide?

We proceed thus to the Fourth Article:—

Objection 1. It would seem that a man ought not to be debarred from receiving Orders on account of homicide. Because our Orders originated with the office of the Levites, as stated in the previous *Distinction* (iv. *Sent.* D. 24). But the Levites consecrated their hands by shedding the blood of their brethren (Exod. xxxii. 29). Therefore neither should anyone in the New Testament be debarred from receiving Orders on account of the shedding of blood.

Obj. 2. Further, no one should be debarred from a sacrament on account of an act of virtue. Now blood is sometimes shed for justice' sake, for instance by a judge; and he who has the office would sin if he did not shed it. Therefore he is not hindered on that account from receiving Orders.

Obj. 3. Further, punishment is not due save for a fault. Now sometimes a person commits homicide without fault, for instance by defending himself, or again by mishap. Therefore he ought not to incur the punishment of irregularity.

On the contrary, Against this there are many canonical statutes,* as also the custom of the Church.

I answer that, All the Orders bear a relation to the sacrament of the Eucharist, which is the sacrament of the peace vouchsafed to us by the shedding of Christ's blood. And since homicide is most opposed to peace, and those who slay are conformed to Christ's slayers rather than to Christ slain, to whom all the ministers of the aforesaid sacrament ought to be conformed, it follows that it is unlawful, although not invalid, for homicides to be raised to Orders.

Reply Obj. 1. The Old Law inflicted the punishment of blood, whereas the New Law does not. Hence the comparison fails between the ministers of the Old Testament and those of the New, which is a sweet yoke and a light burden (Matth. xi. 30).

Reply Obj. 2. Irregularity is incurred not only on account of sin, but chiefly on account of a person being unfit to administer the sacrament of the Eucharist. Hence the judge and all who take part with him in a cause of blood are irregular, because the shedding of blood is unbecoming to the ministers of that sacrament.

Reply Obj. 3. No one does a thing without being the cause thereof, and in man this is something voluntary. Hence he who by mishap slays a man without knowing that it is a man, is not called a homicide, nor does he incur irregularity (unless he was occupying himself in some unlawful manner, or failed to take sufficient care, since in this case the slaying becomes somewhat voluntary). But this is not because he is not in fault, since irregularity is incurred even without fault. Wherefore even he who in a particular case slays a man in self-defense without committing a sin is none the less irregular.†

---

* Cap. *Miror;* cap. *Clericum;* cap. *De his Cler.* dist. 1; cap. *Continebatur,* De homic. volunt.

† S. Thomas is speaking according to the canon law of his time. This is no longer the case now.

FIFTH ARTICLE

Whether Those of Illegitimate Birth Should Be Debarred from Receiving Orders?

We proceed thus to the Fifth Article:—

Objection 1. It would seem that those who are of illegitimate birth should not be debarred from receiving Orders. For the son should not bear the iniquity of the father (Ezech. xviii. 20); and yet he would if this were an impediment to his receiving Orders. Therefore, etc.

Obj. 2. Further, one's own fault is a greater impediment than the fault of another. Now unlawful intercourse does not always debar a man from receiving Orders. Therefore neither should he be debarred by the unlawful intercourse of his father.

On the contrary, It is written (Deut. xxiii. 2): *A mamzer, that is to say, one born of a prostitute, shall not enter into the Church of the Lord until the tenth generation.* Much less therefore should he be ordained.

I answer that, Those who are ordained are placed in a position of dignity over others. Hence by a kind of propriety it is requisite that they should be without reproach, not for the validity but for the lawfulness of the sacrament, namely that they should be of good repute, bedecked with a virtuous life, and not publicly penitent. And since a man's good name is bedimmed by a sinful origin, therefore those also who are born of an unlawful union are debarred from receiving Orders, unless they receive a dispensation; and this is the more difficult to obtain, according as their origin is more discreditable.

Reply Obj. 1. Irregularity is not a punishment due for sin. Hence it is clear that those who are of illegitimate birth do not bear the iniquity of their father through being irregular.

Reply Obj. 2. What a man does by his own act can be removed by repentance and by a contrary act; not so the things which are from nature. Hence the comparison fails between sinful act and sinful origin.

SIXTH ARTICLE

Whether Lack of Members Should Be an Impediment?

We proceed thus to the Sixth Article:—

Objection 1. It would seem that a man ought not to be debarred from receiving Orders on account of a lack of members. For one who is afflicted should not receive additional affliction. Therefore a man ought not to be deprived of the degree of Orders on account of his suffering a bodily defect.

Obj. 2. Further, integrity of discretion is more necessary for the act of Orders than integrity of body. But some can be ordained before the years of discretion. Therefore they can also be ordained though deficient in body.

On the contrary, The like were debarred from the ministry of the Old Law (Levit. xxi. 18 *seqq.*). Much more therefore should they be debarred in the New Law.

We shall speak of bigamy in the treatise on Matrimony (Q. 66).

I answer that, As appears from what we have said above (AA. 3, 4, 5), a man is disqualified from receiving Orders, either on account of an impediment to the act, or on account of an impediment affecting his personal comeliness. Hence he who suffers from a lack of members is debarred from receiving Orders, if the defect be such as to cause a notable blemish, whereby a man's comeliness is bedimmed (for instance if his nose be cut off) or the exercise of his Order imperilled; otherwise he is not debarred. This integrity, however, is necessary for the lawfulness and not for the validity of the sacrament.

This suffices for the *Replies* to the *Objections.*

QUESTION 40

Of the Things Annexed to the Sacrament of Order

(In Seven Articles)

We must now consider the things that are annexed to the sacrament of Order. Under this head there are seven points of inquiry:
(1) Whether those who are ordained ought to be shaven and tonsured in the form of a crown? (2) Whether the tonsure is an Order? (3) Whether by receiving the tonsure one renounces temporal goods? (4) Whether above the priestly Order there should be an episcopal power? (5) Whether the episcopate is an Order? (6) Whether in the Church there can be any power above the episcopate?

(7) Whether the vestments of the ministers are fittingly instituted by the Church?

FIRST ARTICLE

Whether Those Who Are Ordained Ought to Wear the Tonsure?

We proceed thus to the First Article:—

Objection 1. It would seem that those who are ordained ought not to wear the tonsure in the shape of a crown. For the Lord threatened captivity and dispersion to those who were shaven in this way: *Of the captivity of the bare head of the enemies* (Deut. xxxii. 42), and: *I will scatter into every wind them that have their hair cut round* (Jer. xlix. 32). Now the ministers of Christ should not be captives, but free. Therefore shaving and tonsure in the shape of a crown does not become them.

Obj. 2. Further, the truth should correspond to the figure. Now the crown was prefigured in the Old Law by the tonsure of the Nazarenes, as stated in the text (iv. *Sent.* D. 24). Therefore since the Nazarenes were not ordained to the Divine ministry, it would seem that the ministers of the Church should not receive the tonsure or shave the head in the form of a crown. The same would seem to follow from the fact that lay brothers, who are not ministers of the Church, receive a tonsure in the religious orders.

Obj. 3. Further, the hair signifies superabundance, because it grows from that which is superabundant. But the ministers of the Church should cast off all superabundance. Therefore they should shave the head completely and not in the shape of a crown.

On the contrary, According to Gregory, *to serve God is to reign (Super Ps.* ci. 23). Now a crown is the sign of royalty. Therefore a crown is becoming to those who are devoted to the Divine ministry.

Further, according to 1 Cor. xi. 15, hair is given us *for a covering.* But the ministers of the altar should have the mind uncovered. Therefore the tonsure is becoming to them.

I answer that, It is becoming for those who apply themselves to the Divine ministry to be shaven or tonsured in the form of a crown by reason of the shape. Because a crown is the sign of royalty; and of perfection, since it is circular; and those who are appointed to the Divine service acquire a royal dignity and ought to be perfect in virtue. It is also becoming to them as it involves the hair being taken both from the higher part of the head by shaving, lest their mind be hindered by temporal occupations from contemplating Divine things, and from the lower part by clipping, lest their senses be entangled in temporal things.

Reply Obj. 1. The Lord threatens those who did this for the worship of demons.

Reply Obj. 2. The things that were done in the Old Testament represent imperfectly the things of the New Testament. Hence things pertaining to the ministers of the New Testament were signified not only by the offices of the Levites, but also by all those persons who professed some degree of perfection. Now the Nazarenes professed a certain perfection by having their hair cut off, thus signifying their contempt of temporal things, although they

did not have it cut in the shape of a crown, but cut it off completely, for as yet it was not the time of the royal and perfect priesthood. In like manner lay brothers have their hair cut because they renounce temporalities; but they do not shave the head, because they are not occupied in the Divine ministry, so as to have to contemplate Divine things with the mind.

Reply Obj. 3. Not only the renunciation of temporalities, but also the royal dignity has to be signified by the form of a crown; wherefore the hair should not be cut off entirely. Another reason is that this would be unbecoming.

SECOND ARTICLE

Whether the Tonsure Is an Order?

We proceed thus to the Second Article:—

Objection 1. It would seem that the tonsure is an Order. For in the acts of the Church the spiritual corresponds to the corporal. Now the tonsure is a corporal sign employed by the Church. Therefore seemingly there is some interior signification corresponding thereto; so that a person receives a character when he receives the tonsure, and consequently the latter is an order.

Obj. 2. Further, just as Confirmation and the other Orders are given by a bishop alone, so is the tonsure. Now a character is imprinted in Confirmation, and the other Orders. Therefore one is imprinted likewise in receiving the tonsure. Therefore the same conclusion follows.

Obj. 3. Further, Order denotes a degree of dignity. Now a cleric by the very fact of being a cleric is placed on a degree above the people. Therefore the tonsure by which he is made a cleric is an Order.

On the contrary, No Order is given except during the celebration of Mass. But the tonsure is given even outside the office of the Mass. Therefore it is not an Order.

Further, in the conferring of every Order mention is made of some power granted, but not in the conferring of the tonsure. Therefore it is not an Order.

I answer that, The ministers of the Church are severed from the people in order that they may give themselves entirely to the Divine worship. Now in the Divine worship are certain actions that have to be exercised by virtue of certain definite powers, and for this purpose the spiritual power of Order is given; while other actions are performed by the whole body of ministers in common, for instance the recital of the Divine praises. For such things it is not necessary to have the power of Order, but only to be deputed to such an office; and this is done by the tonsure. Consequently it is not an Order but a preamble to Orders.

Reply Obj. 1. The tonsure has some spiritual thing inwardly corresponding to it, as signate corresponds to sign; but this is not a spiritual power. Wherefore a character is not imprinted in the tonsure as in an Order.

Reply Obj. 2. Although a man does not receive a character in the tonsure, nevertheless he is appointed to the Divine worship. Hence this appointment should be made by the supreme minister, namely the bishop, who moreover blesses the vestments and vessels and whatsoever else is employed in the Divine worship.

Reply Obj. 3. A man through being a cleric is in a higher state than a layman; but as regards power he has not the higher degree that is required for Orders.

THIRD ARTICLE

Whether by Receiving the Tonsure a Man Renounces Temporal Goods?

We proceed thus to the Third Article:—

Objection 1. It would seem that men renounce temporal goods by receiving the tonsure, for when they are tonsured they say: *The Lord is the portion of my inheritance.* But, as Jerome says (*Ep. ad Nepot.*), *the Lord disdains to be made a portion together with these temporal things.* Therefore he renounces temporalities.

Obj. 2. Further, the justice of the ministers of the New Testament ought to abound more than that of the ministers of the Old Testament (Matth. v. 20). But the ministers of the Old Testament, namely the Levites, did not receive a portion of inheritance with their brethren (Deut. x; xviii). Therefore neither should the ministers of the New Testament.

Obj. 3. Further, Hugh says (*De Sacram.* ii) that *after a man is made a cleric, he must from thenceforward live on the pay of the Church.* But this would not be so were he to retain his patrimony. Therefore he would seem to renounce it by becoming a cleric.

On the contrary, Jeremias was of the priestly order (Jer. i. 1). Yet he retained possession of his inheritance (*ibid.* xxxii. 8). Therefore clerics can retain their patrimony.

Further, if this were not so there would seem to be no difference between religious and the secular clergy.

I answer that, Clerics by receiving the tonsure, do not renounce their patrimony or other temporalities; since the possession of earthly things is not contrary to the Divine worship to which clerics are appointed, although excessive care for such things is; for as Gregory says (*Moral.* x. 30), *it is not wealth but the love of wealth that is sinful.*

Reply Obj. 1. The Lord disdains to be a portion as being loved equally with other things, so that a man place his end in God and the things of the world. He does not, however, disdain to be the portion of those who so possess the things of the world as not to be withdrawn thereby from the Divine worship.

Reply Obj. 2. In the Old Testament the Levites had a right to their paternal inheritance; and the reason why they did not receive a portion with the other tribes was because they were scattered throughout all the tribes, which would have been impossible if, like the other tribes, they had received one fixed portion of the soil.

Reply Obj. 3. Clerics promoted to holy Orders, if they be poor, must be provided for by the bishop who ordained them; otherwise he is not so bound. And they are bound to minister to the Church in the Order they have received. The words of Hugh refer to those who have no means of livelihood.

FOURTH ARTICLE

Whether above the Priestly Order There Ought to Be an Episcopal Power?

We proceed thus to the Fourth Article:—

Objection 1. It would seem that there ought not to be an episcopal power above the priestly order. For as stated in the text (iv. *Sent.* D. 24) the *priestly Order originated from Aaron.* Now in the Old Law there was no one above Aaron. Therefore neither in the New Law ought there to be any power above that of the priests.

Obj. 2. Further, powers rank according to acts. Now no sacred act can be greater than to consecrate the body of Christ, whereunto the priestly power is directed. Therefore there should not be an episcopal above the priestly power.

Obj. 3. Further, the priest, in offering, represents Christ in the Church, Who offered Himself for us to the Father. Now no one is above Christ in the Church, since He is the Head of the Church. Therefore there should not be an episcopal above the priestly power.

On the contrary, A power is so much the higher according as it extends to more things. Now the priestly power, according to Dionysius (*Eccl. Hier.* v), extends only to cleansing and enlightening, whereas the episcopal power extends both to this and to perfecting. Therefore the episcopal should be above the priestly power.

Further, the Divine ministries should be more orderly than human ministries. Now the order of human ministries requires that in each office there should be one person to preside, just as a general is placed over soldiers. Therefore there should also be appointed over priests one who is the chief priest, and this is the bishop. Therefore the episcopal should be above the priestly power.

I answer that, A priest has two acts: one is the principal, namely to consecrate the body of Christ; the other is secondary, namely to prepare God's people for the reception of this sacrament, as stated above (Q. 37, AA. 2, 4). As regards the first act, the priest's power does not depend on a higher power save God's; but as to the second, it depends on a higher and that a human power. For every power that cannot exercise its act without certain ordinances, depends on the power that makes those ordinances. Now a priest cannot loose and bind, except we presuppose him to have the jurisdiction of authority, whereby those whom he absolves are subject to him. But he can consecrate any matter determined by Christ, nor is anything else required for the validity of the sacrament; although, on account of a certain congruousness, the act of the bishop is pre-required in the consecration of the altar, vestments, and so forth. Hence it is clear that it behooves the episcopal to be above the priestly power, as regards the priest's secondary act, but not as regards his primary act.

Reply Obj. 1. Aaron was both priest and pontiff, that is chief priest. Accordingly the priestly power originated from him, in so far as he was a priest offering sacrifices, which was lawful even to the lesser priests; but it does not originate from him as pontiff, by which power he was able to do certain things; for instance, to enter once a year the Holy of Holies, which it was unlawful for the other priests to do.

Reply Obj. 2. There is no higher power with regard to this act, but with regard to another, as stated above.

Reply Obj. 3. Just as the perfections of all natural things pre-exist in God as their exemplar, so was Christ the exemplar of all ecclesiastical offices. Wherefore each minister of the Church is, in some respect, a copy of Christ, as stated in the text (iv. *Sent.* D. 24). Yet he is the higher who represents Christ according to a greater perfection. Now a priest represents Christ in that He fulfilled a certain ministry by Himself, whereas a bishop represents Him in that He instituted other ministers and founded the Church. Hence it belongs to a bishop to dedicate a thing to the Divine offices, as establishing the Divine worship after the manner of Christ. For this reason also a

* The four Ember Saturdays. † Dist. lxxv, can. *Ordinationes.*

bishop is especially called the bridegroom o the Church even as Christ is.

We proceed thus to the Fifth Article:—

Objection 1. It would seem that the episco pate is an Order. First of all, because Diony sius (*Eccl. Hier.* v) assigns these three Order to the ecclesiastical hierarchy, the bishop, the priest, and the minister. In the text also (iv *Sent.* D. 24) it is stated that the episcopa Order is fourfold.

Obj. 2. Further, Order is nothing else but a degree of power in the dispensing of spiritua things. Now bishops can dispense certain sac raments which priests cannot dispense, namely Confirmation and Order. Therefore the epis copate is an Order.

Obj. 3. Further, in the Church there is no spiritual power other than of Order or juris diction. But things pertaining to the episcopal power are not matters of jurisdiction, else they might be committed to one who is not a bishop, which is false. Therefore they belong to the power of Order. Therefore the bishop has an Order which a simple priest has not and thus the episcopate is an Order.

On the contrary, One Order does not depend on a preceding Order as regards the validity of the sacrament. But the episcopal power depends on the priestly power, since no one can receive the episcopal power unless he have previously the priestly power. Therefore the episcopate is not an Order.

Further, the greater Orders are not conferred except on Saturdays.* But the episcopal power is bestowed on Sundays.† Therefore it is not an Order.

I answer that, Order may be understood in two ways. In one way as a sacrament, and thus, as already stated (Q. 37, AA. 2, 4), every Order is directed to the sacrament of the Eucharist. Wherefore since the bishop has not a higher power than the priest, in this respect the episcopate is not an Order. In another way Order may be considered as an office in relation to certain sacred actions: and thus since in hierarchical actions a bishop has in relation to the mystical body a higher power than the priest, the episcopate is an Order. It is in this sense that the authorities quoted speak.

Hence the *Reply* to the *First Objection* is clear.

Reply Obj. 2. Order considered as a sacrament which imprints a character is specially directed to the sacrament of the Eucharist, in which Christ Himself is contained, because by a character we are made like to Christ Himself.* Hence although at his promotion a bishop receives a spiritual power in respect of certain sacraments, this power nevertheless has not the nature of a character. For this reason the episcopate is not an Order, in the sense in which an Order is a sacrament.

Reply Obj. 3. The episcopal power is one not only of jurisdiction but also of Order, as stated above, taking Order in the sense in which it is generally understood.

SIXTH ARTICLE

Whether in the Church There Can Be Anyone above the Bishops?

We proceed thus to the Sixth Article:—

Objection 1. It would seem that there cannot be anyone in the Church higher than the bishops. For all the bishops are the successors of the apostles. Now the power so given to one of the apostles, namely Peter (Matth. xvi. 19), was given to all the apostles (Jo. xx. 23). Therefore all bishops are equal, and one is not above another.

Obj. 2. Further, the rite of the Church ought to be more conformed to the Jewish rite than to that of the Gentiles. Now the distinction of the episcopal dignity and the appointment of one over another, were introduced by the Gentiles, as stated in the text (iv. *Sent.* D. 24); and there was no such thing in the Old Law. Therefore neither in the Church should one bishop be above another.

Obj. 3. Further, a higher power cannot be conferred by a lower, nor equal by equal, because *without all contradiction that which is less is blessed by the greater* (Vulg.,—*better*); hence a priest does not consecrate a bishop or a priest, but a bishop consecrates a priest. But a bishop can consecrate any bishop, since even the bishop of Ostia consecrates the Pope. Therefore the episcopal dignity is equal in all matters, and consequently one bishop should not be subject to another, as stated in the text (iv. *Sent.* D. 24).

On the contrary, We read in the council of Constantinople: *In accordance with the Scriptures and the statutes and definitions of the canons, we venerate the most holy bishop of ancient Rome the first and greatest of bishops, and after him the bishop of Constantinople.* Therefore one bishop is above another.

Further, the blessed Cyril, bishop of Alexandria, says: *That we may remain members of our apostolic head, the throne of the Roman Pontiffs, of whom it is our duty to seek what we are to believe and what we are to hold, venerating him, beseeching him above others;*

*Cf. P. III, Q. 63, A. 3.

for his it is to reprove, to correct, to appoint, to loose, and to bind in place of Him Who set up that very throne, and Who gave the fulness of His own to no other, but to him alone, to whom by divine right all bow the head, and the primates of the world are obedient as to our Lord Jesus Christ Himself. Therefore bishops are subject to someone even by divine right.

I answer that, Wherever there are several authorities directed to one purpose, there must needs be one universal authority over the particular authorities, because in all virtues and acts the order is according to the order of their ends (*Ethic.* i. 1, 2). Now the common good is more Godlike than the particular good. Wherefore above the governing power which aims at a particular good there must be a universal governing power in respect of the common good, otherwise there would be no cohesion towards the one object. Hence since the whole Church is one body, it behooves, if this oneness is to be preserved, that there be a governing power in respect of the whole Church, above the episcopal power whereby each particular Church is governed, and this is the power of the Pope. Consequently those who deny this power are called schismatics as causing a division in the unity of the Church. Again, between a simple bishop and the Pope there are other degrees of rank corresponding to the degrees of union, in respect of which one congregation or community includes another; thus the community of a province includes the community of a city, and the community of a kingdom includes the community of one province, and the community of the whole world includes the community of one kingdom.

Reply Obj. 1. Although the power of binding and loosing was given to all the apostles in common, nevertheless in order to indicate some order in this power, it was given first of all to Peter alone, to show that this power must come down from him to the others. For this reason He said to him in the singular: *Confirm thy brethren* (Luke xxii. 32), and: *Feed My sheep* (Jo. xxi. 17, i.e. according to Chrysostom: *Be thou the president and head of thy brethren in My stead, that they, putting thee in My place, may preach and confirm thee throughout the world whilst thou sittest on thy throne.*

Reply Obj. 2. The Jewish rite was not spread abroad in various kingdoms and provinces, but was confined to one nation; hence there was no need to distinguish various pontiffs under the one who had the chief power. But the rite of the Church, like that of the Gentiles, is spread abroad through various nations; and consequently in this respect it is necessary for the constitution of the Church to be like the rite of the Gentiles rather than that of the Jews.

Reply Obj. 3. The priestly power is surpassed by the episcopal power, as by a power of a different kind; but the episcopal is surpassed by the papal power as by a power of the same kind. Hence a bishop can perform every hierarchical act that the Pope can; whereas a priest cannot perform every act that a bishop can in conferring the sacraments. Wherefore, as regards matters pertaining to the episcopal order, all bishops are equal, and for this reason any bishop can consecrate another bishop.

SEVENTH ARTICLE

Whether the Vestments of the Ministers Are Fittingly Instituted in the Church?

We proceed thus to the Seventh Article:—

Objection 1. It would seem that the vestments of the ministers are not fittingly instituted in the Church. For the ministers of the New Testament are more bound to chastity than were the ministers of the Old Testament. Now among the vestments of the Old Testament there were the breeches as a sign of chastity. Much more therefore should they have a place among the vestments of the Church's ministers.

Obj. 2. Further, the priesthood of the New Testament is more worthy than the priesthood of the Old. But the priests of the Old Testament had mitres, which are a sign of dignity. Therefore the priests of the New Testament should also have them.

Obj. 3. Further, the priest is nearer than the episcopal Order to the Orders of ministers. Now the bishop uses the vestments of the ministers, namely the dalmatic, which is the deacon's vestment, and the tunic, which is the subdeacon's. Much more therefore should simple priests use them.

Obj. 4. Further, in the Old Law the pontiff wore the ephod,* which signified the burden of the Gospel, as Bede observes *(De Tabernac.* iii). Now this is especially incumbent on our pontiffs. Therefore they ought to wear the ephod.

Obj. 5. Further, *Doctrine and Truth* were inscribed on the *rational* which the pontiffs of the Old Testament wore. Now truth was made known especially in the New Law. Therefore it is becoming to the pontiffs of the New Law.

Obj. 6. Further, the golden plate on which was written the most admirable name of God, was the most admirable of the adornments of the Old Law. Therefore it should especially have been transferred to the New Law.

Obj. 7. Further, the things which the ministers of the Church wear outwardly are signs

* Superhumerale, i.e. over-the-shoulders.

of inward power. Now the archbishop has no other kind of power than a bishop, as stated above (A. 6). Therefore he should not have the pallium which other bishops have not.

Obj. 8. Further, the fulness of power resides in the Roman Pontiff. But he has not a crozier. Therefore other bishops should not have one.

I answer that, The vestments of the ministers denote the qualifications required of them for handling Divine things. And since certain things are required of all, and some are required of the higher, that are not so exacted of the lower ministers, therefore certain vestments are common to all the ministers, while some pertain to the higher ministers only. Accordingly it is becoming to all the ministers to wear the *amice* which covers the shoulders, thereby signifying courage in the exercise of the Divine offices to which they are deputed; and the *alb*, which signifies a pure life, and the *girdle*, which signifies restraint of the flesh. But the subdeacon wears in addition the *maniple* on the left arm; this signifies the wiping away of the least stains, since a maniple is a kind of handkerchief for wiping the face; for they are the first to be admitted to the handling of sacred things. They also have the *narrow tunic,* signifying the doctrine of Christ; wherefore in the Old Law little bells hung therefrom, and subdeacons are the first admitted to announce the doctrine of the New Law. The deacon has in addition the *stole* over the left shoulder, as a sign that he is deputed to a ministry in the sacraments themselves, and the *dalmatic* (which is a full vestment, so called because it first came into use in Dalmatia), to signify that he is the first to be appointed to dispense the sacraments: for he dispenses the blood, and in dispensing one should be generous.

But in the case of the priest the *stole* hangs from both shoulders, to show that he has received full power to dispense the sacraments, and not as the minister of another man, for which reason the stole reaches right down. He also wears the *chasuble,* which signifies charity, because he it is who consecrates the sacrament of charity, namely the Eucharist.

Bishops have nine ornaments besides those which the priest has; these are the *stockings, sandals, succinctory, tunic, dalmatic, mitre, gloves, ring, and crozier,* because there are nine things which they can, but priests cannot, do, namely ordain clerics, bless virgins, consecrate bishops, impose hands, dedicate churches, depose clerics, celebrate synods, consecrate chrism, bless vestments and vessels.

We may also say that the *stockings* signify his upright walk; the *sandals* which cover the feet, his contempt of earthly things; the *suc-*

cinctory which girds the stole with the alb, his love of probity; the *tunic,* perseverance, for Joseph is said (Gen. xxxvii. 23) to have had a long tunic,—*talaric,* because it reached down to the ankles *(talos),* which denote the end of life; the *dalmatic,* generosity in works of mercy; the *gloves,* prudence in action; the *mitre,* knowledge of both Testaments, for which reason it has two crests; the *crozier,* his pastoral care, whereby he has to gather together the wayward (this is denoted by the curve at the head of the crozier), to uphold the weak (this is denoted by the stem of the crozier), and to spur on the laggards (this is denoted by the point at the foot of the crozier). Hence the line:

> Gather, uphold, spur on
> The wayward, the weak, and the laggard.

The *ring* signifies the sacraments of that faith whereby the Church is espoused to Christ. For bishops are espoused to the Church in the place of Christ. Furthermore archbishops have the *pallium* in sign of their privileged power, for it signifies the golden chain which those who fought rightfully were wont to receive.

Reply Obj. 1. The priests of the Old Law were enjoined continency only for the time of their attendance for the purpose of their ministry. Wherefore as a sign of the chastity which they had then to observe, they wore the breeches while offering sacrifices. But the ministers of the New Testament are enjoined perpetual continency; and so the comparison fails.

Reply Obj. 2. The mitre was not a sign of dignity, for it was a kind of hat, as Jerome says *(Ep. ad Fabiol.).* But the diadem which was a sign of dignity was given to the pontiffs alone, as the mitre is now.

Reply Obj. 3. The power of the ministers resides in the bishop as their source, but not in the priest, for he does not confer those Orders. Wherefore the bishop, rather than the priest, wears those vestments.

Reply Obj. 4. Instead of the ephod, they wear the stole, which is intended for the same signification as the ephod.

Reply Obj. 5. The pallium takes the place of the *rational.*

Reply Obj. 6. Instead of that plate our pontiff wears the cross, as Innocent III says *(De Myst. Miss.* i), just as the breeches are replaced by the sandals, the linen garment by the alb, the belt by the girdle, the long or talaric garment by the tunic, the ephod by the amice, the *rational* by the pallium, the diadem by the mitre.

Reply Obj. 7. Although he has not another kind of power he has the same power more fully; and so in order to designate this perfection, he receives the pallium which surrounds him on all sides.

Reply Obj. 8. The Roman Pontiff does not use a pastoral staff because Peter sent his to restore to life a certain disciple who afterwards became bishop of Treves. Hence in the diocese of Treves the Pope carries a crozier but not elsewhere. Or else it is a sign of his not having a restricted power denoted by the curve of the staff.

QUESTION 41

Of the Sacrament of Matrimony As Directed to an Office of Nature

(In Four Articles)

In the next place we must consider matrimony. We must treat of it (1) as directed to an office of nature; (2) as a sacrament; (3) as considered absolutely and in itself. Under the first head there are four points of inquiry: (1) Whether it is of natural law? (2) Whether it is a matter of precept? (3) Whether its act is lawful? (4) Whether its act can be meritorious?

FIRST ARTICLE

Whether Matrimony Is of Natural Law?

We proceed thus to the First Article:—

Objection 1. It would seem that matrimony is not natural. Because *the natural law is what nature has taught all animals.** But in other animals the sexes are united without matrimony. Therefore matrimony is not of natural law.

Obj. 2. Further, that which is of natural law is found in all men with regard to their every state. But matrimony was not in every state of man, for as Tully says *(De Inv. Rhet.)*, *at the beginning men were savages and then no man knew his own children, nor was he bound by any marriage tie,* wherein matrimony consists. Therefore it is not natural.

Obj. 3. Further, natural things are the same among all. But matrimony is not in the same way among all, since its practice varies according to the various laws. Therefore it is not natural.

Obj. 4. Further, those things without which the intention of nature can be maintained would seem not to be natural. But nature intends the preservation of the species by generation which is possible without matrimony, as in the case of fornicators. Therefore matrimony is not natural.

On the contrary, At the commencement of the *Digests* it is stated: *The union of male and female, which we call matrimony, is of natural law.*

Further, the Philosopher *(Ethic.* viii. 12) says that *man is an animal more inclined by nature to connubial than political society.* But *man is naturally a political and gregarious animal,* as the same author asserts *(Polit.* i. 2). Therefore he is naturally inclined to connubial union, and thus the conjugal union or matrimony is natural.

I answer that, A thing is said to be natural

* *Digest.* I, i, *de justitia et jure,* 1.

in two ways. First, as resulting of necessity from the principles of nature; thus upward movement is natural to fire. In this way matrimony is not natural, nor are any of those things that come to pass at the intervention or motion of the free-will. Secondly, that is said to be natural to which nature inclines, although it comes to pass through the intervention of the free-will; thus acts of virtue and the virtues themselves are called natural; and in this way matrimony is natural, because natural reason inclines thereto in two ways. First, in relation to the principal end of matrimony, namely the good of the offspring. For nature intends not only the begetting of offspring, but also its education and development until it reach the perfect state of man as man, and that is the state of virtue. Hence, according to the Philosopher *(Ethic.* viii. 11, 12), we derive three things from our parents, namely *existence, nourishment,* and *education.* Now a child cannot be brought up and instructed unless it have certain and definite parents, and this would not be the case unless there were a tie between the man and a definite woman, and it is in this that matrimony consists. Secondly, in relation to the secondary end of matrimony, which is the mutual services which married persons render one another in household matters. For just as natural reason dictates that men should live together, since one is not self-sufficient in all things concerning life, for which reason man is described as being naturally inclined to political society, so too among those works that are necessary for human life some are becoming to men, others to women. Wherefore nature inculcates that society of man and woman which consists in matrimony. These two reasons are given by the Philosopher *(Ethic.* viii, *loc. cit.).*

Reply Obj. 1. Man's nature inclines to a thing in two ways. In one way, because that thing is becoming to the generic nature, and this is common to all animals; in another way because it is becoming to the nature of the difference, whereby the human species in so far as it is rational overflows the genus; such is an act of prudence or temperance. And just as the generic nature, though one in all animals, yet is not in all in the same way, so neither does it incline in the same way in all, but in a way befitting each one. Accordingly man's nature inclines to matrimony on the part of the difference, as regards the second reason given above; wherefore the Philosopher *(loc. cit.; Polit.* i) gives this reason in men over other animals; but as regards the first reason it inclines on the part of the genus; wherefore he says that the begetting of offspring is common to all animals. Yet nature does not incline thereto in the same way in all animals; since there are animals whose offspring are able to seek food immediately after birth, or are sufficiently fed by their mother; and in these there is no tie between male and female; whereas in those whose offspring needs the support of both parents, although for a short time, there is a certain tie, as may be seen in certain birds. In man, however, since the child needs the parents' care for a long time, there is a very great tie between male and female, to which tie even the generic nature inclines.

Reply Obj. 2. The assertion of Tully may be true of some particular nation, provided we understand it as referring to the proximate beginning of that nation when it became a nation distinct from others; for that to which natural reason inclines is not realized in all things, and this statement is not universally true, since Holy Writ states that there has been matrimony from the beginning of the human race.

Reply Obj. 3. According to the Philosopher *(Ethic.* vii) *human nature is not unchangeable as the Divine nature is.* Hence things that are of natural law vary according to the various states and conditions of men; although those which naturally pertain to things Divine nowise vary.

Reply Obj. 4. Nature intends not only being in the offspring, but also perfect being, for which matrimony is necessary, as shown above.

SECOND ARTICLE

Whether Matrimony Still Comes under a Precept?

We proceed thus to the Second Article:—

Objection 1. It would seem that matrimony still comes under a precept. For a precept is binding so long as it is not recalled. But the primary institution of matrimony came under a precept, as stated in the text (iv. *Sent.* D. 26); nor do we read anywhere that this precept was recalled, but rather that it was confirmed (Matth. xix. 6): *What . . . God hath joined together let no man put asunder.* Therefore matrimony still comes under a precept.

Obj. 2. Further, the precepts of natural law are binding in respect of all time. Now matrimony is of natural law, as stated above (A. 1). Therefore, etc.

Obj. 3. Further, the good of the species is better than the good of the individual, *for the good of the State is more Godlike than the good of one man (Ethic.* i. 2). Now the precept given to the first man concerning the preservation of the good of the individual by the act of the nutritive power is still in force. Much more therefore does the precept concerning matrimony still hold, since it refers to the preservation of the species.

Obj. 4. Further, where the reason of an obligation remains the same, the obligation must remain the same. Now the reason why men were bound to marry in olden times was lest the human race should cease to multiply. Since then the result would be the same, if each one were free to abstain from marriage, it would seem that matrimony comes under a precept.

On the contrary, It is written (1 Cor. vii. 38): *He that giveth not his virgin in marriage, doth better,** namely than he that giveth her in marriage. Therefore the contract of marriage is not now a matter of precept.

Further, no one deserves a reward for breaking a precept. Now a special reward, namely the aureole, is due to virgins.† Therefore matrimony does not come under a precept.

I answer that, Nature inclines to a thing in two ways. In one way as to that which is necessary for the perfection of the individual, and such an obligation is binding on each one, since natural perfections are common to all. In another way it inclines to that which is necessary for the perfection of the community; and since there are many things of this kind, one of which hinders another, such an inclination does not bind each man by way of precept; else each man would be bound to husbandry and building and to such offices as are necessary to the human community; but the inclination of nature is satisfied by the accomplishment of those various offices by various individuals. Accordingly, since the perfection of the human community requires that some should devote themselves to the contemplative life to which marriage is a very great obstacle, the natural inclination to marriage is not binding by way of precept even according to the philosophers. Hence Theophrastus proves that it is not advisable for a wise man to marry, as Jerome relates *(Contra Jovin.* i).

Reply Obj. 1. This precept has not been recalled, and yet it is not binding on each individual, for the reason given above, except at that time when the paucity of men required each one to betake himself to the begetting of children.

The *Replies* to *Objections* 2 and 3 are clear from what has been said.

* Vulg.,—*He that giveth his virgin in marriage doth well, and he that giveth her not doth better.*
† Cf. Q. 96, A. 5.

Reply Obj. 4. Human nature has a general inclination to various offices and acts, as already stated. But since it is variously in various subjects, as individualized in this or that one, it inclines one subject more to one of those offices, and another subject more to another, according to the difference of temperament of various individuals. And it is owing to this difference, as well as to Divine providence which governs all, that one person chooses one office such as husbandry, and another person another. And so it is too that some choose the married life and some the contemplative. Wherefore no danger threatens.

THIRD ARTICLE

Whether the Marriage Act Is Always Sinful?

We proceed thus to the Third Article:—

Objection 1. It would seem that the marriage act is always sinful. For it is written (1 Cor. vii. 29): *That they . . . who have wives, be as if they had none.* But those who are not married do not perform the marriage act. Therefore even those who are married sin in that act.

Obj. 2. Further, *Your iniquities have divided between you and your God.* Now the marriage act divides man from God, wherefore the people who were to see God (Exod. xix. 11) were commanded not to go near their wives (*ibid.* 20); and Jerome says (*Ep. ad Ageruch.: Contra Jovin.* i. 18) that in the marriage act *the Holy Ghost touches not the hearts of the prophets.* Therefore it is sinful.

Obj. 3. Further, that which is shameful in itself can by no means be well done. Now the marriage act is always connected with concupiscence, which is always shameful. Therefore it is always sinful.

Obj. 4. Further, nothing is the object of excuse save sin. Now the marriage act needs to be excused by the marriage blessings, as the Master says (iv. *Sent.* D. 26). Therefore it is a sin.

Obj. 5. Further, things alike in species are judged alike. But marriage intercourse is of the same species as the act of adultery, since its end is the same, namely the human species. Therefore since the act of adultery is a sin, the marriage act is likewise.

Obj. 6. Further, excess in the passions corrupts virtue. Now there is always excess of pleasure in the marriage act, so much so that it absorbs the reason which is man's principal good, wherefore the Philosopher says (*Ethic.* vii. 11) that *in that act it is impossible to understand anything.* Therefore the marriage act is always a sin.

On the contrary, It is written (1 Cor. vii. 28): *If a virgin marry she hath not sinned,* and (1 Tim. v. 14): *I will . . . that the younger should marry,* and *bear children.* But there can be no bearing of children without carnal union. Therefore the marriage act is not a sin; else the Apostle would not have approved of it.

Further, no sin is a matter of precept. But the marriage act is a matter of precept (1 Cor. vii. 3): *Let the husband render the debt to his wife.* Therefore it is not a sin.

I answer that, If we suppose the corporeal nature to be created by the good God, we cannot hold that those things which pertain to the preservation of the corporeal nature and to which nature inclines, are altogether evil; wherefore, since the inclination to beget an offspring whereby the specific nature is preserved is from nature, it is impossible to maintain that the act of begetting children is altogether unlawful, so that it be impossible to find the mean of virtue therein; unless we suppose, as some are mad enough to assert, that corruptible things were created by an evil god, whence perhaps the opinion mentioned in the text is derived (iv. *Sent.* D. 26); wherefore this is a most wicked heresy.

Reply Obj. 1. By these words the Apostle did not forbid the marriage act, as neither did he forbid the possession of things when he said (*loc. cit.,* verse 31): *They that use this world* (let them be) *as if they used it not.* In each case he forbade enjoyment;* which is clear from the way in which he expresses himself; for he did not say *let them not use it,* or *let them not have them,* but let them be *as if they used it not* and *as if they had none.*

Reply Obj. 2. We are united to God by the habit of grace and by the act of contemplation and love. Therefore whatever severs the former of these unions is always a sin, but not always that which severs the latter, since a lawful occupation about lower things distracts the mind so that it is not fit for actual union with God; and this is especially the case in carnal intercourse wherein the mind is withheld by the intensity of pleasure. For this reason those who have to contemplate Divine things or handle sacred things are enjoined not to have to do with their wives for that particular time; and it is in this sense that the Holy Ghost, as regards the actual revelation of hidden things, did not touch the hearts of the prophets at the time of the marriage act.

Reply Obj. 3. The shamefulness of concupiscence that always accompanies the marriage act is a shamefulness not of guilt, but of punishment inflicted for the first sin, inasmuch as the lower powers and the members do not

* *Fruitionem,* i.e. enjoyment of a thing sought as one's last end.

obey reason. Hence the argument does not prove.

Reply Obj. 4. Properly speaking, a thing is said to be excused when it has some appearance of evil, and yet is not evil, or not as evil as it seems, because some things excuse wholly, others in part. And since the marriage act, by reason of the corruption of concupiscence, has the appearance of an inordinate act, it is wholly excused by the marriage blessing, so as not to be a sin.

Reply Obj. 5. Although they are the same as to their natural species, they differ as to their moral species, which differs in respect of one circumstance, namely intercourse with one's wife and with another than one's wife; just as to kill a man by assault or by justice differentiates the moral species, although the natural species is the same; and yet the one is lawful and the other unlawful.

Reply Obj. 6. The excess of passions that corrupts virtue not only hinders the act of reason, but also destroys the order of reason. The intensity of pleasure in the marriage act does not do this, since, although for the moment man is not being directed, he was previously directed by his reason.

FOURTH ARTICLE

Whether the Marriage Act Is Meritorious?

We proceed thus to the Fourth Article:—

Objection 1. It would seem that the marriage act is not meritorious. For Chrysostom* says in his commentary on Matthew: *Although marriage brings no punishment to those who use it, it affords them no meed.* Now merit bears a relation to meed. Therefore the marriage act is not meritorious.

Obj. 2. Further, to refrain from what is meritorious deserves not praise. Yet virginity whereby one refrains from marriage is praiseworthy. Therefore the marriage act is not meritorious.

Obj. 3. Further, he who avails himself of an indulgence granted him, avails himself of a favor received. But a man does not merit by receiving a favor. Therefore the marriage act is not meritorious.

Obj. 4. Further, merit like virtue, consists in difficulty. But the marriage act affords not difficulty but pleasure. Therefore it is not meritorious.

Obj. 5. Further, that which cannot be done without venial sin is never meritorious, for a man cannot both merit and demerit at the same time. Now there is always a venial sin in the marriage act, since even the first movement in such like pleasures is a venial sin. Therefore the aforesaid act cannot be meritorious.

On the contrary, Every act whereby a precept is fulfilled is meritorious if it be done from charity. Now such is the marriage act, for it is said (1 Cor. vii. 3): *Let the husband render the debt to his wife.* Therefore, etc.

Further, every act of virtue is meritorious. Now the aforesaid act is an act of justice, for it is called the rendering of a debt. Therefore it is meritorious.

I answer that, Since no act proceeding from a deliberate will is indifferent, as stated in the Second Book (ii. *Sent.* D. 40, Q. 1, A. 3; I-II, Q. 18, A. 9), the marriage act is always either sinful or meritorious in one who is in a state of grace. For if the motive for the marriage act be a virtue, whether of justice that they may render the debt, or of religion, that they may beget children for the worship of God, it is meritorious. But if the motive be lust, yet not excluding the marriage blessings, namely that he would by no means be willing to go to another woman, it is a venial sin; while if he exclude the marriage blessings, so as to be disposed to act in like manner with any woman, it is a mortal sin. And nature cannot move without being either directed by reason, and thus it will be an act of virtue, or not so directed, and then it will be an act of lust.

Reply Obj. 1. The root of merit, as regards the essential reward, is charity itself; but as regards an accidental reward, the reason for merit consists in the difficulty of an act; and thus the marriage act is not meritorious except in the first way.

Reply Obj. 2. The difficulty required for merit of the accidental reward is a difficulty of labor, but the difficulty required for the essential reward is the difficulty of observing the mean, and this is the difficulty in the marriage act.

Reply Obj. 3. First movements in so far as they are venial sins are movements of the appetite to some inordinate object of pleasure. This is not the case in the marriage act, and consequently the argument does not prove.

---

* *Hom.* i, in the *Opus Imperfectum,* falsely ascribed to S. John Chrysostom.

QUESTION 42

Of Matrimony As a Sacrament

(In Four Articles)

WE must next consider matrimony as a sacrament. Under this head there are four points of inquiry: (1) Whether matrimony is a sacrament? (2) Whether it ought to have been instituted before sin was committed? (3) Whether it confers grace? (4) Whether carnal intercourse belongs to the integrity of matrimony?

FIRST ARTICLE

Whether Matrimony Is a Sacrament?

We proceed thus to the First Article:—

Objection 1. It would seem that matrimony is not a sacrament. For every sacrament of the New Law has a form that is essential to the sacrament. But the blessing given by the priest at a wedding is not essential to matrimony. Therefore it is not a sacrament.

Obj. 2. Further, a sacrament according to Hugh *(De Sacram.* i) is a material element. But matrimony has not a material element for its matter. Therefore it is not a sacrament.

Obj. 3. Further, the sacraments derive their efficacy from Christ's Passion. But matrimony, since it has pleasure annexed to it, does not conform man to Christ's Passion, which was painful. Therefore it is not a sacrament.

Obj. 4. Further, every sacrament of the New Law causes that which it signifies. Yet matrimony does not cause the union of Christ with the Church, which union it signifies. Therefore matrimony is not a sacrament.

Obj. 5. Further, in the other sacraments there is something which is reality and sacrament. But this is not to be found in matrimony, since it does not imprint a character, else it would not be repeated. Therefore it is not a sacrament.

On the contrary, It is written (Eph. v. 32): *This is a great sacrament.* Therefore, etc.

Further, a sacrament is the sign of a sacred thing. But such is Matrimony. Therefore, etc.

I answer that, A sacrament denotes a sanctifying remedy against sin offered to man under sensible signs.* Wherefore since this is the case in matrimony, it is reckoned among the sacraments.

Reply Obj. 1. The words whereby the marriage consent is expressed are the form of this sacrament, and not the priest's blessing, which is a sacramental.

Reply Obj. 2. The sacrament of Matrimony, like that of Penance, is perfected by the act of the recipient. Wherefore just as Penance has no other matter than the sensible acts themselves, which take the place of the material element, so it is in Matrimony.

Reply Obj. 3. Although Matrimony is not conformed to Christ's Passion as regards pain, it is as regards charity, whereby He suffered for the Church who was to be united to Him as His spouse.

Reply Obj. 4. The union of Christ with the Church is not the reality contained in this sacrament, but is the reality signified and not contained,—and no sacrament causes a reality of that kind,—but it has another both contained and signified which it causes, as we shall state further on *(ad* 5). The Master, however (iv. *Sent.* D. 26), asserts that it is a non-contained reality, because he was of opinion that Matrimony has no reality contained therein.

Reply Obj. 5. In this sacrament also those three things† are to be found, for the acts externally apparent are the sacrament only; the bond between husband and wife resulting from those acts is reality and sacrament; and the ultimate reality contained is the effect of this sacrament, while the non-contained reality is that which the Master assigns *(loc. cit.).*

SECOND ARTICLE

Whether This Sacrament Ought to Have Been Instituted before Sin Was Committed?

We proceed thus to the Second Article:—

Objection 1. It would seem that Matrimony ought not to have been instituted before sin. Because that which is of natural law needs not to be instituted. Now such is Matrimony, as stated above (Q. 41, A. 1). Therefore it ought not to have been instituted.

Obj. 2. Further, sacraments are medicines against the disease of sin. But a medicine is not made ready except for an actual disease. Therefore it should not have been instituted before sin.

Obj. 3. Further, one institution suffices for one thing. Now Matrimony was instituted also after sin, as stated in the text (iv. *Sent.* D. 26). Therefore it was not instituted before sin.

Obj. 4. Further, the institution of a sacrament must come from God. Now before sin, the words relating to Matrimony were not definitely said by God but by Adam; the words which God uttered (Gen. i. 22), *In-*

* Cf. P. III, Q. 61, A. 1; Q. 65, A. 1.   † Cf. P. III, Q. 66, A. 1.

crease and multiply, were addressed also to the brute creation where there is no marriage. Therefore Matrimony was not instituted before sin.

Obj. 5. Further, Matrimony is a sacrament of the New Law. But the sacraments of the New Law took their origin from Christ. Therefore it ought not to have been instituted before sin.

On the contrary, It is said (Matth. xix. 4): *Have ye not read that He Who made man from the beginning "made them male and female"?*

Further, Matrimony was instituted for the begetting of children. But the begetting of children was necessary to man before sin. Therefore it behooved Matrimony to be instituted before sin.

I answer that, Nature inclines to marriage with a certain good in view, which good varies according to the different states of man, wherefore it was necessary for matrimony to be variously instituted in the various states of man in reference to that good. Consequently matrimony as directed to the begetting of children, which was necessary even when there was no sin, was instituted before sin; according as it affords a remedy for the wound of sin, it was instituted after sin at the time of the natural law; its institution belongs to the Mosaic Law as regards personal disqualifications; and it was instituted in the New Law in so far as it represents the mystery of Christ's union with the Church, and in this respect it is a sacrament of the New Law. As regards other advantages resulting from matrimony, such as the friendship and mutual services which husband and wife render one another, its institution belongs to the civil law. Since, however, a sacrament is essentially a sign and a remedy, it follows that the nature of sacrament applies to matrimony as regards the intermediate institution; that it is fittingly intended to fulfill an office of nature as regards the first institution; and, as regards the last-mentioned institution, that it is directed to fulfill an office of society.

Reply Obj. 1. Things which are of natural law in a general way, need to be instituted as regards their determination which is subject to variation according to various states; just as it is of natural law that evil-doers be punished, but that such and such a punishment be appointed for such and such a crime is determined by positive law.

Reply Obj. 2. Matrimony is not only for a remedy against sin, but is chiefly for an office of nature; and thus it was instituted before sin, not as intended for a remedy.

Reply Obj. 3. There is no reason why matrimony should not have had several institutions corresponding to the various things that had to be determined in connection with marriage. Hence these various institutions are not of the same thing in the same respect.

Reply Obj. 4. Before sin matrimony was instituted by God, when He fashioned a helpmate for man out of his rib, and said to them: *Increase and multiply.* And although this was said also to the other animals, it was not to be fulfilled by them in the same way as by men. As to Adam's words, he uttered them inspired by God to understand that the institution of marriage was from God.

Reply Obj. 5. As was clearly stated, matrimony was not instituted before Christ as a sacrament of the New Law.

THIRD ARTICLE

Whether Matrimony Confers Grace?

We proceed thus to the Third Article:—

Objection 1. It would seem that matrimony does not confer grace. For, according to Hugh *(De Sacram.* i) *the sacraments, by virtue of their sanctification, confer an invisible grace.* But matrimony has no sanctification essential to it. Therefore grace is not conferred therein.

Obj. 2. Further, every sacrament that confers grace confers it by virtue of its matter and form. Now the acts which are the matter in this sacrament are not the cause of grace (for it would be the heresy of Pelagius to assert that our acts cause grace); and the words expressive of consent are not the cause of grace, since no sanctification results from them. Therefore grace is by no means given in matrimony.

Obj. 3. Further, the grace that is directed against the wound of sin is necessary to all who have that wound. Now the wound of concupiscence is to be found in all. Therefore, if grace were given in matrimony against the wound of concupiscence, all men ought to contract marriage, and it would be very stupid to refrain from matrimony.

Obj. 4. Further, sickness does not seek a remedy where it finds aggravation. Now concupiscence is aggravated by concupiscence, because, according to the Philosopher *(Ethic.* iii. 12), *the desire of concupiscence is insatiable, and is increased by congenial actions.* Therefore it would seem that grace is not conferred in matrimony, as a remedy for concupiscence.

On the contrary, Definition and thing defined should be convertible. Now causality of grace is included in the definition of a sacrament. Since, then, matrimony is a sacrament, it is a cause of grace.

Further, Augustine says *(De Bono Viduit.* viii; *Gen. ad lit.* ix. 7) that *matrimony affords a remedy to the sick.* But it is not a remedy except in so far as it has some efficacy. Therefore it has some efficacy for the repression of concupiscence. Now concupiscence is not repressed except by grace. Therefore grace is conferred therein.

I answer that, There have been three opinions on this point. For some* said that matrimony is nowise the cause of grace, but only a sign thereof. But this cannot be maintained, for in that case it would in no respect surpass the sacraments of the Old Law. Wherefore there would be no reason for reckoning it among the sacraments of the New Law; since even in the Old Law by the very nature of the act it was able to afford a remedy to concupiscence lest the latter run riot when held in too strict restraint.

Hence others† said that grace is conferred therein as regards the withdrawal from evil, because the act is excused from sin, for it would be a sin apart from matrimony. But this would be too little, since it had this also in the Old Law. And so they say that it makes man withdraw from evil, by restraining the concupiscence lest it tend to something outside the marriage blessings, but that this grace does not enable a man to do good works. But this cannot be maintained, since the same grace hinders sin and inclines to good, just as the same heat expels cold and gives heat.

Hence others§ say that matrimony, inasmuch as it is contracted in the faith of Christ, is able to confer the grace which enables us to do those works which are required in matrimony; and this is more probable, since wherever God gives the faculty to do a thing, He gives also the helps whereby man is enabled to make becoming use of that faculty; thus it is clear that to all the soul's powers there correspond bodily members by which they can proceed to act. Therefore, since in matrimony man receives by Divine institution the faculty to use his wife for the begetting of children, he also receives the grace without which he cannot becomingly do so; just as we have said of the sacrament of Orders (Q. 35, A. 1). And thus this grace which is given the last thing contained in this sacrament.

Reply Obj. 1. Just as the baptismal water by virtue of its contact with Christ's body** is able to *touch the body and cleanse the heart,*†† so is matrimony able to do so through Christ having represented it by His Passion, and not principally through any blessing of the priest.

Reply Obj. 2. Just as the water of Baptism together with the form of words results immediately not in the infusion of grace, but in the imprinting of the character, so the outward

acts and the words expressive of consent directly effect a certain tie which is the sacrament of matrimony; and this tie by virtue of its Divine institution works dispositively‡‡ to the infusion of grace.

Reply Obj. 3. This argument would hold if no more efficacious remedy could be employed against the disease of concupiscence; but a yet more powerful remedy is found in spiritual works and mortification of the flesh by those who make no use of matrimony.

Reply Obj. 4. A remedy can be employed against concupiscence in two ways. First, on the part of concupiscence by repressing it in its root, and thus matrimony affords a remedy by the grace given therein. Secondly, on the part of its act, and this in two ways: first, by depriving the act to which concupiscence inclines of its outward shamefulness, and this is done by the marriage blessings which justify carnal concupiscence; secondly, by hindering the shameful act, which is done by the very nature of the act; because concupiscence, being satisfied by the conjugal act, does not incline so much to other wickedness. For this reason the Apostle says (1 Cor. vii. 9): *It is better to marry than to burn.* For though the works congenial to concupiscence are in themselves of a nature to increase concupiscence, yet in so far as they are directed according to reason they repress concupiscence, because like acts result in like dispositions and habits.

FOURTH ARTICLE

Whether Carnal Intercourse Is an Integral Part of This Sacrament?

We proceed thus to the Fourth Article:—

Objection 1. It would seem that carnal intercourse is an integral part of marriage. For at the very institution of marriage it was declared (Gen. ii. 24): *They shall be two in one flesh.* Now this is not brought about save by carnal intercourse. Therefore it is an integral part of marriage.

Obj. 2. Further, that which belongs to the signification of a sacrament is necessary for the sacrament, as we have stated above (A. 2; Q. 9, A. 1). Now carnal intercourse belongs to the signification of matrimony, as stated in the text (iv. *Sent.* D. 26). Therefore it is an integral part of the sacrament.

Obj. 3. Further, this sacrament is directed to the preservation of the species. But the species cannot be preserved without carnal intercourse. Therefore it is an integral part of the sacrament.

Obj. 4. Further, Matrimony is a sacrament

---

* Peter Lombard, iv, *Sent.* D. 2.   † S. Albert Magn., iv, *Sent.* D. 26.   § S. Bonavent., iv, *Sent.* D. 26.
** Cf. P. III, Q. 66, A. 3, *ad* 4.   †† S. Augustine, *Tract.* lxxx, *in Joan.*   ‡‡ Cf. Q. 18, A. 1, where S. Thomas uses the same expression; and Editor's notes at the beginning of the Supplement and on that *Article.*

inasmuch as it affords a remedy against concupiscence; according to the Apostle's saying (1 Cor. vii. 9): *It is better to marry than to burn.* But it does not afford this remedy to those who have no carnal intercourse. Therefore the same conclusion follows as before.

On the contrary, There was matrimony in Paradise, and yet there was no carnal intercourse. Therefore carnal intercourse is not an integral part of matrimony.

Further, a sacrament by its very name denotes a sanctification. But matrimony is holier without carnal intercourse, according to the text (iv. *Sent.* D. 26). Therefore carnal intercourse is not necessary for the sacrament.

I answer that, Integrity is twofold. One regards the primal perfection consisting in the very essence of a thing; the other regards the secondary perfection consisting in operation. Since then carnal intercourse is an operation or use of marriage which gives the faculty for that intercourse, it follows that carnal intercourse belongs to the latter, and not to the former integrity of marriage.*

Reply Obj. 1. Adam expressed the integrity of marriage in regard to both perfections, because a thing is known by its operation.

Reply Obj. 2. Signification of the thing contained is necessary for the sacrament. Carnal intercourse belongs not to this signification, but to the thing not contained, as appears from what was said above (A. 1, *ad* 4, 5).

Reply Obj. 3. A thing does not reach its end except by its own act. Wherefore, from the fact that the end of matrimony is not attained without carnal intercourse, it follows that it belongs to the second and not to the first integrity.

Reply Obj. 4. Before carnal intercourse marriage is a remedy by virtue of the grace given therein, although not by virtue of the act, which belongs to the second integrity.

QUESTION 43

Of Matrimony with Regard to the Betrothal

(In Three Articles)

In the next place we must consider matrimony absolutely; and here we must treat (1) of the betrothal; (2) of the nature of matrimony; (3) of its efficient cause, namely the consent; (4) of its blessings; (5) of the impediments thereto; (6) of second marriages; (7) of certain things annexed to marriage.

Under the first head there are three points of inquiry: (1) What is the betrothal? (2) Who can contract a betrothal? (3) Whether a betrothal can be canceled?

FIRST ARTICLE

Whether a Betrothal Is a Promise of Future Marriage?

We proceed thus to the First Article:—

Objection 1. It would seem that a betrothal is not rightly defined *a promise of future marriage,* as expressed in the words of Pope Nicholas I *(Resp. ad Consul. Bulgar.,* iii). For as Isidore says *(Etym.* iv), *a man is betrothed not by a mere promise, but by giving his troth (spondet) and providing sureties (sponsores).* Now a person is said to be betrothed by reason of his betrothal. Therefore it is wrongly described as a promise.

Obj. 2. Further, whoever promises a thing must be compelled to fulfill his promise. But those who have contracted a betrothal are not compelled by the Church to fulfill the marriage. Therefore a betrothal is not a promise.

Obj. 3. Further, sometimes a betrothal does

*Cf. P. III, Q. 29, A. 2.

not consist of a mere promise, but an oath is added, as also certain pledges. Therefore seemingly it should not be defined as a mere promise.

Obj. 4. Further, marriage should be free and absolute. But a betrothal is sometimes expressed under a condition even of money to be received. Therefore it is not fittingly described as a promise of marriage.

Obj. 5. Further, promising about the future is blamed in James iv *(verse* 13 *seqq.).* But there should be nothing blameworthy about the sacraments. Therefore one ought not to make a promise of future marriage.

Obj. 6. Further, no man is called a spouse except on account of his espousals. But a man is said to be a spouse on account of actual marriage, according to the text (iv. *Sent.* D. 27). Therefore espousals are not always a promise of future marriage.

I answer that, Consent to conjugal union if expressed in words of the future does not make a marriage, but a promise of marriage; and this promise is called *a betrothal from plighting one's troth,* as Isidore says *(loc. cit.).* For before the use of writing-tablets, they used to give pledges of marriage, by which they plighted their mutual consent under the marriage code, and they provided guarantors. This promise is made in two ways, namely absolutely, or conditionally. Absolutely, in four ways: firstly, a mere promise, by saying: *I will take thee for my wife,* and conversely;

secondly, by giving betrothal pledges, such as money and the like; thirdly, by giving an engagement ring; fourthly, by the addition of an oath. If, however, this promise be made conditionally, we must draw a distinction; for it is either an honorable condition, for instance if we say: *I will take thee, if thy parents consent,* and then the promise holds if the condition is fulfilled, and does not hold if the condition is not fulfilled; or else the condition is dishonorable, and this in two ways: for either it is contrary to the marriage blessings, as if we were to say: *I will take thee if thou promise means of sterility,* and then no betrothal is contracted; or else it is not contrary to the marriage blessings, as were one to say: *I will take thee if thou consent to my thefts,* and then the promise holds, but the condition should be removed.

Reply Obj. 1. The betrothal itself and giving of sureties are a ratification of the promise, wherefore it is denominated from these as from that which is more perfect.

Reply Obj. 2. By this promise one party is bound to the other in respect of contracting marriage; and he who fulfills not his promise sins mortally, unless a lawful impediment arise; and the Church uses compulsion in the sense that she enjoins a penance for the sin. But he is not compelled by sentence of the court, because compulsory marriages are wont to have evil results; unless the parties be bound by oath, for then he ought to be compelled, in the opinion of some, although others think differently on account of the reason given above, especially if there be fear of one taking the other's life.

Reply Obj. 3. Such things are added only in confirmation of the promise, and consequently they are not distinct from it.

Reply Obj. 4. The condition that is appended does not destroy the liberty of marriage; for if it be unlawful, it should be renounced; and if it be lawful, it is either about things that are good simply, as were one to say, *I will take thee, if thy parents consent,* and such a condition does not destroy the liberty of the betrothal, but gives it an increase of rectitude; or else it is about things that are useful, as were one to say: *I will marry thee if thou pay me a hundred pounds,* and then this condition is appended, not as asking a price for the consent of marriage, but as referring to the promise of a dowry; so that the marriage does not lose its liberty. Sometimes, however, the condition appended is the payment of a sum of money by way of penalty, and then, since marriage should be free, such a condition does not hold, nor can such a penalty be exacted from a person who is unwilling to fulfill the promise of marriage.

Reply Obj. 5. James does not intend to forbid altogether the making of promises about the future, but the making of promises as though one were certain of one's life; hence he teaches that we ought to add the condition: *If the Lord will,* which, though it be not expressed in words, ought nevertheless to be impressed on the heart.

Reply Obj. 6. In marriage we may consider both the marriage union and the marriage act; and on account of his promise of the first as future a man is called a *spouse* from his having contracted his espousals by words expressive of the future; but from the promise of the second a man is called a *spouse,* even when the marriage has been contracted by words expressive of the present, because by this very fact he promises *(spondet)* the marriage act. However, properly speaking, espousals are so called from the promise *(sponsione)* in the first sense, because espousals are a kind of sacramental annexed to matrimony, as exorcism to baptism.

SECOND ARTICLE

Whether Seven Years Is Fittingly Assigned As the Age for Betrothal?

We proceed thus to the Second Article:—

Objection 1. It would seem that seven years is not fittingly assigned as the age for betrothal. For a contract that can be formed by others does not require discretion in those whom it concerns. Now a betrothal can be arranged by the parents without the knowledge of either of the persons betrothed. Therefore a betrothal can be arranged before the age of seven years as well as after.

Obj. 2. Further, just as some use of reason is necessary for the contract of betrothal, so is there for the consent to mortal sin. Now, as Gregory says *(Dial.* iv), a boy of five years of age was carried off by the devil on account of the sin of blasphemy. Therefore a betrothal can take place before the age of seven years.

Obj. 3. Further, a betrothal is directed to marriage. But for marriage the same age is not assigned to boy and girl.

Obj. 4. Further, one can become betrothed as soon as future marriage can be agreeable to one. Now signs of this agreeableness are often apparent in boys before the age of seven. Therefore they can become betrothed before that age.

Obj. 5. Further, if persons become betrothed before they are seven years old, and subsequently after the age of seven and before the age of maturity renew their promise in words expressive of the present, they are reckoned to be betrothed. Now this is not by virtue of the second contract, since they intend to contract not betrothal but marriage. Therefore it is by the virtue of the first; and thus espousals can be contracted before the age of seven.

Obj. 6. Further, when a thing is done by many persons in common, if one fails he is supplied by another, as in the case of those who row a boat. Now the contract of betrothal is an action common to the contracting parties. Therefore if one be of mature age, he can contract a betrothal with a girl who is not seven years old, since the lack of age in one is more than counterbalanced in the other.

Obj. 7. Further, those who at about the age of puberty, but before it, enter into the marriage contract by words expressive of the present are reputed to be married. Therefore in like manner if they contract marriage by words expressive of the future, before yet close on the age of puberty, they are to be reputed as betrothed.

I answer that, The age of seven years is fixed reasonably enough by law for the contracting of betrothals, for since a betrothal is a promise of the future, as already stated (A. 1), it follows that they are within the competency of those who can make a promise in some way, and this is only for those who can have some foresight of the future, and this requires the use of reason, of which three degrees are to be observed, according to the Philosopher (*Ethic.* i. 4). The first is when a person neither understands by himself nor is able to learn from another; the second stage is when a man can learn from another but is incapable by himself of consideration and understanding; the third degree is when a man is both able to learn from another and to consider by himself. And since reason develops in man by little and little, in proportion as the movement and fluctuation of the humors is calmed, man reaches the first stage of reason before his seventh year; and consequently during that period he is unfit for any contract, and therefore for betrothal. But he begins to reach the second stage at the end of his first seven years, wherefore children at that age are sent to school. But man begins to reach the third stage at the end of his second seven years, as regards things concerning his person, when his natural reason develops; but as regards things outside his person, at the end of his third seven years. Hence before his first seven years a man is not fit to make any contract, but at the end of that period he begins to be fit to make certain promises for the future, especially about those things to which natural reason inclines us more, though he is not fit to bind himself by a perpetual obligation, because as yet he has not a firm will. Hence at that age betrothals can be contracted. But at the end of the second seven years he can already bind himself in matters concerning his person, either to religion or to wedlock. And after the third seven years he can bind himself in other matters also; and according to the laws he is given the power of disposing of his property after his twenty-second year.

Reply Obj. 1. If the parties are betrothed by another person before they reach the age of puberty, either of them or both can demur; wherefore in that case the betrothal does not take effect, so that neither does any affinity result therefrom. Hence a betrothal made between certain persons by some other takes effect, in so far as those between whom the betrothal is arranged do not demur when they reach the proper age, whence they are understood to consent to what others have done.

Reply Obj. 2. Some say that the boy of whom Gregory tells this story was not lost, and that he did not sin mortally; and that this vision was for the purpose of making the father sorrowful, for he had sinned in the boy through failing to correct him. But this is contrary to the express intention of Gregory, who says (*loc. cit.*) that *the boy's father having neglected the soul of his little son, fostered no little sinner for the flames of hell.* Consequently it must be said that for a mortal sin it is sufficient to give consent to something present, whereas in a betrothal the consent is to something future; and greater discretion of reason is required for looking to the future than for consenting to one present act. Wherefore a man can sin mortally before he can bind himself to a future obligation.

Reply Obj. 3. Regarding the age for the marriage contract a disposition is required not only on the part of the use of reason, but also on the part of the body, in that it is necessary to be of an age adapted to procreation. And since a girl becomes apt for the act of procreation in her twelfth year, and a boy at the end of his second seven years, as the Philosopher says (*De Hist. Anim.* vii), whereas the age is the same in both for attaining the use of reason which is the sole condition for betrothal, hence it is that the one age is assigned for both as regards betrothal, but not as regards marriage.

Reply Obj. 4. This agreeableness in regard to boys under the age of seven does not result from the perfect use of reason, since they are not as yet possessed of complete self-control; it results rather from the movement of nature than from any process of reason. Consequently, this agreeableness does not suffice for contracting a betrothal.

Reply Obj. 5. In this case, although the second contract does not amount to marriage, nevertheless the parties show that they ratify their former promise; wherefore the first contract is confirmed by the second.

Reply Obj. 6. Those who row a boat act by way of one cause, and consequently what is lacking in one can be supplied by another. But those who make a contract of betrothal act as distinct persons, since a betrothal can only be between two parties; wherefore it is necessary for each to be qualified to contract, and thus the defect of one is an obstacle to their betrothal, nor can it be supplied by the other.

Reply Obj. 7. It is true that in the matter of betrothal if the contracting parties are close upon the age of seven, the contract of betrothal is valid, since, according to the Philosopher *(Phys.* ii. 56), *when little is lacking it seems as though nothing were lacking.* Some fix the margin at six months; but it is better to determine it according to the condition of the contracting parties, since the use of reason comes sooner to some than to others.

THIRD ARTICLE

Whether a Betrothal Can Be Dissolved?

We proceed thus to the Third Article:—

Objection 1. It would seem that a betrothal cannot be dissolved if one of the parties enter religion. For if I have promised a thing to someone I cannot lawfully pledge it to someone else. Now he who betroths himself promises his body to the woman. Therefore he cannot make a further offering of himself to God in religion.

Obj. 2. Again, seemingly it should not be dissolved when one of the parties leaves for a distant country, because in doubtful matters one should always choose the safer course. Now the safer course would be to wait for him. Therefore she is bound to wait for him.

Obj. 3. Again, neither seemingly is it dissolved by sickness contracted after betrothal, for no man should be punished for being under a penalty. Now the man who contracts an infirmity would be punished if he were to lose his right to the woman betrothed to him. Therefore a betrothal should not be dissolved on account of a bodily infirmity.

Obj. 4. Again, neither seemingly should a betrothal be dissolved on account of a supervening affinity, for instance if the spouse were to commit fornication with a kinswoman of his betrothed; for in that case the affianced bride would be penalized for the sin of her affianced spouse, which is unreasonable.

Obj. 5. Again, seemingly they cannot set one another free; for it would be a proof of greatest fickleness if they contracted together and then set one another free; and such conduct ought not to be tolerated by the Church. Therefore, etc.

Obj. 6. Again, neither seemingly ought a betrothal to be dissolved on account of the fornication of one of the parties. For a betrothal does not yet give the one power over the body of the other; wherefore it would seem that they nowise sin against one another if meanwhile they commit fornication. Consequently a betrothal should not be dissolved on that account.

Obj. 7. Again, neither seemingly on account of his contracting with another woman by words expressive of the present. For a subsequent sale does not void a previous sale. Therefore neither should a second contract void a previous one.

Obj. 8. Again, neither seemingly should it be dissolved on account of deficient age; since what is not cannot be dissolved. Now a betrothal is null before the requisite age. Therefore it cannot be dissolved.

I answer that, In all the cases mentioned above the betrothal that has been contracted is dissolved, but in different ways. For in two of them,—namely when a party enters religion, and when either of the affianced spouses contracts with another party by words expressive of the present,—the betrothal is dissolved by law, whereas in the other cases it has to be dissolved according to the judgment of the Church.

Reply Obj. 1. The like promise is dissolved by spiritual death, for that promise is purely spiritual, as we shall state further on (Q. 61, A. 2).

Reply Obj. 2. This doubt is solved by either party not putting in an appearance at the time fixed for completing the marriage. Wherefore, if it was no fault of that party that the marriage was not completed, he or she can lawfully marry without any sin. But if he or she was responsible for the non-completion of the marriage, this responsibility involves the obligation of doing penance for the broken promise,—or oath if the promise was confirmed by oath,—and he or she can contract with another if they wish it, subject to the judgment of the Church.

Reply Obj. 3. If either of the betrothed parties incur an infirmity which notably weakens the subject (as epilepsy or paralysis), or causes a deformity (as loss of the nose or eyes, and the like), or is contrary to the good of the offspring (as leprosy, which is wont to be transmitted to the children), the betrothal can be dissolved, lest the betrothed be displeasing to one another, and the marriage thus contracted have an evil result. Nor is one punished for being under a penalty, although one incurs a loss from one's penalty, and this is not unreasonable.

Reply Obj. 4. If the affianced bridegroom

has carnal knowledge of a kinswoman of his spouse, or *vice versa,* the betrothal must be dissolved; and for proof it is sufficient that the fact be the common talk, in order to avoid scandal; for causes whose effects mature in the future are voided of their effects, not only by what actually is, but also by what happens subsequently. Hence just as affinity, had it existed at the time of the betrothal, would have prevented that contract, so, if it supervene before marriage, which is an effect of the betrothal, the previous contract is voided of its effect. Nor does the other party suffer in consequence, indeed he or she gains, being set free from one who has become hateful to God by committing fornication.

Reply Obj. 5. Some do not admit this case. Yet they have against them the Decretal (cap. *Præterea,* De spons. et matr.) which says expressly: *Just as those who enter into a contract of fellowship by pledging their faith to one another and afterwards give it back, so it may be patiently tolerated that those who are betrothed to one another should set one another free.* Yet to this they say that the Church allows this lest worse happen rather than because it is according to strict law. But this does not seem to agree with the example quoted by the Decretal.

Accordingly we must reply that it is not always a proof of fickleness to rescind an agreement, since *our counsels are uncertain* (Wis. ix. 14).

Reply Obj. 6. Although when they become betrothed they have not yet given one another power over one another's body, yet if this* were to happen it would make them suspicious of one another's fidelity; and so one can ensure himself against the other by breaking off the engagement.

Reply Obj. 7. This argument would hold if each contract were of the same kind; whereas the second contract of marriage has greater force than the first, and consequently dissolves it.

Reply Obj. 8. Although it was not a true betrothal, there was a betrothal of a kind; and consequently, lest approval should seem to be given when they come to the lawful age, they should seek a dissolution of the betrothal by the judgment of the Church, for the sake of a good example.

QUESTION 44

Of the Definition of Matrimony

(In Three Articles)

WE must now consider the nature of matrimony. Under this head there are three points of inquiry: (1) Whether matrimony is a kind of joining? (2) Whether it is fittingly named? (3) Whether it is fittingly defined?

FIRST ARTICLE

Whether Matrimony Is a Kind of Joining?

We proceed thus to the First Article:—

Objection 1. It would seem that matrimony is not a kind of joining. Because the bond whereby things are tied together differs from their joining, as cause from effect. Now matrimony is the bond whereby those who are joined in matrimony are tied together. Therefore it is not a kind of joining.

Obj. 2. Further, every sacrament is a sensible sign. But no relation is a sensible accident. Therefore since matrimony is a sacrament, it is not a kind of relation, and consequently neither is it a kind of joining.

Obj. 3. Further, a joining is a relation of equiparance as well as of equality. Now according to Avicenna the relation of equality is not identically the same in each extreme. Neither therefore is there an identically same

* Referring to the contention of the *Objection.*

joining; and consequently if matrimony is a kind of joining, there is not only one matrimony between man and wife.

On the contrary, It is by relation that things are related to one another. Now by matrimony certain things are related to one another; for the husband is the wife's husband, and the wife is the husband's wife. Therefore matrimony is a kind of relation, nor is it other than a joining.

Further, the union of two things into one can result only from their being joined. Now such is the effect of matrimony (Gen. ii. 24): *They shall be two in one flesh.* Therefore matrimony is a kind of joining.

I answer that, A joining denotes a kind of uniting, and so wherever things are united there must be a joining. Now things directed to one purpose are said to be united in their direction thereto, thus many men are united in following one military calling or in pursuing one business, in relation to which they are called fellow-soldiers or business partners. Hence, since by marriage certain persons are directed to one begetting and upbringing of children, and again to one family life, it is clear that in matrimony there is a joining in respect of which we speak of husband and wife; and this joining, through being directed to some one thing, is matrimony; while the joining together of bodies and minds is a result of matrimony.

Reply Obj. 1. Matrimony is the bond by which they are tied formally, not effectively, and so it need not be distinct from the joining.

Reply Obj. 2. Although relation is not itself a sensible accident, its causes may be sensible. Nor is it necessary in a sacrament for that which is both reality and sacrament* to be sensible (for such is the relation of the aforesaid joining to this sacrament), whereas the words expressive of consent, which are sacrament only and are the cause of that same joining, are sensible.

Reply Obj. 3. A relation is founded on something as its cause,—for instance likeness is founded on quality,—and on something as its subject,—for instance in the things themselves that are like; and on either hand we may find unity and diversity of relation. Since then it is not the same identical quality that conduces to likeness, but the same specific quality in each of the like subjects, and since, moreover, the subjects of likeness are two in number, and the same applies to equality, it follows that both equality and likeness are in every way numerically distinct in either of the like or equal subjects. But the relations of matrimony, on the one hand, have unity in both extremes, namely on the part of the cause, since it is directed to the one identical begetting; whereas on the part of the subject there is numerical diversity. The fact of this relation having a diversity of subjects is signified by the terms *husband* and *wife*, while its unity is denoted by its being called matrimony.

SECOND ARTICLE

Whether Matrimony Is Fittingly Named?

We proceed thus to the Second Article:—

Objection 1. It would seem that matrimony is unfittingly named. Because a thing should be named after that which ranks higher. But the father ranks above the mother. Therefore the union of father and mother should rather be named after the father.

Obj. 2. Further, a thing should be named from that which is essential to it, since a *definition expresses the nature signified by a name* (*Met.* iv. 28). Now nuptials are not essential to matrimony. Therefore matrimony should not be called nuptials.

Obj. 3. Further, a species cannot take its proper name from that which belongs to the genus. Now a joining (*conjunctio*) is the

genus of matrimony. Therefore it should not be called a conjugal union.

On the contrary, stands the common use of speech.

I answer that, Three things may be considered in matrimony. First, its essence, which is a joining together, and in reference to this it is called the *conjugal union;* secondly, its cause, which is the wedding, and in reference to this it is called the *nuptial union* from *nubo,*† because at the wedding ceremony, whereby the marriage is completed, the heads of those who are wedded are covered with a veil;‡ thirdly, the effect, which is the offspring, and in reference to this it is called *matrimony,* as Augustine says (*Contra Faust.* xix. 26), because *a woman's sole purpose in marrying should be motherhood.* Matrimony may also be resolved into *matris munium,*§ i.e. a mother's duty, since the duty of bringing up the children chiefly devolves on the women; or into *matrem muniens,* because it provides the mother with a protector and support in the person of her husband; or into *matrem monens,* as admonishing her not to leave her husband and take up with another man; or into *materia unius,* because it is a joining together for the purpose of providing the matter of one offspring as though it were derived from μόνος and *materia;* or into *matre* and *nato,* as Isidore says (*Etym.* ix), because it makes a woman the mother of a child.

Reply Obj. 1. Although the father ranks above the mother, the mother has more to do with the offspring than the father has. Or we may say that woman was made chiefly in order to be man's helpmate in relation to the offspring, whereas the man was not made for this purpose. Wherefore the mother has a closer relation to the nature of marriage than the father has.

Reply Obj. 2. Sometimes essentials are known by accidentals, wherefore some things can be named even after their accidentals, since a name is given to a thing for the purpose that it may become known.

Reply Obj. 3. Sometimes a species is named after something pertaining to the genus on account of an imperfection in the species, when namely it has the generic nature completely, yet adds nothing pertaining to dignity; thus the accidental property retains the name of property, which is common to it and to the definition. Sometimes, however, it is on account of a perfection, when we find the generic nature completely in one species and not in another; thus animal is named from soul (*anima*), and this belongs to an animate body, which is the genus of animal; yet ani-

---

* Cf. P. III, Q. 66, A. 1.
‡ This is still done in some countries.

† The original meaning of *nubo* is *to veil.*
§ l.c., *munus.*

mation is not found perfectly in those animate beings that are not animals. It is thus with the case in point; for the joining of husband and wife by matrimony is the greatest of all joinings, since it is a joining of soul and body, wherefore it is called a *conjugal* union.

THIRD ARTICLE

Whether Matrimony Is Fittingly Defined in the Text?

We proceed thus to the Third Article:—

Objection 1. It would seem that matrimony is unfittingly defined in the text* (iv. *Sent.* D. 27). For it is necessary to mention matrimony in defining a husband, since it is the husband who is joined to the woman in matrimony. Now *marital union* is put in the definition of matrimony. Therefore in these definitions there would seem to be a vicious circle.

Obj. 2. Further, matrimony makes the woman the man's wife no less than it makes the man the woman's husband. Therefore it should not be described as a *marital union* rather than an uxorial union.

Obj. 3. Further, habit *(consuetudo)* pertains to morals. Yet it often happens that married persons differ very much in habit. Therefore the words *involving their living together (consuetudinem) in undivided partnership* should have no place in the definition of matrimony.

Obj. 4: Further, we find other definitions given of matrimony, for according to Hugh *(Sum. Sent.* vii. 6), *matrimony is the lawful consent of two apt persons to be joined together.* Also, according to some, *matrimony is the fellowship of a common life and a community regulated by Divine and human law;* and we ask how these definitions differ.

I answer that, As stated above (A. 2), three things are to be considered in matrimony, namely its cause, its essence, and its effect; and accordingly we find three definitions given of matrimony. For the definition of Hugh indicates the cause, namely the consent, and this definition is self-evident. The definition given in the text indicates the essence of matrimony, namely the *union,* and adds determinate subjects by the words *between lawful persons.* It also points to the difference of the contracting parties in reference to the species, by the word *marital,* for since matrimony is a joining together for the purpose of some one thing, this joining together is specified by the purpose to which it is directed, and this is what pertains to the husband *(maritum).* It also indicates the force of this joining,—for it is indissoluble,—by the words *involving,* etc.

The remaining definition indicates the effect to which matrimony is directed, namely the common life in family matters. And since every community is regulated by some law, the code according to which this community is directed, namely Divine and human law, finds a place in this definition; while other communities, such as those of traders or soldiers, are established by human law alone.

Reply Obj. 1. Sometimes the prior things from which a definition ought to be given are not known to us, and consequently certain things are defined from things that are posterior simply, but prior to us; thus in the definition of quality the Philosopher employs the word *such (quale)* when he says (Cap. *De Qualitate)* that *quality is that whereby we are said to be such.* Thus, too, in defining matrimony we say that it is a *marital union,* by which we mean that matrimony is a union for the purpose of those things required by the marital office, all of which could not be expressed in one word.

Reply Obj. 2. As stated (A. 2), this difference indicates the end of the union. And since, according to the Apostle (1 Cor. xi. 9), the *man is not* (Vulg.,—*was not created) for the woman, but the woman for the man,* it follows that this difference should be indicated in reference to the man rather than the woman.

Reply Obj. 3. Just as the civic life denotes not the individual act of this or that one, but the things that concern the common action of the citizens, so the conjugal life is nothing else than a particular kind of companionship pertaining to that common action; wherefore as regards this same life the partnership of married persons is always indivisible, although it is divisible as regards the act belonging to each party.

The *Reply* to the *Fourth Objection* is clear from what has been said above.

---

* The definition alluded to is as follows: *Marriage is the marital union of man and woman involving their living together in undivided partnership.*

QUESTION 45

Of the Marriage Consent Considered in Itself

(In Five Articles)

In the next place we have to consider the consent; and the first point to discuss is the consent considered in itself; the second is the consent confirmed by oath or by carnal intercourse; the third is compulsory consent and conditional consent; and the fourth is the object of the consent.

Under the first head there are five points of inquiry: (1) Whether the consent is the efficient cause of matrimony? (2) Whether the consent needs to be expressed in words? (3) Whether consent given in words expressive of the future makes a marriage? (4) Whether consent given in words expressive of the present, without inward consent, makes a true marriage outwardly? (5) Whether consent given secretly in words expressive of the present makes a marriage?

FIRST ARTICLE

Whether Consent Is the Efficient Cause of Matrimony?

We proceed thus to the First Article:—

Objection 1. It would seem that consent is not the efficient cause of matrimony. For the sacraments depend not on the human will but on the Divine institution, as shown above (iv, *Sent.* D. 2: P. III, Q. 64, A. 2). But consent belongs to the human will. Therefore it is no more the cause of matrimony than of the other sacraments.

Obj. 2. Further, nothing is its own cause. But seemingly matrimony is nothing else than the consent, since it is the consent which signifies the union of Christ with the Church.

Obj. 3. Further, of one thing there should be one cause. Now there is one marriage between two persons, as stated above (Q. 44, A. 1); whereas the consents of the two parties are distinct, for they are given by different persons and to different things, since on the one hand there is consent to take a husband, and on the other hand consent to take a wife. Therefore mutual consent is not the cause of matrimony.

On the contrary, Chrysostom* says: *It is not coition but consent that makes a marriage.*

Further, one person does not receive power over that which is at the free disposal of another, without the latter's consent. Now by marriage each of the married parties receives power over the other's body (1 Cor. vii. 4), whereas hitherto each had free power over his own body. Therefore consent makes a marriage.

I answer that, In every sacrament there is a spiritual operation by means of a material operation which signifies it; thus in Baptism the inward spiritual cleansing is effected by a bodily cleansing. Wherefore, since in matrimony there is a kind of spiritual joining together, in so far as matrimony is a sacrament, and a certain material joining together, in so far as it is directed to an office of nature and of civil life, it follows that the spiritual joining is the effect of the Divine power by means of the material joining. Therefore seeing that the joinings of material contracts are effected by mutual consent, it follows that the joining together of marriage is effected in the same way.

Reply Obj. 1. The first cause of the sacraments is the Divine power which works in them the welfare of the soul; but the second or instrumental causes are material operations deriving their efficacy from the Divine institution, and thus consent is the cause in matrimony.

Reply Obj. 2. Matrimony is not the consent itself, but the union of persons directed to one purpose, as stated above (Q. 44, A. 1), and this union is the effect of the consent. Moreover, the consent, properly speaking, signifies not the union of Christ with the Church, but His will whereby His union with the Church was brought about.

Reply Obj. 3. Just as marriage is one on the part of the object to which the union is directed, whereas it is more than one on the part of the persons united, so too the consent is one on the part of the thing consented to, namely the aforesaid union, whereas it is more than one on the part of the persons consenting. Nor is the direct object of consent a husband, but union with a husband on the part of the wife, even as it is union with a wife on the part of the husband.

SECOND ARTICLE

Whether the Consent Needs to Be Expressed in Words?

We proceed thus to the Second Article:—

Objection 1. It would seem that there is no need for the consent to be expressed in words. For a man is brought under another's

* *Hom.* xxxii, in the *Opus Imperfectum* falsely ascribed to S. John Chrysostom.

power by a vow just as he is by matrimony. Now a vow is binding in God's sight, even though it be not expressed in words. Therefore consent also makes a marriage binding even without being expressed in words.

Obj. 2. Further, there can be marriage between persons who are unable to express their mutual consent in words, through being dumb or of different languages. Therefore expression of the consent by words is not required for matrimony.

Obj. 3. Further, if that which is essential to a sacrament be omitted for any reason whatever, there is no sacrament. Now there is a case of marriage without the expression of words if the maid is silent through bashfulness when her parents give her away to the bridegroom. Therefore the expression of words is not essential to matrimony.

On the contrary, Matrimony is a sacrament. Now a sensible sign is required in every sacrament. Therefore it is also required in matrimony, and consequently there must needs be at least words by which the consent is made perceptible to the senses.

Further, in matrimony there is a contract between husband and wife. Now in every contract there must be expression of the words by which men bind themselves mutually to one another. Therefore in matrimony also the consent must be expressed in words.

I answer that, As stated above (A. 1), the marriage union is effected in the same way as the bond in material contracts. And since material contracts are not feasible unless the contracting parties express their will to one another in words, it follows that the consent which makes a marriage must also be expressed in words, so that the expression of words is to marriage what the outward washing is to Baptism.

Reply Obj. 1. In a vow there is not a sacramental but only a spiritual bond, wherefore there is no need for it to be done in the same way as material contracts, in order that it be binding, as in the case of matrimony.

Reply Obj. 2. Although the like cannot plight themselves to one another in words, they can do so by signs, and such signs count for words.

Reply Obj. 3. According to Hugh of S. Victor *(Tract.* vii, *Sum. Sent.),* persons who are being married should give their consent by accepting one another freely; and this is judged to be the case if they show no dissent when they are being wedded. Wherefore in such a case the words of the parents are taken as being the maid's, for the fact that she does not contradict them is a sign that they are her words.

THIRD ARTICLE

Whether Consent Given in Words Expressive of the Future Makes a Marriage?

We proceed thus to the Third Article:—

Objection 1. It would seem that consent given in words expressive of the future makes a marriage. For as present is to present, so is future to future. But consent given in words expressive of the present makes a marriage in the present. Therefore consent given in words expressive of the future makes a marriage in the future.

Obj. 2. Further, in other civil contracts, just as in matrimony, a certain obligation results from the words expressing consent. Now in other contracts it matters not whether the obligation is effected by words of the present or of the future tense. Therefore neither does it make any difference in matrimony.

Obj. 3. Further, by the religious vow man contracts a spiritual marriage with God. Now the religious vow is expressed in words of the future tense, and is binding. Therefore carnal marriage also can be effected by words of the future tense.

On the contrary, A man who consents in words of the future tense to take a particular woman as his wife, and after, by words of the present tense, consents to take another, according to law must take the second for his wife (cap. *Sicut ex Litteris,* De spons. et matr.). But this would not be the case if consent given in words of the future tense made a marriage, since from the very fact that his marriage with the one is valid, he cannot, as long as she lives, marry another. Therefore consent given in words of the future tense does not make a marriage.

Further, he who promises to do a certain thing does it not yet. Now he who consents in words of the future tense, promises to marry a certain woman. Therefore he does not marry her yet.

I answer that, The sacramental causes produce their effect by signifying it; hence they effect what they signify. Since therefore when a man expresses his consent by words of the future tense, he does not signify that he is marrying, but promises that he will marry, it follows that a consent expressed in this manner does not make a marriage, but a promise *(sponsionem)* of marriage, and this promise is known as a betrothal *(sponsalia).*

Reply Obj. 1. When consent is expressed in words of the present tense, not only are the words actually present, but consent is directed to the present, so that they coincide in point of time; but when consent is given in words of the future tense, although the words are actually present, the consent is directed to a future time, and hence they do not coincide in point of time. For this reason the comparison fails.

Reply Obj. 2. Even in other contracts, a man who uses words referring to the future, does not transfer the power over his property to another person,—for instance if he were to say *I will give thee,*—but only when he uses words indicative of the present.

Reply Obj. 3. In the vow of religious profession it is not the spiritual marriage itself that is expressed in words which refer to the future, but an act of the spiritual marriage, namely obedience or observance of the rule. If, however, a man vow spiritual marriage in the future, it is not a spiritual marriage, for a man does not become a monk by taking such a vow, but promises to become one.

FOURTH ARTICLE

Whether, in the Absence of Inward Consent, a Marriage Is Made by Consent Given in Words of the Present?

We proceed thus to the Fourth Article:—

Objection 1. It would seem that even in the absence of inward consent a marriage is made by consent expressed in words of the present. For *fraud and deceit should benefit no man,* according to the law (cap. *Ex Tenore,* De Rescrip., cap. *Si Vir,* De cognat. spir.). Now he who gives consent in words without consenting in heart commits a fraud. Therefore he should not benefit by it, through being released of the bond of marriage.

Obj. 2. Further, the mental consent of one person cannot be known to another, except in so far as it is expressed in words. If then the expression of the words is not enough, and inward consent is required in both parties, neither of them will be able to know that he is truly married to the other; and consequently whenever he uses marriage he will commit fornication.

Obj. 3. Further, if a man is proved to have consented to take a certain woman to wife in words of the present tense, he is compelled under pain of excommunication to take her as his wife, even though he should say that he was wanting in mental consent, notwithstanding that afterwards he may have contracted marriage with another woman by words expressive of consent in the present. But this would not be the case if mental consent were requisite for marriage. Therefore it is not required.

On the contrary, Innocent III says in a Decretal (cap. *Tua Nos,* De Spons. et matr.) in reference to this case: *Other things cannot complete the marriage bond in the absence of consent.*

Further, intention is necessary in all the sacraments. Now he who consents not in his heart has no intention of contracting marriage; and therefore he does not contract a marriage.

I answer that, The outward cleansing stands in the same relation to baptism as the expression of words to this sacrament, as stated above (A. 2). Wherefore just as were a person to receive the outward cleansing, with the intention, not of receiving the sacrament, but of acting in jest or deceit, he would not be baptized; so, too, expression of words without inward consent makes no marriage.

Reply Obj. 1. There are two things here, namely the lack of consent,—which benefits him in the tribunal of his conscience so that he is not bound by the marriage tie, albeit not in the tribunal of the Church where judgment is pronounced according to the evidence,—and the deceit in the words, which does not benefit him, neither in the tribunal of his conscience nor in the tribunal of the Church, since in both he is punished for this.

Reply Obj. 2. If mental consent is lacking in one of the parties, on neither side is there marriage, since marriage consists in a mutual joining together, as stated above (Q. 44, A. 1). However one may believe that in all probability there is no fraud unless there be evident signs thereof; because we must presume good of everyone, unless there be proof of the contrary. Consequently the party in whom there is no fraud is excused from sin on account of ignorance.

Reply Obj. 3. In such a case the Church compels him to hold to his first wife, because the Church judges according to outward appearances; nor is she deceived in justice or right, although she is deceived in the facts of the case. Yet such a man ought to bear the excommunication rather than return to his first wife; or else he should go far away into another country.

FIFTH ARTICLE

Whether Consent Given Secretly in Words of the Present Makes a Marriage?

We proceed thus to the Fifth Article:—

Objection 1. It would seem that consent given secretly in words of the present does not make a marriage. For a thing that is in one person's power is not transferred to the power of another without the consent of the person in whose power it was. Now the maid is in her father's power. Therefore she cannot by marriage be transferred to a husband's power without her father's consent. Wherefore if consent be given secretly, even though it should be expressed in words of the present, there will be no marriage.

Obj. 2. Further, in penance, just as in matrimony, our act is as it were essential to the sacrament. But the sacrament of penance is not made complete except by means of the ministers of the Church, who are the dispensers of the sacraments. Therefore neither can marriage be perfected without the priest's blessing.

Obj. 3. Further, the Church does not forbid baptism to be given secretly, since one may baptize either privately or publicly. But the Church does forbid the celebration of clandestine marriages (cap. *Cum inhibitio,* De clandest. despons.). Therefore they cannot be done secretly.

Obj. 4. Further, marriage cannot be contracted by those who are related in the second degree, because the Church has forbidden it. But the Church has also forbidden clandestine marriages. Therefore they cannot be valid marriages.

On the contrary, Given the cause the effect follows. Now the sufficient cause of matrimony is consent expressed in words of the present. Therefore whether this be done in public or in private the result is a marriage.

Further, wherever there is the due matter and the due form of a sacrament there is the sacrament. Now in a secret marriage there is the due matter, since there are persons who are able lawfully to contract,—and the due form, since there are the words of the present expressive of consent. Therefore there is a true marriage.

I answer that, Just as in the other sacraments certain things are essential to the sacrament, and if they are omitted there is no sacrament, while certain things belong to the solemnization of the sacrament, and if these be omitted the sacrament is nevertheless validly performed, although it is a sin to omit them; so, too, consent expressed in words of the present between persons lawfully qualified to contract makes a marriage, because these two conditions are essential to the sacrament;

while all else belongs to the solemnization of the sacrament, as being done in order that the marriage may be more fittingly performed. Hence if these be omitted it is a true marriage, although the contracting parties sin, unless they have a lawful motive for being excused.*

Reply Obj. 1. The maid is in her father's power, not as a female slave without power over her own body, but as a daughter, for the purpose of education. Hence, in so far as she is free, she can give herself into another's power without her father's consent, even as a son or daughter, since they are free, may enter religion without their parent's consent.

Reply Obj. 2. In penance our act, although essential to the sacrament, does not suffice for producing the proximate effect of the sacrament, namely forgiveness of sins, and consequently it is necessary that the act of the priest intervene in order that the sacrament be perfected. But in matrimony our acts are the sufficient cause for the production of the proximate effect, which is the marriage bond, because whoever has the right to dispose of himself can bind himself to another. Consequently the priest's blessing is not required for matrimony as being essential to the sacrament.

Reply Obj. 3. It is also forbidden to receive baptism otherwise than from a priest, except in a case of necessity. But matrimony is not a necessary sacrament; and consequently the comparison fails. However, clandestine marriages are forbidden on account of the evil results to which they are liable, since it often happens that one of the parties is guilty of fraud in such marriages; frequently, too, they have recourse to other nuptials when they repent of having married in haste; and many other evils result therefrom, besides which there is something disgraceful about them.

Reply Obj. 4. Clandestine marriages are not forbidden as though they were contrary to the essentials of marriage, in the same way as the marriages of unlawful persons, who are undue matter for this sacrament; and hence there is no comparison.

QUESTION 46

Of the Consent to Which an Oath or Carnal Intercourse Is Appended

(In Two Articles)

WE must now consider the consent to which an oath or carnal intercourse is appended. Under this head there are two points of inquiry: (1) Whether an oath added to the consent that is expressed in words of the future tense makes a marriage? (2) Whether carnal intercourse supervening to such a consent makes a marriage?

---

* Clandestine marriages have since been declared invalid by the Council of Trent (Sess. xxiv). It must be borne in mind that throughout the treatise on marriage S. Thomas gives the Canon Law of his time.

FIRST ARTICLE

Whether an Oath Added to the Consent That Is Expressed in Words of the Future Tense Makes a Marriage?

We proceed thus to the First Article:—

Objection 1. It would seem that if an oath be added to a consent that is expressed in words of the future tense it makes a marriage. For no one can bind himself to act against the Divine law. But the fulfilling of an oath is of Divine law according to Matth. v. 33, *Thou shalt perform thy oaths to the Lord.* Consequently no subsequent obligation can relieve a man of the obligation to keep an oath previously taken. If, therefore, after consenting to marry a woman by words expressive of the future and confirming that consent with an oath, a man binds himself to another woman by words expressive of the present, it would seem that none the less he is bound to keep his former oath. But this would not be the case unless that oath made the marriage complete. Therefore an oath affixed to a consent expressed in words of the future tense makes a marriage.

Obj. 2. Further, Divine truth is stronger than human truth. Now an oath confirms a thing with the Divine truth. Since then words expressive of consent in the present in which there is mere human truth complete a marriage, it would seem that much more is this the case with words of the future confirmed by an oath.

Obj. 3. Further, according to the Apostle (Heb. vi. 16), *An oath for confirmation is the end of all . . . controversy;* wherefore in a court of justice at any rate one must stand by an oath rather than by a mere affirmation. Therefore if a man consent to marry a woman by a simple affirmation expressed in words of the present, after having consented to marry another in words of the future confirmed by oath, it would seem that in the judgment of the Church he should be compelled to take the first and not the second as his wife.

Obj. 4. Further, the simple uttering of words relating to the future makes a betrothal. But the addition of an oath must have some effect. Therefore it makes something more than a betrothal. Now beyond a betrothal there is nothing but marriage. Therefore it makes a marriage.

On the contrary, What is future is not yet. Now the addition of an oath does not make words of the future tense signify anything else than consent to something future. Therefore it is not a marriage yet.

Further, after a marriage is complete, no further consent is required for the marriage. But after the oath there is yet another consent which makes the marriage, else it would be useless to swear to a future marriage. Therefore it does not make a marriage.

I answer that, An oath is employed in confirmation of one's words; wherefore it confirms that only which is signified by the words, nor does it change their signification. Consequently, since it belongs to words of the future tense, by their very signification, not to make a marriage, since what is promised in the future is not done yet, even though an oath be added to the promise, the marriage is not made yet, as the Master says in the text (iv. *Sent.* D. 28).

Reply Obj. 1. The fulfilling of a lawful oath is of Divine law, but not the fulfilling of an unlawful oath. Wherefore if a subsequent obligation makes that oath unlawful, whereas it was lawful before, he who does not keep the oath he took previously does not disobey the Divine law. And so it is in the case in point; since he swears unlawfully who promises unlawfully; and a promise about another's property is unlawful. Consequently the subsequent consent by words of the present, whereby a man transfers the power over his body to another woman, makes the previous oath unlawful which was lawful before.

Reply Obj. 2. The Divine truth is most efficacious in confirming that to which it is applied. Hence the *Reply* to the *Third Objection* is clear.

Reply Obj. 4. The oath has some effect, not by causing a new obligation, but confirming that which is already made, and thus he who violates it sins more grievously.

SECOND ARTICLE

Whether Carnal Intercourse after Consent Expressed in Words of the Future Makes a Marriage?

We proceed thus to the Second Article:—

Objection 1. It would seem that carnal intercourse after consent expressed in words of the future makes a marriage. For consent by deed is greater than consent by word. But he who has carnal intercourse consents by deed to the promise he has previously made. Therefore it would seem that much more does this make a marriage than if he were to consent to mere words referring to the present.

Obj. 2. Further, not only explicit but also interpretive consent makes a marriage. Now there can be no better interpretation of consent than carnal intercourse. Therefore marriage is completed thereby.

Obj. 3. Further, all carnal union outside marriage is a sin. But the woman, seemingly, does not sin by admitting her betrothed to carnal intercourse. Therefore it makes a marriage.

Obj. 4. Further, *Sin is not forgiven unless restitution be made,* as Augustine says *(Ep.* cliii, *ad Macedon.).* Now a man cannot reinstate a woman whom he has violated under the pretense of marriage unless he marry her. Therefore it would seem that even if, after his carnal intercourse, he happen to contract with another by words of the present tense, he is bound to return to the first; and this would not be the case unless he were married to her. Therefore carnal intercourse after consent referring to the future makes a marriage.

On the contrary, Pope Nicholas I says *(Resp. ad Consult. Bulg.* iii; Cap. *Tuas dudum,* De clandest. despons.), *Without the consent to marriage, other things, including coition, are of no effect.*

Further, that which follows a thing does not make it. But carnal intercourse follows the actual marriage, as effect follows cause. Therefore it cannot make a marriage.

I answer that, We may speak of marriage in two ways. First, in reference to the tribunal of conscience, and thus in very truth carnal intercourse cannot complete a marriage the promise of which has previously been made in words expressive of the future, if inward consent is lacking, since words, even though expressive of the present, would not make a marriage in the absence of mental consent, as stated above (Q. 45, A. 4). Secondly, in reference to the judgment of the Church; and since in the external tribunal judgment is given in accordance with external evidence, and since nothing is more expressly significant of consent than carnal intercourse, it follows that

in the judgment of the Church carnal intercourse following on betrothal is declared to make a marriage, unless there appear clear signs of deceit or fraud* (De sponsal. et matrim., cap. *Is qui fidem).*

Reply Obj. 1. In reality he who has carnal intercourse consents by deed to the act of sexual union, and does not merely for this reason consent to marriage except according to the interpretation of the law.

Reply Obj. 2. This interpretation does not alter the truth of the matter, but changes the judgment which is about external things.

Reply Obj. 3. If the woman admit her betrothed, thinking that he wishes to consummate the marriage, she is excused from the sin, unless there be clear signs of fraud; for instance if they differ considerably in birth or fortune, or some other evident sign appear. Nevertheless the affianced husband is guilty of fornication, and should be punished for this fraud he has committed.

Reply Obj. 4. In a case of this kind the affianced husband, before his marriage with the other woman, is bound to marry the one to whom he was betrothed, if she be his equal or superior in rank. But if he has married another woman, he is no longer able to fulfill his obligation, wherefore it suffices if he provide for her marriage. Nor is he bound even to do this, according to some, if her affianced husband is of much higher rank than she, or if there be some evident sign of fraud, because it may be presumed that in all probability she was not deceived but pretended to be.

QUESTION 47

Of Compulsory and Conditional Consent

(In Six Articles)

WE must now consider compulsory and conditional consent. Under this head there are six points of inquiry: (1) Whether compulsory consent is possible? (2) Whether a constant man can be compelled by fear? (3) Whether compulsory consent invalidates marriage? (4) Whether compulsory consent makes a marriage as regards the party using compulsion? (5) Whether conditional consent makes a marriage? (6) Whether one can be compelled by one's father to marry?

FIRST ARTICLE

Whether a Compulsory Consent Is Possible?

We proceed thus to the First Article:—
Objection 1. It would seem that no consent

* According to the pre-Tridentine legislation.

can be compulsory. For, as stated above (ii, Sent. D. 25; I-II, Q. 6, A. 4) the free-will cannot be compelled. Now consent is an act of the free-will. Therefore it cannot be compulsory.

Obj. 2. Further, violent is the same as compulsory. Now, according to the Philosopher *(Ethic.* iii. 1), *a violent action is one the principle of which is without, the patient concurring not at all.* But the principle of consent is always within. Therefore no consent can be compulsory.

Obj. 3. Further, every sin is perfected by consent. But that which perfects a sin cannot be compulsory, for, according to Augustine *(De Lib. Arb.* iii. 18), *no one sins in what he cannot avoid.* Since then violence is defined by jurists (i, ff. *de eo quod vi metusve)* as the *force of a stronger being that cannot be repulsed,* it would seem that consent cannot be compulsory or violent.

Obj. 4. Further, power is opposed to liberty. But compulsion is allied to power, as appears from a definition of Tully's in which he says that *compulsion is the force of one who exercises his power to detain a thing outside its proper bounds.* Therefore the free-will cannot be compelled, and consequently neither can consent which is an act thereof.

On the contrary, That which cannot be, cannot be an impediment. But compulsory consent is an impediment to matrimony, as stated in the text (iv, *Sent.* D. 29). Therefore consent can be compelled.

Further, in marriage there is a contract. Now the will can be compelled in the matter of contracts; for which reason the law adjudges that restitution should be made of the whole, for it does not ratify *that which was done under compulsion or fear (loc. cit.).* Therefore in marriage also it is possible for the consent to be compulsory.

I answer that, Compulsion or violence is twofold. One is the cause of absolute necessity, and violence of this kind the Philosopher calls *(loc. cit.) violent simply,* as when by bodily strength one forces a person to move; the other causes conditional necessity, and the Philosopher calls this a *mixed violence,* as when a person throws his merchandise overboard in order to save himself. In the latter kind of violence, although the thing done is not voluntary in itself, yet taking into consideration the circumstances of place and time it is voluntary. And since actions are about particulars, it follows that it is voluntary simply, and involuntary in a certain respect.* Wherefore this latter violence or compulsion is consistent with consent, but not the former. And since this compulsion results from one's fear of a threatening danger, it follows that this violence coincides with fear which, in a manner, compels the will, whereas the former violence has to do with bodily actions. Moreover, since the law considers not merely internal actions, but rather external actions, consequently it takes violence to mean absolute compulsion, for which reason it draws a distinction between violence and fear. Here, however, it is a question of internal consent which cannot be influenced by compulsion or violence as distinct from fear. Therefore as to the question at issue compulsion and fear are the same. Now, according to lawyers, fear is *the agitation of the mind occasioned by danger imminent or future (loc. cit.).*

This suffices for the *Replies* to the *Objections;* for the first set of arguments consider the first kind of compulsion, and the second set of arguments consider the second.

SECOND ARTICLE

Whether a Constant Man Can Be Compelled by Fear?

We proceed thus to the Second Article:—

Objection 1. It would seem that *a constant man†* cannot be compelled by fear. Because the nature of a constant man is not to be agitated in the midst of dangers. Since then fear is *agitation of the mind occasioned by imminent danger,* it would seem that he is not compelled by fear.

Obj. 2. Further, *Of all fearsome things death is the limit,* according to the Philosopher *(Ethic.* iii. 6), as though it were the most perfect of all things that inspire fear. But the constant man is not compelled by death, since the brave face even mortal dangers. Therefore no fear influences a constant man.

Obj. 3. Further, of all dangers a good man fears most that which affects his good name. But the fear of disgrace is not reckoned to influence a constant man, because, according to the law (vii, ff. *de eo quod metus,* etc.), *fear of disgrace is not included under the ordinance, "That which is done through fear."‡* Therefore neither does any other kind of fear influence a constant man.

Obj. 4. Further, in him who is compelled by fear, fear leaves a sin, for it makes him promise what he is unwilling to fulfill, and thus it makes him lie. But a constant man does not commit a sin, not even a very slight one, for fear. Therefore no fear influences a constant man.

On the contrary, Abraham and Isaac were constant. Yet they were influenced by fear, since on account of fear each said that his wife was his sister (Gen. xii. 12; xxvi. 7).

Further, wherever there is mixed violence, it is fear that compels. But however constant a man may be he may suffer violence of that kind, for if he be on the sea, he will throw his merchandise overboard if menaced with shipwreck. Therefore fear can influence a constant man.

I answer that, By fear influencing a man we mean his being compelled by fear. A man is compelled by fear when he does that which otherwise he would not wish to do, in order to avoid that which he fears. Now the constant differs from the inconstant man in two respects. First, in respect of the quality of the danger feared, because the constant man follows right reason, whereby he knows whether to omit this rather than that, and whether to do this rather than that. Now the lesser evil or the greater good is always to be chosen in

* Cf. I-II, Q. 6, A. 6.   † Cap. *Ad audientiam,* De his quæ vi.   ‡ Dig. iv. 2, *Quod metus causa.*

preference; and therefore the constant man is compelled to bear with the lesser evil through fear of the greater evil, but he is not compelled to bear with the greater evil in order to avoid the lesser. But the inconstant man is compelled to bear with the greater evil through fear of a lesser evil, namely to commit sin through fear of bodily suffering; whereas on the contrary the obstinate man cannot be compelled even to permit or to do a lesser evil, in order to avoid a greater. Hence the constant man is a mean between the inconstant and the obstinate. Secondly, they differ as to their estimate of the threatening evil, for a constant man is not compelled unless for grave and probable reasons, while the inconstant man is compelled by trifling motives: *The wicked man fleeth when no man pursueth* (Prov. xxviii. 1).

Reply Obj. 1. The constant man, like the brave man, is fearless, as the Philosopher states *(Ethic.* iii. 4), not that he is altogether without fear, but because he fears not what he ought not to fear, or where, or when he ought not to fear.

Reply Obj. 2. Sin is the greatest of evils, and consequently a constant man can nowise be compelled to sin; indeed a man should die rather than suffer the like, as again the Philosopher says *(Ethic.* iii. 6, 9). Yet certain bodily injuries are less grievous than certain others; and chief among them are those which relate to the person, such as death, blows, the stain resulting from rape, and slavery. Wherefore the like compel a constant man to suffer other bodily injuries. They are contained in the verse

Rape, status, blows, and death.

Nor does it matter whether they refer to his own person, or to the person of his wife or children, or the like.

Reply Obj. 3. Although disgrace is a greater injury it is easy to remedy it. Hence fear of disgrace is not reckoned to influence a constant man according to law.

Reply Obj. 4. The constant man is not compelled to lie, because at the time he wishes to give; yet afterwards he wishes to ask for restitution, or at least to appeal to the judge, if he promised not to ask for restitution. But he cannot promise not to appeal, for since this is contrary to the good of justice, he cannot be compelled thereto, namely to act against justice.

THIRD ARTICLE

Whether Compulsory Consent Invalidates a Marriage?

We proceed thus to the Third Article:—

Objection 1. It would seem that compulsory consent does not invalidate a marriage

For just as consent is necessary for matrimony, so is intention necessary for Baptism. Now one who is compelled by fear to receive Baptism, receives the sacrament. Therefore one who is compelled by fear to consent is bound by his marriage.

Obj. 2. Further, according to the Philosopher *(Ethic.* iii. 1), that which is done on account of mixed violence is more voluntary than involuntary. Now consent cannot be compelled except by mixed violence. Therefore it is not entirely involutary, and consequently the marriage is valid.

Obj. 3. Further, seemingly he who has consented to marriage under compulsion ought to be counseled to stand to that marriage; because to promise and not to fulfill has an *appearance of evil,* and the Apostle wishes us to refrain from all such things (1 Thess. v. 22). But that would not be the case if compulsory consent invalidated a marriage altogether. Therefore, etc.

On the contrary, A Decretal says (cap. *Cum locum,* De sponsal. et matrim.): *Since there is no room for consent where fear or compulsion enters in, it follows that where a person's consent is required, every pretext for compulsion must be set aside.* Now mutual contract is necessary in marriage. Therefore, etc.

Further, Matrimony signifies the union of Christ with the Church, which union is according to the liberty of love. Therefore it cannot be the result of compulsory consent.

I answer that, The marriage bond is everlasting. Hence whatever is inconsistent with its perpetuity invalidates marriage. Now the fear which compels a constant man deprives the contract of its perpetuity, since its complete rescission can be demanded. Wherefore this compulsion by fear which influences a constant man, invalidates marriage, but not the other compulsion. Now a constant man is reckoned a virtuous man who, according to the Philosopher *(Ethic,* iii. 4), is a measure in all human actions.

However, some say that if there be consent, although compulsory, the marriage is valid in conscience and in God's sight, but not in the eyes of the Church, who presumes that there was no inward consent on account of the fear. But this is of no account, because the Church should not presume a person to sin until it be proved; and he sinned if he said that he consented whereas he did not consent. Wherefore the Church presumes that he did consent, but judges this compulsory consent to be insufficient for a valid marriage.

Reply Obj. 1. The intention is not the efficient cause of the sacrament in baptism, it is merely the cause that elicits the action of the agent; whereas the consent is the efficient cause in matrimony. Hence the comparison fails.

Reply Obj. 2. Not any kind of voluntariness suffices for marriage: it must be completely voluntary, because it has to be perpetual; and consequently it is invalidated by violence of a mixed nature.

Reply Obj. 3. He ought not always to be advised to stand to that marriage, but only when evil results are feared from its dissolution. Nor does he sin if he does otherwise, because there is no appearance of evil in not fulfilling a promise that one has made unwillingly.

FOURTH ARTICLE

Whether Compulsory Consent Makes a Marriage As Regards the Party Who Uses Compulsion?

We proceed thus to the Fourth Article:—

Objection 1. It would seem that compulsory consent makes a marriage, at least as regards the party who uses compulsion. For matrimony is a sign of a spiritual union. But spiritual union which is by charity may be with one who has not charity. Therefore marriage is possible with one who wills it not.

Obj. 2. Further, if she who was compelled consents afterwards, it will be a true marriage. But he who compelled her before is not bound by her consent. Therefore he was married to her by virtue of the consent he gave before.

On the contrary, Matrimony is an equiparant relation. Now a relation of that kind is equally in both terms. Therefore if there is an impediment on the part of one, there will be no marriage on the part of the other.

I answer that, Since marriage is a kind of relation, and a relation cannot arise in one of the terms without arising in the other, it follows that whatever is an impediment to matrimony in the one, is an impediment to matrimony in the other; since it is impossble for a man to be the husband of one who is not his wife, or for a woman to be a wife without a husband, just as it is impossible to be a mother without having a child. Hence it is a common saying that *marriage is not lame.*

Reply Obj. 1. Although the act of the lover can be directed to one who loves not, there can be no union between them, unless love be mutual. Wherefore the Philosopher says (*Ethic.* viii. 2) that friendship which consists in a kind of union requires a return of love.

Reply Obj. 2. Marriage does not result from the consent of her who was compelled before, except in so far as the other party's previous consent remains in force; wherefore if he were to withdraw his consent there would be no marriage.

FIFTH ARTICLE

Whether Conditional Consent Makes a Marriage?

We proceed thus to the Fifth Article:—

Objection 1. It would seem that not even a conditional consent makes a marriage, because a statement is not made simply if it is made subject to a condition. But in marriage the words expressive of consent must be uttered simply. Therefore a conditional consent makes no marriage.

Obj. 2. Further, marriage should be certain But where a statement is made under a condition it is rendered doubtful. Therefore a like consent makes no marriage.

On the contrary, In other contracts an obligation is undertaken conditionally, and holds so long as the condition holds. Therefore since marriage is a contract, it would seem that it can be made by a conditional consent.

I answer that, The condition made is either of the present or of the future. If it is of the present and is not contrary to marriage, whether it be moral or immoral, the marriage holds if the condition is verified, and is invalid if the condition is not verified. If, however, it be contrary to the marriage blessings, the marriage is invalid, as we have also said in reference to betrothals (Q. 43, A. 1). But if the condition refer to the future, it is either necessary, as that the sun will rise tomorrow, —and then the marriage is valid, because such future things are present in their causes,—or else it is contingent, as the payment of a sum of money, or the consent of the parents, and then the judgment about a consent of this kind is the same as about a consent expressed in words of the future tense; wherefore it makes no marriage.

This suffices for the *Replies* to the *Objections.*

SIXTH ARTICLE

Whether One Can Be Compelled by One's Father's Command to Marry?

We proceed thus to the Sixth Article:—

Objection 1. It would seem that one can be compelled by one's father's command to marry. For it is written (Col. iii. 20): *Children, obey your parents in all things.* Therefore they are bound to obey them in this also.

Obj. 2. Further, Isaac charged Jacob (Gen. xxviii. 1) not to take a wife from the daughters of Chanaan. But he would not have charged him thus unless he had the right to command it. Therefore a son is bound to obey his father in this.

Obj. 3. Further, no one should promise, especially with an oath, for one whom he cannot compel to keep the promise. Now parents promise future marriages for their children, and even confirm their promise by oath. Therefore they can compel their children to keep that promise.

Obj. 4. Further, our spiritual father, the Pope to wit, can by his command compel a man to a spiritual marriage, namely to accept a bishopric. Therefore a carnal father can compel his son to marriage.

On the contrary, A son may lawfully enter religion though his father command him to marry. Therefore he is not bound to obey him in this.

Further, if he were bound to obey, a betrothal contracted by the parents would hold good without their children's consent. But this is against the law (cap. *Ex litteris,* De despon. impub.). Therefore, etc.

I answer that, Since in marriage there is a kind of perpetual service, as it were, a father cannot by his command compel his son to marry, since the latter is of free condition: but he may induce him for a reasonable cause; and thus the son will be affected by his father's command in the same way as he is affected by that cause, so that if the cause be compelling as indicating either obligation or fitness, his father's command will compel him in the same measure: otherwise he may not compel him.

Reply Obj. 1. The words of the Apostle do not refer to those matters in which a man is his own master as the father is. Such is marriage by which the son also becomes a father.

Reply Obj. 2. There were other motives why Jacob was bound to do what Isaac commanded him, both on account of the wickedness of those women, and because the seed of Chanaan was to be cast forth from the land which was promised to the seed of the patriarchs. Hence Isaac could command this.

Reply Obj. 3. They do not swear except with the implied condition *if it please them;* and they are bound to induce them in good faith.

Reply Obj. 4. Some say that the Pope cannot command a man to accept a bishopric, because consent should be free. But if this be granted there would be an end of ecclesiastical order, for unless a man can be compelled to accept the government of a church, the Church could not be preserved, since sometimes those who are qualified for the purpose are unwilling to accept unless they be compelled. Therefore we must reply that the two cases are not parallel; for there is no bodily service in a spiritual marriage as there is in the bodily marriage; because the spiritual marriage is a kind of office for dispensing the public weal: *Let a man so account of us as of the ministers of Christ, and the dispensers of the mysteries of God* (1 Cor. iv. 1).

QUESTION 48

Of the Object of the Consent

(In Two Articles)

WE must now consider the object of the consent. Under this head there are two points of inquiry: (1) Whether the consent that makes a marriage is a consent to carnal intercourse? (2) Whether consent to marry a person for an immoral motive makes a marriage?

FIRST ARTICLE

Whether the Consent That Makes a Marriage Is a Consent to Carnal Intercourse?

We proceed thus to the First Article:—

Obj. 1. It would seem that the consent which makes a marriage is a consent to carnal intercourse. For Jerome* says that *for those who have vowed virginity it is wicked, not only to marry, but even to wish to marry.* But it would not be wicked unless it were contrary to virginity, and marriage is not contrary to virginity except by reason of carnal intercourse. Therefore the will's consent in marriage is a consent to carnal intercourse.

Obj. 2. Further, whatever there is in marriage between husband and wife is lawful between brother and sister except carnal intercourse. But there cannot lawfully be a consent to marriage between them. Therefore the marriage consent is a consent to carnal intercourse.

Obj. 3. Further, if the woman say to the man: *I consent to take thee provided however that you know me not,* it is not a marriage consent, because it contains something against the essence of that consent. Yet this would not be the case unless the marriage consent were a consent to carnal intercourse. Therefore, etc.

Obj. 4. Further, in everything the beginning corresponds to the consummation. Now marriage is consummated by carnal intercourse. Therefore, since it begins by the consent, it would seem that the consent is to carnal intercourse.

On the contrary, No one that consents to

* The words quoted are found implicitly in S. Augustine (*De Bono Viduit.* ix).

carnal intercourse is a virgin in mind and body. Yet Blessed John the evangelist after consenting to marriage was a virgin both in mind and body. Therefore he did not consent to carnal intercourse.

Further, the effect corresponds to its cause. Now consent is the cause of marriage. Since then carnal intercourse is not essential to marriage, seemingly neither is the consent which causes marriage a consent to carnal intercourse.

I answer that, The consent that makes a marriage is a consent to marriage, because the proper effect of the will is the thing willed. Wherefore, according as carnal intercourse stands in relation to marriage, so far is the consent that causes marriage a consent to carnal intercourse. Now, as stated above (Q. 44, A. 1; Q. 45, AA. 1, 2), marriage is not essentially the carnal union itself, but a certain joining together of husband and wife ordained to carnal intercourse, and a further consequent union between husband and wife, in so far as they each receive power over the other in reference to carnal intercourse, which joining together is called the nuptial bond. Hence it is evident that they said well who asserted that to consent to marriage is to consent to carnal intercourse implicitly and not explicitly. For carnal intercourse is not to be understood, except as an effect is implicitly contained in its cause, for the power to have carnal intercourse, which power is the object of the consent, is the cause of carnal intercourse, just as the power to use one's own property is the cause of the use.

Reply Obj. 1. The reason why consent to marriage after taking the vow of virginity is sinful, is because that consent gives a power to do what is unlawful: even so would a man sin if he gave another man the power to receive that which he has in deposit, and not only by actually delivering it to him. With regard to the consent of the Blessed Virgin, we have spoken about it above (iv, *Sent.* D. 3; P. III, Q. 29, A. 2).

Reply Obj. 2. Between brother and sister there can be no power of one over the other in relation to carnal intercourse, even as neither can there be lawfully carnal intercourse itself. Consequently the argument does not prove.

Reply Obj. 3. Such an explicit condition is contrary not only to the act but also to the power of carnal intercourse, and therefore it is contrary to marriage.

Reply Obj. 4. Marriage begun corresponds to marriage consummated, as habit or power corresponds to the act which is operation.

The arguments on the contrary side show

that consent is not given explicitly to carnal intercourse; and this is true.

SECOND ARTICLE

Whether Marriage Can Result from One Person's Consent to Take Another for a Base Motive?

We proceed thus to the Second Article:—

Objection 1. It would seem that marriage cannot result from one person's consent to take another for a base motive. For there is but one reason for one thing. Now marriage is one sacrament. Therefore it cannot result from the intention of any other end than that for which it was instituted by God; namely the begetting of children.

Obj. 2. Further, the marriage union is from God, according to Matth. xix. 6, *What . . . God hath joined together let no man put asunder.* But a union that is made for immoral motives is not from God. Therefore it is not a marriage.

Obj. 3. Further, in the other sacraments, if the intention of the Church be not observed, the sacrament is invalid. Now the intention of the Church in the sacrament of matrimony is not directed to a base purpose. Therefore, if a marriage be contracted for a base purpose, it will not be a valid marriage.

Obj. 4. Further, according to Boëthius (De Diff. *Topic.* ii) *a thing is good if its end be good.* But matrimony is always good. Therefore it is not matrimony if it is done for an evil end.

Obj. 5. Further, matrimony signifies the union of Christ with the Church; and in this there can be nothing base. Neither therefore can marriage be contracted for a base motive.

On the contrary, He who baptizes another for the sake of gain baptizes validly. Therefore if a man marries a woman for the purpose of gain it is a valid marriage.

Further, the same conclusion is proved by the examples and authorities quoted in the text (iv, *Sent.* D. 30).

I answer that, The final cause of marriage may be taken as twofold, namely essential and accidental. The essential cause of marriage is the end to which it is by its very nature ordained, and this is always good, namely the begetting of children and the avoiding of fornication. But the accidental final cause thereof is that which the contracting parties intend as the result of marriage. And since that which is intended as the result of marriage is consequent upon marriage, and since that which comes first is not altered by what comes after, but conversely; marriage does not become good or evil by reason of that cause, but the contracting parties to whom this cause is the essential end. And since accidental causes are infinite in number, it follows that there can be an infinite number of such causes in matrimony, some of which are good and some bad.

Reply Obj. 1. This is true of the essential and principal cause; but that which has one essential and principal end may have several secondary essential ends, and an infinite number of accidental ends.

Reply Obj. 2. The joining together can be taken for the relation itself which is marriage, and that is always from God, and is good, whatever be its cause; or for the act of those who are being joined together, and thus it is sometimes evil and is not from God simply. Nor is it unreasonable that an effect be from God, the cause of which is evil, such as a child born of adultery; for it is not from that cause as evil, but as having some good in so far as it is from God, although it is not from God simply.

Reply Obj. 3. The intention of the Church whereby she intends to confer a sacrament is essential to each sacrament, so that if it be not observed, all sacraments are null. But the intention of the Church whereby she intends an advantage resulting from the sacrament belongs to the well-being and not to the essence of a sacrament; wherefore, if it be not observed, the sacrament is none the less valid. Yet he who omits this intention sins; for instance if in baptism one intend not the healing of the mind which the Church intends. In like manner he who intends to marry, although he fail to direct it to the end which the Church intends, nevertheless contracts a valid marriage.

Reply Obj. 4. This evil which is intended is the end not of marriage, but of the contracting parties.

Reply Obj. 5. The union itself, and not the action of those who are united, is the sign of the union of Christ with the Church: wherefore the conclusion does not follow.

QUESTION 49

Of the Marriage Goods *

(In Six Articles)

In the next place we must consider the marriage goods. Under this head there are six points of inquiry: (1) Whether certain goods are necessary in order to excuse marriage? (2) Whether those assigned are sufficient? (3) Whether the sacrament is the principal among the goods? (4) Whether the marriage act is excused from sin by the aforesaid goods? (5) Whether it can ever be excused from sin without them? (6) Whether in their absence it is always a mortal sin?

FIRST ARTICLE

Whether Certain Blessings Are Necessary in Order to Excuse Marriage?

We proceed thus to the First Article:—

Objection 1. It would seem that certain blessings are not necessary in order to excuse marriage. For just as the preservation of the individual which is effected by the nutritive power is intended by nature, so too is the preservation of the species which is effected by marriage; and indeed so much the more as the good of the species is better and more exalted than the good of the individual. But no goods are necessary to excuse the act of the nutritive power. Neither therefore are they necessary to excuse marriage.

Obj. 2. Further, according to the Philosopher *(Ethic.* viii. 12) the friendship between husband and wife is natural, and includes the virtuous, the useful, and the pleasant. But that which is virtuous in itself needs no excuse. Therefore neither should any goods be assigned for the excuse of matrimony.

Obj. 3. Further, matrimony was instituted as a remedy and as an office, as stated above (Q. 42, A. 2). Now it needs no excuse in so far as it is instituted as an office, since then it would also have needed an excuse in paradise, which is false, for there, as Augustine says, *marriage would have been without reproach and the marriage-bed without stain (Gen. ad Lit.* ix). In like manner neither does it need an excuse in so far as it is intended as a remedy, any more than the other sacraments which were instituted as remedies for sin. Therefore matrimony does not need these excuses.

Obj. 4. Further, the virtues are directed to whatever can be done aright. If then marriage can be righted by certain goods, it needs nothing else to right it besides the virtues of the soul; and consequently there is no need to assign to matrimony any goods whereby it is righted, any more than to other things in which the virtues direct us.

On the contrary, Wherever there is indulgence, there must needs be some reason for excuse. Now marriage is allowed in the state of infirmity *by indulgence* (1 Cor. vii. 6).

* *Bona matrimonii,* variously rendered marriage goods, marriage blessings, and advantages of marriage.

Therefore it needs to be excused by certain goods.

Further, the intercourse of fornication and that of marriage are of the same species as regards the species of nature. But the intercourse of fornication is wrong in itself. Therefore, in order that the marriage intercourse be not wrong, something must be added to it to make it right, and draw it to another moral species.

I answer that, No wise man should allow himself to lose a thing except for some compensation in the shape of an equal or better good. Wherefore for a thing that has a loss attached to it to be eligible, it needs to have some good connected with it, which by compensating for that loss makes that thing ordinate and right. Now there is a loss of reason incidental to the union of man and woman, both because the reason is carried away entirely on account of the vehemence of the pleasure, so that it is unable to understand anything at the same time, as the Philosopher says *(Ethic.* vii. 11) ; and again because of the tribulation of the flesh which such persons have to suffer from solicitude for temporal things (1 Cor. vii. 28). Consequently the choice of this union cannot be made ordinate except by certain compensations whereby that same union is righted; and these are the goods which excuse marriage and make it right.

Reply Obj. 1. In the act of eating there is not such an intense pleasure overpowering the reason as in the aforesaid action, both because the generative power, whereby original sin is transmitted, is infected and corrupt, whereas the nutritive power, by which original sin is not transmitted, is neither corrupt nor infected; and again because each one feels in himself a defect of the individual more than a defect of the species. Hence, in order to entice a man to take food which supplies a defect of the individual, it is enough that he feel this defect; but in order to entice him to the act whereby a defect of the species is remedied, Divine providence attached pleasure to that act, which moves even irrational animals in which there is not the stain of original sin. Hence the comparison fails.

Reply Obj. 2. These goods which justify marriage belong to the nature of marriage, which consequently needs them, not as extrinsic causes of its rectitude, but as causing in it that rectitude which belongs to it by nature.

Reply Obj. 3. From the very fact that marriage is intended as an office or as a remedy it has the aspect of something useful and right; nevertheless both aspects belong to it from the fact that it has these goods by which it fulfills the office and affords a remedy to concupiscence.

Reply Obj. 4. An act of virtue may derive its rectitude both from the virtue as its elicitive principle, and from its circumstances as its formal principles; and the goods of marriage are related to marriage as circumstances to an act of virtue which owes it to those circumstances that it can be an act of virtue.

SECOND ARTICLE

Whether the Goods of Marriage Are Sufficiently Enumerated?

We proceed thus to the Second Article:—

Objection 1. It would seem that the goods of marriage are insufficiently enumerated by the Master (iv. *Sent.* D. 31), namely *faith, offspring, and sacrament.* For the object of marriage among men is not only the begetting and feeding of children, but also the partnership of a common life, whereby each one contributes his share of work to the common stock, as stated in *Ethic.* viii. 12. Therefore as the offspring is reckoned a good of matrimony, so also should the communication of works.

Obj. 2. Further, the union of Christ with the Church, signified by matrimony, is the effect of charity. Therefore charity rather than faith should be reckoned among the goods of matrimony.

Obj. 3. Further, in matrimony, just as it is required that neither party have intercourse with another, so is it required that the one pay the marriage debt to the other. Now the former pertains to faith according to the Master *(loc. cit.).* Therefore justice should also be reckoned among the goods of marriage on account of the payment of the debt.

Obj. 4. Further, in matrimony as signifying the union of Christ with the Church, just as indivisibility is required, so also is unity, whereby one man has one wife. But the sacrament which is reckoned among the three marriage goods pertains to indivisibility. Therefore there should be something else pertaining to unity.

Obj. 5. *On the other hand,* it would seem that they are too many. For one virtue suffices to make one act right. Now faith is one virtue. Therefore it was not necessary to add two other goods to make marriage right.

Obj. 6. Further, the same cause does not make a thing both useful and virtuous, since the useful and the virtuous are opposite divisions of the good. Now marriage derives its character of useful from the offspring. Therefore the offspring should not be reckoned among the goods that make marriage virtuous.

Obj. 7. Further, nothing should be reckoned as a property or condition of itself. Now these goods are reckoned to be conditions of marriage. Therefore since matrimony is a sacrament, the sacrament should not be reckoned a condition of matrimony.

I answer that, Matrimony is instituted both as an office of nature and as a sacrament of the Church. As an office of nature it is directed by two things, like every other virtuous act. One of these is required on the part of the agent and is the intention of the due end, and thus the *offspring* is accounted a good of matrimony; the other is required on the part of the act, which is good generically through being about a due matter; and thus we have *faith,* whereby a man has intercourse with his wife and with no other woman. Besides this it has a certain goodness as a sacrament, and this is signified by the very word *sacrament.*

Reply Obj. 1. Offspring signifies not only the begetting of children, but also their education, to which as its end is directed the entire communion of works that exists between man and wife as united in marriage, since parents naturally *lay up* for their *children* (2 Cor. xii. 14); so that the offspring like a principal end includes another, as it were, secondary end.

Reply Obj. 2. Faith is not taken here as a theological virtue, but as part of justice, in so far as faith *(fides)* signifies the suiting of deed to word *(fiant dicta)* by keeping one's promises; for since marriage is a contract it contains a promise whereby this man is assigned to this woman.

Reply Obj. 3. Just as the marriage promise means that neither party is to have intercourse with a third party, so does it require that they should mutually pay the marriage debt. The latter is indeed the chief of the two, since it follows from the power which each receives over the other. Consequently both these things pertain to faith, although the Book of Sentences mentions that which is the less manifest.

Reply Obj. 4. By sacrament we are to understand not only indivisibility, but all those things that result from marriage being a sign of Christ's union with the Church. We may also reply that the unity to which the objection refers pertains to faith, just as indivisibility belongs to the sacrament.

Reply Obj. 5. Faith here does not denote a virtue, but that condition of virtue which is a part of justice and is called by the name of faith.

Reply Obj. 6. Just as the right use of a useful good derives its rectitude not from the useful but from the reason which causes the right use, so too direction to a useful good may cause the goodness of rectitude by virtue of the reason causing the right direction; and in this way marriage, through being directed to the offspring, is useful, and nevertheless righteous, inasmuch as it is directed aright.

Reply Obj. 7. As the Master says (iv. *Sent.* D. 31), sacrament here does not mean matrimony itself, but its indissolubility, which is a sign of the same thing as matrimony is.

We may also reply that although marriage is a sacrament, marriage as marriage is not the same as marriage as a sacrament, since it was instituted not only as a sign of a sacred thing, but also as an office of nature. Hence the sacramental aspect is a condition added to marriage considered in itself, whence also it derives its rectitude. Hence its sacramentality, if I may use the term, is reckoned among the goods which justify marriage; and accordingly this third good of marriage, the sacrament to wit, denotes not only its indissolubility, but also whatever pertains to its signification.

THIRD ARTICLE

Whether the Sacrament Is the Chief of the Marriage Goods?

We proceed thus to the Third Article:—

Objection 1. It would seem that the *sacrament* is not the chief of the marriage goods. For the end is principal in everything. Now the end of marriage is the offspring. Therefore the offspring is the chief marriage good.

Obj. 2. Further, in the specific nature the difference is more important than the genus, even as the form is more important than matter in the composition of a natural thing. Now *sacrament* refers to marriage on the part of its genus, while *offspring* and *faith* refer thereto on the part of the difference whereby it is a special kind of sacrament. Therefore these other two are more important than sacrament in reference to marriage.

Obj. 3. Further, just as we find marriage without *offspring* and without *faith,* so do we find it without indissolubility, as in the case where one of the parties enters religion before the marriage is consummated. Therefore neither from this point of view is *sacrament* the most important marriage good.

Obj. 4. Further, an effect cannot be more important than its cause. Now consent, which is the cause of matrimony, is often changed. Therefore the marriage also can be dissolved, and consequently inseparability is not always a condition of marriage.

Obj. 5. Further, the sacraments which produce an everlasting effect imprint a character. But no character is imprinted in matrimony. Therefore it is not conditioned by a lasting inseparability. Consequently just as there is marriage without *offspring* so is there marriage without *sacrament,* and thus the same conclusion follows as above.

On the contrary, That which has a place in the definition of a thing is most essential thereto. Now inseparability, which pertains to sacrament, is placed in the definition of marriage (Q. 44, A. 3), while offspring and faith are not. Therefore among the other goods sacrament is the most essential to matrimony.

Further, the Divine power which works in the sacraments is more efficacious than human power. But *offspring* and *faith* pertain to matrimony as directed to an office of human nature, whereas *sacrament* pertains to it as instituted by God. Therefore sacrament takes a more important part in marriage than the other two.

I answer that, This or that may be more important to a thing in two ways, either because it is more essential or because it is more excellent. If the reason is because it is more excellent, then *sacrament* is in every way the most important of the three marriage goods, since it belongs to marriage considered as a sacrament of grace; while the other two belong to it as an office of nature; and a perfection of grace is more excellent than a perfection of nature. If, however, it is said to be more important because it is more essential, we must draw a distinction; for *faith* and *offspring* can be considered in two ways. First, in themselves, and thus they regard the use of matrimony in begetting children and observing the marriage compact; while inseparability, which is denoted by *sacrament*, regards the very sacrament considered in itself, since from the very fact that by the marriage compact man and wife give to one another power the one over the other in perpetuity, it follows that they cannot be put asunder. Hence there is no matrimony without inseparability, whereas there is matrimony without *faith* and *offspring*, because the existence of a thing does not depend on its use; and in this sense *sacrament* is more essential to matrimony than *faith* and *offspring*. Secondly, *faith* and *offspring* may be considered as in their principles, so that *offspring* denote the intention of having children, and *faith* the duty of remaining faithful, and there can be no matrimony without these also, since they are caused in matrimony by the marriage compact itself, so that if anything contrary to these were expressed in the consent which makes a marriage, the marriage would be invalid. Taking *faith* and *offspring* in this sense, it is clear that *offspring* is the most essential thing in marriage, secondly *faith*, and thirdly *sacrament;* even as to man it is more essential to be in nature than to be in grace, although it is more excellent to be in grace.

Reply Obj. 1. The end as regards the intention stands first in a thing, but as regards the attainment it stands last. It is the same with *offspring* among the marriage goods;

wherefore in a way it is the most important and in another way it is not.

Reply Obj. 2. Sacrament, even as holding the third place among the marriage goods, belongs to matrimony by reason of its difference; for it is called *sacrament* from its signification of that particular sacred thing which matrimony signifies.

Reply Obj. 3. According to Augustine *(De Bono Conjug.* ix), marriage is a good of mortals, wherefore in the resurrection *they shall neither marry nor be married* (Matth. xxii 30). Hence the marriage bond does not last after the life wherein it is contracted, and consequently it is said to be inseparable, because it cannot be sundered in this life, but either by bodily death after carnal union, or by spiritual death after a merely spiritual union.

Reply Obj. 4. Although the consent which makes a marriage is not everlasting materially, i.e. in regard to the substance of the act, since that act ceases and a contrary act may succeed it, nevertheless formally speaking it is everlasting, because it is a consent to an everlasting bond, else it would not make a marriage, for a consent to take a woman for a time makes no marriage. Hence it is everlasting formally, inasmuch as an act takes its species from its object; and thus it is that matrimony derives its inseparability from the consent.

Reply Obj. 5. In those sacraments wherein a character is imprinted, power is given to perform spiritual actions; but in matrimony, to perform bodily actions. Wherefore matrimony by reason of the power which man and wife receive over one another agrees with the sacraments in which a character is imprinted, and from this it derives its inseparability, as the Master says (iv, *Sent.* D. 31); yet it differs from them in so far as that power regards bodily acts; hence it does not confer a spiritual character.

FOURTH ARTICLE

Whether the Marriage Act Is Excused by the Aforesaid Goods?

We proceed thus to the Fourth Article:—

Objection 1. It would seem that the marriage act cannot be altogether excused from sin by the aforesaid goods. For whoever allows himself to lose a greater good for the sake of a lesser good sins because he allows it inordinately. Now the good of reason which is prejudiced in the marriage act is greater than these three marriage goods. Therefore the aforesaid goods do not suffice to excuse marriage intercourse.

Obj. 2. Further, if a moral good be added to a moral evil the sum total is evil and not good, since one evil circumstance makes an action evil, whereas one good circumstance does not make it good. Now the marriage act is evil in itself, else it would need no excuse. Therefore the addition of the marriage goods cannot make the act good.

Obj. 3. Further, wherever there is immoderate passion there is moral vice. Now the marriage goods cannot prevent the pleasure in that act from being immoderate. Therefore they cannot excuse it from being a sin.

Obj. 4. Further, according to Damascene (*De Fide Orthod.* ii. 15), shame is only caused by a disgraceful deed. Now the marriage goods do not deprive that deed of its shame. Therefore they cannot excuse it from sin.

On the contrary, The marriage act differs not from fornication except by the marriage goods. If therefore these were not sufficient to excuse it marriage would be always unlawful; and this is contrary to what was stated above (Q. 41, A. 3).

Further, the marriage goods are related to its act as its due circumstances, as stated above (A. 1, *ad* 4). Now the like circumstances are sufficient to prevent an action from being evil. Therefore these goods can excuse marriage so that it is nowise a sin.

I answer that, An act is said to be excused in two ways. First, on the part of the agent, so that although it be evil it is not imputed as sin to the agent, or at least not as so grave a sin; thus ignorance is said to excuse a sin wholly or partly. Secondly, an act is said to be excused on its part, so that, namely, it is not evil; and it is thus that the aforesaid goods are said to excuse the marriage act. Now it is from the same cause that an act is not morally evil, and that it is good, since there is no such thing as an indifferent act, as was stated in the Second Book (ii, *Sent.* D. 40; I-II, Q. 18, A. 9). Now a human act is said to be good in two ways. In one way by goodness of virtue, and thus an act derives its goodness from those things which place it in the mean. This is what *faith* and *offspring* do in the marriage act, as stated above (A. 2). In another way, by goodness of the *sacrament*, in which way an act is said to be not only good, but also holy, and the marriage act derives this goodness from the indissolubility of the union, in respect of which it signifies the union of Christ with the Church. Thus it is clear that the aforesaid goods sufficiently excuse the marriage act.

Reply Obj. 1. By the marriage act man does not incur harm to his reason as to habit, but only as to act. Nor is it unfitting that a certain act which is generically better be sometimes interrupted for some less good act; for it is possible to do this without sin, as in the case of one who ceases from the act of contemplation in order meanwhile to devote himself to action.

Reply Obj. 2. This argument would avail if the evil that is inseparable from carnal intercourse were an evil of sin. But in this case it is an evil not of sin but of punishment alone, consisting in the rebellion of concupiscence against reason; and consequently the conclusion does not follow.

Reply Obj. 3. The excess of passion that amounts to a sin does not refer to the passion's quantitative intensity, but to its proportion to reason; wherefore it is only when a passion goes beyond the bounds of reason that it is reckoned to be immoderate. Now the pleasure attaching to the marriage act, while it is most intense in point of quantity, does not go beyond the bounds previously appointed by reason before the commencement of the act, although reason is unable to regulate them during the pleasure itself.

Reply Obj. 4. The turpitude that always accompanies the marriage act and always causes shame is the turpitude of punishment, not of sin, for man is naturally ashamed of any defect.

FIFTH ARTICLE

Whether the Marriage Act Can Be Excused without the Marriage Goods?

We proceed thus to the Fifth Article:—

Objection 1. It would seem that the marriage act can be excused even without the marriage goods. For he who is moved by nature alone to the marriage act, apparently does not intend any of the marriage goods, since the marriage goods pertain to grace or virtue. Yet when a person is moved to the aforesaid act by the natural appetite alone, seemingly he commits no sin, for nothing natural is an evil, since *evil is contrary to nature and order,* as Dionysius says (*Div. Nom.* iv). Therefore the marriage act can be excused even without the marriage goods.

Obj. 2. Further, he who has intercourse with his wife in order to avoid fornication, does not seemingly intend any of the marriage goods. Yet he does not sin apparently, because marriage was granted to human weakness for the very purpose of avoiding fornication (1 Cor. vii. 2, 6). Therefore the marriage act can be excused even without the marriage goods.

Obj. 3. Further, he who uses as he will that which is his own does not act against justice, and thus seemingly does not sin. Now marriage makes the wife the husband's own, and *vice versa.* Therefore, if they use one another at will through the instigation of lust, it would seem that it is no sin; and thus the same conclusion follows.

Obj. 4. Further, that which is good generically does not become evil unless it be done with an evil intention. Now the marriage act whereby a husband knows his wife is generically good. Therfore it cannot be evil unless it be done with an evil intention. Now it can be done with a good intention, even without intending any marriage good, for instance by intending to keep or acquire bodily health. Therefore it seems that this act can be excused even without the marriage goods.

On the contrary, If the cause be removed the effect is removed. Now the marriage goods are the cause of rectitude in the marriage act. Therefore the marriage act cannot be excused without them.

Further, the aforesaid act does not differ from the act of fornication except in the aforesaid goods. But the act of fornication is always evil. Therefore the marriage act also will always be evil unless it be excused by the aforesaid goods.

I answer that, Just as the marriage goods, in so far as they consist in a habit, make a marriage honest and holy, so too, in so far as they are in the actual intention, they make the marriage act honest, as regards those two marriage goods which relate to the marriage act. Hence when married persons come together for the purpose of begetting children, or of paying the debt to one another (which pertains to *faith*), they are wholly excused from sin. But the third good does not relate to the use of marriage, but to its excuse, as stated above (A. 3); wherefore it makes marriage itself honest, but not its act, as though its act were wholly excused from sin, through being done on account of some signification. Consequently there are only two ways in which married persons can come together without any sin at all, namely in order to have offspring, and in order to pay the debt; otherwise it is always at least a venial sin.

Reply Obj. 1. The offspring considered as a marriage good includes something besides the offspring as a good intended by nature. For nature intends offspring as safeguarding the good of the species, whereas the offspring as a good of the sacrament of marriage includes besides this the directing of the child to God. Wherefore the intention of nature which intends the offspring must needs be referred either actually or habitually to the intention of having an offspring, as a good of the sacrament: otherwise the intention would go no further than a creature; and this is always a sin. Consequently whenever nature alone moves a person to the marriage act, he is not wholly excused from sin, except in so far as the movement of nature is further directed actually or habitually to the offspring as a good of the sacrament. Nor does it follow that

the instigation of nature is evil, but that it is imperfect unless it be further directed to some marriage good.

Reply Obj. 2. If a man intends by the marriage act to prevent fornication in his wife, it is no sin, because this is a kind of payment of the debt that comes under the good of *faith*. But if he intends to avoid fornication in himself, then there is a certain superfluity, and accordingly there is a venial sin, nor was the sacrament instituted for that purpose, except by indulgence, which regards venial sins.

Reply Obj. 3. One due circumstance does not suffice to make a good act, and consequently it does not follow that, no matter how one use one's own property, the use is good, but when one uses it as one ought according to all the circumstances.

Reply Obj. 4. Although it is not evil in itself to intend to keep oneself in good health, this intention becomes evil, if one intend health by means of something that is not naturally ordained for that purpose; for instance if one sought only bodily health by the sacrament of baptism, and the same applies to the marriage act in the question at issue.

SIXTH ARTICLE

Whether It Is a Mortal Sin for a Man to Have Knowledge of His Wife, with the Intention Not of a Marriage Good but Merely of Pleasure?

We proceed thus to the Sixth Article:—

Objection 1. It would seem that whenever a man has knowledge of his wife, with the intention not of a marriage good but merely of pleasure, he commits a mortal sin. For according to Jerome (*Comment. in Eph.* v. 25), as quoted in the text (iv, *Sent.* D. 31), *the pleasure taken in the embraces of a wanton is damnable in a husband.* Now nothing but mortal sin is said to be damnable. Therefore it is always a mortal sin to have knowledge of one's wife for mere pleasure.

Obj. 2. Further, consent to pleasure is a mortal sin, as stated in the Second Book (ii, *Sent.* D. 24). Now whoever knows his wife for the sake of pleasure consents to the pleasure. Therefore he sins mortally.

Obj. 3. Further, whoever fails to refer the use of a creature to God enjoys a creature, and this is a mortal sin. But whoever uses his wife for mere pleasure does not refer that use to God. Therefore he sins mortally.

Obj. 4. Further, no one should be excommunicated except for a mortal sin. Now according to the text (*loc. cit.*) a man who knows his wife for mere pleasure is debarred from entering the Church, as though he were excommunicate. Therefore every such man sins mortally.

On the contrary, As stated in the text *(loc. cit.),* according to Augustine *(Contra Jul.* ii. 10; *De Decem Chord.* xi; *Serm.* xli, *de Sanct.),* carnal intercourse of this kind is one of the daily sins, for which we say the *Our Father.* Now these are not mortal sins. Therefore, etc.

Further, it is no mortal sin to take food for mere pleasure. Therefore in like manner it is not a mortal sin for a man to use his wife merely to satisfy his desire.

I answer that, Some say that whenever pleasure is the chief motive for the marriage act it is a mortal sin; that when it is an indirect motive it is a venial sin; and that when it spurns the pleasure altogether and is displeasing, it is wholly void of venial sin; so that it would be a mortal sin to seek pleasure in this act, a venial sin to take the pleasure when offered, but that perfection requires one to detest it. But this is impossible, since according to the Philosopher *(Ethic.* x. 3, 4) the same judgment applies to pleasure as to action, because pleasure in a good action is good, and in an evil action, evil; wherefore, as the marriage act is not evil in itself, neither will it be always a mortal sin to seek pleasure therein. Consequently the right answer to this question is that if pleasure be sought in such a way as to exclude the honesty of marriage, so that, to wit, it is not as a wife but as a woman that a man treats his wife, and that he is ready to use her in the same way if she were not his wife, it is a mortal sin; wherefore such a man is said to be too ardent a lover of his wife, because his ardor carries him away from the goods of marriage. If, however, he seek pleasure within the bounds of marriage, so that it would not be sought in another than his wife, it is a venial sin.

Reply Obj. 1. A man seeks wanton pleasure in his wife when he sees no more in her than he would in a wanton.

Reply Obj. 2. Consent to the pleasure of the intercourse that is a mortal sin is itself a mortal sin; but such is not the consent to the marriage act.

Reply Obj. 3. Although he does not actually refer the pleasure to God, he does not place his will's last end therein; otherwise he would seek it anywhere indifferently. Hence it does not follow that he enjoys a creature; but he uses a creature actually for his own sake, and himself habitually, though not actually, for God's sake.

Reply Obj. 4. The reason for this statement is not that man deserves to be excommunicated for this sin, but because he renders himself unfit for spiritual things, since in that act he becomes flesh and nothing more.

QUESTION 50

Of the Impediments of Marriage, in General

(In One Article)

IN the next place we must consider the impediments of marriage: (1) In general; (2) in particular.

ARTICLE

Whether It Is Fitting That Impediments Should Be Assigned to Marriage?

We proceed thus to this Article:—

Objection 1. It would seem unfitting for impediments to be assigned to marriage. For marriage is a sacrament condivided with the others. But no impediments are assigned to the others. Neither therefore should they be assigned to marriage.

Obj. 2. Further, the less perfect a thing is the fewer its obstacles. Now matrimony is the least perfect of the sacraments. Therefore it should have either no impediments or very few.

Obj. 3. Further, wherever there is disease, it is necessary to have a remedy for the disease. Now concupiscence, a remedy for which is permitted in matrimony (1 Cor. vii. 6), is in all. Therefore there should not be any impediment making it altogether unlawful for a particular person to marry.

Obj. 4. Further, unlawful means against the law. Now these impediments that are assigned to matrimony are not against the natural law, because they are not found to be the same in each state of the human race, since more degrees of kindred come under prohibition at one time than at another. Nor, seemingly, can human law set up impediments against marriage, since marriage, like the other sacraments, is not of human but of Divine institution. Therefore impediments should not be assigned to marriage, making it unlawful for a person to marry.

Obj. 5. Further, lawful and unlawful differ as that which is against the law from that which is not, and between these there is no middle term, since they are opposed according to affirmation and negation. Therefore there cannot be impediments to marriage, placing a person in a middle position between those who are lawful and those who are unlawful subjects of marriage.

Obj. 6. Further, union of man and woman is unlawful save in marriage. Now every unlawful union should be dissolved. Therefore if anything prevent a marriage being contracted, it will *de facto* dissolve it after it has been contracted; and thus impediments should not be assigned to marriage, which hinder it from being contracted, and dissolve it after it has been contracted.

Obj. 7. Further, no impediment can remove from a thing that which is part of its definition. Now indissolubility is part of the definition of marriage. Therefore there cannot be any impediments which annul a marriage already contracted.

Obj. 8. *On the other hand,* it would seem that there should be an infinite number of impediments to marriage. For marriage is a good. Now good may be lacking in an infinite number of ways, as Dionysius says *(Div. Nom.* iii). Therefore there is an infinite number of impediments to marriage.

Obj. 9. Further, the impediments to marriage arise from the conditions of individuals. But such like conditions are infinite in number. Therefore the impediments to marriage are also infinite.

I answer that, In marriage, as in other sacraments, there are certain things essential to marriage, and others that belong to its solemnization. And since even without the things that pertain to its solemnization it is still a true sacrament, as also in the case of the other sacraments, it follows that the impediments to those things that pertain to the solemnization of this sacrament do not derogate from the validity of the marriage. These impediments are said to hinder the contracting of marriage, but they do not dissolve the marriage once contracted; such are the veto of the Church, or the holy seasons. Hence the verse:

> The veto of the Church and holy tide
> Forbid the knot, but loose it not if tied.

On the other hand, those impediments which regard the essentials of marriage make a marriage invalid, wherefore they are said not only to hinder the contracting of marriage, but to dissolve it if contracted; and they are contained in the following verse:

> Error, station, vow, kinship, crime,
> Difference of worship, force, holy orders,
> Marriage bond, honesty, affinity, impotence,
> All these forbid marriage, and annul it though contracted.

The reason for this number may be explained as follows: Marriage may be hindered either on the part of the contract or in regard to the contracting parties. If in the first way, since the marriage contract is made by voluntary consent, and this is incompatible with either ignorance or violence, there will be two impediments to marriage, namely *force,* i.e. compulsion, and *error* in reference to ignorance. Wherefore the Master pronounced on these two impediments when treating of the cause of matrimony (iv, *Sent.* DD. 29, 30). Here, however, he is treating of the impediments as arising from the contracting parties, and these may be differentiated as follows. A person may be hindered from contracting marriage either simply, or with some particular person. If simply, so that he be unable to contract marriage with any woman, this can only be because he is hindered from performing the marriage act. This happens in two ways. First, because he cannot *de facto,* either through being altogether unable,—and thus we have the impediment of *impotence,*—or through being unable to do so freely, and thus we have the impediment of the *condition of slavery.* Secondly, because he cannot do it lawfully, and this because he is bound to continence, which happens in two ways, either through his being bound on account of the office he has undertaken to fulfill,—and thus we have the impediment of *Order,*—or on account of his having taken a vow,—and thus *Vow* is an impediment.

If, however, a person is hindered from marrying, not simply but in reference to a particular person, this is either because he is bound to another person, and thus he who is married to one cannot marry another, which constitutes the impediment of the *bond of marriage,*—or through lack of proportion to the other party, and this for three reasons. First, on account of too great a distance separating them, and thus we have *difference of worship;* secondly, on account of their being too closely related, and thus we have three impediments, namely *kinship,* then *affinity,* which denotes the close relationship between two persons, in reference to a third united to one of them by marriage, and the *justice of public honesty,* where we have a close relationship between two persons arising out of the betrothal of one of them to a third person; thirdly, on account of a previous undue union between him and the woman, and thus the *crime of adultery* previously committed with her is an impediment.

Reply Obj. 1. There may be impediments to the other sacraments also in the omission either of that which is essential, or of that which pertains to the solemnization of the sacrament, as stated above. However, impediments are assigned to matrimony rather than to the other sacraments for three reasons. First, because matrimony consists of two persons, and consequently can be impeded in more ways than the other sacraments which refer to one person taken individually; secondly, because matrimony has its cause in us and in God, while some of the other sacraments have their cause in God alone. Wherefore penance, which in a manner has a cause in us, is assigned certain impediments by the Master (iv, *Sent.* D. 16), such as hypocrisy, the public games, and so forth; thirdly, because other sacraments are objects of command or counsel, as being more perfect goods, whereas marriage is a matter of indulgence, as being a less perfect good (1 Cor. vii. 6). Wherefore, in order to afford an opportunity of proficiency towards a greater good, more impediments are assigned to matrimony than to the other sacraments.

Reply Obj. 2. The more perfect things can be hindered in more ways, in so far as more conditions are required for them. And if an imperfect thing requires more conditions, there will be more impediments to it; and thus it is in matrimony.

Reply Obj. 3. This argument would hold, were there no other and more efficacious remedies for the disease of concupiscence; which is false.

Reply Obj. 4. Persons are said to be unlawful subjects for marriage through being contrary to the law whereby marriage is established. Now marriage as fulfilling an office of nature is established by the natural law; as a sacrament, by the Divine law; as fulfilling an office of society, by the civil law. Consequently a person may be rendered an unlawful subject of marriage by any of the aforesaid laws. Nor does the comparison with the other sacraments hold, for they are sacraments only. And since the natural law is particularized in various ways according to the various states of mankind, and since positive law, too, varies according to the various conditions of men, the Master (iv, *Sent.* D. 34) asserts that at various times various persons have been unlawful subjects of marriage.

Reply Obj. 5. The law may forbid a thing either altogether, or in part and in certain cases. Hence between that which is altogether according to the law and that which is altogether against the law (which are opposed by contrariety and not according to affirmation and negation), that which is somewhat according to the law and somewhat against the law is a middle term. For this reason certain persons hold a middle place between those who are simply lawful subjects and those who are simply unlawful.

Reply Obj. 6. Those impediments which do not annul a marriage already contracted sometimes hinder a marriage from being contracted, by rendering it not invalid but unlawful. And if it be contracted it is a true marriage although the contracting parties sin; just as by consecrating after breaking one's fast one would sin by disobeying the Church's ordinance, and yet it would be a valid sacrament because it is not essential to the sacrament that the consecrator be fasting.

Reply Obj. 7. When we say that the aforesaid impediments annul marriage already contracted, we do not mean that they dissolve a marriage contracted in due form, but that they dissolve a marriage contracted *de facto* and not *de jure.* Wherefore if an impediment supervene after a marriage has been contracted in due form, it cannot dissolve the marriage.

Reply Obj. 8. The impediments that hinder a good accidentally are infinite in number, like all accidental causes. But the causes which of their own nature corrupt a certain good are directed to that effect, and determinate, even as are the causes which produce that good; for the causes by which a thing is destroyed and those by which it is made are either contrary to one another, or the same but taken in a contrary way.

Reply Obj. 9. The conditions of particular persons taken individually are infinite in number, but taken in general, they may be reduced to a certain number; as instanced in medicine and all operative arts, which consider the conditions of particular persons in whom acts are.

QUESTION 51

Of the Impediment of Error

(In Two Articles)

WE must now consider the impediments to matrimony in particular, and in the first place the impediment of error. Under this head there are two points of inquiry: (1) Whether error of its very nature is an impediment to matrimony? (2) What kind of error?

FIRST ARTICLE

Whether It Is Right to Reckon Error As an Impediment to Marriage?

We proceed thus to the First Article:—

Objection 1. It would seem that error should not be reckoned in itself an impediment to marriage. For consent, which is the efficient cause of marriage, is hindered in the same way as the voluntary. Now the voluntary, according to the Philosopher *(Ethic.* iii. 1), may be hindered by ignorance. But ignorance is not the same as error, because ignorance excludes knowledge altogether, whereas error does not, since *error is to approve the false as though it were true,* according to Augustine *(De Trin.* ix. 11). Therefore ignorance rather than error should have been reckoned here as an impediment to marriage.

Obj. 2. Further, that which of its very nature can be an impediment to marriage is in opposition to the good of marriage. But error is not a thing of this kind. Therefore error is not by its very nature an impediment to marriage.

Obj. 3. Further, just as consent is required for marriage, so is intention required for baptism. Now if one were to baptize John, thinking to baptize Peter, John would be baptized none the less. Therefore error does not annul matrimony.

Obj. 4. Further, there was true marriage between Lia and Jacob, and yet, in this case, there was error. Therefore error does not annul a marriage.

On the contrary, It is said in the *Digests (Si per errorem,* ff. De jurisdic. omn. judic.): *What is more opposed to consent than error?* Now consent is required for marriage. Therefore error is an impediment to matrimony.

Further, consent denotes something voluntary. Now error is an obstacle to the voluntary, since *the voluntary,* according to the Philosopher *(Ethic.* iii. 1), Damascene *(De Fide Orthod.* ii. 24), and Gregory of Nyssa* *(De Nat. Hom.* xxxii), *is that which has its principle in one who has knowledge of singulars which are the matter of actions.* But this does not apply to one who is in error. Therefore error is an impediment to matrimony.

I answer that, Whatever hinders a cause, of its very nature hinders the effect likewise. Now consent is the cause of matrimony, as stated above (Q. 45, A. 1). Hence whatever voids the consent, voids marriage. Now consent is an act of the will, presupposing an act of the intellect; and if the first be lacking, the second must needs be lacking also. Hence, when error hinders knowledge, there follows a defect in the consent also, and consequently in the marriage. Therefore it is possible according to the natural law for error to void marriage.

Reply Obj. 1. Speaking simply, ignorance differs from error, because ignorance does not of its very nature imply an act of knowledge, while error supposes a wrong judgment of reason about something. However, as regards

* Nemesius.

being an impediment to the voluntary, it differs not whether we call it ignorance or error, since no ignorance can be an impediment to the voluntary, unless it have error in conjunction with it, because the will's act presupposes an estimate or judgment about something which is the object of the will. Wherefore if there be ignorance there must needs be error; and for this reason error is set down as being the proximate cause.

Reply Obj. 2. Although error is not of itself contrary to matrimony, it is contrary thereto as regards the cause of marriage.

Reply Obj. 3. The character of baptism is not caused directly by the intention of the baptizer, but by the material element applied outwardly; and the intention is effective only as directing the material element to its effect; whereas the marriage tie is caused by the consent directly. Hence the comparison fails.

Reply Obj. 4. According to the Master (iv, *Sent.* D. 30) the marriage between Lia and Jacob was effected not by their coming together, which happened through an error, but by their consent, which followed afterwards. Yet both are clearly to be excused from sin *(ibid.).*

SECOND ARTICLE

Whether Every Error Is an Impediment to Matrimony?

We proceed thus to the Second Article:—

Objection 1. It would seem that every error is an impediment to matrimony, and not, as stated in the text (iv, *Sent.* D. 30), only error about the condition or the person. For that which applies to a thing as such applies to it in all its bearings. Now error is of its very nature an impediment to matrimony, as stated above (A. 1). Therefore every error is an impediment to matrimony.

Obj. 2. Further, if error, as such, is an impediment to matrimony, the greater the error the greater the impediment. Now the error concerning faith in a heretic who disbelieves in this sacrament is greater than an error concerning the person. Therefore it should be a greater impediment than error about the person.

Obj. 3. Further, error does not void marriage except as removing voluntariness. Now ignorance about any circumstance takes away voluntariness *(Ethic.* iii. 1). Therefore it is not only error about condition or person that is an impediment to matrimony.

Obj. 4. Further, just as the condition of slavery is an accident affecting the person, so are bodily or mental qualities. But error regarding the condition is an impediment to matrimony. Therefore error concerning quality or fortune is equally an impediment.

Obj. 5. Further, just as slavery or freedom pertains to the condition of person, so do high and low rank, or dignity of position and the lack thereof. Now error regarding the condition of slavery is an impediment to matrimony. Therefore error about the other matters mentioned is also an impediment.

Obj. 6. Further, just as the condition of slavery is an impediment, so are difference of worship and impotence, as we shall say further on (Q. 52, A. 2; Q. 58, A. 1; Q. 59, A. 1). Therefore just as error regarding the condition is an impediment, so also should error about those other matters be reckoned an impediment.

Obj. 7. *On the other hand,* it would seem that not even error about the person is an impediment to marriage. For marriage is a contract even as a sale is. Now in buying and selling the sale is not voided if one coin be given instead of another of equal value. Therefore a marriage is not voided if one woman be taken instead of another.

Obj. 8. Further, it is possible for them to remain in this error for many years and to beget between them sons and daughters. But it would be a grave assertion to maintain that they ought to be separated then. Therefore their previous error did not void their marriage.

Obj. 9. Further, it might happen that the woman is betrothed to the brother of the man whom she thinks that she is consenting to marry, and that she has had carnal intercourse with him; in which case, seemingly, she cannot go back to the man to whom she thought to give her consent, but should hold on to his brother. Thus error regarding the person is not an impediment to marriage.

I answer that, Just as error, through causing involuntariness, is an excuse from sin, so on the same count is it an impediment to marriage. Now error does not excuse from sin unless it refer to a circumstance the presence or absence of which makes an action lawful or unlawful. For if a man were to strike his father with an iron rod thinking it to be of wood, he is not excused from sin wholly, although perhaps in part; but if a man were to strike his father, thinking to strike his son to correct him, he is wholly excused provided he take due care. Wherefore error, in order to void marriage, must needs be about the essentials of marriage. Now marriage includes two things, namely the two persons who are joined together, and the mutual power over one another wherein marriage consists. The first of these is removed by error concerning the person, the second by error regarding the condition, since a slave cannot freely give power over his body to another, without his master's

consent. For this reason these two errors, and no others, are an impediment to matrimony.

Reply Obj. 1. It is not from its generic nature that error is an impediment to marriage, but from the nature of the difference added thereto; namely from its being error about one of the essentials to marriage.

Reply Obj. 2. An error of faith about matrimony is about things consequent upon matrimony, for instance on the question of its being a sacrament, or of its being lawful. Wherefore such error as these is no impediment to marriage, as neither does an error about baptism hinder a man from receiving the character, provided he intend to receive what the Church gives, although he believe it to be nothing.

Reply Obj. 3. It is not any ignorance of a circumstance that causes the involuntariness which is an excuse from sin, as stated above; wherefore the argument does not prove.

Reply Obj. 4. Difference of fortune or of quality does not make a difference in the essentials to matrimony, as the condition of slavery does. Hence the argument does not prove.

Reply Obj. 5. Error about a person's rank, as such, does not void a marriage, for the same reason as neither does error about a personal quality. If, however, the error about a person's rank or position amounts to an error about the person, it is an impediment to matrimony. Hence, if the woman consent directly to this particular person, her error about his rank does not void the marriage; but if she intend directly to consent to marry the king's son, whoever he may be, then, if another man than the king's son be brought to her, there is error about the person, and the marriage will be void.

Reply Obj. 6. Error is an impediment to matrimony, although it be about other impediments to marriage if it concern those things which render a person an unlawful subject of marriage. But (the Master) does not mention error about such things, because they are an impediment to marriage whether there be error about them or not; so that if a woman contract with a subdeacon, whether she know this or not, there is no marriage; whereas the condition of slavery is no impediment if the slavery be known. Hence the comparison fails.

Reply Obj. 7. In contracts money is regarded as the measure of other things (*Ethic* v. 5), and not as being sought for its own sake. Hence if the coin paid is not what it is thought to be but another of equal value, this does not void the contract. But if there be error about a thing sought for its own sake, the contract is voided, for instance if one were to sell a donkey for a horse; and thus it is in the case in point.

Reply Obj. 8. No matter how long they have cohabited, unless she be willing to consent again, there is no marriage.

Reply Obj. 9. If she did not consent previously to marry his brother, she may hold to the one whom she took in error. Nor can she return to his brother, especially if there has been carnal intercourse between her and the man she took to husband. If, however, she had previously consented to take the first one in words of the present, she cannot have the second while the first lives. But she may either leave the second or return to the first; and ignorance of the fact excuses her from sin, just as she would be excused if after the consummation of the marriage a kinsman of her husband were to know her by fraud since she is not to be blamed for the other's deceit.

QUESTION 52

Of the Impediment of the Condition of Slavery

(In Four Articles)

WE must now consider the impediment of the condition of slavery. Under this head there are four points of inquiry: (1) Whether the condition of slavery is an impediment to matrimony? (2) Whether a slave can marry without his master's consent? (3) Whether a man who is already married can make himself a slave without his wife's consent? (4) Whether the children should follow the condition of their father or of their mother?

FIRST ARTICLE

Whether the Condition of Slavery Is an Impediment to Matrimony?

We proceed thus to the First Article:—

Objection 1. It would seem that the condition of slavery is no impediment to matrimony. For nothing is an impediment to marriage except what is in some way opposed to it. But slavery is in no way opposed to marriage, else there could be no marriage among slaves. Therefore slavery is no impediment to marriage.

Obj. 2. Further, that which is contrary to nature cannot be an impediment to that which is according to nature. Now slavery is contrary to nature, for as Gregory says *(Pastor.* ii. 6), *it is contrary to nature for man to wish to lord it over another man;* and this is also evident from the fact that it was said of man (Gen. i. 26) that he should *have dominion over the fishes of the sea,* but not that he should have dominion over man. Therefore it cannot be an impediment to marriage, which is a natural thing.

Obj. 3. Further, if it is an impediment, this is either of natural law or of positive law. But it is not of natural law, since according to natural law all men are equal, as Gregory says *(loc. cit.),* while it is stated at the beginning of the *Digests (Manumissiones,* ff. de just. et jure.) that slavery is not of natural law; and positive law springs from the natural law, as Tully says *(De Invent.* ii). Therefore, according to law, slavery is not an impediment to any marriage.

Obj. 4. Further, that which is an impediment to marriage is equally an impediment whether it be known or not, as in the case of consanguinity. Now the slavery of one party, if it be known to the other, is no impediment to their marriage. Therefore slavery, considered in itself, is unable to void a marriage; and consequently it should not be reckoned by itself as a distinct impediment to marriage.

Obj. 5. Further, just as one may be in error about slavery, so as to deem a person free who is a slave, so may one be in error about freedom, so as to deem a person a slave whereas he is free. But freedom is not accounted an impediment to matrimony. Therefore neither should slavery be so accounted.

Obj. 7. Further, leprosy is a greater burden to the fellowship of marriage and is a greater obstacle to the good of the offspring than slavery is. Yet leprosy is not reckoned an impediment to marriage. Therefore neither should slavery be so reckoned.

On the contrary, A Decretal says (De conjug. servorum, cap. *Ad nostram)* that *error regarding the condition hinders a marriage from being contracted and voids that which is already contracted.*

Further, marriage is one of the goods that are sought for their own sake, because it is qualified by honesty; whereas slavery is one of the things to be avoided for their own sake. Therefore marriage and slavery are contrary to one another; and consequently slavery is an impediment to matrimony.

I answer that, In the marriage contract one party is bound to the other in the matter of paying the debt; wherefore if one who thus binds himself is unable to pay the debt, ignorance of this inability, on the side of the party to whom he binds himself, voids the contract. Now just as impotence in respect of coition makes a person unable to pay the debt, so that he is altogether disabled, so slavery makes him unable to pay it freely. Therefore, just as ignorance or impotence in respect of coition is an impediment if not known but not if known, as we shall state further on (Q. 58), so the condition of slavery is an impediment if not known, but not if it be known.

Reply Obj. 1. Slavery is contrary to marriage as regards the act to which marriage binds one party in relation to the other, because it prevents the free execution of that act; and again as regards the good of the offspring who become subject to the same condition by reason of the parent's slavery. Since, however, it is free to everyone to suffer detriment in that which is his due, if one of the parties knows the other to be a slave, the marriage is none the less valid. Likewise since in marriage there is an equal obligation on either side to pay the debt, neither party can exact of the other a greater obligation than that under which he lies; so that if a slave marry a bondswoman, thinking her to be free, the marriage is not thereby rendered invalid. It is therefore evident that slavery is no impediment to marriage except when it is unknown to the other party, even though the latter be in a condition of freedom; and so nothing prevents marriage between slaves, or even between a freeman and a bondswoman.

Reply Obj. 2. Nothing prevents a thing being against nature as to the first intention of nature, and yet not against nature as to its second intention. Thus, as stated in *De Cœlo,* ii, all corruption, defect, and old age are contrary to nature, because nature intends being and perfection, and yet they are not contrary to the second intention of nature, because nature, through being unable to preserve being in one thing, preserves it in another which is engendered of the other's corruption. And when nature is unable to bring a thing to a greater perfection it brings it to a lesser; thus when it cannot produce a male it produces a female which is *a misbegotten male (De Gener. Animal.* ii. 3). I say then in like manner that slavery is contrary to the first intention of nature. Yet it is not contrary to the second, because natural reason has this inclination, and nature has this desire,—that everyone should be good; but from the fact that a person sins, nature has an inclination that he should be punished for his sin, and thus slavery was brought in as a punishment of sin. Nor is it unreasonable for a natural thing to be hindered by that which is unnatural in this way; for thus is marriage hindered by impotence of coition, which impotence is contrary to nature in the way mentioned.

Reply Obj. 3. The natural law requires punishment to be inflicted for guilt, and that no one should be punished who is not guilty; but the appointing of the punishment according to the circumstances of person and guilt belongs to positive law. Hence slavery which is a definite punishment is of positive law, and arises out of natural law, as the determinate from that which is indeterminate. And it arises from the determination of the same positive law that slavery if unknown is an impediment to matrimony, lest one who is not guilty be punished; for it is a punishment to the wife to have a slave for husband, and *vice versa.*

Reply Obj. 4. Certain impediments render a marriage unlawful; and since it is not our will that makes a thing lawful or unlawful, but the law to which our will ought to be subject, it follows that the validity or invalidity of a marriage is not affected either by ignorance (such as destroys voluntariness) of the impediment or by knowledge thereof; and such an impediment is affinity or a vow, and others of the same kind. Other impediments, however, render a marriage ineffectual as to the payment of the debt; and since it is within the competency of our will to remit a debt that is due to us, it follows that such impediments, if known, do not invalidate a marriage, but only when ignorance of them destroys voluntariness. Such impediments are slavery and impotence of coition. And, because they have of themselves the nature of an impediment, they are reckoned as special impediments besides error; whereas a change of person is not reckoned a special impediment besides error, because the substitution of another person has not the nature of an impediment except by reason of the intention of one of the contracting parties.

Reply Obj. 5. Freedom does not hinder the marriage act, wherefore ignorance of freedom is no impediment to matrimony.

Reply Obj. 6. Leprosy does not hinder marriage as to its first act, since lepers can pay the debt freely; although they lay a burden upon marriage as to its secondary effects; wherefore it is not an impediment to marriage as slavery is.

SECOND ARTICLE

Whether a Slave Can Marry without His Master's Consent?

We proceed thus to the Second Article:—

Objection 1. It would seem that a slave cannot marry without his master's consent. For no one can give a person that which is another's without the latter's consent. Now a slave is his master's chattel. Therefore he cannot give his wife power over his body by marrying without his master's consent.

Obj. 2. Further, a slave is bound to obey

his master. But his master may command him not to consent to marry. Therefore he cannot marry without his consent.

Obj. 3. Further, after marriage, a slave is bound even by a precept of the Divine law to pay the debt to his wife. But at the time that his wife asks for the debt his master may demand of him a service which he will be unable to perform if he wish to occupy himself in carnal intercourse. Therefore if a slave can marry without his master's consent, the latter would be deprived of a service due to him without any fault of his; and this ought not to be.

Obj. 4. Further, a master may sell his slave into a foreign country, where the latter's wife is unable to follow him, through either bodily weakness, or imminent danger to her faith; for instance if he be sold to unbelievers, or if her master be unwilling, supposing her to be a bondswoman; and thus the marriage will be dissolved, which is unfitting. Therefore a slave cannot marry without his master's consent.

Obj. 5. Further, the burden under which a man binds himself to the Divine service is more advantageous than that whereby a man subjects himself to his wife. But a slave cannot enter religion or receive orders without his master's consent. Much less therefore can he be married without his consent.

On the contrary, In Christ Jesus . . . there is neither bond nor free (Gal. iii. 26, 28): Therefore both freeman and bondsman enjoy the same liberty to marry in the faith of Christ Jesus.

Further, slavery is of positive law; whereas marriage is of natural and Divine law. Since then positive law is not prejudicial to the natural or the Divine law, it would seem that a slave can marry without his master's consent.

I answer that, As stated above (A. 1, *ad* 3), the positive law arises out of the natural law, and consequently slavery, which is of positive law, cannot be prejudicious to those things that are of natural law. Now just as nature seeks the preservation of the individual, so does it seek the preservation of the species by means of procreation; wherefore even as a slave is not so subject to his master as not to be at liberty to eat, sleep, and do such things as pertain to the needs of his body, and without which nature cannot be preserved, so he is not subject to him to the extent of being unable to marry freely, even without his master's knowledge or consent.

Reply Obj. 1. A slave is his master's chattel in matters superadded to nature, but in natural things all are equal. Wherefore, in things pertaining to natural acts, a slave can by marrying give another person power over his body without his master's consent.

Reply Obj. 2. A slave is bound to obey his master in those things which his master can command lawfully; and just as his master cannot lawfully command him not to eat or sleep, so neither can he lawfully command him to refrain from marrying. For it is the concern of the lawgiver how each one uses his own, and consequently if the master command his slave not to marry, the slave is not bound to obey his master.

Reply Obj. 3. If a slave has married with his master's consent, he should omit the service commanded by his master and pay the debt to his wife; because the master, by consenting to his slave's marriage, implicitly consented to all that marriage requires. If, however, the marriage was contracted without the master's knowledge or consent, he is not bound to pay the debt, but in preference to obey his master, if the two things are incompatible. Nevertheless in such matters there are many particulars to be considered, as in all human acts, namely the danger to which his wife's chastity is exposed, and the obstacle which the payment of the debt places in the way of the service commanded, and other like considerations, all of which being duly weighed it will be possible to judge which of the two in preference the slave is bound to obey, his master or his wife.

Reply Obj. 4. In such a case it is said that the master should be compelled not to sell the slave in such a way as to increase the weight of the marriage burden, especially since he is able to obtain anywhere a just price for his slave.

Reply Obj. 5. By entering religion or receiving orders a man is bound to the Divine service for all time; whereas a husband is bound to pay the debt to his wife not always, but at a fitting time; hence the comparison fails. Moreover, he who enters religion or receives orders binds himself to works that are superadded to natural works, and in which his master has power over him, but not in natural works to which a man binds himself by marriage. Hence he cannot vow continence without his master's consent.

THIRD ARTICLE

Whether Slavery Can Supervene to Marriage?

We proceed thus to the Third Article:—

Objection 1. It would seem that slavery cannot supervene to marriage, by the husband selling himself to another as slave. Because what is done by fraud and to another's detriment should not hold. But a husband who sells himself for a slave, does so sometimes to cheat marriage, and at least to the detriment of his wife. Therefore such a sale should not hold as to the effect of slavery.

Obj. 2. Further, two favorable things outweigh one that is not favorable. Now marriage and freedom are favorable things and are contrary to slavery, which in law is not a favorable thing. Therefore such a slavery ought to be entirely annulled in marriage.

Obj. 3. Further, in marriage husband and wife are on a par with one another. Now the wife cannot surrender herself to be a slave without her husband's consent. Therefore neither can the husband without his wife's consent.

Obj. 4. Further, in natural things that which hinders a thing being generated destroys it after it has been generated. Now bondage of the husband, if unknown to the wife, is an impediment to the act of marriage before it is performed. Therefore if it could supervene to marriage it would dissolve it; which is unreasonable.

On the contrary, Everyone can give another that which is his own. Now the husband is his own master since he is free. Therefore he can surrender his right to another.

Further, a slave can marry without his master's consent, as stated above (A. 2). Therefore a husband can in like manner subject himself to a master, without his wife's consent.

I answer that, A husband is subject to his wife in those things which pertain to the act of nature; in these things they are equal, and the subjection of slavery does not extend thereto. Wherefore the husband, without his wife's knowledge, can surrender himself to be another's slave. Nor does this result in a dissolution of the marriage, since no impediment supervening to marriage can dissolve it, as stated above (Q. 50, A. 1, *ad* 7).

Reply Obj. 1. The fraud can indeed hurt the person who has acted fraudulently, but it cannot be prejudicial to another person: wherefore if the husband, to cheat his wife, surrender himself to be another's slave, it will be to his own prejudice, through his losing the inestimable good of freedom; whereas this can nowise be prejudicial to the wife, and he is bound to pay her the debt when she asks, and to do all that marriage requires of him, for he cannot be taken away from these obligations by his master's command.

Reply Obj. 2. In so far as slavery is opposed to marriage, marriage is prejudicial to slavery, since the slave is bound then to pay the debt to his wife, though his master be unwilling.

Reply Obj. 3. Although husband and wife are considered to be on a par in the marriage act and in things relating to nature, to which the condition of slavery does not extend, nevertheless as regards the management of the household, and other such additional matters the husband is the head of the wife and should correct her, and not *vice versa*. Hence the wife cannot surrender herself to be a slave without her husband's consent.

Reply Obj. 4. This argument considers corruptible things; and yet even in these there are many obstacles to generation that are not capable of destroying what is already generated. But in things which have stability it is possible to have an impediment which prevents a certain thing from beginning to be, yet does not cause it to cease to be; as instanced by the rational soul. It is the same with marriage, which is a lasting tie so long as this life lasts.

FOURTH ARTICLE

Whether Children Should Follow the Condition of Their Father?

We now proceed to the Fourth Article:—

Objection 1. It would seem that children should follow the condition of their father. Because dominion belongs to those of higher rank. Now in generating the father ranks above the mother. Therefore, etc.

Obj. 2. Further, the being of a thing depends on the form more than on the matter. Now in generation the father gives the form, and the mother the matter (*De Gener. Animal.* ii. 4). Therefore the child should follow the condition of the father rather than of the mother.

Obj. 3. Further, a thing should follow that chiefly to which it is most like. Now the son is more like the father than the mother, even as the daughter is more like the mother. Therefore at least the son should follow the father in preference, and the daughter the mother.

Obj. 4. Further, in Holy Writ genealogies are not traced through the women but through the men. Therefore the children follow the father rather than the mother.

On the contrary, If a man sows on another's land, the produce belongs to the owner of the land. Now the woman's womb in relation to the seed of man is like the land in relation to the sower. Therefore, etc.

Further, we observe that in animals born from different species the offspring follows the mother rather that the father, wherefore mules born of a mare and an ass are more like mares than those born of a she-ass and a horse. Therefore it should be the same with men.

I answer that, According to civil law (xix, ff. De statu hom. vii, cap. *De rei vendit.*) the offspring follows the womb: and this is reasonable since the offspring derives its formal complement from the father, but the substance of the body from the mother. Now slavery is a condition of the body, since a slave is to the master a kind of instrument in working; wherefore children follow the mother in freedom and bondage; whereas in matters pertaining to dignity as proceeding from a thing's form, they follow the father, for instance in honors, franchise, inheritance and so forth. The canons are in agreement with this (cap. *Liberi*, 32, qu. iv, in gloss.: cap. *Indecens*, De natis ex libero ventre) as also the law of Moses (Exod. xxi).

In some countries, however, where the civil law does not hold, the offspring follows the inferior condition, so that if the father be a slave the children will be slaves although the mother be free; but not if the father gave himself up as a slave after his marriage and without his wife's consent; and the same applies if the case be reversed. And if both be of servile condition and belong to different masters, the children, if several, are divided among the latter, or if one only, the one master will compensate the other in value and will take the child thus born for his slave. However it is incredible that this custom have as much reason in its favor as the decision of the time-honored deliberations of many wise men.

Moreover in natural things it is the rule that what is received is in the recipient according to the mode of the recipient and not according to the mode of the giver; wherefore it is reasonable that the seed received by the mother should be drawn to her condition.

Reply Obj. 1. Although the father is a more noble principle than the mother, nevertheless the mother provides the substance of the body, and it is to this that the condition of slavery attaches.

Reply Obj. 2. As regards things pertaining to the specific nature the son is like the father rather than the mother, but in material conditions should be like the mother rather than the father, since a thing has its specific being from its form, but material conditions from matter.

Reply Obj. 3. The son is like the father in respect of the form which is his, and also the father's, complement. Hence the argument is not to the point.

Reply Obj. 4. It is because the son derives honor from his father rather than from his mother that in the genealogies of Scripture, and according to common custom, children are named after their father rather than from their mother. But in matters relating to slavery they follow the mother by preference.

QUESTION 53

Of the Impediment of Vows and Orders

(In Four Articles)

WE must now consider the impediment of vows and orders. Under this head there are four points of inquiry: (1) Whether a simple vow is a diriment impediment to matrimony? (2) Whether a solemn vow is a diriment impediment? (3) Whether order is an impediment to matrimony? (4) Whether a man can receive a sacred order after being married?

FIRST ARTICLE

Whether Marriage Already Contracted Should Be Annulled by the Obligation of a Simple Vow?

We proceed thus to the First Article:—

Objection 1. It would seem that a marriage already contracted ought to be annulled by the obligation of a simple vow. For the stronger tie takes precedence of the weaker. Now a vow is a stronger tie than marriage, since the latter binds man to man, but the former binds man to God. Therefore the obligation of a vow takes precedence of the marriage tie.

Obj. 2. Further, God's commandment is

* Cf. S. Augustine, *De Bono Viduit.* ix.

no less binding than the commandment of the Church. Now the commandment of the Church is so binding that a marriage is void if contracted in despite thereof; as instanced in the case of those who marry within the degrees of kindred forbidden by the Church. Therefore, since it is a Divine commandment to keep a vow, it would seem that if a person marry in despite of a vow his marriage should be annulled for that reason.

Obj. 3. Further, in marriage a man may have carnal intercourse without sin. Yet he who has taken a simple vow of chastity can never have carnal intercourse with his wife without sin. Therefore a simple vow annuls marriage. The minor is proved as follows. It is clear that it is a mortal sin to marry after taking a simple vow of continence, since according to Jerome* *for those who vow virginity it is damnable not only to marry, but even to wish to marry.* Now the marriage contract is not contrary to the vow of continence, except by reason of carnal intercourse: and therefore he sins mortally the first time he has intercourse with his wife, and for the same reason every other time, because a sin committed in the first instance cannot be an excuse for a subsequent sin.

Obj. 4. Further, husband and wife should be equal in marriage, especially as regards carnal intercourse. But he who has taken a simple vow of continence can never ask for the debt without a sin, for this is clearly against his vow of continence, since he is bound to continence by vow. Therefore neither can he pay the debt without sin.

On the contrary, Pope Clement† says (cap. *Consuluit,* De his qui cler. vel vovent.) that a *simple vow is an impediment to the contract of marriage, but does not annul it after it is contracted.*

I answer that, A thing ceases to be in one man's power from the fact that it passes into the power of another. Now the promise of a thing does not transfer it into the power of the person to whom it is promised, wherefore a thing does not cease to be in a person's power for the reason that he has promised it. Since then a simple vow contains merely a simple promise of one's body to the effect of keeping continence for God's sake, a man still retains power over his own body after a simple vow, and consequently can surrender it to another, namely his wife; and in this surrender consists the sacrament of matrimony, which is indissoluble. Therefore although a simple vow is an impediment to the contracting of a marriage, since it is a sin to marry after taking a simple vow of continence, yet since the contract is valid, the marriage cannot be annulled on that account.

Reply Obj. 1. A vow is a stronger tie than matrimony, as regards that to which man is tied, and the obligation under which he lies; because by marriage a man is tied to his wife, with the obligation of paying the debt, whereas by a vow a man is tied to God, with the obligation of remaining continent. But as to the manner in which he is tied marriage is a stronger tie than a simple vow, since by marriage a man surrenders himself actually to the power of his wife, but not by a simple vow as explained above: and the possessor is always in the stronger position. In this respect a simple vow binds in the same way as a betrothal; wherefore a betrothal must be annulled on account of a simple vow.

Reply Obj. 2. The contracting of a marriage between blood relations is annulled by the commandment forbidding such marriages, not precisely because it is a commandment of God or of the Church, but because it makes it impossible for the body of a kinswoman to be transferred into the power of her kinsman: whereas the commandment forbidding mar-

† Alexander III.

riage after a simple vow has not this effect, as already stated. Hence the argument is void, for it assigns as a cause that which is not cause.

Reply Obj. 3. If after taking a simple vow a man contract marriage by words of the present, he cannot know his wife without mortal sin, because until the marriage is consummated he is still in a position to fulfill the vow of continence. But after the marriage has been consummated, thenceforth through his fault it is unlawful for him not to pay the debt when his wife asks: wherefore this is not covered by his obligation to his vow, as explained above (*ad* 1). Nevertheless he should atone for not keeping continence, by his tears of repentance.

Reply Obj. 4. After contracting marriage he is still bound to keep his vow of continence in those matters wherein he is not rendered unable to do so. Hence if his wife die he is bound to continence altogether. And since the marriage tie does not bind him to ask for the debt, he cannot ask for it without sin, although he can pay the debt without sin on being asked, when once he has incurred this obligation through the carnal intercourse that has already occurred. And this holds whether the wife ask expressly or interpretively, as when she is ashamed and her husband feels that she desires him to pay the debt, for then he may pay it without sin. This is especially the case if he fears to endanger her chastity: nor does it matter that they are equal in the marriage act, since everyone may renounce what is his own. Some say, however, that he may both ask and pay lest the marriage become too burdensome to the wife who has always to ask; but if this be looked into aright, it is the same as asking interpretively.

SECOND ARTICLE

Whether a Solemn Vow Dissolves a Marriage Already Contracted?

We proceed thus to the Second Article:—

Objection 1. It would seem that not even a solemn vow dissolves a marriage already contracted. For according to a Decretal (cap. *Rursus,* De his qui cler. vel vovent.) *in God's sight a simple vow is no less binding than a solemn one.* Now marriage stands or falls by virtue of the Divine acceptance. Therefore since a simple vow does not dissolve marriage, neither will a solemn vow dissolve it.

Obj. 2. Further, a solemn vow does not add the same force to a simple vow as an oath does. Now a simple vow, even though an oath be added thereto, does not dissolve a marriage already contracted. Neither therefore does a solemn vow.

Obj. 3. Further, a solemn vow has nothing that a simple vow cannot have. For a simple vow may give rise to scandal since it may be public, even as a solemn vow. Again the Church could and should ordain that a simple vow dissolves a marriage already contracted, so that many sins may be avoided. Therefore for the same reason that a simple vow does not dissolve a marriage already contracted, neither should a solemn vow dissolve it.

On the contrary, He who takes a solemn vow contracts a spiritual marriage with God, which is much more excellent than a material marriage. Now a material marriage already contracted annuls a marriage contracted afterwards. Therefore a solemn vow does also.

Further, the same conclusion may be proved by many authorities quoted in the text (iv, *Sent.* D. 28).

I answer that, All agree that as a solemn vow is an impediment to the contracting of marriage, so it invalidates the contract. Some assign scandal as the reason. But this is futile, because even a simple vow sometimes leads to scandal since it is at times somewhat public. Moreover the indissolubility of marriage belongs to the truth of life,* which truth is not to be set aside on account of scandal. Wherefore others say that it is on account of the ordinance of the Church. But this again is insufficient, since in that case the Church might decide the contrary, which is seemingly untrue. Wherefore we must say with others that a solemn vow of its very nature dissolves the marriage contract, inasmuch namely as thereby a man has lost the power over his own body, through surrendering it to God for the purpose of perpetual continence. Wherefore he is unable to surrender it to the power of a wife by contracting marriage. And since the marriage that follows such a vow is void, a vow of this kind is said to annul the marriage contracted.

Reply Obj. 1. A simple vow is said to be no less binding in God's sight than a solemn vow, in matters pertaining to God, for instance the separation from God by mortal sin, because he who breaks a simple vow commits a mortal sin just as one who breaks a solemn vow, although it is more grievous to break a solemn vow, so that the comparison be understood as to the genus and not as to the definite degree of guilt. But as regards marriage, whereby one man is under an obligation to another, there is no need for it to be of equal obligation even in general, since a solemn vow binds to certain things to which a simple vow does not bind.

Reply Obj. 2. An oath is more binding than a vow on the part of the cause of the obliga-

*Cf. P. I, Q. 16, A. 4, *ad* 3; Q. 21, A. 2, *ad* 2; II-II, Q. 109, A. 3, *ad* 3.

tion: but a solemn vow is more binding as to the manner in which it binds, in so far as it is an actual surrender of that which is promised; while an oath does not do this actually. Hence the conclusion does not follow.

Reply Obj. 3. A solemn vow implies the actual surrender of one's body, whereas a simple vow does not, as stated above (A. 1). Hence the argument does not suffice to prove the conclusion.

THIRD ARTICLE

Whether Order Is an Impediment to Matrimony?

We proceed thus to the Third Article:—

Objection 1. It would seem that order is not an impediment to matrimony. For nothing is an impediment to a thing except its contrary. But order is not contrary to matrimony. Therefore it is not an impediment thereto.

Obj. 2. Further, orders are the same with us as with the Eastern Church. But they are not an impediment to matrimony in the Eastern Church. Therefore, etc.

Obj. 3. Further, matrimony signifies the union of Christ with the Church. Now this is most fittingly signified in those who are Christ's ministers, those namely who are ordained. Therefore order is not an impediment to matrimony.

Obj. 4. Further, all the orders are directed to spiritual things. Now order cannot be an impediment to matrimony except by reason of its spirituality. Therefore if order is an impediment to matrimony, every order will be an impediment, and this is untrue.

Obj. 5. Further, every ordained person can have ecclesiastical benefices, and can enjoy equally the privilege of clergy. If, therefore, orders are an impediment to marriage, because married persons cannot have an ecclesiastical benefice, nor enjoy the privilege of clergy, as jurists assert (cap. *Joannes* et seqq. De cler. conjug.), then every order ought to be an impediment. Yet this is false, as shown by the Decretal of Alexander III (De cler. conjug., cap. *Si Quis*): and consequently it would seem that no order is an impediment to marriage.

On the contrary, the Decretal says *(ibid.):* *any person whom you shall find to have taken a wife after receiving the subdiaconate or the higher orders, you shall compel to put his wife away.* But this would not be so if the marriage were valid.

Further, no person who has vowed continence can contract marriage. Now some orders have a vow of continence connected with them, as appears from the text (iv, *Sent.* D. 37). Therefore in that case order is an impediment to matrimony.

I answer that, By a certain fittingness the

very nature of holy order requires that it should be an impediment to marriage: because those who are in holy orders handle the sacred vessels and the sacraments: wherefore it is becoming that they keep their bodies clean by continence.* But it is owing to the Church's ordinance that it is actually an impediment to marriage. However it is not the same with the Latins as with the Greeks; since with the Greeks it is an impediment to the contracting of marriage, solely by virtue of order; whereas with the Latins it is an impediment by virtue of order, and besides by virtue of the vow of continence which is annexed to the sacred orders; for although this vow is not expressed in words, nevertheless a person is understood to have taken it by the very fact of his being ordained. Hence among the Greeks and other Eastern peoples a sacred order is an impediment to the contracting of matrimony but it does not forbid the use of marriage already contracted: for they can use marriage contracted previously, although they cannot be married again. But in the Western Church it is an impediment both to marriage and to the use of marriage, unless perhaps the husband should receive a sacred order without the knowledge or consent of his wife, because this cannot be prejudicial to her.

Of the distinction between sacred and non-sacred orders now and in the early Church we have spoken above (Q. 37, A. 3).

Reply Obj. 1. Although a sacred order is not contrary to matrimony as a sacrament, it has a certain incompatibility with marriage in respect of the latter's act which is an obstacle to spiritual acts.

Reply Obj. 2. The objection is based on a false statement: since order is everywhere an impediment to the contracting of marriage, although it has not everywhere a vow annexed to it.

Reply Obj. 3. Those who are in sacred orders signify Christ by more sublime actions, as appears from what has been said in the treatise on orders (Q. 37, AA. 2, 4), than those who are married. Consequently the conclusion does not follow.

Reply Obj. 4. Those who are in minor orders are not forbidden to marry by virtue of their order; for although those orders are entrusted with certain spiritualities, they are not admitted to the immediate handling of sacred things, as those are who are in sacred orders. But according to the laws of the Western Church, the use of marriage is an impediment to the exercise of a non-sacred order, for the sake of maintaining a greater honesty in the offices of the Church. And since the holding of an ecclesiastical benefice

*Cf. Isa. lii. 11.　　†Cf. Q. 61, A. 1.

binds a man to the exercise of his order, and since for this very reason he enjoys the privilege of clergy, it follows that in the Latin Church this privilege is forfeit to a married cleric.

This suffices for the *Reply* to the *last Objection.*

FOURTH ARTICLE

Whether a Sacred Order Can Supervene to Matrimony?

We proceed thus to the Fourth Article:—

Objection 1. It would seem that a sacred order cannot supervene to matrimony. For the stronger prejudices the weaker. Now a spiritual obligation is stronger than a bodily tie. Therefore if a married man be ordained, this will prejudice the wife, so that she will be unable to demand the debt, since order is a spiritual, and marriage a bodily bond. Hence it would seem that a man cannot receive a sacred order after consummating marriage.

Obj. 2. Further, after consummating the marriage, one of the parties cannot vow continence without the other's consent.† Now a sacred order has a vow of continence annexed to it. Therefore if the husband be ordained without his wife's consent, she will be bound to remain continent against her will, since she cannot marry another man during her husband's lifetime.

Obj. 3. Further, a husband may not even for a time devote himself to prayer without his wife's consent (1 Cor. vii. 5). But in the Eastern Church those who are in sacred orders are bound to continence for the time when they exercise their office. Therefore neither may they be ordained without their wife's consent, and much less may the Latins.

Obj. 4. Further, husband and wife are on a par with one another. Now a Greek priest cannot marry again after his wife's death. Therefore neither can his wife after her husband's death. But she cannot be deprived by her husband's act of the right to marry after his death. Therefore her husband cannot receive orders after marriage.

Obj. 5. Further, order is as much opposed to marriage as marriage to order. Now a previous order is an impediment to a subsequent marriage. Therefore, etc.

On the contrary, Religious are bound to continence like those who are in sacred orders. But a man may enter religion after marriage, if his wife die, or if she consent. Therefore he can also receive orders.

Further, a man may become a man's bondsman after marriage. Therefore he can become a bondsman of God by receiving orders.

I answer that, Marriage is not an impediment to the receiving of sacred orders, since if a married man receive sacred orders, even though his wife be unwilling, he receives the character of order: but he lacks the exercise of his order. If, however, his wife consent, or if she be dead, he receives both the order and the exercise.

Reply Obj. 1. The bond of orders dissolves the bond of marriage as regards the payment of the debt, in respect of which it is incompatible with marriage, on the part of the person ordained, since he cannot demand the debt, nor is the wife bound to pay it. But it does not dissolve the bond in respect of the other party, since the husband is bound to pay the debt to the wife if he cannot persuade her to observe continence.

Reply Obj. 2. If the husband receive sacred orders with the knowledge and consent of his wife, she is bound to vow perpetual continence, but she is not bound to enter religion, if she has no fear of her chastity being endangered through her husband having taken a solemn vow: it would have been different, however, if he had taken a simple vow. On the other hand, if he be ordained without her consent, she is not bound in this way, because the result is not prejudicial to her in any way.

Reply Obj. 3. It would seem more probable, although some say the contrary, that even a Greek ought not to receive sacred orders without his wife's consent, since at least at the time of his ministry she would be deprived of the payment of the debt, of which she cannot be deprived according to law if the husband should have been ordained without her consent or knowledge.

Reply Obj. 4. As stated, among the Greeks the wife, by the very fact of consenting to her husband's receiving a sacred order, binds herself never to marry another man, because the signification of marriage would not be safeguarded, and this is especially required in the marriage of a priest. If, however, he be ordained without her consent, seemingly she would not be under that obligation.

Reply Obj. 5. Marriage has for its cause our consent: not so order, which has a sacramental cause appointed by God. Hence matrimony may be impeded by a previous order, so as not to be true marriage: whereas order cannot be impeded by marriage, so as not to be true order, because the power of the sacraments is unchangeable, whereas human acts can be impeded.

QUESTION 54

Of the Impediment of Consanguinity

(In Four Articles)

WE must next consider the impediment of consanguinity. Under this head there are four points of inquiry: (1) Whether consanguinity is rightly defined by some? (2) Whether it is fittingly distinguished by degrees and lines? (3) Whether certain degrees are by natural law an impediment to marriage? (4) Whether the impediment degrees can be fixed by the ordinance of the Church?

FIRST ARTICLE

Whether Consanguinity Is Rightly Defined?

We proceed thus to the First Article:—

Objection 1. It would seem that consanguinity is unsuitably defined by some as follows: *Consanguinity is the tie contracted between persons descending from the same common ancestor by carnal procreation.* For all men descend from the same common ancestor, namely Adam, by carnal procreation. Therefore if the above definition of consanguinity is right, all men would be related by consanguinity: which is false.

Obj. 2. Further, a tie is only between things

*Cf. P. I, Q. 119, A. 2.

in accord with one another, since a tie unites. Now there is not greater accordance between persons descended from a common ancestor than there is between other men, since they accord in species but differ in number, just as other men do. Therefore consanguinity is not a tie.

Obj. 3. Further, carnal procreation, according to the Philosopher (*De Gener. Anim.* ii. 19), is effected from the surplus food.* Now this surplus has more in common with that which is eaten, since it agrees with it in substance, than with him who eats. Since then no tie of consanguinity arises between the person born of semen and that which he eats, neither will there be any tie of kindred between him and the person of whom he is born by carnal procreation.

Obj. 4. Further, Laban said to Jacob (Gen. xxix. 14): *Thou art my bone and my flesh,* on account of the relationship between them. Therefore such a kinship should be called flesh-relationship rather than blood-relationship (*consanguinitas*).

Obj. 5. Further, carnal procreation is common to men and animals. But no tie of consanguinity is contracted among animals from carnal procreation. Therefore neither is there among men.

I answer that, According to the Philosopher *(Ethic.* iii. 11, 12) *all friendship is based on some kind of fellowship.* And since friendship is a knot or union, it follows that the fellowship which is the cause of friendship is called *a tie.* Wherefore in respect of any kind of a fellowship certain persons are denominated as though they were tied together: thus we speak of fellow-citizens who are connected by a common political life, of fellow-soldiers who are connected by the common business of soldiering, and in the same way those who are connected by the fellowship of nature are said to be tied by blood *(consanguinei).* Hence in the above definition *tie* is included as being the genus of consanguinity; the *persons descending from the same common ancestor,* who are thus tied together are the subject of this tie; while *carnal procreation* is mentioned as being its origin.

Reply Obj. 1. An active force is not received into an instrument in the same degree of perfection as it has in the principal agent. And since every moved mover is an instrument, it follows that the power of the first mover in a particular genus when drawn out through many mediate movers fails at length, and reaches something that is moved and not a mover. But the power of a begetter moves not only as to that which belongs to the species, but also as to that which belongs to the individual, by reason of which the child is like the parent even in accidentals and not only in the specific nature. And yet this individual power of the father is not so perfect in the son as it was in the father, and still less so in the grandson, and thus it goes on failing: so that at length it ceases and can go no further. Since then consanguinity results from this power being communicated to many through being conveyed to them from one person by procreation, it destroys itself by little and little, as Isidore says *(Etym.* ix). Consequently in defining consanguinity we must not take a remote common ancestor but the nearest, whose power still remains in those who are descended from him.

Reply Obj. 2. It is clear from what has been said that blood relations agree not only in the specific nature but also in that power peculiar to the individual which is conveyed from one to many: the result being that sometimes the child is not only like his father, but also his grandfather or his remote ancestors *(De Gener. Anim.* iv. 3).

Reply Obj. 3. Likeness depends more on form whereby a thing is actually, than on matter whereby a thing is potentially: for instance, charcoal has more in common with fire than with the tree from which the wood was cut. In like manner food already transformed by the nutritive power into the substance of the person fed has more in common with the subject nourished than with that from which the nourishment was taken. The argument however would hold according to the opinion of those who asserted that the whole nature of a thing is from its matter and that all forms are accidents: which is false.

Reply Obj. 4. It is the blood that is proximately changed into the semen, as proved in *De Gener.* anim. i. 18. Hence the tie contracted by carnal procreation is more fittingly called blood-relationship than flesh-relationship. That sometimes one relation is called the flesh of another, is because the blood which is transformed into the man's seed or into the menstrual fluid is potentially flesh and bone.

Reply Obj. 5. Some say that the reason why the tie of consanguinity is contracted among men through carnal procreation, and not among other animals, is because whatever belongs to the truth of human nature in all men was in our first parent: which does not apply to other animals. But according to this, matrimonial consanguinity would never come to an end. However the above theory was disproved in the Second Book (ii, *Sent.* D. 30: P. I., Q. 119, A. 1). Wherefore we must reply that the reason for this is that animals are not united together in the union of friendship through the begetting of many from one proximate parent, as is the case with men, as stated above.

SECOND ARTICLE

Whether Consanguinity Is Fittingly Distinguished by Degrees and Lines?

We proceed thus to the Second Article:—

Objection 1. It would seem that consanguinity is unfittingly distinguished by degrees and lines. For a line of consanguinity is described as *the ordered series of persons related by blood, and descending from a common ancestor in various degrees.* Now consanguinity is nothing else but a series of such persons. Therefore a line of consanguinity is the same as consanguinity. Now a thing ought not to be distinguished by itself. Therefore consanguinity is not fittingly distinguished into lines.

Obj. 2. Further, that by which a common thing is divided should not be placed in the definition of that common thing. Now descent is placed in the above definition of consanguinity. Therefore consanguinity cannot be divided into ascending, descending and collateral lines.

Obj. 3. Further, a line is defined as being

between two points. But two points make but one degree. Therefore one line has but one degree, and for this reason it would seem that consanguinity should not be divided into lines and degrees.

Obj. 4. Further, a degree is defined as *the relation between distant persons, whereby is known the distance between them.* Now since consanguinity is a kind of propinquity, distance between persons is opposed to consanguinity rather than a part thereof.

Obj. 5. Further, if consanguinity is distinguished and known by its degrees, those who are in the same degree ought to be equally related. But this is false since a man's great-uncle and great-nephew are in the same degree, and yet they are not equally related according to a Decretal (cap. *Porro* and cap. *Parentelæ*, 35, qu. v). Therefore consanguinity is not rightly divided into degrees.

Obj. 6. Further, in ordinary things a different degree results from the addition of one thing to another, even as every additional unity makes a different species of number. Yet the addition of one person to another does not always make a different degree of consanguinity, since father and uncle are in the same degree of consanguinity, for they are side by side. Therefore consanguinity is not rightly divided into degrees.

Obj. 7. Further, if two persons be akin to one another there is always the same measure of kinship between them, since the distance from one extreme to the other is the same either way. Yet the degrees of consanguinity are not always the same on either side, since sometimes one relative is in the third and the other in the fourth degree. Therefore the measure of consanguinity cannot be sufficiently known by its degrees.

I answer that, Consanguinity as stated (A. 1) is a certain propinquity based on the natural communication by the act of procreation whereby nature is propagated. Wherefore according to the Philosopher *(Ethic.* viii. 12) this communication is threefold. One corresponds to the relationship between cause and effect, and this is the consanguinity of father to son, wherefore he says that *parents love their children as being a part of themselves.* Another corresponds to the relation of effect to cause, and this is the consanguinity of son to father, wherefore he says that *children love their parents as being themselves something which owes its existence to them.* The third corresponds to the mutual relation between things that come from the same cause, as brothers, *who are born of the same parents,* as he again says *(ibid.).* And since the movement of a point makes a line, and since a father by procreation may be said to descend to his

son, hence it is that corresponding to these three relationships there are three lines of consanguinity, namely the *descending* line corresponding to the first relationship, the *ascending* line corresponding to the second, and the *collateral* line corresponding to the third. Since however the movement of propagation does not rest in one term but continues beyond, the result is that one can point to the father's father and to the son's son, and so on, and according to the various steps we take we find various degrees in one line. And seeing that the degrees of a thing are parts of that thing, there cannot be degrees of propinquity where there is no propinquity. Consequently identity and too great a distance do away with degrees of consanguinity; since no man is kin to himself any more than he is like himself: for which reason there is no degree of consanguinity where there is but one person, but only when one person is compared to another.

Nevertheless there are different ways of counting the degrees in various lines. For the degree of consanguinity in the ascending and descending line is contracted from the fact that one of the parties whose consanguinity is in question, is descended from the other. Wherefore according to the canonical as well as the legal reckoning, the person who occupies the first place, whether in the ascending or in the descending line, is distant from a certain one, say Peter, in the first degree,— for instance father and son; while the one who occupies the second place in either direction is distant in the second degree, for instance grandfather, grandson and so on. But the consanguinity that exists between persons who are in collateral lines is contracted not through one being descended from the other, but through both being descended from one: wherefore the degrees of consanguinity in this line must be reckoned in relation to the one principle whence it arises. Here, however, the canonical and legal reckonings differ: for the legal reckoning takes into account the descent from the common stock on both sides, whereas the canonical reckoning takes into account only one, that namely on which the greater number of degrees are found. Hence according to the legal reckoning brother and sister, or two brothers, are related in the second degree, because each is separated from the common stock by one degree; and in like manner the children of two brothers are distant from one another in the fourth degree. But according to the canonical reckoning, two brothers are related in the first degree, since neither is distant more than one degree from the common stock: but the children of one brother are distant in the second degree from the other brother, because they are at that distance from the common stock. Hence, according to the canonical reckoning, by whatever degree a person is distant from some higher degree, by so much and never by less is he distant from each person descending from that degree, because *the cause of a thing being so is yet more so.* Wherefore although the other descendants from the common stock be related to some person on account of his being descended from the common stock, these descendants of the other branch cannot be more nearly related to him than he is to the common stock. Sometimes, however, a person is more distantly related to a descendant from the common stock, than he himself is to the common stock, because this other person may be more distantly related to the common stock than he is: and consanguinity must be reckoned according to the more distant degree.

Reply Obj. 1. This objection is based on a false premise: for consanguinity is not the series but a mutual relationship existing between certain persons, the series of whom forms a line of consanguinity.

Reply Obj. 2. Descent taken in a general sense attaches to every line of consanguinity, because carnal procreation whence the tie of consanguinity arises is a kind of descent: but it is a particular kind of descent, namely from the person whose consanguinity is in question, that makes the descending line.

Reply Obj. 3. A line may be taken in two ways. Sometimes it is taken properly for the dimension itself that is the first species of continuous quantity: and thus a straight line contains actually but two points which terminate it, but infinite points potentially, any one of which being actually designated, the line is divided, and becomes two lines. But sometimes a line designates things which are arranged in a line, and thus we have line and figure in numbers, in so far as unity added to unity involves number. Thus every unity added makes a degree in a particular line: and it is the same with the line of consanguinity: wherefore one line contains several degrees.

Reply Obj. 4. Even as there cannot be likeness without a difference, so there is no propinquity without distance. Hence not every distance is opposed to consanguinity, but such as excludes the propinquity of blood-relationship.

Reply Obj. 5. Even as whiteness is said to be greater in two ways, in one way through intensity of the quality itself, in another way through the quantity of the surface, so consanguinity is said to be greater or lesser in two ways. First, intensively by reason of the very nature of consanguinity: secondly, extensively as it were, and thus the degree of consanguinity is measured by the persons between whom there is the propagation of a common blood, and in this way the degrees of consanguinity are distinguished. Wherefore it happens that of two persons related to one person in the same degree of consanguinity, one is more akin to him than the other, if we consider the quantity of consanguinity in the first way: thus a man's father and brother are related to him in the first degree of consanguinity, because in neither case does any person come in between; and yet from the point of view of intensity a man's father is more closely related to him than his brother, since his brother is related to him only because he is of the same father. Hence the nearer a person is to the common ancestor from whom the consanguinity descends, the greater is his consanguinity although he be not in a nearer degree. In this way a man's great-uncle is more closely related to him than his great-nephew, although they are in the same degree.

Reply Obj. 6. Although a man's father and uncle are in the same degree in respect of the root of consanguinity, since both are separated by one degree from the grandfather, nevertheless in respect of the person whose consanguinity is in question, they are not in the same degree, since the father is in the first degree, whereas the uncle cannot be nearer than the second degree, wherein the grandfather stands.

Reply Obj. 7. Two persons are always related in the same degree to one another, although they are not always distant in the same number of degrees from the common ancestor, as explained above.

THIRD ARTICLE

Whether Consanguinity Is an Impediment to Marriage by Virtue of the Natural Law?

We proceed thus to the Third Article:—

Objection 1. It would seem that consanguinity is not by natural law an impediment to marriage. For no woman can be more akin to a man than Eve was to Adam, since of her did he say (Gen. ii. 23): *This now is bone of my bones and flesh of my flesh.* Yet Eve was joined in marriage to Adam. Therefore as regards the natural law no consanguinity is an impediment to marriage.

Obj. 2. Further, the natural law is the same for all. Now among the uncivilized nations no person is debarred from marriage by reason of consanguinity. Therefore, as regards the law of nature, consanguinity is no impediment to marriage.

Obj. 3. Further, the natural law is what *nature has taught all animals,* as stated at the beginning of the *Digests* (i. ff. *De just. et jure*). Now brute animals copulate even with their mother. Therefore it is not of natural law that certain persons are debarred from marriage on account of consanguinity.

Obj. 4. Further, nothing that is not contrary to one of the goods of matrimony is an impediment to marriage. But consanguinity is not contrary to any of the goods of marriage. Therefore it is not an impediment thereto.

Obj. 5. Further, things which are more akin and more similar to one another are better and more firmly united together. Now matrimony is a kind of union. Since then consanguinity is a kind of kinship, it does not hinder marriage but rather strengthens the union.

On the contrary, According to the natural law whatever is an obstacle to the good of the offspring is an impediment to marriage. Now consanguinity hinders the good of the offspring, because in the words of Gregory *(Regist., ep.* xxxi) quoted in the text (iv, *Sent.* D. 40) *We have learnt by experience that the children of such a union cannot thrive.* Therefore according to the law of nature consanguinity is an impediment to matrimony.

Further, that which belongs to human nature when it was first created is of natural law. Now it belonged to human nature from when it was first created that one should be debarred from marrying one's father or mother: in proof of which it was said (Gen. ii. 24): *Wherefore a man shall leave father and mother:* which cannot be understood of cohabitation, and consequently must refer to the union of marriage. Therefore consanguinity is an impediment to marriage according to the natural law.

I answer that, In relation to marriage a thing is said to be contrary to the natural law if it prevents marriage from reaching the end for which it was instituted. Now the essential and primary end of marriage is the good of the offspring; and this is hindered by a certain consanguinity, namely that which is between father and daughter, or son and mother. It is not that the good of the offspring is utterly destroyed, since a daughter can have a child of her father's semen and with the father rear and teach that child in which things the good of the offspring consists, but that it is not effected in a becoming way. For it is out of order that a daughter be mated to her father in marriage for the purpose of begetting and rearing children, since in all things she ought to be subject to her father as proceeding from him. Hence by natural law a father and mother are debarred from marrying their children; and the mother still more than the father, since it is more derogatory to the reverence due to parents if the son marry his mother than if the father marry his daughter; since the wife should be to a certain extent subject to her husband. The secondary essential end of marriage is the curbing of concupiscence; and this end would be forfeit if a man could marry any blood-relation, since a wide scope would be afforded to concupiscence if those who have to live together in the same house were not forbidden to be mated in the flesh. Wherefore the Divine law debars from marriage not only father and mother, but also other kinsfolk who have to live in close intimacy with one another and ought to safeguard one another's modesty. The Divine law assigns this reason (Levit. xviii. 10): *Thou shalt not uncover the nakedness* of such and such a one, *because it is thy own nakedness.*

But the accidental end of marriage is the binding together of mankind and the extension of friendship: for a husband regards his wife's kindred as his own. Hence it would be prejudicial to this extension of friendship if a man could take a woman of his kindred to wife since no new friendship would accrue to anyone from such a marriage. Wherefore, according to human law and the ordinances of the Church, several degrees of consanguinity are debarred from marriage.

Accordingly it is clear from what has been said that consanguinity is by natural law an impediment to marriage in regard to certain persons, by Divine law in respect of some, and by human law in respect of others.

Reply Obj. 1. Although Eve was formed from Adam she was not Adam's daughter, because she was not formed from him after the manner in which it is natural for a man to beget his like in species, but by the Divine operation, since from Adam's rib a horse might have been formed in the same way as Eve was. Hence the natural connection between Eve and Adam was not so great as between daughter and father, nor was Adam the natural principle of Eve as a father is of his daughter.

Reply Obj. 2. That certain barbarians are united carnally to their parents does not come from the natural law but from the passion of concupiscence which has clouded the natural law in them.

Reply Obj. 3. Union of male and female is said to be of natural law, because nature has taught this to animals: yet she has taught this union to various animals in various ways according to their various conditions. But carnal copulation with parents is derogatory to the reverence due to them. For just as nature has instilled into parents solicitude in providing for their offspring, so has it instilled into the offspring reverence towards their parents: yet to no kind of animal save man has she instilled a lasting solicitude for his children or reverence for parents; but to other animals more or less, according as the offspring is more or less necessary to its parents, or the parents to their offspring. Hence as the Philosopher attests *(De Animal.* ix. 47) concerning the camel and the horse, among certain animals the son abhors copulation with its mother as long as he retains knowledge of her and a certain reverence for her. And since all honest customs of animals are united together in man naturally, and more perfectly than in other animals, it follows that man naturally abhors carnal knowledge not only of his mother, but also of his daughter, which is, however, less against nature, as stated above.

Moreover consanguinity does not result from carnal procreation in other animals as in man, as stated above (A. 1, *ad* 5). Hence the comparison fails.

Reply Obj. 4. It has been shown how consanguinity between married persons is contrary to the goods of marriage. Hence the *Objection* proceeds from false premises.

Reply Obj. 5. It is not unreasonable for one of two unions to be hindered by the other, even as where there is identity there is not likeness. In like manner the tie of consanguinity may hinder the union of marriage.

FOURTH ARTICLE

Whether the Degrees of Consanguinity That Are an Impediment to Marriage Could Be Fixed by the Church?

We proceed thus to the Fourth Article:—

Objection 1. It would seem that the degrees of consanguinity that are an impediment to marriage could not be fixed by the Church so as to reach to the fourth degree. For it is written (Matth. xix. 6): *What God hath joined together let no man put asunder.* But God joined those together who are married within the fourth degree of consanguinity, since their union is not forbidden by the Divine law. Therefore they should not be put asunder by a human law.

Obj. 2. Further, matrimony is a sacrament as also is baptism. Now no ordinance of the Church could prevent one who is baptized from receiving the baptismal character, if he be capable of receiving it according to the Divine law. Therefore neither can an ordinance of the Church forbid marriage between those who are not forbidden to marry by the Divine law.

Obj. 3. Further, positive law can neither void nor extend those things which are natural. Now consanguinity is a natural tie which is in itself of a nature to impede marriage. Therefore the Church cannot by its ordinance permit or forbid certain people to marry, any more than she can make them to be kin or not kin.

Obj. 4. Further, an ordinance of positive law should have some reasonable cause, since it is for this reasonable cause that it proceeds from the natural law. But the causes that are assigned for the number of degrees seem altogether unreasonable, since they bear no relation to their effect; for instance, that consanguinity be an impediment as far as the fourth degree on account of the four elements, as far as the sixth degree on account of the six ages of the world, as far as the seventh degree on account of the seven days of which all time is comprised. Therefore seemingly this prohibition is of no force.

Obj. 5. Further, where the cause is the same there should be the same effect. Now the causes for which consanguinity is an impediment to marriage are the good of the offspring, the curbing of concupiscence, and the extension of friendship, as stated above (A. 3), which are equally necessary for all time. Therefore the degrees of consanguinity should have equally impeded marriage at all times: yet this is not true since consanguinity is now an impediment to marriage as far as the fourth degree, whereas formerly it was an impediment as far as the seventh.

Obj. 6. Further, one and the same union cannot be a kind of sacrament and a kind of incest. But this would be the case if the Church had the power of fixing a different number in the degrees which are an impediment to marriage. Thus if certain parties related in the fifth degree were married when that degree was an impediment, their union would be incestuous, and yet this same union would be a marriage afterwards when the Church withdrew her prohibition. And the reverse might happen if certain degrees which were not an impediment were subsequently to be forbidden by the Church. Therefore seemingly the power of the Church does not extend to this.

Obj. 7. Further, human law should copy the Divine law. Now according to the Divine law which is contained in the Old Law, the prohibition of degrees does not apply equally in the ascending and descending lines: since in the Old Law a man was forbidden to marry his father's sister but not his brother's daughter. Therefore neither should there remain now a prohibition in respect of nephews and uncles.

On the contrary, Our Lord said to His disciples (Luke x. 16): *He that heareth you heareth Me.* Therefore a commandment of the Church has the same force as a commandment of God. Now the Church sometimes has forbidden and sometimes allowed certain degrees which the Old Law did not forbid. Therefore those degrees are an impediment to marriage.

Further, even as of old the marriages of pagans were controlled by the civil law, so now is marriage controlled by the laws of the Church. Now formerly the civil law decided which degrees of consanguinity impede marriage, and which do not. Therefore this can be done now by a commandment of the Church.

I answer that, The degrees within which consanguinity has been an impediment to marriage have varied according to various times. For at the beginning of the human race father and mother alone were debarred from marrying their children, because then mankind were few in number, and then it was necessary for the propagation of the human race to be ensured with very great care, and consequently only such persons were to be debarred as were unfitted for marriage even in respect of its principal end which is the good of the offspring, as stated above (A. 3). Afterwards however, the human race having multiplied, more persons were excluded by the law of Moses, for they already began to curb concupiscence. Wherefore as Rabbi Moses says *(Doc. Perp.* iii. 49) all those persons were debarred from marrying one another who are wont to live together in one household, because if a lawful carnal intercourse were possible between them, this would prove a very great incentive to lust. Yet the Old Law permitted other degrees of consanguinity, in fact to a certain extent it commanded them, to wit that each man should take a wife from his kindred, in order to avoid confusion of inheritances: because at that time the Divine worship was handed down as the inheritance of the race. But afterwards more degrees were forbidden by the New Law which is the law of the spirit and of love, because the worship of God is no longer handed down and spread abroad by a carnal birth but by a spiritual grace: wherefore it was necessary that men should be yet more withdrawn from carnal things by devoting themselves to things spiritual, and that love should have a yet wider play. Hence in olden times marriage was forbidden even within the more remote degrees of consanguinity, in order that consanguinity and affinity might be the sources of a wider natural friendship; and this was reasonably extended to the seventh degree, both because beyond this it was difficult to have any recollection of the common stock, and because this was in keeping with the sevenfold grace of the Holy Ghost. Afterwards, however, towards these latter times the prohibition of the Church has been restricted to the fourth degree, because it became useless and dangerous to extend the prohibition to more remote degrees of consanguinity. Useless, because

charity waxed cold in many hearts so that they had scarcely a greater bond of friendship with their more remote kindred than with strangers: and it was dangerous because through the prevalence of concupiscence and neglect men took no account of so numerous a kindred, and thus the prohibition of the more remote degrees became for many a snare leading to damnation. Moreover there is a certain fittingness in the restriction of the above prohibition to the fourth degree. First because men are wont to live until the fourth generation, so that consanguinity cannot lapse into oblivion, wherefore God threatened (Exod. xx. 5) to visit the parent's sins on their children to the third and fourth generation. Secondly, because in each generation the blood, the identity of which causes consanguinity, receives a further addition of new blood, and the more another blood is added the less there is of the old. And because there are four elements, each of which is the more easily mixed with another, according as it is more rarefied, it follows that at the first admixture the identity of blood disappears as regards the first element which is most subtle; at the second admixture, as regards the second element; at the third, as to the third element; at the fourth, as to the fourth element. Thus after the fourth generation it is fitting for the carnal union to be repeated.

Reply Obj. 1. Even as God does not join together those who are joined together against the Divine command, so does He not join together those who are joined together against the commandment of the Church, which has the same binding force as a commandment of God.

Reply Obj. 2. Matrimony is not only a sacrament but also fulfills an office; wherefore it is more subject to the control of the Church's ministers than baptism which is a sacrament only: because just as human contracts and offices are controlled by human laws, so are spiritual contracts and offices controlled by the law of the Church.

Reply Obj. 3. Although the tie of consanguinity is natural, it is not natural that consanguinity forbid carnal intercourse, except as regards certain degrees, as stated above (A. 3). Wherefore the Church's commandment does not cause certain people to be kin or not kin, because they remain equally kin at all times: but it makes carnal intercourse to be lawful or unlawful at different times for different degrees of consanguinity.

Reply Obj. 4. The reasons assigned are given as indicating aptness and congruousness rather than causality and necessity.

Reply Obj. 5. The reason for the impediment of consanguinity is not the same at different times: wherefore that which it was useful to allow at one time, it was beneficial to forbid at another.

Reply Obj. 6. A commandment does not affect the past but the future. Wherefore if the fifth degree which is now allowed were to be forbidden at any time, those in the fifth degree who are married would not have to separate, because no impediment supervening to marriage can annul it; and consequently a union which was a marriage from the first would not be made incestuous by a commandment of the Church. In like manner, if a degree which is now forbidden were to be allowed, such a union would not become a marriage on account of the Church's commandment by reason of the former contract, because they could separate if they wished. Nevertheless, they could contract anew, and this would be a new union.

Reply Obj. 7. In prohibiting the degrees of consanguinity the Church considers chiefly the point of view of affection. And since the reason for affection towards one's brother's son is not less but even greater than the reasons for affection towards one's father's brother, inasmuch as the son is more akin to the father than the father to the son (*Ethic.* viii. 12), therefore did the Church equally prohibit the degrees of consanguinity in uncles and nephews. On the other hand the old law in debarring certain persons looked chiefly to the danger of concupiscence arising from cohabitation; and debarred those persons who were in closer intimacy with one another on account of their living together. Now it is more usual for a niece to live with her uncle than an aunt with her nephew: because a daughter is more identified with her father, being part of him, whereas a sister is not in this way identified with her brother, for she is not part of him but is born of the same parent. Hence there was not the same reason for debarring a niece and an aunt.

QUESTION 55

Of the Impediment of Affinity

(In Eleven Articles)

WE must consider next the impediment of affinity. Under this head there are eleven points of inquiry: (1) Whether affinity results from matrimony? (2) Whether it remains after the death of husband or wife? (3) Whether it is caused through unlawful intercourse? (4) Whether it arises from a betrothal? (5) Whether affinity is caused through affinity? (6) Whether affinity is an impediment to marriage? (7) Whether affinity in itself admits of degrees? (8) Whether its degrees extend as far as the degrees of consanguinity? (9) Whether marriages of persons related to one another by consanguinity or affinity should always be dissolved by divorce? (10) Whether the process for the dissolution of like marriages should always be by way of accusation? (11) Whether witnesses should be called in such a case?

FIRST ARTICLE

Whether a Person Contracts Affinity through the Marriage of a Blood-Relation?

We proceed thus to the First Article:—

Objection 1. It would seem that a person does not contract affinity through the marriage of a blood-relation. For *the cause of a thing being so is yet more so.* Now the wife is not connected with her husband's kindred except by reason of the husband. Since then she does not contract affinity with her husband, neither does she contract it with her husband's kindred.

Obj. 2. Further, if certain things be separate from one another and something be connected with one of them, it does not follow that it is connected with the other. Now a person's blood relations are separate from one another. Therefore it does not follow, if a certain woman be married to a certain man, that she is therefore connected with all his kindred.

Obj. 3. Further, relations result from certain things being united together. Now the kindred of the husband do not become united together by the fact of his taking a wife. Therefore they do not acquire any relationship of affinity.

On the contrary, Husband and wife are made one flesh. Therefore if the husband is related in the flesh to all his kindred, for the same reason his wife will be related to them all.

Further, this is proved by the authorities quoted in the text (iv, *Sent.* D. 41).

I answer that, A certain natural friendship is founded on natural fellowship. Now natural fellowship, according to the Philosopher (*Ethic.* viii. 12), arises in two ways; first, from carnal procreation; secondly, from connection with orderly carnal procreation, wherefore he says (*ibid.*) that the friendship of a husband towards his wife is natural. Consequently even as a person through being connected with another by carnal procreation is bound to him by a tie of natural friendship, so does one person become connected with another through carnal intercourse. But there is a difference in this, that one who is connected with another through carnal procreation, as a son with his father, shares in the same common stock and blood, so that a son is connected with his father's kindred by the same kind of tie as the father was, the tie, namely of consanguinity, albeit in a different degree on account of his being more distant from the stock: whereas one who is connected with another through carnal intercourse does not share in the same stock, but is as it were an extraneous addition thereto: whence arises another kind of tie known by the name of *affinity*. This is expressed in the verse:

> Marriage makes a new kind of connection,
> While birth makes a new degree,

because, to wit, the person begotten is in the same kind of relationship, but in a different degree, whereas through carnal intercourse he enters into a new kind of relationship.

Reply Obj. 1. Although a cause is more potent than its effect, it does not always follow that the same name is applicable to the cause as to the effect, because sometimes that which is in the effect, is found in the cause not in the same but in a higher way; wherefore it is not applicable to both cause and effect under the same name or under the same aspect, as is the case with all equivocal effective causes. Thus, then, the union of husband and wife is stronger than the union of the wife with her husband's kindred, and yet it ought not to be named affinity, but matrimony which is a kind of unity; even as a man is identical with himself, but not with his kinsman.

Reply Obj. 2. Blood-relations are in a way separate, and in a way connected: and it happens in respect of their connection that a person who is connected with one of them is in some way connected with all of them. But on account of their separation and distance from one another it happens that a person who is connected with one of them in one way is connected with another in another way, either as to the kind of connection or as to the degree.

Reply Obj. 3. Further, a relation results sometimes from a movement in each extreme, for instance fatherhood and sonship, and a relation of this kind is really in both extremes. Sometimes it results from the movement of one only, and this happens in two ways. In one way when a relation results from the movement of one extreme without any movement previous or concomitant of the other extreme; as in the Creator and the creature,

the sensible and the sense, knowledge and the knowable object: and then the relation is in one extreme really and in the other logically only. In another way when the relation results from the movement of one extreme without any concomitant movement, but not without a previous movement of the other; thus there results equality between two men by the increase of one, without the other either increasing or decreasing then, although previously he reached his actual quantity by some movement or change, so that this relation is founded really in both extremes. It is the same with consanguinity and affinity, because the relation of brotherhood which results in a grown child on the birth of a boy, is caused without any movement of the former's at the time, but by virtue of that previous movement of his wherein he was begotten; wherefore at the time it happens that there results in him the aforesaid relation through the movement of another. Likewise because this man descends through his own birth from the same stock as the husband, there results in him affinity with the latter's wife, without any new change in him.

SECOND ARTICLE

Whether Affinity Remains after the Death of Husband or Wife?

We proceed thus to the Second Article:—

Objection 1. It would seem that affinity does not remain after the death of husband or wife, between the blood-relations of husband and wife or *vice versa*. Because if the cause cease the effect ceases. Now the cause of affinity was the marriage, which ceases after the husband's death, since then *the woman . . . is loosed from the law of the husband* (Rom. vii. 2). Therefore the aforesaid affinity ceases also.

Obj. 2. Further, consanguinity is the cause of affinity. Now the consanguinity of the husband with his blood-relations ceases at his death. Therefore, the wife's affinity with them ceases also.

On the contrary, Affinity is caused by consanguinity. Now consanguinity binds persons together for all time as long as they live. Therefore affinity does so also: and consequently affinity (between two persons) is not dissolved through the dissolution of the marriage by the death of a third person.

I answer that, A relation ceases in two ways: in one way through the corruption of its subject, in another way by the removal of its cause; thus likeness ceases when one of the like subjects dies, or when the quality that caused the likeness is removed. Now there are certain relations which have for their cause an action, or a passion or movement *(Met.* v. 20): and some of these are caused by movement, through something being moved actually; such is the relation between mover and moved: some of them are caused through something being adapted to movement, for instance the relations between the motive power and the movable, or between master and servant; and some of them result from something having been moved previously, such as the relation between father and son, for the relation between them is caused not by (the son) being begotten now, but by his having been begotten. Now aptitude for movement and for being moved is transitory; whereas the fact of having been moved is everlasting, since what has been moved never ceases having been. Consequently fatherhood and sonship are never dissolved through the removal of the cause, but only through the corruption of the subject, that is of one of the subjects. The same applies to affinity, for this is caused by certain persons having been joined together, not by their being actually joined. Wherefore it is not done away, as long as the persons between whom affinity has been contracted survive, although the person die through whom it was contracted.

Reply Obj. 1. The marriage tie causes affinity not only by reason of actual union, but also by reason of the union having been effected in the past.

Reply Obj. 2. Consanguinity is not the chief cause of affinity, but union with a blood-relation, not only because that union is now, but because it has been. Hence the argument does not prove.

THIRD ARTICLE

Whether Unlawful Intercourse Causes Affinity?

We proceed thus to the Third Article:—

Objection 1. It would seem that unlawful intercourse does not cause affinity. For affinity is an honorable thing. Now honorable things do not result from that which is dishonorable. Therefore affinity cannot be caused by a dishonorable intercourse.

Obj. 2. Further, where there is consanguinity there cannot be affinity; since affinity is a relationship between persons that results from carnal intercourse and is altogether void of blood-relationship. Now if unlawful intercourse were a cause of affinity, it would sometimes happen that a man would contract affinity with his blood-relations and with himself: for instance when a man is guilty of incest with a blood-relation. Therefore affinity is not caused by unlawful intercourse.

Obj. 3. Further, unlawful intercourse is according to nature or against nature. Now affinity is not caused by unnatural unlawful intercourse as decided by law (can. *Extraordinaria,* xxxv. qu. 2, 3). Therefore it is not caused only by unlawful intercourse according to nature.

On the contrary, He who is joined to a harlot is made one body (1 Cor. vi. 16). Now this is the reason why marriage caused affinity. Therefore unlawful intercourse does so for the same reason.

Further, carnal intercourse is the cause of affinity, as shown by the definition of affinity, which definition is as follows: Affinity is the relationship of persons which results from carnal intercourse and is altogether void of blood-relationship. But there is carnal copulation even in unlawful intercourse. Therefore unlawful intercourse causes affinity.

I answer that, According to the Philosopher *(Ethic.* viii. 12) the union of husband and wife is said to be natural chiefly on account of the procreation of offspring, and secondly on account of the community of works: the former of which belongs to marriage by reason of carnal copulation, and the latter, in so far as marriage is a partnership directed to a common life. Now the former is to be found in every carnal union where there is a mingling of seeds, since such a union may be productive of offspring, but the latter may be wanting. Consequently since marriage caused affinity, in so far as it was a carnal mingling, it follows that also an unlawful intercourse causes affinity in so far as it has something of natural copulation.

Reply Obj. 1. In an unlawful intercourse there is something natural which is common to fornication and marriage, and in this respect it causes affinity. There is also something which is inordinate whereby it differs from marriage, and in this respect it does not cause affinity. Hence affinity remains honorable, although its cause is in a way dishonorable.

Reply Obj. 2. There is no reason why diverse relations should not be in the same subject by reason of different things. Consequently there can be affinity and consanguinity between two persons, not only on account of unlawful but also on account of lawful intercourse: for instance if a blood-relation of mine on my father's side marries a blood-relation of mine on my mother's side. Hence in the above definition the words *which is altogether void of blood-relationship* apply to affinity as such. Nor does it follow that a man by having intercourse with his blood-relation contracts affinity with himself, since affinity, like consanguinity, requires diversity of subjects, as likeness does.

Reply Obj. 3. In unnatural copulation there is no mingling of seeds that makes generation possible: wherefore a like intercourse does not cause affinity.

FOURTH ARTICLE

Whether Affinity Is Caused by Betrothal?

We proceed thus to the Fourth Article:—

Objection 1. It would seem that affinity cannot be caused by betrothal. For affinity is a lasting tie: whereas a betrothal is sometimes broken off. Therefore it cannot cause affinity.

Obj. 2. Further, if the hymen be penetrated without the deed being consummated, affinity is not contracted. Yet this is much more akin to carnal intercourse than a betrothal. Therefore betrothal does not cause affinity.

Obj. 3. Further, betrothal is nothing but a promise of future marriage. Now sometimes there is a promise of future marriage without affinity being contracted, for instance if it take place before the age of seven years; or if a man having a perpetual impediment of impotence promise a woman future marriage; or if a like promise be made between persons to whom marriage is rendered unlawful by a vow; or in any other way whatever. Therefore betrothal cannot cause affinity.

On the contrary, Pope Alexander (cap. *Ad audiendam,* De spons. et matrim.) forbade a certain woman to marry a certain man, because she had been betrothed to his brother. Now this would not be the case unless affinity were contracted by betrothal. Therefore, etc.

I answer that, Just as a betrothal has not the conditions of a perfect marriage, but is a preparation for marriage, so betrothal causes not affinity as marriage does, but something like affinity. This is called *the justice of public honesty,* which is an impediment to marriage even as affinity and consanguinity are, and according to the same degrees, and is defined thus: *The justice of public honesty is a relationship arising out of betrothal, and derives its force from ecclesiastical institution by reason of its honesty.* This indicates the reason of its name as well as its cause, namely that this relationship was instituted by the Church on account of its honesty.

Reply Obj. 1. Betrothal, by reason not of itself but of the end to which it is directed, causes this kind of affinity known as *the justice of public honesty:* wherefore just as marriage is a lasting tie, so is the aforesaid kind of affinity.

Reply Obj. 2. In carnal intercourse man and woman become one flesh by the mingling of seeds. Wherefore it is not every invasion or penetration of the hymen that causes affinity to be contracted, but only such as is followed by a mingling of seeds. But marriage causes affinity not only on account of carnal intercourse, but also by reason of the conjugal fellowship, in respect of which also marriage is according to nature. Consequently affinity results from the marriage contract itself expressed in words of the present and before its consummation, and in like manner there results from betrothal, which is a promise of conjugal fellowship, something akin to affinity, namely the justice of public honesty.

Reply Obj. 3. All those impediments which void a betrothal prevent affinity being contracted through a promise of marriage. Hence whether he who actually promises marriage be lacking in age, or be under a solemn vow of continence or any like impediment, no affinity nor anything akin to it results because the betrothal is void. If, however, a minor, laboring under insensibility or malefice, having a perpetual impediment, is betrothed before the age of puberty and after the age of seven years, with a woman who is of age, from such a contract there results the impediment called justice of public honesty, because at the time the impediment was not actual, since at that age the boy who is insensible is equally impotent in respect of the act in question.

FIFTH ARTICLE

Whether Affinity Is a Cause of Affinity?

We proceed thus to the Fifth Article:—

Objection 1. It would seem that affinity also is a cause of affinity. For Pope Julius I says (cap. *Contradicimus,* 35 qu. iii) : *No man may marry his wife's surviving blood-relation:* and it is said in the next chapter (cap. *Porro duorum*) that *the wives of two cousins are forbidden to marry, one after the other, the same husband.* But this is only on account of affinity being contracted through union with a person related by affinity. Therefore affinity is a cause of affinity.

Obj. 2. Further, carnal intercourse makes persons akin even as carnal procreation, since the degrees of affinity and consanguinity are reckoned equally. But consanguinity causes affinity. Therefore affinity does also.

Obj. 3. Further, things that are the same with one and the same are the same with one another. But the wife contracts the same relations with all her husband's kindred. Therefore all her husband's kindred are made one with all who are related by affinity to the wife, and thus affinity is the cause of affinity.

Obj. 4. *On the contrary,* If affinity is

caused by affinity a man who has connection with two women can marry neither of them, because then the one would be related to the other by affinity. But this is false. Therefore affinity does not cause affinity.

Obj. 5. Further, if affinity arose out of affinity a man by marrying another man's widow would contract affinity with all her first husband's kindred, since she is related to them by affinity. But this cannot be the case because he would become especially related by affinity to her deceased husband. Therefore, etc.

Obj. 6. Further, consanguinity is a stronger tie than affinity. But the blood-relations of the wife do not become blood-relations of the husband. Much less, therefore, does affinity to the wife cause affinity to her blood-relations, and thus the same conclusion follows.

I answer that, There are two ways in which one thing proceeds from another: in one way a thing proceeds from another in likeness of species, as a man is begotten of a man: in another way one thing proceeds from another, not in likeness of species; and this process is always towards a lower species, as instanced in all equivocal agents. The first kind of procession, however often it be repeated, the same species always remains: thus if one man be begotten of another by an act of the generative power, of this man also another man will be begotten, and so on. But the second kind of procession, just as in the first instance it produces another species, so it makes another species as often as it is repeated. Thus by movement from a point there proceeds a line and not a point, because a point by being moved makes a line; and from a line moved lineally, there proceeds not a line but a surface, and from a surface a body, and in this way the procession can go no further. Now in the procession of kinship we find two kinds whereby this tie is caused: one is by carnal procreation, and this always produces the same species of relationship; the other is by the marriage union, and this produces a different kind of relationship from the beginning: thus it is clear that a married woman is related to her husband's blood-relations not by blood but by affinity. Wherefore if this kind of process be repeated, the result will be not affinity but another kind of relationship; and consequently a married party contracts with the affines of the other party a relation not of affinity but of some other kind which is called affinity of the second kind. And again if a person through marriage contracts relationship with an affine of the second kind, it will not be affinity of the second kind, but of a third kind, as indicated in the verse quoted above (A. 1). Formerly these two kinds were included in the

prohibition, under the head of the justice of public honesty rather than under the head of affinity, because they fall short of true affinity in the same way as the relationship arising out of betrothal. Now however they have ceased to be included in the prohibition, which now refers only to the first kind of affinity in which true affinity consists.

Reply Obj. 1. A husband contracts affinity of the first kind with his wife's male blood relation, and affinity of the second kind with the latter's wife: wherefore if the latter may dies the former cannot marry his widow on account of the second kind of affinity. Again if a man *A* marry a widow *B*, *C*, a relation of her former husband being connected with *B* by the first kind of affinity, contracts affinity of the second kind with her husband *A ;* and *D*, the wife of this relation *C* being connected by affinity of the second kind, with *B*, this man's wife contracts affinity of the third kind with her husband *A*. And since the third kind of affinity was included in the prohibition on account of a certain honesty more than by reason of affinity, the canon (cap. *Porro duorum*, 35, qu. iii) says: *The justice of public honesty forbids the wives of two cousins to be married to the same man, the one after the other*. But this prohibition is done away with.

Reply Obj. 2. Although carnal intercourse is a cause of people being connected with one another, it is not the same kind of connection.

Reply Obj. 3. The wife contracts the same connection with her husband's relatives as to the degree but not as to the kind of connection.

Since however the arguments in the contrary sense would seem to show that no tie is caused by affinity, we must reply to them lest the time-honored prohibition of the Church seem unreasonable.

Reply Obj. 4. As stated above, a woman does not contract affinity of the first kind with the man to whom she is united in the flesh wherefore she does not contract affinity of the second kind with a woman known by the same man; and consequently if a man marry one of these women, the other does not contract affinity of the third kind with him. And so the laws of bygone times did not forbid the same man to marry successively two women known by one man.

Reply Obj. 5. As a man is not connected with his wife by affinity of the first kind, so he does not contract affinity of the second kind with the second husband of the same wife. Wherefore the argument does not prove.

Reply Obj. 6. One person is not connected with me through another, except they be connected together. Hence through a woman who is affine to me, no person becomes connected with me, except such as is connected with her. Now this cannot be except through carnal procreation from her, or through connection with her by marriage: and according to the olden legislation, I contracted some kind of connection through her in both ways: because her son even by another husband becomes affine to me in the same kind and in a different degree of affinity, as appears from the rule given above: and again her second husband becomes affine to me in the second kind of affinity. But her other blood-relations are not connected with him, but she is connected with them, either as with father or mother, inasmuch as she descends from them, or, as with her brothers, as proceeding from the same principle; wherefore the brother or father of my affine does not become affine to me in any kind of affinity.

SIXTH ARTICLE

Whether Affinity Is an Impediment to Marriage?

We proceed thus to the Sixth Article:—
Objection 1. It would seem that affinity is not an impediment to marriage. For nothing is an impediment to marriage except what is contrary thereto. But affinity is not contrary to marriage since it is caused by it. Therefore it is not an impediment to marriage.

Obj. 2. Further, by marriage the wife becomes a possession of the husband. Now the husband's kindred inherit his possessions after his death. Therefore they can succeed to his wife, although she is affine to them, as shown above (A. 5). Therefore affinity is not an impediment to marriage.

On the contrary, It is written (Lev. xviii. 8): *Thou shalt not uncover the nakedness of thy father's wife.* Now she is only affine. Therefore affinity is an impediment to marriage.

I answer that, Affinity that precedes marriage hinders marriage being contracted and voids the contract, for the same reason as consanguinity. For just as there is a certain need for blood-relations to live together, so is there for those who are connected by affinity: and just as there is a tie of friendship between blood-relations, so is there between those who are affine to one another. If, however, affinity supervene to matrimony, it cannot void the marriage, as stated above (Q. 50, A. 7).

Reply Obj. 1. Affinity is not contrary to the marriage which causes it, but to a marriage being contracted with an affine, in so far as the latter would hinder the extension of friendship and the curbing of concupiscence, which are sought in marriage.

Reply Obj. 2. The husband's possessions

do not become one with him as the wife is made one flesh with him. Wherefore just as consanguinity is an impediment to marriage or union with the husband according to the flesh, so is one forbidder to marry the husband's wife.

SEVENTH ARTICLE

Whether Affinity in Itself Admits of Degrees?

We proceed thus to the Seventh Article:—
Objection 1. It would seem that affinity in itself admits of degrees. For any kind of propinquity can itself be the subject of degrees. Now affinity is a kind of propinquity. Therefore it has degrees in itself apart from the degrees of consanguinity by which it is caused.

Obj. 2. Further, it is stated in the text (iv, *Sent.* D. 41) that the child of a second marriage could not take a consort from within the degrees of affinity of the first husband. But this would not be the case unless the son of an affine were also affine. Therefore affinity like consanguinity admits itself of degrees.

On the contrary, Affinity is caused by consanguinity. Therefore all the degrees of affinity are caused by the degrees of consanguinity: and so it has no degrees of itself.

I answer that, A thing does not of itself admit of being divided except in reference to something belonging to it by reason of its genus: thus animal is divided into rational and irrational and not into white and black. Now carnal procreation has a direct relation to consanguinity, because the tie of consanguinity is immediately contracted through it; whereas it has no relation to affinity except through consanguinity which is the latter's cause. Wherefore since the degrees of relationship are distinguished in reference to carnal procreation, the distinction of degrees is directly and immediately referable to consanguinity, and to affinity through consanguinity. Hence the general rule in seeking the degrees of affinity is that in whatever degree of consanguinity I am related to the husband, in that same degree of affinity I am related to the wife.

Reply Obj. 1. The degrees in propinquity of relationship can only be taken in reference to ascent and descent of propagation, to which affinity is compared only through consanguinity. Wherefore affinity has no direct degrees, but derives them according to the degrees of consanguinity.

Reply Obj. 2. Formerly it used to be said that the son of my affine by a second marriage was affine to me, not directly but accidentally as it were: wherefore he was forbidden to marry on account of the justice of public honesty rather than affinity. And for this reason this prohibition is now revoked.

EIGHTH ARTICLE

Whether the Degrees of Affinity Extend in the Same Way As the Degrees of Consanguinity?

We proceed thus to the Eighth Article:—

Objection 1. It would seem that the degrees of affinity do not extend in the same way as the degrees of consanguinity. For the tie of affinity is less strong than the tie of consanguinity, since affinity arises from consanguinity in diversity of species, as from an equivocal cause. Now the stronger the tie the longer it lasts. Therefore the tie of affinity does not last to the same number of degrees as consanguinity.

Obj. 2. Further, human law should imitate Divine law. Now according to the Divine law certain degrees of consanguinity were forbidden, in which degrees affinity was not an impediment to marriage: as instanced in a brother's wife whom a man could marry although he could not marry her sister. Therefore now too the prohibition of affinity and consanguinity should not extend to the same degrees.

On the contrary, A woman is connected with me by affinity from the very fact that she is married to a blood-relation of mine. Therefore in whatever degree her husband is related to me by blood she is related to me in that same degree by affinity: and so the degrees of affinity should be reckoned in the same number as the degrees of consanguinity.

I answer that, Since the degrees of affinity are reckoned according to the degrees of consanguinity, the degrees of affinity must needs be the same in number as those of consanguinity. Nevertheless, affinity being a lesser tie than consanguinity, both formerly and now, a dispensation is more easily granted in the more remote degrees of affinity than in the remote degrees of consanguinity.

Reply Obj. 1. The fact that the tie of affinity is less than the tie of consanguinity causes a difference in the kind of relationship but not in the degrees. Hence this argument is not to the point.

Reply Obj. 2. A man could not take his deceased brother's wife except, in the case when the latter died without issue, in order to raise up seed to his brother. This was requisite at a time when religious worship was propagated by means of the propagation of the flesh, which is not the case now. Hence it is clear that he did not marry her in his own person as it were, but as supplying the place of his brother.

NINTH ARTICLE

Whether a Marriage Contracted by Persons within the Degrees of Affinity or Consanguinity Should Always Be Annulled?

We proceed thus to the Ninth Article:—

Objection 1. It would seem that a marriage contracted by persons within the degrees of affinity or consanguinity ought not always to be annulled by divorce. For *what God hath joined together let no man put asunder* (Matt. xix. 6). Since then it is understood that what the Church does God does, and since the Church sometimes through ignorance joins such persons together, it would seem that if subsequently this came to knowledge they ought not to be separated.

Obj. 2. Further, the tie of marriage is less onerous than the tie of ownership. Now after a long time a man may acquire by prescription the ownership of a thing of which he was not the owner. Therefore by length of time a marriage becomes good in law, although it was not so before.

Obj 3.. Further, of like things we judge alike. Now if a marriage ought to be annulled on account of consanguinity, in the case when two brothers marry two sisters, if one be separated on account of consanguinity, the other ought to be separated for the same reason; and yet this is not seemly. Therefore a marriage ought not to be annulled on account of afffinity or consanguinity.

On the contrary, Consanguinity and affinity forbid the contracting of a marriage and void the contract. Therefore if affinity or consanguinity be proved, the parties should be separated even though they have actually contracted marriage.

I answer that, Since all copulation apart from lawful marriage is a mortal sin, which the Church uses all her endeavors to prevent, it belongs to her to separate those between whom there cannot be valid marriage, especially those related by blood or by affinity, who cannot without incest be united in the flesh.

Reply Obj. 1. Although the Church is upheld by God's gift and authority, yet in so far as she is an assembly of men there results in her acts something of human frailty which is not Divine. Therefore a union effected in the presence of the Church who is ignorant of an impediment is not indissoluble by Divine authority, but is brought about contrary to Divine authority through man's error, which being an error of fact excuses from sin, as iong as it remains. Hence when the impediment comes to the knowledge of the Church, she ought to sever the aforesaid union.

Reply Obj. 2. That which cannot be done

without sin is not ratified by any prescription, for as Innocent III says (Conc. Later. iv, can. 50: cap. *Non debent,* De consang. et affinit.), *length of time does not diminish sin but increases it:* nor can it in any way legitimize a marriage which could not take place between unlawful persons.

Reply Obj. 3. In contentious suits between two persons the verdict does not prejudice a third party, wherefore although the one brother's marriage with the one sister is annulled on account of consanguinity, the Church does not therefore annul the other marriage against which no action is taken. Yet in the tribunal of the conscience the other brother ought not on this account always to be bound to put away his wife, because such accusations frequently proceed from ill-will, and are proved by false witnesses. Hence he is not bound to form his conscience on what has been done about the other marriage: but seemingly one ought to draw a distinction, because either he has certain knowledge of the impediment of his marriage, or he has an opinion about it, or he has neither. In the first case, he can neither seek nor pay the debt, in the second, he must pay, but not ask, in the third he can both pay and ask.

TENTH ARTICLE

Whether It Is Necessary to Proceed by Way of Accusation for the Annulment of a Marriage Contracted by Persons Related to Each Other by Affinity or Consanguinity?

We proceed thus to the Tenth Article:—

Objection 1. It would seem that one ought not to proceed by way of accusation in order to sever a marriage contracted between persons related by affinity or consanguinity. Because accusation is preceded by inscription * whereby a man binds himself to suffer the punishment of retaliation, if he fail to prove his accusation. But this is not required when a matrimonial separation is at issue. Therefore accusation has no place then.

Obj. 2. Further, in a matrimonial lawsuit only the relatives are heard, as stated in the text (iv, *Sent.* D. 41). But in accusations even strangers are heard. Therefore in a suit for matrimonial separation the process is not by way of accusation.

Obj. 3. Further, if a marriage ought to be denounced this should be done especially where it is least difficult to sever the tie. Now this is when only the betrothal has been contracted, and then it is not the marriage that is denounced. Therefore accusation should never take place at any other time.

Obj. 4. Further, a man is not prevented from accusing by the fact that he does not accuse at once. But this happens in marriage, for if he was silent at first when the marriage was being contracted, he cannot denounce the marriage afterwards without laying himself open to suspicion. Therefore, etc.

On the contrary, Whatever is unlawful can be denounced. But the marriage of relatives by affinity and consanguinity is unlawful. Therefore it can be denounced.

I answer that, Accusation is instituted lest the guilty be tolerated as though they were innocent. Now just as it happens through ignorance of fact that a guilty man is reputed innocent, so it happens through ignorance of a circumstance that a certain fact is deemed lawful whereas it is unlawful. Wherefore just as a man is sometimes accused, so is a fact sometimes an object of accusation. It is in this way that a marriage is denounced, when through ignorance of an impediment it is deemed lawful, whereas it is unlawful.

Reply Obj. 1. The punishment of retaliation takes place when a person is accused of a crime, because then action is taken that he may be punished. But when it is a deed that is accused, action is taken not for the punishment of the doer, but in order to prevent what is unlawful. Hence in a matrimonial suit the accuser does not bind himself to a punishment. Moreover, the accusation may be made either in words or in writing, provided the person who denounces the marriage denounced, and the impediment for which it is denounced, be expressed.

Reply Obj. 2. Strangers cannot know of the consanguinity except from the relatives, since these know with greater probability. Hence when these are silent, a stranger is liable to be suspected of acting from ill-will unless he wish the relatives to prove his assertion. Wherefore a stranger is debarred from accusing when there are relatives who are silent, and by whom he cannot prove his accusation. On the other hand the relatives, however nearly related they be, are not debarred from accusing, when the marriage is denounced on account of a perpetual impediment, which prevents the contracting of the marriage and voids the contract. When, however, the accusation is based on a denial of the contract having taken place, the parents should be debarred from witnessing as being liable to suspicion, except those of the party that is inferior in rank and wealth, for they, one is inclined to think, would be willing for the marriage to stand.

* The accuser was bound by Roman Law to endorse (*se inscribere*) the writ of accusation. Cf. II-II, Q. 33, A. 7.

Reply Obj. 3. If the marriage is not yet contracted and there is only a betrothal, there can be no accusation, for what is not, cannot be accused. But the impediment can be denounced lest the marriage be contracted.

Reply Obj. 4. He who is silent at first is sometimes heard afterwards if he wish to denounce the marriage, and sometimes he is repulsed. This is made clear by the Decretal (cap. *Cum in tua*, De his qui matrim. accus. possunt.) which runs as follows: *If an accuser present himself after the marriage has been contracted, since he did not declare himself when according to custom, the banns were published in church, we may rightly ask whether he should be allowed to voice his accusation. In this matter we deem that a distinction should be made, so that if he who lodges information against persons already married was absent from the diocese at the time of the aforesaid publication, or if for some other reason this could not come to his knowledge, for instance if through exceeding stress of weakness and fever he was not in possession of his faculties, or was of so tender years as to be too young to understand such matters, or if he were hindered by some other lawful cause, his accusation should be heard. Otherwise without doubt he should be repulsed as open to suspicion, unless he swear that the information lodged by him came to his knowledge subsequently and that he is not moved by ill-will to make his accusation.*

ELEVENTH ARTICLE

Whether in a Suit of This Kind One Should Proceed by Hearing Witnesses in the Same Way As in Other Suits?

We proceed thus to the Eleventh Article:—

Objection 1. It would seem that in such a suit one ought not to proceed by hearing witnesses, in the same way as in other suits where any witnesses may be called provided they be unexceptionable. But here strangers are not admitted, although they be unexceptionable. Therefore, etc.

Obj. 2. Further, witnesses who are suspected of private hatred or love are debarred from giving evidence. Now relatives are especially open to suspicion of love for one party, and hatred for the other. Therefore their evidence should not be taken.

Obj. 3. Further, marriage is a more favorable suit than those others in which purely corporeal questions are at stake. Now in these the same person cannot be both accuser and witness. Neither therefore can this be in a matrimonial suit; and so it would appear that it is not right to proceed by hearing witnesses in a suit of this kind.

On the contrary, Witnesses are called in a suit in order to give the judge evidence concerning matters of doubt. Now evidence should be afforded the judge in this suit as in other suits, since he must not pronounce a hasty judgment on what is not proven. Therefore here as in other lawsuits witnesses should be called.

I answer that, In this kind of lawsuit as in others, truth must be unveiled by witnesses: yet, as the lawyers say, there are many things peculiar to this suit; namely that *the same person can be accuser and witness; that evidence is not taken "on oath of calumny," since it is a quasi-spiritual lawsuit; that relatives are allowed as witnesses; that the juridical order is not perfectly observed, since if the denunciation has been made, and the suit is uncontested, the defendant may be excommunicated if contumacious; that hearsay evidence is admitted; and that witnesses may be called after the publication of the names of the witnesses.* All this is in order to prevent the sin that may occur in such a union (cap. *Quoties aliqui:* cap. *Super eo,* De test. et attest.: cap. *Literas,* De juram. calumn.).

This suffices for the *Replies* to the *Objections.*

QUESTION 56

Of the Impediment of Spiritual Relationship

(In Five Articles)

WE must now consider the impediment of spiritual relationship: under which head there are five points of inquiry: (1) Whether spiritual relationship is an impediment to marriage? (2) From what cause is it contracted? (3) Between whom? (4) Whether it passes from husband to wife? (5) Whether it passes to the father's carnal children?

FIRST ARTICLE

Whether Spiritual Relationship Is an Impediment to Marriage?

We proceed thus to the First Article:—

Objection 1. It would seem that spiritual relationship is not an impediment to marriage. For nothing is an impediment to marriage save what is contrary to a marriage good. Now spiritual relationship is not contrary to a marriage good. Therefore it is not an impediment to marriage.

Obj. 2. Further, a perpetual impediment to marriage cannot stand together with marriage. But spiritual relationship sometimes stands together with marriage, as stated in the text (iv, *Sent.* D. 42), as when a man in a case of necessity baptizes his own child, for then he contracts a spiritual relationship with his wife, and yet the marriage is not dissolved. Therefore spiritual relationship is not an impediment to marriage.

Obj. 3. Further, union of the spirit does not pass to the flesh. But marriage is a union of the flesh. Therefore since spiritual relationship is a union of the spirit, it cannot become an impediment to marriage.

Obj. 4. Further, contraries have not the same effects. Now spiritual relationship is apparently contrary to disparity of worship, since spiritual relationship is a kinship resulting from the giving of a sacrament or the intention of so doing:* whereas disparity of worship consists in the lack of a sacrament, as stated above (Q. 50, A. 1). Since then disparity of worship is an impediment to matrimony, it would seem that spiritual relationship has not this effect.

On the contrary, The holier the bond, the more is it to be safeguarded. Now a spiritual bond is holier than a bodily tie: and since the tie of bodily kinship is an impediment to marriage, it follows that spiritual relationship should also be an impediment.

Further, in marriage the union of souls ranks higher than union of bodies, for it precedes it. Therefore with much more reason can a spiritual relationship hinder marriage than bodily relationship does.

I answer that, Just as by carnal procreation man receives natural being, so by the sacraments he receives the spiritual being of grace. Wherefore just as the tie that is contracted by carnal procreation is natural to man, inasmuch as he is a natural being, so the tie that is contracted from the reception of the sacraments is after a fashion natural to man, inasmuch as he is a member of the Church. Therefore as carnal relationship hinders marriage, even so does spiritual relationship by command of the Church. We must however draw a distinction in reference to spiritual relationship, since either it precedes or follows marriage. If it precedes, it hinders the contracting of marriage and voids the contract. If it follows, it does not dissolve the marriage bond: but we must draw a further distinction in reference to the marriage act. For either the

* See next Article, *ad* 3.

spiritual relationship is contracted in a case of necessity, as when a father baptizes his child who is at the point of death—and then it is not an obstacle to the marriage act on either side—or it is contracted without any necessity and through ignorance, in which case if the person whose action has occasioned the relationship acted with due caution, it is the same with him as in the former case—or it is contracted purposely and without any necessity, and then the person whose action has occasioned the relationship, loses the right to ask for the debt; but is bound to pay if asked, because the fault of the one party should not be prejudicial to the other.

Reply Obj. 1. Although spiritual relationship does not hinder any of the chief marriage goods, it hinders one of the secondary goods, namely the extension of friendship, because spiritual relationship is by itself a sufficient reason for friendship: wherefore intimacy and friendship with other persons need to be sought by means of marriage.

Reply Obj. 2. Marriage is a lasting bond, wherefore no supervening impediment can sever it. Hence it happens sometimes that marriage and an impediment to marriage stand together, but not if the impediment precedes.

Reply Obj. 3. In marriage there is not only a bodily but also a spiritual union: and consequently kinship of spirit proves an impediment thereto, without spiritual kinship having to pass into a bodily relationship.

Reply Obj. 4. There is nothing unreasonable in two things that are contrary to one another being contrary to the same thing, as great and small are contrary to equal. Thus disparity of worship and spiritual relationship are opposed to marriage, because in one the distance is greater, and in the other less, than required by marriage. Hence there is an impediment to marriage in either case.

SECOND ARTICLE

Whether Spiritual Relationship Is Contracted by Baptism Only?

We proceed thus to the Second Article:—

Objection 1. It would seem that spiritual relationship is contracted by Baptism only. For as bodily kinship is to bodily birth, so is spiritual kinship to spiritual birth. Now Baptism alone is called spiritual birth. Therefore spiritual kinship is contracted by Baptism only, even as only by carnal birth is carnal kinship contracted.

Obj. 2. Further, a character is imprinted in Order as in Confirmation. But spiritual relationship does not result from receiving Orders. Therefore it does not result from Confirmation but only from Baptism.

Obj. 3. Further, sacraments are more excellent than sacramentals. Now spiritual relationship does not result from certain sacraments, for instance from Extreme Unction. Much less therefore does it result from catechizing, as some maintain.

Obj. 4. Further, many other sacramentals are attached to Baptism besides catechizing. Therefore spiritual relationship is not contracted from catechism any more than from the others.

Obj. 5. Further, prayer is no less efficacious than instruction of catechism for advancement in good. But spiritual relationship does not result from prayer. Therefore it does not result from catechism.

Obj. 6. Further, the instruction given to the baptized by preaching to them avails no less than preaching to those who are not yet baptized. But no spiritual relationship results from preaching. Neither therefore does it result from catechism.

Obj. 7. On the other hand, It is written (1 Cor. iv. 15): *In Christ Jesus by the gospel I have begotten you.* Now spiritual birth causes spiritual relationship. Therefore spiritual relationship results from the preaching of the gospel and instruction, and not only from Baptism.

Obj. 8. Further, as original sin is taken away by Baptism, so is actual sin taken away by Penance. Therefore just as Baptism causes spiritual relationship, so also does Penance.

Obj. 9. Further, *father* denotes relationship. Now a man is called another's spiritual father in respect of Penance, teaching, pastoral care and many other like things. Therefore spiritual relationship is contracted from many other sources besides Baptism and Confirmation.

I answer that, There are three opinions on this question. Some say that as spiritual regeneration is bestowed by the sevenfold grace of the Holy Ghost, it is caused by means of seven things, beginning with the first taste of blessed salt and ending with Confirmation given by the bishop: and they say that spiritual relationship is contracted by each of these seven things. But this does not seem reasonable, for carnal relationship is not contracted except by a perfect act of generation. Wherefore affinity is not contracted except there be mingling of seeds, from which it is possible for carnal generation to follow. Now spiritual generation is not perfected except by a sacrament: wherefore it does not seem fitting for spiritual relationship to be contracted otherwise than through a sacrament. Hence others say that spiritual relationship is only contracted through three sacraments, namely catechism, Baptism and Confirmation, but these do not apparently know the meaning of what

they say, since catechism is not a sacrament, but a sacramental. Wherefore others say that it is contracted through two sacraments only, namely Confirmation and Baptism, and this is the more common opinion. Some however of these say that catechism is a weak impediment, since it hinders the contracting of marriage but does not void the contract.

Reply Obj. 1. Carnal birth is twofold. The first is in the womb, wherein that which is born is a weakling and cannot come forth without danger: and to this birth regeneration by Baptism is likened; wherein a man is regenerated as though yet needing to be fostered in the womb of the Church. The second is birth from out of the womb, when that which was born in the womb is so far strengthened that it can without danger face the outer world which has a natural corruptive tendency. To this is likened Confirmation, whereby man being strengthened goes forth abroad to confess the name of Christ. Hence spiritual relationship is fittingly contracted through both these sacraments.

Reply Obj. 2. The effect of the sacrament of Order is not regeneraiton but the bestowal of power, for which reason it is not conefrred on women, and consequently no impediment to marriage can arise therefrom. Hence this kind of relationship does not count.

Reply Obj. 3. In catechism one makes a profession of future Baptism, just as in betrothal one enters an engagement of future marriage. Wherefore just as in betrothal a certain kind of propinquity is contracted, so is there in catechism, whereby marriage is rendered at least unlawful, as some say; but not in the other sacraments.

Reply Obj. 4. There is not made a profession of faith in the other sacramentals of Baptism, as in catechism: wherefore the comparison fails.

The same answer applies to the *Fifth* and *Sixth Objections.*

Reply Obj. 7. The Apostle had instructed them in the faith by a kind of catechism; and consequently his instruction was directed to their spiritual birth.

Reply Obj. 8. Properly speaking a spiritual relationship is not contracted through the sacrament of Penance. Wherefore a priest's son can marry a woman whose confession the priest has heard, else in the whole parish he could not find a woman whom he could marry. Nor does it matter that by Penance actual sin is taken away, for this is not a kind of birth, but a kind of healing. Nevertheless Penance occasions a kind of bond between the woman penitent and the priest, that has a resemblance to spiritual relationship, so that if he have carnal intercourse with her, he sins as grievously as if she were his spiritual daughter. The reason of this is that the relations between priest and penitent are most intimate, and consequently in order to remove the occasion of sin this prohibition* was made.

Reply Obj. 9. A spiritual father is so called from his likeness to a carnal father. Now as the Philosopher says *(Ethic.* viii. 2) a carnal father gives his child three things, being, nourishment and instruction: and consequently a person's spiritual father is so called from one of these three things. Nevertheless he has not, through being his spiritual father, a spiritual relationship with him, unless he is like a (carnal) father as to generation which is the way to being. This solution may also be applied to the foregoing *Eighth Objection.*

THIRD ARTICLE

Whether Spiritual Relationship Is Contracted between the Person Baptized and the Person Who Raises Him from the Sacred Font?

We proceed thus to the Third Article:—

Objection 1. It would seem that spiritual relationship is not contracted between the person baptized and the person who raises him from the sacred font. For in carnal generation carnal relationship is contracted only on the part of the person of whose seed the child is born, and not on the part of the person who receives the child after birth. Therefore neither is spiritual relationship contracted between the receiver and the received at the sacred font.

Obj. 2. Further, he who raises a person from the sacred font is called ἀνάδοχος by Dionysius *(Eccl. Hier.* ii): and it is part of his office to instruct the child. But instruction is not a sufficient cause of spiritual relationship, as stated above (A. 2). Therefore no relationship is contracted between him and the person whom he raises from the sacred font.

Obj. 3. Further, it may happen that someone raises a person from the sacred font before he himself is baptized. Now spiritual relationship is not contracted in such a case, since one who is not baptized is not capable of spirituality. Therefore raising a person from the sacred font is not sufficient to contract a spiritual relationship.

On the contrary, There is the definition of spiritual relationship quoted above (A. 1), as also the authorities mentioned in the text (iv, *Sent.* D. 42).

I answer that, Just as in carnal generation a person is born of a father and mother, so in spiritual generation a person is born again a son of God as Father, and of the Church as Mother. Now while he who confers the

* Can. *Omnes quos,* and *seqq.,* Caus. xxx.

sacrament stands in the place of God, whose instrument and minister he is, he who raises a baptized person from the sacred font, or holds the candidate for Confirmation, stands in the place of the Church. Therefore spiritual relationship is contracted with both.

Reply Obj. 1. Not only the father, of whose seed the child is born, is related carnally to the child, but also the mother who provides the matter, and in whose womb the child is begotten. So too the godparent who in place of the Church offers and raises the candidate for Baptism and holds the candidate for Confirmation contracts spiritual relationship.

Reply Obj. 2. He contracts spiritual relationship not by reason of the instruction it is his duty to give, but on account of the spiritual birth in which he co-operates.

Reply Obj. 3. A person who is not baptized cannot raise anyone from the sacred font, since he is not a member of the Church whom the godparent in Baptism represents: although he can baptize, because he is a creature of God Whom the baptizer represents. And yet he cannot contract a spiritual relationship, since he is void of spiritual life to which man is first born by receiving Baptism.

FOURTH ARTICLE

Whether Spiritual Relationship Passes from Husband to Wife?

We proceed thus to the Fourth Article:—

Objection 1. It would seem that spiritual relationship does not pass from husband to wife. For spiritual and bodily union are disparate and differ generically. Therefore carnal union which is between husband and wife cannot be the means of contracting a spiritual relationship.

Obj. 2. Further, the godfather and godmother have more in common in the spiritual birth that is the cause of spiritual relationship, than a husband, who is godfather, has with his wife. Now godfather and godmother do not hereby contract spiritual relationship. Therefore neither does a wife contract a spiritual relationship through her husband being godfather to someone.

Obj. 3. Further, it may happen that the husband is baptized, and his wife not, for instance when he is converted from unbelief without his wife being converted. Now spiritual relationship cannot be contracted by one who is not baptized. Therefore it does not always pass from husband to wife.

Obj. 4. Further, husband and wife together can raise a person from the sacred font, since no law forbids it. If therefore spiritual relationship passed from husband to wife, it would follow that each of them is twice godfather or godmother of the same individual: which is absurd.

On the contrary, Spiritual goods are more communicable than bodily goods. But the bodily consanguinity of the husband passes to his wife by affinity. Much more therefore does spiritual relationship.

I answer that, A may become co-parent with B in two ways. First, by the act of another *(B),* who baptizes *A's* child, or raises him in Baptism. In this way spiritual relationship does not pass from husband to wife, unless perchance it be his wife's child, for then she contracts spiritual relationship directly, even as her husband. Secondly, by his own act, for instance when he raises *B's* child from the sacred font, and thus spiritual relationship passes to the wife if he has already had carnal knowledge of her, but not if the marriage be not yet consummated, since they are not as yet made one flesh: and this is by way of a kind of affinity; wherefore it would seem on the same grounds to pass to a woman of whom he has carnal knowledge, though she be not his wife. Hence the verse:

I may not marry my own child's godmother, nor the mother of my godchild: but I may marry the godmother of my wife's child.

Reply Obj. 1. From the fact that corporal and spiritual union differ generically we may conclude that the one is not the other, but not that the one cannot cause the other, since things of different genera sometimes cause one another either directly or indirectly.

Reply Obj. 2. The godfather and godmother of the same person are not united in that person's spiritual birth save accidentally, since one of them would be self-sufficient for the purpose. Hence it does not follow from this that any spiritual relationship results between them whereby they are hindered from marrying one another. Hence the verse:

Of two coparents one is always spiritual, the other carnal: this rule is infallible.

On the other hand, marriage by itself makes husband and wife one flesh: wherefore the comparison fails.

Reply Obj. 3. If the wife be not baptized, the spiritual relationship will not reach her, because she is not a fit subject, and not because spiritual relationship cannot pass from husband to wife through marriage.

Reply Obj. 4. Since no spiritual relationship results between godfather and godmother, nothing prevents husband and wife from raising together someone from the sacred font. Nor is it absurd that the wife become twice godmother of the same person from different causes, just as it is possible for her to be connected in carnal relationship both by affinity and consanguinity to the same person.

FIFTH ARTICLE

Whether Spiritual Relationship Passes to the Godfather's Carnal Children?

We proceed thus to the Fifth Article:—

Objection 1. It would seem that spiritual relationship does not pass to the godfather's carnal children . For no degrees are assigned to spiritual relationship. Yet there would be degrees if it passed from father to son, since the person begotten involves a change of degree, as stated above (Q. 55, A. 5). Therefore it does not pass to the godfather's carnal sons.

Obj. 2. Further, father and son are related in the same degree as brother and brother. If therefore spiritual relationship passes from father to son, it will equally pass from brother to brother: and this is false.

On the contrary, This is proved by authority quoted in the text (iv, *Sent.* D. 42).

I answer that, A son is something of his father and not conversely *(Ethic.* viii. 12): wherefore spiritual relationship passes from father to his carnal son and not conversely. Thus it is clear that there are three spiritual relationships: one called spiritual fatherhood between godfather and godchild; another called co-paternity between the godparent and carnal parent of the same person; and the third is called spiritual brotherhood, between godchild and the carnal children of the same parent. Each of these hinders the contracting of marriage and voids the contract.

Reply Obj. 1. The addition of a person by carnal generation entails a degree with regard to a person connected by the same kind of relationship, but not with regard to one connected by another kind of relationship. Thus a son is connected with his father's wife in the same degree as his father, but by another kind of relationship. Now spiritual relationship differs in kind from carnal. Wherefore a godson is not related to his godfather's carnal son in the same degree as the latter's father is related to him, through whom the spiritual relationship is contracted. Consequently it does not follow that spiritual relationship admits of degrees.

Reply Obj. 2. A man is not part of his brother as a son is of his father. But a wife is part of her husband, since she is made one with him in body. Consequently the relationship does not pass from brother to brother, whether the brother be born before or after spiritual brotherhood.

QUESTION 57

Of Legal Relationship, Which Is by Adoption

(In Three Articles)

WE must now consider legal relationship which is by adoption. Under this head there are three points of inquiry: (1) What is adoption? (2) Whether one contracts through it a tie that is an impediment to marriage? (3) Between which persons is this tie contracted.

FIRST ARTICLE

Whether Adoption Is Rightly Defined?

We proceed thus to the First Article:—

Objection 1. It would seem that adoption is not rightly defined: *Adoption is the act by which a person lawfully takes for his child or grandchild and so on one who does not belong to him.* For the child should be subject to its father. Now, sometimes the person adopted does not come under the power of the adopter. Therefore adoption is not always the taking of someone as a child.

Obj. 2. Further, *Parents should lay up for their children* (2 Cor. xii. 14). But the adoptive father does not always necessarily lay up for his adopted child, since sometimes the adopted does not inherit the goods of the adopter. Therefore adoption is not the taking of someone as a child.

Obj. 3. Further, adoption, whereby someone is taken as a child, is likened to natural procreation whereby a child is begotten naturally. Therefore whoever is competent to beget a child naturally is competent to adopt. But this is untrue, since neither one who is not his own master, nor one who is not twenty-five years of age, nor a woman can adopt, and yet they can beget a child naturally. Therefore, properly speaking, adoption is not the taking of someone as a child.

Obj. 4. Further, to take as one's child one who is not one's own seems necessary in order to supply the lack of children begotten naturally. Now one who is unable to beget, through being a eunuch or impotent, suffers especially from the absence of children of his own begetting. Therefore he is especially competent to adopt someone as his child. But he is not competent to adopt. Therefore adoption is not the taking of someone as one's child.

Obj. 5. Further, in spiritual relationship, where someone is taken as a child without carnal procreation, it is of no consequence whether an older person become the father of a younger, or *vice versa,* since a youth can baptize an old man and *vice versa.* Therefore, if by adoption a person is taken as a child without being carnally begotten, it would make no difference whether an older person adopted a younger, or a younger an older person; which is not true. Therefore the same conclusion follows.

Obj. 6. Further, there is no difference of degree between adopted and adopter. Therefore whoever is adopted, is adopted as a child; and consequently it is not right to say that one may be adopted as a grandchild.

Obj. 7. Further, adoption is a result of love, wherefore God is said to have adopted us as children through charity. Now we should have greater charity towards those who are connected with us than towards strangers. Therefore adoption should be not of a stranger but of someone connected with us.

I answer that, Art imitates nature and supplies the defect of nature where nature is deficient. Hence just as a man begets by natural procreation, so by positive law which is the art of what is good and just, one person can take to himself another as a child in likeness to one that is his child by nature, in order to take the place of the children he has lost, this being the chief reason why adoption was introduced. And since taking implies a term *wherefrom,* for which reason the taker is not the thing taken, it follows that the person taken as a child must be a stranger. Accordingly, just as natural procreation has a term *whereto,* namely the form which is the end of generation, and a term *wherefrom,* namely the contrary form, so legal generation has a term *whereto,* namely a child or grandchild, and a term *wherefrom,* namely, a stranger. Consequently the above definition includes the genus of adoption, for it is described as a *lawful taking,* and the term *wherefrom,* since it is said to be the taking of *a stranger,* and the term *whereto,* because it says, *as a child or grandchild.*

Reply Obj. 1. The sonship of adoption is an imitation of natural sonship. Wherefore there are two species of adoption, one which imitates natural sonship perfectly, and this is called *arrogatio,* whereby the person adopted is placed under the power of the adopter; and one who is thus adopted inherits from his adopted father if the latter die intestate, nor can his father legally deprive him of a fourth part of his inheritance. But no one can adopt in this way except one who is his own master, one namely who has no father or, if he has, is of age. There can be no adoption of this kind without the authority of the sovereign. The other kind of adoption imitates natural sonship imperfectly, and is called *simple adoption,* and by this the adopted does not come under the power of the adopter: so that it is a disposition to perfect adoption, rather than perfect adoption itself. In this way even one who is not his own master can adopt, without the consent of the sovereign and with the authority of a magistrate; and one who is thus adopted does not inherit the estate of the adopter, nor is the latter bound to bequeath to him any of his goods in his will, unless he will.

This suffices for the *Reply* to the *Second Objection.*

Reply Obj. 3. Natural procreation is directed to the production of the species; wherefore anyone in whom the specific nature is not hindered is competent to be able to beget naturally. But adoption is directed to hereditary succession, wherefore those alone are competent to adopt who have the power to dispose of their estate. Consequently one who is not his own master, or who is less than twenty-five years of age, or a woman, cannot adopt anyone, except by special permission of the sovereign.

Reply Obj. 4. An inheritance cannot pass to posterity through one who has a perpetual impediment from begetting: hence for this very reason it ought to pass to those who ought to succeed to him by right of relationship; and consequently he cannot adopt, as neither can he beget. Moreover greater is sorrow for children lost than for children one has never had. Wherefore those who are impeded from begetting need no solace for their lack of children, as those who have had and have lost them, or could have had them but have them not by reason of some accidental impediment.

Reply Obj. 5. Spiritual relationship is contracted through a sacrament whereby the faithful are born again in Christ, in Whom there is no difference between male and female, bondman and free, youth and old age (Gal. iii. 28; Col. iii. 11). Wherefore anyone can indifferently become another's godfather. But adoption aims at hereditary succession and a certain subjection of the adopted to the adopter: and it is not fitting that older persons should be subjected to younger in the care of the household. Consequently a younger person cannot adopt an older; but according to law the adopted person must be so much younger than the adopter, that he might have been the child of his natural begetting.

Reply Obj. 6. One may lose one's grandchildren and so forth even as one may lose one's children. Wherefore since adoption was introduced as a solace for children lost, just as someone may be adopted in place of a child, so may someone be adopted in place of a grandchild and so on.

Reply Obj. 7. A relative ought to succeed by right of relationship; and therefore such a person is not competent to be chosen to succeed by adoption. And if a relative, who is not competent to inherit the estate, be adopted, he is adopted not as a relative, but as a stranger lacking the right of succeeding to the adopter's goods.

SECOND ARTICLE

Whether a Tie That Is an Impediment to Marriage Is Contracted through Adoption?

We proceed thus to the Second Article:—

Objection 1. It would seem that there is not contracted through adoption a tie that is an impediment to marriage. For spiritual care is more excellent than corporeal care. But no tie of relationship is contracted through one's being subjected to another's spiritual care: else all those who dwell in the parish would be related to the parish priest and would be unable to marry his son. Neither therefore can this result from adoption which places the adopted under the care of the adopter.

Obj. 2. Further, no tie of relationship results from persons conferring a benefit on another. But adoption is nothing but the conferring of a benefit. Therefore no tie of relationship results from adoption.

Obj. 3. Further, a natural father provides for his child chiefly in three things, as the Philosopher states (*Ethic.* viii. 11, 12). namely by giving him being, nourishment and education; and hereditary succession is subsequent to these. Now no tie of relationship is contracted by one's providing for a person's nourishment and education, else a person would be related to his nourishers, tutors and masters, which is false. Therefore neither is any relationship contracted through adoption by which one inherits another's estate.

Obj. 4. Further, the sacraments of the Church are not subject to human laws. Now marriage is a sacrament of the Church. Since then adoption was introduced by human law, it would seem that a tie contracted from adoption cannot be an impediment to marriage.

On the contrary, Relationship is an impediment to marriage. Now a kind of relationship results from adoption, namely legal relationship, as evidenced by its definition, for *legal relationship is a connection arising out of adoption.* Therefore adoption results in a tie which is an impediment to marriage.

Further, the same is proved by the authorities quoted in the text (iv, *Sent*. D. 42).

I answer that, The Divine law especially forbids marriage between those persons who have to live together lest, as Rabbi Moses observes (*Doc. Perp.* iii. 49), if it were lawful for them to have carnal intercourse, there should be more room for concupiscence to the repression of which marriage is directed. And since the adopted child dwells in the house of his adopted father like one that is begotten naturally, human laws forbid the contracting of marriage between the like, and this prohibition is approved by the Church. Hence it is that legal adoption is an impediment to marriage. This suffices for the *Replies* to the first three *Objections,* because none of those things entails such a cohabitation as might be an incentive to concupiscence. Therefore they do not cause a relationship that is an impediment to marriage.

Reply Obj. 4. The prohibition of a human law would not suffice to make an impediment to marriage, unless the authority of the Church intervenes by issuing the same prohibition.

THIRD ARTICLE

Whether Legal Relationship Is Contracted Only between the Adopting Father and the Adopted Child?

We proceed thus to the Third Article:—

Objection 1. It would seem that a relationship of this kind is contracted only between the adopting father and the adopted child. For it would seem that it ought above all to be contracted between the adopting father and the natural mother of the adopted, as happens in spiritual relationship. Yet there is no legal relationship between them. Therefore it is not contracted between any other persons besides the adopter and adopted.

Obj. 2. Further, the relationship that impedes marriage is a perpetual impediment. But there is not a perpetual impediment between the adopted son and the naturally begotten daughter of the adopted; because when the adoption terminates at the death of the adopter, or when the adopted comes of age, the latter can marry her. Therefore he was not related to her in such a way as to prevent him from marrying her.

Obj. 3. Further, spiritual relationship passes to no person incapable of being a god-parent; wherefore it does not pass to one who is not baptized. Now a woman cannot adopt, as stated above (A. 1, *ad* 2). Therefore legal relationship does not pass from husband to wife.

Obj. 4. Further, spiritual relationship is stronger than legal. But spiritual relationship does not pass to a grandchild. Neither, therefore, does legal relationship.

On the contrary, Legal relationship is more in agreement with carnal union or procreation than spiritual relationship is. But spiritual relationship passes to another person. Therefore legal relationship does so also.

Further, the same is proved by the authorities quoted in the text (iv, *Sent*. D. 42).

I answer that, Legal relationship is of three kinds. The first is in the descending order as it were, and is contracted between the adoptive father and the adopted child, the latter's child, grandchild and so on; the second is between the adopted child and the naturally begotten child; the third is like a kind of affinity, and is between the adoptive father and the wife of the adopted son, or contrariwise between the adopted son and the wife of the adoptive father. Accordingly the first and third relationships are perpetual impediments to marriage: but the second is not, but only so long as the adopted person remains under the power of the adoptive father, wherefore when the father dies or when the child comes of age, they can be married.

Reply Obj. 1. By spiritual generation the son is not withdrawn from the father's power, as in the case of adoption, so that the godson remains the son of both at the same time, whereas the adopted son does not. Hence no relationship is contracted between the adoptive father and the natural mother or father, as was the case in spiritual relationship.

Reply Obj. 2. Legal relationship is an impediment to marriage on account of the parties dwelling together: hence when the need for dwelling together ceases, it is not unreasonable that the aforesaid tie cease, for instance when he ceases to be under the power of the same father. But the adoptive father and his wife always retain a certain authority over their adopted son and his wife, wherefore the tie between them remains.

Reply Obj. 3. Even a woman can adopt by permission of the sovereign, wherefore legal relationship passes also to her. Moreover the reason why spiritual relationship does not pass to a non-baptized person is not because such a person cannot be a god-parent, but because he is not a fit subject of spirituality.

Reply Obj. 4. By spiritual relationship the son is not placed under the power and care of the godfather, as in legal relationship: because it is necessary that whatever is in the son's power pass under the power of the adoptive father. Wherefore if a father be adopted the children and grandchildren who are in the power of the person adopted are adopted also.

QUESTION 58

Of the Impediments of Impotence, Spell, Frenzy or Madness, Incest and Defective Age

(In Five Articles)

WE must now consider five impediments to marriage, namely the impediments of impotence, spell, frenzy or madness, incest, and defective age. Under this head there are five points of inquiry: (1) Whether impotence is an impediment to marriage? (2) Whether a spell is? (3) Whether frenzy or madness is? (4) Whether incest is? (5) Whether defective age is?

FIRST ARTICLE

Whether Impotence Is an Impediment to Marriage?

We proceed thus to the First Article:—

Objection 1. It would seem that impotence is not an impediment to marriage. For carnal copulation is not essential to marriage, since marriage is more perfect when both parties observe continency by vow. But impotence deprives marriage of nothing save carnal copulation. Therefore it is not a diriment impediment to the marriage contract.

Obj. 2. Further, just as impotence prevents carnal copulation so does frigidity. But frigidity is not reckoned an impediment to marriage. Therefore neither should impotence be reckoned as such.

Obj. 3. Further, all old people are frigid. Yet old people can marry. Therefore, etc.

Obj. 4. Further, if the woman knows the man to be frigid when she marries him, the marriage is valid. Therefore frigidity, considered in itself, is not an impediment to marriage.

Obj. 5. Further, calidity may prove a sufficient incentive to carnal copulation with one who is not a virgin, but not with one who is, because it happens to be so weak as to pass away quickly, and is therefore insufficient for the deflowering of a virgin. Or again it may move a man sufficiently in regard to a beautiful woman, but insufficiently in regard to an uncomely one. Therefore it would seem that frigidity, although it be an impediment in regard to one, is not an impediment absolutely.

Obj. 6. Further, generally speaking woman is more frigid than man. But women are not debarred from marriage. Neither therefore should men be debarred on account of frigidity.

On the contrary, It is stated (Extra, *De Frigidis et Malefic.*, cap. *Quod Sedem*): *Just as a boy who is incapable of marital intercourse is unfit to marry, so also those who are impotent are deemed most unfit for the marriage contract.* Now persons affected with frigidity are the like. Therefore, etc.

Further, no one can bind himself to the impossible. Now in marriage man binds himself to carnal copulation; because it is for this purpose that he gives the other party power over his body. Therefore a frigid person, being incapable of carnal copulation, cannot marry.

I answer that, In marriage there is a contract whereby one is bound to pay the other the marital debt: wherefore just as in other contracts, the bond is unfitting if a person bind himself to what he cannot give or do, so the marriage contract is unfitting, if it be made by one who cannot pay the marital debt. This impediment is called by the general name of impotence as regards coition, and can arise either from an intrinsic and natural cause, or from an extrinsic and accidental cause, for instance spell, of which we shall speak later (A. 2). If it be due to a natural cause, this may happen in two ways. For either it is temporary, and can be remedied by medicine, or by the course of time, and then it does not void a marriage: or it is perpetual and then it voids marriage, so that the party who labors under this impediment remains for ever without hope of marriage, while the other may *marry to whom she will . . . in the Lord* (1 Cor. vii. 39). In order to ascertain whether the impediment be perpetual or not, the Church has appointed a fixed time, namely three years, for putting the matter to a practical proof: and if after three years, during which both parties have honestly endeavored to fulfil their marital intercourse, the marriage remain unconsummated, the Church adjudges the marriage to be dissolved. And yet the Church is sometimes mistaken in this, because three years are sometimes insufficient to prove impotence to be perpetual. Wherefore if the Church find that she has been mistaken, seeing that the subject of the impediment has completed carnal copulation with another or with the same person, she reinstates the former marriage and dissolves the subsequent one, although the latter has been contracted with her permission.*

Reply Obj. 1. Although the act of carnal copulation is not essential to marriage, ability to fulfill the act is essential, because marriage

---

* "Nowadays it is seldom necessary to examine too closely into this matter, as all cases arising from it are treated as far as possible under the form of dispensations of non-consummated marriages" (Catholic Encyclopedia, art. *Canonical Impediments*).

gives each of the married parties power over the other's body in relation to marital intercourse.

Reply Obj. 2. Excessive calidity can scarcely be a perpetual impediment. If, however, it were to prove an impediment to marital intercourse for three years it would be adjudged to be perpetual. Nevertheless, since frigidity is a greater and more frequent impediment (for it not only hinders the mingling of seeds but also weakens the members which co-operate in the union of bodies), it is accounted an impediment rather than calidity, since all natural defects are reduced to frigidity.

Reply Obj. 3. Although old people have not sufficient calidity to procreate, they have sufficient to copulate. Wherefore they are allowed to marry, in so far as marriage is intended as a remedy, although it does not befit them as fulfilling an office of nature.

Reply Obj. 4. In all contracts it is agreed on all hands that anyone who is unable to satisfy an obligation is unfit to make a contract which requires the fulfilling of that obligation. Now this inability is of two kinds. First, because a person is unable to fulfill the obligation *de jure,* and such inability renders the contract altogether void, whether the party with whom he contracts knows of this or not. Secondly, because he is unable to fulfill *de facto;* and then if the party with whom he contracts knows of this and, notwithstanding, enters the contract, this shows that the latter seeks some other end from the contract, and the contract stands. But if he does not know of it the contract is void. Consequently frigidity which causes such an impotence that a man cannot *de facto* pay the marriage debt, as also the condition of slavery, whereby a man cannot *de facto* give his service freely, are impediments to marriage, when the one married party does not know that the other is unable to pay the marriage debt. But an impediment whereby a person cannot pay the marriage debt *de jure,* for instance consanguinity, voids the marriage contract, whether the other party knows of it or not. For this reason the Master holds (iv, *Sent.* D. 34) that these two impediments, frigidity and slavery, make it not altogether unlawful for their subjects to marry.

Reply Obj. 5. A man cannot have a perpetual natural impediment in regard to one person and not in regard to another. But if he cannot fulfill the carnal act with a virgin, while he can with one who is not a virgin, the hymeneal membrane may be broken by a medical instrument, and thus he may have connection with her. Nor would this be contrary to nature, for it would be done not for pleasure

but for a remedy. Dislike for a woman is not a natural cause, but an accidental extrinsic cause: and therefore we must form the same judgment in its regard as about spells, of which we shall speak further on (A. 2).

Reply Obj. 6. The male is the agent in procreation, and the female is the patient, wherefore greater calidity is required in the male than in the female for the act of procreation. Hence the frigidity which renders the man impotent would not disable the woman. Yet there may be a natural impediment from another cause, namely stricture, and then we must judge of stricture in the woman in the same way as of frigidity in the man.

SECOND ARTICLE

Whether a Spell Can Be an Impediment to Marriage?

We proceed thus to the Second Article:—

Objection 1. It would seem that a spell cannot be an impediment to marriage. For the spells in question are caused by the operation of demons. But the demons have no more power to prevent the marriage act than other bodily actions; and these they cannot prevent, for thus they would upset the whole world if they hindered eating and walking and the like. Therefore they cannot hinder marriage by spells.

Obj. 2. Further, God's work is stronger than the devil's. But a spell is the work of the devil. Therefore it cannot hinder marriage which is the work of God.

Obj. 3. Further, no impediment, unless it be perpetual, voids the marriage contract. But a spell cannot be a perpetual impediment, for since the devil has no power over others than sinners, the spell will be removed if the sin be cast out, or by another spell, or by the exorcisms of the Church which are employed for the repression of the demon's power. Therefore a spell cannot be an impediment to marriage.

Obj. 4. Further, carnal copulation cannot be hindered, unless there be an impediment to the generative power which is its principle. But the generative power of one man is equally related to all women. Therefore a spell cannot be an impediment in respect of one woman without being so also in respect of all.

On the contrary, It is stated in the Decretals (XXXIII, qu. 1, cap. iv): *If by sorcerers or witches . . .,* and further on, *if they be incurable, they must be separated.*

Further, the demons' power is greater than man's: *There is no power upon earth that can be compared with him who was made to fear no one* (Job xli. 24). Now through the action of man, a person may be rendered incapable of carnal copulation by some power or by castration; and this is an impediment to marriage. Therefore much more can this be done by the power of a demon.

I answer that, Some have asserted that witchcraft is nothing in the world but an imagining of men who ascribed to spells those natural effects the causes of which are hidden. But this is contrary to the authority of holy men who state that the demons have power over men's bodies and imaginations, when God allows them: wherefore by their means wizards can work certain signs. Now this opinion grows from the root of unbelief or incredulity, because they do not believe that demons exist save only in the imagination of the common people, who ascribe to the demon the terrors which a man conjures from his thoughts, and because, owing to a vivid imagination, certain shapes such as he has in his thoughts become apparent to the senses, and then he believes that he sees the demons. But such assertions are rejected by the true faith whereby we believe that angels fell from heaven, and that the demons exist, and that by reason of their subtle nature they are able to do many things which we cannot; and those who induce them to do such things are called wizards.

Wherefore others have maintained that witchcraft can set up an impediment to carnal copulation, but that no such impediment is perpetual: hence it does not void the marriage contract, and they say that the laws asserting this have been revoked. But this is contrary to actual facts and to the new legislation which agrees with the old.

We must therefore draw a distinction: for the inability to copulate caused by witchcraft is either perpetual and then it voids marriage, or it is not perpetual and then it does not void marriage. And in order to put this to practical proof the Church has fixed the space of three years in the same way as we have stated with regard to frigidity (A. 1). There is, however, this difference between a spell and frigidity, that a person who is impotent through frigidity is equally impotent in relation to one as to another, and consequently when the marriage is dissolved, he is not permitted to marry another woman; whereas through witchcraft a man may be rendered impotent in relation to one woman and not to another, and consequently when the Church adjudges the marriage to be dissolved, each party is permitted to seek another partner in marriage.

Reply Obj. 1. The first corruption of sin whereby man became the slave of the devil was transmitted to us by the act of the generative power, and for this reason God allows the devil to exercise his power of witchcraft in this act more than in others. Even so the power

of witchcraft is made manifest in serpents more than in other animals according to Gen. iii, since the devil tempted the woman through a serpent.

Reply Obj. 2. God's work may be hindered by the devil's work with God's permission; not that the devil is stronger than God so as to destroy His works by violence.

Reply Obj. 3. Some spells are so perpetual that they can have no human remedy, although God might afford a remedy by coercing the demon, or the demon by desisting. For, as wizards themselves admit, it does not always follow that what was done by one kind of witchcraft can be destroyed by another kind, and even though it were possible to use witchcraft as a remedy, it would nevertheless be reckoned to be perpetual, since nowise ought one to invoke the demon's help by witchcraft. Again, if the devil has been given power over a person on account of sin, it does not follow that his power ceases with the sin, because the punishment sometimes continues after the fault has been removed. And again, the exorcisms of the Church do not always avail to repress the demons in all their molestations of the body, if God will it so, but they always avail against those assaults of the demons against which they are chiefly instituted.

Reply Obj. 4. Witchcraft sometimes causes an impediment in relation to all, sometimes in relation to one only: because the devil is a voluntary cause not acting from natural necessity. Moreover, the impediment resulting from witchcraft may result from an impression made by the demon on a man's imagination, whereby he is deprived of the concupiscence that moves him in regard to a particular woman and not to another.

THIRD ARTICLE

Whether Madness Is an Impediment to Marriage?

We proceed thus to the Third Article:—

Objection 1. It would seem that madness is not an impediment to marriage. For spiritual marriage which is contracted in Baptism is more excellent than carnal marriage. But mad persons can be baptized. Therefore they can also marry.

Obj. 2. Further, frigidity is an impediment to marriage because it impedes carnal copulation, which is not impeded by madness. Therefore neither is marriage impeded thereby.

Obj. 3. Further, marriage is not voided save by a perpetual impediment. But one cannot tell whether madness is a perpetual impediment. Therefore it does not void marriage.

Obj. 4. Further, the impediments that hinder marriage are sufficiently contained in the verses given above (Q. 50). But they contain no mention of madness. Therefore, etc.

On the contrary, Madness removes the use of reason more than error does. But error is an impediment to marriage. Therefore madness is also.

Further, mad persons are not fit for making contracts. But marriage is a contract. Therefore, etc.

I answer that, The madness is either previous or subsequent to marriage. If subsequent, it nowise voids the marriage, but if it be previous, then the mad person either has lucid intervals, or not. If he has, then although it is not safe for him to marry during that interval, since he would not know how to educate his children, yet if he marries, the marriage is valid. But if he has no lucid intervals, or marries outside a lucid interval, then, since there can be no consent without use of reason, the marriage will be invalid.

Reply Obj. 1. The use of reason is not necessary for Baptism as its cause, in which way it is necessary for matrimony. Hence the comparison fails. We have, however, spoken of the Baptism of mad persons (P. III, Q. 68, A. 12).

Reply Obj. 2. Madness impedes marriage on the part of the latter's cause which is the consent, although not on the part of the act as frigidity does. Yet the Master treats of it together with frigidity, because both are defects of nature (iv, *Sent.* D. 34).

Reply Obj. 3. A passing impediment which hinders the cause of marriage, namely the consent, voids marriage altogether. But an impediment that hinders the act must needs be perpetual in order to void the marriage.

Reply Obj. 4. This impediment is reducible to error, since in either case there is lack of consent on the part of the reason.

FOURTH ARTICLE

Whether Marriage Is Annulled by the Husband Committing Incest with His Wife's Sister?

We proceed thus to the Fourth Article:—

Objection 1. It would seem that marriage is not annulled by the husband committing incest with his wife's sister. For the wife should not be punished for her husband's sin. Yet she would be punished if the marriage were annulled. Therefore, etc.

Obj. 2. Further, it is a greater sin to know one's own relative, than to know the relative of one's wife. But the former sin is not an impediment to marriage. Therefore neither is the second.

Obj. 3. Further, if this is inflicted as a punishment of the sin, it would seem, if the incestuous husband marry even after his wife's death, that they ought to be separated: which is not true.

Obj. 4. Further, this impediment is not mentioned among those enumerated above (Q. 50). Therefore it does not void the marriage contract.

On the contrary, By knowing his wife's sister he contracts affinity, with his wife. But affinity voids the marriage contract. Therefore the aforesaid incest does also.

Further, by whatsoever a man sinneth, by the same also is he punished. Now such a man sins against marriage. Therefore he ought to be punished by being deprived of marriage.

I answer that, If a man has connection with the sister or other relative of his wife before contracting marriage, even after his betrothal, the marriage should be broken off on account of the resultant affinity. If, however, the connection take place after the marriage has been contracted and consummated, the marriage must not be altogether dissolved: but the husband loses his right to marital intercourse, nor can he demand it without sin. And yet he must grant it if asked, because the wife should not be punished for her husband's sin. But after the death of his wife he ought to remain without any hope of marriage, unless he receive a dispensation on account of his frailty, through fear of unlawful intercourse. If, however, he marry without a dispensation, he sins by contravening the law of the Church, but his marriage is not for this reason to be annulled. This suffices for the *Replies* to the *Objections,* for incest is accounted an impediment to marriage not so much for its being a sin as on account of the affinity which it causes. For this reason it is not mentioned with the other impediments, but is included in the impediment of affinity.

FIFTH ARTICLE

Whether Defective Age Is an Impediment to Marriage?

We proceed thus to the Fifth Article:—

Objection 1. It would seem that deficient age is not an impediment to marriage. For according to the laws children are under the care of a guardian until their twenty-fifth year. Therefore it would seem that before that age their reason is not sufficiently mature to give consent, and consequently that ought seemingly to be the age fixed for marrying. Yet marriage can be contracted before that age. Therefore lack of the appointed age is not an impediment to marriage.

Obj. 2. Further, just as the tie of religion is perpetual so is the marriage tie. Now according to the new legislation (cap. *Non Solum,* De regular. et transeunt.) no one can be professed before the fourteenth year of age. Therefore neither could a person marry if defective age were an impediment.

Obj. 3. Further, just as consent is necessary for marriage on the part of the man, so is it on the part of the woman. Now a woman can marry before the age of fourteen. Therefore a man can also.

Obj. 4. Further, inability to copulate, unless it be perpetual and not known, is not an impediment to marriage. But lack of age is neither perpetual nor unknown. Therefore it is not an impediment to marriage.

Obj. 5. Further, it is not included under any of the aforesaid impediments (Q. 50), and consequently would seem not to be an impediment to marriage.

On the contrary, A Decretal (cap. *Quod Sedem,* De frigid. et malefic.) says that *a boy who is incapable of marriage intercourse is unfit to marry* . But in the majority of cases he cannot pay the marriage debt before the age of fourteen *(De Animal.* vii). Therefore, etc.

Further, *There is a fixed limit of size and growth for all things in nature* according to the Philosopher *(De Anima.* ii. 4) : and consequently it would seem that, since marriage is natural, it must have a fixed age by defect of which it is impeded.

I answer that, Since marriage is effected by way of a contract, it comes under the ordinance of positive law like other contracts. Consequently according to law (cap. *Tua,* De sponsal. impub.) it is determined that marriage may not be contracted before the age of discretion when each party is capable of suffi-

cient deliberation about marriage, and of mutual fulfilment of the marriage debt, and that marriages otherwise contracted are void. Now for the most part this age is the fourteenth year in males and the twelfth year in women: but since the ordinances of positive law are consequent upon what happens in the majority of cases, if anyone reach the required perfection before the aforesaid age, so that nature and reason are sufficiently developed to supply the lack of age, the marriage is not annulled. Wherefore if the parties who marry before the age of puberty have marital intercourse before the aforesaid age, their marriage is none the less perpetually indissoluble.

Reply Obj. 1. In matters to which nature inclines there is not required such a development of reason in order to deliberate, as in other matters: and therefore it is possible after deliberation to consent to marriage before one is able to manage one's own affairs in other matters without a guardian.

Reply Obj. 2. The same answer applies, since the religious vow is about matters outside the inclination of nature, and which offer greater difficulty than marriage.

Reply Obj. 3. It is said that woman comes to the age of puberty sooner than man does *(De Animal.* ix) ; hence there is no parallel between the two.

Reply Obj. 4. In this case there is an impediment not only as to inability to copulate, but also on account of the defect of the reason, which is not yet qualified to give rightly that consent which is to endure in perpetuity.

Reply Obj. 5. The impediment arising from defective age, like that which arises from madness, is reducible to the impediment of error; because a man has not yet the full use of his free-will.

QUESTION 59

Of Disparity of Worship As an Impediment to Marriage

(In Six Articles)

WE must now consider disparity of worship as an impediment to marriage. Under this head there are six points of inquiry: (1) Whether a believer can marry an unbeliever? (2) Whether there is marriage between unbelievers? (3) Whether a husband being converted to the faith can remain with his wife if she be unwilling to be converted? (4) Whether he may leave his unbelieving wife? (5) Whether after putting her away he may take another wife? (6) Whether a husband may put aside his wife on account of other sins as he may for unbelief?

FIRST ARTICLE

Whether a Believer Can Marry an Unbeliever?

We proceed thus to the First Article:—

Objection 1. It would seem that a believer can marry an unbeliever. For Joseph married an Egyptian woman, and Esther married Assuerus: and in both marriages there was disparity of worship, since one was an unbeliever and the other a believer. Therefore disparity of worship previous to marriage is not an impediment thereto.

Obj. 2. Further, the Old Law teaches the

same faith as the New. But according to the Old Law there could be marriage between a believer and an unbeliever, as evidenced by Deut. xxi. 10 *seqq.: If thou go out to the fight . . . and seest in the number of the captives a beautiful woman and lovest her, and wilt have her to wife . . . thou shalt go in unto her, and shalt sleep with her, and she shall be thy wife.* Therefore it is lawful also under the New Law.

Obj. 3. Further, betrothal is directed to marriage. Now there can be a betrothal between a believer and an unbeliever in the case where a condition is made of the latter's future conversion. Therefore under the same condition there can be marriage between them.

Obj. 4. Further, every impediment to marriage is in some way contrary to marriage. But unbelief is not contrary to marriage, since marriage fulfills an office of nature whose dictate faith surpasses. Therefore disparity of worship is not an impediment to marriage.

Obj. 5. Further, there is sometime disparity of worship even between two persons who are baptized, for instance when, after Baptism, a person falls into heresy. Yet if such a person marry a believer, it is nevertheless a valid marriage. Therefore disparity of worship is not an impediment to marriage.

On the contrary, It is written (2 Cor. vi. 14): *What concord hath light with darkness?*[*] Now there is the greatest concord between husband and wife. Therefore one who is in the light of faith cannot marry one who is in the darkness of unbelief.

Further, it is written (Mal. ii. 11): *Juda hath profaned the holiness of the Lord, which he loved, and hath married the daughter of a strange god.* But such had not been the case if they could have married validly. Therefore disparity of worship is an impediment to marriage.

I answer that, The chief good of marriage is the offspring to be brought up to the worship of God. Now since education is the work of father and mother in common, each of them intends to bring up the child to the worship of God according to their own faith. Consequently if they be of different faith, the intention of the one will be contrary to the intention of the other, and therefore there cannot be a fitting marriage between them. For this reason disparity of faith previous to marriage is an impediment to the marriage contract.

Reply Obj. 1. In the Old Law it was allowable to marry with certain unbelievers, and forbidden with others. It was however especially forbidden with regard to inhabitants of the land of Canaan, both because the Lord had commanded them to be slain on account of their obstinacy, and because it was fraught

with a greater danger, lest to wit they should pervert to idolatry those whom they married or their children, since the Israelites were more liable to adopt their rites and customs through dwelling among them. But it was permitted in regard to other unbelievers, especially when there could be no fear of their being drawn into idolatry. And thus Joseph, Moses, and Esther married unbelievers. But under the New Law which is spread throughout the whole world the prohibition extends with equal reason to all unbelievers. Hence disparity of worship previous to marriage is an impediment to its being contracted and voids the contract.

Reply Obj. 2. This law either refers to other nations with whom they could lawfully marry, or to the case when the captive woman was willing to be converted to the faith and worship of God.

Reply Obj. 3. Present is related to present in the same way as future to future. Wherefore just as when marriage is contracted in the present, unity of worship is required in both contracting parties, so in the case of a betrothal, which is a promise of future marriage, it suffices to add the condition of future unity of worship.

Reply Obj. 4. It has been made clear that disparity of worship is contrary to marriage in respect of its chief good, which is the good of the offspring.

Reply Obj. 5. Matrimony is a sacrament: and therefore so far as the sacramental essentials are concerned, it requires purity with regard to the sacrament of faith, namely Baptism, rather than with regard to interior faith. For which reason also this impediment is not called disparity of faith, but disparity of worship which concerns outward service, as stated above (iii, *Sent.* D. 9, Q. 1, A. 1, qu. 1). Consequently if a believer marry a baptized heretic, the marriage is valid, although he sins by marrying her if he knows her to be a heretic: even so he would sin were he to marry an excommunicated woman, and yet the marriage would not be void: whereas on the other hand if a catechumen having right faith but not having been baptized were to marry a baptized believer, the marriage would not be valid.

SECOND ARTICLE

Whether There Can Be Marriage between Unbelievers?

We proceed thus to the Second Article:—

Objection 1. It would seem that there can be no marriage between unbelievers. For matrimony is a sacrament of the Church. Now Baptism is the door of the sacraments. There-

[*] Vulg.,—*What fellowship hath light with darkness? And what concord hath Christ with Belial?*

fore unbelievers, since they are not baptized, cannot marry any more than they can receive other sacraments.

Obj. 2. Further, two evils are a greater impediment to good than one. But the unbelief of only one party is an impediment to marriage. Much more, therefore, is the unbelief of both, and consequently there can be no marriage between unbelievers.

Obj. 3. Further, just as there is disparity of worship between believer and unbeliever, so can there be between two unbelievers, for instance if one be a heathen and the other a Jew. Now disparity of worship is an impediment to marriage, as stated above (A. 1). Therefore there can be no valid marriage at least between unbelievers of different worship.

Obj. 4. Further, in marriage there is real chastity. But according to Augustine *(De Adult. Conjug.* i. 18) *there is no real chastity between an unbeliever and his wife,* and these words are quoted XXVIII, qu. i. can. *Sic enim.* Neither therefore is there a true marriage.

Obj. 5. Further, true marriage excuses carnal intercourse from sin. But marriage contracted between unbelievers cannot do this, since *the whole life of unbelievers is a sin,* as a gloss observes on Rom. xiv. 23, *All that is not of faith is sin.* Therefore there is no true marriage between unbelievers.

On the contrary, It is written (1 Cor. vii. 12): *If any brother hath a wife that believeth not, and she consent to dwell with him, let him not put her away.* But she is not called his wife except by reason of marriage. Therefore marriage between unbelievers is a true marriage.

Further, the removal of what comes after does not imply the removal of what comes first. Now marriage belongs to an office of nature, which precedes the state of grace, the principle of which is faith. Therefore unbelief does not prevent the existence of marriage between unbelievers.

I answer that, Marriage was instituted chiefly for the good of the offspring, not only as to its begetting,—since this can be effected even without marriage,—but also as to its advancement to a perfect state, because everything intends naturally to bring its effect to perfection. Now a twofold perfection is to be considered in the offspring. One is the perfection of nature, not only as regards the body but also as regards the soul, by those means which are of the natural law. The other is the perfection of grace: and the former perfection is material and imperfect in relation to the latter. Consequently, since those things which are for the sake of the end are proportionate to the end, the marriage that tends to the first

perfection is imperfect and material in comparison with that which tends to the second perfection. And since the first perfection can be common to unbelievers and believers, while the second belongs only to believers, it follows that between unbelievers there is marriage indeed, but not perfected by its ultimate perfection as there is between believers.

Reply Obj. 1. Marriage was instituted not only as a sacrament, but also as an office of nature. And therefore, although marriage is not competent to unbelievers, as a sacrament dependent on the dispensation of the Church's ministers, it is nevertheless competent to them as fulfilling an office of nature. And yet even a marriage of this kind is a sacrament after the manner of a habit, although it is not actually since they do not marry actually in the faith of the Church.

Reply Obj. 2. Disparity of worship is an impediment to marriage, not by reason of unbelief, but on account of the difference of faith. For disparity of worship hinders not only the second perfection of the offspring, but also the first, since the parents endeavor to draw their children in different directions, which is not the case when both are unbelievers.

Reply Obj. 3. As already stated (*ad* 1) there is marriage between unbelievers, in so far as marriage fulfills an office of nature. Now those things that pertain to the natural law are determinable by positive law; and therefore if any law among unbelievers forbid the contracting of marriage with unbelievers of a different rite, the disparity of worship will be an impediment to their intermarrying. They are not, however, forbidden by Divine law, because before God, however much one may stray from the faith, this makes no difference to one's being removed from grace: nor is it forbidden by any law of the Church who has not to judge of those who are without.

Reply Obj. 4. The chastity and other virtues of unbelievers are said not to be real, because they cannot attain the end of real virtue, which is real happiness. Thus we say it is not a real wine if it has not the effect of wine.

Reply Obj. 5. An unbeliever does not sin in having intercourse with his wife, if he pays her the marriage debt, for the good of the offspring, or for the troth whereby he is bound to her: since this is an act of justice and of temperance which observes the due circumstance in pleasure of touch; even as neither does he sin in performing acts of other civic virtues. Again, the reason why the whole life of unbelievers is said to be a sin is not that they sin in every act, but because they cannot be delivered from the bondage of sin by that which they do.

THIRD ARTICLE

Whether the Husband, Being Converted to the Faith, May Remain with His Wife if She Be Unwilling to Be Converted?

We proceed thus to the Third Article:—

Objection 1. It would seem that when a husband is converted to the faith he cannot remain with his wife who is an unbeliever and is unwilling to be converted, and whom he had married while he was yet an unbeliever. For where the danger is the same one should take the same precautions. Now a believer is forbidden to marry an unbeliever for fear of being turned away from the faith. Since then if the believer remain with the unbeliever whom he had married previously, the danger is the same, in fact greater, for neophytes are more easily perverted than those who have been brought up in the faith, it would seem that a believer, after being converted, cannot remain with an unbeliever.

Obj. 2. Further, *An unbeliever cannot remain united to her who has been received into the Christian faith* (XXVIII, qu. 1 can. *Judæi*). Therefore a believer is bound to put away a wife who does not believe.

Obj. 3. Further, a marriage contracted between believers is more perfect than one contracted between unbelievers. Now, if believers marry within the degrees forbidden by the Church, their marriage is void. Therefore the same applies to unbelievers, and thus a believing husband cannot remain with an unbelieving wife, at any rate, if as an unbeliever he married her within the forbidden degrees.

Obj. 4. Further, sometimes an unbeliever has several wives recognized by his law. If, then, he can remain with those whom he married while yet an unbeliever, it would seem that even after his conversion he can retain several wives.

Obj. 5. Further, it may happen that after divorcing his first wife he has married a second, and that he is converted during this latter marriage. It would seem therefore that at least in this case he cannot remain with this second wife.

On the contrary, The Apostle counsels him to remain (1 Cor. vii. 12).

Further, no impediment that supervenes upon a true marriage dissolves it. Now it was a true marriage when they were both unbelievers. Therefore when one of them is converted, the marriage is not annulled on that account; and thus it would seem that they may lawfully remain together.

I answer that, The faith of a married person does not dissolve but perfects the marriage. Wherefore, since there is true marriage between unbelievers, as stated above (A. 2, *ad* 1).

the marriage tie is not broken by the fact that one of them is converted to the faith, but sometimes while the marriage tie remains, the marriage is dissolved as to cohabitation and marital intercourse, wherein unbelief and adultery are on a par, since both are against the good of the offspring. Consequently, the husband has the same power to put away an unbelieving wife or to remain with her, as he has to put away an adulterous wife or to remain with her. For an innocent husband is free to remain with an adulterous wife in the hope of her amendment, but not if she be obstinate in her sin of adultery, lest he seem to approve of her disgrace; although even if there be hope of her amendment he is free to put her away. In like manner the believer after his conversion may remain with the unbeliever in the hope of her conversion, if he see that she is not obstinate in her unbelief, and he does well in remaining with her, though not bound to do so: and this is what the Apostle counsels (*loc. cit.*).

Reply Obj. 1. It is easier to prevent a thing being done than to undo what is rightly done. Hence there are many things that impede the contracting of marriage if they precede it, which nevertheless cannot dissolve it if they follow it. Such is the case with affinity (Q. 55, A. 6): and it is the same with disparity of worship.

Reply Obj. 2. In the early Church at the time of the apostles, both Jews and Gentiles were everywhere converted to the faith: and consequently the believing husband could then have a reasonable hope for his wife's conversion, even though she did not promise to be converted. Afterwards, however, as time went on the Jews became more obstinate than the Gentiles, because the Gentiles still continued to come to the faith, for instance, at the time of the martyrs, and at the time of Constantine and thereabouts. Wherefore it was not safe then for a believer to cohabit with an unbelieving Jewish wife, nor was there hope for her conversion as for that of a Gentile wife. Consequently, then, the believer could, after his conversion, cohabit with his wife if she were a Gentile, but not if she were a Jewess, unless she promised to be converted. This is the sense of that decree. Now, however, they are on a par, namely Gentiles and Jews, because both are obstinate; and therefore unless the unbelieving wife be willing to be converted, he is not allowed to cohabit with her, be she Gentile or Jew.

Reply Obj. 3. Non-baptized unbelievers are not bound by the laws of the Church, but they are bound by the ordinances of the Divine law. Hence unbelievers who have married within the degrees forbidden by the Divine law, whether both or one of them be converted to the faith, cannot continue in a like marriage. But if they have married within the degrees forbidden by a commandment of the Church, they can remain together if both be converted, or if one be converted and there be hope of the other's conversion.

Reply Obj. 4. To have several wives is contrary to the natural law by which even unbelievers are bound. Wherefore an unbeliever is not truly married save to her whom he married first. Consequently if he be converted with all his wives, he may remain with the first, and must put the others away. If, however, the first refuse to be converted, and one of the others be converted, he has the same right to marry her again as he would have to marry another. We shall treat of this matter further on (A. 5).

Reply Obj. 5. To divorce a wife is contrary to the law of nature, wherefore it is not lawful for an unbeliever to divorce his wife. Hence if he be converted after divorcing one and marrying another, the same judgment is to be pronounced in this case as in the case of a man who had several wives, because if he wish to be converted he is bound to take the first whom he had divorced and to put the other away.

FOURTH ARTICLE

Whether a Believer Can, after His Conversion, Put Away His Unbelieving Wife if She Be Willing to Cohabit with Him Without Insult to the Creator?

We proceed thus to the Fourth Article:—

Objection 1. It would seem that a believer, after his conversion, cannot put away his unbelieving wife if she be willing to cohabit with him without insult to the Creator. For the husband is more bound to his wife than a slave to his master. But a converted slave is not freed from the bond of slavery, as appears from 1 Cor. vii. 21, 1 Tim. vi. 1. Therefore neither can a believing husband put away his unbelieving wife.

Obj. 2. Further, no one may act to another's prejudice without the latter's consent. Now the unbelieving wife had a right in the body of her unbelieving husband. If, then, her husband's conversion to the faith could be prejudicial to the wife, so that he would be free to put her away, the husband could not be converted to the faith without his wife's consent, even as he cannot receive Orders or vow continence without her consent.

Obj. 3. Further, if a man, whether slave or free, knowingly marry a bondwoman, he cannot put her away on account of her different condition. Since, then, the husband, when he married an unbeliever, knew that she was an unbeliever, it would seem that in like man-

ner he cannot put her away on account of her unbelief.

Obj. 4. Further, a father is in duty bound to work for the salvation of his children. But if he were to leave his unbelieving wife, the children of their union would remain with the mother, because *the offspring follows the womb,* and thus their salvation would be imperiled. Therefore he cannot lawfully put away his unbelieving wife.

Obj. 5. Further, an adulterous husband cannot put away an adulterous wife, even after he has done penance for his adultery. Therefore if an adulterous and an unbelieving husband are to be judged alike, neither can the believer put aside the unbeliever, even after his conversion to the faith.

On the contrary, are the words of the Apostle (1 Cor. vii. 15, 16).

Further, spiritual adultery is more grievous than carnal. But a man can put his wife away, as to cohabitation, on account of carnal adultery. Much more, therefore, can he do so on account of unbelief, which is spiritual adultery.

I answer that, Different things are competent and expedient to man according as his life is of one kind or of another. Wherefore he who dies to his former life is not bound to those things to which he was bound in his former life. Hence it is that he who vowed certain things while living in the world is not bound to fulfill them when he dies to the world by adopting the religious life. Now he who is baptized is regenerated in Christ and dies to his former life, since the generation of one thing is the corruption of another, and consequently he is freed from the obligation whereby he was bound to pay his wife the marriage debt, and is not bound to cohabit with her when she is unwilling to be converted, although in a certain case he is free to do so, as stated above (A. 3), just as a religious is free to fulfill the vows he took in the world, if they be not contrary to his religious profession, although he is not bound to do so.

Reply Obj. 1. Bondage is not inconsistent with the perfection of the Christian religion, which makes a very special profession of humility. But the obligation to a wife, or the conjugal bond, is somewhat derogatory to the perfection of Christian life, the highest state of which is in the possession of the continent: hence the comparison fails. Moreover one married party is not bound to the other as the latter's possession, as a slave to his master, but by way of a kind of partnership, which is unfitting between unbeliever and believer as appears from 2 Cor. vi. 15; hence there is no comparison between a slave and a married person.

Reply Obj. 2. The wife had a right in the

body of her husband only as long as he remained in the life wherein he had married, since also when the husband dies the wife *is delivered from the law of her husband* (Rom. vii. 3). Wherefore if the husband leave her after he has changed his life by dying to his former life, this is nowise prejudicial to her. Now he who goes over to the religious life dies but a spiritual death and not a bodily death. Wherefore if the marriage be consummated, the husband cannot enter religion without his wife's consent, whereas he can before carnal connection when there is only a spiritual connection. On the other hand, he who is baptized is even corporeally buried together with Christ unto death; and therefore he is freed from paying the marriage debt even after the marriage has been consummated.

We may also reply that it is through her own fault in refusing to be converted that the wife suffers prejudice.

Reply Obj. 3. Disparity of worship makes a person simply unfit for lawful marriage, whereas the condition of bondage does not, but only where it is unknown. Hence there is no comparison between an unbeliever and a bondswoman.

Reply Obj. 4. Either the child has reached a perfect age, and then it is free to follow either the believing father or the unbelieving mother, or else it is under age, and then it should be given to the believer notwithstanding that it needs the mother's care for its education.

Reply Obj. 5. By doing penance the adulterer does not enter another life as an unbeliever by being baptized. Hence the comparison fails.

FIFTH ARTICLE

Whether the Believer Who Leaves His Unbelieving Wife Can Take Another Wife?

We proceed thus to the Fifth Article:—

Objection 1. It would seem that the believer who leaves his unbelieving wife cannot take another wife. For indissolubility is of the nature of marriage, since it is contrary to the natural law to divorce one's wife. Now there was true marriage between them as unbelievers. Therefore their marriage can nowise be dissolved. But as long as a man is bound by marriage to one woman he cannot marry another. Therefore a believer who leaves his unbelieving wife cannot take another wife.

Obj. 2. Further, a crime subsequent to marriage does not dissolve the marriage. Now, if the wife be willing to cohabit without insult to the Creator, the marriage tie is not dissolved, since the husband cannot marry another. Therefore the sin of the wife who

refuses to cohabit without insult to the Creator does not dissolve the marriage so that her husband be free to take another wife.

Obj. 3. Further, husband and wife are equal in the marriage tie. Since, then, it is unlawful for the unbelieving wife to marry again while her husband lives, it would seem that neither can the believing husband do so.

Obj. 4. Further, the vow of continence is more favorable than the marriage contract. Now seemingly it is not lawful for the believing husband to take a vow of continence without the consent of his unbelieving wife, since then the latter would be deprived of marriage if she were afterwards converted. Much less therefore is it lawful for him to take another wife.

Obj. 5. Further, the son who persists in unbelief after his father's conversion loses the right to inherit from his father: and yet if he be afterwards converted, the inheritance is restored to him even though another should have entered into possession thereof. Therefore it would seem that in like manner, if the unbelieving wife be converted, her husband ought to be restored to her even though he should have married another wife: yet this would be impossible if the second marriage were valid. Therefore he cannot take another wife.

On the contrary, Matrimony is not ratified without the sacrament of Baptism. Now what is not ratified can be annulled. Therefore marriage contracted in unbelief can be annulled, and consequently, the marriage tie being dissolved, it is lawful for the husband to take another wife.

Further, a husband ought not to cohabit with an unbelieving wife who refuses to cohabit without insult to the Creator. If therefore it were unlawful for him to take another wife he would be forced to remain continent, which would seem unreasonable, since then he would be at a disadvantage through his conversion.

I answer that, When either husband or wife is converted to the faith the other remaining in unbelief, a distinction must be made. For if the unbeliever be willing to cohabit without insult to the Creator—that is without drawing the other to unbelief—the believer is free to part from the other, but by parting is not permitted to marry again. But if the unbeliever refuse to cohabit without insult to the Creator, by making use of blasphemous words and refusing to hear Christ's name, then if she strive to draw him to unbelief, the believing husband after parting from her may be united to another in marriage.

Reply Obj. 1. As stated above (A. 2), the marriage of unbelievers is imperfect, whereas the marriage of believers is perfect and consequently binds more firmly. Now the firmer tie always looses the weaker if it is contrary to it, and therefore the subsequent marriage contracted in the faith of Christ dissolves the marriage previously contracted in unbelief. Therefore the marriage of unbelievers is not altogether firm and ratified, but is ratified afterwards by Christ's faith.

Reply Obj. 2. The sin of the wife who refuses to cohabit without insult to the Creator frees the husband from the tie whereby he was bound to his wife so as to be unable to marry again during her lifetime. It does not however dissolve the marriage at once, since if she were converted from her blasphemy before he married again, her husband would be restored to her. But the marriage is dissolved by the second marriage which the believing husband would be unable to accomplish unless he were freed from his obligation to his wife by her own fault.

Reply Obj. 3. After the believer has married, the marriage tie is dissolved on either side, because the marriage is not imperfect as to the bond, although it is sometimes imperfect as to its effect. Hence it is in punishment of the unbelieving wife rather than by virtue of the previous marriage that she is forbidden to marry again. If however she be afterwards converted, she may be allowed by dispensation to take another husband, should her husband have taken another wife.

Reply Obj. 4. The husband ought not to take a vow of continence nor enter into a second marriage, if after his conversion there be a reasonable hope of the conversion of his wife, because the wife's conversion would be more difficult if she knew she was deprived of her husband. If however there be no hope of her conversion, he can take Holy Orders or enter religion, having first besought his wife to be converted. And then if the wife be converted after her husband has received Holy Orders, her husband must not be restored to her, but she must take it as a punishment of her tardy conversion that she is deprived of her husband.

Reply Obj. 5. The bond of fatherhood is not dissolved by disparity of worship, as the marriage bond is: wherefore there is no comparison between an inheritance and a wife.

SIXTH ARTICLE

Whether Other Sins Dissolve Marriage?

We proceed thus to the Sixth Article:—

Objection 1. It would seem that other sins besides unbelief dissolve marriage. For adultery is seemingly more directly opposed to marriage than unbelief is. But unbelief dissolves marriage in a certain case so that it is lawful to marry again. Therefore adultery has the same effect.

Obj. 2. Further, just as unbelief is spiritual fornication, so is any kind of sin. If, then, unbelief dissolves marriage because it is spiritual fornication, for the same reason any kind of sin will dissolve marriage.

Obj. 3. Further, it is said (Matth. v. 30): *If thy right hand scandalize thee, pluck it off, and cast it from thee,* and a gloss of Jerome says that *by the hand and the right eye we may understand our brother, wife, relatives and children.* Now these become obstacles to us by any kind of sin. Therefore marriage can be dissolved on account of any kind of sin.

Obj. 4. Further, covetousness is idolatry according to Eph. v. 5. Now a wife may be put away on account of idolatry. Therefore in like manner she can be put away on account of covetousness, as also on account of other sins graver than covetousness.

Obj. 5. Further, the Master says this expressly (iv, *Sent.* D. 30).

On the contrary, It is said (Matth. v. 32): *Whosoever shall put away his wife, excepting for the cause of fornication, maketh her to commit adultery.*

Further, if this were true, divorces would be made all day long, since it is rare to find a marriage wherein one of the parties does not fall into sin.

I answer that, Bodily fornication and unbelief have a special contrariety to the goods of marriage, as stated above (A. 3). Hence they are specially effective in dissolving marriages. Nevertheless it must be observed that marriage is dissolved in two ways. In one way as to the marriage tie, and thus marriage cannot be dissolved after it is ratified, neither by unbelief nor by adultery. But if it be not ratified, the tie is dissolved, if the one party remain in unbelief, and the other being converted to the faith has married again. On the other hand the aforesaid tie is not dissolved by adultery, else the unbeliever would be free to give a bill of divorce to his adulterous wife, and having put her away, could take another wife, which is false. In another way marriage is dissolved as to the act, and thus it can be dissolved on account of either unbelief or fornication. But marriage cannot be dissolved even as to the act on account of other sins, unless perchance the husband wish to cease from intercourse with his wife in order to punish her by depriving her of the comfort of his presence.

Reply Obj. 1. Although adultery is opposed to marriage as fulfilling an office of nature, more directly than unbelief, it is the other way about if we consider marriage as a sacrament of the Church, from which source it derives perfect stability, inasmuch as it signifies the indissoluble union of Christ with the Church. Wherefore the marriage that is not ratified can be dissolved as to the marriage tie on account of unbelief rather than on account of adultery.

Reply Obj. 2. The primal union of the soul to God is by faith, and consequently the soul is thereby espoused to God as it were, according to Osee ii. 20, *I will espouse thee to Me in faith.* Hence in Holy Writ idolatry and unbelief are specially designated by the name of fornication: whereas other sins are called spiritual fornications by a more remote signification.

Reply Obj. 3. This applies to the case when the wife proves a notable occasion of sin to her husband, so that he has reason to fear his being in danger: for then the husband can withdraw from living with her, as stated above (A. 5).

Reply Obj. 4. Covetousness is said to be idolatry on account of a certain likeness of bondage, because both the covetous and the idolater serve the creature rather than the Creator; but not on account of likeness of unbelief, since unbelief corrupts the intellect whereas covetousness corrupts the affections.

Reply Obj. 5. The words of the Master refer to betrothal, because a betrothal can be rescinded on account of a subsequent crime. Or, if he is speaking of marriage, they must be referred to the severing of mutual companionship for a time, as stated above, or to the case when the wife is unwilling to cohabit except on the condition of sinning, for instance if she were to say: *I will not remain your wife unless you amass wealth for me by theft,* for then he ought to leave her rather than thieve.

QUESTION 60

Of Wife-Murder

(In Two Articles)

WE must now consider wife-murder, under which head there are two points of inquiry: (1) Whether in a certain case it is lawful to kill one's wife? (2) Whether wife-murder is an impediment to marriage?

FIRST ARTICLE

Whether It Is Lawful for a Man to Kill His Wife if She Be Discovered in the Act of Adultery?

We proceed thus to the First Article:—

Objection 1. It would seem lawful for a man to kill his wife if she be discovered in the act of adultery. For the Divine law commanded adulterous wives to be stoned. Now it is not a sin to fulfill the Divine law. Neither therefore is it a sin to kill one's own wife if she be an adulteress.

Obj. 2. Further, that which the law can rightly do, can be rightly done by one whom the law has commissioned to do it. But the law can rightly kill an adulterous wife or any other person deserving of death. Since then the law has commissioned the husband to kill his wife if she be discovered in the act of adultery, it would seem that he can rightly do so.

Obj. 3. Further, the husband has greater power over his adulterous wife than over the man who committed adultery with her. Now if the husband strike a cleric whom he found with his wife he is not excommunicated. Therefore it would seem lawful for him even to kill his own wife if she be discovered in adultery.

Obj. 4. Further, the husband is bound to correct his wife. But correction is given by inflicting a just punishment. Since then the just punishment of adultery is death, because it is a capital sin, it would seem lawful for a husband to kill his adulterous wife.

On the contrary, It is stated in the text (iv, *Sent.* D. 37) that *the Church of God is never bound by the laws of this world, for she has none but a spiritual sword.* Therefore it would seem that he who wishes to belong to the Church cannot rightly take advantage of the law which permits a man to kill his wife.

Further, husband and wife are judged on a par. But it is not lawful for a wife to kill her husband if he be discovered in adultery. Neither therefore may a husband kill his wife.

I answer that, It happens in two ways that a husband kills his wife. First, by a civil judgment; and thus there is no doubt that a husband, moved by zeal for justice and not by vindictive anger or hatred can, without sin, bring a criminal accusation of adultery upon his wife before a secular court, and demand that she receive capital punishment as appointed by the law; just as it is lawful to accuse a person of murder or any other crime. Such an accusation however cannot be made in an ecclesiastical court, because, as stated in the text (*loc. cit.*), the Church does not wield a material sword. Secondly, a husband can kill his wife himself without her being convicted in court, and thus to kill her outside of the act of adultery is not lawful, neither according to civil law nor according to the law of conscience, whatever evidence he may have of her adultery. The civil law however considers it, as though it were lawful, that he should kill her in the very act, not by commanding him to do so, but by not inflicting on him the punishment for murder, on account of the very great provocation which the husband receives by such a deed to kill his wife. But the Church is not bound in this matter by human laws, neither does she acquit him of the debt of eternal punishment, nor of such punishment as may be awarded him by an ecclesiastical tribunal for the reason that he is quit of any punishment to be inflicted by a secular court. Therefore in no case is it lawful for a husband to kill his wife on his own authority.

Reply Obj. 1. The law has committed the infliction of this punishment not to private individuals, but to public persons, who are deputed to this by their office. Now the husband is not his wife's judge: wherefore he may not kill her, but may accuse her in the judge's presence.

Reply Obj. 2. The civil law has not commissioned the husband to kill his wife by commanding him to do so, for thus he would not sin, just as the judge's deputy does not sin by killing the thief condemned to death: but it has permitted this by not punishing it. For which reason it has raised certain obstacles to prevent the husband from killing his wife.

Reply Obj. 3. This does not prove that it is lawful simply, but that it is lawful as regards immunity from a particular kind of punishment, since excommunication is also a kind of punishment.

Reply Obj. 4. There are two kinds of community: the household, such as a family; and the civil community, such as a city or kingdom. Accordingly, he who presides over the latter kind of community, a king for instance, can punish an individual both by correcting and by exterminating him, for the betterment of the community with whose care he is charged. But he who presides over a community of the first kind, can inflict only corrective punishment, which does not extend beyond the limits of amendment, and these are exceeded by the punishment of death. Wherefore the husband who exercises this kind of control over his wife may not kill her, but he may accuse or chastise her in some other way.

SECOND ARTICLE

Whether Wife-Murder Is an Impediment to Marriage?

We proceed thus to the Second Article:—
Objection 1. It would seem that wife-murder is not an impediment to marriage. For adultery is more directly opposed to marriage than murder is. Now adultery is not an impediment to marriage. Neither therefore is wife-murder.

Obj. 2. Further, it is a more grievous sin to kill one's mother than one's wife, for it is never lawful to strike one's mother, whereas it is sometimes lawful to strike one's wife. But matricide is not an impediment to marriage. Neither therefore is wife-murder.

Obj. 3. Further, it is a greater sin for a man to kill another man's wife on account of adultery than to kill his own wife, inasmuch as he has less motive and is less concerned with her correction. But he who kills another man's wife is not hindered from marrying. Neither therefore is he who kills his own wife.

Obj. 4. Further, if the cause be removed, the effect is removed. But the sin of murder can be removed by repentance. Therefore the consequent impediment to marriage can be removed also: and consequently it would seem that after he has done penance he is not forbidden to marry.

On the contrary, A canon (caus. xxxiii, qu. ii, can. *Interfectores*) says: *The slayers of their own wives must be brought back to penance, and they are absolutely forbidden to marry.* Further, in whatsoever a man sins, in that same must he be punished. But he who kills his wife sins against marriage. Therefore he must be punished by being deprived of marriage.

I answer that, By the Church's decree wife-murder is an impediment to marriage. Sometimes however it forbids the contracting of marriage without voiding the contract, when to wit the husband kills his wife on account of adultery or even through hatred; nevertheless if there be fear lest he should prove incontinent, he may be dispensed by the Church so as to marry lawfully. Sometimes it also voids the contract, as when a man kills his wife in order to marry her with whom he has committed adultery, for then the law declares him simply unfit to marry her, so that if he actually marry her his marriage is void. He is not however hereby rendered simply unfit by law in relation to other women: wherefore if he should have married another, although he sin by disobeying the Church's ordinance, the marriage is nevertheless not voided for this reason.

Reply Obj. 1. Murder and adultery in certain cases forbid the contracting of marriage and void the contract, as we say here in regard to wife-murder, and shall say further on (iv, *Sent.* Q. 62, A. 2) in regard to adultery. We may also reply that wife-murder is contrary to the substance of wedlock, whereas adultery is contrary to the good of fidelity due to marriage. Hence adultery is not more opposed to marriage than wife-murder, and the argument is based on a false premiss.

Reply Obj. 2. Simply speaking it is a more grievous sin to kill one's mother than one's wife, as also more opposed to nature, since a man reveres his mother naturally. Consequently he is less inclined to matricide and more prone to wife-murder; and it is to repress this proneness that the Church has forbidden marriage to the man who has murdered his wife.

Reply Obj. 3. Such a man does not sin against marriage as he does who kills his own wife; wherefore the comparison fails.

Reply Obj. 4. It does not follow that because guilt has been remitted therefore the entire punishment is remitted, as evidenced by irregularity. For repentance does not restore a man to his former dignity, although it can restore him to his former state of grace, as stated above (Q. 38, A. 1, *ad* 3).

QUESTION 61

Of the Impediment to Marriage, Arising from a Solemn Vow

(In Three Articles)

WE must next consider the impediments which supervene to marriage. We shall consider (1) the impediment which affects an unconsummated marriage, namely a solemn vow: (2) the impediment which affects a consummated marriage, namely fornication. Under the first head there are three points of inquiry: (1) Whether either party after the marriage has been consummated can enter religion without the other's consent? (2) Whether they can enter religion before the consummation of the marriage? (3) Whether the wife can take another husband if her former husband has entered religion before the consummation of the marriage?

FIRST ARTICLE

Whether One Party after the Marriage Has Been Consummated Can Enter Religion without the Other's Consent?

We proceed thus to the First Article:—

Objection 1. It would seem that even after the marriage has been consummated one consort can enter religion without the other's consent. For the Divine law ought to be more favorable to spiritual things than human law. Now human law has allowed this. Therefore much more should the Divine law permit it.

Obj. 2. Further, the lesser good does not hinder the greater. But the married state is a lesser good than the religious state, according to 1 Cor. vii. 38. Therefore marriage ought not to hinder a man from being able to enter religion.

Obj. 3. Further, in every form of religious life there is a kind of spiritual marriage. Now it is lawful to pass from a less strict religious order to one that is stricter. Therefore it is also allowable to pass from a less strict—namely a carnal—marriage to a stricter marriage, namely that of the religious life, even without the wife's consent.

On the contrary, Married persons are forbidden (1 Cor. vii. 5) to abstain from the use of marriage even for a time without one another's consent, in order to have time for prayer.

Further, no one can lawfully do that which is prejudicial to another without the latter's consent. Now the religious vow taken by one consort is prejudicial to the other, since the one has power over the other's body. Therefore one of them cannot take a religious vow without the other's consent.

I answer that, No one can make an offering to God of what belongs to another. Wherefore since by a consummated marriage the husband's body already belongs to his wife, he cannot by a vow of continence offer it to God without her consent.

Reply Obj. 1. Human law considers marriage merely as fulfilling an office of nature: whereas the Divine law considers it as a sacrament, by reason of which it is altogether indissoluble. Hence the comparison fails.

Reply Obj. 2. It is not unreasonable that a greater good be hindered by a lesser which is contrary to it, just as good is hindered by evil.

Reply Obj. 3. In every form of religious life marriage is contracted with one person, namely Christ; to Whom, however, a person contracts more obligations in one religious order than in another. But in carnal marriage and religious marriage the contract is not with the same person: wherefore the comparison fails.

SECOND ARTICLE

Whether before the Marriage Has Been Consummated One Consort Can Enter Religion without the Other's Consent?

We proceed thus to the Second Article:—

Objection 1. It would seem that even before the marriage has been consummated one consort cannot enter religion without the other's consent. For the indissolubility of marriage belongs to the sacrament of matrimony, inasmuch, namely, as it signifies the union of Christ with the Church. Now marriage is a true sacrament before its consummation, and after consent has been expressed in words of the present. Therefore it cannot be dissolved by one of them entering religion.

Obj. 2. Further, by virtue of the consent expressed in words of the present, the one consort has given power over his body to the other. Therefore the one can forthwith ask for the marriage debt, and the other is bound to pay: and so the one cannot enter religion without the other's consent.

Obj. 3. Further, it is said (Matth. xix. 6): *What God hath joined together let no man put asunder.* But the union which precedes marital intercourse was made by God. Therefore it cannot be dissolved by the will of man.

On the contrary, According to Jerome* our Lord called John from his wedding.

I answer that, Before marital intercourse there is only a spiritual bond between husband and wife, but afterwards there is a carnal bond between them. Wherefore, just as after marital intercourse marriage is dissolved by carnal death, so by entering religion the bond which exists before the consummation of the marriage is dissolved, because religious life is a kind of spiritual death, whereby a man dies to the world and lives to God.

Reply Obj. 1. Before consummation marriage signifies the union of Christ with the soul by grace, which is dissolved by a contrary spiritual disposition, namely mortal sin. But after consummation it signifies the union of Christ with the Church, as regards the assumption of human nature into the unity of person, which union is altogether indissoluble.

Reply Obj. 2. Before consummation the body of one consort is not absolutely delivered into the power of the other, but conditionally, provided neither consort meanwhile seek the fruit of a better life. But by marital intercourse the aforesaid delivery is completed, because then each of them enters into bodily possession of the power transferred to him. Wherefore also before consummation they are not bound to pay the marriage debt forthwith after contracting marriage by words of the present, but a space of two months is allowed them for three reasons. First that they may deliberate meanwhile about entering religion; secondly, to prepare what is necessary for the solemnization of the wedding; thirdly, lest the husband think little of a gift he has not longed to possess (cap. *Institutum,* caus. xxvi, qu. ii).

* *Prolog. in Joan.*

Reply Obj. 3. The marriage union, before consummation, is indeed perfect as to its primary being, but is not finally perfect as to its second act which is operation. It is like bodily possession and consequently is not altogether indissoluble.

THIRD ARTICLE

Whether the Wife May Take Another Husband If Her Husband Has Entered Religion before the Consummation of the Marriage?

We proceed thus to the Third Article:—

Objection 1. It would seem that the wife may not take another husband, if her husband has entered religion before the consummation of the marriage. For that which is consistent with marriage does not dissolve the marriage tie. Now the marriage tie still remains between those who equally take religious vows. Therefore by the fact that one enters religion, the other is not freed from the marriage tie. But as long as she remains tied to one by marriage, she cannot marry another. Therefore, etc.

Obj. 2. Further, after entering religion and before making his profession the husband can return to the world. If then the wife can marry again when her husband enters religion, he also can marry again when he returns to the world: which is absurd.

Obj. 3. Further, by a new decree (cap. *Non solum,* de regular. et transeunt.) a profession, if made before the expiry of a year, is accounted void. Therefore if he return to his wife after making such a profession, she is bound to receive him. Therefore neither by her husband's entry into religion, nor by his taking a vow, does the wife receive the power to marry again.

On the contrary, No one can bind another to those things which belong to perfection. Now continence is of those things that belong to perfection. Therefore a wife is not bound to continence on account of her husband entering religion, and consequently she can marry.

I answer that, Just as bodily death of the husband dissolves the marriage tie in such a way that the wife may marry whom she will, according to the statement of the Apostle (1 Cor. vii. 39); so too after the husband's spiritual death by entering religion, she can marry whom she will.

Reply Obj. 1. When both consorts take a like vow of continence, neither renounces the marriage tie, wherefore it still remains: but when only one takes the vow, then for his own part he renounces the marriage tie, wherefore the other is freed therefrom.

Reply Obj. 2. A person is not accounted dead to the world by entering religion until he makes his profession, and consequently his wife is bound to wait for him until that time.

Reply Obj. 3. We must judge of a profession thus made before the time fixed by law, as of a simple vow. Wherefore just as when the husband has taken a simple vow his wife is not bound to pay him the marriage debt, and yet has not the power to marry again, so is it in this case.

QUESTION 62

Of the Impediment That Supervenes to Marriage after Its Consummation, Namely Fornication

(In Six Articles)

WE must now consider the impediment that supervenes upon marriage after its consummation, namely fornication, which is an impediment to a previous marriage as regards the act, although the marriage tie remains. Under this head there are six points of inquiry: (1) Whether it is lawful for a husband to put his wife away on account of fornication? (2) Whether he is bound to do so? (3) Whether he may put her away at his own judgment? (4) Whether in this matter husband and wife are of equal condition? (5) Whether, after being divorced, they must remain unmarried? (6) Whether they can be reconciled after being divorced?

FIRST ARTICLE

Whether It Is Lawful for a Husband to Put away His Wife on Account of Fornication?

We proceed thus to the First Article:—

Objection 1. It would seem unlawful for a husband to put away his wife on account of fornication. For we must not return evil for evil. But the husband, by putting away his wife on account of fornication, seemingly returns evil for evil. Therefore this is not lawful.

Obj. 2. Further, the sin is greater if both commit fornication, than if one only commits it. But if both commit fornication, they cannot be divorced on that account. Neither therefore can they be, if only one commits fornication.

Obj. 3. Further, spiritual fornication and certain other sins are more grievous than carnal fornication. But separation from bed cannot be motived by those sins. Neither therefore can it be done on account of fornication.

Obj. 4. Further, the unnatural vice is further removed from the marriage goods than fornication is, the manner of which is natural. Therefore it ought to have been a cause of separation rather than fornication.

On the contrary, are the words of Matth. v. 32.

Further, one is not bound to keep faith with one who breaks his faith. But a spouse by fornication breaks the faith due to the other spouse. Therefore one can put the other away on account of fornication.

I answer that, Our Lord permitted a man to put away his wife on account of fornication, in punishment of the unfaithful party and in favor of the faithful party, so that the latter is not bound to marital intercourse with the unfaithful one. There are however seven cases to be excepted in which it is not lawful to put away a wife who has committed fornication, when either the wife is not to be blamed, or both parties are equally blameworthy. The first is if the husband also has committed fornication; the second is if he has prostituted his wife; the third is if the wife, believing her husband dead on account of his long absence, has married again; the fourth is if another man has fraudulently impersonated her husband in the marriage-bed; the fifth is if she be overcome by force; the sixth is if he has been reconciled to her by having carnal intercourse with her after she has committed adultery; the seventh is if both having been married in the state of unbelief, the husband has given his wife a bill of divorce and she has married again; for then if both be converted the husband is bound to receive her back again.

Reply Obj. 1. A husband sins if through vindictive anger he puts away his wife who has committed fornication, but he does not sin if he does so in order to avoid losing his good name, lest he seem to share in her guilt, or in order to correct his wife's sin, or in order to avoid the uncertainty of her offspring.

Reply Obj. 2. Divorce on account of fornication is effected by the one accusing the other. And since no one can accuse who is guilty of the same crime, a divorce cannot be pronounced when both have committed fornication, although marriage is more sinned against when both are guilty of fornication that when only one is.

Reply Obj. 3. Fornication is directly opposed to the good of marriage, since by it the certainty of offspring is destroyed, faith is broken, and marriage ceases to have its signification when the body of one spouse is given to several others. Wherefore other sins, though perhaps they be more grievous than fornication, are not motives for a divorce. Since, however, unbelief which is called spiritual fornication, is also opposed to the good of marriage consisting in the rearing of the offspring to the worship of God, it is also a motive for divorce, yet not in the same way as bodily fornication. Because one may take steps for procuring a divorce on account of one act of carnal fornication, not, however, on account of one act of unbelief, but on account of inveterate unbelief which is a proof of obstinacy wherein unbelief is perfected.

Reply Obj. 4. Steps may be taken to procure a divorce on account also of the unnatural vice: but this is not mentioned in the same way, both because it is an unmentionable passion, and because it does not so affect the certainty of offspring.

SECOND ARTICLE

Whether the Husband Is Bound by Precept to Put Away His Wife When She Is Guilty of Fornication?

We proceed thus to the Second Article:—

Objection 1. It would seem that the husband is bound by precept to put away his wife who is guilty of fornication. For since the husband is the head of his wife, he is bound to correct his wife. Now separation from bed is prescribed as a correction of the wife who is guilty of fornication. Therefore he is bound to separate from her.

Obj. 2. Further, he who consents with one who sins mortally, is also guilty of mortal sin. Now the husband who retains a wife guilty of fornication would seem to consent with her, as stated in the text (iv, *Sent.* D. 35). Therefore he sins unless he puts her away.

Obj. 3. Further, it is written (1 Cor. vi. 16): *He who is joined to a harlot is made one body:* Now a man cannot at once be a member of a harlot and a member of Christ *(ibid.* 15). Therefore the husband who is joined to a wife guilty of fornication ceases to be a member of Christ, and therefore sins mortally.

Obj. 4. Further, just as relationship voids the marriage tie, so does fornication dissolve the marriage-bed. Now after the husband becomes cognizant of his consanguinity with his wife, he sins mortally if he has carnal intercourse with her. Therefore he also sins mortally if he does so after knowing her to be guilty of fornication.

Obj. 5. *On the contrary,* A gloss on 1 Cor. vii. 11, *Let not the husband put away his wife,* says that *Our Lord permitted a wife to be put away on account of fornication.* Therefore it is not a matter of precept.

Obj. 6. Further, one can always pardon the sin that another has committed against oneself. Now the wife, by committing fornication, sinned against her husband. Therefore the husband may spare her by not putting her away.

I answer that, The putting away of a wife guilty of fornication was prescribed in order that the wife might be corrected by means of that punishment. Now a corrective punishment is not required when amendment has already taken place. Wherefore, if the wife repent of her sin, her husband is not bound to put her away: whereas if she repent not, he is bound to do so, lest he seem to consent to her sin, by not having recourse to her due correction.

Reply Obj. 1. The wife can be corrected for her sin of fornication not only by this punishment but also by words and blows; wherefore if she be ready to be corrected otherwise, her husband is not bound to have recourse to the aforesaid punishment in order to correct her.

Reply Obj. 2. The husband seems to consent with her when he retains her, notwithstanding that she persists in her past sin: if, however, she has mended her ways, he does not consent with her.

Reply Obj. 3. She can no longer be called a harlot since she has repented of her sin. Wherefore her husband, by being joined to her, does not become a member of a harlot. We might also reply that he is joined to her not as a harlot but as his wife.

Reply Obj. 4. There is no parallel, because the effect of consanguinity is that there is no marriage tie between them, so that carnal intercourse between them becomes unlawful. Whereas fornication does not remove the said tie, so that the act remains, in itself, lawful, unless it become accidentally unlawful, in so far as the husband seems to consent to his wife's lewdness.

Reply Obj. 5. This permission is to be understood as an absence of prohibition: and thus it is not in contradistinction with a precept, for that which is a matter of precept is also not forbidden.

Reply Obj. 6. The wife sins not only against her husband, but also against herself and against God, wherefore her husband cannot entirely remit the punishment, unless amendment has followed.

THIRD ARTICLE

Whether the Husband Can on His Own Judgment Put Away His Wife on Account of Fornication?

We proceed thus to the Third Article:—

Objection 1. It would seem that the husband can on his own judgment put away his wife on account of fornication. For when sentence has been pronounced by the judge, it is lawful to carry it out without any further judgment. But God, the just Judge, has pronounced this judgment, that a husband may put his wife away on account of fornication. Therefore no further judgment is required for this.

Obj. 2. Further, it is stated (Matth. i. 19) that Joseph . . . being a just man . . . *was minded to put* Mary *away privately.* Therefore it would seem that a husband may privately pronounce a divorce without the judgment of the Church.

Obj. 3. Further, if after becoming cognizant of his wife's fornication a husband has marital intercourse with his wife, he forfeits the action which he had against the adulteress. Therefore the refusal of the marriage debt, which pertains to a divorce, ought to precede the judgment of the Church.

Obj. 4. Further, that which cannot be proved ought not to be submitted to the judgment of the Church. Now the crime of fornication cannot be proved, since *the eye of the adulterer observeth darkness* (Job xxiv. 15). Therefore the divorce in question ought not to be made on the judgment of the Church.

Obj. 5. Further, accusation should be preceded by inscription,* whereby a person binds himself under the pain of retaliation, if he fails to bring proof. But this is impossible in this matter, because then, in every event the husband would obtain his end, whether he put his wife away, or his wife put him away. Therefore she ought not to be summoned by accusation to receive the judgment of the Church.

Obj. 6. Further, a man is more bound to his wife than to a stranger. Now a man ought not to refer to the Church the crime of another, even though he be a stranger, without previously admonishing him privately (Matth. xviii. 15). Much less therefore may the husband bring his wife's crime before the Church, unless he has previously rebuked her in private.

On the contrary, No one should avenge himself. But if a husband were by his own judgment to put away his wife on account of fornication, he would avenge himself. Therefore this should not be done.

Further, no man is prosecutor and judge in the same cause. But the husband is the prosecutor by suing his wife for the offense she has committed against him. Therefore he cannot be the judge, and consequently he cannot put her away on his own judgment.

I answer that, A husband can put away his wife in two ways. First as to bed only, and thus he may put her away on his own

judgment, as soon as he has evidence of her fornication: nor is he bound to pay her the marriage debt at her demand, unless he be compelled by the Church, and by paying it thus he nowise prejudices his own case. Secondly, as to bed and board, and in this way she cannot be put away except at the judgment of the Church; and if she has been put away otherwise, he must be compelled to cohabit with her unless the husband can at once prove the wife's fornication. Now this putting away is called a divorce: and consequently it must be admitted that a divorce cannot be pronounced except at the judgment of the Church.

Reply Obj. 1. The sentence is an application of the general law to a particular fact. Wherefore God gave out the law according to which the sentence of the court has to be pronounced.

Reply Obj. 2. Joseph was minded to put away the Blessed Virgin not as suspected of fornication, but because in reverence for her sanctity, he feared to cohabit with her. Moreover there is no parallel, because then the sentence at law was not only divorce but also stoning, but not now when the case is brought to the Church for judgment. The *Reply* to the *Third Objection* is clear from what has been said.

Reply Obj. 4. Sometimes when the husband suspects his wife of adultery he watches her secretly that together with witnesses he may discover her in the sin of fornication, and so proceed to accusation. Moreover, if he has no evidence of the fact, there may be strong suspicions of fornication, which suspicions being proved the fornication seems to be proved: for instance if they be found together alone, at a time and place which are open to suspicion, or *nudas cum nuda.*

Reply Obj. 5. A husband may accuse his wife of adultery in two ways. First, he may seek a separation from bed before a spiritual judge, and then there is no need for an inscription to be made under the pain of retaliation, since thus the husband would gain his end, as the objection proves. Secondly, he may seek for the crime to be punished in a secular court, and then it is necessary for inscription* to precede, whereby he binds himself under pain of retaliation if he fail to prove his case.

Reply Obj. 6. According to a Decretal (Extra, De Simonia, cap. *Licet),* there are *three modes of procedure in criminal cases. First, by inquisition, which should be preceded by notoriety; secondly, by accusation, which should be preceded by inscription,* thirdly, by denunciation, which should be preceded by fraternal correction.* Accordingly the saying of our Lord refers to the case where

* Cf. footnote on II-II, Q. 33, A. 7.

the process is by way of denunciation, and not by accusation, because then the end in view is not only the correction of the guilty party, but also his punishment, for the safeguarding of the common good, which would be destroyed if justice were lacking.

FOURTH ARTICLE

Whether in a Case of Divorce Husband and Wife Should Be Judged on a Par with Each Other?

We proceed thus to the Fourth Article:—

Objection 1. It would seem that, in a case of divorce, husband and wife ought not to be judged on a par with each other. For divorce under the New Law takes the place of the divorce *(repudium)* recognized by the Old Law (Matth. v. 31, 32). Now in the *repudium* husband and wife were not judged on a par with each other, since the husband could put away his wife, but not *vice versa*. Therefore neither in divorce ought they to be judged on a par with each other.

Obj. 2. Further, it is more opposed to the natural law that a wife have several husbands than that a husband have several wives: wherefore the latter has been sometimes lawful, but the former never. Therefore the wife sins more grievously in adultery than the husband, and consequently they ought not to be judged on a par with each other.

Obj. 3. Further, where there is greater injury to one's neighbor, there is a greater sin. Now the adulterous wife does a greater injury to her husband, than does the adulterous husband to his wife, since a wife's adultery involves uncertainty of the offspring, whereas the husband's adultery does not. Therefore the wife's sin is the greater, and so they ought not to be judged on a par with each other.

Obj. 4. Further, divorce is prescribed in order to punish the crime of adultery. Now it belongs to the husband who is the head of the wife (1 Cor. xi. 3) to correct his wife, rather than *vice versa*. Therefore they should not be judged on a par with each other for the purpose of divorce, but the husband ought to have the preference.

Obj. 5. *On the contrary*, It would seem in this matter the wife ought to have the preference. For the more frail the sinner the more is his sin deserving of pardon. Now there is greater frailty in women than in men, for which reason Chrysostom* says that *lust is a passion proper to women* and the Philosopher says *(Ethic.* vii. 7) that *properly speaking women are not said to be continent on account of their being easily inclined to concupiscence,* for neither can dumb animals be continent, because they have nothing to stand in the way

of their desires. Therefore women are rather to be spared in the punishment of divorce.

Obj. 6. Further, the husband is placed as the head of the woman in order to correct her. Therefore his sin is greater than the woman's, and so he should be punished the more.

I answer that, In a case of divorce husband and wife are judged on a par with each other, in the sense that the same things are lawful or unlawful to the one as to the other: but they are not judged on a par with each other in reference to those things, since the reason for divorce is greater in one spouse than in the other, although there is sufficient reason for divorce in both. For divorce is a punishment of adultery, in so far as it is opposed to the marriage goods. Now as regards the good of fidelity to which husband and wife are equally bound towards each other, the adultery of one is as great a sin against marriage as the adultery of the other, and this is in either of them a sufficient reason for divorce. But as regards the good of the offspring the wife's adultery is a greater sin against marriage than the husband's wherefore it is a greater reason for divorce in the wife than in the husband: and thus they are under an equal obligation, but not for equal reasons. Nor is this unjust for on either hand there is sufficient reason for the punishment in question, just as there is in two persons condemned to the punishment of death, although one of them may have sinned more grievously than the other.

Reply Obj. 1. The only reason why divorce was permitted, was to avoid murder. And since there was more danger of this in men than in women, the husband was allowed to put away his wife by a bill of divorce, but not *vice versa*.

Reply Objs. 2 *and* 3. These arguments are based on the fact that in comparison with the good of the offspring there is more reason for divorce in an adulterous wife than in an adulterous husband. It does not follow, however, that they are not judged on a par with each other.

Reply Obj. 4. Although the husband is the head of the wife, he is her pilot as it were, and is no more her judge than she is his. Consequently in matters that have to be submitted to a judge, the husband has no more power over his wife, than she over him.

Reply Obj. 5. In adultery there is the same sinful character as in simple fornication, and something more which aggravates it, namely the lesion to marriage. Accordingly if we consider that which is common to adultery and fornication, the sin of the husband and that of the wife are compared the one to the other as that which exceeds to that which is exceeded,

* *Hom.* xl, in the *Opus Imperfectum* falsely ascribed to S. John Chrysostom.

for in women the humors are more abundant, wherefore they are more inclined to be led by their concupiscences, whereas in man there is abundance of heat which excites concupiscence. Simply speaking, however, other things being equal, a man sins more grievously in simple fornication than a woman, because he has more of the good of reason, which prevails over all movements of bodily passions. But as regards the lesion to marriage which adultery adds to fornication and for which reason it is an occasion for divorce, the woman sins more grievously than the man, as appears from what we have said above. And since it is more grievous than simple fornication, it follows that, simply speaking, the adulterous wife sins more grievously than the adulterous husband, other things being equal.

Reply Obj. 6. Although the control which the husband receives over his wife is an aggravating circumstance, nevertheless the sin is yet more aggravated by this circumstance which draws the sin to another species, namely by the lesion to marriage, which lesion becomes a kind of injustice, through the fraudulent substitution of another's child.

FIFTH ARTICLE

Whether a Husband Can Marry Again after Having a Divorce?

We proceed thus to the Fifth Article:—

Objection 1. It would seem that a husband can marry again after having a divorce. For no one is bound to perpetual continence. Now in some cases the husband is bound to put away his wife forever on account of fornication, as stated above (A. 2). Therefore seemingly at least in this case he can marry again.

Obj. 2. Further, a sinner should not be given a greater occasion of sin. But if she who is put away on account of the sin of fornication is not allowed to seek another marriage, she is given a greater occasion of sin: for it is improbable that one who was not continent during marriage will be able to be continent afterwards. Therefore it would seem lawful for her to marry again.

Obj. 3. Further, the wife is not bound to the husband save as regards the payment of the marriage debt and cohabitation. But she is freed from both obligations by divorce. Therefore *she is loosed from the law of her husband.** Therefore she can marry again; and the same applies to her husband.

Obj. 4. Further, it is said (Matth. xix. 9): *Whosoever shall put away his wife, except it be for fornication, and shall marry another, committeth adultery.* Therefore seemingly he does not commit adultery if he marry again

* Rom. vii. 2.

after putting away his wife on account of fornication, and consequently this will be a true marriage.

On the contrary, It is written (1 Cor. vii. 10, 11): *Not I, but the Lord, commandeth that the wife depart not from her husband; and, if she depart, that she remain unmarried.*

Further, no one should gain advantage from sin. But the adulteress would if she were allowed to contract another and more desired marriage; and an occasion of adultery would be afforded those who wish to marry again. Therefore it is unlawful both to the wife and to the husband to contract a second marriage.

I answer that, Nothing supervenient to marriage can dissolve it: wherefore adultery does not make a marriage cease to be valid. For, according to Augustine (*De Nup. et Concup.* i. 10), *as long as they live they are bound by the marriage tie, which neither divorce nor union with another can destroy.* Therefore it is unlawful for one, while the other lives, to marry again.

Reply Obj. 1. Although no one is absolutely bound to continence, he may be bound accidentally; for instance, if his wife contract an incurable disease that is incompatible with carnal intercourse. And it is the same if she labor under a spiritual disease, namely fornication, so as to be incorrigible.

Reply Obj. 2. The very shame of having been divorced ought to keep her from sin: and if it cannot keep her from sin, it is a lesser evil that she alone sin than that her husband take part in her sin.

Reply Obj. 3. Although after divorce the wife is not bound to her husband as regards paying him the marriage debt and cohabiting with him, the marriage tie, whereby she was bound to this, remains, and consequently she cannot marry again during her husband's lifetime. She can, however, take a vow of continence, against her husband's will, unless it seem that the Church has been deceived by false witnesses in pronouncing the divorce; for in that case, even if she has made her vow of profession she ought to be restored to her husband, and would be bound to pay the marriage debt, but it would be unlawful for her to demand it.

Reply Obj. 4. The exception expressed in our Lord's words refers to the putting away of the wife. Hence the objection is based on a false interpretation.

SIXTH ARTICLE

Whether Husband and Wife May Be Reconciled after Being Divorced?

We proceed thus to the Sixth Article:—

Objection 1. It would seem that husband and wife may not be reconciled after being divorced. For the law contains the rule (Can. *Quod bene semel,* Caus. vi. qu. iv): *That which has been once well decided must not be subsequently withdrawn.* Now it has been decided by the judgment of the Church that they ought to be separated. Therefore they cannot subsequently be reconciled.

Obj. 2. Further, if it were allowable for them to be reconciled, the husband would seem bound to receive his wife, especially after she has repented. But he is not bound, for the wife, in defending herself before the judge, cannot allege her repentance against her husband's accusation of fornication. Therefore in no way is reconciliation allowable.

Obj. 3. Further, if reconciliation were allowable, it would seem that the adulterous wife is bound to return to her husband if her husband asks her. But she is not bound, since they are separated by the Church. Therefore, etc.

Obj. 4. Further, if it were lawful to be reconciled to an adulterous wife, this would especially be the case when the husband is found to have committed adultery after the divorce. But in this case the wife cannot compel him to be reconciled, since the divorce has been justly pronounced. Therefore she may nowise be reconciled.

Obj. 5. Further, if a husband whose adultery is unknown put away his wife, who is convicted of adultery by the sentence of the Church, the divorce would seem to have been pronounced unjustly. And yet the husband is not bound to be reconciled to his wife, because she is unable to prove his adultery in court. Much less, therefore, is reconciliation allowable when the divorce has been granted justly.

On the contrary, It is written (1 Cor. vii. 11): *And if she depart, that she remain unmarried, or be reconciled to her husband.*

Further, it is allowable for the husband not to put her away after fornication. Therefore, for the same reason, he can be reconciled to her after divorce.

I answer that, If the wife has mended her ways by repenting of her sin after the divorce, her husband may become reconciled to her; but if she remain incorrigible in her sin, he must not take her back, for the same reason which forbade him to retain her while she refused to desist from sin.

Reply Obj. 1. The sentence of the Church in pronouncing the divorce did not bind them to separate, but allowed them to do so. Therefore reconciliation may be effected or ensue without any withdrawal of the previous sentence.

Reply Obj. 2. The wife's repentance should induce the husband not to accuse or put away the wife who is guilty of fornication. He cannot, however, be compelled to this course of action, nor can his wife oppose her repentance to his accusation, because although she is no longer guilty, neither in act nor in the stain of sin, there still remains something of the debt of punishment, and though this has been taken away in the sight of God, there still remains the debt of punishment to be inflicted by the judgment of man, because man sees not the heart as God does.

Reply Obj. 3. That which is done in a person's favor does him no prejudice. Wherefore since the divorce has been granted in favor of the husband, it does not deprive him of the right of asking for the marriage debt, or of asking his wife to return to him. Hence his wife is bound to pay the debt, and to return to him, if he ask her, unless with his consent she has taken a vow of continence.

Reply Obj. 4. According to strict law, a husband who was previously innocent should not be compelled to receive an adulterous wife on account of his having committed adultery after the divorce. But according to equity, the judge is bound by virtue of his office first of all to admonish him to beware of imperiling his own soul and of scandalizing others; although the wife may not herself seek reconciliation.

Reply Obj. 5. If the husband's adultery is secret, this does not deprive his adulterous wife of the right to allege it in self-defense, although she cannot prove it. Wherefore the husband sins by seeking a divorce, and if, after the sentence of divorce, his wife asks for the marriage debt or for a reconciliation, the husband is bound to both.

QUESTION 63

Of Second Marriages

(In Two Articles)

In the next place we must consider second marriage. Under this head there are two points of inquiry: (1) Whether it is lawful? (2) Whether it is a sacrament?

FIRST ARTICLE

Whether a Second Marriage Is Lawful?

We proceed thus to the First Article:—

Objection 1. It would seem that a second marriage is unlawful. Because we should judge of things according to truth. Now Chrysostom* says that *to take a second husband is in truth fornication,* which is unlawful. Therefore neither is a second marriage lawful.

Obj. 2. Further, whatever is not good is unlawful. Now Ambrose† says that a second marriage is not good. Therefore it is unlawful.

Obj. 3. Further, no one should be debarred from being present at such things as are becoming and lawful. Yet priests are debarred from being present at second marriages, as stated in the text (iv, *Sent.* D. 42). Therefore they are unlawful.

Obj. 4. Further, no one incurs a penalty save for sin. Now a person incurs the penalty of irregularity on account of being married twice. Therefore a second marriage is unlawful.

On the contrary, We read of Abraham having contracted a second marriage (Gen. xxv. 1).

Further, the Apostle says (1 Tim. v. 14): *I will . . . that the younger,* namely widows, *should marry, bear children.* Therefore second marriages are lawful.

I answer that, The marriage tie lasts only until death (Rom. vii. 2), wherefore at the death of either spouse the marriage tie ceases: and consequently when one dies the other is not hindered from marrying a second time on account of the previous marriage. Therefore not only second marriages are lawful, but even third and so on.

Reply Obj. 1. Chrysostom is speaking in reference to the cause which is wont at times to incite a person to a second marriage, namely concupiscence which incites also to fornication.

Reply Obj. 2. A second marriage is stated not to be good, not that it is unlawful, but because it lacks the honor of the signification which is in a first marriage, where one husband has one wife, as in the case of Christ and the Church.

Reply Obj. 3. Men who are consecrated to Divine things are debarred not only from unlawful things, but even from things which have any appearance of turpitude; and consequently they are debarred from second marriages, which lack the decorum which was in a first marriage.

Reply Obj. 4. Irregularity is not always incurred on account of a sin, and may be incurred through a defect in a sacrament.‡ Hence the argument is not to the point.

SECOND ARTICLE

Whether a Second Marriage Is a Sacrament?

We proceed thus to the Second Article:—

Objection 1. It would seem that a second marriage is not a sacrament. For he who repeats a sacrament injures the sacrament. But no sacrament should be done an injury. Therefore if a second marriage were a sacrament, marriage ought nowise to be repeated.

Obj. 2. Further, in every sacrament some kind of blessing is given. But no blessing is given in a second marriage, as stated in the text (iv, *Sent.* D. 42). Therefore no sacrament is conferred therein.

Obj. 3. Further, signification is essential to a sacrament. But the signification of marriage is not preserved in a second marriage, because there is not a union of only one woman with only one man, as in the case of Christ and the Church. Therefore it is not a sacrament.

Obj. 4. Further, one sacrament is not an impediment to receiving another. But a second marriage is an impediment to receiving Orders. Therefore it is not a sacrament.

On the contrary, Marital intercourse is excused from sin in a second marriage even as in a first marriage. Now marital intercourse is excused§ by the marriage goods which are fidelity, offspring, and sacrament. Therefore a second marriage is a sacrament.

Further, irregularity is not contracted through a second and non-sacramental union, such as fornication. Yet irregularity is contracted through a second marriage. Therefore it is a sacramental union.

I answer that, Wherever we find the essentials of a sacrament, there is a true sacrament. Wherefore, since in a second marriage we find all the essentials of the sacrament of marriage (namely the due matter—which results from the parties having the conditions prescribed

---

* *Hom.* xxxii, in the *Opus Imperfectum* falsely ascribed to S. John Chrysostom.   † On 1 Cor. vii. 40, and *De Viduis.*   ‡ *Defectus sacramenti,* i.e. defect of signification. Cf. A. 2, *Obj.* 3.   § Cf. Q. 69, A. 1.

by law—and the due form, which is the expression of the inward consent by words of the present), it is clear that a second marriage is a sacrament even as a first.

Reply Obj. 1. This is true of a sacrament which causes an everlasting effect: for then, if the sacrament be repeated, it is implied that the first was not effective, and thus an injury is done to the first, as is clear in all those sacraments which imprint a character. But those sacraments which have not an everlasting effect can be repeated without injury to the sacrament, as in the case of Penance. And, since the marriage tie ceases with death, no injury is done to the sacrament if a woman marry again after her husband's death.

Reply Obj. 2 Although the second marriage, considered in itself, is a perfect sacrament, yet if we consider it in relation to the first marriage, it is somewhat a defective sacrament, because it has not its full signification, since there is not a union of only one woman with only one man as in the marriage of Christ with the Church. And on account of this defect the blessing is omitted in a second marriage.

This, however, refers to the case when it is a second marriage on the part of both man and woman, or on the part of the woman only. For if a virgin marry a man who has had another wife, the marriage is blessed nevertheless. Because the signification is preserved to a certain extent even in relation to the former marriage, since though Christ has but one Church for His spouse, there are many persons espoused to Him in the one Church. But the soul cannot be espoused to another besides Christ, else it commits fornication with the devil. Nor is there a spiritual marriage. For this reason when a woman marries a second time the marriage is not blessed on account of the defect in the sacrament.

Reply Obj. 3. The perfect signification is found in a second marriage considered in itself, not however if it be considered in relation to the previous marriage, and it is thus that it is a defective sacrament.

Reply Obj. 4. A second marriage in so far as there is a defect in the sacrament, but not as a sacrament, is an impediment to the sacrament of Order.

QUESTION 64

Of the Things Annexed to Marriage, and First of the Payment of the Marriage Debt

(In Seven Articles)

In the next place we must consider those things which are annexed to marriage: (1) the payment of the marriage debt; (2) plurality of wives; (3) bigamy; (4) the bill of divorce; (5) illegitimate children.

Under the first head there are ten points of inquiry: (1) Whether one spouse is bound to pay the marriage debt to the other? (2) Whether one is sometimes bound to pay without being asked? (3) Whether a wife may demand the debt during the menses? (4) Whether she is bound to pay it at that time? (5) Whether husband and wife are equal in this matter? (6) Whether the one without the other's consent may take a vow that prohibits the payment of the debt? (7) Whether it is forbidden to ask for the debt at any particular time? (8) Whether it is a mortal sin to ask for it at a holy time? (9) Whether it is an obligation to pay it at the time of a festival? (10) Whether weddings should be forbidden at certain times?

FIRST ARTICLE

Whether Husband and Wife Are Mutually Bound to the Payment of the Marriage Debt?

We proceed thus to the First Article:—

Objection 1. It would seem that husband

* *Serm. de Esu Agni,* viii.

and wife are not mutually bound, under the obligation of a precept, to the payment of the marriage debt. For no one is forbidden to receive the Eucharist on account of fulfilling a precept. Yet he who has had intercourse with his wife cannot partake of the flesh of the Lamb according to Jerome* quoted in the text (iv, *Sent.* D. 32). Therefore the payment of the debt does not come under the obligation of a precept.

Obj. 2. Further, it is lawful to everyone to abstain from what is hurtful to his person. But it is sometimes harmful to a person to pay the debt when asked, whether on account of sickness, or because they have already paid it. Therefore it would seem allowable to refuse the one who asks.

Obj. 3. Further, it is a sin to render oneself unfit to fulfill an obligation of precept. If, therefore, the payment of the debt comes under the obligation of a precept, it would seem sinful to render oneself unfit for paying the debt, by fasting or otherwise weakening the body: but apparently this is untrue.

Obj. 4. Further, according to the Philosopher *(Ethic.* viii. 12), marriage is directed to the begetting and rearing of children, as well as to the community of life. Now leprosy is opposed to both these ends of marriage, for since it is a contagious disease, the wife is not bound to cohabit with a leprous husband; and besides this disease is often transmitted to the offspring. Therefore it would seem that a wife is not bound to pay the debt to a leprous husband.

On the contrary, As the slave is in the power of his master, so is one spouse in the power of the other (1 Cor. vii. 4). But a slave is bound by an obligation of precept to pay his master the debt of his service according to Rom. xiii. 7, *Render . . . to all men their dues, tribute to whom tribute is due,* etc. Therefore husband and wife are mutually bound to the payment of the marriage debt.

Further, marriage is directed to the avoiding of fornication (1 Cor. vii. 2). But this could not be the effect of marriage, if the one were not bound to pay the debt to the other when the latter is troubled with concupiscence. Therefore the payment of the debt is an obligation of precept.

I answer that, Marriage was instituted especially as fulfilling an office of nature. Wherefore in its act the movement of nature must be observed according to which the nutritive power administers to the generative power that alone which is in excess of what is required for the preservation of the individual: for the natural order requires that a thing should be first perfected in itself, and that afterwards it should communicate of its perfection to others: and this is also the order of charity which perfects nature. And therefore, since the wife has power over her husband only in relation to the generative power and not in relation to things directed to the preservation of the individual, the husband is bound to pay the debt to his wife, in matters pertaining to the begetting of children, with due regard however to his own welfare.

Reply Obj. 1. It is possible through fulfilling a precept to render oneself unfit for the exercise of a sacred duty: thus a judge becomes irregular by sentencing a man to death. In like manner he who pays the marriage debt, in fulfillment of the precept, becomes unfit for the exercise of divine offices, not because the act in question is sinful, but on account of its carnal nature. And so, according to the Master *(loc. cit.),* Jerome is speaking only of the ministers of the Church, and not of others who should be left to use their own discretion, because without sin they may either abstain out of reverence or receive Christ's body out of devotion.

Reply Obj. 2. The wife has no power over her husband's body, except as is consistent with the welfare of his person, as stated above. Wherefore if she go beyond this in her demands, it is not a request for the debt, but an unjust exaction; and for this reason the husband is not bound to satisfy her.

Reply Obj. 3. If the husband be rendered incapable of paying the debt through a cause consequent upon marriage, for instance through having already paid the debt and being unable to pay it, the wife has no right to ask again, and in doing so she behaves as a harlot rather than as a wife. But if he be rendered incapable through some other cause, then if this be a lawful cause, he is not bound, and she cannot ask, but if it be an unlawful cause, then he sins, and his wife's sin, should she fall into fornication on this account, is somewhat imputable to him. Hence he should endeavor to do his best that his wife may remain continent.

Reply Obj. 4. Leprosy voids a betrothal but not a marriage. Wherefore a wife is bound to pay the debt even to a leprous husband. But she is not bound to cohabit with him, because she is not so liable to infection from marital intercourse as from continual cohabitation. And though the child begotten of them be diseased, it is better to be thus than not at all.

SECOND ARTICLE

Whether a Husband Is Bound to Pay the Debt If His Wife Does Not Ask for It?

We proceed thus to the Second Article:—

Objection 1. It would seem that the husband is not bound to pay the marriage debt if his wife does not ask for it. For an affirmative precept is binding only at a certain time. But the time fixed for the payment of the debt can only be when it is asked for. Therefore he is not bound to payment otherwise.

Obj. 2. Further, we ought to presume the better things of everyone. Now even for married people it is better to be continent than to make use of marriage. Therefore unless she ask expressly for the debt, the husband should presume that it pleases her to be continent, and so he is not bound to pay her the debt.

Obj. 3. Further, as the wife has power over her husband, so has a master over his slave. Now a slave is not bound to serve his master save when the latter commands him. Therefore neither is a husband bound to pay the debt to his wife except when she demands it.

Obj. 4. Further, the husband can sometimes request his wife not to exact the debt when she asks for it. Much more therefore may he not pay it when he is not asked.

On the contrary, By the payment of the debt a remedy is afforded against the wife's concupiscence. Now a physician who has the care of a sick person is bound to remedy the disease without being asked. Therefore the husband is bound to pay the debt to his wife although she ask not for it. Further, a superior is bound to apply a remedy for the sins of his subjects even though they rebel against it. But the payment of the debt on the husband's part is directed against the sins of his wife. Therefore sometimes the husband is bound to pay the debt to his wife even though she ask it not of him.

I answer that, The debt may be demanded in two ways. First, explicitly, as when they ask one another by words; secondly, implicitly, when namely the husband knows by certain signs that the wife would wish him to pay the debt, but is silent through shame. And so even though she does not ask for the debt explicitly in words, the husband is bound to pay it, whenever his wife shows signs of wishing him to do so.

Reply Obj. 1. The appointed time is not only when it is demanded but also when on account of certain signs there is fear of danger (to avoid which is the purpose of the payment of the debt) unless it be paid then.

Reply Obj. 2. The husband may presume this of his wife when he perceives in her no signs of the contrary; but it would be foolish of him to admit this presumption if he does see such signs.

Reply Obj. 3. The master is not ashamed to demand of his slave the duty of his service, as a wife is to ask the marriage debt of her husband. Yet if the master were not to demand it, either through ignorance or some other cause, the slave would nevertheless be bound to fulfill his duty, if some danger were threatening. For this is what is meant by *not serving to the eye* (Eph. vi. 6; Col. iii. 22) which is the Apostle's command to servants.

Reply Obj. 4. A husband should not dissuade his wife from asking for the debt, except for a reasonable cause; and even then he should not be too insistent, on account of the besetting danger.

THIRD ARTICLE*

Whether It Is Allowable for a Menstruous Wife to Ask for the Marriage Debt?

We proceed thus to the Third Article:—

Objection 1. It would seem lawful for a menstruous wife to ask for the marriage debt. For in the Law a man who had an issue of seed was unclean, even as a menstruous woman. Yet a man who has an issue of seed may ask for the debt. Therefore a menstruous wife may also.

Obj. 2. Further, leprosy is a worse complaint than suffering from monthly periods, and would seem to cause a greater corruption in the offspring. Yet a leper can ask for the debt. Therefore, etc.

Obj. 3. Further, if a menstruous wife is not allowed to ask for the debt, this can only be because it is feared this may be detrimental to the offspring. Yet if the wife be unfruitful there is no such fear. Therefore

* This and the Fourth Article are omitted in the Leonine edition.

seemingly, at least an unfruitful wife may ask for the debt during her menses.

On the contrary, Thou shalt not approach to a woman having her flowers (Levit. xviii. 19) where Augustine observes: *Although he has already sufficiently forbidden this, he repeats the prohibition here, lest he seem to have spoken figuratively.*

Further, *All our justices* are become *as the rag of a menstruous woman* (Isa. lxiv. 6) where Jerome observes: *Men ought then to keep away from their wives, because thus is a deformed, blind, lame, leprous offspring conceived: so that those parents who are not ashamed to come together in sexual intercourse have their sin made obvious to all:* and thus the same conclusion follows.

I answer that, It was forbidden in the Law to approach to a menstruous woman, for two reasons, both on account of her uncleanness, and on account of the harm that frequently resulted to the offspring from such intercourse. With regard to the first reason, it was a ceremonial precept, but with regard to the second it was a moral precept. For since marriage is chiefly directed to the good of the offspring, all use of marriage which is intended for the good of the offspring is in order. Consequently this precept is binding even in the New Law on account of the second reason, although not on account of the first. Now, the menstrual issue may be natural or unnatural. The natural issue is that to which women are subject at stated periods when they are in good health; and it is unnatural when they suffer from an issue of blood through some disorder resulting from sickness. Accordingly, if the menstrual flow be unnatural it is not forbidden in the New Law to approach to a menstruous woman, both on account of her infirmity since a woman in that state cannot conceive, and because an issue of this kind is lasting and continuous, so that the husband would have to abstain for always. When however the woman is subject to a natural issue of the menstruum, she can conceive; moreover, the said issue lasts only a short time, wherefore it is forbidden to approach to her. In like manner a woman is forbidden to ask for the debt during the period of that issue.

Reply Obj. 1. The issue of seed in a man is the result of infirmity, nor is the seed in this case apt for generation. Moreover, a complaint of this kind is continual or lasting like leprosy: wherefore the comparison fails.

This suffices for the *Reply* to the *Second Objection.*

Reply Obj. 3. As long as a woman is subject to the menses it cannot be certain that she is sterile. For some are sterile in youth, and in course of time become fruitful, and *vice versa,* as the Philosopher observes (*De Gener. Anim.* xvi).

FOURTH ARTICLE

Whether a Menstruous Woman Should or May Lawfully Pay the Marriage Debt to Her Husband If He Ask for It?

We proceed thus to the Fourth Article:—

Objection 1. It would seem that a menstruous wife may not pay the marriage debt to her husband at his asking. For it is written (Lev. xx. 18) that if any man approach to a menstruous woman both shall be put to death. Therefore it would seem that both he who asks and she who grants are guilty of mortal sin.

Obj. 2. Further, *Not only they that do them, but they also that consent to them, are worthy of death* (Rom. i. 32). Now he who knowingly asks for the debt from a menstruous woman sins mortally. Therefore she also sins mortally by consenting to pay the debt.

Obj. 3. Further, a madman must not be given back his sword lest he kill himself or another. Therefore in like manner neither should a wife give her body to her husband during her menses, lest he be guilty of spiritual murder.

On the contrary, The wife hath not power of her own body, but the husband (1 Cor. vii. 4). Therefore at his asking his wife must pay the debt even during her menses.

Further, the menstruous wife should not be an occasion of sin to her husband. But she would give her husband an occasion of sin, if she paid him not the debt at his asking; since he might commit fornication. Therefore, etc.

I answer that, In this regard some have asserted that a menstruous woman may not pay the debt, even as she may not ask for it. For just as she would not be bound to pay it if she had some personal ailment so as to make it dengerous for herself, so is she not bound to pay for fear of danger to the offspring. But this opinion would seem to derogate from marriage, by which the husband is given entire power of his wife's body with regard to the marriage act. Nor is there any parallel between bodily affliction of the offspring and the danger to her own body: since, if the wife be ailing, it is quite certain that she would be endangered by the carnal act, whereas this is by no means so certain with regard to the offspring which perhaps would not be forthcoming.

Wherefore others say that a menstruous woman is never allowed to ask for the debt; and that if her husband ask, he does so either knowingly or in ignorance. If knowingly, she ought to dissuade him by her prayers and admonitions; yet not so insistently as possibly to afford him an occasion of falling into other, and those sinful, practices, if he be deemed that way inclined. If, however, he ask in ignorance, the wife may put forward some motive, or allege sickness as a reason for not paying the debt, unless there be fear of danger to her husband. If, however, the husband ultimately persists in his request, she must yield to his demand. But it would not be safe for her to make known* her disaffection, lest this make her husband entertain a repulsion towards her, unless his prudence may be taken for granted.

Reply Obj. 1. This refers to the case when both willingly consent, but not when the woman pays the debt by force as it were.

Reply Obj. 2. Since there is no consent without the concurrence of the will, the woman is not deemed to consent in her husband's sin unless she pay the debt willingly. For when she is unwilling she is passive rather than consenting.

Reply Obj. 3. A madman should be given back his sword if a greater danger were feared from its not being returned to him: and thus it is in the case in point.

FIFTH ARTICLE

Whether Husband and Wife Are Equal in the Marriage Act?

We proceed thus to the Fifth Article:—

Objection 1. It would seem that husband and wife are not equal in the marriage act. For according to Augustine *(Gen. ad lit.* xii) the agent is more noble than the patient. But in the marriage act the husband is as agent and the wife as patient. Therefore they are not equal in that act.

Obj. 2. Further, the wife is not bound to pay her husband the debt without being asked; whereas he is so bound, as stated above (AA. 1, 2). Therefore they are not equal in the marriage act.

Obj. 3. Further, the woman was made on the man's account in reference to marriage, according to Gen. ii. 18, *Let us make him a help like unto himself.* But that on account of which another thing is, is always the principal. Therefore, etc.

Obj. 4. Further, marriage is chiefly directed to the marriage act. But in marriage *the husband is the head of the wife* (Eph. v. 23). Therefore they are not equal in the aforesaid act.

On the contrary, It is written (1 Cor. vii. 4): *The husband . . . hath not power of his own body,* and the same is said of the wife. Therefore they are equal in the marriage act.

Further, Marriage is a relation of equiparence, since it is a kind of union, as stated above (Q. 44., AA. 1, 3). Therefore husband and wife are equal in the marriage act.

I answer that, Equality is twofold, of quantity and of proportion. Equality of quantity is that which is observed between two quantities of the same measure, for instance a thing two cubits long and another two cubits in length. But equality of proportion is that which is observed between two proportions of the same kind as double to double. Accordingly, speaking of the first equality, husband and wife are not equal in marriage; neither as regards the marriage act, wherein the more noble part is due to the husband, nor as regards the household management, wherein the wife is ruled and the husband rules. But with reference to the second kind of equality, they are equal in both matters, because just as in both the marriage act and in the management of the household the husband is bound to the wife in all things pertaining to the husband, so is the wife bound to the husband in all things pertaining to the wife. It is in this sense that it is stated in the text (iv, *Sent.* D. 32) that they are equal in paying and demanding the debt.

Reply Obj. 1. Although it is more noble to be active than passive, there is the same proportion between patient and passivity as between agent and activity; and accordingly there is equality of proportion between them.

Reply Obj. 2. This is accidental. For the husband having the more noble part in the marriage act, it is natural that he should be less ashamed than the wife to ask for the debt. Hence it is that the wife is not bound to pay the debt to her husband without being asked, whereas the husband is bound to pay it to the wife.

Reply Obj. 3. This proves that they are not equal absolutely, but not that they are not equal in proportion.

Reply Obj. 4. Although the head is the

* *Indicare,* as in the commentary on the Sentences. The Leonine edition reads *judicare.*

principal member, yet just as the members are bound to the head in their own respective capacities, so is the head in its own capacity bound to the members: and thus there is equality of proportion between them.

SIXTH ARTICLE

Whether Husband and Wife Can Take a Vow Contrary to the Marriage Debt without Their Mutual Consent?

We proceed thus to the Sixth Article:—

Objection 1. It would seem that husband and wife may take a vow contrary to the marriage debt without their mutual consent. For husband and wife are equally bound to pay the debt, as stated above (A. 5). Now it is lawful for the husband, even if his wife be unwilling, to take the cross in defense of the Holy Land: and consequently this is also lawful to the wife. Therefore, since this prevents the payment of the debt, either husband or wife may without the other's consent take the aforesaid vow.

Obj. 2. Further, in taking a vow one should not await the consent of another who cannot dissent without sin. Now the husband or wife cannot, without sin, refuse their consent to the other's taking a vow of continence whether absolutely or for a time; because to prevent a person's spiritual progress is a sin against the Holy Ghost. Therefore the one can take a vow of continence either absolutely or for a time, without the other's consent.

Obj. 3. Further, in the marriage act, the debt has to be demanded just as it has to be paid. Now the one can, without the other's consent, vow not to demand the debt, since in this he is within his own rights. Therefore he can equally take a vow not to pay the debt.

Obj. 4. Further, no one can be bound by the command of a superior to do what he cannot lawfully vow or do simply, since one must not obey in what is unlawful. Now the superior authority might command the husband not to pay the debt to his wife for a time, by occupying him in some service. Therefore he might, of his own accord, do or vow that which would hinder him from paying the debt.

On the contrary, It is written (1 Cor. vii. 5): *Defraud not one another, except . . . by consent, for a time, that you may give yourselves to prayer.*

Further, no one can vow that which belongs to another. Now *the husband . . . hath not power of his own body, but the wife* (*ibid.* 4). Therefore, without her consent, the husband cannot take a vow of continence whether absolutely or for a time.

I answer that, A vow is a voluntary act, as

* Cf. Q. 53, AA. 1, 4; Q. 61, A. 1.

its very name implies: and consequently a vow can only be about those goods which are subject to our will, and those in which one person is bound to another do not come under this head. Therefore in matters of this kind one person cannot take a vow without the consent of the one to whom he is bound. Consequently, since husband and wife are mutually bound as regards the payment of the debt which is an obstacle to continence, the one cannot vow continence without the other's consent; and if he take the vow he sins, and must not keep the vow, but must do penance for an ill-taken vow.*

Reply Obj. 1. It is sufficiently probable that the wife ought to be willing to remain continent for a time, in order to succor the need of the universal Church. Hence in favor of the business for which the cross is given to him, it is laid down that the husband may take the cross without his wife's consent, even as he might go fighting without the consent of his landlord whose land he has leased. And yet the wife is not entirely deprived of her right, since she can follow him. Nor is there a parallel between wife and husband: because, since the husband has to rule the wife and not *vice versa*, the wife is bound to follow her husband rather than the husband the wife. Moreover there would be more danger to the wife's chastity as a result of wandering from country to country, than to the husband's, and less profit to the Church. Wherefore the wife cannot take this vow without her husband's consent.

Reply Obj. 2. The one spouse, by refusing to consent to the other's vow of continence, does not sin, because the object of his dissent is to hinder not the other's good, but the harm to himself.

Reply Obj. 3. There are two opinions on this point. For some say that one can without the other's consent vow not to demand the debt, not however not to pay it, because in the former case they are both within their own rights, but not in the second. Seeing, however, that if one were never to ask for the debt, marriage would become too burdensome to the other who would always have to undergo the shame of asking for the debt, others assert with greater probability that neither vow can be lawfully taken by one spouse without the other's consent.

Reply Obj. 4. Just as the wife receives power over her husband's body, without prejudice to the husband's duty to his own body, so also is it without prejudice to his duty to his master. Hence just as a wife cannot ask her husband for the debt to the detriment of his bodily health, so neither can she do this so as to hinder him in his duty to his master.

And yet the master cannot for this reason prevent her from paying the debt.

SEVENTH ARTICLE

Whether It Is Forbidden to Demand the Debt on Holy Days?

We proceed thus to the Seventh Article:—

Objection 1. It would seem that a person ought not to be forbidden to ask for the debt on holy days. For the remedy should be applied when the disease gains strength. Now concupiscence may possibly gain strength on a feast day. Therefore the remedy should be applied then by asking for the debt.

Obj. 2. Further, the only reason why the debt should not be demanded on feast days is because they are devoted to prayer. Yet on those days certain hours are appointed for prayer. Therefore one may ask for the debt at some other time.

On the contrary, Just as certain places are holy because they are devoted to holy things, so are certain times holy for the same reason. But it is not lawful to demand the debt in a holy place. Therefore neither is it lawful at a holy time.

I answer that, Although the marriage act is void of sin, nevertheless since it oppresses the reason on account of the carnal pleasure, it renders man unfit for spiritual things. Therefore, on those days when one ought especially to give one's time to spiritual things, it is not lawful to ask for the debt.

Reply Obj. 1. At such a time other means may be employed for the repression of concupiscence; for instance, prayer and many similar things, to which even those who observe perpetual continence have recourse.

Reply Obj. 2. Although one is not bound to pray at all hours, one is bound throughout the day to keep oneself fit for prayer.

EIGHTH ARTICLE

Whether It Is a Mortal Sin to Ask for the Debt at a Holy Time?

We proceed thus to the Eighth Article:—

Objection 1. It would seem that it is a mortal sin to ask for the debt at a holy time. For Gregory says (*Dial.* i) that the devil took possession of a woman who had intercourse with her husband at night and came in the morning to the procession. But this would not have happened had she not sinned mortally. Therefore, etc.

Obj. 2. Further, whoever disobeys a Divine command commits a mortal sin. Now the Lord commanded (Exod. xix. 15): *Come not near your wives,* when namely they were about to receive the Law. Much more therefore do husbands sin mortally if they have intercourse with their wives at a time when they should be intent on the sacred observances of the New Law.

On the contrary, No circumstance aggravates infinitely. But undue time is a circumstance. Therefore it does not aggravate a sin infinitely, so as to make mortal what was otherwise venial.

I answer that, To ask for the debt on a feast day is not a circumstance drawing a sin into another species; wherefore it cannot aggravate infinitely. Consequently a wife or husband does not sin mortally by asking for the debt on a feast day. It is however a more grievous sin to ask for the sake of mere pleasure, than through fear of the weakness of the flesh.

Reply Obj. 1. This woman was punished not because she paid the debt, but because afterwards she rashly intruded into the divine service against her conscience.

Reply Obj. 2. The authority quoted shows not that it is a mortal sin but that it is unbecoming. For under the Old Law which was given to a carnal people many things were required under an obligation of precept, for the sake of bodily cleanness, which are not required in the New Law which is the law of the spirit.

NINTH ARTICLE

Whether One Spouse Is Bound to Pay the Debt to the Other at a Festal Time?

We proceed thus to the Ninth Article:—

Objection 1. It would seem that neither are they bound to pay the debt at a festal time. For those who commit a sin as well as those who consent thereto are equally punished (Rom. i. 32). But the one who pays the debt consents with the one that asks, who sins. Therefore he sins also.

Obj. 2. Further, it is an affirmative precept that binds us to pray, and therefore we are bound to do so at a fixed time. Therefore one ought not to pay the debt at a time when one is bound to pray, as neither ought one at a time when one is bound to fulfill a special duty towards a temporal master.

On the contrary, It is written (1 Cor. vii. 5): *Defraud not one another, except by consent, for a time,* etc. Therefore when one spouse asks the other must pay.

I answer that, Since the wife has power of her husband's body, and *vice versa,* with regard to the act of procreation, the one is bound to pay the debt to the other, at any season or hour, with due regard to the decorum required in such matters, for this must not be done at once openly.

Reply Obj. 1. As far as he is concerned he

does not consent, but grants unwillingly and with grief that which is exacted of him; and consequently he does not sin. For it is ordained by God, on account of the weakness of the flesh, that the debt must always be paid to the one who asks lest he be afforded an occasion of sin.

Reply Obj. 2. No hour is fixed for praying, but that compensation can be made at some other hour; wherefore the argument is not cogent.

TENTH ARTICLE*

Whether Weddings Should Be Forbidden at Certain Times?

We proceed thus to the Tenth Article:—

Objection 1. It would seem that weddings ought not to be forbidden at certain times. For marriage is a sacrament: and the celebration of the others sacraments is not forbidden at those times. Therefore neither should the celebration of marriage be forbidden then.

Obj. 2. Further, asking for the marriage debt is more unbecoming on feast days than the celebration of marriage. Yet the debt may be asked for on those days. Therefore also marriages may be solemnized.

Obj. 3. Further, marriages that are contracted in despite of the law of the Church ought to be dissolved. Yet marriages are not dissolved if they be contracted at those times. Therefore it should not be forbidden by a commandment of the Church.

On the contrary, It is written (Eccles. iii. 5): *A time to embrace, and a time to be far from embraces.*

I answer that, When the newly married spouse is given to her husband, the minds of husband and wife are taken up with carnal preoccupations by reason of the very newness of things, wherefore weddings are wont to be signalized by much unrestrained rejoicing. On this account it is forbidden to celebrate marriages at those times when men ought especially to arise to spiritual things. Those times are from Advent until the Epiphany because of the Communion which, according to the ancient Canons, is wont to be made at Christmas (as was observed in its proper place, P. III, Q. 30), from Septuagesima until the Octave day of Easter, on account of the Easter Communion, and from the three days before the Ascension until the Octave day of Pentecost, on account of the preparation for Communion to be received at that time.

Reply Obj. 1. The celebration of marriage has a certain worldly and carnal rejoicing connected with it, which does not apply to the other sacraments. Hence the comparison fails.

Reply Obj. 2. There is not such a distraction of minds caused by the payment of a request for the debt as by the celebration of a marriage; and consequently the comparison fails.

Reply Obj. 3. Since time is not essential to a marriage contracted within the forbidden seasons, the marriage is nevertheless a true sacrament. Nor is the marriage dissolved absolutely, but for a time, that they may do penance for having disobeyed the commandment of the Church. It is thus that we are to understand the statement of the Master (iv, *Sent.* D. 33), namely that should a marriage have been contracted or a wedding celebrated at the aforesaid times, those who have done so *ought to be separated.* Nor does he say this on his own authority, but in reference to some canonical ordinance, such as that of the Council of Lerida, which decision is quoted by the Decretals.

QUESTION 65

Of Plurality of Wives

(In Five Articles)

We must now consider the plurality of wives. Under this head there are five points of inquiry: (1) Whether it is against the natural law to have several wives? (2) Whether this was ever lawful? (3) Whether it is against the natural law to have a concubine? (4) Whether it is a mortal sin to have intercourse with a concubine? (5) Whether it was ever lawful to have a concubine?

FIRST ARTICLE

Whether It is Against the Natural Law to Have Several Wives?

We proceed thus to the First Article:—

Objection 1. It would seem that it is not against the natural law to have several wives. For custom does not prejudice the law of nature. But *it was not a sin* to have several wives *when this was the custom* according to Augustine *(De Bono Conjug.* xv) as quoted in the text (iv, *Sent.* D. 33). Therefore it is not contrary to the natural law to have several wives.

Obj. 2. Further, whoever acts in opposition to the natural law, disobeys a commandment, for the law of nature has its commandments even as the written law has. Now Augustine says *(loc. cit.* and *De Civ. Dei.* xv. 38) that *it was not contrary to a commandment* to have several wives, *because by no law was it forbidden.* Therefore it is not against the natural law to have several wives.

Obj. 3. Further, marriage is chiefly directed to the begetting of offspring. But one man may get children of several women, by causing them to be pregnant. Therefore it is not against the natural law to have several wives.

Obj. 4. Further, *Natural right is that which nature has taught all animals,* as stated at the beginning of the *Digests* (1. i. ff. De just. et jure). Now nature has not taught all animals that one male should be united to but one female, since with many animals the one male is united to several females. Therefore it is not against the natural law to have several wives.

Obj. 5. Further, according to the Philosopher *(De Gener. Animal.* i. 20), in the beget-

* This article is omitted in the Leonine edition.

ting of offspring the male is to the female as agent to patient, and as the craftsman is to his material. But it is not against the order of nature for one agent to act on several patients, or for one craftsman to work in several materials. Therefore neither is it contrary to the law of nature for one husband to have many wives.

Obj. 6. *On the contrary,* That which was instilled into man at the formation of human nature would seem especially to belong to the natural law. Now it was instilled into him at the very formation of human nature that one man should have one wife, according to Gen. ii. 24, *They shall be two in one flesh.* Therefore it is of natural law.

Obj. 7. Further, It is contrary to the law of nature that man should bind himself to the impossible, and that what is given to one should be given to another. Now when a man contracts with a wife, he gives her the power of his body, so that he is bound to pay her the debt when she asks. Therefore it is against the law of nature that he should afterwards give the power of his body to another, because it would be impossible for him to pay both were both to ask at the same time.

Obj. 8. Further, *Do not to another what thou wouldst not were done to thyself** is a precept of the natural law. But a husband would by no means be willing for his wife to have another husband. Therefore he would be acting against the law of nature, were he to have another wife in addition.

Obj. 9. Further, whatever is against the natural desire is contrary to the natural law. Now a husband's jealousy of his wife and the wife's jealousy of her husband are natural, for they are found in all. Therefore, since jealousy is *love impatient of sharing the beloved,* it would seem to be contrary to the natural law that several wives should share one husband.

I answer that, All natural things are imbued with certain principles whereby they are enabled not only to exercise their proper actions, but also to render those actions proportionate to their end, whether such actions belong to a thing by virtue of its generic nature, or by virtue of its specific nature: thus it belongs to a magnet to be borne downwards by virtue of its generic nature, and to attract iron by virtue of its specific nature. Now just as in those things which act from natural necessity the principle of action is the form itself, whence their proper actions proceed proportionately to their end, so in things which are endowed with knowledge the principles of action are knowledge and appetite. Hence in the cognitive power there needs to be a natural

* Cf. Tob. iv. 16.

concept, and in the appetitive power a natural inclination, whereby the action befitting the genus or species is rendered proportionate to the end. Now since man, of all animals, knows the aspect of the end, and the proportion of the action to the end, it follows that he is imbued with a natural concept, whereby he is directed to act in a befitting manner, and this is called *the natural law* or *the natural right,* but in other animals *the natural instinct.* For brutes are rather impelled by the force of nature to do befitting actions, than guided to act on their own judgment. Therefore the natural law is nothing else than a concept naturally instilled into man, whereby he is guided to act in a befitting manner in his proper actions, whether they are competent to him by virtue of his generic nature, as, for instance, to beget, to eat, and so on, or belong to him by virtue of his specific nature, as, for instance, to reason and so forth. Now whatever renders an action improportionate to the end which nature intends to obtain by a certain work is said to be contrary to the natural law. But an action may be improportionate either to the principal or to the secondary end, and in either case this happens in two ways. First, on account of something which wholly hinders the end; for instance a very great excess or a very great deficiency in eating hinders both the health of the body, which is the principal end of food, and aptitude for conducting business, which is its secondary end. Secondly, on account of something that renders the attainment of the principal or secondary end difficult, or less satisfactory, for instance eating inordinately in respect of undue time. Accordingly if an action be improportionate to the end, through altogether hindering the principal end directly, it is forbidden by the first precepts of the natural law, which hold the same place in practical matters, as the general concepts of the mind in speculative matters. If, however, it be in any way improportionate to the secondary end, or again to the principal end, as rendering its attainment difficult or less satisfactory, it is forbidden, not indeed by the first precepts of the natural law, but by the second which are derived from the first even as conclusions in speculative matters receive our assent by virtue of self-known principles: and thus the act in question is said to be against the law of nature.

Now marriage has for its principal end the begetting and rearing of children, and this end is competent to man according to his generic nature, wherefore it is common to other animals *(Ethic.* viii. 12), and thus it is that the *offspring* is assigned as a marriage good. But for its secondary end, as the Philosopher says *(ibid.)*, it has, among men alone, the community of works that are a necessity of life, as stated above (Q. 41, A. 1). And in reference to this they owe one another *fidelity* which is one of the goods of marriage. Furthermore it has another end, as regards marriage between believers, namely the signification of Christ and the Church: and thus the *sacrament* is said to be a marriage good. Wherefore the first end corresponds to the marriage of man inasmuch as he is an animal: the second, inasmuch as he is a man; the third, inasmuch as he is a believer. Accordingly plurality of wives neither wholly destroys nor in any way hinders the first end of marriage, since one man is sufficient to get children of several wives, and to rear the children born of them. But though it does not wholly destroy the second end, it hinders it considerably, for there cannot easily be peace in a family where several wives are joined to one husband, since one husband cannot suffice to satisfy the requisitions of several wives, and again because the sharing of several in one occupation is a cause of strife: thus *potters quarrel with one another**, and in like manner the several wives of one husband. The third end, it removes altogether, because as Christ is one, so also is the Church one. It is therefore evident from what has been said that plurality of wives is in a way against the law of nature, and in a way not against it.

Reply Obj. 1. Custom does not prejudice the law of nature as regards the first precepts of the latter, which are like the general concepts of the mind in speculative matters. But those which are drawn like conclusions from these custom enforces, as Tully declares *(De inv. Rhet.* ii), or weakens. Such is the precept of nature in the matter of having one wife.

Reply Obj. 2. As Tully says *(ibid.) fear of the law and religion have sanctioned those things that come from nature and are approved by custom.* Wherefore it is evident that those dictates of the natural law, which are derived from the first principles as it were of the natural law, have not the binding force of an absolute commandment, except when they have been sanctioned by Divine or human law. This is what Augustine means by saying that *they did not disobey the commandments of the law, since it was not forbidden by any law.*

The *Reply* to the *Third Objection* follows from what has been said.

Reply Obj. 4. Natural right has several significations. First a right is said to be natural by its principle, because it is instilled by nature: and thus Tully defines it *(ibid.)* when he says: *Natural right is not the result of opinion but the product of an innate force.*

* Aristot. *(Rhet.* ii. 4.

And since even in natural things certain movements are called natural, not that they be from an intrinsic principle, but because they are from a higher moving principle,—thus the movements that are caused in the elements by the impress of heavenly bodies are said to be natural, as the Commentator states *(De cœlo et mundo* iii. 28)—therefore those things that are of Divine right are said to be of natural right, because they are caused by the impress and influence of a higher principle, namely God. Isidore takes it in this sense, when he says *(Etym.* v) that *the natural right is that which is contained in the Law and the Gospel.* Thirdly, right is said to be natural not only from its principle but also from its matter, because it is about natural things. And since nature is contradistinguished with reason, whereby man is a man, it follows that if we take natural right in its strictest sense, those things which are dictated by natural reason and pertain to man alone are not said to be of natural right, but only those which are dictated by natural reason and are common to man and other animals. Thus we have the aforesaid definition, namely: *Natural right is what nature has taught all animals.* Accordingly plurality of wives, though not contrary to natural right taken in the third sense, is nevertheless against natural right taken in the second sense, because it is forbidden by the Divine law. It is also against natural right taken in the first sense, as appears from what has been said, for such is nature's dictate to every animal according to the mode befitting its nature. Wherefore also certain animals, the rearing of whose offspring demands the care of both, namely the male and female, by natural instinct cling to the union of one with one, for instance the turtle-dove, the dove, and so forth.

The *Reply* to the *Fifth Objection* is clear from what has been said.

Since, however, the arguments adduced *on the contrary* side would seem to show that plurality of wives is against the first principles of the natural law, we must reply to them.

Accordingly we reply to the *Sixth Objection* that human nature was founded without any defect, and consequently it is endowed not only with those things without which the principal end of marriage is impossible of attainment, but also with those without which the secondary end of marriage could not be obtained without difficulty: and in this way it sufficed man when he was first formed to have one wife, as stated above.

Reply Obj. 7. In marriage the husband gives his wife power of his body, not in all respects, but only in those things that are required by marriage. Now marriage does not require the husband to pay the debt every time his wife asks for it, if we consider the principal end for which marriage was instituted, namely the good of the offspring, but only as far as is necessary for impregnation. But in so far as it is instituted as a remedy (which is its secondary end), marriage does require the debt to be paid at all times on being asked for. Hence it is evident that by taking several wives a man does not bind himself to the impossible, considering the principal end of marriage; and therefore plurality of wives is not against the first principles of the natural law.

Reply Obj. 8. This precept of the natural law, *Do not to another what thou wouldst not were done to thyself,* should be understood with the proviso that there be equal proportion. For if a superior is unwilling to be withstood by his subject, he is not therefore bound not to withstand his subject. Hence it does not follow in virtue of this precept that as a husband is unwilling for his wife to have another husband, he must not have another wife: because for one man to have several wives is not contrary to the first principles of the natural law, as stated above: whereas for one wife to have several husbands is contrary to the first principles of the natural law, since thereby the good of the offspring which is the principal end of marriage is, in one respect, entirely destroyed, and in another respect hindered. For the good of the offspring means not only begetting, but also rearing. Now the begetting of offspring, though not wholly voided (since a woman may be impregnated a second time after impregnation has already taken place, as stated in *De gener. animal.* vii. 4), is nevertheless considerably hindered, because this can scarcely happen without injury either to both fetus or to one of them. But the rearing of the offspring is altogether done away, because as a result of one woman having several husbands there follows uncertainty of the offspring in relation to its father, whose care is necessary for its education. Wherefore the marriage of one wife with several husbands has not been sanctioned by any law or custom, whereas the converse has been.

Reply Obj. 9. The natural inclination in the appetitive power follows the natural concept in the cognitive power. And since it is not so much opposed to the natural concept for a man to have several wives as for a wife to have several husbands, it follows that a wife's love is not so averse to another sharing the same husband with her, as a husband's love is to another sharing the same wife with him. Consequently both in man and in other animals the male is more jealous of the female than *vice versa*.

SECOND ARTICLE

Whether It Was Ever Lawful to Have Several Wives?

We proceed thus to the Second Article:—

Objection 1. It would seem that it can never have been lawful to have several wives. For, according to the Philosopher *(Ethic.* v. 7), *The natural law has the same power at all times and places.* Now plurality of wives is forbidden by the natural law, as stated above (A. 1). Therefore as it is unlawful now, it was unlawful at all times.

Obj. 2. Further, if it was ever lawful, this could only be because it was lawful either in itself, or by dispensation. If the former, it would also be lawful now; if the latter, this is impossible, for according to Augustine *(Contra Faust.* xxvi. 3), *as God is the founder of nature, He does nothing contrary to the principles which He has planted in nature.* Since then God has planted in our nature the principle that one man should be united to one wife, it would seem that He has never dispensed man from this.

Obj. 3. Further, if a thing be lawful by dispensation, it is only lawful for those who receive the dispensation. Now we do not read in the Law of a general dispensation having been granted to all. Since then in the Old Testament all who wished to do so, without any distinction, took to themselves several wives, nor were reproached on that account, either by the law or by the prophets, it would seem that it was not made lawful by dispensation.

Obj. 4. Further, where there is the same reason for dispensation, the same dispensation should be given. Now we cannot assign any other reason for dispensation than the multiplying of the offspring for the worship of God, and this is necessary also now. Therefore this dispensation would be still in force, especially as we read nowhere of its having been recalled.

Obj. 5. Further, in granting a dispensation the greater good should not be overlooked for the sake of a lesser good. Now fidelity and the sacrament, which it would seem impossible to safeguard in a marriage where one man is joined to several wives, are greater goods than the multiplication of the offspring. Therefore this dispensation ought not to have been granted with a view to this multiplication.

On the contrary, It is stated (Gal. iii. 19) that the Law *was set because of transgressors* (Vulg.,—*transgressions),* namely in order to prohibit them. Now the Old Law mentions plurality of wives without any prohibition thereof, as appears from Deut. xxi. 15, *If a man have two wives,* etc. Therefore they were not transgressors through having two wives, and so it was lawful.

Further, this is confirmed by the example

of the holy patriarchs, who are stated to have had several wives, and yet were most pleasing to God, for instance Jacob, David, and several others. Therefore at one time it was lawful.

I answer that, As stated above (A. 1, *ad* 7, 8), plurality of wives is said to be against the natural law, not as regards its first precepts, but as regards the secondary precepts, which like conclusions are drawn from its first precepts. Since, however, human acts must needs vary according to the various conditions of persons, times, and other circumstances, the aforesaid conclusions do not proceed from the first precepts of the natural law, so as to be binding in all cases, but only in the majority; for such is the entire matter of Ethics according to the Philosopher (*Ethic.* i. 3, 7). Hence, when they cease to be binding, it is lawful to disregard them. But because it is not easy to determine the above variations, it belongs exclusively to him from whose authority he derives its binding force to permit the non-observance of the law in those cases to which the force of the law ought not to extend, and this permission is called a dispensation. Now the law prescribing the one wife was framed not by man but by God, nor was it ever given by word or in writing, but was imprinted on the heart, like other things belonging in any way to the natural law. Consequently a dispensation in this matter could be granted by God alone through an inward inspiration, vouchsafed originally to the holy patriarchs, and by their example continued to others, at a time when it behooved the aforesaid precept not to be observed, in order to ensure the multiplication of the offspring to be brought up in the worship of God. For the principal end is ever to be borne in mind before the secondary end. Wherefore, since the good of the offspring is the principal end of marriage, it behooved to disregard for a time the impediment that might arise to the secondary ends, when it was necessary for the offspring to be multiplied; because it was for the removal of this impediment that the precept forbidding a plurality of wives was framed, as stated above (A. 1).

Reply Obj. 1. The natural law, considered in itself, has the same force at all times and places; but accidentally on account of some impediment it may vary at certain times and places, as the Philosopher (*ibid.*) instances in the case of other natural things. For at all times and places the right hand is better than the left according to nature, but it may happen accidentally that a person is ambidextrous, because our nature is variable; and the same applies to the natural, just as the Philosopher states (*ibid.*).

* John xix. 2.

Reply Obj. 2. In a Decretal (De divortiis, cap. *Gaudemus*) it is asserted that is was never lawful to have several wives without having a dispensation received through Divine inspiration. Nor is the dispensation thus granted a contradiction to the principles which God has implanted in nature, but an exception to them, because those principles are not intended to apply to all cases but to the majority, as stated. Even so it is not contrary to nature when certain occurrences take place in natural things miraculously, by way of exception to more frequent occurrences.

Reply Obj. 3. Dispensation from a law should follow the quality of the law. Wherefore, since the law of nature is imprinted on the heart, it was not necessary for a dispensation from things pertaining to the natural law to be given under the form of a written law, but by internal inspiration.

Reply Obj. 4. When Christ came it was the time of the fulness of the grace of Christ, whereby the worship of God was spread abroad among all nations by a spiritual propagation. Hence there is not the same reason for a dispensation as before Christ's coming, when the worship of God was spread and safeguarded by a carnal propagation.

Reply Obj. 5. The offspring, considered as one of the marriage goods, includes the keeping of faith with God, because the reason why it is reckoned a marriage good is because it is awaited with a view to its being brought up in the worship of God. Now the faith to be kept with God is of greater import than the faith to be kept with a wife, which is reckoned a marriage good, and than the signification which pertains to the sacrament, since the signification is subordinate to the knowledge of faith. Hence it is not unfitting if something is taken from the two other goods for the sake of the good of the offspring. Nor are they entirely done away, since there remains faith towards several wives; and the sacrament remains after a fashion, for though it did not signify the union of Christ with the Church as one, nevertheless the plurality of wives signified the distinction of degrees in the Church, which distinction is not only in the Church militant but also in the Church triumphant. Consequently their marriages signified somewhat the union of Christ not only with the Church militant, as some say, but also with the Church triumphant where there are *many mansions.**

THIRD ARTICLE

Whether It Is Against the Natural Law to Have a Concubine?

We proceed thus to the Third Article:—

Objection 1. It would seem that to have a concubine is not against the natural law. For the ceremonies of the Law are not of the natural law. But fornication is forbidden (Acts xv. 29) in conjunction with ceremonies of the law which for the time were being imposed on those who were brought to the faith from among the heathens. Therefore simple fornication which is intercourse with a concubine is not against the natural law.

Obj. 2. Further, positive law is an outcome of the natural law, as Tully says *(De Invent.* ii). Now fornication was not forbidden by positive law; indeed according to the ancient laws women used to be sentenced to be taken to brothels. Therefore it is not against the natural law to have a concubine.

Obj. 3. Further, the natural law does not forbid that which is given simply, to be given for a time or under certain restrictions. Now one unmarried woman may give the power of her body for ever to an unmarried man, so that he may use her when he will. Therefore it is not against the law of nature, if she give him power of her body for a time.

Obj. 4. Further, whoever uses his own property as he will, injures no one. But a bondswoman is her master's property. Therefore if her master use her as he will, he injures no one: and consequently it is not against the natural law to have a concubine.

Obj. 5. Further, everyone may give his own property to another. Now the wife has power of her husband's body (1 Cor. vii. 4). Therefore if his wife be willing, the husband can have intercourse with another woman without sin.

On the contrary, According to all laws the children born of a concubine are children of shame. But this would not be so unless the union of which they are born were naturally shameful.

Further, as stated above (Q. 41, A. 1), marriage is natural. But this would not be so if without prejudice to the natural law a man could be united to a woman otherwise than by marriage. Therefore it is against the natural law to have a concubine.

I answer that, As stated above (A. 1), an action is said to be against the natural law, if it is not in keeping with the due end intended by nature, whether through not being directed thereto by the action of the agent, or through being directed thereto by the action of the agent, or through being in itself improportionate to that end. Now the end which nature intends in sexual union is the begetting and rearing of the offspring; and that this good might be sought after, it attached pleasure to the union; as Augustine says *(De Nup. et Concup.* i. 8). Accordingly to make use of sexual intercourse on account of its inherent

* Cf. Q. 44, A. 2.

pleasure, without reference to the end for which nature intended it, is to act against nature, as also is it if the intercourse be not such as may fittingly be directed to that end. And since, for the most part, things are denominated from their end, as being that which is of most consequence to them, just as the marriage union took its name from the good of the offspring,* which is the end chiefly sought after in marriage, so the name of concubine is expressive of that union where sexual intercourse is sought after for its own sake. Moreover even though sometimes a man may seek to have offspring of such an intercourse, this is not befitting to the good of the offspring, which signifies not only the begetting of children from which they take their being, but also their rearing and instruction, by which means they receive nourishment and learning from their parents, in respect of which three things the parents are bound to their children, according to the Philosopher *(Ethic.* viii. 11, 12). Now since the rearing and teaching of the children remain a duty of the parents during a long period of time, the law of nature requires the father and mother to dwell together for a long time, in order that together they may be of assistance to their children. Hence birds that unite together in rearing their young do not sever their mutual fellowship from the time when they first come together until the young are fully fledged. Now this obligation which binds the female and her mate to remain together constitutes matrimony. Consequently it is evident that it is contrary to the natural law for a man to have intercourse with a woman who is not married to him, which is the signification of a concubine.

Reply Obj. 1. Among the Gentiles the natural law was obscured in many points: and consequently they did not think it wrong to have intercourse with a concubine, and in many cases practiced fornication as though it were lawful, as also other things contrary to the ceremonial laws of the Jews, though not contrary to the law of nature. Wherefore the apostles inserted the prohibition of fornication among that of other ceremonial observances, because in both cases there was a difference of opinion between Jews and Gentiles.

Reply Obj. 2. This law was the result of the darkness just mentioned, into which the Gentiles had fallen, by not giving due honor to God as stated in Rom. i. 21, and did not proceed from the instinct of the natural law. Hence, when the Christian religion prevailed, this law was abolished.

Reply Obj. 3. In certain cases no evil results ensue if a person surrenders his right to a thing whether absolutely or for a time, so that in neither case is the surrender against the natural law. But that does not apply to the case in point, wherefore the argument does not prove.

Reply Obj. 4. Injury is opposed to justice. Now the natural law forbids not only injustice, but also whatever is opposed to any of the virtues: for instance it is contrary to the natural law to eat immoderately, although by doing so a man uses his own property without injury to anyone. Moreover although a bondswoman is her master's property that she may serve him, she is not his that she may be his concubine. And again it depends how a person makes use of his property. For such a man does an injury to the offspring he begets, since such a union is not directed to its good, as stated above.

Reply Obj. 5. The wife has power of her husband's body, not simply and in all respects, but only in relation to marriage, and consequently she cannot transfer her husband's body to another to the detriment of the good of marriage.

FOURTH ARTICLE

Whether It Is a Mortal Sin to Have Intercourse with a Concubine?

We proceed thus to the Fourth Article:—

Objection 1. It would seem that it is not a mortal sin to have intercourse with a concubine. For a lie is a greater sin than simple fornication: and a proof of this is that Juda, who did not abhor to commit fornication with Thamar, recoiled from telling a lie, saying (Gen. xxxviii. 23): *Surely she cannot charge us with a lie.* But a lie is not always a mortal sin. Neither therefore is simple fornication.

Obj. 2. Further, a deadly sin should be punished with death. But the Old Law did not punish with death intercourse with a concubine, save in a certain case (Deut. xxii. 25). Therefore it is not a deadly sin.

Obj. 3. Further, according to Gregory *(Moral.* xxxiii. 12), the sins of the flesh are less blameworthy than spiritual sins. Now pride and covetousness, which are spiritual sins, are not always mortal sins. Therefore fornication, which is a sin of the flesh, is not always a mortal sin.

Obj. 4. Further, where the incentive is greater the sin is less grievous, because he sins more who is overcome by a lighter temptation. But concupiscence is the greatest incentive to lust. Therefore since lustful actions are not always mortal sins, neither is simple fornication a mortal sin.

On the contrary, Nothing but mortal sin excludes from the kingdom of God. But fornicators are excluded from the kingdom of God

(1 Cor. vi. 9, 10). Therefore simple fornication is a mortal sin.

Further, mortal sins alone are called crimes. Now all fornication is a crime according to Tob. iv. 13, *Take heed to keep thyself . . . from all fornication, and beside thy wife never endure to know crime.* Therefore, etc.

I answer that, As we have already stated (ii, *Sent.* D. 42, Q. 1, A. 4), those sins are mortal in their genus which violate the bond of friendship between man and God, and between man and man; for such sins are against the two precepts of charity which is the life of the soul. Wherefore since the intercourse of fornication destroys the due relations of the parent with the offspring that is nature's aim in sexual intercourse, there can be no doubt that simple fornication by its very nature is a mortal sin even though there were no written law.

Reply Obj. 1. It often happens that a man who does not avoid a mortal sin, avoids a venial sin to which he has not so great an incentive. Thus, too, Juda avoided a lie while he avoided not fornication. Nevertheless that would have been a pernicious lie, for it would have involved an injury if he had not kept his promise.

Reply Obj. 2. A sin is called deadly, not because it is punished with temporal, but because it is punished with eternal death. Hence also theft, which is a mortal sin, and many other sins are sometimes not punished with temporal death by the law. The same applies to fornication.

Reply Obj. 3. Just as not every movement of pride is a mortal sin, so neither is every movement of lust, because the first movements of lust and the like are venial sins, even sometimes marriage intercourse. Nevertheless some acts of lust are mortal sins, while some movements of pride are venial: since the words quoted from Gregory are to be understood as comparing vices in their genus and not in their particular acts.

Reply Obj. 4. A circumstance is the more effective in aggravating a sin according as it comes nearer to the nature of sin. Hence although fornication is less grave on account of the greatness of its incentive, yet on account of the matter about which it is, it has a greater gravity than immoderate eating, because it is about those things which tighten the bond of human fellowship, as stated above. Hence the argument does not prove.

FIFTH ARTICLE

Whether It Was Ever Lawful to Have a Concubine?

We proceed thus to the Fifth Article:—

Objection 1. It would seem that it has been sometime lawful to have a concubine. For just as the natural law requires a man to have but one wife, so does it forbid him to have a concubine. Yet at times it has been lawful to have several wives. Therefore it has also been lawful to have a concubine.

Obj. 2. Further, a woman cannot be at the same time a slave and a wife; wherefore according to the Law (Deut. xxi. 11 *seqq.*) a bondswoman gained her freedom by the very fact of being taken in marriage. Now we read that certain men who were most beloved of God, for instance Abraham and Jacob, had intercourse with their bondswomen. Therefore these were not wives, and consequently it was sometime lawful to have a concubine.

Obj. 3. Further, a woman who is taken in marriage cannot be cast out, and her son should have a share in the inheritance. Yet Abraham sent Agar away, and her son was not his heir (Gen. xxi. 14). Therefore she was not Abraham's wife.

On the contrary, Things opposed to the precepts of the decalogue were never lawful. Now to have a concubine is against a precept of the decalogue, namely, *Thou shalt not commit adultery.* Therefore it was never lawful.

Further, Ambrose says in his book on the patriarchs *(De Abraham* i. 4): *What is unlawful to a wife is unlawful to a husband.* But it is never lawful for a wife to put aside her own husband and have intercourse with another man. Therefore it was never lawful for a husband to have a concubine.

I answer that, Rabbi Moses says *(Doc. Perp.* iii. 49) that before the time of the Law fornication was not a sin; and he proved his assertion from the fact that Juda had intercourse with Thamar. But this argument is not conclusive. For there is no need to excuse Jacob's sons from mortal sin, since they were accused to their father of a most wicked crime (Gen. xxxvii. 2), and consented kill Joseph and to sell him. Wherefore we must say that since it is against the natural law to have a concubine outside wedlock, as stated above (A. 3), it was never lawful either in itself or by dispensation. For as we have shown *(ibid.)* intercourse with a woman outside wedlock is an action improportionate to the good of the offspring which is the principal end of marriage: and consequently it is against the first precepts of the natural law which admit of no dispensation. Hence wherever in the Old Testament we read of concubines being taken by

such men as we ought to excuse from mortal sin, we must needs understand them to have been taken in marriage, and yet to have been called concubines, because they had something of the character of a wife and something of the character of a concubine. In so far as marriage is directed to its principal end, which is the good of the offspring, the union of wife and husband is indissoluble or at least of a lasting nature, as shown above (A. 1), and in regard to this there is no dispensation. But in regard to the secondary end, which is the management of the household and community of works, the wife is united to the husband as his mate: and this was lacking in those who were known as concubines. For in this respect a dispensation was possible, since it is the secondary end of marriage. And from this point of view they bore some resemblance to concubines, and for this reason they were known as such.

Reply Obj. 1. As stated above (A. 1, *ad* 7, 8) to have several wives is not against the first precepts of the natural law, as it is to have a concubine; wherefore the argument does not prove.

Reply Obj. 2. The patriarchs of old by virtue of the dispensation which allowed them several wives, approached their bondswomen with the disposition of a husband towards his wife. For these women were wives as to the principal and first end of marriage, but not as to the other union which regards the secondary end, to which bondage is opposed, since a woman cannot be at once mate and slave.

Reply Obj. 3. As in the Mosaic law it was allowable by dispensation to grant a bill of divorce in order to avoid wife-murder (as we shall state further on, Q. 67, A. 6), so by the same dispensation Abraham was allowed to send Agar away, in order to signify the mystery which the Apostle explains (Gal. iv. 22 *seqq.*). Again, that this son did not inherit belongs to the mystery, as explained in the same place. Even so Esau, the son of a free woman, did not inherit (Rom. ix. 13 *seqq.*). In like manner on account of the mystery it came about that the sons of Jacob born of bond and free women inherited, as Augustine says *(Tract.* xi, *in Joan.)* because *sons and heirs are born to Christ both of good ministers denoted by the free woman and of evil ministers denoted by the bondswoman.*

QUESTION 66

Of Bigamy and of the Irregularity Contracted Thereby

(In Five Articles)

IN the next place we must consider bigamy and the irregularity contracted thereby. Under this head there are five points of inquiry: (1) Whether irregularity attaches to the bigamy that consists in having two successive wives? (2) Whether irregularity is contracted by one who has two wives at once? (3) Whether irregularity is contracted by marrying one who is not a virgin? (4) Whether bigamy is removed by Baptism? (5) Whether a dispensation can be granted to a bigamous person?

FIRST ARTICLE

Whether Irregularity Attaches to Bigamy?

We proceed thus to the First Article:—

Objection 1. It would seem that irregularity is not attached to the bigamy that consists in having two wives successively. For multitude and unity are consequent upon being. Since then non-being does not cause plurality, a man who has two wives successively, the one in being, the other in non-being, does not thereby become the husband of more than one wife, so as to be debarred, according to the Apostle (1 Tim. iii. 2; Tit. i. 6), from the episcopate.

Obj. 2. Further, a man who commits fornication with several women gives more evidence of incontinence than one who has several wives successively. Yet in the first case a man does not become irregular. Therefore neither in the second should he become irregular.

Obj. 3. Further, if bigamy causes irregularity, this is either because of the sacrament, or because of the carnal intercourse. Now it is not on account of the former, for if a man had contracted marriage by words of the present and, his wife dying before the consummation of the marriage, he were to marry another, he would become irregular, which is against the decree of Innocent III (cap. *Dubium,* De bigamia). Nor again is it on account of the second, for then a man who had committed fornication with several women would become irregular: which is false. Therefore bigamy nowise causes irregularity.

I answer that, By the sacrament of Order a man is appointed to the ministry of the sacraments; and he who has to administer the sacraments to others must suffer from no defect in the sacraments. Now there is a defect in a sacrament when the entire signification of the sacrament is not found therein. And the sacrament of marriage signifies the union of Christ with the Church, which is the union of one with one. Therefore the perfect signification of the sacrament requires the husband to have only one wife, and the wife to have but one husband; and consequently bigamy, which does away with this, causes irregularity. And there are four kinds of bigamy: the first is when a man has several lawful wives successively; the second is when a man has several wives at once, one in law, the other in fact; the third, when he has several successively, one in law, the other in fact; the fourth, when a man marries a widow. Accordingly irregularity attaches to all of these.

There is another consequent reason assigned, since those who receive the sacrament of Order should be signalized by the greatest spirituality, both because they administer spiritual things, namely the sacraments, and because they teach spiritual things, and should be occupied in spiritual matters. Wherefore since concupiscence is most incompatible with spirituality, inasmuch as it makes a man to be wholly carnal, they should give no sign of persistent concupiscence, which does indeed show itself in bigamous persons, seeing that they were unwilling to be content with one wife. The first reason however is the better.

Reply Obj. 1. The multitude of several wives at the same time is a multitude simply, wherefore a multitude of this kind is wholly inconsistent with the significatiton of the sacrament, so that the sacrament is voided on that account. But the multitude of several successive wives is a multitude relatively, wherefore it does not entirely destroy the signification of the sacrament, nor does it void the sacrament in its essence but in its perfection, which is re₁uired of those who are the dispensers of sacraments.

Reply Obj. 2. Although those who are guilty of fornication give proof of greater concupiscence, theirs is not a so persistent concupiscence, since by fornication one party is not bound to the other for ever; and consequently no defect attaches to the sacrament.

Reply Obj. 3. As stated above, bigamy causes irregularity, because it destroys the perfect signification of the sacrament: which signification is seated both in the union of minds, as expressed by the consent, and in the union of bodies. Wherefore bigamy must affect both of these at the same time in order to cause irregularity. Hence the decree of Innocent III disposes of the statement of the

Master (iv, *Sent.* D. 27), namely that consent alone by words of the present is sufficient to cause irregularity.

SECOND ARTICLE

Whether Irregularity Results from Bigamy, When One Husband Has Two Wives, One in Law, the Other in Fact?

We proceed thus to the Second Article:—

Objection 1. It would seem that irregularity does not result from bigamy when one husband has two wives at the same time, one in law and one in fact. For when the sacrament is void there can be no defect in the sacrament. Now when a man marries a woman in fact but not in law there is no sacrament, since such a union does not signify the union of Christ with the Church. Therefore since irregularity does not result from bigamy except on account of a defect in the sacrament, it would seem that no irregularity attaches to bigamy of this kind.

Obj. 2. Further, if a man has intercourse with a woman whom he has married in fact and not in law, he commits fornication if he has not a lawful wife, or adultery if he has. But a man does not become irregular by dividing his flesh among several women by fornication or adultery. Therefore neither does he by the aforesaid kind of bigamy.

Obj. 3. Further, it may happen that a man, before knowing carnally the woman he has married in law, marries another in fact and not in law, and knows her carnally, whether the former woman be living or dead. Now this man has contracted marriage with several women either in law or in fact, and yet he is not irregular, since he has not divided his flesh among several women. Therefore irregularity is not contracted by reason of the aforesaid kind of bigamy.

I answer that, Irregularity is contracted in the two second kinds of bigamy, for although in the one there is no sacrament, there is a certain likeness to a sacrament. Wherefore these two kinds are secondary, and the first is the principal kind in causing irregularity.

Reply Obj. 1. Although there is no sacrament in this case there is a certain likeness to a sacrament, whereas there is no such likeness in fornication or adultery. Hence the comparison fails.

This suffices for the *Reply* to the *Second Objection.*

Reply Obj. 3. In this case the man is not reckoned a bigamist, because the first marriage lacked its perfect signification. Nevertheless if, by the judgment of the Church, he be compelled to return to his first wife and carnally to know her, he becomes irregular forthwith, because the irregularity is the result not of the sin but of imperfect signification.

THIRD ARTICLE

Whether Irregularity Is Contracted by Marrying One Who Is Not a Virgin?

We proceed thus to the Third Article:—

Objection 1. It would seem that irregularity is not contracted by marrying one who is not a virgin. For a man's own defect is a greater impediment to him than the defect of another. But if the man himself who marries is not a virgin he does not become irregular. Therefore much less does he if his wife is not a virgin.

Obj. 2. Further, it may happen that a man marries a woman after corrupting her. Now, seemingly, such a man does not become irregular, since he has not divided his flesh among several, nor has his wife done so, and yet he marries a woman who is not a virgin. Therefore this kind of bigamy does not cause irregularity.

Obj. 3. Further, no man can become irregular except voluntarily. But sometimes a man marries involuntarily one who is not a virgin, for instance when he thinks her a virgin and afterwards, by knowing her carnally, finds that she is not. Therefore this kind does not always cause irregularity.

Obj. 4. Further, unlawful intercourse after marriage is more guilty than before marriage. Now if a wife, after the marriage has been consummated, has intercourse with another man, her husband does not become irregular, otherwise he would be punished for his wife's sin. Moreover, it might happen that, after knowing of this, he pays her the debt at her asking, before she is accused and convicted of adultery. Therefore it would seem that this kind of bigamy does not cause irregularity.

On the contrary, Gregory says *(Regist.* ii. ep. 37): *We command thee never to make unlawful ordinations, nor to admit to holy orders a bigamist, or one who has married a woman that is not a virgin, or one who is unlettered, or one who is deformed in his limbs, or bound to do penance or to perform some civil duty, or who is in any state of subjection.*

I answer that, In the union of Christ with the Church unity is found on either side. Consequently whether we find division of the flesh on the part of the husband, or on the part of the wife, there is a defect of sacrament. There is, however, a difference, because on the part of the husband it is required that he should not have married another wife, but not that he should be a virgin, whereas on the part of the wife it is also required that she be a virgin. The reason assigned by those versed in the Decretals is because the bridegroom signifies the Church militant which is entrusted to the care of a bishop, and in which there are many corruptions, while the spouse signifies Christ Who was a virgin: wherefore virginity on the part of the spouse, but not on the part of the bridegroom, is required in order that a man be made a bishop. This reason, however, is expressly contrary to the words of the Apostle (Eph. v. 25): *Husbands, love your wives, as Christ also loved the Church,* which show that the bride signifies the Church, and the bridegroom Christ; and again he says (*verse 23*): *Because the husband is the head of the wife, as Christ is the head of the Church.* Wherefore others say that Christ is signified by the bridegroom, and that the bride signifies the Church triumphant in which there is no stain. Also that the synagogue was first united to Christ as a concubine; so that the sacrament loses nothing of its signification if the bridegroom previously had a concubine. But this is most absurd, since just as the faith of ancients and of moderns is one, so is the Church one. Wherefore those who served God at the time of the synagogue belonged to the unity of the Church in which we serve God. Moreover this is expressly contrary to Jerem. iii. 14, Ezech. xvi. 8, Osee ii. 16, where the espousals of the synagogue are mentioned explicitly: so that she was not as a concubine but as a wife. Again, according to this, fornication would be the sacred sign (*sacramentum*) of that union, which is absurd. Wherefore heathendom, before being espoused to Christ in the faith of the Church, was corrupted by the devil through idolatry. Hence we must say otherwise that irregularity is caused by a defect in the sacrament itself. Now when a corruption of the flesh occurs outside wedlock on account of a preceding marriage, it causes no defect in the sacrament on the part of the person corrupted, but it causes a defect in the other person, because the act of one who contracts marriage terminates not in himself, but in the other party, wherefore it takes its species from its term, which, moreover, in regard to that act, is the matter as it were of the sacrament. Consequently if a woman were able to receive Orders, just as her husband becomes irregular through marrying one who is not a virgin, but not through his not being a virgin when he marries, so also would a woman become irregular if she were to marry a man who is not a virgin, but not if she were no longer a virgin when she married—unless she had been corrupted by reason of a previous marriage.

This suffices for the *Reply* to the *First Objection.*

Reply Obj. 2. In this case opinions differ. It is, however, more probable that he is not

irregular, because he has not divided his flesh among several women.

Reply Obj. 3. Irregularity is not the infliction of a punishment, but the defect of a sacrament. Consequently it is not always necessary for bigamy to be voluntary in order to cause irregularity. Hence a man who marries a woman, thinking her to be a virgin, whereas she is not, becomes irregular by knowing her carnally.

Reply Obj. 4. If a woman commits fornication after being married, her husband does not become irregular on that account, unless he again knows her carnally after she has been corrupted by adultery, since otherwise the corruption of the wife nowise affects the marriage act of the husband. But though he be compelled by law to pay her the debt, or if he do so at her request, being compelled by his own conscience, even before she is convicted of adultery, he becomes irregular, albeit opinions differ on this point. However, what we have said is more probable, since here it is not a question of sin, but of signification only.

FOURTH ARTICLE
Whether Bigamy Is Removed by Baptism?

We proceed thus to the Fourth Article:—

Objection 1. It would seem that bigamy is removed by Baptism. For Jerome says in his commentary on the Epistle to Titus (i. 6, *the husband of one wife*) that if a man has had several wives before receiving Baptism, or one before and another after Baptism, he is not a bigamist. Therefore bigamy is removed by Baptism.

Obj. 2. Further, he who does what is more, does what is less. Now Baptism removes all sin, and sin is a greater thing than irregularity. Therefore it removes irregularity.

Obj. 3. Further, Baptism takes away all punishment resulting from an act. Now such is the irregularity of bigamy. Therefore, etc.

Obj. 4. Further, a bigamist is irregular because he is deficient in the representation of Christ. Now by Baptism we are fully conformed to Christ. Therefore this irregularity is removed.

Obj. 5. Further, the sacraments of the New Law are more efficacious than the sacraments of the Old Law. But the sacraments of the Old Law removed irregularities according to the Master's statement (iv, *Sent.*). Therefore Baptism also, being the most efficacious of the sacraments of the New Law, removes the irregularity consequent upon bigamy.

On the contrary, Augustine says (*De Bono Conjug.,* xviii): *Those understand the question more correctly who maintain that a man who has married a second wife, though he was a catechumen or even a pagan at the time, cannot be ordained, because it is a question of a sacrament, not of a sin.*

Further, according to the same authority *(ibid.) a woman who has been corrupted while a catechumen or a pagan cannot after Baptism be consecrated among God's virgins.* Therefore in like manner one who was a bigamist before Baptism cannot be ordained.

I answer that, Baptism removes sin, but does not dissolve marriage. Wherefore since irregularity results from marriage, it cannot be removed by Baptism, as Augustine says *(loc. cit.).*

Reply Obj. 1. In this case Jerome's opinion is not followed: unless perhaps he wished to explain that he means that a dispensation should be more easily granted.

Reply Obj. 2. It does not follow that what does a greater thing, does a lesser, unless it be directed to the latter. This is not so in the case in point, because Baptism is not directed to the removal of an irregularity.

Reply Obj. 3. This must be understood of punishments consequent upon actual sin, which are, or have yet to be, inflicted: for one does not recover virginity by Baptism, nor again undivision of the flesh.

Reply Obj. 4. Baptism conforms a man to Christ as regards the virtue of the mind, but not as to the condition of the body, which is effected by virginity or division of the flesh.

Reply Obj. 5. Those irregularities were contracted through slight and temporary causes, and consequently they could be removed by those sacraments. Moreover the latter were ordained for that purpose, whereas Baptism is not.

FIFTH ARTICLE

Whether It Is Lawful for a Bigamist to Receive a Dispensation?

We proceed thus to the Fifth Article:—

Objection 1. It would seem unlawful for a bigamist to be granted a dispensation. For it is said (Extra, De bigamis, cap. *Nuper): It is not lawful to grant a dispensation to clerics who, as far as they could do so, have taken to themselves a second wife.*

Obj. 2. Further, it is not lawful to grant a dispensation from the Divine law. Now whatever is in the canonical writings belongs to the Divine law. Since then in canonical Scripture the Apostle says (1 Tim. iii. 2): *It behooveth ... a bishop to be ... the husband of one wife,* it would seem that a dispensation cannot be granted in this matter.

Obj. 3. Further, no one can receive a dispensation in what is essential to a sacrament. But it is essential to the sacrament of Order

that the recipient be not irregular, since the signification which is essential to a sacrament is lacking in one who is irregular. Therefore he cannot be granted a dispensation in this.

Obj. 4. Further, what is reasonably done cannot be reasonably undone. If, therefore, a bigamist can lawfully receive a dispensation, it was unreasonable that he should be irregular: which is inadmissible.

On the contrary, Pope Lucius granted a dispensation to the bishop of Palermo who was a bigamist, as stated in the gloss on can. *Lector,* dist. 34.

Further, Pope Martin* says: *If a Reader marry a widow, let him remain a Reader, or if there be need for it, he may receive the Sub-diaconate, but no higher order: and the same applies if he should be a bigamist.* Therefore he may at least receive a dispensation as far as the Subdiaconate.

I answer that, Irregularity attaches to bigamy not by natural, but by positive law; nor again is it one of the essentials of Order that a man be not a bigamist, which is evident from the fact that if a bigamist present himself for Orders, he receives the character. Wherefore the Pope can dispense altogether from such an irregularity; but a bishop, only as regards the minor Orders, though some say that in order to prevent religious wandering abroad he can dispense therefrom as regards the major Orders in those who wish to serve God in religion.

Reply Obj. 1. This Decretal shows that there is the same difficulty against granting a dispensation in those who have married several wives in fact, as if they had married them in law; but it does not prove that the Pope has no power to grant a dispensation in such cases.

Reply Obj. 2. This is true as regards things belonging to the natural law, and those which are essential to the sacraments, and to faith. But in those which owe their institution to the apostles, since the Church has the same power now as then of setting up and of putting down, she can grant a dispensation through him who holds the primacy.

Reply Obj. 3. Not every signification is essential to a sacrament, but that alone which belongs to the sacramental effect,† and this is not removed by irregularity.

Reply Obj. 4. In particular cases there is no ratio that applies to all equally, on account of their variety. Hence what is reasonably established for all, in consideration of what happens in the majority of cases, can be with equal reason done away in a certain definite case.

* Martinus Bracarensis: cap. xliii.

† Leonine edition reads *officium,* some read *effectum;* the meaning is the same, and is best rendered as above.

QUESTION 67

Of the Bill of Divorce

(In Seven Articles)

WE must now consider the bill of divorce, under which head there are seven points of inquiry: (1) Whether the indissolubility of marriage is of natural law? (2) Whether by dispensation it may become lawful to put away a wife? (3) Whether it was lawful under the Mosaic law? (4) Whether a wife who has been divorced may take another husband? (5) Whether the husband can marry again the wife whom he has divorced? (6) Whether the cause of divorce was hatred of the wife? (7) Whether the reasons for divorce had to be written on the bill?

FIRST ARTICLE

Whether Inseparableness of the Wife Is of Natural Law?

We proceed thus to the First Article:—

Objection 1. It would seem that inseparableness of the wife is not of natural law. For the natural law is the same for all. But no law save Christ's has forbidden the divorcing of a wife. Therefore inseparableness of a wife is not of natural law.

Obj. 2. Further, the sacraments are not of the natural law. But the indissolubility of marriage is one of the marriage goods. Therefore it is not of the natural law.

Obj. 3. Further, the union of man and woman in marriage is chiefly directed to the begetting, rearing, and instruction of the offspring. But all things are complete by a certain time. Therefore after that time it is lawful to put away a wife without prejudice to the natural law.

Obj. 4. Further, the good of the offspring is the principal end of marriage. But the indissolubility of marriage is opposed to the good of the offspring, because, according to philosophers, a certain man cannot beget offspring of a certain woman, and yet he might beget of another, even though she may have had intercourse with another man. Therefore the indissolubility of marriage is against rather than according to the natural law.

On the contrary, Those things which were assigned to nature when it was well established in its beginning belong especially to the law of nature. Now the indissolubility of marriage is one of these things according to Matth. xix. 4, 6. Therefore it is of natural law.

Further, it is of natural law that man should not oppose himself to God. Yet man would,

in a way, oppose himself to God if he were to sunder *what God hath joined together.* Since then the indissolubility of marriage is gathered from this passage (Matth. xix. 6) it would seem that it is of natural law.

I answer that, By the intention of nature marriage is directed to the rearing of the offspring, not merely for a time, but throughout its whole life. Hence it is of natural law that parents should lay up for their children, and that children should be their parents' heirs (2 Cor. xii. 14). Therefore, since the offspring is the common good of husband and wife, the dictate of the natural law requires the latter to live together for ever inseparably: and so the indissolubility of marriage is of natural law.

Reply Obj. 1. Christ's law alone *brought* mankind *to perfection,** by bringing man back to the state of the newness of nature. Wherefore neither Mosaic nor human laws could remove all that was contrary to the law of nature, for this was reserved exclusively to *the law of the spirit of life.*†

Reply Obj. 2. Indissolubility belongs to marriage in so far as the latter is a sign of the perpetual union of Christ with the Church, and in so far as it fulfills an office of nature that is directed to the good of the offspring, as stated above. But since divorce is more directly incompatible with the signification of the sacrament than with the good of the offspring, with which it is incompatible consequently, as stated above (Q. 65, A. 2, *ad* 5), the indissolubility of marriage is implied in the good of the sacrament rather than in the good of the offspring, although it may be connected with both. And in so far as it is connected with the good of the offspring, it is of the natural law, but not as connected with the good of the sacrament.

Reply Obj. 3. may be gathered from what has been said.

Reply Obj. 4. Marriage is chiefly directed to the common good in respect of its principal end, which is the good of the offspring; although in respect of its secondary end it is directed to the good of the contracting party, in so far as it is by its very nature a remedy for concupiscence. Hence marriage laws consider what is expedient for all rather than what may be suitable for one. Therefore although the indissolubility of marriage hinder the good of the offspring with regard to some individual, it is proportionate with the good

* Cf. Heb. vii. 19.   † Cf. Rom. viii. 2.

of the offspring absolutely speaking: and for this reason the argument does not prove.

SECOND ARTICLE

Whether It May Have Been Lawful by Dispensation to Put Away a Wife?

We proceed thus to the Second Article:—

Objection 1. It seems that it could not be lawful by dispensation to put away a wife. For in marriage anything that is opposed to the good of the offspring is against the first precepts of the natural law, which admit of no dispensation. Now such is the putting away of a wife, as stated above (A. 1). Therefore, etc.

Obj. 2. Further, a concubine differs from a wife especially in the fact that she is not inseparably united. But by no dispensation could a man have a concubine. Therefore by no dispensation could he put his wife away.

Obj. 3. Further, men are as fit to receive a dispensation now as of old. But now a man cannot receive a dispensation to divorce his wife. Neither, therefore, could he in olden times.

On the contrary, Abraham carnally knew Agar with the disposition of a husband towards his wife, as stated above (Q. 65, A. 5, *ad* 2, 3). Now by Divine command he sent her away, and yet sinned not. Therefore it could be lawful by dispensation for a man to put away his wife.

I answer that, In the commandments, especially those which in some way are of natural law, a dispensation is like a change in the natural course of things: and this course is subject to a twofold change. First, by some natural cause whereby another natural cause is hindered from following its course: it is thus in all things that happen by chance less frequently in nature. In this way, however, there is no variation in the course of those natural things which happen always, but only in the course of those which happen frequently. Secondly, by a cause altogether supernatural, as in the case of miracles: and in this way there can be a variation in the course of nature, not only in the course which is appointed for the majority of cases, but also in the course which is appointed for all cases, as instanced by the sun standing still at the time of Josue, and by its turning back at the time of Ezechias, and by the miraculous eclipse at the time of Christ's Passion.* In like manner the reason for a dispensation from a precept of the law of nature is sometimes found in the lower causes, and in this way a dispensation may bear upon the secondary precepts of the natural law, but not on the first precepts be-

* Jos. x. 14; 4 Kings xx. 10; Isa. xxxviii. 8; Matth. xxvii. 15.

cause these are always existent as it were, as stated above (Q. 65, A. 1) in reference to the plurality of wives and so forth. But sometimes this reason is found in the higher causes, and then a dispensation may be given by God even from the first precepts of the natural law, for the sake of signifying or showing some Divine mystery, as instanced in the dispensation vouchsafed to Abraham in the slaying of his innocent son. Such dispensations, however, are not granted to all generally, but to certain individual persons, as also happens in regard to miracles. Accordingly, if the indissolubility of marriage is contained among the first precepts of the natural law, it could only be a matter of dispensation in this second way; but, if it be one of the second precepts of the natural law, it could be a matter of dispensation even in the first way. Now it would seem to belong rather to the secondary precepts of the natural law. For the indissolubility of marriage is not directed to the good of the offspring, which is the principal end of marriage, except in so far as parents have to provide for their children for their whole life, by due preparation of those things that are necessary in life. Now this preparation does not pertain to the first intention of nature, in respect of which all things are common. And therefore it would seem that to put away one's wife is not contrary to the first intention of nature, and consequently that it is contrary not to the first but to the second precepts of the natural law. Therefore, seemingly, it can be a matter of dispensation even in the first way.

Reply Obj. 1. The good of the offspring, in so far as it belongs to the first intention of nature, includes procreation, nourishment, and instruction, until the offspring comes to perfect age. But that provision be made for the children by bequeathing to them the inheritance or other goods belongs seemingly to the second intention of the natural law.

Reply Obj. 2. To have a concubine is contrary to the good of the offspring, in respect of nature's first intention in that good, namely the rearing and instruction of the child, for which purpose it is necessary that the parents remain together permanently; which is not the case with a concubine, since she is taken for a time. Hence the comparison fails. But in respect of nature's second intention, even the having of a concubine may be a matter of dispensation as evidenced by Osee i.

Reply Obj. 3. Although indissolubility belongs to the second intention of marriage as fulfilling an office of nature, it belongs to its first intention as a sacrament of the Church. Hence, from the moment it was made a sacrament of the Church, as long as it remains such it cannot be a matter of dispensation, except perhaps by the second kind of dispensation.

THIRD ARTICLE

Whether It Was Lawful to Divorce a Wife Under the Mosaic Law?

We proceed thus to the Third Article:—

Objection 1. It would seem that it was lawful to divorce a wife under the Mosaic law. For one way of giving consent is to refrain from prohibiting when one can prohibit. It is also unlawful to consent to what is unlawful. Since then the Mosaic law did not forbid the putting away of a wife and did no wrong by not forbidding it, for *the law . . . is holy* (Rom. vii. 12), it would seem that divorce was at one time lawful.

Obj. 2. Further, the prophets spoke inspired by the Holy Ghost, according to 2 Pet. i. 21. Now it is written (Mal. ii. 16): *When thou shalt hate her, put her away.* Since then that which the Holy Ghost inspires is not unlawful, it would seem that it was not always unlawful to divorce a wife.

Obj. 3. Further, Chrysostom* says that even as the apostles permitted second marriages, so Moses allowed the bill of divorce. But second marriages are not sinful. Therefore neither was it sinful under the Mosaic law to divorce a wife.

Obj. 4. *On the contrary,* Our Lord said (Matth. xix. 8) that Moses granted the Jews the bill of divorce by reason of the hardness of their heart. But their hardness of heart did not excuse them from sin. Neither therefore did the law about the bill of divorce.

Obj. 5. Further, Chrysostom† says (*ibid.*) that *Moses, by granting the bill of divorce, did not indicate the justice of God, but deprived their sin of its guilt, for while the Jews acted as though they were keeping the law, their sin seemed to be no sin.*

I answer that, On this point there are two opinions. For some say that under the Law those who put away their wives, after giving them a bill of divorce, were not excused from sin, although they were excused from the punishment which they should have suffered according to the Law: and that for this reason Moses is stated to have permitted the bill of divorce. Accordingly they reckon four kinds of permission: one by absence of precept, so that when a greater good is not prescribed, a lesser good is said to be permitted: thus the Apostle by not prescribing virginity, permitted marriage (1 Cor. vii). The second is by absence of prohibition: thus venial sins are said

to be permitted because they are not forbidden. The third is by absence of prevention, and thus all sins are said to be permitted by God, in so far as He does not prevent them, whereas He can. The fourth is by omission of punishment, and in this way the bill of divorce was permitted in the Law, not indeed for the sake of obtaining a greater good, as was the dispensation to have several wives, but for the sake of preventing a greater evil, namely wife-murder to which the Jews were prone on account of the corruption of their irascible appetite. Even so they were allowed to lend money for usury to strangers, on account of corruption in their concupiscible appetite, lest they should exact usury of their brethren; and again on account of the corruption of suspicion in the reason they were allowed the sacrifice of jealousy, lest mere suspicion should corrupt their judgment. But because the Old Law, though it did not confer grace, was given that it might indicate sin, as the saints are agreed in saying, others are of opinion that if it had been a sin for a man to put away his wife, this ought to have been indicated to him, at least by the law or the prophets: *Show My people their wicked doings* (Isa. lviii. 1): else they would seem to have been neglected, if those things which are necessary for salvation and which they knew not were never made known to them: and this cannot be admitted, because the righteousness of the Law observed at the time of the Law would merit eternal life. For this reason they say that although to put away one's wife is wrong in itself, it nevertheless became lawful by God's permitting it, and they confirm this by the authority of Chrysostom, who says (*loc. cit.*) that *the Lawgiver by permitting divorce removed the guilt from the sin.* Although this opinion has some probability the former is more generally held: wherefore we must reply to the arguments on both sides.†

Reply Obj. 1. He who can forbid, sins not by omitting to forbid if he has no hope of correcting, but fears by forbidding to furnish the occasion of a greater evil. Thus it happened to Moses: wherefore acting on Divine authority he did not forbid the bill of divorce.

Reply Obj. 2. The prophets, inspired by the Holy Ghost, said that a wife ought to be put away, not as though this were a command of the Holy Ghost, but as being permitted lest greater evils should be perpetrated.

Reply Obj. 3. This likeness of permission must not be applied to every detail, but only to the cause which was the same in both cases, since both permissions were granted in order to avoid some form of wickedness.

---

* *Hom.* xxxii, in the *Opus Imperfectum* falsely ascribed to S. John Chrysostom.
† Cf. I-II, Q. 105, A. 4, *ad* 8; Q. 108, A. 3, *ad* 2. *Contra Gentes* iii, cap. 123.

Reply Obj. 4. Although their hardness of heart excused them not from sin, the permission given on account of that hardness excused them. For certain things are forbidden those who are healthy in body, which are not forbidden the sick, and yet the sick sin not by availing themselves of the permission granted to them.

Reply Obj. 5. A good may be omitted in two ways. First, in order to obtain a greater good, and then the omission of that good becomes virtuous by being directed to a greater good; thus Jacob rightly omitted to have only one wife, on account of the good of the offspring. In another way a good is omitted in order to avoid a greater evil, and then if this is done with the authority of one who can grant a dispensation, the omission of that good is not sinful, and yet it does not also become virtuous. In this way the indissolubility of marriage was suspended in the law of Moses in order to avoid a greater evil, namely wife-murder. Hence Chrysostom says that *he removed the guilt from the sin.* For though divorce remained inordinate, for which reason it is called a sin, it did not incur the debt of punishment, either temporal or eternal, in so far as it was done by Divine permission: and thus its guilt was taken away from it. And therefore he says again *(ibid.)* that *divorce was permitted, an evil indeed, yet lawful.* Those who hold the first opinion understand by this only that divorce incurred the debt of temporal punishment.

FOURTH ARTICLE

Whether It Was Lawful for a Divorced Wife to Have Another Husband?

We proceed thus to the Fourth Article:—

Objection 1. It would seem that it was lawful for a divorced wife to have another husband. For in divorce the husband did a greater wrong by divorcing his wife than the wife by being divorced. But the husband could, without sin, marry another wife. Therefore the wife could without sin, marry another husband.

Obj. 2. Further, Augustine, speaking about bigamy, says *(De Bono Conjug.* xv, xviii) that *when it was the manner it was no sin.* Now at the time of the Old Law it was the custom for a wife after divorce to marry another husband: *When she is departed and marrieth another husband,* etc. Therefore the wife sinned not by marrying another husband.

Obj. 3. Further, our Lord showed that the justice of the New Testament is superabundant in comparison with the justice of the Old Testament (Matth. v). Now He said that it belongs to the superabundant justice of the New Testament that the divorced wife marry not another husband *(ibid.* 32). Therefore it was lawful in the Old Law.

Obj. 4. *On the contrary,* are the words of Matth. v. 32, *He that shall marry her that is put away committeth adultery.* Now adultery was never permitted in the Old Law. Therefore it was not lawful for the divorced wife to have another husband.

Obj. 5. Further, it is written (Deut. xxiv. 3) that a divorced woman who marries another husband *is defiled, and is become abominable before the Lord.* Therefore she sinned by marrying another husband.

I answer that, According to the first above-mentioned opinion (A. 3), she sinned by marrying another husband after being divorced, because her first marriage still held good. For *the woman . . . whilst her husband liveth, is bound to the law* of her husband (Rom. vii. 2): and she could not have several husbands at one time. But according to the second opinion, just as it was lawful by virtue of the Divine dispensation for a husband to divorce his wife, so could the wife marry another husband, because the indissolubility of marriage was removed by reason of the divine dispensation: and as long as that indissolubility remains the saying of the Apostle holds.

Accordingly to reply to the arguments on either side,—

Reply Obj. 1. It was lawful for a husband to have several wives at one time by virtue of the divine dispensation: wherefore having put one away he could marry another even though the former marriage were not dissolved. But it was never lawful for a wife to have several husbands. Wherefore the comparison fails.

Reply Obj. 2. In this saying of Augustine manner *(mos)* does not signify custom but good manners; in the same sense a person is said to have manners *(morigeratus)* because he has good manners; and *moral* philosophy takes its name from the same source.

Reply Obj. 3. Our Lord shows the superabundance of the New Law over the Old in respect of the counsels, not only as regards those things which the Old Law permitted, but also as regards those things which were forbidden in the Old Law, and yet were thought by many to be permitted on account of the precepts being incorrectly explained,—for instance that of the hatred towards our enemies: and so is it in the matter of divorce.

Reply Obj. 4. The saying of our Lord refers to the time of the New Law, when the aforesaid permission was recalled. In the same way we are to understand the statement of Chrysostom*, who says that *a man who divorces his*

* *Hom.* xii, in the *Opus Imperfectum* falsely ascribed to S. John Chrysostom.

wife according to the law is guilty of four crimes: for in God's sight he is a murderer, in so far as he has the purpose of killing his wife unless he divorce her; *and because he divorces her without her having committed fornication,* in which case alone the law of the Gospel allows a man to put away his wife; *and again, because he makes her an adulteress, and the man whom she marries an adulterer.*

Reply Obj. 5. A gloss observes here: *She is defiled and abominable, namely in the judgment of him who first put her away as being defiled,* and consequently it does not follow that she is defiled absolutely speaking. Or she is said to be defiled just as a person who had touched a dead or leprous body was said to be unclean with the uncleanness, not of sin, but of a certain legal irregularity. Wherefore a priest could not marry a widow or a divorced woman.

FIFTH ARTICLE

Whether a Husband Could Lawfully Take Back the Wife He Had Divorced?

We proceed thus to the Fifth Article:—

Objection 1. It would seem that a husband could lawfully take back the wife he had divorced. For it is lawful to undo what was ill done. But for the husband to divorce his wife was ill done. Therefore it was lawful for him to undo it, by taking back his wife.

Obj. 2. Further, it has always been lawful to be indulgent to the sinner, because this is a moral precept, which obtains in every law. Now the husband by taking back the wife he had divorced was indulgent to one who had sinned. Therefore this also was lawful.

Obj. 3. Further, the reason given (Deut. xxiv. 4) for its being unlawful to take back a divorced wife was *because she is defiled.* But the divorced wife is not defiled except by marrying another husband. Therefore at least it was lawful to take back a divorced wife before she married again.

On the contrary, It is said (Deut. xxiv. 4) that *the former husband cannot take her again,* etc.

I answer that, In the law concerning the bill of divorce two things were permitted, namely for the husband to put away the wife, and for the divorced wife to take another husband; and two things were commanded, namely that the bill of divorce should be written, and secondly that the husband who divorced his wife could not take her back. According to those who hold the first opinion (A. 3) this was done in punishment of the woman who married again, and that it was by this sin that she was defiled: but according to the others it was done that a husband might not be too ready to di-

vorce his wife if he could nowise take her back afterwards.

Reply Obj. 1. In order to prevent the evil committed by a man in divorcing his wife, it was ordered that the husband could not take back his divorced wife, as stated above: and for this reason it was ordered by God.

Reply Obj. 2. It was always lawful to be indulgent to the sinner as regards the unkindly feelings of the heart, but not as regards the punishment appointed by God.

Reply Obj. 3. There are two opinions on this point. For some say that it was lawful for a divorced wife to be reconciled to her husband, unless she were joined in marriage to another husband. For then, on account of the adultery to which she had voluntarily yielded, it was assigned to her in punishment that she should not return to her former husband. Since, however, the law makes no distinction in its prohibition, others say that from the moment that she was put away she could not be taken back, even before marrying again, because the defilement must be understood not in reference to sin, but as explained above (A. 4, *ad* 3).

SIXTH ARTICLE

Whether the Reason for Divorce Was Hatred for the Wife?

We proceed thus to the Sixth Article:—

Objection 1. It would seem that the reason for divorce was hatred for the wife. For it is written (Mal. ii. 16): *When thou shalt hate her put her away.* Therefore, etc.

Obj. 2. Further, it is written (Deut. xxiv. 1): *If . . . she find not favor in his eyes, for some uncleanness,* etc. Therefore the same conclusion follows as before.

Obj. 3. *On the contrary,* Barrenness and fornication are more opposed to marriage than hatred. Therefore they ought to have been reasons for divorce rather than hatred.

Obj. 4. Further, hatred may be caused by the virtue of the person hated. Therefore, if hatred is a sufficient reason, a woman could be divorced on account of her virtue, which is absurd.

Obj. 5. Further, *If a man marry a wife and afterwards hate her, and seek occasions to put her away** alleging that she was not a virgin when he married her, should he fail to prove this, he shall be beaten, and shall be condemned in a hundred sicles of silver, and he shall be unable to put her away all the days of his life (Deut. xxii. 13-19). Therefore hatred is not a sufficient reason for divorce.

I answer that, It is the general opinion of holy men that the reason for permission being

* The rest of the passage is apparently quoted from memory.

given to divorce a wife was the avoidance of wife-murder. Now the proximate cause of murder is hatred: wherefore the proximate cause of divorce was hatred. But hatred proceeds, like love, from a cause. Wherefore we must assign to divorce certain remote causes which were a cause of hatred. For Augustine says in his gloss (*De Serm. Dom. in Monte*, i. 14): *In the Law there were many causes for divorcing a wife: Christ admitted none but fornication: and He commands other grievances to be borne for conjugal fidelity and chastity*. Such causes are imperfections either of body, as sickness or some notable deformity, or in soul as fornication or the like which amounts to moral depravity. Some, however, restrict these causes within narrower limits, saying with sufficient probability that it was not lawful to divorce a wife except for some cause subsequent to the marriage; and that not even then could it be done for any such cause, but only for such as could hinder the good of the offspring, whether in body as barrenness, or leprosy and the like, or in soul, for instance if she were a woman of wicked habits which her children through continual contact with her would imitate. There is however a gloss on Deut. xxiv. 1, *If . . . she find not favor in his eyes*, which would seem to restrict them yet more, namely to sin, by saying that there *uncleanness* denotes sin: but *sin* in the gloss refers not only to the morality of the soul but also to the condition of the body. Accordingly we grant the first two objections.

Reply Obj. 3. Barrenness and other like things are causes of hatred, and so they are remote causes of divorce.

Reply Obj. 4. No one is hateful on account of virtue as such, because goodness is the cause of love. Wherefore the argument does not hold.

Reply Obj. 5. The husband was punished in that case by being unable to put away his wife for ever, just as in the case when he had corrupted a maid (Deut. xxii. 28-30).

SEVENTH ARTICLE

Whether the Causes of Divorce Had to Be Written in the Bill?

We proceed thus to the Seventh Article:—

Objection 1. It would seem that the causes of divorce had to be written in the bill: because the husband was absolved from the punishment of the law by the written bill of divorce. But this would seem altogether unjust, unless sufficient causes were alleged for a divorce. Therefore it was necessary for them to be written in the bill.

Obj. 2. Further, seemingly this document was of no use except to show the causes for divorce. Therefore, if they were not written down, the bill was delivered for no purpose.

Obj. 3. Further, the Master says that it was so in the text (iv, *Sent.* D. 33).

On the contrary, The causes for divorce were either sufficient or not. If they were sufficient, the wife was debarred from a second marriage, though this was allowed her by the Law. If they were insufficient, the divorce was proved to be unjust, and therefore could not be effected. Therefore the causes for divorce were by no means particularized in the bill.

I answer that, The causes for divorce were not particularized in the bill, but were indicated in a general way, so as to prove the justice of the divorce. According to Josephus (*Antiq.* iv. 6) this was in order that the woman, having the written bill of divorce, might take another husband, else she would not have been believed. Wherefore according to him it was written in this wise: *I promise never to have thee with me again.* But according to Augustine (*Contra Faust.* xix. 26) the bill was put into writing in order to cause a delay, and that the husband might be dissuaded by the counsel of the notaries to refrain from his purpose of divorce.

This suffices for the *Replies* to the *Objections*.

QUESTION 68

Of Illegitimate Children

(In Three Articles)

WE must now consider children of illegitimate birth. Under this head there are three points of inquiry: (1) Whether those born out of true marriage are illegitimate? (2) Whether children should suffer any loss through being illegitimate? (3) Whether they can be legitimized?

FIRST ARTICLE

Whether Children Born out of True Marriage Are Illegitimate?

We proceed thus to the First Article:—

Objection 1. It would seem that children born out of true marriage are legitimate. For he that is born according to law is called a legitimate son. Now everyone is born according to law, at least the law of nature, which has more force than any other. Therefore every child is to be called legitimate.

Obj. 2. Further, it is the common saying that a legitimate child is one born of a legitimate marriage, or of a marriage that is deemed legitimate in the eyes of the Church. Now it happens sometimes that a marriage is deemed legitimate in the eyes of the Church, whereas there is some impediment affecting its validity; which impediment may be known to the parties who marry in the presence of the Church: or they may marry in secret and be ignorant of the impediment, in which case their marriage would seem legitimate in the eyes of the Church, for the very reason that it is not prevented by the Church. Therefore children born out of true marriage are not illegitimate.

On the contrary, Illegitimate is that which is against the law. Now those who are born out of wedlock are born contrary to the law. Therefore they are illegitimate.

I answer that, Children are of four conditions. Some are natural and legitimate, for instance those who are born of a true and lawful marriage; some are natural and illegitimate, as those who are born of fornication; some are legitimate and not natural, as adopted children; some are neither legitimate nor natural; such are those born of adultery or incest, for these are born not only against the positive law, but against the express natural law. Hence we must grant that some children are illegitimate.

Reply Obj. 1. Although those who are born of an unlawful intercourse are born according to the nature common to man and all animals, they are born contrary to the law of nature which is proper to man: since fornication, adultery, and the like are contrary to the law of nature. Hence the like are not legitimate by any law.

Reply Obj. 2. Ignorance, unless it be affected, excuses unlawful intercourse from sin. Wherefore those who contract together in good faith in the presence of the Church, although there be an impediment, of which however they are ignorant, sin not, nor are their children illegitimate. If, however, they know of the impediment, although the Church upholds their marriage because she knows not of the impediment, they are not excused from sin, nor do their children avoid being illegitimate. Neither are they excused if they know not of the impediment and marry secretly, because such ignorance would appear to be affected.

SECOND ARTICLE

Whether Children Should Suffer Any Loss through Being Illegitimate?

We proceed thus to the Second Article:—

Objection 1. It would seem that children ought not to suffer any loss through being illegitimate. For a child should not be punished on account of his father's sin, according to the Lord's saying (Ezech. xviii. 20). But it is not his own but his father's fault that he is born of an unlawful union. Therefore he should not incur a loss on this account.

Obj. 2. Further, human justice is copied from Divine. Now God confers natural goods equally on legitimate and illegitimate children. Therefore illegitimate should be equalled to legitimate children according to human laws.

On the contrary, It is stated (Gen. xxv. 5, 6) that *Abraham gave all his possessions to Isaac, and that to the children of the concubines he gave gifts:* and yet the latter were not born of an unlawful intercourse. Much more, therefore, ought those born of an unlawful intercourse to incur loss by not inheriting their father's property.

I answer that, A person is said to incur a loss for some cause in two ways: First, because he is deprived of his due, and thus an illegitimate child incurs no loss. Secondly, because something is not due to him, which might have been due otherwise, and thus an illegitimate son incurs a twofold loss. First, because he is excluded from legitimate acts, such as offices and dignities, which require a certain respectability in those who perform them. Secondly, he incurs a loss by not succeeding to his father's inheritance. Nevertheless natural sons can inherit a sixth only, whereas spurious children cannot inherit any portion, although by natural law their parents are bound to provide for their needs. Hence it is part of a bishop's care to compel both parents to provide for them.

Reply Obj. 1. To incur a loss in this second way is not a punishment. Hence we do not say that a person is punished by not succeeding to the throne through not being the king's son. In like manner it is no punishment to an illegitimate child that he has no right to that which belongs to the legitimate children.

Reply Obj. 2. Illegitimate intercourse is contrary to the law, not as an act of the generative power, but as proceeding from a wicked will. Hence an illegitimate son incurs a loss, not in those things which come to him by his natural origin, but in those things which are dependent on the will for being done or possessed.

Whether an Illegitimate Son Can Be Legitimized?

We proceed thus to the Third Article:—

Objection 1. It would seem that an illegitimate son cannot be legitimized. For the legitimate child is as far removed from the illegitimate as the illegitimate from the legitimate. But a legitimate child is never made illegitimate. Neither, therefore, is an illegitimate child ever made legitimate.

Obj. 2. Further, illegitimate intercourse begets an illegitimate child. But illegitimate intercourse never becomes legitimate. Neither, therefore, can an illegitimate son become legitimate.

On the contrary, What is done by the law can be undone by the law. Now the illegitimacy of children is an effect of positive law. Therefore an illegitimate child can be legitimized by one who has legal authority.

I answer that, An illegitimate child can be legitimized, not so that he be born of a legitimate intercourse, because this intercourse is a thing of the past and can never be legitimized from the moment that it was once illegitimate. But the child is said to be legitimized, in so far as the losses which an illegitimate child ought to incur are withdrawn by the authority of the law.

There are six ways of becoming legitimate: two according to the canons (Cap. *Conquestus* and Cap. *Tanta),* namely when a man marries the woman of whom he has an unlawful child (if it were not a case of adultery), and by special indulgence and dispensation of the lord Pope. The other four ways are according to the laws: (1) If the father offer his natural son to the emperor's court, for by this very fact the son is legitimate on account of the reputation of the court; (2) if the father designate him in his will as his legitimate heir, and the son afterwards offer the will to the emperor; (3) if there be no legitimate son and the son himself offer himself to the emperor; (4) if the father designate him as legitimate in a public document or in a document signed by three witnesses, without calling him natural.

Reply Obj. 1. A favor may be bestowed on a person without injustice, but a person cannot be damnified except for a fault. Hence an illegitimate child can be legitimized rather than *vice versa;* for although a legitimate son is sometimes deprived of his inheritance on account of his fault, he is not said to be illegitimate, because he was legitimately begotten.

Reply Obj. 2. Illegitimate intercourse has an inherent inseparable defect whereby it is opposed to the law: and consequently it cannot be legitimized. Nor is there any comparison with an illegitimate child who has no such defect.

RESURRECTION OF THE BODY—LIFE EVERLASTING

QUESTION 69

Of Matters Concerning the Resurrection, and First of the Place Where Souls Are after Death

(In Seven Articles)

IN sequence to the foregoing we must treat of matters concerning the state of resurrection: for after speaking of the sacraments whereby man is delivered from the death of sin, we must next speak of the resurrection whereby man is delivered from the death of punishment. The treatise on the resurrection offers a threefold consideration, namely the things that precede, those that accompany, and those that follow the resurrection. Consequently we must speak (1) of those things which partly, though not wholly, precede the resurrection; (2) of the resurrection itself and its circumstances; (3) of the things which follow it.

Among the things which precede the resurrection we must consider (1) the places appointed for the reception of bodies after death; (2) the quality of separated souls, and the punishment inflicted on them by fire; (3) the suffrages whereby the souls of the departed are assisted by the living; (4) the prayers of the saints in heaven; (5) the signs preceding the general judgment; (6) the fire of the world's final conflagration which will precede the appearance of the Judge.

Under the first head there are seven points of inquiry: (1) Whether any places are appointed to receive souls after death? (2) Whether souls are conveyed thither immediately after death? (3) Whether they are able to leave those places? (4) Whether the limbo of hell is the same as Abraham's bosom? (5) Whether limbo is the same as the hell of the damned? (6) Whether the limbo of the patriarchs is the same as the limbo of children? (7) Whether so many places should be distinguished?

FIRST ARTICLE

Whether Places Are Appointed to Receive Souls after Death?

We proceed thus to the First Article:—

Objection 1. It would seem that places are not appointed to receive souls after death. For as Boëthius says *(De Hebdom.): Wise men are agreed that incorporeal things are not in a place,* and this agrees with the words of Augustine *(Gen. ad lit.* xii. 32): *We can answer without hesitation that the soul is not conveyed to corporeal places, except with a body, or that it is not conveyed locally.* Now

* *Hexaem.* i, ad Gen. i. 2.

the soul separated from the body is without a body, as Augustine also says *(ibid.).* Therefore it is absurd to assign any places for the reception of souls.

Obj. 2. Further, whatever has a definite place has more in common with that place than with any other. Now separated souls, like certain other spiritual substances, are indifferent to all places; for it cannot be said that they agree with certain bodies, and differ from others, since they are utterly removed from all corporeal conditions. Therefore places should not be assigned for their reception.

Obj. 3. Further, nothing is assigned to separated souls after death, except what conduces to their punishment or to their reward. But a corporeal place cannot conduce to their punishment or reward, since they receive nothing from bodies. Therefore definite places should not be assigned to receive them.

On the contrary, The empyrean heaven is a corporeal place, and yet as soon as it was made it was filled with the holy angels, as Bede* says. Since then angels even as separated souls are incorporeal, it would seem that some place should also be assigned to receive separated souls.

Further, this appears from Gregory's statement *(Dial.* iv) that souls after death are conveyed to various corporeal places, as in the case of Paschasius whom Germanus, Bishop of Capua, found at the baths, and of the soul of King Theodoric, which he asserts to have been conveyed to hell. Therefore after death souls have certain places for their reception.

I answer that, Although spiritual substances do not depend on a body in respect of their being, nevertheless the corporeal world is governed by God by means of the spiritual world, as asserted by Augustine *(De Trin.* iii. 4) and Gregory *(Dial.* iv. 6). Hence it is that there is a certain fittingness by way of congruity of spiritual substances to corporeal substances, in that the more noble bodies are adapted to the more noble substances: wherefore also the philosophers held that the order of separate substances is according to the order of movables. And though after death souls have no bodies assigned to them whereof they be the forms or determinate motors, nevertheless certain corporeal places are appointed to them by way of congruity in reference to their degree of nobility (wherein they are as though in a place, after the manner in which incorporeal things can be in a place), according as they more or less approach to the first substance (to which the highest place it fittingly assigned), namely God, whose throne the Scriptures proclaim heaven to be (Ps. cii. 19, Isa. lxvi. 1). Wherefore we hold that those souls that have a perfect share of the Godhead are in heaven, and that those souls that are deprived of that share are assigned to a contrary place.

Reply Obj. 1. Incorporeal things are not in place after a manner known and familiar to us, in which way we say that bodies are properly in place; but they are in place after a manner befitting spiritual substances, a manner that cannot be fully manifest to us.

Reply Obj. 2. Things have something in common with or a likeness to one another in two ways. First, by sharing a same quality: thus hot things have something in common, and incorporeal things can have nothing in common with corporeal things in this way. Secondly, by a kind of proportionateness, by reason of which the Scriptures apply the corporeal world to the spiritual metaphorically. Thus the Scriptures speak of God as the sun, because He is the principle of spiritual life, as the sun is of corporeal life. In this way certain souls have more in common with certain places: for instance, souls that are spiritually enlightened, with luminous bodies, and souls that are plunged in darkness by sin, with dark places.

Reply Obj. 3. The separated soul receives nothing directly from corporeal places in the same way as bodies which are maintained by their respective places: yet these same souls, through knowing themselves to be appointed to such places, gather joy or sorrow therefrom; and thus their place conduces to their punishment or reward.

SECOND ARTICLE

Whether Souls Are Conveyed to Heaven or Hell Immediately after Death?

We proceed thus to the Second Article:—

Objection 1. It would seem that no souls are conveyed to heaven or hell immediately after death. For a gloss on Ps. xxxvi. 10, *Yet a little while and the wicked shall not be,* says that *the saints are delivered at the end of life; yet after this life they will not yet be where the saints will be* when it is said to them: *Come ye blessed of My Father.* Now those saints will be in heaven. Therefore after this life the saints do not go immediately up to heaven.

Obj. 2. Further, Augustine says *(Enchir.*

* Vulg.,—*eternal in heaven.* Cf. 1 Pet. i 4.

cix) that *the time which lies between man's death and the final resurrection holds the souls in secret receptacles according as each one is worthy of rest or of suffering.* Now these secret abodes cannot denote heaven and hell, since also after the final resurrection the souls will be there together with their bodies: so that he would have no reason to distinguish between the time before and the time after the resurrection. Therefore they will be neither in hell nor in heaven until the day of judgment.

Obj. 3. Further, the glory of the soul is greater than that of bodies. Now the glory of the body is awarded to all at the same time, so that each one may have the greater joy in the common rejoicing of all, as appears from a gloss on Heb. xi. 40, *God providing some better thing for us—that the common joy may make each one rejoice the more.* Much more, therefore, ought the glory of souls to be deferred until the end, so as to be awarded to all at the same time.

Obj. 4. Further, punishment and reward, being pronounced by the sentence of the judge, should not precede the judgment. Now hell fire and the joys of heaven will be awarded to all by the sentence of Christ judging them, namely at the last judgment, according to Matth. xxv. Therefore no one will go up to heaven or down to hell before the day of judgment.

On the contrary, It is written (2 Cor. v. 1): *If our earthly house of this habitation be dissolved, that we have . . . a house not made with hands, but reserved in heaven.** Therefore, after the body's dissolution, the soul has an abode, which had been reserved for it in heaven.

Further, the Apostle says (Philip. i. 23): *I desire* (Vulg.,—*Having a desire) to be dissolved and to be with Christ.* From these words Gregory argues as follows *(Dial.* iv. 25): *If there is no doubt that Christ is in heaven, it cannot be denied that Paul's soul is in heaven likewise.* Now it cannot be gainsaid that Christ is in heaven, since this is an article of faith. Therefore neither is it to be denied that the souls of the saints are borne to heaven. That also some souls go down to hell immediately after death is evident from Luke xvi. 22, *And the rich man died, and he was buried in hell.*

I answer that, Even as in bodies there is gravity or levity whereby they are borne to their own place which is the end of their movement, so in souls there is merit or demerit whereby they reach their reward or punishment, which are the ends of their deeds. Wherefore just as a body is conveyed at once to its place, by its gravity or levity, unless there be an obstacle, so too the soul, the bonds of the flesh being broken, whereby it was detained in the state of the way, receives at once its reward or punishment, unless there be an obstacle. Thus sometimes venial sin, though needing first of all to be cleansed, is an obstacle to the receiving of the reward; the result being that the reward is delayed. And since a place is assigned to souls in keeping with their reward or punishment, as soon as the soul is set free from the body it is either plunged into hell or soars to heaven, unless it be held back by some debt, for which its flight must needs be delayed until the soul is first of all cleansed. This truth is attested by the manifest authority of the canonical Scriptures and the doctrine of the holy Fathers; wherefore the contrary must be judged heretical as stated in *Dial.* iv. 25, and in *De Eccl. Dogm.* xlvi.

Reply Obj. 1. The gloss explains itself: for it expounds the words, *They will not yet be where the saints will be*, etc., by saying immediately afterwards: *That is to say, they will not have the double stole which the saints will have at the resurrection.*

Reply Obj. 2. Among the secret abodes of which Augustine speaks, we must also reckon hell and heaven, where some souls are detained before the resurrection. The reason why a distinction is drawn between the time before and the time after the resurrection is because before the resurrection they are there without the body whereas afterwards they are with the body, and because in certain places there are souls now which will not be there after the resurrection.

Reply Obj. 3. There is a kind of continuity among men as regards the body, because in respect thereof is verified the saying of Acts xvii. 24, 26, *God . . . hath made of one all mankind:* whereas He has fashioned souls independently of one another. Consequently it is not so fitting that all men should be glorified together in the soul as that they should be glorified together in the body. Moreover the glory of the body is not so essential as the glory of the soul; wherefore it would be more derogatory to the saints if the glory of the soul were delayed, than that the glory of the body be deferred: nor could this detriment to their glory be compensated on account of the joy of each one being increased by the common joy.

Reply Obj. 4. Gregory proposes and solves this very difficulty *(Dial.* iv. l.c.): *If then*, he says, *the souls of the just are in heaven now, what will they receive in reward for their justice on the judgment day?* And he answers: *Surely it will be a gain to them at the judgment, that whereas now they enjoy only the* happiness of the soul, afterwards they will enjoy also that of the body, so as to rejoice also in the flesh wherein they bore sorrow and torments for the Lord. The same is to be said in reference to the damned.

THIRD ARTICLE

Whether the Souls Who Are in Heaven or Hell Are Able to Go from Thence?

We proceed thus to the Third Article:—

Objection 1. It would seem that the souls in heaven or hell are unable to go from thence. For Augustine says *(De Cura pro Mort.* xiii): *If the souls of the dead took any part in the affairs of the living, to say nothing of others, there is myself whom not for a single night would my loving mother fail to visit since she followed me by land and sea in order to abide with me:* and from this he concludes that the souls of the departed do not mingle in the affairs of the living. But they would be able to do so if they were to leave their abode. Therefore they do not go forth from their abode.

Obj. 2. Further, it is written (Ps. xxvi. 4): *That I may dwell in the house of the Lord all the days of my life,* and (Job vii. 9): *He that shall go down to hell shall not come up.* Therefore neither the good nor the wicked quit their abode.

Obj. 3. Further, as stated above (A. 2), abodes are awarded to souls after death as a reward or punishment. Now after death neither the rewards of the saints nor the punishments of the damned are increased. Therefore they do not quit their abodes.

On the contrary, Jerome writing against Vigilantius addresses him thus: *For thou sayest that the souls of the apostles and martyrs have taken up their abode either in Abraham's bosom or in the place of refreshment, or under the altar of God, and that they are unable to visit their graves when they will. Wouldst thou then lay down the law for God? Wouldst thou put the apostles in chains, imprison them until the day of judgment, and forbid them to be with their Lord, them of whom it is written: They follow the Lamb whithersoever He goeth? And if the Lamb is everywhere, therefore we must believe that those also who are with Him are everywhere.* Therefore it is absurd to say that the souls of the departed do not leave their abode.

Further, Jerome argues as follows *(ibid.): Since the devil and the demons wander throughout the whole world, and are everywhere present with wondrous speed, why should the martyrs, after shedding their blood, be imprisoned and unable to go forth?* Hence we may infer that not only the good sometimes leave their abode, but also the wicked, since their damnation does not exceed that of the demons who wander about everywhere.

Further, the same conclusion may be gathered from Gregory *(Dial.* iv), where he relates many cases of the dead having appeared to the living.

I answer that, There are two ways of understanding a person to leave hell or heaven. First, that he goes from thence simply, so that heaven or hell be no longer his place: and in this way no one who is finally consigned to hell or heaven can go from thence, as we shall state further on (Q. 71, A. 5, *ad* 5). Secondly, they may be understood to go forth for a time: and here we must distinguish what befits them according to the order of nature, and what according to the order of Divine providence; for as Augustine says *(De Cura pro Mort.* xvi): *Human affairs have their limits other than have the wonders of the Divine power, nature's works differ from those which are done miraculously.* Consequently, according to the natural course, the separated souls consigned to their respective abodes are utterly cut off from communication with the living. For according to the course of nature men living in mortal bodies are not immediately united to separate substances, since their entire knowledge arises from the senses: nor would it be fitting for them to leave their abode for any purpose other than to take part in the affairs of the living. Nevertheless, according to the disposition of Divine providence separated souls sometimes come forth from their abode and appear to men, as Augustine, in the book quoted above, relates of the martyr Felix who appeared visibly to the people of Nola when they were besieged by the barbarians. It is also credible that this may occur sometimes to the damned, and that for man's instruction and intimidation they be permitted to appear to the living; or again in order to seek our suffrages, as to those who are detained in purgatory, as evidenced by many instances related in the fourth book of the *Dialogues.* There is, however, this difference between the saints and the damned, that the saints can appear when they will to the living, but not the damned; for even as the saints while living in the flesh are able by the gifts of gratuitous grace to heal and work wonders, which can only be done miraculously by the Divine power, and cannot be done by those who lack this gift, so it is not unfitting for the souls of the saints to be endowed with a power in virtue of their glory, so that they are able to appear wondrously to the living, when they will: while others are unable to do so unless they be sometimes permitted.

Reply Obj. 1. Augustine, as may be gathered from what he says afterwards, is speaking according to the common course of nature. And

yet it does not follow, although the dead be able to appear to the living as they will, that they appear as often as when living in the flesh: because when they are separated from the flesh, they are either wholly conformed to the divine will, so that they may do nothing but what they see to be agreeable with the Divine dispostion, or else they are so overwhelmed by their punishments that their grief for their unhappiness surpasses their desire to appear to others.

Reply Obj. 2. The authorities quoted speak in the sense that no one comes forth from heaven or hell simply, and do not imply that one may not come forth for a time.

Reply Obj. 3 As stated above (A. 1, *ad* 3) the soul's place conduces to its punishment or reward in so far as the soul, through being consigned to that place, is affected either by joy or by grief. Now this joy or grief at being consigned to such a place remains in the soul even when it is outside that place. Thus a bishop who is given the honor of sitting on a throne in the church incurs no dishonor when he leaves the throne, for though he sits not therein actually, the place remains assigned to him.

We must also reply to the arguments in the contrary sense.

Reply Obj. 4. Jerome is speaking of the apostles and martyrs in reference to that which they gain from their power of glory, and not to that which befits them as due to them by nature. And when he says that they are everywhere, he does not mean that they are in several places or everywhere at once, but that they can be wherever they will.

Reply Obj. 5. There is no parity between demons and angels on the one hand and the souls of the saints and of the damned on the other. For the good or bad angels have alotted to them the office of presiding over men, to watch over them or to try them; but this cannot be said of the souls of men. Nevertheless, according to the power of glory, it is competent to the souls of the saints that they can be where they will; and this is what Jerome means to say.

Reply Obj. 6. Although the souls of the saints or of the damned are sometimes actually present where they appear, we are not to believe that this is always so: for sometimes these apparitions occur to persons whether asleep or awake by the activity of good or wicked angels in order to instruct or deceive the living. Thus sometimes even the living appear to others and tell them many things in their sleep; and yet it is clear that they are not present, as Augustine proves from many instances *(De Cura pro Mort.* xi, xii).

FOURTH ARTICLE

Whether the Limbo of Hell Is the Same As Abraham's Bosom?

We proced thus to the Fourth Article:—

Objection 1. It would seem that the limbo of hell is not the same as Abraham's bosom. For according to Augustine *(Gen. ad lit.* xxxiii): *I have not yet found Scripture mentioning hell in a favorable sense.* Now Abraham's bosom is taken in a favorable sense, as Augustine goes on to say *(ibid.)*: *Surely no one would be allowed to give an unfavorable signification to Abraham's bosom and the place of rest whither the godly poor man was carried by the angels.* Therefore Abraham's bosom is not the same as the limbo of hell.

Obj. 2. Further, those who are in hell see not God. Yet God is seen by those who are in Abraham's bosom, as may be gathered from Augustine *(Conf.* ix. 3) who, speaking of Nebridius, says: *Whatever that be, which is signified by that bosom, there lives my Nebridius,* and further on: *Now lays he not his ear to my mouth, but his spiritual mouth unto Thy fountain, and drinketh as much as he can receive wisdom in proportion to his thirst, endlessly happy.* Therefore Abraham's bosom is not the same as the limbo of hell.

Obj. 3. Further, the Church prays not that a man be taken to hell: and yet she prays that the angels may carry the departed soul to Abraham's bosom. Therefore it would seem that Abraham's bosom is not the same as limbo.

On the contrary, The place whither the beggar Lazarus was taken is called Abraham's bosom. Now he was taken to hell, for as a gloss* on Job xxx. 23, *Where a house is appointed for every one that liveth,* says: *Hell was the house of all the living until the coming of Christ.* Therefore Abraham's bosom is the same as limbo.

Further, Jacob said to his sons *(Gen.* xliv. 38): *You will bring down my grey hairs with sorrow to hell:* wherefore Jacob knew that he would be taken to hell after his death. Therefore Abraham likewise was taken to hell after his death; and consequently Abraham's bosom would seem to be a part of hell.

I answer that, After death men's souls cannot find rest save by the merit of faith, because *he that cometh to God must believe* (Heb. xi. 6). Now the first example of faith was given to men in the person of Abraham, who was the first to sever himself from the body of unbelievers, and to receive a special sign of faith: for which reason *the place of rest given to men after death is called Abraham's bosom,* as Augustine declares *(Gen. ad Lit.* xii). But the souls of the saints have not at all times

* S. Gregory *(Moral.* xx). † Allusion to Osee xiii. 14.

had the same rest after death; because, since Christ's coming they have had complete rest through enjoying the vision of God, whereas before Christ's coming they had rest through being exempt from punishment, but their desire was not set at rest by their attaining their end. Consequently the state of the saints before Christ's coming may be considered both as regards the rest it afforded, and thus it is called Abraham's bosom, and as regards its lack of rest, and thus it is called the limbo of hell. Accordingly, before Christ's coming the limbo of hell and Abraham's bosom were one place accidentally and not essentially: and consequently, nothing prevents Abraham's bosom from being after Christ's coming, and from being altogether distinct from limbo, since things that are one accidentally may be parted from one another.

Reply Obj. 1. The state of the holy Fathers as regards what was good in it was called Abraham's bosom, but as regards its deficiencies it was called hell. Accordingly, neither is Abraham's bosom taken in an unfavorable sense, nor hell in a favorable sense, although in a way they are one.

Reply Obj. 2. The place of rest of the holy Fathers was called Abraham's bosom before as well as after Christ's coming, but in different ways. For since before Christ's coming the saints' rest had a lack of rest attached to it, it was called both hell and Abraham's bosom, wherefore God was not seen there. But since after the coming of Christ the saints' rest is complete through their seeing God, this rest is called Abraham's bosom, but not hell by any means. It is to this bosom of Abraham that the Church prays for the faithful to be brought.

Hence the *Reply* to the *Third Objection* is evident: and the same meaning applies to a gloss on Luke xvi. 22, *It came to pass that the beggar died,* etc., which says: *Abraham's bosom is the rest of the blessed poor, whose is the kingdom of heaven.*

FIFTH ARTICLE

Whether Limbo Is the Same As the Hell of the Damned?

We proceed thus to the Fifth Article:—

Objection 1. It would seem that the limbo of hell is the same as the hell of the damned. For Christ is said to have *bitten*† hell, but not to have swallowed it, because He took some from thence but not all. Now He would not be said to have *bitten* hell if those whom He set free were not part of the multitude shut up in hell. Therefore since those whom He set free were shut up in hell, the same were shut up in limbo and in hell. Therefore limbo is either the same as hell, or is a part of hell.

Obj. 2. Further, in the Creed Christ is said to have descended into hell. But He did not descend save to the limbo of the Fathers. Therefore the limbo of the Fathers is the same as hell.

Obj. 3. Further, it is written (Job xvii. 16): *All that I have shall go down into the deepest hell* (Douay,—*pit*). Now since Job was a holy and just man, he went down to limbo. Therefore limbo is the same as the deepest hell.

On the contrary, In hell there is no redemption.* But the saints were redeemed from limbo. Therefore limbo is not the same as hell.

Further, Augustine says *(Gen. ad lit.* xii): *I do not see how we can believe that the rest which Lazarus received was in hell.* Now the soul of Lazarus went down into limbo. Therefore limbo is not the same as hell.

I answer that, The abodes of souls after death may be distinguished in two ways; either as to their situation, or as to the quality of the places, inasmuch as souls are punished or rewarded in certain places. Accordingly if we consider the limbo of the Fathers and hell in respect of the aforesaid quality of the places, there is no doubt that they are distinct, both because in hell there is sensible punishment, which was not in the limbo of the Fathers, and because in hell there is eternal punishment, whereas the saints were detained but temporally in the limbo of the Fathers. On the other hand, if we consider them as to the situation of the place, it is probable that hell and limbo are the same place, or that they are continuous as it were, yet so that some higher part of hell be called the limbo of the Fathers. For those who are in hell receive diverse punishments according to the diversity of their guilt, so that those who are condemned are consigned to darker and deeper parts of hell according as they have been guilty of graver sins, and consequently the holy Fathers in whom there was the least amount of sin were consigned to a higher and less darksome part than all those who were condemned to punishment.

Reply Obj. 1. When Christ, by His descent, delivered the Fathers from limbo, He is said to have *bitten* hell and to have descended into hell, in so far as hell and limbo are the same as to situation.

This suffices for the *Reply* to the *Second Objection.*

Reply Obj. 3. Job descended, not to the hell of the damned, but to the limbo of the Fathers. The latter is called the deepest place, not in reference to the places of punishment, but in comparison with other places, as includ-

* Office of the Dead, *Resp.* vii.

ing all penal places under one head.—Again we may reply with Augustine *(Gen. ad lit.* xii): who says of Jacob: *When Jacob said to his sons, "You will bring down my grey hairs with sorrow to hell," he seems to have feared most, lest he should be troubled with so great a sorrow as to obtain, not the rest of good men, but the hell of sinners.* The saying of Job may be expounded in the same way, as being the utterance of one in fear, rather than an assertion.

SIXTH ARTICLE

Whether the Limbo of Children Is the Same As the Limbo of the Fathers?

We proceed thus to the Sixth Article:—

Objection 1. It would seem that the limbo of children is the same as the limbo of the Fathers. For punishment should correspond to sin. Now the Fathers were detained in limbo for the same sin as children, namely for original sin. Therefore the place of punishmen should be the same for both.

Obj. 2. Further, Augustine says *(Enchir.* xciii): *The punishment of children who die in none but original sin is most lenient.* But no punishment is more lenient than that of the holy Fathers. Therefore the place of punishment is the same for both.

On the contrary, Even as temporal punishment in purgatory and eternal punishment in hell are due to actual sin, so temporal punishment in the limbo of the Fathers and eternal punishment in the limbo of the children were due to original sin. If, therefore, hell and purgatory be not the same it would seem that neither are the limbo of children and the limbo of the Fathers the same.

I answer that, The limbo of the Fathers and the limbo of children, without any doubt, differ as to the quality of punishment or reward. For children have no hope of the blessed life, as the Fathers in limbo had, in whom, moreover, shone forth the light of faith and grace. But as regards their situation, there is reason to believe that the place of both is the same; except that the limbo of the Fathers is placed higher than the limbo of children, just as we have stated in reference to limbo and hell (A. 5).

Reply Obj. 1. The Fathers did not stand in the same relation to original sin as children. For in the Fathers original sin was expiated in so far as it infected the person, while there remained an obstacle on the part of nature, on account of which their satisfaction was not yet complete. On the other hand, in children there is an obstacle both on the part of the person and on the part of nature: and for this reason different abodes are appointed to the Fathers and to children.

Reply Obj. 2. Augustine is speaking of punishments due to some one by reason of his person. Of these the most lenient are due to those who are burdened with none but original sin. But lighter still is the punishment due to those who are debarred from the reception of glory by no personal defect but only by a defect of nature, so that this very delay of glory is called a kind of punishment.

SEVENTH ARTICLE

Whether So Many Abodes Should Be Distinguished?

We proceed thus to the Seventh Article:—

Objection 1. It would seem that we should not distinguish so many abodes. For after death, just as abodes are due to souls on account of sin, so are they due on account of merit. Now there is only one abode due on account of merit, namely paradise. Therefore neither should there be more than one abode due on account of sin, namely hell.

Obj. 2. Further, abodes are appointed to souls after death on account of merits or demerits. Now there is one place where they merit or demerit. Therefore only one abode should be assigned to them after death.

Obj. 3. Further, the places of punishment should correspond to the sins. Now there are only three kinds of sin, namely original, venial, and mortal. Therefore there should only be three penal abodes.

Obj. 4. *On the other hand,* it would seem that there should be many more than those assigned. For this darksome air is the prison house of the demons (2 Pet. ii. 17), and yet it is not reckoned among the five abodes which are mentioned by certain authors. Therefore there are more than five abodes.

Obj. 5. Further, the earthly paradise is distinct from the heavenly paradise. Now some were borne away to the earthly paradise after this state of life, as is related of Enoch and Elias. Since then the earthly paradise is not counted among the five abodes, it would seem that there are more than five.

Obj. 6. Further, some penal place should correspond to each state of sinners. Now if we suppose a person to die in original sin who has committed only venial sins, none of the assigned abodes will be befitting to him. For it is clear that he would not be in heaven, since he would be without grace, and for the same reason neither would he be in the limbo of the Fathers; nor again, would he be in the limbo of children, since there is no sensible punishment there, which is due to such a person by reason of venial sin: nor would he be in purgatory, where there is none but temporal punishment, whereas everlasting punishment is due to him: nor would he be in the hell of

the damned, since he is not guilty of actual mortal sin. Therefore a sixth abode should be assigned.

Obj. 7. Further, rewards and punishments vary in quantity according to the differences of sins and merits. Now the degrees of merit and sin are infinite. Therefore we should distinguish an infinite number of abodes, in which souls are punished or rewarded after death.

Obj. 8. Further, souls are sometimes punished in the places where they sinned, as Gregory states *(Dial.* iv. 55). But they sinned in the place which we inhabit. Therefore this place should be reckoned among the abodes, especially since some are punished for their sins in this world, as the Master said above (iv. *Sent.* D. 21).

Obj. 9. Further, just as some die in a state of grace and have some venial sins for which they deserve punishment, so some die in mortal sin and have some good for which they would deserve a reward. Now to those who die in grace with venial sins an abode is assigned where they are punished ere they receive their reward, which abode is purgatory. Therefore, on the other hand, there should be equally an abode for those who die in mortal sin together with some good works.

Obj. 10. Further, just as the Fathers were delayed from obtaining full glory of the soul before Christ's coming, so are they now detained from receiving the glory of the body. Therefore as we distinguish an abode of the saints before the coming of Christ from the one where they are received now, so ought we to distinguish the one in which they are received now from the one where they will be received after the resurrection.

I answer that, The abodes of souls are distinguished according to the souls' various states. Now the soul united to a mortal body is in the state of meriting, while the soul separated from the body is in the state of receiving good or evil for its merits; so that after death it is either in the state of receiving its final reward, or in the state of being hindered from receiving it. If it is in the state of receiving its final retribution, this happens in two ways: either in the respect of good, and then it is in paradise; or in respect of evil, and thus as regards actual sin it is hell, and as regards original sin it is the limbo of children. On the other hand, if it be in the state where it is hindered from receiving its final reward, this is either on account of a defect of the person, and thus we have purgatory where souls are detained from receiving their reward at once on account of the sins they have committed, or else it is on account of a defect of nature, and thus we have the limbo of the Fathers, where the Fathers were detained from obtaining glory on account of the guilt of human nature which could not yet be expiated.

Reply Obj. 1. *Good happens in one way, but evil in many ways,* according to Dionysius (*Div. Nom.* iv) and the Philosopher (*Ethic.* ii. 6): wherefore it is not unfitting if there be one place of blissful reward and several places of punishment.

Reply Obj. 2. The state of meriting and demeriting is one state, since the same person is able to merit and demerit: wherefore it is fitting that one place should be assigned to all: whereas of those who receive according to their merits there are various states, and consequently the comparison fails.

Reply Obj. 3. One may be punished in two ways for original sin, as stated above, either in reference to the person, or in reference to nature only. Consequently there is a twofold limbo corresponding to that sin.

Reply Obj. 4. This darksome air is assigned to the demons, not as the place where they receive retribution for their merits, but as a place befitting their office, in so far as they are appointed to try us. Hence it is not reckoned among the abodes of which we are treating now: since hell fire is assigned to them in the first place (Matth. xxv).

Reply Obj. 5. The earthly paradise belongs to the state of the wayfarer rather than to the state of those who receive for their merits; and consequently it is not reckoned among the abodes whereof we are treating now.

Reply Obj. 6. This supposition is impossible.* If, however, it were possible, such a one would be punished in hell eternally: for it is accidental to venial sin that it be punished temporally in purgatory, through its having grace annexed to it: wherefore if it be annexed to a mortal sin, which is without grace, it will be punished eternally in hell. And since this one who dies in original sin has a venial sin without grace, it is not unfitting to suppose that he be punished eternally.

Reply Obj. 7. Diversity of degrees in punishments or rewards does not diversify the state, and it is according to the diversity of state that we distinguish various abodes. Hence the argument does not prove.

Reply Obj. 8. Although separated souls are sometimes punished in the place where they dwell, it does not follow that this is their proper place of punishment: but this is done for our instruction, that seeing their punishment we may be deterred from sin. That souls while yet in the flesh are punished here for their sins has nothing to do with the question, because a punishment of this kind does not place a man outside the state of meriting or demeriting: whereas we are treating now of the abodes to which souls are assigned after the state of merit or demerit.

Reply Obj. 9. It is impossible for evil to be pure and without the admixture of good, just as the supreme good is without any admixture of evil. Consequently those who are to be conveyed to beatitude which is a supreme good must be cleansed of all evil; wherefore there must needs be a place where such persons are cleansed if they go hence without being perfectly clean. But those who will be thrust into hell will not be free from all good: and consequently the comparison fails, since those who are in hell can receive the reward of their goods, in so far as their past goods avail for the mitigation of their punishment.

Reply Obj. 10. The essential reward consists in the glory of the soul, but the body's glory, since it overflows from the soul, is entirely founded as it were on the soul: and consequently lack of the soul's glory causes a difference of state, whereas lack of the body's glory does not. For this reason, too, the same place, namely the empyrean, is assigned to the holy souls separated from their bodies and united to glorious bodies: whereas the same place was not assigned to the souls of the Fathers both before and after the glorification of souls.

QUESTION 70

Of the Quality of the Soul after Leaving the Body, and of the Punishment Inflicted on It by Material Fire

(In Three Articles)

WE must next consider the general quality of the soul after leaving the body, and the punishment inflicted on it by material fire. Under this head there are three points of inquiry: (1) Whether the sensitive powers remain in the separated soul? (2) Whether the acts of the aforesaid powers remain in the soul? (3) Whether the separated soul can suffer from a material fire?

* Cf. I-II, Q. 89, A. 6.   † Cf. P. I, Q. 77, A. 8.

FIRST ARTICLE

Whether the Sensitive Powers Remain in the Separated Soul? †

We proceed thus to the First Article:—

Objection 1. It would seem that the sensitive powers remain in the sensitive soul. For Augustine says (*De Spir. et Anim.* xv): *The soul withdraws from the body taking all with itself, sense and imagination, reason, under-*

standing and intelligence, the concupiscible and irascible powers. Now sense, imagination, concupiscible and irascible are sensitive powers. Therefore the sensitive powers remain in the separated soul.

Obj. 2. Further, Augustine says (*De Eccl. Dogm.* xvi): *We believe that man alone has a substantial soul, which lives though separated from the body, and clings keenly to its senses and wits.* Therefore the soul retains its senses after being separated from the body.

Obj. 3. Further, the soul's powers are either its essential parts as some maintain, or at least are its natural properties. Now that which is in a thing essentially cannot be separated from it, nor is a subject severed from its natural properties. Therefore it is impossible for the soul to lose any of its powers after being separated from the body.

Obj. 4. Further, a whole is not entire if one of its parts be lacking. Now the soul's powers are called its parts. Therefore, if the soul lose any of its powers after death, it will not be entire after death: and this is unfitting.

Obj. 5. Further, the soul's powers co-operate in merit more even than the body, since the body is a mere instrument of action, while the powers are principles of action. Now the body must of necessity be rewarded together with the soul, since it co-operated in merit. Much more, therefore, is it necessary that the powers of the soul be rewarded together with it. Therefore the separated soul does not lose them.

Obj. 6. Further, if the soul after separation from the body loses its sensitive power, that must needs come to naught. For it cannot be said that it is dissolved into some matter, since it has no matter as a part of itself. Now that which entirely comes to naught is not restored in identity; wherefore at the resurrection the soul will not have the same identical sensitive powers. Now according to the Philosopher (*De Anima,* ii. 1), as the soul is to the body so are the soul's powers to the parts of the body, for instance the sight to the eye. But if it were not identically the same soul that returns to the body, it would not be identically the same man. Therefore for the same reason it would not be identically the same eye, if the visual power were not identically the same; and in like manner no other part would rise again in identity, and consequently neither would the whole man be identically the same. Therefore it is impossible for the separated soul to lose its sensitive powers.

Obj. 7. Further, if the sensitive powers were to be corrupted when the body is corrupted, it would follow that they are weakened when the body is weakened. Yet this is not the case, for according to *De Anima,* i, *if an old man*

were given the eye of a young man, he would, without doubt, see as well as a young man. Therefore neither are the sensitive powers corrupted when the body is corrupted.

On the contrary, Augustine says (*De Eccl. Dogm.* xix): *Of two substances alone does man consist, soul and body; the soul with its reason, and the body with its senses.* Therefore the sensitive powers belong to the body: and consequently when the body is corrupted the sensitive powers remain not in the soul.

Further, the Philosopher, speaking of the separation of the soul, expresses himself thus (*Met.* xi. 3): *If, however, anything remain at last, we must ask what this is: because in certain subjects it is not impossible, for instance if the soul be of such a disposition, not the whole soul but the intellect; for as regards the whole soul this is probably impossible.* Hence it seems that the whole soul is not separated from the body, but only the intellective powers of the soul, and consequently not the sensitive or vegetative powers.

Further, the Philosopher, speaking of the intellect, says (*De Anima,* ii. 2): *This alone is ever separated, as the everlasting from the corruptible: for it is hereby clear that the remaining parts are not separable as some maintain.* Therefore the sensitive powers do not remain in the separated soul.

I answer that, There are many opinions on this question. For some, holding the view that all the powers are in the soul in the same way as color is in a body, hold that the soul separated from the body takes all its powers away with it: because, if it lacked any one of them, it would follow that the soul is changed in its natural properties, since these cannot change so long as their subject remains. But the aforesaid view is false, for since a power is so called because it enables us to do or suffer something, and since to do and to be able belong to the same subject, it follows that the subject of a power is the same as that which is agent or patient. Hence the Philosopher says (*De Somn. et Vigil.*) that *where we find power there we find action.* Now it is evident that certain operations, whereof the soul's powers are the principles, do not belong to the soul properly speaking but to the soul as united to the body, because they are not performed except through the medium of the body,—such as to see, to hear, and so forth. Hence it follows that such like powers belong to the united soul and body as their subject, but to the soul as their quickening principle, just as the form is the principle of the properties of a composite being. Some operations, however, are performed by the soul without a bodily organ,—for instance to understand, to consider, to will: wherefore, since these actions are proper to the soul, the powers that are the principles thereof belong to the soul not only as their principle but also as their subject. Therefore, since so long as the proper subject remains its proper passions must also remain, and when it is corrupted they also must be corrupted, it follows that these powers which use no bodily organ for their actions must needs remain in the separated body, while those which use a bodily organ must needs be corrupted when the body is corrupted: and such are all the powers belonging to the sensitive and the vegetative soul. On this account some draw a distinction in the sensitive powers of the soul: for they say that they are of two kinds—some being acts of organs and emanating from the soul into the body are corrupted with the body; others, whence the former originate, are in the soul, because by them the soul sensitizes the body for seeing, hearing, and so on; and these primary powers remain in the separated soul. But this statement seems unreasonable: because the soul, by its essence and not through the medium of certain other powers, is the origin of those powers which are the acts of organs, even as any form, from the very fact that by its essence it informs its matter, is the origin of the properties which result naturally in the composite. For were it necessary to suppose other powers in the soul, by means of which the powers that perfect the organs may flow from the essence of the soul, for the same reason it would be necessary to suppose other powers by means of which these mean powers flow from the essence of the soul, and so on to infinity, and if we have to stop it is better to do so at the first step.

Hence others say that the sensitive and other like powers do not remain in the separated soul except in a restricted sense, namely radically, in the same way as a result is in its principle: because there remains in the separated soul the ability to produce these powers if it should be reunited to the body; nor is it necessary for this ability to be anything in addition to the essence of the soul, as stated above. This opinion appears to be the more reasonable.

Reply Obj. 1. This saying of Augustine is to be understood as meaning that the soul takes away with it some of those powers actually, namely understanding and intelligence, and some radically, as stated above.*

Reply Obj. 2. The senses which the soul takes away with it are not these external senses, but the internal, those, namely, which pertain to the intellective part, for the intellect is sometimes called sense, as Basil states in his commentary on the Proverbs, and again the Philosopher (*Ethic.* vi. 11). If, however, he

* Cf. P. I, Q. 77, A. 8, *ad* 1, and *infra* A. 2, *ad* 1.

means the external senses we must reply as above to the first objection.

Reply Obj. 3. As stated above, the sensitive powers are related to the soul, not as natural passions to their subject, but as compared to their origin: wherefore the conclusion does not follow.

Reply Obj. 4. The powers of the soul are not called its integral but its potential parts. Now the nature of such like wholes is that the entire energy of the whole is found perfectly in one of the parts, but partially in the others; thus in the soul the soul's energy is found perfectly in the intellective part, but partially in the others. Wherefore, as the powers of the intellective part remain in the separated soul, the latter will remain entire and undiminished, although the sensitive powers do not remain actually: as neither is the king's power decreased by the death of a mayor who shared his authority.

Reply Obj. 5. The body co-operates in merit, as an essential part of the man who merits. The sensitive powers, however, do not co-operate thus, since they are of the genus of accidents. Hence the comparison fails.

Reply Obj. 6. The powers of the sensitive soul are said to be acts of the organs, not as though they were the essential forms of those organs, except in reference to the soul whose powers they are. But they are the acts of the organs, by perfecting them for their proper operations, as heat is the act of fire by perfecting it for the purpose of heating. Wherefore, just as a fire would remain identically the same, although another individual heat were in it (even so the cold of water that has been heated returns not identically the same, although the water remains the same in identity), so the organs will be the same identically, although the powers be not identically the same.

Reply Obj. 7. The Philosopher is speaking there of these powers as being rooted in the soul. This is clear from his saying that *old age is an affection not of the soul, but of that in which the soul is,* namely the body. For in this way the powers of the soul are neither weakened nor corrupted on account of the body.

SECOND ARTICLE

Whether the Acts of the Sensitive Powers Remain in the Separated Soul?

We proceed thus to the Second Article:—

Objection 1. It would seem that the acts of the sensitive powers remain in the separated soul. For Augustine says (*De Spiritu et Anima,* xv): *When the soul leaves the body it derives pleasure or sorrow through being affected with these* (namely the imagination, and the concupiscible and irascible faculties) *according to its merits*. But the imagination, the concupiscible, and the irascible are sensitive powers. Therefore the separated soul will be affected as regards the sensitive powers, and consequently will be in some act by reason of them.

Obj. 2. Further, Augustine says *(Gen. ad lit.* xii) that *the body feels not, but the soul through the body,* and further on: *The soul feels certain things, not through the body but without the body.* Now that which befits the soul without the body can be in the soul separated from the body. Therefore the soul will then be able to feel actually.

Obj. 3. Further, to see images of bodies, as occurs in sleep, belongs to imaginary vision which is in the sensitive part. Now it happens that the separated soul sees images of bodies in the same way as when we sleep. Thus Augustine says *(Gen. ad lit.* xii): *For I see not why the soul has an image of its own body when, the body lying senseless, yet not quite dead, it sees some things which many have related after returning to life from this suspended animation and yet has it not when it has left the body through death having taken place.* For it is unintelligible that the soul should have an image of its body, except in so far as it sees that image: wherefore he said before of those who lie senseless that *they have a certain image of their own body, by which they are able to be borne to corporeal places and by means of sensible images to take cognizance of such things as they see.* Therefore the separated soul can exercise the acts of the sensitive powers.

Obj. 4. Further, the memory is a power of the sensitive part, as proved in *De Memor. et Remin.* i. Now separated souls will actually remember the things they did in this world: wherefore it is said to the rich glutton (Luke xvi. 25): *Remember that thou didst receive good things in thy lifetime.* Therefore the separated soul will exercise the act of a sensitive power.

Obj. 5. Further, according to the Philosopher *(De Anima,* iii. 9) the irascible and concupiscible are in the sensitive part. But joy and sorrow, love and hatred, fear and hope, and similar emotions which according to our faith we hold to be in separated souls, are in the irascible and concupiscible. Therefore separated souls will not be deprived of the acts of the sensitive powers.

On the contrary, That which is common to soul and body cannot remain in the separated soul. Now all the operations of the sensitive powers are common to the soul and body: and this is evident from the fact that no sensitive power exercises an act except through a bodily

organ. Therefore the separated soul will be deprived of the acts of the sensitive powers.

Further, the Philosopher says *(De Anima,* i. 4), that *when the body is corrupted, the soul neither remembers nor loves,* and the same applies to all the acts of the sensitive powers. Therefore the separated soul does not exercise the act of any sensitive power.

I answer that, Some distinguish two kinds of acts in the sensitive powers: external acts which the soul exercises through the body; and these do not remain in the separated soul: and internal acts which the soul performs by itself; and these will be in the separated soul. This statement would seem to have originated from the opinion of Plato, who held that the soul is united to the body, as a perfect substance nowise dependant on the body, and merely as a mover is united to the thing moved. This is an evident consequence of transmigration which he held. And since according to him nothing is in motion except what is moved, and lest he should go on indefinitely, he said that the first mover moves itself, and he maintained that the soul is the cause of its own movement. Accordingly there would be a twofold movement of the soul, one by which it moves itself, and another whereby the body is moved by the soul: so that this act *to see* is first of all in the soul itself as moving itself, and secondly in the bodily organ in so far as the soul moves the body. This opinion is refuted by the Philosopher *(De Anima,* i. 3) who proves that the soul does not move itself, and that it is nowise moved in respect of such operations as seeing, feeling, and the like, but that such operations are movements of the composite only. We must therefore conclude that the acts of the sensitive powers nowise remain in the separated soul, except perhaps as in their remote origin.

Reply Obj. 1. Some deny that this book is Augustine's: for it is ascribed to a Cistercian who compiled it from Augustine's works and added things of his own. Hence we are not to take what is written there, as having authority. If, however, its authority should be maintained, it must be said that the meaning is that the separated soul is affected with imagination and other like powers, not as though such affection were the act of the aforesaid powers, but in the sense that the soul will be affected in the future life for good or ill, according to the things which it committed in the body through the imagination and other like powers: so that the imagination and such like powers are not supposed to elicit that affection, but to have elicited in the body the merit of that affection.

Reply Obj. 2. The soul is said to feel through the body, not as though the act of feeling belonged to the soul by itself, but as belonging to the whole composite by reason of the soul, just as we say that heat heats. That which is added, namely that the soul feels some things without the body, such as fear and so forth, means that it feels such things without the outward movement of the body that takes place in the acts of the proper senses: since fear and like passions do not occur without any bodily movement.

It may also be replied that Augustine is speaking according to the opinion of the Platonists who maintained this as stated above.

Reply Obj. 3. Augustine speaks there as nearly throughout that book, as one inquiring and not deciding. For it is clear that there is no comparison between the soul of a sleeper and the separated soul: since the soul of the sleeper uses the organ of imagination wherein corporeal images are impressed; which cannot be said of the separated soul. Or we may reply that images of things are in the soul, both as to the sensitive and imaginative power and as to the intellective power, with greater or lesser abstraction from matter and material conditions. Wherefore Augustine's comparison holds in this respect that just as the images of corporeal things are in the soul of the dreamer or of one who is carried out of his mind, imaginatively, so are they in the separated soul intellectively: but not that they are in the separated soul imaginatively.

Reply Obj. 4. As stated in the first book (D. 3, qu. 4), memory has a twofold signification. Sometimes it means a power of the sensitive part, in so far as its gaze extends over past time; and in this way the act of the memory will not be in the separated soul. Wherefore the Philosopher says (*De Anima*, i. 4) that *when this*, the body to wit, *is corrupted, the soul remembers not.* In another way memory is used to designate that part of the imagination which pertains to the intellective faculty, in so far namely as it abstracts from all differences of time, since it regards not only the past but also the present, and the future as Augustine says (*De Trin.* xiv. 11). Taking memory in this sense the separated soul will remember.*

Reply Obj. 5. Love, joy, sorrow, and the like, have a twofold signification. Sometimes they denote passions of the sensitive appetite, and thus they will not be in the separated soul, because in this way they are not exercised without a definite movement of the heart. In another way they denote acts of the will which is in the intellective part: and in this way they will be in the separated soul, even as delight will be there without bodily movement, even as it is in God, namely in so far

* Cf. P. I, Q. 77, A. 8; Q. 89, A. 6.

as it is a simple movement of the will. In this sense the Philosopher says (*Ethic.* vii. 14) that *God's joy is one simple delight.*

THIRD ARTICLE

Whether the Separated Soul Can Suffer from a Bodily Fire?

We proceed thus to the Third Article:—

Objection 1. It would seem that the separated soul cannot suffer from a bodily fire. For Augustine says (*Gen. ad lit.* xii): *The things that affect the soul well or ill after its separation from the body, are not corporeal but resemble corporeal things.* Therefore the separated soul is not punished with a bodily fire.

Obj. 2. Further, Augustine (*ibid.*) says that *the agent is always more excellent than the patient.* But it is impossible for any body to be more excellent than the separated soul. Therefore it cannot suffer from a body.

Obj. 3. Further, according to the Philosopher (*De Gener.* i) and Boëthius (*De Duab. Natur.*) only those things that agree in matter are active and passive in relation to one another. But the soul and corporeal fire do not agree in matter, since there is no matter common to spiritual and corporeal things: wherefore they cannot be changed into one another, as Boëthius says (*ibid.*). Therefore the separated soul does not suffer from a bodily fire.

Obj. 4. Further, whatsoever is patient receives something from the agent. Therefore if the soul suffer from the bodily fire, it will receive something therefrom. Now whatsoever is received in a thing is received according to the mode of the recipient. Therefore that which is received in the soul from the fire, is in it not materially but spiritually. Now the forms of things existing spiritually in the soul are its perfections. Therefore though it be granted that the soul suffer from the bodily fire, this will not conduce to its punishment, but rather to its perfection.

Obj. 5. Further, if it be said that the soul is punished merely by seeing the fire, as Gregory would seem to say (*Dial.* iv. 29); on the contrary,—If the soul sees the fire of hell, it cannot see it save by intellectual vision, since it has not the organs by which sensitive or imaginative vision is effected. But it would seem impossible for intellectual vision to be the cause of sorrow, since *there is no sorrow contrary to the pleasure of considering,* according to the Philosopher (*Top.* i. 13). Therefore the soul is not punished by that vision.

Obj. 6. Further, if it be said that the soul suffers from the corporeal fire, through being held thereby, even as now it is held by the body while living in the body; on the contrary, —The soul while living in the body is held by the body in so far as there results one thing from the soul and the body, as from form and matter. But the soul will not be the form of that corporeal fire. Therefore it cannot be held by the fire in the manner aforesaid.

Obj. 7. Further, every bodily agent acts by contact. But a corporeal fire cannot be in contact with the soul, since contact is only between corporeal things whose bounds come together. Therefore the soul suffers not from that fire.

Obj. 8. Further, an organic agent does not act on a remote object, except through acting on the intermediate objects; wherefore it is able to act at a fixed distance in proportion to its power. But souls, or at least the demons to whom this equally applies, are sometimes outside the place of hell, since sometimes they appear to men even in this world: and yet they are not then free from punishment, for just as the glory of the saints is never interrupted, so neither is the punishment of the damned. And yet we do not find that all the intermediate things suffer from the fire of hell: nor again is it credible that any corporeal thing of an elemental nature has such a power that its action can reach to such a distance. Therefore it does not seem that the pains suffered by the souls of the damned are inflicted by a corporeal fire.

On the contrary, The possibility of suffering from a corporeal fire is equally consistent with separated souls and with demons. Now demons suffer therefrom since they are punished by that fire into which the bodies of the damned will be cast after the resurrection, and which must needs be as corporeal fire. This is evident from the words of our Lord (Matth. xxv. 41), *Depart from Me, you cursed, into everlasting fire, which was prepared for the devil,* etc. Therefore separated souls also can suffer from that fire.

Further, punishment should correspond to sin. Now in sinning the soul subjected itself to the body by sinful concupiscence. Therefore it is just that it should be punished by being made subject to a bodily thing by suffering therefrom.

Further, there is greater union between form and matter than between agent and patient. Now the diversity of spiritual and corporeal nature does not hinder the soul from being the form of the body. Therefore neither is it an obstacle to its suffering from a body.

I answer that, Given that the fire of hell is not so called metaphorically, nor an imaginary fire, but a real corporeal fire, we must needs say that the soul will suffer punishment from a corporeal fire, since our Lord said (Matth. xxv. 41) that this fire was prepared for the devil and his angels, who are incorporeal even as the soul. But how it is that they can thus suffer is explained in many ways.

For some have said that the mere fact that the soul sees the fire makes the soul suffer from the fire: wherefore Gregory (*Dial.* iv. 29) says: *The soul suffers from the fire by merely seeing it.* But this does not seem sufficient, because whatever is seen, from the fact that it is seen, is a perfection of the seer; wherefore it cannot conduce to his punishment, as seen. Sometimes, however, it is of a penal or unpleasant nature accidentally, in so far, to wit, as it is apprehended as something hurtful, and consequently, besides the fact that the soul sees the fire, there must needs be some relation of the soul to the fire, according to which the fire is hurtful to the soul.

Hence others have said that although a corporeal fire cannot burn the soul, the soul nevertheless apprehends it as hurtful to itself, and in consequence of this apprehension is seized with fear and sorrow, in fulfillment of Ps. xiii. 5, *They have trembled for fear, where there was no fear.* Hence Gregory says (*Dial.* iv. l.c.) that *the soul burns through seeing itself aflame.* But this, again, seems insufficient, because in this case the soul would suffer from the fire, not in reality but only in apprehension: for although a real passion of sorrow or pain may result from a false imagination, as Augustine observes (*Gen. ad lit.* xii), it cannot be said in relation to that passion that one really suffers from the thing, but from the image of the thing that is present to one's fancy. Moreover, this kind of suffering would be more unlike real suffering than that which results from imaginary vision, since the latter is stated to result from real images of things, which images the soul carries about with it, whereas the former results from false fancies which the erring soul imagines: and furthermore, it is not probable that separated souls or demons, who are endowed with keen intelligence, would think it possible for a corporeal fire to hurt them, if they were nowise distressed thereby.

Hence others say that it is necessary to admit that the soul suffers even really from the corporeal fire: wherefore Gregory says (*Dial.* iv. l. c.): *We can gather from the words of the Gospel, that the soul suffers from the fire not only by seeing it, but also by feeling it.* They explain the possibility of this as follows. They say that this corporeal fire can be considered in two ways. First, as a corporeal thing, and thus it has not the power to act on the soul. Secondly, as the instrument of the vengeance of Divine justice. For the order of Divine justice demands that the soul which by sinning subjected itself to corporeal things should be subjected to them also in punishment. Now an instrument acts not only in virtue of its own nature, but also in virtue of the principal agent: wherefore it is not unreasonable if that fire, seeing that it acts in virtue of a spiritual agent, should act on the spirit of a man or demon, in the same way as we have explained the sanctification of the soul by the sacraments (P. III, Q. 62, AA. 1, 4).

But, again, this does not seem to suffice, since every instrument, in acting on that on which it is used instrumentally, has its own connatural action besides the action whereby it acts in virtue of the principal agent: in fact it is by fulfilling the former that it effects the latter action, even as, in Baptism, it is by laving the body that water sanctifies the soul, and the saw by cutting wood produces the shape of a house.

Hence we must allow the fire to exercise on the soul an action connatural to the fire, in order that it may be the instrument of Divine justice in the punishment of sin: and for this reason we must say that a body cannot naturally act on a spirit, nor in any way be hurtful or distressful to it, except in so far as the latter is in some way united to a body: for thus we observe that *the corruptible body is a load upon the soul* (Wis. ix. 15). Now a spirit is united to a body in two ways. In one way as form to matter, so that from their union there results one thing simply: and the spirit that is thus united to a body both quickens the body and is somewhat burdened by the body: but it is not thus that the spirit of man or demon is united to the corporeal fire. In another way as the mover is united to the things moved, or as a thing placed is united to place, even as incorporeal things are in a place. In this way created incorporeal spirits are confined to a place, being in one place in such a way as not to be in another. Now although of its nature a corporeal thing is able to confine an incorporeal spirit to a place, it is not able of its nature to detain an incorporeal spirit in the place to which it is confined, and so to tie it to that place that it be unable to seek another, since a spirit is not by nature in a place so as to be subject to place. But the corporeal fire is enabled as the instrument of the vengeance of Divine justice thus to detain a spirit; and thus it has a penal effect on it, by hindering it from fulfilling its own will, that is by hindering it from acting where it will and as it will.

This way is asserted by Gregory *(Dial.* iv. l.c.). For in explaining how the soul can suffer from that fire by feeling it, he expresses himself as follows: *Since Truth declares the rich sinner to be condemned to fire, will any wise man deny that the souls of the wicked*

are imprisoned in flames? Julian* says the same as quoted by the Master (iv. *Sent. D.* 44): *If the incorporeal spirit of a living man is held by the body, why shall it not be held after death by a corporeal fire?* and Augustine says *(De Civ. Dei,* xxi. 10) that *just as, although the soul is spiritual and the body corporeal, man is so fashioned that the soul is united to the body as giving it life, and on account of this union conceives a great love for its body, so it is chained to the fire, as receiving punishment therefrom, and from this union conceives a loathing.*

Accordingly we must unite all the aforesaid modes together, in order to understand perfectly how the soul suffers from a corporeal fire: so as to say that the fire of its nature is able to have an incorporeal spirit united to it as a thing placed is united to a place; that as the instrument of Divine justice it is enabled to detain it enchained as it were, and in this respect this fire is really hurtful to the spirit, and thus the soul seeing the fire as something hurtful to it is tormented by the fire. Hence Gregory *(Dial.* iv. l.c.) mentions all these in order, as may be seen from the above quotations.

Reply Obj. 1. Augustine speaks there as one inquiring: wherefore he expresses himself otherwise when deciding the point, as quoted above *(De Civ. Dei,* xxi).—Or we may reply that Augustine means to say that the things which are the proximate occasion of the soul's pain or sorrow are spiritual, since it would not be distressed unless it apprehended the fire as hurtful to it: wherefore the fire as apprehended is the proximate cause of its distress, whereas the corporeal fire which exists outside the soul is the remote cause of its distress.

Reply Obj. 2. Although the soul is simply more excellent than the fire, the fire is relatively more excellent than the soul, in so far, to wit, as it is the instrument of Divine justice.

Reply Obj. 3. The Philosopher and Boëthius are speaking of the action whereby the patient is changed into the nature of the agent. Such is not the action of the fire on the soul: and consequently the argument is not conclusive.

Reply Obj. 4. By acting on the soul the fire bestows nothing on it but detains it, as stated above. Hence the argument is not to the point.

Reply Obj. 5. In intellectual vision sorrow is not caused by the fact that something is seen, since the thing seen as such can nowise be contrary to the intellect. But in the sensible vision the thing seen, by its very action on the sight so as to be seen, there may be accidentally something corruptive of the sight, in so far as it destroys the harmony of the organ. Nevertheless, intellectual vision may cause

* Bishop of Toledo, *Prognostic* ii. 17.

sorrow, in so far as the thing seen is apprehended as hurtful, not that it hurts through being seen, but in some other way no matter which. It is thus that the soul in seeing the fire is distressed.

Reply Obj. 6. The comparison does not hold in every respect, but it does in some, as explained above.

Reply Obj. 7. Although there is no bodily contact between the soul and body, there is a certain spiritual contact between them (even as the mover of the heaven, being spiritual, touches the heaven, when it moves it, with a spiritual contact) in the same way as a *painful object is said to touch,* as stated in *De Generat.* i. This mode of contact is sufficient for action.

Reply Obj. 8. The souls of the damned are never outside hell, except by Divine permission, either for the instruction or for the trial of the elect. And wherever they are outside hell they nevertheless always see the fire

thereof as prepared for their punishment. Wherefore, since this vision is the immediate cause of their distress, as stated above, wherever they are, they suffer from hell-fire. Even so prisoners, though outside the prison, suffer somewhat from the prison, seeing themselves condemned thereto. Hence just as the glory of the elect is not diminished, neither as to the essential, nor as to the accidental reward, if they happen to be outside the empyrean, in fact this somewhat conduces to their glory, so the punishment of the damned is nowise diminished, if by God's permission they happen to be outside hell for a time. A gloss on James iii. 6, *inflameth the wheel of our nativity,* etc., is in agreement with this, for it is worded thus: *The devil, wherever he is, whether in the air or under the earth, drags with him the torments of his flames.* But the objection argues as though the corporeal fire tortured the spirit immediately in the same way as it torments bodies.

QUESTION 71

Of the Suffrages for the Dead

(In Fourteen Articles)

WE must now consider the suffrages for the dead. Under this head there are fourteen points of inquiry: (1) Whether suffrages performed by one person can profit others? (2) Whether the dead can be assisted by the works of the living? (3) Whether the suffrages of sinners profit the dead? (4) Whether suffrages for the dead profit those who perform them? (5) Whether suffrages profit those who are in hell? (6) Whether they profit those who are in purgatory? (7) Whether they avail the children in limbo? (8) Whether in any way they profit those who are heaven? (9) Whether the prayer of the Church, the Sacrament of the altar, and almsgiving profit the departed? (10) Whether indulgences granted by the Church profit them? (11) Whether the burial service profits the departed? (12) Whether suffrages for one dead person profit that person more than others? (13) Whether suffrages for many avail each one as much as if they were offered for each individual? (14) Whether general suffrages avail those for whom special suffrages are not offered, as much as special and general suffrages together avail those for whom they are offered?

FIRST ARTICLE

Whether the Suffrages of One Person Can Profit Others?

We proceed thus to the First Article:—
Objection 1. It would seem that the suf-

frages of one person cannot profit others. For it is written (Gal. vi. 8): *What things a man shall sow, those also shall he reap.* Now if one person reaped fruit from the suffrages of another, he would reap from another's sowing. Therefore a person receives no fruit from the suffrages of others.

Obj. 2. Further, it belongs to God's justice, that each one should receive according to his merits, wherefore the psalm (lxi. 13) says: *Thou wilt render to every man according to his works.* Now it is impossible for God's justice to fail. Therefore it is impossible for one man to be assisted by the works of another.

Obj. 3. Further, a work is meritorious on the same count as it is praiseworthy, namely inasmuch as it is voluntary. Now one man is not praised for the work of another. Therefore neither can the work of one man be meritorious and fruitful for another.

Obj. 4. Further, it belongs to Divine justice to repay good for good in the same way as evil for evil. But no man is punished for the evildoings of another; indeed, according to Ezech. xviii. 4, *the soul that sinneth, the same shall die.* Therefore neither does one person profit by another's good.

On the contrary, It is written (Ps. cxviii. 63): *I am a partaker with all them that fear Thee,* etc.

Further, all the faithful united together by charity are members of the one body of the

Church. Now one member is assisted by another. Therefore one man can be assisted by the merits of another.

I answer that, Our actions can avail for two purposes. First, for acquiring a certain state; thus by a meritorious work a man obtains the state of bliss. Secondly, for something consequent upon a state; thus by some work a man merits an accidental reward, or a rebate of punishment. And for both these purposes our actions may avail in two ways: first, by way of merit; secondly, by way of prayer: the difference being that merit relies on justice, and prayer on mercy; since he who prays obtains his petition from the mere liberality of the one he prays. Accordingly we must say that the work of one person nowise can avail another for acquiring a state by way of merit, so that, to wit, a man be able to merit eternal life by the works which I do, because the share of glory is awarded according to the measure of the recipient, and each one is disposed by his own and not by another's actions,—disposed, that is to say, by being worthy of reward. By way of prayer, however, the work of one may profit another while he is a wayfarer, even for acquiring a state; for instance, one man may obtain the first grace for another:* and since the impetration of prayer depends on the liberality of God Whom we pray, it may extend to whatever is ordinately subject to the Divine power. On the other hand, as regards that which is consequent upon or accessory to a state, the work of one may avail another, not only by way of prayer but even by way of merit: and this happens in two ways. First, on account of their communion in the root of the work, which root is charity in meritorious works. Wherefore all who are united together by charity acquire some benefit from one another's works, albeit according to the measure of each one's state, since even in heaven each one will rejoice in the goods of others. Hence it is that the communion of saints is laid down as an article of faith. Secondly, through the intention of the doer who does certain works specially for the purpose that they may profit such persons: so that those works become somewhat the works of those for whom they are done, as though they were bestowed on them by the doer. Wherefore they can avail them either for the fulfillment of satisfaction or for some similar purpose that does not change their state.

Reply Obj. 1. This reaping is the receiving of eternal life, as stated in Jo. iv. 36, *And he that reapeth . . . gathereth fruit unto life everlasting.* Now a share of eternal life is not given to a man save for his own works, for

* Cf. I-II, Q. 114, A. 6.

although we may impetrate for another that he obtain life, this never happens except by means of his own works, when namely, at the prayers of one, another is given the grace whereby he merits eternal ilfe.

Reply Obj. 2. The work that is done for another becomes his for whom it is done: and in like manner the work done by a man who is one with me is somewhat mine. Hence it is not contrary to Divine justice if a man receives the fruit of the works done by a man who is one with him in charity, or of works done for him. This also happens according to human justice, so that the satisfaction offered by one is accepted in lieu of another's.

Reply Obj. 3. Praise is not given to a person save according to his relation to an act, wherefore praise is *in relation to something (Ethic.* i. 12). And since no man is made or shown to be well or ill disposed to something, by another's deed, it follows that no man is praised for another's deeds save accidentally, in so far as he is somewhat the cause of those deeds, by giving counsel, assistance, inducement, or by any other means. On the other hand, a work is meritorious to a person, not only by reason of his disposition, but also in view of something consequent upon his disposition or state, as evidenced by what has been said.

Reply Obj. 4. It is directly contrary to justice to take away from a person that which is his due: but to give a person what is not his due is not contrary to justice, but surpasses the bounds of justice, for it is liberality. Now a person cannot be hurt by the ills of another, unless he be deprived of something of his own. Consequently it is not becoming that one should be punished for another's sins, as it is that one should acquire some advantage from deeds of another.

SECOND ARTICLE

Whether the Dead Can Be Assisted by the Works of the Living?

We proceed thus to the Second Article:—

Objection 1. It would seem that the dead cannot be assisted by the works of the living. First, because the Apostle says (2 Cor. v. 10): *We must all be manifested before the judgment seat of Christ, that every one may receive the proper things of the body, according as he hath done.* Therefore nothing can accrue to a man from the works of others, which are done after his death and when he is no longer in the body.

Obj. 2. Further, this also seems to follow from the words of Apoc. xiv. 13, *Blessed are the dead who die in the Lord . . . for their works follow them.*

Obj. 3. Further, it belongs only to one who is on the way to advance on account of some deed. Now after death men are no longer wayfarers, because to them the words of Job xix. 8, refer: *He hath hedged in my path round about, and I cannot pass.* Therefore the dead cannot be assisted by a person's suffrages.

Obj. 4. Further, no one is assisted by the deed of another, unless there be some community of life between them. Now there is no community of life between the dead and the living, as the Philosopher says *(Ethic.* i. 11). Therefore the suffrages of the living do not profit the dead.

On the contrary are the words of 2 Machab. xii. 46: *It is ... a holy and wholesome thought to pray for the dead that they may be loosed from sins.* But this would not be profitable unless it were a help to them. Therefore the suffrages of the living profit the dead.

Further, Augustine says *(De Cura pro Mort.* i): *Of no small weight is the authority of the Church whereby she clearly approves of the custom whereby a commendation of the dead has a place in the prayers which the priests pour forth to the Lord God at His altar.* This custom was established by the apostles themselves according to the Damascene in a sermon on suffrages for the dead,* where he expresses himself thus: *Realizing the nature of the Mysteries the disciples of the Saviour and His holy apostles sanctioned a commemoration of those who had died in the faith, being made in the awe-inspiring and life-giving Mysteries.* This is also confirmed by the authority of Dionysius *(Hier. Eccl.),* where he mentions the rite of the Early Church in praying for the dead, and, moreover, asserts that the suffrages of the living profit the dead. Therefore we must believe this without any doubt.

I answer that, Charity, which is the bond uniting the members of the Church, extends not only to the living, but also to the dead who die in charity. For charity which is the life of the soul, even as the soul is the life of the body, has no end: *Charity never falleth away* (1 Cor. xiii. 8). Moreover, the dead live in the memory of the living: wherefore the intention of the living can be directed to them. Hence the suffrages of the living profit the dead in two ways even as they profit the living, both on account of the bond of charity and on account of the intention being directed to them. Nevertheless, we must not believe that the suffrages of the living profit them so as to change their state from unhappiness to happiness or *vice versa;* but they avail for the diminution of punishment or something of the kind that involves no change in the state of the dead.

* *De his qui in fide dormierunt,* 3.

Reply Obj. 1. Man while living in the body merited that such things should avail him after death. Wherefore if he is assisted thereby after this life, this is, nevertheless, the result of the things he has done in the body.

Or we may reply, according to John Damascene, in the sermon quoted above, that these words refer to the retribution which will be made at the final judgment, of eternal glory or eternal unhappiness: for then each one will receive only according as he himself has done in the body. Meanwhile, however, he can be assisted by the suffrages of the living.

Reply Obj. 2. The words quoted refer expressly to the sequel of eternal retribution as is clear from the opening words: *Blessed are the dead,* etc. Or we may reply that deeds done on their behalf are somewhat their own, as stated above.

Reply Obj. 3. Although, strictly speaking, after death souls are not in the state of the way, yet in a certain respect they are still on the way, in so far as they are delayed awhile in their advance towards their final award. Wherefore, strictly speaking, their way is hedged in round about, so that they can no more be changed by any works in respect of the state of happiness or unhappiness. Yet their way is not so hedged around that they cannot be helped by others in the matter of their being delayed from receiving their final award, because in this respect they are still wayfarers.

Reply Obj. 4. Although the communion of civic deeds whereof the Philosopher speaks, is impossible between the dead and the living, because the dead are outside civic life, the communication of the spiritual life is possible between them, for that life is founded on charity towards God, to Whom the spirits of the dead live.

THIRD ARTICLE

Whether Suffrages Performed by Sinners Profit the Dead?

We proceed thus to the Third Article:—

Objection 1. It would seem that suffrages performed by sinners do not profit the dead. For, according to Jo. ix. 31, *God doth not hear sinners.* Now if their prayers were to profit those for whom they pray, they would be heard by God. Therefore the suffrages performed by them do not profit the dead.

Obj. 2. Further, Gregory says *(Pastoral,* i. 11) that *when an offensive person is sent to intercede, the wrath of the angered party is provoked to harsher measures.* Now every sinner is offensive to God. Therefore God is not inclined to mercy by the suffrages of sinners, and consequently their suffrages are of no avail.

Obj. 3. Further, a person's deed would seem to be more fruitful to the doer than to another. But a sinner merits naught for himself by his deeds. Much less, therefore, can he merit for another.

Obj. 4. Further, every meritorious work must be a living work, that is to say, informed by charity. Now works done by sinners are dead. Therefore the dead for whom they are done cannot be assisted thereby.

Obj. 5. *On the contrary,* No man can know for certain about another man whether the latter be in a state of sin or of grace. If, therefore, only those suffrages were profitable that are done by those who are in a state of grace, a man could not know of whom to ask suffrages for his dead, and consequently many would be deterred from obtaining suffrages.

Obj. 6. Further, according to Augustine (*Enchir.* cix), as quoted in the text (iv. *Sent.* D. 45), the dead are assisted by suffrages according as while living they merited to be assisted after death. Therefore the worth of suffrages is measured according to the disposition of the person for whom they are performed. Therefore it would appear that it differs not whether they be performed by good or by wicked persons.

I answer that, Two things may be considered in the suffrages performed by the wicked. First, the deed done, for instance the sacrifice of the altar. And since our sacraments have their efficacy from themselves independently of the deed of the doer, and are equally efficacious by whomsoever they are performed, in this respect the suffrages of the wicked profit the departed. Secondly, we may consider the deed of the doer, and then we must draw a distinction; because the deed of a sinner who offers suffrage may be considered—in one way in so far as it is his own deed, and thus it can nowise be meritorious either to himself or to another; in another way in so far as it is another's deed, and this happens in two ways. First, when the sinner, offering suffrages, represents the whole Church; for instance a priest when he performs the burial service in church. And since one in whose name or in whose stead a thing is done is understood to do it himself as Dionysius asserts (*Cœl. Hier.* xiii), it follows that the suffrages of that priest, albeit a sinner, profit the departed. Secondly, when he acts as the instrument of another: for the work of the instrument belongs more to the principal agent. Wherefore, although he who acts as the instrument of another be not in a state of merit, his act may be meritorious on account of the principal agent: for instance

if a servant being in sin do any work of mercy at the command of his master who has charity. Hence, if a person dying in charity command suffrages to be offered for him, or if some other person having charity prescribe them, those suffrages avail for the departed, even though the persons by whom they are performed be in sin. Nevertheless they would avail more if those persons were in charity, because then those works would be meritorious on two counts.

Reply Obj. 1. The prayer offered by a sinner is sometimes not his but another's, and consequently in this respect is worthy to be heard by God. Nevertheless, God sometimes hears sinners, when, to wit, they ask for something acceptable to God. For God dispenses His goods not only to the righteous but also to sinners (Matth. v. 45), not indeed on account of their merits, but of His loving kindness. Hence a gloss on Jo. ix. 31, *God doth not hear sinners,* says that *he speaks as one unanointed and as not seeing clearly.*

Reply Obj. 2. Although the sinner's prayer is not acceptable in so far as he is offensive, it may be acceptable to God on account of another in whose stead or at whose command he offers the prayer.

Reply Obj. 3. The reason why the sinner who performs these suffrages gains nothing thereby is because he is not capable of profiting by reason of his own indisposition. Nevertheless, as stated above, it may in some way profit another, who is disposed.

Reply Obj. 4. Although the sinner's deed is not living in so far as it is his own, it may be living in so far as it is another's, as stated above.

Since, however, the arguments in the contrary sense would seem to show that it matters not whether one obtain suffrages from good or from evil persons, we must reply to them also.

Reply Obj. 5. Although one cannot know for certain about another whether he be in the state of salvation, one may infer it with probability from what one sees outwardly of a man: for a tree is known by its fruit (Matth. vii. 16).

Reply Obj. 6. In order that suffrage avail another, it is requisite that the one for whom it is performed be capable of availing by it: and a man has become capable of this by his own works which he did in his life-time This is what Augustine means to say. Nevertheless, those works must be such that they can profit him, and this depends not on the person for whom the suffrage is performed, but rather on the one who offers the suffrages whether by performing them or by commanding them.

FOURTH ARTICLE

Whether Suffrages Offered by the Living for the Dead Profit Those Who Offer Them?

We proceed thus to the Fourth Article:—

Objection 1. It would seem that suffrages offered by the living for the dead do not profit those who offer them. For according to human justice a man is not absolved from his own debt if he pay a debt for another man. Therefore a man is not absolved from his own debt for the reason that by offering suffrages he has paid the debt of the one for whom he offered them.

Obj. 2. Further, whatever a man does, he should do it as best he can. Now it is better to assist two than one. Therefore if one who by suffrages has paid the debt of a dead person is freed from his own debt, it would seem that one ought never to satisfy for oneself, but always for another.

Obj. 3. Further, if the satisfaction of one who satisfies for another profits him equally with the one for whom he satisfies, it will likewise equally profit a third person if he satisfy for him at the same time, and likewise a fourth and so on. Therefore he might satisfy for all by one work of satisfaction; which is absurd.

On the contrary, It is written (Ps. xxxiv. 13): *My prayer shall be turned into my bosom.* Therefore, in like manner, suffrages that are offered for others profit those who satisfy.

Further, the Damascene says in the sermon *On those who fell asleep in the faith: Just as when about to anoint a sick man with the ointment or other holy oil, first of all he,* namely the anointer, *shares in the anointing and thus proceeds to anoint the patient, so whoever strives for his neighbor's salvation first of all profits himself and afterwards his neighbor.* And thus the question at issue is answered.

I answer that, The work of suffrage that is is done for another may be considered in two ways. First, as expiating punishment by way of compensation which is a condition of satisfaction: and in this way the work of suffrage that is counted as belonging to the person for whom it is done, while absolving him from the debt of punishment, does not absolve the performer from his own debt of punishment, because in this compensation we have to consider the equality of justice: and this work of satisfaction can be equal to the one debt without being equal to the other, for the debts of two sinners require a greater satisfaction than the debt of one. Secondly, it may be considered as meriting eternal life, and this it has as proceeding from its root, which is charity: and in this way it profits not only the person

* De his qui in fide dormierunt.

for whom it is done, but also and still more the doer.

This suffices for the *Replies* to the *Objections:* for the first considered the work of suffrage as a work of satisfaction, while the others consider it as meritorious.

FIFTH ARTICLE

Whether Suffrages Profit Those Who Are in Hell?

We proceed thus to the Fifth Article:—

Objection 1. It would seem that suffrages profit those who are in hell. For it is written (2 Machab. xii. 40): *They found under the coats of the slain some of the donaries of the idols . . ., which the law forbiddeth to the Jews,* and yet we read further on (*verse* 43) that Judas *sent twelve thousand drachms of silver to Jerusalem . . . to be offered for the sins of the dead.* Now it is clear that they sinned mortally through acting against the Law, and consequently that they died in mortal sin, and were taken to hell. Therefore suffrages profit those who are in hell.

Obj. 2. Further, the text (iv. *Sent.* D. 45) quotes the saying of Augustine (*Enchir.* cx) that *those whom suffrages profit gain either entire forgiveness, or at least an abatement of their damnation.* Now only those who are in hell are said to be damned. Therefore suffrages profit even those who are in hell.

Obj. 3. Further, Dionysius says (*Eccl. Hier.*): *If here the prayers of the righteous avail those who are alive, how much more do they, after death, profit those alone who are worthy of their holy prayers?* Hence we may gather that suffrages are more profitable to the dead than to the living. Now they profit the living even though they be in mortal sin, for the Church prays daily for sinners that they be converted to God. Therefore suffrages avail also for the dead who are in mortal sin.

Obj. 4. Further, in the Lives of the Fathers (iii. 172: vi. 3) we read, and the Damascene relates in his sermon* that Macarius discovered the skull of a dead man on the road, and that after praying he asked whose head it was, and the head replied that it had belonged to a pagan priest who was condemned to hell; and yet he confessed that he and others were assisted by the prayers of Macarius. Therefore the suffrages of the Church profit even those who are in hell.

Obj. 5. Further, the Damascene in the same sermon relates that Gregory, while praying for Trajan, heard a voice from heaven saying to him: *I have heard thy voice, and I pardon Trajan:* and of this fact the Damascene adds in the same sermon, *the whole East and West are witnesses.* Yet it is clear that Trajan was in hell, since *he put many martyrs to a cruel death (ibid.).* Therefore the suffrages of the Church avail even for those who are in hell.

On the contrary, Dionysius says *(Eccl. Hier.* vii): *The high priest prays not for the unclean, because by so doing he would act counter to the Divine order,* and consequently he says *(ibid.)* that *he prays not that sinners be forgiven, because his prayer for them would not be heard.* Therefore suffrages avail not those who are in hell.

Further, Gregory says *(Moral.* xxxiv. 19): *There is the same reason for not praying then* (namely after the judgment day) *for men condemned to the everlasting fire, as there is now for not praying for the devil and his angels who are sentenced to eternal punishment, and for this reason the saints pray not for dead unbelieving and wicked men, because, forsooth, knowing them to be already condemned to eternal punishment, they shrink from pleading for them by the merit of their prayers before they are summoned to the presence of the just Judge.*

Further, the text (iv. *Sent.* D. 45) quotes the words of Augustine *(De Verb. Apost. Serm.* xxxii): *If a man depart this life without the faith that worketh by charity and its sacraments, in vain do his friends have recourse to such like acts of kindness.* Now all the damned come under that head. Therefore suffrages profit them not.

I answer that, There have been three opinions about the damned. For some have said that a twofold distinction must be made in this matter. First, as to time; for they said that after the judgment day no one in hell will be assisted by any suffrage, but that before the judgment day some are assisted by the suffrages of the Church. Secondly, they made a distinction among those who are detained in hell. Some of these, they said, are very bad, those namely who have died without faith and the sacraments, and these, since they were not of the Church, neither *by grace nor, by name,** can the suffrages of the Church avail; while others are not very bad, those namely who belonged to the Church as actual members, who had the faith, frequented the sacraments and performed works generically good, and for these the suffrages of the Church ought to avail. Yet they were confronted with a difficulty which troubled them, for it would seem to follow from this (since the punishment of hell is finite in intensity although infinite in duration) that a multiplicity of suffrages would take away that punishment altogether, which is the error of Origen *(Peri Archon.* i; cf. Gregory, *Moral.* xxxiv): and consequently

endeavored in various ways to avoid this difficulty.

Præpositivus† said that suffrages for the damned can be so multiplied that they are entirely freed from punishment, not absolutely as Origen maintained, but for a time, namely till the judgment day: for their souls will be reunited to their bodies, and will be cast back into the punishments of hell without hope of pardon. But this opinion seems incompatible with Divine providence, which leaves nothing inordinate in the world. For guilt cannot be restored to order save by punishment: wherefore it is impossible for punishment to cease, unless first of all guilt be expiated: so that, as guilt remains for ever in the damned, their punishment will nowise be interrupted.

For this reason the followers of Gilbert de la Porrée devised another explanation. These said that the process in the diminution of punishments by suffrages is as the process in dividing a line, which though finite, is indefinitely divisible, and is never destroyed by division, if it be diminished not by equal but by proportionate quantities, for instance if we begin by taking away a quarter of the whole, and secondly, a quarter of that quarter, and then a quarter of this second quarter, and so on indefinitely. In like manner, they say by the first suffrage a certain proportion of the punishment is taken away, and by the second an equally proportionate part of the remainder. But this explanation is in many ways defective. First, because it seems that indefinite division which is applicable to continuous quantity cannot be transferred to spiritual quantity: secondly, because there is no reason why the second suffrage, if it be of equal worth, should diminish the punishment less than the first: thirdly, because punishment cannot be diminished unless guilt be diminished, even as it cannot be done away unless the guilt be done away: fourthly, because in the division of a line we come at length to something which is not sensible, for a sensible body is not indefinitely divisible: and thus it would follow that after many suffrages the remaining punishment would be so little as not to be felt, and thus would no longer be a punishment.

Hence others found another explanation. For Antissiodorensis‡ (iv. *Sent. Tract.* 14) said that suffrages profit the damned not by diminishing or interrupting their punishment, but by fortifying the person punished: even as a man who is carrying a heavy load might bathe his face in water, for thus he would be enabled to carry it better, and yet his load would be none the lighter. But this again is

---

* Cf. *Oratio ad Vesperas, Fer. ii, post Dom. Pass.*
A. D. 1205-9.   ‡ William of Auxerre, Archdeacon of Beauvais.

† Gilbert Prévostin, Chancellor of the See of Paris,

impossible, because according to Gregory (*Moral.* ix) a man suffers more or less from the eternal fire according as his guilt deserves; and consequently some suffer more, some less, from the same fire; wherefore since the guilt of the damned remains unchanged, it cannot be that he suffers less punishment. Moreover, the aforesaid opinion is presumptuous, as being in opposition to the statements of holy men, and groundless as being based on no authority. It is also unreasonable. First, because the damned in hell are cut off from the bond of charity in virtue of which the departed are in touch with the works of the living. Secondly, because they have entirely come to the end of life, and have received the final award for their merits, even as the saints who are in heaven. For the remaining punishment or glory of the body does not make them to be wayfarers, since glory essentially and radically resides in the soul. It is the same with the unhappiness of the damned, wherefore their punishment cannot be diminished as neither can the glory of the saints be increased as to the essential reward.

However, we may admit, in a certain measure, the manner in which, according to some, suffrages profit the damned, if it be said that they profit neither by diminishing nor interrupting their punishment, nor again by diminishing their sense of punishment, but by withdrawing from the damned some matter of grief, which matter they might have if they knew themselves to be so outcast as to be a care to no one; and this matter of grief is withdrawn from them when suffrages are offered for them. Yet even this is impossible according to the general law, because as Augustine says (*De Cura pro Mort.* xiii)—and this applies especially to the damned—*the spirits of the departed are where they see nothing of what men do or of what happens to them in this life,* and consequently they know not when suffrages are offered for them, unless this relief be granted from above to some of the damned in spite of the general law. This, however, is a matter of great uncertainty; wherefore it is safer to say simply that suffrages profit not the damned, nor does the Church intend to pray for them, as appears from the authors quoted above.

Reply Obj. 1. The donaries to the idols were not found on those dead so that they might be taken as a sign that they were carried off in reverence to the idols: but they took them as conquerors because they were due to them by right of war. They sinned, however, venially by covetousness: and consequently they were not damned in hell, and thus suffrages could profit them. Or we may say, according to some, that in the midst of fighting,

seeing they were in danger, they repented of their sin, according to Ps. lxxvii. 34, *When He slew them, then they sought Him:* and this is a probable opinion. Wherefore the offering was made for them.

Reply Obj. 2. In these words damnation is taken in a broad sense for any kind of punishment, so as to include also the punishment of purgatory which is sometimes entirely expiated by suffrages, and sometimes not entirely, but diminished.

Reply Obj. 3. Suffrage for a dead person is more acceptable than for a living person, as regards his being in greater want, since he cannot help himself as a living person can. But a living person is better off in that he can be taken from the state of mortal sin to the state of grace, which cannot be said of the dead. Hence there is not the same reason for praying for the dead as for the living.

Reply Obj. 4. This assistance did not consist in a diminishment of their punishment, but in this alone (as stated in the same place) that when he prayed they were permitted to see one another, and in this they had a certain joy, not real but imaginary, in the fulfillment of their desire. Even so the demons are said to rejoice when they draw men into sin, although this nowise diminishes their punishment, as neither is the joy of the angels diminished by the fact that they take pity on our ills.

Reply Obj. 5. Concerning the incident of Trajan it may be supposed with probability that he was recalled to life at the prayers of blessed Gregory, and thus obtained the grace whereby he received the pardon of his sins and in consequence was freed from punishment. The same applies to all those who were miraculously raised from the dead, many of whom were evidently idolaters and damned. For we must needs say likewise of all such persons that they were consigned to hell, not finally, but as was actually due to their own merits according to justice: and that according to higher causes, in view of which it was foreseen that they would be recalled to life, they were to be disposed of otherwise.

Or we may say with some that Trajan's soul was not simply freed from the debt of eternal punishment, but that his punishment was suspended for a time, that is, until the judgment day. Nor does it follow that this is the general result of suffrages, because things happen differently in accordance with the general law from that which is permitted in particular cases and by privilege. Even so the bounds of human affairs differ from those of the miracles of the Divine power as Augustine says (*De Cura pro Mort.* xvi).

SIXTH ARTICLE

Whether Suffrages Profit Those Who Are in Purgatory?

We proceed thus to the Sixth Article:—

Objection 1. It would seem that suffrages do not profit even those who are in purgatory. For purgatory is a part of hell. Now *there is no redemption in hell,** and it is written Ps. vi. 6), *Who shall confess to Thee in hell?* Therefore suffrages do not profit those who are in purgatory.

Obj. 2. Further, the punishment of purgatory is finite. Therefore if some of the punishment is abated by suffrages, it would be possible to have such a great number of suffrages, that the punishment would be entirely remitted, and consequently the sin entirely unpunished: and this would seem incompatible with Divine justice.

Obj. 3. Further, souls are in purgatory in order that they may be purified there, and being pure may come to the kingdom. Now nothing can be purified, unless something be done to it. Therefore suffrages offered by the living do not diminish the punishment of purgatory.

Obj. 4. Further, if suffrages availed those who are in purgatory, those especially would seem to avail them which are offered at their behest. Yet these do not always avail: for instance, if a person before dying were to provide for so many suffrages to be offered for him that if they were offered they would suffice for the remission of his entire punishment. Now supposing these suffrages to be delayed until he is released from punishment, they will profit him nothing. For it cannot be said that they profit him before they are discharged; and after they are fulfilled, he no longer needs them, since he is already released. Therefore suffrages do not avail those who are in purgatory.

On the contrary, As quoted in the text (iv. *Sent.* D. 45), Augustine says (*Enchir.* cx): *Suffrages profit those who are not very good or not very bad.* Now such are those who are detained in purgatory. Therefore, etc.

Further, Dionysius says (*Eccl. Hier.* vii) that the *godlike priest in praying for the departed prays for those who lived a holy life, and yet contracted certain stains through human frailty.* Now such persons are detained in purgatory. Therefore, etc.

I answer that, The punishment of purgatory is intended to supplement the satisfaction which was not fully completed in the body. Consequently, since, as stated above (AA. 1, 2: Q. 13, A. 2), the works of one person can avail for another's satisfaction, whether the latter

be living or dead, the suffrages of the living, without any doubt, profit those who are in purgatory.

Reply Obj. 1. The words quoted refer to those who are in the hell of the damned, where there is no redemption for those who are finally consigned to that punishment. We may also reply with Damascene (*Serm. de his qui in fide dorm.*) that such statements are to be explained with reference to the lower causes, that is according to the demands of the merits of those who are consigned to those punishments. But according to the Divine mercy which transcends human merits, it happens otherwise through the prayers of the righteous, than is implied by the expressions quoted in the aforesaid authorities. Now *God changes His sentence but not his counsel,* as Gregory says (*Moral.* xx): wherefore the Damascene (*loc. cit.*) quotes as instances of this the Ninevites, Achab and Ezechias, in whom it is apparent that the sentence pronounced against them by God was commuted by the Divine mercy.†

Reply Obj. 2. It is not unreasonable that the punishment of those who are in purgatory be entirely done away by the multiplicity of suffrages. But it does not follow that the sins remain unpunished, because the punishment of one undertaken in lieu of another is credited to that other.

Reply Obj. 3. The purifying of the soul by the punishment of purgatory is nothing else than the expiation of the guilt that hinders it from obtaining glory. And since, as stated above (Q. 13, A. 2), the guilt of one person can be expiated by the punishment which another undergoes in his stead, it is not unreasonable that one person be purified by another satisfying for him.

Reply Obj. 4. Suffrages avail on two counts, namely the action of the agent‡ and the action done. By action done I mean not only the sacrament of the Church, but the effect incidental to that action,—thus from the giving of alms there follow the relief of the poor and their prayer to God for the deceased. In like manner the action of the agent may be considered in relation either to the principal agent or to the executor. I say, then, that the dying person, as soon as he provides for certain suffrages to be offered for him, receives the full meed of those suffrages, even before they are discharged, as regards the efficacy of the suffrages that results from the action as proceeding from the principal agent. But as regards the efficacy of the suffrages arising from the action done or from the action as proceeding from the executor, he does not receive the fruit before the suffrages are discharged. And

* Office of the dead, *Resp.* vii.　　† Cf. P. I, Q. 19, A. 7, *ad* 2.　　‡ *Ex opere operante* and *ex opere operato.*

if, before this, he happens to be released from his punishment, he will in this respect be deprived of the fruit of the suffrages, and this will fall back upon those by whose fault he was then defrauded. For it is not unreasonable that a person be defrauded in temporal matters by another's fault,—and the punishment of purgatory is temporal,—although as regards the eternal retribution none can be defrauded save by his own fault.

SEVENTH ARTICLE

Whether Suffrages Avail the Children Who Are in Limbo?

We proceed thus to the Seventh Article:—

Objection 1. It would seem that suffrages avail the children who are in limbo. For they are not detained there except for another's sin. Therefore it is most becoming that they should be assisted by the suffrages of others.

Obj. 2. Further, in the text (iv. *Sent.* D. 45) the words of Augustine *(Enchir.* cx) are quoted: *The suffrages of the Church obtain forgiveness for those who are not very bad.* Now children are not reckoned among those who are very bad, since their punishment is very light. Therefore the suffrages of the Church avail them.

On the contrary, The text *(ibid.)* quotes Augustine as saying *(Serm.* xxxii, *De Verb Ap.)* that *suffrages avail not those who have departed hence without the faith that works by love.* Now the children departed thus. Therefore suffrages avail them not.

I answer that, Unbaptized children are not detained in limbo save because they lack the state of grace. Hence, since the state of the dead cannot be changed by the works of the living, especially as regards the merit of the essential reward or punishment, the suffrages of the living cannot profit the children in limbo.

Reply Obj. 1. Although original sin is such that one person can be assisted by another on its account, nevertheless the souls of the children in limbo are in such a state that they cannot be assisted, because after this life there is no time for obtaining grace.

Reply Obj. 2. Augustine is speaking of those who are not very bad, but have been baptized. This is clear from what precedes: *Since these sacrifices, whether of the altar or of any alms whatsoever, are offered for those who have been baptized, etc.*

EIGHTH ARTICLE

Whether Suffrages Profit the Saints in Heaven?

We proceed thus to the Eighth Article:—

Objection 1. It would seem that in some

* Postcommunion, Feast of S. Andrew, Apostle.

way suffrages profit the saints in heaven; on account of the words of the Collect in the Mass:* *Even as they* (i.e. the sacraments) *avail thy saints unto glory, so may they profit us unto healing.* Now foremost among all suffrages is the sacrifice of the altar. Therefore suffrages profit the saints in heaven.

Obj. 2. Further, the sacraments cause what they signify. Now the third part of the host, that namely which is dropped into the chalice, signifies those who lead a happy life in heaven. Therefore the suffrages of the Church profit those who are in heaven.

Obj. 3. Further, the saints rejoice in heaven not only in their own goods, but also in the goods of others: hence it is written (Luke xv. 10): *There is* (Vulg.,—*shall be) joy before the angels of God upon one sinner doing penance.* Therefore the joy of the saints in heaven increases on account of the good works of the living: and consequently our suffrages also profit them.

Obj. 4. Further, the Damascene says *(Serm. de his qui in fide dorm.)* quoting the words of Chrysostom: *For if the heathens,* he says, *burn the dead together with what has belonged to them, how much more shouldst thou, a believer, send forth a believer together with what has belonged to him, not that they also may be brought to ashes like him, but that thou mayest surround him with greater glory by so doing; and if he be a sinner who has died, that thou mayest loose him from his sins, and if he be righteous, that thou mayest add to his meed and reward!* And thus the same conclusion follows.

On the contrary, As quoted in the text (iv. *Sent.* D. 15), Augustine says *(De Verb. Ap. Serm.* xvii): *It is insulting to pray for a martyr in church, since we ought to commend ourselves to his prayers.*

Further, to be assisted belongs to one who is in need. But the saints in heaven are without any need whatever. Therefore they are not assisted by the suffrages of the Church.

I answer that, Suffrage by its very nature implies the giving of some assistance, which does not apply to one who suffers no default: since no one is competent to be assisted except he who is in need. Hence, as the saints in heaven are free from all need, being inebriated with the plenty of God's house (Ps. xxxv. 10), they are not competent to be assisted by suffrages.

Reply Obj. 1. Such like expressions do not mean that the saints receive an increase of glory in themselves through our observing their feasts, but that we profit thereby in celebrating their glory with greater solemnity. Thus, through our knowing or praising God, and through His glory thus increasing somewhat in us, there accrues something, not to God, but to us.

Reply Obj. 2. Although the sacraments cause what thy signify, they do not produce this effect in respect of everything that they signify: else, since they signify Christ, they would produce something in Christ (which is absurd). But they produce their effect on the recipient of the sacrament in virtue of that which is signified by the sacrament. Thus it does not follow that the sacrifices offered for the faithful departed profit the saints, but that by the merits of the saints which we commemorate, or which are signified in the sacrament, they profit others for whom they are offered.

Reply Obj. 3. Although the saints in heaven rejoice in all our goods, it does not follow, that if our joys be increased their joy is also increased formally, but only materially, because every passion is increased formally in respect of the formal aspect of its object. Now the formal aspect of the saints' joy, no matter what they rejoice in, is God Himself, in Whom they cannot rejoice more and less, for otherwise their essential reward, consisting of their joy in God, would vary. Hence from the fact that the goods are multiplied, wherein they rejoice with God as the formal aspect of their joy, it does not follow that their joy is intensified, but that they rejoice in more things. Consequently it does not follow that they are assisted by our works.

Reply Obj. 4. The sense is not that an increase of meed or reward accrues to the saint from the suffrages offered by a person, but that this accrues to the offerer. Or we may reply that the blessed departed may derive a reward from suffrages through having, while living, provided for suffrage to be offered for himself, and this was meritorious for him.

NINTH ARTICLE

Whether the Prayers of the Church, the Sacrifice of the Altar and Alms Profit the Departed?

We proceed thus to the Ninth Article:—

Objection 1. It would seem that the souls of the departed are not assisted only by the prayers of the Church, the sacrifice of the altar and alms, or that they are not assisted by them chiefly. For punishment should compensate for punishment. Now fasting is more penal than almsgiving or prayer. Therefore fasting profits more as suffrage than any of the above.

Obj. 2. Further, Gregory reckons fasting together with these three, as stated in the Decretals (xiii, Q. ii, Cap. 22): *The souls of the departed are released in four ways, either by the offerings of priests, or the alms of their friends, or the prayers of the saints, or the fasting of their kinsfolk.* Therefore the three mentioned above are insufficiently reckoned by Augustine (*De Cura pro Mort.* xviii).

Obj. 3. Further, Baptism is the greatest of the sacraments, especially as regards its effect. Therefore Baptism and other sacraments ought to be offered for the departed equally with or more than the Sacrament of the altar.

Obj. 4. Further, this would seem to follow from the words of 1 Cor. xv. 29, *If the dead rise not again at all, why are they then baptized for them?* Therefore Baptism avails as suffrage for the dead.

Obj. 5. Further, in different Masses there is the same Sacrifice of the altar. If, therefore, sacrifice, and not the Mass, be reckoned among the suffrages, it would seem that the effect would be the same whatever Mass be said for a deceased person, whether in honor of the Blessed Virgin or of the Holy Ghost, or any other. Yet this seems contrary to the ordinance of the Church which has appointed a special Mass for the dead.

Obj. 6. Further, the Damascene (*Serm. de his qui in fide dorm.*) teaches that candles and oil should be offered for the dead. Therefore not only the offering of the sacrifice of the altar, but also other offerings should be reckoned among suffrages for the dead.

I answer that, The suffrages of the living profit the dead in so far as the latter are united to the living in charity, and in so far as the intention of the living is directed to the dead. Consequently those whose works are by nature best adapted to assist the dead, which pertain chiefly to the communication of charity, or to the directing of one's intention to another person. Now the sacrament of the Eucharist belongs chiefly to charity, since it is the sacrament of ecclesiastical unity, inasmuch as it contains Him in Whom the whole Church is united and incorporated, namely Christ: wherefore the Eucharist is as it were the origin and bond of charity. Again, chief among the effects of charity is the work of almsgiving: wherefore on the part of charity these two, namely the sacrifice of the Church and almsgiving are the chief suffrages for the dead. But on the part of the intention directed to the dead the chief suffrage is prayer, because prayer by its very nature implies relation not only to the person who prays, even as other works do, but more directly still to that which we pray for. Hence these three are reckoned the principal means of succoring the dead, although we must allow that any other goods whatsoever that are done out of charity for the dead are profitable to them.

Reply Obj. 1. When one person satisfies for another, the point to consider, in order that the effect of his satisfaction reach the other, is the thing whereby the satisfaction of one passes to another, rather than even the punishment undergone by way of satisfaction; although the punishment expiates more the guilt of the one who satisfies, in so far as it is a kind of medicine. And consequently the three aforesaid are more profitable to the departed than fasting.

Reply Obj. 2. It is true that fasting can profit the departed by reason of charity, and on account of the intention being directed to the departed. Nevertheless, fasting does not by its nature contain anything pertaining to charity or to the directing of the intention, and these things are extrinsic thereto as it were, and for this reason Augustine did not reckon, while Gregory did reckon, fasting among the suffrages for the dead.

Reply Obj. 3. Baptism is a spiritual regeneration, wherefore just as by generation being does not accrue save to the object generated, so Baptism produces its effect only in the person baptized, as regards the deed done: and yet as regards the deed of the doer whether of the baptizer or of the baptized, it may profit others even as other meritorious works. On the other hand, the Eucharist is the sign of ecclesiastical unity, wherefore by reason of the deed done its effect can pass to another, which is not the case with the other sacraments.

Reply Obj. 4. According to a gloss this passage may be expounded in two ways. First, thus: *If the dead rise not again, nor did Christ rise again, why are they baptized for them?* i.e. *for sins, since they are not pardoned if Christ rose not again, because in Baptism not only Christ's passion but also His resurrection operates, for the latter is in a sense the cause of our spiritual resurrection.* Secondly, thus: There have been some misguided persons who were baptized for those who had departed this life without baptism, thinking that this would profit them: and according to this explanation the Apostle is speaking, in the above words, merely according to the opinion of certain persons.

Reply Obj. 5. In the office of the Mass there is not only a sacrifice but also prayers. Hence the suffrage of the Mass contains two of the things mentioned by Augustine *(loc. cit.),* namely *prayer* and *sacrifice.* As regards the sacrifice offered the Mass profits equally the departed, no matter in whose honor it be said: and this is the principal thing done in the Mass. But as regards the prayers, that Mass is most profitable in which the prayers are appointed for this purpose. Nevertheless, this defect may be supplied by the greater devotion, either of the one who says Mass, or of the one who orders the Mass to be said,

* Cf. Q. 25, A. 2.

or again, by the intercession of the saint whose suffrage is besought in the Mass.

Reply Obj. 6. This offering of candles or oil may profit the departed in so far as they are a kind of alms: for they are given for the worship of the Church or for the use of the faithful.

TENTH ARTICLE

Whether the Indulgences of the Church Profit the Dead?

We proceed thus to the Tenth Article:—

Objection 1. It would seem that the indulgences granted by the Church profit even the dead. First, on account of the custom of the Church, who orders the preaching of a crusade in order that some one may gain an indulgence for himself and for two or three and sometimes even ten souls, both of the living and of the dead. But this would amount to a deception unless they profited the dead. Therefore indulgences profit the dead.

Obj. 2. Further, the merit of the whole Church is more efficacious than that of one person. Now personal merit serves as a suffrage for the departed, for instance in the case of almsgiving. Much more therefore does the merit of the Church whereon indulgences are founded.

Obj. 3. Further, the indulgences of the Church profit those who are members of the Church. Now those who are in purgatory are members of the Church, else the suffrages of the Church would not profit them. Therefore it would seem that indulgences profit the departed.

On the contrary, In order that indulgences may avail a person, there must be a fitting cause for granting the indulgence.* Now there can be no such cause on the part of the dead, since they can do nothing that is of profit to the Church, and it is for such a cause that indulgences are chiefly granted. Therefore, seemingly, indulgences profit not the dead.

Further, indulgences are regulated according to the decision of the party who grants them. If, therefore, indulgences could avail the dead, it would be in the power of the party granting them to release a deceased person entirely from punishment: which is apparently absurd.

I answer that, An indulgence may profit a person in two ways: in one way, principally; in another, secondarily. It profits principally the person who avails himself of an indulgence, who, namely, does that for which the indulgence is granted, for instance one who visits the shrine of some saint. Hence since the dead can do none of those things for which indulgences are granted, indulgences cannot avail them directly. However, they profit secondarily and indirectly the person for whom one does that which is the cause of the indulgence. This is sometimes feasible and sometimes not, according to the different forms of indulgence. For if the form of indulgence be such as this: *Whosoever does this or that shall gain so much indulgence,* he who does this cannot transfer the fruit of the indulgence to another, because it is not in his power to apply to a particular person the intention of the Church who dispenses the common suffrages whence indulgences derive their value, as stated above (Q. 27, A. 3, *ad* 2). If, however, the indulgence be granted in this form: *Whosoever does this or that, he, his father, or any other person connected with him and detained in purgatory, will gain so much indulgence,* an indulgence of this kind will avail not only a living but also a deceased person. For there is no reason why the Church is able to transfer the common merits, whereon indulgences are based, to the living and not to the dead. Nor does it follow that a prelate of the Church can release souls from purgatory just as he lists, since for indulgences to avail there must be a fitting cause for granting them, as stated above (Q. 26, A. 3).

ELEVENTH ARTICLE

Whether the Burial Service Profits the Dead?

We proceed thus to the Eleventh Article:—

Objection 1. It would seem that the burial service profits the dead. For Damascene *(Serm. de his qui in fide dorm.)* quotes Athanasius as saying: *Even though he who has departed in godliness be taken up to heaven, do not hesitate to call upon God and to burn oil and wax at his tomb; for such things are pleasing to God and receive a great reward from Him.* Now the like pertain to the burial service. Therefore the burial service profits the dead.

Obj. 2. Further, according to Augustine *(De Cura pro mort.* iii), *In olden times the funerals of just men were cared for with dutiful piety, their obsequies celebrated, their graves provided, and themselves while living charged their children touching the burial or even the translation of their bodies.* But they would not have done this unless the tomb and things of this kind conferred something on the dead. Therefore the like profit the dead somewhat.

Obj. 3. Further, no one does a work of mercy on some one's behalf unless it profit him. Now burying the dead is reckoned among the works of mercy, therefore Augustine says *(ibid.)*: *Tobias, as attested by the angel, is declared to have found favor with God by burying the dead.* Therefore such like burial observances profit the dead.

Obj. 4. Further, it is unbecoming to assert that the devotion of the faithful is fruitless. Now some, out of devotion, arrange for their burial in some religious locality. Therefore the burial service profits the dead.

Obj. 5. Further, God is more inclined to pity than to condemn. Now burial in a sacred place is hurtful to some if they be unworthy: wherefore Gregory says *(Dial.* iv): *If those who are burdened with grievous sins are buried in the church this will lead to their more severe condemnation rather than to their release.* Much more, therefore, should we say that the burial service profits the good.

On the contrary, Augustine says *(De Cura pro Mort.* iii): *Whatever service is done the body is no aid to salvation, but an office of humanity.*

Further, Augustine says *(ibid.; De Civ. Dei,* i): *The funereal equipment, the disposition of the grace, the solemnity of the obsequies are a comfort to the living rather than a help to the dead.*

Further, Our Lord said (Luke xii. 4): *Be not afraid of them who kill the body, and after that have no more that they can do.* Now after death the bodies of the saints can be hindered from being buried, as we read of having been done to certain martyrs at Lyons in Gaul (Eusebius, *Eccl. Hist.* v. 1). Therefore the dead take no harm if their bodies remain unburied: and consequently the burial service does not profit them.

I answer that, We have recourse to burial for the sake of both the living and the dead. For the sake of the living, lest their eyes be revolted by the disfigurement of the corpse, and their bodies be infected by the stench, and this as regards the body. But it profits the living also spiritually inasmuch as our belief in the resurrection is confirmed thereby. It profits the dead in so far as one bears the dead in mind and prays for them through looking on their burial place, wherefore a *monument* takes its name from remembrance, for a monument is something that recalls the mind *(monens mentem)*, as Augustine observes *(De Civ. Dei,* i; *De Cura pro Mort.* iv). It was, however, a pagan error that burial was profitable to the dead by procuring rest for his soul: for they believed that the soul could not be at rest until the body was buried, which is altogether ridiculous and absurd.

That, moreover, burial in a sacred place profits the dead, does not result from the action done, but rather from the action itself of the doer: when, to wit, the dead person himself, or another, arranges for his body to be buried in a sacred place, and commends him to the patronage of some saint, by whose prayers we must believe that he is assisted, as well as to the suffrages of those who serve the holy place, and pray more frequently and more specially for those who are buried in their midst. But such things as are done for the display of the obsequies are profitable to the living, as being a consolation to them; and yet they can also profit the dead, not directly but indirectly, in so far as men are aroused to pity thereby and consequently to pray, or in so far as the outlay on the burial brings either assistance to the poor or adornment to the church: for it is in this sense that the burial of the dead is reckoned among the works of mercy.

Reply Obj. 1. By bringing oil and candles to the tombs of the dead we profit them indirectly, either as offering them to the Church and as giving them to the poor, or as doing this in reverence of God. Hence, after the words quoted we read: For oil and candles are a holocaust.

Reply Obj. 2. The fathers of old arranged for the burial of their bodies, so as to show that the bodies of the dead are the object of Divine providence, not that there is any feeling in a dead body, but in order to confirm the belief in the resurrection, as Augustine says (De Civ. Dei, i. 13). Hence, also, they wished to be buried in the land of promise, where they believed Christ's birth and death would take place, Whose resurrection is the cause of our rising again.

Reply Obj. 3. Since flesh is a part of man's nature, man has a natural affection for his flesh, according to Eph. v. 29, No man ever hated his own flesh. Hence in accordance with this natural affection a man has during life a certain solicitude for what will become of his body after death: and he would grieve if he had a presentiment that something untoward would happen to his body. Consequently those who love a man, through being conformed to the one they love in his affection for himself, treat his body with loving care. For as Augustine says (De Civ. Dei, i. 13): If a father's garment and ring, and whatever such like is the more dear to those whom they leave behind the greater their affection is towards their parents, in no wise are the bodies themselves to be spurned which truly we wear in more familiar and close conjunction than anything else we put on.

Reply Obj. 4. As Augustine says (De Cura pro Mort. iv), the devotion of the faithful is not fruitless when they arrange for their friends to be buried in holy places, since by so doing they commend their dead to the suffrages of the saints, as stated above.

Reply Obj. 5. The wicked man dead takes no harm by being buried in a holy place, ex-

* S. Augustine, Enchiridion cx.

cept in so far as he rendered such a burial place unfitting for him by reason of human glory.

TWELFTH ARTICLE

Whether Suffrages Offered for One Deceased Person Profit the Person for Whom They Are Offered More Than Others?

We proceed thus to the Twelfth Article:—

Objection 1. It would seem that suffrages offered for one deceased person are not more profitable to the one for whom they are offered, than to others. For spiritual light is more communicable than a material light. Now a material light, for instance of a candle, though kindled for one person only, avails equally all those who are gathered together, though the candle be not lit for them. Therefore, since suffrages are a kind of spiritual light, though they be offered for one person in particular, do not avail him any more than the others who are in purgatory.

Obj. 2. Further, as stated in the text (iv, Sent. D. 45), suffrages avail the dead in so far as during this life they merited that they might avail them afterwards.* Now some merited that suffrages might avail them more than those for whom they are offered. Therefore they profit more by those suffrages, else their merits would be rendered unavailing.

Obj. 3. Further, the poor have not so many suffrages given them as the rich. Therefore if the suffrages offered for certain people profit them alone, or profit them more than others, the poor would be worse off: yet this is contrary to our Lord's saying (Luke vi. 20): Blessed are ye poor, for yours is the kingdom of God.

On the contrary, Human justice is copied from Divine justice. But if a person pay another's debt human justice releases the latter alone. Therefore since he who offers suffrages for another pays the debt, in a sense, of the person for whom he offers them, they profit this person alone.

Further, just as a man by offering suffrages satisfies somewhat for a deceased person, so, too, sometimes a person can satisfy for a living person. Now where one satisfies for a living person the satisfaction counts only for the person for whom it is offered. Therefore one also who offers suffrages profits him alone for whom he offers them.

I answer that, There have been two opinions on this question. Some, like Præpositivus, have said that suffrages offered for one particular person do avail chiefly, not the person for whom they are offered, but those who are most worthy. And they instanced a candle which is lit for a rich man and profits those who are with him no less than the rich man himself, and perhaps even more, if they have keener sight. They also gave the instance of a lesson which profits the person to whom it is given no more than others who listen with him, but perhaps profits these others more, if they be more intelligent. And if it were pointed out to them that in this case the Church's ordinance in appointing certain special prayers for certain persons is futile, they said that the Church did this to excite the devotion of the faithful, who are more inclined to offer special than common suffrages, and pray more fervently for their kinsfolk than for strangers.

Others, on the contrary, said that suffrages avail more those for whom they are offered. Now both opinions have a certain amount of truth: for the value of suffrages may be gauged from two sources. For their value is derived in the first place from the virtue of charity, which makes all goods common, and in this respect they avail more the person who is more full of charity, although they are not offered specially for him. In this way the value of suffrages regards more a certain inward consolation by reason of which one who is in charity rejoices in the goods of another after death in respect of the diminution of punishment; for after death there is no possibility of obtaining or increasing grace, whereas during life the works of others avail for this purpose by the virtue of charity. In the second place suffrages derive their value from being applied to another person by one's intention. In this way the satisfaction of one person counts for another, and there can be no doubt that thus they avail more the person for whom they are offered: in fact, they avail him alone in this way, because satisfaction, properly speaking, is directed to the remission of punishment. Consequently, as regards the remission of punishment, suffrages avail chiefly the person for whom they are offered, and accordingly there is more truth in the second opinion than in the first.

Reply Obj. 1. Suffrages avail, after the manner of a light, in so far as they reach the dead, who thereby receive a certain amount of consolation: and this is all the greater according as they are endowed with a greater charity. But in so far as suffrages are a satisfaction applied to another by the intention of the offerer, they do not resemble a light, but rather the payment of a debt: and it does not follow, if one person's debt be paid, that the debt of others is paid likewise.

Reply Obj. 2. Such a merit is conditional, for in this way they merited that suffrages would profit them if offered for them, and this was merely to render themselves fit recipients of those suffrages. It is therefore clear that they did not directly merit the assistance of those suffrages, but made themselves fit by their preceding merits to receive the fruit of suffrages. Hence it does not follow that their merit is rendered unavailing.

Reply Obj. 3. Nothing hinders the rich from being in some respects better off than the poor, for instance as regards the expiation of their punishment. But this is as nothing in comparison with the kingdom of heaven, where the poor are shown to be better off by the authority quoted.

THIRTEENTH ARTICLE

Whether Suffrages Offered for Several Are of As Much Value to Each One As If They Had Been Offered for Each in Particular?

We proceed thus to the Thirteenth Article:—

Objection 1. It would seem that suffrages offered for several are of as much value to each one as if they had been offered for each in particular. For it is clear that if one person receives a lesson he loses nothing if others receive the lesson with him. Therefore in like manner a person for whom a suffrage is offered loses nothing if some one else is reckoned together with him: and consequently if it be offered for several, it is of as much value to each one as if it were offered for each in particular.

Obj. 2. Further, it is to be observed that according to the common practice of the Church, when Mass is said for one deceased person, other prayers are added for other deceased persons. Now this would not be done, if the dead person for whom the Mass is said were to lose something thereby. Therefore the same conclusion follows as above.

Obj. 3. Further, suffrages, especially of prayers, rely on the Divine power. But with God, just as it makes no difference whether He helps by means of many or by means of a few, so it differs not whether He assists many or a few. Therefore if the one same prayer be said for many, each one of them will receive as much assistance as one person would if that same prayer were said for him alone.

On the contrary, It is better to assist many than one. If therefore a suffrage offered for several is of as much value to each one as if it were offered for one alone, it would seem that the Church ought not to have appointed a Mass and prayer to be said for one person in particular, but that Mass ought always to be said for all the faithful departed: and this is evidently false.

Further, a suffrage has a finite efficiency. Therefore if it be divided among many it avails less for each one than if it were offered for one only.

I answer that, If the value of suffrages be

considered according as it is derived from the virtue of charity uniting the members of the Church together, suffrages offered for several persons avail each one as much as if they were offered for one alone, because charity is not diminished if its effect be divided among many, in fact rather is it increased; and in like manner joy increases through being shared by many, as Augustine says *(Conf.* viii). Consequently many in purgatory rejoice in one good deed no less than one does. On the other hand, if we consider the value of suffrages, inasmuch as they are a kind of satisfaction applied to the dead by the intention of the person offering them, then the suffrage for some person in particular avails him more than that which is offered for him in common with many others; for in this case the effect of the suffrages is divided in virtue of Divine justice among those for whom the suffrages are offered. Hence it is evident that this question depends on the first; and, moreover, it is made clear why special suffrages are appointed to be offered in the Church.

Reply Obj. 1. Suffrages considered as works of satisfaction do not profit after the manner of an action as teaching does; for teaching, like any other action, produces its effect according to the disposition of the recipient. But they profit after the manner of the payment of a debt, as stated above (A. 12, *ad* 1); and so the comparison fails.

Reply Obj. 2. Since suffrages offered for one person avail others in a certain way, as stated (A. 1), it follows that when Mass is said for one person, it is not unfitting for prayers to be said for others also. For these prayers are said, not that the satisfaction offered by one suffrage be applied to those others chiefly, but that the prayer offered for them in particular may profit them also.

Reply Obj. 3. Prayer may be considered both on the part of the one who prays, and on the part of the person prayed: and its effect depends on both. Consequently though it is no more difficult to the Divine power to absolve many than to absolve one, nevertheless the prayer of one who prays thus is not as satisfactory for many as for one.

FOURTEENTH ARTICLE

Whether General Suffrages Avail Those for Whom Special Suffrages Are Not Offered, As Much As Special Suffrages Avail Those for Whom They Are Offered in Addition to General Suffrages?

We proceed thus to the Fourteenth Article:—

Objection 1. It would seem that general suffrages avail those for whom special suffrages are not offered. as much as special suffrages avail those for whom they are offered in addition to general suffrages. For in the life to come each one will be rewarded according to his merits. Now a person for whom no suffrages are offered merited to be assisted after death as much as one for whom special suffrages are offered. Therefore the former will be assisted by general suffrages as much as the latter by special and general suffrages.

Obj. 3. Further, the Eucharist is the chief of the suffrages of the Church. Now the Eucharist, since it contains Christ whole, has infinite efficacy so to speak. Therefore one offering of the Eucharist for all in general is of sufficient value to release all who are in purgatory: and consequently general suffrages alone afford as much assistance as special and general suffrages together.

On the contrary, Two goods are more eligible than one. Therefore special suffrages, together with general suffrages, are more profitable to the person for whom they are offered than general suffrages alone.

I answer that, The reply to this question depends on that which is given to the twelfth inquiry (A. 12): for if the suffrages offered for one person in particular avail indifferently for all, then all suffrages are common; and consequently one for whom the special suffrages are not offered will be assisted as much as the one for whom they are offered, if he be equally worthy. On the other hand, if the suffrages offered for a person do not profit all indifferently, but those chiefly for whom they are offered, then there is no doubt that general and special suffrages together avail a person more than general suffrages alone. Hence the Master, in the text (iv. *Sent.* D. 45), mentions two opinions: one, when he says that a rich man derives from general, together with special suffrages, an equal profit to that which a poor man derives from special suffrages alone; for although the one receives assistance from more sources than the other, he does not receive a greater assistance: the other opinion he mentions when he says that a person for whom special suffrages are offered obtains a more speedy but not a more complete release, because each will be finally released from all punishment.

Reply Obj. 1. As stated above (A. 12, *ad* 2) the assistance derived from suffrages is not directly and simply an object of merit, but conditionally as it were: hence the argument does not prove.

Reply Obj. 2. Although the power of Christ Who is contained in the Sacrament of the Eucharist is infinite, yet there is a definite effect to which that sacrament is directed. Hence it does not follow that the whole punishment of those who are in purgatory is expiated by one sacrifice of the altar: even so, by the one sacrifice which a man offers, he is not released from the whole satisfaction due for his sins, wherefore sometimes several Masses are enjoined in satisfaction for one sin. Nevertheless, if any thing from special suffrages be left over for those for whom they are offered (for instance if they need them not) we may well believe that by God's mercy this is granted to others for whom those suffrages are not offered, if they need them: as affirmed by Damascene *(Serm. de his qui in fide dorm.)* who says: *Truly God, forasmuch as He is just, will adapt ability to the disabled, and will arrange for an exchange of deficiencies:* and this exchange is effected when what is lacking to one is supplied by another.

QUESTION 72

Of Prayers with Regard to the Saints in Heaven

(In Three Articles)

WE must now consider prayer with regard to the saints in heaven. Under this head there are three points of inquiry: (1) Whether the saints have knowledge of our prayers? (2) Whether we should beseech them to pray for us? (3) Whether the prayers they pour forth for us are always granted?

FIRST ARTICLE

Whether the Saints Have Knowledge of Our Prayers?

We proceed thus to the First Article:—

Objection 1. It would seem that the saints have no knowledge of our prayers. For a gloss on Isa. lxii. 16, *Thou art our father and Abraham hath not known us, and Israel hath been ignorant of us,* says that *the dead saints know not what the living, even their own children, are doing,* This is taken from Augustine *(De Cura pro Mort.* xiii), where he quotes the aforesaid authority, and the following are his words: *If such great men as the patriarchs knew not what was happening to the people begotten of them, how can the dead occupy themselves in watching and helping the affairs and actions of the living?* Therefore the saints cannot be cognizant of our prayers.

Obj. 2. Further, the following words are addressed to King Joas (4 Kings xxii. 20): *Therefore* (i.e. because thou hast wept before Me), *I will gather thee to thy fathers . . . that thy eyes may not see all the evils which I will bring upon this place.* But Joas would have gained no such advantage from his death if he were to know after death what was happening to his people. Therefore the saints after death know not our actions, and thus they are not cognizant of our prayers.

Obj. 3. Further, the more perfect a man is in charity, the more he succors his neighbor when the latter is in danger. Now the saints, in this life, watch over their neighbor, especially their kinsfolk, when these are in danger, and manifestly assist them. Since then, after death, their charity is much greater, if they

*Cf. P. I, Q. 106, A. 1.

were cognizant of our deeds, much more would they watch over their friends and kindred and assist them in their needs: and yet, seemingly, they do not. Therefore it would seem that our deeds and prayers are not known to them.

Obj. 4. Further, even as the saints after death see the Word, so do the angels of whom it is stated (Matth. xviii. 10) that *their angels in heaven always see the face of My Father.* Yet the angels through seeing the Word do not therefore know all things, since the lower angels are cleansed from their lack of knowledge by the higher angels,* as Dionysius declares *(Cœl. Hier.* vii). Therefore although the saints see the Word, they do not see therein our prayers and other things that happen in our regard.

Obj. 5. Further, God alone is the searcher of hearts. Now prayer is seated chiefly in the heart. Therefore it belongs to God alone to know our prayers. Therefore our prayers are unknown to the saints.

On the contrary, Gregory, commenting on Job xiv. 21, *Whether his children come to honor or dishonor, he shall not understand,* says *(Moral.* xii): *This does not apply to the souls of the saints, for since they have an insight of Almighty God's glory we must nowise believe that anything outside that glory is unknown to them.* Therefore they are cognizant of our prayers.

Further, Gregory says *(Dial.* ii): *All creatures are little to the soul that sees God: because however little it sees of the Creator's light, every created thing appears foreshortened to it.* Now apparently the chief obstacle to the souls of the saints being cognizant of our prayers and other happenings in our regard is that they are far removed from us. Since then distance does not prevent these things, as appears from the authority quoted, it would seem that the souls of the saints are cognizant of our prayers and of what happens here below.

Further, unless they were aware of what happens in our regard they would not pray for us, since they would be ignorant of our needs.

But this is the error of Vigilantius, as Jerome asserts in his letter against him. Therefore the saints are cognizant of what happens in our regard.

I answer that, The Divine essence is a sufficient medium for knowing all things, and this is evident from the fact that God, by seeing His essence, sees all things. But it does not follow that whoever sees God's essence knows all things, but only those who comprehend the essence of God:* even as the knowledge of a principle does not involve the knowledge of all that follows from that principle unless the whole virtue of the principle be comprehended. Wherefore, since the souls of the saints do not comprehend the Divine essence, it does not follow that they know all that can be known by the Divine essence,—for which reason the lower angels are taught concerning certain matters by the higher angels, though they all see the essence of God; but each of the blessed must needs see in the Divine essence as many other things as the perfection of his happiness requires. For the perfection of a man's happiness requires him to have whatever he will, and to will nothing amiss: and each one wills with a right will, to know what concerns himself. Hence since no rectitude is lacking to the saints, they wish to know what concerns themselves, and consequently it follows that they know it in the Word. Now it pertains to their glory that they assist the needy for their salvation: for thus they become God's co-operators, *than which nothing is more Godlike,* as Dionysius declares (*Cœl. Hier.* iii). Wherefore it is evident that the saints are cognizant of such things as are required for this purpose; and so it is manifest that they know in the Word the vows, devotions, and prayers of those who have recourse to their assistance.

Reply Obj. 1. The saying of Augustine is to be understood as referring to the natural knowledge of separated souls, which knowledge is devoid of obscurity in holy men. But he is not speaking of their knowledge in the Word, for it is clear that when Isaias said this, Abraham had no such knowledge, since no one had come to the vision of God before Christ's passion.

Reply Obj. 2. Although the saints, after this life, know what happens here below, we must not believe that they grieve through knowing the woes of those whom they loved in this world: for they are so filled with heavenly joy, that sorrow finds no place in them. Wherefore if after death they know the woes of their friends, their grief is forestalled by their removal from this world before their woes occur. Perhaps, however, the non-glorified souls would grieve somewhat, if they were aware of the

* Cf. P. I, Q. 12, AA. 7, 8.

distress of their dear ones: and since the soul of Josias was not glorified as soon as it went out from his body, it is in this respect that Augustine uses this argument to show that the souls of the dead have no knowledge of the deeds of the living.

Reply Obj. 3. The souls of the saints have their will fully conformed to the Divine will even as regards the things willed; and consequently, although they retain the love of charity towards their neighbor, they do not succor him otherwise than they see to be in conformity with the disposition of Divine justice. Nevertheless, it is to be believed that they help their neighbor very much by interceding for him to God.

Reply Obj. 4. Although it does not follow that those who see the Word see all things in the Word, they see those things that pertain to the perfection of their happiness, as stated above.

Reply Obj. 5. God alone of Himself knows the thoughts of the heart: yet others know them, in so far as these are revealed to them, either by their vision of the Word or by any other means.

SECOND ARTICLE

Whether We Ought to Call Upon the Saints to Pray for Us?

We proceed thus to the Second Article:—

Objection 1. It would seem that we ought not to call upon the saints to pray for us. For no man asks anyone's friends to pray for him, except in so far as he believes he will more easily find favor with them. But God is infinitely more merciful than any saint, and consequently His will is more easily inclined to give us a gracious hearing, than the will of a saint. Therefore it would seem unnecessary to make the saints mediators between us and God, that they may intercede for us.

Obj. 2. Further, if we ought to beseech them to pray for us, this is only because we know their prayer to be acceptable to God. Now among the saints the holier a man is, the more is his prayer acceptable to God. Therefore we ought always to bespeak the greater saints to intercede for us with God, and never the lesser ones.

Obj. 3. Further, Christ, even as man, is called the *Holy of Holies,* and, as man, it is competent to Him to pray. Yet we never call upon Christ to pray for us. Therefore neither should we ask the other saints to do so.

Obj. 4. Further, whenever one person intercedes for another at the latter's request, he presents his petition to the one with whom he intercedes for him. Now it is unnecessary to present anything to one to whom all things are present. Therefore it is unnecessary to make the saints our intercessors with God.

Obj. 5. Further, it is unnecessary to do a thing if, without doing it, the purpose for which it is done would be achieved in the same way, or else not achieved at all. Now the saints would pray for us just the same, or would not pray for us at all, whether we pray to them or not: for if we be worthy of their prayers, they would pray for us even though we prayed not to them, while if we be unworthy they pray not for us even though we ask them to. Therefore it seems altogether unnecessary to call on them to pray for us.

On the contrary, It is written (Job. v. 1): *Call . . . if there be any that will answer thee, and turn to some of the saints.* Now, as Gregory says *(Moral.* v. 30) on this passage, *we call upon God when we beseech Him in humble prayer.* Therefore when we wish to pray God, we should turn to the saints, that they may pray God for us.

Further, the saints who are in heaven are more acceptable to God than those who are on the way. Now we should make the saints, who are on the way, our intercessors with God, after the example of the Apostle, who said (Rom. xv. 30): *I beseech you . . . brethren, through our Lord Jesus Christ, and by the charity of the Holy Ghost, that you help me in your prayers for me to God.* Much more, therefore, should we ask the saints who are in heaven to help us by their prayers to God.

Further, an additional argument is provided by the common custom of the Church which asks for the prayers of the saints in the Litany.

I answer that, According to Dionysius *(Eccl. Hier.* v) the order established by God among things is that *the last should be led to God by those that are midway between.* Wherefore, since the saints who are in heaven are nearest to God, the order of the Divine law requires that we, who while we remain in the body are pilgrims from the Lord, should be brought back to God by the saints who are between us and Him: and this happens when the Divine goodness pours forth its effect into us through them. And since our return to God should correspond to the outflow of His boons upon us, just as the Divine favors reach us by means of the saints intercession, so should we, by their means, be brought back to God, that we may receive His favors again. Hence it is that we make them our intercessors with God, and our mediators as it were, when we ask them to pray for us.

Reply Obj. 1. It is not on account of any defect in God's power that He works by means of second causes, but it is for the perfection of the order of the universe, and the more manifold outpouring of His goodness on things,

through His bestowing on them not only the goodness which is proper to them, but also the faculty of causing goodness in others. Even so it is not through any defect in His mercy, that we need to bespeak His clemency through the prayers of the saints, but to the end that the aforesaid order in things be observed.

Reply Obj. 2. Although the greater saints are more acceptable to God than the lesser, it is sometimes profitable to pray to the lesser; and this for five reasons. First, because sometimes one has greater devotion for a lesser saint than for a greater, and the effect of prayer depends very much on one's devotion. Secondly, in order to avoid tediousness, for continual attention to one thing makes a person weary; whereas by praying to different saints, the fervor of our devotion is aroused anew as it were. Thirdly, because it is granted to some saints to exercise their patronage in certain special cases, for instance to Saint Anthony against the fire of hell. Fourthly, that due honor be given by us to all. Fifthly, because the prayers of several sometimes obtain that which would not have been obtained by the prayers of one.

Reply Obj. 3. Prayer is an act, and acts belong to particular persons *(supposita).* Hence, were we to say: *Christ, pray for us,* except we added something, this would seem to refer to Christ's person, and consequently to agree with the error either of Nestorius, who distinguished in Christ the person of the son of man from the person of the Son of God, or of Arius, who asserted that the person of the Son is less than the Father. Wherefore to avoid these errors the Church says not: *Christ, pray for us,* but *Christ, hear us,* or *have mercy on us.*

Reply Obj. 4. As we shall state further on (A. 3) the saints are said to present our prayers to God, not as though they notified things unknown to Him, but because they ask God to grant those prayers a gracious hearing, or because they seek the Divine truth about them, namely what ought to be done according to His providence.

Reply Obj. 5. A person is rendered worthy of a saint's prayers for him by the very fact that in his need he has recourse to him with pure devotion. Hence it is not unnecessary to pray to the saints.

THIRD ARTICLE

Whether the Prayers Which the Saints Pour Forth to God for Us Are Always Granted?

We proceed thus to the Third Article:—

Objection 1. It would seem that the prayers which the saints pour forth to God for us are not always granted. For if they were always granted, the saints would be heard especially in regard to matters concerning themselves. But they are not heard in reference to these things; wherefore it is stated in the Apocalypse (vi. 11) that on the martyrs beseeching vengeance on them that dwell on earth, *it was said to them that they should rest for a little while till the number of their brethren should be filled up.** Much less therefore, are they heard in reference to matters concerning others.

Obj. 2. Further, it is written (Jer. xv. 1): *If Moses and Samuel shall stand before Me, My soul is not towards this people.* Therefore, the saints are not always heard when they pray God for us.

Obj. 3. Further, the saints in heaven are stated to be equal to the angels of God (Matth. xxii. 30). But the angels are not always heard in the prayers which they offer up to God. This is evident from Dan. x. 12, 13, where it is written: *I am come for thy words: but the prince of the kingdom of the Persians resisted me one-and-twenty days.* But the angel who spoke had not come to Daniel's aid except by asking of God to be set free; and yet the fulfillment of his prayer was hindered. Therefore neither are other saints always heard by God when they pray for us.

Obj. 4. Further, whosoever obtains something by prayer merits it in a sense. But the saints in heaven are not in the state of meriting. Therefore they cannot obtain anything for us from God by their prayers.

Obj. 5. Further, the saints, in all things, conform their will to the will of God. Therefore they will nothing but what they know God to will. But no one prays save for what he wills. Therefore they pray not save for what they know God to will. Now that which God wills would be done even without their praying for it. Therefore their prayers are not efficacious for obtaining anything.

Obj. 6. Further, the prayers of the whole heavenly court, if they could obtain anything, would be more efficacious than all the petitions of the Church here below. Now if the suffrages of the Church here below for some one in purgatory were to be multiplied, he would be wholly delivered from punishment. Since then the saints in heaven pray for those who are in purgatory on the same account as for us, if they obtain anything for us, their prayers would deliver entirely from punishment those who are in purgatory. But this is not true because, then the Church's suffrages for the dead would be unnecessary.

On the contrary, It is written (2 Machab. xv. 14): *This is he that prayeth much for the people, and for all the holy city, Jeremias*

the prophet of God: and that his prayer was granted is clear from what follows *(verse 15): Jeremias stretched forth his right hand, and gave to Judas a sword of gold, saying: Take this holy sword, a gift from God,* etc.

Further, Jerome says *(Ep. contra Vigilant.): Thou sayest in thy pamphlets, that while we live, we can pray for one another, but that when we are dead no one's prayer for another will be heard:* and afterwards he refutes this in the following words: *If the apostles and martyrs while yet in the body can pray for others, while they are still solicitous for themselves, how much more can they do so when the crown, the victory, the triumph is already theirs!*

Further, this is confirmed by the custom of the Church, which often asks to be assisted by the prayers of the saints.

I answer that, The saints are said to pray for us in two ways. First, by *express* prayer, when by their prayers they seek a hearing of the Divine clemency on our behalf: secondly, by *interpretive* prayer, namely by their merits which, being known to God, avail not only them unto glory, but also us as suffrages and prayers, even as the shedding of Christ's blood is said to ask pardon for us. In both ways the saints' prayers considered in themselves avail to obtain what they ask, yet on our part they may fail so that we obtain not the fruit of their prayers, in so far as they are said to pray for us by reason of their merits availing on our behalf. But in so far as they pray for us by asking something for us in their prayers, their prayers are always granted, since they will only what God wills, nor do they ask save for what they will to be done; and what God wills is always fulfilled,—unless we speak of His *antecedent* will, whereby *He wishes all men to be saved.†* For this will is not always fulfilled; wherefore no wonder if that also which the saints will according to this kind of will be not fulfilled sometimes.

Reply Obj. 1. This prayer of the martyrs is merely their desire to obtain the robe of the body and the fellowship of those who will be saved, and their consent to God's justice in punishing the wicked. Hence a gloss on Apoc. vi. 11, *How long, O Lord,* says: *They desire an increase of joy and the fellowship of the saints, and they consent to God's justice.*

Reply Obj. 2. The Lord speaks there of Moses and Samuel according to their state in this life. For we read that they withstood God's anger by praying for the people. And yet even if they had been living at the time in question, they would have been unable to placate God towards the people by their prayers, on account of the wickedness of this same people: and it is thus that we are to understand this passage.

Reply Obj. 3. This dispute among the good angels does not mean that they offered contradictory prayers to God, but that they submitted contrary merits on various sides to the Divine inquiry, with a view of God's pronouncing sentence thereon. This, in fact, is what Gregory says *(Moral.* xvii) in explanation of the aforesaid words of Daniel: *The lofty spirits that are set over the nations never fight in behalf of those that act unjustly, but they justly judge and try their deeds. And when the guilt or innocence of any particular nation is brought into the debate of the court above, the ruling spirit of that nation is said to have won or lost in the conflict. Yet the supreme will of their Maker is victorious over all, for since they have it ever before their eyes, they will not what they are unable to obtain,* wherefore neither do they seek for it. And consequently it is clear that their prayers are always heard.

Reply Obj. 4. Although the saints are not in a state to merit for themselves, when once they are in heaven, they are in a state to merit for others, or rather to assist others by reason of their previous merit: for while living they merited that their prayers should be heard after their death.

Or we may reply that prayer is meritorious on one count, and impetratory on another. For merit consists in a certain equation of the act to the end for which it is intended, and which is given to it as its reward; while the impetration of a prayer depends on the liberality of the person supplicated. Hence prayer sometimes, through the liberality of the person supplicated, obtains that which was not merited either by the suppliant, or by the person supplicated for: and so, although the saints are not in the state of meriting, it does not follow that they are not in the state of impetrating.

Reply Obj. 5. As appears from the authority of Gregory quoted above *(ad* 3), the saints and angels will nothing but what they see to be in the Divine will :and so neither do they pray for aught else. Nor is their prayer fruitless, since as Augustine says *(De Præd Sanct.**): The prayers of the saints profit the predestinate, because it is perhaps pre-ordained that they shall be saved through the prayers of those who intercede for them: and consequently God also wills that what the saints see Him to will shall be fulfilled through their prayers.

Reply Obj. 6. The suffrages of the Church for the dead are as so many satisfactions of the living in lieu of the dead: and accordingly they free the dead from the punishment which the latter have not paid. But the saints in heaven are not in the state of making satisfaction; and consequently the parallel fails between their prayers and the suffrages of the Church.

QUESTION 73

Of the Signs That Will Precede the Judgment

(In Three Articles)

WE must next consider the signs that will precede the judgment: and under this head there are three points of inquiry: (1) Whether any signs will precede the Lord's coming to judgment? (2) Whether in very truth the sun and moon will be darkened? (3) Whether the powers of the heavens will be moved when the Lord shall come?

FIRST ARTICLE

Whether Any Signs Will Precede the Lord's Coming to Judgment?

We proceed thus to the First Article:—

Objection 1. It would seem that the Lord's coming to judgment will not be preceded by any signs. Because it is written (1 Thess. v. 3): *When they shall say: Peace and security; then shall sudden destruction come upon them.* Now there would be no peace and security if men were terrified by previous signs. Therefore signs will not precede that coming.

Obj. 2. Further, signs are ordained for the manifestation of something. But His coming is to be hidden; wherefore it is written (1 Thess. v. 2): *The day of the Lord shall come as a thief in the night.* Therefore signs ought not to precede it.

Obj. 3. Further, the time of His first coming was foreknown by the prophets, which does not apply to His second coming. Now no such signs preceded the first coming of Christ. Therefore neither will they precede the second.

On the contrary, It is written (Luke xxi. 25): *There shall be signs in the sun, and in the moon, and in the stars,* etc.

Further, Jerome† mentions fifteen signs preceding the judgment. He says that on the

---

* *De Dono Persever.* xxii.
† S. Peter Damian, *Opuscul.* xlix. 4. *He quotes S. Jerome,* but the reference is not known.

first day all the seas will rise fifteen cubits above the mountains; in the *second* day all the waters will be plunged into the depths, so that scarcely will they be visible; on the *third* day they will be restored to their previous condition; on the *fourth* day all the great fishes and other things that move in the waters will gather together and, raising their heads above the sea, roar at one another contentiously; on the *fifth* day, all the birds of the air will gather together in the fields, wailing to one another, with neither bite nor sup; on the *sixth* day rivers of fire will arise towards the firmament rushing together from the west to the east; on the *seventh* day all the stars, both planets and fixed stars, will throw out fiery tails like comets; on the *eighth* day there will be a great earthquake, and all animals will be laid low; on the *ninth* day all the plants will be bedewed as it were with blood; on the *tenth* day all stones, little and great, will be divided into four parts dashing against one another; on the *eleventh* day all hills and mountains and buildings will be reduced to dust; on the *twelfth* day all animals will come from forest and mountain to the fields, roaring and tasting of nothing; on the *thirteenth* day all graves from east to west will open to allow the bodies to rise again; on the *fourteenth* day all men will leave their abode, neither understanding nor speaking, but rushing hither and thither like madmen; on the *fifteenth* day all will die and will rise again with those who died long before.

I answer that, When Christ shall come to judge He will appear in the form of glory, on account of the authority becoming a judge. Now it pertains to the dignity of judicial power to have certain signs that induce people to reverence and subjection: and consequently many signs will precede the advent of Christ when He shall come to judgment, in order that the hearts of men be brought to subjection to the coming judge, and be prepared for the judgment, being forewarned by those signs. But it is not easy to know what these signs may be: for the signs of which we read in the gospels, as Augustine says, writing to Hesychius about the end of the world (*Ep.* lxxx), refer not only to Christ's coming to judgment, but also to the time of the sack of Jerusalem, and to the coming of Christ in ceaselessly visiting His Church. So that, perhaps, if we consider them carefully, we shall find that none of them refers to the coming advent, as he remarks: because these signs that are mentioned in the gospels, such as wars, fears, and so forth, have been from the beginning of the human race: unless perhaps we say that at that time they will be more prevalent: although it is uncertain in what degree this increase will foretell the imminence of the ad-

vent. The signs mentioned by Jerome are not asserted by him; he merely says that he found them written in the annals of the Hebrews: and, indeed, they contain very little likelihood.

Reply Obj. 1. According to Augustine (*Ad Hesych., loc. cit.*) towards the end of the world there will be a general persecution of the good by the wicked: so that at the same time some will fear, namely the good, and some will be secure, namely the wicked. The words: *When they shall say: Peace and security,* refer to the wicked, who will pay little heed to the signs of the coming judgment: while the words of Luke xxi. 26, *men withering away,* etc., should be referred to the good.

We may also reply that all these signs that will happen about the time of the judgment are reckoned to occur within the time occupied by the judgment, so that the judgment day contains them all. Wherefore although men be terrified by the signs appearing about the judgment day, yet before those signs begin to appear the wicked will think themselves to be in peace and security, after the death of Antichrist and before the coming of Christ, seeing that the world is not at once destroyed, as they thought hitherto.

Reply Obj. 2. The day of the Lord is said to come as a thief, because the exact time is not known, since it will not be possible to know it from those signs: although, as we have already said, all these most manifest sings which will precede the judgment immediately may be comprised under the judgment day.

Reply Obj. 3. At His first advent Christ came secretly, although the appointed time was known beforehand by the prophets. Hence there was no need for such signs to appear at His first coming, as will appear at His second advent, when He will come openly, although the appointed time is hidden.

SECOND ARTICLE

Whether towards the Time of the Judgment the Sun and Moon Will Be Darkened in Very Truth?

We proceed thus to the Second Article:—

Objection 1. It would seem that towards the time of the judgment the sun and moon will be darkened in very truth. For, as Rabanus says, commenting on Matth. xxiv. 29, *nothing hinders us from gathering that the sun, moon, and stars will then be deprived of their light, as we know happened to the sun at the time of our Lord's passion.*

Obj. 2. Further, the light of the heavenly bodies is directed to the generation of inferior bodies, because by its means and not only by their movement they act upon this lower world, as Averroës says (*De Subst. Orbis.*). But generation will cease then. Therefore neither will light remain in the heavenly bodies.

Obj. 3. Further, according to some the inferior bodies will be cleansed of the qualities by which they act. Now heavenly bodies act not only by movement, but also by light, as stated above *(Obj.* 2). Therefore as the movement of heaven will cease, so will the light of the heavenly bodies.

On the contrary, According to astronomers the sun and moon cannot be eclipsed at the same time. But this darkening of the sun and moon is stated to be simultaneous, when the Lord shall come to judgment. Therefore the darkening will not be in very truth due to a natural eclipse.

Further, it is not seemly for the same to be the cause of a thing's failing and increasing. Now when our Lord shall come the light of the luminaries will increase according to Isa. xxx. 26, *The light of the moon shall be as the light of the sun, and the light of the sun shall be sevenfold.* Therefore it is unfitting for the light of these bodies to cease when our Lord comes.

I answer that, If we speak of the sun and moon in respect of the very moment of Christ's coming, it is not credible that they will be darkened through being bereft of their light, since when Christ comes and the saints rise again the whole world will be renewed, as we shall state further on (Q. 74). If, however, we speak of them in respect of the time immediately preceding the judgment, it is possible that by the Divine power the sun, moon, and other luminaries of the heavens will be darkened, either at various times or all together, in order to inspire men with fear.

Reply Obj. 1. Rabanus is speaking of the time preceding the judgment: wherefore he adds that when the judgment day is over the words of Isaias shall be fulfilled.

Reply Obj. 2. Light is in the heavenly bodies not only for the purpose of causing generation in these lower bodies, but also for their own perfection and beauty. Hence it does not follow that where generation ceases, the light of the heavenly bodies will cease, but rather that it will increase.

Reply Obj. 3. It does not seem probable that the elemental qualities will be removed from the elements, although some have asserted this. If, however, they be removed, there would still be no parallel between them and light, since the elemental qualities are in opposition to one another, so that their action is corruptive: whereas light is a principle of action not by way of opposition, but by way of a principle regulating things in opposition to one another and bringing them back to

* Cf. P. I, Q. 108, A. 5, *ad* 1.

harmony. Nor is there a parallel with the movement of heavenly bodies, for movement is the act of that which is imperfect, wherefore it must needs cease when the imperfection ceases: whereas this cannot be said of light.

THIRD ARTICLE

Whether the Virtues of Heaven Will Be Moved When Our Lord Shall Come?

We proceed thus to the Third Article:—

Objection 1. It would seem that the virtues of heaven will not be moved when our Lord shall come. For the virtues of heaven can denote only the blessed angels. Now immobility is essential to blessedness. Therefore it will be impossible for them to be moved.

Obj. 2. Further, ignorance is the cause of wonder *(Met.* i. 2). Now ignorance, like fear, is far from the angels, for as Gregory says *(Dial.* iv. 33; *Moral.* ii. 3), *what do they not see, who see Him Who sees all.* Therefore it will be impossible for them to be moved with wonder, as stated in the text (iv. *Sent.* D. 48).

Obj. 3. Further, all the angels will be present at the Divine judgment; wherefore it is stated (Apoc. vii. 11): *All the angels stood round about the throne.* Now the virtues denote one particular order of angels. Therefore it should not be said of them rather than of others, that they are moved.

On the contrary, It is written (Job xxvi. 11): *The pillars of heaven tremble, and dread at His beck.* Now the pillars of heaven can denote only the virtues of heaven. Therefore the virtues of heaven will be moved.

Further, it is written (Matth. xxiv. 29): *The stars shall fall from heaven, and the virtues* (Douay,—*powers*) *of heaven shall be moved.*

I answer that, Virtue is twofold as applied to the angels,* as Dionysius states *(Cœl. Hier.* xi). For sometimes the name of *virtues* is appropriated to one order, which according to him, is the middle order of the middle hierarchy, but according to Gregory *(Hom. in Ev.* xxxiv) is the highest order of the lowest hierarchy. In another sense it is employed to denote all the angels: and then they are said to the question at issue it may be taken either way. For in the text *(loc. cit.)* it is explained according to the second acceptation, so as to denote all the angels: and then they are said to be moved through wonder at the renewing of the world, as stated in the text. It can also be explained in reference to virtue as the name of a particular order; and then that order is said to be moved more than the others by reason of the effect, since according to Gregory *(loc. cit.)* we ascribe to that order the working of miracles which especially will be worked about that time: or again, because that order

—since, according to Dionysius *(loc. cit.)*, it belongs to the middle hierarchy—is not limited in its power, wherefore its ministry must needs regard universal causes. Consequently the proper office of the virtues is seemingly to move the heavenly bodies which are the cause of what happens in nature here below. And again the very name denotes this, since they are called the *virtues of heaven.* Accordingly they will be moved then, because they will no more produce their effect, by ceasing to move the heavenly bodies: even as the angels who are appointed to watch over men will no longer fulfill the office of guardians.

Reply Obj. 1. This movement changes nothing pertaining to their state; but refers either to their effects which may vary without any change on their part, or to some new con-

sideration of things which hitherto they were unable to see by means of their concreated species, which change of thought is not taken from them by their state of blessedness. Hence Augustine says *(Gen. ad lit.* viii. 20) that *God moves the spiritual creature through time.*

Reply Obj. 2. Wonder is wont to be about things surpassing our knowledge or ability: and accordingly the virtues of heaven will wonder at the Divine power doing such things, in so far as they fail to do or comprehend them. In this sense the blessed Agnes said that the *sun and moon wonder at His beauty:* and this does not imply ignorance in the angels, but removes the comprehension of God from them.

The *Reply* to the *Third Objection* is clear from what has been said.

QUESTION 74

Of the Fire of the Final Conflagration

(In Nine Articles)

We must now consider the fire of the final conflagration: and under this head there are nine points of inquiry: (1) Whether any cleansing of the world is to take place? (2) Whether it will be effected by fire? (3) Whether that fire is of the same species as elemental fire? (4) Whether that fire will cleanse also the higher heavens? (5) Whether that fire will consume the other elements? (6) Whether it will cleanse all the elements? (7) Whether that fire precedes or follows the judgment? (8) Whether men are to be consumed by that fire? (9) Whether the wicked will be involved therein?

FIRST ARTICLE

Whether the World Is to Be Cleansed?

We proceed thus to the First Article:—

Objection 1. It would seem that there is not to be any cleansing of the world. For only that which is unclean needs cleansing. Now God's creatures are not unclean, wherefore it is written (Acts x. 15): *That which God hath cleansed, do not thou call common,* i.e. unclean. Therefore the creatures of the world shall not be cleansed.

Obj. 2. Further, according to Divine justice cleansing is directed to the removal of the uncleanness of sin, as instanced in the cleansing after death. But there can be no stain of sin in the elements of this world. Therefore, seemingly, they need not to be cleansed.

Obj. 3. Further, a thing is said to be cleansed when any foreign matter that depreciates it is removed therefrom: for the removal of that

* S. Augustine, *De Civ. Dei,* xx. 16.

which ennobles a thing is not called a cleansing, but rather a diminishing. Now it pertains to the perfection and nobility of the elements that something of a foreign nature is mingled with them, since the form of a mixed body is more noble than the form of a simple body. Therefore it would seem nowise fitting that the elements of this world can possibly be cleansed.

On the contrary, All renewal is effected by some kind of cleansing. But the elements will be renewed; hence it is written (Apoc. xxi. 1): *I saw a new heaven and a new earth: for the first heaven and the first earth was gone.* Therefore the elements shall be cleansed.

Further, a gloss* on 1 Cor. vii. 31, *The fashion of this earth passeth away,* says: *The beauty of this world will perish in the burning of worldly flames.* Therefore the same conclusion follows.

I answer that, Since the world was, in a way, made for man's sake, it follows that, when man shall be glorified in the body, the other bodies of the world shall also be changed to a better state, so that it is rendered a more fitting place for him and more pleasant to look upon. Now in order that man obtain the glory of the body, it behooves first of all those things to be removed which are opposed to glory. There are two, namely the corruption and stain of sin,— because according to 1 Cor. xv. 50, *neither shall corruption possess incorruption,* and all the unclean shall be without the city of glory (Apoc. xxii. 15),—and again, the elements require to be cleansed from the contrary dispositions, ere they be brought to the newness of glory, proportionately to what we have said with regard to man. Now although, properly speaking, a corporeal thing cannot be the subject of the stain of sin, nevertheless, on account of sin corporeal things contract a certain unfittingness for being appointed to spiritual purposes; and for this reason we find that places where crimes have been committed are reckoned unfit for the performance of sacred actions therein, unless they be cleansed beforehand. Accordingly that part of the world which is given to our use contracts from men's sins a certain unfitness for being glorified, wherefore in this respect it needs to be cleansed. In like manner with regard to the intervening space, on account of the contact of the elements, there are many corruptions, generations and alterations of the elements, which diminish their purity: wherefore the elements need to be cleansed from these also, so that they be fit to receive the newness of glory.

Reply Obj. 1. When it is asserted that every creature of God is clean we are to understand this as meaning that its substance contains no alloy of evil, as the Manichees maintained, saying that evil and good are two substances in some places severed from one another, in others mingled together. But it does not exclude a creature from having an admixture of a foreign nature, which in itself is also good, but is inconsistent with the perfection of that creature. Nor does this prevent evil from being accidental to a creature, although not mingled with it as part of its substance.

Reply Obj. 2. Although corporeal elements cannot be the subject of sin, nevertheless, from the sin that is committed in them they contract a certain unfitness for receiving the perfection of glory.

Reply Obj. 3. The form of a mixed body and the form of an element may be considered in two ways: either as regards the perfection of the species, and thus a mixed body is more perfect,—or as regards their continual endurance; and thus the simple body is more noble, because it has not in itself the cause of corruption, unless it be corrupted by something extrinsic: whereas a mixed body has in itself the cause of its corruption, namely the composition of contraries. Wherefore a simple body, although it be corruptible in part is incorruptible as a whole, which cannot be said of a mixed body. And since incorruption belongs to the perfection of glory, it follows that the perfection of a simple is more in keeping with the perfection of glory, than the perfection of a mixed body, unless the mixed body has also in itself some principle of incorruption, as the human body has, the form of which is incorruptible. Nevertheless, although a mixed body is somewhat more noble than a simple body, a simple body that exists by itself has a more noble being than if it exist in a mixed body, because in a mixed body simple bodies are somewhat in potentiality, whereas, existing by themselves, they are in their ultimate perfection.

SECOND ARTICLE

Whether the Cleansing of the World Will Be Effected by Fire?

We proceed thus to the Second Article:—

Objection 1. It would seem that this cleansing will not be effected by fire. For since fire is a part of the world, it needs to be cleansed like the other parts. Now, the same thing should not be both cleanser and cleansed. Therefore it would seem that the cleansing will not be by fire.

Obj. 2. Further, just as fire has a cleansing virtue so has water. Since then all things are not capable of being cleansed by fire, and some need to be cleansed by water,—which distinction is moreover observed by the old law,—it would seem that fire will not at any rate cleanse all things.

Obj. 3. Further, this cleansing would seem to consist in purifying the parts of the world by separating them from one another. Now the separation of the parts of the world from one another at the world's beginning was effected by God's power alone, for the work of distinction was carried out by that power: wherefore Anaxagoras asserted that the separation was effected by the act of the intellect which moves all things (cf. Arist. *Phys.* viii. 9). Therefore it would seem that at the end of the world the cleansing will be done immediately by God and not by fire.

On the contrary, It is written (Ps. xlix. 3): *A fire shall burn before Him, and a mighty tempest shall be around Him;* and afterwards in reference to the judgment *(verse* 4): *He shall call heaven from above, and the earth to judge His people.* Therefore it would seem that the final cleansing of the world will be by means of fire.

Further, it is written (2 Pet. iii. 12): *The heavens being on fire will be dissolved, and the elements shall melt with the burning heat.* Therefore this cleansing will be effected by fire.

I answer that, As stated above (A. 1) this cleansing of the world will remove from it the stain contracted from sin, and the impurity resulting from mixture, and will be a disposition to the perfection of glory; and consequently in this threefold respect it will be most fitting for it to be effected by fire. First, because since fire is the most noble of the elements, its natural properties are more like the properties of glory, and this is especially clear in regard to light. Secondly, because fire, on account of the efficacy of its active virtue, is not as susceptible as the other elements to the admixture of a foreign matter. Thirdly, because the sphere of fire is far removed from our abode; nor are we so familiar with the use of fire as with that of earth, water, and air, so that it is not so liable to depreciation. Moreover, it is most efficacious in cleansing and in separating by a process of rarefaction.

Reply Obj. 1. Fire is not employed by us in its proper matter (since thus it is far removed from us), but only in a foreign matter: and in this respect it will be possible for the world to be cleansed by fire as existing in its pure state. But in so far as it has an admixture of some foreign matter it will be possible for it to be cleansed; and thus it will be cleanser and cleansed under different aspects; and this is not unreasonable.

Reply Obj. 2. The first cleansing of the world by the deluge regarded only the stain of sin. Now the sin which was most prevalent then was the sin of concupiscence, and consequently it was fitting that the cleansing should be by means of its contrary, namely water. But the second cleansing regards both the stain of sin and the impurity of mixture, and in respect of both it is more fitting for it to be effected by fire than by water. For the power of water tends to unite rather than to separate; wherefore the natural impurity of the elements could not be removed by water as by fire. Moreover, at the end of the world the prevalent sin will be that of tepidity, as though the world were already growing old, because then, according to Matth. xxiv. 12, *the charity of many shall grow cold,* and consequently the cleansing will then be fittingly effected by fire. Nor is there any thing that cannot in some way be cleansed by fire: some things, however, cannot be cleansed by fire without being destroyed themselves, such as cloths and wooden vessels, and these the Law ordered to be cleansed with water; yet all these things will be finally destroyed by fire.

Reply Obj. 3. By the work of distinction things received different forms whereby they are distinct from one another: and consequently this could only be done by Him Who is the author of nature. But by the final cleansing things will be restored to the purity wherein they were created, wherefore created nature will be able to minister to its Creator to this effect; and for this reason is a creature employed as a minister, that it is ennobled thereby.

THIRD ARTICLE

Whether the Fire Whereby the World Will Be Cleansed Will Be of the Same Species with Elemental Fire?

We proceed thus to the Third Article:—
Objection 1. It would seem that the fire in

question is not of the same species as elemental fire. For nothing consumes itself. But that fire will consume the four elements according to a gloss on 2 Pet. iii. 12. Therefore that fire will not be of the same species as elemental fire.

Obj. 2. Further, as power is made known by operation, so is nature made known by power. Now that fire will have a different power from the fire which is an element: because it will cleanse the universe, whereas this fire cannot do that. Therefore it will not be of the same species as this.

Obj. 3. Further, in natural bodies those that are of the same species have the same movement. But that fire will have a different movement from the fire that is an element, because it will move in all directions so as to cleanse the whole. Therefore it is not of the same species.

On the contrary, Augustine says (*De Civ. Dei,* xx. 16), and his words are contained in a gloss on 1 Cor. vii. 31, that *the fashion of this world will perish in the burning of worldly flames.* Therefore that fire will be of the same nature as the fire which is now in the world.

Further, just as the future cleansing is to be by fire, so was the past cleansing by water: and they are both compared to one another, 2 Pet. iii. 5. Now in the first cleansing the water was of the same species with elemental water. Therefore in like manner the fire of the second cleansing will be of the same species with elemental fire.

I answer that, We meet with three opinions on this question. For some say that the element of fire which is in its own sphere will come down to cleanse the world: and they explain this descent by way of multiplication, because the fire will spread through finding combustible matter on all sides. And this will result all the more then, since the virtue of the fire will be raised over all the elements. Against this, however, would seem to be not only the fact that this fire will come down, but also the statement of the saints that it will rise up; thus (2 Pet. iii. 10) it is declared that the fire of the judgment will rise as high as the waters of the deluge; whence it would seem to follow that this fire is situated towards the middle of the place of generation. Hence others say that this fire will be generated towards the intervening space through the focusing together of the rays of the heavenly bodies, just as we see them focused together in a burning-glass; for at that time in lieu of glasses there will be concave clouds, on which the rays will strike. But this again does not seem probable: for since the effects of heavenly bodies depend on certain fixed positions and aspects, if this fire resulted from the virtue of the heavenly bodies, the time of this cleansing would be known to those who observe the movements of the stars, and this is contrary to the authority of Scripture. Consequently others, following Augustine, say that *just as the deluge resulted from an outpouring of the waters of the world, so the fashion of this world will perish by a burning of worldly flames (De Civ. Dei,* xx. 16). This burning is nothing else but the assembly of all those lower and higher causes that by their nature have a kindling virtue: and this assembly will take place not in the ordinary course of things, but by the Divine power: and from all these causes thus assembled the fire that will burn the surface of this world will result. If we consider aright these opinions, we shall find that they differ as to the cause producing this fire and not as to its species. For fire, whether produced by the sun or by some lower heating cause, is of the same species as fire in its own sphere, except in so far as the former has some admixture of foreign matter. And this will of necessity be the case then, since fire cannot cleanse a thing, unless this become its matter in some way. Hence we must grant that the fire in question is simply of the same species as ours.

Reply Obj. 1. The fire in question, although of the same species as ours, is not identically the same. Now we see that of two fires of the same species one destroys the other, namely the greater destroys the lesser, by consuming its matter. In like manner that fire will be able to destroy our fire.

Reply Obj. 2. Just as an operation that proceeds from the virtue of a thing is an indication of that virtue, so is its virtue an indication of its essence or nature, if it proceed from the essential principles of the thing. But an operation that does not proceed from the virtue of the operator does not indicate its virtue. This appears in instruments: for the action of an instrument shows forth the virtue of the mover rather than that of the instrument, since it shows forth the virtue of the agent in so far as the latter is the first principle of the action, whereas it does not show forth the virtue of the instrument, except in so far as it is susceptive of the influence of the principal agent as moving that instrument. In like manner a virtue that does not proceed from the essential principles of a thing does not indicate the nature of that thing except in the point of susceptibility. Thus the virtue whereby hot water can heat is no indication of the nature of water except in the point of its being receptive of heat. Consequently nothing prevents water that has this virtue from being of the same species as water that has it not. In like manner it is not unreasonable that this fire, which will

have the power to cleanse the surface of the world, will be of the same species as the fire to which we are used, since the heating power therein arises, not from its essential principles but from the divine power or operation: whether we say that this power is an absolute quality, such as heat in hot water, or a kind of intention as we have ascribed to instrumental virtue (iv. *Sent.* D. 1, qu. 1, A. 4).* The latter is more probable since that fire will not act save as the instrument of the Divine power.

Reply Obj. 3. Of its own nature fire tends only upwards; but in so far as it pursues its matter, which it requires when it is outside its own sphere, it follows the site of combustible matter. Accordingly it is not unreasonable for it to take a circular or a downward course, especially in so far as it acts as the instrument of the Divine power.

FOURTH ARTICLE

Whether That Fire Will Cleanse Also the Higher Heavens?

We proceed thus to the Fourth Article:—

Objection 1. It would seem that that fire will cleanse also the higher heavens. For it is written (Ps. ci. 26, 27): *The heavens are the works of Thy hands: they shall perish but Thou remainest.* Now the higher heavens also are the work of God's hands. Therefore they also shall perish in the final burning of the world.

Obj. 2. Further, it is written (2 Pet. iii. 12): *The heavens being on fire shall be dissolved, and the elements shall melt with the burning heat of fire.* Now the heavens that are distinct from the elements are the higher heavens, wherein the stars are fixed. Therefore it would seem that they also will be cleansed by that fire.

Obj. 3. Further, the purpose of that fire will be to remove from bodies their indisposition to the perfection of glory. Now in the higher heaven we find this indisposition both as regards guilt, since the devil sinned there, and as regards natural deficiency, since a gloss on Rom. viii. 22, *We know that every creature groaneth and is in labor even until now,* says: *All the elements fulfill their duty with labor: even as it is not without labor that the sun and moon travel their appointed course.* Therefore the higher heavens also will be cleansed by that fire.

On the contrary, The heavenly bodies are not receptive of impressions from without.†

Further, a gloss on 2 Thess. i. 8, *In a flame of fire giving vengeance,* says: *There will be in the world a fire that shall precede Him, and shall rise in the air to the same height as did*

* Cf. P. III, Q. 62, A. 4, *ad* 1.   † *Sent. Philosop. ex Arist. collect.* lit. c.—Among the works of Bede.

the waters of the deluge. But the waters of the deluge did not rise to the height of the higher heavens but only 15 cubits higher than the mountain summits (Gen. vii. 20). Therefore the higher heavens will not be cleansed by that fire.

I answer that, The cleansing of the world will be for the purpose of removing from bodies the disposition contrary to the perfection of glory, and this perfection is the final consummation of the universe: and this disposition is to be found in all bodies, but differently in different bodies. For in some this indisposition regards something inherent to their substance: as in these lower bodies which by being mixed together fall away from their own purity. In others this indisposition does not regard something inherent to their substance; as in the heavenly bodies, wherein nothing is to be found contrary to the final perfection of the universe, except movement which is the way to perfection, and this not any kind of movement, but only local movement, which changes nothing intrinsic to a thing, such as its substance, quantity, or quality, but only its place which is extrinsic to it. Consequently there is no need to take anything away from the substance of the higher heavens, but only to set its movement at rest. Now local movement is brought to rest not by the action of a counter agent, but by the mover ceasing to move; and therefore the heavenly bodies will not be cleansed, neither by fire nor by the action of any creature, but in lieu of being cleansed they will be set at rest by God's will alone.

Reply Obj. 1. As Augustine says *(De Civ. Dei,* xx. 18, 24): Those words of the psalm refer to the aerial heavens which will be cleansed by the fire of the final conflagration. Or we may reply that if they refer also to the higher heavens, these are said to perish as regards their movement whereby now they are moved without cessation.

Reply Obj. 2. Peter explains himself to which heavens he refers. For before the words quoted, he had said *(verses 5-7): The heavens ... first, and the earth ... through water ... perished ... which ... now, by the same word are kept in store, reserved unto fire unto the day of judgment.** Therefore the heavens to be cleansed are those which before were cleansed by the waters of the deluge, namely the aerial heavens.

Reply Obj. 3. This labor and service of the creature, that Ambrose ascribes to the heavenly bodies, is nothing else than the successive movements whereby they are subject to time, and the lack of that final consummation which they will attain in the end. Nor did the empyrean heaven contract any stain from the sin

of the demons, because they were expelled from that heaven as soon as they sinned.

Whether That Fire Will Consume the Other Elements?

We proceed thus to the Fifth Article:—

Objection 1. It would seem that the fire in question will consume the other elements. For a gloss of Bede on 2 Pet. iii. 12 says: *This exceeding great fire will engulf the four elements whereof the world consists: yet it will not so engulf all things that they will cease to be, but it will consume two of them entirely, and will restore two of them to a better fashion.* Therefore it would seem that at least two of the elements are to be entirely destroyed by that fire.

Obj. 2. Further, it is written (Apoc. xxi. 1): *The first heaven and the first earth have passed away and the sea is no more.* Now the heaven here denotes the air, as Augustine states *(De Civ. Dei,* xx. 18); and the sea denotes the gathering together of the waters. Therefore it would seem that these three elements will be wholly destroyed.

Obj. 3. Further, fire does not cleanse except in so far as other things are made to be its matter. If, then, fire cleanses the other elements, they must needs become its matter.' Therefore they must pass into its nature, and consequently be voided of their own nature.

Obj. 4. Further, the form of fire is the most noble of the forms to which elemental matter can attain. Now all things will be brought to the most noble state by this cleansing. Therefore the other elements will be wholly transformed into fire.

On the contrary, A gloss on 1 Cor. vii. 31, *The fashion of this world passeth away,* says: *The beauty, not the substance, passeth.* But the very substance of the elements belongs to the perfection of the world. Therefore the elements will not be consumed as to their substance.

Further, this final cleansing that will be effected by fire will correspond to the first cleansing which was effected by water. Now the latter did not corrupt the substance of the elements. Therefore neither will the former which will be the work of fire.

I answer that, There are many opinions on this question. For some say that all the elements will remain as to their matter, while all will be changed as regards their imperfection; but that two of them will retain their respective substantial form, namely air and earth, while two of them, namely fire and water, will not retain their substantial form but will be changed to the form of heaven. In

* The entire text differs somewhat from S. Thomas's quotation; but the sense is the same.

this way three elements, namely air, fire, and water, will be called *heaven;* although air will retain the same substantial form as it has now, since even now it is called *heaven.* Wherefore (Apoc. xxi. 1) only heaven and earth are mentioned: *I saw,* says he, *a new heaven and a new earth.* But this opinion is altogether absurd: for it is opposed both to philosophy— which holds it impossible for the lower bodies to be in potentiality to the form of heaven, since they have neither a common matter, nor mutual contrariety—and to theology, since according to this opinion the perfection of the universe with the integrity of its parts will not be assured on account of two of the elements being destroyed.

Consequently *heaven* is taken to denote the fifth body, while all the elements are designated by *earth,* as expressed in Ps. cxlviii. 7, 8, *Praise the Lord from the earth* and afterwards, *Fire, hail, snow, ice,* etc.

Hence others say that all the elements will remain as to their substance, but that their active and passive qualities will be taken from them: even as they say too, that in a mixed body the elements retain their substantial form without having their proper qualities, since these are reduced to a mean, and a mean is neither of the extremes. And seemingly the following words of Augustine *(De Civ. Dei,* xx. 16) would seem in agreement with this: *In this conflagration of the world the qualities of the corruptible elements that were befitting our corruptible bodies will entirely perish by fire: and the substance itself will have those qualities that become an immortal body.*

However, this does not seem probable, for since the proper qualities of the elements are the effects of their substantial form, it seems impossible, as long as the substantial forms remain, for the aforesaid qualities to be changed, except for a time by some violent action: thus in hot water we see that by virtue of its species it returns to the cold temperature which it had lost by the action of fire, provided the species of water remain. Moreover, these same elemental qualities belong to the second perfection of the elements, as being their proper passions: nor is it probable that in this final consummation the elements will lose anything of their natural perfection.

Wherefore it would seem that the reply to this question should be that the elements will remain as to their substance and proper qualities, but that they will be cleansed both from the stain which they contracted from the sins of men, and from the impurity resulting in them through their mutual action and passion: because when once the movement of the first movable body ceases, mutual action and passion will be impossible in the lower elements:

and this is what Augustine calls the *qualities of corruptible elements,* namely their unnatural dispositions by reason of which they come near to corruption.

Reply Obj. 1. That fire is said to engulf the four elements in so far as in some way it will cleanse them. But when it is said further that *it will consume two entirely,* this does not mean that two of the elements are to be destroyed as to their substance, but that two will be more changed from the property which they have now. Some say that these two are fire and water which excel the others in their active qualities, namely heat and cold, which are the chief principles of corruption in other bodies; and since then there will be no action of fire and water which surpass the others in activity, they would seem especially to be changed from the virtue which they have now. Others, however, say that these two are air and water, on account of the various movements of these two elements, which movements they derive from the movement of the heavenly bodies. And since these movements will cease (such as the ebb and flow of the sea, and the disturbances of winds and so forth), therefore these elements especially will be changed from the property which they have now.

Reply Obj. 2. As Augustine says *(De Civ. Dei,* xx. 16), when it is stated: *And the sea is no more,* by the sea we may understand the present world of which he had said previously (xx. 13): *The sea gave up the dead that were in it.* If, however, the sea be taken literally we must reply that by the sea two things are to be understood, namely the substance of the waters, and their disposition, as containing salt and as to the movement of the waves. The sea will remain, not as to this second, but as to the first.

Reply Obj. 3. This fire will not act save as the instrument of God's providence and power; wherefore it will not act on the other elements so as to consume them but only so as to cleanse them. Nor is it necessary for that which becomes the matter of fire, to be voided of its proper species entirely, as instanced by incandescent iron, which by virtue of its species that remains returns to its proper and former state as soon as it is taken from the furnace. It will be the same with the elements after they are cleansed by fire.

Reply Obj. 4. In the elemental parts we must consider not only what is befitting a part considered in itself, but also what is befitting it in its relation to the whole. I say, then, that although water would be more noble if it had the form of fire, as likewise would earth and air, yet the universe would be more imperfect, if all elemental matter were to assume the form of fire.

SIXTH ARTICLE

Whether All the Elements Will Be Cleansed by That Fire?

We proceed thus to the Second Article:—

Objection 1. It would seem that neither will all the elements be cleansed by that fire. Because that fire, as stated already (A. 3), will not rise higher than the waters of the deluge. But the waters of the deluge did not reach to the sphere of fire. Therefore neither will the element of fire be cleansed by the final cleansing.

Obj. 2. Further, a gloss on Apoc. xxi. 1, *I saw a new heaven*, etc., says: *There can be no doubt that the transformation of the air and earth will be caused by fire; but it is doubtful about water, since it is believed to have the power of cleansing itself.* Therefore at least it is uncertain that all the elements will be cleansed.

Obj. 3. Further, a place where there is an everlasting stain is never cleansed. Now there will always be a stain in hell. Since, then, hell is situated among the elements, it would seem that the elements will not be wholly cleansed.

Obj. 4. Further, the earthly paradise is situated on the earth. Yet it will not be cleansed by fire, since not even the waters of the deluge reached it, as Bede says *(Hexaem.* i, *ad Gen. ii.* 8), as is stated in ii, *Sent.* D. 7. Therefore it would seem that the elements will not all be wholly cleansed.

On the contrary, The gloss quoted above (A. 5, *Obj.* 1) on 2 Pet. iii. 12 declares that *this fire will engulf the four elements.*

I answer that, Some* say that the fire in question will rise to the summit of the space containing the four elements: so that the elements would be entirely cleansed both from the stain of sin by which also the higher parts of the elements were infected (as instanced by the smoke of idolatry which stained the higher regions), and again from corruption, since the elements are corruptible in all their parts. But this opinion is opposed to the authority of Scripture, because it is written (2 Pet. iii. 7) that those heavens are *kept in store unto fire,* which were cleansed by water; and Augustine says *(De Civ. Dei,* xx. 18) that *the same world which perished in the deluge is reserved unto fire.* Now it is clear that the waters of the deluge did not rise to the summit of the space occupied by the elements, but only 15 cubits above the mountain tops; and moreover it is known that vapors or any smoke whatever rising from the earth cannot pierce the entire sphere of fire so as to reach its summit; and so the stain of sin did not reach the aforesaid space. Nor can the elements be cleansed from

_____
* S. Bonaventure, iv. *Sent.* D. 47, A. 2, Q. 3.

corruptibility by the removal of something that might be consumed by fire: whereas it will be possible for the impurities of the elements arising from their mingling together to be consumed by fire. And these impurities are chiefly round about the earth as far as the middle of the air: wherefore the fire of the final conflagration will cleanse up to that point, since the waters of the deluge rose to a height which can be approximately calculated from the height of the mountains which they surpassed in a fixed measure.

We therefore grant the *First Objection.*

Reply Obj. 2. The reason for doubt is expressed in the gloss, because, to wit, water is believed to have in itself the power of cleansing, yet not such a power as will be competent to the future state, as stated above (A. 5; A. 2, *ad* 2).

Reply Obj. 3. The purpose of this cleansing will be chiefly to remove all imperfection from the abode of the saints; and consequently in this cleansing all that is foul will be brought together to the place of the damned: so hell will not be cleansed, and the dregs of the whole earth will be brought thither, according to Ps. lxxiv. 9, *The dregs thereof are not emptied, all the sinners of the earth shall drink.*

Reply Obj. 4. Although the sin of the first man was committed in the earthly paradise, this is not the place of sinners, as neither is the empyrean heaven: since from both places, man and devil were expelled forthwith after their sin. Consequently that place needs no cleansing.

SEVENTH ARTICLE

Whether the Fire of the Final Conflagration Is to Follow the Judgment?

We proceed thus to the Seventh Article:—

Objection 1. It would seem that the fire of the final conflagration is to follow the judgment. For Augustine *(De Civ. Dei,* xx. 30) gives the following order of the things to take place at the judgment, saying: *At this judgment we have learned that the following things will occur. Elias the Thesbite will appear, the Jews will believe, Antichrist will persecute, Christ will judge, the dead shall rise again, the good shall be separated from the wicked, the world shall be set on fire and shall be renewed.* Therefore the burning will follow the judgment.

Obj. 2. Further, Augustine says *(ibid.* 16): *After the wicked have been judged, and cast into everlasting fire, the figure of this world will perish in the furnace of worldly flames.* Therefore the same conclusion follows.

Obj. 3. Further, when the Lord comes to judgment He will find some men living, as appears from the words of 1 Thess. iv. 16, where the Apostle speaking in their person says: *Then we who are alive, who remain unto the coming of the Lord.** But it would not be so, if the burning of the world were to come first, since they would be destroyed by the fire. Therefore this fire will follow the judgment.

Obj. 4. Further, it is said that our Lord will come to judge the earth by fire, and consequently the final conflagration would seem to be the execution of the sentence of Divine judgment. Now execution follows judgment. Therefore that fire will follow the judgment.

On the contrary, It is written (Ps. xcvi. 3): *A fire shall go before Him.*

Further, the resurrection will precede the judgment, else every eye would not see Christ judging. Now the burning of the world will precede the resurrection, for the saints who will rise again will have spiritual and impassible bodies, so that it will be impossible for the fire to cleanse them, and yet the text (iv. *Sent.* D. 47) quotes Augustine *(De Civ. Dei,* xx. 18) as saying that *whatever needs cleansing in any way shall be cleansed by that fire.* Therefore that fire will precede the judgment.

I answer that, The fire in question will in reality, as regards its beginning, precede the judgment. This can clearly be gathered from the fact that the resurrection of the dead will precede the judgment, since according to 1 Thess. iv. 13-16, those who have slept *shall be taken up . . . in the clouds . . . into the air . . . to meet Christ* coming to judgment. Now the general resurrection and the glorification of the bodies of the saints will happen at the same time; for the saints in rising again will assume a glorified body, as evidenced by 1 Cor. xv. 43, *It is sown in dishonor, it shall rise in glory:* and at the same time as the saints' bodies shall be glorified, all creatures shall be renewed, each in its own way, as appears from the statement (Rom. viii. 21) that *the creature . . . itself shall be delivered from the servitude of corruption into the liberty of the glory of the children of God.* Since then the burning of the world is a disposition to the aforesaid renewal, as stated above (AA. 1, 4); it can clearly be gathered that this burning, so far as it shall cleanse the world, will precede the judgment, but as regards a certain action thereof, whereby it will engulf the wicked, it will follow the judgment.

Reply Obj. 1 Augustine is speaking not as one who decides the point, but as expressing an opinion. This is clear from his continuing thus: *That all these things are to happen is a matter of faith, but how and in what order we shall learn more then by experience of the things themselves than now by seeking a defi-* nite conclusion by arguing about them. Methinks, however, they will occur in the order I have given. Hence it is clear that he is speaking as offering his opinion. The same answer applies to the *Second Objection.*

Reply Obj. 3. All men shall die and rise again: yet those are said to be found alive who will live in the body until the time of the conflagration.

Reply Obj. 4. That fire will not carry out the sentence of the judge except as regards the engulfing of the wicked: in this respect it will follow the judgment.

EIGHTH ARTICLE

Whether That Fire Will Have Such an Effect on Men As Is Described?

We proceed thus to the Eighth Article:—

Objection 1. It would seem that this fire will not have such an effect on men as is described in the text (iv. *Sent.* D. 47). For a thing is said to be consumed when it is reduced to naught. Now the bodies of the wicked will not be reduced to naught, but will be kept for eternity, that they may bear an eternal punishment. Therefore this fire will not consume the wicked, as stated in the text.

Obj. 2. Further, if it be said that it will consume the bodies of the wicked by reducing them to ashes; on the contrary, as the bodies of the wicked, so will those of the good be brought to ashes: for it is the privilege of Christ alone that His flesh see not corruption. Therefore it will consume also the good who will then be found.

Obj. 3. Further, the stain of sin is more abundant in the elements, as combining together to the formation of the human body wherein is the corruption of the fomes† even in the good, than in the elements existing outside the human body. Now the elements existing outside the human body will be cleansed on account of the stain of sin. Much therefore will the elements in the human body whether of the good or of the wicked need to be cleansed, and consequently the bodies of both will need to be destroyed.

Obj. 4. Further, as long as the state of the way lasts the elements act in like manner on the good and the wicked. Now the state of the way will still endure in that conflagration, since after this state of the way death will not be natural, and yet it will be caused by that fire. Therefore that fire will act equally on good and wicked; and consequently it does not seem that any distinction is made between them as to their being affected by that fire, as stated in the text.

* Vulg.,—*who are left, shall be taken . . . to meet Christ*—the words *who remain,* etc., are from *verse* 14.
† Cf. I-II, Q. 83, A. 3; Q. 91, A. 6.

Obj. 5. Further, this fire will have done its work in a moment as it were. Yet there will be many among the living in whom there will be many things to be cleansed. Therefore that fire will not suffice for their cleansing.

I answer that, This fire of the final conflagration, in so far as it will precede the judgment, will act as the instrument of Divine justice as well as by the natural virtue of fire. Accordingly, as regards its natural virtue, it will act in like manner on the wicked and good who will be alive, by reducing the bodies of both to ashes. But in so far as it acts as the instrument of Divine justice, it will act differently on different people as regards the sense of pain. For the wicked will be tortured by the action of the fire; whereas the good in whom there will be nothing to cleanse will feel no pain at all from the fire, as neither did the children in the fiery furnace (Dan. iii); although their bodies will not be kept whole, as were the bodies of the children: and it will be possible by God's power for their bodies to be destroyed without their suffering pain. But the good, in whom matter for cleansing will be found, will suffer pain from that fire, more or less according to their different merits.

On the other hand, as regards the action which this fire will have after the judgment, it will act on the damned alone, since the good will all have impassible bodies.

Reply Obj. 1. Consumption there signifies being brought, not to nothing, but to ashes.

Reply Obj. 2. Although the bodies of the good will be reduced to ashes by the fire, they will not suffer pain thereby, as neither did the children in the Babylonian furnace. In this respect a distinction is drawn between the good and the wicked.

Reply Obj. 3. The elements that are in human bodies, even in the bodies of the elect, will be cleansed by fire. But this will be done, by God's power, without their suffering pain.

Reply Obj. 4. This fire will act not only according to the natural power of the element, but also as the instrument of Divine justice.

Reply Obj. 5. There are three reasons why those who will be found living will be able to be cleansed suddenly. One is because there will be few things in them to be cleansed, since they will be already cleansed by the previous fears and persecutions. The second is because they will suffer pain both while living and of their own will: and pain suffered in this life voluntarily cleanses much more than pain inflicted after death, as in the case of the martyrs, because *if anything needing to be cleansed be found in them, it is cut off by the sickle of suffering,* as Augustine says *(De Unic. Bap.* xiii), although the pain of martyrdom is of short duration in comparison with the pain en-

dured in purgatory. The third is because the heat will gain in intensity what it loses in shortness of time.

NINTH ARTICLE

Whether That Fire Will Engulf the Wicked?

We proceed thus to the Ninth Article:—

Objection 1. It would seem that that fire will not engulf the wicked. For a gloss on Mal. iii. 3, *He shall purify the sons of Levi,* says that *it is a fire consuming the wicked and refining the good;* and a gloss on 1 Cor. iii. 13, *Fire shall try every man's work,* says: *We read that there will be a twofold fire, one that will cleanse the elect and will precede the judgment, another that will torture the wicked.* Now the latter is the fire of hell that shall engulf the wicked, while the former is the fire of the final conflagration. Therefore the fire of the final conflagration will not be that which will engulf the wicked.

Obj. 2. Further, that fire will obey God in the cleansing of the world: therefore it should receive its reward like the other elements, especially since fire is the most noble of the elements. Therefore it would seem that it ought not to be cast into hell for the punishment of the damned.

Obj. 3. Further, the fire that will engulf the wicked will be the fire of hell: and this fire was prepared from the beginning of the world for the damned; hence it is written (Matth. xxv. 41): *Depart . . . you cursed . . . into everlasting fire which was prepared for the devil,* etc., and (Isa. xxx. 33): *Tophet is prepared from yesterday, prepared by the king,* etc., where a gloss observes: *From yesterday,* i.e. *from the beginning—Tophet,* i.e. *the valley of hell.* But this fire of the final conflagration was not prepared from the beginning, but will result from the meeting together of the fires of the world. Therefore that fire is not the fire of hell which will engulf the wicked.

On the contrary, are the words of Ps. xcvi. 3, where it is said of this fire that it *shall burn His enemies round about.*

Further, it is written (Dan. vii. 10): *A swift stream of fire issued forth from before Him;* and a gloss adds, *to drag sinners into hell.* Now the passage quoted refers to that fire of which we are now speaking, as appears from a gloss which observes on the same words: *In order to punish the wicked and cleanse the good.* Therefore the fire of the final conflagration will be plunged into hell together with the wicked.

I answer that, The entire cleansing of the world and the renewal for the purpose of cleansing will be directed to the renewal of man: and consequently the cleansing and renewal of the world must needs correspond with the cleansing and renewal of mankind. Now mankind will be cleansed in one way by the separation of the wicked from the good: wherefore it is said (Luke iii. 17): *Whose fan is in His hand, and He will purge His floor, and will gather the wheat,* i.e. the elect, *into His barn, but the chaff,* i.e. the wicked, *He will burn with unquenchable fire.* Hence it will be thus with the cleansing of the world, so that all that is ugly and vile will be cast with the wicked into hell, and all that is beautiful and noble will be taken up above for the glory of the elect: and so too will it be with the fire of that conflagration, as Basil says in Ps. xxviii. 7, *The voice of the Lord divideth the flame of fire,* because whatever fire contains of burning heat and gross matter will go down into hell for the punishment of the wicked, and whatever is subtle and lightsome will remain above for the glory of the elect.

Reply Obj. 1. The fire that will cleanse the elect before the judgment will be the same as the fire that will burn the world, although some say the contrary. For it is fitting that man, being a part of the world, be cleansed with the same fire as the world. They are, however, described as two fires, that will cleanse the good, and torture the wicked, both in reference to their respective offices, and somewhat in reference to their substance: since the substance of the cleansing fire will not all be cast into hell, as stated above.

Reply Obj. 2. This fire will be rewarded because whatever it contains of gross matter will be separated from it, and cast into hell.

Reply Obj. 3. The punishment of the wicked, even as the glory of the elect, will be greater after the judgment than before. Wherefore, just as charity will be added to the higher creature in order to increase the glory of the elect, so too whatever is vile in creatures will be thrust down into hell in order to add to the misery of the damned. Consequently it is not unbecoming that another fire be added to the fire of the damned that was prepared from the beginning of the world.

QUESTION 75

Of the Resurrection

(In Three Articles)

IN the next place we must consider things connected with and accompanying the resurrection. Of these the first to be considered will be the resurrection itself; the second will be the cause of the resurrection; the third its time and manner; the fourth its term *wherefrom*; the fifth the condition of those who rise again.

Under the first head there will be three points of inquiry: (1) Whether there is to be a resurrection of the body? (2) Whether it is universally of all bodies? (3) Whether it is natural or miraculous?

FIRST ARTICLE

Whether There Is to Be a Resurrection of the Body?

We proceed thus to the First Article:—

Objection 1. It would seem that there is not to be a resurrection of the body: for it is written (Job xiv. 12): *Man, when he is fallen asleep, shall not rise again till the heavens be broken.* But the heavens shall never be broken, since the earth, to which seemingly this is still less applicable, *standeth for ever* (Eccles. i. 4). Therefore the man that is dead shall never rise again.

Obj. 2. Further, Our Lord proves the resurrection by quoting the words: *I am the God of Abraham, and the God of Isaac, and the God of Jacob. He is not the God of the dead but of the living* (Matth. xxii. 32; Exod. iii. 6).

But it is clear that when those words were uttered, Abraham, Isaac, and Jacob lived not in body, but only in the soul. Therefore there will be no resurrection of bodies but only of souls.

Obj. 3. Further, the Apostle (1 Cor. xv) seemingly proves the resurrection from the reward for labors endured by the saints in this life. For if they trusted in this life alone, they would be the most unhappy of all men. Now there can be sufficient reward for labor in the soul alone: since it is not necessary for the instrument to be repaid together with the worker, and the body is the soul's instrument. Wherefore even in purgatory, where souls will be punished for what they did in the body, the soul is punished without the body. Therefore there is no need to hold a resurrection of the body, but it is enough to hold a resurrection of souls, which consists in their being taken from the death of sin and unhappiness to the life of grace and glory.

Obj. 4. Further, the last state of a thing is the most perfect, since thereby it attains its end. Now the most perfect state of the soul is to be separated from the body, since in that state it is more conformed to God and the angels, and is more pure, as being separated from any extraneous nature. Therefore separation from the body is its final state, and consequently it returns not from this state to the body, as neither does a man end in becoming a boy.

Obj. 5. Further, bodily death is the punishment inflicted on man for his own transgression, as appears from Gen. ii, even as spiritual death, which is the separation of the soul from God, is inflicted on man for mortal sin. Now man never returns to life from spiritual death after receiving the sentence of his damnation. Therefore neither will there be any return from bodily death to bodily life, and so there will be no resurrection.

On the contrary, It is written (Job xix. 25-26): *I know that my Redeemer liveth, and in the last day I shall rise out of the earth, and I shall be clothed again with my skin,* etc. Therefore there will be a resurrection of the body.

Further, the gift of Christ is greater than the sin of Adam, as appears from Rom. v. 15. Now death was brought in by sin, for if sin had not been, there had been no death. Therefore by the gift of Christ man will be restored from death to life.

Further, the members should be conformed to the head. Now our Head lives and will live eternally in body and soul, since *Christ rising again from the dead dieth now no more* (Rom. vi. 8). Therefore men who are His members will live in body and soul; and consequently there must needs be a resurrection of the body.

I answer that, According to the various opinions about man's last end there have been various opinions holding or denying the resurrection. For man's last end which all men desire naturally is happiness. Some have held that man is able to attain this end in this life: wherefore they had no need to admit another life after this, wherein man would be able to attain to his perfection: and so they denied the resurrection.

This opinion is confuted with sufficient probability by the changeableness of fortune, the weakness of the human body, the imperfection and instability of knowledge and virtue, all of which are hindrances to the perfection of happiness, as Augustine argues at the end of *De Civ. Dei* (xxii. 22).

Hence others maintained that after this there is another life wherein, after death, man lives according to the soul only, and they held that such a life sufficed to satisfy the natural desire to obtain happiness: wherefore Porphyrius said as Augustine states (*De Civ. Dei*, xxii. 26): *The soul, to be happy, must avoid all bodies:* and consequently these did not hold the resurrection.

This opinion was based by various people on various false foundations. For certain heretics asserted that all bodily things are from the

evil principle, but that spiritual things are from the good principle: and from this it follows that the soul cannot reach the height of its perfection unless it be separated from the body, since the latter withdraws it from its principle, the participation of which makes it happy. Hence all those heretical sects that hold corporeal things to have been created or fashioned by the devil deny the resurrection of the body. The falsehood of this principle has been shown at the beginning of the Second Book (ii. *Sent.* D. 4, qu. 1, *A.* 3).*

Others said that the entire nature of man is seated in the soul, so that the soul makes use of the body as an instrument, or as a sailor uses his ship: wherefore according to this opinion, it follows that if happiness is attained by the soul alone, man would not be balked in his natural desire for happiness, and so there is no need to hold the resurrection. But the Philosopher sufficiently destroys this foundation (*De Anima*, ii. 2), where he shows that the soul is united to the body as form to matter. Hence it is clear that if man cannot be happy in this life, we must of necessity hold the resurrection.

Reply Obj. 1. The heavens will never be broken as to their substance, but as to the effect of their power whereby their movement is the cause of generation and corruption of lower things: for this reason the Apostle says (1 Cor. vii. 31): *The fashion of this world passeth away.*

Reply Obj. 2. Abraham's soul, properly speaking, is not Abraham himself, but a part of him (and the same as regards the others). Hence life in Abraham's soul does not suffice to make Abraham a living being, or to make the God of Abraham the God of a living man. But there needs to be life in the whole composite, *i.e.* the soul and body: and although this life were not actually when these words were uttered, it was in each part as ordained to the resurrection. Wherefore our Lord proves the resurrection with the greatest subtlety and efficacy.

Reply Obj. 3. The soul is compared to the body, not only as a worker to the instrument with which he works, but also as form to matter: wherefore the work belongs to the composite and not to the soul alone, as the Philosopher shows (*De Anima*, i. 4). And since to the worker is due the reward of the work, it behooves man himself, who is composed of soul and body, to receive the reward of his work. Now as venial offenses are called sins as being dispositions to sin, and not as having simply and perfectly the character of sin, so the punishment which is awarded to them in purgatory is not a retribution simply, but rather a cleansing, which is wrought sepa-

* Cf. P. I, Q. 49, A. ?.

rately in the body, by death and by its being reduced to ashes, and in the soul by the fire of purgatory.

Reply Obj. 4. Other things being equal, the state of the soul in the body is more perfect than outside the body, because it is a part of the whole composite; and every integral part is material in comparison to the whole: and though it were conformed to God in one respect, it is not simply. Because, strictly speaking, a thing is more conformed to God when it has all that the condition of its nature requires, since then most of all it imitates the Divine perfection. Hence the heart of an animal is more conformed to an immovable God when it is in movement than when it is at rest, because the perfection of the heart is in its movement, and its rest is its undoing.

Reply Obj. 5. Bodily death was brought about by Adam's sin which was blotted out by Christ's death: hence its punishment lasts not for ever. But mortal sin which causes everlasting death through impenitence will not be expiated hereafter. Hence that death will be everlasting.

SECOND ARTICLE

Whether the Resurrection Will Be for All Without Exception?

We proceed thus to the Second Article:—

Objection 1. It would seem that the resurrection will not be for all without exception. For it is written (Ps. i. 5): *The wicked shall not rise again in judgment.* Now men will not rise again except at the time of the general judgment. Therefore the wicked shall in no way rise again.

Obj. 2. Further, it is written (Dan. xii. 2): *Many of those that sleep in the dust of the earth shall awake.* But these words imply a restriction. Therefore all will not rise again.

Obj. 3. Further, by the resurrection men are conformed to Christ rising again; wherefore the Apostle argues (1 Cor. xv. 12, *seqq.*) that if Christ rose again, we also shall rise again. Now those alone should be conformed to Christ rising again who have borne His image, and this belongs to the good alone. Therefore they alone shall rise again.

Obj. 4. Further, punishment is not remitted unless the fault be condoned. Now bodily death is the punishment of original sin. Therefore, as original sin is not forgiven to all, all will not rise again.

Obj. 5. Further, as we are born again by the grace of Christ, even so shall we rise again by His grace. Now those who die in their mother's womb can never be born again: therefore neither can they rise again, and consequently all will not rise again.

* John iii. 18.

On the contrary, It is said (Jo. v. 28, 25): *All that are in the graves shall hear the voice of the Son of God, . . . and they that hear shall live.* Therefore the dead shall all rise again.

Further, it is written (1 Cor. xv. 51): *We shall all indeed rise again,* etc.

Further, the resurrection is necessary in order that those who rise again may receive punishment or reward according to their merits. Now either punishment or reward is due to all, either for their own merits, as to adults, or for others' merits, as to children. Therefore all will rise again.

I answer that, Those things, the reason of which comes from the nature of a species, must needs be found likewise in all the members of that same species. Now such is the resurrection: because the reason thereof, as stated above (A. 1), is that the soul cannot have the final perfection of the human species, so long as it is separated from the body. Hence no soul will remain for ever separated from the body. Therefore it is necessary for all, as well as for one, to rise again.

Reply Obj. 1. As a gloss expounds these words, they refer to the spiritual resurrection whereby the wicked shall not rise again in the particular judgment. Or else they refer to the wicked who are altogether unbelievers, who will not rise again to be judged, since they are already judged.*

Reply Obj. 2. Augustine (*De Civ. Dei,* xx. 23) explains *many* as meaning *all*: in fact, this way of speaking is often met with in Holy Writ. Or else the restriction may refer to the children consigned to limbo who, although they shall rise again, are not properly said to awake, since they will have no sense either of pain or of glory, and waking is the unchaining of the senses.

Reply Obj. 3. All, both good and wicked, are conformed to Christ, while living in this life, as regards things pertaining to the nature of the species, but not as regards matters pertaining to grace. Hence all will be conformed to Him in the restoration of natural life, but not in the likeness of glory, except the good alone.

Reply Obj. 4. Those who have died in original sin have, by dying, discharged the obligation of death which is the punishment of original sin. Hence, notwithstanding original sin, they can rise again from death: for the punishment of original sin is to die, rather than to be detained by death.

Reply Obj. 5. We are born again by the grace of Christ that is given to us, but we rise again by the grace of Christ whereby it came about that He took our nature, since it is by this that we are conformed to Him in natural things. Hence those who die in their mother's womb, although they are not born again by receiving grace, will nevertheless rise again on account of the conformity of their nature with Him, which conformity they acquired by attaining to the perfection of the human species.

THIRD ARTICLE

Whether the Resurrection Is Natural?

We proceed thus to the Third Article:—

Objection 1. It would seem that the resurrection is natural. For, as the Damascene says *(De Fide Orthod.* iii. 14), *that which is commonly observed in all, marks the nature of the individuals contained under it.* Now resurrection applies commonly to all. Therefore it is natural.

Obj. 2. Further, Gregory says *(Moral.* xiv. 55): *Those who do not hold the resurrection on the principle of obedience ought certainly to hold it on the principle of reason. For what does the world every day but imitate, in its elements, our resurrection?* And he offers as examples the light which *as it were dies . . . and is withdrawn from our sight . . . and again rises anew, as it were, and is recalled—the shrubs which lose their greenery, and again by a kind of resurrection are renewed—and the seeds which rot and die and then sprout and rise again as it were:* which same example is adduced by the Apostle (1 Cor. xv. 36). Now from the works of nature nothing can be known save what is natural. Therefore the resurrection is natural.

Obj. 3. Further, things that are against nature abide not for long, because they are violent, so to speak. But the life that is restored by the resurrection will last for ever. Therefore the resurrection will be natural.

Obj. 4. Further, that to which the entire expectation of nature looks forward would seem to be natural. Now such a thing is the resurrection and the glorification of the saints according to Rom. viii. 19. Therefore the resurrection will be natural.

Obj. 5. Further, the resurrection is a kind of movement towards the everlasting union of soul and body. Now movement is natural if it terminate in a natural rest *(Phys.* v. 6): and the everlasting union of soul and body will be natural, for since the soul is the body's proper mover, it has a body proportionate to it: so that the body is likewise for ever capable of being quickened by it, even as the soul lives for ever. Therefore the resurrection will be natural.

On the contrary, There is no natural return from privation to habit. But death is privation of life. Therefore the resurrection whereby one returns from death to life is not natural.

Further, things of the one species have one fixed way of origin: wherefore animals begotten of putrefaction are never of the same species as those begotten of seed, as the Commentator says on *Phys.* viii. Now the natural way of man's origin is for him to be begotten of a like in species: and such is not the case in the resurrection. Therefore it will not be natural.

I answer that, A movement or an action stands related to nature in three ways. For there is a movement or action whereof nature is neither the principle nor the term: and such a movement is sometimes from a principle above nature as in the case of a glorified body; and sometimes from any other principle whatever; for instance, the violent upward movement of a stone which terminates in a violent rest. Again, there is a movement whereof nature is both principle and term: for instance, the downward movement of a stone. And there is another movement whereof nature is the term, but not the principle, the latter being sometimes something above nature (as in giving sight to a blind man, for sight is natural, but the principle of the sight-giving is above nature), and sometimes something else, as in the forcing of flowers or fruit by artificial process. It is impossible for nature to be the principle and not the term, because natural principles are appointed to definite effects, beyond which they cannot extend.

Accordingly the action or movement that is related to nature in the first way can nowise be natural, but is either miraculous if it come from a principle above nature, or violent if from any other principle. The action or movement that is related to nature in the second way is simply natural: but the action that is related to nature in the third way cannot be described as natural simply, but as natural in a restricted sense, in so far, to wit, as it leads to that which is according to nature: but it is called either miraculous or artificial or violent. For, properly speaking, natural is that which is according to nature, and a thing is according to nature if it has that nature and whatever results from that nature *(Phys.* ii. 1). Consequently, speaking simply, movement cannot be described as natural unless its principle be natural.

Now nature cannot be the principle of resurrection, although resurrection terminates in the life of nature. For nature is the principle of movement in the thing wherein nature is,— either the active principle, as in the movement of heavy and light bodies and in the natural alterations of animals,—or the passive principle, as in the generation of simple bodies. The passive principle of natural generation is the natural passive potentiality which always has an active principle corresponding to it in nature, according to *Met*. viii. 1: nor as to this does it matter whether the active principle in nature correspond to the passive principle in respect of its ultimate perfection, namely the form; or in respect of a disposition in virtue of which it demands the ultimate form, as in the generation of a man according to the teaching of faith, or in all other generations according to the opinions of Plato and Avicenna. But in nature there is no active principle of the resurrection, neither as regards the union of the soul with the body, nor as regards the disposition which is the demand for that union: since such a disposition cannot be produced by nature, except in a definite way by the process of generation from seed. Wherefore even granted a passive potentiality on the part of the body, or any kind of inclination to its union with the soul, it is not such as to suffice for the conditions of natural movement. Therefore the resurrection, strictly speaking, is miraculous and not natural except in a restricted sense, as we have explained.

Reply Obj. 1. The Damascene is speaking of those things that are found in all individuals and are caused by the principles of nature. For supposing by a divine operation all men to be made white, or to be gathered together in one place, as happened at the time of the deluge, it would not follow that whiteness or existence in some particular place is a natural property of man.

Reply Obj. 2. From natural things one does not come by a demonstration of reason to know non-natural things, but by the induction of reason one may know something above nature, since the natural bears a certain resemblance to the supernatural. Thus the union of soul and body resembles the union of the soul with God by the glory of fruition, as the Master says (ii. *Sent*. D. 1): and in like manner the examples, quoted by the Apostle and Gregory, are confirmatory evidences of our faith in the resurrection.

Reply Obj. 3. This argument regards an operation which terminates in something that is not natural but contrary to nature. Such is not the resurrection, and hence the argument is not to the point.

Reply Obj. 4. The entire operation of nature is subordinate to the Divine operation, just as the working of a lower art is subordinate to the working of a higher art. Hence just as all the work of a lower art has in view an end unattainable save by the operation of the higher art that produces the form, or makes use of what has been made by art: so the last end which the whole expectation of nature has in view is unattainable by the operation of nature, and for which reason the attaining thereto is not natural.

Reply Obj. 5. Although there can be no natural movement terminating in a violent rest, there can be a non-natural movement terminating in a natural rest, as explained above.

QUESTION 76

Of the Cause of the Resurrection

(In Three Articles)

WE must next consider the cause of our resurrection. Under this head there are three points of inquiry: (1) Whether Christ's resurrection is the cause of our resurrection? (2) Whether the sound of the trumpet is? (3) Whether the angels are?

FIRST ARTICLE

Whether the Resurrection of Christ Is the Cause of Our Resurrection?

We proceed thus to the First Article:—

Objection 1. It would seem that the resurrection of Christ is not the cause of our resurrection. For, given the cause, the effect follows. Yet given the resurrection of Christ the resurrection of the other dead did not follow at once. Therefore His resurrection is not the cause of ours.

Obj. 2. Further, an effect cannot be unless the cause precede. But the resurrection of the dead would be even if Christ had not risen again: for God could have delivered man in some other way. Therefore Christ's resurrection is not the cause of ours.

Obj. 3. Further, the same thing produces the one effect throughout the one same species. Now the resurrection will be common to all men. Since then Christ's resurrection is not its own cause, it is not the cause of the resurrection of others.

Obj. 4. Further, an effect retains some likeness to its cause. But the resurrection, at least of some, namely the wicked, bears no likeness to the resurrection of Christ. Therefore Christ's resurrection will not be the cause of theirs.

On the contrary, In every genus that which is first is the cause of those that come after it (Met. ii. 1). Now Christ, by reason of His bodily resurrection, is called *the firstfruits of them that sleep* (1 Cor. xv. 20), and *the first-begotten of the dead* (Apoc. i. 5). Therefore His resurrection is the cause of the resurrection of others.

Further, Christ's resurrection has more in common with our bodily resurrection than with our spiritual resurrection which is by justification. But Christ's resurrection is the cause of our justification, as appears from Rom. iv. 25, where it is said that He *rose again for our justification.* Therefore Christ's resurrection is the cause of our bodily resurrection.

I answer that, Christ by reason of His nature is called the mediator of God and men: wherefore the Divine gifts are bestowed on men by means of Christ's humanity. Now just as we cannot be delivered from spiritual death save by the gift of grace bestowed by God, so neither can we be delivered from bodily death except by resurrection wrought by the Divine power. And therefore as Christ, in respect of His human nature, received the firstfruits of grace from above, and His grace is the cause of our grace, because *of His fulness we all have received . . . grace for grace* (Jo. i. 16), so in Christ has our resurrection begun, and His resurrection is the cause of ours. Thus Christ as God is, as it were, the equivocal cause of our resurrection, but as God and man rising again, He is the proximate and, so to say, the univocal cause of our resurrection. Now a univocal efficient cause produces its effect in likeness to its own form, so that not only is it an efficient, but also an exemplar cause in relation to that effect. This happens in two ways. For sometimes this very form, whereby the agent is likened to its effect, is the direct principle of the action by which the effect is produced, as heat in the fire that heats: and sometimes it is not the form in respect of which this likeness is observed, that is primarily and directly the principle of that action, but the principles of that form. For instance, if a white man beget a white man, the whiteness of the begetter is not the principle of active generation, and yet the whiteness of the begetter is said to be the cause of the whiteness of the begotten, because the principles of whiteness in the begetter are the generative principles causing whiteness in the begotten. In this way the resurrection of Christ is the cause of our resurrection, because the same thing that wrought the resurrection of Christ, which is the univocal efficient cause of our resurrection, is the active cause of our resurrection, namely the power of Christ's Godhead which is common to Him and the Father. Hence it is written (Rom. viii. 11): *He that raised up Jesus Christ from the dead shall quicken also your mortal bodies.* And this very resurrection of Christ by virtue of His indwelling God-head is the quasi-instrumental cause of our resurrection: since the Divine operations were wrought by means of Christ's flesh, as though it were a kind of organ; thus the Damascene instances as an example *(De Fide Orthod.* iii. 15) the touch of His body whereby He healed the leper (Matth. viii. 3).

Reply Obj. 1. A sufficient cause produces at once its effect to which it is immediately directed, but not the effect to which it is directed by means of something else, no matter how sufficient it may be: thus heat, however intense it be, does not cause heat at once in the first instant, but it begins at once to set up a movement towards heat, because heat is its effect by means of movement. Now Christ's resurrection is said to be the cause of ours, in that it works our resurrection, not immediately, but by means of its principle, namely the Divine power which will work our resurrection in likeness to the resurrection of Christ. Now God's power works by means of His will which is nearest to the effect; hence it is not necessary that our resurrection should follow straightway after He has wrought the resurrection of Christ, but that it should happen at the time which God's will has decreed.

Reply Obj. 2. God's power is not tied to any particular second causes, but that He can produce their effects either immediately or by means of other causes: thus He might work the generation of lower bodies even though there were no movement of the heaven: and yet according to the order which He has established in things, the movement of the heaven is the cause of the generation of the lower bodies. In like manner according to the order appointed to human things by Divine providence, Christ's resurrection is the cause of ours: and yet He could have appointed another order, and then our resurrection would have had another cause ordained by God.

Reply Obj. 3. This argument holds when all the things of one species have the same order to the first cause of the effect to be produced in the whole of that species. But it is not so in the case in point, because Christ's humanity is nearer to His Godhead, Whose power is the first cause of the resurrection, than is the humanity of others. Hence Christ's Godhead caused His resurrection immediately, but it causes the resurrection of others by means of Christ-man rising again.

Reply Obj. 4. The resurrection of all men will bear some resemblance to Christ's resurrection, as regards that which pertains to the life of nature, in respect of which all were conformed to Christ. Hence all will rise again to immortal life; but in the saints who were conformed to Christ by grace, there will be conformity as to things pertaining to glory.

SECOND ARTICLE

Whether the Sound of the Trumpet Will Be the Cause of Our Resurrection?

We proceed thus to the Second Article:—

Objection 1. It would seem that the sound of the trumpet will not be the cause of our resurrection. For the Damascene says *(De Fide Orthod.* iv) : *Thou must believe that the resurrection will take place by God's will, power, and nod.* Therefore since these are a sufficient cause of our resurrection, we ought not to assign the sound of the trumpet as a cause thereof.

Obj. 2. Further, it is useless to make sounds to one who cannot hear. But the dead will not have hearing. Therefore it is unfitting to make a sound to arouse them.

Obj. 3. Further, if any sound is the cause of the resurrection, this will only be by a power given by God to the sound: wherefore a gloss on Ps. lxvii. 34, *He will give to His voice the voice of power,* says,—*to arouse our bodies.* Now from the moment that a power is given to a thing, though it be given miraculously, the act that ensues is natural, as instanced in the man born blind who, after being restored to sight, saw naturally. Therefore if a sound be the cause of resurrection, the resurrection would be natural: which is false.

On the contrary, It is written (1 Thess. iv. 15) : *The Lord Himself will come down from heaven . . . with the trumpet of God; and the dead who are in Christ shall rise.*

Further, it is written (Jo. v. 28) that they *who are in the graves shall hear the voice of the Son of God . . . and* (verse 25) *they that hear shall live.* Now this voice is called the trumpet, as stated in the text (iv. *Sent.* D. 43). Therefore, etc.

I answer that, Cause and effect must needs in some way be united together, since mover and moved, maker and made, are simultaneous *(Phys.* vii. 2). Now Christ rising again is the univocal cause of our resurrection: wherefore at the resurrection of bodies, it behooves Christ to work the resurrection at the giving of some common bodily sign. According to some this sign will be literally Christ's voice commanding the resurrection, even as He commanded the sea and the storm ceased (Matth. viii. 26). Others say that this sign will be nothing else than the manifest appearance of the Son of God in the world, according to the words of Matth. xxiv. 27 : *As lightning cometh out of the east, and appeareth even into the west, so shall also the coming of the Son of man be.* These rely on the authority of Gregory* who says that *the*

sound *of the trumpet is nothing else but the Son appearing to the world as judge.* According to this, the visible presence of the Son of God is called His voice, because as soon as He appears all nature will obey His command in restoring human bodies: hence He is described as coming *with commandment* (1 Thess. iv. 15). In this way His appearing, in so far as it has the force of a command, is called His voice: which voice, whatever it be, is sometimes called a cry,† as of a crier summoning to judgment; sometimes the sound of a trumpet,‡ either on account of its distinctness, as stated in the text (iv. *Sent.* D. 43), or as being in keeping with the use of the trumpet in the Old Testament: for by the trumpet they were summoned to the council, stirred to the battle, and called to the feast; and those who rise again will be summoned to the council of judgment, to the battle in which *the world shall fight . . . against the unwise* (Wis. v. 21), and to the feast of everlasting solemnity.

Reply Obj. 1. In those words the Damascene touches on three things respecting the material cause of the resurrection: to wit, the Divine will which commands, the power which executes, and the ease of execution, when he adds *bidding,* in resemblance to our own affairs: since it is very easy for us to do what is done at once at our word. But the ease is much more evident, if before we say a word, our servants execute our will at once at the first sign of our will, which sign is called a nod: and this nod is a kind of cause of that execution, in so far as others are led thereby to accomplish our will. And the Divine nod, at which the resurrection will take place, is nothing but the sign given by God, which all nature will obey by concurring in the resurrection of the dead. This sign is the same as the sound of the trumpet, as explained above.

Reply Obj. 2. As the forms of the Sacrament have the power to sanctify, not through being heard, but through being spoken: so this sound, whatever it be, will have an instrumental efficacy of resuscitation, not through being perceived, but through being uttered. Even so a sound by the pulsation of the air arouses the sleeper, by loosing the organ of perception, and not because it is known: since judgment about the sound that reaches the ears is subsequent to the awakening and is not its cause.

Reply Obj. 3. This argument would avail, if the power given to that sound were a complete being in nature: because then that which would proceed therefrom would have for principle a power already rendered natural. But this power is not of that kind but such as we

---

* *Moral.* xxxi, as quoted by S. Albert the Great, iv, *Sent.* D. 42, A. 4.

† Matth. xxv. 6.

‡ 1 Cor. xv. 52; 1 Thess. iv. 15.

have ascribed above to the forms of the Sacraments (iv. *Sent.* D. 1; P. iii, Q. 62, AA. 1, 4).

THIRD ARTICLE

Whether the Angels Will Do Anything towards the Resurrection?

We proceed thus to the Third Article:—

Objection 1. It would seem that the angels will do nothing at all towards the resurrection. For raising the dead shows a greater power than does begetting men. Now when men are begotten, the soul is not infused into the body by means of the angels. Therefore neither will the resurrection, which is reunion of soul and body, be wrought by the ministry of the angels.

Obj. 2. Further, if this is to be ascribed to the instrumentality of any angels at all, it would seem especially referable to the virtues, to whom it belongs to work miracles. Yet it is referred, not to them, but to the archangels, according to the text (iv. *Sent.* D. 43). Therefore the resurrection will not be wrought by the ministry of the angels.

On the contrary, It is stated (1 Thess. iv. 15) that *the Lord . . . shall come down from heaven . . . with the voice of an archangel . . . and the dead shall rise again.* Therefore the resurrection of the dead will be accomplished by the angelic ministry.

I answer that, According to Augustine (*De Trin.* iii. 4) *just as the grosser and inferior bodies are ruled in a certain order by the more subtle and more powerful bodies, so are all bodies ruled by God by the rational spirit of life:* and Gregory speaks in the same sense (*Dial.* iv. 6). Consequently in all God's bodily works, He employs the ministry of the angels. Now in the resurrection there is something pertaining to the transmutation of the bodies, to wit the gathering together of the mortal remains and the disposal thereof for the restoration of the human body; wherefore in this respect God will employ the ministry of the angels in the resurrection. But the soul, even as it is immediately created by God, so will it be reunited to the body immediately by God without any operation of the angels: and in like manner He Himself will glorify the body without the ministry of the angels, just as He immediately glorifies man's soul. This ministry of the angels is called their voice, according to one explanation given in the text (iv. *Sent.* D. 43).

Hence the *Reply* to the *First Objection* is evident from what has been said.

Reply Obj. 2. This ministry will be exercised chiefly by one Archangel, namely Michael, who is the prince of the Church as he was of the Synagogue (Dan. x. 13, 21). Yet he will act under the influence of the Virtues and the other higher orders: so that what he shall do, the higher orders will, in a way, do also. In like manner the lower angels will co-operate with him as to the resurrection of each individual to whose guardianship they were appointed: so that this voice can be ascribed either to one or to many angels.

QUESTION 77

Of the Time and Manner of the Resurrection

(In Four Articles)

WE must now consider the time and manner of the resurrection. Under this head there are four points of inquiry. (1) Whether the time of the resurrection should be delayed until the end of the world? (2) Whether that time is hidden? (3) Whether the resurrection will occur at night-time? (4) Whether it will happen suddenly?

FIRST ARTICLE

Whether the Time of Our Resurrection Should Be Delayed Till the End of the World?

We proceed thus to the First Article:—

Objection 1. It would seem that the time of the resurrection ought not to be delayed till the end of the world, so that all may rise together. For there is more conformity between head and members than between one member and another, as there is more between cause and effect than between one effect and another. Now Christ, Who is our Head, did not delay His resurrection until the end of the world, so as to rise again together with all men. Therefore there is no need for the resurrection of the early saints to be deferred until the end of the world, so that they may rise again together with the others.

Obj. 2. Further, the resurrection of the Head is the cause of the resurrection of the members. But the resurrection of certain members that desire nobility from their being closely connected with the Head was not delayed till the end of the world, but followed immediately after Christ's resurrection, as is piously believed concerning the Blessed Virgin and John the Evangelist.* Therefore the resurrection of others will be so much nearer Christ's resur-

* *Ep. de Assump. B.V.,* cap. ii, among S. Jerome's works.

rection, according as they have been more conformed to Him by grace and merit.

Obj. 3. Further, the state of the New Testament is more perfect, and bears a closer resemblance to Christ, than the state of the Old Testament. Yet some of the fathers of the Old Testament rose again when Christ rose, according to Matth. xxvii. 52: *Many of the bodies of the saints, that had slept, arose.* Therefore it would seem that the resurrection of the Old Testament saints should not be delayed till the end of the world, so that all may rise together.

Obj. 4. Further, there will be no numbering of years after the end of the world. Yet after the resurrection of the dead, the years are still reckoned until the resurrection of others, as appears from Apoc. xx. 4, 5. For it is stated there that *I saw . . . the souls of them that were beheaded for the testimony of Jesus, and for the word of God,* and further on: *And they lived and reigned with Christ a thousand years.* And *the rest of the dead lived not till the thousand years were finished.* Therefore the resurrection of all is not delayed until the end of the world, that all may rise together.

On the contrary, It is written (Job xiv. 12): *Man when he is fallen asleep shall not rise again till the heavens be broken, he shall not wake, nor rise out of his sleep,* and it is a question of the sleep of death. Therefore the resurrection of men will be delayed until the end of the world when the heavens shall be broken.

Further, it is written (Heb. xi. 39): *All these being approved by the testimony of faith received not the promise, i.e.* full beatitude of soul and body, since *God has provided something better for us, lest they should be consummated, i.e.* perfected, *without us,—in order that,* as a gloss observes, *through all rejoicing each one might rejoice the more.* But the resurrection will not precede the glorification of bodies, because *He will reform the body of our lowness made like to the body of His glory* (Phil. iii. 21), and the children of the resurrection will be *as the angels . . . in heaven* (Matth. xxii. 30). Therefore the resurrection will be delayed till the end of the world, when all shall rise together.

I answer that, As Augustine states *(De Trin.* iii. 4) *Divine providence decreed that the grosser and lower bodies should be ruled in a certain order by the more subtle and powerful bodies:* wherefore the entire matter of the lower bodies is subject to variation according to the movement of the heavenly bodies. Hence it would be contrary to the order established in things by Divine providence if the matter of lower bodies were brought to the state of

incorruption, so long as there remains movement in the higher bodies. And since, according to the teaching of faith, the resurrection will bring men to immortal life conformably to Christ Who *rising again from the dead dieth now no more* (Rom. vi. 9), the resurrection of human bodies will be delayed until the end of the world when the heavenly movement will cease. For this reason, too, certain philosophers, who held that the movement of the heavens will never cease, maintained that human souls will return to mortal bodies such as we have now,—whether, as Empedocles, they stated that the soul would return to the same body at the end of the great year, or that it would return to another body; thus Pythagoras asserted that *any soul will enter any body,* as stated in *De Anima,* i. 3.

Reply Obj. 1. Although the head is more conformed to the members by conformity of proportion (which is requisite in order that it have influence over the members) than one member is to another, yet the head has a certain causality over the members which the members have not; and in this the members differ from the head and agree with one another. Hence Christ's resurrection is an exemplar of ours, and through our faith therein there arises in us the hope of our own resurrection. But the resurrection of one of Christ's members is not the cause of the resurrection of other members, and consequently Christ's resurrection had to precede the resurrection of others who have all to rise again at the consummation of the world.

Reply Obj. 2. Although among the members some rank higher than others and are more conformed to the Head, they do not attain to the character of headship so as to be the cause of others. Consequently greater conformity to Christ does not give them a right to rise again before others as though they were exemplar and the others exemplate, as we have said in reference to Christ's resurrection: and if it has been granted to others that their resurrection should not be delayed until the general resurrection, this has been by special privilege of grace, and not as due on account of conformity to Christ.

Reply Obj. 3. Jerome, in a sermon on the Assumption,* seems to be doubtful of this resurrection of the saints with Christ, namely as to whether, having been witnesses to the resurrection, they died again, so that theirs was a resuscitation (as in the case of Lazarus who died again) rather than a resurrection such as will be at the end of the world,—or really rose again to immortal life, to live for ever in the body, and to ascend bodily into heaven with Christ, as a gloss says on Matth.

---

* *Ep. x, ad Paul. et Eustoch.,* now recognized as spurious.

xxvii. 52. The latter seems more probable, because, as Jerome says *(ibid.)*, in order that they might bear true witness to Christ's true resurrection, it was fitting that they should truly rise again. Nor was their resurrection hastened for their sake, but for the sake of bearing witness to Christ's resurrection: and that by bearing witness thereto they might lay the foundation of the faith of the New Testament: wherefore it was more fitting that it should be borne by the fathers of the Old Testament, than by those who died after the foundation of the New. It must, however, be observed that, although the Gospel mentions their resurrection before Christ's, we must take this statement as made in anticipation, as is often the case with writers of history. For none rose again with a true resurrection before Christ, since He is the *firstfruits of them that sleep* (1 Cor. xv. 20), although some were resuscitated before Christ's resurrection, as in the case of Lazarus.

Reply Obj. 4. On account of these words, as Augustine relates *(De Civ. Dei, xx. 7)*, certain heretics asserted that there will be a first resurrection of the dead that they may reign with Christ on earth for a thousand years; whence they were called *chiliasts* or *millenarians.* Hence Augustine says *(ibid.)* that these words are to be understood otherwise, namely of the spiritual resurrection, whereby men shall rise again from their sins to the gift of grace: while the second resurrection is of bodies. The reign of Christ denotes the Church wherein not only martyrs but also the other elect reign, the part denoting the whole; or they reign with Christ in glory as regards all, special mention being made of the martyrs, because they especially reign after death who fought for the truth, even unto death. The number of a thousand years denotes not a fixed number, but the whole of the present time wherein the saints now reign with Christ, because the number 1,000 designates universality more than the number 100, since 100 is the square of 10, whereas 1,000 is a cube resulting from the multiplication of ten by its square, for $10 \times 10 = 100$, and $100 \times 10 = 1,000$. Again in Ps. civ. 8, *The word which He commanded to a thousand, i.e. all, generations.*

SECOND ARTICLE

Whether the Time of Our Resurrection Is Hidden?

We proceed thus to the Second Article:—

Objection 1. It would seem that this time is not hidden. Because when we know exactly the beginning of a thing, we can know its end exactly, since *all things are measured by a certain period (De Generat.* ii). Now the beginning of the world is known exactly. There-

fore its end can also be known exactly. But this will be the time of the resurrection and judgment. Therefore that time is not hidden.

Obj. 2. Further, it is stated (Apoc. xii. 6) that *the woman who represents the Church had a place prepared by God, that there she might feed* (Vulg.,—*they should feed her) a thousand two hundred sixty days.* Again (Dan. xii. 11), a certain fixed number of days is mentioned, which apparently signify years, according to Ezech. iv. 6: *A day for a year, yea a day for a year I have appointed to thee.* Therefore the time of the end of the world and of the resurrection can be known exactly from Holy Writ.

Obj. 3. Further, the state of the New Testament was foreshadowed in the Old Testament. Now we know exactly the time wherein the state of the Old Testament endured. Therefore we can also know exactly the time wherein the state of the New Testament will endure. But the state of the New Testament will last to the end of the world, wherefore it is said (Matth. xxviii. 20): *Behold I am with you . . . to the consummation of the world.* Therefore the time of the end of the world and of the resurrection can be known exactly.

On the contrary, That which is unknown to the angels will be much more unknown to men: because those things to which men attain by natural reason are much more clearly and certainly known to the angels by their natural knowledge. Moreover revelations are not made to men save by means of the angels as Dionysius asserts *(Cœl. Hier.* iv). Now the angels have no exact knowledge of that time, as appears from Matth. xxiv. 36: *Of that day and hour no one knoweth, no not the angels of heaven.* Therefore that time is hidden from men.

Further, the apostles were more cognizant of God's secrets than others who followed them, because they had *the firstfruits of the spirit* (Rom. viii. 23),—*before others in point of time and more abundantly,* as a gloss observes. And yet when they questioned our Lord about this very matter, He answered them (Acts i. 7): *It is not for you to know the times or moments which the Father hath put in His own power.* Much more, therefore, is it hidden from others.

I answer that, As Augustine says *(Qq. lxxxiii, qu.* 58) as to the last age of the human race, which begins from our Lord's coming and lasts until the end of the world, it is uncertain of how many generations it will consist: even so old age, which is man's last age, has no fixed time according to the measure of the other ages, since sometimes alone it lasts as long a time as all the others.* The reason of this is because the exact length of future time cannot be known except either by revelation or by natural reason: and the time until the resurrection cannot be reckoned by natural reason, because the resurrection and the end of the heavenly movement will be simultaneous as stated above (A. 1). And all things that are foreseen by natural reason to happen at a fixed time are reckoned by movement: and it is impossible from the movement of the heaven to reckon its end, for since it is circular, it is for this very reason able by its nature to endure for ever: and consequently the time between this and the resurrection cannot be reckoned by natural reason. Again it cannot be known by revelation, so that all may be on the watch and ready to meet Christ: and for this reason when the apostles asked Him about this, Christ answered (Acts i. 7): *It is not for you to know the times or moments which the Father hath put in His own power*, whereby, as Augustine says *(De Civ. Dei*, xviii. 53): *He scatters the fingers of all calculators and bids them be still.* For what He refused to tell the apostles, He will not reveal to others: wherefore all those who have been misled to reckon the aforesaid time have so far proved to be untruthful; for some, as Augustine says *(ibid.)*, stated that from our Lord's Ascension to His last coming 400 years would elapse, others 500, others 1,000. The falseness of these calculators is evident, as will likewise be the falseness of those who even now cease not to calculate.

Reply Obj. 1. When we know a thing's beginning and also its end it follows that its measure is known to us: wherefore if we know the beginning of a thing the duration of which is measured by the movement of the heaven, we are able to know its end, since the movement of heaven is known to us. But the measure of the duration of the heavenly movement is God's ordinance alone, which is unknown to us. Wherefore however much we may know its beginning, we are unable to know its end.

Reply Obj. 2. The thousand two hundred sixty days mentioned in the Apocalypse *(loc. cit.)* denote all the time during which the Church endures, and not any definite number of years. The reason whereof is because the preaching of Christ on which the Church is built lasted three years and a half, which time contains almost an equal number of days as the aforesaid number. Again the number of days appointed by Daniel does not refer to a number of years to elapse before the end of the world or until the preaching of Antichrist, but to the time of Antichrist's preaching and the duration of his persecution.

Reply Obj. 3. Although the state of the New Testament in general is foreshadowed by the state of the Old Testament it does not follow that individuals correspond to individuals: especially since all the figures of the Old Testament were fulfilled in Christ. Hence Augustine *(De Civ. Dei*, xviii. 52) answers certain persons who wished to liken the number of persecutions suffered by the Church to the number of the plagues of Egypt, in these words: *I do not think that the occurrences in Egypt were in their signification prophetic of these persecutions, although those who think so have shown nicety and ingenuity in adapting them severally the one to the other, not indeed by a prophetic spirit, but by the guess-work of the human mind, which sometimes reaches the truth and sometimes not.* The same remarks would seem applicable to the statements of Abbot Joachim, who by means of such conjectures about the future foretold some things that were true, and in others was deceived.

THIRD ARTICLE

Whether the Resurrection Will Take Place at Night-Time?

We proceed thus to the Third Article:—

Objection 1. It would seem that the resurrection will not be at night-time. For the resurrection will not be *till the heavens be broken* (Job xiv. 12). Now when the heavenly movement ceases, which is signified by its breaking, there will be no time, neither night nor day. Therefore the resurrection will not be at night-time.

Obj. 2. Further, the end of a thing ought to be most perfect. Now the end of time will be then: wherefore it is said (Apoc. x. 6) that *time shall be no longer.* Therefore time ought to be then in its most perfect disposition and consequently it should be the daytime.

Obj. 3. Further, the time should be such as to be adapted to what is done therein: wherefore (John xiii. 30) the night is mentioned as being the time when Judas went out from the fellowship of the light. Now, all things that are hidden at the present time will then be made most manifest, because when the Lord shall come He *will bring to light the hidden things of darkness, and will make manifest the counsels of the hearts* (1 Cor. iv. 5). Therefore it ought to be during the day.

On the contrary, Christ's resurrection is the exemplar of ours. Now Christ's resurrection was at night, as Gregory says in a homily for Easter (xxi, *in Ev.*). Therefore our resurrection will also be at night-time.

Further, the coming of our Lord is compared to the coming of a thief into the house (Luke xii. 39, 40). But the thief comes to the house at night-time. Therefore our Lord will also come in the night. Now, when He comes the resurrection will take place, as stated above (Q. 76, A. 2). Therefore the resurrection will be at night-time.

I answer that, The exact time and hour at which the resurrection will be cannot be known for certain, as stated in the text (iv. *Sent.* D. 43). Nevertheless some assert with sufficient probability that it will be towards the twilight, the moon being in the east and the sun in the west; because the sun and moon are believed to have been created in these positions, and thus their revolutions will be altogether completed by their return to the same point. Wherefore it is said that Christ arose at such an hour.

Reply Obj. 1. When the resurrection occurs, it will not be time but the end of time; because at the very instant that the heavens will cease to move the dead will rise again. Nevertheless the stars will be in the same position as they occupy now at any fixed hour: and accordingly it is said that the resurrection will be at this or that hour.

Reply Obj. 2. The most perfect disposition of time is said to be midday, on account of the light given by the sun. But then the city of God will need neither sun nor moon, because the glory of God will enlighten it (Apoc. xxii. 5). Wherefore in this respect it matters not whether the resurrection be in the day or in the night.

Reply Obj. 3. That time should be adapted to manifestation as regards the things that will happen then, and to secrecy as regards the fixing of the time. Hence either may happen fittingly, namely that the resurrection be in the day or in the night.

FOURTH ARTICLE

Whether the Resurrection Will Happen Suddenly or by Degrees?

We proceed thus to the Fourth Article:—

Objection 1. It would seem that the resurrection will not happen suddenly but by degrees. For the resurrection of the dead is foretold (Ezech. xxxvii. 7, 8) where it is written: *The bones came together . . . and I saw and behold the sinews and the flesh came up upon them, and the skin was stretched out over them, but there was no spirit in them.* Therefore the restoration of the bodies will precede in time their reunion with the souls, and thus the resurrection will not be sudden.

Obj. 2. Further, a thing does not happen suddenly if it require several actions following one another. Now the resurrection requires several actions following one another, namely the gathering of the ashes, the refashioning of

the body, the infusion of the soul. Therefore the resurrection will not be sudden.

Obj. 3. Further, all sound is measured by time. Now the sound of the trumpet will be the cause of the resurrection, as stated above (Q. 76, A. 2). Therefore the resurrection will take time and will not happen suddenly.

Obj. 4. Further, no local movement can be sudden as stated in *De Sensu et Sensato,* vii. Now the resurrection requires local movement in the gathering of the ashes. Therefore it will not happen suddenly.

On the contrary, It is written (1 Cor. xv. 51, 52): *We shall all indeed rise again . . . in a moment, in the twinkling of an eye.* Therefore the resurrection will be sudden.

Further, infinite power works suddenly. But the Damascene says *(De Fide Orthod.* iv): *Thou shalt believe in the resurrection to be wrought by the power of God,* and it is evident that this is infinite. Therefore the resurrection will be sudden.

I answer that, At the resurrection something will be done by the ministry of the angels, and something immediately by the power of God, as state dabove (Q. 76, A. 3). Accordingly that which is done by the ministry of the angels, will not be instantaneous, if by instant we mean an indivisible point of time, but it will be instantaneous if by instant we mean an imperceptible time. But that which will be done immediately by God's power will happen suddenly, namely at the end of the time wherein the work of the angels will be done, because the higher power brings the lower to perfection.

Reply Obj. 1. Ezechiel spoke, like Moses, to a rough people, and therefore, just as Moses divided the works of the six days into days, in order that the uncultured people might be able to understand, although all things were made together according to Augustine *(Gen. ad Lit.* iv), so Ezechiel expressed the various things that will happen in the resurrection, although they will all happen together in an instant.

Reply Obj. 2. Although these actions follow one another in nature, they are all together in time: because either they are together in the same instant, or one is in the instant that terminates the other.

Reply Obj. 3. The same would seem to apply to that sound as to the forms of the sacraments, namely that the sound will produce its effect in its last instant.

Reply Obj. 4. The gathering of the ashes which cannot be without local movement will be done by the ministry of the angels. Hence it will be in time though imperceptible on account of the facility of operation which is competent to the angels.

QUESTION 78

Of the Term "Wherefrom" of the Resurrection

(In Three Articles)

WE must now consider the term *wherefrom* of the resurrection; and under this head there are three points of inquiry: (1) Whether death is the term *wherefrom* of the resurrection in every case? (2) Whether ashes are, or dust? (3) Whether this dust has a natural inclination towards the soul?

FIRST ARTICLE

Whether Death Will Be the Term Wherefrom of the Resurrection in All Cases?

We proceed thus to the First Article:—

Objection 1. It would seem that death will not be the term *wherefrom* of the resurrection in all cases. Because some shall not die but shall be clothed with immortality: for it is said in the creed that our Lord *will come to judge the living and the dead.* Now this cannot refer to the time of judgment, because then all will be alive; therefore this distinction must refer to the previous time, and consequently all will not die before the judgment.

Obj. 2. Further, a natural and common desire cannot be empty and vain, but is fulfilled in some cases. Now according to the Apostle (2 Cor. v. 4) it is a common desire that *we would not be unclothed but clothed upon.* Therefore there will be some who will never be stripped of the body by death, but will be arrayed in the glory of the resurrection.

Obj. 3. Further, Augustine says *(Enchir.* cxv) that the four last petitions of the Lord's prayer refer to the present life: and one of them is: *Forgive us our debts* (Douay,—*trespasses).* Therefore the Church prays that all debts may be forgiven her in this life. Now the Church's prayer cannot be void and not granted: *If you ask the Father anything in My name, He will give it you* (Jo. xvi. 23). Therefore at some time of this life the Church will receive the remission of all debts: and one of the debts to which we are bound by the sin of our first parent is that we be born in original sin. Therefore at some time God will grant to the Church that men be born without original sin. But death is the punishment of original sin. Therefore at the end of the world there will be some men who will not die: and so the same conclusion follows.

Obj. 4. Further, the wise man should always choose the shortest way. Now the shortest way is for the men who shall be found living to be transferred to the impassibility of the resurrection, than for them to die first, and afterwards rise again from death to immortality. Therefore God Who is supremely wise will choose this way for those who shall be found living.

On the contrary, It is written (1 Cor. xv. 36): *That which thou sowest is not quickened except it die first,* and he is speaking of the resurrection of the body as compared to the seed.

Further, it is written *(ibid.* 22): *As in Adam all die, so also in Christ all shall be made alive.* Now all shall be made alive in Christ. Therefore all shall die in Adam: and so all shall rise again from death.

I answer that, The saints differ in speaking on this question, as may be seen in the text (iv. *Sent.* D. 43). However, the safer and more common opinion is that all shall die and rise again from death: and this for three reasons. First, because it is more in accord with Divine justice, which condemned human nature for the sin of its first parent, that all who by the act of nature derive their origin from him should contract the stain of original sin, and consequently be the debtors of death. Secondly, because it is more in agreement with Divine Scripture which foretells the resurrection of all; and resurrection is not predicted properly except of that *which has fallen and perished,* as the Damascene says *(De Fide Orthod.* iv). Thirdly, because it is more in harmony with the order of nature where we find that what is corrupted and decayed is not renewed except by means of corruption: thus vinegar does not become wine unless the vinegar be corrupted and pass into the juice of the grape. Wherefore since human nature has incurred the defect of the necessity of death, it cannot return to immortality save by means of death. It is also in keeping with the order of nature for another reason, because, as it is stated in *Phys.* viii. 1, *the movement of heaven is as a kind of life to all existing in nature,* just as the movement of the heart is a kind of life of the whole body: wherefore even as all the members become dead on the heart ceasing to move, so when the heavenly movement ceases nothing can remain living with that life which was sustained by the influence of that movement. Now such is the life by which we live now: and therefore it follows that those who shall live after the movement of the heaven comes to a standstill must depart from this life.

Reply Obj. 1. This distinction of the dead and the living does not apply to the time itself of the judgment, nor to the whole preceding time, since all who are to be judged were living at some time, and dead at some time: but it applies to that particular time which shall precede the judgment immediately, when, to wit, the signs of the judgment shall begin to appear.

Reply Obj. 2. The perfect desire of the saints cannot be void; but nothing prevents their conditional desire being void. Such is the desire whereby we would not be *unclothed,* but *clothed upon,* namely if that be possible: and this desire is called by some a *velleity.*

Reply Obj. 3. It is erroneous to say that any one except Christ is conceived without original sin, because those who would be conceived without original sin would not need the redemption which was wrought by Christ, and thus Christ would not be the Redeemer of all men.* Nor can it be said that they needed not this redemption, because it was granted to them that they should be conceived without sin. For, this grace was vouchsafed,—either to their parents, that the sin of nature might be healed in them (because so long as that sin remained they were unable to beget without communicating original sin),—or to nature itself which was healed. Now we must allow that every one needs the redemption of Christ personally, and not only by reason of nature, and one cannot be delivered from an evil or absolved from a debt unless one incur the debt or incur the evil: and consequently all could not reap in themselves the fruit of the Lord's prayer, unless all were born debtors and subject to evil. Hence the forgiveness of debts or delivery from evil cannot be applied to one who is born without a debt or free from evil, but only to one who is born with a debt and is afterwards delivered by the grace of Christ. Nor does it follow, if it can be asserted without error that some die not, that they are born without original sin, although death is a punishment of original sin; because God can of His mercy remit the punishment which one has incurred by a past fault, as He forgave the adulterous woman without punishment (Jo. viii): and in like manner He can deliver from death those who have contracted the debt of death by being born in original sin. And thus it does not follow that if they die not, therefore they were born without original sin.

Reply Obj. 4. The shortest way is not always the one to be chosen, but only when it is more or equally adapted for attaining the end. It is not so here, as is clear from what we have said.

* See Editor's note p. 2155

SECOND ARTICLE

Whether All Will Rise Again from Ashes?

We proceed thus to the Second Article:—

Objection 1. It would seem that all will not rise again from ashes. For Christ's resurrection is the exemplar of ours. Yet His resurrection was not from ashes, for His flesh saw not corruption according to Ps. xv. 10; Acts ii. 27, 31. Therefore neither will all rise again from ashes.

Obj. 2. Further, the human body is not always burned. Yet a thing cannot be reduced to ashes unless it be burned. Therefore not all will rise again from ashes.

Obj. 3. Further, the body of a dead man is not reduced to ashes immediately after death. But some will rise again at once after death, according to the text (iv. *Sent.* D. 43), namely those who will be found living. Therefore all will not rise again from ashes.

Obj. 4. Further, the term *wherefrom* corresponds to the term *whereto.* Now the term *whereto* of the resurrection is not the same in the good as in the wicked: *We shall all indeed rise again, but we shall not all be changed* (1 Cor. xv. 51). Therefore the term *wherefrom* is not the same. And thus, if the wicked rise again from ashes, the good will not rise again from ashes.

On the contrary, Haymo says (on Rom. v. 10, *For if when we were enemies*): *All who are born in original sin lie under the sentence: Earth thou art and into earth shalt thou go.* Now all who shall rise again at the general resurrection were born in original sin, either at their birth within the womb or at least at their birth from the womb. Therefore all will rise again from ashes.

Further, there are many things in the human body that do not truly belong to human nature. But all these will be removed. Therefore all bodies must needs be reduced to ashes.

I answer that, The same reasons by which we have shown (A. 1) that all rise again from death prove also that at the general resurrection all will rise again from ashes, unless the contrary, such as the hastening of their resurrection, be vouchsafed to certain persons by a special privilege of grace. For just as holy writ foretells the resurrection, so does it foretell the reformation of bodies (Phil. iii. 21). And thus it follows that even as all die that the bodies of all may be able truly to rise again, so will the bodies of all perish that they may be able to be reformed. For just as death was inflicted by Divine justice as a punishment on man, so was the decay of the body, as appears from Gen. iii. 19, *Earth thou art and into earth shalt thou go.*†

† Vulg.,—*Dust thou art and into dust thou shalt return.*

Moreover the order of nature requires the dissolution not only of the union of soul and body, but also of the mingling of the elements: even as vinegar cannot be brought back to the quality of wine unless it first be dissolved into the prejacent matter: for the mingling of the elements is both caused and preserved by the movement of the heaven, and when this ceases all mixed bodies will be dissolved into pure elements.

Reply Obj. 1. Christ's resurrection is the exemplar of ours as to the term *whereto,* but not as to the term *wherefrom.*

Reply Obj. 2. By ashes we mean all the remains that are left after the dissolution of the body,—for two reasons. First, because it was the common custom in olden times to burn the bodies of the dead, and to keep the ashes, whence it became customary to speak of the remains of a human body as ashes. Secondly, on account of the cause of dissolution, which is the flame of the fomes* whereby the human body is radically infected. Hence, in order to be cleansed of this infection the human body must needs be dissolved into its primary components: and when a thing is destroyed by fire it is said to be reduced to ashes; wherefore the name of ashes is given to those things into which the human body is dissolved.

Reply Obj. 3. The fire that will cleanse the face of the earth will be able to reduce suddenly to ashes the bodies of those that will be found living, even as it will dissolve other mixed bodies into their prejacent matter.

Reply Obj. 4. Movement does not take its species from its term *wherefrom* but from its term *whereto.* Hence the resurrection of the saints which will be glorious must needs differ from the resurrection of the wicked which will not be glorious, in respect of the term *whereto,* and not in respect of the term *wherefrom.* And it often happens that the term *whereto* is not the same, whereas the term *wherefrom* is the same,—for instance, a thing may be moved from blackness to whiteness and to pallor.

THIRD ARTICLE

Whether the Ashes from Which the Human Body Will Be Restored Have any Natural Inclination towards the Soul Which Will Be United to Them?

We proceed thus to the Third Article:—

Objection 1. It would seem that the ashes from which the human body will be restored will have a natural inclination towards the soul which will be united to them. For if they had no inclination towards the soul, they would stand in the same relation to that soul as other ashes. Therefore it would make no difference

--- *Cf. I-II, Q. 82, A. 3.

whether the body that is to be united to that soul were restored from those ashes or from others: and this is false.

Obj. 2. Further, the body is more dependent on the soul than the soul on the body. Now the soul separated from the body is still somewhat dependent on the body, wherefore its movement towards God is retarded on account of its desire for the body, as Augustine says *(Gen. ad Lit.* xii). Much more, therefore, has the body when separated from the soul, a natural inclination towards that soul.

Obj. 3. Further, it is written (Job xx. 11): *His bones shall be filled with the vices of his youth, and they shall sleep with him in the dust.* But vices are only in the soul. Therefore there will still remain in those ashes a natural inclination towards the soul.

On the contrary, The human body can be dissolved into the very elements, or changed into the flesh of other animals. But the elements are homogeneous, and so is the flesh of a lion or other animal. Since then in the other parts of the elements or animals there is no natural inclination to that soul, neither will there be an inclination towards the soul in those parts into which the human body has been changed. The first proposition is made evident on the authority of Augustine *(Enchir.* lxxxviii): *The human body, although changed into the substance of other bodies or even into the elements, although it has become the food and flesh of any animals whatsoever, even of man, will in an instant return to that soul which erstwhile animated it, making it a living and growing man.*

Further, to every natural inclination there corresponds a natural agent: else nature would fail in necessaries. Now the aforesaid ashes cannot be reunited to the same soul by any natural agent. Therefore there is not in them any natural inclination to the aforesaid reunion.

I answer that, Opinion is threefold on this point. For some say that the human body is never dissolved into its very elements; and so there always remains in the ashes a certain force besides the elements, which gives a natural inclination to the same soul. But this assertion is in contradiction with the authority of Augustine quoted above, as well as with the senses and reason: since whatever is composed of contraries can be dissolved into its component parts. Wherefore others say that these parts of the elements into which the human body is dissolved retain more light, through having been united to the soul, and for this reason have a natural inclination to human souls. But this again is nonsensical, since the parts of the elements are of the same nature and have an equal share of light and darkness. Hence we must say differently that in those ashes there is no natural inclination to resurrection, but only by the ordering of Divine providence, which decreed that those ashes should be reunited to the soul: it is on this account that those parts of the elements shall be reunited and not others.

Hence the *Reply* to the *First Objection* is clear.

Reply Obj. 2. The soul separated from the body remains in the same nature that it has when united to the body. It is not so with the body, and consequently the comparison fails.

Reply Obj. 3. These words of Job do not mean that the vices actually remain in the ashes of the dead, but that they remain according to the ordering of Divine justice, whereby those ashes are destined to the restoration of the body which will suffer eternally for the sins committed.

QUESTION 79

Of the Conditions of Those Who Rise Again, and First of Their Identity

(In Three Articles)

IN the next place we must consider the conditions of those who rise again. Here we shall consider: (1) Those which concern the good and wicked in common; (2) those which concern the good only; (3) those which concern only the wicked. Three things concern the good and wicked in common, namely their identity, their integrity, and their quality: and we shall inquire (1) about their identity; (2) about their integrity; (3) about their quality.

Under the first head there are three points of inquiry: (1) Whether the body will rise again identically the same? (2) Whether it will be the selfsame man? (3) Whether it is necessary that the same ashes should return to the same parts in which they were before?

FIRST ARTICLE

Whether in the Resurrection the Soul Will Be Reunited to the Same Identical Body?

We proceed thus to the First Article:—

Objection 1. It would seem that the soul will not be reunited to the same identical body at the resurrection, for *thou sowest not the body that shall be, but bare grain* (1 Cor. xv. 37). Now the Apostle is there comparing death to sowing and resurrection to fructifying. Therefore the same body that is laid aside in death is not resumed at the resurrection.

Obj. 2. Further, to every form some matter is adapted according to its condition, and likewise to every agent some instrument. Now the body is compared to the soul as matter to form, and as instrument to agent. Since then at the resurrection the soul will not be of the same condition as now (for it will be either entirely borne away to the heavenly life to which it adhered while living in the world, or will be cast down into the life of the brutes, if it lived as a brute in this world) it would seem that it will not resume the same body, but either a heavenly or a brutish body.

Obj. 3. Further, after death, as stated above (Q. 78, A. 3), the human body is dissolved into the elements. Now these elemental parts into which the human body has been dissolved do not agree with the human body dissolved into them, except in primary matter, even as any other elemental parts agree with that same body. But if the body were to be formed from those other elemental parts, it would not be described as identically the same. Therefore neither will it be the selfsame body if it be restored from these parts.

Obj. 4. Further, there cannot be numerical identity where there is numerical distinction of essential parts. Now the form of the mixed body, which form is an essential part of the human body, as being its form, cannot be resumed in numerical identity. Therefore the body will not be identically the same. The minor is proved thus: That which passes away into complete nonentity cannot be resumed in identity. This is clear from the fact that there cannot be identity where there is distinction of existence: and existence, which is the act of a being, is differentiated by being interrupted, as is any interrupted act. Now the form of a mixed body passes away into complete nonentity by death, since it is a bodily form, and so also do the contrary qualities from which the mixture results. Therefore the form of a mixed body does not return in identity.

On the contrary, It is written (Job xix. 26): *In my flesh I shall see God my Saviour* (Vulg., —*my God*), where he is speaking of the vision after the resurrection, as appears from the preceding words: *In the last day I shall rise out of the earth.* Therefore the selfsame body will rise again.

Further, the Damascene says *(De Fide Orthod.* iv. 27): *Resurrection is the second rising of that which has fallen.* But the body which we have now fell by death. Therefore it will rise again the same identically.

I answer that, On this point the philosophers erred and certain modern heretics err. For some of the philosophers allowed that souls separated from bodies are reunited to bodies, yet they erred in this in two ways. First, as to the mode of reunion, for some held the separated soul to be naturally reunited to a body by the way of generation. Secondly, as to the body to which it was reunited, for they held that this second union was not with the selfsame body that was laid aside in death, but with another, sometimes of the same, sometimes of a different species. Of a different species when the soul while existing in the body had led a life contrary to the ordering of reason: wherefore it passed after death from the body of a man into the body of some other animal to whose manner of living it had conformed in this life, for instance into the body of a dog on account of lust, into the body of a lion on account of robbery and violence, and so forth,—and into a body of the same species when the soul has led a good life in the body, and having after death experienced some happiness, after some centuries began to wish to return to the body; and thus it was reunited to a human body.

This opinion arises from two false sources. The first of these is that they said that the soul is not united to the body essentially as form to matter, but only accidentally, as mover to the thing moved,* or as a man to his clothes. Hence it was possible for them to maintain that the soul pre-existed before being infused into the body begotten of natural generation, as also that it is united to various bodies. The second is that they held intellect not to differ from sense except accidentally, so that man would be said to surpass other animals in intelligence, because the sensitive power is more acute in him on account of the excellence of his bodily complexion; and hence it was possible for them to assert that man's soul passes into the soul of a brute animal, especially when the human soul has been habituated to brutish actions. But these two sources are refuted by the Philosopher *(De Anima,* ii. 1), and in consequence of these being refuted, it is clear that the above opinion is false.

In like manner the errors of certain heretics are refuted. Some of them fell into the aforesaid opinions of the philosophers: while others held that souls are reunited to heavenly bodies, or again to bodies subtle as the wind, as Gregory relates of a certain Bishop of Constantinople, in his exposition of Job xix. 26, *In my flesh I shall see my God,* etc. Moreover these same errors of heretics may be refuted by the fact that they are prejudicial to the truth of resurrection as witnessed to by Holy

*Cf. P. I, Q. 76, A. 1.

Writ. For we cannot call it resurrection unless the soul return to the same body, since resurrection is a second rising, and the same thing rises that falls: wherefore resurrection regards the body which after death falls rather than the soul which after death lives. And consequently if it be not the same body which the soul resumes, it will not be a resurrection, but rather the assuming of a new body.

Reply Obj. 1. A comparison does not apply to every particular, but to some. For in the sowing of grain, the grain sown and the grain that is born thereof are neither identical, nor of the same condition, since it was first sown without a husk, yet is born with one: and the body will rise again identically the same, but of a different condition, since it was mortal and will rise in immortality.

Reply Obj. 2. The soul rising again and the soul living in this world differ, not in essence but in respect of glory and misery, which is an accidental difference. Hence it follows that the body in rising again differs, not in identity, but in condition, so that a difference of bodies corresponds proportionally to the difference of souls.

Reply Obj. 3. That which is understood as though it were in matter before its form remains in matter after corruption, because when that which comes afterwards is removed that which came before may yet remain. Now, as the Commentator observes on the First Book of *Physics* and in *De Substantia Orbis,* in the matter of things subject to generation and corruption, we must presuppose undeterminate dimensions, by reason of which matter is divisible, so as to be able to receive various forms in its various parts. Wherefore after the separation of the substantial form from matter, these dimensions still remain the same: and consequently the matter existing under those dimensions, whatever form it receive, is more identified with that which was generated from it, than any other part of matter existing under any form whatever. Thus the matter that will be brought back to restore the human body will be the same as that body's previous matter.

Reply Obj. 4. Even as a simple quality is not the substantial form of an element, but its proper accident, and the disposition whereby its matter is rendered proper to such a form; so the form of a mixed body, which form is a quality resulting from simple qualities reduced to a mean, is not the substantial form of the mixed body, but its proper accident, and the disposition whereby the matter is in need of the form. Now the human body has no substantial form besides this form of the mixed body, except the rational soul, for if it had any previous substantial form, this would give it substantial being, and would establish it in the genus of substance: so that the soul would be united to a body already established in the genus of substance, and thus the soul would be compared to the body as artificial forms are to their matter, in respect of their being established in the genus of substance by their matter. Hence the union of the soul to the body would be accidental, which is the error of the ancient philosophers refuted by the Philosopher *(De Anima,* ii. 2) * It would also follow that the human body and each of its parts would not retain their former names in the same sense, which is contrary to the teaching of the Philosopher *(ibid.* 1). Therefore since the rational soul remains, no substantial form of the human body falls away into complete nonentity. And the variation of accidental forms does not make a difference of identity. Therefore the selfsame body will rise again, since the selfsame matter is resumed as stated in a previous reply *(ad* 2).

SECOND ARTICLE
Whether It Will Be Identically the Same Man That Shall Rise Again?

We proceed thus to the Second Article:—

Objection 1. It would seem that it will not be identically the same man that shall rise again. For according to the Philosopher *(De Gener.* ii): *Whatsoever things are changed in their corruptible substance are not repeated identically.* Now such is man's substance in his present state. Therefore after the change wrought by death the selfsame man cannot be repeated.

Obj. 2. Further, where there is a distinction of human nature there is not the same identical man: wherefore Socrates and Plato are two men and not one man, since each has his own distinct human nature. Now the human nature of one who rises again is distinct from that which he has now. Therefore he is not the same identical man. The minor can be proved in two ways. First, because human nature which is the form of the whole is not both form and substance as the soul is, but is a form only. Now such like forms pass away into complete nonentity, and consequently they cannot be restored. Secondly, because human nature results from union of parts. Now the same identical union as that which was heretofore cannot be resumed, because repetition is opposed to identity, since repetition implies number, whereas identity implies unity, and these are incompatible with one another. But resurrection is a repeated union: therefore the union is not the same, and consequently there is not the same human nature nor the same man.

* Cf. P. I, Q. 76, A. 1.

Obj. 3. Further, one same man is not several animals: wherefore if it is not the same animal it is not the same identical man. Now where sense is not the same, there is not the same animal, since animal is defined from the primary sense, namely touch. But sense, as it does not remain in the separated soul (as some maintain), cannot be resumed in identity. Therefore the man who rises again will not be the same identical animal, and consequently he will not be the same man.

Obj. 4. Further, the matter of a statue ranks higher in the statue than the matter of a man does in man: because artificial things belong to the genus of substance by reason of their matter, but natural things by reason of their form, as appears from the Philosopher *(Phys.* ii. 1), and again from the Commentator *(De Anima,* ii). But if a statue is remade from the same brass, it will not be the same identically. Therefore much less will it be identically the same man if he be reformed from the same ashes.

On the contrary, It is written (Job. xix. 27): *Whom I myself shall see . . . and not another,* and he is speaking of the vision after the resurrection. Therefore the same identical man will rise again.

Further, Augustine says *(De Trin.* viii. 5) that *to rise again is naught else but to live again.* Now unless the same identical man that died return to life, he would not be said to live again. Therefore he would not rise again, which is contrary to faith.

I answer that, The necessity of holding the resurrection arises from this,—that man may obtain the last end for which he was made; for this cannot be accomplished in this life, nor in the life of the separated soul, as stated above (Q. 75, AA. 1, 2): otherwise man would have been made in vain, if he were unable to obtain the end for which he was made. And since it behooves the end to be obtained by the selfsame thing that was made for that end, lest it appear to be made without purpose, it is necessary for the selfsame man to rise again; and this is effected by the selfsame soul being united to the selfsame body. For otherwise there would be no resurrection properly speaking, if the same man were not reformed. Hence to maintain that he who rises again is not the selfsame man is heretical, since it is contrary to the truth of Scripture which proclaims the resurrection.

Reply Obj. 1. The Philosopher is speaking of repetition by movement or natural change. For he shows the difference between the recurrence that occurs in generation and corruption and that which is observed in the movement of the heavens. Because the selfsame heaven by local movement returns to the beginning of its movement, since it has a moved incorruptible substance. On the other hand, things subject to generation and corruption return by generation to specific but not numerical identity, because from man blood is engendered, from blood seed, and so on until a man is begotten, not the selfsame man, but the man specifically. In like manner from fire comes air, from air water, from water earth, whence fire is produced, not the selfsame fire, but the same in species. Hence it is clear that the argument, so far as the meaning of the Philosopher is concerned, is not to the point.

We may also reply that the form of other things subject to generation and corruption is not subsistent of itself, so as to be able to remain after the corruption of the composite, as it is with the rational soul. For the soul, even after separation from the body, retains the being which accrues to it when in the body, and the body is made to share that being by the resurrection, since the being of the body and the being of the soul in the body are not distinct from one another, otherwise the union of soul and body would be acidental. Consequently there has been no interruption in the substantial being of man, as would make it impossible for the selfsame man to return on account of an interruption in his being, as is the case with other things that are corrupted, the being of which is interrupted altogether, since their form remains not, and their matter remains under another being.

Nevertheless neither does the selfsame man recur by natural generation, because the body of the man begotten is not composed of the whole body of his begetter: hence his body is numerically distinct, and consequently his soul and the whole man.

Reply Obj. 2. There are two opinions about humanity and about any form of a whole. For some say that the form of the whole and the form of the part are really one and the same: but that it is called the form of the part inasmuch as it perfects the matter, and the form of the whole inasmuch as the whole specific nature results therefrom. According to this opinion humanity is really nothing else than the rational soul: and so, since the selfsame rational soul is resumed, there will be the same identical humanity, which will remain even after death, albeit not under the aspect of humanity, because the composite does not derive the specific nature from a separated humanity.

The other opinion, which seems nearer the truth, is Avicenna's, according to whom the form of the whole is not the form of a part only, nor some other form besides the form of the part, but is the whole resulting from the composition of form and matter, embracing both within itself. This form of the whole is called the essence or quiddity. Since then at the resurrection there will be the selfsame body, and the selfsame rational soul, there will be, of necessity, the same humanity.

The first argument proving that there will be a distinction of humanity was based on the supposition that humanity is some distinct form supervening form and matter; which is false.

The second reason does not disprove the identity of humanity, because union implies action or passion, and though there be a different union, this cannot prevent the identity of humanity, because the action and passion from which humanity resulted are not of the essence of humanity, wherefore a distinction on their part does not involve a distinction of humanity: for it is clear that generation and resurrection are not the selfsame movement. Yet the identity of the rising man with the begotten man is not hindered for this reason: and in like manner neither is the identity of humanity prevented, if we take union for the relation itself: because this relation is not essential to but concomitant with humanity, since humanity is not one of those forms that are composition or order *(Phys. ii. 1)*, as are the forms of things produced by art, so that if there be another distinct composition there is another distinct form of a house.

Reply Obj. 3. This argument affords a very good proof against those who held a distinction between the sensitive and rational souls in man: because in that case the sensitive soul in man would not be incorruptbile, as neither is it in other animals; and consequently in the resurrection there would not be the same sensitive soul, and consequently neither the same animal nor the same man.

But if we assert that in man the same soul is by its substance both rational and sensitive, we shall encounter no difficulty in this question, because animal is defined from sense, i.e. the sensitive soul as from its essential form: whereas from sense, i.e. the sensitive power, we know its definition as from an accidental form *that contributes more than any other to our knowledge of the quiddity (De Anima,* i. 1). Accordingly after death there remains the sensitive soul, even as the rational soul, according to its substance: whereas the sensitive powers, according to some, do not remain. And since these powers are accidental properties, diversity on their part cannot prevent the identity of the whole animal, not even of the animal's parts: nor are powers to be called perfections or acts of organs unless as principles of action, as heat in fire.

Reply Obj. 4. A statue may be considered in two ways. either as a particular substance, or as something artificial. And since it is placed in the genus of substance by reason of its matter, it follows that if we consider it as a particular substance, it is the selfsame statue that is remade from the same matter. On the other hand, it is placed in the genus of artificial things inasmuch as it has an accidental form which, if the statue be destroyed, passes away also. Consequently it does not return identically the same, nor can the statue be identically the same. But man's form, namely the soul, remains after the body has perished: wherefore the comparison fails.

THIRD ARTICLE

Whether the Ashes of the Human Body Must Needs, by the Resurrection, Return to the Same Parts of the Body That Were Dissolved into Them?

We proceed thus to the Third Article:—

Objection 1. It would seem necessary for the ashes of the human body to return, by the resurrection, to the same parts that were dissolved into them. For, according to the Philosopher, *as the whole soul is to the whole body, so is a part of the soul to a part of the body, as sight to the pupil (De Anima,* ii. 1). Now it is necessary that after the resurrection the body be resumed by the same soul. Therefore it is also necessary for the same parts of the body to return to the same limbs, in which they were perfected by the same parts of the soul.

Obj. 2. Further, difference of matter causes difference of identity. But if the ashes return not to the same parts, each part will not be remade from the same matter of which it consisted before. Therefore they will not be the same identically. Now if the parts are different the whole will also be different, since parts are to the whole as matter is to form *(Phys.* ii. 3). Therefore it will not be the selfsame man; which is contrary to the truth of the resurrection.

Obj. 3. Further, the resurrection is directed to the end that man may receive the meed of his works. Now different parts of the body are employed in different works, whether of merit or of demerit. Therefore at the resurrection each part must needs return to its former state that it may be rewarded in due measure.

On the contrary, Artificial things are more dependent on their matter than natural things. Now in artificial things, in order that the same artificial thing be remade, from the same matter, there is no need for the parts to be brought back to the same position. Neither therefore is it necessary in man.

Further, change of an accident does not cause a change of identity. Now the situation of parts is an accident. Therefore its change in a man does not cause a change of identity.

I answer that, In this question it makes a difference whether we ask what can be done without prejudice to identity, and what will be done for the sake of congruity. As regards the first it must be observed that in man we may speak of parts in two ways: first as of the various parts of a homogeneous whole, for instance the various parts of flesh, or the various parts of bone; secondly, as of various parts of various species of a heterogeneous whole, for instance bone and flesh. Accordingly if it be said that one part of matter will return to another part of the same species, this causes no change except in the position of the parts: and change of position of parts does not change the species in homogeneous wholes: and so if the matter of one part return to another part, this is nowise prejudicial to the identity of the whole. Thus is it in the example given in the text (iv. *Sent.* D. 44), because a statue, after being remade, is identically the same, not as to its form, but as to its matter, in respect of which it is a particular substance, and in this way a statue is homogeneous, although it is not according to its artificial form. But if it be said that the matter of one part returns to another part of another species, it follows of necessity that there is a change not only in the position of parts, but also in their identity: yet so that the whole matter, or something belonging to the truth of human nature in one is transferred to another; but not if what was superfluous in one part is transferred to another. Now the identity of parts being taken away, the identity of the whole is removed, if we speak of essential parts, but not if we speak of accidental parts, such as hair and nails, to which apparently Augustine refers *(De Civ. Dei,* xxii). It is thus clear how the transference of matter from one part of another destroys the identity, and how it does not.

But speaking of the congruity, it is more probable that even the parts will retain their position at the resurrection, especially as regards the essential and organic parts, although perhaps not as regards the accidental parts, such as nails and hair.

Reply Obj. 1. This argument considers organic or heterogeneous parts, but no homogeneous or like parts.

Reply Obj. 2. A change in the position of the parts of matter does not cause a change of identity, although difference of matter does.

Reply Obj. 3. Operation, properly speaking, is not ascribed to the part but to the whole, wherefore the reward is due, not to the part but to the whole.

QUESTION 80

Of the Integrity of the Bodies in the Resurrection

(In Five Articles)

WE must next consider the integrity of the bodies in the resurrection. Under this head there are five points of inquiry: (1) Whether all the members of the human body will rise again therein? (2) Whether the hair and nails will? (3) Whether the humors will? (4) Whether whatever the body contained belonging to the truth of human nature will rise again? (5) Whether whatever it contained materially will rise again?

FIRST ARTICLE

Whether All the Members of the Human Body Will Rise Again?

We proceed thus to the First Article:—

Objection 1. It would seem that not all the members of the human body will rise again. For if the end be done away it is useless to repair the means. Now the end of each member is its act. Since then nothing useless is done in the Divine works, and since the use of certain members is not fitting to man after the resurrection, especially the use of the genital members, for then they *shall neither marry, nor be married* (Matth. xxii. 30), it would seem that not all the members shall rise again.

Obj. 2. Further, the entrails are members: and yet they will not rise again. For they can neither rise full, since thus they contain impurities, nor empty, since nothing is empty in nature. Therefore the members shall not all rise again.

Obj. 3. Further, the body shall rise again that it may be rewarded for the works which the soul did through it. Now the member of which a thief has been deprived for theft, and who has afterwards done penance and is saved, cannot be rewarded at the resurrection, neither for any good deed, since it has not co-operated in any, nor for evil deeds, since the punishment of the member would redound to the punishment of man. Therefore the members will not all rise again.

On the contrary, The other members belong more to the truth of human nature than hair and nails. Yet these will be restored to man at the resurrection according to the text (iv. *Sent.* D. 4). Much more therefore does this apply to the other members.

Further, *The works of God are perfect* (Deut. xxxii. 4). But the resurrection will be the work of God. Therefore man will be re-made perfect in all his members.

I answer that, As stated in *De Anima,* ii. 4, the soul stands in relation to the body not only as its form and end, but also as efficient cause, For the soul is compared to the body as art to the thing made by art, as the Philosopher says *(De Anim. Gener.* ii. 4), and whatever is shown forth explicitly in the product of art is all contained implicitly and originally in the art. In like manner whatever appears in the parts of the body is all contained originally and, in a way, implicitly in the soul. Thus just as the work of an art would not be perfect, if its product lacked any of the things contained in the art, so neither could man be perfect, unless the whole that is contained enfolded in the soul be outwardly unfolded in the body, nor would the body correspond in full proportion to the soul. Since then at the resurrection it behooves man's body to correspond entirely to the soul, for it will not rise again except according to the relation it bears to the rational soul, it follows that man also must rise again perfect, seeing that he is thereby repaired in order that he may obtain his ultimate perfection. Consequently all the members that are now in man's body must needs be restored at the resurrection.

Reply Obj. 1. The members may be considered in two ways in relation to the soul: either according to the relation of matter to form, or according to the relation of instrument to agent, since *the whole body is compared to the whole soul in the same way as one part is to another (De Anima,* ii. 1). If then the members be considered in the light of the first relationship, their end is not operation, but rather the perfect being of the species, and this is also required after the resurrection: but if they be considered in the light of the second relationship, then their end is operation. And yet it does not follow that when the operation fails the instrument is useless, because an instrument serves not only to accomplish the operation of the agent, but also to show its virtue. Hence it will be necessary for the virtue of the soul's powers to be shown in their bodily instruments, even though they never proceed to action, so that the wisdom of God be thereby glorified.

Reply Obj. 2. The entrails will rise again in the body even as the other members: and they will be filled not with vile superfluities but with goodly humors.

Reply Obj. 3. The acts whereby we merit are not the acts, properly speaking, of hand or foot but of the whole man; even as the work of art is ascribed not to the instrument but to the craftsman. Therefore though the member which was cut off before a man's repentance did not co-operate with him in the state wherein he merits glory, yet man himself merits that the whole man may be rewarded, who with his whole being serves God.

SECOND ARTICLE

Whether the Hair and Nails Will Rise Again in the Human Body?

We proceed thus to the Second Article:—

Objection 1. It would seem that the hair and nails will not rise again in the human body. For just as hair and nails result from the surplus of food, so do urine, sweat and other superfluities or dregs. But these will not rise again with the body. Neither therefore will hair and nails.

Obj. 2. Further, of all the superfluities that are produced from food, seed comes nearest to the truth of human nature, since though superfluous it is needed. Yet seed will not rise again in the human body. Much less therefore will hair and nails.

Obj. 3. Further, nothing is perfected by a rational soul that is not perfected by a sensitive soul. But hair and nails are not perfected by a sensitive soul, for *we do not feel with them (De Anima,* i. 5: iii. 13). Therefore since the human body rises not again except because it is perfected by a rational soul, it would seem that the hair and nails will not rise again.

On the contrary, It is written (Luke xxi. 18): *A hair of your head shall not perish.*

Further, hair and nails were given to man as an ornament. Now the bodies of men, especially of the elect, ought to rise again with all their adornment. Therefore they ought to rise again with the hair.

I answer that, The soul is to the animated body, as art is to the work of art, and is to the parts of the body as art to its instruments: wherefore an animated body is called an organic body. Now art employs certain instruments for the accomplishment of the work intended, and these instruments belong to the primary intention of art: and it also uses other instruments for the safe-keeping of the principal instruments, and these belong to the secondary intention of art: thus the art of warfare employs a sword for fighting, and a sheath for the safe-keeping of the sword. And so among the parts of an animated body, some are directed to the accomplishment of the souls' operations, for instance the heart, liver, hand, foot; while others are directed to the safe-keeping of the other parts as leaves to cover fruit; and thus hair and nails are in man for the protection of other parts. Consequently,

although they do not belong to the primary perfection of the human body, they belong to the secondary perfection: and since man will rise again with all the perfections of his nature, it follows that hair and nails will rise again in him.

Reply Obj. 1. Those superfluities are voided by nature, as being useful for nothing. Hence they do not belong to the perfection of the human body. It is not so with the superfluities which nature reserves for the production of hair and nails which she needs for the protection of the members.

Reply Obj. 2. Seed is not required for the perfection of the individual, as hair and nails are, but only for the protection of the species.

Reply Obj. 3. Hair and nails are nourished and grow, and so it is clear that they share in some operation, which would not be possible unless they were parts in some way perfected by the soul. And since in man there is but one soul, namely the rational soul, it is clear that they are perfected by the rational soul, although not so far as to share in the operation of sense, as neither do bones, and yet it is certain that these will rise again and that they belong to the integrity of the individual.

THIRD ARTICLE

Whether the Humors Will Rise Again in the Body?

We proceed thus to the Third Article:—

Objection 1. It would seem that the humors will not rise again in the body. For it is written (1 Cor. xv. 50): *Flesh and blood cannot possess the kingdom of God.* Now blood is the chief humor. Therefore it will not rise again in the blessed, who will possess the kingdom of God, and much less in others.

Obj. 2. Further, humors are intended to make up for the waste. Now after the resurrection there will be no waste. Therefore the body will not rise again with humors.

Obj. 3. Further, that which is in process of generation in the human body is not yet perfected by the rational soul. Now the humors are still in process of generation because they are potentially flesh and bone. Therefore they are not yet perfected by the rational soul. Now the human body is not directed to the resurrection except in so far as it is perfected by the rational soul. Therefore the humors will not rise again.

On the contrary, Whatever enters into the constitution of the human body will rise again with it. Now this applies to the humors, as appears from the statement of Augustine *(De Spir. et Anima,* xv) that *the body consists of functional members; the functional members of homogeneous parts; and the homogeneous parts of humors.* Therefore the humors will rise again in the body.

Further, our resurrection will be conformed to the resurrection of Christ. Now in Christ's resurrection His blood rose again, else the wine would not now be changed into His blood in the Sacrament of the altar. Therefore the blood will rise again in us also, and in like manner the other humors.

I answer that, Whatever belongs to the integrity of human nature in those who take part in the resurrection will rise again, as stated above (AA. 1, 2). Hence whatever humidity of the body belongs to the integrity of human nature must needs rise again in man. Now there is a threefold humidity in man. There is one which occurs as receding from the perfection of the individual,—either because it is on the way to corruption, and is voided by nature, for instance urine, sweat, matter, and so forth,—or because it is directed by nature to the preservation of the species in some individual, either by the act of the generative power, as seed, or by the act of the nutritive power, as milk. None of these humidities will rise again, because they do not belong to the perfection of the person rising again.

The second kind of humidity is one that has not yet reached its ultimate perfection, which nature achieves in the individual, yet it is directed thereto by nature: and this is of two kinds. For there is one kind that has a definite form and is contained among the parts of the body, for instance the blood and the other humors which nature has directed to the members that are produced or nourished therefrom: and yet they have certain definite forms like the other parts of the body, and consequently will rise again with the other parts of the body: while another kind of humidity is in transition from form to form, namely from the form of humor to the form of member. Humidities of this kind will not rise again, because after the resurrection each part of the body will be established in its form, so that one will not pass into another. Wherefore this humidity that is actually in transition from one form to another will not rise again. Now this humidity may be considered in a twofold state,—either as being at the beginning of its transformation, and thus it is called *ros,* namely the humidity that is found in the cavities of the smaller veins,—or as in the course of transformation and already beginning to undergo alteration, and thus it is called *cambium:* but in neither state will it rise again. The third kind of humidity is that which has already reached its ultimate perfection that nature intends in the body of the individual, and has already undergone transformation and become incorporate with the members. This

is called *gluten,* and since it belongs to the members it will rise again just as the members will.

Reply Obj. 1. In these words of the Apostle flesh and blood do not denote the substance of flesh and blood but deeds of flesh and blood, which are either deeds of sin or the operations of the animal life. Or we may say with Augustine in his letter to Consentius (*Ep.* cxlvi) that *flesh and blood here signify the corruption which is now predominant in flesh and blood;* wherefore the Apostle's words continue: *Neither shall corruption possess incorruption.*

Reply Obj. 2. Just as the members that serve for generation will be after the resurrection for the integrity of human nature, and not for the operation accomplished now by them, so will the humors be in the body not to make up for waste, but to restore the integrity of human nature and to show forth its natural power.

Reply Obj. 3. Just as the elements are in the course of generation in relation to mixed bodies, because they are their matter, yet not so as to be always in transition when in the mixed body, so too are the humors in relation to the members. And for this reason as the elements in the parts of the universe have definite forms, by reason of which they, like mixed bodies, belong to the perfection of the universe, so too the humors belong to the perfection of the human body, just as the other parts do, although they do not reach its entire perfection, as the other parts do, and although the elements have not perfect forms as mixed bodies have. But as all the parts of the universe receive their perfection from God, not equally, but each one according to its mode, so too the humors are in some way perfected by the rational soul, yet not in the same measure as the more perfect parts.

FOURTH ARTICLE

Whether Whatever in the Body Belonged to the Truth of Human Nature Will Rise Again in It?

We proceed thus to the Fourth Article:—

Objection 1. It would seem that what was in the body, belonging to the truth of human nature, will not all rise again in it. For food is changed into the truth of human nature. Now sometimes the flesh of the ox or of other animals is taken as food. Therefore if whatever belonged to the truth of human nature will rise again, the flesh of the ox or of other animals will also rise again: which is inadmissible.

Obj. 2. Further, Adam's rib belonged to the truth of human nature in him, as ours does in us. But Adam's rib will rise again not in Adam but in Eve, else Eve would not rise again at all since she was made from that rib. Therefore whatever belonged in man to the truth of human nature will not all rise again in him.

Obj. 3. Further, it is impossible for the same thing from different men to rise again. Yet it is possible for something in different men to belong to the truth of human nature, for instance if a man were to partake of human flesh which would be changed into his substance. Therefore there will not rise again in man whatever belonged in him to the truth of human nature.

Obj. 4. Further, if it be said that not all the flesh partaken of belongs to the truth of human nature, and that consequently some of it may possibly rise again in the one man and some in the other,—on the contrary: That which is derived from one's parents would especially seem to belong to the truth of human nature. But if one who partook of nothing but human flesh were to beget children, that which his child derives from him must needs be of the flesh of other men partaken of by his father, since the seed is from the surplus of food, as the Philosopher proves (*De Gen. Animal.* i). Therefore what belongs to the truth of human nature in that child belonged also to the truth of human nature in other men of whose flesh his father had partaken.

Obj. 5. Further, if it be said that what was changed into seed was not that which belonged to the truth of human nature in the flesh of the men eaten, but something not belonging to the truth of human nature,—on the contrary: Let us suppose that some one is fed entirely on embryos in which seemingly there is nothing but what belongs to the truth of human nature, since whatever is in them is derived from the parents. If then the surplus food be changed into seed, that which belonged to the truth of human nature in the embryos—and after these have received a rational soul, the resurrection applies to them—must needs belong to the truth of human nature in the child begotten of that seed. And thus, since the same cannot rise again in two subjects, it will be impossible for whatever belonged to the truth of human nature in both to rise again in both of them.

On the contrary, Whatever belonged to the truth of human nature was perfected by the rational soul. Now it is through being perfected by the rational soul that the human body is directed to the resurrection. Therefore whatever belonged to the truth of human nature will rise again in each one.

Further, if anything belonging to the truth of human nature in a man be taken from his body, this will not be the perfect body of a man. Now all imperfection of a man will be removed at the resurrection, especially in the elect, to whom it was promised (Luke xxi. 18) that not a hair of their head should perish. Therefore whatever belonged to the truth of human nature in a man will rise again in him.

I answer that, Everything is related to truth in the same way as to being (Met. ii), because a thing is true when it is as it appears to him who actually knows it. For this reason Avicenna (*Met.* ii) says that *the truth of anything is a property of the being immutably attached thereto.* Accordingly a thing is said to belong to the truth of human nature, because it belongs properly to the being of human nature, and this is what shares the form of human nature, just as true gold is what has the true form of gold whence gold derives its proper being. In order therefore to see what it is that belongs to the truth of human nature, we must observe that there have been three opinions on the question For some have maintained that nothing begins anew to belong to the truth of human nature, and that whatever belongs to the truth of human nature, all of it belonged to the truth of human nature when this was created; and that this multiplies by itself, so that it is possible for the seed whereof the child is begotten to be detached therefrom by the begetter, and that again the detached part multiplies in the child, so that he reaches perfect quantity by growth, and so on; and that thus was the whole human race multiplied. Wherefore according to this opinion, whatever is produced by nourishment, although it seem to have the appearance of flesh and blood, does not belong to the truth of human nature.

Others held that something new is added to the truth of human nature by the natural transformation of the food into the human body, if we consider the truth of human nature in the species to the preservation of which the act of the generative power is directed: but that if we consider the truth of human nature in the individual, to the preservation and perfection of which the act of the nutritive power is directed, that which is added by food belongs to the truth of the human nature of the individual, not primarily but secondarily. For they assert that the truth of human nature, first and foremost, consists in the radical humor, that namely which is begotten of the seed of which the human race was originally fashioned: and that what is changed from food into true flesh and blood does not belong principally to the truth of human nature in this particular individual, but secondarily: and that nevertheless this can belong principally to the truth of human nature in another individual who is begotten of the seed of the former. For they assert that seed is the surplus from food, either mingled with something belonging principally to the truth of human nature in the begetter, according to some, or without any such admixture, as others maintain. And thus the nutrimental humor in one becomes the radical humor in another.

The third opinion is that something new begins to belong principally to the truth of human nature even in this individual, because distinction in the human body does not require that any signate material part must needs remain throughout the whole lifetime; any signate part one may take is indifferent to this, whereas it remains always as regards what belongs to the species in it, albeit as regards what is material therein it may ebb and flow. And thus the nutrimental humor is not distinct from the radical on the part of its principle (so that it be called radical when begotten of the seed, and nutrimental when produced by the food), but rather on the part of the term, so that it be called radical when it reaches the term of generation by the act of the generative, or even nutritive power, but nutrimental, when it has not yet reached this term, but is still on the way to give nourishment.

These three opinions have been more fully exposed and examined in the Second Book (ii. *Sent.* D. 30); wherefore there is no need for repetition here, except in so far as the question at issue is concerned. It must accordingly be observed that this question requires different answers according to these opinions.

For the first opinion on account of its explanation of the process of multiplication is able to admit perfection of the truth of human nature, both as regards the number of individuals and as regards the due quantity of each individual, without taking into account that which is produced from food; for this is not added except for the purpose of resisting the destruction that might result from the action of natural heat, as lead is added to silver lest it be destroyed in melting. Wherefore since at the resurrection it behooves human nature to be restored to its perfection, nor does the natural heat tend to destroy the natural humor, there will be no need for anything resulting from food to rise again in man, but that alone will rise again which belonged to the truth of the human nature of the individual, and this reaches the aforesaid perfection in number and quantity by being detached and multiplied.

The second opinion, since it maintains that what is produced from food is needed for the perfection of quantity in the individual and for the multiplication that results from generation, must needs admit that something of this product from food shall rise again: not all, however, but only so much as is required for

the perfect restoration of human nature in all its individuals. Hence this opinion asserts that all that was in the substance of the seed will rise again in this man who was begotten of this seed; because this belongs chiefly to the truth of human nature in him: while of that which afterwards he derives from nourishment, only so much will rise again in him as is needed for the perfection of his quantity; and not all, because this does not belong to the perfection of human nature, except in so far as nature requires it for the perfection of quantity. Since however this nutrimental humor is subject to ebb and flow the restoration will be effected in this order, that what first belonged to the substance of a man's body, will all be restored, and of that which was added secondly, thirdly, and so on, as much as is required to restore quantity. This is proved by two reasons. First, because that which was added was intended to restore what was wasted at first, and thus it does not belong principally to the truth of human nature to the same extent as that which came first. Secondly, because the addition of extraneous humor to the first radical humors results in the whole mixture not sharing the truth of the specific nature as perfectly as the first did: and the Philosopher instances as an example *(De Gener.* i) the mixing of water with wine, which always weakens the strength of the wine, so that in the end the wine becomes watery: so that although the second water be drawn into the species of wine, it does not share the species of wine as perfectly as the first water added to the wine. Even so that which is secondly changed from food into flesh does not so perfectly attain to the species of flesh as that which was changed first, and consequently does not belong in the same degree to the truth of human nature nor to the resurrection. Accordingly it is clear that this opinion maintains that the whole of what belongs to the truth of human nature principally will rise again, but not the whole of what belongs to the truth of human nature secondarily.

The third opinion differs somewhat from the second and in some respects agrees with it. It differs in that it maintains that whatever is under the form of flesh and bone all belongs to the truth of human nature, because this opinion does not distinguish as remaining in man during his whole lifetime any signate matter that belongs essentially and primarily to the truth of human nature, besides something ebbing and flowing, that belongs to the truth of human nature merely on account of the perfection of quantity, and not on account of the primary being of the species, as the second opinion asserted. But it states that all the parts that are not beside the intention of the nature generated belong to the truth of human nature, as regards what they have of the species, since thus they remain; but not as regards what they have of matter, since thus they are indifferent to ebb and flow: so that we are to understand that the same thing happens in the parts of one man as in the whole population of a city, for each individual is cut off from the population by death, while others take their place: wherefore the parts of the people flow back and forth materially, but remain formally, since these others occupy the very same offices and positions from which the former were withdrawn, so that the commonwealth is said to remain the selfsame. In like manner, while certain parts are on the ebb and others are being restored to the same shape and position, all the parts flow back and forth as to their matter, but remain as to their species; and nevertheless the selfsame man remains.

On the other hand, The third opinion agrees with the second, because it holds that the parts which come secondly do not reach the perfection of the species so perfectly as those which come first: and consequently the third opinion asserts that the same thing rises again in man as the second opinion maintains, but not for quite the same reason. For it holds that the whole of what is produced from the seed will rise again, not because it belongs to the truth of human nature otherwise than that which comes after, but because it shares the truth of human nature more perfectly: which same order the second opinion applied to those things that are produced afterwards from food, in which point also these two opinions agree.

Reply Obj. 1. A natural thing is what it is, not from its matter but from its form: wherefore, although that part of matter which at one time was under the form of bovine flesh rises again in man under the form of human flesh, it does not follow that the flesh of an ox rises again, but the flesh of a man: else one might conclude that the clay from which Adam's body was fashioned shall rise again. The second opinion, however, grants this argument.

Reply Obj. 2. That rib did not belong to the perfection of the individual in Adam, but was directed to the multiplication of the species. Hence it will rise again not in Adam but in Eve, just as the seed will rise again, not in the begetter, but in the begotten.

Reply Obj. 3. According to the first opinion it is easy to reply to this argument, because the flesh that is eaten never belonged to the truth of human nature in the eater, but it did belong to the truth of human nature in him whose flesh was eaten: and thus it will rise again in the latter but not in the former. But according to the second and third opinions, each one will rise again in that wherein he approached nearest to the perfect participation of the virtue of the species, and if he approached equally in both, he will rise again in that wherein he was first, because in that he first was directed to the resurrection by union with the rational soul of that man. Hence if there were any surplus in the flesh eaten, not belonging to the truth of human nature in the first man, it will be possible for it to rise again in the second: otherwise what belonged to the resurrection in the first will rise again in him and not in the second; but in the second its place is taken either by something of that which was the product from other food, or if he never partook of any other food than human flesh, the substitution is made by Divine power so far as the perfection of quantity requires, as it does in those who die before the perfect age. Nor does this derogate from numerical identity, as neither does the ebb and flow of parts.

Reply Obj. 4. According to the first opinion this argument is easily answered. For that opinion asserts that the seed is not from the surplus food: so that the flesh eaten is not changed into the seed whereof the child is begotten. But according to the other two opinions we must reply that it is impossible for the whole of the flesh eaten to be changed into seed, because it is after much separation that the seed is distilled from the food, since seed is the ultimate surplus of food. That part of the eaten flesh which is changed into seed belongs to the truth of human nature in the one born of the seed more than in the one of whose flesh the seed was the product. Hence, according to the rule already laid down (*ad* 3), whatever was changed into the seed will rise again in the person born of the seed; while the remaining matter will rise again in him of whose flesh the seed was the product.

Reply Obj. 5. The embryo is not concerned with the resurrection before it is animated by a rational soul, in which state much has been added to the seminal substance from the substance of food, since the child is nourished in the mother's womb. Consequently on the supposition that a man partook of such food, and that some one were begotten of the surplus thereof, that which was in the seminal substance will indeed rise again in the one begotten of that seed; unless it contain something that would have belonged to the seminal substance in those from whose flesh being eaten the seed was produced, for this would rise again in the first but not in the second. The remainder of the eaten flesh, not being changed into seed, will clearly rise again in the first, the Divine power supplying deficiences in both,

The first opinion is not troubled by this objection, since it does not hold the seed to be from the surplus food: but there are many other reasons against it as may be seen in the Second Book (ii. *Sent.* D. 30; P. I, Q. 119, A. 2).

FIFTH ARTICLE

Whether Whatever Was Materially in a Man's Members Will All Rise Again?

We proceed thus to the Fifth Article:—

Objection 1. It would seem that whatever was materially in a man's members will all rise again. For the hair, seemingly, is less concerned in the resurrection than the other members. Yet whatever was in the hair will all rise again, if not in the hair, at least in other parts of the body, as Augustine says *(De Civ. Dei,* xxii) quoted in the text (iv. *Sent.* D. 44). Much more therefore whatever was materially in the other members will all rise again.

Obj. 2. Further, just as the parts of the flesh are perfected as to species by the rational soul, so are the parts as to matter. But the human body is directed to the resurrection through being perfected by a rational soul. Therefore not only the parts of species but also the parts of matter will all rise again.

Obj. 3. Further, the body derives its totality from the same cause as it derives its divisibility into parts. But division into parts belongs to a body in respect of matter the disposition of which is quantity in respect of which it is divided. Therefore totality is ascribed to the body in respect of its parts of matter. If then all the parts of matter rise not again, neither will the whole body rise again: which is inadmissible.

On the contrary, The parts of matter are not permanent in the body but ebb and flow, as stated in *De Gener.* i. If, therefore, all the parts of matter, which remain not but ebb and flow, rise again, either the body of one who rises again will be very dense, or it will be immoderate in quantity.

Further, whatever belongs to the truth of human nature in one man can all be a part of matter in another man, if the latter were to partake of his flesh. Therefore if all the parts of matter in one man were to rise again it follows that in one man there will rise again that which belongs to the truth of human nature in another: which is absurd.

I answer that, What is in man materially, is not directed to the resurrection, except in so far as it belongs to the truth of human nature, because it is in this respect that it bears a relation to the human souls. Now all that is in man materially belongs indeed to the truth of human nature in so far as it has something of the species, but not all, if we consider the totality of matter; because all the matter that was in a man from the beginning of his life to the end would surpass the quantity due to his species, as the third opinion states, which opinion seems to me more probable than the others. Wherefore the whole of what is in man will rise again, if we speak of the totality of the species which is dependent on quantity, shape, position and order of parts, but the whole will not rise again if we speak of the totality of matter. The second and first opinions, however, do not make this distinction, but distinguish between parts both of which have the species and matter. But these two opinions agree in that they both state what is produced from the seed will all rise again even if we speak of totality of matter: while they differ in this that the first opinion maintains that nothing will rise again of that which was engendered from food, whereas the second holds that something, but not all, thereof will rise again, as stated above (A. 4).

Reply Obj. 1. Just as all that is in the other parts of the body will rise again, if we speak of the totality of the species, but not if we speak of material totality, so is it with the hair. In the other parts something accrues from nourishment which causes growth, and this is reckoned as another part, if we speak of totality of species, since it occupies another place and position in the body, and is under other parts of dimension: and there accrues something which does not cause growth, but serves to make up for waste by nourishing; and this is not reckoned as another part of the whole considered in relation to the species, since it does not occupy another place or position in the body than that which was occupied by the part that has passed away: although it may be reckoned another part if we consider the totality of matter. The same applies to the hair. Augustine, however, is speaking of the cutting of hair that was a part causing growth of the body; wherefore it must needs rise again, not however as regards the quantity of hair, lest it should be immoderate, but it will rise again in other parts as deemed expedient by Divine providence. Or else he refers to the case when something will be lacking to the other parts, for then it will be possible for this to be supplied from the surplus of hair.

Reply Obj. 2. According to the third opinion parts of species are the same as parts of matter: for the Philosopher does not make this distinction *(De Gener.* i) in order to distinguish different parts, but in order to show that the same parts may be considered both in respect of species, as to what belongs to the form and species in them, and in respect of matter, as to that which is under the form and species. Now it is clear that the matter of the flesh has no relation to the rational soul except in so far as it is under such a form, and consequently by reason thereof it is directed to the resurrection. But the first and second opinions which draw a distinction between parts of species and parts of matter say that although the rational soul perfects both parts, it does not perfect parts of matter except by means of the parts of species, wherefore they are not equally directed to the resurrection.

Reply Obj. 3. In the matter of things subject to generation and corruption it is necessary to presuppose indefinite dimensions before the reception of the substantial form. Consequently division which is made according to these dimensions belongs properly to matter. But complete and definite quantity comes to matter after the substantial form; wherefore division that is made in reference to definite quantity regards the species especially when definite position of parts belongs to the essence of the species, as in the human body.

QUESTION 81

Of the Quality of Those Who Rise Again

(In Four Articles)

WE must now consider the quality of those who rise again. Under this head there are four points of inquiry: (1) Whether all will rise again in the youthful age? (2) Whether they will be of equal stature? (3) Whether all will be of the same sex? (4) Whether they will rise again to the animal life?

FIRST ARTICLE

Whether All Will Rise Again of the Same Age?

We proceed thus to the First Article:—

Objection 1. It would seem that all will not rise again of the same, namely the youthful age. Because God will take nothing pertaining to man's perfection from those who rise again, especially from the blessed. Now age pertains to the perfection of man, since old age is the age that demands reverence. Therefore the old will not rise again of a youthful age.

Obj. 2. Further, age is reckoned according to the length of past time. Now it is impossible for past time not to have passed. Therefore it is impossible for those who were of greater age to be brought back to a youthful age.

Obj. 3. Further, that which belonged most to the truth of human nature in each individual will especially rise again in him. Now the sooner a thing was in man the more would it seem to have belonged to the truth of human nature, because in the end, through the strength of the species being weakened the human body is likened to watery wine according to the Philosopher (*De Gener.* i). Therefore if all are to rise again of the same age, it is more fitting that they should rise again in the age of childhood.

On the contrary, It is written (Eph. iv. 13): *Until we all meet . . . unto a perfect man, unto the measure of the age of the fulness of Christ.*

Now Christ rose again of youthful age, which begins about the age of thirty years, as Augustine says (*De Civ. Dei*, xxii). Therefore others also will rise again of a youthful age.

Further, man will rise again at the most perfect stage of nature. Now human nature is at the most perfect stage in the age of youth. Therefore all will rise again of that age.

I answer that, Man will rise again without any defect of human nature, because as God founded human nature without a defect, even so will He restore it without defect. Now human nature has a twofold defect. First, because it has not yet attained to its ultimate perfection. Secondly, because it has already gone back from its ultimate perfection. The first defect is found in children, the second in the aged: and consequently in each of these human nature will be brought by the resurrection to the state of its ultimate perfection which is in the youthful age, at which the movement of growth terminates, and from which the movement of decrease begins.

Reply Obj. 1. Old age calls for reverence, not on account of the state of the body which is at fault; but on account of the soul's wisdom which is taken for granted on account of its being advanced in years. Wherefore in the elect there will remain the reverence due to old age on account of the fulness of Divine wisdom which will be in them, but the defect of old age will not be in them.

Reply Obj. 2. We speak of age not as regards the number of years, but as regards the state which the human body acquires from years. Hence Adam is said to have been formed in the youthful age on account of the particular condition of body which he had at the first day of his formation. Thus the argument is not to the point.

Reply Obj. 3. The strength of the species is said to be more perfect in a child than in a young man, as regards the ability to transform nourishment in a certain way, even as it is more perfect in the seed than in the mature man. In youth, however, it is more perfect as regards the term of completion. Wherefore that which belonged principally to the truth of human nature will be brought to that perfection which it has in the age of youth, and not to that perfection which it has in the age of a child, wherein the humors have not yet reached their ultimate disposition.

SECOND ARTICLE

Whether All Will Rise Again of the Same Stature?

We proceed thus to the Second Article:—

Objection 1. It would seem that all will rise again of the same stature. For just as man is measured by dimensive quantity, so is he by the quantity of time. Now the quantity of time will be reduced to the same measure in all, since all will rise again of the same age. Therefore the dimensive quantity will also be reduced to the same measure in all, so that all will rise again of the same stature.

Obj. 2. Further, the Philosopher says *(De Anima,* ii. 4) that *all things in nature have a certain limit and measure of size and growth.* Now this limitation can only arise by virtue of the form, with which the quantity as well as all the other accidents ought to agree. Therefore since all men have the same specific form, there should be the same measure of quantity in respect of matter in all, unless an error should occur. But the error of nature will be set right at the resurrection. Therefore all will rise again of the same stature.

Obj. 3. Further, it will be impossible for man in rising again to be of a quantity proportionate to the natural power which first formed his body; for otherwise those who could not be brought to a greater quantity by the power of nature will never rise again of a greater quantity, which is false. Therefore that quantity must needs be proportionate to the power which will restore the human body by the resurrection, and to the matter from which it is restored. Now the selfsame, namely the Divine, power will restore all bodies; and all the ashes from which the human bodies will be restored are equally disposed to receive the action of that power. Therefore the resurrection of all men will bring them to the same quantity: and so the same conclusion follows.

On the contrary, Natural quantity results from each individual's nature. Now the nature of the individual will not be altered at the resurrection. Therefore neither will its natural quantity. But all are not of the same natural quantity. Therefore all will not rise again of the same stature.

Further, human nature will be restored by resurrection unto glory or unto punishment. But there will not be the same quantity of glory or punishment in all those who rise again. Neither therefore will there be the same quantity of stature.

I answer that, At the resurrection human nature will be restored not only in the selfsame species but also in the selfsame individual: and consequently we must observe in the resurrection what is requisite not only to the specific but also to the individual nature. Now the specific nature has a certain quantity which it neither exceeds nor fails without error, and yet this quantity has certain degrees of latitude and is not to be attached to one fixed measure; and each individual in the human species aims at some degree of quantity befitting his individual nature within the bounds of that latitude, and reaches it at the end of his growth, if there has been no error in the working of nature, resulting in the addition of something to or the subtraction of something from the aforesaid quantity: the measure whereof is gauged according to the proportion of heat as expanding, and of humidity as expansive, in point of which all are not of the same power. Therefore all will not rise again of the same quantity, but each one will rise again of that quantity which would have been his at the end of his growth if nature had not erred or failed: and the Divine power will subtract or supply what was excessive or lacking in man.

Reply Obj. 1. It has already been explained (A. 1, *ad* 2) that all are said to rise again of the same age, not as though the same length of time were befitting to each one, but because the same state of perfection will be in all, which state is indifferent to a great or small quantity.

Reply Obj. 2. The quantity of a particular individual corresponds not only to the form of the species, but also to the nature or matter of the individual: wherefore the conclusion does not follow.

Reply Obj. 3. The quantity of those who will be raised from the dead is not proportionate to the restoring power, because the latter does not belong to the power of the body,—nor to the ashes, as to the state in which they are before the resurrection,— but to nature which the individual had at first. Nevertheless if the formative power on account of some defect was unable to effect the due quantity that is befitting to the species, the Divine power will supply the defect at the resurrection, as in dwarfs, and in like manner in those who by immoderate size have exceeded the due bounds of nature.

THIRD ARTICLE

Whether All Will Rise Again of the Male Sex?

We proceed thus to the Third Article:—

Objection 1. It would seem that all will rise again of the male sex. For it is written (Ephes. iv. 13) that we shall all meet *unto a perfect man,* etc. Therefore there will be none but the male sex.

Obj. 2. Further, in the world to come all pre-eminence will cease, as a gloss observes on 1 Cor. xv. 24. Now woman is subject to man in the natural order. Therefore women will rise again not in the female but in the male sex.

Obj. 3. Further, that which is produced incidentally and beside the intention of nature will not rise again, since all error will be removed at the resurrection. Now the female sex is produced beside the intention of nature, through a fault in the formative power of the seed, which is unable to bring the matter of the fetus to the male form: wherefore the Philosopher says *(De Animal.* xvi, i.e. *De Generat. Animal.* ii) that *the female is a misbegotten male.* Therefore the female sex will not rise again.

On the contrary, Augustine says *(De Civ. Dei,* xxii): *Those are wiser, seemingly, who doubt not that both sexes will rise again.*

Further, at the resurrection God will restore man to what He made him at the creation. Now He made woman from the man's rib (Gen. ii. 22). Therefore He will also restore female sex at the resurrection.

I answer that, Just as, considering the nature of the individual, a different quantity is due to different men, so also, considering the nature of the individual, a different sex is due to different men. Moreover, this same diversity is becoming to the perfection of the species, the different degrees whereof are filled by this very difference of sex and quantity. Wherefore just as men will rise again of various stature, so will they rise again of different sex. And though there be difference of sex there will be no shame in seeing one another, since there will no lust to invite them to shameful deeds which are the cause of shame.

Reply Obj. 1. When it is said: We shall all meet *Christ unto a perfect man,* this refers not to the male sex but to the strength of soul which will be in all, both men and women.

Reply Obj. 2. Woman is subject to man on account of the frailty of nature, as regards both vigor of soul and strength of body. After the resurrection, however, the difference in those points will be not on account of the difference of sex, but by reason of the difference of merits. Hence the conclusion does not follow.

Reply Obj. 3. Although the begetting of a woman is beside the intention of a particular nature, it is in the intention of universal nature, which requires both sexes for the perfection of the human species. Nor will any defect result from sex as stated above *(ad 2).*

FOURTH ARTICLE

Whether All Will Rise Again to Animal Life So As to Exercise the Functions of Nutrition and Generation?

We proceed thus to the Fourth Article:—

Objection 1. It would seem that they will rise again to the animal life, or in other words that they will make use of the acts of the nutritive and generative powers. For our resurrection will be conformed to Christ's. But Christ is said to have ate after His resurrection (Jo. xxi, Luke xxiv). Therefore, after the resurrection men will eat, and in like manner beget.

Obj. 2. Further, the distinction of sexes is directed to generation; and in like manner the instruments which serve the nutritive power are directed to eating. Now man will rise again with all these. Therefore he will exercise the acts of the generative and nutritive powers.

Obj. 3. Further, the whole man will be beatified both in soul and in body. Now beatitude or happiness, according to the Philosopher *(Ethic.* i. 7), consists in a perfect operation. Therefore it must needs be that all the powers of the soul and all the members should have their respective acts after the resurrection. And so the same conclusion follows as above.

Obj. 4. Further, after the resurrection there will be perfect joy in the blessed. Now such a joy includes all pleasures, since *happiness* according to Boëthius *is a state rendered perfect by the accumulation of all goods (De Consol.* iii), and the perfect is that which lacks nothing. Since then there is much pleasure in the act of the generative and nutritive powers it would seem that such acts belonging to animal life will be in the blessed, and much more in others, who will have less spiritual bodies.

On the contrary, It is written (Matth. xxii. 30): *In the resurrection they shall neither marry nor be married.*

Further, generation is directed to supply the defect resulting from death, and to the multiplication of the human race: and eating is directed to make up for waste, and to increase quantity. But in the state of the resurrection the human race will already have the number of individuals preordained by God, since generation will continue up to that point. In like manner each man will rise again in due quantity; neither will death be any more, nor any waste affect the parts of man. Therefore the acts of the generative and nutritive powers would be void of purpose.

I answer that, The resurrection will not be necessary to man on account of his primary perfection, which consists in the integrity of those things that belong to his nature, since man can attain to this in his present state of life by the action of natural causes; but the necessity of the resurrection regards the attainment of his ultimate perfection, which consists in his reaching his ultimate end. Consequently those natural operations which are directed to cause or preserve the primary perfection of human nature will not be in the resurrection: such are the actions of the animal life in man, the action of the elements on one another, and the movement of the heavens; wherefore all these will cease at the resurrection. And since to eat, drink, sleep, beget, pertain to the animal life, being directed to the primary perfection of nature, it follows that they will not be in the resurrection.

Reply Obj. 1. When Christ partook of that meal, His eating was an act, not of necessity as though human nature needed food after the resurrection, but of power, so as to prove that He had resumed the true human nature which He had in that state wherein He ate and drank with His disciples. There will be no need of such proof at the general resurrection, since it will be evident to all. Hence Christ is said to have ate by dispensation in the sense in which lawyers say that a *dispensation is a relaxation of the general law*: because Christ made an exception to that which is common

to those who rise again (namely not to partake of food) for the aforesaid motive. Hence the argument does not prove.

Reply Obj. 2. The distinction of sexes and the difference of members will be for the restoration of the perfection of human nature both in the species and in the individual. Hence it does not follow that they are without purpose, although they lack their animal operations.

Reply Obj. 3. The aforesaid operations do not belong to man as man, as also the Philosopher states *(Ethic.* x. 7), wherefore the happiness of the human body does not consist therein. But the human body will be glorified by an overflow from the reason whereby man is man, inasmuch as the body will be subject to reason.

Reply Obj. 4. As the Philosopher says *(Ethic.* vii. 12, x. 5), the pleasures of the body are medicinal, because they are applied to man for the removal of weariness; or again, they are unhealthy, in so far as man indulges in those pleasures inordinately, as though they were real pleasures: just as a man whose taste is vitiated delights in things which are not delightful to the healthy. Consequently it does not follow that such pleasures as these belong to the perfection of beatitude, as the Jews and Turks maintain, and certain heretics known as the Chiliasts asserted; who, moreover, according to the Philosopher's teaching, would seem to have an unhealthy appetite, since according to him none but spiritual pleasures are pleasures simply, and to be sought for their own sake: wherefore these alone are requisite for beatitude.

QUESTION 82

Of the Impassibility of the Bodies of the Blessed after Their Resurrection

(In Four Articles)

WE must now consider the conditions under which the blessed rise again, and (1) the impassibility of their bodies: (2) their subtlety: (3) their agility: (4) their clarity. Under the first head there are four points of inquiry: rise again impassible in body? (2) Whether all will be equally impassible? (3) Whether this impassibility renders the glorious bodies (1) Whether at the resurrection the saints will insensible? (4) Whether in them all the senses are in act?

FIRST ARTICLE

Whether the Bodies of the Saints Will Be Impassible After the Resurrection?

We proceed thus to the First Article:—

Objection 1. It seems that the bodies of the saints will not be impassible after the

resurrection. For everything mortal is passible. But man, after the resurrection, will be *a mortal rational animal,* for such is the definition of man, which will never be dissociated from him. Therefore the body will be passible.

Obj. 2. Further, whatever is in potentiality to have the form of another thing is passible in relation to something else; for this is what is meant by being passive to another thing *(De Gener.* i). Now the bodies of the saints will be in potentiality to the form of another thing after the resurrection; since matter, according as it is under one form, does not lose its potentiality to another form. But the bodies of the saints after the resurrection will have matter in common with the elements, because they will be restored out of the same matter of which they are now composed. Therefore they will be in potentiality to another form, and thus will be passible.

Obj. 3. Further, according to the Philosopher (*De Gener.* i), contraries have a natural inclination to be active and passive towards one another. Now the bodies of the saints will be composed of contraries after the resurrection, even as now. Therefore they will be passible.

Obj. 4. Further, in the human body the blood and humors will rise again, as stated above (Q. 80, AA. 3, 4). Now, sickness and such like passions arise in the body through the antipathy of the humors. Therefore the bodies of the saints will be passible after the resurrection.

Obj. 5. Further, actual defect is more inconsistent with perfection than potential defect. But possibility denotes merely potential defect. Since then there will be certain actual defects in the bodies of the blessed, such as the scars of the wounds in the martyrs, even as they were in Christ, it would seem that their perfections will not suffer, if we grant their bodies to be passible.

On the contrary, Everything passible is corruptible, because *increase of passion results in loss of substance.** Now the bodies of the saints will be incorruptible after the resurrection, according to 1 Cor. xv. 42, *It is sown in corruption, it shall rise in incorruption.* Therefore they will be impassible.

Further, the stronger is not passive to the weaker. But no body will be stronger than the bodies of the saints, of which it is written (1 Cor. xv. 43): *It is sown in weakness, it shall rise in power.* Therefore they will be impassible.

I answer that, We speak of a thing being *passive* in two ways.† First in a broad sense, and thus every reception is called a passion, whether the thing received be fitting to the receiver and perfect it, or contrary to it and corrupt it. The glorious bodies are not said to be impassible by the removal of this kind of passion, since nothing pertaining to perfection is to be removed from them. In another way we use the word *passive* properly, and thus the Damascene defines passion (*De Fide Orthod.* ii. 22) as being *a movement contrary to nature.* Hence an immoderate movement of the heart is called its passion, but a moderate movement is called its operation. The reason of this is that whatever is patient is drawn to the bounds of the agent, since the agent assimilates the patient to itself, so that, therefore, the patient as such is drawn beyond its own bounds within which it was confined. Accord-

ingly taking passion in its proper sense there will be no potentiality to passion in the bodies of the saints after resurrection; wherefore they are said to be impassible.

The reason however of this impassibility is assigned differently by different persons. Some ascribe it to the condition of the elements, which will be different then from what it is now. For they say that the elements will remain, then, as to substance, yet that they will be deprived of their active and passive qualities. But this does not seem to be true: because the active and passive qualities belong to the perfection of the elements, so that if the elements were restored without them in the body of the man that rises again, they would be less perfect than now. Moreover since these qualities are the proper accidents of the elements, being caused by their form and matter, it would seem most absurd for the cause to remain and the effect to be removed. Wherefore others say that the qualities will remain, but deprived of their proper activities, the Divine power so doing for the preservation of the human body. This however would seem to be untenable, since the action and passion of the active and passive qualities is necessary for the mixture (of the elements), and according as one or the other preponderates the mixed (bodies) differ in their respective complexions, and this must apply to the bodies of those who rise again, for they will contain flesh and bones and like parts, all of which demand different complexions. Moreover, according to this, impassibility could not be one of their gifts, because it would not imply a disposition in the impassible substance, but merely an external preventive to passion, namely the power of God, which might produce the same effect in a human body even in this state of life. Consequently others say that in the body itself there will be something preventing the passion of a glorified body, namely the nature of a fifth‡ or heavenly body, which they maintain enters into the composition of a human body, to the effect of blending the elements together in harmony so as to be fitting matter for the rational soul; but that in this state of life, on account of the preponderance of the elemental nature, the human body is passible like other elements, whereas in the resurrection the nature of the fifth body will predominate, so that the human body will be made impassible in likeness to the heavenly body. But this cannot stand, because the fifth body does not enter materially into the composition of a human body, as was proved above (ii. *Sent.* D. 12, Q. I, A. 1). Moreover it is absurd to say that a natural power, such as the power

---

* Aristotle, *Topic.* vi. 1.   † Cf. I-II, Q. 22, A. 1.   ‡ The other four being the elements. This fifth element was known to the peripatetic philosophers as the quintessence, of which they held heavenly bodies to be formed.

of a heavenly body, should endow the human body with a property of glory, such as the impassibility of a glorified body, since the Apostle ascribes to Christ's power the transformation of the human body, because *such as is the heavenly, such also are they that are heavenly* (1 Cor. xv. 48), and *He will reform the body of our lowness, made like to the body of His glory, according to the operation whereby also He is able to subdue all things unto Himself* (Phil. iii. 21). And again, a heavenly nature cannot exercise such power over the human body as to take from it its elemental nature which is passible by reason of its essential constituents. Consequently we must say otherwise that all passion results from the agent overcoming the patient, else it would not draw it to its own bounds. Now it is impossible for agent to overcome patient except through the weakening of the hold which the form of the patient has over its matter, if we speak of the passion which is against nature, for it is of passion in this sense that we are speaking now: for matter is not subject to one of two contraries, except through the cessation or at least the diminution of the hold which the other contrary has on it. Now the human body and all that it contains will be perfectly subject to the rational soul, even as the soul will be perfectly subject to God. Wherefore it will be impossible for the glorified body to be subject to any change contrary to the disposition whereby it is perfected by the soul; and consequently those bodies will be impassible.

Reply Obj. 1. According to Anselm *(Cur Deus Homo,* ii. 11), *mortal is included in the philosophers' definition of man, because they did not believe that the whole man could be ever immortal,* for they had no experience of man otherwise than in this state of mortality. Or we may say that since, according to the Philosopher *(Met.* vi. 12), essential differences are unknown to us, we sometimes employ accidental differences in order to signify essential differences from which the accidental differences result. Hence *mortal* is put in the definition of man, not as though mortality were essential to man, but because that which causes passibility and mortality in the present state of life, namely composition of contraries, is essential to man, but it will not cause it then, on account of the triumph of the soul over the body.

Reply Obj. 2. Potentiality is twofold, tied and free: and this is true not only of active but also of passive potentiality. For the form ties the potentiality of matter, by determining it to one thing, and it is thus that It overcomes it. And since in corruptible things form does not perfectly overcome matter, it cannot tie

it completely so as to prevent it from sometimes receiving a disposition contrary to the form through some passion. But in the saints after the resurrection, the soul will have complete dominion over the body, and it will be altogether impossible for it to lose this dominion, because it will be immutably subject to God, which was not the case in the state of innocence. Consequently those bodies will retain substantially the same potentiality as they have now to another form; yet that potentiality will remain tied by the triumph of the soul over the body, so that it will never be realized by actual passion.

Reply Obj. 3. The elemental qualities are the instruments of the soul, as stated in *De Anima,* ii, text. 38, *seq.,* for the heat of fire in an animal's body is directed in the act of nutrition by the soul's power. When, however, the principal agent is perfect, and there is no defect in the instrument, no action proceeds from the instrument, except in accordance with the disposition of the principal agent. Consequently in the bodies of the saints after the resurrection, no action or passion will result from the elemental qualities that is contrary to the disposition of the soul which has the preservation of the body in view.

Reply Obj. 4. According to Augustine *(Ep. ad Consent.* cxlvi) *the Divine power is able to remove* whatever qualities He will *from this visible and tangible body, other qualities remaining.* Hence even as in a certain respect *He deprived the flames of the Chaldees' furnace of the power to burn, since the bodies of the children were preserved without hurt, while in another respect that power remained, since those flames consumed the wood, so will He remove passibility from the humors while leaving their nature unchanged.* It has been explained in the Article how this is brought about.

Reply Obj. 5. The scars of wounds will not be in the saints, nor were they in Christ, in so far as they imply a defect, but as signs of the most steadfast virtue whereby the saints suffered for the sake of justice and faith: so that this will increase their own and others' joy (cf. P. III, Q. 54, A. 4, *ad* 3). Hence Augustine says *(De Civ. Dei,* xxii. 19) : *We feel an undescribable love for the blessed martyrs so as to desire to see in that kingdom the scars of the wounds in their bodies, which they bore for Christ's name. Perchance indeed we shall see them, for this will not make them less comely but more glorious. A certain beauty will shine in them, a beauty though in the body, yet not of the body but of virtue.* Nevertheless those martyrs who have been maimed and deprived of their limbs will not be without those limbs in the resurrection of the dead, for to them it is said (Luke xxi. 18): *A hair of your head shall not perish.*

SECOND ARTICLE

Whether All Will Be Equally Impassible?

We proceed thus to the Second Article:—

Objection 1. It would seem that all will be equally impassible. For a gloss on 1 Cor. xv. 42, *It is sown in corruption,* says that *all have equal immunity from suffering.* Now the gift of impassibility consists in immunity from suffering. Therefore all will be equally impassible.

Obj. 2. Further, negations are not subject to be more or less. Now impassibility is a negation or privation of passibility. Therefore it cannot be greater in one subject than in another.

Obj. 3. Further, a thing is more white if it have less admixture of black. But there will be no admixture of passibility in any of the saints' bodies. Therefore they will all be equally impassible.

On the contrary, Reward should be proportionate to merit. Now some of the saints were greater in merit than others. Therefore, since impassibility is a reward, it would seem to be greater in some than in others.

Further, impassibility is condivided with the gift of clarity. Now the latter will not be equal in all, according to 1 Cor. xv. 41. Therefore neither will impassibility be equal in all.

I answer that, Impassibility may be considered in two ways, either in itself, or in respect of its cause. If it be considered in itself, since it denotes a mere negation or privation, it is not subject to be more or less, but will be equal in all the blessed. On the other hand, if we consider it in relation to its cause, thus it will be greater in one person than in another. Now its cause is the dominion of the soul over the body, and this dominion is caused by the soul's unchangeable enjoyment of God. Consequently in one who enjoys God more perfectly, there is a greater cause of impassibility.

Reply Obj. 1. This gloss is speaking of impassibility in itself and not in relation to its cause.

Reply Obj. 2. Although negations and privations considered in themselves are not increased nor diminished, yet they are subject to increase and diminution in relation to their causes. Thus a place is said to be more darksome from having more and greater obstacles to light.

Reply Obj. 3. Some things increase not only by receding from their contrary, but also by approach to a term: thus light increases. Con-

sequently impassibility also is greater in one subject than in another, although there is no passibility remaining in any one.

THIRD ARTICLE

Whether Impassibility Excludes Actual Sensation from Glorified Bodies?

We proceed thus to the Third Article:—

Objection 1. It would seem that impassibility excludes actual sensation from glorified bodies. For according to the Philosopher (*De Anima,* ii. 11), *sensation is a kind of passion.* But the glorified bodies will be impassible. Therefore they will not have actual sensation.

Obj. 2. Further, natural alteration precedes spiritual* alteration, just as natural being precedes intentional being. Now glorified bodies, by reason of their impassibility, will not be subject to natural alteration. Therefore they will not be subject to spiritual alteration which is requisite for sensation.

Obj. 3. Further, whenever actual sensation is due to a new perception, there is a new judgment. But in that state there will be no new judgment, because *our thoughts will not then be unchangeable,* as Augustine says (*De Trin.* xv. 16). Therefore there will be no actual sensation.

Obj. 4. Further, when the act of one of the soul's powers is intense, the acts of the other powers are remiss. Now the soul will be supremely intent on the act of the contemplative power in contemplating God. Therefore the soul will have no actual sensation whatever.

On the contrary, It is written (*Apoc.* i. 7): *Every eye shall see Him.* Therefore there will be actual sensation.

Further, according to the Philosopher (*De Anima,* i. 2) *the animate is distinct from the inanimate by sensation and movement.* Now there will be actual movement since they *shall run to and fro like sparks among the reeds* (Wis. iii. 7). Therefore there will also be actual sensation.

I answer that, All are agreed that there is some sensation in the bodies of the blessed: else the bodily life of the saints after the resurrection would be likened to sleep rather than to vigilance. Now this is not befitting that perfection, because in sleep a sensible body is not in the ultimate act of life, for which reason sleep is described as half-life.† But there is a difference of opinion as to the mode of sensation.

For some say that the glorified bodies will be impassible, and consequently *not suscep-*

---

* *Animalem,* as though it were derived from *animus*—the mind. Cf. P. I-II, Q. 50, A. 1, 3ᵐ ; Q. 52, A. 1, 3ᵐ.

† This is what Aristotle says: *The good and the bad are in sleep least distinguishable: hence men say that for half their lives there is no difference between the happy and the unhappy* (*Ethic.* i. 13).

tible to impressions from without,* and much less so than the heavenly bodies, because they will have actual sensations, not by receiving species from sensibles, but by emission of species. But this is impossible, since in the resurrection the specific nature will remain the same in man and in all his parts. Now the nature of sense is to be a passive power as the Philosopher proves (*De Anima,* ii, text. 51, 54). Wherefore if the saints, in the resurrection, were to have sensations by emitting and not by receiving species, sense in them would be not a passive but an active power, and thus it would not be the same specifically with sense as it is now, but would be some other power bestowed on them; for just as matter never becomes form, so a passive power never becomes active. Consequently others say that the senses will be actualized by receiving species, not indeed from external sensibles, but by an outflow from the higher powers, so that as now the higher powers receive from the lower, so on the contrary the lower powers will then receive from the higher. But this mode of reception does not result in real sensation, because every passive power, according to its specific nature, is determined to some special active principle, since a power as such bears relation to that with respect to which it is said to be the power. Wherefore since the proper active principle in external sensation is a thing existing outside the soul and not an intention thereof existing in the imagination or reason, if the organ of sense be not moved by external things, but by the imagination or other higher powers, there will be no true sensation. Hence we do not say that madmen or other witless persons (in whom there is this kind of outflow of species towards the organs of sense, on account of the powerful influence of the imagination) have real sensations, but that it seems to them that they have sensations. Consequently we must say with others that sensation in glorified bodies will result from the reception of things outside the soul. It must, however, be observed that the organs of sense are transmuted by things outside the soul in two ways. First by a natural transmutation, when namely the organ is disposed by the same natural quality as the thing outside the soul which acts on that organ: for instance, when the hand is heated by touching a hot object, or becomes fragrant through contact with a fragrant object. Secondly, by a spiritual transmutation, as when a sensible quality is received in an instrument, according to a spiritual mode of being, when, namely, the species or the intention of a quality, and not the quality itself is received: thus the pupil receives the species of whiteness and yet

* Cf. Q. 74, A. 4, *On the Contrary.*

does not itself become white. Accordingly the first reception does not cause sensation, properly speaking, because the senses are receptive of species in matter but without matter; that is to say without the material *being* which the species had outside the soul (*De Anima,* ii, text. 121). This reception transmutes the nature of the recipient, because in this way the quality is received according to its material *being.* Consequently this kind of reception will not be in the glorified bodies, but the second, which of itself causes actual sensation, without changing the nature of the recipient.

Reply Obj. 1. As already explained, by this passion that takes place in actual sensation and is no other than the aforesaid reception of species, the body is not drawn away from natural quality, but is perfected by a spiritual change. Wherefore the impassibility of glorified bodies does not exclude this kind of passion.

Reply Obj. 2. Every subject of passion receives the action of the agent according to its mode. Accordingly if there be a thing that is naturally adapted to be altered by an active principle, with a natural and a spiritual alteration, the natural alteration precedes the spiritual alteration, just as natural precedes intentional being. If however a thing be naturally adapted to be altered only with a spiritual alteration it does not follow that it is altered naturally. For instance the air is not receptive of color, according to its natural being, but only according to its spiritual being, wherefore in this way alone is it altered: whereas, on the contrary, inanimate bodies are altered by sensible qualities only naturally and not spiritually. But in the glorified bodies there cannot be any natural alteration, and consequently there will be only spiritual alteration.

Reply Obj. 3. Just as there will be new reception of species in the organs of sensation, so there will be new judgment in the common sense: but there will be no new judgment on the point in the intellect; such is the case with one who sees what he knew before. The saying of Augustine, that *there our thoughts will not be changeable,* refers to the thoughts of the intellectual part: therefore it is not to the point.

Reply Obj. 4. When one of two things is the type of the other, the attention of the soul to the one does not hinder or lessen its attention to the other: thus a physician while considering urine is not less but more able to bear in mind the rules of his art concerning the colors of urine. And since God is apprehended by the saints as the type of all things that will be done or known by them, their attention to perceiving sensibles, or to contemplating or doing anything else will nowise hinder their contemplation of God, nor conversely. Or we may say that the reason why one power is hindered in its act when another power is intensely engaged is because one power does not alone suffice for such an intense operation, unless it be assisted by receiving from the principle of life the inflow that the other powers or members should receive. And since in the saints all the powers will be most perfect, one will be able to operate intensely without thereby hindering the operation of another power even as it was with Christ.

FOURTH ARTICLE

Whether in the Blessed, after the Resurrection, All the Senses Will Be in Act?

We proceed thus to the Fourth Article:—

Objection 1. It would seem that all the senses are not in act there. For touch is the first of all the senses (*De Anima*, ii. 2). But the glorified body will lack the actual sense of touch, since the sense of touch becomes actual by the alteration of an animal body by some external body preponderating in some one of the active or passive qualities which touch is capable of discerning: and such an alteration will then be impossible. Therefore all the senses will not be in act there.

Obj. 2. Further, the sense of taste assists the action of the nutritive power. Now after the resurrection there will be no such action, as stated above (Q. 81, A. 4). Therefore taste would be useless there.

Obj. 3. Further, nothing will be corrupted after the resurrection because the whole creature will be invested with a certain virtue of incorruption. Now the sense of smell cannot have its act without some corruption having taken place, because smell is not perceived without a volatile evaporation consisting in a certain dissolution. Therefore the sense of smell is not there in its act.

Obj. 4. Further, *Hearing assists teaching* (*De Sensu et Sensato,* i). But the blessed, after the resurrection, will require no teaching by means of sensible objects, since they will be filled with Divine wisdom by the very vision of God. Therefore hearing will not be there.

Obj. 5. Further, seeing results from the pupil receiving the species of the thing seen. But after the resurrection this will be impossible in the blessed. Therefore there will be no actual seeing there, and yet this is the most noble of the senses. The minor is proved thus: —That which is actually lightsome is not receptive of a visible species; and consequently a mirror placed under the sun's rays does not reflect the image of a body opposite to it. Now the pupil like the whole body will be endowed with clarity. Therefore it will not receive the image of a colored body.

Obj. 6. Further, according to the science of perspective, whatever is seen is seen at an angle. But this does not apply to the glorified bodies. Therefore they will not have actual sense of sight. The minor is proved thus: Whenever a thing is seen at an angle, the angle must be proportionate to the distance of the object seen: because what is seen from a greater distance is less seen and at a lesser angle, so that the angle may be so small that nothing is seen of the object. Therefore if the glorified eye sees at an angle, it follows that it sees things within a certain distance, and that consequently it does not see a thing from a greater distance than we see now: and this would seem very absurd. And thus it would seem that the sense of sight will not be actual in glorified bodies.

On the contrary, A power conjoined to its act is more perfect than one not so conjoined. Now human nature in the blessed will be in its greatest perfection. Therefore all the senses will be actual there.

Further, the sensitive powers are nearer to the soul than the body is. But the body will be rewarded or punished on account of the merits or demerits of the soul. Therefore all the senses in the blessed will also be rewarded, and in the wicked will be punished, with regard to pleasure and pain or sorrow which consist in the operation of the senses.

I answer that, There are two opinions on this question. For some say that in the glorified bodies there will be all the sensitive powers, but that only two senses will be in act, namely touch and sight; nor will this be owing to defective senses, but from lack of medium and object; and that the senses will not be useless, because they will conduce to the integrity of human nature and will show forth the wisdom of their Creator. But this is seemingly untrue, because the medium in these senses is the same as in the others. For in the sight the medium is the air, and this is also the medium in hearing and smelling (*De Anima,* ii. 7). Again, the taste, like the touch, has the medium in contact, since taste is a kind of touch (*ibid.* 9). Smell also which is the object of the sense of smell will be there, since the Church sings that the bodies of the saints will be a most sweet smell. There will also be vocal praise in heaven; hence a gloss says on Ps. cxlix. 6, *The high praises of God shall be in their mouth,* that *hearts and tongues shall not cease to praise God.* The same is had on the authority of a gloss on 2 Esdr. xii. 27, *With singing and with cymbals.* Wherefore, according to others we may say that smelling and hearing will be in act there, but taste will not be in act, in the sense of being affected by the taking of food or drink, as appears from what we have said (Q. 81, A. 4): unless perchance we say that there will be taste in act through the tongue being affected by some neighboring humor.

Reply Obj. 1. The qualities perceived by the touch are those which constitute the animal body. Wherefore the body of an animal has, through its tangible qualities according to the present state of life, a natural aptitude to be affected with a natural and spiritual alteration by the object of touch. For this reason the touch is said to be the most material of the senses, since it has a greater measure of material alteration connected with it. Yet material alteration is only accidentally related to the act of sensation which is effected by a spiritual alteration. Consequently the glorified bodies, which by reason of their impassibility are immune from natural alteration, will be subject only to spiritual alteration by tangible qualities. Thus it was with the body of Adam, which could neither be burned by fire, nor pierced by sword, although he had the sense of such things.

Reply Obj. 2. Taste, in so far as it is the perception of food, will not be in act; but perhaps it will be possible in so far as it is cognizant of flavors in the way mentioned above.

Reply Obj. 3. Some have considered smell to be merely a volatile evaporation. But this opinion cannot be true; which is evident from the fact that vultures hasten to a corpse on perceiving the odor from a very great distance, whereas it would be impossible for an evaporation to travel from the corpse to a place so remote, even though the whole corpse were to be dissolved into vapor. This is confirmed by the fact that sensible objects at an equal distance exercise their influence in all directions: so that smell affects the medium sometimes, and the instrument of sensation with a spiritual alteration, without any evaporation reaching the organ. That some evaporation should be necessary is due to the fact that smell in bodies is mixed with humidity; wherefore it is necessary for dissolution to take place in order for the smell to be perceived. But in the glorified bodies odor will be in its ultimate perfection, being nowise hampered by humidity: wherefore it will affect the organ with a spiritual alteration, like the odor of a volatile evaporation. Such will be the sense of smell

in the saints, because it will not be hindered by any humidity: and it will take cognizance not only of the excellences of odors, as happens with us now on account of the very great humidity of the brain, but also of the minutest differences of odors.

Reply Obj. 4. In heaven there will be vocal praise (though indeed some think otherwise), and in the blessed it will affect the organ of hearing by a merely spiritual alteration. Nor will it be for the sake of learning whereby they may acquire knowledge, but for the sake of the perfection of the sense and for the sake pleasure. How it is possible for the voice to give sound there, we have already stated (ii. *Sent.* D. 2; Q. 2, A. 2, *ad* 5).

Reply Obj. 5. The intensity of light does not hinder the spiritual reception of the image of color, so long as the pupil retains its diaphanous nature; thus it is evident that however much the air be filled with light, it can be the medium of sight, and the more it is illumined, the more clearly are objects seen through it, unless there be a fault through defective sight. The fact that the image of an object placed in opposition to a mirror directly opposite the sun's rays does not appear therein, is not due to the reception being hindered, but to the hindering of reflection: because for an image to appear in a mirror it must needs be thrown back by an opaque body, for which reason lead is affixed to the glass in a mirror. The sun's ray dispels this opacity so that no image can appear in the mirror. But the clarity of a glorified body does not destroy the diaphanous nature of the pupil, since glory does not destroy nature; and consequently the greatness of clarity in the pupil renders the sight keen rather than defective.

Reply Obj. 6. The more perfect the sense the less does it require to be altered in order to perceive its object. Now the smaller the angle at which the sight is affected by the visible object, the less is the organ altered. Hence it is that a stronger sight can see from a distance more than a weaker sight; because the greater the distance the smaller the angle at which a thing is seen. And since the sight of a glorified body will be most perfect it will be able to see by the very least alteration (of the organ); and consequently at a very much smaller angle than now, and therefore from a much greater distance.

QUESTION 83

Of the Subtlety of the Bodies of the Blessed

(In Six Articles)

WE must now consider the subtlety of the bodies of the blessed. Under this head there are six points of inquiry: (1) Whether subtlety is a property of the glorified body? (2) Whether by reason of this subtlety it can be in the same place with another not glorified body? (3) Whether by a miracle two bodies can be in the same place? (4) Whether a glorified body can be in the same place with another glorified body? (5) Whether a glorified body necessarily requires a place equal to itself? (6) Whether a glorified body is palpable?

FIRST ARTICLE

Whether Subtlety Is a Property of the Glorified Body?

We proceed thus to the First Article:—

Objection 1. It would seem that subtlety is not a property of the glorified body. For the properties of glory surpass the properties of nature, even as the clarity of glory surpasses the clarity of the sun, which is the greatest in nature. Accordingly if subtlety be a property of the glorified body, it would seem that the glorified body will be more subtle than anything which is subtle in nature, and thus it will be *more subtle than the wind and the air*, which was condemned by Gregory in the city of Constantinople, as he relates *(Moral.* xiv. 56).

Obj. 2. Further, as heat and cold are simple qualities of bodies, *i.e.* of the elements, so is subtlety. But heat and other qualities of the elements will not be intensified in the glorified bodies any more than they are now, in fact, they will be more reduced to the mean. Neither, therefore, will subtlety be in them more than it is now.

Obj. 3. Further, subtlety is in bodies as a result of scarcity of matter, wherefore bodies that have less matter within equal dimensions are said to be more subtle; as fire in comparison with air, and air as compared with water, and water as compared with earth. But there will be as much matter in the glorified bodies as there is now, nor will their dimensions be greater. Therefore they will not be more subtle then than now.

On the contrary, It is written (1 Cor. xv. 44): *It is sown a corruptible body, it shall rise a spiritual, i.e.* a spirit-like, *body.* But the subtlety of a spirit surpasses all bodily subtlety. Therefore the glorified bodies will be most subtle.

Further, the more subtle a body is the more

exalted it is. But the glorified bodies will be most exalted. Therefore they will be most subtle.

I answer that, Subtlety takes its name from the power to penetrate. Hence it is said in *De Gener.* ii that *a subtle thing fills all the parts and the parts of parts.* Now that a body has the power of penetrating may happen through two causes. First, through smallness of quantity, especially in respect of depth and breadth, but not of length, because penetration regards depth, wherefore length is not an obstacle to penetration. Secondly, through paucity of matter, wherefore rarity is synonymous with subtlety: and since in rare bodies the form is more predominant over the matter, the term *subtlety* has been transferred to those bodies which are most perfectly subject to their form, and are most fully perfected thereby: thus we speak of subtlety in the sun and moon and like bodies, just as gold and similar things may be called subtle, when they are most perfectly complete in their specific being and power. And since incorporeal things lack quantity and matter, the term *subtlety* is applied to them, not only by reason of their substance, but also on account of their power. For just as a subtle thing is said to be penetrative, for the reason that it reaches to the inmost part of a thing, so is an intellect said to be subtle because it reaches to the insight of the intrinsic principles and the hidden natural properties of a thing. In like manner a person is said to have subtle sight, because he is able to perceive by sight things of the smallest size: and the same applies to the other senses. Accordingly people have differed by ascribing subtlety to the glorified bodies in different ways.

For certain heretics, as Augustine relates *(De Civ. Dei,* xiii. 22), ascribed to them the subtlety whereby spiritual substances are said to be subtle: and they said that at the resurrection the body will be transformed into a spirit, and that for this reason the Apostle describes as being *spiritual* the bodies of those who rise again (1 Cor. xv. 44). But this cannot be maintained. First, because a body cannot be changed into a spirit, since there is no community of matter between them: and Boëthius proves this *(De duab. Nat.).* Secondly, because, if this were possible, and one's body were changed into a spirit, one would not rise again a man, for a man naturally consists of a soul and body. Thirdly, because if this were the Apostle's meaning, just as he speaks of spiritual bodies, so would he speak of natural *(animale)* bodies, as being changed into souls *(animam)*: and this is clearly false.

Hence certain heretics said that the body will remain at the resurrection, but that it will be endowed with subtlety by means of rarefaction, so that human bodies in rising again will be like the air or the wind, as Gregory relates *(Moral.* xiv. 1.c.). But this again cannot be maintained, because our Lord had a palpable body after the Resurrection, as appears from the last chapter of Luke, and we must believe that His body was supremely subtle. Moreover the human body will rise again with flesh and bones, as did the body of our Lord, according to Luke xxiv. 39, *A spirit hath not flesh and bones as you see Me to have,* and Job xix. 26, *In my flesh I shall see God,* my Saviour: and the nature of flesh and bone is incompatible with the aforesaid rarity.

Consequently another kind of subtlety must be assigned to glorified bodies, by saying that they are subtle on account of the most complete perfection of the body. But this completeness is explained by some in relation to the fifth, or heavenly, essence, which will be then predominant in them. This, however, is impossible, since first of all the fifth essence can nowise enter into the composition of a body, as we have shown above (ii. *Sent.* D. 12, qu. 1). Secondly, because granted that it entered into the composition of the human body, it would be impossible to account for its having a greater predominance over the elemental nature then than now, unless,—either the amount of the heavenly nature in human bodies were increased (thus human bodies would not be of the same stature, unless perhaps elemental matter in man were decreased, which is inconsistent with the integrity of those who rise again),—or unless elemental nature were endowed with the properties of the heavenly nature through the latter's dominion over the body, and in that case a natural power would be the cause of a property of glory, which seems absurd.

Hence others say that the aforesaid completeness by reason of which human bodies are said to be subtle will result from the dominion of the glorified soul (which is the form of the body) over the body, by reason of which dominion the glorified body is said to be *spiritual*, as being wholly subject to the spirit. The first subjection whereby the body is subject to the soul is to the effect of its participating in its specific being, in so far as it is subject to the soul as matter to form; and secondly it is subject to the soul in respect of the other opera-

tions of the soul, in so far as the soul is a principle of movement. Consequently the first reason for spirituality in the body is subtlety, and, after that, agility and the other properties of a glorified body. Hence the Apostle, as the masters expound, in speaking of spirituality indicates subtlety: wherefore Gregory says (Moral. xiv. 1.c.) that *the glorified body is said to be subtle as a result of a spiritual power.*

This suffices for the *Replies* to the *Objections* which refer to the subtlety of rarefaction.

SECOND ARTICLE

Whether by Reason of This Subtlety a Glorified Body Is Able to Be in the Same Place with Another Body Not Glorified?

We proceed thus to the Second Article:—

Objection 1. It would seem that by reason of this subtlety a body is able to be in the same place with another body not glorified. For according to Philip. iii. 21, He *will reform the body of our lowness made like to the body of His glory.* Now the body of Christ was able to be in the same place with another body, as appears from the fact that after His Resurrection He went in to His disciples, the doors being shut (Jo. xx. 19, 26). Therefore also the glorified bodies by reason of their subtlety will be able to be in the same place with other bodies not glorified.

Obj. 2. Further, glorified bodies will be superior to all other bodies. Yet by reason of their superiority certain bodies, to wit the solar rays, are able now to occupy the same place together with other bodies. Much more therefore is this befitting glorified bodies.

Obj. 3. Further, a heavenly body cannot be severed, at least as regards the substance of the spheres: hence it is written (Job xxxvii. 18) that *the heavens . . . are most strong, as if they were of molten brass.* If then the subtlety of a glorified body will not enable it to be in the same place together with another body, it will never be able to ascend to the empyrean,* and this is erroneous.

Obj. 4. Further, a body which is unable to be in the same place with another body can be hindered in its movement or even surrounded by others standing in its way. But this cannot happen to glorified bodies. Therefore they will be able to be together in the same place with other bodies.

Obj. 5. Further, as point is to point, so is line to line, surface to surface, and body to body. Now two points can be coincident, as in the case of two lines touching one another, and two lines when two surfaces are in contact with one another, and two surfaces when

---

* The empyrean was the highest of the concentric spheres or heavens, and was identified by Christian writers with the abode of God. Cf. P. I, Q. 56, A. 3.

two bodies touch one another, because *contiguous things are those whose boundaries coincide (Phys.* vi. 6). Therefore it is not against the nature of a body to be in the same place together with another body. Now whatever excellence is competent to the nature of a body will all be bestowed on the glorified body. Therefore a glorified body, by reason of its subtlety, will be able to be in the same place together with another body.

On the contrary, Boëthius says (De Trin. i): *Difference of accidents makes distinction in number. For three men differ not in genus, nor in species, but in their accidents. If we were to remove absolutely every accident from them, still each one has a different place; and it is quite conceivable that they should all occupy the same place.* Therefore if we suppose two bodies to occupy the same place, there will be but one body numerically.

I answer that, It cannot be maintained that a glorified body, by reason of its subtlety, is able to be in the same place with another body, unless the obstacle to its being now in the same place with another body be removed by that subtlety. Some say that in the present state this obstacle is its grossness by virtue of which it is able to occupy a place; and that this grossness is removed by the gift of subtlety. But there are two reasons why this cannot be maintained. First, because the grossness which the gift of subtlety removes is a kind of defect, for instance an inordinateness of matter in not being perfectly subject to its form. For all that pertains to the integrity of the body will rise again in the body, both as regards the matter and as regards the form. And the fact that a body is able to fill a place belongs to it by reason of that which pertains to its integrity, and not on account of any defect of nature. For since fulness is opposed to vacancy, that alone does not fill a place, which being put in a place, nevertheless leaves a place vacant. Now a vacuum is defined by the Philosopher *(Phys.* iv. 6, 7) as being *a place not filled by a sensible body.* And a body is said to be sensible by reason of its matter, form, and natural accidents, all of which pertain to the integrity of nature. It is also plain that the glorified body will be sensible even to touch, as evidenced by the body of our Lord (Luke xxiv. 39): nor will it lack matter, or form, or natural accidents, namely heat, cold, and so forth. Hence it is evident that the glorified body, the gift of subtlety notwithstanding, will fill a place: for it would seem madness to say that the place in which there will be a glorified body will be empty. Secondly their aforesaid argument does not avail, because to hinder the co-existence of a body in the same place is more than to fill a place. For

if we suppose dimensions separate from matter, those dimensions do not fill a place. Hence some who held the possibility of a vacuum, said that a vacuum is a place wherein such like dimensions exist apart from a sensible body; and yet those dimensions hinder another body from being together with them in the same place. This is made clear by the Philosopher *(Phys.* iv. 1, 8; *Met.* ii. 2), where he considers it impossible for a mathematical body, which is nothing but separate dimensions, to be together with another natural sensible body. Consequently, granted that the subtlety of a glorified body hindered it from filling a place, nevertheless it would not follow that for this reason it is able to be in the same place with another body, since the removal of the lesser does not involve the removal of the greater.

Accordingly we must say that the obstacle to our body's being now in the same place with another body can nowise be removed by the gift of subtlety. For nothing can prevent a body from occupying the same place together with another body, except something in it that requires a different place: since nothing is an obstacle to identity, save that which is a cause of distinction. Now this distinction of place is not required by any quality of the body, because a body demands a place, not by reason of its quality: wherefore if we remove from a body the fact of its being hot or cold, heavy or light, it still retains the necessity of the aforesaid distinction, as the Philosopher proves *(Phys.* iv), and as is self-evident. In like manner neither can matter cause the necessity of the aforesaid distinction, because matter does not occupy a place except through its dimensive quantity. Again neither does form occupy a place, unless it have a place through its matter. It remains therefore that the necessity for two bodies occupying each a distinct place results from the nature of dimensive quantity, to which a place is essentially befitting. For this forms part of its definition, since dimensive quantity is quantity occupying a place. Hence it is that if we remove all else in a thing from it, the necessity of this distinction is found in its dimensive quantity alone. Thus take the example of a separate line, supposing there to be two such lines, or two parts of one line, they must needs occupy distinct places, else one line added to another would not make something greater, and this is against common sense. The same applies to surfaces and mathematical bodies. And since matter demands place, through being the subject of dimension, the aforesaid necessity results in placed matter, so that just as it is impossible for there to be two lines, or two parts of a line, unless they occupy distinct places, so is it impossible for there to be two matters, or two parts of matter, without there be distinction of place. And since distinction of matter is the principle of the distinction between individuals, it follows that, as Boëthius says *(De Trin.)*, *we cannot possibly conceive two bodies occupying one place*, so that this distinction of individuals requires this difference of accidents. Now subtlety does not deprive the glorified body of its dimension; wherefore it nowise removes from it the aforesaid necessity of occupying a distinct place from another body. Therefore the subtlety of a glorified body will not enable it to be in the same place together with another body, but it will be possible for it to be together with another body by the operation of the Divine power: even as the body of Peter had the power whereby the sick were healed at the passing of Peter's shadow (Acts v. 15) not through any inherent property, but by the power of God for the upbuilding of the faith. Thus will the Divine power make it possible for a glorified body to be in the same place together with another body for the perfection of glory.

Reply Obj. 1. That Christ's body was able to be together with another body in the same place was not due to its subtlety, but resulted from the power of His Godhead after His resurrection, even as in His birth.* Hence Gregory says *(Hom.* xxvi *in Ev.)*: *The same body went into His disciples the doors being shut, which to human eyes came from the closed womb of the Virgin at His birth.* Therefore there is no reason why this should be befitting to glorified bodies on account of their subtlety.

Reply Obj. 2. Light is not a body as we have said above (ii. *Sent.* Q. 13, A. 3; P. I, Q. 67, A. 2): hence the objection proceeds on a false supposition.

Reply Obj. 3. The glorified body will pass through the heavenly spheres without severing them, not by virtue of its subtlety, but by the Divine power, which will assist them in all things at will.

Reply Obj. 4. From the fact that God will come to the aid of the blessed at will in whatever they desire, it follows that they cannot be surrounded or imprisoned.

Reply Obj. 5. As stated in *Phys.* iv. 5, *a point is not in a place*: hence if it be said to be in a place, this is only accidental, because the body of which it is a term is in a place. And just as the whole place corresponds to the whole body, so the term of the place corresponds to the term of the body. But it happens that two places have one term, even as two lines terminate in one point. And consequently though two bodies must needs be in distinct places, yet the same term of two places

* Cf. P. III, Q. 28, A. 2, *ad 3.*

corresponds to the two terms of the two bodies. It is in this sense that the bounds of contiguous bodies are said to coincide.

THIRD ARTICLE

Whether It Is Possible, by a Miracle, for Two Bodies to Be in the Same Place?

We proceed thus to the Third Article:—

Objection 1. It would seem that not even by a miracle is it possible for two bodies to be in the same place. For it is not possible that, by a miracle, two bodies be at once two and one, since this would imply that contradictions are true at the same time. But if we suppose two bodies to be in the same place, it would follow that those two bodies are one. Therefore this cannot be done by a miracle. The minor is proved thus. Suppose two bodies A and B to be in the same place. The dimensions of A will either be the same as the dimensions of the place, or they will differ from them. If they differ, then some of the dimensions will be separate: which is impossible, since the dimensions that are within the bounds of a place are not in a subject unless they be in a placed body. If they be the same, then for the same reason the dimensions of B will be the same as the dimensions of the place. Now *things that are the same with one and the same thing are the same with one another.* Therefore the dimensions of A and B are the same. But two bodies cannot have identical dimensions just as they cannot have the same whiteness. Therefore A and B are one body and yet they were two. Therefore they are at the same time one and two.

Obj. 2. Further, a thing cannot be done miraculously either against the common principles,—for instance that the part be not less than the whole; since what is contrary to common principles implies a direct contradiction:—or contrary to the conclusions of geometry which are infallible deductions from common principles,—for instance that the three angles of a triangle should not be equal to two right angles. In like manner nothing can be done to a line that is contrary to the definition of a line, because to sever the definition from the defined is to make two contradictories true at the same time. Now it is contrary to common principles, both to the conclusions of geometry and to the definition of a line, for two bodies to be in the same place. Therefore this cannot be done by a miracle. The minor is proved as follows: It is a conclusion of geometry that two circles touch one another only at a point. Now if two circular bodies were in the same place, the two circles described in them would touch one another as a whole. Again it is contrary to the definition of a line that there be more than one straight line between two points: yet this would be the case were two bodies in the same place, since between two given points in the various surfaces of the place, there would be two straight lines corresponding to the two bodies in that place.

Obj. 3. Further, it would seem impossible that by a miracle a body which is enclosed within another should not be in a place, for then it would have a common and not a proper place, and this is impossible. Yet this would follow if two bodies were in the same place. Therefore this cannot be done by a miracle. The minor is proved thus. Supposing two bodies to be in the same place, the one being greater than the other as to every dimension, the lesser body will be enclosed in the greater, and the place occupied by the greater body will be its common place; while it will have no proper place, because no given surface of the body will contain it, and this is essential to place. Therefore it will not have a proper place.

Obj. 4. Further, place corresponds in proportion to the thing placed. Now it can never happen by a miracle that the same body is at the same time in different places, except by some kind of transformation, as in the Sacrament of the Altar. Therefore it can nowise happen by a miracle that two bodies be together in the same place.

On the contrary, The Blessed Virgin gave birth to her Son by a miracle. Now in this hallowed birth it was necessary for two bodies to be together in the same place, because the body of her child when coming forth did not break through the enclosure of her virginal purity. Therefore it is possible for two bodies to be miraculously together in the same place.

Further, this may again be proved from the fact that our Lord went in to His disciples, the doors being shut (Jo. xx. 19, 26).

I answer that, As shown above (A. 2) the reason why two bodies must needs be in two places is that distinction in matter requires distinction in place. Wherefore we observe that when two bodies merge into one, each loses its distinct being, and one indistinct being accrues to the two combined, as in the case of mixtures. Hence it is impossible for two bodies to remain two and yet be together unless each retain its distinct being which it had hitherto, in so much as each of them was a being undivided in itself and distinct from others. Now this distinct being depends on the essential principles of a thing as on its proximate causes, but on God as on the first cause. And since the first cause can preserve a thing in being, though the second causes be done

away, as appears from the first proposition of *De Causis,* therefore by God's power and by that alone it is possible for an accident to be without substance as in the Sacrament of the Altar. Likewise by the power of God, and by that alone, it is possible for a body to retain its distinct being from that of another body, although its matter be not distinct as to place from the matter of the other body: and thus it is possible by a miracle for two bodies to be together in the same place.

Reply Obj. 1. This argument is sophistical because it is based on a false supposition, or begs the question. For it supposes the existence, between two opposite superficies of a place, of a dimension proper to the place, with which dimension a dimension of the body put in occupation of the place would have to be identified: because it would then follow that the dimensions of two bodies occupying a place would become one dimension, if each of them were identified with the dimension of the place. But this supposition is false, because if it were true whenever a body acquires a new place, it would follow that a change takes place in the dimensions of the place or of thing placed: since it is impossible for two things to become one anew, except one of them be changed. Whereas if, as is the case in truth, no other dimensions belong to a place than those of the thing occupying the place, it is clear that the argument proves nothing, but begs the question, because according to this nothing else has been said, but that the dimensions of a thing placed are the same as the dimensions of the place; excepting that the dimensions of the thing placed are contained within the bounds of the place, and that the distance between the bounds of a place is commensurate with the distance between the bounds of the thing placed, just as the former would be distant by their own dimensions if they had them. Thus that the dimensions of two bodies be the dimensions of one place is nothing else than that two bodies be in the same place, which is the chief question at issue.

Reply Obj. 2. Granted that by a miracle two bodies be together in the same place, nothing follows either against common principles, or against the definition of a line, or against any conclusions of geometry. For, as stated above (A. 2), dimensive quantity differs from all other accidents in that it has a special reason of individuality and distinction, namely on account of the placing of the parts, besides the reason of individuality and distinction which is common to it and all other accidents, arising namely from the matter which is its subject. Thus then one line may be understood as being distinct from another, either because it is in another subject (in which case we are considering a material line), or because it is placed at a distance from another (in which case we are considering a mathematical line, which is understood apart from matter). Accordingly if we remove matter, there can be no distinction between lines save in respect of a different placing: and in like manner neither can there be a distinction of points, nor of superficies, nor of any dimensions whatever. Consequently geometry cannot suppose one line to be added to another, as being distinct therefrom unless it be distinct as to place. But supposing by a Divine miracle a distinction of subject without a distinction of place, we can understand a distinction of lines; and these are not distant from one another in place, on account of the distinction of subjects. Again we can understand a difference of points, and thus different lines described on two bodies that are in the same place are drawn from different points to different points; for the point that we take is not a point fixed in the place, but in the placed body, because a line is not said to be drawn otherwise than from a point which is its term. In like manner the two circles described in two spherical bodies that occupy the same place are two, not on account of the difference of place, else they could not touch one another as a whole, but on account of the distinction of subjects, and thus while wholly touching one another they still remain two. Even so a circle described by a placed spherical body touches, as a whole, the other circle described by the locating body.

Reply Obj. 3. God could make a body not to be in a place; and yet supposing this, it would not follow that a certain body is not in a place, because the greater body is the place of the lesser body, by reason of its superficies which is described by contact with the terms of the lesser body.

Reply Obj. 4. It is impossible for one body to be miraculously in two places locally (for Christ's body is not locally on the altar), although it is possible by a miracle for two bodies to be in the same place. Because to be in several places at once is incompatible with the individual, by reason of its having being undivided in itself, for it would follow that it is divided as to place. On the other hand, to be in the same place with another body is incompatible with the individual as distinct from aught else. Now the nature of unity is perfected in indivision *(Met.* v), whereas distinction from others is a result of the nature of unity. Wherefore that one same body be locally in several places at once implies a contradiction, even as for a man to lack reason, while for two bodies to be in the same place does not imply a contradiction, as explained above. Hence the comparison fails.

FOURTH ARTICLE

Whether One Glorified Body Can Be in the Same Place Together with Another Glorified Body?

We proceed thus to the Fourth Article:—

Objection 1. It would seem that a glorified body can be in the same place together with another glorified body. Because where there is greater subtlety there is less resistance. If then a glorified body is more subtle than a non-glorified body, it will offer less resistance to a glorified body: and so if a glorified body can be in the same place with a non-glorified body, much more can it with a glorified body.

Obj. 2. Further, even as a glorified body will be more subtle than a non-glorified body, so will one glorified body be more subtle than another. Therefore if a glorified body can be in the same place with a non-glorified body, a more subtle glorified body can be in the same place with a less subtle glorified body.

Obj. 3. Further, the body of heaven is subtle, and will then be glorified. Now the glorified body of a saint will be able to be in the same place with the body of heaven, since the saints will be able at will to travel to and from earth. Therefore two glorified bodies will be able to occupy the same place.

On the contrary, The glorified bodies will be spiritual, that is like spirits in a certain respect. Now two spirits cannot be in the same place, although a body and a spirit can be in the same place, as stated above (i. *Sent.* D. 37, Q. 3, A. 3; P. I, Q. 52, A. 3). Therefore neither will two glorified bodies be able to be in the same place.

Further, if two bodies occupy the same place, one is penetrated by the other. But to be penetrated is a mark of imperfection which will be altogether absent from the glorified bodies. Therefore it will be impossible for two glorified bodies to be in the same place.

I answer that, The property of a glorified body does not make it able to be in the same place with another glorified body, nor again to be in the same place with a non-glorified body. But it would be possible by the Divine power for two glorified bodies or two non-glorified bodies to be in the same place, even as a glorified body with a non-glorified body. Nevertheless it is not befitting for a glorified body to be in the same place with another glorified body, both because a becoming order will be observed in them, which demands distinction, and because one glorified body will not be in the way of another. Consequently two glorified bodies will never be in the same place.

Reply Obj. 1. This argument supposes that a glorified body is able by reason of its subtlety to be in the same place with another body: and this is not true.

The same answer applies to the *Second Objection.*

Reply Obj. 3. The body of heaven and the other bodies will be said equivocally to be glorified, in so far as they will have a certain share in glory, and not as though it were becoming for them to have the gifts of glorified human bodies.

FIFTH ARTICLE

Whether by Virtue of Its Subtlety a Glorified Body Will No Longer Need to Be in an Equal Place?

We proceed thus to the Fifth Article:—

Objection 1. It would seem that by virtue of its subtlety, a glorified body will no longer need to be in an equal place. For the glorified bodies will be made like to the body of Christ according to Phil. iii. 21. Now Christ's body is not bound by this necessity of being in an equal place: wherefore it is contained whole under the small or great dimensions of a consecrated host. Therefore the same will be true of the glorified bodies.

Obj. 2. Further, the Philosopher proves *(Phys.* iv. 6), that two bodies are not in the same place, because it would follow that the greatest body would occupy the smallest place, since its various parts could be in the same part of the place: for it makes no difference whether two bodies or however many be in the same place. Now a glorified body will be in the same place with another body, as is commonly admitted. Therefore it will be possible for it to be in any place however small.

Obj. 3. Further, even as a body is seen by reason of its color, so is it measured by reason of its quantity. Now the glorified body will be so subject to the spirit that it will be able at will to be seen, and not seen, especially by a non-glorified eye, as evidenced in the case of Christ. Therefore its quantity will be so subject to the spirit's will that it will be able to be in a little or great place, and to have a little or great quantity at will.

On the contrary, The Philosopher says *(Phys.* iv, text. 30) that *whatever is in a place occupies a place equal to itself.* Now the glorified body will be in a place. Therefore it will occupy a place equal to itself.

Further, the dimensions of a place and of that which is in that place are the same, as shown in *Phys.* iv, text. 30, 76, 77. Therefore if the place were larger than that which is in the place the same thing would be greater and smaller than itself, which is absurd.

I answer that, A body is not related to place save through the medium of its proper dimensions, in respect of which a located body is confined through contact with the locating body. Hence it is not possible for a body to occupy a place smaller than its quantity, unless its proper quantity be made in some way less than itself: and this can only be understood in two ways. First, by a variation in quantity in respect of the same matter, so that in fact the matter which at first is subject to a greater quantity is afterwards subject to a lesser. Some have held this to be the case with the glorified bodies, saying that quantity is subject to them at will, so that when they list, they are able to have a great quantity, and when they list, a small quantity. But this is impossible, because no movement affecting that which is intrinsic to a thing is possible without passion to the detriment* of its substance. Hence in incorruptible, *i.e.* heavenly, bodies, there is only local movement, which is not according to something intrinsic. Thus it is clear that change of quantity in respect of matter would be incompatible with the impassibility and incorruptibility of a glorified body. Moreover, it would follow that a glorified body would be sometimes rarer and sometimes denser, because since it cannot be deprived of any of its matter, sometimes the same matter would be under great dimensions and sometimes under small dimensions, and thus it would be rarefied and densified, which is impossible. Secondly, that the quantity of a glorified body become smaller than itself may be understood by a variation of place; so, to wit, that the parts of a glorified body insinuate themselves into one another, so that it is reduced in quantity however small it may become. And some have held this to be the case, saying that by reason of its subtlety a glorified body will be able to be in the same place with a non-glorified body: and that in like manner its parts can be one within the other, so much so that a whole glorified body will be able to pass through the minutest opening in another body: and thus they explain how Christ's body came out of the Virgin's womb; and how it went into His disciples, the doors being shut. But this is impossible; both because the glorified body will not be able, by reason of its subtlety, to be in the same place with another body, and because, even if it were able to be in the same place with another body, this would not be possible if the other were a glorified body, as many say; and again because this would be inconsistent with the right disposition of the human body, which requires the parts to be in a certain fixed place and at a certain fixed distance from one another. Wherefore this will never happen, not even by a miracle. Consequently we must say that the glorified body will always be in a place equal to itself.

* Cf. I-II, Q. 22, A. 1; Q. 41, A. 1.

Reply Obj. 1. Christ's body is not locally in the Sacrament of the Altar, as stated above (iv. *Sent.* D. 10, Q. 1, A. 1, *ad* 5; P. III, Q. 77, A. 5).

Reply Obj. 2. The Philosopher's argument is that for the same reason one part might permeate another. But this permeation of the parts of a glorified body into one another is impossible, as stated above. Therefore the objection does not prove.

Reply Obj. 3. A body is seen because it acts on the sight: but that it does or does not act on the sight causes no change in the body. Hence it is not unfitting, if it can be seen when it will, and not seen when it will.* On the other hand, being in a place is not an action proceeding from a body by reason of its quantity, as being seen is by reason of its color. Consequently the comparison fails.

SIXTH ARTICLE

Whether the Glorified Body, by Reason of Its Subtlety, Will Be Impalpable?

We proceed thus to the Sixth Article:—

Objection 1. It would seem that the glorified body, by reason of its subtlety, is impalpable. For Gregory says *(Hom.* xxv *in Ev.)*: *What is palpable must needs be corruptible.* But the glorified body is incorruptible. Therefore it is impalpable.

Obj. 2. Further, whatever is palpable resists one who handles it. But that which can be in the same place with another does not resist it. Since then a glorified body can be in the same place with another body, it will not be palpable.

Obj. 3. Further, every palpable body is tangible. Now every tangible body has tangible qualities in excess of the qualities of the one touching it. Since then in the glorified bodies the tangible qualities are not in excess but are reduced to a supreme degree of equality, it would seem that they are impalpable.

On the contrary, Our Lord rose again with a glorified body; and yet His body was palpable, as appears from Luke xxiv. 39: *Handle, and see; for a spirit hath not flesh and bones.* Therefore the glorified bodies also will be palpable.

Further, this is the heresy of Eutychius, Bishop of Constantinople, as Gregory states *(Moral.* xxiv): for he said that in the glory of the resurrection our bodies will be impalpable.

I answer that, Every palpable body is tangible, but not conversely. For every body is tangible that has qualities whereby the sense of touch has a natural aptitude to be affected:

* Cf. P. III, Q. 55, A. 4.

wherefore air, fire, and the like are tangible bodies: but a palpable body, in addition to this, resists the touch; wherefore the air which never resists that which passes through it, and is most easily pierced, is tangible indeed but not palpable. Accordingly it is clear that a body is said to be palpable for two reasons, namely on account of its tangible qualities, and on account of its resisting that which touches it, so as to hinder it from piercing it. And since the tangible qualities are hot and cold and so forth, which are not found save in heavy and light bodies, which through being contrary to one another are therefore corruptible, it follows that the heavenly bodies, which by their nature are incorruptible, are sensible to the sight but not tangible, and therefore neither are they palpable. This is what Gregory means when he says *(loc. cit. Obj.* 1) that *whatever is palpable must needs be corruptible.* Accordingly the glorified body has by its nature those qualities which have a natural aptitude to affect the touch, and yet since the body is altogether subject to the spirit, it is in its power thereby to affect or not to affect the touch. In like manner it is competent by its nature to resist any other passing body, so that the latter cannot be in the same place together with it: although, according to its pleasure, it may happen by the Divine power that it occupy the same place with another body, and thus offer no resistance to a passing body. Wherefore according to its nature the glorified body is palpable, but it is competent for it to be impalpable to a non-glorified body by a supernatural power. Hence Gregory says *(loc. cit.)* that *our Lord offered His flesh to be handled, which He had brought in through the closed doors, so as to afford a complete proof that after His resurrection His body was unchanged in nature though changed in glory.*

Reply Obj. 1. The incorruptibility of a glorified body does not result from the nature of its component parts; and it is on account of that nature that whatever is palpable is corruptible, as stated above. Hence the argument does not prove.

Reply Obj. 2. Although in a way it is possible for a glorified body to be in the same place with another body: nevertheless the glorified body has it in its power to resist at will any one touching it, and thus it is palpable.

Reply Obj. 3. In the glorified bodies the tangible qualities are not reduced to the real mean that is measured according to equal distance from the extremes, but to the proportionate mean, according as is most becoming to the human complexion in each part. Wherefore the touch of those bodies will be most delightful, because a power always delights in a becoming object, and is grieved by excess.

QUESTION 84

Of the Agility of the Bodies of the Blessed

(In Three Articles)

WE must now consider the agility of the bodies of the blessed in the resurrection. Under this head there are three points of inquiry: (1) Whether the glorified bodies will be agile? (2) Whether they will move? (3) Whether they will move instantaneously?

FIRST ARTICLE

Whether the Glorified Bodies Will Be Agile?

We proceed thus to the First Article:—

Objection 1. It would seem that the glorified bodies will not be agile. For that which is agile by itself needs not to be carried in order to move. But the glorified bodies will, after the resurrection, be taken up by the angels (according to a gloss) in the clouds *to meet Christ, into the air* (1 Thess. iv. 16). Therefore the glorified bodies will not be agile.

Obj. 2. Further, no body that moves with labor and pain can be said to be agile. Yet the glorified bodies will move thus, since the principle of their movement, namely the soul, moves them counter to their nature, else they would always move in the same direction. Therefore they are not agile.

Obj. 3. Further, of all the animal operations sense surpasses movement in nobility and priority. Yet no property is ascribed to glorified bodies as perfecting them in sensation. Therefore neither should agility be ascribed to them as perfecting them in movement.

Obj. 4. Further, nature gives different animals instruments of different disposition according to their different powers: hence she does not give instruments of the same disposition to slow as to fleet animals. Now God's works are much more orderly than those of nature. Since then the glorified body's members will have the same disposition, shape and quantity as they now have, it would seem that it will have no agility other than it has now.

On the contrary, It is written (1 Cor. xv. 43): *It is sown in weakness, it shall rise in power,* that is, according to a gloss, *mobile and living.* But mobility can only signify agility in movement. Therefore the glorified bodies will be agile.

Further, slowness of movement would seem especially inconsistent with the nature of a spirit. But the glorified bodies will be most spiritual according to 1 Cor. xv. 44. Therefore they will be agile.

I answer that, The glorified body will be altogether subject to the glorified soul, so that not only will there be nothing in it to resist the will of the spirit, for it was even so in the case of Adam's body, but also from the glorified soul there will flow into the body a certain perfection, whereby it will become adapted to that subjection: and this perfection is called *the gift of the glorified body.* Now the soul is united to body not only as its form, but also as its mover; and in both ways the glorified body must needs be most perfectly subject to the glorified soul. Wherefore even as by the gift of subtlety the body is wholly subject to the soul as its form, whence it derives its specific being, so by the gift of agility it is subject to the soul as its mover, so that it is prompt and apt to obey the spirit in all the movements and actions of the soul.

Some, however, ascribe the cause of this agility to the fifth, *i.e.* the heavenly essence, which will then be predominant in the glorified bodies. But of this we have frequently observed that it does not seem probable (Q. 82, A. 1; Q. 83, A. 1). Wherefore it is better to ascribe it to the soul, whence glory flows to the body.

Reply Obj. 1. Glorified bodies are said to be borne by the angels and also on the clouds, not as though they needed them, but in order to signify the reverence which both angels and all creatures will show them.

Reply Obj. 2. The more the power of the moving soul dominates over the body, the less is the labor of movement, even though it be counter to the body's nature. Hence those in whom the motive power is stronger, and those who through exercise have the body more adapted to obey the moving spirit, labor less in being moved. And since, after the resurrection, the soul will perfectly dominate the body, both on account of the perfection of its own power, and on account of the glorified body's aptitude resulting from the outflow of glory which it receives from the soul, there will be no labor in the saints' movements, and thus it may be said that the bodies of the saints' will be agile.

Reply Obj. 3. By the gift of agility the glorified body will be rendered apt not only for local movement but also for sensation, and for the execution of all the other operations of the soul.

Reply Obj. 4. Even as nature gives to fleeter animals instruments of a different disposition in shape and quantity, so God will give to the bodies of the saints a disposition other than that which they have now, not indeed in shape and quantity, but in that property of glory which is called agility.

SECOND ARTICLE

Whether the Saints Will Never Use Their Agility for the Purpose of Movement?

We proceed thus to the Second Article:—

Objection 1. It would seem that the saints will never use their agility for the purpose of movement. For, according to the Philosopher *(Phys.* iii. 2), *movement is the act of the imperfect.* But there will be no imperfection in glorified bodies. Neither therefore will there be any movement.

Obj. 2. Further, all movement is on account of some need, because whatever is in motion is moved for the sake of obtaining some end. But glorified bodies will have no need, since as Augustine says *(De Spiritu et Anima,* lxiii),* *all thou willest will be there, and nothing that thou willest not.* Therefore they will not move.

Obj. 3. Further, according to the Philosopher *(De Cœlo et Mundo,* ii), *that which shares the Divine goodness without movement shares it more excellently than that which shares it with movement.* Now the glorified body shares the Divine goodness more excellently than any other body. Since then certain bodies, like the heavenly bodies, will remain altogether without movement, it seems that much more will human bodies remain so.

Obj. 4. Further, Augustine says *(De Vera Relig.* xii) that the soul being established in God will in consequence establish its body. Now the soul will be so established in God, that in no way will it move away from Him. Therefore in the body there will be no movement caused by the soul.

Obj. 5. Further, the more noble a body is, the more noble a place is due to it: wherefore Christ's body which is the most exalted of all has the highest place of all, according to Heb. vii. 26, *Made higher than the heavens,* where a gloss† says, *in place and dignity.* And again each glorified body will, in like manner, have a place befitting it according to the measure of its dignity. Now a fitting place is one of the conditions pertaining to glory. Since then after the resurrection the glory of the saints will never vary, neither by increase nor by decrease, because they will then have reached the final term of all, it would seem that their bodies will never leave the place assigned to them, and consequently will not be moved.

On the contrary, It is written (Isa. xl. 31): *They shall run and not be weary, they shall walk and not faint;* and (Wis. iii. 7): *(The just) shall run to and fro like sparks among*

the reeds. Therefore there will be some movement in glorified bodies.

I answer that, It is necessary to suppose that the glorified bodies are moved sometimes, since even Christ's body was moved in His ascension, and likewise the bodies of the saints, which will arise from the earth, will ascend to the empyrean.‡ But even after they have climbed the heavens, it is likely that they will sometimes move according as it pleases them; so that by actually putting into practice that which is in their power, they may show forth the excellence of Divine wisdom, and that furthermore their vision may be refreshed by the beauty of the variety of creatures, in which God's wisdom will shine forth with great evidence: for sense can only perceive that which is present, although glorified bodies can perceive from a greater distance than non-glorified bodies. And yet movement will nowise diminish their happiness which consists in seeing God, for He will be everywhere present to them; thus Gregory says of the angels *(Hom.* xxxiv *in Ev.)* that *wherever they are sent their course lies in God.*

Reply Obj. 1. Local movement changes nothing that is intrinsic to a thing, but only that which is without, namely place. Hence that which is moved locally is perfect as to those things which are within *(Phys.* viii. 7), although it has an imperfection as to place, because while it is in one place it is in potentiality with regard to another place, since it cannot be in several places at the same time, for this belongs to God alone. But this defect is not inconsistent with the perfection of glory, as neither is the defect whereby a creature is formed from nothing. Hence such like defects will remain in glorified bodies.

Reply Obj. 2. A person is said to need a thing in two ways, namely absolutely and relatively. One needs absolutely that without which one cannot retain one's being or one's perfection: and thus movement in glorified bodies will not be on account of a need, because their happiness will suffice them for all such things. But we need a thing relatively when without it some end we have in view cannot be obtained by us, or not so well, or not in some particular way. It is thus that movement will be in the blessed on account of need, for they will be unable to show forth their motive power practically, unless they be in motion, since nothing prevents a need of this kind being in glorified bodies.

Reply Obj. 3. This argument would prove if the glorified body were unable even without movement to share the Divine goodness much more perfectly than the heavenly bodies, which is untrue. Hence glorified bodies will be moved.

* Cf. Q. 70, A. 2, *ad* 1.   † Gloss on Heb. i. 3, *On the right hand of the majesty.*   ‡ Cf. footnote Q. 83, A. 2.

not in order to gain a perfect participation in the Divine goodness (since they have this through glory), but in order to show the soul's power. On the other hand, the movement of the heavenly bodies could not show their power, except the power they have in moving lower bodies to generation and corruption, which is not becoming to that state. Hence the argument does not prove.

Reply Obj. 4. Local movement takes nothing away from the stability of the soul that is established in God, since it does not affect that which is intrinsic to a thing, as stated above (*ad* 1).

Reply Obj. 5. The fitting place assigned to each glorified body according to the degree of its dignity belongs to the accidental reward. Nor does it follow that this reward is diminished whenever the body is outside its place; because that place pertains to reward, not as actually containing the body located therein (since nothing flows therefrom into the glorified body, but rather does it receive splendor therefrom), but as being due to merits. Wherefore, though out of that place, they will still continue to rejoice in it.

THIRD ARTICLE

Whether the Movement of the Saints Will Be Instantaneous?

We proceed thus to the Third Article:—

Objection 1. It would seem that movement of the saints will be instantaneous. For Augustine says *(De Civ. Dei,* xxii. 30) that *wherever the spirit listeth there will the body be.* Now the movement of the will, whereby the spirit wishes to be anywhere, is instantaneous. Therefore the body's movement will be instantaneous.

Obj. 2. Further, the Philosopher *(Phys.* iv. 8) proves that there is no movement through a vacuum, because it would follow that something moves instantaneously, since a vacuum offers no resistance whatever to a thing that is in motion, whereas the plenum offers resistance; and so there would be no proportion between the velocity of movement in a vacuum and that of movement in a plenum, since the ratio of movements in point of velocity is as the ratio of the resistance offered by the medium. Now the velocities of any two movements that take place in time must needs be proportional, since any one space of time is proportional to any other. But in like manner no full place can resist a glorified body since this can be in the same place with another body, no matter how this may occur; even as neither can a vacuum resist a body. Therefore if it moves at all, it moves instantaneously.

Obj. 3. Further, the power of a glorified

soul surpasses the power of a non-glorified soul, out of all proportion so to speak. Now the non-glorified soul moves the body in time. Therefore the glorified soul moves the body instantaneously.

Obj. 4. Further, whatever is moved equally soon to what is near and what is distant, is moved instantaneously. Now such is the movement of a glorified body, for however distant the space to which it is moved, the time it takes to be moved is imperceptible: wherefore Augustine says (QQ. *De Resurrectione, Ep.* cii, qu. 1) that *the glorified body reaches equally soon to any distance, like the sun's ray.* Therefore the glorified body is moved instantaneously.

Obj. 5. Further, whatever is in motion is moved either in time or in an instant. Now after the resurrection the glorified body will not be moved in time, since time will not be then according to Apoc. x. 6. Therefore this movement will be instantaneous.

On the contrary, In local movement space, movement and time are equally divisible, as is demonstrated in *Phys.* vi. 4. Now the space traversed by a glorified body in motion is divisible. Therefore both the movement and the time are divisible. But an instant is indivisible. Therefore this movement will not be instantaneous.

Further, a thing cannot be at the same time wholly in one place and partly in another place, since it would follow that the remaining part is in two places at the same time, which is impossible. But whatever is in motion is partly in a term *wherefrom* and partly in a term *whereto,* as is proved in *Phys.* vi. 6: while whatever has been in motion is wholly in the term whereto the movement is directed; and it is impossible at the same time for it to be moved and to have been moved. Now that which is moved instantaneously is being moved and has been moved at the same time. Therefore the local movement of a glorified body cannot be instantaneous.

I answer that, Opinion is much divided on this point. For some say that a glorified body passes from one place to another without passing through the interval, just as the will passes from one place to another without passing through the interval, and that consequently it is possible for the movement of a glorified body like that of the will to be instantaneous. But this will not hold: because the glorified body will never attain to the dignity of the spiritual nature, just as it will never cease to be a body. Moreover, when the will is said to move from one place to another, it is not essentially transferred from place to place, because in neither place is it contained essentially, but it is directed to one place after being directed by the intention to another: and in this sense it is said to move from one place to another.

Hence others* say that it is a property of the nature of a glorified body, since it is a body, to pass through the interval and consequently to be moved in time, but that by the power of glory, which raises it to a certain infinitude above the power of nature, it is possible for it not to pass through the interval, and consequently to be moved instantaneously. But this is impossible since it implies a contradiction: which is proved as follows. Suppose a body which we will call Z to be in motion from A to B. It is clear that Z, as long as it is wholly in A is not in motion; and in like manner when it is wholly in B, because then the movement is past. Therefore if it is at any time in motion it must needs be neither wholly in A nor wholly in B. Therefore while it is in motion, it is either nowhere, or partly in A and partly in B, or wholly in some other intervening place, say C, or partly in A and C and partly in C and B. But it is impossible for it to be nowhere, for then there would be a dimensive quantity without a place, which is impossible. Nor again is it possible for it to be partly in A and partly in B without being in some way in the intervening space; for since B is a place distant from A, it would follow that in the intervening space the part of Z which is in B is not continuous with the part which is in A. Therefore it follows that it is either wholly in C, or partly in C, and partly in some other place that intervenes between C and A, say D, and so forth. Therefore it follows that Z does not pass form A to B unless first of all it be in all the intervening places: unless we suppose that it passes from A to B without ever being moved, which implies a contradiction, because the very succession of places is local movement. The same applies to any change whatever having two opposite terms, each of which is a positive entity, but not to those changes which have only one positive term, the other being a pure privation, since between affirmation and negation or privation there is no fixed distance: wherefore that which is in the negation may be nearer to or more remote from affirmation, and conversely, by reason of something that causes either of them or disposes thereto: so that while that which is moved is wholly under a negation it is changed into affirmation, and vice versa; wherefore in such things *to be changing precedes to be changed,* as is proved in *Phys.* vi. 5. Nor is there any comparison with the movement of an angel, because being in a place is predicated equivocally of a body and an angel. Hence it is clear that it is

* Alexander of Hales, *Sum. Th.* III, Q. 23, mem. 3.

altogether impossible for a body to pass from one place to another, unless it pass through every interval.

Wherefore others grant this, and yet they maintain that the glorified body is moved instantaneously. But it follows from this that a glorified body is at the same instant in two or more places together, namely in the ultimate term, and in all the intervening places, which is impossible.

To this, however, they reply that, although it is the same instant really, it is not the same logically, like a point at which different lines terminate. But this is not enough, because an instant measures the instantaneous, according to its reality and not according to our way of considering it. Wherefore an instant through being considered in a different way is not rendered capable of measuring things that are not simultaneous in time, just as a point through being considered in a different way does not make it possible for one point of place to contain things that are locally distant from one another.

Hence others with greater probability hold that a glorified body moves in time, but that this time is so short as to be imperceptible; and that nevertheless one glorified body can pass through the same space in less time than another, because there is no limit to the divisibility of time, no matter how short a space we may take.

Reply Obj. 1. That which is little lacking is as it were not lacking at all (Phys. ii. 5); wherefore we say: *I do so and so at once,* when it is to be done after a short time. It is in this sense that Augustine speaks when he says that *wheresoever the will shall be, there shall the body be forthwith.* Or we may say that in the blessed there will never be an inordinate will: so that they never will wish their body to be instantaneously where it cannot be, and consequently whatever instant the will shall choose, at that same instant the body will be in whatever place the will shall determine.

Reply Obj. 2. Some have demurred to this proposition of the Philosopher's, as the Commentator thereon observes. They say that the ratio of one whole movement to another whole movement is not necessarily as the ratio of one resisting medium to another resisting medium, but that the ratio of the intervening mediums gives us the ratio of retardations attending the movements on account of the resistance of the medium. For every movement has a certain fixed speed, either fast or slow, through the mover overcoming the movable, although there be no resistance on the part of the medium; as evidenced in heavenly bodies, which have nothing to hinder their movement; and yet they do not move instantaneously, but in a fixed time proportionate to the power of the mover in comparison with the movable. Consequently it is clear that even if we suppose something to move in a vacuum, it does not follow that it moves instantaneously, but that nothing is added to the time which that movement requires in the aforesaid proportion of the mover to the movable, because the movement is not retarded.

But this reply, as the Commentator observes (ibid.), proceeds from an error in the imagination; for it is imagined that the retardation resulting from the resistance of the medium is a part of movement added to the natural movement, the quantity of which is in proportion to the mover in comparison with the movable, as when one line is added to another: for the proportion of one total to the other is not the same as the proportion of the lines to which an addition has been made.* And so there would not be the same proportion between one whole sensible movement and another, as between the retardations resulting from the resistance of the medium. This is an error of the imagination, because each part of a movement has as much speed as the whole movement: whereas not every part of a line has as much of the dimensive quantity as the whole line has. Hence any retardation or acceleration affecting the movement affects each of its parts, which is not the case with lines: and consequently the retardation that comes to a movement is not another part of the movement, whereas in the case of the lines that which is added is a part of the total line.

Consequently, in order to understand the Philosopher's argument, as the Commentator explains (ibid.), we must take the whole as being one, that is we must take not only the resistance of the movable to the moving power, but also the resistance of the medium through which the movement takes place, and again the resistance of anything else, so that we take the amount of retardation in the whole movement as being proportionate to the moving power in comparison with the resisting movable, no matter in what way it resist, whether by itself or by reason of something extrinsic. For the movable must needs always resist the mover somewhat, since mover and moved, agent and patient, as such, are opposed to one another. Now sometimes it is to be observed that the moved resists the mover by itself, either because it has a force inclining it to a contrary movement, as appears in violent movements, or at least because it has a place contrary to the place which is in the intention of the mover; and such like resistance even heavenly bodies offer their movers. Sometimes the movable resists the power of the mover, by reason only of something else and not by itself. This is seen in the natural movement of heavy and light things, because by their very form they are inclined to such a movement: for the form is an impression of their generator, which is the mover as regards heavy and light bodies. On the part of matter we find no resistance, neither of a force inclining to a contrary movement nor of a contrary place, since place is not due to matter except in so far as the latter, being circumscribed by its dimensions, is perfected by its natural form. Hence there can be no resistance save on the part of the medium, and this resistance is connatural to their movement. Sometimes again the resistance results from both, as may be seen in the movements of animals.

Accordingly when in a movement there is no resistance save on the part of the movable, as in the heavenly bodies, the time of the movement is measured according to the proportion of the mover to the movable, and the Philosopher's argument does not apply to these, since if there be no medium at all their movement is still a movement in time. On the other hand, in those movements where there is resistance on the part of the medium only, the measure of time is taken only according to the obstacle on the part of the medium, so that if the medium be removed there will be no longer an obstacle; and so either it will move instantaneously, or it will move in an equal time through a vacuum and through a plenum, because granted that it moves in time through a vacuum, that time will bear some proportion to the time in which it moves through a plenum. Now it is possible to imagine another body more subtle in the same proportion than the body which filled the space, and then if this body fill some other equal space it will move in as little time through that plenum as it did previously through a vacuum, since by as much as the subtlety of the medium is increased by so much is the length of time decreased, and the more subtle the medium the less it resists. But in those other movements where resistance is offered by both the movable and the medium, the quantity of time must be proportionate to the power of the mover as compared with the resistance of both movable and medium together. Hence granted that the medium be taken away altogether, or that it cease to hinder, it does not follow that the movement is instantaneous, but that the time is measured according only to the resistance of the movable. Nor will there be any inconsistency if it move in an equal time through a vacuum, and through a space filled with the most subtle body imaginable, since

* The same applies to mathematical quantities: for instance the ratio $2 + 1$ to $4 + 1$ is not as 2 to 4.

the greater the subtlety we ascribe to the medium the less is it naturally inclined to retard the movement. Wherefore it is possible to imagine so great a subtlety, as will naturally retard the movement less than does the resistance of the movable, so that the resistance of the medium will add no retardation to the movement.

It is therefore evident that although the medium offer no resistance to the glorified bodies, in so far as it is possible for them to be in the same place with another body, nevertheless their movement will not be instantaneous, because the movable body itself will resist the motive power, from the very fact that it has a determinate place, as we have said in reference to the heavenly bodies.

Reply Obj. 3. Although the power of a glorified soul surpasses immeasurably the power of a non-glorified soul, it does not surpass it infinitely, because both powers are finite: hence it does not follow that it causes instantaneous movement. And even if its power were simply infinite, it would not follow that it causes an instantaneous movement, unless the resistance of the movable were overcome altogether. Now although the resistance of the movable to the mover, that results from opposition to such a movement by reason of its being inclined to a contrary movement, can be altogether overcome by a mover of infinite power, never-theless the resistance it offers through contrariety towards the place which the mover intends by the movement cannot be overcome altogether, except by depriving it of its being in such and such a place or position. For just as white resists black by reason of whiteness, and all the more according as whiteness is the more distant from blackness, so a body resists a certain place through having an opposite place, and its resistance is all the greater, according as the distance is greater. Now it is impossible to take away from a body its being in some place or position, except one deprive it of its corporeity, by reason of which it requires a place or position: wherefore so long as it retains the nature of a body, it can nowise be moved instantaneously, however greater be the motive power. Now the glorified body will never lose its corporeity, and therefore it will never be possible for it to be moved instantaneously.

Reply Obj. 4. In the words of Augustine, the speed is said to be equal because the excess of one over the other is imperceptible, just as the time taken by the whole movement is imperceptible.

Reply Obj. 5. Although after the resurrection the time which is the measure of the heaven's movement will be no more, there will nevertheless be time resulting from the before and after in any kind of movement.

QUESTION 85

Of the Clarity of the Beatified Bodies

(In Three Articles)

WE must now consider the clarity of the beatified bodies at the resurrection. Under this head there are three points of inquiry: (1) Whether there will be clarity in the glorified bodies? (2) Whether this clarity will be visible to the non-glorified eye? (3) Whether a glorified body will of necessity be seen by a non-glorified body?

FIRST ARTICLE

Whether Clarity Is Becoming to the Glorified Body?

We proceed thus to the First Article:—

Objection 1. It would seem that clarity is unbecoming to the glorified body. Because according to Avicenna *(Natural.* vi. 2), *every luminous body consists of transparent parts.* But the parts of a glorified body will not be transparent, since in some of them, such as flesh and bones, earth is predominant. Therefore glorified bodies are not lightsome.

Obj. 2. Further, every lightsome body hides one that is behind it; wherefore one luminary behind another is eclipsed, and a flame of fire prevents one seeing what is behind it. But the glorified bodies will not hide that which is within them, for as Gregory says on Job xxviii. 17, *Gold or crystal cannot equal it (Moral.* xviii. 48). *There,* that is in the heavenly country, *the grossness of the members will not hide one's mind from another's eyes, and the very harmony of the body will be evident to the bodily sight.* Therefore those bodies will not be lightsome.

Obj. 3. Further, light and color require a contrary disposition in their subject, since *light is the extreme point of visibility in an indeterminate body; color, in a determinate body (De Sensu et Sensato,* iii). But glorified bodies will have color, for as Augustine says *(De Civ. Dei,* xxii. 3), *the body's beauty is harmony of parts with a certain charm of color:* and it will be impossible for the glorified bodies to lack beauty. Therefore the glorified bodies will not be lightsome.

Obj. 4. Further, if there be clarity in the

glorified bodies, it will need to be equal in all the parts of the body, just as all the parts will be equally impassible, subtle and agile. But this is not becoming, since one part has a greater disposition to clarity than another, for instance the eye than the hand, the spirits* than the bones, the humors than the flesh or nerves. Therefore it would seem unfitting for those bodies to be lightsome.

On the contrary, It is written (Matth. xiii. 43): *The just shall shine as the sun in the kingdom of their Father,* and (Wis. iii. 7): *The just shall shine, and shall run to and fro like sparks among the reeds.*

Further, it is written (1 Cor. xv. 43): *It is sown in dishonor, it shall rise in glory,* which refers to clarity, as evidenced by the previous context where the glory of the rising bodies is compared to the clarity of the stars. Therefore the bodies of the saints will be lightsome.

I answer that, It is necessary to assert that after the resurrection the bodies of the saints will be lightsome, on account of the authority of Scripture which makes this promise. But the cause of this clarity is ascribed by some to the fifth or heavenly essence, which will then predominate in the human body. Since, however, this is absurd, as we have often remarked (Q. 84, A. 1), it is better to say that this clarity will result from the overflow of the soul's glory into the body. For whatever is received into anything is received not according to the mode of the source whence it flows, but according to the mode of the recipient. Wherefore clarity which in the soul is spiritual is received into the body as corporeal. And consequently according to the greater clarity of the soul by reason of its greater merit, so too will the body differ in clarity, as the Apostle affirms (1 Cor. xv. 41). Thus in the glorified body the glory of the soul will be known, even as through a crystal is known the color of a body contained in a crystal vessel, as Gregory says on Job xxviii. 17, *Gold or crystal cannot equal it.*

Reply Obj. 1. Avicenna is speaking of a body that has clarity through the nature of its component parts. It is not thus but rather by merit of virtue that the glorified body will have clarity.

Reply Obj. 2. Gregory compares the glorified body to gold on account of clarity, and to crystal on account of its transparency. Wherefore seemingly we should say that they will be both transparent and lightsome; for that a lightsome body be not transparent is owing to the fact that the clarity of that body results from the density of the lightsome parts, and density is opposed to transparency. Then, however, clarity will result from another cause,

* Cf. footnote, Q. 82, A. 3.

as stated above: and the density of the glorified body will not deprive it of transparency, as neither does the density of a crystal deprive crystal.

Some, on the other hand, say that they are compared to crystal, not because they are transparent, but on account of this likeness, for as much as that which is enclosed in crystal is visible, so the glory of the soul enclosed in the glorified body will not be hidden. But the first explanation is better, because it safeguards better the dignity of the glorified body, and is more consistent with the words of Gregory.

Reply Obj. 3. The glory of the body will not destroy nature but will perfect it. Wherefore the body will retain the color due to it by reason of the nature of its component parts, but in addition to this it will have clarity resulting from the soul's glory. Thus we see bodies which have color by their nature aglow with the resplendence of the sun, or from some other cause extrinsic or intrinsic.

Reply Obj. 4. Even as the clarity of glory will overflow from the soul into the body according to the mode of the body, and is there otherwise than in the soul, so again it will overflow into each part of the soul according to the mode of that part. Hence it is not unreasonable that the different parts should have clarity in different ways, according as they are differently disposed thereto by their nature. Nor is there any comparison with the other gifts of the body, for the various parts of the body are not differently disposed in their regard.

SECOND ARTICLE

Whether the Clarity of the Glorified Body Is Visible to the Non-Glorified Eye?

We proceed thus to the Second Article:—

Objection 1. It would seem that the clarity of the glorified body is invisible to the nonglorified eye. For the visible object should be proportionate to the sight. But a non-glorified eye is not proportionate to see the clarity of glory, since this differs generically from the clarity of nature. Therefore the clarity of the glorified body will not be seen by a non-glorified eye.

Obj. 2. Further, the clarity of the glorified body will be greater than the clarity of the sun is now, since the clarity of the sun also will then be greater than it is now, according to Isa. xxx. 26, and the clarity of the glorified body will be much greater still, for which reason the sun and the entire world will receive greater clarity. Now a non-glorified eye is unable to gaze on the very orb of the sun on account of the greatness of its clarity. Therefore still less will it be able to gaze on the clarity of a glorified body.

Obj. 3. Further, a visible object that is opposite the eyes of the seer must needs be seen, unless there be some lesion to the eye. But the clarity of a glorified body that is opposite to non-glorified eyes is not necessarily seen by them: which is evident in the case of the disciples who saw our Lord's body after the resurrection, without witnessing its clarity. Therefore this clarity will be invisible to a non-glorified eye.

On the contrary, A gloss on Philip. iii. 21, *Made like to the body of His glory,* says: *It will be like the clarity which He had in the Transfiguration.* Now this clarity was seen by the non-glorified eyes of the disciples. Therefore the clarity of the glorified body will be visible to non-glorified eyes also.

Further, the wicked will be tortured in the judgment by seeing the glory of the just, according to Wis. v. 2. But they would not fully see their glory unless they gazed on their clarity. Therefore, etc.

I answer that, Some have asserted that the clarity of the glorified body will not be visible to the non-glorified eye, except by a miracle. But this is impossible, unless this clarity were so named equivocally, because light by its essence has a natural tendency to move the sight, and sight by its essence has a natural tendency to perceive light, even as the true is in relation to the intellect, and the good to the appetite. Wherefore if there were a sight altogether incapable of perceiving a light, either this sight is so named equivocally, or else this light is. This cannot be said in the point at issue, because then nothing would be made known to us when we are told that the glorified bodies will be lightsome: even so a person who says that a dog* is in the heavens conveys no knowledge to one who knows no other dog than the animal. Hence we must say that the clarity of a glorified body is naturally visible to the non-glorified eye.

Reply Obj. 1. The clarity of glory will differ generically from the clarity of nature, as to its cause, but not as to its species. Hence just as the clarity of nature is, by reason of its species, proportionate to the sight, so too will the clarity of glory be.

Reply Obj. 2. Just as a glorified body is not passible to a passion of nature but only to a passion of the soul,† so in virtue of its property of glory it acts only by the action of the soul. Now intense clarity does not disturb the sight, in so far as it acts by the action of the soul, for thus it rather gives delight, but it disturbs it in so far as it acts by the action of nature by heating and destroying the organ

of sight, and by scattering the spirits‡ asunder. Hence, though the clarity of a glorified body surpasses the clarity of the sun, it does not by its nature disturb the sight but soothes it: wherefore this clarity is compared to the jasper-stone (Apoc. xxi. 11).

Reply Obj. 3. The clarity of the glorified body results from the merit of the will and therefore will be subject to the will, so as to be seen or not seen according to its command. Therefore it will be in the power of the glorified body to show forth its clarity or to hide it: and this was the opinion of Præpositivus

THIRD ARTICLE

Whether a Glorified Body Will Be Necessarily Seen by a Non-Glorified Body?

We proceed thus to the Third Article:—

Objection 1. It would seem that a glorified body will be necessarily seen by a non-glorified body. For the glorified bodies will be lightsome. Now a lightsome body reveals itself and other things. Therefore the glorified bodies will be seen of necessity.

Obj. 2. Further, every body which hides other bodies that are behind it is necessarily perceived by the sight, from the very fact that the other things behind it are hidden. Now the glorified body will hide other bodies that are behind it from being seen, because it will be a colored body. Therefore it will be seen of necessity.

Obj. 3. Further, just as quantity is something in a body, so is the quality whereby a body is seen. Now quantity will not be subject to the will, so that the glorified body be able to be of greater or smaller quantity. Therefore neither will the quality of visibility be subject to the will, so that a body be able not to be seen.

On the contrary, Our body will be glorified in being made like to the body of Christ after the resurrection. Now after the resurrection Christ's body was not necessarily seen; in fact it vanished from the sight of the disciples at Emmaus (Luke xxiv. 31). Therefore neither will the glorified body be necessarily seen.

Further, there the body will be in complete obedience to the will. Therefore as the soul lists the body will be visible or invisible.

I answer that, A visible object is seen, inasmuch as it acts on the sight. Now there is no change in a thing through its acting or. not acting on an external object. Wherefore a glorified body may be seen or not seen without any property pertaining to its perfection being changed. Consequently it will be in the power of a glorified soul for its body to be seen or

---

* The dog star.　　† Cf. Q. 82, A. 1.　　‡ Cf. footnote, Q. 82, A. 3.

not seen, even as any other action of the body will be in the soul's power; else the glorified body would not be a perfectly obedient instrument of its principal agent.

Reply Obj. 1. This clarity will be obedient to the glorified body so that this will be able to show it or hide it.

Reply Obj. 2. A body's color does not prevent its being transparent except in so far as it affects the sight, because the sight cannot be affected by two colors at the same time, so as to perceive them both perfectly. But the color of the glorified body will be completely in the power of the soul, so that it can thereby act or not act on the sight. Hence it will be in its power to hide or not to hide a body that is behind it.

Reply Obj. 3. Quantity is inherent to the glorified body itself, nor would it be possible for the quantity to be altered at the soul's bidding without the glorified body suffering some alteration incompatible with its impassibility. Hence there is no comparison between quantity and visibility, because even this quality whereby it is visible cannot be removed at the soul's bidding, but the action of that quality will be suspended, and thus the body will be hidden at the soul's command.

QUESTION 86

Of the Conditions under Which the Bodies of the Damned Will Rise Again

(In Three Articles)

WE must next consider the conditions in which the bodies of the damned will rise again. Under this head there are three points of inquiry: (1) Whether the bodies of the damned will rise again with their deformities? (2) Whether their bodies will be corruptible? (3) Whether they will be impassible?

FIRST ARTICLE

Whether the Bodies of the Damned Will Rise Again With Their Deformities?

We proceed thus to the First Article:—

Objection 1. It would seem that the bodies of the damned will rise again with their deformities. For that which was appointed as a punishment for sin should not cease except the sin be forgiven. Now the lack of limbs that results from mutilation, as well as all other bodily deformities, are appointed as punishments for sin. Therefore these deformities will not be taken away from the damned, seeing that they will not have received the forgiveness of their sins.

Obj. 2. Further, just as the saints will rise again to final happiness, so the wicked will rise again to final unhappiness. Now when the saints rise again nothing will be taken from them that can pertain to their perfection, therefore nothing pertaining to the defect or unhappiness of the wicked will be taken from them at the resurrection. But such are their deformities. Therefore, etc.

Obj. 3. Further, just as deformity is a defect of the passible body, so is slowness of movement. Now slowness of movement will not be taken from the bodies of the damned at the resurrection, since their bodies will not be agile. Therefore for the same reason neither will their deformity be taken away.

On the contrary, It is written (1 Cor. xv. 52): *The dead shall rise again incorruptible;* where a gloss says: *The dead, i.e. sinners, or all the dead in general shall rise again incorruptible, i.e. without the loss of any limbs.* Therefore the wicked will rise again without their deformities.

Further, there will be nothing in the damned to lessen the sense of pain. But sickness hinders the sense of pain by weakening the organ of sense, and in like manner the lack of a limb would prevent pain from affecting the whole body. Therefore the damned will rise again without these defects.

I answer that, Deformity in the human body is of two kinds. One arises from the lack of a limb: thus we say that a mutilated person is deformed, because he lacks due proportion of the parts to the whole. Deformities of this kind, without any doubt, will not be in the bodies of the damned, since all bodies of both wicked and good will rise again whole. Another deformity arises from the undue disposition of the parts, by reason of undue quantity, quality, or place,—which deformity is, moreover, incompatible with due proportion of parts to whole. Concerning these deformities and like defects such as fevers and similar ailments which sometimes result in deformity, Augustine remained undecided and doubtful *(Enchir.* xcii) as the Master remarks (iv. *Sent.* D. 44). Among modern masters, however, there are two opinions on this point. For some say that such like deformities and defects will remain in the bodies of the damned, because they consider that those who are damned are sentenced to utmost unhappiness wherefrom no affliction should be rebated. But this would seem unreasonable. For in the restoration of the rising body we look to its natural perfection rather than to its previous condition: wherefore those who die under perfect age will rise again in the stature of youth, as stated above (Q. 81, A. 1). Consequently those who had natural defects in the body, or deformities resulting therefrom, will be restored without those defects or deformities at the resurrection, unless the demerit of sin prevent; and so if a person rise again with such defects and deformities, this will be for his punishment. Now the mode of punishment is according to the measure of guilt. And a sinner who is about to be damned may be burdened with less grievous sins and yet have deformities and defects which one who is about to be damned has not, while burdened with more grievous sins. Wherefore if he who had deformities in this life rise again with them, while the other who had them not in this life, and therefore, as is clear, will rise again without them, though deserving of greater punishment, the mode of the punishment would not correspond to the amount of guilt; in fact it would seem that a man is more punished on account of the pains which he suffered in this world; which is absurd.

Hence others say with more reason, that He Who fashioned nature will wholly restore the body's nature at the resurrection. Wherefore whatever defect or deformity was in the body through corruption, or weakness of nature or of natural principles (for instance fever, purblindness, and so forth) will be entirely done away at the resurrection: whereas those defects in the human body which are the natural result of its natural principles, such as heaviness, passibility, and the like, will be in the bodies of the damned, while they will be removed from the bodies of the elect by the glory of the resurrection.

Reply Obj. 1. Since in every tribunal punishment is inflicted according to the jurisdiction of the tribunal, the punishments which in this temporal life are inflicted for some particular sin are themselves temporal, and extend not beyond the term of this life. Hence although the damned are not pardoned their sins, it does not follow that there they will undergo the same punishments as they have in this world: but the Divine justice demands that there they shall suffer more severe punishment for eternity.

Reply Obj. 2. There is no parity between the good and the wicked, because a thing can be altogether good, but not altogether evil. Hence the final happiness of the saints requires that they should be altogether exempt from all evil; whereas the final unhappiness of the wicked will not exclude all good, because *if a thing be wholly evil it destroys itself,* as the Philosopher says *(Ethic.* iv. 5). Hence it is necessary for the good of their nature to under-

lie the unhappiness of the damned, which good is the work of their perfect Creator, Who will restore that same nature to the perfection of its species.

Reply Obj. 3. Slowness of movement is one of those defects which are the natural result of the principles of the human body; but deformity is not, and consequently the comparison fails.

SECOND ARTICLE

Whether the Bodies of the Damned Will Be Incorruptible?

We proceed thus to the Second Article:—

Objection 1. It would seem that the bodies of the damned will be corruptible. For everything composed of contraries must necessarily be corruptible. Now the bodies of the damned will be composed of the contraries whereof they are composed even now, else they would not be the same, neither specifically nor, in consequence, numerically. Therefore they will be corruptible.

Obj. 2. Further, if the bodies of the damned will not be corruptible, this will be due either to nature, or to grace, or to glory. But it will not be by nature, since they will be of the same nature as now; nor will it be by grace or glory, since they will lack these things altogether. Therefore they will be corruptible.

Obj. 3. Further, it would seem inconsistent to withdraw the greatest of punishments from those who are in the highest degree of unhappiness. Now death is the greatest of punishments, as the Philosopher declares *(Ethic.* iii. 6). Therefore death should not be withdrawn from the damned, since they are in the highest degree of unhappiness. Therefore their bodies will be corruptible.

On the contrary, It is written (Apoc. ix. 6): *In those days men shall seek death, and shall not find it, and they shall desire to die, and death shall fly from them.*

Further, the damned will be punished with an everlasting punishment both in soul and body (Matth. xxv. 46): *These shall go into everlasting punishment.* But this would not be possible if their bodies were corruptible. Therefore their bodies will be incorruptible.

I answer that, Since in every movement there must needs be a principle of movement, movement or change may be withdrawn from a movable in two ways: first through absence of a principle of movement, secondly through an obstacle to the principle of movement. Now corruption is a kind of change: and consequently a body which is corruptible on account of the nature of its principles may be rendered incorruptible in two ways. First by the total removal of the principle which leads to corruption, and in this way the bodies of the damned will be incorruptible. For since the heaven is the first principle of alteration in virtue of its local movement, and all other secondary agents act in virtue thereof and as though moved thereby, it follows that at the cessation of the heavenly movement there is no longer any agent that can change the body by altering it from its natural property. Wherefore after the resurrection, and the cessation of the heavenly movement, there will be no quality capable of altering the human body from its natural quality. Now corruption, like generation, is the term of alteration. Hence the bodies of the damned will be incorruptible, and this will serve the purpose of Divine justice, since living for ever they will be punished for ever. This is in keeping with the demands of Divine justice, as we shall state further on (A. 3), even as now the corruptibility of bodies serves the purpose of Divine providence, by which through the corruption of one thing another is generated.

Secondly, this happens through the principle of corruption being hindered, and in this way the body of Adam was incorruptible, because the conflicting qualities that exist in man's body were withheld by the grace of innocence from conducing to the body's dissolution: and much more will they be withheld in the glorified bodies, which will be wholly subject to the spirit. Thus after the general resurrection the two aforesaid modes of incorruptibility will be united together in the bodies of the blessed.

Reply Obj. 1. The contraries of which bodies are composed are conducive to corruption as secondary principles. For the first active principle thereof is the heavenly movement: wherefore given the movement of the heaven, it is necessary for a body composed of contraries to be corrupted unless some more powerful cause prevent it: whereas if the heavenly movement be withdrawn, the contraries of which a body is composed do not suffice to cause corruption, even in accordance with nature, as explained above. But the philosophers were ignorant of a cessation in the heavenly movement; and consequently they held that a body composed of contraries is without fail corrupted in accordance with nature.

Reply Obj. 2. This incorruptibility will result from nature, not as though there were some principle of incorruption in the bodies of the damned, but on account of the cessation of the active principle of corruption, as shown above.

Reply Obj. 3. Although death is simply the greatest of punishments, yet nothing prevents death conducing, in a certain respect, to a cessation of punishments; and consequently the removal of death may contribute to the increase of punishment. For as the Philosopher says (*Ethic.* ix. 9), *Life is pleasant to all, for all desire to be. . . . But we must not apply this to a wicked or corrupt life, nor one passed in sorrow.* Accordingly just as life is simply pleasant, but not the life that is passed in sorrows, so too death, which is the privation of life, is painful simply, and the greatest of punishments, inasmuch as it deprives one of the primary good, namely being, with which other things are withdrawn. But in so far as it deprives one of a wicked life, and of such as is passed in sorrow, it is a remedy for pains, since it puts an end to them; and consequently the withdrawal of death leads to the increase of punishments by making them everlasting. If however we say that death is penal by reason of the bodily pain which the dying feel, without doubt the damned will continue to feel a far greater pain: wherefore they are said to be in *everlasting death,* according to the Psalm (xlviii. 15): *Death shall feed upon them.*

THIRD ARTICLE

Whether the Bodies of the Damned Will Be Impassible?

We proceed thus to the Third Article:—

Objection 1. It would seem that the bodies of the damned will be impassible. For, according to the Philosopher (*Topic.* vi), *increase of passion results in loss of substance.* Now *if a finite thing be continually lessened, it must needs at length be done away* (*Phys.* i. 4). Therefore if the bodies of the damned will be passible, and will be ever suffering, they will at length be done away and corrupted: and this has been shown to be false (A. 2). Therefore they will be impassible.

Obj. 2. Further, every agent likens the patient to itself. If then the bodies of the damned are passive to the fire the fire will liken them to itself. Now fire does not consume bodies except in so far as in likening them to itself it disintegrates them. Therefore if the bodies of the damned will be passible they will at length be consumed by the fire, and thus the same conclusion follows as before.

Obj. 3. Further, those animals, for instance the salamander, which are said to remain living in fire without being destroyed, are not distressed by the fire: because an animal is not distressed by bodily pain, unless the body in some way is hurt thereby. If therefore the bodies of the damned can, like the aforesaid animals, remain in the fire without being corrupted, as Augustine asserts (*De Civ. Dei,* xxi. 2, 4), it would seem that they will suffer no distress there: which would not be the case unless their bodies were impassible. Therefore, etc.

Obj. 4. Further, if the bodies of the damned

be passible, the pain resulting from their suffering, seemingly, will surpass all present bodily pain, even as the joy of the saints will surpass all present joy. Now in this life it sometimes happens that the soul is severed from the body through excess of pain. Much more therefore if those bodies will be passible, the souls will be separate from the bodies through excess of pain, and thus those bodies will be corrupted: which is false. Therefore those bodies will be impassible.

On the contrary, It is written (1 Cor. xv. 52): *And we shall be changed:* and a gloss says: *We,—the good alone,—will be changed with the unchangeableness and impassibility of glory.*

Further, even as the body co-operates with the soul in merit, so does it co-operate in sin. Now on account of the former co-operation not only the soul but also the body will be rewarded after the resurrection. Therefore in like manner the bodies of the damned will be punished; which would not be the case were they impassible. Therefore they will be passible.

I answer that, The principal cause of the bodies of the damned not being consumed by fire will be the Divine justice by which their bodies will be consigned to everlasting punishment. Now the Divine justice is served also by the natural disposition, whether on the part of the passive body or on the part of the active causes; for since passiveness is a kind of receptiveness, there are two kinds of passion, corresponding to two ways in which one thing is receptive of another. For a form may be received into a subject materially according to its natural being, just as the air receives heat from fire materially; and corresponding to this manner of reception there is a kind of passion which we call *passion of nature.* In another way one thing is received into another spiritually by way of an *intention,* just as the likeness of whiteness is received into the air and in the pupil: this reception is like that whereby the soul receives the likeness of things: wherefore corresponding to this mode of reception is another mode of passion which we call *passion of the soul.* Since therefore after the resurrection and the cessation of the heavenly movement it will be impossible for a body to be altered by its natural quality, as stated above (A. 2), it will not be possible for any body to be passive with a passion of nature. Consequently as regards this mode of passion the bodies of the damned will be impassible even as they will be incorruptible. Yet after the heaven has ceased to move, there will still remain the passion which is after the manner of the soul, since the air will both receive light from the sun, and will convey the variety of colors to the sight. Wherefore in respect of

this mode of passion the bodies of the damned will be passible. But the glorified bodies, albeit they receive something, and are in a manner patient to sensation, will nevertheless not be passive, since they will receive nothing to distress or hurt them, as will the bodies of the damned, which for this reason are said to be passible.

Reply Obj. 1. The Philosopher is speaking of the passion whereby the patient is changed from its natural disposition. But this kind of passion will not be in the bodies of the damned, as stated above.

Reply Obj. 2. The likeness of the agent is in the patient in two ways. First, in the same way as in the agent, and thus it is in all univocal agents, for instance a thing that is hot makes another thing hot, and fire generates fire. Secondly, otherwise than in the agent, and thus it is in all equivocal agents. In these it happens sometimes that a form which is in the agent spiritually is received into the patient materially: thus the form of the house built by the craftsman is materially in itself, but spiritually in the mind of the craftsman. On the other hand, sometimes it is in the agent materially, but is received into the patient spiritually: thus whiteness is materially on the wall wherein it is received, whereas it is spiritually in the pupil and in the transferring medium. And so it is in the case at issue, because the species which is in the fire materially is received spiritually into the bodies of the damned; thus it is that the fire will assimilate the bodies of the damned to itself, without consuming them withal.

Reply Obj. 3. According to the Philosopher (*De Prop. Element.*), *no animal can live in fire.* Galen also (*De simp. medic.*) says *that there is no body which at length is not consumed by fire;* although sometimes certain bodies may remain in fire without hurt, such as ebony. The instance of the salamander is not altogether apposite, since it cannot remain in the fire without being at last consumed, as do the bodies of the damned in hell. Nor does it follow that because the bodies of the damned suffer no corruption from the fire, they therefore are not tormented by the fire, because the sensible object has a natural aptitude to please or displease the senses, not only as regards its natural action of stimulating or injuring the organ, but also as regards its spiritual action: since when the sensible object is duly proportionate to the sense, it pleases, whereas the contrary is the result when it is in excess or defect. Hence subdued colors and harmonious sounds are pleasing, whereas discordant sounds displease the hearing.

Reply Obj. 4. Pain does not sever the soul from the body, in so far as it is confined to a power of the soul which feels the pain, but in so far as the passion of the soul leads to the body being changed from its natural disposition. Thus it is that we see that through anger the body becomes heated, and through fear, chilled: whereas after the resurrection it will be impossible for the body to be changed from its natural disposition, as stated above (A. 2). Consequently, however great the pain will be, it will not sever the body from the soul.

QUESTION 87

Of the Knowledge Which, after Rising Again, Men Will Have at the Judgment concerning Merits and Demerits

(In Three Articles)

In the next place we must treat of those things which follow the resurrection. The first of these to be considered will be the knowledge, which after rising again, men will have at the judgment, concerning merits and demerits; the second will be the general judgment itself, as also the time and place at which it will be; thirdly we shall consider who will judge and who will be judged; fourthly we shall treat of the form wherein the judge will come to judge; and fifthly we shall consider what will be after the judgment, the state of the world and of those who will have risen again.

Under the first head there are three points of inquiry: (1) Whether at the judgment every man will know all his sins? (2) Whether every one will be able to read all that is on another's conscience? (3) Whether one will be able at one glance to see all merits and demerits?

FIRST ARTICLE

Whether after the Resurrection Every One Will Know What Sins He Has Committed?

We proceed thus to the First Article:—

Objection 1. It seems that after the resurrection everyone will not be able to know all the sins he has committed. For whatever we know, either we receive it anew through the senses, or we draw it from the treasure house of the memory. Now after the resurrection men will be unable to perceive their sins by means of sense, because they will be things of the past, while sense perceives only the present: and many sins will have escaped the sinner's memory, and he will be unable to recall them from the treasure house of his memory. Therefore after rising again one will not be cognizant of all the sins one has committed.

Obj. 2. Further, it is stated in the text (iv *Sent.* D. 43), that *there are certain books of the conscience, wherein each one's merits are inscribed.* Now one cannot read a thing in a book, unless it be marked down in the book: and sin leaves its mark upon the conscience

according to a gloss of Origen on Rom. ii. 15, *Their conscience bearing witness,* etc., which mark, seemingly, is nothing else than the guilt or stain. Since then in many persons the guilt or stain of many sins is blotted out by grace, it would seem that one cannot read in one's conscience all the sins one has committed: and thus the same conclusion follows as before.

Obj. 3. Further, the greater the cause the greater the effect. Now the cause which makes us grieve for the sins which we recall to memory is charity. Since then charity is perfect in the saints after the resurrection, they will grieve exceedingly for their sins, if they recall them to memory: yet this is impossible, seeing that according to Apoc. xxi. 4, *Sorrow and mourning shall flee away from them.** Therefore they will not recall their own sins to memory.

Obj. 4. Further, at the resurrection the damned will be to the good they once did as the blessed to the sins they once committed. Now seemingly the damned after rising again will have no knowledge of the good they once did, since this would alleviate their pain considerably. Neither therefore will the blessed have any knowledge of the sins they had committed.

On the contrary, Augustine says (*De Civ. Dei,* xx) that *a kind of Divine energy will come to our aid, so that we shall recall all of our sins to mind.*

Further, as human judgment is to external evidence, so is the Divine judgment to the witness of the conscience, according to 1 Kings xvi. 7, *Man seeth those things that appear, but the Lord beholdeth the heart.* Now man cannot pass a perfect judgment on a matter unless evidence be taken on all the points that need to be judged. Therefore, since the Divine judgment is most perfect, it is necessary for the conscience to witness to everything that has to be judged. But all works, both good and evil, will have to be judged (2 Cor. v. 10): *We must all be manifested before the judgment seat of Christ, that every one may receive*

---

* The quotation is from Isa. xxxv. 10. The text of the Apocalypse has: *Nor mourning, nor crying, nor sorrow shall be any more.*

the proper things of the body, according as he hath done, whether it be good or evil. Therefore each one's conscience must needs retain all the works he has done, whether good or evil.

I answer that, According to Rom. ii. 15, 16, *In the day when God shall judge* each one's conscience will bear witness to him, and his thoughts will accuse and defend him. And since in every judicial hearing, the witness, the accuser, and the defendant need to be acquainted with the matter on which judgment has to be pronounced, and since at the general judgment all the works of men will be submitted to judgment, it will behoove every man to be cognizant then of all his works. Wherefore each man's conscience will be as a book containing his deeds on which judgment will be pronounced, even as in the human court of law we make use of records. Of these books it is written in the Apocalypse (xx. 12): *The books were opened: and another book was opened, which is the book of life; and the dead were judged by those things which were written in the books* (Vulg.,—*book*) *according to their works.* According to Augustine's exposition *(De Civ. Dei,* xx) the books which are here said to be opened *denote the saints of the New and Old Testaments in whom God's commandments are exemplified.* Hence Richard of S. Victor *(De judic. potest.)* says: *Their hearts will be like the code of law.* But the book of life, of which the text goes on to speak, signifies each one's conscience, which is said to be one single book, because the one Divine power will cause all to recall their deeds, and this energy, in so far as it reminds a man of his deeds, is called the *book of life.** Or else we may refer the first books to the conscience, and by the second book we may understand the Judge's sentence as expressed in His providence.

Reply Obj. 1. Although many merits and demerits will have escaped our memory, yet there will be none of them but will remain somewhat in its effect, because those merits which are not deadened will remain in the reward accorded to them, while those that are deadened remain in the guilt of ingratitude, which is increased through the fact that a man sinned after receiving grace. In like manner those demerits which are not blotted out by repentance remain in the debt of punishment due to them, while those which have been blotted out by repentance remain in the remembrance of repentance, which they will recall together with their other merits. Hence in each man there will be something whereby he will be able to recollect his deeds. Nevertheless, as Augustine says *(loc. cit.),* the Divine energy will especially conduce to this.

* Cf. P. I, Q. 24, A. 1, *ad* 1.   † Cf. P. I, Q. 107.

Reply Obj. 2. Each one's conscience will bear certain marks of the deeds done by him; and it does not follow that these marks are the guilt alone, as stated above.

Reply Obj. 3. Although charity is now the cause of sorrow for sin, yet the saints in heaven will be so full of joy, that they will have no room for sorrow; and so they will not grieve for their sins, but rather will they rejoice in the Divine mercy, whereby their sins are forgiven them. Even so do the angels rejoice now in the Divine justice whereby those whom they guard fall headlong into sin through being abandoned by grace; and whose salvation none the less they eagerly watch over.

Reply Obj. 4. The wicked will know all the good they have done, and this will not diminish their pain; indeed, it will increase it, because the greatest sorrow is to have lost many goods: for which reason Boëthius says *(De Consol.* ii) that *the greatest misfortune is to have been happy.*

SECOND ARTICLE

Whether Every One Will Be Able to Read All That Is in Another's Conscience

We proceed thus to the Second Article:—

Objection 1. It seems that it will be impossible for every one to read all that is in another's conscience. For the knowledge of those who rise again will not be clearer than that of the angels, equality with whom is promised us after the resurrection (Matth. xxii. 30). Now angels cannot read one another's thoughts in matters dependent on the free-will, wherefore they need to speak in order to notify such things to one another.† Therefore after rising again we shall be unable to read what is contained in another's conscience.

Obj. 2. Further, whatever is known is known either in itself, or in its cause, or in its effect. Now the merits or demerits contained in a person's conscience cannot be known by another in themselves, because God alone enters the heart and reads its secrets. Neither will it be possible for them to be known in their cause, since all will not see God Who alone can act on the will, whence merits and demerits proceed. Nor again will it be possible to know them from their effect, since there will be many demerits, which through being wholly blotted out by repentance will leave no effect remaining. Therefore it will not be possible for every one to know all that is in another's conscience.

Obj. 3. Further, Chrysostom says *(Hom.* xxxi *in Ep. ad Hebr.),* as we have quoted before (iv. *Sent.* D. 17): *If thou remember thy sins now, and frequently confess them before God and beg pardon for them, thou wilt very soon blot them out; but if thou forget them, thou wilt then remember them unwillingly, when they will be made public, and declared before all thy friends and foes, and in the presence of the holy angels.* Hence it follows that this publication will be the punishment of man's neglect in omitting to confess his sins. Therefore the sins which a man has confessed will not be made known to others.

Obj. 4. Further, it is a relief to know that one has had many associates in sin, so that one is less ashamed thereof. If therefore every one were to know the sin of another, each sinner's shame would be much diminished, which is unlikely. Therefore every one will not know the sins of all.

On the contrary, A gloss on 1 Cor. iv. 5, *will . . . bring to light the hidden things of darkness,* says: *Deeds and thoughts both good and evil will then be revealed and made known to all.*

Further, the past sins of all the good will be equally blotted out. Yet we know the sins of some saints, for instance of Magdalen, Peter, and David. Therefore in like manner the sins of the other elect will be known, and much more those of the damned.

I answer that, At the last and general judgment it behooves the Divine justice, which now is in many ways hidden, to appear evidently to all. Now the sentence of one who condemns or rewards cannot be just, unless it be delivered according to merits and demerits. Therefore just as it behooves both judge and jury to know the merits of a case, in order to deliver a just verdict, so is it necessary, in order that the sentence appear to be just, that all who know the sentence should be acquainted with the merits. Hence, since every one will know of his reward or condemnation, so will every one else know of it, and consequently as each one will recall his own merits or demerits, so will he be cognizant of those of others. This is the more probable and more common opinion, although the Master (iv *Sent.* D. 43) says the contrary, namely that a man's sins blotted out by repentance will not be made known to others at the judgment. But it would follow from this that neither would his repentance for these sins be perfectly known, which would detract considerably from the glory of the saints and the praise due to God for having so mercifully delivered them.

Reply Obj. 1. All the preceding merits or demerits will come to a certain amount in the glory or unhappiness of each one rising again. Consequently through eternal things being seen, all things in their consciences will be visible, especially as the Divine power will conduce to this so that the Judge's sentence may appear just to all.

Reply Obj. 2. It will be possible for a man's merits or demerits to be made known by their effects as stated above (A. 1, *ad* 1), or by the power of God, although the power of the created intellect is not sufficient for this.

Reply Obj. 3. The manifestation of his sins to the confusion of the sinner is a result of his neglect in omitting to confess them. But that the sins of the saints be revealed cannot be to their confusion or shame, as neither does it bring confusion to Mary Magdalen that her sins are publicly recalled in the Church, because shame is *fear of disgrace,* as Damascene says (*De Fide Orthod.* ii), and this will be impossible in the blessed. But this manifestation will bring them great glory on account of the penance they did, even as the confessor hails a man who courageously confesses great crimes. Sins are said to be blotted out because God sees them not for the purpose of punishing them.

Reply Obj. 4. The sinner's confusion will not be diminished, but on the contrary increased, through his seeing the sins of others, for in seeing that others are blameworthy he will all the more acknowledge himself to be blamed. For that confusion be diminished by a cause of this kind is owing to the fact that shame regards the esteem of men, who esteem more lightly that which is customary. But then confusion will regard the esteem of God, which weighs every sin according to the truth, whether it be the sin of one man or of many.

THIRD ARTICLE

Whether All Merits and Demerits, One's Own As Well As Those of Others, Will Be Seen by Anyone at a Single Glance?

We proceed thus to the Third Article:—

Objection 1. It would seem that not all merits and demerits, one's own as well as those of others, will be seen by anyone at a single glance. For things considered singly are not seen at one glance. Now the damned will consider their sins singly and will bewail them, wherefore they say (Wis. v. 8): *What hath pride profited us?* Therefore they will not see them all at a glance.

Obj. 2. Further, the Philosopher says (*Topic.* ii) that *we do not arrive at understanding several things at the same time.* Now merits and demerits, both our own and those of others, will not be visible save to the intellect. Therefore it will be impossible for them all to be seen at the same time.

Obj. 3. Further, the intellect of the damned after the resurrection will not be clearer than the intellect of the blessed and of the angels is now, as to the natural knowledge whereby they know things by innate species. Now by such knowledge the angels do not see several things at the same time. Therefore neither will the damned be able then to see all their deeds at the same time.

On the contrary, A gloss on Job viii. 22, *They . . . shall be clothed with confusion,* says: *As soon as they shall see the Judge, all their evil deeds will stand before their eyes.* Now they will see the Judge suddenly. Therefore in like manner will they see the evil they have done, and for the same reason all others.

Further, Augustine *(De Civ. Dei,* xx) considers it unfitting that at the judgment a material book should be read containing the deeds of each individual written therein, for the reason that it would be impossible to measure the size of such a book, or the time it would take to read. But in like manner it would be impossible to estimate the length of time one would require in order to consider all one's merits and demerits and those of others, if one saw these various things one after the other. Therefore we must admit that each one sees them all at the same time.

I answer that, There are two opinions on this question. For some say that one will see all merits and demerits, both one's own and those of others, at the same time in an instant. This is easily credible with regard to the blessed, since they will see all things in the Word: and consequently it is not unreasonable that they should see several things at the same time. But with regard to the damned, a difficulty presents itself, since their intellect is not raised so that they can see God and all else in Him. Wherefore others say that the wicked will see all their sins and those of others generically at the same time: and this suffices for the accusation or absolution necessary for the judgment; but that they will not see them all down to each single one at the same time. But neither does this seem consonant with the words of Augustine *(De Civ. Dei* xx), who says that they will count them all with one glance of the mind; and what is known generically is not counted. Hence we may choose a middle way, by holding that they will consider each sin not instantaneously, but in a very short time, the Divine power coming to their aid. This agrees with the saying of Augustine *(ibid.)* that *they will be discerned with wondrous rapidity.* Nor is this impossible, since in a space of time, however short, is potentially an infinite number of instants. This suffices for the replies to the objections on either side of the question.

QUESTION 88

Of the General Judgment, As to the Time and Place at Which It Will Be

(In Four Articles)

WE must next consider the general judgment, as to the time and place at which it will be. Under this head there are four points of inquiry: (1) Whether there will be a general judgment? (2) Whether as regards the debate it will be conducted by word of mouth? (3) Whether it will take place at an unknown time? (4) Whether it will take place in the valley of Josaphat?

FIRST ARTICLE

Whether There Will Be a General Judgment?

We proceed thus to the First Article:—

Objection 1. It would seem that there will not be a general judgment. For according to Nahum i. 9, following the Septuagint version, *God will not judge the same thing a second time.* But God judges now of mans' every work, by assigning punishments and rewards to each one after death, and also by rewarding and punishing certain ones in this life for their good or evil deeds. Therefore it would seem that there will be no other judgment.

Obj. 2. Further, in no judicial inquiry is the sentence carried out before judgment is pronounced. But the sentence of the Divine judgment on man regards the acquisition of the kingdom or exclusion from the kingdom (Matth. xxv. 34, 41). Therefore since some obtain possession of the kingdom now, and some are excluded from it for ever, it would seem that there will be no other judgment.

Obj. 3. Further, the reason why certain things are submitted to judgment is that we may come to a decision about them. Now before the end of the world each of the damned is awarded his damnation, and each of the blessed his beatitude. Therefore, etc.

On the contrary, It is written (Matth. xii. 41): *The men of Nineve shall rise in judgment with this generation, and shall condemn it.* Therefore there will be a judgment after the resurrection.

Further, it is written (Jo. v. 29): *They that have done good things shall come forth unto the resurrection of life, but they that have done evil, unto the resurrection of judgment.* Therefore it would seem that after the resurrection there will be a judgment.

I answer that, Just as operation refers to the beginning wherefrom things receive their being, so judgment belongs to the term, wherein they are brought to their end. Now we distinguish a twofold operation in God. One is that whereby He first gave things their being, by fashioning their nature and by establishing the distinctions which contribute to the perfection thereof: from this work God is stated to have rested (Gen. ii. 2). His other operation is that whereby He works in governing creatures; and of this it is written (Jo. v. 17): *My Father worketh until now; and I work.* Hence we distinguish in Him a twofold judgment, but in the reverse order. One corresponds to the work of governance which cannot be without judgment: and by this judgment each one is judged individually according to his works, not only as adapted to himself, but also as adapted to the government of the universe. Hence one man's reward is delayed for the good of others (Heb. xi. 13, 39, 40), and the punishment of one conduces to the profit of another. Consequently it is necessary that there should be another, and that a general judgment corresponding on the other hand with the first formation of things in being, in order that, to wit, just as then all things proceeded immediately from God, so at length the world will receive its ultimate complement, by each one receiving finally his own personal due. Hence at this judgment the Divine justice will be made manifest in all things, whereas now it remains hidden, for as much as at times some persons are dealt with for the profit of others, otherwise than their manifest works would seem to require. For this same reason there will then be a general separation of the good from the wicked, because there will be no further motive for the good to profit by the wicked, or the wicked by the good: for the sake of which profit the good are meanwhile mingled with the wicked, so long as this state of life is governed by Divine providence.

Reply Obj. 1. Each man is both an individual person and a part of the whole human race: wherefore a twofold judgment is due to him. One, the particular judgment, is that to which he will be subjected after death, when he will receive according as he hath done in the body,* not indeed entirely but only in part, since he will receive not in the body but only in the soul. The other judgment will be passed on him as a part of the human race: thus a man is said to be judged according to human justice, even when judgment is pronounced on the community of which he is a part. Hence at the general judgment of the whole human race by the general separation of the good from the wicked, it follows that each one will be judged. And yet God will not judge *the same thing a second time*, since He will not inflict

* Cf. 2 Cor. v. 10.

two punishments for one sin, and the punishment which before the judgment was not inflicted completely will be completed at the last judgment, after which the wicked will be tormented at the same time in body and soul.

Reply Obj. 2. The sentence proper to this general judgment is the general separation of the good from the wicked, which will not precede this judgment. Yet even now, as regards the particular sentence on each individual, the judgment does not at once take full effect, since even the good will receive an increase of reward after the judgment, both from the added glory of the body and from the completion of the number of the saints. The wicked also will receive an increase of torment from the added punishment of the body and from the completion of the number of damned to be punished, because the more numerous those with whom they will burn, the more will they themselves burn.

Reply Obj. 3. The general judgment will regard more directly the generality of men than each individual to be judged, as stated above. Wherefore although before that judgment each one will be certain of his condemnation or reward, he will not be cognizant of the condemnation or reward of everyone else. Hence the necessity of the general judgment.

SECOND ARTICLE

Whether the Judgment Will Take Place by Word of Mouth?

We proceed thus to the Second Article:—

Objection 1. It would seem that this judgment, as regards the inquiry and sentence, will take place by word of mouth. For according to Augustine (*De Civ. Dei*, xx) *it is uncertain how many days this judgment will last.* But it would not be uncertain if the things we are told will take place at the judgment were to be accomplished only in the mind. Therefore this judgment will take place by word of mouth and not only in the mind.

Obj. 2. Further, Gregory says (*Moral.* xxvi): *Those at least will hear the words of the Judge, who have confessed their faith in Him by words.* Now this cannot be understood as referring to the inner word, because thus all will hear the Judge's words, since all the deeds of other men will be known to all both good and wicked. Therefore it seems that this judgment will take place by word of mouth.

Obj. 3. Further, Christ will judge according to His human form, so as to be visible in the body to all. Therefore in like manner it seems that He will speak with the voice of the body, so as to be heard by all.

On the contrary, Augustine says (*De Civ.*

Dei, xx) that the book of life which is mentioned Apoc. xx. 12, 15 *is a kind of Divine energy enabling each one to remember all his good or evil works, and to discern them with the gaze of the mind, with wondrous rapidity, his knowledge accusing or defending his conscience, so that all and each will be judged at the same moment.* But if each one's merits were discussed by word of mouth, all and each could not be judged at the same moment. Therefore it would seem that this judgment will not take place by word of mouth.

Further, the sentence should correspond proportionately to the evidence. Now the evidence both of accusation and of defense will be mental, according to Rom. ii. 15, 16, *Their conscience bearing witness to them, and their thoughts between themselves accusing or also defending one another in the day when God shall judge the secrets of men.* Therefore seemingly, this sentence and the entire judgment will take place mentally.

I answer that, It is not possible to come to any certain conclusion about the truth of this question. It is, however, the more probable opinion that the whole of this judgment, whether as regards the inquiry, or as regards the accusation of the wicked and the approval of the good, or again as regards the sentence on both, will take place mentally. For if the deeds of each individual were to be related by word of mouth, this would require an inconceivable length of time. Thus Augustine says *(loc. cit.)* that *if we suppose the book, from the pages of which all will be judged according to Apoc. xx, to be a material book, who will be able to conceive its size and length? or the length of time required for the reading of a book that contains the entire life of every individual?* Nor is less time requisite for telling by word of mouth the deeds of each individual, than for reading them if they were written in a material book. Hence, probably we should understand that the details set forth in Matth. xxv will be fulfilled not by word of mouth but mentally.

Reply Obj. 1. The reason why Augustine says that *it is uncertain how many days this judgment will last* is precisely because it is not certain whether it will take place mentally or by word of mouth. For if it were to take place by word of mouth, a considerable time would be necessary; but if mentally, it is possible for it to be accomplished in an instant.

Reply Obj. 2. Even if the judgment is accomplished solely in the mind, the saying of Gregory stands, since though all will be cognizant of their own and of others' deeds, as a result of the Divine energy which the Gospel describes as speech (Matth. xxv. 34-46), never-

theless those who have had the faith which they received through God's words will be judged from those very words, for it is written (Rom. ii. 12): *Whosoever have sinned in the Law shall be judged by the Law.* Hence in a special way something will be said to those who had been believers, which will not be said to unbelievers.

Reply Obj. 3. Christ will appear in body, so that the Judge may be recognized in the body by all, and it is possible for this to take place suddenly. But speech which is measured by time would require an immense length of time, if the judgment took place by word of mouth.

THIRD ARTICLE

Whether the Time of the Future Judgment Is Unknown?

We proceed thus to the Third Article:—

Objection 1. It would seem that the time of the future judgment is not unknown. For just as the holy Fathers looked forward to the first coming, so do we look forward to the second. But the holy Fathers knew the time of the first coming, as proved by the number of weeks mentioned in Dan. ix: wherefore the Jews are reproached for not knowing the time of Christ's coming (Luke xii. 56): *You hypocrites, you know how to discern the face of the heaven and of the earth, but how is it that you do not discern this time?* Therefore it would seem that the time of the second coming when God will come to judgment should also be certified to us.

Obj. 2. Further, we arrive by means of signs at the knowledge of the things signified. Now many signs of the coming judgment are declared to us in Scripture (Matth. xxiv, Mark xiii, Luke xxi). Therefore we can arrive at the knowledge of that time.

Obj. 3. Further, the Apostle says (1 Cor. x. 11): *It is on us* that the ends of the world are come,* and (1 Jo. ii. 18): *Little children, it is the last hour,* etc. Since then it is a long time since these things were said, it would seem that now at least we can know that the last judgment is nigh.

Obj. 4. Further, there is no need for the time of the judgment to be hidden, except that each one may be careful to prepare himself for judgment, being in ignorance of the appointed time. Yet the same care would still be necessary even were the time known for certain, because each one is uncertain about the time of his death, of which Augustine says *(Ep. ad Hesych.* cxcix) that *as each one's last day finds him, so will the world's last day find him.*

---

* *These things . . . are written for our correction, upon whom the ends of the world are come.*

Therefore there is no necessity for the time of the judgment to be uncertain.

On the contrary, It is written (Mark xiii. 32): *Of that day or hour no man knoweth, neither the angels in heaven, nor the Son, but the Father.* The Son, however, is said not to know in so far as He does not impart the knowledge to us.

Further, it is written (1 Thess. v. 2): *The day of the Lord shall so come as a thief in the night.* Therefore seemingly, as the coming of a thief in the night is altogether uncertain, the day of the last judgment is altogether uncertain.

I answer that, God is the cause of things by His knowledge.* Now He communicates both these things to His creatures, since He both endows some with the power of action on others whereof they are the cause, and bestows on some the knowledge of things. But in both cases He reserves something to Himself, for He operates certain things wherein no creature co-operates with Him, and again He knows certain things which are unknown to any mere creature. Now this should apply to none more than to those things which are subject to the Divine power alone, and in which no creature co-operates with Him. Such is the end of the world when the day of judgment will come. For the world will come to an end by no created cause, even as it derived its existence immediately from God. Wherefore the knowledge of the end of the world is fittingly reserved to God. Indeed our Lord seems to assign this very reason when He said (Acts i. 7): *It is not for you to know the times or moments which the Father hath put in His own power,* as though He were to say, *which are reserved to His power alone.*

Reply Obj. 1. At His first coming Christ came secretly according to Isa. xlv. 15, *Verily Thou art a hidden God, the God of Israel, the Saviour.* Hence, that He might be recognized by believers, it was necessary for the time to be fixed beforehand with certainty. On the other hand, at the second coming, He will come openly, according to Ps. xlix. 3, *God shall come manifestly.* Consequently there can be no error affecting the knowledge of His coming. Hence the comparison fails.

Reply Obj. 2. As Augustine says, in his letter to Hesychius concerning the day of judgment *(Ep.* cxcix), *the signs mentioned in the Gospels do not all refer to the second advent which will happen at the end of the world, but some of them belong to the time of the sack of Jerusalem, which is now a thing of the past, while some, in fact many of them, refer to the advent whereby He comes daily to the Church, whom He visits spiritually when*

*Cf. P. I, Q. 14, A. 8.

He dwells in us by faith and love. Moreover, the details mentioned in the Gospels and Epistles in connection with the last advent are not sufficient to enable us to determine the time of the judgment, for the trials that are foretold as announcing the proximity of Christ's coming occurred even at the time of the Early Church, in a degree sometimes more sometimes less marked; so that even the days of the apostles were called the last days (Acts ii. 17) when Peter expounded the saying of Joel ii. 28, *It shall come to pass in the last days,* etc., as referring to that time. Yet it was already a long time since then: and sometimes there were more and sometimes less afflictions in the Church. Consequently it is impossible to decide after how long a time it will take place, nor fix the month, year, century, or thousand years as Augustine says in the same book *(loc. cit.).* And even if we are to believe that at the end these calamities will be more frequent, it is impossible to fix what amount of such calamities will immediately precede the judgment day or the coming of Antichirst, since even at the time of the Early Church persecutions were so bitter, and the corruptions of error were so numerous, that some looked forward to the coming of Antichrist as being near or imminent; as related in Eusebius' *History of the Church* (vi. 7) and in Jerome's book *De Viris Illustribus,* lii.

Reply Obj. 3. The statement, *It is the last hour* and similar expressions that are to be found in Scripture do not enable us to know the exact length of time. For they are not intended to indicate a short length of time, but to signify the last state of the world, which is the last age of all, and it is not stated definitely how long this will last. Thus neither is fixed duration appointed to old age, which is the last age of man, since sometimes it is seen to last as long as or even longer than all the previous ages, as Augustine remarks *(Qq. 83, qu.* lviii). Hence also the Apostle (2 Thess. ii. 2) disclaims the false signification which some had given to his words, by believing that the day of the Lord was already at hand.

Reply Obj. 4. Notwithstanding the uncertainty of death, the uncertainty of the judgment conduces to watchfulness in two ways. First, as regards the thing ignored, since its delay is equal to the length of man's life, so that on either side uncertainty provokes him to greater care. Secondly, for the reason that a man is careful not only of his own person, but also of his family, or of his city or kingdom, or of the whole Church, the length of whose duration is not dependent on the length of man's life. And yet it behooves each of these to be so ordered that the day of the Lord find us not unprepared.

FOURTH ARTICLE

Whether the Judgment Will Take Place in the Valley of Josaphat?

We proceed thus to the Fourth Article:—

Objection 1. It would seem that the judgment will not take place in the valley of Josaphat or in the surrounding locality. For at least it will be necessary for those to be judged to stand on the ground, and those alone to be raised aloft whose business it will be to judge. But the whole land of promise would not be able to contain the multitude of those who are to be judged. Therefore it is impossible for the judgment to take place in the neighborhood of that valley.

Obj. 2. Further, to Christ in His human form judgment is given that He may judge justly, since He was judged unjustly in the court of Pilate, and bore the sentence of an unjust judgment on Golgotha. Therefore these places would be more suitably appointed for the judgment.

Obj. 3. Further, clouds result from the exhalation of vapors. But then there will be no evaporation or exhalation. Therefore it will be impossible for the just to be *taken up . . . in the clouds to meet Christ, into the air:* and consequently it will be necessary for both good and wicked to be on the earth, so that a much larger place than this valley will be required.

On the contrary, It is written (Joel iii. 2): *I will gather together all nations and will bring them down into the valley of Josaphat, and I will plead with them there.*

Further, it is written (Acts i. 11): *(This Jesus) . . . shall so come as you have seen Him going into heaven.* Now He ascended into heaven from Mount Olivet which overlooks the valley of Josaphat. Therefore He will come to judge in the neighborhood of that place.

I answer that, We cannot know with any great certainty the manner in which this judgment will take place, nor how men will gather together to the place of judgment; but it may be gathered from Scripture that in all probability He will descend in the neighborhood of Mount Olivet, even as He ascended from there, so as to show that He who descends is the same as He who ascended.

Reply Obj. 1. A great multitude can be enclosed in a small space. And all that is required is that in the neighborhood of that locality there be a space, however great, to contain the multitude of those who are to be judged, provided that Christ can be seen thence, since being raised in the air, and shining with exceeding glory, He will be visible from a great distance.

Reply Obj. 2. Although through being sentenced unjustly Christ merited His judiciary power, He will not judge with the appearance of infirmity wherein He was judged unjustly, but under the appearance of glory wherein He ascended to the Father. Hence the place of His ascension is more suitable to the judgment than the place where He was condemned.

Reply Obj. 3. In the opinion of some the name of clouds is here given to certain condensations of the light shining from the bodies of the saints, and not to evaporations from earth and water. Or we may say that those clouds will be produced by Divine power in order to show the parallel between His coming to judge and His ascension; so that He Who ascended in a cloud may come to judgment in a cloud.

Again the cloud on account of its refreshing influence indicates the mercy of the Judge.

QUESTION 89

Of Those Who Will Judge and of Those Who Will Be Judged at the General Judgment

(In Eight Articles)

WE must next consider who will judge and who will be judged at the general judgment. Under this head there are eight points of inquiry: (1) Whether any men will judge together with Christ? (2) Whether the judicial power corresponds to voluntary poverty? (3) Whether the angels also will judge? (4) Whether the demons will carry out the Judge's sentence on the damned? (5) Whether all men will come up for judgment? (6) Whether any of the good will be judged? (7) Whether any of the wicked will be judged? (8) Whether the angels also will be judged?

FIRST ARTICLE

Whether Any Men Will Judge Together with Christ?

We proceed thus to the First Article:—

Objection 1. It would seem that no men will judge with Christ. For it is written (Jo. v. 22, 23): *The Father . . . hath given all judgment to the Son, that all men may honor the Son.* Therefore, etc.

Obj. 2. Further, whoever judges has authority over that which he judges. Now those things about which the coming judgment will have to be, such as human merits and demerits, are subject to Divine authority alone. Therefore no one is competent to judge of those things.

Obj. 3. Further, this judgment will take place not vocally but mentally. Now the publication of merits and demerits in the hearts of all men (which is like an accusation or approval), or the repayment of punishment and reward (which is like the pronouncement of the sentence) will be the work of God alone. Therefore none but Christ Who is God will judge.

On the contrary, It is written (Matth. xix. 28): *You also shall sit on twelve seats judging the twelve tribes of Israel.* Therefore, etc.

Further, *The Lord will enter into judgment with the ancients of His people* (Isa. iii. 14). Therefore it would seem that others also will judge together with Christ.

I answer that, To judge has several significations. First it is used causally as it were, when we say it of that which proves that some person ought to be judged. In this sense the expression is used of certain people in comparison, in so far as some are shown to be deserving of judgment through being compared with others: for instance (Matth. xii. 41): *The men of Nineve shall rise in judgment with this generation, and shall condemn it.* To rise in judgment thus is common to the good and the wicked. Secondly, the expression *to judge* is used equivalently, so to say; for consent to an action is considered equivalent to doing it. Wherefore those who will consent with Christ the Judge, by approving His sentence, will be said to judge. In this sense it will belong to all the elect to judge: wherefore it is written (Wis. iii. 7, 8): *The just . . . shall judge nations.* Thirdly, a person is said to judge assessorially and by similitude, because he is like the judge in that his seat* is raised above the others: and thus assessors are said to judge. Some say that the perfect to whom judiciary power is promised (Matth. xix. 28) will judge in this sense, namely that they will be raised to the dignity of assessors, because they will appear above others at the judgment, and go forth *to meet Christ, into the air.* But this apparently does not suffice for the fulfilment of our Lord's promise *(ibid.)*: *You shall sit . . . judging,* for He would seem to make *judging* something additional to *sitting.* Hence there is a fourth way of judging, which will be competent to perfect men as containing the decrees of Divine justice according to which men will be judged: thus a book containing the law might be said to judge: wherefore it is written (Apoc. xx. 12): *(Judgment took her*

seat)†and the books were opened. Richard of S. Victor expounds this judging in this way *(De judic. potest.),* wherefore he says: *Those who persevere in Divine contemplation, who read every day the book of wisdom, transcribe, so to speak, in their hearts whatever they grasp by their clear insight of the truth;* and further on: *What else are the hearts of those who judge, divinely instructed in all truth, but a codex of the law?* Since, however, judging denotes an action exercised on another person, it follows that, properly speaking, he is said to judge who pronounces judgment on another. But this happens in two ways. First, by his own authority: and this belongs to the one who has dominion and power over others, and to whose ruling those who are judged are subject, wherefore it belongs to him to pass judgment on them. In this sense to judge belongs to God alone. Secondly, to judge is to acquaint others of the sentence delivered by another's authority, that is to announce the verdict already given. In this way perfect men will judge, because they will lead others to the knowledge of Divine justice, that these may know what is due to them on account of their merits: so that this very revelation of justice is called judgment. Hence Richard of S. Victor says *(loc. cit.)* that for the judges to open the books of their decree in the presence of those who are to be judged signifies that they open their hearts to the gaze of all those who are below them, and that they reveal their knowledge in whatever pertains to the judgment.

Reply Obj. 1. This objection considers the judgment of authority which belongs to Christ alone: and the same answer applies to the *Second Objection.*

Reply Obj. 3. There is no reason why some of the saints should not reveal certain things to others, either by way of enlightenment, as the higher angels enlighten the lower,‡ or by way of speech as the lower angels speak to the higher.§

SECOND ARTICLE

Whether the Judicial Power Corresponds to Voluntary Poverty?

We proceed thus to the Second Article:—

Objection 1. It would seem that the judicial power does not correspond to voluntary poverty. For it was promised to none but the twelve apostles (Matth. xix. 28): *You shall sit on twelve seats, judging,* etc. Since then those who are voluntarily poor are not all apostles, it would seem that the judicial power is not competent to all.

---

* An *assessor* is one who *sits by* the judge.   † The words in brackets are not in the Vulgate. Verse 4 we find: *I saw seats, and they sat upon them and judgment was given to them.*
‡ Cf. P. I, Q. 106.   § Cf. P. I, Q. 107, A. 2.

Obj. 2. Further, to offer sacrifice to God of one's own body is more than to do so of outward things. Now martyrs and also virgins offer sacrifice to God of their own body; whereas the voluntarily poor offer sacrifice of outward things. Therefore the sublimity of the judicial power is more in keeping with martyrs and virgins than with those who are voluntarily poor.

Obj. 3. Further, it is written (Jo. v. 45): *There is one that accuseth you, Moses in whom you trust:—because you believe not his voice,* according to a gloss, and *(ibid.* xii. 48): *The word that I have spoken shall judge him in the last day.* Therefore the fact that a man propounds a law, or exhorts men by word to lead a good life, gives him the right to judge those who scorn his utterances. But this belongs to doctors. Therefore it is more competent to doctors than to those who are poor voluntarily.

Obj. 4. Further, Christ through being judged unjustly merited as man to be judge of all in His human nature,* according to Jo. v. 27, *He hath given Him power to do judgment, because He is the Son of man.* Now those who suffer persecution for justice' sake are judged unjustly. Therefore the judicial power is competent to them rather than to the voluntarily poor.

Obj. 5. Further, a superior is not judged by his inferior. Now many who will have made lawful use of riches will have greater merit than many of the voluntarily poor. Therefore the voluntarily poor will not judge where those are to be judged.

On the contrary, It is written (Job xxxvi. 6): *He saveth not the wicked, and He giveth judgment to the poor.*

Further, a gloss on Matth. xix. 28, *You who have left all things*† says: *Those who left all things and followed God will be the judges; those who made right use of what they had lawfully will be judged,* and thus the same conclusion follows as before.

I answer that, The judicial power is due especially to poverty on three counts. First, by reason of congruity, since voluntary poverty belongs to those who despise all the things of the world and cleave to Christ alone. Consequently there is nothing in them to turn away their judgment from justice, so that they are rendered competent to be judges as loving the truth of justice above all things. Secondly, by reason of merit, since exaltation corresponds by way of merit to humility. Now of all the things that make man contemptible in this world humility is the chief: and for this reason the excellence of judicial power is promised to the poor, so that he who humbles

himself for Christ's sake shall be exalted. Thirdly, because poverty disposes a man to the aforesaid manner of judging. For the reason why one of the saints will be said to judge, as stated above (A. 1), is that he will have the heart instructed in all Divine truth which he will be thus able to make known to others. Now in the advancement to perfection, the first thing that occurs to be renounced is external wealth, because this is the last thing of all to be acquired. And that which is last in the order of generation is the first in the order of destruction: wherefore among the beatitudes whereby we advance to perfection, the first place is given to poverty. Thus judicial power corresponds to poverty, in so far as this is the disposition to the aforesaid perfection. Hence also it is that this same power is not promised to all who are voluntarily poor, but to those who leave all and follow Christ in accordance with the perfection of life.

Reply Obj. 1. According to Augustine *(De Civ. Dei,* xx), *we must not imagine that because He says that they will sit on twelve seats, only twelve men will judge with Him; else since we read that Matthias was appointed apostle in the place of the traitor Judas, Paul who worked more than the rest will have nowhere to sit as judge.* Hence *the number twelve,* as he states *(ibid.), signifies the whole multitude of those who will judge, because the two parts of seven, namely three and four, being multiplied together make twelve.* Moreover twelve is a perfect number, being the double of six, which is a perfect number.

Or, speaking literally, He spoke to the twelve apostles in whose person he made this promise to all who follow them.

Reply Obj. 2. Virginity and martyrdom do not dispose man to retain the precepts of Divine justice in his heart in the same degree as poverty does: even so, on the other hand, outward riches choke the word of God by the cares which they entail (Luke viii. 14). Or we may reply that poverty does not suffice alone to merit judicial power, but is the fundamental part of that perfection to which the judicial power corresponds. Wherefore among those things regarding perfection which follow after poverty we may reckon both virginity and martyrdom and all the works of perfection: yet they do not rank as high as poverty, since the beginning of a thing is its chief part.

Reply Obj. 3. He who propounded the law or urged men to good will judge, in the causal‡ sense, because others will be judged in reference to the words he has uttered or- propounded. Hence the judicial power does not properly correspond to preaching or teaching. Or we may reply that, as some say, three things

---

* Cf. P. III, Q. 59, A. 6.   † Vulg.,—*You who have followed Me.*   ‡ Cf. A. 1.

are requisite for the judicial power; first, that one renounce temporal cares, lest the mind be hindered from the contemplation of wisdom; secondly that one possess Divine justice by way of habit both as to knowledge and as to observance; thirdly that one should have taught others this same justice; and this teaching will be the perfection whereby a man merits to have judicial power.

Reply Obj. 4. Christ humbled Himself in that He was judged unjustly; for *He was offered because it was His own will* (Isa. liii. 7): and by His humility He merited His exaltation to judicial power, since all things are made subject to Him (Philip. ii. 8, 9). Hence, judicial power is more due to them who humble themselves of their own will by renouncing temporal goods, on account of which men are honored by worldlings, than to those who are humbled by others.

Reply Obj. 5. An inferior cannot judge a superior by his own authority, but he can do so by the authority of a superior, as in the case of a judge-delegate. Hence it is not unfitting that it be granted to the poor as an accidental reward to judge others, even those who have higher merit in respect of the essential reward.

THIRD ARTICLE

Whether the Angels Will Judge?

We proceed thus to the Third Article:—

Objection 1. It would seem that the angels will judge. For it is written (Matth. xxv. 31): *When the Son of man shall come in His majesty, and all the angels with Him.* Now He is speaking of His coming to judgment. Therefore it would seem that also the angels will judge.

Obj. 2. Further, the orders of the angels take their names from the offices which they fulfill. Now one of the angelic orders is that of the Thrones, which would seem to pertain to the judicial power, since a throne is the *judicial bench, a royal seat, a professor's chair.** Therefore some of the angels will judge.

Obj. 3. Further, equality with the angels is promised the saints after this life (Matth. xxii. 30). If then men will have this power of judging, much more will the angels have it.

On the contrary, It is written (Jo. v. 27): *He hath given Him power to judgment, because He is the Son of man.* But the angels have not the human nature in common with Him. Neither therefore do they share with Him in the judicial power.

Further, the same person is not judge and judge's minister. Now in this judgment the angels will act as ministers of the Judge and,

according to Matth. xiii. 41: *The Son of man shall send His angels and they shall gather out of His kingdom all scandals.* Therefore the angels will not judge.

I answer that, The judge's assessors must be conformed to the judge. Now judgment is ascribed to the Son of man because He will appear to all, both good and wicked, in His human nature, although the whole Trinity will judge by authority. Consequently it behooves also the Judge's assessors to have the human nature, so as to be visible to all, both good and wicked. Hence it is not fitting for the angels to judge, although in a certain sense we may say that the angels will judge, namely by approving the sentence.†

Reply Obj. 1. As a gloss on this passage observes, the angels will come with Christ, not to judge, but *as witnesses of men's deeds, because it was under their guardianship that men did well or ill.*

Reply Obj. 2. The name of Thrones is given to angels in reference to the judgment which God is ever pronouncing, by governing all things with supreme justice: of which judgment angels are in a way the executors and promulgators. On the other hand, the judgment of men by the man Christ will require human assessors.

Reply Obj. 3. Equality with angels is promised to men as regards the essential reward. But nothing hinders an accidental reward from being bestowed on men to the exclusion of the angels, as in the case of the virgins' and martyrs' crowns: and the same may be said of the judicial power.

FOURTH ARTICLE

Whether the Demons Will Carry Out the Sentence of the Judge on the Damned?

We proceed thus to the Fourth Article:—

Objection 1. It would seem that the demons will not carry out the sentence of the Judge on the damned after the day of judgment. For, according to the Apostle (1 Cor. xv. 24): *He will then bring to nought‡ all principality, and power, and virtue.* Therefore all supremacy will cease then. But the carrying out of the Judge's sentence implies some kind of supremacy. Therefore after the judgment day the demons will not carry out the Judge's sentence.

Obj. 2. Further, the demons sinned more grievously than men. Therefore it is not just that men should be tortured by demons.

Obj. 3. Further, just as the demons suggest evil things to men, so good angels suggest good things. Now it will not be the duty of the good angels to reward the good, but this

---

* S. Isidore, *Etym.* vii. 5.　　† Cf. A. 1.　　‡Vulg.,—*When He shall have brought to naught,* etc.

will be done by God, immediately by Himself. Therefore neither will it be the duty of the demons to punish the wicked.

On the contrary, Sinners have subjected themselves to the devil by sinning. Therefore it is just that they should be subjected to him in their punishments, and punished by him as it were.

I answer that, The Master in the text of iv. *Sent.* D. 47 mentions two opinions on this question, both of which seem consistent with Divine justice, because it is just for man to be subjected to the devil for having sinned, and yet it is unjust for the demon to be over him. Accordingly the opinion which holds that after the judgment day the demons will not be placed over men to punish them, regards the order of Divine justice on the part of the demons punishing; while the contrary opinion regards the order of Divine justice on the part of the men punished.

Which of these opinions is nearer the truth we cannot know for certain. Yet I think it truer to say that just as, among the saved, order will be observed so that some will be enlightened and perfected by others (because all the orders of the heavenly hierarchies will continue for ever),* so, too, will order be observed in punishments, men being punished by demons, lest the Divine order, whereby the angels are placed between the human nature and the Divine, be entirely set aside. Wherefore just as the Divine illuminations are conveyed to men by the good angels, so too the demons execute the Divine justice on the wicked. Nor does this in any way diminish the punishment of the demons, since even in torturing others they are themselves tortured, because then the fellowship of the unhappy will not lessen but will increase unhappiness.

Reply Obj. 1. The supremacy which, it is declared, will be brought to nought by Christ in the time to come must be taken in the sense of the supremacy which is in keeping with the state of this world: wherein men are placed over men, angels over men, angels over angels, demons over demons, and demons over men; in every case so as either to lead towards the end or to lead astray from the end. But then, when all things will have attained to that end, there will be no supremacy to lead astray from the end or to lead to it, but only that which maintains in the end, good or evil.

Reply Obj. 2. Although the demerit of the demons does not require that they be placed over men, since they made men subject to them unjustly, yet this is required by the order of their nature in relation to human nature: since *natural goods remain in them unimpaired* as Dionysius says *(Div. Nom.* iv).

* Cf. P. I, Q. 108, AA. 7, 8.   † Cf. P. I, Q. 108, A. 8.

Reply Obj. 3. The good angels are not the cause of the principal reward in the elect, because all receive this immediately from God. Nevertheless the angels are the cause of certain accidental rewards in men, in so far as the higher angels enlighten those beneath them, both angels and men, concerning certain hidden things of God, which do not belong to the essence of beatitude. In like manner the damned will receive their principal punishment immediately from God, namely the everlasting banishment from the Divine vision: but there is no reason why the demons should not torture men with other sensible punishments. There is, however, this difference: that merit exalts, whereas sin debases. Wherefore since the angelic nature is higher than the human, some on account of the excellence of their merit will be so far exalted as to be raised above the angels both in nature and rewards,† so that some angels will be enlightened by some men. On the other hand, no human sinners will, on account of a certain degree of virtue, attain to the eminence that attaches to the nature of the demons.

FIFTH ARTICLE

Whether All Men Will Be Present at the Judgment?

We proceed thus to the Fifth Article:—

Objection 1. It would seem that men will not all be present at the judgment. For it is written (Matth. xix. 28): *You . . . shall sit on twelve seats, judging the twelve tribes of Israel.* But all men do not belong to those twelve tribes. Therefore it would seem that men will not all be present at the judgment.

Obj. 2. Further, the same apparently is to be gathered from Ps. i. 5, *The wicked shall not rise again in judgment.*

Obj. 3. Further, a man is brought to judgment that his merits may be discussed. But some there are who have acquired no merits, such as children who died before reaching the perfect age. Therefore they need not be present at the judgment. Now there are many such. Therefore it would seem that not all will be present.

On the contrary, It is written (Acts x. 42) that Christ *was appointed by God to be judge of the living and of the dead.* Now this division comprises all men, no matter how the living be distinct from the dead. Therefore all men will be present at the judgment.

Further, it is written (Apoc. i. 7): *Behold He cometh with the clouds, and every eye shall see Him.* Now this would not be so unless all were present at the judgment. Therefore, etc.

I answer that, The judicial power was bestowed on Christ as man, in reward for the humility which He showed forth in His passion. Now in His passion He shed His blood for all in point of sufficiency, although through meeting with an obstacle in some, it had not its effect in all. Therefore it is fitting that all men should assemble at the judgment, to see His exaltation in His human nature, in respect of which *He was appointed by God to be judge of the living and of the dead.*

Reply Obj. 1. As Augustine says (*De Civ. Dei,* xx. 5), *it does not follow from the saying, 'Judging the twelve tribes of Israel,' that the tribe of Levi, which is the thirteenth, is not to be judged, or that they will judge that people alone, and not other nations.* The reason why all other nations are denoted by the twelve tribes is because they were called by Christ to take the place of the twelve tribes.

Reply Obj. 2. The words, *The wicked shall not rise in judgment,* if referred to all sinners, mean that they will not arise to judge. But if the wicked denote unbelievers, the sense is that they will not arise to be judged, because they are *already judged* (Jo. iii. 18). All, however, will rise again to assemble at the judgment and witness the glory of the Judge.

Reply Obj. 3. Even children who have died before reaching the perfect age will be present at the judgment, not to be judged, but to see the Judge's glory.

SIXTH ARTICLE

Whether the Good Will Be Judged at the Judgment?

We proceed thus to the Sixth Article:—

Objection 1. It would seem that none of the good will be judged at the judgment. For it is declared (Jo. iii. 18) that *he that believeth in Him is not judged.* Now all the good believed in Him. Therefore they will not be judged.

Obj. 2. Further, those who are uncertain of their bliss are not blessed: whence Augustine proves (*Gen. ad Lit.* xi) that the demons were never blessed. But the saints are now blessed. Therefore they are certain of their bliss. Now what is certain is not submitted to judgment. Therefore the good will not be judged.

Obj. 3. Further, fear is incompatible with bliss. But the last judgment, which above all is described as terrible, cannot take place without inspiring fear into those who are to be judged. Hence Gregory observes on Job xli. 16, *When he shall raise him up, the angels shall fear,* etc. (*Moral.* xxxiv): *Consider how the conscience of the wicked will then be troubled, when even the just are disturbed about their life.* Therefore the blessed will not be judged.

On the contrary, It would seem that all

* Cf. I-II, Q. 89, A. 2.

the good will be judged, since it is written (2 Cor. v. 10): *We must all be manifested before the judgment seat of Christ, that every one may receive the proper things of the body, according as he hath done, whether it be good or evil.* Now there is nothing else to be judged. Therefore all, even the good, will be judged.

Further, the *general* includes all. Now this is called the general judgment. Therefore all will be judged.

I answer that, The judgment comprises two things, namely the discussion of merits and the payment of rewards. As regards the payment of rewards, all will be judged, even the good, since the Divine sentence will appoint to each one the reward corresponding to his merit. But there is no discussion of merits save where good and evil merits are mingled together. Now those who build on the foundation of faith, *gold, silver, and precious stones* (1 Cor. iii. 12), by devoting themselves wholly to the Divine service, and who have no notable admixture of evil merit, are not subjected to a discussion of their merits. Such are those who have entirely renounced the things of the world and are solicitously thoughtful of the things that are of God: wherefore they will be saved but will not be judged. Others, however, build on the foundation of faith, wood, hay, stubble*; they, in fact, love worldly things and are busy about earthly concerns, yet so as to prefer nothing to Christ, but strive to redeem their sins with alms, and these have an admixture of good with evil merits. Hence they are subjected to a discussion of their merits, and consequently in this account will be judged, and yet they will be saved.

Reply Obj. 1. Since punishment is the effect of justice, while reward is the effect of mercy, it follows that punishment is more especially ascribed antonomastically to judgment which is the act of justice; so that judgment is sometimes used to express condemnation. It is thus that we are to understand the words quoted, as a gloss on the passage remarks.

Reply Obj. 2. The merits of the elect will be discussed, not to remove the uncertainty of their beatitude from the hearts of those who are to be judged, but that it may be made manifest to us that their good merits outweigh their evil merits, and thus God's justice be proved.

Reply Obj. 3. Gregory is speaking of the just who will still be in mortal flesh, wherefore he had already said: *Those who will still be in the body, although already brave and perfect, yet through being still in the flesh must needs be troubled with fear in the midst of such a whirlwind of terror.* Hence it is clear that this fear refers to the time immediately before the judgment, most terrible indeed to the wicked, but not to the good, who will have no apprehension of evil.

The arguments in the contrary sense consider judgment as regards the payment of rewards.

SEVENTH ARTICLE

Whether the Wicked Will Be Judged?

We proceed thus to the Seventh Article:—

Objection 1. It would seem that none of the wicked will be judged. For even as damnation is certain in the case of unbelievers, so is it in the case of those who die in mortal sin. Now it is declared because of the certainty of damnation (Jo. iii. 18): *He that believeth not is already judged.* Therefore in like manner neither will other sinners be judged.

Obj. 2. Further, the voice of the Judge is most terrible to those who are condemned by His judgment. Now according to the text of iv. *Sent.* D. 47 and in the words of Gregory (*Moral.* xxvi) *the Judge will not address Himself to unbelievers.* If therefore He were to address Himself to the believers about to be condemned, the unbelievers would reap a benefit from their unbelief, which is absurd.

On the contrary, It would seem that all the wicked are to be judged, because all the wicked will be sentenced to punishment according to the degree of their guilt. But this cannot be done without a judicial pronouncement. Therefore all the wicked will be judged.

I answer that, The judgment as regards the sentencing to punishment for sin concerns all the wicked; whereas the judgment as regards the discussion of merits concerns only believers. Because in unbelievers the foundation of faith is lacking, without which all subsequent works are deprived of the perfection of a right intention, so that in them there is no admixture of good and evil works or merits requiring discussion. But believers in whom the foundation of faith remains, have at least a praiseworthy act of faith, which though it is not meritorious without charity, yet is in itself directed to merit, and consequently they will be subjected to the discussion of merits. Consequently, believers who were at least counted as citizens of the City of God will be judged as citizens, and sentence of death will not be passed on them without a discussion of their merits; whereas unbelievers will be condemned as foes, who are wont among men to be exterminated without their merits being discussed.

Reply Obj. 1. Although it is certain that those who die in mortal sin will be damned, nevertheless since they have an admixture of certain things connected with meriting well,

it behooves, for the manifestation of Divine justice, that their merits be subjected to discussion, in order to make it clear that they are justly banished from the city of the saints, of which they appeared outwardly to be citizens.

Reply Obj. 2. Considered under this special aspect the words addressed to the believers about to be condemned will not be terrible, because they will reveal in them certain things pleasing to them, which it will be impossible to find in unbelievers, since *without faith it is impossible to please God* (Heb. xi. 6). But the sentence of condemnation which will be passed on them all will be terrible to all of them.

The argument in the contrary sense considered the judgment of retribution.

EIGHTH ARTICLE

Whether at the Coming Judgment the Angels Will Be Judged?

We proceed thus to the Eighth Article:—

Objection 1. It would seem that the angels will be judged at the coming judgment. For it is written (1 Cor. vi. 3): *Know you not that we shall judge angels?* But this cannot refer to the state of the present time. Therefore it should refer to the judgment to come.

Obj. 2. Further, it is written concerning Behemoth or Leviathan, whereby the devil is signified (Job xl. 28): *In the sight of all he shall be cast down;* and (Mark i. 24)* the demon cried out to Christ: *Why art Thou come to destroy us before the time?* for, according to a gloss, *the demons seeing our Lord on earth thought they were to be judged forthwith.* Therefore it would seem that a final judgment is in store for them.

Obj. 3. Further, it is written (2 Pet. ii. 4): *God spared not the angels that sinned, but delivered them drawn down by infernal ropes to the lower hell, unto torments, to be reserved unto judgment.* Therefore it seems that the angels will be judged.

On the contrary, It is written (Nahum i. 9) according to the Septuagint version: *God will not judge the same thing a second time.* But the wicked angels are already judged, wherefore it is written (Jo. xvi. 11): *The prince of this world is already judged.* Therefore the angels will not be judged in the time to come.

Further, goodness and wickedness are more perfect in the angels than in men who are wayfarers. Now some men, good and wicked, will not be judged as stated in the text of iv. *Sent.* D. 47. Therefore neither will good or wicked angels be judged.

I answer that, The judgment of discussion nowise concerns either the good or the wicked

---

* The reference should be Matth. viii. 29: *Art Thou come hither to torment us before the time?* The text of Mark reads: *Art Thou come to destroy us?*

angels, since neither is any evil to be found in the good angels, nor is any good liable to judgment to be found in the wicked angels. But if we speak of the judgment of retribution, we must distinguish a twofold retribution. One corresponds to the angels' personal merits and was made to both from the beginning, when some were raised to bliss, and others plunged into the depths of woe. The other corresponds to the merits, good or evil, procured through the angels, and this retribution will be made in the judgment to come, because the good angels will have an increased joy in the salvation of those whom they have prompted to deeds of merit, while the wicked will have an increase of torment through the manifold downfall of those whom they have incited to evil deeds. Consequently the judg-ment will not regard the angels directly, neither as judging nor as judged, but only men; but it will regard the angels indirectly somewhat, in so far as they were concerned in men's deeds.

Reply Obj. 1. This saying of the Apostle refers to the judgment of comparison, because certain men will be found to be placed higher than the angels.

Reply Obj. 2. The demons will then be cast down in the sight of all because they will be imprisoned for ever in the dungeon of hell, so that they will no more be free to go out, since this was permitted to them only in so far as they were directed by Divine providence to try the life of man.

The same answer applies to the *Third Objection.*

QUESTION 90

Of the Form of the Judge in Coming to the Judgment

(In Three Articles)

WE must now consider the form of the Judge in coming to the judgment. Under this head there are three points of inquiry: (1) Whether Christ will judge under the form of His humanity? (2) Whether He will appear under the form of His glorified humanity? (3) Whether His Godhead can be seen without joy?

FIRST ARTICLE

Whether Christ Will Judge under the Form of His Humanity?

We proceed thus to the First Article:—

Objection 1. It would seem that Christ will not judge under the form of His humanity. For judgment requires authority in the judge. Now Christ has authority over the quick and the dead as God, for thus is He the Lord and Creator of all. Therefore He will judge under the form of His Godhead.

Obj. 2. Further, invincible power is requisite in a judge; wherefore it is written (Eccles. vii. 6): *Seek not to be made a judge, unless thou have strength enough to extirpate iniquities.* Now invincible power belongs to Christ as God. Therefore He will judge under the form of the Godhead.

Obj. 3. Further, it is written (John v. 22, 23): *The Father . . . hath given all judgment to the Son, that all men may honor the Son, as they honor the Father.* Now equal honor to that of the Father is not due to the Son in respect of His human nature. Therefore He will not judge under His human form.

Obj. 4. Further, it is written (Dan. vii. 9): *I beheld till thrones were placed and the An-cient of days sat.* Now the thrones signify judicial power, and God is called the Ancient by reason of His eternity, according to Dionysius *(Div. Nom.* x). Therefore it becomes the Son to judge as being eternal; and consequently not as man.

Obj. 5. Further, Augustine says *(Tract.* xix *in Joan.)* that *the resurrection of the soul is the work of the Word the Son of God, and the resurrection of the body is the work of the Word made the Son of man in the flesh.* Now that last judgment regards the soul rather than the body. Therefore it becomes Christ to judge as God rather than as man.

On the contrary, It is written (Jo. v. 27): *He hath given Him power to do judgment, because He is the Son of man.*

Further, it is written (Job xxxvi. 17): *Thy cause hath been judged as that of the wicked,* —*by Pilate* according to a gloss—therefore, *cause and judgment thou shalt recover,*—*that thou mayest judge justly,* according to the gloss. Now Christ was judged by Pilate with regard to His human nature. Therefore He will judge under the human nature.

Further, to Him it belongs to judge who made the law. Now Christ gave us the law of the Gospel while appearing in the human nature. Therefore He will judge under that same nature.

I answer that, Judgment requires a certain authority in the judge. Wherefore it is written (Rom. xiv. 4): *Who art thou that judgest another man's servant?* Hence it is becoming that Christ should judge in respect of His having authority over men to whom chiefly the last judgment will be directed. Now He is our Lord, not only by reason of the Creation, since *the Lord He is God, He made us and not we ourselves* (Ps. xcix. 3), but also by reason of the Redemption, which pertains to Him in respect of His human nature. Wherefore *to this end Christ died and rose again, that He might be Lord both of the dead and of the living* (Rom. xiv. 9). But the goods of the Creation would not suffice us to obtain the reward of eternal life, without the addition of the boon of the Redemption, on account of the obstacle accruing to created nature through the sin of our first parent. Hence, since the last judgment is directed to the admission of some to the kingdom, and the exclusion of others therefrom, it is becoming that Christ should preside at that judgment under the form of His human nature, since it is by favor of that same nature's Redemption that man is admitted to the kingdom. In this sense it is stated (Acts x. 42) that *He . . . was appointed by God to be Judge of the living and of the dead*. And forasmuch as by redeeming mankind He restored not only man but all creatures without exception,—inasmuch as all creatures are bettered through man's restoration, according to Coloss. i. 20, *Making peace through the blood of His cross, both as to things on earth, and the things that are in heaven*,—it follows that through His Passion Christ merited lordship and judicial power not over man alone, but over all creatures, according to Matth. xxviii. 18, *All power is given to Me, in heaven and in earth.**

Reply Obj. 1. Christ, in respect of His Divine nature, has authority of lordship over all creatures by right of creation; but in respect of His human nature He has authority of lordship merited through His Passion. The latter is secondary so to speak and acquired, while the former is natural and eternal.

Reply Obj. 2. Although Christ as man has not of Himself invincible power resulting from the natural power of the human species, nevertheless there is also in His human nature an invincible power derived from His Godhead, whereby all things are subjected under His feet (1 Cor. xv. 25-28; Heb. ii. 8, 9). Hence He will judge in His human nature indeed, but by the power of His Godhead.

Reply Obj. 3. Christ would not have sufficed for the redemption of mankind, had He been a mere man. Wherefore from the very fact that He was able as man to redeem mankind, and thereby obtained judicial power, it is evident that He is God, and consequently is to be honored equally with the Father, not as man but as God.

Reply Obj. 4. In that vision of Daniel the

* Cf. P. III, Q. 59. † Cf. P. III, Q. 56, A. 2, *ad* 1.

whole order of the judicial power is clearly expressed. This power is in God Himself as its first origin, and more especially in the Father Who is the fount of the entire Godhead; wherefore it is stated in the first place that the *Ancient of days sat.* But the judicial power was transmitted from the Father to the Son, not only from eternity in respect of the Divine nature, but also in time in respect of the human nature wherein He merited it. Hence in the aforesaid vision it is further stated *(verses 13, 14): Lo, one like the Son of man came with the clouds of heaven, and He came even to the Ancient of days. . . . And He gave Him power and glory, and a kingdom.*

Reply Obj. 5. Augustine is speaking by a kind of appropriation, so as to trace the effects which Christ wrought in the human nature to causes somewhat similar to them. And since we are made to the image and likeness of God in respect of our soul, and are of the same species as the man Christ in respect of our body, he ascribes to the Godhead the effects wrought by Christ in our souls, and those which He wrought or will work in our bodies he ascribes to His flesh; although His flesh, as being the instrument of His Godhead, has also its effect on our souls as Damascene asserts *(De Fide Orthod.* iii. 15), according to the saying of Heb. ix. 14, that His *blood* hath cleansed *our conscience from dead works.* And thus that *the Word was made flesh* is the cause of the resurrection of souls; wherefore also according to His human nature He is becomingly the Judge not only of bodily but also of spiritual goods.†

SECOND ARTICLE

Whether at the Judgment Christ Will Appear in His Glorified Humanity?

We proceed thus to the Second Article:—

Objection 1. It would seem that at the judgment Christ will not appear in His glorified humanity. For a gloss‡ on Jo. xix. 37, *They shall look on him whom they pierced,* says: *Because He will come in the flesh wherein He was crucified.* Now He was crucified in the form of weakness. Therefore He will appear in the form of weakness and not in the form of glory.

Obj. 2. Further, it is stated (Matth. xxiv. 30) that *the sign of the Son of man shall appear in heaven,* namely, *the sign of the cross,* as Chrysostom says *(Hom.* lxxvii *in Matth.),* for *Christ when coming to the judgment will show not only the scars of His wounds but even His most shameful death.* Therefore it seems that He will not appear in the form of glory.

Obj. 3. Further, Christ will appear at the

‡ S. Augustine *(Tract.* cxx, *in Joan.).*

judgment under that form which can be gazed upon by all. Now Christ will not be visible to all, good and wicked, under the form of His glorified humanity: because the eye that is not glorified is seemingly unproportionate to see the clarity of a glorified body. Therefore He will not appear under a glorified form.

Obj. 4. Further, that which is promised as a reward to the righteous is not granted to the unrighteous. Now it is promised as a reward to the righteous that they shall see the glory of His humanity (Jo. x. 9): *He shall go in, and go out, and shall find pastures, i.e. refreshment in His Godhead and humanity,* according to the commentary of Augustine,* and Isa. xxxiii. 17: *His eyes shall see the King in his beauty.* Therefore He will not appear to all in His glorified form.

Obj. 5. Further, Christ will judge in the form wherein He was judged: wherefore a gloss† on Jo. v. 21, *So the Son also giveth life to whom He will,* says: *He will judge justly in the form wherein He was judged unjustly, that He may be visible to the wicked.* Now He was judged in the form of weakness. Therefore He will appear in the same form at the judgment.

On the contrary, It is written (Luke xxi. 27): *Then they shall see the Son of man coming in a cloud with great power and majesty.* Now majesty and power pertain to glory. Therefore He will appear in the form of glory.

Further, he who judges should be more conspicuous than those who are judged. Now the elect who will be judged by Christ will have a glorified body. Much more therefore will the Judge appear in a glorified form.

Further, as to be judged pertains to weakness, so to judge pertains to authority and glory. Now at His first coming when Christ came to be judged, He appeared in the form of weakness. Therefore at the second coming, when He will come to judge, He will appear in the form of glory.

I answer that, Christ is called the mediator of God and men (1 Tim. ii. 5) inasmuch as He satisfies for men and intercedes for them to the Father, and confers on men things which belong to the Father, according to Jo. xvii. 22, *The glory which Thou hast given Me, I have given to them.* Accordingly then both these things belong to Him in that He communicates with both extremes: for in that He communicates with men, He takes their part with the Father, and in that He communicates with the Father, He bestows the Father's gifts on men. Since then at His first coming He came in order to make satisfaction for us to the Father, He came in the form of our weak-

ness. But since at His second coming He will come in order to execute the Father's justice on men, He will have to show forth His glory which is in Him by reason of His communication with the Father: and therefore He will appear in the form of glory.

Reply Obj. 1. He will appear in the same flesh, but not under the same form.

Reply Obj. 2. The sign of the cross will appear at the judgment, to denote not a present but a past weakness: so as to show how justly those were condemned who scorned so great mercy, especially those who persecuted Christ unjustly. The scars which will appear in His body will not be due to weakness, but will indicate the exceeding power whereby Christ overcame His enemies by His Passion and infirmity. He will also show forth His most shameful death, not by bringing it sensibly before the eye, as though He suffered it there; but by the things which will appear then, namely the signs of His past Passion, He will recall men to the thought of His past death.

Reply Obj. 3. A glorified body has it in its power to show itself or not to show itself to an eye that is not glorified, as stated above (Q. 85, A. 2, *ad* 3). Hence Christ will be visible to all in His glorified form.

Reply Obj. 4. Even as our friend's glory gives us pleasure, so the glory and power of one we hate is most displeasing to us. Hence as the sight of the glory of Christ's humanity will be a reward to the righteous, so will it be a torment to Christ's enemies: wherefore it is written (Isa. xxvi. 11): *Let the envious people see and be confounded and let fire (i.e.* envy) *devour Thy enemies.*

Reply Obj. 5. Form is taken there for human nature wherein He was judged and likewise will judge; but not for a quality of nature, namely of weakness, which will not be the same in Him when judging as when judged (Cf. *ad* 2).

THIRD ARTICLE

Whether the Godhead Can Be Seen by the Wicked Without Joy?

We proceed thus to the Third Article:—

Objection 1. It would seem that the Godhead can be seen by the wicked without joy. For there can be no doubt that the wicked will know with the greatest certainty that Christ is God. Therefore they will see His Godhead, and yet they will not rejoice in seeing Christ. Therefore it will be possible to see it without joy.

---

* *De Spiritu et Anima,* work of an unknown author. S. Thomas (*De Anima*) ascribes it to Alcherus, a Cistercian monk; see above, Q. 70, A. 2, *ad* 1.   † S. Augustine (*Tract. xix, in Joan.*).

Obj. 2. Further, the perverse will of the wicked is not more adverse to Christ's humanity than to His Godhead. Now the fact that they will see the glory of His humanity will conduce to their punishment, as stated above (A. 2, *ad* 4). Therefore if they were to see His Godhead, there would be much more reason for them to grieve rather than rejoice.

Obj. 3. Further, the course of the affections is not a necessary sequel to that which is in the intellect: wherefore Augustine says *(In Ps.* cxviii: conc. 8): *The intellect precedes, the affections follow slowly or not at all.* Now vision regards the intellect, whereas joy regards the affections. Therefore it will be possible to see the Godhead without joy.

Obj. 4. Further, whatever is received into *a thing is received according to the mode of the receiver and not of the received.* But whatever is seen is, in a way, received into the seer. Therefore although the Godhead is in itself supremely enjoyable, nevertheless when seen by those who are plunged in grief, it will give no joy but rather displeasure.

Obj. 5. Further, as sense is to the sensible object, so is the intellect to the intelligible object. Now in the senses, *to the unhealthy palate bread is painful, to the healthy palate sweet,* as Augustine says *(Conf.* vii), and the same happens with the other senses. Therefore since the damned have the intellect indisposed, it would seem that the vision of the uncreated light will give them pain rather than joy.

On the contrary, It is written (Jo. xvii. 3): *This is eternal life: That they may know Thee, the . . . true God.* Wherefore it is clear that the essence of bliss consists in seeing God. Now joy is essential to bliss. Therefore the Godhead cannot be seen without joy.

Further, the essence of the Godhead is the essence of truth. Now it is delightful to every one to see the truth, wherefore *all naturally desire to know,* as stated at the beginning of the *Metaphysics.* Therefore it is impossible to see the Godhead without joy.

Further, if a certain vision is not always delightful, it happens sometimes to be painful. But intellective vision is never painful since *the pleasure we take in objects of understanding has no grief opposed to it,* according to the Philosopher *(Top.* ii). Since then the Godhead cannot be seen save by the intellect, it seems that the Godhead cannot be seen without joy.

I answer that, In every object of appetite or of pleasure two things may be considered, namely the thing which is desired or which gives pleasure, and the aspect of appetibility

* Cf. II-II, Q. 34, A. 1.

or pleasurableness in that thing. Now according to Boëthius *(De Hebdom.)* that *which is can have something besides what it is, but 'being' itself has no admixture of aught else beside itself.* Hence that which is desirable or pleasant can have an admixture of something rendering it undesirable or unpleasant; but the very aspect of pleasurableness has not and cannot have anything mixed with it rendering it unpleasant or undesirable. Now it is possible for things that are pleasurable, by participation of goodness which is the aspect of appetibility or pleasurableness, not to give pleasure when they are apprehended, but it is impossible for that which is good by its essence not to give pleasure when it is apprehended. Therefore since God is essentially His own goodness, it is impossible for the Godhead to be seen without joy.

Reply Obj. 1. The wicked will know most clearly that Christ is God, not through seeing His Godhead, but on account of the most manifest signs of His Godhead.

Reply Obj. 2. No one can hate the Godhead considered in itself, as neither can one hate goodness itself. But God is said to be hated by certain persons in respect of some of the effects of the Godhead, in so far as He does or commands something contrary to their will.* Therefore the vision of the Godhead can be painful to no one.

Reply Obj. 3. The saying of Augustine applies when the thing apprehended previously by the intellect is good by participation and not essentially, such as all creatures are; wherefore there may be something in them by reason of which the affections are not moved. In like manner God is known by wayfarers through His effects, and their intellect does not attain to the very essence of His goodness. Hence it is not necessary that the affections follow the intellect, as they would if the intellect saw God's essence which is His goodness.

Reply Obj. 4. Grief denotes not a disposition but a passion. Now every passion is removed if a stronger contrary cause supervene, and does not remove that cause. Accordingly the grief of the damned would be done away if they saw God in His essence.

Reply Obj. 5. The indisposition of an organ removes the natural proportion of the organ to the object that has a natural aptitude to please, wherefore the pleasure is hindered. But the indisposition which is in the damned does not remove the natural proportion whereby they are directed to the Divine goodness, since its image ever remains in them. Hence the comparison fails.

QUESTION 91

Of the Quality of the World after the Judgment

(In Five Articles)

WE must next discuss the quality which the world and those who rise again will have after the judgment. Here a threefold matter offers itself to our consideration: (1) The state and quality of the world. (2) The state of the blessed. (3) The state of the wicked.

Under the first head there are five points of inquiry: (1) Whether there will be a renewal of the world? (2) Whether the movement of the heavenly bodies will cease? (3) Whether the heavenly bodies will be more brilliant? (4) Whether the elements will receive an additional clarity? (5) Whether the animals and plants will remain?

FIRST ARTICLE

Whether the World Will Be Renewed?

We proceed thus to the First Article: —

Objection 1. It would seem that the world will never be renewed. For nothing will be but what was at some time as to its species: *What is it that hath been? the same thing that shall be* (Eccles. i. 9). Now the world never had any disposition other than it has now as to essential parts, both genera and species. Therefore it will never be renewed.

Obj. 2. Further, renewal is a kind of alteration. But it is impossible for the universe to be altered; because whatever is altered argues some alterant that is not altered, which nevertheless is a subject of local movement: and it is impossible to place such a thing outside the universe. Therefore it is impossible for the world to be renewed.

Obj. 3. Further, it is stated (Gen. ii. 2) that *God . . . rested on the seventh day from all His work which He had done,* and holy men explain that *He rested from forming new creatures.* Now when things were first established, the mode imposed upon them was the same as they have now in the natural order. Therefore they will never have any other.

Obj. 4. Further, the disposition which things have now is natural to them. Therefore if they be altered to another disposition, this disposition will be unnatural to them. Now whatever is unnatural and accidental cannot last for ever *(De Cœlo et Mundo,* i). Therefore this disposition acquired by being renewed will be taken away from them; and thus there will be a cycle of changes in the world as Empedocles and Origen *(Peri Archon.* ii. 3) maintained, and after this world there will be another, and after that again another.

* Ps. viii. 5 *seq.*

Obj. 5. Further, newness of glory is given to the rational creature as a reward. Now where there is no merit, there can be no reward. Since then insensible creatures have merited nothing, it would seem that they will not be renewed.

On the contrary, It is written (Isa. lxv. 17): *Behold I create new heavens and a new earth, and the former things shall not be in remembrance;* and (Apoc. xxi. 1): *I saw a new heaven and a new earth. For the first heaven and the first earth was gone.*

Further, the dwelling should befit the dweller. But the world was made to be man's dwelling. Therefore it should befit man. Now man will be renewed. Therefore the world will be likewise.

Further, *Every beast loveth its like* (Ecclus. xiii. 19), wherefore it is evident that likeness is the reason of love. Now man has some likeness to the universe, wherefore he is called *a little world.* Hence man loves the whole world naturally and consequently desires its good. Therefore, that man's desire be satisfied the universe must needs also be made better.

I answer that, We believe all corporeal things to have been made for man's sake, wherefore all things are stated to be subject to him.* Now they serve man in two ways, first, as sustenance to his bodily life, secondly, as helping him to know God, inasmuch as man sees the invisible things of God by the things that are made (Rom. i. 20). Accordingly glorified man will nowise need creatures to render him the first of these services, since his body will be altogether incorruptible, the Divine power effecting this through the soul which it will glorify immediately. Again man will not need the second service as to intellective knowledge, since by that knowledge he will see God immediately in His essence. The carnal eye, however, will be unable to attain to this vision of the Essence; wherefore that it may be fittingly comforted in the vision of God, it will see the Godhead in Its corporeal effects, wherein manifest proofs of the Divine majesty will appear, especially in Christ's flesh, and secondarily in the bodies of the blessed, and afterwards in all other bodies. Hence those bodies also will need to receive a greater inflow from the Divine goodness than now, not indeed so as to change their species, but so as to add a certain perfection of glory: and such will be the renewal of the world. Wherefore at the one same time, the world will be renewed, and man will be glorified.

Reply Obj. 1. Solomon is speaking there of the natural course: this is evident from his adding: *Nothing under the sun is new.* For since the movement of the sun follows a circle, those things which are subject to the sun's power must needs have some kind of circular movement. This consists in the fact that things which were before return the same in species but different in the individual *(De Generat.* i). But things belonging to the state of glory are not *under the sun.*

Reply Obj. 2. This argument considers natural alteration which proceeds from a natural agent, which acts from natural necessity. For such an agent cannot produce different dispositions, unless it be itself disposed differently. But things done by God proceed from freedom of will, wherefore it is possible, without any change in God Who wills it, for the universe to have at one time one disposition, and another at another time. Thus this renewal will not be reduced to a cause that is moved, but to an immovable principle, namely God.

Reply Obj. 3. God is stated to have ceased on the seventh day forming new creatures, for as much as nothing was made afterwards that was not previously in some likeness* either generically, or specifically, or at least as in a seminal principle, or even as in an obediential potentiality.† I say then that the future renewal of the world preceded in the works of the six days by way of a remote likeness, namely in the gliory and grace of the angels. Moreover it preceded in the obediential potentiality which was then bestowed on the creature to the effect of its receiving this same renewal by the Divine agency.

Reply Obj. 4. This disposition of newness will be neither natural nor contrary to nature, but above nature (just as grace and glory are above the nature of the soul): and it will proceed from an everlasting agent which will preserve it for ever.

Reply Obj. 5. Although, properly speaking, insensible bodies will not have merited this glory, yet man merited that this glory should be bestowed on the whole universe, in so far as this conduces to man's increase of glory. Thus a man merits to be clothed in more splendid robes, which splendor the robes nowise merited themselves.

SECOND ARTICLE

Whether the Movement of the Heavenly Bodies Will Cease?

We proceed thus to the Second Article:—

Objection 1. It seems that when the world is thus renewed the movement of the heavenly bodies will not cease. For it is written (Gen. viii. 22): *All the days of the earth . . . cold and heat, summer and winter, night and day shall not cease.* Now night and day, summer and winter result from the movement of the sun. Therefore the movement of the sun will never cease.

Obj. 2. Further, it is written (Jerem. xxxi. 35, 36): *Thus saith the Lord Who giveth the sun for the light of the day, the order of the moon and of the stars for the light of the night: Who stirreth up the sea, and the waves thereof roar . . . If these ordinances shall fail before Me . . . then also the seed of Israel shall fail, so as not to be a nation before Me for ever.* Now the seed of Israel shall never fail, but will remain for ever. Therefore the laws of day and of the sea waves, which result from the heavenly movement, will remain for ever. Therefore the movement of the heaven will never cease.

Obj. 3. Further, the substance of the heavenly bodies will remain for ever. Now it is useless to admit the existence of a thing unless you admit the purpose for which it was made: and the heavenly bodies were made in order *to divide the day and the night;* and to be *for signs, and for seasons, and for days and for years* (Gen. i. 14). But they cannot do this except by movement. Therefore their movement will remain for ever, else those bodies would remain without a purpose.

Obj. 4. Further, in this renewal of the world the whole world will be bettered. Therefore no body will be deprived of what pertains to its perfection. Now movement belongs to the perfection of a heavenly body, because, as stated in *De Cœlo et Mundo,* ii, *those bodies participate of the Divine goodness by their movement.* Therefore the movement of the heaven will not cease.

Obj. 5. Further, the sun successively gives light to the various parts of the world, by reason of its circular movement. Therefore if the circular movement of the heaven ceases, it follows that in some part of the earth's surface there will be perpetual darkness, which is unbecoming to the aforesaid renewal.

Obj. 6. Further, if the movement were to cease, this could only be because movement causes some imperfection in the heaven, for instance wear and tear, which is impossible, since this movement is natural, and the heavenly bodies are impassible, wherefore they are not worn out by movement *(De Cœlo et Mundo,* ii). Therefore the movement of the heaven will never cease.

Obj. 7. Further, a potentiality is useless if it be not reduced to act. Now in whatever position the heavenly body is placed it is in

* Cf. P. I, Q. 73, A. 1.　　† Cf. P. I, Q. 115, A. 2, *ad* 4; P. III. Q. 11, A. 1.

potentality to another position. Therefore unless this potentiality be reduced to act, it would remain useless, and would always be imperfect. But it cannot be reduced to act save by local movement. Therefore it will always be in motion.

Obj. 8. Further, if a thing is indifferent in relation to more than one alternation, either both are ascribed to it, or neither. Now the sun is indifferent to being in the east or in the west, else its movement would not be uniform throughout, since it would move more rapidly to the place which is more natural to it. Therefore either neither position is ascribed to the sun, or both. But neither both nor neither can be ascribed to it, except successively by movement; for if it stand still, it must needs stand in some position. Therefore the solar body will always be in motion, and in like manner all other heavenly bodies.

Obj. 9. Further, the movement of the heaven is the cause of time. Therefore if the movement of the heaven fail, time must needs fail: and if this were to fail, it would fail in an instant. Now an instant is defined *(Phys.* viii) *the beginning of the future and the end of the past.* Consequently there would be time after the last instant of time, which is impossible. Therefore the movement of the heavens will never cease.

Obj. 10. Further, glory does not remove nature. But the movement of the heaven is natural. Therefore it is not deprived thereof by glory.

On the contrary, It is stated (Apoc. x. 6) that the angel who appeared, *swore by him that liveth for ever and ever . . . that time shall be no longer,* namely after the seventh angel shall have sounded the trumpet, at the sound of which *the dead shall rise again* (1 Cor. xv. 52). Now if time be not, there is no movement of the heaven. Therefore the movement of the heaven will cease.

Further: *Thy sun shall go down no more, and thy moon shall not decrease* (Isa. lx. 20). Now the setting of the sun and the phases of the moon are caused by the movement of the heavens. Therefore the heavenly movement will cease at length.

Further, it is shown in *De Gener.* ii that *the movement of the heaven is for the sake of continual generation in this lower world.* But generation will cease when the number of the elect is complete. Therefore the movement of the heaven will cease.

Further, all movement is for some end *(Met.* ii). But all movement for an end ceases when the end is obtained. Therefore either the movement of the heaven will never obtain its end, and thus it would be useless, or it will cease at length.

Further, rest is more noble than movement, because things are more likened to God, Who is supremely immovable, by being themselves unmoved. Now the movement of lower bodies terminates naturally in rest. Therefore since the heavenly bodies are far nobler, their movement terminates naturally in rest.

I answer that, There are three opinions touching this question. The first is of the philosophers who assert that the movement of the heaven will last for ever. But this is not in keeping with our faith, which holds that the elect are in a certain number preordained by God, so that the begetting of men will not last for ever, and for the same reason, neither will other things that are directed to the begetting of men, such as the movement of the heaven and the variations of the elements. Others say that the movement of the heaven will cease naturally. But this again is false, since every body that is moved naturally has a place wherein it rests naturally, whereto it is moved naturally, and whence it is not moved except by violence. Now no such place can be assigned to the heavenly body, since it is not more natural to the sun to move towards a point in the east than to move away from it, wherefore either its movement would not be altogether natural, or its movement would not naturally terminate in rest. Hence we must agree with others who say that the movement of the heaven will cease at this renewal of the world, not indeed by any natural cause, but as a result of the will of God. For the body in question, like other bodies, was made to serve man in the two ways above mentioned (A. 1): and hereafter in the state of glory man will no longer need one of these services, that namely in respect of which the heavenly bodies serve man for the sustenance of his bodily life. Now in this way the heavenly bodies serve man by their movement, in so far as by the heavenly movement the human race is multiplied, plants and animals needful for man's use generated, and the temperature of the atmosphere rendered conducive to health. Therefore the movement of the heavenly body will cease as soon as man is glorified.

Reply Obj. 1. These words refer to the earth in its present state, when it is able to be the principle of the generation and corruption of plants. This is evident from its being said there: *All the days of the earth, seed time and harvest,* etc. And it is simply to be granted that as long as the earth is fit for seed time and harvest, the movement of the heaven will not cease.

We reply in like manner to *Obj.* 2 that the Lord is speaking there of the duration of the seed of Israel with regard to the present state. This is evident from the words: *Then also the seed of Israel shall fail, so as not to be a nation before Me for ever.* For after this state there will be no succession of days: wherefore the laws also which He had mentioned will cease after this state.

Reply Obj. 3. The end which is there assigned to the heavenly bodies is their proximate end, because it is their proper act. But this act is directed further to another end, namely the service of man, which is shown by the words of Deut. iv. 19: *Lest perhaps lifting up thy eyes to heaven, thou see the sun and the moon and all the stars of heaven, and being deceived by error thou adore and serve them, which the Lord thy God created for the service of all the nations, that are under heaven.* Therefore we should form our judgment of the heavenly bodies from the service of man, rather than from the end assigned to them in Genesis. Moreover the heavenly bodies, as stated above, will serve glorified man in another way; hence it does not follow that they will remain without a purpose.

Reply Obj. 4. Movement does not belong to the perfection of a heavenly body, except in so far as thereby it is the cause of generation and corruption in this lower world: and in that respect also this movement makes the heavenly body participate in the Divine goodness by way of a certain likeness of causality. But movement does not belong to the perfection of the substance of the heaven, which substance will remain. Wherefore it does not follow that, when this movement ceases, the substance of the heaven will lose something of its perfection.

Reply Obj. 5. All the elemental bodies will have in themselves a certain clarity of glory. Hence though part of the surface of the earth be not lit up by the sun, there will by no means be any darkness there.

Reply Obj. 6. A gloss of Ambrose on Rom. viii. 22, *Every creature groaneth,* etc. says explicitly that *all the elements labor to fulfill their offices: thus the sun and moon fill the places appointed to them not without work: this is for our sake, wherefore they will rest when we are taken up to heaven.* This work, in my opinion, does not signify that any stress or passion occurs to these bodies from their movement, since this movement is natural to them and nowise violent, as is proved in *De Cœlo et Mundo,* i. But work here denotes a defect in relation to the term to which a thing tends. Hence since this movement is ordained by Divine providence to the completion of the number of the elect, it follows that as long as the latter is incomplete, this movement has not reached the term whereto it was ordained: hence it is said metaphorically to labor, as a man who has not what he intends to have.

This defect will be removed from the heaven when the number of the elect is complete. Or it may refer to the desire of the future renewal, which it awaits from the Divine disposal.

Reply Obj. 7. In a heavenly body there is no potentiality that can be perfected by place, or that is made for this end which is to be in such and such a place. But potentiality to situation in a place is related to a heavenly body, as the craftsman's potentiality to construct various houses of one kind: for if he construct one of these he is not said to have the potentiality uselessly, and in like manner in whatever situation a heavenly body be placed, its potentiality to be in a place will not remain incomplete or without a purpose.

Reply Obj. 8. Although a heavenly body, so far as regards its nature, is equally inclined to every situation that it can possibly occupy, nevertheless in comparison with things outside it, it is not equally inclined to every situation: but in respect of one situation it has a more noble disposition in comparison with certain things than in respect of another situation; thus in our regard the sun has a more noble disposition at daytime than at night-time. Hence it is probable, since the entire renewal of the world is directed to man, that the heaven will have in this renewal the most noble situation possible in relation to our dwelling there. Or, according to some, the heaven will rest in that situation wherein it was made, else one of its revolutions would remain incomplete. But this argument seems improbable, for since a revolution of the heaven takes no less than 36,000 years to complete, it would follow that the world must last that length of time, which does not seem probable. Moreover according to this it would be possible to know when the world will come to an end. For we may conclude with probability from astronomers in what position the heavenly bodies were made, by taking into consideration the number of years that have elapsed since the beginning of the world: and in the same way it would be possible to know the exact number of years it would take them to return to a like position: whereas the time of the world's end is stated to be unknown.

Reply Obj. 9. Time will at length cease, when the heavenly movement ceases. Yet that last *now* will not be the beginning of the future. For the definition quoted applies to the *now* only as continuous with the parts of time, not as terminating the whole of time.

Reply Obj. 10. The movement of the heaven is said to be natural, not as though it were part of nature in the same way as we speak of natural principles; but because it has its principle in the nature of a body, not indeed its active but its receptive principle. Its active principle is a spiritual substance, as the Commentator says on *De Cœlo et Mundo;* and consequently it is not unreasonable for this movement to be done away by the renewal of glory, since the nature of the heavenly body will not alter through the cessation of that movement.

We grant the other objections which argue in the contrary sense, namely the first three, because they conclude in due manner. But since the remaining two seem to conclude that the movement of heaven will cease naturally, we must reply to them.

To the first, then, we reply that movement ceases when its purpose is attained, provided this is a sequel to, and does not accompany the movement. Now the purpose of the heavenly movement, according to philosophers, accompanies that movement, namely the imitation of the Divine goodness in the causality of that movement with respect to this lower world. Hence it does not follow that this movement ceases naturally.

To the second we reply that although immobility is simply nobler than movement, yet movement in a subject which thereby can acquire a perfect participation of the Divine goodness is nobler than rest in a subject which is altogether unable to acquire that perfection by movement. For this reason the earth which is the lowest of the elements is without movement: although God Who is exalted above all things is without movement, by Whom the more noble bodies are moved. Hence also it is that the movements of the higher bodies might be held to be perpetual, so far as their natural power is concerned, and never to terminate in rest, although the movement of lower bodies terminates in rest.

THIRD ARTICLE

Whether the Brightness of the Heavenly Bodies Will Be Increased at This Renewal?

We proceed thus to the Third Article:—

Objection 1. It would seem that the brightness of the heavenly bodies will not be increased at this renewal. For this renewal as regards the lower bodies will be caused by the cleansing fire. But the cleansing fire will not reach the heavenly bodies. Therefore the heavenly bodies will not be renewed by receiving an increase of brightness.

Obj. 2. Further, just as the heavenly bodies are the cause of generation in this lower world by their movement, so are they by their light. But, when generation ceases, movement will cease as stated above (A. 2). Therefore in like manner the light of the heavenly bodies will cease rather than increase.

Obj. 3. Further, if the heavenly bodies will

be renewed when man is renewed, it follows that when man deteriorated they deteriorated likewise. But this does not seem probable, since these bodies are unalterable as to their substance. Therefore neither will they be renewed when man is renewed.

Obj. 4. Further, if they deteriorated then, it follows that their deterioration was on a par with the amelioration which, it is said, will accrue to them at man's renewal. Now it is written (Isa. xxx. 26) that *the light of the moon shall be as the light of the sun.* Therefore in the original state before sin the moon shone as much as the sun does now. Therefore whenever the moon was over the earth, it made it to be day as the sun does now: which is proved manifestly to be false from the statement of Gen. i. 16 that the moon was made *to rule the night.* Therefore when man sinned, the heavenly bodies were not deprived of their light; and so their light will not be increased, so it seems, when man is glorified.

Obj. 5. Further, the brightness of the heavenly bodies, like other creatures, is directed to the use of man. Now, after the resurrection, the brightness of the sun will be of no use to man: for it is written (Isa. lx. 19): *Thou shalt no more have the sun for thy light by day, neither shall the brightness of the moon enlighten thee,* and (Apoc. xxi. 23): *The city hath no need of the sun, nor of the moon to shine in it.* Therefore their brightness will not be increased.

Obj. 6. Further, it were not a wise craftsman who would make very great instruments for the making of a small work. Now man is a very small thing in comparison with the heavenly bodies, which by their huge bulk surpass the size of man almost beyond comparison: in fact the size of the whole earth in comparison with the heaven is as a point compared with a sphere, as astronomers say. Since then God is most wise it would seem that man is not the end of the creation of the heavens, and so it is unseemly that the heaven should deteriorate when he sinned, or that it should be bettered when he is glorified.

On the contrary, It is written (Isa. xxx. 26): *The light of the moon shall be as the light of the sun, and the light of the sun shall be sevenfold.*

Further, the whole world will be renewed for the better. But the heaven is the more noble part of the corporeal world. Therefore it will be altered for the better. But this cannot be unless it shine out with greater brightness. Therefore its brightness will be bettered and will increase.

Further, *every creature that groaneth and travaileth in pain, awaiteth the revelation of the glory of the children of God* (Rom. viii.

21, 22).* Now such are the heavenly bodies, as a gloss says on the same passage. Therefore they await the glory of the saints. But they would not await it unless they were to gain something by it. Therefore their brightness will increase thereby, since it is its chief beauty.

I answer that, The renewal of the world is directed to the end that, after this renewal has taken place, God may become visible to man by signs so manifest as to be perceived as it were by his senses. Now creatures lead to the knowledge of God chiefly by their comeliness and beauty, which show forth the wisdom of their Maker and Governor; wherefore it is written (Wis. xiii. 5): *By the greatness of the beauty and of the creature, the Creator of them may be seen, so as to be known thereby.* And the beauty of the heavenly bodies consists chiefly in light; wherefore it is written (Ecclus. xliii. 10): *The glory of the stars is the beauty of heaven, the Lord enlighteneth the world on high.* Hence the heavenly bodies will be bettered, especially as regards their brightness. But to what degree and in what way this betterment will take place is known to Him alone Who will bring it about.

Reply Obj. 1. The cleansing fire will not cause the form of the renewal, but will only dispose thereto, by cleansing from the vileness of sin and the impurity resulting from the mingling of bodies, and this is not to be found in the heavenly bodies. Hence although the heavenly bodies are not to be cleansed by fire, they are nevertheless to be Divinely renewed.

Reply Obj. 2. Movement does not denote perfection in the thing moved, considered in itself, since movement is the act of that which is imperfect: although it may pertain to the perfection of a body in so far as the latter is the cause of something. But light belongs to the perfection of a lightsome body, even considered in its substance: and consequently after the heavenly body has ceased to be the cause of generation, its brightness will remain, while its movement will cease.

Reply Obj. 3. A gloss on Isa. xxx. 26, *The light of the moon shall be as the light of the sun,* says: *All things made for man's sake deteriorated at his fall, and sun and moon diminished in light.* This diminishment is understood by some to mean a real lessening of light. Nor does it matter that the heavenly bodies are by nature unalterable, because this alteration was brought about by the Divine power. Others, however, with greater probability, take this diminishment to mean, not a real lessening of light, but a lessening in reference to man's use; because after sin man did not receive as

much benefit from the light of the heavenly bodies as before. In the same sense we read (Gen. iii. 17, 18): *Cursed is the earth in thy work. . . . Thorns and thistles shall it bring forth to thee;* although it would have brought forth thorns and thistles before sin, but not as a punishment to man. Nor does it follow that, supposing the light of the heavenly bodies not to have been lessened essentially through man sinning, it will not really be increased at man's glorification, because man's sin wrought no change upon the state of the universe, since both before and after sin man had an animal life, which needs the movement and generation of a corporeal creature; whereas man's glorification will bring a change upon the state of all corporeal creatures, as stated above (Q. 76, A. 7). Hence there is no comparison.

Reply Obj. 4. This diminution, according to the more probable opinion, refers not to the substance but to the effect. Hence it does not follow that the moon while over the earth would have made it to be day, but that man would have derived as much benefit from the light of the moon then as now from the light of the sun. After the resurrection, however, when the light of the moon will be increased in very truth, there will be night nowhere on earth but only in the center of the earth, where hell will be, because then, as stated, the moon will shine as brightly as the sun does now; the sun seven times as much as now, and the bodies of the blessed seven times more than the sun, although there be no authority or reason to prove this.

Reply Obj. 5. A thing may be useful to man in two ways. First, by reason of necessity, and thus no creature will be useful to man because he will have complete sufficiency from God. This is signified (Apoc. xxi. 23) by the words quoted, according to which that *city hath no need of the sun,* nor *of the moon.* Secondly, on account of a greater perfection, and thus man will make use of other creatures, yet not as needful to him in order to obtain his end, in which way he makes use of them now.

Reply Obj. 6. This is the argument of Rabbi Moses who endeavors to prove (*Dux errantium* iii) that the world was by no means made for man's use. Wherefore he maintains that what we read in the Old Testament about the renewal of the world, as instanced by the quotations from Isaias, is said metaphorically: and that even as the sun is said to be darkened in reference to a person when he encounters a great sorrow so as not to know what to do (which way of speaking is customary to Scripture), so on the other hand the sun is said

---

* *The creature also itself shall be delivered from the servitude of corruption, into the liberty of the children of God. For we know that every creature groaneth and travaileth in pain,* etc.

to shine brighter for a person, and the whole world to be renewed, when he is brought from a state of sorrow to one of very great joy. But this is not in harmony with the authority and commentaries of holy men. Consequently we must answer this argument by saying that although the heavenly bodies far surpass the human body, yet the rational soul surpasses the heavenly bodies far more than these surpass the human body. Hence it is not unreasonable to say that the heavenly bodies were made for man's sake; not, however, as though this were the principal end, since the principal end of all things is God.

FOURTH ARTICLE

Whether the Elements Will Be Renewed by an Addition of Brightness?

We proceed thus to the Fourth Article:—

Obj. 1. It would seem that the elements will not be renewed by receiving some kind of brightness. For just as light is a quality proper to a heavenly body, so are hot and cold, wet and dry, qualities proper to the elements. Therefore as the heaven is renewed by an increase of brightness, so ought the elements to be renewed by an increase of active and passive qualities.

Obj. 2. Further, rarity, and density are qualities of the elements, and the elements will not be deprived of them at this renewal. Now the rarity and density of the elements would seem to be an obstacle to brightness, since a bright body needs to be condensed, for which reason the rarity of the air seems incompatible with brightness, and in like manner the density of the earth which is an obstacle to transparency. Therefore it is impossible for the elements to be renewed by the addition of brightness.

Obj. 3. Further, it is agreed that the damned will be in the earth. Yet they will be in darkness not only internal but also external. Therefore the earth will not be endowed with brightness in this renewal, nor for the same reason will the other elements.

Obj. 4. Further, increase of brightness in the elements implies an increase of heat. If therefore at this renewal the brightness of the elements be greater than it is now, their heat will likewise be greater; and thus it would seem that they will be changed from their natural qualities, which are in them according to a fixed measure: and this is absurd.

Obj. 5. Further, the good of the universe which consists in the order and harmony of the parts is more excellent than the good of any individual creature. But if one creature be bettered, the good of the universe is done

away, since there will no longer be the same harmony. Therefore if the elemental bodies, which according to their natural degree in the universe should be devoid of brightness, were to be endowed with brightness, the perfection of the universe would be diminished thereby rather than increased.

On the contrary, It is written (Apoc. xxi. 1): *I saw a new heaven and a new earth.* Now the heaven will be renewed by an increase of brightness. Therefore the earth and likewise the other elements will also.

Further, the lower bodies, like the higher, are for man's use. Now the corporeal creature will be rewarded for its services to man, as a gloss of Ambrose seems to say on Rom. viii. 22, *Every creature groaneth,* and a gloss of Jerome on Isa. xxx. 26, *And the light of the moon shall be,* etc. Therefore the elements will be glorified as well as the heavenly bodies.

Further, man's body is composed of the elements. Therefore the elemental particles that are in man's body will be glorified by the addition of brightness when man is glorified. Now it is fitting that whole and part should have the same disposition. Therefore it is fitting that the elements themselves should be endowed with brightness.

I answer that, Just as there is a certain order between the heavenly spirits and the earthly or human spirits, so is there an order between heavenly bodies and earthly bodies. Since then the corporeal creature was made for the sake of the spiritual and is ruled thereby, it follows that corporeal things are dealt with similarly to spiritual things. Now in this final consummation of things the lower spirits will receive the properties of the higher spirits, because men will be as the angels in heaven (Matth. xxii. 30): and this will be accomplished by conferring the highest degree of perfection on that in which the human spirit agrees with the angelic. Wherefore, in like manner, since the lower bodies do not agree with the heavenly bodies except in the nature of light and transparency (*De Anima,* ii), it follows that the lower bodies are to be perfected chiefly as regards brightness. Hence all the elements will be clothed with a certain brightness, not equally, however, but according to their mode: for it is said that the earth on its outward surface will be as transparent as glass, water as crystal, the air as heaven, fire as the lights of heaven.

Reply Obj. 1. As stated above (A. 1), the renewal of the world is directed to the effect that man even by his senses may as it were see the Godhead by manifest signs. Now the most spiritual and subtle of our senses is the sight. Consequently all the lower bodies need to be bettered, chiefly as regards the visible qualities the principle of which is light. On the other hand, the elemental qualities regard the touch, which is the most material of the senses, and the excess of their contrariety is more displeasing than pleasant; whereas excess of light will be pleasant, since it has no contrariety, except on account of a weakness in the organ, such as will not be then.

Reply Obj. 2. The air will be bright, not as casting forth rays, but as an enlightened transparency; while the earth, although it is opaque through lack of light, yet by the Divine power its surface will be clothed with the glory of brightness, without prejudice to its density.

Reply Obj. 3. The earth will not be glorified with brightness in the infernal regions; but instead of this glory, that part of the earth will have the rational spirits of men and demons, who though weak by reason of sin are nevertheless superior to any corporeal quality by the dignity of their nature. Or we may say that, though the whole earth be glorified, the wicked will nevertheless be in exterior darkness, since even the fire of hell, while shining for them in one respect, will be unable to enlighten them in another.

Reply Obj. 4. This brightness will be in these bodies even as it is in the heavenly bodies, in which it causes no heat, because these bodies will then be unalterable, as the heavenly bodies are now.

Reply Obj. 5. The order of the universe will not be done away by the betterment of the elements, because all the other parts will also be bettered, and so the same harmony will remain.

FIFTH ARTICLE

Whether the Plants and Animals Will Remain in This Renewal?

We proceed thus to the Fifth Article:—

Objection 1. It would seem that the plants and animals will remain in this renewal. For the elements should be deprived of nothing that belongs to their adornment. Now the elements are said to be adorned by the animals and plants.* Therefore they will not be removed in this renewal.

Obj. 2. Further, just as the elements served man, so also did animals, plants and mineral bodies. But on account of this service the elements will be glorified. Therefore both animals and plants and mineral bodies will be glorified likewise.

Obj. 3. Further, the universe will remain imperfect if anything belonging to its perfection be removed. Now the species of animals,

* Cf. Gen. i. 11, 12, 20, 21, 24, 25.

plants, and mineral bodies belong to the perfection of the universe. Since then we must not say that the world will remain imperfect when it is renewed, it seems that we should assert that the plants and animals will remain.

Obj. 4. Further, animals and plants have a more noble form than the elements. Now the world, at this final renewal, will be changed for the better. Therefore animals and plants should remain rather than the elements, since they are nobler.

Obj. 5. Further, it is unseemly to assert that the natural appetite will be frustrated. But by their natural appetite animals and plants desire to be for ever, if indeed not as regards the individual, at least as regards the species: and to this end their continual generation is directed (*De Generat.* ii). Therefore it is unseemly to say that these species will at length cease to be.

On the contrary, If plants and animals are to remain, either all of them will, or some of them. If all of them, then dumb animals, which had previously died, will have to rise again just as men will rise again. But this cannot be asserted for since their form comes to nothing, they cannot resume the same identical form. On the other hand if not all but some of them remain, since there is no more reason for one of them remaining for ever rather than another, it would seem that none of them will. But whatever remains after the world has been renewed will remain for ever, generation and corruption being done away. Therefore plants and animals will altogether cease after the renewal of the world.

Further, according to the Philosopher (*De Generat.* ii) the species of animals, plants and such like corruptible things, are not perpetuated except by the continuance of the heavenly movement. Now this will cease then. Therefore it will be impossible for those species to be perpetuated.

Further, if the end cease, those things which are directed to the end should cease. Now animals and plants were made for the upkeep of human life; wherefore it is written (Gen. ix. 3): *Even as the green herbs have I delivered all flesh†* to you. Therefore when man's animal life ceases, animals and plants should cease. But after this renewal animal life will cease in man. Therefore neither plants nor animals ought to remain.

I answer that, Since the renewal of the world will be for man's sake it follows that it should be conformed to the renewal of man. Now by being renewed man will pass from the state of corruption to incorruptibility and to a state of everlasting rest, wherefore it is written (1 Cor. xv. 53): *This corruptible must put on*

† Vulg.,—*have I delivered them all to you.*

incorruption, and this mortal must put on immortality; and consequently the world will be renewed in such a way as to throw off all corruption and remain for ever at rest. Therefore it will be impossible for anything to be the subject of that renewal, unless it be a subject of incorruption. Now such are the heavenly bodies, the elements, and man. For the heavenly bodies are by their very nature incorruptible both as to their whole and as to their part: the elements are corruptible as to their parts but incorruptible as a whole: while men are corruptible both in whole and in part, but this is on the part of their matter not on the part of their form, the rational soul to wit, which will remain incorrupt after the corruption of man. On the other hand, dumb animals, plants, and minerals, and all mixed bodies, are corruptible both in their whole and in their parts, both on the part of their matter which loses its form, and on the part of their form which does not remain actually; and thus they are in no way subjects of incorruption. Hence they will not remain in this renewal, but those things alone which we have mentioned above.

Reply Obj. 1. These bodies are said to adorn the elements, inasmuch as the general active and passive forces which are in the elements are applied to specific actions: hence they adorn the elements in their active and passive state. But this state will not remain in the elements: wherefore there is no need for animals or plants to remain.

Reply Obj. 2. Neither animals nor plants nor any other bodies merited anything by their services to man, since they lack free-will. However, certain bodies are said to be rewarded in so far as man merited that those things should be renewed which are adapted to be renewed. But plants and animals are not adapted to the renewal of incorruption, as stated above. Wherefore for this very reason man did not merit that they should be renewed, since no one can merit for another, or even for himself, that which another or himself is incapable of receiving. Hence, granted even that dumb animals merited by serving man, it would not follow that they are to be renewed.

Reply Obj. 3. Just as several kinds of perfection are ascribed to man (for there is the perfection of created nature and the perfection of glorified nature), so also there is a twofold perfection of the universe, one corresponding to this state of changeableness, the other corresponding to the state of a future renewal. Now plants and animals belong to its perfection according to the present state, and not according to the state of this renewal, since they are not capable thereof.

Reply Obj. 4. Although animals and plants as to certain other respects are more noble than the elements, the elements are more noble in relation to incorruption, as explained above.*

Reply Obj. 5. The natural desire to be for ever that is in animals and plants must be understood in reference to the movement of the heaven, so that they may continue in being as long as the movement of the heaven lasts: since there cannot be an appetite for an effect to last longer than its cause. Wherefore if at the cessation of movement in the first movable body, plants and animals cease as to their species, it does not follow that the natural appetite is frustrated.

QUESTION 92

Of the Vision of the Divine Essence in Reference to the Blessed†

(In Three Articles)

IN the next place we must consider matters concerning the blessed after the general judgment. We shall consider: (1) Their vision of the Divine essence, wherein their bliss consists chiefly. (2) Their bliss and their mansions. (3) Their relations with the damned. (4) Their gifts, which are contained in their bliss. (5) The crowns which perfect and adorn their happiness.

Under the first head there are three points of inquiry: (1) Whether the saints will see God in His essence? (2) Whether they will see Him with the eyes of the body? (3) Whether in seeing God they will see all that God sees?

* Cf. Q. 74, A. 1, *ad* 3.   † Cf. P. I, Q. 12.

FIRST ARTICLE

Whether the Human Intellect Can Attain to the Vision of God in His Essence?

We proceed thus to the First Article:—

Objection 1. It would seem that the human intellect cannot attain to the vision of God in His essence. For it is written (Jo. i. 18): *No man hath seen God at any time;* and Chrysostom in his commentary says (*Hom.* xiv. *in Joan.*) that *not even the heavenly essences, namely the Cherubim and Seraphim, have ever been able to see Him as He is.* Now, only equality with the angels is promised to men (Matth. xxii. 30): *They . . . shall be as the angels of God in heaven.* Therefore neither will the saints in heaven see God in His essence.

Obj. 2. Further, Dionysius argues thus *(Div. Nom.* i): Knowledge is only of existing things. Now whatever exists is finite, since it is confined to a certain genus: and therefore God, since He is infinite, is above all existing things. Therefore there is no knowledge of Him, and He is above all knowledge.

Obj. 3. Further, Dionysius *(De Myst. Theol.* i) shows that the most perfect way in which our intellect can be united to God is when it is united to Him as to something unknown. Now that which is seen in its essence is not unknown. Therefore it is impossible for our intellect to see God in His essence.

Obj. 4. Further, Dionysius says *(Ep. ad Caium Monach.)* that *the darkness,*—for thus he calls the abundance of light,—*which screens God is impervious to all illuminations, and hidden from all knowledge: and if anyone in seeing God understood what he saw, he saw not God Himself, but one of those things that are His.* Therefore no created intellect will be able to see God in His essence.

Obj. 5. Further, according to Dionysius *(Ep. ad Hieroth.) God is invisible on account of His surpassing glory.* Now His glory surpasses the human intellect in heaven even as on the way. Therefore since He is invisible on the way, so will He be in heaven.

Obj. 6. Further, since the intelligible object is the perfection of the intellect, there must needs be proportion between intelligible and intellect, as between the visible object and the sight. But there is no possible proportion between our intellect and the Divine essence, since an infinite distance separates them. Therefore our intellect will be unable to attain to the vision of the Divine essence.

Obj. 7. Further, God is more distant from our intellect than the created intelligible is from our senses. But the senses can nowise attain to the sight of a spiritual creature. Therefore neither will our intellect be able to attain to the vision of the Divine essence.

Obj. 8. Further, whenever the intellect understands something actually it needs to be informed with the likeness of the object understood, which likeness is the principle of the intellectual operation terminating in that object, even as heat is the principle of heating. Accordingly if our intellect understands God, this must be by means of some likeness informing the intellect itself. Now this cannot be the very essence of God, since form and thing informed must needs have one being, while the Divine essence differs from our intellect in essence and being. Therefore the form whereby our intellect is informed in understanding God must needs be a likeness impressed by God on

our intellect. But this likeness, being something created, cannot lead to the knowledge of God, except as an effect leads to the knowledge of its cause. Therefore it is impossible for our intellect to see God except through His effect. But to see God through His effect is not to see Him in His essence. Therefore our intellect will be unable to see God in His essence.

Obj. 9. Further, the Divine essence is more distant from our intellect than any angel or intelligence. Now according to Avicenna *(Met.* iii), *the existence of an intelligence in our intellect does not imply that its essence is in our intellect,* because in that case our knowledge of the intelligence would be a substance and not an accident, *but that its likeness is impressed on our intellect.* Therefore neither is God in our intellect, to be understood by us, except in so far as an impression of Him is in our intellect. But this impression cannot lead to the knowledge of the Divine essence, for since it is infinitely distant from the Divine essence, it degenerates to another image much more than if the image of a white thing were to degenerate to the image of a black thing. Therefore, just as a person in whose sight the image of a white thing degenerates to the image of a black thing, on account of an indisposition in the organ, is not said to see a white thing, so neither will our intellect be able to see God in His essence, since it understands God only by means of this impression.

Obj. 10. Further, *In things devoid of matter that which understands is the same as that which is understood (De Anima,* iii). Now God is supremely devoid of matter. Since then our intellect, which is created, cannot attain to be an uncreated essence, it is impossible for our intellect to see God in His essence.

Obj. 11. Further, whatever is seen in its essence is known as to what it is. But our intellect cannot know of God what He is, but only what He is not as Dionysius *(Cœl. Hier.* ii) and Damascene *(De Fide Orthod.* i) declare. Therefore our intellect will be unable to see God in His essence.

Obj. 12. Further, every infinite thing, as such, is unknown. But God is in every way infinite. Therefore He is altogether unknown. Therefore it will be impossible for Him to be seen in His essence by a created intellect

Obj. 13. Further, Augustine says *(De Videndo Deo: Ep.* cxlvii): *God is by nature invisible.* Now that which is in God by nature cannot be otherwise. Therefore it is impossible for Him to be seen in His essence.

Obj. 14. Further, whatever is in one way and is seen in another way is not seen as it is. Now God is in one way and will be seen in another way by the saints in heaven: for He is according to His own mode, but will be seen by the saints according to their mode. Therefore He will not be seen by the saints as He is, and thus will not be seen in His essence.

Obj. 15. Further, that which is seen through a medium is not seen in its essence. Now God will be seen in heaven through a medium which is the light of glory, according to Ps. xxxv. 10, *In Thy light we shall see light.* Therefore He will not be seen in His essence.

Obj. 16. Further, in heaven God will be seen face to face, according to 1 Cor. xiii. 12. Now when we see a man face to face, we see him through his likeness. Therefore in heaven God will be seen through His likeness, and consequently not in His essence.

On the contrary, It is written (1 Cor. xiii. 12): *We see now through a glass in a dark manner, but then face to face.* Now that which is seen face to face is seen in its essence. Therefore God will be seen in His essence by the saints in heaven.

Further, it is written (1 Jo. iii. 2): *When He shall appear we shall be like to Him, because we shall see Him as He is.* Therefore we shall see Him in His essence.

Further, a gloss on 1 Cor. xv. 24, *When He shall have delivered up the kingdom to God and the Father,* says: *Where, i.e.* in heaven, *the essence of Father, Son, and Holy Ghost shall be seen: this is given to the clean of heart alone and is the highest bliss.* Therefore the blessed will see God in His essence.

Further, it is written (Jo. xiv. 21): *He that loveth Me shall be loved of My Father; and I will love him, and will manifest Myself to him.* Now that which is manifested is seen in its essence. Therefore God will be seen in His essence by the saints in heaven.

Further, Gregory commenting (*Moral.* xviii) on the words of Exod. xxxiii. 20, *Man shall not see Me and live,* disapproves of the opinion of those who said that *in this abode of bliss God can be seen in His glory but not in His nature; for His glory differs not from His nature.* But His nature is His essence. Therefore He will be seen in His essence.

Further, the desire of the saints cannot be altogether frustrated. Now the common desire of the saints is to see God in His essence, according to Exod. xxxiii. 13, *Show me Thy glory;* Ps. lxxix. 20, *Show Thy face and we shall be saved;* and Jo. xiv. 8, *Show us the Father and it is enough for us.* Therefore the saints will see God in His essence.

I answer that, Even as we hold by faith that the last end of man's life is to see God, so the philosophers maintained that man's ultimate happiness is to understand immaterial substances according to their being. Hence in reference to this question we find that philosophers and theologians encounter the same difficulty and the same difference of opinion. For some philosophers held that our passive intellect can never come to understand separate substances; thus Alfarabius expresses himself at the end of his *Ethics,* although he says the contrary in his book *On the Intelligence,* as the Commentator attests (*De Anima,* iii). In like manner certain theologians held that the human intellect can never attain to the vision of God in His essence. On either side they were moved by the distance which separates our intellect from the Divine essence and from separate substances. For since the intellect in act is somewhat one with the intelligible object in act, it would seem difficult to understand how the created intellect is made to be an uncreated essence. Wherefore Chrysostom says (*Hom.* xiv *in Joan.*); *How can the creature see the uncreated?* Those who hold the passive intellect to be the subject of generation and corruption, as being a power dependent on the body, encounter a still greater difficulty not only as regards the vision of God but also as regards the vision of any separate substances. But this opinion is altogether untenable. First, because it is in contradiction to the authority of canonical scripture, as Augustine declares (*De Videndo Deo: Ep.* cxlvii). Secondly, because, since understanding is an operation most proper to man, it follows that his happiness must be held to consist in that operation when perfected in him. Now since the perfection of an intelligent being as such is the intelligible object, if in the most perfect operation of his intellect man does not attain to the vision of the Divine essence, but to something else, we shall be forced to conclude that something other than God is the object of man's happiness: and since the ultimate perfection of a thing consists in its being united to its principle, it follows that something other than God is the effective principle of man, which is absurd, according to us, and also according to the philosophers who maintain that our souls emanate from the separate substances, so that finally we may be able to understand these substances. Consequently, according to us, it must be asserted that our intellect will at length attain to the vision of the Divine essence, and according to the philosophers, that it will attain to the vision of separate substances.

It remains, then, to examine how this may come about. For some, like Alfarabius and Avempace, held that from the very fact that our intellect understands any intelligible objects whatever, it attains to the vision of a separate substance. To prove this they employ two arguments. The first is that just as the specific nature is not diversified in various individuals, except as united to various individuating principles, so the idea understood is not diversified in me and you, except in so far as it is united to various imaginary forms: and consequently when the intellect separates the idea understood from the imaginary forms, there remains a quiddity understood, which is one and the same in the various persons understanding it, and such is the quiddity of a separate substance. Hence, when our intellect attains to the supreme abstraction of any intelligible quiddity, it thereby understands the quiddity of the separate substance that is similar to it. The second argument is that our intellect has a natural aptitude to abstract the quiddity from all intelligible objects having a quiddity. If, then, the quiddity which it abstracts from some particular individual be a quiddity without a quiddity, the intellect by understanding it understands the quiddity of the separate substance which has a like disposition, since separate substances are subsisting quiddities without quiddities; for the quiddity of a simple thing is the simple thing itself, as Avicenna says (Met. iii). On the other hand if the quiddity abstracted from this particular sensible be a quiddity that has a quiddity, it follows that the intellect has a natural aptitude to abstract this quiddity, and consequently since we cannot go on indefinitely, we shall come to some quiddity without a quiddity, and this is what we understand by a separate quiddity.*

But this reasoning is seemingly inconclusive. First, because the quiddity of the material substance, which the intellect abstracts, is not of the same nature as the quiddity of the separate substances, and consequently from the fact that our intellect abstracts the quiddities of material substances and knows them, it does not follow that it knows the quiddity of a separate substance, especially of the Divine essence, which more than any other is of a different nature from any created quiddity. Secondly, because granted that it be of the same nature, nevertheless the knowledge of a composite thing would not lead to the knowledge of a separate substance, except in the point of the most remote genus, namely substance: and such a knowledge is imperfect unless it reach to the properties of a thing. For to know a man only as an animal is to know him only in a restricted sense and potentially: and much less is it to know only the nature of substance in him. Hence to know God thus, or other separate substances, is not to see the essence of God or the quiddity of a separate substance, but to know Him in His effect and in a mirror as it were. For this

* Cf. P. I, Q. 88, A. 2.

reason Avicenna in his Metaphysics propounds another way of understanding separate substances, to wit that separate substances are understood by us by means of intentions of their quiddities, such intentions being images of their substances, not indeed abstracted therefrom, since they are immaterial, but impressed thereby on our souls. But this way also seems inadequate to the Divine vision which we seek. For it is agreed that whatever is received into any thing is therein after the mode of the recipient: and consequently the likeness of the Divine essence impressed on our intellect will be according to the mode of our intellect: and the mode of our intellect falls short of a perfect reception of the Divine likeness. Now the lack of perfect likeness may occur in as many ways, as unlikeness may occur. For in one way there is a deficient likeness, when the form is participated according to the same specific nature, but not in the same measure of perfection: such is the defective likeness in a subject that has little whiteness in comparison with one that has much. In another way the likeness is yet more defective, when it does not attain to the same specific nature but only to the same generic nature: such is the likeness of an orange-colored or yellowish object in comparison with a white one. In another way, still more defective is the likeness when it does not attain to the same generic nature, but only to a certain analogy or proportion: such is the likeness of whiteness to man, in that each is a being: and in this way every likeness received into a creature is defective in comparison with the Divine essence. Now in order that the sight know whiteness, it is necessary for it to receive the likeness of whiteness according to its specific nature, although not according to the same manner of being, because the form has a manner of being in the sense other from that which it has in the thing outside the soul: for if the form of yellowness were received into the eye, the eye would not be said to see whiteness. In like manner in order that the intellect understand a quiddity, it is necessary for it to receive its likeness according to the same specific nature, although there may possibly not be the same manner of being on either side: for the form which is in the intellect or sense is not the principle of knowledge according to its manner of being on both sides, but according to its common ratio with the external object. Hence it is clear that by no likeness received in the created intellect can God be understood, so that His essence be seen immediately. And for this reason those who held the Divine essence to be seen in this way alone, said that the essence itself will not be seen, but a certain brightness, as it were a radiance thereof. Consequently neither does this way suffice for the Divine vision that we seek.

Therefore we must take the other way, which also certain philosophers held, namely Alexander and Averroes *(De Anima,* iii.). For since in every knowledge some form is required whereby the object is known or seen, this form by which the intellect is perfected so as to see separate substances is neither a quiddity abstracted by the intellect from composite things, as the first opinion maintained, nor an impression left on our intellect by the separate substance, as the second opinion affirmed; but the separate substance itself united to our intellect as its form, so as to be both that which is understood, and that whereby it is understood. And whatever may be the case with other separate substances, we must nevertheless allow this to be our way of seeing God in His essence, because by whatever other form our intellect were informed, it could not be led thereby to the Divine essence. This, however, must not be understood as though the Divine essence were in reality the form of our intellect, or as though from its conjunction with our intellect there resulted one being simply, as in natural things from the natural form and matter: but the meaning is that the proportion of the Divine essence to our intellect is as the proportion of form to matter. For whenever two things, one of which is the perfection of the other, are received into the same recipient, the proportion of one to the other, namely of the more perfect to the less perfect, is as the proportion of form to matter: thus light and color are received into a transparent object, light being to color as form to matter. When therefore intellectual light is received into the soul, together with the indwelling Divine essence, though they are not received in the same way, the Divine essence will be to the intellect as form to matter: and that this suffices for the intellect to be able to see the Divine essence by the Divine essence itself may be shown as follows:

As from the natural form (whereby a thing has being) and matter, there results one thing simply, so from the form whereby the intellect understands, and the intellect itself, there results one thing intelligibly. Now in natural things a self-subsistent thing cannot be the form of any matter, if that thing has matter as one of its parts, since it is impossible for matter to be the form of a thing. But if this self-subsistent thing be a mere form, nothing hinders it from being the form of some matter and becoming that whereby the composite itself is,* as instanced in the soul. Now in the intellect we must take the intellect itself in

potentiality as matter, and the intelligible species as form; so that the intellect actually understanding will be the composite as it were resulting from both. Hence if there be a self-subsistent thing, that has nothing in itself besides that which is intelligible, such a thing can by itself be the form whereby the intellect understands. Now a thing is intelligible in respect of its actuality and not of its potentiality *(Met.* ix): in proof of which an intelligible form needs to be abstracted from matter and from all the properties of matter. Therefore, since the Divine essence is pure act, it will be possible for it to be the form whereby the intellect understands: and this will be the beatific vision. Hence the Master says (ii. *Sent.* D. 1) that the union of the body with the soul is an illustration of the blissful union of the spirit with God.

Reply Obj. 1. The words quoted can be explained in three ways, according to Augustine *(De Videndo Deo: Ep.* cxlvii.). In one way as excluding corporeal vision, whereby no one ever saw or will see God in His essence; secondly, as excluding intellectual vision of God in His essence from those who dwell in this mortal flesh; thirdly, as excluding the vision of comprehension from a created intellect. It is thus that Chrysostom understands the saying, wherefore he adds: *By seeing, the evangelist means a most clear perception, and such a comprehension as the Father has of the Son.* This also is the meaning of the evangelist, since he adds: *The only-begotten Son Who is in the bosom of the Father, He hath declared Him:* his intention being to prove the Son to be God from His comprehending God.

Reply Obj. 2. Just as God, by His infinite essence, surpasses all existing things which have a determinate being, so His knowledge, whereby He knows, is above all knowledge. Wherefore as our knowledge is to our created essence, so is the Divine knowledge to His infinite essence. Now two things contribute to knowledge, to wit, the knower and the thing known. Again, the vision whereby we shall see God in His essence is the same whereby God sees Himself, as regards that whereby He is seen, because as He sees Himself in His essence, so shall we also see Him. But as regards the knower there is the difference that is between the Divine intellect and ours. Now in the order of knowledge the object known follows the form by which we know, since by the form of a stone we see a stone: whereas the efficacy of knowledge follows the power of the knower: thus he who has stronger sight sees more clearly. Consequently in that vision we shall see the same thing that God sees, namely His essence, but not so effectively.

* Literally,—and becoming the *whereby-it-is* of the composite itself.

Reply obj. 3. Dionysius is speaking there of the knowledge whereby wayfarers know God by a created form, whereby our intellect is informed so as to see God. But as Augustine says (*loc. cit.*), *God evades every form of our intellect,* because whatever form our intellect conceive, that form is out of proportion to the Divine essence. Hence He cannot be fathomed by our intellect: but our most perfect knowledge of Him as wayfarers is to know that He is above all that our intellect can conceive, and thus we are united to Him as to something unknown. In heaven, however, we shall see Him by a form which is His essence, and we shall be united to Him as to something known.

Reply Obj. 4. God is light (Jo. i. 9). Now illumination is the impression of light on an illuminated object. And since the Divine essence is of a different mode from any likeness thereof impressed on the intellect, he (Dionysius) says that the *Divine darkness is impervious to all illumination,* because, to wit, the Divine essence, which he calls *darkness* on account of its surpassing brightness, remains undemonstrated by the impression on our intellect, and consequently *is hidden from all knowledge.* Therefore if anyone in seeing God conceives something in his mind, this is not God but one of God's effects.

Reply Obj. 5. Although the glory of God surpasses any form by which our intellect is informed now, it does not surpass the Divine essence, which will be the form of our intellect in heaven: and therefore although it is invisible now, it will be visible then.

Reply Obj. 6. Although there can be no proportion between finite and infinite, since the excess of the infinite over the finite is indeterminate, there can be proportionateness or a likeness to proportion between them: for as a finite thing is equal to some finite thing, so is an infinite thing equal to an infinite thing. Now in order that a thing be known totally, it is sometimes necessary that there be proportion between knower and known, because the power of the knower needs to be adequate to the knowableness of the thing known, and equality is a kind of proportion. Sometimes, however, the knowableness of the thing surpasses the power of the knower, as when we know God, or conversely when He knows creatures: and then there is no need for proportion between knower and known, but only for proportionateness; so that, to wit, as the knower is to the knowable object, so is the knowable object to the fact of its being known: and this proportionateness suffices for the infinite to be known by the finite, or conversely.

We may also reply that proportion according to the strict sense in which it is employed signifies a ratio of quantity to quantity based on a certain fixed excess or equality; but is further transferred to denote any ratio of any one thing to another; and in this sense we say that matter should be proportionate to its form. In this sense nothing hinders our intellect, although finite, being described as proportionate to the vision of the Divine essence; but not to the comprehension thereof, on account of its immensity.

Reply Obj. 7. Likeness and distance are twofold. One is according to agreement in nature; and thus God is more distant from the created intellect than the created intelligible is from the sense. The other is according to proportionateness; and thus it is the other way about, for sense is not proportionate to the knowledge of the immaterial, as the intellect is proportionate to the knowledge of any immaterial object whatsoever. It is this likeness and not the former that is requisite for knowledge, for it is clear that the intellect understanding a stone is not like it in its natural being; thus also the sight apprehends red honey and red gall, though it does not apprehend sweet honey, for the redness of gall is more becoming to honey as visible, than the sweetness of honey to honey.

Reply Obj. 8. In the vision wherein God will be seen in His essence, the Divine essence itself will be the form, as it were, of the intellect, by which it will understand: nor is it necessary for them to become one in being, but only to become one as regards the act of understanding.

Reply Obj. 9. We do not uphold the saying of Avicenna as regards the point at issue, for in this other philosophers also disagree with him. Unless perhaps we might say that Avicenna refers to the knowledge of separate substances, in so far as they are known by the habits of speculative sciences and the likeness of other things. Hence he makes this statement in order to prove that in us knowledge is not a substance but an accident. Nevertheless, although the Divine essence is more distant, as to the property of its nature, from our intellect, than is the substance of an angel, it surpasses it in the point of intelligibility, since it is pure act without any admixture of potentiality, which is not the case with other separate substances. Nor will that knowledge whereby we shall see God in His essence be in the genus of accident as regards that whereby He will be seen, but only as regards the act of the one who understands Him, for this act will not be the very substance either of the person understanding or of the thing understood.

Reply Obj. 10. A substance that is separate from matter understands both itself and other things; and in both cases the authority quoted can be verified. For since the very essence of a separate substance is of itself intelligible and actual, through being separate from matter, it is clear that when a separate substance understands itself, that which understands and that which is understood are absolutely identical, for it does not understand itself by an intention abstracted from itself, as we understand material objects. And this is apparently the meaning of the Philosopher (De Anima, iii.) as indicated by the Commentator (loc. cit.). But when it understands other things, the object actually understood becomes one with the intellect in act, in so far as the form of the object understood becomes the form of the intellect, for as much as the intellect is in act; not that it becomes identified with the essence of the intellect, as Avicenna proves (De Natural. vi.), because the essence of the intellect remains one under two forms whereby it understands two things in succession, in the same way as primary matter remains one under various forms. Hence also the Commentator (De Anima. iii.) compares the passive intellect, in this respect, to primary matter. Thus it by no means follows that our intellect in seeing God becomes the very essence of God, but that the latter is compared to it as its perfection or form.

Reply Obj. 11. These and all like authorities must be understood to refer to the knowledge whereby we know God on the way, for the reason given above.

Reply Obj. 12. The infinite is unknown if we take it in the privative sense, as such, because it indicates removal of completion whence knowledge of a thing is derived. Wherefore the infinite amounts to the same as matter subject to privation, as stated in *Phys.* iii. But if we take the infinite in the negative sense, it indicates the absence of limiting matter, since even a form is somewhat limited by its matter. Hence the infinite in this sense is of itself most knowable; and it is in this way that God is infinite.

Reply Obj. 13. Augustine is speaking of bodily vision, by which God will never be seen. This is evident from what proceeds: *For no man hath seen God at any time, nor can any man see Him as these things which we call visible are seen: in this way He is by nature invisible even as He is incorruptible.* As, however, He is by nature supremely being, so He is in Himself supremely intelligible. But that He be for a time not understood by us is owing to our defect: wherefore that He be seen by us after being unseen is owing to a change not in Him but in us.

* Cf. P. I, Q. 12, A. 5.

Reply Obj. 14. In heaven God will be seen by the saints as He is, if this be referred to the mode of the object seen, for the saints will see that God has the mode which He has. But if we refer the mode to the knower, He will not be seen as He is, because the created intellect will not have so great an efficacy in seeing, as the Divine essence has to the effect of being seen.

Reply Obj. 15. There is a threefold medium both in bodily and in intellectual vision. The first is the medium *under which* the object is seen, and this is something perfecting the sight so as to see in general, without determining the sight to any particular object. Such is bodily light in relation to bodily vision; and the light of the active intellect in relation to the passive intellect, in so far as this light is a medium. The second is the light *by which* the object is seen, and this is the visible form, whereby either sight is determined to a special object, for instance by the form of a stone to know a stone. The third is the medium *in which* it is seen; and this is something by gazing on which the sight is led to something else: thus by looking in a mirror it is led to see the things reflected in the mirror, and by looking at an image it is led to the thing represented by the image. In this way, too, the intellect from knowing an effect is led to the cause, or conversely. Accordingly in the heavenly vision there will be no third medium, so that, to wit, God be known by the images of other things, as He is known now, for which reason we are said to see now in a glass: nor will there be the second medium, because the essence itself of God will be that whereby our intellect will see God. But there will only be the first medium, which will upraise our intellect so that it will be possible for it to be united to the uncreated substance in the aforesaid manner. Yet this medium will not cause that knowledge to be mediate, because it does not come in between the knower and the thing known, but is that which gives the knower the power to know.*

Reply Obj. 16. Corporeal creatures are not said to be seen immediately, except when that which in them is capable of being brought into conjunction with the sight is in conjunction therewith. Now they are not capable of being in conjunction with the sight of their essence on account of their materiality: hence they are seen immediately when their image is in conjunction with the sight. But God is able to be united to the intellect by His essence: wherefore He would not be seen immediately, unless His essence were united to the intellect: and this vision, which is effected immediately, is called *vision of face.* Moreover the likeness of the corporeal object is received into the sight according to the same ratio as it is in the object, although not according to the same mode of being. Wherefore this likeness leads to the object directly: whereas no likeness can lead our intellect in this way to God, as shown above: and for this reason the comparison fails.

SECOND ARTICLE

Whether after the Resurrection the Saints Will See God with the Eyes of the Body? *

We proceed thus to the Second Article:—

Objection 1. It would seem that after the resurrection the saints will see God with the eyes of the body. Because the glorified eye has greater power than one that is not glorified. Now the blessed Job saw God with his eyes (Job xlii. 5): *With the hearing of the ear, I have heard Thee, but now my eye seeth Thee.* Much more therefore will the glorified eye be able to see God in His essence.

Obj. 2. Further, it is written (Job xix. 26): *In my flesh I shall see God my Saviour* (Vulg.,—*my God*). Therefore in heaven God will be seen with the eyes of the body.

Obj. 3. Further, Augustine, speaking of the sight of the glorified eyes, expresses himself as follows (*De Civ. Dei*, xxii): *A greater power will be in those eyes, not to see more keenly, as certain serpents or eagles are reported to see (for whatever acuteness of vision is possessed by these animals they can see only corporeal things), but to see even incorporeal things.* Now any power that is capable of knowing incorporeal things can be upraised to see God. Therefore the glorified eyes will be able to see God.

Obj. 4. Further, the disparity of corporeal to incorporeal things is the same as of incorporeal to corporeal. Now the incorporeal eye can see corporeal things. Therefore the corporeal eye can see the incorporeal: and consequently the same conclusion follows:

Obj. 5. Further, Gregory, commenting on Job iv. 16, *There stood one whose countenance I knew not,* says (*Moral.* v): *Man who, had he been willing to obey the command, would have been spiritual in the flesh, became, by sinning, carnal even in mind.* Now through becoming carnal in mind, *he thinks only of those things which he draws to his soul by the images of bodies (ibid).* Therefore when he will be spiritual in the flesh (which is promised to the saints after the resurrection), he will be able even in the flesh to see spiritual things. Therefore the same conclusion follows:

Obj. 6. Further, man can be beatified by God alone. Now he will be beatified not only in soul but also in body. Therefore God will

* Cf. P. I, Q. 12, A. 3.

be visible not only to his intellect but also to his flesh.

Obj. 7. Further, even as God is present to the intellect by His essence, so will He be to the senses, because He will be *all in all* (1 Cor. xv. 28). Now He will be seen by the intellect through the union of His essence therewith. Therefore He will also be visible to the sense.

On the contrary, Ambrose, commenting on Luke i. 2, *There appeared to him an angel,* says: *God is not sought with the eyes of the body, nor surveyed by the sight, nor clasped by the touch.* Therefore God will by no means be visible to the bodily sense.

Further, Jerome, commenting on Isa. vi. 1, *I saw the Lord sitting,* says: *The Godhead not only of the Father, but also of the Son and of the Holy Ghost is visible, not to carnal eyes, but only to the eyes of the mind, of which it is said: Blessed are the pure in heart.*

Further, Jerome says again (as quoted by Augustine, *Ep.* cxlvii): *An incorporeal thing is invisible to a corporeal eye.* But God is supremely incorporeal. Therefore, etc.

Further, Augustine says (*De Videndo Deo, Ep.* cxlvii): *No man hath seen God as He is at any time, neither in this life, nor in the angelic life, in the same way as these visible things which are seen with the corporeal sight.* Now the angelic life is the life of the blessed, wherein they will live after the resurrection. Therefore, etc.

Further, according to Augustine (*De Trin.* xiv.), *man is said to be made to God's image inasmuch as he is able to see God.* But man is in God's image as regards his mind, and not as regards his flesh. Therefore he will see God with his mind and not with his flesh.

I answer that, A thing is perceptible to the senses of the body in two ways, directly and indirectly. A thing is perceptible directly if it can act directly on the bodily senses. And a thing can act directly either on sense as such or on a particular sense as such. That which acts directly in this second way on a sense is called a proper sensible, for instance color in relation to the sight, and sound in relation to the hearing. But as sense as such makes use of a bodily organ, nothing can be received therein except corporeally, since whatever is received into a thing is therein after the mode of the recipient. Hence all sensibles act on the sense as such, according to their magnitude: and consequently magnitude and all its consequences, such as movement, rest, number, and the like, are called common sensibles, and yet they are direct objects of sense.

An indirect object of sense is that which does not act on the sense, neither as sense nor as a particular sense, but is annexed to those things that act on sense directly: for instance

Socrates; the son of Diares; a friend and the like which are the direct object of the intellect's knowledge in the universal, and in the particular are the object of the cogitative power in man, and of the estimative power in other animals. The external sense is said to perceive things of this kind, although indirectly, when the apprehensive power (whose province it is to know directly this thing known), from that which is sensed directly, apprehends them at once and without any doubt or discourse (thus we see that a person is alive from the fact that he speaks): otherwise the sense is not said to perceive it even indirectly.

I say then that God can nowise be seen with the eyes of the body, or perceived by any of the senses, as that which is seen directly, neither here, nor in heaven: for if that which belongs to sense as such be removed from sense, there will be no sense, and in like manner if that which belongs to sight as sight be removed therefrom, there will be no sight. Accordingly seeing that sense as sense perceives magnitude, and sight as such a sense perceives color, it is impossible for the sight to perceive that which is neither color nor magnitude, unless we call it a sense equivocally. Since then sight and sense will be specifically the same in the glorified body, as in a non-glorified body, it will be impossible for it to see the Divine essence as an object of direct vision; yet it will see it as an object of indirect vision, because on the one hand the bodily sight will see so great a glory of God in bodies, especially in the glorified bodies and most of all in the body of Christ, and, on the other hand, the intellect will see God so clearly, that God will be perceived in things seen with the eye of the body, even as life is perceived in speech. For although our intellect will not then see God from seeing His creatures, yet it will see God in His creatures seen corporeally. This manner of seeing God corporeally is indicated by Augustine (*De Civ. Dei*, xxii), as is clear if we take note of his words, for he says: *It is very credible that we shall so see the mundane bodies of the new heaven and the new earth, as to see most clearly God everywhere present, governing all corporeal things, not as we now see the invisible things of God as understood by those that are made, but as when we see men . . . we do not believe but see that they live.*

Reply Obj. 1. This saying of Job refers to the spiritual eye, of which the Apostle says (Eph. i. 18): *The eyes of our* (Vulg,—*your*) *heart enlightened.*

Reply Obj. 2. The passage quoted does not mean that we are to see God with the

* Cf. P. I, Q. 12, AA. 7, 8.

eyes of the flesh, but that, in the flesh, we shall see God.

Reply Obj. 3. In these words Augustine speaks as one inquiring and conditionally. This appears from what he had said before: *Therefore they will have an altogether different power, if they shall see that incorporeal nature:* and then he goes on to say: *Accordingly a greater power,* etc., and afterwards he explains himself.

Reply Obj. 4. All knowledge results from some kind of abstraction from matter. Wherefore the more a corporeal form is abstracted from matter, the more is it a principle of knowledge. Hence it is that a form existing in matter is in no way a principle of knowledge, while a form existing in the senses is somewhat a principle of knowledge, in so far as it is abstracted from matter, and a form existing in the intellect is still better a principle of knowledge. Therefore the spiritual eye, whence the obstacle to knowledge is removed, can see a corporeal object: but it does not follow that the corporeal eye, in which the cognitive power is deficient as participating in matter, be able to know perfectly incorporeal objects of knowledge.

Reply Obj. 5. Although the mind that has become carnal cannot think but of things received from the senses, it thinks of them immaterially. In like manner whatever the sight apprehends it must always apprehend it corporeally: wherefore it cannot know things which cannot be apprehended corporeally.

Reply Obj. 6. Beatitude is the perfection of man as man. And since man is man not through his body but through his soul, and the body is essential to man, in so far as it is perfected by the soul: it follows that man's beatitude does not consist chiefly otherwise than in an act of the soul, and passes from the soul on to the body by a kind of overflow, as explained above (Q. 85., A. 1). Yet our body will have a certain beatitude from seeing God in sensible creatures: and especially in Christ's body.

Reply Obj. 7. The intellect can perceive spiritual things, whereas the eyes of the body cannot: wherefore the intellect will be able to know the Divine essence united to it, but the eyes of the body will not.

THIRD ARTICLE

Whether the Saints, Seeing God, See All That God Sees? *

We proceed thus to the Third Article:—

Objection 1. It would seem that the saints, seeing God in His essence, see all that God sees in Himself. For as Isidore says (*De Sum. Bon.* 1.): *The angels know all things in the*

World of God, before they happen. Now the saints will be equal to the angels of God (Matth. xxii. 30). Therefore the saints also in seeing God see all things.

Obj. 2. Further, Gregory says *(Dial.* iv.) : *Since all see God there with equal clearness, what do they not know, who know Him Who knows all things?* and he refers to the blessed who see God in His essence. Therefore those who see God in His essence know all things.

Obj. 3. Further, it is stated in *De Anima,* iii., text. 7, that *when an intellect understands the greatest things, it is all the more able to understand the least things.* Now God is the greatest of intelligible things. Therefore the power of the intellect is greatly increased by understanding Him. Therefore the intellect seeing Him understands all things.

Obj. 4. Further, the intellect is not hindered from understanding a thing except by this surpassing it. Now no creature surpasses the intellect that understands God, since, as Gregory says *(Dial.* ii.), *to the soul which sees its Creator all creatures are small.* Therefore those who see God in His essence know all things.

Obj. 5. Further, every passive power that is not reduced to act is imperfect. Now the passive intellect of the human soul is a power that is passive as it were to the knowledge of all things, since *the passive intellect is in which all are in potentiality (De Anima,* iii., text. 18). If then in that beatitude it were not to understand all things, it would remain imperfect, which is absurd.

Obj. 6. Further, whoever sees a mirror sees the things reflected in the mirror. Now all things are reflected in the Word of God as in a mirror, because He is the type and image of all. Therefore the saints who see the Word in its essence see all created things.

Obj. 7. Further, according to Prov. x. 24, *to the just their desire shall be given.* Now the just desire to know all things, since *all men desire naturally to know,* and nature is not done away by glory. Therefore God will grant them to know all things.

Obj. 8. Further, ignorance is one of the penalties of the present life.* Now all penalty will be removed from the saints by glory. Therefore all ignorance will be removed: and consequently they will know all.

Obj. 9. Further, the beatitude of the saints is in their soul before being in their body. Now the bodies of the saints will be reformed in glory to the likeness of Christ's body (Philip. iii. 21). Therefore their souls will be perfected in likeness to the soul of Christ. Now Christ's soul sees all things in the Word.

* Cf. I-II, Q. 85, A. 3.

Therefore all the souls of the saints will also see all things in the Word.

Obj. 10. Further, the intellect, like the senses, knows all the things with the image of which it is informed. Now the Divine essence shows a thing forth more clearly than any other image thereof. Therefore since in that blessed vision the Divine essence becomes the form as it were of our intellect, it would seem that the saints seeing God see all.

Obj. 11. Further, the Commentator says *(De Anima,* iii.), that *if the active intellect were the form of the passive intellect, we should understand all things.* Now the Divine essence represents all things more clearly than the active intellect. Therefore the intellect that sees God in His essence knows all things.

Obj. 12. Further, the lower angels are enlightened by the higher about the things they are ignorant of, for the reason that they know not all things. Now after the day of judgment, one angel will not enlighten another; for then all superiority will cease, as a gloss observes on 1 Cor. xv. 24, *When He shall have brought to nought,* etc. Therefore the lower angels will then know all things, and for the same reason all the other saints who will see God in His essence.

On the contrary, Dionysius says *(Hier. Eccles.* vi.) : *The higher angels cleanse the lower angels from ignorance.* Now the lower angels see the Divine essence. Therefore an angel while seeing the Divine essence may be ignorant of certain things. But the soul will not see God more perfectly than an angel. Therefore the souls seeing God will not necessarily see all things.

Further, Christ alone has the spirit not *by measure* (Jo. iii. 34). Now it becomes Christ, as having the spirit without measure, to know all things in the Word: wherefore it is stated in the same place *(verse 35)* that *the Father ... hath given all things into His hand.* Therefore none but Christ is competent to know all things in the Word.

Further, the more perfectly a principle is known, the more of its effects are known thereby. Now some of those who see God in His essence will know God more perfectly than others. Therefore some will know more things than others, and consequently every one will not know all.

I answer that, God by seeing his essence knows all things whatsoever that are, shall be, or have been: and He is said to know these things by His *knowledge of vision,* because He knows them as though they were present in likeness to corporeal vision. Moreover by seeing this essence He knows all that He can do, although He never did them, nor ever will: else He would not know His power perfectly; since a power cannot be known unless its objects be known: and this is called His *science* or *knowledge of simple intelligence*. Now it is impossible for a created intellect, by seeing the Divine essence, to know all that God can do, because the more perfectly a principle is known, the more things are known in it; thus in one principle of demonstration one who is quick of intelligence sees more conclusions than one who is slow of intelligence. Since then the extent of the Divine power is measured according to what it can do, if an intellect were to see in the Divine essence all that God can do, its perfection in understanding would equal in extent the Divine power in producing its effects, and thus it would comprehend the Divine power, which is impossible for any created intellect to do. Yet there is a created intellect, namely the soul of Christ,* which knows in the Word all that God knows by the knowledge of vision. But regarding others who see the Divine essence there are two opinions. For some say that all who see God in His essence see all that God sees by His knowledge of vision. This, however, is contrary to the sayings of holy men, who hold that angels are ignorant of some things; and yet it is clear that according to faith all the angels see God in His essence. Wherefore others say that others than Christ, although they see God in His essence, do not see all that God sees because they do not comprehend the Divine essence. For it is not necessary that he who knows a cause should know all its effects, unless he comprehend the cause: and this is not in the competency of a created intellect. Consequently of those who see God in His essence, each one sees in His essence so much the more things according as he sees the Divine essence the more clearly: and hence it is that one is able to instruct another concerning these things. Thus the knowledge of the angels and of the souls of the saints can go on increasing until the day of judgment, even as other things pertaining to the accidental reward. But afterwards it will increase no more, because then will be the final state of things, and in that state it is possible that all will know everything that God knows by the knowledge of vision.

Reply Obj. 1. The saying of Isidore, that *the angels know in the Word all things before they happen*, cannot refer to those things which God knows only by the knowledge of simple intelligence, because those things will never happen; but it must refer to those things which God knows only by the knowledge of vision. Even of these he does not say that all the angels know them all, but that perhaps

* Cf. P. III, Q. 16, A. 2.

some do; and that even those who know do not know all perfectly. For in one and the same thing there are many intelligible aspects to be considered, such as its various properties and relations to other things: and it is possible that while one thing is known in common by two persons, one of them perceives more aspects, and that the one learns these aspects from the other. Hence Dionysius says (*Div. Nom.* iv) that *the lower angels learn from the higher angels the intelligible aspects of things.* Wherefore it does not follow that even the angels who know all creatures are able to see all that can be understood in them.

Reply Obj. 2. It follows from this saying of Gregory that this blessed vision suffices for the seeing of all things on the part of the Divine essence, which is the medium by which one sees, and whereby God sees all things. That all things, however, are not seen is owing to the deficiency of the created intellect which does not comprehend the Divine essence.

Reply Obj. 3. The created intellect sees the Divine essence not according to the mode of that same essence, but according to its own mode which is finite. Hence its efficacy in knowing would need to be infinitely increased by reason of that vision in order for it to know all things.

Reply Obj. 4. Defective knowledge results not only from excess and deficiency of the knowable object in relation to the intellect, but also from the fact that the aspect of knowableness is not united to the intellect: thus sometimes the sight sees not a stone, through the image of the stone not being united to it. And although the Divine essence which is the type of all things is united to the intellect of one who sees God, it is united thereto not as the type of all things, but as the type of some and of so much the more according as one sees the Divine essence more fully.

Reply Obj. 5. When a passive power is perceptible by several perfections in order, if it be perfected with its ultimate perfection, it is not said to be imperfect, even though it lack some of the preceding dispositions. Now all knowledge by which the created intellect is perfected is directed to the knowledge of God as its end. Wherefore he who sees God in His essence, even though he know nothing else, would have a perfect intellect: nor is his intellect more perfect through knowing something else besides Him, except in so far as it sees Him more fully. Hence Augustine says (*Conf.* v.): *Unhappy is he who knoweth all these* (namely, creatures), *and knoweth not Thee: but happy whoso knoweth Thee, though he know not these. And whoso knoweth both Thee and them is not the happier for them, but for Thee only.*

Reply Obj. 6. This mirror has a will: and even as He will show Himself to whom He will, so will He show in Himself whatsoever He will. Nor does the comparison with a material mirror hold, for it is not in its power to be seen or not to be seen.

We may also reply that in a material mirror both object and mirror are seen under their proper image; although the mirror be seen through an image received from the thing itself, whereas the stone is seen through its proper image reflected in some other thing, where the reason for seeing the one is the reason for seeing the other. But in the uncreated mirror a thing is seen through the form of the mirror, just as an effect is seen through the image of its cause and conversely. Consequently it does not follow that whoever sees the eternal mirror sees all that is reflected in that mirror: since he who sees the cause does not of necessity see all its effects, unless he comprehend the cause.

Reply Obj. 7. The desire of the saints to know all things will be fulfilled by the mere fact of their seeing God: just as their desire to possess all good things will be fulfilled by their possessing God. For as God suffices the affections in that He has perfect goodness, and by possessing Him we possess all goods as it were, so does the vision of Him suffice the intellect: *Lord, show us the Father and it is enough for us* (Jo. xiv. 8).

Reply Obj. 8. Ignorance properly so called denotes a privation and thus it is a punishment: for in this way ignorance is nescience of things, the knowledge of which is a duty or a necessity. Now the saints in heaven will not be ignorant of any of these things. Sometimes, however, ignorance is taken in a broad sense of any kind of nescience: and thus the angels and saints in heaven will be ignorant of certain things. Hence Dionysius says *(loc. cit.)* that *the angels will be cleansed from their ignorance.* In this sense ignorance is not a penalty but a defect. Nor is it necessary for all such defects to be done away by glory: for thus we might say that it was a defect in Pope Linus that he did not attain to the glory of Peter.

Reply Obj. 9. Our body will be conformed to the body of Christ in glory, in likeness but not in equality, for it will be endowed with clarity even as Christ's body, but not equally.

* Vulg.,—*hath enlightened it.*

In like manner our soul will have glory in likeness to the soul of Christ, but not in equality thereto: thus it will have knowledge even as Christ's soul, but not so great, so as to know all as Christ's soul does.

Reply Obj. 10. Although the Divine essence is the type of all things knowable, it will not be united to each created intellect according as it is the type of all. Hence the objection proves nothing.

Reply Obj. 11. The active intellect is a form proprotionate to the passive intellect; even as the passive power of matter is proportionate to the power of the natural agent, so that whatsoever is in the passive power of matter or the passive intellect is in the active power of the active intellect or of the natural agent. Consequently if the active intellect become the form of the passive intellect, the latter must of necessity know all those things to which the power of the active intellect extends. But the Divine essence is not a form proportionate to our intellect in this sense. Hence the comparison fails.

Reply Obj. 12. Nothing hinders us from saying that after the judgment day, when the glory of men and angels will be consummated once for all, all the blessed will know all that God knows by the knowledge of vision, yet so that not all will see all in the Divine essence. Christ's soul, however, will see clearly all things therein, even as it sees them now; while others will see therein a greater or lesser number of things according to the degree of clearness wherewith they will know God: and thus Christ's soul will enlighten all other souls concerning those things which it sees in the Word better than others. Hence it is written (Apoc. xxi. 23): *The glory of God shall enlighten the city of Jerusalem,* and the Lamb is the lamp thereof.* In like manner the higher souls will enlighten the lower (not indeed with a new enlightening, so as to increase the knowledge of the lower), but with a kind of continued enlightenment; thus we might understand the sun to enlighten the atmosphere while at a standstill. Wherefore it is written (Dan. xii. 3): *They that instruct many to justice* shall shine *as stars for all eternity.* The statement that the superiority of the orders will cease refers to their present ordinate ministry in our regard, as is clear from the same gloss.

QUESTION 93

Of the Happiness of the Saints and of Their Mansions

(In Three Articles)

WE must next consider the happiness of the saints and their mansions. Under this head there are three points of inquiry: (1) Whether the happiness of the saints will increase after the judgment? (2) Whether the degrees of happiness should be called mansions? (3) Whether the various mansions differ according to various degrees of charity?

FIRST ARTICLE

Whether the Happiness of the Saints Will Be Greater after the Judgment Than Before?

We proceed thus to the First Article:—

Objection 1. It would seem that the happiness of the saints will not be greater after the judgment than before. For the nearer a thing approaches to the Divine likeness, the more perfectly does it participate happiness. Now the soul is more like God when separated from the body than when united to it. Therefore its happiness is greater before being reunited to the body than after.

Obj. 2. Further, power is more effective when it is united than when divided. Now the soul is more united when separated from the body than when it is joined to the body. Therefore it has then greater power for operation, and consequently has a more perfect share of happiness, since this consists in action.*

Obj. 3. Further, beatitude consists in an act of the speculative intellect. Now the intellect, in its act, makes no use of a bodily organ; and consequently by being reunited to the body the soul does not become capable of more perfect understanding. Therefore the soul's happiness is not greater after than before the judgment.

Obj. 4. Further, nothing can be greater than the infinite, and so the addition of the finite to the infinite does not result in something greater than the infinite by itself. Now the beatified soul before its reunion with the body is rendered happy by rejoicing in the infinite good, namely God; and after the resurrection of the body it will rejoice in nothing else except perhaps the glory of the body, and this is a finite good. Therefore their joy after the resumption of the body will not be greater than before.

On the contrary, A gloss on Apoc. vi. 9, *I saw under the altar the souls of them that were slain,* says: *At present the souls of the saints are under the altar, i.e. less exalted than they will be.* Therefore their happiness will be greater after the resurrection than after their death.

Further, just as happiness is bestowed on the good as a reward, so is unhappiness awarded to the wicked. But the unhappiness of the wicked after reunion with their bodies will be greater than before, since they will be punished not only in the soul but also in the body. Therefore the happiness of the saints will be greater after the resurrection of the body than before.

I answer that, It is manifest that the happiness of the saints will increase in extent after the resurrection, because their happiness will then be not only in the soul but also in the body. Moreover, the soul's happiness also will increase in extent, seeing that the soul will rejoice not only in its own good, but also in that of the body. We may also say that the soul's happiness will increase in intensity.† For man's body may be considered in two ways: first, as being dependent on the soul for its completion; secondly, as containing something that hampers the soul in its operations, through the soul not perfectly completing the body. As regards the first way of considering the body, its union with the soul adds a certain perfection to the soul, since every part is imperfect, and is completed in its whole; wherefore the whole is to the part as form to matter. Consequently the soul is more perfect in its natural being, when it is in the whole—namely, man who results from the union of soul and body—than when it is a separate part. But as regards the second consideration the union of the body hampers the perfection of the soul, wherefore it is written (Wis. ix. 15) that *the corruptible body is a load upon the soul.* If, then, there be removed from the body all those things wherein it hampers the soul's action, the soul will be simply more perfect while existing in such a body than when separated therefrom. Now the more perfect a thing is in being, the more perfectly is it able to operate: wherefore the operation of the soul united to such a body will be more perfect than the operation of the separated soul. But the glorified body will be a body of this description, being altogether subject to the spirit. Therefore, since beatitude consists in an operation,‡ the soul's

*Cf. I-II, Q. 3, A. 2.   † Cf. I-II, Q. 4, A. 5, *ad* 5, where S. Thomas retracts this statement.

‡ Cf. I-II, Q. 3, A. 2 *seqq.*

happiness after its reunion with the body will be more perfect than before. For just as the soul separated from a corruptible body is able to operate more perfectly than when united thereto, so after it has been united to a glorified body, its operation will be more perfect than while it was separated. Now every imperfect thing desires its perfection. Hence the separated soul naturally desires reunion with the body, and on account of this desire which proceeds from the soul's imperfection, its operation whereby it is borne towards God is less intense. This agrees with the saying of Augustine (*Gen. ad Lit.* xii. 35) that *on account of the body's desire it is held back from tending with all its might to that sovereign good.*

Reply Obj. 1. The soul united to a glorified body is more like to God than when separated therefrom, in so far as when united it has more perfect being. For the more perfect a thing is the more it is like to God: even so the heart, the perfection of whose life consists in movement, is more like to God while in movement than while at rest, although God is never moved.

Reply Obj. 2. A power which by its own nature is capable of being in matter is more effective when subjected in matter than when separated from matter, although absolutely speaking a power separate from matter is more effective.

Reply Obj. 3. Although in the act of understanding the soul does not make use of the body, the perfection of the body will somewhat conduce to the perfection of the intellectual operation in so far as through being united to a glorified body, the soul will be more perfect in its nature, and consequently more effective in its operation, and accordingly the good itself of the body will conduce instrumentally, as it were, to the operation wherein happiness consists: thus the Philosopher asserts (*Ethic.* i. 8, 10) that external goods conduce instrumentally to the happiness of life.

Reply Obj. 4. Although finite added to infinite does not make a greater thing, it makes more things, since finite and infinite are two things, while infinite taken by itself is one. Now the greater extent of joy regards not a greater thing but more things. Wherefore joy is increased in extent, through referring to God and to the body's glory, in comparison with the joy which referred to God. Moreover, the body's glory will conduce to the intensity of the joy that refers to God, in so far as it will conduce to the more perfect operation whereby the soul tends to God: since the more perfect is a becoming operation, the greater the delight,* as stated in *Ethic.* x. 8.

* Cf. I-II, Q. 32, A. 1.

SECOND ARTICLE

Whether the Degrees of Beatitude Should Be Called Mansions?

We proceed thus to the Second Article:—

Objection 1. It would seem that the degrees of beatitude should not be called mansions. For beatitude implies the notion of a reward: whereas mansion denotes nothing pertaining to a reward. Therefore the various degrees of beatitude should not be called mansions.

Obj. 2. Further, mansion seemingly denotes a place. Now the place where the saints will be beatified is not corporeal but spiritual namely God Who is one. Therefore there is but one mansion: and consequently the various degrees of beatitude should not be called mansions.

Obj. 3. Further, as in heaven there will be men of various merits, so are there now in purgatory, and were in the limbo of the fathers. But various mansions are not distinguished in purgatory and limbo. Therefore in like manner neither should they be distinguished in heaven.

On the contrary, It is written (Jo. xiv. 2): *In My Father's house there are many mansions:* and Augustine expounds this in reference to the different degrees of rewards (*Tract.* lxvii. *in Joan.*).

Further, in every well-ordered city there is a distinction of mansions. Now the heavenly kingdom is compared to a city (Apoc. xxi. 2). Therefore we should distinguish various mansions there according to the various degrees of beatitude.

I answer that, Since local movement precedes all other movements, terms of movement, distance and the like are derived from local movement to all other movements according to the Philosopher (*Phys., liber* viii, 7). Now the end of local movement is a place, and when a thing has arrived at that place it remains there at rest and is maintained therein. Hence in every movement this very rest at the end of the movement is called an establishment (*collocatio*) or mansion. Wherefore since the term movement is transferred to the actions of the appetite and will, the attainment of the end of an appetitive movement is called a mansion or establishment: so that the unity of a house corresponds to the unity of beatitude, which unity is on the part of the object, and the plurality of mansions corresponds to the differences of beatitude on the part of the blessed: even so we observe in natural things that there is one same place above to which all light objects tend, whereas each one reaches it more closely, according as it is lighter, so that they have various mansions corresponding to their various lightness.

Reply Obj. 1. Mansion implies the notion of end and consequently of reward which is the end of merit.

Reply Obj. 2. Though there is one spiritual place, there are different degrees of approaching thereto: and the various mansions correspond to these.

Reply Obj. 3. Those who were in limbo or are now in purgatory have not yet attained to their end. Wherefore various mansions are not distinguished in purgatory or limbo, but only in heaven and hell, wherein is the end of the good and of the wicked.

THIRD ARTICLE

Whether the Various Mansions Are Distinguished According to the Various Degrees of Charity?

We proceed thus to the Third Article:—

Objection 1. It would seem that the various mansions are not distinguished according to the various degrees of charity. For it is written (Matth. xxv. 15): *He gave to every one according to his proper virtue* (Douay,—*ability*). Now the proper ability of a thing is its natural power. Therefore the gifts also of grace and glory are distributed according to the different degrees of natural power.

Obj. 2. Further, it is written (Ps. lxi. 12): *Thou wilt render to every man according to his works.* Now that which is rendered is the measure of beatitude. Therefore the degrees of beatitude are distinguished according to the diversity of works and not according to the diversity of charity.

Obj. 3. Further, reward is due to act and not to habit: hence *it is not the strongest who are crowned but those who engage in the conflict (Ethic.* i. 8) and *he . . . shall not be* (Vulg.,—*is not) crowned except he strive lawfully.* Now beatitude is a reward. Therefore the various degrees of beatitude will be according to the various degrees of works and not according to the various degrees of charity.

On the contrary, The more one will be united to God the happier will one be. Now the measure of charity is the measure of one's union with God. Therefore the diversity of beatitude will be according to the difference of charity.

Further, *if one thing simply follows from another thing simply, the increase of the former follows from the increase of the latter.*

Now to have beatitude follows from having charity. Therefore to have greater beatitude follows from having greater charity.

I answer that, The distinctive principle of the mansions or degrees of beatitude is twofold, namely proximate and remote. The proximate principle is the difference of disposition which will be in the blessed, whence will result the difference of perfection in them in respect to the beatific operation: while the remote principle is the merit by which they have obtained that beatitude. In the first way the mansions are distinguished according to the charity of heaven, which the more perfect it will be in any one, the more will it render him capable of the Divine clarity, on the increase of which will depend the increase in perfection of the Divine vision. In the second way the mansions are distinguished according to the charity of the way. For our actions are meritorious, not by the very substance of the action, but only by the habit of virtue with which they are informed. Now every virtue obtains its meritorious efficacy from charity,* which has the end itself for its object.† Hence the diversity of merit is all traced to the diversity of charity, and thus the charity of the way will distinguish the mansions by way of merit.

Reply Obj. 1. In this passage *virtue* denotes not the natural ability alone, but the natural ability together with the endeavour to obtain grace.‡ Consequently virtue in this sense will be a kind of material disposition to the measure of grace and glory that one will receive. But charity is the formal complement of merit in relation to glory, and therefore the distinction of degrees in glory depends on the degrees of charity rather than on the degrees of the aforesaid virtue.

Reply Obj. 2. Works in themselves do not demand the payment of a reward, except as informed by charity: and therefore the various degrees of glory will be according to the various degrees of charity.

Reply Obj. 3. Although the habit of charity or of any virtue whatever is not a merit to which a reward is due, it is none the less the principle and reason of merit in the act: and consequently according to its diversity is the diversity of rewards. This does not prevent our observing a certain degree of merit in the act considered generically, not indeed in relation to the essential reward which is joy in God, but in relation to some accidental reward, which is joy in some created good.

* Cf. I-II, Q. 114, A. 4.   † Cf. II-II, Q. 24, A. 3, *ad* **1.**   ‡ Cf. II-II, Q. 23, A. 8.

QUESTION 94

Of the Relations of the Saints Towards the Damned

(In Three Articles)

WE must next consider the relations of the saints towards the damned. Under this head there are three points of inquiry: (1) Whether the saints see the sufferings of the damned? (2) Whether they pity them? (3) Whether they rejoice in their sufferings?

FIRST ARTICLE

Whether the Blessed in Heaven Will See the Sufferings of the Damned?

We proceed thus to the First Article:—

Objection 1. It would seem that the blessed in heaven will not see the sufferings of the damned. For the damned are more cut off from the blessed than wayfarers. But the blessed do not see the deeds of wayfarers: wherefore a gloss on Isa. lxiii. 16, *Abraham hath not known us,* says: *The dead, even the saints, know not what the living, even their own children, are doing.** Much less therefore do they see the sufferings of the damned.

Obj. 2. Further, perfection of vision depends on the perfection of the visible object: wherefore the Philosopher says (*Ethic.* x. 4) that *the most perfect operation of the sense of sight is when the sense is most disposed with reference to the most beautiful of the objects which fall under the sight.* Therefore, on the other hand, any deformity in the visible object redounds to the imperfection of the sight. But there will be no imprefection in the blessed. Therefore they will not see the sufferings of the damned wherein there is extreme deformity.

On the contrary, It is written (Isa. lxvi. 24): *They shall go out and see the carcasses of the men that have transgressed against Me;* and a gloss says: *The elect will go out by understanding or seeing manifestly, so that they may be urged the more to praise God.*

I answer that, Nothing should be denied the blessed that belongs to the perfection of their beatitude. Now everything is known the more for being compared with its contrary, because when contraries are placed beside one another they become more conspicuous. Wherefore in order that the happiness of the saints may be more delightful to them and that they may render more copious thanks to God for it, they are allowed to see perfectly the sufferings of the damned.

Reply Obj. 1. This gloss speaks of what

* S. Augustine, *De cura pro mortuis* xiii, xv.
‡ Cf. II-II, Q. 30.

the departed saints are able to do by nature: for it is not necessary that they should know by natural knowledge all that happens to the living. But the saints in heaven know distinctly all that happens both to wayfarers and to the damned. Hence Gregory says (*Moral.* xii) that Job's words (xiv. 21), '*Whether his children come to honour or dishonour, he shall not understand,*' do not apply to the souls of the saints, because since they possess the glory of God within them, we cannot believe that external things are unknown to them.†

Reply Obj. 2. Although the beauty of the thing seen conduces to the perfection of vision, there may be deformity of the thing seen without imperfection of vision: because images of things whereby the soul knows contraries are not themselves contrary. Wherefore also God Who has most perfect knowledge sees all things, beautiful and deformed.

SECOND ARTICLE

Whether the Blessed Pity the Unhappiness of the Damned?

We proceed thus to the Second Article:—

Objection 1. It would seem that the blessed pity the unhappiness of the damned. For pity proceeds from charity; ‡ and charity will be most perfect in the blessed. Therefore they will most especially pity the sufferings of the damned.

Obj. 2. Further, the blessed will never be so far from taking pity as God is. Yet in a sense God compassionates our afflictions, wherefore He is said to be merciful.

On the contrary, Whoever pities another shares somewhat in his unhappiness. But the blessed cannot share in any unhappiness. Therefore they do not pity the afflictions of the damned.

I answer that, Mercy or compassion may be in a person in two ways: first by way of passion, secondly by way of choice. In the blessed there will be no passion in the lower powers except as a result of the reason's choice. Hence compassion or mercy will not be in them, except by the choice of reason. Now mercy or compassion comes of the reason's choice when a person wishes another's evil to be dispelled: wherefore in those things which, in accordance with reason, we do not wish to be dispelled, we have no such com-

† Concerning this *Reply* cf. P. I, Q. 89, A. 8.

passion. But so long as sinners are in this world they are in such a state that without prejudice to the Divine justice they can be taken away from a state of unhappiness and sin to a state of happiness. Consequently it is possible to have compassion on them both by the choice of the will,—in which sense God, the angels and the blessed are said to pity them by desiring their salvation,—and by passion, in which way they are pitied by the good men who are in the state of wayfarers. But in the future state it will be impossible for them to be taken away from their unhappiness: and consequently it will not be possible to pity their sufferings according to right reason. Therefore the blessed in glory will have no pity on the damned.

Reply Obj. 1. Charity is the principle of pity when it is possible for us out of charity to wish the cessation of a person's unhappiness. But the saints cannot desire this for the damned, since it would be contrary to Divine justice. Consequently the argument does not prove.

Reply Obj. 2. God is said to be merciful, in so far as He succors those whom it is befitting to be released from their afflictions in accordance with the order of wisdom and justice: not as though He pitied the damned, except perhaps in punishing them less than they deserve.

THIRD ARTICLE

Whether the Blessed Rejoice in the Punishment of the Wicked?

We proceed thus to the Third Article:—

Objection 1. It would seem that the blessed do not rejoice in the punishment of the wicked. For rejoicing in another's evil pertains to hatred. But there will be no hatred in the blessed. Therefore they will not rejoice in the unhappiness of the damned.

Obj. 2. Further, the blessed in heaven will be in the highest degree conformed to God. Now God does not rejoice in our afflictions. Therefore neither will the blessed rejoice in the afflictions of the damned.

Obj. 3. Further, that which is blameworthy in a wayfarer has no place whatever in a comprehensor. Now it is most repre-

* Douay,—*They shall be a loathsome sight to all flesh.*

hensible in a wayfarer to take pleasure in the pains of others, and most praiseworthy to grieve for them. Therefore the blessed nowise rejoice in the punishment of the damned.

On the contrary, It is written (Ps. lvii. 11): *The just shall rejoice when he shall see the revenge.*

Further, it is written (Isa. lvi. 24): *They shall satiate* the sight of all flesh.* Now satiety denotes refreshment of the mind. Therefore the blessed will rejoice in the punishment of the wicked.

I answer that, A thing may be a matter of rejoicing in two ways. First directly, when one rejoices in a thing as such: and thus the saints will not rejoice in the punishment of the wicked. Secondly, indirectly, by reason namely of something annexed to it: and in this way the saints will rejoice in the punishment of the wicked, by considering therein the order of Divine justice and their own deliverance, which will fill them with joy. And thus the Divine justice and their own deliverance will be the direct cause of the joy of the blessed: while the punishment of the damned will cause it indirectly.

Reply Obj. 1. To rejoice in another's evil as such belongs to hatred, but not to rejoice in another's evil by reason of something annexed to it. Thus a person sometimes rejoices in his own evil as when we rejoice in our own afflictions, as helping us to merit life: *My brethren, count it all joy when you shall fall into divers temptations* (Jas. i. 2).

Reply Obj. 2. Although God rejoices not in punishments as such, He rejoices in them as being ordered by His justice.

Reply Obj. 3. It is not praiseworthy in a wayfarer to rejoice in another's afflictions as such: yet it is praiseworthy if he rejoice in them as having something annexed. However it is not the same with a wayfarer as with a comprehensor, because in a wayfarer the passions often forestall the judgment of reason, and yet sometimes such passions are praiseworthy, as indicating the good disposition of the mind, as in the case of shame, pity and repentance for evil: whereas in a comprehensor there can be no passion but such as follows the judgment of reason.

QUESTION 95

Of the Gifts* of the Blessed

(In Five Articles)

WE must now consider the gifts of the blessed; under which head there are five points of inquiry: (1) Whether any gifts should be assigned to the blessed? (2) Whether a gift differs from beatitude? (3) Whether it is fitting for Christ to have gifts? (4) Whether this is competent to the angels? (5) Whether three gifts of the soul are rightly assigned?

FIRST ARTICLE

Whether Any Gifts Should Be Assigned As Dowry to the Blessed?

We proceed thus to the First Article:—

Objection 1. It would seem that no gifts should be assigned as dowry to the blessed. For a dowry (Cod. v. 12, *De jure dot.,* 20: Dig. xxiii. 3, *De jure dot.)* is given to the bridegroom for the upkeep of the burdens of marriage. But the saints resemble not the bridegroom but the bride, as being members of the Church. Therefore they receive no dowry.

Obj. 2. Further, the dowry is given not by the bridegroom's father, but by the father of the bride (Cod. v. 11, *De dot. promiss.,* 7: Dig. xxiii. 2, *De rit. nup.).* Now all the beatific gifts are bestowed on the blessed by the father of the bridegroom, *i.e.* Christ: *Every best gift and every perfect gift is from above coming down from the Father of lights.* Therefore these gifts which are bestowed on the blessed should not be called a dowry.

Obj. 3. Further, in carnal marriage a dowry is given that the burdens of marriage may be the more easily borne. But in spiritual marriage there are no burdens, especially in the state of the Church triumphant. Therefore no dowry should be assigned to that state.

Obj. 4. Further, a dowry is not given save on the occasion of marriage. But a spiritual marriage is contracted with Christ by faith in the state of the Church militant. Therefore if a dowry is befitting the blessed, for the same reason it will be befitting the saints who are wayfarers. But it is not befitting the latter: and therefore neither is it befitting the blessed.

Obj. 5. Further, a dowry pertains to external goods, which are styled goods of fortune: whereas the reward of the blessed will consist of internal goods. Therefore they should not be called a dowry.

* The Latin *dos* signifies a dowry.

On the contrary, It is written (Eph. v. 32): *This is a great sacrament: but I speak in Christ and in the Church.* Hence it follows that the spiritual marriage is signified by the carnal marriage. But in a carnal marriage the dowered bride is brought to the dwelling of the bridegroom. Therefore since the saints are brought to Christ's dwelling when they are beatified, it would seem that they are dowered with certain gifts.

Further, a dowry is appointed to carnal marriage for the ease of marriage. But the spiritual marriage is more blissful than the carnal marriage. Therefore a dowry should be especially assigned thereto.

Further, the adornment of the bride is part of the dowry. Now the saints are adorned when they are taken into glory, according to Isa. lxi. 10, *He hath clothed me with the garments of salvation . . . as a bride adorned with her jewels.* Therefore the saints in heaven have a dowry.

I answer that, Without doubt the blessed when they are brought into glory are dowered by God with certain gifts for their adornment, and this adornment is called their dowry by the masters. Hence the dower of which we speak now is defined thus: *The dowry is the everlasting adornment of soul and body, adequate to life, lasting for ever in eternal bliss.* This description is taken from a likeness to the material dowry whereby the bride is adorned and the husband provided with an adequate support for his wife and children, and yet the dowry remains inalienable from the bride, so that if the marriage union be severed it reverts to her. As to the reason of the name there are various opinions. For some say that the name *dowry* is taken not from a likeness to the corporeal marriage, but according to the manner of speaking whereby any perfection or adornment of any person whatever is called an endowment; thus a man who is proficient in knowledge is said to be endowed with knowledge, and in this sense Ovid employed the word *endowment (De Arte Amandi,* i. 538): *By whatever endowment thou canst please, strive to please.* But this does not seem quite fitting, for whenever a term is employed to signify a certain thing principally, it is not usually transferred to another save by reason of some likeness. Wherefore since by its primary signification a dowry refers to carnal marriage, it follows that in every other application of the term we must observe some kind of likeness to its principal signification. Consequently others say that the likeness consists in the fact that in carnal marriage a dowry is properly a gift bestowed by the bridegroom on the bride for her adornment when she is taken to the bridegroom's dwelling: and that this is shown by the words of Sichem to Jacob and his sons (Gen. xxxiv. 12): *Raise the dowry, and ask gifts*, and from Exod. xxii. 16: *If a man seduce a virgin . . . and lie with her, he shall endow her, and have her to wife*. Hence the adornment bestowed by Christ on the saints, when they are brought into the abode of glory, is called a dowry. But this is clearly contrary to what jurists say, to whom it belongs to treat of these matters. For they say that a dowry, properly speaking, is a donation on the part of the wife made to those who are on the part of the husband, in view of the marriage burden which the husband has to bear; while that which the bridegroom gives the bride is called *a donation in view of marriage*. In this sense dowry is taken (3 Kings ix. 16) where it is stated that *Pharoa, the king of Egypt, took Gezer . . . and gave it for a dowry to his daughter, Solomon's wife*. Nor do the authorities quoted prove anything to the contrary. For although it is customary for a dowry to be given by the maiden's parents, it happens sometimes that the bridegroom or his father gives the dowry instead of the bride's father; and this happens in two ways: either by reason of his very great love for the bride as in the case of Sichem's father Hemor, who on account of his son's great love for the maiden, wished to give the dowry which he had a right to receive; or as a punishment on the bridegroom, that he should out of his own possessions give a dowry to the virgin seduced by him, whereas he should have received it from the girl's father. In this sense Moses speaks in the passage quoted above. Wherefore in the opinion of others we should hold that in carnal marriage a dowry, properly speaking, is that which is given by those on the wife's side to those on the husband's side, for the bearing of the marriage burden, as stated above. Yet the difficulty remains how this signification can be adapted to the case in point, since the heavenly adornments are given to the spiritual spouse by the Father of the Bridegroom. This shall be made clear by replying to the objections.

Reply Obj. 1. Although in carnal marriage the dowry is given to the bridegroom for his use, yet the ownership and control belong to the bride: which is evident by the fact that if the marriage be dissolved, the dowry reverts to the bride according to law (Cap. 1, 2,

* Cf. P. I, Q. 38, A. 2.

3, *De donat. inter virum et uxorem*). Thus also in spiritual marriage, the very adornments bestowed on the spiritual bride, namely the Church in her members, belong indeed to the Bridegroom, in so far as they conduce to His glory and honor, yet to the bride as adorned thereby.

Reply Obj. 2. The Father of the Bridegroom, that is of Christ, is the Person of the Father alone: while the Father of the bride is the whole Trinity, since that which is effected in creatures belongs to the whole Trinity. Hence in spiritual marriage these endowments, properly speaking, are given by the Father of the bride rather than by the Father of the Bridegroom. Nevertheless, although this endowment is made by all the Persons, it may be in a manner appropriated to each Person. To the Person of the Father, as endowing, since He possesses authority; and fatherhood in relation to creatures is also appropriated to Him, so that He is Father of both Bridegroom and bride. To the Son it is appropriated, inasmuch as it is made for His sake and through Him: and to the Holy Ghost, inasmuch as it is made in Him and according to Him, since love is the reason of all giving.*

Reply Obj. 3. That which is effected by the dowry belongs to the dowry by its nature, and that is the ease of marriage: while that which the dowry removes, namely the marriage burden which is lightened thereby, belongs to it accidentally: thus it belongs to grace by its nature to make a man righteous, but accidentally to make an ungodly man righteous. Accordingly, though there are no burdens in the spiritual marriage, there is the greatest gladness; and that this gladness may be perfected the bride is dowered with gifts, so that by their means she may be happily united with the bridegroom.

Reply Obj. 4. The dowry is usually settled on the bride not when she is espoused, but when she is taken to the bridegroom's dwelling, so as to be in the presence of the bridegroom, since *while we are in the body we are absent from the Lord* (2 Cor. v. 6). Hence the gifts bestowed on the saints in this life are not called a dowry, but those which are bestowed on them when they are received into glory, where the Bridegroom delights them with His presence.

Reply Obj. 5. In spiritual marriage inward comeliness is required, wherefore it is written (Ps. xliv. 14): *All the glory of the king's daughter is within*, etc. But in carnal marriage outward comeliness is necessary. Hence there is no need for a dowry of this kind to be appointed in spiritual marriage as in carnal marriage.

SECOND ARTICLE

Whether the Dowry Is the Same As Beatitude? *

We proceed thus to the Second Article:—

Objection 1. It would seem that the dowry is the same as beatitude. For as appears from the definition of dowry (A. 1), the dowry is *the everlasting adornment of body and soul in eternal happiness.* Now the happiness of the soul is an adornment thereof. Therefore beatitude is a dowry.

Obj. 2. Further, a dowry signifies something whereby the union of bride and bridegroom is rendered delightful. Now such is beatitude in the spiritual marriage. Therefore beatitude is a dowry.

Obj. 3. Further, according to Augustine *(In Ps.* xcii) vision is *the whole essence of beatitude.* Now vision is accounted one of the dowries. Therefore beatitude is a dowry.

Obj. 4. Further, fruition gives happiness. Now fruition is a dowry. Therefore a dowry gives happiness and thus beatitude is a dowry.

Obj. 5. Further, according to Boëthius *(De Consol.* iii), *beatitude is a state made perfect by the aggregate of all good things.* Now the state of the blessed is perfected by the dowries. Therefore the dowries are part of beatitude.

On the contrary, The dowries are given without merits: whereas beatitude is not given, but is awarded in return for merits. Therefore beatitude is not a dowry.

Further, beatitude is one only, whereas the dowries are several. Therefore beatitude is not a dowry.

Further, beatitude is in man according to that which is principal in him *(Ethic.* x. 7): whereas a dowry is also appointed to the body. Therefore dowry and beatitude are not the same.

I answer that, There are two opinions on this question. For some say that beatitude and dowry are the same in reality but differ in aspect: because dowry regards the spiritual marriage between Christ and the soul, whereas beatitude does not. But seemingly this will not stand, since beatitude consists in an operation, whereas a dowry is not an operation, but a quality or disposition. Wherefore according to others it must be stated that beatitude and dowry differ even in reality, beatitude being the perfect operation itself by which the soul is united to God, while the dowries are habits or dispositions or any other qualities directed to this same perfect operation, so that they are directed to beatitude instead of being in it as parts thereof.

Reply Obj. 1. Beatitude, properly speaking, is not an adornment of the soul, but something resulting from the soul's adornment, since it is an operation, while its adornment is a certain comeliness of the blessed themselves.

Reply Obj. 2. Beatitude is not directed to the union but is the union itself of the soul with Christ. This union is by an operation, whereas the dowries are gifts disposing to this same union.

Reply Obj. 3. Vision may be taken in two ways. First, actually, *i.e.* for the act itself of vision; and thus vision is not a dowry, but beatitude itself. Secondly, it may be taken habitually, *i.e.* for the habit whereby this act is elicited, namely the clarity of glory, by which the soul is enlightened from above to see God: and thus it is a dowry and the principle of beatitude, but not beatitude itself. The same answer applies to *Obj.* 4.

Reply Obj. 5. Beatitude is the sum of all goods not as though they were essential parts of beatitude, but as being in a way directed to beatitude, as stated above.

THIRD ARTICLE

Whether It Is Fitting That Christ Should Receive a Dowry?

We proceed thus to the Third Article:—

Objection 1. It would seem fitting that Christ should receive a dowry. For the saints will be conformed to Christ through glory, according to Philip. iii. 21, *Who will reform the body of our lowness made like to the body of His glory.* Therefore Christ also will have a dowry.

Obj. 2. Further, in the spiritual marriage a dowry is given in likeness to a carnal marriage. Now there is a spiritual marriage in Christ, which is peculiar to Him, namely of the two natures in one Person, in regard to which the human nature in Him is said to have been espoused by the Word, as a gloss† has it on Ps. xviii. 6, *He hath set His tabernacle in the sun,* etc., and Apoc. xxi. 3, *Behold the tabernacle of God with men.* Therefore it is fitting that Christ should have a dowry.

Obj. 3. Further, Augustine says *(De Doctr. Christ.* iii) that Christ, according to the *Rule‡* of Tyconius, on account of the unity of the mystic body that exists between the head and its members, calls Himself also the Bride and not only the Bridegroom, as may be gathered from Isa. lxi. 10, *As a bridegroom decked with a crown, and as a bride adorned with her jewels.* Since then a dowry is due to the bride, it would seem that Christ ought to receive a dowry.

Obj. 4. Further, a dowry is due to all the

---

* Cf. P. I, Q. 12, A. 7, *ad* 1; I-II, Q. 4, A. 3.   † S. Augustine, *De Consensu Evang.* i. 40.   ‡ *Liber regularum.*

members of the Church, since the Church is the spouse. But Christ is a member of the Church according to 1 Cor. xii. 27, *You are the body of Christ, and members of member,* i.e. *of Christ,* according to a gloss. Therefore the dowry is due to Christ.

Obj. 5. Further, Christ has perfect vision, fruition, and joy. Now these are the dowries. Therefore, etc.

On the contrary, A distinction of persons is requisite between the bridegroom and the bride. But in Christ there is nothing personally distinct from the Son of God Who is the Bridegroom, as stated in John iii. 29, *He that hath the bride is the bridegroom.* Therefore since the dowry is allotted to the bride or for the bride, it would seem unfitting for Christ to have a dowry.

Further, the same person does not both give and receive a dowry. But it is Christ Who gives spiritual dowries. Therefore it is not fitting that Christ should have a dowry.

I answer that, There are two opinions on this point. For some say that there is a threefold union in Christ. One is the union of concord, whereby He is united to God in the bond of love; another is the union of condescension, whereby the human nature is united to the Divine; the third is the union whereby Christ is united to the Church. They say, then, that as regards the first two unions it is fitting for Christ to have the dowries as such, but as regards the third, it is fitting for Him to have the dowries in the most excellent degree, considered as to that in which they consist, but not considered as dowries; because in this union Christ is the bridegroom and the Church the bride, and a dowry is given to the bride as regards property and control, although it is given to the bridegroom as to use. But this does not seem congruous. For in the union of Christ with the Father by the concord of love, even if we consider Him as God, there is not said to be a marriage, since it implies no subjection such as is required in the bride towards the bridegroom. Nor again in the union of the human nature with the Divine, whether we consider the Personal union or that which regards the conformity of will, can there be a dowry, properly speaking, for three reasons. First, because in a marriage where a dowry is given there should be likeness of nature between bridegroom and bride, and this is lacking in the union of the human nature with the Divine; secondly, because there is required a distinction of persons, and the human nature is not personally distinct from the Word; thirdly, because a dowry is given when the bride is first taken to the dwelling

* Cf. P. III, Q. 8, A. 1.

of the bridegroom and thus would seem to belong to the bride, who from being not united becomes united; whereas the human nature, which was assumed into the unity of Person by the Word, never was otherwise than perfectly united. Wherefore in the opinion of others we should say that the notion of dowry is either altogether unbecoming to Christ, or not so properly as to the saints; but that the things which we call dowries befit Him in the highest degree.

Reply Obj. 1. This conformity must be understood to refer to the thing which is a dowry and not to the notion of a dowry being in Christ: for it is not requisite that the thing in which we are conformed to Christ should be in the same way in Christ and in us.

Reply Obj. 2. Human nature is not properly said to be a bride in its union with the Word, since the distinction of persons, which is requisite between bridegroom and bride, is not observed therein. That human nature is sometimes described as being espoused in reference to its union with the Word is because it has a certain act of the bride, in that it is united to the Bridegroom inseparably, and in this union is subject to the Word and ruled by the Word, as the bride by the bridegroom.

Reply Obj. 3. If Christ is sometimes spoken of as the Bride, this is not because He is the Bride in very truth, but in so far as He personifies His spouse, namely the Church, who is united to Him spiritually. Hence nothing hinders Him, in this way of speaking, from being said to have the dowries, not that He Himself is dowered, but the Church.

Reply Obj. 4. The term Church is taken in two senses. For sometimes it denotes the body only, which is united to Christ as its Head. In this way alone has the Church the character of spouse: and in this way Christ is not a member of the Church, but is the Head from which all the members receive. In another sense the Church denotes the head and members united together; and thus Christ is said to be a member of the Church, inasmuch as He fulfills an office distinct from all others, by pouring forth life into the other members: although He is not very properly called a member, since a member implies a certain restriction, whereas in Christ spiritual good is not restricted but is absolutely entire,* so that He is the entire good of the Church, nor is He together with others anything greater than He is by Himself. Speaking of the Church in this sense, the Church denotes not only the bride, but the bridegroom and bride, in so far as one thing results from their spiritual union. Consequently although Christ be called a member of the Church in a certain sense, He can by no means be called a member of the bride; and therefore the idea of a dowry is not becoming to Him.

Reply Obj. 5. There is here a fallacy of *accident;* for these things are not befitting to Christ if we consider them under the aspect of dowry.

FOURTH ARTICLE

Whether the Angels Receive the Dowries?

We proceed thus to the Fourth Article:—

Objection 1. It would seem that the angels receive dowries. For a gloss on Cant. vi. 8, *One is my dove,* says: *One is the Church among men and angels.* But the Church is the bride, wherefore it is fitting for the members of the Church to have the dowries. Therefore the angels have the dowries.

Obj. 2. Further, a gloss on Luke xii. 36, *And you yourselves like to men who wait for their lord, when he shall return from the wedding,* says: *Our Lord went to the wedding when after His resurrection the new Man espoused to Himself the angelic host.* Therefore the angelic hosts are the spouse of Christ and consequently it is fitting that they should have the dowries.

Obj. 3. Further, the spiritual marriage consists in a spiritual union. Now the spiritual union between the angels and God is no less than between beatified men and God. Since, then, the dowries of which we treat now are assigned by reason of a spiritual marriage, it would seem that they are becoming to the angels.

Obj. 4. Further, a spiritual marriage demands a spiritual bridegroom and a spiritual bride. Now the angels are by nature more conformed than men to Christ as the supreme spirit. Therefore a spiritual marriage is more possible between the angels and Christ than between men and Christ.

Obj. 5. Further, a greater conformity is required between the head and members than between bridegroom and bride. Now the conformity between Christ and the angels suffices for Christ to be called the Head of the angels. Therefore for the same reason it suffices for Him to be called their bridegroom.

On the contrary, Origen at the beginning of the prologue to his commentary on the Canticles, distinguishes four persons, namely *the bridegroom with the bride, the young maidens, and the companions of the bridegroom:* and he says that *the angels are the companions of the bridegroom.* Since then

the dowry is due only to the bride, it would seem that the dowries are not becoming to the angels.

Further, Christ espoused the Church by His Incarnation and Passion: wherefore this is foreshadowed in the words (Exod. iv. 25), *A bloody spouse thou art to me.* Now by His Incarnation and Passion Christ was not otherwise united to the angels than before. Therefore the angels do not belong to the Church, if we consider the Church as spouse. Therefore the dowries are not becoming to the angels.

I answer that, Without any doubt, whatever pertains to the endowments of the soul is befitting to the angels as it is to men. But considered under the aspect of dowry they are not as becoming to the angels as to men, because the character of bride is not so properly becoming to the angels as to men. For there is required a conformity of nature between bridegroom and bride, to wit that they should be of the same species. Now men are in conformity with Christ in this way, since He took human nature, and by so doing became conformed to all men in the specific nature of man. On the other hand, He is not conformed to the angels in unity of species, neither as to His Divine nor as to His human nature. Consequently the notion of dowry is not so properly becoming to angels as to men. Since, however, in metaphorical expressions, it is not necessary to have a likeness in every respect, we must not argue that one thing is not to be said of another metaphorically on account of some lack of likeness; and consequently the argument we have adduced does not prove that the dowries are simply unbecoming to the angels, but only that they are not so properly befitting to angels as to men, on account of the aforesaid lack of likeness.

Reply Obj. 1. Although the angels are included in the unity of the Church, they are not members of the Church according to conformity of nature, if we consider the Church as bride: and thus it is not properly fitting for them to have the dowries.

Reply Obj. 2. Espousal is taken there in a broad sense, for union without conformity of specific nature: and in this sense nothing prevents our saying that the angels have the dowries taking these in a broad sense.

Reply Obj. 3. In the spiritual marriage although there is no other than a spiritual union, those whose union answers to the idea of a perfect marriage should agree in specific nature. Hence espousal does not properly befit the angels.

Reply Obj. 4. The conformity between the angels and Christ as God is not such as suffices for the notion of a perfect marriage, since so far are they from agreeing in species that there is still an infinite distance between them.

Reply Obj. 5. Not even is Christ properly called the Head of the angels, if we consider the head as requiring conformity of nature with the members. We must observe, however, that although the head and the other members are parts of an individual of one species, if we consider each one by itself, it is not of the same species as another member, for a hand is another specific part from the head. Hence, speaking of the members in themselves, the only conformity required among them is one of proportion, so that one receive from another, and one serve another. Consequently the conformity between God and the angels suffices for the notion of head rather than for that of bridegroom.

FIFTH ARTICLE

Whether Three Dowries of the Soul Are Suitably Assigned?

We proceed thus to the Fifth Article:—

Objection 1. It would seem unfitting to assign to the soul three dowries, namely, *vision, love* and *fruition.* For the soul is united to God according to the mind wherein is the image of the Trinity in respect of the memory, understanding, and will. Now love regards the will, and vision the understanding. Therefore there should be something corresponding to the memory, since fruition regards not the memory but the will.

Obj. 2. Further, the beatific dowries are said to correspond to the virtues of the way, which united us to God: and these are faith, hope, and charity, whereby God Himself is the object. Now love corresponds to charity, and vision to faith. Therefore there should be something corresponding to hope, since fruition corresponds rather to charity.

Obj. 3. Further, we enjoy God by love and vision only, since *we are said to enjoy those things which we love for their own sake,* as Augustine says *(De Doctr. Christ.* i. 4). Therefore fruition should not be reckoned a distinct dowry from love.

Obj. 4. Further, comprehension is required for the perfection of beatitude: *So run that you may comprehend* (1 Cor. ix. 24). Therefore we should reckon a fourth dowry.

Obj. 5. Further, Anselm says *(De Simil.* xlviii.) that the following pertain to the soul's beatitude: *wisdom, friendship, concord, power, honor, security, joy:* and consequently the aforesaid dowries are reckoned unsuitably.

* Cf. I-II. Q. 4, A. 3.

Obj. 6. Further, Augustine says *(De Civ. Dei,* xxii) that *in that beatitude God will be seen unendingly, loved without wearying, praised untiringly.* Therefore praise should be added to the aforesaid dowries.

Obj. 7. Further, Boëthius reckons five things pertaining to beatitude *(De Consol.* iii) and these are: Sufficiency which wealth offers, joy which pleasure offers, celebrity which fame offers, security which power offers, reverence which dignity offers. Consequently it seems that these should be reckoned as dowries rather than the aforesaid.

I answer that, All agree in reckoning three dowries of the soul, in different ways however. For some say that the three dowries of the soul are vision, love, and fruition; others reckon them to be vision, comprehension, and fruition; others, vision, delight, and comprehension. However, all these reckonings come to the same, and their number is assigned in the same way. For it has been said (A. 2) that a dowry is something inherent to the soul, and directing it to the operation in which beatitude consists. Now two things are requisite in this operation: its essence which is vision, and its perfection which is delight: since beatitude must needs be a perfect operation. Again, a vision is delightful in two ways: first, on the part of the object, by reason of the thing seen being delightful; secondly, on the part of the vision, by reason of the seeing itself being delightful, even as we delight in knowing evil things, although the evil things themselves delight us not. And since this operation wherein ultimate beatitude consists must needs be most perfect, this vision must needs be delightful in both ways. Now in order that this vision be delightful on the part of the vision, it needs to be made connatural to the seer by means of a habit; while for it to be delightful on the part of the visible object, two things are necessary, namely that the visible object be suitable, and that it be united to the seer. Accordingly for the vision to be delightful on its own part a habit is required to elicit the vision, and thus we have one dowry, which all call vision. But on the part of the visible object two things are necessary. First, suitableness, which regards the affections,—and in this respect some reckon love as a dowry, others fruition (in so far as fruition regards the affective part) since what we love most we deem most suitable. Secondly, union is required on the part of the visible object, and thus some reckon comprehension, which is nothing else than to have God present and to hold Him within ourself;* while others reckon fruition, not of hope, which is ours while on the way, but of possession* which is in heaven.

Thus the three dowries correspond to the three theological virtues, namely vision to faith, comprehension (or fruition in one sense) to hope, and fruition (or delight according to another reckoning to charity. For perfect fruition such as will be had in heaven includes delight and comprehension, for which reason some take it for the one, and some for the other.

Others, however, ascribe these three dowries to the three powers of the soul, namely vision to the rational, delight to the concupiscible, and fruition to the irascible, seeing that this fruition is acquired by a victory. But this is not said properly, because the irascible and concupiscible powers are not in the intellective but in the sensitive part, whereas the dowries of the soul are assigned to the mind.

Reply Obj. 1. Memory and understanding have but one act: either because understanding is itself an act of memory, or—if understanding denote a power—because memory does not proceed to act save through the medium of the understanding, since it belongs to the memory to retain knowledge. Consequently there is only one habit, namely knowledge, corresponding to memory and understanding: wherefore only one dowry, namely vision, corresponds to both.

Reply Obj. 2. Fruition corresponds to hope, in so far as it includes comprehension which will take the place of hope: since we hope for that which we have not yet; wherefore hope chafes somewhat on account of the distance of the beloved: for which reason it will not remain in heaven† but will be succeeded by comprehension.

Reply Obj. 3. Fruition as including comprehension is distinct from vision and love, but otherwise than love from vision. For love and vision denote different habits, the one belonging to the intellect, the other to the affective faculty. But comprehension, or fruition as denoting comprehension, does not signify a habit distinct from those two, but the removal of the obstacles which made it impossible for the mind to be united to God by actual vision. This is brought about by the habit of glory freeing the soul from all defects; for instance by making it capable of knowledge without phantasms, of complete control over the body, and so forth, thus re-

* Literally *of the reality,—non spei . . . sed rei.*

moving the obstacles which result in our being pilgrims from the Lord.

Reply Obj. 4 is clear from what has been said.

Reply Obj. 5. Properly speaking, the dowries are the immediate principles of the operation in which perfect beatitude consists and whereby the soul is united to Christ. The things mentioned by Anselm do not answer to this description; but they are such as in any way accompany or follow beatitude, not only in relation to the Bridegroom, to Whom *wisdom* alone of the things mentioned by him refers, but also in relation to others. They may be either one's equals, to whom *friendship* refers as regards the union of affections, and *concord* as regards consent in actions, or one's inferiors, to whom *power* refers, so far as inferior things are ordered by superior, and *honor* as regards that which inferiors offer to their superiors. Or again (they may accompany or follow beatitude) in relation to oneself: to this *security* refers as regards the removal of evil, and *joy* as regards the attainment of good.

Reply Obj. 6. Praise, which Augustine mentions as the third of those things which will obtain in heaven, is not a disposition to beatitude but rather a sequel to beatitude: because from the very fact of the soul's union with God, wherein beatitude consists, it follows that the soul breaks forth into praise. Hence praise has not the necessary conditions of a dowry.

Reply Obj. 7. The five things aforesaid mentioned by Boëthius are certain conditions of beatitude, but not dispositions to beatitude or to its act, because beatitude by reason of its perfection has of itself alone and undividedly all that men seek in various things, as the Philosopher declares (*Ethic.* i. 7, x 7, 8). Accordingly Boëthius shows that these five things obtain in perfect beatitude, because they are what men seek in temporal happiness. For they pertain either, as *security*, to immunity from evil, or to the attainment either of the suitable good, as *joy*, or of the perfect good, as *sufficiency*, or to the manifestation of good, as *celebrity*, inasmuch as the good of one is made known to others, or as *reverence*, as indicating that good or the knowledge thereof, for reverence is the showing of honor which bears witness to virtue. Hence it is evident that these five should not be called dowries, but conditions of beatitude.

† Cf. II-II, Q. 18, A. 2.

QUESTION 96

Of the Aureoles

(In Thirteen Articles)

IN the next place we must consider the aureoles. Under this head there are thirteen points of inquiry: (1) Whether the aureoles differ from the essential reward? (2) Whether they differ from the fruit? (3) Whether a fruit is due to the virtue of continence only? (4) Whether three fruits are fittingly assigned to the three parts of continence? (5) Whether an aureole is due to virgins? (6) Whether it is due to martyrs? (7) Whether it is due to doctors? (8) Whether it is due to Christ? (9) Whether to the angels? (10) Whether it is due to the human body? (11) Whether three aureoles are fittingly assigned? (12) Whether the virgin's aureole is the greatest? (13) Whether one has the same aureole in a higher degree than another?

FIRST ARTICLE

Whether the Aureole Is the Same As the Essential Reward Which Is Called the Aurea?

We proceed thus to the First Article:—

Objection 1. It would seem that the aureole is not distinct from the essential reward which is called the *aurea*. For the essential reward is beatitude itself. Now according to Boëthius *(De Consol.* iii), beatitude is *a state rendered perfect by the aggregate of all goods.* Therefore the essential reward includes every good possessed in heaven; so that the aureole is included in the *aurea*.

Obj. 2. Further, *more* and *less* do not change a species. But those who keep the counsels and commandments receive a greater reward than those who keep the commandments only, nor seemingly does their reward differ, except in one reward being greater than another. Since then the aureole denotes the reward due to works of perfection it would seem that it does not signify something distinct from the *aurea*.

Obj. 3. Further, reward corresponds to merit. Now charity is the root of all merit. Since then the *aurea* corresponds to charity, it would seem that there will be no reward in heaven other than the *aurea*.

Obj. 4. Further, *All the blessed are taken into the angelic orders* as Gregory declares *(Hom.* xxxiv. *in Ev.).* Now as regards the angels, *though some of them receive certain gifts in a higher degree, nothing is possessed by any of them exclusively, for all gifts are*

in all of them, though not equally, because some are endowed more highly than others with gifts which, however, they all possess, as Gregory says *(ibid.).* Therefore as regards the blessed, there will be no reward other than that which is common to all. Therefore the aureole is not a distinct reward from the *aurea*.

Obj. 5. Further, a higher reward is due to higher merit. If, then, the *aurea* is due to works which are of obligation, and the aureole to works of counsel, the aureole will be more perfect than the *aurea*, and consequently should not be expressed by a diminutive.* Therefore it would seem that the aureole is not a distinct reward from the *aurea*.

On the contrary, A gloss† on Exod. xxv. 24, 25, *Thou shalt make . . . another little golden crown (coronam aureolam),* says: *This crown denotes the new hymn which the virgins alone sing in the presence of the Lamb.* Wherefore apparently the aureole is a crown awarded, not to all, but especially to some: whereas the aurea is awarded to all the blessed. Therefore the aureole is distinct from the *aurea*.

Further, a crown is due to the fight which is followed by victory: *He . . . is not crowned except he strive lawfully* (2 Tim. ii. 5). Hence where there is a special kind of conflict, there should be a special crown. Now in certain works there is a special kind of conflict. Therefore they deserve a special kind of crown, which we call an aureole.

Further, the Church militant comes down from the Church triumphant: *I saw the Holy City,* etc. (Apoc. xxi. 2). Now in the Church militant special rewards are given to those who perform special deeds, for instance a crown to the conqueror, a prize to the runner. Therefore the same should obtain in the Church triumphant.

I answer that, Man's essential reward, which is his beatitude, consists in the perfect union of the soul with God, inasmuch as it enjoys God perfectly as seen and loved perfectly. Now this reward is called a *crown* or *aurea* metaphorically, both with reference to merit which is gained by a kind of conflict, —since *the life of man upon earth is a warfare* (Job vii. 1),—and with reference to the reward whereby in a way man is made a participator of the Godhead, and consequently endowed with regal power: *Thou hast made*

* *Aureola, i.e.,* a little *aurea.*　　　† Ven. Bede, *De Tabernaculis* i. 6.

us to our God a kingdom, etc. (Apoc. v. 10) ; for a crown is the proper sign of regal power.

In like manner the accidental reward which is added to the essential has the character of a crown. For a crown signifies some kind of perfection, on account of its circular shape, so that for this very reason it is becoming to the perfection of the blessed. Since, however, nothing can be added to the essential, but what is less than it, the additional reward is called an *aureole.* Now something may be added in two ways to this essential reward which we call the *aurea.* First, in consequence of a condition attaching to the nature of the one rewarded: thus the glory of the body is added to the beatitude of the soul, wherefore this same glory of the body is sometimes called an *aureole.* Thus a gloss of Bede on Exod. xxv. 25, *Thou . . . shalt make another little golden crown,* says that *finally the aureole is added, when it is stated in the Scriptures that a higher degree of glory is in store for us when our bodies are resumed.* But it is not in this sense that we speak of an aureole now. Secondly, in consequence of the nature of the meritorious act. Now this has the character of merit on two counts, whence also it has the character of good. First, to wit, from its root which is charity, since it is referred to the last end, and thus there is due to it the essential reward, namely the attainment of the end, and this is the *aurea.* Secondly, from the very genus of the act which derives a certain praiseworthiness from its due circumstances, from the habit eliciting it and from its proximate end, and thus is due to it a kind of accidental reward which we call an *aureole*: and it is in this sense that we regard the aureole now. Accordingly it must be said that an *aureole* denotes something added to the *aurea,* a kind of joy, to wit, in the works one has done, in that they have the character of a signal victory: for this joy is distinct from the joy in being united to God, which is called the *aurea.* Some, however, affirm that the comomn reward, which is the *aurea,* receives the name of *aureole,* according as it is given to virgins, martyrs, or doctors: even as money receives the name of debt through being due to some one, though the money and the debt are altogether the same. And that nevertheless this does not imply that the essential reward is any greater when it is called an *aureole;* but that it corresponds to a more excellent act, more excellent not in intensity of merit but in the manner of meriting; so that although two persons may have the Divine vision with equal clearness, it is called an *aureole* in one and not in the other, in so far as it corresponds to higher merit as regards the way of meriting. But this would seem contrary to the meaning of the gloss quoted above. For if *aurea* and *aureole* were the same, the *aureole* would not be described as added to the *aurea.* Moreover, since reward corresponds to merit, a more excellent reward must needs correspond to this more excellent way of meriting: and it is this excellence that we call an *aureole.* Hence it follows that an *aureole* differs from the *aurea.*

Reply Obj. 1. Beatitude includes all the goods necessary for man's perfect life consisting in his perfect operation. Yet some things can be added, not as being necessary for that perfect operation as though it were impossible without them, but as adding to the glory of beatitude. Hence they regard the well-being of beatitude and a certain fitness thereto. Even so civic happiness is embellished by nobility and bodily beauty and so forth, and yet it is possible without them as stated in *Ethic.* i. 8: and thus is the aureole in comparison with the happiness of heaven.

Reply Obj. 2. He who keeps the counsels and the commandments always merits more than he who keeps the commandments only, if we gather the notion of merit in works from the very genus of those works; but not always if we gauge the merit from its root, charity: since sometimes a man keeps the commandments alone out of greater charity than one who keeps both commandments and counsels. For the most part, however, the contrary happens, because the *proof of love is in the performance of deeds,* as Gregory says *(Hom.* xxx. *in Ev.).* Wherefore it is not the more excellent essential reward that is called an aureole, but that which is added to the essential reward without reference to the essential reward of the possessor of an aureole being greater, or less than, or equal to the essential reward of one who has no aureole.

Reply Obj. 3. Charity is the first principle of merit: but our actions are the instruments, so to speak, whereby we merit. Now in order to obtain an effect there is requisite not only a due disposition in the first mover, but also a right disposition in the instrument. Hence something principal results in the effect with reference to the first mover, and something secondary with reference to the instrument. Wherefore in the reward also there is something on the part of charity, namely the *aurea,* and something on the part of the kind of work, namely the *aureole.*

Reply Obj. 4. All the angels merited their beatitude by the same kind of act namely by turning to God: and consequently no particular reward is found in anyone which another has not in some way. But men merit beatitude by different kinds of acts: and so the comparison fails.

Nevertheless among men what one seems to have specially, all have in common in some way, in so far as each one, by charity, deems another's good his own. Yet this joy whereby one shares another's joy cannot be called an aureole, because it is not given him as a reward for his victory, but regards more the victory of another: whereas a crown is awarded the victors themselves and not to those who rejoice with them in the victory.

Reply Obj. 5. The merit arising from charity is more excellent than that which arises from the kind of action: just as the end to which charity directs us is more excellent than the things directed to that end, and with which our actions are concerned. Wherefore the reward corresponding to merit by reason of charity, however little it may be, is greater than any reward corresponding to an action by reason of its genus. Hence *aureole* is used as a diminutive in comparison with *aurea.*

SECOND ARTICLE

Whether the Aureole Differs from the Fruit?

We proceed thus to the Second Article:—

Objection 1. It would seem that the aureole does not differ from the fruit. For different rewards are not due to the same merit. Now the aureole and the hundredfold fruit correspond to the same merit, according to a gloss on Matth. xiii. 8, *Some a hundredfold.* Therefore the aureole is the same as the fruit.

Obj. 2. Further, Augustine says (*De Virgin* xlv) that the *hundredfold fruit is due to the martyrs, and also to virgins.* Therefore the fruit is a reward common to virgins and martyrs. But the aureole also is due to them. Therefore the aureole is the same as the fruit.

Obj. 3. Further, there are only two rewards in beatitude, namely the essential, and the accidental which is added to the essential. Now that which is added to the essential reward is called an aureole, as evidenced by the statement (Exod. xxv. 25) that the little crown *(aureola)* is added to the crown. But the fruit is not the essential reward, for in that case it would be due to all the blessed. Therefore it is the same as the aureole.

On the contrary, Things which are not divided in the same way are not of the same nature. Now fruit and aureole are not divided in the same way, since aureole is divided into the aureole of virgins, of martyrs, and of doctors: whereas fruit is divided into the fruit of the married, of widows, and of virgins. Therefore fruit and aureole are not the same.

Further, if fruit and aureole were the same,

* *De Parad.* xiii.   † Cf. I-II, Q. 70, A. 1 *ad* 2.

the aureole would be due to whomsoever the fruit is due. But this is manifestly untrue, since a fruit is due to widowhood, while an aureole is not. Therefore, etc.

I answer that, Metaphorical expressions can be taken in various ways, according as we find resemblances to the various properties of the thing from which the comparison is taken. Now since fruit, properly speaking, is applied to material things born of the earth, we employ it variously in a spiritual sense, with reference to the various conditions that obtain in material fruits. For the material fruit has sweetness whereby it refreshes so far as it is used by man: again it is the last thing to which the operation of nature attains: moreover it is that to which husbandry looks forward as the result of sowing or any other process. Accordingly fruit is taken in a spiritual sense sometimes for that which refreshes, as being the last end: and according to this signification we are said to enjoy *(frui)* God perfectly in heaven, and imperfectly on the way. From this signification we have fruition which is a dowry: but we are not speaking of fruit in this sense now. Sometimes fruit signifies spiritually that which refreshes only, though it is not the last end; and thus the virtues are called fruits, inasmuch as *they refresh the mind with genuine sweetness,* as Ambrose says.* In this sense fruit is taken (Gal. vi. 22): *The fruit of the Spirit is charity, joy,* etc. Nor again is this the sense in which we speak of fruit now; for we have treated of this already.†

We may, however, take spiritual fruit in another sense, in likeness to material fruit, inasmuch as material fruit is a profit expected from the labor of husbandry: so that we call fruit that reward which man acquires from his labor in this life: and thus every reward which by our labors we shall acquire for the future life is called a *fruit.* In this sense fruit is taken (Rom. vi. 22): *You have your fruit unto sanctification, and the end life everlasting.* Yet neither in this sense do we speak of fruit now, but we are treating of fruit as being the product of seed: for it is in this sense that our Lord speaks of fruit (Matth. xiii. 23), where He divides fruit into thirtyfold, sixtyfold, and hundredfold. Now fruit is the product of seed in so far as the seed power is capable of transforming the humors of the soil into its own nature; and the more efficient this power, and the better prepared the soil, the more plentiful fruit will result. Now the spiritual seed which is sown in us is the Word of God: wherefore the more a person is transformed into a spiritual nature by withdrawing from carnal things, the greater is the fruit of the Word in him. Accordingly the fruit of the

Word of God differs from the aurea and the aureole, in that the *aurea* consists in the joy one has in God, and the *aureole* in the joy one has in the perfection of one's works, whereas the *fruit* consists in the joy that the worker has in his own disposition as to his degree of spirituality to which he has attained through the seed of God's Word.

Some, however, distinguish between aureole and fruit, by saying that the aureole is due to the fighter, according to 2 Tim. ii. 5, *He . . . shall not be crowned, except he strive lawfully;* whereas the fruit is due to the laborer, according to the saying of Wisdom iii. 15, *The fruit of good labors is glorious.* Others again say that the *aurea* regards conversion to God, while the *aureole* and the *fruit* regard things directed to the end; yet so that the fruit regards the will rather, and the aureole the body. Since, however, labor and strife are in the same subject and about the same matter, and since the body's reward depends on the soul's, these explanations of the difference between fruit, aurea and aureole would only imply a logical difference: and this cannot be, since fruit is assigned to some to whom no aureole is assigned.

Reply Obj. 1. There is nothing incongruous if various rewards correspond to the same merit according to the various things contained therein. Wherefore to virginity corresponds the aurea in so far as virginity is kept for God's sake at the command of charity; the aureole, in so far as virginity is a work of perfection having the character of a signal victory; and the fruit, in so far as by virginity a person acquires a certain spirituality by withdrawing from carnal things.

Reply Obj. 2. Fruit, according to the proper acceptation as we are speaking of it now, does not denote the reward common to martyrdom and virginity, by that which corresponds to the three degrees of continency. This gloss which states that the hundredfold fruit corresponds to martyrs takes fruit in a broad sense, according as any reward is called a fruit, the hundredfold fruit thus denoting the reward due to any perfect works whatever.

Reply Obj. 3. Although the aureole is an accidental reward added to the essential reward, nevertheless not every accidental reward is an aureole, but only that which is assigned to works of perfection, whereby man is most conformed to Christ in the achievement of a perfect victory. Hence it is not unfitting that another accidental reward, which is called the fruit, be due sometimes to the withdrawal from a carnal life.

THIRD ARTICLE

Whether a Fruit Is Due to the Virtue of Continence Alone?

We proceed thus to the Third Article:—

Objection 1. It would seem that a fruit is not due to the virtue of continence alone. For a gloss on 1 Cor. xv. 41, *One is the glory of the sun,* says that *the worth of those who have the hundredfold fruit is compared to the glory of the sun; to the glory of the moon those who have the sixtyfold fruit; and to the stars those who have the thirtyfold fruit.* Now this difference of glory, in the meaning of the Apostle, regards any difference whatever of beatitude. Therefore the various fruits should correspond to none but the virtue of continence.

Obj. 2. Further, fruits are so called from fruition. But fruition belongs to the essential reward which corresponds to all the virtues. Therefore, etc.

Obj. 3. Further, fruit is due to labor: *The fruit of good labors is glorious* (Wis. iii. 15). Now there is greater labor in fortitude than in temperance or continence. Therefore fruit does not correspond to continence alone.

Obj. 4. Further, it is more difficult not to exceed the measure in food which is necessary for life, than in sexual matters without which life can be sustained: and thus the labor of frugality is greater than that of continence. Therefore fruit corresponds to frugality rather than to continence.

Obj. 5. Further, fruit implies delight, and delight regards especially the end. Since then the theological virtues have the end for their object, namely God Himself, it would seem that to them especially the fruit should correspond.

On the contrary, is the statement of the gloss on Matth. xiii. 23, *The one a hundredfold,* which assigns the fruits to virginity, widowhood, and conjugal continence, which are parts of continence.

I answer that, A fruit is a reward due to a person in that he passes from the carnal to the spiritual life. Consequently a fruit corresponds especially to that virtue which more than any other frees man from subjection to the flesh. Now this is the effect of continence, since it is by sexual pleasures that the soul is especially subject to the flesh; so much so that in the carnal act, according to Jerome (*Ep. ad Ageruch.*), *not even the spirit of prophecy touches the heart of the prophet,* nor *is it possible to understand anything in the midst of that pleasure,* as the Philosopher says (*Ethic.* vii. 11). Therefore fruit corresponds to continence rather than to another virtue.

Reply Obj. 1. This gloss takes fruit in a broad sense, according as any reward is called a fruit.

Reply Obj. 2. Fruition does not take its name from fruit by reason of any comparison with fruit in the sense in which we speak of it now, as evidenced by what has been said.

Reply Obj. 3. Fruit, as we speak of it now, corresponds to labor not as resulting in fatigue, but as resulting in the production of fruit. Hence a man calls his crops his labor, inasmuch as he labored for them, or produced them by his labor. Now the comparison to fruit, as produced from seed, is more adapted to continence than to fortitude, because man is not subjected to the flesh by the passions of fortitude, as he is by the passions with which continence is concerned.

Reply Obj. 4. Although the pleasures of the table are more necessary than the pleasures of sex, they are not so strong: wherefore the soul is not so much subjected to the flesh thereby.

Reply Obj. 5. Fruit is not taken here in the sense in which fruition applies to delight in the end; but in another sense as stated above (A. 2). Hence the argument proves nothing.

FOURTH ARTICLE

Whether Three Fruits Are Fittingly Assigned to the Three Parts of Continence?

We proceed thus to the Fourth Article:—

Objection 1. It would seem that three fruits are unfittingly assigned to the three parts of continence: because twelve fruits of the Spirit are assigned, *charity, joy, peace,* etc. (Gal. v. 22). Therefore seemingly we should reckon only three.

Obj. 2. Further, fruit denotes a special reward. Now the reward assigned to virgins, widows, and married persons is not a special reward, because all who are to be saved are comprised under one of these three, since no one is saved who lacks continence, and continence is adequately divided by these three. Therefore three fruits are unfittingly assigned to the three aforesaid.

Obj. 3. Further, just as widowhood surpasses conjugal continence, so does virginity surpass widowhood. But the excess of sixtyfold over thirtyfold is not as the excess of a hundredfold over sixtyfold; neither in arithmetical proportion, since sixty exceeds thirty by thirty, and a hundred exceeds sixty by forty; nor in geometrical proportion, since sixty is twice thirty and a hundred surpasses sixty as containing the whole and two-thirds thereof. Therefore the fruits are unfittingly adapted to the degrees of continence.

Obj. 4. Further, the statements contained in Holy Writ stand for all time: *Heaven and earth shall pass away, but My words shall not pass away* (Luke xxi. 33): whereas human institutions are liable to change every day. Therefore human institutions are not to be taken as a criterion of the statements of Holy Writ: and it would seem in consequence that the explanation of these fruits given by Bede is unfitting. For he says (*Expos. in Luc.* iii. 8) that *the thirtyfold fruit is assigned to married persons, because in the signs drawn on the 'abacus' the number* 30 *is denoted by the thumb and index finger touching one another at the tips as though kissing one another: so that the number* 30 *denotes the embraces of married persons. The number* 60 *is denoted by the contact of the index finger above the middle joint of the thumb, so that the index finger by lying over the thumb and weighing on it, signifies the burden which widows have to bear in this world. When, however, in the course of enumeration we come to the number* 100 *we pass from the left to the right hand, so that the number* 100 *denotes virginity, which has a share in the angelic excellence; for the angels are on the right hand, i.e. in glory, while we are on the left on account of the imperfection of the present life.*

I answer that, By continence, to which the fruit corresponds, man is brought to a kind of spiritual nature, by withdrawing from carnal things. Consequently various fruits are distinguished according to the various manners of the spirituality resulting from continence. Now there is a certain spirituality which is necessary, and one which is superabundant. The spirituality that is necessary consists in the rectitude of the spirit not being disturbed by the pleasures of the flesh: and this obtains when one makes use of carnal pleasures according to the order of right reason. This is the spirituality of married persons. Spirituality is superabundant when a man withdraws himself entirely from those carnal pleasures which stifle the spirit. This may be done in two ways: either in respect of all time past, present, and future, and this is the spirituality of virgins; or in respect of a particular time, and this is the spirituality of widows. Accordingly to those who keep conjugal continence, the thirtyfold fruit is awarded; to those who keep the continence of widows, the sixtyfold fruit; and to those who keep virginal continence, the hundredfold fruit: and this for the reason given by Bede quoted above, although another motive may be found in the very nature of the numbers. For 30 is the product of 3 multiplied by 10. Now 3 is the number of everything, as stated in *De Cœlo et Mundo,* i., and contains a certain perfection common to all, namely of beginning, middle, and end. Wherefore the number 30 is fittingly assigned to married persons, in whom no other perfection is added to the observance of the Decalogue, signified by the number 10, than the common perfection without which there is no salvation. The number six the multiplication of which by 10 amounts to 60 has perfection from its parts, being the aggregate of all its parts taken together; wherefore it corresponds fittingly to widowhood, wherein we find perfect withdrawal from carnal pleasures as to all its circumstances (which are the parts so to speak of a virtuous act), since widowhood uses no carnal pleasures in connection with any person, place, or any other circumstance; which was not the case with conjugal continence. The number 100 corresponds fittingly to virginity; because the number 10 of which 100 is a multiple is the limit of numbers: and in like manner virginity occupies the limit of spirituality, since no further spirituality can be added to it. The number 100 also being a square number has perfection from its figure: for a square figure is prefect through being equal on all sides, since all its sides are equal: wherefore it is adapted to virginity wherein incorruption is found equally as to all times.

Reply Obj. 1. Fruit is not taken there in the sense in which we are taking it now.

Reply Obj. 2. Nothing obliges us to hold that fruit is a reward that is not common to all who will be saved. For not only the essential reward is common to all, but also a certain accidental reward, such as joy in those works without which one cannot be saved. Yet it may be said that the fruits are not becoming to all who will be saved, as is evidently the case with those who repent in the end after leading an incontinent life, for to such no fruit is due but only the essential reward.

Reply Obj. 3. The distinction of the fruits is to be taken according to the species and figures of the numbers rather than according to their quantity. Nevertheless even if we regard the excess in point of quantity, we may find an explanation. For the married man abstains only from one that is not his, the widow from both hers and not hers, so that in the latter case we find the notion of double, just as 60 is the double of 30. Again 100 is 60 × 40, which latter number is the product of 4 × 10, and the number 4 is the first solid and square number. Thus the addition of this number is fitting to virginity, which adds perpetual incorruption to the perfection of widowhood.

     * Cf. P. III, Q. 27, A. 3.

Reply Obj. 4. Although these numerical signs are a human institution, they are founded somewhat on the nature of things, in so far as the numbers are denoted in gradation, according to the order of the aforesaid joints and contacts.

FIFTH ARTICLE

Whether an Aureole Is Due on Account of Virginity?

We proceed thus to the Fifth Article:—

Objection 1. It would seem that an aureole is not due on account of virginity. For where there is greater difficulty in the work, a greater reward is due. Now widows have greater difficulty than virgins in abstaining from the works of the flesh. For Jerome says (*Ep. ad Ageruch.*) that the greater difficulty certain persons experience in abstaining from the allurements of pleasure, the greater their reward, and he is speaking in praise of widows. Moreover, the Philosopher says (*De Anim. Hist.* vii) that *young women who have been deflowered desire sexual intercourse the more for the recollection of the pleasure.* Therefore the aureole which is the greatest reward is due to widows more than to virgins.

Obj. 2. Further, if an aureole were due to virginity, it would be especially found where there is the most perfect virginity. Now the most prefect virginity is in the Blessed Virgin, wherefore she is called the Virgin of virgins: and yet no aureole is due to her because she experienced no conflict in being continent, for she was not infected with the corruption of the fomes.* Therefore an aureole is not due to virginity.

Obj. 3. Further, a special reward is not due to that which has not been at all times praiseworthy. Now it would not have been praiseworthy to observe virginity in the state of innocence, since then was it commanded: *Increase and multiply and fill the earth* (Gen. i. 28): nor again during the time of the Law, since the barren were accursed. Therefore an aureole is not due to virginity.

Obj. 4. Further, the same reward is not due to virginity observed, and virginity lost. Yet an aureole is sometimes due to lost virginity; for instance if a maiden be violated unwillingly at the order of a tyrant for confessing Christ. Therefore an aureole is not due to virginity.

Obj. 5. Further, a special reward is not due to that which is in us by nature. But virginity is inborn in every man both good and wicked. Therefore an aureole is not due to virginity.

Obj. 6. Further, as widowhood is to the sixtyfold fruit, so is virginity to the hundredfold fruit, and to the aureole. Now the sixty-fold fruit is not due to every widow, but only, as some say, to one who vows to remain a widow. Therefore it would seem that neither is the aureole due to any kind of virginity, but only to that which is observed by vow.

Obj. 7. Further, reward is not given to that which is done of necessity, since all merit depends on the will. But some are virgins of necessity, such as those who are naturally cold-blooded, and eunuchs. Therefore an aureole is not always due to virginity.

On the contrary, A gloss on Exod. xxv. 25: *Thou shalt also make a little golden crown (coronam aureolam)* says: *This crown denotes the new hymn which the virgins sing in the presence of the Lamb, those, to wit, who follow the Lamb whithersoever He goeth.* Therefore the reward due to virginity is called an aureole.

Further, It is written (Isa. lvi. 4): *Thus saith the Lord to the eunuchs:* and the text continues (*verse* 5): *I will give to them . . . a name better than sons and daughters:* and a gloss* says: *This refers to their peculiar and transcendent glory.* Now the eunuchs *who have made themselves eunuchs for the kingdom of heaven* (Matth. xix. 12) denote virgins. Therefore it would seem that some special reward is due to virginity, and this is called the aureole.

I answer that, Where there is a notable kind of victory, a special crown is due. Wherefore since by virginity a person wins a signal victory over the flesh, against which a continuous battle is waged: *The flesh lusteth against the spirit,* etc. (Gal. v. 17), a special crown called the aureole is due to virginity. This indeed is the common opinion of all; but all are not agreed as to the kind of virginity to which it is due. For some say that the aureole is due to the act. So that she who actually remains a virgin will have the aureole provided she be of the number of the saved. But this would seem unreasonble, because in this case those who have the will to marry and nevertheless die before marrying would have the aureole. Hence others hold that the aureole is due to the state and not to the act: so that those virgins alone merit the aureole who by vow have placed themselves in the state of observing perpetual virginity. But this also seems unreasonable, because it is possible to have the same intention of observing virginity without a vow as with a vow. Hence it may be said otherwise that merit is due to every virtuous act commanded by charity. Now virginity comes under the genus of virtue in so far as perpetual incorruption of mind and

body is an object of choice, as appears from what has been said above (iv. *Sent.* D. 33, Q. 3, AA. 1, 2).† Consequently the aureole is due to those virgins alone, who had the purpose of observing perpetual virginity, whether or no they have confirmed this purpose by vow,—and this I say with reference to the aureole in its proper signification of a reward due to merit,—although this purpose may at some time have been interrupted, integrity of the flesh remaining withal, provided it be found at the end of life, because virginity of the mind may be restored, although virginity of the flesh cannot. If, however, we take the aureole in its broad sense for any joy added to the essential joy of heaven, the aureole will be applicable even to those who are incorrupt in flesh, although they had not the purpose of observing perpetual virginity. For without doubt they will rejoice in the incorruption of their body, even as the innocent will rejoice in having been free from sin, although they had no opportunity of sinning, as in the case of baptized children. But this is not the proper meaning of an aureole, although it is very commonly taken in this sense.

Reply Obj. 1. In some respects virgins experience a greater conflict in remaining continent; and in other respects, widows, other things being equal. For virgins are inflamed by concupiscence, and by the desire of experience, which arises from a certain curiosity as it were, which makes man more willing to see what he has never seen. Sometimes, moreover, this concupiscence is increased by their esteeming the pleasure to be greater than it is in reality, and by their failing to consider the grievances attaching to this pleasure. In these respects widows experience the lesser conflict, yet theirs is the greater conflict by reason of their recollection of the pleasure. Moreover, in different subjects one motive is stronger than another, according to the various conditions and dispositions of the subject, because some are more susceptible to one, and others to another. However, whatever we may say of the degree of conflict, this is certain,—that the virgin's victory is more perfect than the widow's, for the most perfect and most brilliant kind of victory is never to have yielded to the foe: and the crown is due, not to the battle but to the victory gained by the battle.

Reply Obj. 2. There are two opinions about this. For some say that the Blessed Virgin has not an aureole in reward of her virginity, if we take aureole in the proper sense as referring to a conflict, but that she has something more than an aureole, on account of her most perfect purpose of observing virginity. Others

* S. Augustine, *De Virginit.* xxv.   † Cf. II-II, Q. 152, AA. 1, 3.

say that she has an aureole even in its proper signification, and that a most transcendent one: for though she experienced no conflict, she had a certain conflict of the flesh, but owing to the exceeding strength of her virtue, her flesh was so subdued that she did not feel this conflict. This, however, would seem to be said without reason, for since we believe the Blessed Virgin to have been altogether immune from the inclination of the fomes on account of the perfection of her sanctification, it is wicked to suppose that there was in her any conflict with the flesh, since such like conflict is only from the inclination of the fomes, nor can temptation from the flesh be without sin, as declared by a gloss* on 2 Cor. xii. 7, *There was given me a sting of my flesh.* Hence we must say that she has an aureole properly speaking, so as to be conformed in this to those other members of the Church in whom virginity is found: and although she had no conflict by reason of the temptation which is of the flesh, she had the temptation which is of the enemy, who feared not even Christ (Matth. iv).

Reply Obj. 3. The aureole is not due to virginity except as adding some excellence to the other degrees of continence. If Adam had not sinned, virginity would have had no perfection over conjugal continence, since in that case marriage would have been honorable, and the marriage-bed unsullied, for it would not have been dishonored by lust: hence virginity would not then have been observed, nor would an aureole have been due to it. But the condition of human nature being changed, virginity has a special beauty of its own, and consequently a special reward is assigned to it.

During the time of the Mosaic law, when the worship of God was to be continued by means of the carnal act, it was not altogether praiseworthy to abstain from carnal intercourse: wherefore no special reward would be given for such a purpose unless it came from a Divine inspiration, as is believed to have been the case with Jeremias and Elias, of whose marriage we do not read.

Reply Obj. 4. If a virgin is violated, she does not forfeit the aureole, provided she retain unfailingly the purpose of observing perpetual virginity, and nowise consent to the act. Nor does she forfeit virginity thereby; and be this said, whether she be violated for the faith, or for any other cause whatever. But if she suffer this for the faith, this will count to her for merit, and will be a kind of martyrdom: wherefore Lucy said: *If thou causest me to be violated against my will, my chastity will receive a double crown;*† not

that she has two aureoles of virginity, but that she will receive a double reward, one for observing virginity, the other for the outrage she has suffered. Even supposing that one thus violated should conceive, she would not for that reason forfeit her virginity: nor would she be equal to Christ's mother, in whom there was integrity of the flesh together with integrity of the mind.‡

Reply Obj. 5. Virginity is inborn in us as to that which is material in virginity: but the purpose of observing perpetual incorruption, whence virginity derives its merit, is not inborn, but comes from the gift of grace.

Reply Obj. 6. The sixtyfold fruit is due, not to every widow, but only to those who retain the purpose of remaining widows, even though they do not make it the matter of a vow, even as we have said in regard to virginity.

Reply Obj. 7. If cold-blooded persons and eunuchs have the will to observe perpetual incorruption even though they were capable of sexual intercourse, they must be called virgins and merit the aureole: for they make a virtue of necessity. If, on the other hand, they have the will to marry if they could, they do not merit the aureole. Hence Augustine says *(De Sancta Virgin.,* xxiv): *For those like eunuchs whose bodies are so formed that they are unable to beget, it suffices when they become Christians and keep the commandments of God, that they have a mind to have a wife if they could, in order to rank with the faithful who are married.*

SIXTH ARTICLE

Whether an Aureole Is Due to Martyrs?

We proceed thus to the Sixth Article:—

Objection 1. It would seem that an aureole is not due to martyrs. For an aureole is a reward given for works of supererogation, wherefore Bede commenting on Exod. xxv. 25, *Thou shalt also make another . . . crown,* says: *This may be rightly referred to the reward of those who by freely choosing a more perfect life go beyond the general commandments.* But to die for confessing the faith is sometimes an obligation, and not a work of supererogation as appears from the words of Rom. x. 10, *With the heart, we believe unto justice, but with the mouth confession is made unto salvation.* Therefore an aureole is not always due to martyrdom.

Obj. 2. Further, according to Gregory *(Moral.* ix)§ *the freer the service, the more acceptable it is.* Now martyrdom has a minimum of freedom, since it is a punishment in-

* S. Augustine, *De Civ. Dei.* xix. 4.   † Office of S. Lucy; *lect.* vi (Dominican Breviary, December 13th).

‡ Cf. II-II, Q. 64, A. 3, *ad* 3; Q. 124, A. 4, *ad* 2; Q. 152, A. 1.   § Cf. S. Augustine, *De Adult. Conjug.,* i. 14.

flicted by another person with force. Therefore an aureole is not due to martyrdom, since it is accorded to surpassing merit.

Obj. 3. Further, martyrdom consists not only in suffering death externally, but also in the interior act of the will: wherefore Bernard in a sermon on the Holy Innocents distinguishes three kinds of martyr,—in will and not in death, as John; in both will and death, as Stephen; in death and not in will, as the Innocents. Accordingly if an aureole were due to martyrdom, it would be due to voluntary rather than external martyrdom, since merit proceeds from will. Yet such is not the case. Therefore an aureole is not due to martyrdom.

Obj. 4. Further, bodily suffering is less than mental, which consists of internal sorrow and affliction of soul. But internal suffering is also a kind of martyrdom: wherefore Jerome says in a sermon on the Assumption:* *I should say rightly that the Mother of God was both virgin and martyr, although she ended her days in peace, wherefore: Thine own soul a sword hath pierced — namely for her Son's death.* Since then no aureole corresponds to interior sorrow, neither should one correspond to outward suffering.

Obj. 5. Further, penance itself is a kind of martyrdom, wherefore Gregory says (*Hom. iii in Ev.)*: *Although persecution has ceased to offer the opportunity, yet the peace we enjoy is not without its martyrdom; since even if we no longer yield the life of the body to the sword, yet do we slay fleshly desires in the soul with the sword of the spirit.* But no aureole is due to penance which consists in external works. Neither therefore is an aureole due to every external martyrdom.

Obj. 6. Further, an aureole is not due to an unlawful work. Now it is unlawful to lay hands on oneself, as Augustine declares (*De Civ. Dei,* i), and yet the Church celebrates the martyrdom of some who laid hands upon themselves in order to escape the fury of tyrants, as in the case of certain women at Antioch (Eusebius,—*Eccles. Hist.* viii. 24). Therefore an aureole is not always due to martyrdom.

Obj. 7. Further, it happens at times that a person is wounded for the faith, and survives for some time. Now it is clear that such a one is a martyr, and yet seemingly an aureole is not due to him, since his conflict did not last until death. Therefore an aureole is not always due to martyrdom.

Obj. 8. Further, some suffer more from the loss of temporal goods than from the affliction even of their own body and this is shown by their bearing many afflictions for the sake of gain. Therefore if they be despoiled of their temporal goods for Christ's sake they would seem to be martyrs, and yet an aureole is not apparently due to them. Therefore the same conclusion follows as before.

Obj. 9. Further, a martyr would seem to be no other than one who dies for the faith, wherefore Isidore says (*Etym.* vii): *They are called martyrs in Greek, witnesses in Latin: because they suffered in order to bear witness to Christ, and strove unto death for the truth.* Now there are virtues more excellent than faith, such as justice, charity, and so forth, since these cannot be without grace, and yet no aureole is due to them. Therefore seemingly neither is an aureole due to martyrdom.

Obj. 10. Further, even as the truth of faith is from God, so is all other truth, as Ambrose† declares, since *every truth by whomsoever uttered is from the Holy Ghost.* Therefore if an aureole is due to one who suffers death for the truth of faith, in like manner it is also due to those who suffer death for any other virtue: and yet apparently this is not the case.

Obj. 11. Further, the common good is greater than the good of the individual. Now if a man die in a just war in order to save his country, an aureole is not due to him. Therefore even though he be put to death in order to keep the faith that is in himself, no aureole is due to him: and consequently the same conclusion follows as above.

Obj. 12. Further, all merit proceeds from the free will. Yet the Church celebrates the martyrdom of some who had not the use of the free will. Therefore they did not merit an aureole: and consequently an aureole is not due to all martyrs.

On the contrary, Augustine says (*De Sancta Virgin.* xlvi): *No one, methinks, would dare prefer virginity to martyrdom.* Now an aureole is due to virginity, and consequently also to martyrdom.

Further, the crown is due to one who has striven. But in martyrdom the strife presents a special difficulty. Therefore a special aureole is due thereto.

I answer that, Just as in the spirit there is a conflict with the internal concupiscences, so is there in man a conflict with the passion that is inflicted from without. Wherefore, just as a special crown, which we call an aureole, is due to the most perfect victory whereby we triumph over the concupiscences of the flesh, in a word to virginity, so too an aureole is due to the most perfect victory that is won against external assaults. Now the most perfect victory over passion caused from without is considered from two points of view. First from the greatness of the passion. Now among all passions inflicted from without, death holds the first place, just as sexual concupiscences

---

* *Ep. ad Paul. et Eustoch.*   † Spurious work on 1 Cor. xii. 3, *No man can say,* etc.

are chief among internal passions. Consequently, when a man conquers death and things directed to death, his is a most perfect victory. Secondly, the perfection of victory is considered from the point of view of the motive of conflict, when, to wit, a man strives for the most honorable cause; which is Christ Himself. Both these things are to be found in martyrdom, which is death suffered for Christ's sake: for *it is not the pain but the cause that makes the martyr,* as Augustine says *(Contra Crescon.* iii). Consequently an aureole is due to martyrdom as well as to virginity.

Reply Obj. 1. To suffer death for Christ's sake, is absolutely speaking, a work of supererogation; since every one is not bound to confess his faith in the face of a persecutor: yet in certain cases it is necessary for salvation, when, to wit, a person is seized by a persecutor and interrogated as to his faith which he is then bound to confess. Nor does it follow that he does not merit an aureole. For an aureole is due to a work of supererogation, not as such, but as having a certain perfection. Wherefore so long as this perfection remains, even though the supererogation cease, one merits the aureole.

Reply Obj. 2. A reward is due to martyrdom, not in respect of the exterior infliction, but because it is suffered voluntarily: since we merit only through that which is in us. And the more that which one suffers voluntarily is difficult and naturally repugnant to the will, the more is the will that suffers it for Christ's sake shown to be firmly established in Christ, and consequently a higher reward is due to him.

Reply Obj. 3. There are certain acts which, in their very selves, contain intense pleasure or difficulty: and in such the act always adds to the character of merit or demerit, for as much as in the performance of the act the will, on account of the aforesaid intensity, must needs undergo an alteration from the state in which it was before. Consequently, other things being equal, one who performs an act of lust sins more than one who merely consents in the act, because in the very act the will is increased. In like manner since in the act of suffering martyrdom there is a very great difficulty, the will to suffer martyrdom does not reach the degree of merit due to actual martyrdom by reason of its difficulty: although, indeed it may possibly attain to a higher reward, if we consider the root of merit, since the will of one man to suffer martyrdom may possibly proceed from a greater charity than another man's act of martyrdom. Hence one who is willing to be a martyr may by his

* Cf. II-II, Q. 64, A. 5.

will merit an essential reward equal to or greater than that which is due to an actual martyr. But the aureole is due to the difficulty inherent to the conflict itself of martyrdom: wherefore it is not due to those who are martyrs only in will.

Reply Obj. 4. Just as pleasures of touch, which are the matter of temperance, hold the chief place among all pleasures both internal and external, so pains of touch surpass all other pains. Consequently an aureole is due to the difficulty of suffering pains of touch, for instance, from blows and so forth, rather than to the difficulty of bearing internal sufferings, by reason of which, however, one is not properly called a martyr, except by a kind of comparison. It is in this sense that Jerome speaks.

Reply Obj. 5. The sufferings of penance are not a martyrdom properly speaking, because they do not consist in things directed to the causing of death, since they are directed merely to the taming of the flesh: and if any one go beyond this measure, such afflictions will be deserving of blame. However such afflictions are spoken of as a martyrdom by a kind of comparison; and they surpass the sufferings of martyrdom in duration but not in intensity.

Reply Obj. 6. According to Augustine *(De Civ. Dei,* i) it is lawful to no one to lay hands on himself for any reason whatever; unless perchance it be done by Divine instinct as an example of fortitude that others may despise death. Those to whom the objection refers are believed to have brought death on themselves by Divine instinct, and for this reason the Church celebrates their martyrdom.*

Reply Obj. 7. If any one receive a mortal wound for the faith and survive, without doubt he merits the aureole: as instanced in blessed Cecilia who survived for three days, and many martyrs who died in prison. But, even if the wound he receives be not mortal, yet be the occasion of his dying, he is believed to merit the aureole: although some say that he does not merit the aureole if he happen to die through his own carelessness or neglect. For this neglect would not have occasioned his death, except on the supposition of the wound which he received for the faith: and consequently this wound previously received for the faith is the original occasion of his death, so that he would not seem to lose the aureole for that reason, unless his neglect were such as to involve a mortal sin, which would deprive him of both aurea and aureole. If, however, by some chance or other he were not to die of the mortal wound received, or again if the wounds received were not mortal, and he were to die while in prison, he would still merit the aureole. Hence the martyrdom of some saints is celebrated in the Church for that they died in prison, having been wounded long before, as in the case of Pope Marcellus. Accordingly in whatever way suffering for Christ's sake be continued unto death, whether death ensue or not, a man becomes a martyr and merits the aureole. If, however, it be not continued unto death, this is not a reason for calling a person a martyr, as in the case of the blessed Sylvester, whose feast the Church does not solemnize as a martyr's, since he ended his days in peace, although previously he had undergone certain sufferings.

Reply Obj. 8. Even as temperance is not about pleasures of money, honors, and the like, but only about pleasures of touch as being the principal of all, so fortitude is about dangers of death as being the greatest of all (*Ethic.* iii. 6). Consequently the aureole is due to such injuries only as are inflicted on a person's own body and are of a nature to cause death. Accordingly whether a person lose his temporalities, or his good name, or anything else of the kind, for Christ's sake, he does not for that reason become a martyr, nor merit the aureole. Nor is it possible to love ordinately external things more than one's body; and inordinate love does not help one to merit an aureole: nor again can sorrow for the loss of corporeal things be equal to the sorrow for the slaying of the body and other like things.*

Reply Obj. 9. The sufficient motive for martyrdom is not only confession of the faith, but any other virtue, not civic but infused, that has Christ for its end. For one becomes a witness of Christ by any virtuous act, inasmuch as the works which Christ perfects in us bear witness to His goodness. Hence some virgins were slain for virginity which they desired to keep, for instance blessed Agnes and others whose martyrdom is celebrated by the Church.

Reply Obj. 10 The truth of faith has Christ for end and object; and therefore the confession thereof, if suffering be added thereto, merits an aureole, not only on the part of the end but also on the part of the matter. But the confession of any other truth is not a sufficient motive for martyrdom by reason of its matter, but only on the part of the end; for instance if a person were willing to be slain for Christ's sake rather than sin against Him by telling any lie whatever.

Reply Obj. 11. The uncreated good surpasses all created good. Hence any created end, whether it be the common or a private good, cannot confer so great a goodness on an act as can the uncreated end, when, to wit,

an act is done for God's sake. Hence when a person dies for the common good without referring it to Christ, he will not merit the aureole; but if he refer it to Christ he will merit the aureole and he will be a martyr; for instance, if he defend his country from the attack of an enemy who designs to corrupt the faith of Christ, and suffer death in that defense.

Reply Obj. 12. Some say that the use of reason was by the Divine power accelerated in the Innocents slain for Christ's sake, even as in John the Baptist while yet in his mother's womb: and in that case they were truly martyrs in both act and will, and have the aureole. Others say, however, that they were martyrs in act only and not in will: and this seems to be the opinion of Bernard, who distinguishes three kinds of martyrs, as stated above (*Obj.* 3). In this case the Innocents, even as they do not fulfill all the conditions of martyrdom, and yet are martyrs in a sense, in that they died for Christ, so too they have the aureole, not in all its perfection, but by a kind of participation, in so far as they rejoice in having been slain in Christ's service; thus it, was stated above (A. 5) in reference to baptized children, that they will have a certain joy in their innocence and carnal integrity.†

SEVENTH ARTICLE

Whether an Aureole Is Due to Doctors?

We proceed thus to the Seventh Article:—

Objection 1. It would seem that an aureole is not due to doctors. For every reward to be had in the life to come will correspond to some act of virtue. But preaching or teaching is not the act of a virtue. Therefore an aureole is not due to teaching or preaching.

Obj. 2. Further, teaching and preaching are the result of studying and being taught. Now the things that are rewarded in the future life are not acquired by a man's study, since we merit not by our natural and acquired gifts. Therefore no aureole will be merited in the future life for teaching and preaching.

Obj. 3. Further, exaltation in the life to come corresponds to humiliation in the present life, because *he that humbleth himself shall be exalted* (Matth. xxiii. 12). But there is no humiliation in teaching and preaching, in fact they are occasions of pride; for a gloss on Matth. iv. 5, *Then the devil took Him up,* says that *the devil deceives many who are puffed up with the honor of the master's chair.* Therefore it would seem that an aureole is not due to preaching and teaching.

On the contrary, A gloss on Eph. i. 18, 19,

---

* Cf. II-II, Q. 124, A. 5.

† Cf. II-II, Q. 124, A. 1, *ad* 1, where S. Thomas declares that the Holy Innocents were truly martyrs.

That you may know . . . what is the exceeding greatness, etc., says: *The holy doctors will have an increase of glory above that which all have in common.* Therefore, etc.

Further, a gloss on Cant. viii. 12, *My vineyard is before me,* says: *He describes the peculiar reward which He has prepared for His doctors.* Therefore doctors will have a peculiar reward: and we call this an aureole.

I answer that, Just as by virginity and martyrdom a person wins a most perfect victory over the flesh and the world, so is a most perfect victory gained over the devil, when a person not only refuses to yield to the devil's assaults, but also drives him out, not from himself alone, but from others also. Now this is done by preaching and teaching: wherefore an aureole is due to preaching and teaching, even as to virginity and martyrdom. Nor can we admit, as some affirm, that it is due to prelates only, who are competent to preach and teach by virtue of their office; but it is due to all whosoever exercise this act lawfully. Nor is it due to prelates, although they have the office of preaching, unless they actually preach, since a crown is due not to the habit, but to the actual strife, according to 2 Tim. ii. 5, *He . . . shall not be* (Vulg.,—*is not*) *crowned, except he strive lawfully.*

Reply Obj. 1. Preaching and teaching are acts of a virtue, namely mercy, wherefore they are reckoned among the spiritual alms deeds.*

Reply Obj. 2. Although ability to preach and teach is sometimes the outcome of study, the practice of teaching comes from the will, which is informed with charity infused by God: and thus its act can be meritorious.

Reply Obj. 3. Exaltation in this life does not lessen the reward of the other life, except for him who seeks his own glory from that exaltation: whereas he who turns that exaltation to the profit of others acquires thereby a reward for himself. Still, when it is stated that an aureole is due to teaching, this is to be understood of the teaching of things pertaining to salvation, by which teaching the devil is expelled from men's hearts, as by a kind of spiritual weapon, of which it is said (2 Cor. x. 4): *The weapons of our warfare are not carnal but spiritual* (Vulg.,—*but mighty to God*).

EIGHTH ARTICLE

Whether an Aureole Is Due to Christ?

We proceed thus to the Eighth Article:—

Objection 1. It would seem that an aureole is due to Christ. For an aureole is due to virginity, martyrdom, and teaching. Now these three were pre-eminently in Christ. Therefore an aureole is especially due to Him.

* Cf. II-II, Q. 32, A. 2.

Obj. 2. Further, whatever is most perfect in human things must be especially ascribed to Christ. Now an aureole is due as the reward of most excellent merits. Therefore it is also due to Christ.

Obj. 3. Further, Cyprian says (*De Habit. Virg.*) that *virginity bears a likeness to God.* Therefore the exemplar of virginity is in God. Therefore it would seem that an aureole is due to Christ even as God.

On the contrary, An aureole is described as *joy in being conformed to Christ.* Now no one is conformed or likened to himself, as the Philosopher says (*Metaph., lib.* ix. 3). Therefore an aureole is not due to Christ.

Further, Christ's reward was never increased. Now Christ had no aureole from the moment of His conception, since then He had never fought. Therefore He never had an aureole afterwards.

I answer that, There are two opinions on this point. For some say that Christ has an aureole in its strict sense, seeing that in Him there is both conflict and victory, and consequently a crown in its proper acceptation. But if we consider the question carefully, although the notion of aurea or crown is becoming to Christ, the notion of aureole is not. For from the very fact that aureole is a diminutive term it follows that it denotes something possessed by participation and not in its fulness. Wherefore an aureole is becoming to those who participate in the perfect victory by imitating Him in Whom the fulness of perfect victory is realized. And therefore, since in Christ the notion of victory is found chiefly and fully, for by His victory others are made victors,—as shown by the words of John xvi. 33, *Have confidence, I have overcome the world,* and Apoc. v. 5, *Behold the lion of the tribe of Juda . . . hath prevailed,*—it is not becoming for Christ to have an aureole, but to have something from which all aureoles are derived. Hence it is written (Apoc. iii. 21): *To him that shall overcome, I will give to sit with Me in My throne, as I also have overcome, and am set down in My Father's throne* (Vulg.,—*With My Father in His throne*). Therefore we must say with others that although there is nothing of the nature of an aureole in Christ, there is nevertheless something more excellent than any aureole.

Reply Obj. 1. Christ was most truly virgin, martyr, and doctor; yet the corresponding accidental reward in Christ is a negligible quantity in comparison with the greatness of His essential reward. Hence He has not an aureole in its proper sense.

Reply Obj. 2. Although the aureole is due to a most perfect work, yet with regard to us, so far as it is a diminutive term, it denotes the participation of a perfection derived from one in whom that perfection is found in its fulness. Accordingly it implies a certain inferiority, and thus it is not found in Christ in Whom is the fulness of every perfection.

Reply Obj. 3. Although in some way virginity has its exemplar in God, that exemplar is not homogeneous. For the incorruption of God, which virginity imitates, is not in God in the same way as in a virgin.

NINTH ARTICLE

Whether an Aureole Is Due to the Angels?

We proceed thus to the Ninth Article:—

Objection 1. It would seem that an aureole is due to the angels. For Jerome (*Serm. de Assump.*)* speaking of virginity says: *To live without the flesh while living in the flesh is to live as an angel rather than as a man:* and a gloss on 1 Cor. vii. 26, *For the present necessity,* says that *virginity is the portion of the angels.* Since then an aureole corresponds to virginity, it would seem due to the angels.

Obj. 2. Further, incorruption of the spirit is more excellent than incorruption of the flesh. Now there is incorruption of spirit in the angels, since they never sinned. Therefore an aureole is due to them rather than to men incorrupt in the flesh and who have sinned at some time.

Obj. 3. Further, an auroele is due to teaching. Now angels teach us by cleansing, enlightening, and perfecting† us, as Dionysius says (*Hier. Eccles.* vi). Therefore at least the aureole of doctors is due to them.

On the contrary, It is written (2 Tim. ii. 5): *He . . . shall not be* (Vulg.,—*is not*) *crowned, except he strive lawfully.* But there is no conflict in the angels. Therefore an aureole is not due to them.

Further, an aureole is not due to an act that is not performed through the body: wherefore it is not due to lovers of virginity, martyrdom, or teaching, if they do not practice them outwardly. But angels are incorporeal spirits. Therefore they have no aureole.

I answer that, An aureole is not due to the angels. The reason of this is that an aureole, properly speaking, corresponds to some perfection of surpassing merit. Now those things which make for perfect merit in man are connatural to angels, or belong to their state in general, or to their essential reward. Wherefore the angels have not an aureole in the same sense as an aureole is due to men.

Reply Obj. 1. Virginity is said to be an angelic life, in so far as virgins imitate by grace what angels have by nature. For it is

not owing to a virtue that angels abstain altogether from pleasures of the flesh, since they are incapable of such pleasures.

Reply Obj. 2. Perpetual incorruption of the spirit in the angels merits their essential reward: because it is necessary for their salvation, since in them recovery is impossible after they have fallen.‡

Reply Obj. 3. The acts whereby the angels teach us belong to their glory and their common state: wherefore they do not merit an aureole thereby.

TENTH ARTICLE

Whether an Aureole Is Also Due to the Body?

We proceed thus to the Tenth Article:—

Objection 1. It would seem that an aureole is also due to the body. For the essential reward is greater than the accidental. But the dowries which belong to the essential reward are not only in the soul but also in the body. Therefore there is also an aureole which pertains to the accidental reward.

Obj. 2. Further, punishment in soul and body corresponds to sin committed through the body. Therefore a reward both in soul and in body is due to merit gained through the body. But the aureole is merited through works of the body. Therefore an aureole is also due to the body.

Obj. 3. Further, a certain fulness of virtue will shine forth in the bodies of martyrs, and will be seen in their bodily scars: wherefore Augustine says (*De Civ. Dei,* xxii): *We feel an undescribable love for the blessed martyrs so as to desire to see in that kingdom the scars of the wounds in their bodies, which they bore for Christ's name. Perchance indeed we shall see them, for this will not make them less comely, but more glorious. A certain beauty will shine in them, a beauty, though in the body, yet not of the body but of virtue.* Therefore it would seem that the martyr's aureole is also in his body; and in like manner the aureoles of others.

On the contrary, The souls now in heaven have aureoles; and yet they have no body. Therefore the proper subject of an aureole is the soul and not the body.

Further, all merit is from the soul. Therefore the whole reward should be in the soul.

I answer that, Properly speaking the aureole is in the mind: since it is joy in the works to which an aureole is due. But even as from the joy in the essential reward, which is the aurea, there results a certain comeliness in the body, which is the glory of the body, so from the joy in the aureole there results a certain bodily comeliness: so that the aureole is

* *Ep. ad Paul. et Eustoch.,* ix.   † Cf. P. I, Q. 111, A. 1.   ‡ Cf. P. I, Q. 64, A. 2.

chiefly in the mind, but by a kind of overflow it shines forth in the body.

This suffices for the *Replies* to the *Objections*. It must be observed, however, that the beauty of the scars which will appear in the bodies of the martyrs cannot be called an aureole, since some of the martyrs will have an aureole in which such scars will not appear, for instance those who were put to death by drowning, starvation, or the squalor of prison.

ELEVENTH ARTICLE

Whether Three Aureoles Are Fittingly Assigned, Those of Virgins, of Martyrs, and of Doctors?

We proceed thus to the Eleventh Article:—

Objection 1. It would seem that the three aureoles of virgins, martyrs, and doctors are unfittingly assigned. For the aureole of martyrs corresponds to their virtue of fortitude, the aureole of virgins to the virtue of temperance, and the aureole of doctors to the virtue of prudence. Therefore it seems that there should be a fourth aureole corresponding to the virtue of justice.

Obj. 2. Further, a gloss on Exod. xxv. 25: *A polished crown*, etc., says that a golden (*aurea*) crown is added, when the Gospel promises eternal life to those who keep the commandments: '*If thou wilt enter into life, keep the commandments*' (Matth. xix. 17). *To this is added the little golden crown (aureola) when it is said: 'If thou wilt be perfect, go and sell all that thou hast, and give to the poor' (ibid.* 21). Therefore an aureole is due to poverty.

Obj. 3. Further, a man subjects himself wholly to God by the vow of obedience: wherefore the greatest perfection consists in the vow of obedience. Therefore it would seem that an aureole is due thereto.

Obj. 4. Further, there are also many other works of supererogation in which one will rejoice in the life to come. Therefore there are many aureoles besides the aforesaid three.

Obj. 5. Further, just as a man spreads the faith by preaching and teaching, so does he by publishing written works. Therefore a fourth aureole is due to those who do this.

I answer that, An aureole is an exceptional reward corresponding to an exceptional victory: wherefore the three aureoles are assigned in accordance with the exceptional victories in the three conflicts which beset every man. For in the conflict with the flesh, he above all wins the victory who abstains altogether from sexual pleasures which are the chief of this kind; and such is a virgin. Wherefore an aureole is due to virginity. In the conflict with the world, the chief victory is to suffer the world's persecution even until death: wherefore the

second aureole is due to martyrs who win the victory in this battle. In the conflict with the devil, the chief victory is to expel the enemy not only from oneself but also from the hearts of others: this is done by teaching and preaching, and consequently the third aureole is due to doctors and preachers.

Some, however, distinguish the three aureoles in accordance with the three powers of the soul, by saying that the three aureoles correspond to the three chief acts of the soul's three highest powers. For the act of the rational power is to publish the truth of faith even to others, and to this act the aureole of doctors is due: the highest act of the irascible power is to overcome even death for Christ's sake, and to this act the aureole of martyrs is due: and the highest act of the concupiscible power is to abstain altogether from the greatest carnal pleasures, and to this act the aureole of virgins is due.

Others again, distinguish the three aureoles in accordance with those things whereby we are most signally conformed to Christ. For He was the mediator between the Father and the world. Hence He was a doctor, by manifesting to the world the truth which He had received from the Father; He was a martyr, by suffering the persecution of the world; and He was a virgin, by His personal purity. Wherefore doctors, martyrs and virgins are most perfectly conformed to Him: and for this reason an aureole is due to them.

Reply Obj. 1. There is no conflict to be observed in the act of justice as in the acts of the other virtues. Nor is it true that to teach is an act of prudence: in fact rather is it an act of charity or mercy,—inasmuch as it is by such like habits that we are inclined to the practice of such an act,—or again of wisdom, as directing it.

We may also reply, with others, that justice embraces all the virtues, wherefore a special aureole is not due to it.

Reply Obj. 2. Although poverty is a work of perfection, it does not take the highest place in a spiritual conflict, because the love of temporalities assails a man less than carnal concupiscence or persecution whereby his own body is broken. Hence an aureole is not due to poverty; but judicial power by reason of the humiliation consequent upon poverty. The gloss quoted takes aureole in the broad sense for any reward given for excellent merit.

We reply in the same way to the *Third* and *Fourth Objections*.

Reply Obj. 5. An aureole is due to those who commit the sacred doctrine to writing: but it is not distinct from the aureole of doctors, since the compiling of writing is a way of teaching.

TWELFTH ARTICLE

Whether the Virgin's Aureole Is the Greatest of All?

We proceed thus to the Twelfth Article:—

Objection 1. It would seem that the virgin's aureole is the greatest of all. For it is said of virgins (Apoc. xiv. 4) that they *follow the Lamb whithersoever He goeth,* and *(ibid.* 3) that *no* other *man could say the canticle* which the virgins sang. Therefore virgins have the most excellent aureole.

Obj. 2. Further, Cyprian *(De Habit. Virg.)* says of virgins that they are *the more illustrious portion of Christ's flock.* Therefore the greater aureole is due to them.

Obj. 3. Again, it would seem that the martyr's aureole is the greatest. For Aymo, commenting on Apoc. xiv. 3, *No man could say the hymn,* says that *virgins do not all take precedence of married folk; but only those who in addition to the observance of virginity are by the tortures of their passion on a par with married persons who have suffered martyrdom.* Therefore martyrdom gives virginity its precedence over other states: and consequently a greater aureole is due to virginity.

Obj. 4. Again, it would seem that the greatest aureole is due to doctors. Because the Church militant is modelled after the Church triumphant. Now in the Church militant the greatest honor is due to doctors (1 Tim v. 17): *Let the priests that rule well be esteemed worthy of double honor, especially they who labor in the word and doctrine.* Therefore a greater aureole is due to them in the Church triumphant.

I answer that, Precedence of one aureole over another may be considered from two standpoints. First, from the point of view of the conflicts, that aureole being considered greater which is due to the more strenuous battle. Looking at it thus the martyr's aureole takes precedence of the others in one way, and the virgin's in another. For the martyr's battle is more strenuous in itself, and more intensely painful; while the conflict with the flesh is fraught with greater danger, inasmuch as it is more lasting and threatens us at closer quarters. Secondly, from the point of view of the things about which the battle is fought: and thus the doctor's aureole takes precedence of all others, since this conflict is about intelligible goods; while the other conflicts are about sensible passions. Nevertheless, the precedence that is considered in view of the conflict is more essential to the aureole; since the aureole, according to its proper character, regards the victory and the battle, and the difficulty of fighting which is viewed from the standpoint of the battle is of greater importance than that which is considered from our standpoint through the conflict being at closer quarters. Therefore the martyr's aureole is simply the greatest of all: for which reason a gloss on Matth. v. 10, says that *all the other beatitudes are perfected in the eighth, which refers to the martyrs,* namely, *Blessed are they that suffer persecution.* For this reason, too, the Church in enumerating the saints together places the martyrs before the doctors and virgins. Yet nothing hinders the other aureoles from being more excellent in some particular way. And this suffices for the *Replies* to the *Objections.*

THIRTEENTH ARTICLE

Whether One Person Has an Aureole More Excellently Than Another Person?

We proceed thus to the Thirteenth Article:—

Objection 1. It would seem that one person has not the aureole either of virginity, or of martyrdom, or of doctrine more perfectly than another person. For things which have reached their term are not subject to intension or remission. Now the aureole is due to works which have reached their term of perfection. Therefore an aureole is not subject to intension or remission.

Obj. 2. Further, virginity is not subject to being more or less, since it denotes a kind of privation; and privations are not subject to intension or remission. Therefore neither does the reward of virginity, the virgin's aureole to wit, receive intension or remission.

On the contrary, The aureole is added to the aurea. But the aurea is more intense in one than in another. Therefore the aureole is also.

I answer that, Since merit is somewhat the cause of reward, rewards must needs be diversified, according as merits are diversified: for the intension or remission of a thing follows from the intension or remission of its cause. Now the merit of the aureole may be greater or lesser: wherefore the aureole may also be greater or lesser.

We must observe, however, that the merit of an aureole may be intensified in two ways: first, on the part of its cause, secondly on the part of the work. For there may happen to be two persons, one of whom, out of lesser charity, suffers greater torments of martyrdom, or is more constant in preaching, or again withdraws himself more from carnal pleasures. Accordingly, intension not of the aureole but of the aurea corresponds to the intension of merit derived from its root; while intension of the aureole corresponds to intension of merit derived from the kind of act. Consequently it is possible for one who merits less in martyrdom as to his essential reward, to receive a greater aureole for his martyrdom.

Reply Obj. 1. The merits to which an aureole is due do not reach the term of their perfection simply, but according to their species: even as fire is specifically the most subtle of bodies. Hence nothing hinders one aureole being more excellent than another, even as one fire is more subtle than another.

Reply Obj. 2. The virginity of one may be greater than the virginity of another, by reason of a greater withdrawal from that which is contrary to virginity: so that virginity is stated to be greater in one who avoids more the occasions of corruption. For in this way privations may increase, as when a man is said to be more blind, if he be removed further from the possession of sight.

QUESTION 97

Of the Punishment of the Damned

(In Seven Articles)

IN due sequence we must consider those things that concern the damned after the judgment: (1) The punishment of the damned, and the fire by which their bodies will be tormented; (2) matters relating to their will and intellect; (3) God's justice and mercy in regard to the damned.

Under the first head there are seven points of inquiry: (1) Whether in hell the damned are tormented with the sole punishment of fire? (2) Whether the worm by which they are tormented is corporeal? (3) Whether their weeping is corporeal? (4) Whether their darkness is material? (5) Whether the fire whereby they are tormented is corporeal? (6) Whether it is of the same species as our fire? (7) Whether this fire is beneath the earth?

FIRST ARTICLE

Whether in Hell the Damned Are Tormented by the Sole Punishment of Fire?

We proceed thus to the First Article:—

Objection 1. It would seem that in hell the damned are tormented by the sole punishment of fire; because Matth. xxv. 41, where their condemnation is declared, mention is made of fire only, in the words: *Depart from Me, you cursed, into everlasting fire.*

Obj. 2. Further, even as the punishment of purgatory is due to venial sin, so is the punishment of hell due to mortal sin. Now no other punishment but that of fire is stated to be in purgatory, as appears from the words of 1 Cor. iii. 13: *The fire shall try every man's work, of what sort it is.* Therefore neither in hell will there be a punishment other than of fire.

Obj. 3. Further, variety of punishment affords a respite, as when one passes from heat to cold. But we can admit no respite in the damned. Therefore there will not be various punishments, but that of fire alone.

On the contrary, It is written (Ps. x. 7):

Fire and brimstone and storms of winds shall be the portion of their cup.

Further, it is written (Job. xxiv. 19): *Let him pass from the snow waters to excessive heat.*

I answer that, According to Basil (*Homilia* vi, *in Hexaemeron,* and *Hom.* i, *in Ps.* xxviii), at the final cleansing of the world, there will be a separation of the elements, whatever is pure and noble remaining above for the glory of the blessed, and whatever is ignoble and sordid being cast down for the punishment of the damned: so that just as every creature will be to the blessed a matter of joy, so will all the elements conduce to the torture of the damned, according to Wis. v. 21, *the whole world will fight with Him against the unwise.* This is also becoming to Divine justice, that whereas they departed from One by sin, and placed their end in material things which are many and various, so should they be tormented in many ways and from many sources.

Reply Obj. 1. It is because fire is most painful, through its abundance of active force, that the name of fire is given to any torment if it be intense.

Reply Obj. 2. The punishment of purgatory is not intended chiefly to torment, but to cleanse: wherefore it should be inflicted by fire alone which is above all possessed of cleansing power. But the punishment of the damned is not directed to their cleansing. Consequently the comparison fails.

Reply Obj. 3. The damned will pass from the most intense heat to the most intense cold, without this giving them any respite: because they will suffer from external agencies, not by the transmutation of their body from its original natural disposition, and the contrary passion affording a respite by restoring an equable or moderate temperature, as happens now, but by a spiritual action, in the same way as sensible objects act on the senses, being perceived by impressing the organ with their forms according to their spiritual and not their material being.

SECOND ARTICLE

Whether the Worm of the Damned Is Corporeal?

We proceed thus to the Second Article:—

Objection 1. It would seem that the worm by which the damned are tormented is corporeal. Because flesh cannot be tormented by a spiritual worm. Now the flesh of the damned will be tormented by a worm: *He will give fire and worms into their flesh* (Judith xvi. 21), and: *The vengeance on the flesh of the ungodly is fire and worms* (Ecclus. vii. 19). Therefore that worm will be corporeal.

Obj. 2. Further, Augustine says (*De Civ. Dei,* xxi. 9): . . . *Both, namely fire and worm, will be the punishment of the body.* Therefore, etc.

On the contrary, Augustine says (*De Civ. Dei,* xx. 22): *The unquenchable fire and the restless worm in the punishment of the damned are explained in various ways by different persons. Some refer both to the body, some, both to the soul: others refer the fire, in the literal sense, to the body, the worm to the soul metaphorically: and this seems the more probable.*

I answer that, After the day of judgment, no animal or mixed body will remain in the renewed world except only the body of man, because the former are not directed to incorruption,* nor after that time will there be generation or corruption. Consequently the worm ascribed to the damned must be understood to be not of a corporeal but of a spiritual nature: and this is the remorse of conscience, which is called a worm because it originates from the corruption of sin, and torments the soul, as a corporeal worm born of corruption torments by gnawing.

Reply Obj. 1. The very souls of the damned are called their flesh for as much as they were subject to the flesh. Or we may reply that the flesh will be tormented by the spiritual worm, according as the afflictions of the soul overflow into the body, both here and hereafter.

Reply Obj. 2. Augustine speaks by way of comparison. For he does not wish to assert absolutely that this worm is material, but that it is better to say that both are to be understood materially, than that both should be understood only in a spiritual sense: for then the damned would suffer no bodily pain. This is clear to anyone that examines the context of his words in this passage.

THIRD ARTICLE

Whether the Weeping of the Damned Will Be Corporeal?

We proceed thus to the Third Article:—

Objection 1. It would seem that the weep-

* Cf. Q. 91, A. 5.

ing of the damned will be corporeal. For a gloss on Luke xiii. 28, *There will be weeping,* says that *the weeping with which our Lord threatens the wicked is a proof of the resurrection of the body.* But this would not be the case if that weeping were merely spiritual. Therefore, etc.

Obj. 2. Further, the pain of the punishment corresponds to the pleasure of the sin, according to Apoc. xviii. 7: *As much as she hath glorified herself and lived in delicacies, so much torment and sorrow give ye to her.* Now sinners had internal and external pleasure in their sin. Therefore they will also have external weeping.

On the contrary, Corporeal weeping results from dissolving into tears. Now there cannot be a continual dissolution from the bodies of the damned, since nothing is restored to them by food; for everything finite is consumed if something be continually taken from it. Therefore the weeping of the damned will not be corporeal.

I answer that, Two things are to be observed in corporeal weeping. One is the resolution of tears: and as to this corporeal weeping cannot be in the damned, since after the day of judgment, the movement of the first movable being being at an end, there will be neither generation, nor corruption, nor bodily alteration: and in the resolution of tears that humor needs to be generated which is shed forth in the shape of tears. Wherefore in this respect it will be impossible for corporeal weeping to be in the damned. The other thing to be observed in corporeal weeping is a certain commotion and disturbance of the head and eyes, and in this respect weeping will be possible in the damned after the resurrection: for the bodies of the damned will be tormented not only from without, but also from within, according as the body is affected at the instance of the soul's passion towards good or evil. In this sense weeping is a proof of the body's resurrection, and corresponds to the pleasure of sin, experienced by both soul and body.

This suffices for the *Replies* to the *Objections.*

FOURTH ARTICLE

Whether the Damned Are in Material Darkness?

We proceed thus to the Fourth Article:—

Objection 1. It would seem that the damned are not in material darkness. For commenting on Job x. 22, *But everlasting horror dwelleth,* Gregory says (*Moral.* ix): *Although that fire will give no light for comfort, yet, that it may torment the more it does give light for a purpose, for by the light of its flame the wicked will see their followers whom they have drawn thither from the world.* Therefore the darkness there is not material.

Obj. 2. Further, the damned see their own punishment, for this increases their punishment. But nothing is seen without light. Therefore there is no material darkness there.

Obj. 3. Further, there the damned will have the power of sight after being reunited to their bodies. But this power would be useless to them unless they see something. Therefore, since nothing is seen unless it be in the light, it would seem that they are not in absolute darkness.

On the contrary, It is written (Matth. xxii. 13): *Bind his hands and his feet, and cast him into the exterior darkness.* Commenting on these words Gregory says *(Moral.* ix): If this fire gave any light, *he would by no means be described as cast into exterior darkness.*

Further, Basil says *(Hom.* i, *in Ps.* xxviii. 7, *The voice of the Lord divideth the flame of fire)* that *by God's might the brightness of the fire will be separated from its power of burning, so that its brightness will conduce to the joy of the blessed, and the heat of the flame to the torment of the damned.* Therefore the damned will be in material darkness.

Other points relating to the punishment of the damned have been decided above (Q. 86).

I answer that, The disposition of hell will be such as to be adapted to the utmost unhappiness of the damned. Wherefore accordingly both light and darkness are there, in so far as they are most conducive to the unhappiness of the damned. Now seeing is in itself pleasant for, as stated in *Metaph.* i, *the sense of sight is most esteemed, because thereby many things are known.* Yet it happens accidentally that seeing is painful, when we see things that are hurtful to us, or displeasing to our will. Consequently in hell the place must be so disposed for seeing as regards light and darkness, that nothing be seen clearly, and that only such things be dimly seen as are able to bring anguish to the heart. Wherefore, simply speaking, the place is dark. Yet by Divine disposition, there is a certain amount of light, as much as suffices for seeing those things which are capable of tormenting the soul. The natural situation of the place is enough for this, since in the centre of the earth, where hell is said to be, fire cannot be otherwise than thick and cloudy, and reeky as it were.

Some hold that this darkness is caused by the massing together of the bodies of the damned, which will so fill the place of hell with their numbers, that no air will remain, so that there will be no translucid body that can be the subject of light and darkness, ex-

cept the eyes of the damned, which will be darkened utterly.

This suffices for the *Replies* to the *Objections.*

FIFTH ARTICLE

Whether the Fire of Hell Will Be Corporeal?

We proceed thus to the Fifth Article:—

Objection 1. It would seem that the fire of hell whereby the bodies of the damned will be tormented will not be corporeal. For Damascene says *(De Fide Orthod.* iv): The devil, and *demons, and his man,** namely Antichrist, *together with the ungodly and sinners, will be cast into everlasting fire, not material fire, such as that which we have, but such as God knoweth.* Now everything corporeal is material. Therefore the fire of hell will not be corporeal.

Obj. 2. Further, the souls of the damned when severed from their bodies are cast into hell fire. But Augustine says *(Gen. ad Lit.* xii. 32): *In my opinion the place to which the soul is committed after death is spiritual and not corporeal.* Therefore, etc.

Obj. 3. Further, corporeal fire in the mode of its action does not follow the mode of guilt in the person who is burned at the stake, rather does it follow the mode of humid and dry: for in the same corporeal fire we see both good and wicked suffer. But the fire of hell, in its mode of torture or action, follows the mode of guilt in the person punished; wherefore Gregory says *(Dial.* iv. 63): *There is indeed but one hell fire, but it does not torture all sinners equally. For each one will suffer as much pain according as his guilt deserves.* Therefore this fire will not be corporeal.

On the contrary, He says *(Dial.* iv. 29): *I doubt not that the fire of hell is corporeal, since it is certain that bodies are tortured there.*

Further, it is written (Wis. v. 21): *The . . . world shall fight . . . against the unwise.* But the whole world would not fight against the unwise if they were punished with a spiritual and not a corporeal punishment. Therefore they will be punished with a corporeal fire.

I answer that, There have been many opinions about the fire of hell. For some philosophers, as Avicenna, disbelieving in the resurrection, thought that the soul alone would be punished after death. And as they considered it impossible for the soul, being incorporeal, to be punished with a corporeal fire, they denied that the fire whereby the wicked are punished is corporeal, and pretended that all statements as to souls being punished in future after death by any corporeal means are to be taken metaphorically. For just as the

---

* Cf. 2 Thess. ii. 3, *And the man of sin be revealed, the son of perdition.*

joy and happiness of good souls will not be about any corporeal object, but about something spiritual, namely the attainment of their end, so will the torment of the wicked be merely spiritual, in that they will be grieved at being separated from their end, the desire whereof is in them by nature. Wherefore, just as all descriptions of the soul's delight after death that seem to denote bodily pleasure,—for instance, that they are refreshed, that they smile, and so forth,—must be taken metaphorically, so also are all such descriptions of the soul's suffering as seem to imply bodily punishment,—for instance, that they burn in fire, or suffer from the stench, and so forth. For as spiritual pleasure and pain are unknown to the majority, these things need to be declared under the figure of corporeal pleasures and pains, in order that men may be moved the more to the desire or fear thereof. Since, however, in the punishment of the damned there will be not only pain of loss corresponding to the aversion that was in their sin, but also pain of sense corresponding to the conversion, it follows that it is not enough to hold the above manner of punishment. For this reason Avicenna himself (*Met.* ix) added another explanation, by saying that the souls of the wicked are punished after death, not by bodies but by images of bodies; just as in a dream it seems to a man that he is suffering various pains on account of such like images being in his imagination. Even Augustine seems to hold this kind of punishment (*Gen. ad Lit.* xii. 32), as is clear from the text. But this would seem an unreasonable statement. For the imagination is a power that makes use of a bodily organ: so that it is impossible for such visions of the imagination to occur in the soul separated from the body, as in the soul of the dreamer. Wherefore Avicenna also, that he might avoid this difficulty, said that the soul separated from the body uses as an organ some part of the heavenly body, to which the human body needs to be conformed, in order to be perfected by the rational soul, which is like the movers of the heavenly body,—thus following somewhat the opinion of certain philosophers of old, who maintained that souls return to the stars that are their compeers. But this is absolutely absurd according to the Philosopher's teaching, since the soul uses a definite bodily organ, even as art uses definite instruments, so that it cannot pass from one body to another, as Pythagoras is stated (*De Anima* i, text. 53) to have maintained. As to the statement of Augustine we shall say below how it is to be answered (*ad* 2). However, whatever we may say of the fire that torments the separated souls, we must admit that the fire which will torment the

bodies of the damned after the resurrection is corporeal, since one cannot fittingly apply a punishment to a body unless that punishment itself be bodily. Wherefore Gregory (*Dial.* iv) proves the fire of hell to be corporeal from the very fact that the wicked will be cast thither after the resurrection. Again Augustine, as quoted in the text of iv. *Sent.* D. 44, clearly admits (*De Civ. Dei*, xxi. 10) that the fire by which the bodies are tormented is corporeal. And this is the point at issue for the present. We have said elsewhere (Q. 70, A. 3) how the souls of the damned are punished by this corporeal fire.

Reply Obj. 1. Damascene does not absolutely deny that this fire is material, but that it is material as our fire, since it differs from ours in some of its properties. We may also reply that since that fire does not alter bodies as to their matter, but acts on them for their punishment by a kind of spiritual action, it is for this reason that it is stated not to be material, not as regards its substance, but as to its punitive effect on bodies and, still more, on souls.

Reply Obj. 2. The assertion of Augustine may be taken in this way, that the place whither souls are conveyed after death be described as incorporeal, in so far as the soul is there, not corporeally, i.e. as bodies are in a place, but in some other spiritual way, as angels are in a place. Or we may reply that Augustine is expressing an opinion without deciding the point, as he often does in those books.

Reply Obj. 3. That fire will be the instrument of Divine justice inflicting punishment. Now an instrument acts not only by its own power and in its own way, but also by the power of the principal agent, and as directed thereby. Wherefore although fire is not able, of its own power, to torture certain persons more or less, according to the measure of sin, it is able to do so nevertheless in so far as its action is regulated by the ordering of Divine justice: even so the fire of the furnace is regulated by the forethought of the smith, according as the effect of his art requires.

SIXTH ARTICLE

Whether the Fire of Hell Is of the Same Species As Ours?

We proceed thus to the Sixth Article:—

Objection 1. It would seem that this fire is not of the same species as the corporeal fire which we see. For Augustine says (*De Civ. Dei*, xx. 16): *In my opinion no man knows of what kind is the everlasting fire, unless the Spirit of God has revealed it to anyone.* But all or nearly all know the nature of this fire of ours. Therefore that fire is not of the same species as this.

Obj. 2. Further, Gregory commenting on Job xx. 26, *A fire that is not kindled shall devour him,* says (*Moral.* xv): *Bodily fire needs bodily fuel in order to become fire; neither can it be except by being kindled, nor live unless it be renewed.* On the other hand the fire of hell, since it is a bodily fire, and burns in a bodily way the wicked cast therein, is neither kindled by human endeavor, nor kept alive with fuel, but once created endures unquenchably; at one and the same time it needs no kindling, and lacks not heat. Therefore it is not of the same nature as the fire that we see.

Obj. 3. Further, the everlasting and the corruptible differ essentially, since they agree not even in genus, according to the Philosopher (*Metaph.* x). But this fire of ours is corruptible, whereas the other is everlasting: *Depart from Me, you cursed, into everlasting fire* (Matth. xxv. 41). Therefore they are not of the same nature.

Obj. 4. Further, it belongs to the nature of this fire of ours to give light. But the fire of hell gives no light, hence the saying of Job xviii. 5: *Shall not the light of the wicked be extinguished?* Therefore . . . as above.

On the contrary, According to the Philosopher (*Top.* i. 6), *every water is of the same species as every other water.* Therefore in like manner every fire is of the same species as every other fire.

Further, it is written (Wis. xi. 17): *By what things a man sinneth by the same also he is tormented.* Now men sin by the sensible things of this world. Therefore it is just that they should be punished by those same things.

I answer that, As stated in *Meteor.* iv. 1, fire has other bodies for its matter, for the reason that of all the elements it has the greatest power of action. Hence fire is found under two conditions: in its own matter, as existing in its own sphere, and in a strange matter, whether of earth, as in burning coal, or of air, as in the flame. Under whatever conditions however fire be found, it is always of the same species, so far as the nature of fire is concerned, but there may be a difference of species as to the bodies which are the matter of fire. Wherefore flame and burning coal differ specifically, and likewise burning wood and red-hot iron; nor does it signify, as to this particular point, whether they be kindled by force, as in the case of iron, or by a natural intrinsic principle, as happens with sulphur. Accordingly it is clear that the fire of hell is of the same species as the fire we have, so far as the nature of fire is concerned. But whether that fire subsists in its proper matter, or if it

subsists in a strange matter, what that matter may be, we know not. And in this way it may differ specifically from the fire we have, considered materially. It has, however, certain properties differing from our fire, for instance that it needs no kindling, nor is kept alive by fuel. But the differences do not argue a difference of species as regards the nature of the fire.

Reply Obj. 1. Augustine is speaking of that fire with regard to its matter, and not with regard to its nature.

Reply Obj. 2. This fire of ours is kept alive with fuel, and is kindled by man, because it is introduced into a foreign matter by art and force. But that other fire needs no fuel to keep it alive, because either it subsists in its own matter, or is in a foreign matter, not by force but by nature from an intrinsic principle. Wherefore it is kindled not by man but by God, Who fashioned its nature. This is the meaning of the words of Isaias (xxx. 33): *The breath of the Lord is as a torrent of brimstone kindling it.*

Reply Obj. 3. Even as the bodies of the damned will be of the same species as now, although now they are corruptible, whereas then they will be incorruptible, both by the ordering of Divine justice, and on account of the cessation of the heavenly movement, so is it with the fire of hell whereby those bodies will be punished.

Reply Obj. 4. To give light does not belong to fire according to any mode of existence, since in its own matter it gives no light; wherefore it does not shine in its own sphere according to the philosophers: and in like manner in certain foreign matters it does not shine, as when it is in an opaque earthly substance such as sulphur. The same happens also when its brightness is obscured by thick smoke. Wherefore that the fire of hell gives no light is not sufficient proof of its being of a different species.

SEVENTH ARTICLE

Whether the Fire of Hell Is Beneath the Earth?

We proceed thus to the Seventh Article:—

Objection 1. It would seem that this fire is not beneath the earth. For it is said of the damned (Job xviii. 18), *And God shall remove him out of the globe* (Douay,—*world*). Therefore the fire whereby the damned will be punished is not beneath the earth but outside the globe.

Obj. 2. Further, nothing violent or accidental can be everlasting. But this fire will be in hell for ever. Therefore it will be there, not by force but naturally. Now fire cannot be under the earth save by violence. Therefore the fire of hell is not beneath the earth.

Obj. 3. Further, after the day of judgment the bodies of all the damned will be tormented in hell. Now those bodies will fill a place. Consequently, since the multitude of the damned will be exceeding great, for *the number of fools is infinite* (Eccles. i. 15), the space containing that fire must also be exceeding great. But it would seem unreasonable to say that there is so great a hollow within the earth, since all the parts of the earth naturally tend to the center. Therefore that fire will not be beneath the earth.

Obj. 4. Further, *By what things a man sinneth, by the same also he is tormented* (Wis. xi. 17). But the wicked have sinned on the earth. Therefore the fire that punishes them should not be under the earth.

On the contrary, It is witten (Isa. xiv. 9): *Hell below was in an uproar to meet Thee at Thy coming.* Therefore the fire of hell is beneath us.

Further, Gregory says *(Dial.* iv): *I see not what hinders us from believing that hell is beneath the earth.*

Further, a gloss on Jonas ii. 4, *Thou hast cast me forth . . . into the heart of the sea,* says, *i.e. into hell,* and in the Gospel (Matth. xii. 40) the words *in the heart of the earth* have the same sense, for as the heart is in the middle of an animal, so is hell supposed to be in the middle of the earth.

I answer that, As Augustine says *(De Civ. Dei,* xv. 16), *I am of opinion that no one knows in what part of the world hell is situated, unless the Spirit of God has revealed this to some one.* Wherefore Gregory *(Dial.* iv) having been questioned on this point answers: *About this matter I dare not give a rash decision. For some have deemed hell to be in some part of the earth's surface; others think it to be beneath the earth.* He shows the latter opinion to be the more probable for two reasons. First from the very meaning of the word. These are his words: *If we call it the nether regions (infernus),** for the reason that it is beneath us (inferius), what earth is in relation to heaven, such should be hell in relation to earth.* Secondly, from the words of Apoc. v. 3: *No man was able, neither in heaven, nor on earth, nor under the earth, to open the book:* where the words *in heaven* refer to the angels, *on earth* to men living in the body, and *under the earth* to souls in hell. Augustine too *(Gen. ad Lit.* xii. 34) seems to indicate two reasons for the congruity of hell being under the earth. One is that *whereas the souls of the departed sinned through love of the flesh, they should be treated as the dead flesh is wont to be*

treated, by being buried beneath the earth. The other is that heaviness is to the body what sorrow is to the spirit, and joy (of spirit) is as lightness (of body). Wherefore *just as in reference to the body, all the heavier things are beneath the others, if they be placed in order of gravity, so in reference to the spirit, the lower place is occupied by whatever is more sorrowful;* and thus even as the empyrean is a fitting place for the joy of the elect, so the lowest part of the earth is a fitting place for the sorrow of the damned. Nor does it signify that Augustine *(ibid.)* says that *hell is stated or believed to be under the earth,* because he withdraws this *(Retract.* ii. 29) where he says: *Methinks I should have said that hell is beneath the earth, rather than have given the reason why it is stated or believed to be under the earth.* However, some philosophers have maintained that hell is situated beneath the terrestrial orb, but above the surface of the earth, on that part which is opposite to us. This seems to have been the meaning of Isidore when he asserted that *the sun and the moon will stop in the place wherein they were created, lest the wicked should enjoy this light in the midst of their torments.* But this is no argument, if we assert that hell is under the earth. We have already stated how these words may be explained (Q. 91, A. 2).

Pythagoras held the place of punishment to be in a fiery sphere situated, according to him, in the middle of the whole world: and he called it the prison-house of Jupiter as Aristotle relates *(De Cœlo et Mundo,* ii). It is, however, more in keeping with Scripture to say that it is beneath the earth.

Reply Obj. 1. The words of Job, *God shall remove him out of the globe,* refer to the surface of the earth,† *i.e.* from this world. This is how Gregory expounds it *(Moral.* xiv) where he says: *He is removed from the globe when, at the coming of the heavenly judge, he is taken away from this world wherein he now prides himself in his wickedness.* Nor does globe here signify the universe, as though the place of punishment were outside the whole universe.

Reply Obj. 2. Fire continues in that place for all eternity by the ordering of Divine justice although according to its nature an element cannot last for ever outside its own place, especially if things were to remain in this state of generation and corruption. The fire there will be of the very greatest heat, because its heat will be all gathered together from all parts, through being surrounded on all sides by the cold of the earth.

Reply Obj. 3. Hell will never lack sufficient room to admit the bodies of the damned: since

* The Latin for *hell.*   † *De orbe terrarum,* which might be rendered *from the land of the living.*

hell is accounted one of the three things that *never are satisfied* (Prov. xxx. 15, 16). Nor is it unreasonable that God's power should maintain within the bowels of the earth a hollow great enough to contain all the bodies of the damned.

Reply Obj. 4. It does not follow of necessity that *by what things a man sinneth, by the same also he is tormented,* except as regards the principal instruments of sin: for as much as man having sinned in soul and body will be punished in both. But it does not follow that a man will be punished in the very place where he sinned, because the place due to the damned is other from that due to wayfarers. We may also reply that these words refer to the punishments inflicted on man on the way: according as each sin has its corresponding punishment, since *inordinate love is its own punishment,* as Augustine states *(Conf.* i. 12).

QUESTION 98

Of the Will and Intellect of the Damned

(In Nine Articles)

WE must next consider matters pertaining to the will and intellect of the damned. Under this head there are nine points of inquiry: (1) Whether every act of will in the damned is evil? (2) Whether they ever repent of the evil they have done? (3) Whether they would rather not be than be? (4) Whether they would wish others to be damned? (5) Whether the wicked hate God? (6) Whether they can demerit? (7) Whether they can make use of the knowledge acquired in this life? (8) Whether they ever think of God? (9) Whether they see the glory of the blessed?

FIRST ARTICLE

Whether Every Act of Will in the Damned Is Evil?

We proceed thus to the First Article:—

Objection 1. It would seem that not every act of will in the damned is evil. For according to Dionysius *(Div. Nom.* iv), *the demons desire the good and the best, namely to be, to live, to understand.* Since, then, men who are damned are not worse off than the demons, it would seem that they also can have a good will.

Obj. 2. Further, as Dionysius says *(ibid.),* *evil is altogether involuntary.* Therefore if the damned will anything, they will it as something good or apparently good. Now a will that is directly ordered to good is itself good. Therefore the damned can have a good will.

Obj. 3. Further, some will be damned who, while in this world, acquired certain habits of virtue, for instance heathens who had civic virtues. Now a will elicits praiseworthy acts by reason of virtuous habits. Therefore there may be praiseworthy acts of the will in some of the damned.

On the contrary, An obstinate will can never be inclined except to evil. Now men who are damned will be obstinate even as the demons.* Therefore their will can never be good.

Further, as the will of the damned is in relation to evil, so is the will of the blessed in regard to good. But the blessed never have an evil will. Neither therefore have the damned any good will.

I answer that, A twofold will may be considered in the damned, namely the deliberate will and the natural will. Their natural will is theirs not of themselves but of the Author of nature, Who gave nature this inclination which we call the natural will. Wherefore since nature remains in them, it follows that the natural will in them can be good. But their deliberate will is theirs of themselves, inasmuch as it is in their power to be inclined by their affections to this or that. This will is in them always evil: and this because they are completely turned away from the last end of a right will, nor can a will be good except it be directed to that same end. Hence even though they will some good, they do not will it well so that one be able to call their will good on that account.

Reply Obj. 1. The words of Dionysius must be understood of the natural will, which is nature's inclination to some particular good. And yet this natural inclination is corrupted by their wickedness, in so far as this good which they desire naturally is desired by them under certain evil circumstances.†

Reply Obj. 2. Evil, as evil, does not move the will, but in so far as it is thought to be good. Yet it comes of their wickedness that they esteem that which is evil as though it were good. Hence their will is evil.

Reply Obj. 3. The habits of civic virtue do not remain in the separated soul, because those virtues perfect us only in the civic life which will not remain after this life. Even though they remained, they would never come into action, being enchained, as it were, by the obstinacy of the mind.

* Cf. P. I, Q. 64, A. 2.   † Cf. P. I, Q. 64, A. 2, *ad 5.*

SECOND ARTICLE

Whether the Damned Repent of the Evil They Have Done?

We proceed thus to the Second Article:—

Objection 1. It would seem that the damned never repent of the evil they have done. For Bernard says on the Canticle* that *the damned ever consent to the evil they have done.* Therefore they never repent of the sins they have committed.

Obj. 2. Further, to wish one had not sinned is a good will. But the damned will never have a good will. Therefore the damned will never wish they had not sinned: and thus the same conclusion follows as above.

Obj. 3. Further, according to Damascene *(De Fide Orthod.* ii), *death is to man what their fall was to the angels.* But the angel's will is irrevocable after his fall, so that he cannot withdraw from the choice whereby he previously sinned.† Therefore the damned also cannot repent of the sins committed by them.

Obj. 4. Further, the wickedness of the damned in hell will be greater than that of sinners in the world. Now in this world some sinners repent not of the sins they have committed, either through blindness of mind, as heretics, or through obstinacy, as those *who are glad when they have done evil, and rejoice in most wicked things* (Prov. ii. 14). Therefore, etc.

On the contrary, It is said of the damned (Wis. v. 3): *Repenting within themselves* (Vulg.,—*Saying within themselves, repenting*).

Further, the Philosopher says *(Ethic.* ix. 4) that *the wicked are full of repentance; for afterwards they are sorry for that in which previously they took pleasure.* Therefore the damned, being most wicked, repent all the more.

I answer that, A person may repent of sin in two ways: in one way directly, in another way indirectly. He repents of a sin directly who hates sin as such: and he repents indirectly who hates it on account of something connected with it, for instance punishment or something of that kind. Accordingly the wicked will not repent of their sins directly, because consent in the malice of sin will remain in them; but they will repent indirectly, inasmuch as they will suffer from the punishment inflicted on them for sin.

Reply Obj. 1. The damned will wickedness, but shun punishment: and thus indirectly they repent of wickedness committed.

Reply Obj. 2. To wish one had not sinned on account of the shamefulness of vice is a good will: but this will not be in the wicked.

Reply Obj. 3. It will be possible for the damned to repent of their sins without turning their will away from sin, because in their sins they will shun, not what they heretofore desired, but something else, namely the punishment.

Reply Obj. 4. However obstinate men may be in this world, they repent of the sins indirectly, if they be punished for them. Thus Augustine says (QQ. 83, *qu.* 36): *We see the most savage beasts are deterred from the greatest pleasures by fear of pain.*

THIRD ARTICLE

Whether the Damned by Right and Deliberate Reason Would Wish Not to Be?

We proceed thus to the Third Article:—

Objection 1. It would seem impossible for the damned, by right and deliberate reason, to wish not to be. For Augustine says *(De Lib. Arb.* iii. 7): *Consider how great a good it is to be; since both the happy and the unhappy will it; for to be and yet to be unhappy is a greater thing than not to be at all.*

Obj. 2. Further, Augustine argues thus *(ibid.* 8): Preference supposes election. But *not to be* is not eligible; since it has not the appearance of good, for it is nothing. Therefore *not to be* cannot be more desirable to the damned than *to be.*

Obj. 3. Further, the greater evil is the more to be shunned. Now *not to be* is the greatest evil, since it removes good altogether, so as to leave nothing. Therefore *not to be* is more to be shunned than to be unhappy: and thus the same conclusion follows as above.

On the contrary, It is written (Apoc. ix. 6): *In those days men . . . shall desire to die, and death shall fly from them.*

Further, the unhappiness of the damned surpasses all unhappiness of this world. Now in order to escape the unhappiness of this world, it is desirable to some to die, wherefore it is written (Ecclus. xli. 3, 4): *O death, thy sentence is welcome to the man that is in need, and to him whose strength faileth; who is in a decrepit age, and that is in care about all things, and to the distrustful that loseth wisdom* (Vulg.,—*patience*). Much more, therefore, is *not to be* desirable to the damned according to their deliberate reason.

I answer that, Not to be may be considered in two ways. First, in itself, and thus it can nowise be desirable, since it has no aspect of good, but is pure privation of good. Secondly, it may be considered as a relief from a painful life or from some unhappiness: and thus *not to be* takes on the aspect of good, since *to lack an evil is a kind of good* as the Philosopher says *(Ethic.* v. 1). In this way it is

* Cf. *De Consideratione* v. 12, and *De Gratia et Libero Arbitrio* ix.   † Cf. P. I, Q. 64, A. 2.

better for the damned not to be than to be unhappy. Hence it is said (Matth. xxvi. 24): *It were better for him, if that man had not been born*, and (Jerem. xx. 14): *Cursed be the day wherein I was born*, where a gloss of Jerome observes: *It is better not to be than to be evilly*. In this sense the damned can prefer *not to be* according to their deliberate reason.*

Reply Obj. 1. The saying of Augustine is to be understood in the sense that *not to be* is eligible, not in itself but accidentally, as putting an end to unhappiness. For when it is stated that *to be* and *to live* are desired by all naturally, we are not to take this as referable to an evil and corrupt life, and a life of unhappiness, as the Philosopher says *(Ethic.* ix. 4), but absolutely.

Reply Obj. 2. Non-existence is eligible, not in itself, but only accidentally, as stated already.

Reply Obj. 3. Although *not to be* is very evil, in so far as it removes being, it is very good, in so far as it removes unhappiness, which is the greatest of evils, and thus it is preferred *not to be*.

FOURTH ARTICLE

Whether in Hell the Damned Would Wish Others Were Damned Who Are Not Damned?

We proceed thus to the Fourth Article:—

Objection 1. It would seem that in hell the damned would not wish others were damned who are not damned. For it is said (Luke xvi. 27, 28) of the rich man that he prayed for his brethren, lest they should come *into the place of torments*. Therefore in like manner the other damned would not wish, at least, their friends in the flesh to be damned in hell.

Obj. 2. Further, the damned are not deprived of their inordinate affections. Now some of the damned loved inordinately some who are not damned. Therefore they would not desire their evil, *i.e.* that they should be damned.

Obj. 3. Further, the damned do not desire the increase of their punishment. Now if more were damned, their punishment would be greater, even as the joy of the blessed is increased by an increase in their number. Therefore the damned desire not the damnation of those who are saved.

On the contrary, A gloss on Isa. xiv. 9, *are risen up from their thrones*, says: *The wicked are comforted by having many companions in their punishment.*

Further, envy reigns supreme in the damned. Therefore they grieve for the happiness of the blessed, and desire their damnation.

* Cf. P. I, Q. 5, A. 2, *ad* 3.

I answer that, Even as in the blessed in heaven there will be most perfect charity, so in the damned there will be the most perfect hate. Wherefore as the saints will rejoice in all goods, so will the damned grieve for all goods. Consequently the sight of the happiness of the saints will give them very great pain; hence it is written (Isa. xxvi. 11): *Let the envious people see and be confounded, and let fire devour Thy enemies.* Therefore they will wish all the good were damned.

Reply Obj. 1. So great will be the envy of the damned that they will envy the glory even of their kindred, since they themselves are supremely unhappy, for this happens even in this life, when envy increases. Nevertheless they will envy their kindred less than others, and their punishment would be greater if all their kindred were damned, and others saved, than if some of their kindred were saved. For this reason the rich man prayed that his brethren might be warded from damnation: for he knew that some are guarded therefrom. Yet he would rather that his brethren were damned as well as all the rest.

Reply Obj. 2. Love that is not based on virtue is easily voided, especially in evil men, as the Philosopher says *(Ethic.* ix. 4). Hence the damned will not preserve their friendship for those whom they loved inordinately. Yet the will of them will remain perverse, because they will continue to love the cause of their inordinate loving.

Reply Obj. 3. Although an increase in the number of the damned results in an increase of each one's punishment, so much the more will their hatred and envy increase that they will prefer to be more tormented with many rather than less tormented alone.

FIFTH ARTICLE

Whether the Damned Hate God?

We proceed thus to the Fifth Article:—

Objection 1. It would seem that the damned do not hate God. For, according to Dionysius *(Div. Nom.* iv), *the beautiful and good that is the cause of all goodness and beauty is beloved of all.* But this is God. Therefore God cannot be the object of anyone's hate.

Obj. 2. Further, no one can hate goodness itself, as neither can one will badness itself, since *evil is altogether involuntary*, as Dionysius asserts *(Div. Nom.* iv). Now God is goodness itself. Therefore no one can hate Him.

On the contrary, It is written (Ps. lxxiii. 23): *The pride of them that hate Thee ascendeth continually.*

I answer that, The appetite is moved by good or evil apprehended. Now God is apprehended in two ways, namely in Himself, as by the blessed, who see Him in His essence; and in His effects, as by us and by the damned. Since, then, He is goodness by His essence, He cannot in Himself be displeasing to any will; wherefore whoever sees Him in His essence cannot hate Him. On the other hand, some of His effects are displeasing to the will in so far as they are opposed to any one: and accordingly a person may hate God not in Himself, but by reason of His effects. Therefore the damned, perceiving God in His punishment, which is the effect of His justice, hate Him, even as they hate the punishment inflicted on them.*

Reply Obj. 1. The saying of Dionysius refers to the natural appetite; and even this is rendered perverse in the damned, by that which is added thereto by their deliberate will, as stated above (A. 1).†

Reply Obj. 2. This argument would prove if the damned saw God in Himself, as being in His essence.

SIXTH ARTICLE

Whether the Damned Demerit?

We proceed thus to the Sixth Article:—

Objection 1. It would seem that the damned demerit. For the damned have an evil will, as stated in the last *Distinction* of iv, *Sent.* But they demerited by the evil will that they had here. Therefore if they demerit not there, their damnation is to their advantage.

Obj. 2. Further, the damned are on the same footing as the demons. Now the demons demerit after their fall, wherefore God inflicted a punishment on the serpent, who induced man to sin (Gen. iii. 14, 15). Therefore the damned also demerit.

Obj. 3. Further, an inordinate act that proceeds from a deliberate will is not excused from demerit, even though there be necessity of which one is oneself the cause: for the *drunken man deserves a double punishment,* if he commit a crime through being drunk (*Ethic.* iii). Now the damned were themselves the cause of their own obstinacy, owing to which they are under a kind of necessity of sinning. Therefore since their act proceeds from their free will, they are not excused from demerit.

On the contrary, Punishment is contradistinguished from fault.‡ Now the perverse will of the damned proceeds from their obstinacy which is their punishment. Therefore the perverse will of the damned is not a fault whereby they may demerit.

Further, after reaching the last term there is no further movement, or advancement in good or evil. Now the damned, especially after the judgment day, will have reached the last term of their damnation, since then there *will cease to be two cities,* according to Augustine (*Enchir.* cxi). Therefore after the judgment day the damned will not demerit by their perverse will, for if they did their damnation would be augmented.

I answer that, We must draw a distinction between the damned before the judgment day and after. For all are agreed that after the judgment day there will be neither merit nor demerit. The reason for this is because merit or demerit is directed to the attainment of some further good or evil: and after the day of judgment good and evil will have reached their ultimate consummation, so that there will be no further addition to good or evil. Consequently, good will in the blessed will not be a merit but a reward, and evil will in the damned will be not a demerit but a punishment only. For works of virtue belong especially to the state of happiness, and their contraries to the state of unhappiness (*Ethic.* i. 9, 10).

On the other hand, some say that, before the judgment day, both the good merit and the damned demerit. But this cannot apply to the essential reward or to the principal punishment, since in this respect both have reached the term. Possibly, however, this may apply to the accidental reward, or secondary punishment, which are subject to increase until the day of judgment. Especially may this apply to the demons, or to the good angels, by whose activities some are drawn to salvation, whereby the joy of the blessed angels is increased, and some to damnation, whereby the punishment of the demons is augmented.§

Reply Obj. 1. It is in the highest degree unprofitable to have reached the highest degree of evil, the result being that the damned are incapable of demerit. Hence it is clear that they gain no advantage from their sin.

Reply Obj. 2. Men who are damned are not occupied in drawing others to damnation, as the demons are, for which reason the latter demerit as regards their secondary punishment.§

Reply Obj. 3. The reason why they are not excused from demerit is not because they are under the necessity of sinning, but because they have reached the highest of evils.

However, the necessity of sinning whereof we are ourselves the cause, in so far as it is a necessity, excuses from sin, because every

---

* Cf. Q. 90, A. 3, *ad* 2, and II-II, Q. 34, A. 1.   † Cf. II-II, Q. 34, A. 1, *ad* 1, where S. Thomas gives another answer.   ‡ Cf. P. I, Q. 48, A. 5.   § Cf. P. I, Q. 62, A. 9, *ad* 3 : II-II, Q. 13, A. 4, *ad* 2 ; where S. Thomas tacitly retracts the opinion expressed here as to merit or demerit.

sin needs to be voluntary: but it does not excuse, in so far as it proceeds from a previous act of the will: and consequently the whole demerit of the subsequent sin would seem to belong to the previous sin.

SEVENTH ARTICLE

Whether the Damned Can Make Use of the Knowledge They Had in This World? *

We proceed thus to the Seventh Article:—

Objection 1. It would seem that the damned are unable to make use of the knowledge they had in this world. For there is very great pleasure in the consideration of knowledge. But we must not admit that they have any pleasure. Therefore they cannot make use of the knowledge they had heretofore, by applying their consideration thereto.

Obj. 2. Further, the damned suffer greater pains than any pains of this world. Now in this world, when one is in very great pain, it is impossible to consider any intelligible conclusions, through being distracted by the pains that one suffers. Much less therefore can one do so in hell.

Obj. 3. Further, the damned are subject to time. But *length of time is the cause of forgetfulness (Phys. lib. iv. 13).* Therefore the damned will forget what they knew here.

On the contrary, It is said to the rich man who was damned (Luke xvi. 25): *Remember that thou didst receive good things in thy lifetime,* etc. Therefore they will consider about the things they knew here.

Further, the intelligible species remain in the separated soul, as stated above (Q. 70, A. 2, *ad* 3; P. I, Q. 89, AA. 5, 6). Therefore, if they could not use them, these would remain in them to no purpose.

I answer that, Even as in the saints, on account of the perfection of their glory, there will be nothing but what is a matter of joy, so there will be nothing in the damned but what is a matter and cause of sorrow; nor will anything that can pertain to sorrow be lacking, so that their unhappiness is consummate. Now the consideration of certain things known brings us joy, in some respect, either on the part of the things known, because we love them, or on the part of the knowledge, because it is fitting and perfect. There may also be a reason for sorrow both on the part of the things known, because they are of a grievous nature, and on the part of the knowledge, if we consider its imperfection; for instance a person may consider his defective knowledge about a certain thing, which he would desire to know perfectly. Accordingly, in the damned there will be actual consideration of the things they

* Cf. P. I, Q. 89.

knew heretofore as matters of sorrow, but not as a cause of pleasure. For they will consider both the evil they have done, and for which they were damned, and the delightful goods they have lost, and on both counts they will suffer torments. Likewise they will be tormented with the thought that the knowledge they had of speculative matters was imperfect, and that they missed its highest degree of perfection which they might have acquired.

Reply Obj. 1. Although the consideration of knowledge is delightful in itself, it may accidentally be the cause of sorrow, as explained above.

Reply Obj. 2. In this world the soul is united to a corruptible body, wherefore the soul's consideration is hindered by the suffering of the body. On the other hand, in the future life the soul will not be so drawn by the body, but however much the body may suffer, the soul will have a most clear view of those things that can be a cause of anguish to it.

Reply Obj. 3. Time causes forgetfulness accidentally, in so far as the movement whereof it is the measure is the cause of change. But after the judgment day there will be no movement of the heavens; wherefore neither will it be possible for forgetfulness to result from any lapse of time however long. Before the judgment day, however, the separated soul is not changed from its disposition by the heavenly movement.

EIGHTH ARTICLE

Whether the Damned Will Ever Think of God?

We proceed thus to the Eighth Article:—

Objection 1. It would seem that the damned will sometimes think of God. For one cannot hate a thing actually, except one think about it. Now the damned will hate God, as stated in the text of iv. *Sent.* in the last *Distinction.* Therefore they will think of God sometimes.

Obj. 2. Further, the damned will have remorse of conscience. But the conscience suffers remorse for deeds done against God. Therefore they will sometimes think of God.

On the contrary, Man's most perfect thoughts are those which are about God: whereas the damned will be in a state of the greatest imperfection. Therefore they will not think of God.

I answer that, One may think of God in two ways. First, in Himself and according to that which is proper to Him, namely that He is the fount of all goodness: and thus it is altogether impossible to think of Him without delight, so that the damned will by no means think of Him in this way. Secondly, according to something accidental as it were to Him in His effects, such as His punishments, and so forth, and in this respect the thought of God can bring sorrow, so that in this way the damned will think of God.

Reply Obj. 1. The damned do not hate God except because He punishes and forbids what is agreeable to their evil will: and consequently they will think of Him only as punishing and forbidding. This suffices for the *Reply* to the *Second Objection*, since conscience will not have remorse for sin except as forbidden by the Divine commandment.

NINTH ARTICLE

Whether the Damned See the Glory of the Blessed?

We proceed thus to the Ninth Article:—

Objection 1. It would seem that the damned do not see the glory of the blessed. For they are more distant from the glory of the blessed than from the happenings of this world. But they do not see what happens in regard to us: hence Gregory commenting on Job xiv. 21, *Whether his children come to honor* etc. says (*Moral.* xii): *Even as those who still live know not in what place are the souls of the dead; so the dead who have lived in the body know not the things which regard the life of those who are in the flesh.* Much less, therefore, can they see the glory of the blessed.

Obj. 2. Further, that which is granted as a great favor to the saints in this life is never granted to the damned. Now it was granted as a great favor to Paul to see the life in which the saints live for ever with God (2 Cor. xii). Therefore the damned will not see the glory of the saints.

On the contrary, It is stated (Luke xvi. 23) that the rich man in the midst of his torments *saw Abraham . . . and Lazarus in his bosom.*

I answer that, The damned, before the judgment day, will see the blessed in glory, in such a way as to know, not what that glory is like, but only that they are in a state of glory that surpasses all thought. This will trouble them, both because they will, through envy, grieve for their happiness, and because they have forfeited that glory. Hence it is written (Wis. v. 2) concerning the wicked: *Seeing it they shall be troubled with terrible fear.* After the judgment day, however, they will be altogether deprived of seeing the blessed: nor will this lessen their punishment, but will increase it; because they will bear in remembrance the glory of the blessed which they saw at or before the judgment: and this will torment them. Moreover they will be tormented by finding themselves deemed unworthy even to see the glory which the saints merit to have.

Reply Obj. 1. The happenings of this life would not, if seen, torment the damned in hell as the sight of the glory of the saints; wherefore the things which happen here are not shown to the damned in the same way as the saints' glory; although also of the things that happen here those are shown to them which are capable of causing them sorrow.

Reply Obj. 2. Paul looked upon that life wherein the saints live with God,* by actual experience thereof and by hoping to have it more perfectly in the life to come. Not so the damned; wherefore the comparison fails.

QUESTION 99

Of God's Mercy and Justice Towards the Damned

(In Five Articles)

WE must next consider God's justice and mercy towards the damned: under which head there are five points of inquiry: (1) Whether by Divine justice an eternal punishment is inflicted on sinners? (2) Whether by God's mercy all punishment both of men and of demons comes to an end? (3) Whether at least the punishment of men comes to an end? (4) Whether at least the punishment of Christians has an end? (5) Whether there is an end to the punishment of those who have performed works of mercy?

FIRST ARTICLE

Whether by Divine Justice an Eternal Punishment Is Inflicted on Sinners?†

We proceed thus to the First Article:—

Objection 1. It would seem that an eternal

punishment is not inflicted on sinners by Divine justice. For the punishment should not exceed the fault: *According to the measure of the sin shall the measure also of the stripes be* (Deut. xxv. 2). Now fault is temporal. Therefore the punishment should not be eternal.

Obj. 2. Further, of two mortal sins one is greater than the other; and therefore one should receive a greater punishment than the other. But no punishment is greater than eternal punishment, since it is infinite. Therefore eternal punishment is not due to every sin; and if it is not due to one, it is due to none, since they are not infinitely distant from one another.

Obj. 3. Further, a just judge does not punish except in order to correct, wherefore it is stated (*Ethic.* ii. 3) that *punishments are a*

---

* Cf. II-II, Q. 185, A. 3, *ad* 2.   † Cf. I-II, Q. 87, AA. 3, 4.

kind of medicine. Now, to punish the wicked eternally does not lead to their correction, nor to that of others, since then there will be no one in future who can be corrected thereby. Therefore eternal punishment is not inflicted for sins according to Divine justice.

Obj. 4. Further, no one wishes that which is not desirable for its own sake, except on account of some advantage. Now God does not wish punishment for its own sake, for He delights not in punishments.* Since then no advantage can result from the perpetuity of punishment, it would seem that He ought not to inflict such a punishment for sin.

Obj. 5. Further, nothing accidental lasts for ever *(De Cœlo et Mundo,* i). But punishment is one of those things that happen accidentally, since it is contrary to nature. Therefore it cannot be everlasting.

Obj. 6. Further, the justice of God would seem to require that sinners should be brought to naught: because on account of ingratitude a person deserves to lose all benefits; and among other benefits of God there is *being* itself. Therefore it would seem just that the sinner who has been ungrateful to God should lose his being. But if sinners be brought to naught, their punishment cannot be everlasting. Therefore it would seem out of keeping with Divine justice that sinners should be punished for ever.

On the contrary, It is written (Matth. xxv. 46): *These,* namely the wicked, *shall go into everlasting punishment.*

Further, as reward is to merit, so is punishment to guilt. Now, according to Divine justice, an eternal reward is due to temporal merit: *Every one who seeth the Son and believeth in Him hath* (Vulg.,—*that everyone . . . may have) life everlasting.* Therefore according to Divine justice an everlasting punishment is due to temporal guilt.

Further, according to the Philosopher *(Ethic.* v. 5), punishment is meted according to the dignity of the person sinned against, so that a person who strikes one in authority receives a greater punishment than one who strikes anyone else. Now whoever sins mortally sins against God, Whose commandments he breaks, and Whose honor he gives another, by placing his end in some one other than God. But God's majesty is infinite. Therefore whoever sins mortally deserves infinite punishment; and consequently it seems just that for a mortal sin a man should be punished for ever.

I answer that, Since punishment is measured in two ways, namely according to the degree of its severity, and according to its length of time, the measure of punishment corresponds to the measure of fault, as regards the degree of severity, so that the more grievously a person sins the more grievously is he punished: *As much as she hath glorified herself and lived in delicacies, so much torment and sorrow give ye to her* (Apoc. xviii. 7). The duration of the punishment does not, however, correspond with the duration of the fault, as Augustine says *(De Civ. Dei,* xxi. 11), for adultery which is committed in a short space of time is not punished with a momentary penalty even according to human laws.† But the duration of punishment regards the disposition of the sinner: for sometimes a person who commits an offense in a city is rendered by his very offense worthy of being cut off entirely from the fellowship of the citizens, either by perpetual exile or even by death: whereas sometimes he is not rendered worthy of being cut off entirely from the fellowship of the citizens; wherefore in order that he may become a fitting member of the State, his punishment is prolonged or curtailed, according as is expedient for his amendment, so that he may live in the city in a becoming and peaceful manner. So too, according to Divine justice, sin renders a person worthy to be altogether cut off from the fellowship of God's city, and this is the effect of every sin committed against charity, which is the bond uniting this same city together. Consequently, for mortal sin which is contrary to charity a person is expelled for ever from the fellowship of the saints and condemned to everlasting punishment, because as Augustine says *(loc. cit.),* as *men are cut off from this perishable city by the penalty of the first death, so are they excluded from that imperishable city by the punishment of the second death.* That the punishment inflicted by the earthly state is not deemed everlasting is accidental, either because man endures not for ever, or because the state itself comes to an end. Wherefore if man lived for ever, the punishment of exile or slavery, which is pronounced by human law, would remain in him for ever. On the other hand, as regards those who sin in such a way as not to deserve to be entirely cut off from the fellowship of the saints, such as those who sin venially, their punishment will be so much the shorter or longer according as they are more or less fit to be cleansed, through sin clinging to them more or less: this is observed in the punishments of this world and of purgatory according to Divine justice.

We find also other reasons given by the saints why some are justly condemned to everlasting punishment for a temporal sin. One

---

* The allusion is to Wis. i. 13, *Neither hath He pleasure in the destruction of the living,* as may be gathered from I-II, Q. 87, A. 3, *Obj.* 3. † Cf. I-II, Q. 87, A. 3, *ad* 1.

is because they sinned against an eternal good by despising eternal life. This is mentioned by Augustine *(ibid.* 12): *He is become worthy of eternal evil, who destroyed in himself a good which could be eternal.* Another reason is because man sinned in his own eternity;* wherefore Gregory says *(Dial.* iv), *it belongs to the great justice of the judge that those should never cease to be punished, who in this life never ceased to desire sin.* And if it be objected that some who sin mortally propose to amend their life at some time, and that these accordingly are seemingly not deserving of eternal punishment, it must be replied according to some that Gregory speaks of the will that is made manifest by the deed. For he who falls into mortal sin of his own will puts himself in a state whence he cannot be rescued, except God help him: wherefore from the very fact that he is willing to sin, he is willing to remain in sin for ever. For man is *a wind that goeth,* namely to sin, *and returneth not* by his own power (Ps. lxxvii. 39). Thus if a man were to throw himself into a pit whence he could not get out without help, one might say that he wished to remain there for ever, whatever else he may have thought himself. Another and a better answer is that from the very fact that he commits a mortal sin, he places his end in a creature; and since the whole of life is directed to its end, it follows that for this very reason he directs the whole of his life to that sin, and is willing to remain in sin for ever, if he could do so with impunity. This is what Gregory says on Job. xli. 23, *He shall esteem the deep as growing old (Moral.* xxxiv): *The wicked only put an end to sinning because their life came to an end: they would indeed have wished to live for ever, that they might continue in sin for ever, for they desire rather to sin than to live.* Still another reason may be given why the punishment of mortal sin is eternal: because thereby one offends God Who is infinite. Wherefore since punishment cannot be infinite in intensity, because the creature is incapable of an infinite quality, it must needs be infinite at least in duration. And again there is a fourth reason for the same: because guilt remains for ever, since it cannot be remitted without grace, and men cannot receive grace after death; nor should punishment cease so long as guilt remains.

Reply Obj. 1. Punishment has not to be equal to fault as to the amount of duration, as is seen to be the case also with human laws. We may also reply with Gregory *(Dial.* xliv) that although sin is temporal in act, it is eternal in will.

Reply Obj. 2. The degree of intensity in the punishment corresponds to the degree of gravity in the sin; wherefore mortal sins unequal in gravity will receive a punishment unequal in intensity but equal in duration.

Reply Obj. 3. The punishments inflicted on those who are not altogether expelled from the society of their fellow-citizens are intended for their correction: whereas those punishments, whereby certain persons are wholly banished from the society of their fellow-citizens, are not intended for their correction; although they may be intended for the correction and tranquillity of the others who remain in the state. Accordingly the damnation of the wicked is for the correction of those who are now in the Church; for punishments are intended for correction, not only when they are being inflicted, but also when they are decreed.

Reply Obj. 4. The everlasting punishment of the wicked will not be altogether useless. For they are useful for two purposes. First, because thereby the Divine justice is safeguarded which is acceptable to God for its own sake. Hence Gregory says *(Dial.* iv): *Almighty God on account of His loving kindness delights not in the torments of the unhappy, but on account of His justice. He is for ever unappeased by the punishment of the wicked.* Secondly, they are useful, because the elect rejoice therein, when they see God's justice in them, and realize that they have escaped them. Hence it is written (Ps. lvii. 12): *The just shall rejoice when he shall see the revenge,* etc., and (Isa. lxvi. 24): *They,* namely the wicked, *shall be a loathsome sight†** to all flesh,* namely to the saints, as a gloss says. Gregory expresses himself in the same sense *(Dial.* iv): *The wicked are all condemned to eternal punishment, and are punished for their own wickedness. Yet they will burn to some purpose, namely that the just may all both see in God the joys they receive, and perceive in them the torments they have escaped: for which reason they will acknowledge themselves for ever the debtors of Divine grace, the more that they will see how the evils which they overcame by its assistance are punished eternally.*

Reply Obj. 5. Although the punishment relates to the soul accidentally, it relates essentially to the soul infected with guilt. And since guilt will remain in the soul for ever, its punishment also will be everlasting.

Reply Obj. 6. Punishment corresponds to fault, properly speaking, in respect of the inordinateness in the fault, and not of the dignity in the person offended: for if the latter

---

* Cf. I-II, Q. 87, A. 3, *ad* 1.

† *Ad satietatem visionis,* which S. Thomas takes to signify being satiated with joy. Cf. Q. 94, A. 3.

were the case, a punishment of infinite intensity would correspond to every sin. Accordingly, although a man deserves to lose his being from the fact that he has sinned against God the author of his being, yet, in view of the inordinateness of the act itself, loss of being is not due to him, since being is presupposed to merit and demerit, nor is being lost or corrupted by the inordinateness of sin:* and consequently privation of being cannot be the punishment due to any sin.

SECOND ARTICLE

Whether by God's Mercy All Punishment of the Damned, Both Men and Demons, Comes to an End?

We proceed thus to the Second Article:—

Objection 1. It would seem that by God's mercy all punishment of the damned, both men and demons, comes to an end. For it is written (Wis. xi. 24): *Thou hast mercy upon all, O Lord, because Thou canst do all things.* But among all things the demons also are included, since they are God's creatures. Therefore also their punishment will come to an end.

Obj. 2. Further, *God hath concluded all in sin* (Vulg.,—*unbelief*), *that He may have mercy on all* (Rom. xi. 32). Now God has concluded the demons under sin, that is to say, He permitted them to be concluded. Therefore it would seem that in time He has mercy even on the demons.

Obj. 3. Further, as Anselm says (*Cur Deus Homo* ii), *it is not just that God should permit the utter loss of a creature which He made for happiness.* Therefore, since every rational creature was created for happiness, it would seem unjust for it to be allowed to perish altogether.

On the contrary, It is written (Matth. xxv. 41): *Depart from Me, you cursed, into everlasting fire, which is prepared for the devil and his angels.* Therefore they will be punished eternally.

Further, just as the good angels were made happy through turning to God, so the bad angels were made unhappy through turning away from God. Therefore if the unhappiness of the wicked angels comes at length to an end, the happiness of the good will also come to an end, which is inadmissible.

I answer that, As Augustine says (*De Civ. Dei,* xxi) *Origen†* erred in maintaining that the demons will at length, through God's mercy, be delivered from their punishment. But this error has been condemned by the Church for two reasons. First because it is clearly contrary to the authority of Holy Writ (Apoc. xx. 9, 10): *The devil who seduced them*

was cast into the pool of fire and brimstone, where both the beasts and the false prophets‡ shall be tormented day and night for ever and ever, which is the Scriptural expression for eternity. Secondly, because this opinion exaggerated God's mercy in one direction and depreciated it in another. For it would seem equally reasonable for the good angels to remain in eternal happiness, and for the wicked angels to be eternally punished. Wherefore just as he maintained that the demons and the souls of the damned are to be delivered at length from their sufferings, so he maintained that the angels and the souls of the blessed will at length pass from their happy state to the unhappiness of this life.

Reply Obj. 1. God, for His own part, has mercy on all. Since, however, His mercy is ruled by the order of His wisdom, the result is that it does not reach to certain people who render themselves unworthy of that mercy, as do the demons and the damned who are obstinate in wickedness. And yet we may say that even in them His mercy finds a place, in so far as they are punished less than they deserve condignly, but not that they are entirely delivered from punishment.

Reply Obj. 2. In the words quoted the distribution (of the predicate) regards the genera and not the individuals: so that the statement applies to men in the state of wayfarer, inasmuch as He had mercy both on Jews and on Gentiles, but not on every Gentile or every Jew.

Reply Obj. 3. Anselm means that it is not just in the sense of becoming God's goodness, and is speaking of the creature generically. For it becomes not the Divine goodness that a whole genus of creature fail of the end for which it was made: wherefore it is unbecoming for all men or all angels to be damned. But there is no reason why some men or some angels should perish for ever, because the intention of the Divine will is fulfilled in the others who are saved.

THIRD ARTICLE

Whether God's Mercy Suffers at Least Men to Be Punished Eternally?

We proceed thus to the Third Article:—

Objection 1. It would seem that God's mercy does not suffer at least men to be punished eternally. For it is written (Gen. vi. 3): *My spirit shall not remain in man for ever, because he is flesh;* where *spirit* denotes indignation, as a gloss observes. Therefore, since God's indignation is not distinct from His punishment, man will not be punished eternally.

---

*Cf. I-II, Q. 85, A. 1. † Cf. P. I, Q. 64, A. 2. ‡ Vulg.,—*the beast and false prophet,* etc.

Obj. 2. Further, the charity of the saints in this life makes them pray for their enemies. Now they will have more perfect charity in that life. Therefore they will pray then for their enemies who are damned. But the prayers of the saints cannot be in vain, since they are most acceptable to God. Therefore at the saints' prayers the Divine mercy will in time deliver the damned from their punishment.

Obj. 3. Further, God's foretelling of the punishment of the damned belongs to the prophecy of commination. Now the prophecy of commination is not always fulfilled: as appears from what was said of the destruction of Nineve (Jonas iii); and yet it was not destroyed as foretold by the prophet, who also was troubled for that very reason (iv. 1). Therefore it would seem that much more will the threat of eternal punishment be commuted by God's mercy for a more lenient punishment, when this will be able to give sorrow to none but joy to all.

Obj. 4. Further, the words of Ps. lxxvi. 8 are to the point, where it is said: *Will God then be angry for ever?** But God's anger is His punishment. Therefore, etc.

Obj. 5. Further, a gloss on Isa. xiv. 19, *But thou art cast out,* etc., says: *Even though all souls shall have rest at last, thou never shalt:* and it refers to the devil. Therefore it would seem that all human souls shall at length have rest from their pains.

On the contrary, It is written (Matth. xxv. 46) of the elect conjointly with the damned: *These shall go into everlasting punishment: but the just, into life everlasting.* But it is inadmissible that the life of the just will ever have an end. Therefore it is inadmissible that the punishment of the damned will ever come to an end.

Further, as Damascene says *(De Fide Orthod.* ii) *death is to men what their fall was to the angels.* Now after their fall the angels could not be restored.† Therefore neither can man after death: and thus the punishment of the damned will have no end.

I answer that, As Augustine says *(De Civ. Dei,* xxi. 17, 18), some evaded the error of Origen by asserting that the demons are punished everlastingly, while holding that all men, even unbelievers, are at length set free from punishment. But this statement is altogether unreasonable. For just as the demons are obstinate in wickedness and therefore have to be punished for ever, so too are the souls of men who die without charity, since *death is to men what their fall was to the angels,* as Damascene says.

Reply Obj. 1. This saying refers to man generically, because God's indignation was at

length removed from the human race by the coming of Christ. But those who were unwilling to be included or to remain in this reconciliation effected by Christ, perpetuated the Divine anger in themselves, since no other way of reconciliation is given to us save that which is through Christ.

Reply Obj. 2. As Augustine *(De Civ. Dei,* xxi. 24) and Gregory *(Moral.* xxxiv) say, the saints in this life pray for their enemies, that they may be converted to God, while it is yet possible for them to be converted. For if we knew that they were foreknown to death, we should no more pray for them than for the demons. And since for those who depart this life without grace there will be no further time for conversion, no prayer will be offered for them, neither by the Church militant, nor by the Church triumphant. For that which we have to pray for them is, as the Apostle says (2 Tim. ii. 25, 26), that *God may give them repentance to know the truth, and they may recover themselves from the snares of the devil.*

Reply Obj. 3. A punishment threatened prophetically is only then commuted when there is a change in the merits of the person threatened. Hence: *I will suddenly speak against a nation and against a kingdom, to root out and to pull down and to destroy it. If that nation . . . shall repent of their evil, I also will repent of the evil that I have thought to do to them* (Jer. xviii. 7). Therefore, since the merits of the damned cannot be changed, the threatened punishment will ever be fulfilled in them. Nevertheless the prophecy of commination is always fulfilled in a certain sense, because as Augustine says *(ibid.): Nineve has been overthrown, that was evil, and a good Nineve is built up, that was not: for while the walls and the houses remained standing, the city was overthrown in its wicked ways.*

Reply Obj. 4. These words of the Psalm refer to the vessels of mercy, which have not made themselves unworthy of mercy, because in this life (which may be called God's anger on account of its unhappiness) He changes vessels of mercy into something better. Hence the Psalm continues *(verse 11): This is the change of the right hand of the most High.* We may also reply that they refer to mercy as granting a relaxation but not setting free altogether if it be referred also to the damned. Hence the Psalm does not say: *Will He from His anger shut up His mercies?* but *in His anger,* because the punishment will not be done away entirely; but His mercy will have effect by diminishing the punishment while it continues.

* Vulg.,—*Will God then cast off for ever?*   † Cf. P. I, Q. 64, A. 2.

Reply Obj. 5. This gloss is speaking not absolutely but on an impossible supposition in order to throw into relief the greatness of the devil's sin, or of Nabuchodonosor's.

FOURTH ARTICLE

Whether the Punishment of Christians Is Brought to an End by the Mercy of God?

We proceed thus to the Fourth Article:—

Objection 1. It would seem that at least the punishment of Christians is brought to an end by the mercy of God. *For he that believeth and is baptized shall be saved* (Mark xvi. 16). Now this applies to every Christian. Therefore all Christians will at length be saved.

Obj. 2. Further, it is written (Jo. vi. 55): *He that eateth My body and drinketh My blood hath eternal life.* Now this is the meat and drink whereof Christians partake in common. Therefore all Christians will be saved at length.

Obj. 3. Further, *If any man's work burn, he shall suffer loss: but he himself shall be saved, yet so as by fire* (1 Cor. iii. 15), where it is a question of those who have the foundation of the Christian faith. Therefore all such persons will be saved in the end.

On the contrary, It is written (1 Cor. vi. 9): *The unjust shall not possess the kingdom of God.* Now some Christians are unjust. Therefore Christians will not all come to the kingdom of God, and consequently they will be punished for ever.

Further, it is written (2 Pet. ii. 21): *It had been better for them not to have known the way of justice, than after they have known it, to turn back from that holy commandment which was delivered to them.* Now those who know not the way of truth will be punished for ever. Therefore Christians who have turned back after knowing it will also be punished for ever.

I answer that, According to Augustine *(De Civ. Dei,* xxi. 20; 21), there have been some who predicted a delivery from eternal punishment not for all men, but only for Christians; although they stated the matter in different ways. For some said that whoever received the sacraments of faith would be immune from eternal punishment. But this is contrary to the truth, since some receive the sacraments of faith, and yet have not faith, without which *it is impossible to please God* (Heb. xi. 6). Wherefore others said that those alone will be exempt from eternal punishment who have received the sacraments of faith, and professed the Catholic faith. But against this it would seem to be that at one time some people pro-

fess the Catholic faith, and afterwards abandon it, and these are deserving not of a lesser but of a greater punishment, since according to 2 Pet. ii. 21, *it had been better for them not to have known the way of justice than, after they have known it, to turn back.* Moreover it is clear that heresiarchs who renounce the Catholic faith and invent new heresies sin more grievously than those who have conformed to some heresy from the first. And therefore some have maintained that those alone are exempt from eternal punishment, who persevere to the end in the Catholic faith, however guilty they may have been of other crimes. But this is clearly contrary to Holy Writ, for it is written (James ii. 20): *Faith without works is dead,* and (Matth. vii. 21) *Not every one that saith to Me, Lord, Lord, shall enter into the kingdom of heaven: but he that doth the will of My Father Who is in heaven:* and in many other passages Holy Scripture threatens sinners with eternal punishment. Consequently those who persevere in the faith unto the end will not all be exempt from eternal punishment, unless in the end they prove to be free from other crimes.

Reply Obj. 1. Our Lord speaks there of formed faith* *that worketh by love* (Vulg.,— charity, Gal. v. 6): wherein whosoever dieth shall be saved. But to this faith not only is the error of unbelief opposed, but also any mortal sin whatsoever.

Reply Obj. 2. The saying of our Lord refers not to those who partake only sacramentally, and who sometimes by receiving unworthily *eat and drink judgment* to themselves (1 Cor. xi. 29), but to those who eat spiritually and are incorporated with Him by charity, which incorporation is the effect of the sacramental eating, in those who approach worthily.† Wherefore, so far as the power of the sacrament is concerned, it brings us to eternal life, although sin may deprive us of that fruit, even after we have received worthily.

Reply Obj. 3. In this passage of the Apostle the foundation denotes formed faith, upon which whosoever shall build venial sins‡ *shall suffer loss,* because he will be punished for them by God; yet *he himself shall be saved in the end by fire,* either of temporal tribulation, or of the punishment of purgatory which will be after death.

FIFTH ARTICLE

Whether All Those Who Perform Works of Mercy Will Be Punished Eternally?

We proceed thus to the Fifth Article:—

Objection 1. It would seem that all who perform works of mercy will not be punished

*Cf. II-II, Q. 4, A. 3.   † Cf. P. III, Q. 80, AA. 1, 2, 3.   ‡ Cf. I-II, Q. 89, A. 2.

eternally, but only those who neglect those works. For it is written (James ii. 13): *Judgment without mercy to him that hath not done mercy;* and Matth. v. 7): *Blessed are the merciful for they shall obtain mercy.*

Obj. 2. Further, (Matth. xxv. 35-46) we find a description of our Lord's discussion with the damned and the elect. But this discussion is only about works of mercy. Therefore eternal punishment will be awarded only to such as have omitted to practice works of mercy: and consequently the same conclusion follows as before.

Obj. 3. Further, it is written (Matth. vi. 12): *Forgive us our debts, as we also forgive our debtors,* and further on *(verse* 14): *For if you will forgive men their offenses, your heavenly Father will forgive you also your offenses.* Therefore it would seem that the merciful, who forgive others their offenses, will themselves obtain the forgiveness of their sins, and consequently will not be punished eternally.

Obj. 4. Further, a gloss of Ambrose on 1 Tim. iv. 8, *Godliness is profitable to all things,* says: *The sum total of a Christian's rule of life consists in mercy and godliness. Let a man follow this, and though he should suffer from the inconstancy of the flesh, without doubt he will be scourged, but he will not perish: whereas he who can boast of no other exercise but that of the body will suffer everlasting punishment.* Therefore those who persevere in works of mercy, though they be shackled with fleshly sins, will not be punished eternally: and thus the same conclusion follows as before.

On the contrary, It is written (1 Cor. vi. 9, 10): *Neither fornicators, . . . nor adulterers,* etc., *shall possess the kingdom of God.* Yet many are such who practice works of mercy. Therefore the merciful will not all come to the eternal kingdom: and consequently some of them will be punished eternally.

Further, it is written (James ii. 10): *Whosoever shall keep the whole law, but offend in one point, is become guilty of all.* Therefore whoever keeps the law as regards the works of mercy and omits other works, is guilty of transgressing the law, and consequently will be punished eternally.

I answer that, As Augustine says in the book quoted above *(De Civ. Dei,* xxi. 22), some have maintained that not all who have professed the Catholic faith will be freed from eternal punishment, but only those who persevere in works of mercy, although they be guilty of other crimes. But this cannot stand, because without charity nothing can be acceptable to God, nor does anything profit unto eternal life in the absence of charity. Now it happens that certain persons persevere in works of mercy without having charity. Wherefore nothing profits them to the meriting of eternal life, or to exemption from eternal punishment, as may be gathered from 1 Cor. xiii. 3. Most evident is this in the case of those who lay hands on other people's property, for after seizing on many things, they nevertheless spend something in works of mercy. We must therefore conclude that all whosoever die in mortal sin, neither faith nor works of mercy will free them from eternal punishment, not even after any length of time whatever.

Reply Obj. 1. Those will obtain mercy who show mercy in an ordinate manner. But those who while merciful to others are neglectful of themselves do not show mercy ordinately, rather do they strike at themselves by their evil actions. Wherefore such persons will not obtain the mercy that sets free altogether, even if they obtain that mercy which rebates somewhat their due punishment.

Reply Obj. 2. The reason why the discussion refers only to the works of mercy is not because eternal punishment will be inflicted on none but those who omit those works, but because eternal punishment will be remitted to those who after sinning have obtained forgiveness by their works of mercy, making unto themselves *friends of the mammon of iniquity* (Luke xvi. 9).

Reply Obj. 3. Our Lord said this to those who ask that their debt be forgiven, but not to those who persist in sin. Wherefore the repentant alone will obtain by their works of mercy the forgiveness that sets them free altogether.

Reply Obj. 4. The gloss of Ambrose speaks of the inconstancy that consists in venial sin, from which a man will be freed through the works of mercy after the punishment of purgatory, which he calls a scourging. Or, if he speaks of the inconstancy of mortal sin, the sense is that those who while yet in this life fall into sins of the flesh through frailty are disposed to repentance by works of mercy. Wherefore such a one will not perish, that is to say, he will be disposed by those works not to perish, through grace bestowed on him by our Lord, Who is blessed for evermore. Amen.

THE following two questions were compiled by Nicolai from St. Thomas's commentary on the Sentences, and by him included in the supplement between Questions 70 and 71.

QUESTION 1
Of the Quality of Those Souls Who Depart This Life with Original Sin Only

(In Two Articles)

WE must next consider the various qualities of souls that are stripped of their bodies, according to their respective states; and first we shall treat of the souls which depart this life with original sin only.

Under this head there are two points of inquiry: (1) Whether these souls suffer from a bodily fire, and are inflicted with punishment by fire? (2) Whether these souls suffer from a spiritual torment within themselves?

FIRST ARTICLE

Whether Those Souls Which Depart with Original Sin Alone, Suffer from a Bodily Fire, and Are Punished by Fire?

We proceed thus to the First Article:—

Objection 1. It would seem that souls which depart with none but original sin, suffer from a bodily fire and are punished by fire. For Augustine* says: *Hold firmly and doubt not that children who depart this life without the sacrament of Baptism will be punished everlastingly.* Now punishment denotes sensible pain. Therefore souls which depart this life with original sin alone, suffer from a bodily fire and are tormented with the pain of fire.

Obj. 2. Further, a greater fault deserves a greater punishment. Now original sin is greater than venial, because it contains more aversion, since it deprives its subject of grace, whereas venial sin is compatible with grace; and again because original sin is punished eternally, whereas venial sin is punished temporally. Seeing then that venial sin is deserving of the punishment of fire, much more so is original sin.

Obj. 3. Further, sins are more severely punished after this life than during lifetime, for in this life there is room for mercy. Now, sensible punishment corresponds to original sin in this life, for children who have only original sin are justly subject to many sensible punishments. Therefore sensible punishment is due to it after this life.

Obj. 4. Further, even as in actual sin there is aversion and conversion, so in original sin

* Fulgentius, *De Fide ad Petrum*, xxvii.

there is something corresponding to aversion, namely the privation of original justice, and something corresponding to conversion, namely concupiscence. Now the punishment of fire is due to actual sin by reason of the conversion. Therefore it is also due to original sin by reason of concupiscence.

Obj. 5. Further, after the resurrection the bodies of children will be either passible or impassible. If they be impassible — and no human body can be impassible except either on account of the gift of impassibility (as in the blessed) or by reason of original justice (as in the state of innocence)—it follows that the bodies of children will either have the gift of impassibility, and thus will be glorious, so that there will be no difference between baptized and non-baptized children, which is heretical, or else they will have original justice, and thus will be without original sin, and will not be punished for original sin, which is likewise heretical. If, on the other hand, they be passible, since everything passible suffers of necessity in the presence of the active, it follows that in the presence of active sensible bodies they will suffer sensible punishment.

On the contrary, Augustine says (*Enchir.* xxiii) that the mildest punishment of all will be for those who are burdened with original sin only. But this would not be so, if they were tormented with sensible punishment, because the pain of hell fire is most grievous. Therefore they will not suffer sensible punishment.

Further, the grief of sensible punishment corresponds to the pleasure of sin (Apoc. xviii. 7): *As much as she hath glorified herself and lived in delicacies, so much torment and sorrow give ye to her.* But there is no pleasure in original sin, as neither is there operation, for pleasure follows operation, as stated in *Ethic.* x. 4. Therefore punishment by fire is not due to original sin.

Further, Gregory Nazianzen in his fortieth sermon, which is entitled *On Holy Baptism,* distinguishes three classes of unbaptized persons: those namely who refuse to be baptized, those who through neglect have put off being baptized until the end of life and have been surprised by sudden death, and those who, like infants, have failed to receive it through no fault of theirs. Of the first he says that they will be punished not only for their other sins, but also for their contempt of Baptism; of the second, that they will be punished, though less severely than the first, for having neglected it; and of the last he says that *a just and eternal Judge will consign them neither to heavenly glory nor to the eternal pains of hell, for although they have not been signed with Baptism, they are without wickedness and malice, and have suffered rather than caused their loss of Baptism.* He also gives the reason why, although they do not reach the glory of heaven, they do not therefore suffer the eternal punishment suffered by the damned: *Because there is a mean between the two, since he who deserves not honor and glory is not for that reason worthy of punishment, and on the other hand he who is not deserving of punishment is not for that reason worthy of glory and honor.*

I answer that, Punishment should be proportionate to fault, according to the saying of Isaias xxvii. 8, *In measure against measure, when it shall be cast off, thou shalt judge it.* Now the defect transmitted to us through our origin, and having the character of a sin does not result from the withdrawal or corruption of a good consequent upon human nature by virtue of its principles, but from the withdrawal or corruption of something that had been superadded to nature. Nor does this sin belong to this particular man, except in so far as he has such a nature, that is deprived of this good, which in the ordinary course of things he would have had and would have been able to keep. Wherefore no further punishment is due to him, besides the privation of that end to which the gift withdrawn destined him, which gift human nature is unable of itself to obtain. Now this is the divine vision; and consequently the loss of this vision is the proper and only punishment of original sin after death: because, if any other sensible punishment were inflicted after death for original sin, a man would be punished out of proportion to his guilt, for sensible punishment is inflicted for that which is proper to the person, since a man undergoes sensible punishment in so far as he suffers in his person. Hence, as his guilt did not result from an action of his own, even so neither should he be punished by suffering himself, but only by losing that which his nature was unable to obtain. On the other hand, those who are under sentence for original sin will suffer no loss whatever in other kinds of perfection and goodness which are consequent upon human nature by virtue of its principles.

Reply Obj. 1. In the authority quoted punishment denotes, not pain of sense, but only pain of loss, which is the privation of the divine vision, even as in Scripture the word *fire* is often wont to signify any kind of punishment.

Reply Obj. 2. Of all sins original sin is the least, because it is the least voluntary; for it is voluntary not by the will of the person, but only by the will of the origin of our nature. But actual sin, even venial, is voluntary by the will of the person in which it is; wherefore a lighter punishment is due to original than to venial sin. Nor does it matter that original sin is incompatible with grace; because privation of grace has the character, not of sin, but of punishment, except in so far as it is voluntary: for which reason that which is less voluntary is less sinful. Again it matters not that actual venial sin is deserving of temporal punishment, since this is accidental, for as much as he who falls venially has sufficient grace to attenuate the punishment. For if venial sin were in a person without grace, it would be punished eternally.

Reply Obj. 3. There is no parity between pain of sense before and after death, since before death the pain of sense results from the power of the natural agent, whether the pain of sense be interior as fever or the like, or exterior as burning and so forth. Whereas after death nothing will act by natural power, but only according to the order of divine justice, whether the object of such action be the separate soul, on which it is clear that fire cannot act naturally, or the body after resurrection, since then all natural action will cease, through the cessation of the first movable which is the cause of all bodily movement and alteration.

Reply Obj. 4. Sensible pain corresponds to sensible pleasure, which is in the conversion of actual sin: whereas habitual concupiscence, which is in original sin, has no pleasure. Hence, sensible pain does not correspond thereto as punishment.

Reply Obj. 5. The bodies of children will be impassible, not through their being unable in themselves to suffer, but through the lack of an external agent to act upon them: because, after the resurrection, no body will act on another, least of all so as to induce corruption by the action of nature, but there will only be action to the effect of punishing them by order of the divine justice. Wherefore those bodies to which pain of sense is not due by divine justice will not suffer punishment. On the other hand, the bodies of the saints will be impassible, because they will lack the capability of suffering; hence impassibility in them will be a gift, but not in children.

SECOND ARTICLE

Whether These Same Souls Suffer Spiritual Affliction on Account of the State in Which They Are?

We proceed thus to the Second Article:—

Objection 1. It would seem that the souls in question suffer spiritual affliction on account of the state wherein they are, because as Chrysostom says *(Hom.* xxiii, *in Matth.),* the punishment of God in that they will be deprived of seeing God will be more painful than their being burned in hell fire. Now these souls will be deprived of seeing God. Therefore they will suffer spiritual affliction thereby.

Obj. 2. Further, one cannot, without suffering, lack what one wishes to have. But these souls would wish to have the divine vision, else their will would be actually perverse. Therefore since they are deprived of it, seemingly they also suffer.

Obj. 3. Further, if it be said that they do not suffer, because they know that through no fault of theirs they are deprived thereof, on the contrary: — Freedom from fault does not lessen but increases the pain of punishment: for a man does not grieve less for that he is disinherited or deprived of a limb through no fault of his. Therefore these souls likewise, albeit deprived of so great a good through no fault of theirs, suffer none the less.

Obj. 4. Further, as baptized children are in relation to the merit of Christ, so are unbaptized children to the demerit of Adam. But baptized children receive the reward of eternal life by virtue of Christ's merit. Therefore the unbaptized suffer pain through being deprived of eternal life on account of Adam's demerit.

Obj. 5. Further, separation from what we love cannot be without pain. But these children will have natural knowledge of God, and for that very reason will love Him naturally. Therefore since they are separated from Him for ever, seemingly they cannot undergo this separation without pain.

On the contrary, If unbaptized children have interior sorrow after death, they will grieve either for their sin or for their punishment. If for their sin, since they cannot be further cleansed from that sin, their sorrow will lead them to despair. Now sorrow of this kind in the damned is the worm of conscience. Therefore these children will have the worm of conscience, and consequently theirs would not be the mildest punishment, as Augustine says it is.* If, on the other hand, they grieve for their punishment, it follows, since their punishment is justly inflicted by God, that their will opposes itself to divine justice, and thus would be actually inordinate, which is

* Cf. Art. 1, *On the contrary,* . . .

not to be granted. Therefore they will feel no sorrow.

Further, right reason does not allow one to be disturbed on account of what one was unable to avoid; hence Seneca proves (Ep. lxxxv, and *De ira* ii. 6) that *a wise man is not disturbed.* Now in these children there is right reason deflected by no actual sin. Therefore they will not be disturbed for that they undergo this punishment which they could nowise avoid.

I answer that, On this question there are three opinions. Some say that these children will suffer no pain, because their reason will be so much in the dark that they will not know that they lack what they have lost. It, however, seems improbable that the soul freed from its bodily burden should ignore things which, to say the least, reason is able to explore, and many more besides. Hence others say that they have perfect knowledge of things subject to natural reason, and know God, and that they are deprived of seeing Him, and that they feel some kind of sorrow on this account but that their sorrow will be mitigated, in so far as it was not by their will that they incurred the sin for which they are condemned. Yet this again would seem improbable, because this sorrow cannot be little for the loss of so great a good, especially without the hope of recovery: wherefore their punishment would not be the mildest. Moreover the very same reason that impugns their being punished with pain of sense, as afflicting them from without, argues against their feeling sorrow within, because the pain of punishment corresponds to the pleasure of sin; wherefore, since original sin is void of pleasure, its punishment is free of all pain. Consequently others say that they will know perfectly things subject to natural knowledge, and both the fact of their being deprived of eternal life and the reason for this privation, and that nevertheless this knowledge will not cause any sorrow in them. How this may be possible we must explore.

Accordingly, it must be observed that if one is guided by right reason one does not grieve through being deprived of what is beyond one's power to obtain, but only through lack of that which, in some way, one is capable of obtaining. Thus no wise man grieves for being unable to fly like a bird, or for that he is not a king or an emperor, since these things are not due to him; whereas he would grieve if he lacked that to which he had some kind of claim. I say, then, that every man who has the use of free-will is adapted to obtain eternal life, because he can prepare himself for grace whereby to merit eternal life;† so that if he fail in this, his grief will be very great, since

† Cf. I-II, Q. 109, AA. 5, 6.

he has lost what he was able to possess. But children were never adapted to possess eternal life, since neither was this due to them by virtue of their natural principles, for it surpasses the entire faculty of nature, nor could they perform acts of their own whereby to obtain so great a good. Hence they will nowise grieve for being deprived of the divine vision; nay, rather will they rejoice for that they will have a large share of God's goodness and their own natural perfections. Nor can it be said that they were adapted to obtain eternal life, not indeed by their own action, but by the actions of others around them, since they could be baptized by others, like other children of the same condition who have been baptized and obtained eternal life: for this is of superabundant grace that one should be rewarded without any act of one's own. Wherefore the lack of such a grace will not cause sorrow in children who die without Baptism, any more than the lack of many graces accorded to others of the same condition makes a wise man to grieve.

Reply Obj. 1. In those who, having the use of free-will, are damned for actual sin, there was aptitude to obtain eternal life, but not in children, as stated above. Consequently there is no parity between the two.

Reply Obj. 2. Although the will may be directed both to the possible and to the impossible as stated in *Ethic.* iii. 5, an ordinate and complete will is only of things which in some way are proportionate to our capability; and we grieve if we fail to obtain this will, but not if we fail in the will that is of impossibilities, and which should be called *velleity** rather than *will;* for one does not will such things absolutely, but one would if they were possible.

Reply Obj. 3. Everyone has a claim to his own inheritance or bodily members, wherefore it is not strange that he should grieve at their loss, whether this be through his own or another's fault: hence it is clear that the argument is not based on a true comparison.

Reply Obj. 4. The gift of Christ surpasses the sin of Adam, as stated in Rom. v. 15 *seqq.* Hence it does not follow that unbaptized children have as much of evil as the baptized have of good.

Reply Obj. 5. Although unbaptized children are separated from God as regards the union of glory, they are not utterly separated from Him: in fact they are united to Him by their share of natural goods, and so will also be able to rejoice in Him by their natural knowledge and love.

QUESTION 2

Of the Quality of Souls Who Expiate Actual Sin or Its Punishment in Purgatory

(In Six Articles)

WE must next treat of the souls which after this life expiate the punishment of their actual sins in the fire of Purgatory.

Under this head there are six points of inquiry: (1) Whether the pain of Purgatory surpasses all the temporal pains of this life? (2) Whether that punishment is voluntary? (3) Whether the souls in Purgatory are punished by the demons? (4) Whether venial sin as regards its guilt is expiated by the pains of Purgatory? (5) Whether the fire of Purgatory frees from the debt of punishment? (6) Whether one is freed from that punishment sooner than another?

FIRST ARTICLE

Whether the Pains of Purgatory Surpass All the Temporal Pains of This Life?

We proceed thus to the First Article:—

Objection 1. It would seem that the pains of Purgatory do not surpass all the temporal pains of this life. Because the more passive

* Cf. I-II, Q. 13, A. 5 *ad* 1; III, Q. 21, A. 4.

a thing is the more it suffers if it has the sense of being hurt. Now the body is more passive than the separate soul, both because it has contrariety to a fiery agent, and because it has matter which is susceptive of the agent's quality: and this cannot be said of the soul. Therefore the pain which the body suffers in this world is greater than the pain whereby the soul is cleansed after this life.

Obj. 2. Further, the pains of Purgatory are directly ordained against venial sins. Now since venial sins are the least grievous, the lightest punishment is due to them, if the measure of the stripes is according to the measure of the fault. Therefore the pain of Purgatory is the lightest of all.

Obj. 3. Further, since the debt of punishment is an effect of sin, it does not increase unless the sin increases. Now sin cannot increase in one whose sin is already remitted. Therefore if a mortal sin has been remitted in a man who has not fully paid the debt of punishment, this debt does not increase when he dies. But while he lived he was not in debt to the extent of the most grievous punishment. Therefore the pain that he will suffer after this life will not be more grievous to him than all other pains of this life.

On the contrary, Augustine says in a sermon (xli, *de Sanctis*): *This fire of Purgatory will be more severe than any pain that can be felt, seen or conceived in this world.*

Further, the more universal a pain is the greater it is. Now the whole separate soul is punished, since it is simple: which is not the case with the body. Therefore this, being the punishment of the separate soul, is greater than any pain suffered by the body.

I answer that, In Purgatory there will be a twofold pain; one will be the pain of loss, namely the delay of the divine vision, and the pain of sense, namely punishment by corporeal fire. With regard to both the least pain of Purgatory surpasses the greatest pain of this life. For the more a thing is desired the more painful is its absence. And since after this life the holy souls desire the Sovereign Good with the most intense longing,—both because their longing is not held back by the weight of the body, and because, had there been no obstacle, they would already have gained the goal of enjoying the Sovereign Good,—it follows that they grieve exceedingly for their delay. Again, since pain is not hurt, but the sense of hurt, the more sensitive a thing is, the greater the pain caused by that which hurts it: wherefore hurts inflicted on the more sensible parts cause the greatest pain. And, because all bodily sensation is from the soul, it follows of necessity that the soul feels the greatest pain when a hurt is inflicted on the soul itself. That the soul suffers pain from the bodily fire is at present taken for granted, for we shall treat of this matter further on.* Therefore it follows that the pain of Purgatory, both of loss and of sense, surpasses all the pains of this life.

Some, however, prove this from the fact that the whole soul is punished, and not the body. But this is to no purpose, since in that case the punishment of the damned would be milder after the resurrection than before, which is false.

Reply Obj. 1. Although the soul is less passive than the body, it is more cognizant of actual suffering *(passionis)*: and where the sense of suffering is greater, there is the greater pain, though the suffering be less.

Reply Obj. 2. The severity of that punishment is not so much a consequence of the degree of sin, as of the disposition of the person punished, because the same sin is more severely punished then than now. Even so a person who has a better temperament is pun-

* Cf. Suppl., Q. 70, A. 3.

ished more severely by the same sentence than another; and yet the judge acts justly in condemning both for the same crimes to the same punishment.

This suffices for the Reply to the Third Objection.

SECOND ARTICLE

Whether This Punishment Is Voluntary?

We proceed thus to the Second Article:—

Objection 1. It would seem that this punishment is voluntary. For those who are in Purgatory are upright in heart. Now uprightness in heart is to conform one's will to God's, as Augustine says *(Serm.* i, *in* Ps. xxxii). Therefore, since it is God's will that they be punished, they will suffer that punishment voluntarily.

Obj. 2. Further, every wise man wills that without which he cannot obtain the end he has in view. Now those who are in Purgatory know that they cannot obtain glory, unless they be punished first. Therefore they are punished willingly.

On the contrary, No one asks to be freed from a punishment that he suffers willingly. Now those who are in Purgatory ask to be set free, as appears from many incidents related in the *Dialogue* of Gregory (iv. 40, 65). Therefore they will not undergo that punishment voluntarily.

I answer that, A thing is said to be voluntary in two ways. First, by an absolute act of the will; and thus no punishment is voluntary, because the very notion of punishment is that it be contrary to the will. Secondly, a thing is said to be voluntary by a conditional act of the will: thus cautery is voluntary for the sake of regaining health. Hence a punishment may be voluntary in two ways. First, because by being punished we obtain some good, and thus the will itself undertakes a punishment, as instanced in satisfaction, or when a man accepts a punishment gladly, and would not have it not to be, as in the case of martyrdom. Secondly, when, although we gain no good by the punishment, we cannot obtain a good without being punished, as in the case of natural death: and then the will does not undertake the punishment, and would be delivered from it; but it submits to it, and in this respect the punishment is said to be voluntary. In this latter sense the punishment of Purgatory is said to be voluntary.

Some, however, say that it is not voluntary in any way, because the souls in Purgatory are so replete with suffering, that they know not that they are being cleansed by their pains, and deem themselves damned. But this is false, for did they not know that they will be set free, they would not ask for prayers, as they often do.

This suffices for the Replies to the Objections.

THIRD ARTICLE

Whether the Souls in Purgatory Are Punished by the Demons?

We proceed thus to the Third Article:—

Objection 1. It would seem that the souls in Purgatory are punished by the demons. for, according to the Master, *they will have for torturers in their pains, those who were their tempters in sin.* Now the demons tempt us to sin, not only mortal, but also venial when they fail in the former. Therefore in Purgatory also they will torture souls on account of venial sins.

Obj. 2. Further, the just are competent to be cleansed from sin both in this life and afterwards. Now, in this life, they are cleansed by pains inflicted by the devil, as was the case with Job. Therefore after this life also, those who have to be cleansed will be punished by the demons.

On the contrary, It were unjust that he who has triumphed over someone, should be subjected to him after victory. Now those who are in Purgatory have triumphed over the demons, since they died without mortal sin. Therefore they will not be subjected to them through being punished by them.

I answer that, As after the Judgment day the Divine justice will kindle the fire with which the damned will be punished for ever, even so now the elect are cleansed after this life by the Divine justice alone, and neither by the ministry of the demons whom they have vanquished, nor by the ministry of the angels who would not inflict such tortures on their fellow-citizens. It is, however, possible that they take them to the place of punishment: also that even the demons, who rejoice in the punishment of man, accompany them and stand by while they are being cleansed, both that they may be sated with their pains, and that when these leave their bodies, they may find something of their own in them. But in this life, while there is yet time for the combat, men are punished both by the wicked angels as foes, as instanced in Job, and by the good angels, as instanced in Jacob, the sinew of whose thigh shrank at the angel's touch.* Moreover, Dionysius says explicitly that the good angels sometimes inflict punishment.

This suffices for the Replies to the Objections.

FOURTH ARTICLE

Whether Venial Sin Is Expiated by the Pains of Purgatory As Regards the Guilt?

We proceed thus to the Fourth Article:—

Objection 1. It would seem that venial sin is not expiated by the pains of Purgatory as regards the guilt. For a gloss† on 1 John v. 16, *There is a sin unto death,* etc., says: *It is vain to ask pardon after death for what was not amended in this life.* Therefore no sin is remitted as to guilt after this life.

Obj. 2. Further, the same subject is freed from sin as falls into sin. But after death the soul cannot sin venially. Therefore neither can it be loosed from venial sin.

Obj. 3. Further, Gregory says‡ that every man will be at the judgment as he was when he left the body, because *the tree . . . wheresoever it shall fall, there shall it be.*§ If, then, a man go forth from this life with venial sin, he will be with venial sin at the judgment: and consequently one does not atone for venial sin in Purgatory.

Obj. 4. Further, it has been stated (Suppl. ii. 3) that actual sin is not blotted out save by contrition. But there will be no contrition after this life, because it is a meritorious act.⸱ For then there will be neither merit nor demerit since, according to the Damascene,¶ *death is to men what the fall was to the angels.* Therefore, after this life, venial sin is not remitted in Purgatory as to its guilt.

Obj. 5. Further, venial sin is not in us except on account of the fomes. Wherefore in the original state Adam would not have sinned venially, as was stated (2 *Sent.* xxi. 2). Now after this life there will be no sensuality; because the fomes will cease when the soul is separated, since it is called the *law of the flesh* (Rom. vii). Hence there will be no venial sin then, and consequently it cannot be expiated by the fire of Purgatory.

On the contrary, Gregory** and Augustine†† say that certain slight sins will be remitted in the life to come. Nor can this be understood of the punishment: because thus all sins, however grave they be, are expiated by the fire of Purgatory, as regards the debt of punishment. Therefore venial sins are cleansed by the fire of Purgatory as to their guilt.

Further, wood, hay, stubble (1 Cor. iii. 12) denote venial sins, as we have said (I-II, Q. 89, A. 2). Now wood, hay, stubble are consumed in Purgatory. Therefore venial sins are remitted after this life.

I answer that, Some have asserted that no sin is remitted after this life, as regards the guilt: that if a man die with mortal sin, he

---

* Gen. xxxii. 25.   † St. Gregory (*Moral.* xvi. 28).   ‡ *Dial.* iv. 39.   § Eccles. xi. 3.
¶ *De Fide Orthod.* ii. 4.   ** *Dial.* iv. 39.   †† *De vera et falsa pœnit.* iv, xviii, by some other author.

is damned and incapable of being forgiven; and that it is not possible for a man to die with a venial sin and without mortal sin, since the final grace washes the venial sin away. They assign as reason for this that venial sin is excessive love of a temporal thing, in one who has his foundation in Christ, which excess results from the corruption of concupiscence. Wherefore if grace entirely overcome the corruption of concupiscence, as in the Blessed Virgin, there is no room for venial sin. Hence, since this concupiscence is altogether abated and removed, the powers of the soul are wholly subject to grace, and venial sin is cast out. But this opinion is nonsensical in itself and in its proof. In itself, because it is opposed to the statements of holy men and of the Gospel, which cannot be expounded as referring to the remission of venial sins as to their punishment, as the Master says in the text,* because in this way both light and grave sins are remitted in the life to come: while Gregory † declares that light sins alone are remitted after this life. Nor does it suffice for them to say, that this is said expressly of light sins, lest we should think that we shall suffer nothing grievous on their account: because the remission of sin diminishes punishment rather than aggravates it. As to the proof, it is shown to be worthless, since bodily defect, such as obtains at the last moment of life, does not remove the corruption of concupiscence; nor does it diminish it in its root but in its act, as instanced in those who lie dangerously ill; nor again does it calm the powers of the soul, so as to subject them to grace, because tranquillity of the powers, and their subjection to grace, is effected when the lower powers obey the higher which delight together in God's law. But this cannot happen in that state, since the acts of both kinds of powers are impeded; unless tranquillity denote the absence of combat, as occurs even in those who are asleep; and yet sleep is not said, for this reason, to diminish concupiscence, or to calm the powers of the soul, or to subject them to grace. Moreover, granted that the aforesaid defect diminish concupiscence radically, and that it subject the powers to grace, it would still be insufficient to wash away venial sin already committed, although it would suffice in order to avoid it in the future. Because actual sin, even if it be venial, is not remitted without an actual movement of contrition, as stated above (Suppl., Q. 2, A. 3), however much the latter be in the habitual intention. Now it happens sometimes that a man dies in his sleep,

being in a state of grace and yet having a venial sin when he went to sleep: and such a man cannot make an act of contrition for his venial sin before he dies. Nor may we say, as they do, that if he repented neither by act nor by intention, neither in general nor in particular, his venial sin becomes mortal, for that "venial becomes mortal when it is an object of complacency"; because not all complacency in venial sin makes it mortal (else all venial sin would be mortal, since every venial sin pleases for as much as it is voluntary), but only that complacency which amounts to enjoyment, wherein all human wickedness consists, in that *we enjoy what we should use*, as Augustine says. ‡ Hence the complacency which makes a sin mortal is actual complacency, for every mortal sin consists in an act. Now it may happen that a man, after committing a venial sin, has no actual thought of being forgiven or of remaining in that sin, but thinks perhaps about a triangle having its three angles equal to two right angles, and while engaged in this thought falls asleep, and dies.

It is therefore clear that this opinion is utterly unreasonable: and consequently we must say with others that venial sin in one who dies in a state of grace, is remitted after this life by the fire of Purgatory: because this punishment so far as it is voluntary, will have the power, by virtue of grace, to expiate all such guilt as is compatible with grace. §

Reply Obj. 1. The gloss refers to mortal sin. Or it may be replied that although, in this life, it is not amended in itself, it is amended in merits, because a man merited here that his punishment should be meritorious to him there.

Reply Obj. 2. Venial sin arises from the corruption of the fomes, which will no longer be in the separate soul that is in Purgatory, wherefore this soul cannot sin venially. On the other hand, the remission of venial sin proceeds from the will informed by grace, which will be in the separate soul in Purgatory. Hence the comparison fails.

Reply Obj. 3. Venial sins do not alter a man's state, for they neither destroy nor diminish charity, according to which the amount of the soul's gratuitous goodness is measured. Hence the soul remains such as it was before, notwithstanding the remission or commission of venial sins.

Reply Obj. 4. After this life there can be no merit in respect of the essential reward, but there can be in respect of some accidental re-

---

*4 *Sent.* D. xxi.   † *l. c.*   ‡ *De Trin.* x. 10.

§ St. Thomas expresses himself differently, *De Malo*, Q. 7, A. 2 *ad* 9 and *ad* 17: *Guilt is not remitted by punishment, but venial sin as to its guilt is remitted in Purgatory by virtue of grace, not only as existing in the habit, but also as proceeding to the act of charity in detestation of venial sin.*

ward, so long as man remains in the state of the way, in a sense. Consequently in Purgatory there can be a meritorious act in respect of the remission of venial sin.

Reply Obj. 5. Although venial sin arises from the proneness of the fomes, sin results in the mind; wherefore even when the fomes is no more, sin can still remain.

FIFTH ARTICLE

Whether the Fire of Purgatory Delivers from the Debt of Punishment?

We proceed thus to the Fifth Article:—

Objection 1. It would seem that the fire of Purgatory does not deliver from the debt of punishment. For every cleansing is in respect of some uncleanness. But punishment does not imply uncleanness. Therefore the fire of Purgatory does not deliver from punishment.

Obj. 2. Further, a contrary is not cleansed save by its contrary. But punishment is not contrary to punishment. Therefore one is not cleansed from the debt of punishment by the punishment of Purgatory.

Obj. 3. Further, a gloss on 1 Cor. iii. 15, *He shall be saved, yet so,* etc., says: *This fire is the trial of tribulation of which it is written* (Ecclus. xxvii. 6): *The furnace tries the potter's vessels,* etc. Therefore man expiates every punishment by the pains of this world, at least by death, which is the greatest punishment of all, and not by the fire of Purgatory.

On the contrary, The pains of Purgatory are more grievous than all the pains of this world, as stated above (A. 3). Now the satisfactory punishment which one undergoes in this life atones for the debt of punishment. Much more therefore is this effected by the punishment of Purgatory.

I answer that, Whosoever is another's debtor, is freed from his indebtedness by paying the debt. And, since the obligation incurred by guilt is nothing else than the debt of punishment, a person is freed from that obligation by undergoing the punishment which he owed. Accordingly the punishment of Purgatory cleanses from the debt of punishment.

Reply Obj. 1. Although the debt of punishment does not in itself imply uncleanness, it bears a relation to uncleanness by reason of its cause.

Reply Obj. 2. Although punishment is not contrary to punishment, it is opposed to the debt of punishment, because the obligation to punishment remains from the fact that one has

not undergone the punishment that was due.

Reply Obj. 3. Many meanings underlie the same words of Holy Writ. Hence this fire may denote both the present tribulation and the punishment to come, and venial sins can be cleansed from both of these. That natural death is not sufficient for this, has been stated above (4 *Sent.* D. xx).

SIXTH ARTICLE

Whether One Person Is Delivered from This Punishment Sooner Than Another?

We proceed thus to the Sixth Article:—

Objection 1. It would seem that one person is not delivered from this punishment sooner than another. For the more grievous the sin, and the greater the debt, the more severely is it punished in Purgatory. Now there is the same proportion between severer punishment and graver fault, as between lighter punishment and less grievous fault. Therefore one is delivered from this punishment as soon as another.

Obj. 2. Further, in point of duration unequal merits receive equal retribution both in heaven and in hell. Therefore seemingly it is the same in Purgatory.

On the contrary, is the comparison of the Apostle, who denotes the differences of venial sins by wood, hay, and stubble. Now it is clear that wood remains longer in the fire than hay and stubble. Therefore one venial sin is punished longer in Purgatory than another.

I answer that, Some venial sins cling more persistently than others, according as the affections are more inclined to them, and more firmly fixed in them. And since that which clings more persistently is more slowly cleansed, it follows that some are tormented in Purgatory longer than others, for as much as their affections were steeped in venial sins.

Reply Obj. 1. Severity of punishment corresponds properly speaking to the amount of guilt: whereas the length corresponds to the firmness with which sin has taken root in its subject. Hence it may happen that one may be delayed longer who is tormented less, and *vice versa.*

Reply Obj. 2. Mortal sin which deserves the punishment of hell, and charity which deserves the reward of heaven, will, after this life, be immovably rooted in their subject. Hence as to all there is the same duration in either case. It is otherwise with venial sin which is punished in Purgatory, as stated above (A. 6).

TWO ARTICLES ON PURGATORY

FIRST ARTICLE

Whether There Is a Purgatory after This Life?

We proceed thus to the First Article:—

Objection 1. It would seem that there is not a Purgatory after this life. For it is said (Apoc. xiv. 13): *Blessed are the dead who die in the Lord. From henceforth now, saith the Spirit, that they may rest from their labors.* Therefore after this life no cleansing labor awaits those who die in the Lord, nor those who do not die in the Lord, since they cannot be cleansed. Therefore there is no Purgatory after this life.

Obj. 2. Further, as charity is to an eternal reward, so is mortal sin to eternal punishment. Now those who die in mortal sin are forthwith consigned to eternal punishment. Therefore those who die in charity go at once to their reward; and consequently no Purgatory awaits them after this life.

Obj. 3. Further, God Who is supremely merciful is more inclined to reward good than to punish evil. Now just as those who are in the state of charity, do certain evil things which are not deserving of eternal punishment, so those who are in mortal sin, at times perform actions, generically good, which are not deserving of an eternal reward. Therefore since these good actions are not rewarded after this life in those who will be damned, neither should those evil actions be punished after this life. Hence the same conclusion follows.

On the contrary, It is said (2 Machab. xii. 46): *It is a holy and wholesome thought to pray for the dead, that they may be loosed from sins.* Now there is no need to pray for the dead who are in heaven, for they are in no need; nor again for those who are in hell, because they cannot be loosed from sins. Therefore after this life, there are some not yet loosed from sins, who can be loosed therefrom; and the like have charity, without which sins cannot be loosed, for *charity covereth all sins.** Hence they will not be consigned to everlasting death, since *he that liveth and believeth in Me, shall not die for ever :*† nor will they obtain glory without being cleansed, because nothing unclean shall obtain it, as stated in the last chapter of the Apocalypse *(verse 14).* Therefore some kind of cleansing remains after this life.

Further, Gregory of Nyssa‡ says: *If one who loves and believes in Christ,* has failed to wash away his sins in this life, *he is set free after death by the fire of Purgatory.* Therefore there remains some kind of cleansing after this life.

I answer that, From the conclusions we have drawn above (III, Q. 86, AA. 4, 5 : Suppl., Q. 12, A. 1) it is sufficiently clear that there is a Purgatory after this life. For if the debt of punishment is not paid in full after the stain of sin has been washed away by contrition, nor again are venial sins always removed when mortal sins are remitted, and if justice demands that sin be set in order by due punishment, it follows that one who after contrition for his fault and after being absolved, dies before making due satisfaction, is punished after this life. Wherefore those who deny Purgatory speak against the justice of God: for which reason such a statement is erroneous and contrary to faith. Hence Gregory of Nyssa, after the words quoted above, adds: *This we preach, holding to the teaching of truth, and this is our belief; this the universal Church holds, by praying for the dead that they may be loosed from sins.* This cannot be understood except as referring to Purgatory: and whosoever resists the authority of the Church, incurs the note of heresy.

Reply Obj. 1. The authority quoted is speaking of the labor of working for merit, and not of the labor of suffering to be cleansed.

Reply Obj. 2. Evil has not a perfect cause, but results from each single defect: whereas good arises from one perfect cause, as Dionysius asserts.§ Hence each defect is an obstacle to the perfection of good; while not every good hinders some consummation of evil, since there is never evil without some good. Consequently venial sin prevents one who has charity from obtaining the perfect good, namely eternal life, until he be cleansed; whereas mortal sin cannot be hindered by some conjoined good from bringing a man forthwith to the extreme of evils.

Reply Obj. 3. He that falls into mortal sin, deadens all the good he has done before, and what he does, while in mortal sin, is dead: since by offending God he deserves to lose all the good he has from God. Wherefore no reward after this life awaits him who dies in mortal sin, whereas sometimes punishment awaits him who dies in charity, which does not always wash away the sin which it finds, but only that which is contrary to it.

* Prov. x. 12.   † John xi. 26.   ‡ *De iis qui in fide dormiunt.*   § *Div. Nom.* iv. 4.

SECOND ARTICLE

Whether It Is the Same Place Where Souls Are Cleansed, and the Damned Punished?

We proceed thus to the Second Artilce:—

Objection 1. It would seem that it is not the same place where souls are cleansed and the damned punished. For the punishment of the damned is eternal, according to Matth. xxv. 46, *These shall go into everlasting punishment* (Vulg.,—*fire*). But the fire of Purgatory is temporary, as the Master says (4 *Sent.* D. xxi). Therefore the former and the latter are not punished together in the same place: and consequently these places must needs be distinct.

Obj. 2. The punishment of hell is called by various names, as in Ps. x. 7, *Fire and brimstone, and storms of winds*, etc., whereas the punishment of Purgatory is called by one name only, namely fire. Therefore they are not punished with the same fire and in the same place.

Obj. 3. Further, Hugh of St. Victor says *(De Sacram.* ii. 16): *It is probable that they are punished in the very places where they sinned.* And Gregory relates *(Dial.* iv. 40) that Germanus, Bishop of Capua, found Paschasius being cleansed in the baths. Therefore they are not cleansed in the same place as hell, but in this world.

On the contrary, Gregory says:* *Even as in the same fire gold glistens and straw smokes, so in the same fire the sinner burns and the elect is cleansed.* Therefore the fire of Purgatory is the same as the fire of hell: and hence they are in the same place.

Further, the holy fathers, before the coming of Christ, were in a more worthy place than that wherein souls are now cleansed after death, since there was no pain of sense there. Yet that place was joined to hell, or the same as hell: otherwise Christ when descending into Limbo would not be said to have descended into hell. Therefore Purgatory is either close to, or the same place as, hell.

* The quotation is from St. Augustine *(De Civ. Dei* i. 8).

I answer that, Nothing is clearly stated in Scripture about the situation of Purgatory, nor is it possible to offer convincing arguments on this question. It is probable, however, and more in keeping with the statements of holy men and the revelations made to many, that there is a twofold place of Purgatory. One, according to the common law; and thus the place of Purgatory is situated below and in proximity to hell, so that it is the same fire which torments the damned in hell and cleanses the just in Purgatory; although the damned being lower in merit, are to be consigned to a lower place. Another place of Purgatory is according to dispensation: and thus sometimes, as we read, some are punished in various places, either that the living may learn, or that the dead may be succored, seeing that their punishment being made known to the living may be mitigated through the prayers of the Church.

Some say, however, that according to the common law the place of Purgatory is where man sins. This does not seem probable, since a man may be punished at the same time for sins committed in various places. And others say that according to the common law they are punished above us, because they are between us and God, as regards their state. But this is of no account, for they are not punished for being above us, but for that which is lowest in them, namely sin.

Reply Obj. 1. The fire of Purgatory is eternal in its substance, but temporary in its cleansing effect.

Reply Obj. 2. The punishment of hell is for the purpose of affliction, wherefore it is called by the names of things that are wont to afflict us here. But the chief purpose of the punishment of Purgatory is to cleanse us from the remains of sin; and consequently the pain of fire only is ascribed to Purgatory, because fire cleanses and consumes.

Reply Obj. 3. This argument considers the point of special dispensation and not that of the common law.

A chart of the "Summa theologica" showing the organization of all the treatises and the numeration of the questions for all three parts.

	Question 1
1. Sacred doctrine.	1
2. The one God.	2–26
3. The Most Holy Trinity.	27–43
4. The creation.	44–46
5. The distinction of things in general.	47
6. The distinction of good and evil.	48–49
7. The angels.	50–64
8. The creature purely corporeal.	65–74
9. On man.	75–102
10. The conservation and government of creatures.	103–119
11. The end of man and beatitude.	1–5
12. Human acts.	6–21
13. The passions.	22–48
14. Habits in general.	49–54
15. The virtues.	55–70
16. On vices and sins.	71–89
17. On laws.	90–108
18. On grace.	109–114
19. Faith.	1–16
20. Hope.	17–22
21. Charity.	23–46
22. Prudence.	47–56
23. Justice.	57–122
24. Fortitude.	123–140
25. Temperance.	141–170
26. Graces gratuitously given.	171–178
27. The active and contemplative life.	179–182
28. The various offices and conditions of men.	183–189
29. The Incarnation.	1–59
30. The Sacraments in general.	60–65
31. Baptism.	66–71
32. Confirmation.	72
33. Eucharist.	73–83
34. Penance, Qu. 84–90. Supplement	1–28
35. Extreme Unction.	29–33
36. Orders.	34–40
37. Matrimony.	41–68
38. The Resurrection and Four Last Things.	69–99

Part 1

Sacred Doctrine. What it is and to what it extends. All things are treated in it, under the idea of God, either because they are God Himself or because they have some relation to God.

1. GOD (Threefold consideration)
- 1st Concerning things that pertain to the divine essence.
- 2d Concerning things that pertain to the distinction of Persons.
- 3d Concerning those things that pertain to the PRODUCTION of CREATURES by GOD.
  - 1st The PRODUCTION OF CREATURES.
  - 2d The DISTINCTION of CREATURES.
    - 1st The distinction of things in general.
    - 2d The distinction of things in particular.
      - (a) The distinction of good and evil.
      - (b) The distinction of corporeal and spiritual creatures.
        - 1st The creature purely spiritual.
        - 2d The creature purely corporeal.
        - 3d The creature composed of body and spirit, i.e., man.
  - 3d The PRESERVATION and GOVERNMENT of CREATURES.

Part 2

2. The ADVANCE of the RATIONAL CREATURE to GOD. (Twofold consideration)

Those things should be considered by means of which man attains to or deviates from his end, i.e., HUMAN ACTS.

But because singular things are the objects of operations and acts, therefore every operative science is perfected by the consideration of things in particular. Therefore a moral consideration of human acts must be given:

1a 2ae — THE END OF MAN. In GENERAL

- 1st The ACTS THEMSELVES. Some acts are peculiar to man; some are common to man and other living creatures; and since beatitude is the peculiar good of man inasmuch as he is rational, the acts that are peculiar to him have a more intimate connection with that good than those that are common to man and living creatures.
  - (a) Acts that are PECULIAR TO MAN.
  - (b) Acts that are COMMON TO MAN and other ANIMALS.
- 2d The PRINCIPLES of ACTS. The intrinsic principles are POWERS of the soul and HABITS; but powers have already been treated in the 1st part. Therefore, now the consideration of HABITS:
  - (a) INTRINSIC PRINCIPLES
    - 1st HABITS IN GENERAL.
    - 2d HABITS in PARTICULAR.
      - Good habits, i.e., virtues.
      - Evil habits, i.e., vices.
  - (b) EXTRINSIC PRINCIPLES. The extrinsic principle of GOOD is GOD, who instructs man by His law and helps and moves man by grace. The external principle of EVIL is the DEVIL. But he was treated in the 1st part; therefore it remains to treat of:
    - 1st Laws.
    - 2d Grace.

2a 2ae — In PARTICULAR

- 1st ACTS that pertain to ALL CONDITIONS of life (the virtues and vices affecting all men).
  - (a) THEOLOGICAL VIRTUES
    - In the intellect: Faith.
    - In the will: Hope. Charity.
  - (b) CARDINAL VIRTUES
    - Prudence.
    - Justice.
    - Fortitude.
    - Temperance.
- 2d ACTS that pertain in a SPECIAL MANNER to SOME men.
  - (a) Graces gratuitously given (gratiae gratis datae).
  - (b) Active and contemplative life.
  - (c) The various offices and conditions of men.

Part 3

3. CHRIST

Since Our Lord and Savior Jesus Christ, redeeming His people from their sins, has shown in Himself the way of truth, by which man, arising from the dead, is able to arrive at the happiness of immortal life, it is necessary to sustain the scope of all theology, after considering the final end of men and the virtues and vices, to consider the Savior of all and the benefits He has offered on man. Therefore, a consideration of:

- 1st The SAVIOR HIMSELF, i.e., the mystery of the Incarnation, what He did and suffered.
  - (a) In GENERAL.
  - (b) In PARTICULAR.
- 2d The SACRAMENTS, which have their efficacy from the Incarnate Word.
- 3d IMMORTAL LIFE, the end man attains through Christ, both God and man, suffering, dying, and rising from the dead.

Reprinted from *The New Catholic Encyclopedia*, Vol. 16, by permission of the Catholic University of America, Washington, D.C.